CASTLEFORD RUGBY LEAGUE FOOTBALL CLUB

A Ninety Years Statistical and Pictorial Record

1926 – 2016

Ian & Roy Garbett
(In Memory of Len Garbett)

FOREWORD

Alan Hardisty
Player, Captain, Coach & President of Castleford Players Association

 My rugby career almost finished before it had started. I broke two collar bones when I was ten years old, and my parents suggested quite forcefully that I was not to play rugby any more. I was a quiet, shy, 'stand-backer' as a kid; and I didn't have the build to be a budding rugby player.

I guess you never know what's in front of you when you are just ten years old. I think it has a lot to do with the school you go to and the teachers you meet up with along the way. I was lucky. My Sports Master was a big Rugby League man and he was very good at what he did.

Rugby League must have been something I had inbuilt as I spent most of my time playing it.

When I left school I joined Glasshoughton Under 16s team. I was lucky enough to meet up with Keith Hepworth, who turned out to be my half-back playing partner for the rest of my career.

After Glasshoughton we decided to go and play with the Castleford Under 17s team. When we arrived at the Cas Ground we were told that we had come on the wrong night; and I feel that that was where fate played its' part. We were told that we could train with Castleford's Second Team. A week later we were asked if we would like to play in a pre-season warm-up game against the First Team.

After the game the First Team Coach, who was Harry Street at that time, took me into his van and asked if I would be interested in signing for Castleford Rugby League Club. I immediately said "Yes". He locked me in the van and came back after seeing the Club's Directors, with a Signing-On form for me. It offered me £150 to sign on, £300 if I was ever selected to play for Yorkshire and £500 if I was selected for Great Britain. I would have signed for nothing, but I didn't tell him that.

The Club went on to sign a lot of young local talent and became known as "Classy Cas" in the Sixties and competed with all the top teams.

Keith and I went on to realise all our ambitions. I was given the honour of being made Captain of the Club, and I made it to play at the Great Wembley Stadium in 1969 and 1970. The pinnacle of my career was when I was made Captain of the Great Britain team to play France in 1968.

I feel I had a great career and to have it with my own Castleford Rugby League Club, and to do it with so much local talent, and some of the great players it produced, made it so much more special.

Steve Gill
Director and CEO Castleford Rugby League Football Club

I guess my love for Castleford started on the 1st of March 1969, when was rescued by my uncle from sitting in the hairdressers with my mum one Saturday afternoor in Castleford town centre. I know we beat Leeds 9-5 that day and went on to beat Salford at Wembley, so I realise how spoilt we were back then, especially with the team we had, but I never in a mill on years would have imagined what Castleford Tigers had in store for me in the coming years.

My first employment at the club was doing the old scoreboard (where the SKY screen now stands) which paid 20p a game including A team matches. After a couple of seasons doing that I did the Ball Boy's jcb (who rescued the balls after they had been kicked over the stands) for that I was paid 30p and given a torch. I guess at a young age I saw the demise of a squad that had given us so much pleasure, but always believed that we could win any game.

My next employment with the club came around 2000 when I was coaching at Smawthorne Panthers (a side that included Brett Ferres, Michael Shenton and Andy Kain). It was to assist Dean Sampson with the under 17s whilst he was still playing. From there it was a progression to 18s assistant coach to 18s head coach. In 2005 I was lucky enough to be asked to assist Dave Woocs in the fight to get back into Super League, which we accomplished with a great win over at Widnes against Whitehaven. I played it a little smart that year in resigning on the day after, just before I was sacked, as I had seen the vultures gather ng before we had even got to the final.

I wanted to walk away from any employment at the club at that time as sometimes you are better off not seeing what goes on behind the scenes, especially when you love the club as I do. Anyway, after a while I was asked to return as Scholarship Manager, then an opportunity arose to do the Head of Youth Development and then finally CEO.

It's been one hell of a journey, I've seen some good things and not so good things, and maybe one day that's another book that needs to be written!

Daryl Powell
Head Coach Castleford Rugby League Football Club

Castleford has always been my team and always will be. Unfortunately I wasn't able to play for Castleford during my younger days, however the ability to coach my boyhood team is a dream come true, and I'm enjoying my time at the club massively. I am hopeful of driving the current team to huge success on the field which I hope will continue the great name of everything that has gone before, both in the success and in the way it is done. The club has exciting times ahead both on the field and when the new stadium is built, in the meantime I hope we can get the best out of Wheldon Road and add to the special memories of this great place. I will enjoy reading this book and reflecting on what a special club we all belong to.

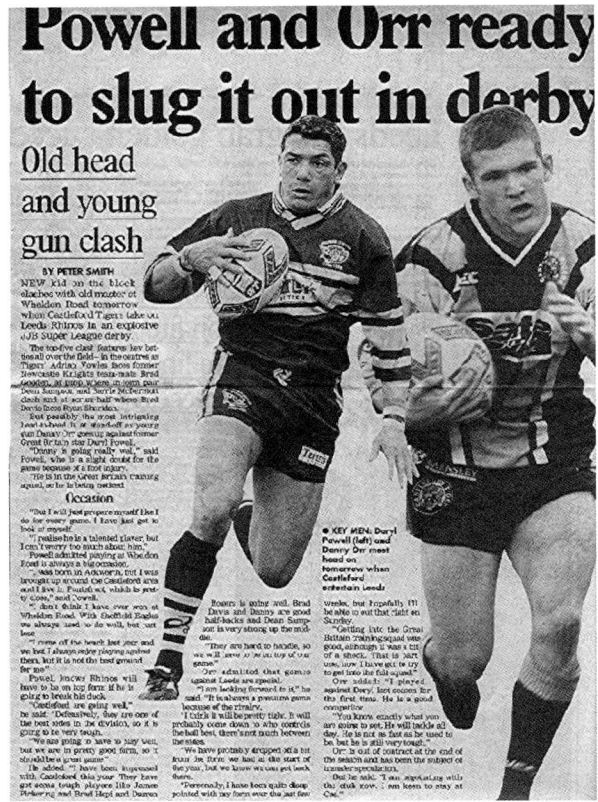

Head Coach and Assistant Coach

Daryl and Danny in their Playing Days !!

CASTLEFORD R.L.F.C. - A 90 YEAR RECORD

This book has been written and produced by Ian and Roy Garbett to commemorate Ninety Years of Castleford Rugby League Football Club and as a tribute to their parents Len Garbett and Sue Garbett.

Both our parents were born and bred 'down the Lane' and their love for each other and the Castleford Club led to a huge archive of club related material; match statistics, programmes, scrapbooks, photographs, a record of the names, pictures, and facts and figures that record the playing careers of all those who have worn the Castleford jersey in a first team fixture since Castleford RLFC joined the semi-professional world of Rugby League from the start of the 1926/27 season until the last match of the 2016 season. This book records details of all those who have played, from the magnificent career of John Joyner who made 613 appearances to those who made just one appearance.

We know the excitement, sheer pleasure and, yes, the heartache that being a Cas fan brings and has brought to our family and many other similar families in Castleford and the surrounding areas. Our grandchildren are the fifth generation of the Garbett/Liversidge family to be season ticket holders at Castleford RLFC.

We also wish to express in writing our sincere thanks, and pay our own personal tribute to the Fulton Family, the late Jack and Bridie, and their children James Ian and Janet Elaine for their considerable financial support over many years, and which as been crucial to the Club's survival and its place and recent success in the Super League era.

The decision to produce a book detailing the history of our great club now, and not when we leave the Wheldon Road ground to move to a new stadium, which will inevitably herald the end of an era, was taken because of our involvement with the Castleford Tigers Trust Heritage Lottery funded project to provide a virtual history of the Club and its place in the local Castleford community.

As a 'not for profit book', all proceeds raised through its sales, after publishing costs have been paid, will go to Castleford Tigers and/or the Heritage Trust to further their work.

We wish to acknowledge the help and assistance we have received from other members of our family and from those involved with the Heritage Project. We would have wished that the current sponsors of the Club could have sponsored the book, but we did not want this to conflict with their financial support for the Club. We wish to acknowledge the financial contribution made by Directors,

Shareholders, all those who have sponsored the Club, been Patrons or Season Ticket holders, and regular supporters over the years.

Our personal thanks go to Norman Carr, a fellow Castleford RLFC Historian, for his help to our father and latterly to ourselves in trying to ensure that the records in this book are as accurate as humanly possible.

Members of the Steering Group that have championed this book

Ian and Roy Garbett

Geoff Smith

Stephen Ball

LEONARD GARBETT   1919 –2009
Boot Boy to President

Len Garbett was born at 32 Princess Street, Wheldon Road, the youngest of nine children born to William and Rosina Garbett (nee Doidge).

The rear back bedrooms of the even numbers on Princess Street overlooked the rugby ground providing young Len, his family and neighbours, free viewing at every home game.   Eventually the Directors decided to take action to stop this and had posts erected along the length of the field, then on the morning of a game Billy Rhodes, who was a great servant of the Club over many years, and his assistant George Wainwright, would fasten lengths of sacking to the posts, putting an end to free viewing.

At the age of eleven Len passed the School Certificate Examination entitling him to go to Castleford Grammar School, where he played Rugby Union as a scrum half; they did not play rugby league in those days. On leaving school he was invited to play for Castleford RUFC 'A' team, playing just one game against Sandal at Aketon Road, the teams changing in the King William IV Hotel (King Billy).

On leaving school he joined the ground staff at the Club. The Company Secretary, Captain J A Pickles, told him he would not get paid but that the Club would pay his National Insurance stamp so that he was not considered to be unemployed.

After a year in his dream job his Mother, Rosina, decided he should have a 'proper job' and gained him employment with Mr Alfred Beedle, a local Estate Agent, as a Clerk and Rent and Debt Collector, his initial duties being rent collection. He had never ridden a bicycle, but on his first day was allocated one and told to cycle to Normanton and collect certain rents that were due.

In July 1935, just weeks after Castleford's Wembley triumph he signed semi-professional forms for the Club. Like most players he did not receive a signing on fee. Legend has it that one of our greatest players, Arthur Atkinson, received a pork pie from Stanley Hirst, a local butcher and Club Director, when he signed. Leslie (Juicy) Adams was the first team scrum half at the time, he was one of the very best, and sadly went missing in action on an air raid with the RAF over Burma.

Len eventually made his first team debut at York on Easter Monday 1938 and also played the following day, away against Leeds. His rugby career was effectively ended when war was declared against Germany, as he was called up for National Service on 20th October 1938 into the 2nd Battalion Glasgow Highlanders (Highland Light Infantry). He was issued with a kilt, which he very proudly wore at his wedding to Susan Liversidge on 11th July 1942.

Being ranked as a semi-professional player when called up gave him some privileges, and he was selected for the Battalion's rugby union, soccer, cricket and boxing teams. Whilst playing left full back for the Company football team on a very muddy pitch with a wet and heavy leather ball, he suffered concussion through heading it out of defence too many times. When the opposition mounted another attack the Goalkeeper punched the ball clear, Len caught it, evaded a couple of tackles and dived over the line for a try. Unfortunately the referee gave a penalty against him for handling the ball and they lost 1-0. It did, however, mean that he featured in the next issue of the Battalion magazine.

In 1944, in preparation for 'D Day', the Battalion relocated from Scotland to Bingley in Yorkshire, marching the whole way over three days. During his stay in Bingley Len decided to try and get a game with Keighley as a guest player. He went along one Saturday when they were at home to Huddersfield. The Huddersfield team that day already included four guest players from Castleford - the Wembley front row of Pat McManus, Harold Haley and Tommy Taylor plus second row forward Frank Wagstaff. Castleford did not have a team in the Emergency War League owing to so many players being called up for National Service, but due to that chance meeting he went on to play a number of matches for Huddersfield.

Ironically for a rugby man, he broke his big toe playing football, and this was closely followed by an operation for acute obstructed appendix. These two incidents probably saved his life as the Battalion lost nearly a third of its members in their first action after 'D Day'. Had he been fit and well he would have been involved in those Normandy landings.

He was demobbed on 1st February 1946 after over six years National Service, and returned to his old job of Clerk and Rent Collector for local Estate Agent Harry Harrison, who had become a Director of the Club. After a while he obtained a post with Castleford Borough Council as a Clerk in the Rates Office. The main benefit of that for a sports lover was that he did not have to work on Saturday afternoons.

After playing only two 'A' Team games he realised that, after his National Service, he was not fit enough to be a professional rugby player, but wishing to keep an involvement with the game he loved he decided he would try refereeing. He wrote to Bill Fallowfield, the then Secretary of The Rugby Football League, asking for his advice on this and he suggested Len should contact George Butler, Secretary of Castleford Amateur Rugby Football League. He did this and subsequently received an appointment to referee a cup final between Kippax and Wheldale Colliery.

He was a founder member of the Pontefract and Castleford Rugby League Referees' Society; he followed George Butler as Honorary Secretary of the Castleford & District ARL, later becoming Chairman and eventually Honorary Life Member. With a view to refereeing at a higher grade he sat and passed the Referees' Examination at RL headquarters in Leeds and became a Grade 5 referee. In 1953 Len was upgraded to Grade 2 which meant he became the first Castlefordian to referee a first team rugby league game.

With no car his refereeing career was made difficult by having to travel on public transport, which for matches in Lancashire and Cumberland was very time consuming. He was very intolerant of indiscipline of any description which inevitably resulted in the sending off of offenders - seven in one amateur game and both teams in another!

Whilst refereeing Len was still on the lookout for talent to recommend to the Castleford club. One such recommendation was a young centre playing for local amateur club Lock Lane, his name was John Sheridan who became a great servant of the Club as player, captain and First and 'A' team coach and one of the finest rugby brains to ever grace our game. In the 1957/58 season John played in all 41 matches scoring 27 tries, just one less than the Club record at that time. His playing record was 300 appearances plus 1 as substitute, scoring 82 tries, 2 goals, and 1 drop goal for 264 points.

Len resigned from refereeing after receiving a request to become Castleford RLFC's 'A' Team coach. He took up his duties in November 1955 and when Earnest Ward resigned as first team coach in January 1956 he took over that position. Unfortunately he was not able to improve the team's fortune and we remember hanging a banner out of our bedroom window after their first league win.

Ken Holmes, Club Secretary, resigned on 17th December 1957 and a few days later Albert Dobson the former referee and by now a Club Director and Len went to Harewood House Parks Department to offer the position of First Team Coach to former international loose forward Harry Street, a Gardener on the estate. After the Christmas Day 1957 fixture Len resigned as Coach, and the following day became

Company Secretary for the Club. Many older supporters still believe that it was Harry Street who put the "class" into the team that throughout the 1960's was known as "Classy Cas".

So began a career as Company Secretary which lasted for over fourteen years. In the early 1960s he was instrumental in the Club starting its own U17 and U19 teams. Club Director George Gregory, John Sheridan and the Secretary watched many local amateur matches which led to the Club signing a considerable number of very good local youngsters.

Soon after Len became Secretary Roy volunteered to answer fan mail from supporters requesting programmes or information about the Club or players. A letter was received from a young person asking for details which neither the Club nor our father were able to provide. This set him thinking he should try to collate the details and statistics of the Club's history and record it for future reference; he received help and assistance and collaborated with Norman Carr in ensuring their records were accurate.

Some older supporters may have a copy of Len Garbett's "*Castleford RLFC - A Sixty Years History*". This new book includes details not available when the 1986 book was produced; every match played, players of both teams, the scorers and referee, and also statistics for each season and each player.

In the first three months of 1963 a considerable number of sporting events were postponed due to frozen grounds. Castleford had been drawn at home against Leeds in the first round of the Challenge Cup to be played on 9th February. The Castleford Chairman, at that time Harry Clarkson, wanted the tie to go ahead, so straw bales were acquired and about 50 braziers and these were kept burning on the pitch, day and night, for several days leading up to match day by Albert Lunn the Castleford player and Groundsman, with the help of a large number of volunteers. The referee declared the pitch playable and 11,000 spectators turned up to watch the only match played that day. Castleford were leading 8–5 deep into the second half when Leeds' Welsh Wizard Lewis Jones broke through towards the line. Albert Lunn was a good tackler and was waiting for him at full back when Jones decided to kick over Albert, the ball bounced off Albert's chest and back into the hands of Jones who scored under the posts. Cas lost 8–10 and Albert Lunn retired shortly after that game due to ill health, having played in 363 games scoring 40 tries and 875 goals - a Club record of 1,870 points despite not always being the regular goal kicker.

Another notable Challenge Cup event took place in the second round of the 1967/68 season, when the Club were drawn away to Hull KR; a match that ended in a score of 9 points apiece with two drop goals from one of our greatest players, Alan Hardisty, meaning a replay at home. Hull KR refused to play an evening match, insisting they would be at a disadvantage as they did not have floodlights at that time. What happened on that day, 1st March 1967, was remarkable, 22,582 paying spectators were joined by several thousand non-paying spectators. Such was the interest in the replay many shops, factories, businesses and some schools decided to close early so that supporters were able to attend. Unfortunately they all arrived at the ground at about the same time. Hull KR refused to delay kick off by thirty minutes as this would have resulted in playing the latter part of the match under the floodlights. When those outside heard the match begin, the perimeter walls and fencing were breached. Fortunately the Castleford players did not need any advantage and a fantastic display against a very good Hull KR team resulted in a 13–6 win for the home team. Len made an appeal in the local papers to request those who had seen a fantastic game for free to make a financial donation. A small number did, including his brother Tom, but most did not!

Although Castleford won the BBC 2 Floodlit Competition three years running in the mid-1960s, the highlight for players, supporters, and Directors, were the two Wembley wins in 1969 and 1970.

Len was responsible for organising all aspects of the Club's two visits to Wembley, an enjoyable and proud experience for him. Whenever the winning players were invited to show off the Cup he was there, and the Cup went home with him afterwards where he placed it under his bed for safe keeping.

During his years as Secretary Len wrote and produced the programme for all home games and for several years he wrote a weekly article for *"The Rugby Leaguer"* newspaper, called *"Castleford Comments"*.

Len became a Director of the Club in January 1970, whilst still working full-time as a Rating Officer. Undertaking the Castleford RLFC Secretary's duties for what was in reality a full-time post the inevitable happened, and sadly he suffered his first coronary thrombosis followed shortly after by a second heart attack, and had little choice but to resign as Secretary on health grounds in August 1971.

He became Vice-Chairman in May 1973 and served as Chairman for a few months in 1978. Once again he was forced to resign for health reasons and subsequently resigned from the Castleford RLFC Board of Directors and the Management Committee of the Yorkshire Senior Competition, of which he had been a member for four years, in December 1978, and was then made an Honorary Life Member of the Club.

In July 1975 Len called a meeting of all former players, 23 attended the inaugural meeting forming the Castleford Rugby League Players' Association, and he became the Secretary/Organizer, resigning from this position due to ill health in July 1991, and becoming a Life Member and Vice President.

Over many years he was a regular member of The Queen's Park Bowling Club, and served as Secretary and President and eventually, again, becoming a Life Member.

Probably his proudest moment came when he was invited to become President of Castleford RLFC. He regarded it as a great honour, becoming only the third President following Gideon Shaw and Ronnie Simpson and he remained as President until his death in August 2009 which brought to a close his 74 year association with the Club. His wife of over 67 years, Sue, deserves great credit for the love and support which enabled him to fulfil his passion for Castleford RLFC despite him suffering with heart problems for many, many years.

He would proudly tell everyone his association with the Club took him from 'Boot Boy to President'. However he always said he wished his epitaph to read "He was the ideal family man, with an ideal family".

Len passed away in 2009 and Sue in 2014, leaving Sons Ian and Roy; their wives Barbara and Anne; Grandchildren Jill, Martin, Richard and Helen; their Spouses Stuart, Samantha and Lindsey; and Great Grandchildren Archie, Adam, Zak, Kate, Max and Rosa with very fond memories of a very loving couple.

(Reproduced From)
Castleford RLFC
A 60 Years History 1926 – 1986
By Len Garbett

It is generally accepted that Rugby League Football started in Castleford in 1926, but this however was only the year that the present Club became members of The Northern Rugby Football League. Records show that 1896 was a very significant year for Rugby in Castleford. Prior to and of course after 1896 there was a successful Rugby Union team in Castleford which provided many players for England such as H. Speed, R. Walton, E.J. Walton, J. W. Ward, J. T. Taylor, A. Starks and J. Rhodes.

On Tuesday, 13th May, 1896 a meeting was held in The George and Dragon Hotel, Bridge Street, Castleford — the sole purpose of the meeting to discuss the possibility of breaking away from Rugby Union, and joining the Northern Union, as Rugby League was known at that time. The meeting decided, amongst other things, that a Northern Union Football Club be formed under the title of Castleford Football Club. At a later meeting, on 2nd September, 1896 the team was selected to play the first match — RADCLIFFE at home (Lock Lane) — from A. Townend, A. Kettlewell, T. Needham, I. Wilson, T. Heptinstall, T. Farley, I. Clarke, F. T. Hunt, T. Barker, H. Speed (Captain), J. Rhodes, W. Holland, W. Dooley, J. Wood, J. Turner, H. Hall, R. Hanson, G. Shaw, J. VV. Wade. Minutes from various meetings show that the team played in the Second Division, wore jerseys with blue and yellow quarters, blue knickers and black stockings and played teams such as Radcliffe, Wakefield, Halifax, Bramley, Leeds, Hull, Holbeck Hall, Allerton, St. Helens, Batley Purlwell, Brighouse Rangers, Monk Fryston, Ripon, Morley, and Leeds Parish Church. Statistics show that the team played in the Second Division in 1902/3 finishing Fourth from the bottom, seventh from the top in 1903/4 and ninth from the top in 1904/5.

The present Club was formed in 1912, but no records are available, and eventually a team was entered in the Yorkshire Senior Competition in 1922

Playing in the Yorkshire Senior Competition in 1922/23 Castleford's record was: Played 26; Won 15; Drawn 2; Lost 9; Points For 264; Points Against 195. R.L. Challenge Cup 1st Round - 17th February1923 - Salford 16versus Castleford 0.

1923/24: Played 18; Won 14; Drawn 0; Lost 4; Points For 263; Points Against 94. Yorkshire Cup 1st Round - 13th October 1923 - Castleford 3 versus Batley 17. R.L. Cup 1st Round - 16th February 1924 - Hull Kingston Rovers 24 versus Castleford 2

1924/25: Played 32; Won 22; Drawn 3; Lost 7; Points For 403; Points Against188. Yorkshire Cup 1st Round-11th October1924 -Leeds 24 versus Castleford 10. R.L. Cup 1st Round - 14th February1925 - Hunslet 25 versus Castleford 0.

1925/26: Played 23; Won 14; Drawn 1; Lost 8; Points For 230; Points Against 191 Yorkshire Cup 1st Round - 10th October 1925 — Bradford 9 versus Castleford 9. Replay — 13th October 1925 — Castleford 5 versus Bradford Northern 11. R.L. Cup 1st Round - 13th February 1926 — Castleford 12 versus St. Helens Recs. 18 (played on Castleford Town F.C. ground at Wheldon Road).

It is known that the Club had various grounds in those early days, playing at Cutsyke — on a ground between the river and the canal over Lock Lane — a ground near The Aire and Calder Hotel, Wheldon Road — eventually moving to The Sandy Desert, Lock Lane, where they played their first season as members of the Northern Rugby Football League in 1926/27. However, The Sandy Desert was not up to Yorkshire Senior Competition standards especially as from time to time the adjoining River Aire overflowed its banks and flooded the playing area. Everyone connected with the Club set to work to improve the situation. The playing area was re-turfed, fencing and turnstiles were erected, two ex-army huts were bought for Dressing Rooms, and an old double deck bus was installed. The top deck was used as a Press Box, and the lower deck as a tea room. The players' pay in those days was 7/6 for a win and 5/- (*Old Money*) for losing.

Meanwhile, efforts were being made to become members of The Northern Rugby Football League. An application in 1923 was rejected out of hand - in 1924 the voting was 23 to 5 against, and the third application in 1925 saw joy, drama and tragedy. The voting was 12 for Castleford and 12 against them, and to Castleford's delight the Chairman gave his casting vote to Castleford. Jubilation turned to dismay when the Leeds Member pointed out that the Chairman had already voted for Bramley and therefore could not vote for Castleford. Undismayed, Castleford's representatives — Charlie Penfold and Walter Smith prepared for the next meeting on Wednesday, 17th February, 1926 at The Belle Vue Hotel, Bradford, and this time they were successful.

The next step was to form a Limited Company and at 7.30 p.m. on Wednesday, 7th July, 1926 the first meeting of the Directors took place in The North Eastern Hotel, Station Road, Castleford. Present were F. Scatchard (Chairman), F. Briggs, W. Smith, J. H. Williams, P. A.J. Fell, C. O'Rourke, A. E. Smith, T. Appleyard, S. Bolderson and A. Wyke. Mr. P. R. Appleyard was appointed Secretary, with the office of the Company being registered as Court Chambers, Jessop Street, Castleford, and F. W. Hanson appointed Auditor.

WITH THE YORKSHIRE SENIOR COMPETITION CHAMPIONSHIP SHIELD
Back Row: F Scratchard J Palliser W Smith <u>R Nicholls(9)</u> <u>L Wilson(28)</u> <u>G Hinton(31)</u>
<u>J Wormold(12)</u> F A Dabbage J Bamford F Goodward F S Grant
Middle Row: R C Holland <u>H Minton(3)</u> J Whitwell <u>T Needham(6)</u> G A Naylor J W Hardwick
W Taylor C S Beardmore
Front Row: J W Shirley J Kelly

Players who went on to play from 1926-27 onwards are underlined and with their Debut nunber in brackets. George (Gagger) Hinton who only played in the clubs first season had a benefit game on the 10 December 1927 (1927-28) therefore he must have played a number of season for the Club before they were granted full membership of the Rugby Football League.

The following is additional information on the early seasons since the above extract was published.

Season	P	W	D	L	FOR	AGT	PTS	PST	OF	Comp
1896-97	30	11	6	13	178	161	28	9	16	YSC
1897-98	30	16	1	13	256	208	33	6	16	YSC
1898-99	30	10	4	16	159	214	24	12	16	YSC
1899-00	30	11	3	16	155	199	25	11	16	YSC
1900-01	30	5	4	21	92	331	14	15	16	YSC
1901-02							21	9	14	YSC
1902-03	34	9	4	21	105	268	22	15	18	DIV 2
1903-04	32	18	3	11	185	194	39	7	17	DIV 2
1904-05	26	9	3	14	104	199	21	9	14	DIV 2
1905-06	20	3	2	15	45	325	8	28	31	I DIV
1906-07	WITHDREW FROM LEAGUE									

Team's Seasons
1926-27 to 2016

Players making their Debut are signified by their full name being in UPPERCASE letters followed by their Debut number in brackets.

Players playing in their final ever game are signified by their full name in Title Case and Underlined.

Players playing in only one game are signified by their full name being in UPPERCASE and Underlined.

Players leaving the Club and then retuning to make a second/third Debut retain their original Debut Number, their first 'last match' and subsequent debut are not signified.

S/O after a name signifies that the player was Sent Off.

S/B after a name signifies that the player was Sin Binned.

For all Full time and Half Time scores Castleford's score is always first.

From season 1965-66 to 2002 substitutes are indicated by the player's name in brackets following the name of the player he replaced.

From season 2003 onwards substitutes are named separately as it would have been too complicated to do otherwise.

The Statistics of many 'Friendlies' are shown throughout the Seasons, but they are not included in the Players Records. The matches that are included in the Players Records are shown in the Summary after the Players Seasons Records.

The photographs included in this book have been collected over the years from various sources. These will include pictures donated from publications such as:-

Bradford Telegraph and Argus	*Rugby Leaguer*
Castleford RLFC programmes	*Rugby Leaguer and League Express*
Castleford RLFC website	*Rugby League Weekly*
Other Rugby League Teams'	*Yorkshire Evening News*
programmes and websites	*Yorkshire Evening Post*
Other Club's Historians	*Yorkshire Post*
Pontefract and Castleford Express	*Malcolm Billingham*
Rugby League Journal	*SWPix*

There has never been any intention to breach anyone's copyright, and we apologise if anyone feels we have done so. As Historians we have only attempted to collect a photograph of any player that has played for Castleford Rugby League Football Club from any source we could.

SEASON 1926-27

Sat 28 Aug 1926 HULL away lost nil - 22
HULL - Jenny: Collins Davies A.N.Other Gwynne: Witty
Casewell: Beasty Pickering Bowman Smallwood Taylor
Bateson:
Tries - Bateson(3) Gwynne(2) Taylor: Goals - Bateson
Taylor:
CASTLEFORD - WILLIAM HARGRAVE(1): WILLIAM
SKELTON(2) HARRY MINTON(3) THOMAS DAVIES(4)
HARRY HUDSON(5): THOMAS NEEDHAM(6) ARTHUR JIM
TREVIS(CAPT)(7): JACK LEAKE(8) ROBERT NICHOLLS(9)
WILLIAM RENTON(10) JOSEPH MALKIN(11) JACK
WORMALD(12) JOSEPH(PAT)KELLY(13):
Referee T Johnson (Bramley) Att - 5000 H.T. 8 - nil

**Wed 1 Sept 1926 ROCHDALE HORNETS home
lost nil - 3**
CASTLEFORD - Hargrave: Hudson Davies Minton Skelton:
Needham Trevis: Leake Nicholls Renton
HARRY(DANNY)RUSSELL(14) Malkin Kelly:
ROCHDALE H - Wild: W.Evans H.Evans Walker Longshaw:
May Heaton: Harris Millard Wood Edwards Tetlow
Cooper: Try - Tetlow:
Referee C Denham (Broughton) Att - 2000 H.T. nil - 3

Sat 4 Sept 1926 HUNSLET home lost 3 - 12
CASTLEFORD - Hargrave: HARRY TAYLOR(15) Minton
Davies WILLIAM(NAT)ASQUITH(16): Needham Trevis:
THOMAS SHERWOOD(17) Nicholls Renton Malkin Russell
Kelly:
Try - Minton:
HUNSLET - Chapman: Coulson Dawson Davies
Broughton: Young Jones: Band Wood Jenkins Keating
Crowther Clarkson:
Tries - Clarkson Jenkins Broughton Keating:
Referee H Swift (Halifax) Att - 2000 H.T. 3 - 6

Mon 6 Sept 1926 LEEDS away lost 3 - 15
LEEDS - Rosser: Smith Brough Lloyd James: Williams
Banks: Litt Hall Mason McCade Kibbler Davies:
Tries - Lloyd(2) Smith: Goals - Litt(3):
CASTLEFORD - Skelton: Asquith ELIJAH HUNTER(18)
Davies ALBERT E KEMP(19): Trevis JAMES NASH(20): T
Sherwood Nicholls Renton Russell Malkin Kelly:
Try - Asquith:
Referee F Chambers (Huddersfield) Att - 3000 H.T. nil -3

**Sat 11 Sept 1926 ROCHDALE HORNETS away
lost 5 - 33**
ROCHDALE H - Wild: W.Evans H.Evans Walker Langshaw:
May Heaton: Harris Millard Valentine Edwards Tetlow
Hinam:
Tries - Langshaw(4) W.Evans(2) May Millard Edwards:
Goals - May(2) Wild:
CASTLEFORD - Skelton: Kemp Hunter ARTHUR
ATKINSON(21) WILLIAM BROWN(22): Nash Minton: T
Sherwood Nicholls Renton RICHARD WALTON(23) Russell
Kelly:
Try - Nicholls: Goal Hunter:
Referee H Swift (Halifax) Att - 4000 H.T. nil - 19

**Sat 18 Sept 1926 BRADFORD NORTHERN home
won 37 - 25**
CASTLEFORD - ARTHUR FELTHAM(24): Skelton Hargrave
Needham Hudson: Nash ALBERT DICKINSON(25): T
Sherwood Nicholls Renton Malkin Russell Kelly:
Tries - Hudson(3) Dickinson(2) Nicholls(2) Needham
Hargrave:
Goals - Hargrave(4) Feltham:
BRADFORD N - Brierley: Vowles Perkins Redmond
Johnson: Melling Gledhill: Smith Hardaker Wilson Craven
Lowery Young:
Tries - Johnson(2) Young(2) Perkins: Goals - Melling(5):
Referee W G Rees (Leeds) Att - 4000 H.T. 14 - 3

Sat 25 Sept 1926 YORK away lost 10 - 21
YORK - Owen: Hook T.Mills J.Corsi Van Heerden: W.Mills
Brittain: Mirfield Myers Betteridge Keech Dawson Cooper:
Tries - Owen T.Mills Corsi Brittain Cooper: Goals -
Keech(3):
CASTLEFORD - Feltham: Hudson Hargrave Needham
Kemp: Dickinson Nash: T Sherwood WILLIAM
SHERWOOD(26): Renton Malkin Russell Kelly:
Tries - Hargrave (2): Goals - Hargrave (2):
Referee F Peel (Bradford) Att - 3000 H.T. 5 - 10

Sat 2 Oct 1926 HUDDERSFIELD home lost 2 - 12
CASTLEFORD - Feltham: Hudson Needham Hargrave
Dickinson: Nash Trevis: Leake OWEN ROBERTS(27)
Renton Malkin Russell T.Sherwood:
Goal - Hargrave:
HUDDERSFIELD - Walmsley: Walker Oliver Edmondson
Watts: H.JonesE.Reed: H.Sherwood Barlow Lumb
Cracknell Phillips Tiffany:
Tries - Barlow Cracknell: Goals Oliver(2) Walmsley:
Referee F Peel (Bradford) Att - 4000 H.T. 2 - 10

**Sat 9 Oct 1926 YORK away lost 2 - 24
YORKSHIRE CUP ROUND 1**
YORK - Owen: Hook T.Mills Corsi Van Heerden: W.Mills
Brittain: Myers Mirfield Betteridge Keech Dawson Cooper:
Tries - Van Heerden(3) Hook T.Mills Dawson: Goals -
Owen(2) Keech:
CASTLEFORD - Feltham: Hudson Elijah Hunter
Hargrave(S/O)Minton: Needham Trevis: Leake Nicholls
Renton Malkin Russell JOHN(LINA)WILSON(28):
Goal - Hargrave:
Referee J Eddon (Swinton) Att - 2685 H.T. 2 - 6

**Sat 16 Oct 1926 FEATHERSTONE ROVERS away
lost 9 - 24**
FEATHERSTONE R - S.Denton: Broom Hirst T.C.Askin
Taylor: Annable Morgan: Barraclough Lorriman Woolley
Smith Clements Ashton:
Tries - Morgan Ashton Askin Taylor Lorriman Hirst: Goals
- Denton(3)
CASTLEFORD - Feltham: Harry Minton Hargrave
Needham Atkinson: CLARENCE MANN(29) Dickinson:
Renton Nicholls Leake Malkin Russell Taylor:
Try - Taylor: Goals - Feltham(3):
Referee H Horsfall (Batley) Att - 4000 H.T. 7 - 8

Sat 23 Oct 1926 DEWSBURY home lost 5 - 15

CASTLEFORD - Feltham: Atkinson Davies Trevis Dickinson:
Mann TONY MUSCROFT(30):
GEORGE(GAGGER)HINTON(31) Nicholls Renton Malkin
Russell Harry Taylor:
Try - Malkin: Goals - Feltham(DG):
DEWSBURY - Stocks: Raywood Smith Jim Lyman Roberts:
McLoughlin Stockley: Brown Rhodes Lee Ryan Westerdale
Joe Lyman:
Tries - Raywood(3): Goals - Joe Lyman(2) Raywood:
Referee T Johnson (Bramley) Att - 4000 H.T. 3 - 7

Sat 30 Oct 1926 HALIFAX away lost 6 - 18

HALIFAX - Davies: Murchison Rhodes Beeby Peckett: King
Watkins: Rawbone Halliday Brown Swan Evans Rees:
Tries - Murchison(2) Peckett Swan: Goals - Davies(3):
CASTLEFORD - Skelton: Atkinson Davies Needham Albert
E.Kemp: Nash Feltham: Hinton Nicholls Renton Malkin
T.Sherwood Kelly: Tries - Atkinson Malkin:
Referee G Rees (Leeds) Att - 4000 H.T. nil - 18

Sat 6 Nov 1926 SALFORD home won 10 - 3

CASTLEFORD - Feltham: Atkinson Davies Skelton
Hargrave: Needham Nash: Hinton Nicholls Renton Malkin
T.Sherwood Kelly:
Tries - Malkin Kelly: Goals - Feltham(2):
SALFORD - Clegg: Southward Peacock Somerville Boyd:
Mannison Meek: Skamper Grice Pemberton Muir Burgess
Gore: Try - Boyd:
Referee F Fairhirst (Wigan) Att - 5000 H.T. 5 - nil

Sat 13 Nov 1926 HUNSLET away lost 6 - 16

HUNSLET - Chapman: Coulson Dawson Davies Buck:
Young Haworth: Wood Band Keating Crowther Guerin
Clarkson:
Tries - Dawson Coulson Clarkson Guerin: Goals -
Guerin(1)(DG):
CASTLEFORD - Feltham: Atkinson Davies Hargrave
Malkin: Needham Clarence Mann: Hinton Nicholls Renton
NORMAN DIXON(32) T.Sherwood Kelly:
Goals - Feltham(3):
Referee F H Chambers (Hud'field) Att - 4000 H.T. 2 - 13

Sat 20 Nov 1926 HALIFAX home lost 4 - 8

CASTLEFORD - Feltham: Hargrave HARRY SYLVESTER(33)
Davies Atkinson: Nash Needham: Hinton Nicholls Renton
Malkin T.Sherwood Kelly:
Goals - Feltham (1)(DG):
HALIFAX - Davies: Murdison Kitson W.Young H.Young:
Todd Watkins: Rawbone Halliday Brown Swan Douglas
Townend:
Tries - W.Young Kitson: Goal - W.Young:
Referee A Brown (Wakefield) Att - 5000 H.T. 2 - nil

Sat 27 Nov 1926 DEWSBURY away lost 5 - 7

DEWSBURY - Stocks: Lyons Jim Lyman Smith Coates: Hirst
Roberts: Rhodes Mitchell Lee Ryan Donnelly Joe Lyman:
Try - Smith: Goals - Joe Lyman(2):
CASTLEFORD - Feltham: Skelton Davies Hargrave
Dickinson: Needham Trevis: T.Sherwood Nicholls Renton
Malkin Dixon Kelly:
Try - Feltham: Goal - Feltham
Referee F J Peel (Bradford) Att - 2000 H.T. 5 - 7
Abandoned After 50 Minutes (Replayed 28 Dec1926)

Sat 4 Dec 1926 LEEDS home won 10 - 9

CASTLEFORD - Feltham: Skelton Davies Hargrave
Dickinson: Needham Trevis: T.Sherwood Nicholls Renton
Malkin Dixon Kelly:
Tries - Needham Malkin: Goals - Feltham(2):
LEEDS - Rosser: Bacon Brough Williams Jenkins: Swift
Lloyd: Wharville Thomas Litt Thompson Davies Watkins:
Try - Thomas: Goals - Thomoson(3):
Referee F Chambers (Huddersfield) Att - 4000 H.T. 5 - 4

Sat 11 Dec 1926 LEIGH home lost 3 - 16

CASTLEFORD - Feltham: Skelton Davies Hargrave
Dickinson: Nash Trevis: T.Sherwood Nicholls Renton
Malkin Wormald Kelly:
Try - Trevis:
LEIGH - Clarkson: Roberts Emery Osborne Baldwin:
Russell Moss: Winstanley Leyland Worrell Myers Wood
Blackburn:
Tries - Roberts Emery Moss Blackburn:
Goals - Clarkson(2):
Referee W Marshall (Widnes) Att - 2000 H.T. nil - 8

Sat 18 Dec 1926 HUDDERSFIELD away lost 12 - 27

HUDDERSFIELD - Walmsley: Walker Fisher Bowkett Smart:
H.Jones Williams: H.Sherwood Barlow Lumb Cracknell
Phillips Tiffany:
Tries - Walker(3) Smart(2) Walmsley Bowkett: Goals -
Walmsley(3)
CASTLEFORD - Feltham: Dickinson JOSEPH McTIGHE(34)
Davies Hargrave: Needham Trevis: Renton Nicholls
T.Sherwood Malkin Wormald Dixon:
Tries - Dickinson Needham: Goals - Feltham(3):
Referee G Rees (Leeds) Att - 4000 H.T. nil - 11

Sat 25 Dec 1926 BRAMLEY away lost nil - 8

BRAMLEY - Powell: T.Davidson H.Roberts Witherington
Carter: Gadsby E.Pashley: Tasker A.Firth Pickles Mann
Hesketh Bowden:
Tries - Gadsby Firth: Goal - Powell:
CASTLEFORD - Feltham: Dickinson McTighe Davies
Hargrave: Needham Trevis: Renton Nicholls T.Sherwood
Russell Wormald Dixon:
Referee A Brown (Wakefield) Att   H.T.

Mon 27 Dec 1926 HULL KINGSTON ROVERS home draw 5 - 5

CASTLEFORD - Hargrave: HARRY(NABS)OWEN(35)
McTighe Feltham Davies: Needham Trevis: Renton
Nicholls T.Sherwood Malkin Wormald Russell:
Try - Feltham: Goal - Feltham:
HULL K R - Osborne: Harris Cook Spamer Austin: Hoult
McIntyre: J.R.Wilkinson Britton J.M.Wilkinson Westerdale
Bielby Feetham:
Try - Bielby: Goal - Osborne:
Referee F Peel (Bradford) Att - 5000 H.T. 5 - 5

SEASON 1926-27

Tuesday 28 Dec 1926 DEWSBURY away lost 6 - 12
DEWSBURY - Joe Lyman: Rayner McLaughlin Moss Smith:
First Coates: Mitchell Rhodes Lee Ryan Fox Donnelly:
Tries - Smith(2): Goals - Coates(2) Joe Lyman:
CASTLEFORD - Feltham: Owen Asquith Davies McTighe:
Needham Trevis: Renton Nicholls T.Sherwood Malkin
Wormald Russell: Tries - Owen Asquith:
Referee F Peel (Bradford) Att - 2000 H.T. nil - 8

Sat 1 Jan 1927 BATLEY away lost 12 - 34
BATLEY - H.Scott: Stacey McGraw Smith Wale: W.Scott
Fowler: Leeming Demaine Middlemass Collins Carter
Gallagher:
Tries - Wale(3) Carter(3) Stacey McGraw:
Goals - H.Scott(4)Fowler:
CASTLEFORD - Hargrave: Owen McTighe Feltham Davies:
Needham Trevis: Renton Nicholls Wormald Malkin
T.Sherwood Russell:
Tries - Davies Trevis: Goals - Feltham(3): 2000 H.T. 2- nil
Referee Rev F H Chambers(Hud'field) Att -

Sat 8 Jan 1927 WAKEFIELD TRINITY home lost nil -8
CASTLEFORD - Feltham: Owen Hudson McTighe ALBERT
MARSHALL(36): Needham Trevis: Renton Nicholls(S/O)
Wormald Malkin T.Sherwood Kelly:
WAKEFIELD T - Ward: Bateson Davies Pickup C.Pollard:
Parkin Pearce: Kendall White(S/O) Waters Cole Maidment
Gossop: Tries - Pickup Bateson: Goal - Pollard:
Referee H Horsfall (Batley) Att - 6000 H.T. nil - 3

**Sat 15 Jan 1927 BROUGHTON RANGERS home
lost nil - 14**
CASTLEFORD - Feltham: Atkinson McTighe Needham
Davies: D.J.ALDRIDGE(37) Trevis: Renton THOMAS
H.JDSON(38) Wormald Malkin Russell Kelly:
BROUGHTON R - Bevan: Evans Condrew Dingsdale
Bentham: Lomas Davies: Dixon Curren Scott Bestwick
Smith Phillips:
Tries - Bentham Phillips Evans Dingsdale: Goal - Bevan:
Referee R Jones (Widnes) Att - 3500 H.T. nil - 3

**Sat 22 Jan 1927 BRADFORD NORTHERN away
lost 18 - 19**
BRADFORD N - Robinson: J.Smith Catterall T.R.Smith
Hughes: Melling Rowlands: H.Smith Moran Lowry
Woodruffe Wright Youmg:
Tries - J.Smith(2) Young(2) Rowlands: Goals - Catterall(2):
CASTLEFORD - Feltham: McTighe Malkin Dickinson
H Hudson: Needham Trevis: Hinton JAMES PLIMMER(39)
Leake Wormald Renton T.Sherwood:
Goals - Feltham(3):
Referee A Brown (Wakefield) Att - 2000 H.T. 14 - nil

Sat 29 Jan 1927 LEIGH away lost 5 - 15
LEIGH - Clarkson: Unsworth Emery Osborne Baldwin:
Bithell Moss: Leyland Winstanley: Worrall Myers Wood
Blackburn: Tries - Baldwin(3) Unsworth Osborne:
CASTLEFORD - Hargrave: McTighe Feltham Thomas
Davies H.Hudson: Trevis Nash: Renton Nicholls Leake

Malkin Wormald T.Sherwood:
Try - Renton: Goal - Feltham:
Referee F Peel (Bradford) Att - 3000 H.T. nil - 5

Sat 5 Feb 1927 YORK home won 6 - 3
CASTLEFORD - Hargrave: H.Hudson Feltham WILLIAM
BATTEN(40) WILLIAM R.HARRIS(41): Trevis McTighe:
Leake Nicholls Renton Malkin Wormald T.Sherwood:
Goals - Feltham(3):
YORK - Tordoff: Hook Mills Corsi Perkins: Pickard Hodges:
Davies Mirfield Betteridge Dawson Cooper Van Heerde:
Try - Mills:
Referee G Rees (Leeds) Att - 3000 H.T. 2 - nil

**Sat 12 Feb 1927 BROUGHTON RANGERS home
lost 5 - 18 CHALLENGE CUP ROUND 1**
CASTLEFORD - Hargrave: H.Hudson Feltham Batten
William R.Harris Trevis McTighe: Leake Nicholls Renton
Malkin Wormald Russell:
Try - Batten: Goal - Feltham:
BROUGHTON R - Bevan: Evans Condren Dingsdale
Bentham: Lomas Davies: Dixon Curran Smith Bestwick
Larkin Phillips:
Tries - Evans(2) Condren Dingsdale: Goals - Bevan(3):
Referee B Ennion (Wigan) Att - 7336 H.T. nil - 9

Wed 23 Feb 1927 BRAMLEY home lost 9 - 12
CASTLEFORD - Feltham: H.Hudson Batten Sylvester
Hargrave: Needham McTighe: Renton Plimmer Wormald
Malkin ERNEST HOBSON(42) Kelly:
Try - McTighe: Goals - Feltham(2) Hargrave(DG):
BRAMLEY - Parkinson: A.Davidson Gadsby Withington
T.Davidson: Judd Marsden: Pickles Bowden Hesketh
Tasker Sykes Moore:
Tries - A.Davidson Gadsby: Goals - Sykes(3):
Referee F H Chambers (Hud.field) Att - 1000 H.T. 2 - 7

**Sat 5 Mar 1927 WAKEFIELD TRINITY away
lost 14 - 17**
WAKEFIELD T - C.Pollard: Bateson E.Pollard Siswick Jones:
Parkin Pickup: Gibson White Waters Cowes Horton
Absalom
Tries - Bateson(2) Horton: Goals - C.Pollard(2) E.Pollard(2):
CASTLEFORD - Feltham: Owen Batten Hargrave Atkinson:
Needham McTighe: Leake Plimmer Hinton Malkin
Joseph(Pat)Kelly VICTOR KINSEY(43):
Tries - Hargrave(2) McTighe Leake: Goal - Hargrave:
Referee G Rees (Leeds) Att - 5000 H.T. 6 - 13

Sat 12 Mar 1927 KEIGHLEY home won 32 - 5
CASTLEFORD - Feltham: H.Hudson Batten Hargrave
Atkinson: Needham McTighe: Hinton Nicholls Leake
Malkin(S/O)Renton Kinsey:
Tries - Kinsey(3) Leake H.Hudson Needham: Goals -
Feltham(4)Hargrave(3):
KEIGHLEY - White: Kendall Pearson H.Burton Craven:
Phillips Fowler: Trusler Watson Langhorn Thompson
C.Burton Stamper: Try - Stamper: Goal - Kendall:
Referee R Robinson (Bradford) Att - H.T. 15 - 2

SEASON 1926-27

Sat 19 Mar 1927 HULL home lost 12 - 22
CASTLEFORD - Feltham: H.Hudson Batten Hargrave
Atkinson: Needham McTighe: Hinton Nicholls Leake
Malkin Renton Kinsey:
Tries - Feltham Hargrave: Goals - Hargrave(3):
HULL - Jenny: Collins Davies Beardshaw Gwynne: Caswell
Whitty: Bowman Pickering Bolderson Smallwood
Errington Bateson:
Tries - Collins(2) Davies Gwynne Beardshaw Bateson:
Goals - Bateson(2):
Referee H Swift (Halifax) Att - 4000 H.T. nil - 11

Sat 2 Apr 1927 BATLEY home lost 9 - 11
CASTLEFORD - Feltham: H.Hudson Batten Hargrave
Atkinson: Needham McTighe: Hinton Nicholls Leake
Plimmer Renton Kinsey:
Try - Hinton: Goals - Hargrave(3):
BATLEY - Oliver: Wale Davidge Davies Scott: Rees Fowler:
Leeming Demaine Douglas Collins Middlemass Carter:
Tries - Wale Davies Carter: Goal - Scott:
Referee T Johnson (Bramley) Att - 3000 H.T. 9 - 6

**Sat 9 Apr 1927 HULL KINGSTON ROVERS away
lost 4 - 18**
HULL K R - Osborne: Harris Cook Spamer Austin: McIntyre
Raynor: J.R.Wilkinson Boagey J.H.Wilkinson Bielby
Westerdale Feetham:
Tries - Feetham(2) Harris Austin: Goals - Osborne(3):
CASTLEFORD - Feltham: H.Hudson William Batten
Hargrave Atkinson: Nash McTighe: Hinton Nicholls Leake
Plimmer Renton Kinsey:
Goals - Hargrave Feltham(DG):
Referee W Lynch (Leeds) Att -1000 H.T. nil - 2

**Fri 15 Apr 1927 BROUGHTON RANGERS away
lost 7 - 32**
BROUGHTON R - Bevan: Evans Lomas Dingsdale
Bentham: Sharrocks Davies: Tonge Rothwell Eland
Simpson Smith Phillips:
Tries - Phillips(2) Evans(2) Dingsdale Rothwell Bentham
Simpson: Goals - Bevan(4):

CASTLEFORD - Feltham: Atkinson Hargrave Needham
Owen: Nash McTighe: Hinton Nicholls Leake Renton
Plimmer Kinsey Try - McTighe: Goals - Feltham(2):
Referee H Swift (Halifax) Att - 3000 H.T. 2 - 14

Sat 16 Apr 1927 KEIGHLEY away lost nil - 14
KEIGHLEY - J.Davies: Blaymire White Holmes Spedding:
Pearson Hanson: Langhorn Trusler Stamper Thompson
Burton McGoun:
Tries - Burton(2) Holmes Blaymire: Goal - Pearson:
CASTLEFORD - Atkinson: Owen Hargrave Feltham
H.Hudson: McTighe Needham: Hinton Nicholls Leake
Renton Malkin Kinsey:
Referee F H Chambers (Hud'field) Att - 3500 H.T. nil - nil

**Mon 18 Apr 1927 FEATHERSTONE ROVERS home
lost 3 - 13**
CASTLEFORD - Atkinson: Malkin Feltham Hargrave
H.Hudson: Nash Needham: Hinton Nicholls Leake Renton
Russell(S/O) Kinsey:
Try - Malkin:
FEATHERSTONE R - S.Denton: J.Denton Taylor Askin
Cartwright: Annable Williams: Woolley Barraclough
Hepworth Haigh Clements Ashton:
Tries - Cartwright Haigh Annable:
Goals - J.Denton Clements:
Referee R Robinson (Bradford) Att -   H.T. 3 - 3

Sat 23 Apr 1927 SALFORD away lost 7 - 9
SALFORD - Williams: Davies Peacock Garland Southward:
Mannion Meek: Mann Price Butterworth Muir Haines
Gore:
Tries - Garland Southward Gore:
CASTLEFORD - Atkinson: Malkin H.Hudson Feltham
William Skelton: Nash ROBERT MATTICK(44):
George(Gagger)Hinton Nicholls Leake Plimmer Renton
Kinsey:
Try - H.Hudson: Goals - Feltham(2):
Referee F Peel (Bradford) Att - 3000 H.T.

William Hargrave
D. No 1
19626-27 to 1929-30

Harry Hudson
D. No 5
1926-27 to 1932-33

Tommy Needham
D. No 6
1926-27 to 1928-29

Arthur J Trevis
First Captain
D. No 7
1926-27 to 1929-30

Jack Leake
D. No 8
1926-27 to 1928-29

Bob Nicholls
D. No 9
1926-27 to 1930-31

Bill Renton
D. No 10
1926-27 to 1928-29

Joe Malkin
D. No 11
1926-27 to 1932-33

Jack Wormald
D. No 12
1926-27 to 1929-30

Harry(Danny) Russell
D. No 14
1926-27 to 1933-34

William (Nat) Asquith
D. No 16
1926-27 to 1930-31

Thomas Sherwood
D. No 17
1926-27 to 1927-28

James Nash
D. no 20
1926-27 to 1927-28

Arthur Atkinson
D. No 21
1926-27 to 1941-42

Richard (Dick) Walton
D. No 23
1926-27 to 1939-40

Arthur Feltham
D. No 24
1926-27 to 1929-30

George (Gagger Hinton
D. No 31
1926-27

James Plimmer
D. No 39
1926-27 to 1935-36

SEASON 1926-27

D.N	PLAYER		DEBUT	L MATCH	APP	SUB	T.AP	TR'S	G'LS	D.G	P'TS
1	HARGRAVE	WILLIAM	28/08/1926		30	0	30	6	19	1	58
2	SKELTON	WILLIAM	28/08/1926	23/04/1927	11	0	11	0	0	0	0
3	MINTON	HARRY	28/08/1926	16/10/1926	6	0	6	1	0	0	3
4	DAVIES	THOMAS	28/08/1926	29/01/1927	19	0	19	1	0	0	3
5	HUDSON	HARRY	28/08/1926		19	0	19	5	0	0	15
6	NEEDHAM	THOMAS	28/08/1926		30	0	30	5	0	0	15
7	TREVIS	ARTHUR	28/08/1926		21	0	21	3	0	0	9
8	LEAKE	JACK	28/08/1926		18	0	18	3	0	0	9
9	NICHOLLS	ROBERT	28/08/1926		33	0	33	3	0	0	9
10	RENTON	WILLIAM	28/08/1926		38	0	38	1	0	0	3
11	MALKIN	JOSEPH	28/08/1926		34	0	34	5	0	0	15
12	WORMALD	JACK	28/08/1926		14	0	14	0	0	0	0
13	KELLY	JOSEPH (PAT)	28/08/1926	5/03/1927	18	0	18	1	0	0	3
14	RUSSELL	HARRY (DANNY)	1/09/1926		17	0	17	0	0	0	0
15	TAYLOR	HARRY	4/09/1926	23/10/1926	3	0	3	1	0	0	3
16	ASQUITH	WILLIAM (NAT)	4/09/1926		3	0	3	2	0	0	6
17	SHERWOOD	THOMAS	4/09/1926		22	0	22	1	0	0	3
18	HUNTER	ELIJAH	6/09/1926	9/10/1926	3	0	3	0	1	0	2
19	KEMP	ALBERT E.	6/09/1926	30/10/1926	4	0	4	0	0	0	0
20	NASH	JAMES	6/09/1926		14	0	14	0	0	0	0
21	ATKINSON	ARTHUR	11/09/1926		17	0	17	1	0	0	3
22	BROWN	WILLIAM	11/09/1926	11/09/1926	1	0	1	0	0	0	0
23	WALTON	RICHARD	11/09/1926		1	0	1	0	0	0	0
24	FELTHAM	ARTHUR	18/09/1926		34	0	34	3	38	3	91
25	DICKINSON	ALBERT	18/09/1926		11	0	11	3	0	0	9
26	SHERWOOD	WILLIAM	25/09/1926		1	0	1	0	0	0	0
27	ROBERTS	OWEN	2/10/1926	2/10/1926	1	0	1	0	0	0	0
28	WILSON	JOHN (LINA)	9/10/1926	9/10/1926	1	0	1	0	0	0	0
29	MANN	CLARENCE	16/10/1926	13/11/1926	3	0	3	0	0	0	0
30	MUSCROFT	TONY	23/10/1926	23/10/1926	1	0	1	0	0	0	0
31	HINTON	GEORGE (GAGGER)	23/10/1926	23/04/1927	15	0	15	1	0	0	3
32	DIXON	NORMAN	13/11/1926		5	0	5	0	0	0	0
33	SYLVESTER	HARRY	20/11/1926		2	0	2	0	0	0	0
34	McTIGHE	JOSEPH	18/12/1926		19	0	19	3	0	0	9
35	OWEN	HARRY (NABS)	27/12/1926		7	0	7	1	0	0	3
36	MARSHALL	ALBERT	8/01/1927		1	0	1	0	0	0	0
37	ALDRIDGE	D J	15/01/1927	15/01/1927	1	0	1	0	0	0	0
38	HUDSON	THOMAS	15/01/1927	15/01/1927	1	0	1	0	0	0	0
39	PLIMMER	JAMES	22/01/1927		7	0	7	0	0	0	0
40	BATTEN	WILLIAM	5/02/1927	9/04/1927	8	0	8	1	0	0	3
41	HARRIS	WILLIAM R.	5/02/1927	12/02/1927	2	0	2	0	0	0	0
42	HOBSON	ERNEST	23/02/1927	23/02/1927	1	0	1	0	0	0	0
43	KINSEY	VICTOR	5/03/1927		9	0	9	3	0	0	9
44	MATTICK	ROBERT	23/04/1927		1	0	1	0	0	0	0
44			**44**	**18**	**507**	**0**	**507**	**54**	**58**	**4**	**286**

COMPETITION		P	W	D	L	FOR	AGT
LEAGUE	POSITION 29 OF 29	36	5	1	30	274	550
YORK'S CUP		1	0	0	1	2	24
RL CUP		1	0	0	1	5	18
MATCH VOID DEWSBURY		1	0	0	1	5	7
PLAYERS RECORDS		**39**	**5**	**1**	**33**	**286**	**599**

The other 28 members of the Northern Rugby Football League in our first season were: -Barrow, Batley, Bradford Northern, Bramley, Broughton Rangers, Dewsbury, Featherstone Rovers, Halifax, Huddersfield, Hull KR, Hull, Hunslet, Keighley, Leeds, Leigh, Oldham, Pontypridd, Rochdale Hornets, Salford, St Helens Recs, St Helens, Swinton, Wakefield Trinity, Warrington, Widnes, Wigan Highfield, Wigan, and York.

Clubs did not play the same number of games, as clubs from the same county played each other home and away and then arranged their own inter-county fixtures, therefore league positions were decided on percentages.

The Castleford home games for this season only were played at the 'Sandy Desert' pitch on Lock Lane, and Bill Hargrave set the mark for the most points in a League game at 11, v Bradford N at home on 18 September 1926.

The first trainer was William H (Billy) Rhodes.

Sat 27 Aug 1927 HUDDERSFIELD home lost nil - 3
CASTLEFORD - Atkinson: Harry(Nabs)Owen Feltham
Sylvester Hudson: Needham Trevis: Renton Nicholls Leake
A.R.RUSHWORTH(45) Sherwood Kinsey:
HUDDERSFIELD - Brook: Mills Bowkett Fisher Smart:
Williams Reed: Gee Tiffany Dyson Ryan Kibbler Phillips:
Try - Mills:
Referee R Robinson (Bradford) Att - 5000 H.T. nil - nil

Sat 3 Sep 1927 HULL away lost 10 - 19
HULL - Jenny: Garvey Batten Whitty Gwynne: Hall Caswell:
Oliver Pickering Bowman Smallwood R.Taylor Bateson:
Tries - Gwynne(2) Taylor Smallwood Bateson:
Goals - Bateson(2):
CASTLEFORD - Feltham: McTighe Hudson Atkinson
Sylvester: Needham Mattick: Leake Nicholls Renton BEN
RUSSELL(46) Sherwood Kinsey:
Tries - McTighe Renton: Goals - Feltham(2):
Referee J Johnson (Bramley) Att -   H.T. 5 - 14

Sat 10 Sep 1927 DEWSBURY home won 9 - 5
CASTLEFORD - Feltham: McTighe Hudson Atkinson
Sylvester: Needham Trevis: Renton Nicholls Leake Dixon
Rushworth Kinsey:
Try - Trevis: Goals - Feltham(2) Atkinson:
DEWSBURY - Stocks: Raywood Smith Layhe Midgley:
Coates Roberts: Mitchell Rhodes Hobson Bland Donnelly
Fox: Try - Layhe: Goal - Roberts(DG):
Referee F Peel (Bradford) Att - 4000 H.T. 7 - 5

Sat 17 Sep 1927 BRAMLEY away won 15 - nil
BRAMLEY - Parkinson: Carter Casey Gadsby Davidson:
Pashley Marsden: Sykes Bowden Tasker Firth Pearson
Moore:
CASTLEFORD - Hargrave: Hudson McTighe Atkinson
Sylvester: Needham Trevis: Renton Nicholls Leake
B Russell Malkin Kinsey: Tries - Sylvester Trevis Renton:
Goals - Atkinson(2) Hargrave(DG):
Referee B Laughlin (Batley) Att - 3400 H.T. 10 - nil

Sat 24 Sep 1927 PONTYPRIDD home won 26 - 6
CASTLEFORD - Hargrave: Hudson McTighe Atkinson
Sylvester: Needham Trevis: Renton Nicholls Leake Malkin
Rushworth Kinsey:
Tries - Needham(2) Atkinson Trevis Nicholls Kinsey:
Goals - Hargrave(2) Atkinson Needham:
PONTYPRIDD - F.Thomas: Garside Mills J.Thomas
Loveluck: Fairfax Rees: Green White Rellings Coleman
Jones Kay: Tries - Loveluck(2):
Referee G Rees (Leeds) Att - 3000 H.T. 13 - nil

Sat 1 Oct 1927 WIGAN HIGHFIELD away lost 2 - 22
WIGAN H - Osbaldestin: Cowley Catterall Winstanley
Binkhorn: Parkinson Grimes: Bentham Longshaw Norburn
Green Thompson Lyon: Tries - Parkinson(2)Winstanley
Binkhorn Bentham Norburn: Goals - Osbaldestin(2):
CASTLEFORD - Hargrave: Hudson McTighe Atkinson
Sylvester: Needham Trevis: Renton Nicholls Malkin Kinsey
Leake FRED CARTER(47): Goal - Hargrave:
Referee H Swift (Halifax) Att -   H.T. nil - 11

Sat 8 Oct 1927 BRAMLEY home won 22 - nil
YORKSHIRE CUP ROUND 1
CASTLEFORD - Hargrave: McTighe Atkinson JOSEPH
A.(JIM) BACON(48) Hudson: Needham Trevis: Renton
Nicholls Leake Kinsey Malkin Carter:
Tries - Hudson(2) Leake Kinsey:
Goals - Atkinson(3) Hargrave McTighe:
BRAMLEY - Parkinson: Marsden Casey Withington Carter:
Gadsby Cooper Hesketh Bowden Reed Firth Tanner
Ward:
Referee W Wood (Oldham) Att – 6000 H.T. 8 - nil

Sat 15 Oct 1927 BRADFORD NORTHERN away
lost 10 - 12
BRADFORD N - Dalby: Cox T.Smith Brogden J.Smith:
Melling W.Smith: Moran Hardaker Wood Thorber Hulme
Woodruffe: Tries - Cox J.Smith: Goals - Melling(3):
CASTLEFORD - Hargrave: McTighe Atkinson Bacon
Hudson: Needham Trevis: Renton Nicholls Leake Kinsey
Wormald Carter:
Tries - Bacon Carter: Goals - Atkinson(2):
Referee F H Chambers (Hud'field) Att - 6000 H.T. 4 - 2

Thu 20 Oct 1927 HULL away draw 7 - 7
YORKSHIRE CUP ROUND 2
HULL - Jenny: Gwynne Batten Whitty Davies: Hall Caswell:
Bowman Balderson Short Errington Smallwpood Bateson:
Try - Gwynne: Goals - Bateson(2):
CASTLEFORD - Hargrave: McTighe Atkinson Bacon
Sylvester: Needham Trevis: Renton Nicholls Leake
Wormald Malkin Carter:
Try - Sylvester: Goals - Atkinson(2):
Referee F Fairhurst (Wigan) Att - 3000 H.T. 5 - 5

Sat 22 Oct 1927 LEEDS home lost 3 - 13
CASTLEFORD - Hargrave: McTighe Atkinson Bacon
Sylvester: Needham Trevis: Renton Nicholls Leake
Wormald A.R.Rushworth Kinsey: Try - Leake:
LEEDS - Brough Andrews O'Rourke Watkins Bailey:
Williams Moores: Hall Thomas Slater Pascoe Davies
Woolmore:
Tries - Davies(2) Andrews: Goals - Pascoe(2):
Referee R Robinson (Bradford) Att - 3000 H.T. 3 - 7

Wed 26 Oct 1927 HULL home lost nil - 3
YORKSHIRE CUP ROUND 2 REPLAY
CASTLEFORD - Hargrave: Hudson Bacon Atkinson
Sylvester: Needham Trevis: Renton Nicholls(S/O) Leake
Wormald Malkin Carter:
HULL - Jenny: Gwynne Batten Whitty Davies: Caswell Hall:
Bowman Balderson Short Errington Smallwood Bateson:
Try - Bateson:
Referee F Fairhurst (Wigan) Att - 6000 H.T. nil - 3

Sat 29 Oct 1927 HULL KINGSTON ROVERS away
lost nil - 31
HULL K R - Rainton: Harris Spamer Jordan Austin: Hall
McIntyre: Wilkinson Boagey Westerdale Binks Britton
Bielby:
Tries - Spamer(2) Bielby(2) Harris Jordan Westerdale:

Goals - Rainton(5):
CASTLEFORD - Hargrave: Asquith Atkinson McTighe
Sylvester: Nash Needham: Renton Plimmer Leake
Wormald Ben Russell H.Russell:
Referee T Johnson (Bramley) Att - 4500 H.T. nil - 16

Sat 5 Nov 1927 LEIGH Home lost 2 - 14
CASTLEFORD - Feltham: Hargrave Bacon Atkinson
Sylvester: Needham McTighe: Renton Nicholls Leake
Wormald Sherwood Russell: Goal - Atkinson:
LEIGH - Clarkson: France Emery Van Heerden Bithell:
Hurcombe Moss: Winstanley Leyland Worrall Darwell
Wood Hartley:
Tries - Emery(2): Goals - Clarkson(3)(DG):
Referee B Ennion (Swinton) Att - 1000 H.T. nil - 7

Sat 12 Nov 1927 HUNSLET away lost nil - 17
HUNSLET - Place: Broughton Walkington Beverley
Dobing: Young Coulson: Guerin G.Tootles Moss Crowther
Dawson Chapman:
Tries - Broughton(2) Dawson Walkington Guerin:
Goal - Walkington:
CASTLEFORD - Feltham: Sylvester Atkinson Bacon
Dickinson: Trevis Needham: Renton Plimmer Leake
Wormald Thomas Sherwood Kinsey:
Referee H W Bateman   Att - 3000 H.T. nil - 6

**Sat 19 Nov 1927 WIGAN HIGHFIELD home
won 10 - 2**
CASTLEFORD - Feltham: Atkinson Sylvester Hargrave
Hudson: Trevis Needham: Renton Plimmer Wormald
Walton Russell Carter:
Tries - Atkinson Carter: Goals - Feltham(1) Needham(DG):
WIGAN H - Osbaldestin: Cowley Catterall Hunter
Blinkhorn: Parkinson Grimes: Bentham Thompson
Longshaw Green Norburn Lyon: Goal - Osbaldestin:
Referee C Denham   Att - 2000 H.T. 5 - nil

Sat 26 Nov 1927 LEIGH away lost 9 - 17
LEIGH - Clarkson: Thomas Emery Osborne Baldwin: Bithell
Moss: Leyland Winstanley Worrall Daewell Myers
Blackburn:
Tries - Bithell(2) Baldwin: Goals - Clarkson(4):
CASTLEFORD - Hudson: Atkinson Sylvester Hargrave
Bacon: Trevis Needham: Renton Plimmer Wormald
Walton Russell Carter:
Try - Atkinson: Goals - Hargrave(3):
Referee F H Chambers (Hud'field) Att - 5000 H.T. nil - 15

**Sat 3 Dec 1927 BRADFORD NORTHERN home
won 10 - nil**
CASTLEFORD - Hargrave: Hudson Bacon Atkinson
Sylvester: Trevis Needham: Renton Plimmer Wormald
Russell Walton Carter:
Tries - Needham Carter: Goals - Hargrave Atkinson:
BRADFORD N - J.Smith: Cox Brogden Thornber Speak:
Melling W.Smith: Hardaker Hulme Woodruffe Wood
Malone Young:
Referee T Johnson (Bramley) Att   H.T. 5 - nil

**Sat 10 Dec 1927 CASTLEFORD 9 - J BACON's X111 13
GEORGE HINTON BENEFIT MATCH - FRIENDLY**
CASTLEFORD - Feltham: Chapman Atkinson Skelton
Burdin(Knottingley): Needham Trevis: Wormald Plimmer
Walton Russell Asquith T.Kinsey:
Tries - Asquith Kinsey Needham:
J BACON's Xlll - Hudson: Lyons(Dewsbury) Bacon
Sylvester Harrison(Scarborough): Mattick Dickinson:
Hinton Nicholls Leake Ambler Drury Russell:
Tries - Lyons Bacon Dickinson: Goals - Bacon Sylvester:
Referee   Att -   H.T.

Sat 17 Dec 1927 HALIFAX away lost 3 - 25
HALIFAX - Davies: Adams Murdison Haigh Smith: Gledhill
Todd: Rathbone Holliday H.Smith Evans Douglas
Townend:
Tries - Murdison(4) Douglas: Goals - Adams(5):
CASTLEFORD - Feltham: Atkinson Bacon Hargrave
Sylvester: Trevis Needham: Renton Plimmer Wormald
Russell Walton Carter: Try - Atkinson:
Referee A Brown (Wakefield) Att - 5000 H.T. nil - 17

Sat 24 Dec 1927 HUNSLET home won 13 - 2
CASTLEFORD - Hargrave: Sylvester Bacon Atkinson
Hudson: Trevis Needham: Renton Nicholls Wormald
Leake Russell Carter:
Tries - Bacon Renton Wormald: Goals - Hargrave(2):
HUNSLET - Place: Broughton Walkington Davies Buck:
Coulson Young: Jenkins Moss Guerin Crowther G Tootles
Chapman: Goal - Guerin:
Referee H Horsfall (Batley) Att -   H.T. 5 - 2

**Mon 26 Dec 1927 FEATHERSTONE ROVERS away
lost 5 - 11**
FEATHERSTONE R - S.Denton: J.Denton Hirst Askin Taylor:
Whittaker Rudd: Woolley Smith Barraclough Haigh
Ashton Flaherty:
Tries - Hirst Whittaker Haigh: Goal - J.Denton:
CASTLEFORD - Hargrave: Sylvester Bacon Atkinson
Hudson: Trevis Needham: Renton Nicholls Wormald
Leake Russell Carter:
Try - Leake: Goal - Hargrave:
Referee F H Chambers (Hud'field) Att - 3000 H.T. nil - 8

**Tuesday 27 Dec 1927 WAKEFIELD TRINITY home
lost 2 - 5**
CASTLEFORD - Hargrave: WILLIAM E.LYONS(49) Bacon
Atkinson Hudson: Trevis Needham: Renton Nicholls Leake
Walton Russell Carter:
Goal - Hargrave:
WAKEFIELD T - C.Pollard: Bateson Ward Davies Pickup:
E.Pollard Parkin: Gibson Field White L.Higson Waters
Glossop:
Try - Bateson: Goal - C.Pollard:
Referee G Rees (Leeds) Att - 6000 H.T. nil - 5

Sat 7 Jan 1928 HULL home lost 12 - 13
CASTLEFORD - Hargrave Hudson Needham Bacon
Atkinson: Trevis Mattick: Renton Nicholls Leake Russell
Walton Carter:

Tries - Hudson Leake: Goals - Hargrave(3):
HULL - Jenny: Davies Gwynne Whitty Gardiner: Phillipson
Caswell: Bowman Balderson Short Taylor Errington
Bateson
Tries - Gwynne Taylor Phillipson: Goals - Jenny Bateson:
Referee F Chambers (Dewsbury)   Att -   H.T.10 - 0

Wed 11 Jan 1928 HUDDERSFIELD away lost 5 - 39
HUDDERSFIELD - Scott: Mills Harris Bowkett Smart:
Williams Brook: Rudd Gee Dyson Tiffany Carr Clark:
Tries - Mills(3) Smart(3) Harris Brook Carr:
Goals - Bowkett(4)Harris Brook:
CASTLEFORD - Hargrave: EDWARD PARKER(50) Atkinson
Bacon Hudson: Trevis Nash: Renton Nicholls Leake
Norman Dixon Russell Carter:
Try - Atkinson: Goal - Hargrave:
Referee   Att - 3000 H.T. 3 - 5

Sat 14 Jan 1928 YORK away lost 5 - 13
YORK - Tindall: Van Heerden Hoult Aspinall Mills: Pickard
Brittain: Mirfield Myers Betteridge Cooper Dawson
Johnson:
Tries - Hoult Brittain Cooper: Goals - Tindall(2):
CASTLEFORD - GEORGE A PEARCE(51): Hargrave Bacon
Atkinson Hudson: Nash Mattick: Renton Plimmer Leake
Walton Russell Carter: Try - Nash: Goal Hargrave:
Referee H Horsfall (Batley) Att - 1000 H.T. nil - 5

Sat 21 Jan 1928 BRAMLEY home lost nil - 5
CASTLEFORD - George A.Pearce: ALBERT SHAW(52)
Bacon Hargrave Sylvester: Nash Joseph McTighe: Renton
Plimmer Leake Walton Russell Carter:
BRAMLEY - Parkinson: Carter Withington Davidson
Vowles: Gadsby Whelan: Reed Bowden Hesketh Tucker
Moore Rowan: Try - Rowan: Goal - Parkinson:
Referee T Johnson (Bramley) Att -   H.T. nil - 5

Sat 28 Jan 1928 KEIGHLEY away lost nil - 8
KEIGHLEY - Davies: Holmes Collins Phillips W.Foster:
L Foster Fowler: Thompson Moore Langhorn Firth
McGoun Burton: Tries - Phillips W.Foster: Goal - Davies:
CASTLEFORD - Hargrave: Hudson Malkin Bacon EPHRAIM
MALSOM(53): Mattick Nash(S/O): Leake Nicholls Renton
Carter MACK ARNOLD(54) Russell:
Referee F H Chambers (Hud'field) Att - 3000 H.T. nil - 8

Sat 4 Feb 1928 BATLEY home draw 5 - 5
CASTLEFORD - Hargrave: Hudson Bacon Atkinson
Asquith: Nash Mattick: Renton Malkin Leake Wormald
Russell Carter: Try - Carter: Goal - Hargrave:
BATLEY - Oliver: Wale Fisher Morton Murray: Davies
Fowler: Demaine Douglas Fairhurst Collins Leeming
Wright Try - Leeming: Goal - Murray:
Referee G Rees (Leeds) Att -   H.T. 5 - nil

Sat 11 Feb 1928 SALFORD away won 7 - 3
CHALLENGE CUP ROUND 1
SALFORD - L.Williams: Boyd Southward Manning Lindley:
Mannion Meek: W.Williams Price Butterworth Price
Haines Gore: Try - Haines:

CASTLEFORD - Hargrave: Malkin Bacon Atkinson Trevis:
Nash Mattick: Fenton Nicholls Leake Wormald Russell
Carter: Try - Leake: Goals - Hargrave(2):
Referee T Johnson (Bramley) Att - 2945 H.T. 5 - nil

Sat 18 Feb 1928 HALIFAX home won 11 - 3
CASTLEFORD - Hargrave: RALPH PANTHER(55) Bacon
Needham Atkinson: Trevis Mattick: Renton Nicholls Leake
Wormald Russell Carter:
Tries - Atkinson(2) Bacon: Goal - Hargrave:
HALIFAX - Davies: Stacey Murdison Haigh M.Smith: Todd
Gledhill: Rawbone Halliday Swan Douglas Beattie
Rushworth: Try - Murdison:
Referee T Johnson (Bramley) Att - 4000 H.T. nil - 3

Sat 25 Feb 1928 FEATHERSTONE ROVERS home
won 3 - nil CHALLENGE CUP ROUND 2
CASTLEFORD - Hargrave: Atkinson Trevis Needham
Sylvester: Nash Mattick: Renton Nicholls Leake Wormald
Russell Carter: Try - Leake:
FEATHERSTONE R - S.Denton: J.Denton Hirst Askin Taylot:
J.Morgan Whittaker: Barraclough Hall Woolley Smith
Haigh Ashton:
Referee R Jones (Widnes) Att - 12500 H.T. 3 - nil

Sat 3 Mar 1928 WAKEFIELD TRINITY away
lost 3 - 44
WAKEFIELD T - Ward: Bateson Pickup E.Pollard Smith:
Parkin Pearce: Gibson Field Moss Horton Clements
Glossop: Tries - Bateson(6) Smith Glossop Pickup Pollard:
Goals - Pollard(4) Pearce Bateson Horton:
CASTLEFORD - Ralph Panther: Atkinson Needham Trevis
Sylvester: Nash Mattick: Renton Nicholls Leake Wormald
Russell Carter: Try - Leake:
Referee F H Chambers (Hud'field) Att - 5000 H.T. nil - 28

Sat 10 Mar 1928 SWINTON home lost nil - 3
CHALLENGE CUP ROUND 3
CASTLEFORD - Hargrave: Sylvester Needham Bacon
Atkinson: Trevis Mattick: Renton Nicholls Leake Wormald
Russell Carter:
SWINTON - Pearson: F.Evans Halsall Sulway Brookbank:
B.Evans Rees: Strong Blower Morris Hodgson Cracknell
Beswick: Try - F.Evans:
Referee B Ennion (Wigan) Att - 11299 H.T. nil - 3
**The match when Atkinson(Castleford) was running in
the clear for a certain try when Strong (Swinton) was
receiving treatment off the field and he ran on to the
field and tackled Atkinson.**

Sat 17 Mar 1928 LEEDS away lost 4 - 20
LEEDS - Brough: Lloyd O'Rourke Desmond Andrews:
Moores Williams: Watson Thompson Smith Pascoe Davies
Gallagher:
Tries - Lloyd(2) O'Rourke Andrews: Goals - Thompson(4):
CASTLEFORD - Hargrave: Sylvester Needham Bacon
Atkinson: Trevis Mattick: Renton Nicholls Leake Wormald
Russell Carter: Goals - Hargrave(2):
Referee F Peel (Bradford) Att - 7000 H.T. nil - 8

SEASON 1927-28

Sat 24 Mar 1928 KEIGHLEY home won 24 - 9
CASTLEFORD - Hargrave: Hudson Trevis Needham
Atkinson: Mattick James Nash: Renton Nicholls Leake
Russell Wormald Carter:
Tries - Hudson Trevis Needham Atkinson Nash Wormald:
Goals - Hargrave(3):
KEIGHLEY - Davies: Holmes Collins White Craven: Pearson
L.Foster: Thompson Moore Langhorn Firth Wade Burton:
Try - Holmes: Goals - Davies(3):
Referee G Rees (Leeds) Att - 2000 H.T. 10 - 7

Sat 31 Mar 1928 BATLEY away lost 7 - 13
BATLEY - Dewhirst: Wale Oliver Davies Morton: Chappell
Fowler: Douglas Demaine Fairhurst Collins Leeming
Wright:
Tries - Wale Morton Collins: Goals - Wale(2):
CASTLEFORD - Atkinson: Hudson Trevis Needham
Ephraim Malsom: SAMMY STONES(56) Mattick: Renton
PERCY RAYNOR(57) Leake Wormald Malkin Russell:
Try - Hudson: Goals - Atkinson(2):
Referee T Johnson (Bramley) Att - 2000 H.T. 6 - 2

Fri 6 Apr 1928 FEATHERSTONE ROVERS home draw 4 - 4
CASTLEFORD - Hargrave: Atkinson Needham Bacon
Hudson: Trevis Mattick: Renton Nicholls Leake Russell
Wormald Carter:
Goals - Hargrave Atkinson:
FEATHERSTONE R - S.Denton: J.Denton Askin Whittaker
Taylor: Williams Hirst: Hall Smith Blakeley Haigh Morgan
Ashton:
Goals - Williams(2):
Referee F H Chambers (Hud'field) Att - 2000 H.T. 4 - nil

Mon 9 Apr 1928 DEWSBURY away won 5 - 2
DEWSBURY - Stocks: Raywood G.Smith Gates Joe Lyman:
Hirst Roberts: Rhodes Mitchell Hobson Bland Booth Fox:
Goal - Joe Lyman:
CASTLEFORD - Atkinson: Carter Needham Bacon
HAROLD CHAPMAN(58): Trevis: Mattick: Renton Nicholls
Leake Wormald Malkin Russell:
Try - Bacon: Goal - Atkinson:
Referee G Rees (Leeds) Att - 2000 H.T. 2 - 2

Tue 10 Apr 1928 YORK home won 21 - 5
CASTLEFORD - Atkinson: Carter Needham Bacon
Chapman: Trevis Mattick: Renton Nicholls Leake Wormald
Malkin Russell:
Tries - Mattick(2) Carter Bacon Russell:
Goals - Atkinson(3)
YORK - Owen: Van Heerden Flint Cooper Lickiss: Barnard
Pickard: Myers Betteridge Mirfield Dawson Hampton
Cooper:
Try - Pickard: Goal - Owen
Referee B Robinson (Bradford) Att - H.T. 3 - 5

Sat 28 Apr 1928 HULL KINGSTON ROVERS home draw 8 - 8
CASTLEFORD - Hargrave: Atkinson Bacon Needham
Chapman: Trevis Mattick: Renton Nicholls(S/O) Leake
Wormald Russell Carter:
Tries - Chapman Carter: Goal - Hargrave:
HULL K R - Osborne: Bateman Spamer Jordan
Scarborough: Saul McIntyre: Wilkinson Brittain Binks
Roberts Saddington Feetham(S/O):
Tries - Bateman McIntyre: Goal Osborne:
Referee T Johnson (B'ramey) Att - 2000 H.T. 8 – 5

Fred Carter
D. No 47
1927-28 to 1928-29

Joshua (Jim) Bacon
D. No 48
1927-28 to 1929-30

Harold Chapman
D. No 58
1927-28 to 1933-34

D,N	PLAYER		DEBUT	L MATCH	APP	SL B	T.AP	TR'S	G'LS	D.G	P'TS
1	HARGRAVE	WILLIAM			31	0	31	0	28	1	58
5	HUDSON	HARRY			23	0	23	5	0	0	15
6	NEEDHAM	THOMAS			33	0	33	4	1	1	16
7	TREVIS	ARTHUR.JAMES			32	0	32	4	0	0	12
8	LEAKE	JACK			35	0	35	7	0	0	21
9	NICHOLLS	ROBERT			29	0	29	1	0	0	3
10	RENTON	WILLIAM			39	0	39	3	0	0	9
11	MALKIN	JOSEPH			12	0	12	0	0	0	0
12	WORMALD	JACK			26	0	26	2	0	0	6
14	RUSSELL	HARRY (DANNY)			27	0	27	1	0	0	3
16	ASQUITH	WILLIAM (NAT)			2	0	2	0	0	0	0
17	SHERWOOD	THOMAS		12/11/1927	4	0	4	0	0	0	0
20	NASH	JAMES		24/03/1928	10	0	10	2	0	0	6
21	ATKINSON	ARTHUR			37	0	37	8	20	0	64
23	WALTON	RICHARD			8	0	8	0	0	0	0
24	FELTHAM	ARTHUR			7	0	7	0	5	0	10
25	DICKINSON	ALBERT			1	0	1	0	0	0	0
32	DIXON	NORMAN		11/01/1928	2	0	2	0	0	0	6
33	SYLVESTER	HARRY			23	0	23	2	0	0	5
34	McTIGHE	JOSEPH		21/01/1928	12	0	12	1	1	0	0
35	OWEN	HARRY (NABS)		27/08/1927	1	0	1	0	0	0	0
39	PLIMMER	JAMES			8	0	8	0	0	0	6
43	KINSEY	VICTOR			10	0	10	2	0	0	0
44	MATTICK	ROBERT			17	0	17	2	0	0	15
45	RUSHWORTH	A R	27/08/1927	22/10/1927	4	0	4	0	0	0	18
46	RUSSELL	BEN	03/09/1927	29/10/1927	3	0	3	0	0	0	3
47	CARTER	FRED	01/10/1927		29	0	29	6	0	0	0
48	BACON	JOSHUA (JIM)	08/10/1927		27	0	27	5	0	0	6
49	LYONS	WILLIAM E.	27/12/1927	27/12/1927	1	0	1	0	0	0	0
50	PARKER	EDWARD	11/01/1928	11/01/1928	1	0	1	0	0	0	0
51	PEARCE	GEORGE	14/01/1928	21/01/1928	2	0	2	0	0	0	0
52	SHAW	ALBERT	21/01/1928	21/01/1928	1	0	1	0	0	0	0
53	MALSOM	EPHRAIM	28/01/1928	31/03/1928	2	0	2	0	0	0	0
54	ARNOLD	MACK	28/01/1928	28/01/1928	1	0	1	0	0	0	0
55	PANTHER	RALPH	18/02/1928	03/03/1928	2	0	2	0	0	0	0
56	STONES	SAMMY	31/03/1928		1	0	1	0	0	0	0
57	RAYNOR	PERCY	31/03/1928	31/03/1928	1	0	1	0	0	0	0
58	CHAPMAN	HAROLD	09/04/1928		3	0	3	1	0	0	0
	38		**14**	**15**	**507**	**0**	**507**	**56**	**55**	**2**	**282**

	COMPETITION		P	W	D	L	FOR	AGT
	LEAGUE	POSITION 25 OF 28	32	9	3	20	217	389
	YORK'S CUP		3	1	1	1	29	10
	RL CUP		3	2	0	1	10	6
	MATCH VOID PONTIPRIDD		1	1	0	0	26	6
	PLAYERS RECORDS		**39**	**13**	**4**	**22**	**282**	**411**

When the Club moved to the former Castleford Town FC ground in Wheldon Road it took over a ground that would probably not be recognised today. The present practise pitch and car park were allotments and on the present main stand side of the ground stood a double decker bus, which was used as a Press Box and Tea Room. There was no Supporters' stand and when the old main stand burnt down Billy Rhodes had to rescue his Alsatian dog, Billo.

The Welsh side Pontypridd, left the league after playing only eight games their playing record being deleted from the league table. However, one of those eight games was against Castleford and appearances and scorers in that one game are included in the Club's statistics.

Billy Rhodes left to take up the position of Trainer at Dewsbury and former International Jim Bacon was appointed as Castleford's Trainer/Player.

Sat 18 Aug 1928 YORKSHIRE home lost 18 - 23
CASTLEFORD WAR MEMORIAL MATERNITY HOME
CUP - FRIENDLY
CASTLEFORD - Hargrave: Chapman Bacon Needham
Panther:Trevis Mattick: Leake Walton Plimmer Malkin
Russell Carter
Tries - Carter(2) Trevis Mattick: Goals - Hargrave(3):
YORKSHIRE - Chapman(Hunslet): Broom(Featherstone R)
Feltham(Castleford) Broughton(Hunslet)
Coulson(Hunslet): Melling(Bradford N) Rudd(Featherstone
R): Smith (Featherstone R) Haigh (Featherstone R) Traill
(Hunslet) White(Hunslet) Wood(Bradford N) Ward(York):
Tries - Haigh(2) Coulson Smith Ward: Goals - Chapman(2)
Feltham(2 DG)
Referee A Brown (Wakefield) Att - 3000 H.T. 15 - 15

Sat 25 Aug 1928 HULL away lost nil - 22
HULL - Jenney: Carney Caswell Gardiner Whitty: Phillipson
Hall: Longbottom Smallwood Taylor Short Bolderson
Errington:
Tries - Phillipson(3) Whitty: Goals - Phillipson(5):
CASTLEFORD - Feltham: Chapman Bacon Hargrave
Sylvester: Trevis Mattick: Malkin Walton Leake Russell
Kinsey Albert Dickinson:
Referee G Rees (Leeds) Att - 4000 H.T. nil - 12

Sat 1 Sep 1928 KEIGHLEY home won 21 - 9
CASTLEFORD - Feltham: Chapman Bacon Atkinson
Hargrave: Trevis WILLIAM SHERWOOD(59): HARRY
WOODALL(60) Walton Leake Russell Malkin Carter:
Tries - Hargrave(2) Carter(2) Bacon: Goals - Hargrave(2)
Feltham:
KEIGHLEY - Davies: Thorpe Kendall Collins E.Holmes:
Pearson Foster: Thompson Moore Langhorn Firth
McGoun Burton:
Try - Kendall: Goals - Davies(2) Kendall:
Referee R Robinson (Bradford) Att - 1000 H.T. 8 - 9

Wed 5 Sep 1928 LEEDS away lost nil - 49
LEEDS - Goldie: Lloyd O'Rourke Deasmond Bailey: Casey
Wlliams: Demaine Satterthwaite Davies Pascoe Thomas
Woolmore:
Tries - Woolmore(3) Lloyd(2) Desmond(2) O'Rourke Casey
Pascoe Thomas: Goals - Pascoe(8):
CASTLEFORD - Feltham: Chapman Bacon Atkinson
Hargrave: Trevis Mattick: Harry Woodall Leake Walton
Russell Malkin Carter:
Referee B Laughlin (Batley) Att - H.T. nil - 20

Sat 15 Sep 1928 HUDDERSFIELD home lost 13 - 15
CASTLEFORD - MILLWARD BEDWORTH(61): Chapman
Sylvester Atkinson Hargrave: Needham Mattick: Renton
Leake ARTHUR SHERWOOD(62) Walton Russell Carter:
Tries - Sylvester Hargrave Walton: Goals - Hargrave
Atkinson:
HUDDERSFIELD - Brooks: Mills Harris Parker Smart: Jones
Williams: Rudd Barlow Morton Tiffany Gee Carr:
Tries - Smart(2) Parker: Goals - Brooks(3):
Referee G Rees (Leeds) Att - 3000 H.T. 13 - 7

Sat 22 Sep 1928 BROUGHTON RANGERS away
lost 3 - 5
BROUGHTON R - Stowell: Lomas Doran Sharrocks
Holland: Melling Howarth: Bestwick Curran Dixon Hope
Smith Whatmough
Try - Melling: Goal - Melling:
CASTLEFORD - EDWIN JONES(63): Chapman Harry
Sylvester Atkinson Asquith: Mattick Hargrave: Renton
Walton Sherwood Russell Wormald Carter:
Try - Hargrave:
Referee H Jones (Widnes) Att - 5000 H.T. nil - nil

Sat 29 Sep 1928 BRAMLEY home won 9 - nil
CASTLEFORD - Jones: Chapman Hargrave Atkinson
Asquith: Trevis Mattick: Renton Sherwood Wormald
Walton Russell Carter:
Try - Hargrave: Goals - Hargrave(3):
BRAMLEY - Parkinson: Vowles Ballantine Witherington
Peters: Gadsby Gill: Rees Bowden Pickles Tasker Walker
Rowan
Referee F Peel (Bradford) Att - 2500 H.T. 9 - nil

Sat 6 Oct 1928 BRADFORD NORTHERN away
won 13 - 10
BRADFORD N - Bevan: Fordham Brogden T.R.Smith
W.R.Smith: Gledhill "Evans": Hume Rooks Woodruff
Jefferson Cox Young:
Tries - Brogden(2): Goals - Bevan Gledhill:
CASTLEFORD - Jones: Asquith Hargrave Atkinson
Chapman: Trevis Needham: Renton Nicholls Sherwood
Wormald Walton Carter:
Tries - Hargrave Sherwood Carter: Goals - Atkinson(2):
Referee H Horsfall (Batley) Att - H.T. 7 - nil

Sat 13 Oct 1928 KEIGHLEY home won 19 - 4
YORKSHIRE CUP ROUND 1
CASTLEFORD - Jones: Asquith Hargrave Atkinson
Chapman: Trevis Needham: Renton Nicholls Sherwood
Wormald Russell Carter:
Tries - Atkinson(2) Hargrave Chapman Needham:
Goals - Hargrave Atkinson:
KEIGHLEY - Taylor: Thorpe Burton Collins Buttle: Pearson
Kelly: Thompson Moore Langhorn Firth McGoun Wade:
Goals - Taylor(2):
Referee R Jones (Widnes) Att - 4000 H.T. 8 - 2

Sat 20 Oct 1928 WIGAN HIGHFIELD away lost 5 - 10
WIGAN H - Bennett: Blinkhorn Osbaldestin O.Cowley
N.Cowley: Hunter Chisnall: Connelly Thompson Baines
Morley Longshaw Gore:
Tries - Hunter(2): Goals - Blinkhorn(2):
CASTLEFORD - Atkinson: Chapman Hargrave Asquith
EDWIN THOMAS(64): Trevis Needham: Renton Nicholls
Sherwood Wormald Russell Carter:
Try - Carter: Goal - Atkinson:
Referee T Johnson (Bramley) Att - 500 H.T. nil - 2

Wed 24 Oct 1928 YORK away won 8 - nil
YORKSHIRE CUP ROUND 2
YORK - Owen: T.Mills Roberts Hoult Austin: W.Mills

Brittain: Myers Mirfield Keech Johnson Bielby Cooper:
CASTLEFORD - Hargrave: Carter Bacon Atkinson Asquith:
Trevis Needham: Renton Nicholls Sherwood Wormald
Walton Russell:
Tries - Asquith Needham: Goal - Atkinson:
Referee J Eddon (Swinton) Att - 3000 H.T. 5 - nil

Sat 27 Oct 1928 WAKEFIELD TRINITY home
draw 10 - 10
CASTLEFORD - Hargrave: Carter Bacon Atkinson Asquith:
Trevis Needham: Renton Nicholls Sherwood Wormald
Walton Russell:
Tries - Trevis Needham: Goals - Atkinson(2):
WAKEFIELD T - C.Pollard: Bateson Siswick Maidment
Smith: Davies Parkin: Gibson Field Quinn Horton Higson
Glossop:
Tries - Bateson(2): Goals - Pollard(2):
Referee R Robinson (Bradford) Att - 4000 H.T. 8 - nil

Sat 3 Nov 1928 LEIGH away lost 6 - 21
LEIGH - Clarkson: Higson Crook Bithell Kenny: Hurcombe
Houghton: Leyland Ogden Worrall Darwell Myers Hartley:
Tries - Kenny(2) Higson Bithell Worrall:
Goals - Clarkson(3):
CASTLEFORD - Jones: BENJAMIN T.HODGSON(65)
Asquith Atkinson Chapman: Trevis Needham: Wormald
Nicholls Sherwood Walton Russell Carter:
Tries - Asquith Carter:
Referee R Robinson (Bradford) Att - 6000 H.T. 5 - nil

Wed 7 Nov 1928 FEATHERSTONE ROVERS away
lost 6 – 10 YORKSHIRE CUP SEMI-FINAL
FEATHERSTONE R - S.Denton: J.Denton Hirst Whittaker
Taylor: Williams Annable: Smith Flaherty Rogerson Haigh
Shirley J.Morgan:
Tries - Whittaker Annable: Goals - J.Denton Williams:
CASTLEFORD - Hargrave: Chapman Bacon Atkinson
Asquith: Trevis Needham: Renton Nicholls Sherwood
Wormald Russell Fred Carter:
Goals - Atkinson(3):
Referee F Fairhurst (Wigan) Att -   H.T. nil - 5

Sat 10 Nov 1928 HUNSLET home lost 2 - 23
CASTLEFORD - Hargrave: Benjamin T Hodgson Asquith
Atkinson(S/O) Bacon: Trevis Needham: Renton Nicholls
Sherwood Wormald Walton Russell:
Goal - Atkinson:
HUNSLET - Place: Broughton Coulson Dawson Rhodea:
Young Todd: Jenkins White(S/O) Litt Traill Crowther
Chapman:
Tries - Broughton(2) Place Coulson Rhodes: Goals - Litt(4):
Referee H Horsfall (Batley) Att - 2500 H.T. 2 - 5

Sat 17 Nov 1928 WAKEFIELD TRINITY away
lost 10 - 11
WAKEFIELD T - C.Pollard: Bateson Beardshaw Davies Ray:
Pearce Parkin: Gibson Field Quinn Maidment Horton
Glossop:
Tries - Bateson(2) Maidment: Goal - Pollard:
CASTLEFORD - Jones: Chapman Atkinson Asquith Mattick:

Trevis Stones: Renton Nicholls Sherwood Wormald
RAYMONDAYD MASKILL(66) Russell:
Tries - Atkinson(2): Goals - Atkinson(2):
Referee F Peel (Bradford) Att - 5000 H.T. 5 - 11
**Castleford were a player short at kick off Mattick
brought from the 'A'team**

Sat 24 Nov 1928 HALIFAX away lost 4 - 11
HALIFAX - Davies: Stacey Fletcher Rhoades Smith: Hanson
Atkinson: Rawbone Bentham Gelder Swan Moxon
Townend:
Tries - Stacey Smith Townend: Goal - Davies:
CASTLEFORD - Edwin Jones: Chapman Asquith Hargrave
Trevis: HERBERT WHITEHOUSE(67) WILLIAM WRAITH(68):
William Renton Nicholls Sherwood Wormald Walton
Russell:
Goals - Hargrave(2):
Referee J Eddon (Swinton) Att - 3000 H.T. nil - 11
**Kick-off delayed for 20 minutes - Castleford being
delayed**

Sat 1 Dec 1928 LEIGH home lost 3 - 11
CASTLEFORD - Hargrave: Stones Atkinson Asquith
Chapman: Herbert Whitehouse Wraith: Leake Nicholls
Walton Maskill Wormald Russell:
Try - Chapman:
LEIGH - Clarkson: Osborne Crook Bithell Kenny: Green
Houghton: Ogden Leyland Worrall Wood Barwell
Blackburn:
Tries - Kenny Green Houghton: Goal - Clarkson:
Referee F Fairhurst (Wigan) Att - 3500 H.T. nil - 6

Sat 8 Dec 1928 BRADFORD NORTHERN home
won 16 - nil
CASTLEFORD - Hargrave: Thomas Asquith Atkinson
Chapman: Stones Wraith: Sherwood Nicholls Walton
Wormald Maskill Russell:
Tries - Chapman(2) Thomas Asquith: Goals - Atkinson(2):
BRADFORD N - Gledhill: Fordham Brogden Thornber
T.R.Smith: Brearley Wilcock: Wood Hume Moran Cox
Woodruff Malone:
Referee A Brown (Wakefield) Att - 1000 H.T. 8 - nil

Sat 22 Dec 1928 BATLEY away lost 10 - 21
BATLEY - Lyman: Kingsley H.Rees Fowler J.Davies:
Chappell W.Davies: Brook Tootles Bailey Collins Donnelly
McCade:
Tries - W.Davies(2) Rees Chappell McCade:
Goals - Lyman(3):
CASTLEFORD - Hargrave: Thomas Atkinson Asquith
Chapman: Stones Wraith: Sherwood Nicholls Walton
Wormald Maskill Russell:
Tries - Chapman Wraith: Goals - Atkinson(2):
Referee H Swift (Halifax) Att - 2000 H.T. 10 - 15

Tue 25 Dec 1928 FEATHERSTONE ROVERS home
won 8 - 3
CASTLEFORD - Bacon: Hargrave Atkinson Asquith
Chapman: JOHN CASEY(69) Stones: Sherwood Nicholls
Leake Wormald Walton Russell:

SEASON 1928-29

Tries - Hargrave(2): Goal - Hargrave:
FEATHERSTONE R - S.Denton: Johnson Whittaker Askin
Hirst: Williams Annable: Barraclough Flaherty Smith
Rogerson Shirley Morgan:
Try - Johnson:
Referee A Brown (Wakefield) Att - 6000 H.T. 3 - 3

Wed 26 Dec 1928 HUNSLET away lost 4 - 11
HUNSLET - Place: Broughton Thornton Coulson
Walkington: Young Todd: Jenkins White Traill Crowther
Moss Chapman:
Tries - Coulson Crowther Chapman: Goal - Walkington:
CASTLEFORD - Mattick: Hargrave Atkinson Asquith
Chapman: Stones William Wraith: Sherwood Plimmer
Leake Wormald Walton Russell:
Goals - Hargrave(2)
Referee H Horsfall (Batley) Att - 3000 H.T. 2 - 5

**Sat 29 Dec 1928 HULL KINGSTON ROVERS home
draw 5 - 5**
CASTLEFORD - Mattick: Hargrave Atkinson Asquith
Chapman: Casey Stones: Sherwood Nicholls Leake
Wormald Walton Russell:
Try - Hargrave: Goal - Hargrave:
HULL K R - Osborne: Bateman Cook Jordan Spamer:
McIntyre Dale: Binns Sharp Britton Westerdale
Saddington Feetham:
Try - Bateman: Goal - Osborne:
Referee B Laughlin (Batley) Att - H.T. 2 - 5

Sat 12 Jan 1929 BRAMLEY away draw 2 - 2
BRAMLEY - Parkinson: Whitham Ballantyne Bowan
Witherington: Gadsby Hughes: Bowen Reed Wilkinson
Sykes Tasker Moore: Goal - Parkinson(DG):
CASTLEFORD - Feltham: Hargrave Atkinson Asquith
Chapman: Casey Stones: Sherwood Leake Nicholls
Wormald Walton Russell:
Goal - Atkinson:
Referee R Robinson (Bradford) Att-3000 H.T. nil - nil

Sat 19 Jan 1929 YORK home won 5 - 2
CASTLEFORD - Feltham: Hargrave Atkinson Asquith
Stones: Casey Mattick: Sherwood Nicholls Leake Wormald
Walton Russell:
Try - Asquith: Goal - Atkinson:
YORK - Owen: T.Mills Hoult Batten Barnard: W.Mills
Pickard: Myers Mason Johnson Iveson Aspinall Bielby:
Goal - Hoult(DG):
Referee T Johnson (Bramley) Att - 2500 H.T. 5 - nil

Sat 26 Jan 1929 YORK away won 8 - 5
YORK - Owen: Hoult T.Mills Batten Spiller: W.Mills Pickard:
Myers Johnson Mason Iveson Aspinall Bielby:
Try - Spiller: Goal - Hoult(DG):
CASTLEFORD - Feltham: Hargrave Atkinson Asquith
Stones: Trevis Needham: Sherwood Leake Nicholls
Wormald Walton Russell:
Tries - Hargrave Needham: Goal - Atkinson:
Referee H Horsfall (Batley) Att - 3000 H.T. nil - 3

Sat 2 Feb 1929 HALIFAX home lost nil - 2
CASTLEFORD - Feltham: Hargrave Atkinson Asquith
Chapman: Casey Stones: Sherwood Nicholls Walton
Wormald Plimmer Russell:
HALIFAX - Davies: Stacey Murdison Rhoades Smith: Haigh
Hanson: Rawbone Bentham Renton D.Rees Evans
Townend:
Goal - Murdison:
Referee R Robinson (Bradford) Att - 1250 H.T. nil - 2

**Sat 9 Feb 1929 WHITEHAVEN RECS home won 31 - 7
CHALLENGE CUP ROUND 1**
CASTLEFORD - Feltham: Hargrave Atkinson Asquith
Chapman: Casey Needham: Sherwood Nicholls Walton
Wormald Plimmer Russell:
Tries - Atkinson(3) Hargrave(2) Casey(2):
Goals - Hargrave(4) Feltham:
WHITEHAVEN R - G.Fearon: R.Fearon Biggs H.Atkinson
Graham: B.Atkinson Smith: Dand Berwick McAdam Strong
Barnes Lowry:
Try - Biggs: Goals - B.Atkinson(2):
Referee A E Harding (Man'ster) Att - 2500 H.T. 8 - nil

**Sat 23 Feb 1929 HUDDERSFIELD home won 8 - nil
CHALLENGE CUP ROUND 2**
CASTLEFORD - Feltham: Hargrave Atkinson Asquith
Chapman: Casey Trevis: Sherwood Nicholls Leake
Wormald Walton Russell:
Tries - Casey Wormald: Goal - Feltham:
HUDDERSFIELD - Stocks: Mills Harris Parker Smart:
Williams Bowkett: Rudd Halliday Clark Gee Tiffany Young:
Referee J Eddon (Swinton) Att - 9000 H.T. 5 - nil

Sat 2 Mar 1929 BATLEY home won 9 - 2
CASTLEFORD - Feltham: Hargrave Atkinson Asquith
Chapman: Casey Trevis: Sherwood Nicholls Leake
Wormald Walton Plimmer:
Tries - Atkinson Chapman Plimmer:
BATLEY - Rogers: H.Pratt Rees Iyman D.C.Davies: Chappell
W.J.Davies: Leeming Brook Fairhurst McCade Collins
Donnelly:
Goal - Rees:
Referee A Brown (Wakefield) Att - 3000 H.T. 3 - 2

**Sat 9 Mar 1929 WIGAN HIGHFIELD home
won 8 - nil CHALLENGE CUP ROUND 3**
CASTLEFORD - Feltham: Hargrave Atkinson Asquith
Chapman: Casey Trevis: Sherwood Nicholls Leake
Wormald Walton Plimmer:
Tries - Atkinson Asquith: Goal - Hargrave:
WIGAN H - Osbaldestin: Ashcroft Catterall Hunter
Maloney: Parkinson Chisnall: Lowe Thompson Baines
Morley Smith Gore:
Referee R Jones (Widnes) Att - 11700 H.T. nil - nil

Sat 16 Mar 1929 HUDDERSFIELD away lost nil - 7
HUDDERSFIELD - Stocks: Mills Brook Bowkett Smart:
Spencer Williams: Morton Holliday Gee Carter Tiffany
Young:
Try - Spencer: Goals - Brook Morton(DG):

SEASON 1928-29

CASTLEFORD - Feltham: Hargrave Atkinson Asquith Chapman: Casey Trevis: Sherwood Nicholls Wormald Walton Plimmer Needham:
Referee T Johnson (Bramley) Att -   H.T. 2 - nil

Tue 19 Mar 1929 KEIGHLEY away lost nil - 5
KEIGHLEY - Taylor: E.Holmes L.Foster Collins Kendall: Midgley Fowler: Thompson Firth Langhorn Burton McGoun Fox: Try - Kendall: Goal - Langhorn:
CASTLEFORD - Feltham: Hargrave Stones Asquith Chapman: Casey Needham: Sherwood Nicholls Leake Wormald Walton Plimmer:
Referee R Robinson (Bradford) Att - 1500 H.T. 5 - nil

Sat 23 Mar 1929 WIGAN HIGHFIELD home lost 7 -12
CASTLEFORD - Feltham: Hargrave Atkinson Stones Asquith: Casey Trevis: Sherwood Nicholls Leake Walton Plimmer Thomas Needham:
Try - Hargrave: Goals - Atkinson(2)
WIGAN H - Osbaldestin: Maloney Cowley Grimes Hunter: Chiswell Parkinson: Lowe Thompson Baines Morley Smith Gore: Tries - Grimes(3) Gore:
Referee A E Harding (Man'ster) Att - 2500 H.T. 2 - 6

Sat 29 Mar 1929 FEATHERSTONE ROVERS away won 15 - 6
FEATHERSTONE R - S.Denton: J.Denton Hirst Whittaker F.Smith: Annable Pickup: Barraclough Hepworth Rogerson Gronow Haigh J.Morgan:
Goals - Gronow(2) Plus I Goal - kicker not known:
CASTLEFORD - Feltham: Asquith Atkinson Hargrave Chapman: Casey Stones: Sherwood Nicholls JAMES FOWELL(70) Wormald Walton Plimmer:
Tries - Asquith(2) Atkinson: Goals - Hargrave(2) Atkinson:
Referee B Laughlin (Batley) Att - 6000 H.T. 10 - 4

Sat 30 Mar 1929 BROUGHTON RANGERS home draw 16 - 16
CASTLEFORD - Feltham: Asquith Atkinson HARRY HIRST(71) Chapman: Casey Stones: Sherwood Plimmer Leake Wormald Powell Walton:
Tries - Asquith(2) Atkinson Leake: Goals - Feltham Atkinson:
BROUGHTON R - Price: Stowell Doran Maddock Condron: Sharrock Atkinson: Woodcock Curran McGhie Smith Dixon Butters:
Tries - Maddock Condron: Goals - Stowell(5):
Referee – B Ennion (Wigan) Att - 3000 H.T. 5 - 7

Mon 1 Apr 1929 DEWSBURY home lost 9 - 15
CASTLEFORD - Feltham: Walton Trevis Hirst Chapman: Casey Stones: Sherwood HERBERT WHARVILLE(72) Powell Wormald Leake Plimmer:
Try - Leake: Goals - Feltham(3):
DEWSBURY - Fortis: Craven Layhe Sperrett Coates: H.Mitchell Hirst: Mitchell Hobson Rhodes Booth Bland Evans: Tries - Craven Coates H.Mitchell: Goals - Coates(3)
Referee F Peel (Bradford) Att - 5000 H.T. 7 - 5

Sat 6 Apr 1929 DEWSBURY lost 3 - 9
CHALLENGE CUP SEMI-FINAL - at Huddersfield
CASTLEFORD - Feltham: Asquith Atkinson Hargrave Chapman: Casey Trevis: Sherwood Nicholls Jack Leake Walton Wormald Russell:
Try - Leake:
DEWSBURY - Davies: Bailey Layhe Hirst Coates: Rudd Joe Lyman: Brown Hobson Rhodes Bland Malkin Sperrett:
Try - Layhe: Goals - Lyman(2) Coates(DG):
Referee F Fairhurst (Wigan) Att - 24728 H.T. nil - 2

Sat 13 Apr 1929 LEEDS home lost 4 - 17
CASTLEFORD - Hargrave: Asquith Atkinson Trevis Chapman: Casey Stones: Sherwood WALTER ROOKES(73) Powell Wormald Plimmer Russell:
Goals - Atkinson(2):
LEEDS - Brown: Andrews O'Rourke Rosser Lloyd: Moore Swift: Demaine Pascoe Thompson Davies Thomas Gallagher:
Tries - O'Rourke(2) Lloyd(2) Andrews: Goal - Thompson:
Referee W Horsfall (Batley) Att - 4500 H.T. 4 - 3

Sat 20 Apr 1929 HULL KINGSTON ROVERS away lost nil - 13
HULL K R - Osborne: Bateman Cook Jordan Spamer: McIntyre Dale: Britton Sharpe C.Westerdale Binks F.Westerdale Feetham:
Tries - Spamer Feetham F.Westerdale: Goals - Osborne(2):
CASTLEFORD - JOSEPH WALKER(74): Chapman Trevis Atkinson Asquith: Casey Stones: Sherwood Plimmer Wormald Russell GEORGE H.DEVONSHIRE(75) Hirst:
Referee H Swift (Halifax) Att - 4500 H.T. nil - nil

Mon 22 Apr 1929 DEWSBURY away won 23 - 13
DEWSBURY - Davies: Coates "Jones" Hirst Craven: H.Mitchell Fortis: G.Mitchell Rhodes Hobson Bland Brown Sperrett:
Tries - Coates(2) Craven: Goals - Coates(2)
CASTLEFORD - Hargrave: Chapman Trevis Atkinson Asquith: Casey Stones: Sherwood Plimmer Wormald Russell Walton Hirst:
Tries - Stones(2) Atkinson Casey Chapman: Goals - Hargrave(4):
Referee A Brown (Wakefield) Att - 1500 H.T. 12 - 5

Sat 27 Apr 1929 HULL home won 28 – 5
CASTLEFORD - Walker: Asquith Atkinson Hargrave Chapman: Casey Stones: Sherwood Plimmer Wormald Russell Walton Hirst:
Tries - Asquith Atkinson Hargrave Chapman Casey Sherwood:
Goals - Hargrave(3) Atkinson Walker(DG):
HULL - Jenney: Davies Lyon Oliver Gwynne: Phillipson Caswell: Bowman Pickering Short Bateson Longbottom Carmichael:
Try - Bateson: Goal - Oliver:
Referee A Brown (Wakefield) Att - 3000 H.T. 10 - nil

Arthur Sherwood
D. No 62
1928 29 to 1933-34

James Powell
D. No 70
1928-29 to 1930-31

**Sat 6 October 1928
BRADFORD
NORTHERN away won
13 - 10**
Back Row – Tommy
Needham Jack Wormold
Bob Nichols Fred Carter
Bill Renton Dick Walton
Arthur Sherwood
Front Row – Harold
Chapman Bill Asquith
Arthur Atkinson William
(Bill) Hargrave Edwin
Jones Arthur (Jim)Trevis

Sat 6 Apr 1929 CHALLENGE CUP SEMI-FINAL – v DEWSBURY at Huddersfield lost 3 – 9
Back Row – Charlie Dell (Ambulance Man) Jack Leake Dick Walton Harry Russell Arthur Sherwood Bob Nichols Jack
Wormold Jim Plimmer (Reserve)
Front Row – Jim Bacon (Trainer) Harold Chapman Bill Hargrave Arthur Atkinson (Captain) Bill Asquith Arthur Feltham
John Casey Jim Trevis

SEASON 1928-29

D,N	PLAYER		DEBUT	L MATCH	APP	SUB	T.AP	TR'S	G'LS	D.GS	P'TS
1	HARGRAVE	WILLIAM			36	0	36	15	27	0	99
6	NEEDHAM	THOMAS		23/03/1929	14	0	14	4	0	0	12
7	TREVIS	ARTHUR			25	0	25	1	0	0	3
8	LEAKE	JACK		06/04/1929	19	0	19	3	0	0	9
9	NICHOLLS	ROBERT			28	0	28	0	0	0	0
10	RENTON	WILLIAM		24/11/1928	12	0	12	0	0	0	0
11	MALKIN	JOSEPH			3	0	3	0	0	0	0
12	WORMALD	JACK			36	0	36	1	0	0	3
14	RUSSELL	HARRY (DANNY)			32	0	32	0	0	0	0
16	ASQUITH	WILLIAM (NAT)			36	0	36	10	0	0	30
21	ATKINSON	ARTHUR			37	0	37	13	28	0	95
23	WALTON	RICHARD			35	0	35	1	0	0	3
24	FELTHAM	ARTHUR			18	0	18	0	7	0	14
25	DICKINSON	ALBERT		25/08/1928	1	0	1	0	0	0	0
33	SYLVESTER	HARRY		22/09/1928	3	0	3	1	0	0	3
39	PLIMMER	JAMES			15	0	15	1	0	0	3
43	KINSEY	VICTOR			1	0	1	0	0	0	0
44	MATTICK	ROBERT			9	0	9	0	0	0	0
47	CARTER	FRED		07/11/1928	12	0	12	5	0	0	15
48	BACON	JOSHUA (JIM)			8	0	8	1	0	0	3
56	STONES	SAMMY			20	0	20	2	0	0	6
58	CHAPMAN	HAROLD			35	0	35	8	0	0	24
59	SHERWOOD	WILLIAM	01/09/1928	01/09/1928	1	0	1	0	0	0	0
60	WOODALL	HARRY	01/09/1928	05/09/1928	2	0	2	0	0	0	0
61	BEDWORTH	MILLWARD	15/09/1928	15/09/1928	1	0	1	0	0	0	0
62	SHERWOOD	ARTHUR	15/09/1928		37	0	37	2	0	0	6
63	JONES	EDWIN	22/09/1928	24/11/1928	7	0	7	0	0	0	0
64	THOMAS	EDWIN	20/10/1928		3	0	3	1	0	0	3
65	HODGSON	BENJAMIN T.	03/11/1928	10/11/1928	2	0	2	0	0	0	0
66	MASKILL	RAYMOND	17/11/1928		4	0	4	0	0	0	0
67	WHITEHOUSE	HERBERT	24/11/1928	01/12/1928	2	0	2	0	0	0	0
68	WRAITH	WILLIAM	24/11/1928	26/12/1928	5	0	5	1	0	0	3
69	CASEY	JOHN	25/12/1928		20	0	20	5	0	0	15
70	POWELL	JAMES	29/03/1929		4	0	4	0	0	0	0
71	HIRST	HARRY	30/03/1929		5	0	5	0	0	0	0
72	WHARVILLE	HERBERT	01/04/1929	01/04/2029	1	0	1	0	0	0	0
73	ROOKES	WALTER	13/04/1929	13/04/1929	1	0	1	0	0	0	0
74	WALKER	JOSEPH	20/04/1929		2	0	2	0	0	1	2
75	DEVONSHIRE	GEORGE H.	20/04/1929		1	0	1	0	0	0	0
39			**17**	**15**	**533**	**●**	**533**	**75**	**62**	**1**	**351**

COMPETITION		P	W	D	L	FOR	AGT
LEAGUE	POSITION 21 OF 28	34	11	4	19	268	369
YORK'S CUP		3	2	0	1	33	14
RL CUP		4	3	0	1	50	16
PLAYERS RECORDS		**41**	**16**	**4**	**21**	**351**	**399**

In the League Carlisle were admitted, but disbanded after only ten matches with their results being expunged from the records.

This season brought the Club's first representative honours. William Renton playing for Yorkshire in their 10-33 defeat by Lancashire at Halifax on 3 November 1928, and Arthur Atkinson playing for England in their 21–20 victory against an Other Nationalities team played at Leeds on 20 March 1929.

Bill Hargrave set the record for scoring most points in a Cup game to 14 against Whitehaven at home in the R.L. Challenge Cup on the 9 February 1929.

**Sat 24 Aug 1929 A T LAZENBY X111 Won 63 - 8
GREGORY CUP -FRIENDLY**
CASTLEFORD - Walker: Chapman Bacon Atkinson
Asquith: Casey Stones: Sherwood Plimmer Powell
Wormald Walton Russell:
Tries - Atkinson(5) Casey(3) Chapman(2) Stones(2) Bacon
Sherwood Wormald:
Goals - Atkinson(5) Stones(2) Sherwood Walton:
A T LAZENBY team not known:
Tries - Mattick Rudd: Goal - Rudd:
Referee   Att - 2000 H.T. 31 - nil

**Sat 31 Aug 1929 BRADFORD NORTHERN home
won 11 - 8**
CASTLEFORD - Walker: Chapman Bacon Atkinson
Asquith: Casey Stones: Sherwood Plimmer Powell
Wormald Walton Russell:
Tries - Chapman Atkinson Wormald: Goal - Atkinson:
BRADFORD N - Reed: Fordham W.R.Smith Gledhill Sims:
Preston Sharpe: Spencer Dolan Woodruffe Cox Hume
Malone: Goals - Reed(2) Gledhill(2):
Referee H Swift (Halifax) Att - 2000 H.T. nil - 6

Tue 3 Sep 1929 WAKEFIELD TRINITY home lost 7 - 8
CASTLEFORD - Walker: Stones Asquith Bacon Chapman:
Casey Robert Mattick: Sherwood THOMAS TOOTLES(76)
Wormald GEORGE STAFFORD(77) Russell Hirst:
Try - Casey: Goals - Casey Stones:
WAKEFIELD T - Ward: Bateson Jones E.Pollard Ray:
Metcalfe Pearce: Moss White Higson Horton Exley
Glossop: Tries - Bateson Ray: Goal - Pollard:
Referee R Robinson (Bradford) Att – 3000 H.T. 2 - 2

Sat 7 Sep 1929 HUNSLET away lost 9 - 35
HUNSLET - Walkington: Broughton Coulson Beverley
Kitching: Howarth Todd: Jenkins White Traill Dawson
Crowther Chapman:
Tries - Coulson(2) Kitching(2) Chapman(2) Broughton
Howarth Dawson: Goals - Traill(4):
CASTLEFORD - Bacon: Chapman Hirst Asquith WILLIAM
JAMES(78): Casey Stones: Sherwood Tootles Wormald
Stafford Kinsey Russell: Tries - James(2) Chapman:
Referee A Brown (Wakefield) Att - 5500 H.T. 3 - 14

Sat 14 Sep 1929 DEWSBURY home draw 13 - 13
CASTLEFORD - Joseph Walker: James Atkinson Asquith
Chapman: Casey Stones: Sherwood Thomas Tootles
Wormald Russell Stafford Harry Hirst:
Tries - James Asquith Casey:
Goals - Sherwood Stones(DG):
DEWSBURY - Osbaldestin: Raywood Hirst Layhe Smith:
Coates Grimes: Rhodes Brown Hobson Malkin Evans
Orford:
Tries - Layhe Smith Grimes: Goals - Coates Malkin:
Referee J McEwan (York) Att - 4000 H.T. 6 - nil

Sat 21 Sep 1929 LEIGH away lost 2 - 37
LEIGH - Clarkson: Slater Osborne Nolan Kenny: Green
Crook: Leyland Rudd Worrall Wood Prescott Hurtley:
Tries - Kenny(3) Green(2) Slater Osborne Prescott Hurtley:

Goals - Hurtley(5):
CASTLEFORD - GEORGE LEWIS(79): James Atkinson
Asquith Chapman: Casey Stones: Sherwood Plimmer
Powell Wormald Russell Stafford:
Goal - Atkinson:
Referee B Laughlin (Batley) Att - 3000 H.T. 2 - 24

Sat 28 Sep 1929 HALIFAX home lost 4 - 6
CASTLEFORD - Arthur Feltham: James Atkinson Asquith
Casey: Trevis Stones: Sherwood Plimmer Walton Wormald
Stafford AUGUSTINE GORMAN(80):
Goals - Atkinson(2):
HALIFAX - Davies: Gill Rhodes Haigh Adams: Fletcher
Gledhill: Gelder Bentham Crabtree Swan Briggs Rees:
Tries - Haigh Adams:
Referee H Horsfall (Batley) Att - 3000 H.T. 2 - 3

Sat 5 Oct 1929 BRAMLEY away lost nil - 9
BRAMLEY - Parkinson: Vowles Morgan Hughes
Witherington: Gadsby Ballantyne: Bowden Reed
Wilkinson Walker Tasker Rowan:
Try - Rowan: Goals - Parkinson (1)(DG) Walker:
CASTLEFORD - Atkinson: James JOHN CAYSER(81)
Asquith Chapman: Trevis Stones: Sherwood Plimmer
Walton Wormald Russell Gorman:
Referee H Horsfall (Batley) Att - 3000 H.T. nil - nil

Wed 9 Oct 1929 AUSTRALIA lost 2 - 53
CASTLEFORD - Stones: James Atkinson Asquith Chapman:
Trevis Casey: Sherwood(S/O) Plimmer Walton Wormald
Russell Gorman: Goal - Atkinson:
AUSTRALIA - Upton: Ridley Laws Holmes Finch: Kadwell
Weisel: Madsen Justice Root Dempsey(S/O) Kingston
Sellars: Tries - Ridley(5) Finch(3) Kingston(2) Kadwell
Upton Justice: Goals - Weisel(5) Kadwell(2):
Referee W Wood (Oldham) Att - 4000 H.T. 2 - 13

Sat 12 Oct 1929 YORK home lost 8 - 17
CASTLEFORD - WILLIAM GLEDHILL(82): James Atkinson
Asquith Chapman: Casey Trevis: Sherwood Plimmer
Walton Stafford Russell Gorman:
Tries - Chapman(2): Goal - Atkinson:
YORK - Owen: Thompson Batten Hoult Sherburn: Mills
Pickard: Mirfield Myers Collins Aspinall Gregory Bielby:
Tries - Thompson Mills Bielby: Goals - Sherburn(4):
Referee F Peel (Bradford) Att - 3000 H.T. 3 - 7

**Sat 19 Oct 1929 HALIFAX away lost 5 - 18
YORKSHIRE CUP ROUND 1**
HALIFAX - Davies: Gill Atkinson Haigh M.Smith: Fletcher
Gledhill: Gelder Bentham Crabtree H.Smith Renton Rees:
Tries - Gill Atkinson Fletcher Gledhill: Goals - Davies(3):
CASTLEFORD - Hargrave: James Atkinson Asquith
Chapman: Trevis Stones: Walton Plimmer Wormald
Russell Stafford Gorman:
Try - Atkinson: Goal - Atkinson:
Referee A E Harding (Man'ster) Att - 9000 H.T. 5 - 2

SEASON 1929-30

Sat 26 Oct 1929 ST HELENS away won 20 - 10
ST HELENS - Lewis: Hardgrave Frodsham R.Jones
Robinson: T.Jones H.Frodsham: Atkin Bailey Houghton
Hutt Halfpenny Shaw: Goals - Lewis(5):
CASTLEFORD - Gledhill: Asquith Atkinson Trevis James:
JOHN WINSTANLEY(83) Stones: Wormald Plimmer
Walton Russell Gorman Bacon:
Tries - Asquith Bacon: Goals Atkinson(6) Stones:
Referee H Swift (Batley) Att - 3000 H.T. 8 - 7
**Atkinson's third goal was kicked from 75 yards giving
Castleford the lead at 9 - 8 and is the longest goal
kicked in a Rugby League match.
Guinness Book Of Records 1995.**

Sat 2 Nov 1929 KEIGHLEY home lost 6 - 14
CASTLEFORD - Gledhill: Asquith Atkinson Trevis James:
Casey Stones: Sherwood Plimmer Walton Wormald
Russell Bacon: Tries - Asquith Atkinson:
KEIGHLEY - Taylor: Holmes Collins Oates Kendall: Foster
Holmes: Langhorn Moore Firth McGoun Burton Fox:
Tries - Kendall Collins: Goals - Kendall(3) Taylor:
Referee J E Taylor (Hull) Att - 2000 H.T. 6 - 2

Sat 9 Nov 1929 HULL away lost 9 - 41
HULL - Courtney: Lyon Davies Oliver Gwynne: Whitty
Everett: Howlett Pickering Short Carmichael Milner(S/O)
Longbottom:
Tries - Oliver(2) Carmichael(2) Lyon Davies Gwynne
Howlett Milner: Goals - Oliver(7):
CASTLEFORD - Gledhill: Asquith Hargrave Trevis
Chapman: Casey WILSON HALL(84): ALBERT LEESE(85)
Nicholls Walton(S/O) Russell Gorman Joshua(Jim)Bacon:
Try - Asquith: Goals - Hargrave(3):
Referee J McEwan (York) Att - 2000 H.T. nil - 21

Sat 23 Nov 1929 BATLEY home won 11 - 6
CASTLEFORD - Gledhill: Asquith Atkinson James
Hargrave: Hall Stones: Sherwood Plimmer Wormald
Stafford Gorman Russell:
Tries - Asquith James Gorman: Goal - Atkinson:
BATLEY - Lyman: Broom Caswell Hall Stenton: Wood
Whittaker: Brook Litt Bennett Baxter Shirley Kendall:
Tries - Broom Baxter:
Referee A Brown (Wakefield) Att -   H.T. 5 - nil

Wed 27 Nov 1929 LEEDS away lost 8 - 34
LEEDS - Rosser: O'Rourke Moores Askin Andrews:
Williams Swift: Demaine Pascoe Thomas Douglas Jenkins
Evans: Tries - Moores(4) Evans(2) Swift Jenkins:
Goals - Pascoe(4) Moores:
CASTLEFORD - Gledhill: Chapman Atkinson Asquith
Hargrave: James Hall: Powell Plimmer Wormald
Devonshire Gorman Russell:
Tries - James Hall: Goal - Hargrave:
Referee B Laughlin (Batley) Att - 5000 H.T. 8 – 15

**Sat 7 Dec 1929 HULL KINGSTON ROVERS home
draw nil - nil**
CASTLEFORD - Gledhill: Chapman Hargrave Asquith
Stones: James Hall: Sherwood Plimmer Walton Stafford

Gorman Russel :
HULL K R - Osborne: Bateman Cook Jordan Rainton: Dale
Spamer: Britten Sharpe Roberts Binks Westerdale
Williams:
Referee H Horsfall (Batley) Att -   H.T.

Sat 14 Dec 1929 BATLEY away won 19 - 5
BATLEY - Rogers: Broom Hall Chisnall Arran: Wood
Whittaker: Dyson Wilkinson Litt Shirley Green Baxter:
Try - Broom: Goal - Litt:
CASTLEFORD - Gledhill: Chapman Hargrave Asquith
Stones: James Hall: Sherwood Plimmer Wormald Stafford
Gorman Russell:
Tries - Hargrave Stones Hall: Goals - Hargrave(3) James(2)
Referee R W Bateman (Hull) Att - 2000 H.T. 10 - 5

Sat 21 Dec 1929 HUDDERSFIELD home lost 2 - 22
CASTLEFORD - William Gledhill: Stones Atkinson WALLY
DESMOND(86) Hargrave: James Hall: Sherwood Plimmer
Wormald Stafford Gorman Russell:
Goal - Hargrave:
HUDDERSFIELD - Stocks: Mills Brook Brogden Smart:
Bowkett Thompson: Rudd Halliday Gee Tiffany T.Banks
Morton:
Tries - Mills(4) Brogden Thompson: Goals - Brook(2)
Referee J McEwan (York) Att - 2000 H.T. 2 - 6

**Wed 25 Dec 1929 FEATHERSTONE ROVERS away
lost 4 - 11**
FEATHERSTONE R - S.Denton: J.Denton Smith Hirst
Pickup: Whittaker Annable: Barraclough P.Morris
Rogerson Norbury Darlison Bradley:
Tries - Hirst(2) Pickup: Goal - J.Denton:
CASTLEFORD - Hargrave: Stones Atkinson Wally
Desmond James: Casey Hall: Walton Plimmer Jack
Wormald Stafford Victor Kinsey Russell:
Goals - Atkinson (2):
Referee F Peel (Bradford) Att -   H.T. 4 - 5

Thu 26 Dec 1929 HUNSLET home lost 3 - 7
CASTLEFORD - Lewis: Stones Atkinson Asquith Hargrave:
James Hall: Sherwood Gorman Walton Stafford STANLEY
JENNINGS(87) Russell:
Try - Atkinson:
HUNSLET - Walkington: Broughton Beverley Coulson
Rhodes: Todd Thornton: Jenkins White Smith Moss
Dawson Chapman:
Try - Todd: Goals Walkington(1)(DG):
Referee   Att - 4500 H.T. nil - 5

Sat 28 Dec 1929 ST HELENS home won 5 - nil
CASTLEFORD - Lewis: Thomas Asquith Atkinson Stones:
James Hall: Sherwood Plimmer Walton Stafford Jennings
Russell:
Try - Atkinson: Goal - Stones:
ST HELENS - Crooks: Hardgrave Lewis Mercer Ellaby:
Dennett Dowdal : Atkin Unwin Haughton Hall Halfpenny
Greaves:
Referee A E Harding (Man'ster) Att - 1000 H.T. 5 - nil

SEASON 1929-30

Sat 4 Jan 1930 HALIFAX away won 3 - 2
HALIFAX - Higgins: Gill Rhodes Haigh M.Smith: Gledhill
Werrett: Gelder Rawnsley Crabtree Norcliffe Rees
Townend: Goal - Higgins:
CASTLEFORD - Lewis: Stones Asquith Trevis Thomas:
James Hall: Sherwood Plimmer Walton Jennings Stafford
Russell: Try - Asquith:
Referee H Horsfall (Batley) Att - 6000 H.T. 3 - nil

Sat 11 Jan 1930 LEEDS home lost 2 - 22
CASTLEFORD - Lewis: Thomas Asquith Atkinson Stones:
James Hall: Sherwood Plimmer Walton Jennings Russell
George H.Devonshire: Goal - James:
LEEDS - Goldie: O'Rourke Moores Rosser Smith: Williams
Adams: Demaine Pascoe Thompson Thomas Douglas
Evans:
Tries - Rosser(2) Moores Thompson: Goals Thompson(5):
Referee B Laughlin (Batley) Att - 5000 H.T. nil - 12

Sat 18 Jan 1930 KEIGHLEY away lost nil - 2
KEIGHLEY - Taylor: Collins Holmes Oakes Paley: Hall
Foster: Thompson Moore Firth McGoun Burton Fox:
Goal - Taylor:
CASTLEFORD - Hargrave: Stones Atkinson James Asquith:
Arthur J.Trevis Hall: Sherwood Plimmer Walton Russell
Jennings Gorman:
Referee R Robinson (Bradford) Att - 3500 H.T. nil - nil

Sat 25 Jan 1930 HULL home won 8 - 3
CASTLEFORD - William Hargrave: Asquith Atkinson
Chapman James: Stones Hall: Sherwood Plimmer Powell
Walton Jennings Russell:
Tries - Stones Walton: Goal - Hargrave:
HULL - Jenney: Hartley Courtney Oliver Gwynne:
Phillipson Metcalfe: Bowman Pickering Short Carmichael
Eastburn Bateson: Try - Bowman:
Referee A McEwan (York) Att - 3000 H.T. nil - nil

**Sat 1 Feb 1930 BRADFORD NORTHERN away
lost 2 - 9**
BRADFORD N - W.Sherwood: Raymond W.R.Smith
T.R.Smith Abson: Pearson Gledhill: Coates Dolan Fay Cox
Malone Thornber: Tries - Abson(3):
CASTLEFORD - Lewis: Stones Marshall Asquith Chapman:
Casey Hall: Sherwood Plimmer Powell Walton Jennings
Russell:
Goal - Sherwood:
Referee J E Taylor (Wakefield) Att -   H.T. 2 - 3

**Sat 8 Feb 1930 BRAMLEY home won 11 - 4
CHALLENGE CUP ROUND 1**
CASTLEFORD - Lewis: Stones Atkinson Asquith Chapman:
James Hall: Sherwood Plimmer Walton Stafford Jennings
Gorman:
Tries - Stafford(2) Asquith: Goal - Stones:
BRAMLEY - Parkinson: Whitham Morgan Roberts Vowles:
Whelan Ballantine: Rhodes Bowden Rees Wilkinson
Harrison Rowan:
Goals - Parkinson(1)(DG):
Referee F Fairhurst (Wigan) Att - 5500 H.T. 8 - 2

Sat 15 Feb 1930 BRAMLEY home won 14 - 6
CASTLEFORD - Lewis: Stones Atkinson Asquith MEL
ROSSER(88): James Hall: Sherwood Plimmer Walton
Stafford Jennings Gorman:
Try - Atkinson Hall Sherwood Gorman: Goal - Atkinson:
HULL - Jenney: Winsor Oliver Davies Gwynne: Mills
Caswell: Bowman Pickering Howlett Bateson Errington
Carmichael:
Goal - Bateson(2) Oliver:
Referee J Eddon (Swinton) Att - 7500 H.T. nil - 4

**Sat 22 Feb 1930 HULL home lost 3 - 6
CHALLENGE CUP ROUND 2**
CASTLEFORD - Lewis: Stones Atkinson Asquith Chapman:
James Hall: Sherwood Plimmer Walton Stafford Jennings
Gorman:
Try - Asquith:
HULL - Jenney: Winsor Oliver Davies Gwynne: Mills
Caswell: Bowman Pickering Howlett Bateson Errington
Carmichael:
Goals - Bateson(2) Oliver:
Referee J Eddon (Swinton) Att - 7500 H.T. nil - 4

**Sat 1 Mar 1930 HULL KINGSTON ROVERS away
lost 3 - 39**
HULL K R - Carmichael: Bateman McIntyre Jordan
Rainton: Dale Spamer: Britten Roberts Westerdale Binks
Brindle Williams:
Tries - Dale(2) Williams(2) Bateman McIntyre Spamer
Britten Westerdale: Goals - Carmichael(6):
CASTLEFORD - Lewis: Chapman Asquith Atkinson James:
Casey Stones: Sherwood Plimmer Walton Stafford
Jennings Russell:
Try - Walton:
Referee A Brown (Wakefield) Att - 3000 H.T. nil - 29

Sat 15 Mar 1930 HUDDERSFIELD away lost 5 - 34
HUDDERSFIELD - Turton: Mills Brook Brogden Smart: Gee
Bates: Thompson Halliday Rudd Tiffany Morton Young:
Tries - Mills(2) Brogden(2) Tiffany(2) Smart Halliday
Young Morton: Goals - Brook(2):
CASTLEFORD - Lewis: Thomas Atkinson Asquith
Chapman: WILLIAM R.SMITH(89)Hall: Sherwood WILLIAM
DOLAN(90) Walton Stafford Russell Gorman:
Try - Smith: Goal - Sherwood:
Referee H Swift (Halifax) Att - 2000 H.T. 5 - 14

**Sat 22 Mar 1930 WIGAN HIGHFIELD home
lost 7 - 14**
CASTLEFORD - Lewis: Chapman Asquith Smith Thomas:
James Hall: Sherwood Plimmer Powell Walton Jennings
Russell:
Try - Hall: Goals - Sherwood Lewis(DG):
WIGAN H - Unsworth: Maloney Hunter Walker Colley:
Burkhill Winstanley: Lowe Fairhurst Worsley Green Gore
Hilton:
Tries - Colley(2) Hunter Burkhill: Goal - Hunter:
Referee W Wood (Oldham) Att - 2500 H.T. nil - 6

SEASON 1929-30

Wed 26 Mar 1930 WARRINGTON home lost 10 - 17
CASTLEFORD - Lewis: Asquith Atkinson Marshall Chapman: DON ROBINSON(91) Stones: Sherwood Plimmer Walton Russell Stafford Gorman:
Tries - Atkinson(2): Goals - Sherwood(2):
WARRINGTON - Holding;Blinkhorn Perkins Dingsdale Thompson: Flynn Davies: Miller Bentham Cunliffe Williams Meredith Jones:
Tries - Dingsdale(2) Thompson: Goals - Holding(4):
Referee A E Harding (Man'ster) Att - 1500 H.T. 5 - 10

Sat 29 Mar 1930 YORK away lost nil - 5
YORK - Owen: Sherburn Layhe Batten Lloyd: W.J.Davies Thomas: Myers Johnson Mason H.Davies Bielby Battersby:
Try - Myers: Goal - Sherburn:
CASTLEFORD - Lewis: Asquith Atkinson Marshall Chapman: Robinson Hall: Sherwood Plimmer Walton Russell Stafford Gorman:
Referee A Brown (Wakefield) Att - 5000 H.T. nil - 5

Sat 5 Apr 1930 WARRINGTON away lost 7 - 22
WARRINGTON - Holding: Blinkhorn Griffiths Dingsdale Thompson: Flynn Davies: Miller Bentham Cunliffe Williams Meredith Jones:
Tries - Blinkhorn Dingsdale Davies Williams:
Goals Holding(5):
CASTLEFORD - Lewis: Asquith Atkinson Marshall Chapman: J.Winstanley Hall: Sherwood Plimmer Walton Russell Stafford Gorman:
Try - Asquith: Goals - Sherwood Lewis(DG):
Referee J McEwan (York) Att - 4000 H.T. 2 - 4

Wed 9 Apr 1930 WAKEFIELD TRINITY away won 6 - 2
WAKEFIELD T - Warrington: C.Pollard E.Pollard Jones Herberts: Davies Parkin: Moss White Higson Horton Exley Glossop: Goal - C.Pollard:
CASTLEFORD - Atkinson: Lewis Asquith Marshall Chapman: J.Winstanley A.N.OTHER(92): Sherwood Plimmer Walton Stafford Russell Gorman:
Tries - Chapman Walton:
Referee R Robinson (Bradford) Att - H.T. 3 - 2

Sat 12 Apr 1930 LEIGH home lost 5 - 6
CASTLEFORD - Atkinson: Lewis Asquith Marshall Chapman: J.Winstanley THOMAS WINSTANLEY(93): Sherwood Plimmer Walton Russell Jennings Gorman:
Try - Atkinson: Goal - Atkinson:
LEIGH - Clarkson: Baxter Crook Tolan Kenny: Green Keegan: Lewyland Rudd Worrall Griffin Waterworth Hurtley: Tries - Kenny(2):
Referee E Houghton (Warr'gton) Att - 2000 H.T. nil - 3

Fri 18 Apr 1930 FEATHERSTONE ROVERS home won 11 - 3
CASTLEFORD - Lewis: Chapman Atkinson William R.Smith Asquith: J.Winstanley Hall: Sherwood Plimmer Walton Jennings Stafford Russell:
Try - Atkinson: Goals - Atkinson(4)
FEATHERSTONE R - S.Denton: J.Denton Hirst Whittaker F.Smith: Owens Howarth: S.Smith Morris Rogerson Norbury L.Morgan J.Morgan: Try - Owens:
Referee F Peel (Bradford) Att - 4000 H.T. 11 - nil

Sat 19 Apr 1930 WIGAN HIGHFIELD away lost 6 - 46
WIGAN H - Bennett: Maloney Hunter Bradbury Cowley: Burkhill Whittle: Lowe Fairhurst Worsley Green Smith Gore:
Tries - Hunter(4) Maloney(2) Bradbury(2) Cowley Green: Goals - Bennett(5) Smith(2):
CASTLEFORD - Lewis: Chapman Atkinson Marshall Stones: J.Winstanley Hall: Walton Plimmer Stafford Jennings Russell Gorman: Tries Atkinson(2):
Referee H Horsfall (Batley) Att H.T. nil - 22

Tue 22 Apr 1930 DEWSBURY away lost nil - 20
DEWSBURY - Osbaldestin: Raywood Smith Hoult Hirst: Coates Grimes: Connolly Booth Evans Woolmore Malkin Joe Lyman:
Tries - Hirst(2) Osbaldestin Evans: Goals - Lynam(4):
CASTLEFORD - Marshall: Chapman Atkinson(S/O) Asquith Casey: J.Winstanley Stones: Sherwood Plimmer Walton Jennings Russell Gorman:
Referee F Peel (Bradford) Att - 3000 H.T. nil – 5

William (Billy) James
D. No 78
1929-30 to 1934-35

George Lewis
D. No 79
1929-30 to 1944-45

Wilson Hall
D. No 84
1929-30 to 1934-35

SEASON 1929-30

D.N	PLAYER		DEBUT	L MATCH	APP	SUB	T.AP	TR'S	G'LS	D.G	P'TS
1	HARGRAVE	WILLIAM		25/01/1930	11	0	11	1	9	0	21
7	TREVIS	ARTHUR		18/01/1930	10	0	10	0	0	0	0
9	NICHOLLS	ROBERT			1	0	1	0	0	0	0
12	WORMALD	JACK		25/12/1929	16	0	16	1	0	0	3
14	RUSSELL	HARRY (DANNY)			36	0	36	0	0	0	0
16	ASQUITH	WILLIAM (NAT)			37	0	37	9	0	0	27
21	ATKINSON	ARTHUR			32	0	32	12	22	0	80
23	WALTON	RICHARD			32	0	32	3	0	0	9
24	FELTHAM	ARTHUR		28/09/1929	1	0	1	0	0	0	0
36	MARSHALL	ALBERT			8	0	8	0	0	0	0
39	PLIMMER	JAMES			34	0	34	0	0	0	0
43	KINSEY	VICTOR		25/12/1929	2	0	2	0	0	0	0
44	MATTICK	ROBERT		03/09/2029	1	0	1	0	0	0	0
48	BACON	JOSHUA (JIM)		09/11/2029	6	0	6	1	0	0	3
56	STONES	SAMMY			30	0	30	2	4	1	16
58	CHAPMAN	HAROLD			28	0	28	5	0	0	15
62	SHERWOOD	ARTHUR			34	0	34	1	7	0	17
64	THOMAS	EDWIN			5	0	5	0	0	0	0
69	CASEY	JOHN			14	0	14	2	1	0	8
70	POWELL	JAMES			6	0	6	0	0	0	0
71	HIRST	HARRY		14/09/1929	3	0	3	0	0	0	0
74	WALKER	JOSEPH		14/09/1929	3	0	3	0	0	0	0
75	DEVONSHIRE	GEORGE H.		11/01/1930	2	0	2	0	0	0	0
76	TOOTLES	THOMAS	03/09/1929	14/09/1929	3	0	3	0	0	0	0
77	STAFFORD	GEORGE	03/09/1929		26	0	26	2	0	0	6
78	JAMES	WILLIAM	07/09/1929		27	0	27	5	3	0	21
79	LEWIS	GEORGE	21/09/1929		19	0	19	0	0	2	4
80	GORMAN	AUGUSTINE	28/09/1929		25	0	25	2	0	0	6
81	CAYSER	JOHN	05/10/1929	05/10/1929	1	0	1	0	0	0	0
82	GLEDHILL	WILLIAM	12/10/1929	21/12/1929	9	0	9	0	0	0	0
83	WINSTANLEY	JOHN	26/10/1929		7	0	7	0	0	0	0
84	HALL	WILSON	09/11/1929		23	0	23	4	0	0	12
85	LEESE	ALBERT	09/11/1929		1	0	1	0	0	0	0
86	DESMOND	WALLY	21/12/1929	25/12/1929	2	0	2	0	0	0	0
87	JENNINGS	STANLEY	26/12/1929		16	0	16	0	0	0	0
88	ROSSER	MEL	15/02/1930	15/02/1930	1	0	1	0	0	0	0
89	SMITH	WILLIAM	15/03/1930	18/04/1930	3	0	3	1	0	0	3
90	DOLAN	WILLIAM	15/03/1930	15/03/1930	1	0	1	0	0	0	0
91	ROBINSON	DONALD	26/03/1930		2	0	2	0	0	0	0
92	A.N.OTHER		09/04/1930	09/04/1930	1	0	1	0	0	0	0
93	WINSTANLEY	THOMAS	12/04/1930	12/04/1930	1	0	1	0	0	0	0
	41		**18**	**19**	**520**	**0**	**520**	**51**	**46**	**3**	**251**

	COMPETITION		P	W	D	L	FOR	AGT
	LEAGUE	POSITION 26 OF 28	36	10	2	24	230	535
	YORK'S CUP		1	0	0	1	5	18
	RL CUP		2	1	0	1	14	10
	AUSTRALIA		1	0	0	1	2	53
	PLAYERS RECORDS		**40**	**11**	**2**	**27**	**251**	**616**

This season will be remembered for Castleford signing its first overseas player – Augustine (Gus) Gorman, an Australian loose forward who made his debut against Halifax at home on 28 September 1928 losing 4–6. He was followed by two New Zealanders, scrum half Wilson Hall who made his debut in the 9-41 away defeat by Hull on 9 November 1929, and stand off Wally Desmond who made his debut in the 2-21 home defeat by Huddersfield on 21 December 1929.

When Arthur Atkinson kicked his 75 yard goal at St Helens we had been awarded a penalty for a foul on Arthur and it is thought that he was still dazed when he took the kick at goal..

Former Widnes Player Dick Silcock was appointed Trainer replacing Jim Bacon.

SEASON 1930-31

5at 23 Aug 1930 FEATHERSTONE ROVERS away lost 5 - 11 LYON CUP - FRIENDLY

FEATHERSTONE R - S.Denton: J.Denton Whittaker Winter Smith: Shaw Stott: Barraclough P.Morris L.Morgan Darlison Norbury J.Morgan:
Tries - Winter Smith L.Morgan: Goal - Stott:
CASTLEFORD - Hargrave: Lewis Marshall Asquith Chapman: Winstanley Hall: Sherwood Plimmer Walton Maskill Stafford Russell: Try - Stafford: Goal - Hargrave:
Referee A S Dobson (Featherstone) Att 3000 H.T. 5 - 3

Sat 30 Aug 1930 DEWSBURY away lost 8 - 51

DEWSBURY - Osbaldestin: F.W.Hobson Smith Hoult Hirst: Coates Grimes: Connolly Booth Evans Marsden Woolmore Joe Lyman: Tries - Hobson(5) Smith(2) Hoult Hirst Woolmore Lyman: Goals - Lyman(9):
CASTLEFORD - JAMES HIGO(94): Chapman Marshall Asquith Sammy Stones: Don Robinson Hall: Sherwood Plimmer Powell Walton Maskill Russell:
Tries - Chapman Robinson: Goal - Sherwood:
Referee J McEwan (York) Att - 3000 H.T. nil - 24

Sat 6 Sep 1930 BRADFORD NORTHERN home won 31 - 2

CASTLEFORD - Lewis: Chapman Atkinson James Asquith: Casey Hall: Walton Plimmer Sherwood Russell Maskill Stafford: Tries - Chapman(3) James(2) Atkinson Asquith: Goals - James(5):
BRADFORD N - Gledhill: Haigh Kay W.Sherwood Elsworth: Sykes McQuade: Fay Beard Appleyard Woodruff Hume Thornber: Goal - Gledhill:
Referee J Taylor (Wakefield) Att - 2000 H.T. 17 - 2

Wed 10 Sep 1930 HULL home won 16 - 4

CASTLEFORD - Lewis: Chapman Atkinson James Asquith: Casey Hall: Walton Plimmer Sherwood Russell Maskill Stafford: Tries - Chapman(2) Atkinson(2):
Goals - Atkinson Sherwood:
HULL - Courtney: Harsley Oliver Phillipson Sharpe: Mills Metcalfe: Thompson Pickering Short Bateson Bowman Longbottom: Goals - Oliver(2):
Referee F Peel (Bradford) Att - 2000 H.T. 8 - 4

Sat 13 Sep 1930 HUDDERSFIELD away lost 5 - 9

HUDDERSFIELD - Stocks: Mills Brogden Brook Bowkett: Spencer Thompson: Rudd Halliday Gee Tiffany Banks Young: Try - Gee: Goals - Stocks(2) Brook:
CASTLEFORD - Lewis: Chapman Atkinson Asquith HAROLD SPAWFORTH(95): Casey Hall: Walton Plimmer Sherwood Russell Maskill Stafford:
Try - Chapman: Goal - Atkinson:
Referee B Laughlin (Batley) Att - 5000 H.T. 2 - 3

Sat 20 Sep 1930 LEEDS home won 6 - 5

CASTLEFORD - Lewis: Chapman Marshall Asquith Spawforth: Casey Hall: Sherwood Plimmer Walton Russell Maskill Stafford: Tries - Marshall Hall:
LEEDS - Goldie: Cox O'Rourke Jones Eastwood: Swift Adams: Rawling Watson Thompson Evans Douglas Gill:
Try - Jones: Goal - Thompson:

Referee R Brown (Wakefield) Att - 4000 H.T. 3 - 5

Sat 27 Sep 1930 ROCHDALE HORNETS home won 3 - 2

CASTLEFORD - Lewis: Chapman Marshall Asquith Spawforth: Casey Hall: Sherwood Plimmer Walton Russell Maskill Stafford   Try - Casey:
ROCHDALE H - Gowers: Hall H.Evans Lindley Simpson: Whittle: Hill Miram Welsby Milne Whitehead Beattie Iveson: Goal - Gowers:
Referee F Fairhurst (Wigan) Att - 3000 H.T. nil - nil

Sat 4 Oct 1930 WIGAN HIGHFIELD away lost 3 - 24

WIGAN H - Bennett: Maloney Hunter Bradbury Cowley:Birkhill Whittle: Lowe Catterall Worsley Gore Green Hilton: Tries - Bennett Bradbury Cowley Lowe: Goals - Whittle(5) Green:
CASTLEFORD - Lewis: Chapman Atkinson Marshall Asquith: Casey Hall: Sherwood Plimmer Walton Russell Maskill Stafford   Try - Asquith:
Referee J McEwan (York) Att -   H.T. 3 - 6

Sat 11 Oct 1930 BRAMLEY away won 9 - 4 YORKSHIRE CUP ROUND 1

BRAMLEY - Laughton: Whitham Morgan Ballantine Paterson: Whelan Raynor: Reed Bowden Rhodes Parkinson Walker Rowan: Goals - Laughton(2):
CASTLEFORD - Lewis: Chapman Atkinson James Asquith: Casey Hall: Sherwood Plimmer Walton Russell Maskill Stafford: Try - James: Goals - James(3):
Referee J Molloy   Att - 5019 H.T. 2 - 2

Sat 18 Oct 1930 YORK home lost 10 - 11

CASTLEFORD - Lewis: Marshall John Winstanley James Asquith: Casey Hall: Sherwood CLIFFORD HARLING(96) Maskill Stafford Jennings Russell:
Tries - Asquith Maskill: Goals - James(2):
YORK - Owen: Sherburn Batten Lloyd Taylor: W.J.Davies Thomas: Myers Betteridge Pascoe Layhe Allen Johnson: Tries - Lloyd(2) Layhe: Goal - Pascoe:
Referee J Laughin (Batley) Att - 4000 H.T. 10 - 3

Thu 23 Oct 1930 HULL away lost 8 - 12 YORKSHIRE CUP ROUND 2

HULL - Ellerington: Bateman Oliver Lyon Windsor: Mills Metcalfe: Bowman Adamson Errington Larven Eastburn Bateson:
Tries - Bateman Oliver: Goals - Oliver(2) Bateson:
CASTLEFORD - Lewis: Chapman Atkinson Asquith James: Casey Hall: Sherwood Plimmer Stafford Maskill Jennings Russell: Goals - James(4):
Referee J Eddon (Swinton) Att - 5000 H.T. 4 - 5

Sat 25 Oct 1930 BRAMLEY away won 8 - 5

BRAMLEY - Taylor: Whitham Morgan Ballantyne Paterson: Hansell Rayner: Read Bowden Wilkinson Ingham Walker Parkinson: Try - Hansell: Goal - Walker:
CASTLEFORD - Marshall: Chapman James Asquith Spawforth: Casey Hall: Sherwood Plimmer Stafford Maskill KENNETH JUBB(97) Russell:

SEASON 1930-31

Tries - Casey Russell: Goal - James:
Referee H Swift (Wakefield) Att   H.T. 5 - 5

Sat 1 Nov 1930 WIDNES home lost 3 - 10
CASTLEFORD - Lewis: Chapman Marshall James Asquith:
Casey Hall: Walton Plimmer Stafford Maskill Jennings
Russell: Try - Asquith:
WIDNES - Bradley: A.Higgins Ratcliffe Topping Marshall:
Coyne Shannon: Kelsall Stevens Silcock Van Rooyen
J.Higgins Hoey:
Tries - Shannon(2): Goals - Ratcliffe Hoey:
Referee A E Harding (Man'ster) Att - 3000 H.T. nil - 8

Sat 8 Nov 1930 WIDNES away lost 4 - 6
WIDNES - Bradley: Marshall Topping Ratcliffe Owen:
Coyne Shannon: Kelsall Silcock Higgins Millington Hoey
McCafferty: Tries - Marshall Silcock:
CASTLEFORD - Marshall: Thomas James Lewis Asquith:
Casey Hall: Walton Plimmer Stafford Maskill Jennings
Russell: Goals - James(2):
Referee   Att -   H.T.

Sat 15 Nov 1930 HUNSLET home won 21 - 15
CASTLEFORD - Marshall: Chapman Atkinson THOMAS
C.ASKIN(98) James:Casey Hall: Walton Plimmer Stafford
Maskill Jennings Russell:
Tries - Atkinson(2) Casey: Goals - James(6):
HUNSLET - Walkington: Broughton Wilson Leach Adams:
Todd Thornton: Moss White Traill Dawson Smith
Chapman: Tries - Broughton Adams Dawson:
Goals - Walkington(2)(DG):
Referee J McEwen (York) Att - 5000 H.T. 12 - 12

Sat 22 Nov 1930 YORK away lost 5 - 11
YORK - Jordan: Taylor J.Davies Thomas Batten: W.J.Davies
Calvert: Myers Pascoe W.Davies Layhe H.Davies Johnson:
Tries - Taylor J.Davies Calvert: Goal - Pascoe:
CASTLEFORD - Lewis: Chapman Atkinson Askin Asquith:
Casey Hall: Walton Plimmer Stafford Maskill Jennings
Russell: Try - Lewis: Goal - Lewis:
Referee H Horsfall (Batley) Att - 1500 H.T. nil - 8

Sat 29 Nov 1930 BRAMLEY home won 22 - 3
CASTLEFORD - Lewis: Chapman Askin Asquith James:
Casey Hall: Sherwood Plimmer Stafford Walton Jennings
Russell:
Tries - Askin(2) Chapman Jennings: Goals - James(5):
BRAMLEY - Laughton: Whitham Morgan Withington
Sellars: Hansell Hughes: Reed Bowden Wilkinson
Parkinson Rowan Morrell: Try - Hughes:
Referee H Horsfall (Batley) Att - 1500 H.T. 4 - 3

Sat 6 Dec 1930 BARROW away lost 5 - 17
BARROW - Miller: Scott Carr Doyle Woods: J.McGarry
Curtis: Banks Burgess McManus Braithwaite Strong
McDowell: Tries - Carr(2) Scott: Goals - Burgess(4):
CASTLEFORD - Lewis: Chapman Askin Asquith James:
Casey Hall: Sherwood Plimmer Stafford Walton Jennings
Russell: Try - Chapman: Goal - James:
Referee B Laughlin (Batley) Att - 3000 H.T. 3 - 2

Sat 13 Dec 1930 WARRINGTON away lost 3 - 27
WARRINGTON - Holding: Hodgetts Perkins Dingsdale
Thompson: Flynn Kirk: Marsden(S/O) Jones Williams
Bentham Mason Seeling: Tries - Thompson(2) Dingsdale
Kirk Williams: Goals - Holding(6):
CASTLEFORD - Lewis: Chapman Askin Asquith James:
Casey Hall: Sherwood Plimmer Stafford(S/O) Walton
Jennings Russell: Try - Walton:
Referee J McEwan (York) Att -   H.T. nil - 9

Sat 20 Dec 1930 HULL KINGSTON ROVERS home won 14 - 7
CASTLEFORD - Lewis: Asquith Atkinson Askin James:
Casey:Hall: Sherwood Plimmer Walton Gorman Jennings
Russell: Tries - Atkinson(2) James(2): Goal - James:
HULL K R - Osborne: Blazier Spamer Hill Rhoades:
McIntyre Parkin: Britton Sharpe Binks Saddington Brindle
Westerdale: Try - Spamer: Goals - Osborne(2):
Referee F Peel (Bradford) Att - 4000 H.T. 5 - 5

Thu 25 Dec 1930 FEATHERSTONE ROVERS home won 7 - nil
CASTLEFORD - Lewis James Askin Atkinson Chapman
Casey Hall Sherwood Plimmer Walton Jennings(S/O)
Gorman William(Nat)Asquith
Try - Atkinson : Goals - Atkinson(2)
FEATHERSTONE R - S.Denton: J.Denton Winter F.Smith
J.Morris: Annable Stott: Darlison P.Morris Rogerson
L.Morgan S.Smith J.Morgan:
Referee W Hemmings   Att - 6000 H.T. 5 - nil

Fri 26 Dec 1930 HUNSLET away lost 9 - 10
HUNSLET - Walkington: Adams Johnson Coulson Wilson:
Todd Thornton: Jenkins White Traill Crowther Moss
Dawson: Tries - Todd Dawson: Goal - Walkington(2):
CASTLEFORD - Marshall: James Askin Atkinson Chapman:
Casey Hall: Sherwood Plimmer Walton Jennings Gorman
Stafford: Try - Stafford: Goals - James(3):
Referee R Robinson (Bradford) Att - 4000 H.T. 2 - 2

Sat 27 Dec 1930 HULL away lost 2 - 6
HULL - Jenney: Harsley Lyon Oliver Winsor: Phillipson
Metcalfe:Bowman Adamson Eastburn Bateson Errington
Carmichael: Goals - Oliver(3):
CASTLEFORD - Marshall: James Askin Atkinson Lewis:
Casey Hall: HARRY(MICK)HAND(99) Plimmer Walton
Gorman Jennings Stafford: Goal - James:
Referee A Brown (Wakefield) Att - 3000 H.T. 2 - 2

Sat 10 Jan 1931 BRADFORD NORTHERN away lost 12 - 15
BRADFORD N - Reed: Sykes Smith Eastwood Bailey: Rudd
Howarth: Appleyard(S/O) Watson Coates H.Tasker
Malone Thornber:
Tries - Eastwood(2) Howarth: Goals - Reed(3):
CASTLEFORD - Marshall: James Askin Atkinson Lewis:
Casey Hall: Sherwood Plimmer(S/O) Stafford Hand
Walton Russell: Tries - Askin Atkinson: Goals - James(3):
Referee B Laughlin (Batley) Att - 6000 H.T. 10 - 13

SEASON 1930-31

Sat 17 Jan 1931 WAKEFIELD TRINITY home won 5 -4
CASTLEFORD - Lewis: GEORGE ANDREWS(100)James
Askin Thomas: Casey Hall: Sherwood Plimmer Walton
Russell Stafford ARTHUR(CANDY)EVANS9(101):
Try - Stafford: Goal - Lewis(DG):
WAKEFIELD T - C.Pollard: Ray Jones Robinson Smart:
Pearce E.Pollard: Hudson White Field Horton Exley
Glossop: Goals - C.Pollard(2):
Referee B Horsfall (Batley) Att - 7000 H.T. nil - 4

Sat 24 Jan 1931 WARRINGTON home won 10 - 5
CASTLEFORD - Lewis: Andrews Atkinson Askin Thomas:
Casey Hall: Sherwood Plimmer Walton Russell Stafford
Evans: Tries - Hall(2): Goals - Atkinson(2):
WARRINGTON - Holding: Thompson Perkins Blinkhorne
Hodgetts: Flynn Davies: Mason Bentham Williams
Marsden Jones Seeling: Try - Flynn: Goal - Holding:
Referee A E Harding (Manchester) Att - 5000 H.T. 5 - 5

Sat 31 Jan 1931 SALFORD away lost 4 - 32
SALFORD - Risman: Boyd Dobing Fisher Hudson:
Matthews Meek: W.A.Williams Shaw Muir Middleton
Haines Dalton: Tries - Hudson(3) Risman Boyd Dobing
Muir Haines: Goals - Hudson(4)
CASTLEFORD - Lewis: Andrews Atkinson Askin Thomas:
James Hall: Sherwood Harling Walton Russell Stafford
Evans: Goals - James(2):
Referee J McEwen (York) Att - 5000 H.T. 2 - 3
Match Abandoned After 70 Minutes

**Sat 7 Feb 1931 HULL home draw nil - nil
CHALLENGE CUP ROUND 1**
CASTLEFORD - Lewis: James Atkinson Askin Thomas:
Casey Hall: Sherwood Harling Walton Stafford Russell
Evans:
HULL - Jenney: Winsor Oliver Lyon Harsley: Caswell
Mills:Bowman Adamson Thompson Errington Wood
Carmichael:
Referee J W Webb (Manchester) Att - 6000 H.T. nil - nil

**Thu 12 Feb 1931 HULL away won 5 - 4
CHALLENGE CUP ROUND 1 REPLAY**
HULL - Jenney: Bateman Oliver Lyon Winsor: Caswell
Mills: Bowman Adamson Errington Thompson Wood
A.Carmichael: Goals - Oliver(2):
CASTLEFORD - Lewis: Chapman Atkinson Askin Thomas:
James Hall: Sherwood Plimmer Walton Stafford Jennings
Russell: Try - Sherwood: Goal - James:
Referee J W Webb (Manchester) Att - 7000 H.T. 2 - 4

Sat 14 Feb 1931 BARROW home lost 5 - 6
CASTLEFORD - Lewis: Chapman Atkinson Askin Andrews:
James Hall: Walton Plimmer Stafford Jennings Evans
Russell: Try - Hall: Goal - James:
BARROW - Miller: Woods Carr Doyle Scott: Curtis
Fletcher: McKenna Troup McManus Strong Braithwaite
Pratt: Tries - Fletcher McManus:
Referee J Eddon (Swinton) Att - 5000 H.T. nil - 6

**Sat 21 Feb 1931 ST HELENS home lost 2 - 8
CHALLENGE CUP ROUND 2**
CASTLEFORD - Lewis: Chapman Atkinson Askin Andrews:
James Hall: Sherwood Harling Walton Evans Stafford
Russell: Goal - James:
ST HELENS - Lewis: Hardgrave Carr Mercer Ellaby: Groves
Fairclough: Hill Cotton Fildes Halfpenny Hutt Turner:
Tries - Ellaby Fairclough: Goal - Lewis:
Referee F Fairhurst (Wigan) Att - 13327 H.T. nil - 3

Sat 28 Feb 1931 KEIGHLEY away won 7 - 5
KEIGHLEY - Taylor: Jones Collings Manning Kendall:Oakes
Hanson: Fuller Moore G.Thompson McGoun Burton Fox:
Try - Burton: Goal - Fox:
CASTLEFORD - Lewis: Thomas James Askin Andrews:
Casey Hall: Sherwood Harling Walton Evans Stafford
Russell: Try - Sherwood: Goals - James(2):
Referee J McEwan (York) Att - 1000 H.T. 5 - 7

Wed 4 Mar 1931 KEIGHLEY home won 19 - 14
CASTLEFORD - James: Andrews Askin Atkinson Thomas:
Casey Hall: Sherwood Harling Walton Evans Stafford
Russell: Tries - Atkinson(4) Askin: Goals - James(2):
KEIGHLEY - Taylor: Jones Collings Manning Kendall:
A.N.Other Hanson: Fuller Moore Firth McGoun Burton
Fox: Tries - Hanson Burton: Goals - Taylor(4):
Referee J E Taylor (Wakefield) Att - 1000 H.T. 11 - 2

Sat 7 Mar 1931 LEEDS away lost 8 - 24
LEEDS - Brough: Harris Moores Goulthorpe S.Smith:
Williams Busch: Demaine Thompson Thomas R.Smith
Jenkins Gill: Tries - Harris(2) Moores S.Smith Williams
Busch: Goals - Thompson(3):
CASTLEFORD - Lewis: Chapman Askin James George
Andrews: Casey Hall: Sherwood Harling Walton Evans
Stafford Russell: Tries - Chapman Casey: Goal - James:
Referee H Swift (Halifax) Att - 6000 H.T. 3 - 9

Sat 14 Mar 1931 HUDDERSFIELD home lost 8 - 17
CASTLEFORD - Lewis: Chapman Atkinson Askin James:
Casey Hall: Sherwood Robert Nicholls Walton Hand
Stafford Evans: Tries - Askin Evans: Goal - James:
HUDDERSFIELD - Stocks: Mills Bowkett Brogden Walker:
Thompson Royston: Rudd Halliday Sherwood T Banks
Tiffany Young:
Tries - Mills(2) Walker Royston Tiffany: Goal - Bowkett:
Referee F Peel (Bradford) Att - 4000 H.T. 3 - 3

**Sat 21 Mar 1931 HULL KINGSTON ROVERS away
lost 6 - 32**
HULL K R - Osborne: Carmichael Batten Spamer Hill:
Parkin Dale: Britton Binks Westerdale Saddington Sharpe
Brindle: Tries - Batten(2) Westerdale(2) Carmichael
Parkin Dale Brindle:
Goals - Parkin(2) Osborne Saddington:
CASTLEFORD - James: Lewis Askin Atkinson Chapman:
Casey Hall: Sherwood James Powell Walton Stafford Hand
Marshall: Goals - James(3):
Referee J Devine (Leeds) Att - 4000 H.T. 2 - 14

SEASON 1930-31

Sat 28 Mar 1931 SALFORD home lost 10 - 22
CASTLEFORD - Marshall: James Askin Atkinson Spawforth:
Casey Hall: Sherwood Plimmer Walton Stafford Evans
Russell: Tries - Atkinson Stafford: Goals - James(2):
SALFORD - Risman: J.Williams Fisher Boyd Hudson: Miller
Meek: W.A.Williams Shaw Muir Middleton Dalton
Feetham: Tries - Hudson(2) Boyd Middleton Dalton
Feetham: Goals - Hudson(2):
Referee A Holbrook (Warrington) Att - 2000 H.T. 3 - 3

**Fri 3 Apr 1931 FEATHERSTONE ROVERS away
won 22 - 6**
FEATHERSTONE R - S.Denton: Barker Smith Emery Ward:
Evans J.Denton: Barraclough Morris Lister Norbury
L.Morgan Darlison: Goals - J.Denton(3):
CASTLEFORD - James: Thomas Atkinson Askin Chapman:
Lewis Hall: Walton Plimmer Stafford Evans Russell JOSEPH
KENDALL(102):
Tries - Atkinson(2) Thomas Lewis: Goals - James(5):
Referee F Peel (Bradford) Att - 2500 H.T. 10 - 4

Sat 4 Apr 1931 ROCHDALE HORNETS away lost 8 -28
ROCHDALE H - Gowers: Edmonds Aynsley Halton Walker:
Hill Lindley: Mahon Anderton Hyman Beattie Ivison
Campbell:
Tries - Halton(3) Edmonds Walker Hill: Goals - Gowers(5):
CASTLEFORD - James: Chapman Askin Atkinson Thomas:
Lewis Hall: Stafford Harling Walton Evans Kendall Russell:
Tries - Chapman Thomas: Goal - James:
Referee A Brown (Wakefield) Att - 3000 H.T. nil - 20

Mon 6 Apr 1931 DEWSBURY home lost 7 - 20
CASTLEFORD - James: Thomas Atkinson Chapman Harold
Spawforth: Askin Hall Walton Plimmer Sherwood Stafford
Evans Russell Try - Askin: Goals - James(1)(DG):
DEWSBURY - Lyman: F.W.Hobson C.Smith Grimes Hirst:
Coates Davies: J.Hobson Surguy Evans Booth Cracknell
Woolmore: Tries - F.W.Hobson Grimes Surguy
Woolmore: Goals - Lyman(4):
Referee J R Taylor (Wakefield) Att - 2500 H.T. 2 - 5

Sat 11 Apr 1931 WAKEFIELD TRINITY away lost 10 -46
WAKEFIELD T - C.Pollard: Ray Robinson Davies Smart:
Raynard Herbert: Hudson Field Close Horton Exley
Glossop: Tries - Horton(2) Ray Robinson Smart Field
Herbert Exley: Goals - Pollard(11):
CASTLEFORD - James: Thomas Atkinson Askin Chapman:
HERBERT WOOD(103) Hall: Walton Plimmer Stafford
Russell Jubb Evans:
Tries - Atkinson Walton: Goals - James (2):
Referee B Laughlin (Batley) Att - 3000 H.T. nil - 14

Mon 20 Apr 1931 BATLEY home won 13 - 4
CASTLEFORD - Marshall: Chapman Atkinson Lewis
Thomas: James Hall: Sherwood Plimmer(S/O) Stafford
Evans BEN BEAUMONT(104) Russell:
Tries Atkinson(2) Thomas: Goals - Atkinson James:
BATLEY - Addison: Broom Desmond Nunn Oliver: Swift
Murray: Oates Wilkinson Leeming Lomas Stephens Jones:
Goals - Addison(2):

Referee J E Taylor (Wakefield) Att - H.T. 8 - 2

Sat 25 Apr 1931 BATLEY away lost nil - 15
BATLEY - Addison: Oliver Nunn Desmond Broom: Honey
Swift: Lomas Wilkinson Leeming Oates Stephen Jones:
Tries - Oliver Nunn Swift: Goals - Addison(3):
CASTLEFORD - Marshall: Chapman Atkinson Lewis
Thomas: James A.N.OTHER(105): Sherwood Plimmer
Evans Beaumont Stafford Kendall:
Referee J E Taylor (Wakefield) Att - H.T. nil - 7

**Wed 29 Apr 1931 WIGAN HIGHFIELD home
lost 12 - 19**
CASTLEFORD - Lewis: Thomas Atkinson
Arthur(Candy)Evans James: Casey Hall: Sherwood Harling
WILLIAM HARRISON(106) Ben Beaumont Stafford
Kendall: Tries - Atkinson Stafford: Goals - James(3):
WIGAN H - Bennett: Maloney Hunter Lowe Jnr. Cowley:
Whittle Helme: Lowe Snr. Fairhurst Baines Gray Morley
Collier:
Tries - Maloney Lowe Jnr. Whittle: Goals - Whittle(5):
Referee A E Harding (Manchester) Att - 1000 H.T. 8 – 5

Cliff Harling
D. No 96
1930-31 to 1933-34

Ken Jubb
D. No 97
1930-31 to 1932-33

Thomas Askin
D. No 98
1930-31 to 1936-37

SEASON 1930-31

D.NO	PLAYER		DEBUT	L MATCH	APP	S JB	T.AP	TR'S	G'LS	D.G	P'TS
9	NICHOLLS	ROBERT		14/03/1931	1	0	1	0	0	0	0
14	RUSSELL	HARRY (DANNY)			36	0	36	1	0	0	3
16	ASQUITH	WILLIAM (NAT)		25/12/1930	19	0	19	4	0	0	12
21	ATKINSON	ARTHUR			30	0	30	20	7	0	74
23	WALTON	RICHARD			37	0	37	2	0	0	6
36	MARSHALL	ALBERT			16	0	16	1	0	0	3
39	PLIMMER	JAMES			32	0	32	0	0	0	0
56	STONES	SAMMY		30/08/1930	1	0	1	0	0	0	0
58	CHAPMAN	HAROLD			30	0	30	11	0	0	33
62	SHERWOOD	ARTHUR			34	0	34	2	2	0	10
64	THOMAS	EDWIN			15	0	15	3	0	0	9
66	MASKILL	RAYMOND			15	0	15	1	0	0	3
69	CASEY	JOHN			32	0	32	4	0	0	12
70	POWELL	JAMES		21/03/1931	2	0	2	0	0	0	0
77	STAFFORD	GEORGE			40	0	40	4	0	0	12
78	JAMES	WILLIAM			36	0	36	5	66	1	149
79	LEWIS	GEORGE			35	0	35	2	1	1	10
80	GORMAN	AUGUSTINE			4	0	4	0	0	0	0
83	WINSTANLEY	JOHN		18/10/1930	1	0	1	0	0	0	0
84	HALL	WILSON			42	0	42	4	0	0	12
87	JENNINGS	STANLEY			15	0	15	1	0	0	3
91	ROBINSON	DONALD		30/08/1930	1	0	1	1	0	0	3
94	HIGO	JAMES	30/08/1930	30/08/1930	1	0	1	0	0	0	0
95	SPAWFORTH	HAROLD	13/09/1930	06/04/1931	6	0	6	0	0	0	0
96	HARLING	CLIFFORD	18/10/1930		9	0	9	0	0	0	0
97	JUBB	KENNETH	25/10/1930		2	0	2	0	0	0	0
98	ASKIN	THOMAS C	15/11/1930		27	0	27	6	0	0	18
99	HAND	HARRY (MICK)	27/12/1930		4	0	4	0	0	0	0
100	ANDREWS	GEORGE	17/01/1931	07/03/1931	8	0	8	0	0	0	0
101	EVANS	ARTHUR	17/01/1931	29/04/1931	18	0	18	1	0	0	3
102	KENDALL	JOSEPH	03/04/1931		4	0	4	0	0	0	0
103	WOOD	HERBERT	11/04/1931	11/04/1931	1	0	1	0	0	0	0
104	BEAUMONT	BEN	20/04/1931	29/04/1931	3	0	3	0	0	0	0
105	A.N.OTHER		25/04/1931	25/04/1931	1	0	1	0	0	0	0
106	HARRISON	WILLIAM	29/04/1931	29/04/1931	1	0	1	0	0	0	0
	35		**13**	**14**	**559**	**0**	**559**	**73**	**76**	**2**	**375**

COMPETITION		P	W	D	L	FOR	AGT
LEAGUE	POSITION 20 OF 28	38	15	0	23	351	539
YORK'S CUP		2	1	0	1	17	16
RL CUP		3	1	1	1	7	12
PLAYERS RECORDS		**43**	**17**	**1**	**25**	**375**	**567**

The League's format was amended; all clubs now played the same number of games on a formula basis, with two points for a win and one point for a draw. The top four teams on a point basis; 1st v 4th and 2nd v 3rd played off, the winners playing off to be crowned Champions, therefore percentages were no longer applicable.

Former Featherstone player William Clements was appointed Trainer replacing Dick Silcock.

William (Billy) James increased the record for most points scored in a League game to 16 against Bradford N on 6 September 1930.

SEASON 1931-32

Sat 22 Aug 1931 FEATHERSTONE ROVERS home won 18 - 12 LYON CUP - FRIENDLY
CASTLEFORD - Goldie(Leeds): Thomas Atkinsom Askin
Chapman: Lewis Hall: Walton Swales Taylor Wadsworth
Stafford Kendall:
Tries - Thomas(2) Atkinson Askin: Goals - Atkinson(3):
FEATHERSTONE R - S.Denton: Barker Killingbeck Stott
Taylor: J.Evans W.Evans: Barraclough Morris L.Morgan
Darlison Norbury J.Morgan:
Tries - J.Evans W.Evans: Goals - Stott(2) Denton(DG):
Referee A S Dobson (Pontefract) Att - 3000 H.T. 3 - 5

Sat 29 Aug 1931 DEWSBURY home won 7 - 5
CASTLEFORD - Lewis: Thomas Atkinson Askin Chapman:
James Hall: Sherwood Walton Stafford J.WILLIAM
WINN(107) Hand Russell: Try - Winn: Goals - James(2):
DEWSBURY - Thomas: Raywood C.Smith Manning Grimes:
A.Smith Matthews: Evans Surguy Booth Malkin Woolmore
Fox: Try - Raywood: Goal - Manning:
Referee F Peel (Bradford) Att - 4000 H.T. 4 - 2

Sat 5 Sep 1931 WIGAN away lost 9 - 48
WIGAN - Sullivan: Falwasser Davies Kinnear Brown:
Spillane Bennett: Houghton Welsby Morgan Mason
Jennion Sherrington: Tries - Falwasser(3) Brown(3) Davies
Kinnear Bennett Morgan: Goals - Sullivan(9):
CASTLEFORD - Marshall: Thomas Atkinson Askin
Chapman: James Hall: Sherwood Hand Walton Stafford
Winn Kendall: Try - Chapman: Goals - Atkinson(2) James:
Referee E Devine (Leeds) Att - H.T. 4 - 29

Wed 9 Sep 1931 DEWSBURY away lost 6 - 11
DEWSBURY - Thomas: Raywood C.Smith Manning
F.W.Hobson: Matthews Werrett: Targett Green J.A.Hobson
Malkin Orford Fox:
Tries - Raywood Matthews F W Hobson: Goal - Green:
CASTLEFORD - FRED KNOWLING(108): Thomas Atkinson
James Chapman: Hall WILLIAMHAYES(109):
Sherwood(S/O) Plimmer Walton Hand Stafford Kendall:
Tries - Atkinson Chapman:
Referee F Peel (Bradford) Att - 2500 H.T. nil - 5

Sat 12 Sep 1931 HULL KINGSTON ROVERS home lost 5 - 15
CASTLEFORD - Fred Knowling: Thomas Atkinson Askin
Chapman: James Hayes: Hand Plimmer Walton Stafford
J.William Winn Hall: Try - Askin: Goal - James:
HULL K R - Osborne: Batten Spamer Smith Hill: Parkin
Dale: Horton Binks Westerdale Sharpe Tattersfield
Williams: Tries - Batten Hill Dale: Goals - Osborne(3):
Referee H Horsfall (Batley) Att - 3000 H.T. 5 - 10

Sat 19 Sep 1931 WIGAN HIGHFIELD away lost 3 - 18
WIGAN H - Parkinson: J.Lowe Walker Hunter Maloney:
Helme Whittle: Fairhurst Bentham Worsley Gray Collier
Stock:
Tries - Maloney Helme Whittle Gray: Goals - Whittle(3):
CASTLEFORD - James: Chapman Marshall Atkinson
Thomas: Askin Hall: Sherwood Plimmer Hand Walton
Jubb Gorman: Try - Chapman:

Referee R Robinson (Bradford) Att - H.T. nil - 3

Sat 26 Sep 1931 WIGAN home lost 9 - 25
CASTLEFORD - James: Thomas Atkinson Askin Chapman:
CHARLES ANNABLE(110) WILLIAM H.DAVIES(111): Walton
Plimmer(S/O)Stafford FRED WADSWORTH(112) Jubb
Gorman: Try - Stafford: Goals - James(3):
WIGAN - Sullivan: Ring Davies Kinnear Jones: Spillane
Abram: Houghton Welsby Morgan Mason Dixon Jennion:
Tries - Ring Houghton Dixon: Goals - Sullivan(8):
Referee J Eddon (Swinton) Att - 6000 H.T. 2 - 16

Sat 3 Oct 1931 SALFORD away lost 6 - 36
SALFORD - Osbaldestin: Boyd Dobing Risman Hudson:
Meek Watkins: Williams Shaw Bradbury Marsden Dalton
Middleton: Tries - Risman(3) Boyd(2) Dobing Hudson
Meek Watkins Williams: Goals - Hudson(2) Risman:
CASTLEFORD - James: Thomas Atkinson Askin Chapman:
Annable Davies: Walton Plimmer Raymond Maskill
Stafford Gorman: Joseph Kendall:
Goals - James(2) Atkinson:
Referee J E Taylor (Wakefield) Att - 8000 H.T. 2 - 22

Sat 10 Oct 1931 DEWSBURY home lost 4 - 12 YORKSHIRE CUP ROUND 1
CASTLEFORD - Albert Marshall: Askin James Atkinson
Chapman: Annable Davies: Sherwood Plimmer Hand Jubb
Augustine Gorman Stafford: Goals - James(2):
DEWSBURY - Thomas: Raywood Smith Hoult F.Hobson:
Matthews Hall: Golby J.Hudson Targett Green Booth
Manning:
Tries - Raywood Hall: Goals - Green(2) Matthews:
Referee A Holbrook (Warrington) Att 6000 H.T. 2 - 8

Sat 17 Oct 1931 KEIGHLEY home won 21 - 3
CASTLEFORD - James: Thomas Askin Davies Lewis:
Annable Hall: Sherwood Harling(S/O) Hand Malkin
Stafford Russell: Tries - James Thomas Lewis Stafford
Malkin: Goals - James(3):
KEIGHLEY - Holmes: W.Jones Hutchinson Foster Kendall:
Schofield Davies: Simmons H.Jones(S/O) Lee Fuller
McGoun Thompson: Try - Davies:
Referee E Devine (Leeds) Att - H.T. 10 - 3

Sat 24 Oct 1931 LEIGH away lost 7 - 9
LEIGH - Unsworth: Higson Johnson Bithell Smith: Green
A.N.Other: Worrall Hilton Richardson Griffin Flannery
Hurtley: Try - Hurtley: Goals - Johnson(2) Hurtley:
CASTLEFORD - James: Lewis Atkinson Davies Askin:
Annable Hall: Sherwood Harling Hand Stafford Malkin
Russell: Try - Davies: Goals - James(2):
Referee B Laughlin (Batley) Att - 2000 H.T. nil - 7

Sat 31 Oct 1931 ST HELENS RECS home won 21 - 6
CASTLEFORD - James: Lewis Atkinson Davies Askin:
Annable Hall: Sherwood Plimmer Hand Stafford Malkin
Russell:
Tries - Atkinson(3) Lewis Davies: Goals - James(3):
ST HELENS R - Dingsdale: Graham Abbott Heaton Wilson:
Bowen Green: Doran Thompson Highcock Smith Green

Grundy: Tries - Abbott Highcock:
Referee A E Harding (Man'ster) Att - 3000 H.T. 11 - 6

Sat 7 Nov 1931 BRADFORD NORTHERN away lost 5 - 18

BRADFORD N - Reed: Holmes Berry Thornburrow
Shackleton: Martin Binks: Coates Hulme Swan Monaghan
Malone Thornber:
Tries - Holmes(2) Berry Binks: Goals - Berry(2) Coates:
CASTLEFORD - James: Lewis Atkinson Davies Askin:
Annable Hall: Sherwood Plimmer Hand Stafford Malkin
Russell: Try - Atkinson: Goal - James:
Referee A Brown (Wakefield) Att - 1500 H.T. 2 - 5

Sat 14 Nov 1931 BRADFORD NORTHERN home won 13 - 5

CASTLEFORD - James: Askin Davies Atkinson Lewis:
Annable Hall: Sherwood Plimmer Hand Walton(S/O)
Wadsworth Stafford:
Tries - Atkinson Lewis Sherwood: Goals - James Atkinson:
BRADFORD N - Reed: Holmes Berry Thornburrow
Shackleton: Martin Binks: Coates Hulme Swan Monaghan
Malone(S/O) Thornber: Try - Thornburrow: Goal - Berry:
Referee H Swift (Halifax) Att - 2000 H.T. 8 - 5

Sat 28 Nov 1931 LEEDS home won 22 - 13

CASTLEFORD - James: Lewis Atkinson Davies Askin:
Annable Hall: Sherwood Plimmer J.J.STOBART(113)
Stafford Jubb Russell:
Tries - Atkinson Davies Hall Russell: Goals - James(5):
LEEDS - Brough: Harris Goulthorpe S.Smith Williams:
Busch Adams: Lowe Thompson Douglas R.Smith Cox
Glossop:
Tries - Harris Adams Goulthorpe: Goals - Thompson(2):
Referee A Brown (Wakefield) Att - 6000 H.T. 12 - 10

Sat 5 Dec 1931 ST HELENS RECS away lost 4 - 16

ST HELENS R - Dingsdale: Potter Frodsham Martin Bailey:
Bowen Greenall: Dolan Thompson Lipton Highcock(S/O)
Smith Green:
Tries - Potter(2) Frodsham Greenall: Goals - Dingsdale(2):
CASTLEFORD - James: Lewis Atkinson Davies Askin:
Annable Hall: Sherwood Plimmer Stobart Malkin Jubb
Russell: Goals - James(2):
Referee B Laughlin (Batley) Att - 2000 H.T. 2 - 5

Sat 12 Dec 1931 SALFORD home lost 8 - 13

CASTLEFORD - James: Lewis Atkinson Davies Askin:
Annable Hall: Sherwood Plimmer Stobart Stafford Jubb
Russell: Tries - Atkinson(2): Goal - James:
SALFORD - Miller: Boyd Southward Risman Hudson:
Jenkins Meek: Williams Shaw Bradbury Dalton Feetham
Cresswell:
Tries - Feetham(2) Risman: Goals - Southward(2):
Referee F Fairhurst (Wigan) Att - 5000 H.T. nil - 8

Sat 19 Dec 1931 KEIGHLEY away lost 2 - 5

KEIGHLEY - Holmes: W.Jones Fisher Oakes A.N.Other:
Schofield Hurcombe: Fuller Watson Thompson McGoun
H.Jones Pybus: Try - W.Jones: Goal - Hurcombe:

CASTLEFORD - James: Lewis Atkinson Davies Askin:
Annable Hall: Sherwood Plimmer Stobart Stafford Jubb
Russell: Goal - James:
Referee E Devine (Leeds) Att - 2000 H.T. nil - 3

Fri 25 Dec 1931 FEATHERSTONE ROVERS away lost 8 - 15

FEATHERSTONE R - S.Denton: Barker J.Denton Winter
Killingbeck: Johnson Evans: Barraclough Morris L.Morgan
Darlison Norbury Fox:
Tries - Barker Fox Barraclough: Goals - Johnson(3):
CASTLEFORD - James: Lewis Atkinson Davies Askin: Casey
Hall: Sherwood Plimmer J.J.Stobart Jubb Stafford Russell:
Tries - Askin(2) Goal - James:
Referee H Swift (Halifax) Att - 6000 H.T. 5 - 7

Sat 26 Dec 1931 HUNSLET home won 5 - 3

CASTLEFORD - Lewis: ALBERT McGONIGLE(114) Atkinson
Davies Askin: James Hall: Sherwood Plimmer Malkin Jubb
Walton Russell: Try - Askin: Goal - James:
HUNSLET - Walkington: Adams Johnson Cornell Wilson:
Thorndon Morrell: Jenkins White Smith Crowther Dawson
Beverley: Try - Wilson:
Referee R Robinson (Bradford) Att 6500 H.T. nil - nil

Sat 2 Jan 1932 HULL home won 17 - 3

CASTLEFORD - Lewis: James Atkinson McGonigle Askin:
Davies Hall: Sherwood Plimmer Walton Malkin Jubb
Russell:
Tries - James Atkinson Davies Hall Russell: Goal - Malkin:
HULL - Teall: Bateman Oliver Ellerington Lyon: Fifield
Metcalfe: Errington Pickering Thompson Wood
Carmichael Gillyon: Try - Fifield:
Referee H Horsfall (Batley) Att - 3500 H.T. 9 - nil

Sat 9 Jan 1932 HUNSLET away lost 9 - 12

HUNSLET - Walkington: Broughton Coulson Higgins
Wilson: Todd Thornton: Jenkins White Moss Dawson
Smith Beverley: Tries - Wilson Beverley:
Goals - Walkington(1)(DG) Higgins:
CASTLEFORD - Lewis: James Atkinson McGonigle Askin:
Davies Hall: Sherwood Harling Walton Malkin Jubb
Russell: Try - McGonigle: Goals - Atkinson(2) James:
Referee R Robinson (Bradford) Att - 7000 H.T. 7 - 7

Sat 16 Jan 1932 WIGAN HIGHFIELD home won 27 - 15

CASTLEFORD - Lewis: ALBERT BENNETT(115) Atkinson
Askin Stafford: Davies Hall: Sherwood Harling Walton
Jubb Malkin Russell: Tries - Bennett(2) Atkinson(2)
Stafford(2) Sherwood: Goals - Atkinson(3):
WIGAN H - Barnes: Walker Hunter Lowe Hilton: Bush
Helme: Fairhurst Patterson Woodward Wood Worsley
Gore: Tries - Walker Lowe Helme: Goals - Lowe(3):
Referee J W Webb (Broughton) Att - 3000 H.T. 14 - nil

Wed 20 Jan 1932 BRAMLEY away lost 3 - 7

BRAMLEY - Desmond: Glynne Maudsley Ballantyne
Witham: Hughes Whittaker: Tasker Bowden Harrison
Parkinson Morrell Rowan:

SEASON 1931-32

Try - Ballantyne: Goals - Desmond(2):
CASTLEFORD - Lewis: Bennett Atkinson Askin Thomas:
Davies Hall: Sherwood Harling Walton Jubb Malkin
Russell: Try - Thomas:
Referee F Peel (Bradford) Att -   H.T. 3 - 4

Sat 23 Jan 1932 HUDDERSFIELD away lost 15 - 31
HUDDERSFIELD - Bowkett: Mills Brogden Parker Walker:
Wistanley Thompson: Rudd Halliday Sherwood Tiffany
Morton Talbot:
Tries - Mills(5) Walker Tiffany: Goals - Bowkett(5):
CASTLEFORD - James: Lewis Thomas Atkinson McGonigle:
Annable Hall: Sherwood Plimmer Stafford Walton Malkin
Jubb: Tries - Lewis Malkin Hall: Goals - James(3):
Referee J E Taylor (Wakefield) Att - 5000 H.T. 5 - 13

Sat 30 Jan 1932 BRAMLEY home won 38 - 5
CASTLEFORD - James: Lewis Atkinson Davies Askin:
Annable Hall: Sherwood Plimmer Walton Malkin Jubb
Russell: Tries - Askin(4) Atkinson Hall Walton Malkin:
Goals - James(7):
BRAMLEY - Desmond: Witham Ballantyne Maudsley
Evans: Hansen Hudson: Reed Woodhead Tasker
Parkinson Morrrell Rowan:
Try - Parkinson: Goal - Desmond:
Referee B Laughlin (Batley) Att - 3500 H.T. 15 - nil

**Sat 6 Feb 1932 FEATHERSTONE ROVERS home
won 6 - 2   CHALLENGE CUP ROUND 1**
CASTLEFORD - James: Lewis Atkinson Davies Askin:
Annable Hall: Sherwood Plimmer Walton Malkin Jubb
Russell: Goals - Atkinson(3):
FEATHERSTONE R - S.Denton: Killingbeck Winter J.Denton
Barker: Johnson Evans: Barraclough Morris L.Morgan
Norbury Darlison J.Morgan: Goals - J.Denton (DG):
Referee J W Webb (Broughton) Att - 10000 H.T. 2 - 2

**Sat 13 Feb 1932 WAKEFIELD TRINITY away
lost 10 - 35**
WAKEFIELD T - Owen: Griffiths Robinson E.Pollard Smart:
Pearce Herberts: Moss Gee Maskill Higson Exley
Wilkinson: Tries - Smart(2) Higson(2) Robinson Pollard
Pearce Herberts Wilkinson: Goals - Pollard(3) Robinson:
CASTLEFORD - Lewis: Askin Davies James Thomas:
Annable Hall: Sherwood Plimmer Walton Jubb Russell
Malkin: Tries - Thomas(2): Goals - James(2):
Referee J W Webb (Broughton) Att - 4000 H.T. 4 - 6

**Sat 20 Feb 1932 ST HELENS RECS away won 11 - 8
CHALLENGE CUP ROUND 2**
ST HELENS R - Graham: Wilson Frodsham Abbott Bailey:
Greenall W.Bowen: Dolan Thompson Liptrot Highcock
F.Bowen Smith: Tries - Smith(2): Goal - Frodsham:
CASTLEFORD - Lewis: Askin Atkinson James Thomas:
McGonigle Hall: Sherwood Plimmer Walton Jubb Malkin
Stafford: Tries - Malkin(2) James: Goal - James:
Referee H Swift (Halifax) Att - 7253 H.T. 5 - nil

Sat 27 Feb 1932 ST HELENS home won 5 - nil
CASTLEFORD - Lewis: Askin James Atkinson Davies:
McGonigle Hall: Sherwood Plimmer Walton Jennings
Malkin Russell: Try - Jennings: Goal - James:
ST HELENS - Jones: Hardgrave Mercer Lewis Ellaby:
Garvey Frodsham: Cotton Atkin Hill Fildes Halfpenny
Groves:
Referee J Eddon (Swinton) Att - 5000 H.T. 5 - nil

**Sat 5 Mar 1932 SWINTON home lost 2 - 10
CHALLENGE CUP ROUND 3**
CASTLEFORD - Lewis: Davies James Atkinson Askin: Albert
McGonigle Hall: Sherwood Plimmer Walton Jubb Malkin
Stafford: Goal - Atkinson:
SWINTON - Scott: Buckingham Whittaker H.Evans Kenny:
B.Evans Rees: Strong Armitt Wright Hodgson Beswick
Butters: Tries - Beswick Butters: Goals - Hodgson(2):
Referee A Holbrook (Warrington) Att - 14500 H.T. 2 - 5

Sat 12 Mar 1932 BATLEY away lost 10 - 11
BATLEY - J.Lyman: Brown Firth Evans Nunn: Hick Swift:
Wilkinson Dyson Oates Earnshaw Walker Chapman:
Try - Swift: Goals - Lyman(4):
CASTLEFORD - Lewis: Thomas Atkinson James Askin:
Davies Hall: Walton Plimmer Malkin Jubb Jennings
Wadsworth: Tries - James Wadsworth:
Goals - Atkinson(2):
Referee J E Taylor (Wake'ld) Att - 2500 H.T. nil – 6

Sat 19 Mar 1932 BATLEY home won 24 - 14
CASTLEFORD - Lewis: Thomas Atkinson Davies James:
Casey Annable: Walton Plimmer THOMAS L.TAYLOR(116)
Malkin Jennings Wadsworth
Tries - Davies(2) James Casey: Goals - James(6)
BATLEY - J.Lyman: Broom Evans Firth Nunn: Brook Swift:
Dyson Wilkinson Leeming Earnshaw Oates Chapman:
Tries - Nunn(2): Goals - Lyman(4)
Referee A Brown (Wakefield) Att - 2000 H.T. 6 - 9

**Fri 25 Mar 1932 FEATHERSTONE ROVERS home
Won 9 - 5**
CASTLEFORD - Lewis: Thomas Atkinson James Casey:
Davies Hall: Taylor Plimmer Walton Jubb Malkin
Wadsworth: Tries - Atkinson James Malkin:
FEATHERSTONE R - S.Denton: J.Denton Killingbeck Winter
Barker: Hayes Evans: Barraclough Morris L.Morgan Easter
Norbury J.Morgan:
Try - Hayes(Obstruction): Goal - J.Denton:
Referee E Devine (Leeds) Att - 4000 H.T. 9 - nil

Sat 26 Mar 1932 ST HELENS away lost 6 - 24
ST HELENS - Jones: Hardgrave Mercer Winnard Butler:
Frodsham Garvey: Atkin Halfpenny Hutt Awkwright Fildes
Groves: Tries - Arkwright Winnard Fildes Hardgrave:
Goals - Winnard(6):
CASTLEFORD - Lewis: Thomas Atkinson Davies Malkin:
Casey Hall: Walton Plimmer Taylor Jubb Jennings
Wadsworth: Goals - Atkinson(3):
Referee A Hill (Leeds) Att - 6000 H.T. 2 - 9

46

SEASON 1931-32

Mon 28 Mar 1932 HULL away draw 10 - 10
HULL - Teall: Bateman Oliver Fifield Lyons: Everitt
Ellerington: Thompson Pickering: Stead Bowman
Carmichael Courteney:
Tries - Fifield Lyon: Goals - Teall Oliver:
CASTLEFORD - Lewis: Casey Atkinson James Bennett:
Davies Hall: Sherwood Plimmer Taylor AMBROSE
ASKIN(117) Jubb Wadsworth: Tries - Atkinson Jubb:
Goals - James(2):
Referee R Robinson (Bradford) Att -   H.T. 5 - 5

Tue 29 Mar 1932 HUDDERSFIELD home lost 5 - 13
CASTLEFORD - Lewis: Albert Bennett Atkinson Davies
Casey: Annable Hall: Walton Plimmer Taylor Jubb Malkin
Wadsworth: Try - Casey: Goal - Atkinson:
HUDDERSFIELD - Turton: Mills Brogden Towill Walker:
Winstanley Thompson: Rudd Halliday Sherwood Banks
Tiffany Young:
Tries - Thompson(2) Mills: Goals - Turton Thompson:
Referee F Peel (Bradford) Att - 3000 H.T. 2 - 10

Sat 2 April 1932 WAKEFIELD TRINITY home won 20 - nil
CASTLEFORD - Lewis: Casey Atkinson Davies T.C.Askin:
Annable Hall: Taylor Plimmer Walton Jubb Malkin
Wadsworth: Tries - Casey Annable Jubb Wadsworth:
Goals - Lewis(2) Atkinson(2):
WAKEFIELD T - Owen: Bateson Griffiths Jones Smart:
Pearce Herbert: Moss Field Maskill Wilkinson Higson
Exley:
Referee E Devine (Leeds) Att - 5000 H.T. 3 - nil

Wed 6 Apr 1932 LEIGH home won 10 - 6
CASTLEFORD - Lewis: T.C.Askin Atkinson Davies Casey:
Annable Hall: Walton Plimmer Taylor Jubb A.Askin
Wadsworth:
Tries - Casey Walton: Goals - Lewis Atkinson:
LEIGH - Unsworth: Johnson Harris Critchley Stringman:
Downs Keegan: Worrall Richardson Edwards Griffin
Flannery Jones: Goals - Johnson(3):
Referee L Greenwood (Rochdale) Att - 1000 H.T. 7 - 4

Sat 9 Apr 1932 YORK home lost 4 - 9
CASTLEFORD - Lewis: Casey Atkinson Davies T.C.Askin:
Annable Hall: Walton Plimmer Taylor Jubb Malkin
Wadsworth: Goals - Atkinson(2):
YORK - Owen: Brown Rosser Jordan Smith: Rees Pickard:
Myers John A.G.Thomas Wayne Coldrick Allen:
Try - Thomas: Goals - Allen(2) Owen(DG)
Referee H Horsfall (Batley) Att - 3000 H.T. 4 - nil

Sat 16 Apr 1932 LEEDS away lost nil - 20
LEEDS - Brough: Harris Moores O'Rourke Goulthorpe:
Williams Busch: Demaine Satterthwaite E.Smith Douglas
Cox Jones: Tries - Harris O'Rourke Goulthorpe Busch:
Goals - Jones(4):
CASTLEFORD - Lewis: T.C.Askin James Davies Casey:
Annable Hall: Taylor Plimmer Walton Jubb Malkin
Wadsworth:
Referee H Swift (Batley) Att - 7500 H.T. nil - 13

Thu 21 Apr 1932 HULL KINGSTON ROVERS away lost 11 - 18
HULL K R - Carmichael: Batten Spamer Brien McCloud:
Dale Parkin: Britton Binks Blossom Eddom Sharpe Brindle:
Tries - Carmichael Batten Dale Sharpe:
Goals - Carmichael(3):
CASTLEFORD - James: A.N.OTHER(118) Davies Lewis
Hudson: Casey Hall: Walton Malkin Taylor Jubb Russell
Wadsworth: Tries - Hudson James Casey: Goal - James:
Referee F Peel (Bradford) Att - 3000 H.T. 3 - 6

Tue 26 Apr 1932 YORK away lost 8 - 13
YORK - Owen: Brown Rosser Jordan H.Thomas: Taylor
W.Thomas: G.Thomas Johnson John H.Davies Coldrick
Allen:
Tries - Brown H.Thomas W.Thomas: Goals - Taylor(2):
CASTLEFORD - James: Casey Davies Lewis Hudson:
Annable Hall: Taylor Plimmer Jubb Russell Malkin A.Askin:
Tries - Hudson A.Askin: Goal - James:
Referee R Robinson (Bradford) Att - 4317 H.T. 3 – 5

William (Billy) Davies
D. No 111
1931-32 to 1936-37

Tommy Taylor
D. No 116
1931-32 to 1945-46

Ambrose Askin
D. No 117
1931-32 to 1936-37

SEASON 1931-32

D.N	PLAYER		DEBUT	L MATCH	APP	SUB	T.AP	TR'S	G'LS	D.G	P'TS
5	HUDSON	HARRY			2	0	2	2	0	0	6
11	MALKIN	JOSEPH			27	0	27	6	1	0	20
14	RUSSELL	HARRY (DANNY)			21	0	21	2	0	0	6
21	ATKINSON	ARTHUR			37	0	37	15	24	0	93
23	WALTON	RICHARD			30	0	30	2	0	0	6
36	MARSHALL	ALBERT		10/10/1931	3	0	3	0	0	0	0
39	PLIMMER	JAMES			34	0	34	0	0	0	0
58	CHAPMAN	HAROLD			8	0	8	3	0	0	9
62	SHERWOOD	ARTHUR			28	0	28	2	0	0	6
64	THOMAS	EDWIN			16	0	16	4	0	0	12
66	MASKILL	RAYMOND		03/10/1931	1	0	1	0	0	0	0
69	CASEY	JOHN			12	0	12	5	0	0	15
77	STAFFORD	GEORGE			20	0	20	4	0	0	12
78	JAMES	WILLIAM			35	0	35	7	57	0	135
79	LEWIS	GEORGE			35	0	35	4	3	0	18
80	GORMAN	AUGUSTINE		10/10/1931	4	0	4	0	0	0	0
84	HALL	WILSON			38	0	38	4	0	0	12
87	JENNINGS	STANLEY			4	0	4	1	0	0	3
96	HARLING	CLIFFORD			5	0	5	0	0	0	0
97	JUBB	KENNETH			30	0	30	2	0	0	6
98	ASKIN	THOMAS C.			33	0	33	8	0	0	24
99	HAND	HARRY (MICK)			11	0	11	0	0	0	0
102	KENDALL	JOSEPH		03/10/1931	3	0	3	0	0	0	0
107	WINN	JOHN WILLIAM	29/08/1931	12/09/1931	3	0	3	1	0	0	3
108	KNOWLING	FRED	09/09/1931	12/09/1931	2	0	2	0	0	0	0
109	HAYES		09/09/1931	12/09/1931	2	0	2	0	0	0	0
110	ANNABLE	CHARLES	26/09/1931		23	0	23	1	0	0	3
111	DAVIES	WILLIAM H	26/09/1931		35	0	35	6	0	0	18
112	WADSWORTH	FRED	26/09/1931		13	0	13	2	0	0	6
113	STOBART	J. J.	28/11/1931	25/12/1931	5	0	5	0	0	0	0
114	McGONIGLE	ALBERT	26/12/1931	05/09/1932	7	0	7	1	0	0	3
115	BENNETT	ALBERT	16/01/1932	29/03/1932	4	0	4	2	0	0	6
116	TAYLOR	THOMAS L.	19/03/1932		11	0	11	0	0	0	0
117	ASKIN	AMBROSE	28/03/1932		3	0	3	1	0	0	3
118	A.N.OTHER		21/04/1932	21/04/1932	1	0	1	0	0	0	0
	35		**12**	**11**	**546**	**0**	**546**	**85**	**85**	**0**	**425**

COMPETITION		P	W	D	L	FOR	AGT
LEAGUE	POSITION 22 OF 28	38	14	1	23	402	515
YORK'S CUP		1	0	0	1	4	12
RL CUP		3	2	0	1	19	20
PLAYERS RECORDS		**42**	**16**	**1**	**25**	**425**	**547**

Arthur Atkinson became the first Castleford player to be chosen for the Great Britain team to tour Australasia. He played in all three Test matches in Australia and all three in New Zealand.

Sat 20 Aug 1932 FEATHERSTONE ROVERS away
lost 3 - 12   LYON CUP - FRIENDLY
FEATHERSTONE R - Johnson: Price Killingbeck Winter
Anderson: W.Evans Stott: Barraclough Morris Darlison
Taylor Norbury J.Morgan:
Tries - W.Evans Darlison: Goals - Johnson(2)(DG):
CASTLEFORD - Lewis: T.C.Askin Davies Hoult Chapman:
Annable Hall: Taylor Plimmer Walton Jubb A.Askin
Russell: Try - T.C.Askin:
Referee A S Dobson (Pontefract) Att - 1500 H.T. 3 - nil

Sat 27 Aug 1932 HUDDERSFIELD away won 7 - 2
HUDDERSFIELD - Bowkett: Mills Parker Towill Peck:
Richards Spence: Rudd Halliday Sherwood Tiffany Banks
Young: Goal - Bowkett:
CASTLEFORD - Lewis: Hudson Davies JACK HOULT(119)
T.C.Askin: Casey Hall: Taylor Plimmer Sherwood Stafford
A.Askin Russell: Try - Casey: Goals - Lewis(2):
Referee F Peel (Bradford) Att - 4000 H.T. 2 - 2

Sat 3 Sept 1932 BROUGHTON RANGERS home
lost 4 - 15
CASTLEFORD - Lewis: Hudson Davies Hoult T.C.Askin:
Casey Hall: Taylor Plimmer Sherwood Stafford A.Askin
Russell: Goals - Lewis(2):
BROUGHTON R - Barlow: H.Dennett Bunter Davies
Parkinson: G.Bennett McCarrigan: Woodcock Walsh
Whitehead Hill Tetley W.Brown: Tries - Parkinson
McCarrigan Brown: Goals - Woodcock(3):
Referee F Fairhurst (Wigan) Att -   H.T. 2 - 3

Sat 10 Sept 1932 HUNSLET away lost nil - 13
HUNSLET - Walkington: Broughton Goulthorpe Higgins
Johnson: Todd Thornton: Traill Leonard(S/O) Moss
Dawson Crowther Beverley: Tries - Broughton
Goulthorpe Beverley: Goals - Walkington(2):
CASTLEFORD - Lewis: Harry Hudson Davies Hoult
T.C.Askin: John Casey Annable: Sherwood Plimmer Taylor
Jubb(S/O) A.Askin Stafford(S/O):
Referee H Swift (Halifax) Att - 5000 H.T. nil - 2

Sat 17 Sept 1932 WIGAN HIGHFIELD away lost 3 -15
WIGAN H - Barnes: Walker Lowe Hunter McGregor: Wills
Ashcroft: Fairhurst Travis Wood Cayser Gray Stocks:
Tries - McGregor Ashcroft Cayser:
Goals - Lowe(2) Ashcroft:
CASTLEFORD - Lewis: Chapman Davies Hoult JOHN
JOHNSON(120): Annable T.C.Askin: Sherwood Plimmer
Taylor Jubb A.Askin Wadsworth: Try - Johnson:
Referee B Laughlin (Batley) Att -   H.T. nil - 2

Sat 24 Sept 1932 HUDDERSFIELD home won 14 - 10
CASTLEFORD - Lewis: T.C.Askin Atkinson Davies Hoult:
Annable Hall: Sherwood Plimmer Walton Jubb Malkin
Taylor: Tries - T.C.Askin Hall: Goals - Lewis(2) Atkinson(2):
HUDDERSFIELD - Bowkett: Mills Lockwood Parker Peck:
Richards Thompson: Rudd Halliday Sherwood Tiffany
Banks Talbot:
Tries - Thompson(2): Goals - Bowkett(1)(DG):
Referee F Peel (Bradford) Att - 6000 H.T. 5 - 5

Thu 29 Sept 1932 HULL KINGSTON ROVERS away
lost 4 - 18
HULL K R - Carmichael: Smith Spamer Hill Batten: Dale
Fridlington: Sharpe Binks Blossom Tattersfield Williams
Brindle:
Tries - Smith(2) Spamer Brindle: Goals - Carmichael(3):
CASTLEFORD - Lewis: T.C.Askin Atkinson Davies Hoult:
Annable Hall: Sherwood Plimmer Walton Jubb Malkin
Taylor: Goals - Lewis Atkinson:
Referee J E Taylor (Wakefield) Att - 3000 H.T. 2 - 12

Sat 1 Oct 1932 HULL away lost 5 - 13
HULL - Teall: Bateman Sowerby Fifield Winsor: Ellerington
Phillipson: Steac Wilkinson Bowman Dawson Carmichael
Milner: Tries - Bateman(3): Goals - Teall Phillipson:
CASTLEFORD - Lewis: Edwin Thomas Davies Hoult
T.C.Askin: Annable Hall: Taylor Plimmer Walton Jubb
Joseph Malkin Wadsworth: Try - Hoult: Goal - Lewis:
Referee W E Smith (Dewsbury) Att - 1500 H.T. nil - 5

Sat 8 Oct 1932 SWINTON home won 9 - 8
FRIENDLY
CASTLEFORD - Lewis: T.C.Askin Atkinson Hoult Davies:
Dennis Hall: Sherwood Plimmer Taylor A.Askin Stafford
Jubb: Try - Hall: Goals - Atkinson(2) Lewis:
SWINTON - Scott: Buckingham Whittaker H.Evans Kenny:
Atkinson Rees: Strong Armitt Wright Hodgson Beswick
Butters: Tries - Kenny(2): Goal - Hodgson:
Referee J Roberts (Leeds) Att -   H.T. 7 - 3

Wed 12 Oct 1932 BRADFORD NORTHERN home
won 26 - 9   YORKSHIRE CUP ROUND 2
CASTLEFORD - Lewis: T.C.Askin Atkinson Hoult Davies:
THOMAS DENNIS(121) Hall: Sherwood Plimmer Taylor
A.Askin Stafford Jubb: Tries - T.C.Askin(2) Davies(2)
Hoult Stafford: Goals - Lewis(2) Atkinson(2):
BRADFORD N - Stocks: Smith Thornburrow Reed Bright:
Binks Gledhill: Litt Mclester Sutton Cracknell Woolmore
Sherwood: Try - Sherwood: Goals - Litt(3):
Referee J W Webb (Broughton) Att - 4500 H.T.

Sat 15 Oct 1932 HULL KINGSTON ROVERS home
won 13 - 2
CASTLEFORD - Lewis: T.C.Askin Atkinson Hoult Davies:
Dennis Hall Sherwood(S/O) Plimmer(S/O) Taylor A.Askin
Stafford Jubb: Try - Jubb: Goals - Atkinson(5):
HULL K R - Carmichael: Hill Brindle Spamer Smith: Dale
Fridlington: Sharpe Binks Blossom Williams Tattersfield
Saddington: Goal - Carmichael:
Referee E Devine (Leeds) Att - 4000 H.T. 4 - nil

Wed 19 Oct 1932 LEEDS away lost 2 - 9
YORKSHIRE CUP SEMI FINAL
LEEDS - Brough: Harris Moores O'Rourke S.Smith:
Williams Busch: Thompson Lowe Jenkins R.Smith Douglas
Glossop: Try - Harris: Goals - Thompson(3):
CASTLEFORD - Lewis: T.C.Askin Atkinson Hoult Davies:
Dennis Hall: Sherwood Plimmer(S/O) Taylor A.Askin
Stafford Jubb: Goal - Atkinson:
Referee J Eddon (Swinton) Att - 6700 H.T. 2 - 7

SEASON 1932-33

Sat 22 Oct 1932 DEWSBURY home won 29 - 4
CASTLEFORD - Lewis: T.C.Askin Atkinson Hoult Davies:
Dennis Hall: Sherwood Plimmer Walton Taylor
A.Askin(S/O) Jubb: Tries - T.C.Askin(2) Atkinson(2)
Davies - Atkinson(5) Lewis(2):
DEWSBURY - Owen: Hobson(S/O) Morgan Oakland
Raywood: Manning Werrett: Golby Banks Targett Green
Booth Orford: Goals - Owen(2):
Referee W H Eastman (Hull) Att - 3000 H.T. 7 - 2

Sat 29 Oct 1932 LEEDS away lost 5 - 26
LEEDS - Brough: Harris Moores O'Rourke Grainge:
Williams Adams: Lowe Thompson Jenkins Dyer Douglas
Jones: Tries - Harris(3) Moores(2) O'Rourke Grainge
Adams: Goal - Thompson:
CASTLEFORD - JOHN.T.BIRD(122): T.C.Askin James Hoult
Dennis: Annable Hall: Walton HAROLD HALEY(123) Taylor
Stafford FRANK SMITH(124) Jennings:
Try - Jennings: Goal - James:
Referee A Brown (Wakefield) Att - 3000 H.T. 5 - 14

Sat 5 Nov 1932 OLDHAM home lost 6 - 18
CASTLEFORD - Lewis: T.C.Askin Atkinson Hoult Davies:
Charles Annable Hall: Walton Haley Taylor Stafford Jubb
Jennings: Goals - Lewis(2) Atkinson:
OLDHAM - Foote: Williams Bardsley Stephens Lewis:
Houghton Reybould: Reed Scaife Entwistle Thomas
Hathway Ashworth: Tries - Stephens(2) Williams
Hatheway: Goals - Stephens(2) Reybould:
Referee L Greenwood (Rochdale) Att - 4000 H.T. 3 - 4

Sat 12 Nov 1932 WIGAN away lost 8 - 11
WIGAN - Sullivan: Twose Davies Wilson Morley: Rees
Howarth: Hall Vernon Morgan Dixon Mason Griffiths:
Tries - Twose Davies Morley: Goal - Sullivan:
CASTLEFORD - James: T.C.Askin Atkinson Lewis Hoult:
Davies Hall: Walton Harling Taylor Jubb Jennings Russell:
Tries - Atkinson(2): Goal - James:
Referee J E Taylor (Wakefield) Att -   H.T. 5 - 8

Sat 19 Nov 1932 WIGAN home lost 10 - 13
CASTLEFORD - James: T.C.Askin Atkinson Lewis Hoult:
Davies Hall: Sherwood Haley Taylor Jennings A.Askin
Jubb: Tries - T.C.Askin A.Askin: Goals - James Atkinson:
WIGAN - Sullivan: Twose Davies Wilson Morley: Howarth
Gee: Hall Vernon Morgan Dixon Mason Griffiths:
Tries - Twose Morley Howarth: Goals - Sullivan(2):
Referee J W Webb (Broughton) Att - 4500 H.T. 2 - 8

**Sat 26 Nov 1932 BROUGHTON RANGERS away
lost 6 - 10**
BROUGHTON R - Williams: Cumberbatch Davies Rix
Bunter: Dennett McCarrigan: Whitehead Thomas Axon
Hill Tetlow Doran:
Tries - Cumberbatch(2): Goals - Williams(2):
CASTLEFORD - Lewis: T.C.Askin Atkinson James Hoult:
Davies Hall: Sherwood Haley Taylor Jennings A.Askin
Jubb: Tries - Jubb Hoult:
Referee F Peel (Bradford) Att -   H.T.

Sat 3 Dec 1932 ST HELENS home lost 7 - 10
CASTLEFORD - Lewis: T.C.Askin Atkinson Davies Hoult:
Dennis Hall: Sherwood Haley(S/O) Taylor A.Askin
Jennings Jubb: Try - Taylor: Goals - Lewis(2):
ST HELENS - Jones: Hardgrave Butler Winnard Ellaby:
Garvey Frodsham: Cotton(S/O) Atkin Halfpenny Hill
Arkwright Groves:
Tries - Ellaby Halfpenny: Goals - Winnard(2):
Referee E Houghton (Warrington) Att - 4000 H.T. 3 - 10

Sat 10 Dec 1932 YORK away draw 4 - 4
YORK - Dingsdale: Brown Higgins J.Davies H.Thomas:
Smith W.Thomas: Bland Myers Crabtree John Coldrick
Fender: Goals - Dingsdale Higgins:
CASTLEFORD - Lewis: T.C.Askin Atkinson James Hoult:
Davies Hall: Sherwood Plimmer Taylor Jubb A.Askin
Russell: Goals - Atkinson(2):
Referee W Eastman (Hull) Att - 5000 H.T. 4 - 2

Sat 17 Dec 1932 HULL home won 13 - 2
CASTLEFORD - Lewis: Jubb Atkinson DONALD
KNOWLES(125) Hoult: Davies Hall: Sherwood Plimmer
Taylor A.Askin Russell Walton:
Tries - Atkinson Taylor Sherwood: Goals - Lewis Atkinson:
HULL - Teall: Bateman Oliver Fifield Winsor: Curtis
Ellerington: Thompson Wilkinson Stead Dawson Milner
Carmichael: Goal - Oliver:
Referee T Hesketh (Wigan) Att - 3000 H.T. 11 - 2

Sat 24 Dec 1932 BRAMLEY away draw 13 - 13
BRAMLEY - Parkinson: Whittaker Rees Marshall Desmond:
Ballantyne Wood: Reed Bowden Harrison Maudsley
Morrell Blackburn:
Try - Desmond: Goals - Rees(3) Marshall(2):
CASTLEFORD - Lewis: T.C.Askin Atkinson Knowles Hoult:
Davies Hall: George Stafford Plimmer Taylor A.Askin Jubb
Russell: Tries - T.C.Askin(2) Russell: Goals - Lewis(2):
Referee H Swift (Halifax) Att -   H.T. 8 - 2

**Mon 26 Dec 1932 FEATHERSTONE ROVERS home
won 13 - nil**
CASTLEFORD - Lewis: T.C.Askin Atkinson James Hoult:
Davies Hall: Sherwood Plimmer Taylor A.Askin Jubb
Russell: Tries - Jubb(2) T.C.Askin: Goals - Atkinson(2):
FEATHERSTONE R - Johnson: Killingbeck Winter Stott
Ward: W.Evans Hayes: Barraclough Morgan Padgett
Williams Norbury J.Evans:
Referee H Swift (Halifax) Att - 4000 H.T. 5 - nil

Tue 27 Dec 1932 OLDHAM away won 9 - 6
OLDHAM - Hilton: L.Lewis Marner Stephens L.Williams:
Houghton Foote: Entwistle Scaife Reed Thomas Ashworth
Hathway: Tries - Williams(2):
CASTLEFORD - Lewis: Hoult James Atkinson T.C.Askin:
Davies Hall: Sherwood Haley Taylor A.Askin Jubb Russell:
Try - Atkinson: Goals - Atkinson(2) Lewis(DG):
Referee J Roberts (Leeds) Att - 4500 H.T. 5 - 3

Sat 31 Dec 1932 YORK home draw 2 - 2
CASTLEFORD - Lewis: T.C.Askin Atkinson James Hoult:

Davies Hall: Sherwood Plimmer Taylor A.Askin(S/O) Jubb
Russell: Goal - Atkinson:
YORK - Dingsdale: Brown Higgins Rosser H.Thomas: Rees
W.Thomas: Bland Myers Crabtree(S/O) Fender Coldrick
Aspinall: Goal - Dingsdale:
Referee J E Taylor (Wakefield) Att - 5500 H.T. nil - nil

Sat 7 Jan 1933 KEIGHLEY home won 10 - 8

CASTLEFORD - Lewis: T.C.Askin Atkinson James Hoult:
Davies Hall: Sherwood Plimmer Taylor A.Askin Jubb
Russell: Tries - T.C.Askin Hoult: Goals - Atkinson(2):
KEIGHLEY - Rainton: W.Jones Sherburn Briggs Oakes:
Davies Spillane: H.Jones Watson Pascoe McGoun Ashton
Gill: Tries - W.Jones Briggs: Goal - Sherburn:
Referee F Peel (Bradford) Att - 4000 H.T. 5 - 6

Sat 14 Jan 1933 DEWSBURY away won 25 - 2

DEWSBURY - Owen: Hirst Morgan Chester Hobson:
Coates Smith: Surguy Johnson Targett Green Orford
Manning: Goal - Hirst:
CASTLEFORD - Lewis: T.C.Askin Knowles James Hoult:
Davies Hall: Sherwood Harling Taylor Stanley Jennings
Smith Russell: Tries - T.C.Askin(2) Harling(2) Knowles
James Hoult: Goals - Lewis(2):
Referee J E Taylor (Wakefield) Att - 2500 H.T. 6 - 2

Sat 28 Jan 1933 KEIGHLEY away draw 5 - 5

KEIGHLEY - Holmes: Oakes Foster Sherburn W.Jones:
Davies Spillane: Thompson Watson Pascoe H.Jones
McGoun Gill: Try - Davies: Goal - Sherburn:
CASTLEFORD - Lewis: T.C.Askin Atkinson James Hoult:
Davies Hall: Sherwood Harling Taylor Jubb Smith Russell:
Try - Hoult: Goal - Atkinson:
Referee E Devine (Leeds) Att - 4500 H.T. 2 - 5

Wed 1 Feb 1933 BRADFORD NORTHERN home won 14 - 2

CASTLEFORD - Lewis: T.C.Askin Atkinson James Hoult:
Davies Hall: Sherwood Harling Taylor Jubb Smith Russell:
Tries - Hoult(2) T.C.Askin James: Goal - Atkinson:
BRADFORD N - Stocks: Tetlow Thornburrow Mullens
Walker: Bush Binks: Litt McLester Coates Collins
Woolmore Sherwood: Goal - Litt:
Referee W Eastman (Hull) Att - 2000 H.T. 11 - 2

Sat 4 Feb 1933 WIGAN HIGHFIELD home won 29 - 6

CASTLEFORD - Lewis: T.C.Askin Atkinson James Hoult:
Davies Hall: Sherwood Haley Taylor Jubb Smith Russell:
Tries - Hoult(4) T.C.Askin Atkinson Davies:
Goals - Atkinson(3) Lewis:
WIGAN H - Barnes: Jas Walker Fey Winnard Hanson:
J.Walker Bradbury: Gray Wood Davies Cayser Halsall
Stocks: Tries - Winnard Davies:
Referee A Holbrook (Warrington) Att - 4000 H.T. 16 - 3

Sat 11 Feb 1933 SALFORD away lost nil - 11
CHALLENGE CUP ROUND 1

SALFORD - Risman: Boyd Miller Brown Hudson: Jenkins
Watkins: Williams Day Bradbury Casewell Middleton
Feetham: Tries - Boyd Hudson Casewell: Goal - Risman:

CASTLEFORD - Lewis: T.C.Askin James Hoult A.Askin:
Davies Hall: Sherwood Haley Taylor Jubb Smith Russell:
Referee E Devine (Leeds) Att - 14000 H.T. nil - nil

Sat 18 Feb 1933 BRADFORD NORTHERN away won 8 - 5

BRADFORD N - Stocks: Tetlow Thornburrow Mullens
Smith: Bush Gledhill: Litt McLester Sutton Collins Davies
Sherwood: Try - Smith: Goal - Litt:
CASTLEFORD - Dennis: T.C.Askin Lewis James Hoult:
Davies Hall: Sherwood Haley Taylor Smith A.Askin Jubb:
Tries - T.C.Askin Hoult: Goal - James:
Referee W Eastman (Hull) Att - H.T. 5 - 3

Sat 4 Mar 1933 BRAMLEY home won 20 - 3

CASTLEFORD - Lewis: Knowles T.C.Askin James Hoult:
Davies Hall: Sherwood Haley Taylor A.Askin Jubb Russell:
Tries - James(2) Knowles T.C.Askin Hoult Davies:
Goal - Lewis:
BRAMLEY - Knowling: Whittaker Marshall Ballantyne
Desmond: E.Reed Wood: G.Reed Bowden Harrison
Ingham Malkin Rowan: Try - Whittaker:
Referee A Brown (Wakefield) Att - 2750 H.T. 11 - 3

Sat 11 Mar 1933 LEIGH home won 17 - 5

CASTLEFORD - Lewis: Knowles T.C.Askin James Hoult:
Davies Hall: Sherwood Plimmer Taylor A.Askin Jubb
Russell:
Tries - Knowles Hoult Taylor: Goals - Lewis(3) James:
LEIGH - Baxter: Stringman Harris Osborne Houghton:
Smith Davies: Worrall Richardson Edwards Flannery
Morley Langford: Try - Houghton: Goal - Baxter:
Referee F Fairhurst (Wigan) Att - 4750 H.T. 10 - nil

Sat 18 Mar 1933 WAKEFIELD TRINITY away won 10 - nil

WAKEFIELD T - Farrar: Gorner Lingard Pollard Smart:
Thompson Pearce: Rudd Field Hobson Exley Wilkinson
Horton:
CASTLEFORD - Lewis: Knowles T.C.Askin James Hoult:
Davies Hall: Sherwood Plimmer Taylor A.Askin Jubb
Russell: Tries - A.Askin Jubb: Goals - Lewis(2):
Referee B Laughlin (Batley) Att - 5000 H.T. 5 - nil

Wed 29 Mar 1933 BATLEY away won 12 - 8

BATLEY - Goldie: Broom Thomas Evans Nunn: Shirley
Swift: Dyson Hall Leeming Jones Hopton Glossop:
Tries - Nunn(2): Goal - Goldie:
CASTLEFORD - Lewis: Atkinson T.C.Askin James Hoult:
Davies Hall: Sherwood Plimmer Taylor A.Askin Jubb
Russell: Tries - Atkinson Russell: Goals - Atkinson(2) Lewis:
Referee F Peel (Bradford) Att - H.T. 10 - nil

Sat 1 Apr 1933 WAKEFIELD TRINITY home won 7 -3

CASTLEFORD - Lewis: T.C.Askin Atkinson James Hoult:
Davies Hall: Sherwood Plimmer Taylor Smith A.Askin
Russell: Try - James: Goals - Lewis Atkinson:
WAKEFIELD T - Bonner: Newman Exley Owen Smart:
Thompson Reynard: Rudd Field Hobson Horton Higson
Wilkinson: Try - Reynard:

SEASON 1932-33

Referee B Laughlin (Batley) Att - 5000 H.T. 2 - 3

Fri 14 Apr 1933 FEATHERSTONE ROVERS away won 25 - nil
FEATHERSTONE R - Lockwood: Rowley Denton Stott Barker: W.Evans Hayes: Barraclough Morgan Darlison Norbury Easter J.Evans:
CASTLEFORD - Lewis: T.C.Askin Atkinson James Hoult: Davies Hall: Sherwood Haley Taylor A.Askin Jubb Russell:
Tries - T.C.Askin Atkinson Hoult Taylor Jubb:
Goals - Atkinson(3)Lewis(2):
Referee H Swift (Batley) Att - 9334 H.T. 2 - nil

Sat 15 Apr 1933 LEIGH away lost 7 - 8
LEIGH - Baxter: Stringman Harris Smith Houghton: Green Davies: Worrall Hilton Edwards Morley Prescott Griffin:
Tries - Prescott(2): Goal - Baxter:
CASTLEFORD - Lewis: T.C.Askin Atkinson James Hoult: Davies Hall: Walton Plimmer Leese A.Askin Smith Fred Wadsworth: Try - Wadsworth: Goals - Atkinson(2):
Referee F Peel (Bradford) Att - 4000 H.T. 2 - 3

Mon 17 Apr 1933 LEEDS home won 12 - 10
CASTLEFORD - Lewis: T.C.Askin Atkinson James Hoult: Davies Hall: Sherwood Haley Taylor A.Askin Jubb Russell:
Tries - T.C.Askin A.Askin: Goals - Atkinson(2) James:
LEEDS - Pollard: Harris Brough O'Rourke Grainge: Williams Busch: Jenkins Lowe Satterthwaite Dyer Douglas Davies: Tries - Harris Douglas: Goals - Williams(2):
Referee H Swift (Batley) Att - 9000 H.T. 5 - nil

Tue 18 Apr 1933 HUNSLET home won 10 - 5
CASTLEFORD - Lewis: Knowles Atkinson T.C.Askin Hoult: Davies Hall: Sherwood Haley Taylor A.Askin Jubb Russell:
Tries - T.C.Askin Hall: Goals - Lewis(1)(DG):
HUNSLET - Walkington: Cornell Winter Goulthorpe Broughton: Thornton Morrell: Traill White Moss Dawson Smith Beverley: Try - Smith: Goal - Thornton:
Referee J E Taylor (Wakefield) Att - 9540 H.T. 8 - 5

Sat 22 Apr 1933 BATLEY home won 12 - 10
CASTLEFORD - Lewis: Knowles James Hoult A.Askin:
T.C.Askin Hall: Sherwood Haley Taylor Jubb Smith Russell:
Tries - T.C.Askin Hall: Goals - Lewis(2) Smith:
BATLEY - Goldie: Broom A.N.Other A.N.Other Nunn:
Shirley Hick: Dyson Hall Earnshaw Oates Jones Glossop:
Tries - Hick Earnshaw: Goals - Goldie(2):
Referee A Brown (Wakefield) Att - 4000 H.T. 5 - 5

Sat 29 Apr 1933 ST HELENS away lost 5 - 39
ST HELENS - Lewis: Hardgrave Mercer Winnard Butler: Garvey Frodsham: A.N.Other Cotton Hargrave Fildes Arkwright 'A.Newman'
Tries - Hardgrave(5) Winnard Butler Garvey A.Newman:
Goals - Lewis(3) A.Newman(3):
CASTLEFORD - Lewis: Hoult Knowles James JOSEPH ALLAN(125): T.C.Askin Hall: Leese Haley Taylor A.Askin Kenneth Jubb Russell: Try - T.C.Askin: Goal - Lewis:
Referee J E Taylor (Wakefield) Att - 3000 H.T. nil - 8

Donald Knowles
D. No 125
1932-33 to 1935-36

Harold Haley
D. No 123
1932-33 to 1947-48

Frank Smith Snr
D. No 124
1932-33 to 1946-47

YORKSHIRE LEAGUE CHAMPIONS1932-33
Back Row F Briggs (Director) H Haley A Smith(Director) A Askin A Sherwood T Taylor F Smith K Jubb H Russell
H Atkins (Director) T Appleyard (Director) A Pickles (Secretary)
Middle Row – W Smith (Director) T Askin G Lewis A Atkinson (Captain) G Shaw (Chairman) B James J Hoult
D Knowles W Rhodes (Trainer) Front Row – Billy Davies Wilson Hall

SEASON 1932-33

D.N	PLAYER		DEBUT	L MATCH	APP	SLB	T.AP	TR'S	G'LS	D.G	P'TS
5	HUDSON	HARRY		10/09/1932	3	0	3	0	0	0	0
11	MALKIN	JOSEPH		01/10/1932	3	0	3	0	0	0	0
14	RUSSELL	HARRY (DANNY)			25	0	25	2	0	0	6
21	ATKINSON	ARTHUR			27	0	27	9	43	0	113
23	WALTON	RICHARD			9	0	9	0	0	0	0
39	PLIMMER	JAMES			22	0	22	0	0	0	0
58	CHAPMAN	HAROLD			1	0	1	0	0	0	0
62	SHERWOOD	ARTHUR			34	0	34	1	0	0	3
64	THOMAS	EDWIN		01/10/1932	1	0	1	0	0	0	0
69	CASEY	JOHN		10/09/1932	3	0	3	1	0	0	3
77	STAFFORD	GEORGE		24/12/1932	9	0	9	1	0	0	3
78	JAMES	WILLIAM			25	0	25	5	6	0	27
79	LEWIS	GEORGE			40	0	40	0	36	2	76
84	HALL	WILSON			39	0	39	3	0	0	9
85	LEESE	ALBERT			2	0	2	0	0	0	0
87	JENNINGS	STANLEY		14/01/1933	7	0	7	1	0	0	3
96	HARLING	CLIFFORD			4	0	4	2	0	0	6
97	JUBB	KENNETH		29/04/1933	35	0	35	6	0	0	18
98	ASKIN	THOMAS C.			40	0	40	21	0	0	63
110	ANNABLE	CHARLES		05/11/1932	7	0	7	0	0	0	0
111	DAVIES	WILLIAM H.			38	0	38	5	0	0	15
112	WADSWORTH	FRED		15/04/1933	3	0	3	1	0	0	3
116	TAYLOR	THOMAS L.			40	0	40	4	0	0	12
117	ASKIN	AMBROSE			31	0	31	3	0	0	9
119	HOULT	JACK	27/08/1932		41	0	41	16	0	0	48
120	JOHNSON	JOHN	17/09/1932		1	0	1	1	0	0	3
121	DENNIS	THOMAS	12/10/1932		7	0	7	0	0	0	0
122	BIRD	JOHN T.	29/10/1932	29/10/1932	1	0	1	0	0	0	0
123	HALEY	HAROLD	29/10/1932		15	0	15	0	0	0	0
124	SMITH	FRANK Snr.	29/10/1932		10	0	10	0	1	0	2
125	KNOWLES	DONALD	17/12/1932		9	0	9	3	0	0	9
126	ALLAN	JOSEPH	29/04/1933	29/04/1933	1	0	1	0	0	0	0
	32		8	11	533	0	533	85	86	2	431

COMPETITION		P	W	D	L	FOR	AGT
LEAGUE	POSITION 8 OF 28	38	21	4	13	403	326
YORK'S CUP		2	1	0	1	28	18
RL CUP		1	0	0	1	0	11
PLAYERS RECORDS		41	22	4	15	431	355

Billy Rhodes returned to take over the Trainer's duties again from Billy Clements, retaining this position until 1951.

History was created this season with the Club winning its first trophy, being crowned the Yorkshire League Champions. This was achieved with six players who played in that first 1926/27 season: Arthur Atkinson; Harry Hudson; Joe Malkin; Jim Plimmer; Harry (Danny) Russell; and Dick Walton.

The Yorkshire League was a competition within a competition, as the normal league results against the other Yorkshire teams were collated in a separate table with the winner being decided in the usual manner, with two points for a win and one for a draw.

It was during this season that Castleford set the record of being unbeaten in 18 consecutive League matches. The run started with a four all draw away at York on 10 December 1932 and included a further three drawn games and ended with an 18-7 defeat at Leigh. We also won the next three games before losing the final game of the season away at St Helens.

Arthur Atkinson equalled the record for most point scored in a League game at 16 against Dewsbury at home on the 22 October 1932.

**Sat 19 Aug 1933 FEATHERSTONE ROVERS home
won 21 - 15 LYON CUP - FRIENDLY**
CASTLEFORD - Lewis: Johnson Atkinson James Hoult:
Davies Hall: Sherwood Haley Taylor Sam Walton Smith
Russell:
Tries - Lewis James Davies Hall Taylor: Goals - James(3):
FEATHERSTONE R - Lockwood: Rowley Plenderleith Stott
Barker: Evans Hayes: Barraclough Morgan Padgett Easter
Taylor Fox:
Tries - Stott(2) Rowley: Goals - Lockeood(2) Stott:
Referee J E Taylor (Wakefield) Att - 2000 H.T. 8 - 5

Sat 26 Aug 1933 HUNSLET home won 24 - 10
CASTLEFORD - Lewis: T.C.Askin Atkinson James Hoult:
Davies Hall: Walton Haley Taylor Smith A.Askin Russell:
Tries - Hall(2) T.C.Askin Hoult: Goals - James(5) Lewis(DG):
HUNSLET - Walkington: Dennis Winter Goulthorpe
Broughton: Thornton Morrell: Traill White Moss Smith
Dawson Beverley:
Tries - Winter Goulthorpe: Goals - Traill(2):
Referee W Eastman (Hull) Att - 5000 H.T. 5 - 3

Wed 30 Aug 1933 BATLEY home won 21 - 9
CASTLEFORD - Lewis: T.C.Askin Atkinson James Hoult:
Davies Hall: Walton Haley Taylor Smith A.Askin Russell:
Tries - Atkinson Davies Walton: Goals - James(5)
Atkinson:
BATLEY - Goldie: Nunn Smith Thomas Broom: Swift
Shirley: Dyson Hall Earnshaw Hopton Oates Glossop:
Tries - Dyson Oates Glossop:
Referee J E Taylor (Wakefield) Att - 4000 H.T. 9 - 3

**Sat 2 Sept 1933 BRADFORD NORTHERN away
lost 14 - 17**
BRADFORD N - Whittle: Tetlow Townsend Thornburrow
Walker: Bradbury Bush: Litt McLester Sutton Parr Elson
Sherwood:
Tries - Thornburrow Bradbury Parr: Goals - Litt(4):
CASTLEFORD - Lewis: T.C.Askin Atkinson James Hoult:
Davies Hall: Walton Plimmer Taylor A.Askin Smith Russell:
Tries - Atkinson Smith: Goals - James(4):
Referee A Brown (Wakefield) Att - 3500 H.T. 5 - 14

Sat 9 Sept 1933 BRAMLEY home Won 26 - 10
CASTLEFORD - Lewis: T.C.Askin Atkinson James Hoult:
Davies Hall: Sherwood Haley Taylor Walton A.Askin
HAROLD YOUNG(127):
Tries - Atkinson(3) Hoult(2) Young: Goals - Atkinson(2)
James(2):
BRAMLEY - Leach: Whittaker Davidson Rees Gee: Abram
Curtiss: Reed Bowden Harrison Ingham Hulme Rowan:
Tries - Gee Abram: Goals - Rees(2):
Referee J A Armstrong (Hud'field) Att - 3500 H.T. 13 -nil

**Mon 11 Sept 1933 HALIFAX away lost 5 - 14
ROYAL INFIRMARY CHARITY CUP - FRIENDLY**
HALIFAX - J.Irvine: Gill Kitson Haigh Jones: Davies
Hanson: Renton Morris Thomas Morgan H.Irving Cox:
Tries - Cox Morgan: Goals - Irving(4):
CASTLEFORD - Pollitt: T.C.Askin Atkinson James Lewis:

Davies Hall: Hand Haley Taylor A.Askin Walton Russell:
Try - Walton: Goal - James:
Referee A E Harding (Manchester) Att - 7000   H.T.

Sat 16 Sept 1933 KEIGHLEY away lost 9 - 14
KEIGHLEY - Rainton: Sherburn W.Jones Davies Oakes:
A.N.Other Spillane: Pascoe Watson H.Jones McGoun
Dixon Gill:
Tries - Sherburn W.Jones: Goals - Pascoe(4):
CASTLEFORD - JOHN POLLITT(128): Johnson Atkinson
James Hoult: T.C.Askin Hall: Walton Haley Taylor Smith
Russell Young:
Try - Hall: Goals - Atkinson(3):
Referee W Eastman (Hull) Att - 6500 H.T. 7 - 6

Wed 20 Sept 1933 BATLEY away won 7 - 4
BATLEY - Goldie: Nunn Smith Cook Broom: Hick Swift:
Dyson Hall Earnshaw Hopton Oates Glossop:
Goals - Goldie Hick:
CASTLEFORD - Lewis: T.C.Askin Atkinson James Johnson:
Davies Hall: Walton Haley Taylor Smith Russell Young:
Try - Atkinson: Goals - James(1)(DG):
Referee F Peel (Bradford) Att - 2000 H.T. 5 - 4

Sat 23 Sept 1933 SWINTON home won 22 - 9
CASTLEFORD - Pollitt: T.C.Askin Lewis James Johnson:
Davies Hall: Walton Haley Taylor Smith Russell Young:
Tries - T.C.Askin Lewis Johnson Smith: Goals - Pollitt(2)
James(2) Davies(DG):
SWINTON - Scott: McGregor Whittaker H.Evans Kenny:
Rees Holland: Armitt Sulway Hodgson Woodall Beswick
Spruce:
Try - Kenny: Goals - Hodgson(2) Whittaker(DG):
Referee F Fairhurst (Wigan) Att - 5000 H.T. 5 - nil

Wed 27 Sept 1933 AUSTRALIA lost 6 - 39
CASTLEFORD - Pollitt: T.C.Askin Lewis James Johnson:
Davies Hall: Walton Haley Hand Smith Russell Young:
Goals - Pollitt(3):
AUSTRALIA - Smith: Ridley Pearce Brown Neumann:
Doonar Thickness: Madsen Dempsey Curran Gibbs
0'Connor Prigg:
Tries - Ridley(4) Prigg Thicknesse Gibb 0'Connor Brown:
Goals - Brown(6):
Referee J Eddon (Swinton) Att - 6000 H.T. nil - 12

Sat 30 Sept 1933 LEEDS away lost 3 - 30
LEEDS - Davies: Atkinson Pollard O'Rourke Grainge: Ralph
Busch: Lowe Green Jenkins Aspinall Jubb Isaac:
Tries - Atkinson(2) Pollard(2) Grainge(2) O'Rourke Isaac:
Goals - Grange(2) Green:
CASTLEFORD - Pollitt: Johnson James Lewis T.C.Askin:
Davies Hall: Walton Plimmer Harry(Mick)Hand Smith
J.H.WILLIAMS(129) Russell:
Try - T.C.Askin:
Referee A Holbrook (War'gton) Att - 9500 H.T. nil - 13

SEASON 1933-34

Sat 7 Oct 1933 BRADFORD NORTHERN home won 18 - 7
CASTLEFORD - Pollitt: T.C.Askin Lewis James ALFRED JAMES CROSTON(130): Thomas Dennis Hall: Walton Haley Sherwood Smith Russell Johnson:
Tries - T.C.Askin Croston Hall Johnson: Goals - Pollitt(2) James:
BRADFORD N - Taylor: Smith Halton Berry Walker: Bradbury Bush: Collins Turber Sutton Elson Woolmore Sherwood:
Try - Bradbury: Goals - Taylor Sherwood:
Referee W Eastman (Hull) Att -   H.T. 5 - 2

Sat 14 Oct 1933 HUNSLET home won 10 - 9
YORKSHIRE CUP ROUND 1
CASTLEFORD - Lewis: Johnson T.C.Askin James Hoult: Davies Hall: Walton Haley Sherwood Smith Russell Young:
Tries - T.C.Askin Russell: Goals - James(2):
HUNSLET - Walkington: Dennis Winter Morrell Broughton: Todd Thornton: Traill White Moss Dawson Crowther Whitehead:
Try - Thornton: Goals - Walkington(3):
Referee A Holbrook (Warrington) Att 8000 H..T..5 - 9

Sat 21 Oct 1933 ROCHDALE HORNETS away lost 4 - 6
ROCHDALE H - Gowers: Skinner Gaunt Davies Tolan: Beattie Helme: Milne Lister Thompson Walker Reed Armbruster:
Tries - Skinner Gaunt:
CASTLEFORD - Lewis: Johnson T.C.Askin James Hoult: Davies Hall: Walton Haley Sherwood Smith Russell Knowles:
Goals - James(2):
Referee C Ramsden (Doncaster) Att - 4000 H.T 4 - 6

Wed 25 Oct 1933 HALIFAX away lost 2 - 18
YORKSHIRE CUP ROUND 2
HALIFAX - C.Davies: H.Thomas Cutbush R.Thomas Jones: I.Davies Burrows: Renton Morris Baynham Cox H.Irvine Higgs:
Tries - H.Thomas(2) Cutbush Higgs: Goals - Jones(3):
CASTLEFORD - Lewis: Johnson James Croston T.C.Askin: Davies Hall: Sherwood Haley Walton Smith Russell Knowles:
Goal - James:
Referee A E Harding (Manchester) Att - 6200 H.T. 2 - 10

Sat 28 Oct 1933 DEWSBURY home won 26 - 11
CASTLEFORD - Lewis: T.C.Askin James Croston Hoult: Davies Hall: Walton Haley Taylor Smith Russell Knowles:
Tries - Hall(4) Croston Davies: Goals - James(4):
DEWSBURY - Thomas: Whitehead Killingbeck Hogan Hobson: Rees Herbert: Banks Golby Targett Evans Malkin Oakland:
Try - Evans: Goals - Whitehead(2) Thomas Rees(DG):
Referee W Eastman (Hull) Att - 3000 H.T. 12 - 8

Sat 4 Nov 1933 WIGAN away lost 9 - 21
WIGAN - Sullivan: Morley Wilson G.Davies Merritt: Bennett Gee: Hall Leonard Gaskell Mason A.Davies Griffith:
Tries - Morley(2) Wilson: Goals - Sullivan(6):
CASTLEFORD - Lewis: Hoult James Croston T.C.Askin: Davies Hall: Walton Haley(S/O) Taylor Smith Russell Knowles:
Try - T.C.Askin: Goals - James(3):
Referee J Armstrong (Hud'field) Att - 4800 H.T. 7 - 12

Sat 11 Nov 1933 KEIGHLEY home lost 9 - 14
CASTLEFORD - Lewis: T.C.Askin Atkinson Croston James: Davies Hall: Walton Plimmer Taylor Smith Russell Harold Young:
Try - T.C.Askin Goals - James(2) Atkinson:
KEIGHLEY - Rainton: Sherburn Foster Davies W.Jones: Phelps Spillane: Pascoe Watson H.Jones Dixon Fuller Gill:
Tries - Foster Gill: Goals - Sherburn(2) Pascoe Phelps(DG):
Referee B Laughlin (Batley) Att - 6000 H.T. 4 - nil

Sat 18 Nov 1933 HUNSLET away lost 4 - 12
HUNSLET - Walkington: Dennis Winter Morrell Broughton: Todd Thornton: Traill White Smith Dawson Crowther Wh tehead:
Tries - Winter Morrell Broughton Traill:
CASTLEFORD - Lewis: T.C.Askin Atkinson Croston Johnson: Davies Hall: Walton Plimmer Taylor Smith Russell Knowles:
Goals - Atkinson Lewis:
Referee W H Eastman (Hull) Att - 3000 H.T. 2 - 9

Sat 25 Nov 1933 HULL home won 17 - 12
CASTLEFORD - Lewis: T.C.Askin Atkinson Croston John Johnson: Davies Hall: Leese Harling Taylor Smith Walton Knowles:
Tries - Croston(2) Atkinson: Goals - Atkinson(3) Lewis:
HULL - Miller: Winsor Oliver Sowerby Sheard: Fifield Metcalfe: Bowman Wilkinson Barlow Dawson Stead Carmichael:
Tries - Sheard Dawson: Goals - Oliver(3):
Referee F Peel (Bradford) Att - 5000 H.T. 10 - 7

Sat 9 Dec 1933 HULL KINGSTON ROVERS home Won 20 - 7
CASTLEFORD - Lewis: T.C.Askin Atkinson Croston Hoult: Davies Hal : Walton Haley Taylor Amith Leese Russell:
Tries - T.C.Askin Atkinson Croston Russell:
Goals - Lewis(4):
HULL K R - Carmichael: Deeley Spamer Hill Tattersfield: Woodcock Beaumont: Britton Binks Eddoms Blossom Sharpe Saddington:
Try - Blossom: Goals - Carmichael(2):
Referee J E Taylor (Wakefield) Att - 4000 H.T. 13 - 2

Sat 16 Dec 1933 DEWSBURY away lost 5 - 7
DEWSBURY - Thomas: Rees Whitehead Killingbeck S.Ward: Large D.Ward: Golby Targett Malkin Orford Evans Oakland: Try - S.Ward: Goals Thomas (2):
CASTLEFORD - Lewis: T.C.Askin James Croston Jack Hoult: Davies Hall: Walton Haley Taylor Smith Leese Russell
Try - Croston: Goal - Lewis
Referee _ E Taylor (Wakefield) Att - 2000 H.T. 5 - 2

SEASON 1933-34

Sat 23 Dec 1933 WIDNES home won 13 - 3

CASTLEFORD - Pollitt: T.C.Askin Atkinson Croston
Knowles: Davies Hall: Walton Haley Taylor Smith Leese
Russell:
Tries - Atkinson Smith Leese: Goals - Pollitt(2):
WIDNES - Bradley: Owens Robinson Taylor Gallimore:
Jacks McCue: Silcock Jones Higgins McDowell Hoey
Millington: Try - Higgins:
Referee J Eddon (Swinton) Att - 4000 H.T. 3 - nil

Mon 25 Dec 1933 FEATHERSTONE ROVERS away won 22 - 3

FEATHERSTONE R - Johnson: J.Denton Lingard Malpass
Asquith: W.Evans Hayes: Morgan Taylor Flaherty
Barraclough Plenderleith Price:
Try - Asquith:
CASTLEFORD - Pollitt: JAMES GILL(131) Croston Atkinson
T.C.Askin: Davies Hall: Walton Haley Taylor Smith Leese
Russell:
Tries - Atkinson(2) Croston Davies:
Goals - Pollitt(3) Atkinson(2):
Referee A Brown (Wakefield) Att - 5000 H.T. 7 - 3

Tue 26 Dec 1933 YORK home won 11 - 10

CASTLEFORD - Pollitt: T.C.Askin Atkinson Croston Gill:
Davies Hall: Walton Haley Taylor Smith Leese Russell:
Try - Croston: Goals - Pollitt(2) Atkinson Davies(DG):
YORK - Dingsdale: Higgins Smith Moores Brown: Rees
Thomas: Bland Myers Crabtree Elias John Fender:
Tries - Moores Rees: Goals - Higgins(2):
Referee F Peel (Bradford) Att - 9000 H.T. 2 - 2

Sat 30 Dec 1933 BRAMLEY away won 26 - 2

BRAMLEY - Eccles: Gee Senior Rees Whittaker: Abrams
Curtis: G.Reed Bowden Litt Hulme Ballantyne Rowan:
Goal - Litt:
CASTLEFORD - Pollitt: T.C.Askin Atkinson Croston Gill:
Davies Hall: Walton Haley Taylor Smith Russell A.Askin:
Tries - T.C.Askin(3) Gill Atkinson A.Askin: Goals - Pollitt(4):
Referee C Ramsden (Askern) Att - 2000 H.T. 8 - nil

Mon 1 Jan 1934 LEIGH away won 20 - 15

LEIGH - Johnson: Stringman Harris Critchley Spencer:
Green Walsh: Worrall Richardson Waterworth Flannery
Blackburn Langford:
Tries - Critchley(3): Goals - Flannery(2) Green(DG):
CASTLEFORD - Pollitt: T.C.Askin Croston James Knowles:
Davies Hall: Walton Haley Taylor Smith Russell A.Askin:
Tries - Croston Knowles Taylor Smith: Goals - Pollitt(4):
Referee F Peel (Bradford) Att - 4000 H.T. 5 - l2

Sat 6 Jan 1934 LEEDS home lost 9 - 10

CASTLEFORD - Pollitt: T.C.Askin Atkinson Croston Gill:
Davies Hall: Walton Haley Taylor Smith Albert Leese
Knowles:
Try - T.C.Askin: Goals - Pollitt(3):
LEEDS - Davies: Harris Pollard Grainge Atkinson: Ralph
Busch: Jenkins Lowe Satterthwaite Jubb Aspinall Isaac:
Tries - Harris(2): Goals - Pollard Satterthwaite:
Referee B Laughlin (Batley) Att - 9000 H.T. 6 - 2

Sat 13 Jan 1934 HUDDERSFIELD away lost 3 - 27

HUDDERSFIELD - Lockwood: Mills Brogden Parker
Markham: Fiddes Spencer: Roberts Halliday Sherwood
Tiffany Talbot Brindle:
Tries - Brogden(3) Markham(2): Goals - Sherwood(5)
Lockwood:
CASTLEFORD - Pollitt: T.C.Askin James Croston Gill:
Davies JAMES PHILLIPS(132): Walton Haley Smith Taylor
Knowles A.Askin: Try - Pollitt:
Referee J E Taylor (Wakefield) Att - 4000 H.T. 3 - 5

Sat 20 Jan 1934 WIGAN home lost 7 - 9

CASTLEFORD - Pollitt: T.C.Askin Atkinson Croston Gill:
Davies LESLIE ADAMS(133): Sherwood Haley Taylor Smith
Russell A.Askin:
Try - Croston: Goals - Pollitt(2):
WIGAN - Sullivan: Morley G.Davies Howarth Case:
Bennett Gee: Targett Golby Edwards Mason H.Davies
Hathaway:
Try - Bennett: Goals - Sullivan(3):
Referee L Greenwood (Rochdale) Att - 9000 H.T. 2 - nil

Sat 27 Jan 1934 WIDNES away lost 7 - 9

WIDNES - Bradley: Owen Robinson Taylor Gallimore:
Jacks McCue: Higgins Jones Silcock Ratcliffe McDowall
Millington:
Try - Robinson: Goals - Jacks(3):
CASTLEFORD - Pollitt: Knowles T.C.Askin Croston Gill:
Davies Adams: Sherwood Haley Taylor Smith A.Askin
Russell:
Try - Croston: Goals - Pollitt(2):
Referee B Laughlin (Batley) Att - 3000 H.T. 2 - 2

Sat 3 Feb 1934 HULL away lost 8 - 12

HULL - Miller: Bateman Oliver Fifield Sowerby: Collins
Metcalfe: Bowman Wilkinson Thacker Dawson Carmichael
Courtney:
Tries - Bateman Metcalfe: Goals - Miller(2)(DG):
CASTLEFORD - Pollitt: Knowles T.C.Askin Croston Gill:
Davies Adams: Sherwood Haley Taylor A.Askin Russell
EDWARD L.SADLER(134):
Tries - Gill(2): Goal - Pollitt:
Referee J Armitage (Huddersfield) Att - 5000 H.T. 3 - 10

Sat.10 Feb 1934 BROUGHTON RANGERS away won 9 - 3 CHALLENGE CUP ROUND 1

BROUGHTON R - Teall: Cumberbatch J.Evans Stott
Parkinson: Kelly Thompson: Thomas Jones Hill Tetlow
Bunter Manning:
Try - Thompson:
CASTLEFORD - Lewis: T.C.Askin Atkinson Croston Gill:
Davies Adams: Sherwood Haley Taylor A.Askin Russell
Sadler:
Try - Gill: Goals - Lewis Atkinson(1)(DG):
Referee F Peel (Bradford) Att - 9278 H.T. 2 - 3

Sat 17 Feb 1934 WAKEFIELD TRINITY home won 15 – 3 LEAGUE MATCH - ALLOCATED TO ARTHUR ATKINSON'S BENEFIT

CASTLEFORD - Pollitt: T.C.Askin Lewis Croston Gill: Davies

SEASON 1933-34

Adams: Sherwood Haley Walton A.Askin Russell Sadler:
Tries - Croston(2) Gill: Goals - Pollitt(3):
WAKEFIELD T - Bonner: Milner Smith Moore Smart:
Pickard Raynard: Higson Field Hobson Exley Ramsden
Wilkinson:
Try - Higson:
Referee W Eastman (Hull) Att - 8000 H.T. 10 - 3

**Sat 24 Feb 1934 HUNSLET home draw 4 - 4
CHALLENGE CUP ROUND 2**
CASTLEFORD - Lewis: T.C.Askin Atkinson Croston Gill:
Davies Adams: Sherwood Harling Walton A.Askin Russell
Sadler:
Goals - Lewis(l)(DG):
HUNSLET - Walkington: Dennis Winter Morrell
Broughton: Todd Thornton: Smith White Tolson Dawson
Crowther Beverley:
Goals - Tolson(2):
Referee A E Harding (Manchester) Att - 23000 H.T.

**Wed 28 Feb 1934 HUNSLET away lost nil - 23
CHALLENGE CUP ROUND 2 REPLAY**
HUNSLET - Walkington: Dennis Winter Morrell
Broughton: Todd Thornton: Tolson White Traill Smith
Crowther Beverley:
Tries - Crowther(2) Dennis Traill Beverley:
Goals - Tolson(4):
CASTLEFORD - Pollitt: T.C.Askin Atkinson Lewis James:
Davies Adams: Sherwood Harling Taylor Russell A.Askin
Sadler:
Referee J W Webb (Manchester) Att - 19000 H.T. nil - 13

Sat 3 Mar 1934 HUDDERSFIELD home lost 3 - 27
CASTLEFORD - Lewis: T.C.Askin Sadler Adams Knowles:
BERNARD CUNNIFFE(135) Hall: Walton Clifford Harling
Taylor Smith JAMES.M.CROSSLEY(136) Russell:
Try - Taylor:
HUDDERSFIELD - Scourfield: Mills Bowkett Fiddes
Markham: Richards Spencer: Roberts Halliday Sherwood
Tiffany Norcliffe Brindle:
Tries - Tiffany(3) Fiddes Markham: Goals - Bowkett(6):
Referee J E Taylor (Wakefield) Att - 4000 H.T. nil - 7

Sat 10 Mar 1934 SALFORD home lost 5 - 19
CASTLEFORD - Atkinson: Davies T.C.Askin Croston Gill:
Adams Hall: Walton Plimmer Smith A.Askin
Harry(Danny)Russell Sadler:
Try - Smith: Goal - Atkinson:
SALFORD - Risman: Hudson Miller Dobing Brown: Evans
Watkins: Williams Day Bradbury Casewell Feetham
Dalton:
Tries - Brown(2) Hudson: Goals - Risman(5):
Referee P Cowell (Warrington) Att - 2000 H.T. nil - 6

**Sat 17 Mar 1934 WAKEFIELD TRINITY away
draw 13 - 13**
WAKEFIELD T - Bonner: Batten Smith Moore Smart:
Richards Herbert: Higson Field Hobson Horton Exley
Wilkinson:
Tries - Smart(2) Exley: Goals - Bonner(2):

CASTLEFORD - Lewis: Chapman Croston WILLIAM
HENSHAW(137): T.C.Askin: Davies Adams: Walton Haley
Taylor Smith A.Askin Sadler:
Tries - Sadler(2) Adams: Goals - Lewis(2):
Referee J Eddon (Swinton) Att - 4000 H.T. 8 - 8

Sat 24 Mar 1934 LEIGH home lost 11 - 17
CASTLEFORD - Lewis: ROSSLYN KAYE(138) Croston
T.C.Askin Chapman: Davies Adams: Walton Haley Taylor
Smith A.Askin Sadler:
Tries - Kaye T.C.Askin Chapman: Goal - Lewis:
LEIGH - Meadows: Stringman Harris Johnson Spensley:
Green Walsh: Worrall Richardson Montford Prescott
Edwards Langford:
Tries - Stringman Harris Walsh Worrall Prescott:
Goal - Green:
Referee J Eddon (Swinton) Att - 2000 H.T. 11 - 6

**Fri 30 Mar 1934 FEATHERSTONE ROVERS home
won 20 - 3**
CASTLEFORD - Pollitt: T.C.Askin Atkinson Henshaw
Chapman: Croston Adams: Walton Haley Taylor A.Askin
Smith Sadler:
Tries - T.C.Askin Chapman Smith Sadler: Goals - Pollitt(4):
FEATHERSTONE R - Lockwood: Evans Malpass J.Dennis
Hammond: T.Dennis Ward: Barraclough Lomas Flaherty
Morgan Taylor Plenderleith:
Try - T.Dennis:
Referee J E Taylor (Wakefield) Att - 4000 H.T. 3 - nil

**Sat 31 Mar 1934 ROCHDALE HORNETS home
won 13 - 10**
CASTLEFORD - Pollitt: Chapman Henshaw Croston
T.C.Askin: James Adams: Sherwood Haley Walton Smith
A.Askin Sadler:
Tries - Chapman Croston Sadler: Goals - Pollitt(2):
ROCHDALE H - Gowers: Williams Abbott Gaunt Beattie:
Burkill Helme: Thompson Lister Moore Walker Mills
Campbell:
Tries - Williams Gaunt: Goals - Gowers(2):
Referee J Orford (St Helens) Att - 4000 H.T. 3 - 5

Mon 2 Apr 1934 YORK away lost 10 - 20
YORK - Dingsdale: Brown Rees Rosser Waudby: Thomas
Kelleher: Sharpe Myers Crabtree Saddington Coldrick
Fender:
Tries - Waudby(2) Rees Brown: Goals - Dingsdale(4):
CASTLEFORD - Pollitt: T.C.Askin Croston Henshaw
Chapman: James Adams: Sherwood Haley Walton Taylor
Smith Sadler:
Goals - Pollitt(5):
Referee W Eastman (Hull) Att - 9000 H.T. 10 - 2

Sat 7 Apr 1934 SWINTON away lost 15 - 21
SWINTON - Scott: McGregor Whittaker Green Kenny:
H.Evans B.Evans: Wright Armitt Stoddart Spruce Woodall
Butters:
Tries - Kenny(3) H.Evans Woodall: Goals - Scott(3):
CASTLEFORD - Pollitt: T.C.Askin Croston Davies Harold
Chapman James Adams: Sherwood Haley Walton Smith

SEASON 1933-34

Taylor Sadler:
Tries - T.C.Askin Smith Sadler: Goals - Pollitt(3):
Referee C Ramsden (Doncaster) Att -5000 H.T. nil - 18

Wed 11 Apr 1934 HALIFAX home lost 2 - 6
WILLIAM(NAT)ASQUITH BENEFIT MATCH - FRIENDLY
CASTLEFORD - Wilfred Newbould: T.C.Askin Henshaw
Croston Smith: Cunniffe James: Wood Haley Walton
A.Askin Taylor Sadler:
Goal - James:
HALIFAX - Schofield: Morgan Jayne C.Davies Daniels:
Cutbush Ball: Thomas Fairbanks Caley Sparkes Briggs
Chadwick: Tries - Davies Caley:
Referee A S Dobson (Pontefract) Att 1000 H.T. 2 - 3

Sat 14 Apr 1934 SALFORD away lost nil - 18
SALFORD - Osbaldestin: Pearson Miller Dobing Brown:
Evans Watkins: Williams Day Bradbury Casewell
Middleton Feetham:
Tries - Brown(4) Goals - Dobing(2) Osbaldestin:
CASTLEFORD - Pollitt: T.C.Askin Croston Henshaw Gill:
James Adams: Walton Haley Taylor A.Askin Smith Sadler:
Referee A Brown (Wakefield) Att - 27000 H.T. nil - 6

Thu 19 Apr 1934 HULL KINGSTON ROVERS away
lost 7 - 17
HULL K R - Carmichael: Deely Walsham Sanderson Hill:
Eastwood Gibson: Shillito Eddoms Brown L.Beaumont
Jackson Williams:
Tries - Hill Eastwood Beaumont: Goals - Carmichael(4):
CASTLEFORD - Pollitt: T.C.Askin Croston William Henshaw
Gill: James Hall: Arthur Sherwood Haley Walton Taylor
Smith A.Askin:
Try - Gill: Goals - Pollitt James:
Referee   Att - 3000 H.T.

A J (Jimmy) Croston
D. No 130
1933-34 to 1944-45

Leslie (Juicy) Adams
D. No 133
- 1933-34 to 1941-42

Edward (Ted) Sadler
D. No 134
1933-34 to 1939-40

Bernard Cunniffe
D.No135
1933-34 to 1945-46

James (Jim) Crossley
D. No 136
1933-34 to 1948-49

D.N	PLAYER		DEBUT	L MATCH	APP	SU3S	T.AP	TR'S	G'LS	D.G	P'TS
14	RUSSELL	HARRY (DANNY)		10/03/1934	32	0	32	2	0	0	6
21	ATKINSON	ARTHUR			21	0	21	12	16	1	70
23	WALTON	RICHARD			39	0	39	1	0	0	3
39	PLIMMER	JAMES			5	0	5	0	0	0	0
58	CHAPMAN	HAROLD		07/04/1934	6	0	6	3	0	0	9
62	SHERWOOD	ARTHUR		19/04/1934	16	0	16	0	0	0	0
78	JAMES	WILLIAM			25	0	25	0	35	1	72
79	LEWIS	GEORGE			26	0	26	1	13	1	31
84	HALL	WILSON			29	0	29	8	0	0	24
85	LEESE	ALBERT		06/01/1934	7	0	7	1	0	0	3
96	HARLING	CLIFFORD		03/03/1934	4	0	4	0	0	0	0
98	ASKIN	THOMAS C.			44	0	44	15	0	0	45
99	HAND	HARRY (MICK)		30/09/1933	2	0	2	0	0	0	0
111	DAVIES	WILLIAM H.			36	0	36	3	0	2	13
116	TAYLOR	THOMAS L.			34	0	34	2	0	0	6
117	ASKIN	AMBROSE			21	0	21	1	0	0	3
119	HOULT	JACK		16/12/1933	11	0	11	3	0	0	9
120	JOHNSON	JOHN		25/11/1933	11	0	11	2	0	0	6
121	DENNIS	THOMAS		07/10/1933	1	0	1	0	0	0	0
123	HALEY	HAROLD			35	0	35	0	0	0	0
124	SMITH	FRANK (Snr)			38	0	38	7	0	0	21
125	KNOWLES	DONALD			13	0	13	1	0	0	3
127	YOUNG	HAROLD	09/09/1933	11/11/1933	7	0	7	1	0	0	3
128	POLLITT	JOHN	16/09/1933		23	0	23	1	48	0	99
129	WILLIAMS	J.H.	30/09/1933	30/09/1933	1	0	1	0	0	0	0
130	CROSTON	ALFRED JAMES	07/10/1933		31	0	31	14	0	0	42
131	GILL	JAMES	25/12/1933		14	0	14	6	0	0	18
132	PHILLIPS	JAMES	13/01/1934	13/01/1934	1	0	1	0	0	0	0
133	ADAMS	LESLIE	20/01/1934		16	0	16	1	0	0	3
134	SADLER	EDWARD L.	03/02/1934		14	0	14	5	0	0	15
135	CUNNIFFE	BERNARD	03/03/1934		1	0	1	0	0	0	0
136	CROSSLEY	JAMES M.	03/03/1934		-	0	1	0	0	0	0
137	HENSHAW	WILLIAM	17/03/1934	19/04/1934	6	0	6	0	0	0	0
138	KAYE	ROSSLYN	24/03/1934		1	0	1	1	0	0	3
	34		**12**	**13**	**572**	**0**	**572**	**91**	**112**	**5**	**507**

COMPETITION		P	W	D	L	FOR	AGT
LEAGUE	POSITION 16 OF 28	38	17	1	20	476	468
YORK'S CUP		2	1	0	1	12	27
RL CUP		3	1	1	1	13	30
AUSTRALIA		1	0	0	1	6	39
PLAYERS RECORDS		**44**	**19**	**2**	**23**	**507**	**564**

In the league Wigan Highfield changed their name to London Highfield and relocated to London to become the first rugby league team to be based in the capital.

This season also saw the first visit of an Australian team to Wheldon Road on 27 September 1933, the tourists winning 39-6.

SEASON 1934-35

Sat 18 Aug 1934 FEATHERSTONE ROVERS away won 48 - 19 LYON CUP - FRIENDLY
FEATHERSTONE R - Lockwood: Noble Plenderleith
Malpass Rowley: Dennis Ward: Padgett Taylor
Cunningham Sutcliffe Dyson Smith:
Tries - Noble Rowley Dennis Padgett Smith: Goals -
Lockwood(2):
CASTLEFORD - Lewis: T.C.Askin Croston James Gill: Ward
Adams: McManus Haley Walton A.Askin Smith Sadler:
Tries - McManus(2) A.Askin(2) Lewis Croston James Gill
Ward Adams Walton Smith: Goals - Ward(5) James:
Referee A S Dobson (Pontefract) Att - 2300 H.T. 17 - 5

Sat 25 Aug 1934 HUNSLET away lost 10 - 20
HUNSLET - Walkington: Dennis Winter Goulthorpe
Broughton: Todd Thornton: Benson White Smith Dawson
Crowther Beverley:
Tries - Todd(2) Dennis Beverley: Goals - Walkington(4):
CASTLEFORD - Lewis: ERIC ENGLAND(139) Davies
T.C.Askin Gill: JOHN WARD(140) Adams: PATRICK
B.McMANUS(141) Haley Walton A.Askin Smith Sadler:
Tries - Ward Sadler: Goals - Ward(2):
Referee B Laughlin (Batley) Att - 5000 H.T. nil - 13

Sat 1 Sept 1934 ROCHDALE HORNETS home won 16 - 5
CASTLEFORD - Lewis: Cunniffe Davies Croston Gill: Ward
Adams: McManus Haley Taylor Smith A.Askin Sadler:
Tries - Croston(2) Davies Adams: Goals - Lewis(2):
ROCHDALE H - Gowers: Williams Beattie Gaunt Skillen:
Aynsley Helme: Thompson Lister Moore Mills Reed
Selway: Try - Beattie: Goal - Gowers:
Referee A E Harding (Manchester) Att - 4000 H.T. 3 - 5

Sat 8 Sept 1934 BRADFORD NORTHERN home draw 9 - 9 YORKSHIRE CUP ROUND 1
CASTLEFORD - Lewis: Atkinson Croston Davies Cunniffe:
Ward Adams: NcManus Haley Walton Taylor Smith
Sadler: Try - Cunniffe: Goals - Atkinson(3):
BRADFORD N - Hirst: Bradbury Winnard Hutchinson
Walker: Hayes Marsh: Cotton Green Turner Morgan
Edson Sherwood: Try - Hayes: Goals - Winnard(3):
Referee J Orford (St Helens) Att - 4000 H.T. 4 - nil

Tue 12 Sept 1934 BRADFORD NORTHERN away won 16 - 13 YORKSHIRE CUP ROUND 1 REPLAY
BRADFORD N - Hirst: Bradbury Winnard Hutchinson
Walker: Hayes Marsh: Cotton Green Turner Morgan
Edson Sherwood:
Tries - Winnard Walker Hayes: Goals - Winnard(2):
CASTLEFORD - Lewis: Gill Atkinson Croston Cunniffe:
Davies Adams: McManus Haley Walton A.Askin Smith
Sadler:
Tries - Cunniffe(2) Atkinson Sadler: Goals - Lewis(1)(DG):
Referee A Holbrook (Warrington) Att - 12000 H.T. 7 - 7

Sat 15 Sept 1934 DEWSBURY away won 20 - 19
DEWSBURY - Allen: Daniel Jayne Killingbeck Hobson:
Davies Werrett: Briggs Harling Jenkins Orford Thomas
Oakland:

Tries - Killingbeck(2) Orford: Goals - Killingbeck(5):
CASTLEFORD - Lewis: Gill Atkinson Croston Cunniffe:
Davies Hall: McManus Haley Walton Taylor A.Askin
Sadler:
Tries - Atkinson(3) Gill: Goals - Atkinson(3) Lewis:
Referee J E Taylor (Wakefield) Att - 5000 H.T. 16 - nil

Tue 19 Sept 1934 HUDDERSFIELD away draw 6 - 6 YORKSHIRE CUP ROUND 2
HUDDERSFIELD - Scourfield: Mills Bowkett Fiddes
Markham: Richards Spencer: Norcliffe Halliday Sherwood
Tiffany Talbot Brindle: Goals - Bowkett(2) Scourfield(DG):
CASTLEFORD - Lewis: Cunniffe Atkinson Croston HAROLD
TURNER(142): Davies Adams: McManus Haley Walton
Taylor Smith Sadler: Goals - Atkinson(2) Lewis:
Referee F Fairhurst (Wigan) Att - 6204 H.T. 2 - nil

Sat 22 Sept 1934 BROUGHTON RANGERS home lost nil - 3
CASTLEFORD - Lewis: Cunniffe T.C.Askin Croston Harold
Turner: Davies Adams: McManus Haley Walton Taylor
Smith Sadler:
BROUGHTON R - Teall: Mills Kenny Stott Cumberbatch:
Garvet Thompson: Sulway Jones D.Thomas Cambridge
Bunter Saddington: Try - Garvey:
Referee P Cowell (Warrington) Att - 4000 H.T. nil - nil

Tue 26 Sept 1934 HUDDERSFIELD home won 3 - 2 YORKSHIRE CUP ROUND 2 REPLAY
CASTLEFORD - Lewis: Cunniffe Atkinson Croston
T.C.Askin: Davies Adams: McManus Haley Walton Taylor
Smith Sadler: Try - Cunniffe:
HUDDERSFIELD - Scourfield: Mills Bowkett Fiddes
Markham: Richards Matthews: Norcliffe Halliday
Sherwood Tiffany Talbot Brindle: Goal - Bowkett:
Referee J W Webb (Manchester) Att - 9000 H.T. nil - 2

Sat 29 Sept 1934 BRAMLEY away draw 4 - 4
BRAMLEY - Reed: Gee Abram Eccles Hardy: Annable
Hardy: Ingham Bowden Litt Parkinson Larvin Ballantyne:
Goals - Litt(2):
CASTLEFORD - Lewis: Cunniffe James Croston T.C.Askin:
Davies Hall: McManus Haley Walton Smith A.Askin Sadler:
Goals - Lewis(2):
Referee J Armstrong (Huddersfield) Att - H.T. 2 - 4

Tue 3 Oct 1934 WAKEFIELD TRINITY home lost nil - 10 YORKSHIRE CUP SEMI-FINAL
CASTLEFORD - Lewis: Cunniffe Atkinson Croston
T.C.Askin: Davies Adams: McManus Haley Walton Smith
Taylor Sadler:
WAKEFIELD T - Johnson: Farrar Smith Moore Smart:
Pollard Pickard: Hammond Field Hobson Horton Exley
Rowan: Tries - Moore Pollard: Goals - Pollard(2):
Referee A E Harding (Man'ster) Att - 11000 H.T. nil - 5

Sat 6 Oct 1934 BRAMLEY home won 24 - 5
CASTLEFORD - Lewis: Cunniffe Atkinson Davies Croston:
Ward Adams: McManus Haley Taylor Smith Crossley
Sadler:

Tries - Cunniffe(2) Croston(2) Lewis Atkinson: Goals - Ward(2) Atkinson:
BRAMLEY - Reed: Gee Rees Abram Eccles: Senior Bardy: Addinghall Ingham Litt Thompson Larvin Ballantyne: Try - Abram: Goal - Litt:
Referee J E Taylor (Wakefield) Att - 2000 H.T. 14 - 2

Sat 13 Oct 1934 BROUGHTON RANGERS away lost 7 - 12
BROUGHTON R - Teall: Kenny Davies Stott Mills: Garvey Thompson: Sulway G.Jones Cambridge T.Thomas Bunter Manning: Tries - Mills Thomas: Goals - Stott(2) Davies:
CASTLEFORD - Lewis: Cunniffe Atkinson Davies Croston: Ward Adams: McManus Haley Taylor Crossley Smith Walton: Try - Cunniffe: Goals - Atkinson Lewis:
Referee B Laughlin (Batley) Att - 5000 H.T. 2 - 3

Sat 20 Oct 1934 DEWSBURY home won 44 - 9
CASTLEFORD - Lewis: Cunniffe Atkinson Davies Croston: Ward Adams: McManus Haley Taylor Crossley Smith Sadler:
Tries - Cunniffe(2) Atkinson(2) Crossley(2) Adams(2) McManus Sadler: Goals - Ward(6) Atkinson:
DEWSBURY - S.Ward: Large Hogan Jayne Whitehead: Chester Werrett: Jenkins Harling Banks Evans Morgan Oakland: Try - Hogan: Goals - Chester(3):
Referee F Peel (Bradford) Att - H.T. 22 - 4

Sat 27 Oct 1934 WIDNES away won 16 - 5
WIDNES - Bradley: Owen Topping Noon Taylor: Jacks McCue: Silcock Jones Higgins J.Hoey Sherratt Millington: Try - Owen: Goal - Hoey:
CASTLEFORD - Lewis: Cunniffe Atkinson Croston England: Ward Adams: McManus Haley Taylor Crossley Smith Sadler:
Tries - Smith Atkinson Cunniffe Croston: Goals - Ward(2): Referee L Thorpe (Wakefield) Att - 2000 H.T. 10 - nil

Sat 3 Nov 1934 HUNSLET home won 10 - 4
CASTLEFORD - James: Cunniffe Atkinson Croston England: Ward Adams: McManus Haley Taylor Smith Crossley Sadler: Tries - Cunniffe(2): Goals - James Ward:
HUNSLET - Walkington: Dennis Thornton Grainge Broughton: Todd Jackson: Tolson White Benson Crowther Dawson Beverley: Goals - Walkington(2):
Referee W H Eastman (Hull) Att - H.T. 10 - nil

Sat 10 Nov 1934 HALIFAX away draw 3 - 3
HALIFAX - Lockwood: Thomas Rule Treen Jones: Broadhead Gascoigne: Sparkes Meek Baynham Thorber Cox Shaw: Try - Shaw:
CASTLEFORD - Lewis: Cunniffe Atkinson Davies Croston: Ward Adams(S/O): McManus Haley Taylor Smith Crossley Sadler: Try - Adams:
Referee W H Eastman (Hull) Att - 7000 H.T. 3 - 3

Sat 17 Nov 1934 LEEDS home lost 6 - 17
CASTLEFORD - Lewis: Cunniffe Atkinson Croston T.C.Askin: Ward Adams: McManus Haley Taylor Crossley Smith Sadler: Goals - Atkinson Ward(1)(DG):
LEEDS - Brown: Harris Brogden Parker Smith: Williams

Busch: Dyer Lowe Aspinall Jubb Jones Whitehead: Tries - Harris(2) Smith: Goals - Whitehead(4): Referee J E Taylor (Wakefield) Att - 10000 H.T. 6 - 2

Sat 24 Nov 1934 ROCHDALE HORNETS away lost 7 - 19
ROCHDALE H - Sayer: Williams Abbott Davies Gaunt: Aynsley Burkhill. Thompson Lister Moore Sutcliffe Knapton Mills:
Tries - Williams 2) Gaunt(2) Davies: Goals - Williams(2):
CASTLEFORD - Lewis: Cunniffe Atkinson Davies Croston: Ward Adams: McManus Haley Taylor Crossley Smith Sadler: Try - Ward: Goals - Lewis(2):
Referee J E Tay or (Wakefield) Att - 5000 H.T. 2 - 3

Sat 1 Dec 1934 WIDNES home won 26 - 3
CASTLEFORD - Lewis: Cunniffe Croston Davies T.C.Askin: WILLIAM ECCLESTONE(143) Hall: McManus Haley Taylor Smith Crossley Sadler:
Tries - Croston T.C.Askin Cunniffe Hall Taylor Sadler: Goals - Lewis(2) Crossley(2):
WIDNES - Bradley: Owen Taylor Jacks Gallimore: Shannon McCue: Chatterton Jones Silcock Sherratt Ratcliffe Millington: Try - Jacks:
Referee J Eddon (Swinton) Att - 4000 H.T. 7 - 3

Sat 8 Dec 1934 ST HELENS away lost 11 - 19
ST HELENS - Butler: Smith Bradbury Mercer Davies: Frodsham Glover: Atkin Cotton Lemon Hill Hall Griffiths: Tries - Smith(3) Glover Griffiths: Goals - Davies(2):
CASTLEFORD - Lewis: Cunniffe Croston Davies T.C.Askin: William Ecclestone Wilson Hall: McManus Haley Taylor Smith Crossley Sadler:
Try - McManus: Goals - Crossley(3) Lewis:
Referee L Thorpe (Wakefield) Att - 2500 H.T. 7 - 5

Sat 15 Dec 1934 LIVERPOOL STANLEY home won 18 - 5
CASTLEFORD - Lewis: Cunniffe Atkinson Croston T.C.Askin: Davies Adams: Mcmanus Haley Taylor Smith Crossley Sadler:
Tries - T.C.Askin Adams McManus Sadler: Goals - Smith(3):
LIVERPOOL S - Belshaw: Robinson Martin Howarth Maloney: Kirk Oyster: Welsby Oakley Woods Smith Grey Stock: Try - Kirk: Goal - Woods:
Referee J W Webb (Manchester) Att - 4000 H.T. 5 - 5

Sat 22 Dec 1934 BRADFORD NORTHERN away Abandoned After 51 Minutes Owing To Fog - Bradford Winning 9 – 3
BRADFORD N - Carmichael: Hutchinson Winnard Wilson Filling: Hayes Bush: Dilorenzo Griffiths Morgan Green Webb Young: Try - Young: Goals - Carmichael(3):
CASTLEFORD - Lewis: Cunniffe Atkinson Croston T.C.Askin: Davies Adams: McManus Haley Taylor Smith Crossley Sadler: Try - Adams:
Referee J Eddon (Swinton) Att - H.T. nil - 7
Replayed Tue 23 Jan 1935 Cas Winning 20 - 11

Tue 25 Dec 1934 FEATHERSTONE ROVERS home won 28 - 3
CASTLEFORD - Lewis: Cunniffe Atkinson Croston
T.C.Askin: Davies Adams: McManus(S/O) Haley Taylor
Smith Crossley Sadler:
Tries - Cunniffe(2) T.C.Askin(2) Lewis Croston Adams
Crossley: Goals - Lewis(2):
FEATHERSTONE R - Lockwood: Asquith Dennis Noble
Rowley: Johnson Evans: Padgett Taylor Flaherty Sutcliffe
Dyson Smith: Try - Asquith:
Referee A Brown (Wakefield) Att - 4000 H.T. 19 - 3

Tue 26 Dec 1934 YORK away won 18 - 9
YORK - Dingsdale: Waudby Rosser Whittaker Hardgrave:
Rees Thomas: Banks Myers Prosser Sharpe Coldrick
Fender: Try - Rosser: Goals - Dingsdale(3):
CASTLEFORD - Lewis: Cunniffe Atkinson Croston
T.C.Askin: Davies Adams: McManus Haley Taylor Smith
Crossley Sadler:
Tries - Cunniffe Atkinson Croston Haley: Goals - Lewis(3):
Referee A Hill (Leeds) Att - 13000 H.T. 10 - 3

Sat 29 Dec 1934 HUDDERSFIELD home won 12 - 9
CASTLEFORD - Lewis: Cunniffe Atkinson Croston
T.C.Askin: Davies Adams: McManus Haley Taylor Smith
Crossley Sadler:
Tries - Atkinson Adams: Goals - Lewis(3):
HUDDERSFIELD - Scourfield: Mills Towill Barrow
Markham: Richards Spencer: Sherwood Watson Norcliffe
Tiffany Fuller Brindle: Tries - Towill(2) Markham:
Referee F Peel (Bradford) Att - 5000 H.T. 5 - 6

Sat 5 Jan 1935 HULL home won 18 - 10
CASTLEFORD - Lewis: Cunniffe Atkinson Croston
T.C.Askin: Davies Adams: McManus Haley Taylor Smith
Crossley Sadler:
Tries - Atkinson T.C.Askin Cunniffe Adams:
Goals - Lewis(3):
HULL - Miller: Bateman Oliver Fifield Wilson: Herbert
Cooling: Carmichael G.Barlow Stead Dawson L.Barlow
Ellerington: Tries - Bateman L.Barlow: Goals - Oliver(2):
Referee B Laughlin (Batley) Att - 5000 H.T. 10 - 7

Sat 12 Jan 1935 WAKEFIELD TRINITY away won 28 - 8
WAKEFIELD T - Knowles: Farrar Moore Pollard Hughes:
Goodfellow Burrows: Wilkinson Field Robson Hammond
Turton Rowan: Tries - Rowan Hughes: Goals - Knowles):
CASTLEFORD - Lewis: Cunniffe Atkinson Davies T.C.Askin:
Ward Adams: Taylor Haley Smith Crossley Knowles Sadler:
Tries - Cunniffe(3) Knowles(2) Atkinson Ward Adams:
Goals - Lewis Crossley:
Referee A Hill (Leeds) Att - 5000 H.T. 6 - 5

Sat 19 Jan 1935 WAKEFIELD TRINITY home lost 3 - 5
CASTLEFORD - Lewis: Cunniffe Atkinson Croston
T.C.Askin: Davies Adams: Smith Haley Taylor Crossley
Knowles Sadler: Try - Sadler:
WAKEFIELD T - Knowles: Batten Farrar Moore Appleyard:
Pollard Herbert: Hammond Carter Hobson Horton Field

Rowan: Try - Moore: Goal - Knowles:
Referee A Hill (Leeds) Att - 6000 H.T. nil - nil

Tue 23 Jan 1935 BRADFORD NORTHERN away won 20 - 11
BRADFORD N - Carmichael: Walker Winnard Wilson
Goulthorpe: Hayes Spillane: Dilorenzo Griffiths Morgan
Green Hutchinson Young:
Tries - Winnard(2) Spillane: Goal - Carmichael:
CASTLEFORD - Lewis: Cunniffe Atkinson Croston
T.C.Askin: Davies Adams: McManus Haley Taylor Smith
Crossley Sadler:
Tries - Atkinson T.C.Askin Smith Sadler: Goals - Lewis(4):
Referee J Eddon (Swinton) Att - 5000 H.T. 7 - 3

Sat 26 Jan 1935 BATLEY away won 20 - 9
BATLEY - Johnson: Nunn Smith Kitson Peck: Brown Swift:
Dyson Earnshaw Booth Bradley Oates Foley:
Tries - Nunn(2) Foley:
CASTLEFORD - Lewis: Cunniffe Atkinson Croston
T.C.Askin: Davies Adams: Smith Haley Taylor Crossley
Knowles Sadler:
Tries Cunniffe(2) Davies(2) Atkinson Croston: Goal - Lewis:
Referee A Brown (Wakefield) Att - 4000 H.T. 6 - 3

Sat 2 Feb 1935 KEIGHLEY home won 12 - 2
CASTLEFORD - Lewis: Cunniffe Atkinson Croston
T.C.Askin: Davies Adams: McManus Haley Taylor Smith
Crossley Sadler:
Tries - Cunniffe Atkinson T.C.Askin Adams:
KEIGHLEY - Herbert: Sherburn Foster Bainton Orchard:
Jackson Meek: Houghton Kenyon Jones McGoun Dixon
Gill: Goal - Sherburn:
Referee F Peel (Bradford) Att - 7000 H.T. 9 - nil

Sat 9 Feb 1935 ASTLEY & TYLDESLEY home on 33 – 4 CHALLENGE CUP ROUND 1
CASTLEFORD - Lewis: Cunniffe Atkinson Croston
T.C.Askin: Davies Adams: Smith Haley Taylor Crossley
Knowles Sadler:
Tries - Croston(2)Adams(2) Cunniffe Davies T.C.Askin
Crossley Sadler: Goals - Lewis(2) Davies(DG):
ASTLEY & TYLDESLEY - Clarke: Squires Davies Disley
Sutton: Gunning Higson: Openshaw Hilton Price O'Neil
Sanderson Lewis: Goals - Clarke(2):
Referee A Holbrook (Warrington) Att - 6400 H.T. 16 - 4

Sat 16 Feb 1935 HUDDERSFIELD away lost 3 - 5
HUDDERSFIELD - Bowkett: Mills Mountain Barrow
Markham: Matthews Davies: Roberts Watson Sherwood
Talbot Norcliffe Fuller:
Try - Barrow: Goal - Bowkett:
CASTLEFORD - Lewis: Cunniffe Atkinson Croston
T.C.Askin: Davies Ward: McManus Haley Taylor Smith
Crossley Sadler:
Try - Cunniffe:
Referee B Laughlin (Batley) Att 1000 H.T. 3 - nil

SEASON 1934-35

**Sat 23 Feb 1935 LIVERPOOL STANLEY away
won 8 - 2 CHALLENGE CUP ROUND 2**
LIVERPOOL S - McNamara: Robinson Martin Belshaw
Maloney: Howarth Kirk: Davies Welsby Woods Cayser
Smith Stock(S/O):   Goal - Belshaw:
CASTLEFORD - Lewis: Cunniffe Atkinson Croston
T.C.Askin: Davie Adams: McManus Haley Taylor Smith
Crossley Sadler:
Tries - T.C.Askin Davies: Goal - Davies(DG):
Referee A Brown (Wakefield) Att - 8802 H.T. 2 - nil

Sat 2 Mar 1935 ST HELENS home won 14 - 4
CASTLEFORD - Lewis: Cunniffe Atkinson Croston
T.C.Askin: Davies Adams: McManus Haley Taylor Smith
Crossley Sadler:
Tries - Atkinson T.C.Askin: Goals - Lewis(3) Smith:
ST HELENS - Lewis: Davies Bradbury Mercer Stephen:
Frodsham Glover: Atkin Cotton Lemon Hall Blackburn
Griffiths: Goals - Davies(2):
Referee J Molloy (Wigan) Att - 6000 H.T. 2 - nil

**Sat 9 Mar 1935 HUNSLET home won 10 - 3
CHALLENGE CUP ROUND 3**
CASTLEFORD - Lewis: Cunniffe Atkinson T.C.Askin
Knowles: Davies Adams: McManus Haley Taylor Smith
Crossley Sadler:
Tries - Atkinson Knowles: Goals - Lewis Smith:
HUNSLET - Walkington: Dennis Yates Morrell Grainge:
Todd Thornton: Tolson White Dawson Smith Plenderleith
Beverley: Try - Yates:
Referee A E Harding (Manchester)
Att - 25449 (Ground Record) H.T. 2 - nil

Sat 16 Mar 1935 HULL away lost 5 - 12
HULL - Bateman: Oliver Wilson Corner Fifield: Collings
Stead: G.Barlow Carmichael Stead Dawson L.Barlow
Ellerington: Tries - Corner(2): Goals - Oliver(3):
CASTLEFORD - Cunniffe Atkinson Croston T.C.Askin Rosslyn
Kaye: Davies Adams: Taylor Haley Smith Crossley Knowles
Sadler: Try - Sadler: Goal - Lewis:
Referee F Peel (Bradford) Att - 14000 H.T. 5 - 5

Tue 20 Mar 1935 LEEDS away lost 8 - 13
LEEDS - Brough: E.Harris F.Harris Parker Brogden: Ralph
Richards: Satterthwaite Lowe Casewell Jubb Aspinall Isaac:
Tries - E.Harris Brogden Aspinall: Goals - Brough
Ralph(DG):
CASTLEFORD - Lewis: Cunniffe Atkinson Croston
T.C.Askin: Davies Adams: McManus Haley Taylor Smith
Crossley Sadler: Tries - Sadler(2): Goal - Lewis:
Referee J E Taylor (Wakefield) Att - 9000 H.T. 3 - nil

**Sat 23 Mar 1935 LIVERPOOL STANLEY away
lost 3 - 20**
LIVERPOOL S - McNamara: Robinson Martin Belshaw
Maloney: Howarth Salmon: Davies Welsby Gray Cayser
Wood Stocks:
Tries - Martin(2) Belshaw Howarth Woods Maloney:
Goal - Belshaw:
CASTLEFORD - Lewis: Knowles Atkinson Croston England:

Davies T.C.Askin McManus Haley Taylor Smith Crossley
Sadler: Try - Atkinson:
Referee A Hill (Leeds) Att - few hundred H.T. nil - 3

**Sat 30 Mar 1935 BARROW (at Swinton) Won 11 - 5
CHALLENGE CUP SEMI-FINAL**
CASTLEFORD - Lewis Cunniffe Atkinson Croston T.C.Askin:
Davies Adams: McManus Haley Taylor Knowles Smith
Sadler:
Tries - T.C.Askin Croston Knowles: Goal - Lewis:
BARROW - Bennett: Johnson Barton Gummer Harris:
Maddock Little: Yarr Martin Skelly Troop Ayres Mattison:
Try - Little: Goa - Troop:
Referee J E Taylor (Wakefield) Att - 24508 H.T. 8 - 3

**Sat 6 Apr 1935 HULL KINGSTON ROVERS home
lost 9 - 13**
CASTLEFORD - Pollitt: Cunniffe Atkinson Lewis T.C.Askin:
Davies E.(BILL) HUGGETT(144): McManus Haley Taylor
Smith Crossley Sadler:
Try - McManus: Goals - Pollitt(2)(DG):
HULL K R - McWatt: Winsor Spamer Walshaw Eastwood:
McGowan Dale: Reach Ramsden Thompson Shillito
Tattersfield Moores:
Tries - Dale Shillito Moores: Goals - McWatt(2):
Referee J Orford (St Helens) Att - If time 2 - 10

Mon 8 Apr 1935 HALIFAX home draw 10 - 10
CASTLEFORD - Pollitt: England T.C.Askin HERBERT
SMITH(145): HARRY MALKIN(146): Ward Huggett:
McManus Haley Taylor F.Smith Crossley Sadler:
Tries - Ward Sadler: Goals - Pollitt Ward(DG):
HALIFAX - Lockwood: Cutbush Rule Treen Mills: Irving
Hanson: Baynham Meek H.Irving Chadwick Thornber Cox:
Tries - Treen Cox: Goals - Lockwood(2):
Referee J E Taylor (Wakefield) Att - 2000 H.T. 2 - nil

**Sat 13 Apr 1935 HULL KINGSTON ROVERS away
lost 14 - 25**
HULL K R - McWatt: Winsor Spamer Walshaw Eastwood:
McGowan Dale: Riach Jordan Thompson Shillito
Tattersfield Moores
Tries - Eastwood(2) Moores(2) Dale: Goals - McWatt(5):
CASTLEFORD - Lewis: Cunniffe Davies T.C.Askin H.Smith:
John Ward Huggett: McManus Haley Taylor F.Smith
Crossley Sadler: Tries - Cunniffe F.Smith: Goals - Lewis(4):
Referee B Laughlin (Batley) Att - 6000 H.T. 9 - 10

**Fri 19 Apr 1935 FEATHERSTONE ROVERS away
won 19 - 10**
FEATHERSTONE R - Lockwood: Ling Noble Hammond
Asquith: Johnson Ward: Flaherty Morris Hemingway
Taylor Smith Price:
Tries - Johnson Ward: Goals - Lockwood(2):
CASTLEFORD - Lewis: Cunniffe Atkinson Croston
T.C.Askin: Davies Adams: McManus Haley Taylor F Smith
Crossley Sadler:
Tries - Cunniffe Atkinson Haley Crossley Sadler:
Goals - Lewis(2):
Referee F Peel (Bradford) Att - H.T. 11 - 5

SEASON 1934-35

Sat 20 Apr 1935 KEIGHLEY away won 13 - nil
KEIGHLEY - Herbert: Sherburn Foster Rainton Orchard:
Davies Meek: Houghton Kenyon Jones McGoun Dixon
Sykes:
CASTLEFORD - Lewis: Cunniffe Atkinson Croston England:
Davies T.C.Askin: McManus Haley Taylor F Smith Crossley
Knowles: Tries Atkinson(2) T.C.Askin: Goals - Lewis(2):
Referee L Thorpe (Wakefield) Att - 6000 H.T. 3 - nil

Mon 22 Apr 1935 YORK home lost 7 - 10
CASTLEFORD - Lewis: Cunniffe Atkinson Croston Knowles:
Davies T.C.Askin: McManus Haley Taylor F Smith Crossley
Sadler: Try - Taylor: Goals - Atkinson(2):
YORK - Dingsdale: Haigh Rosser Moores Whittaker: Rees
Thomas: Prosser Myers Banks Sharpe Coldrick Walsh:
Tries - Whittaker Walsh: Goals Dingsdale(2):
Referee A Hill (Leeds) Att - 3000 H.T. 7 - 2

Tue 23 Apr 1935 BATLEY home won 19 - 7
CASTLEFORD - Lewis: Cunniffe Atkinson T.C.Askin
England: Davies Huggett: McManus Haley Taylor Knowles
F Smith Sadler:
Tries - Cunniffe Atkinson England Davies McManus: Goals
F Smith(2):
BATLEY - Johnson: Smith Nunn C.Dyson Peck: Shirley
Swift: W.Dyson Hall Booth A.N.Other Oates Foley:
Try - Peck: Goals - Booth(2):
Referee A Brown (Wakefield) Att - 4000 H.T. 9 - 4

**Sat 27 Apr 1935 BRADFORD NORTHERN home
lost 7 - 8**
CASTLEFORD - Lewis: T.C.Askin Herbert Smith William
James England: Davies Huggett: McManus Haley Taylor
F.Smith Crossley Knowles:
Try - England: Goals - Lewis F.Smith:
BRADFORD N - Carmichael: Gray Hutchinson Winnard
Walker: Marsh Spillane: Griffiths Dilorenzo Green Dennis
Webb Orford:
Tries - Hutchinson Walker: Goal - Carmichael:
Referee B Laughlin (Batley) Att - 2500 H.T. 2 - 3

**Sat 4 May 1935 HUDDERSFIELD won 11 - 8
CHALLENGE CUP FINAL - AT WEMBLEY STADIUM
LONDON**
CASTLEFORD - Lewis: Cunniffe Atkinson Croston
T.C.Askin: Davies Adams: McManus Haley Taylor Smith
Crossley Sadler:
Tries - Cunniffe T.C.Askin Adams: Goal - Atkinson:
HUDDERSFIELD - Scourfield: Mountain Towill Fiddes
Markham: Richards Davies: Roberts Watson Sherwood
Tiffany Fuller Talbot:
Tries - Towill Fiddes: Goal - Sherwood
Referee A E Harding (Broughton) Att - 39000 H.T. 5 - 3
**Cup Presented By Mr J Lewthwaite - Rugby League
Chairman**

**Sunday 12 May 1935 LYONS VILLEURBANNE away
won 24 - 21 FRIENDLY - AT STADE BUFFALO PARIS
FRANCE**
LYONS VILLEURBANNE - Marty: Lambert Barbazanges
Amila Barnoud: Sematan Mathon: Perrin Ancladge Lafont
Piany Griffard Genovet:
Tries - Sematan(2) Lambert Barbazanges Barnoud:
Goals - Amila(3):
CASTLEFORD - Lewis: Cunniffe Atkinson Croston
T.C.Askin: Davies Adams: McManus Haley Taylor Smith
Crossley Sadler:
Tries - Sadler(2) Atkinson(2) Cunniffe Croston:
Goals - Lewis(2) Atkinson:
Referee A S Dobson (Pontefract) Att - 5000 H.T. 21 – 11

Eric England
D. No 139
1934-35 to 1937-38

Patrick B McManus
D. No 141
1934-35-to 1946-47

1934-35 R.L Challenge Cup Final V Huddersfield
Won 11 – 8 at Wembley Stadium

Top - Arthur Atkinson with the Cup
Bottom – Tommy Taylor Pat Mcmanus Harold Haley

Arthur Atkinson George Lewis Billy Davies Harold Haley Bernard Cunniffe Jim Crossley Jim Croston Leslie Adams

SEASON 1934-35

D.N	PLAYER		DEBUT	L MATCH	APP	SUB	T.AP	TR'S	G'LS	D.G	P'TS
21	ATKINSON	ARTHUR			40	0	40	22	15	0	96
23	WALTON	RICHARD			10	0	10	0	0	0	0
78	JAMES	WILLIAM		27/04/1935	3	0	3	0	1	0	2
79	LEWIS	GEORGE			47	0	47	2	48	1	104
84	HALL	WILSON		08/12/1934	4	0	4	1	0	0	3
98	ASKIN	THOMAS C.			37	0	37	13	0	0	39
111	DAVIES	WILLIAM H.			45	0	45	6	0	2	22
116	TAYLOR	THOMAS L.			46	0	46	2	0	0	6
117	ASKIN	AMBROSE			5	0	5	0	0	0	0
123	HALEY	HAROLD			49	0	49	2	0	0	6
124	SMITH	FRANK Snr			48	0	48	3	8	0	25
125	KNOWLES	DONALD			12	0	12	4	0	0	12
128	POLLITT	JOHN			2	0	2	0	4	0	8
130	CROSTON	ALFRED JAMES			40	0	40	12	0	0	36
131	GILL	JAMES			4	0	4	1	0	0	3
133	ADAMS	LESLIE			36	0	36	14	0	0	42
134	SADLER	EDWARD L.			46	0	46	13	0	0	39
135	CUNNIFFE	BERNARD			45	0	45	29	0	0	87
136	CROSSLEY	JAMES M.			37	0	37	5	6	0	27
138	KAYE	ROSSLYN		16/03/1935	1	0	1	0	0	0	0
139	ENGLAND	ERIC	25/08/1934		8	0	8	2	0	0	6
140	WARD	JOHN	25/08/1934	13/04/1935	15	0	15	4	14	2	44
141	McMANUS	PATRICK B.	25/08/1934		44	0	44	5	0	0	15
142	TURNER	HAROLD	19/09/1934	22/09/1934	2	0	2	0	0	0	0
143	ECCLESTONE	WILLIAM	01/12/1934	08/12/1934	2	0	2	0	0	0	0
144	HUGGETT	WILLIAM E.(BILL)	06/04/1935		5	0	5	0	0	0	0
145	SMITH	HERBERT	08/04/1935	27/04/1935	3	0	3	0	0	0	0
146	MALKIN	HARRY	08/04/1935	08/04/1935	1	0	1	0	0	0	0
	28			**8**	**8**	**637**	**0**	**637**	**140**	**96**	**5**	**622**

COMPETITION		P	W	D	L	FOR	AGT
LEAGUE	POSITION 9 OF 28	38	20	3	15	512	355
YORK'S CUP		5	2	2	1	34	40
RL CUP		5	5	0	0	73	22
VOID MATCH BRADFORD		1	0	0	1	3	9
PLAYERS RECORDS		**49**	**27**	**5**	**17**	**622**	**426**

In the league, London Highfield changed their name to Liverpool Stanley and returned to the North of England after only one season in the Capital.

This was truly an historic season and still ranks today as one of "THE" seasons in the Club's entire history; it was of course the season that brought our first Challenge Cup Final victory.

The Final at Wembley on Saturday, 4 May 1935, saw Castleford outplaying and beating the overwhelming favourites and star studded team from Huddersfield 11–8 before a crowd of 39,000. The three try scorers were Bernard Cunniffe, Tommy Askin and Leslie (Juicy) Adams, with Captain Arthur Atkinson kicking a goal.

The following week brought another piece of rugby league history when Castleford became the first British team to play in France. The opponents were Lyons-Villeurbanne, the venue Stade Buffalo, Paris on the 12 May 1935. Castleford running out victors 24–21, before 5000 spectators. The referee that day was Mr Albert Dobson of Pontefract who later became a Castleford Director.

The third round tie on Saturday 9 March 1935 created a record attendance for a Castleford home match when 25,449 spectators saw Castleford beat Hunslet 10–3, the official record attendance which still stands today (although probably surpassed in 1966-67 when the fences where pulled down in the RL Cup replay against Hull K.R.

SEASON 1935-36

Sat 24 Aug 1935 FEATHERSTONE ROVERS home won 48 - 12 LYON CUP - FRIENDLY
CASTLEFORD - Lewis: Cunniffe Atkinson Croston
T.C.Askin: Davies Adams: McManus Haley Taylor Smith
Crossley Sadler: Tries - Cunniffe(4) Atkinson(3) Croston(3)
Askin Crossley: Goals - Lewis(6):
FEATHERSTONE R - Lockwood: Gamble Asquith Lingard
Rowley: Johnson Ward: Padgett Morris Hemingay Taylor
Dyson Smith:
Tries - Lingard Ward: Goals - Lockwood(2) Johnson:
Referee A S Dobson (Pontefract) Att–2000 H.T. 28 - 6

Sat 31 Aug 1935 HUNSLET home won 44 - nil
CASTLEFORD - Lewis: Cunniffe Atkinson Croston
T.C.Askin: Davies Adams: McManus Haley Taylor Smith
Crossley Sadler: Tries - Cunniffe(2) Atkinson(2)
Croston(2) Lewis T.C.Askin Adams Sadler: Goals - Lewis(7):
HUNSLET - Walkington: Dennis Morrell Winter Yates:
Todd Thornton: Tolson White Benson Dawson Stansfield
Beverley:
Referee J E Taylor (Wakefield) Att – 7000 H.T. 17 - nil

Mon 2 Sep 1935 BATLEY away lost 2 - 10
BATLEY - Goldie: Shirley Smith Kitson Peck: Pollard
Dooler: Dyson Lockwood Earnshaw Hudson Myers Brown:
Tries - Peck Brown: Goals - Brown Goldie(DG):
CASTLEFORD - Lewis: Cunniffe Atkinson Croston
T.C.Askin: Davies Adams: McManus Haley Taylor Smith
Crossley Sadler: Goal - Lewis:
Referee A Hill (Leeds) Att - 3000 H.T. 2 - 3

Sat 7 Sep 1935 KEIGHLEY away won 22 - 11
KEIGHLEY - Taylor: Sherburn Foster Rainton Orchard:
Davies Meek: Traill Halliday Jones McGoun Dixon Gill:
Try - Gill: Goals - Taylor(3) Davies(DG):
CASTLEFORD - Lewis: Cunniffe Atkinson Croston
T.C.Askin: Davies Adams: McManus James Plimmer Taylor
Smith Crossley Sadler:
Tries - Croston Cunniffe Adams Smith: Goals - Lewis(5):
Referee F Peel (Bradford) Att - 6500 H.T. 7 - 4

**Sat l4 Sep 1935 DEWSBURY home lost 8 - 11
YORKSHIRE CUP ROUND 1**
CASTLEFORD - Lewis: Cunniffe Atkinson Croston
T.C.Askin: Davies Adams: McManus Haley Taylor Smith
Crossley Sadler: Goals - Lewis(3) Davies(DG):
DEWSBURY - Chester: Hobson Killingbeck Jayne
Whitehead: Davies Werrett: Thomas Morgan Pearson
Jenkins Evans Oakland:
Try - Hobson: Goals - Chester(2) Killingbeck(2):
Referee F Fairhurst (Wigan) Att - 9000 H.T. 4 - 4

Wed 18 Sep 1935 WAKEFIELD TRINITY home won 9-8
CASTLEFORD - Lewis: Cunniffe Atkinson Croston
T.C.Askin: Davies Adams: McManus Haley Taylor Smith
Crossley Sadler: Try - Haley: Goals - Lewis(3):
WAKEFIELD T - Knowles: Farrar Ryan Pollard Smart:
Burrows Herbert: Wilkinson Carter Hobson Horton Exley
Rowan: Tries - Ryan Horton: Goal - Knowles:
Referee J F Armitage (Hull) Att - 6000 H.T. 5 - 5

Sat 21 Sep 1935 LYONS VILLEURBANNE home won 18 - 8 FRIENDLY
CASTLEFORD - Lewis: Cunniffe Atkinson T.C.Askin:
England: Davies Huggett: Taylor Haley Smith Crossley
Knowles Sadler:
Tries - Atkinson(2) Davies Sadler: Goals - Lewis(3):
LYON V - Burnchom: Lambert Barbazanges Amila
Barnoud: Font Mathon: Piany Anaiade Arioulou Petit
Griffard Barcella: Tries - Barcella Amila: Goal - Amila:
Referee A Brown (Wakefield) Att - 3000 H.T. 5 - nil

Sat 28 Sep 1935 WIGAN away lost 15 - 23
WIGAN - Sullivan: Morley Innes Davies Ellaby: Bennett
H.Gee: Targett Davies K.Gee Hall Edwards Seeling:
Tries - Innes(2) H.Gee(2) Ellaby: Goals - Sullivan(4):
CASTLEFORD - Lewis: Cunniffe Atkinson T.C.Askin
England: THOMAS HARDY(147) Huggett: McManus Haley
Smith Crossley Knowles Sadler:
Try - Atkinson Goals - Lewis(6):
Referee A Brown (Wakefield) Att - 7000 H.T. 11 - 15

Sat 5 Oct 1935 SWINTON home lost 7 - 10
CASTLEFORD - Lewis: Cunniffe Atkinson Croston
T.C.Askin: Hardy Adams: McManus Haley Taylor Smith
Crossley Sadler: Try - Sadler: Goals - Lewis(2):
SWINTON - Scott: Buckingham Hickman Shaw McGregor:
H.Evans Green: Wright Armitt Hughes Hodgson Spruce
Sullivan: Tries - Hickman Evans: Goals - Hodgson(2):
Referee A Holbrook (Warrington) Att - 10000 H.T. 2 - 10

Sat 12 Oct 1935 BRAMLEY away lost 17 - 20
BRAMLEY – A N Other: Hodgkiss Lingard Rees Davidson:
Abram Bardy: Kirk Bowden Graham Pearson Maudsley
Ballantyne:
Tries - Bardy(2) Hodgkiss Lingard: Goals - Rees(4):
CASTLEFORD - Pollitt: Cunniffe Lewis James Gill England:
T.C.Askin Huggett: McManus Haley Crossley Smith
Knowles Sadler: Tries - England(2) Sadler: Goals - Lewis(4):
Referee J F Armitage (Hud'field) Att - 2000 H.T. 10 - 7

Sat 19 Oct 1935 ST HELENS RECS home won 11 - nil
CASTLEFORD - Lewis: England FRANK WALKER(148)
Croston T.C.Askin: Davies Adams: McManus Haley Taylor
Smith Crossley Sadler:
Tries - Sadler(2) Croston: Goal - Lewis:
ST HELENS R - Johnson: Forber Frodsham Bailey Balmer:
? ? : Bowen Dolan Liptrot Randolph Atherton Jennison:
Referee F Fairhurst (Wigan) Att - H.T. 3 - nil

Sat 26 Oct 1935 ACTON & WILLESDEN away won 13 -9
ACTON & WILLESDEN - Addison: Roberts James Cutbush
Veysey: Bibby Jenkins: Walton Murphy Atherton Avery
Morgan Cayser:
Try - Veysey: Goals - James(2) Addison:
CASTLEFORD - Lewis: England Walker Croston T.C.Askin:
Davies Adams: McManus Haley Taylor Smith Crossley
A.Askin:
Tries - Croston(2) Davies: Goals - Lewis(2):
Referee B Laughlin (Batley) Att - 12000 H.T. 8 - 7

Wed 30 Oct 1935 HULL KINGSTON ROVERS home won 12 - 8
CASTLEFORD - Lewis: DON CRAVEN(149) T.C.Askin Croston England: Davies Adams: McManus Haley Taylor Smith A.Askin Crossley:
Tries - Craven A.Askin: Goals - Smith(2) Lewis:
HULL K R - White: Wood Spamer McWatt Winsor: H.Beaumont McGowan: Riach Eddom Thompson Brown Blanchard L.Beaumont: Tries - Spamer McGoun: Goal - McWatt:
Referee A Brown (Wakefield) Att - 2000 H.T. 2 - 2

Sat 2 Nov 1935 HULL home lost 6 - 8
CASTLEFORD - Lewis:Craven Atkinson Croston T.C.Askin: Davies Adams: McManus Haley Taylor Smith A.Askin Crossley: Goals - Lewis(3):
HULL - Miller: Gouldstone Oliver Fifield Corner: Colling Herbert: Stead G.Barlow Thacker Dawson L.Barlow Ellerington: Tries - Fifield G.Barlow: Goal - Oliver:
Referee J E Taylor (Wakefield) Att - 7000 H.T. 6 - 3

Sat 9 Nov 1935 HUDDERSFIELD away won 9 - 3
HUDDERSFIELD - Scourfield: Frost Mountain Fiddes Markham: Richards Pepperell: Sherwood Watson Fuller Tiffany Senior Gronow: Try - Fiddes:
CASTLEFORD - Lewis: Cunniffe Atkinson Croston T.C.Askin: Davies Adams: McManus Haley Taylor Smith A.Askin Knowles: Tries - Cunniffe Smith Davies:
Referee J E Taylor (Wakefield) Att - 8000 H.T. 6 - nil

Sat 16 Nov 1935 ACTON & WILLESDEN home won 28 - 5
CASTLEFORD - Lewis: Cunniffe Atkinson Croston Walker: Davies Adams: McManus Haley Taylor Smith A.Askin Donald Knowles:
Tries - Smith(2) Lewis Croston Walker Davies: Goals - Lewis(5):
ACTON & WILLESDEN - Addison: Madden Roberts Cutbush Veysey: Bibby Jenkins: Walton Murphy Atherton Morgan Sutcliffe Cayser: Try - Roberts: Goal - Addison:
Referee P Cowell (Warrington) Att - 5000 H.T. 13 - 2

Sat 23 Nov 1935 SALFORD away won 9 - 2
SALFORD - White: Evans Brown Miller Hudson: Jenkins Schofield: Williams Day Bradbury Dalton Harris Feetham: Goal - White:
CASTLEFORD - Lewis: Cunniffe Atkinson Croston Walker: Davies Adams: McManus Haley Taylor Smith A.Askin Crossley: Try - Atkinson: Goals - Lewis(3):
Referee A Hill (Leeds) Att -   H.T. 4 - 2

Sat 30 Nov 1935 DEWSBURY home won 17 - 10
CASTLEFORD - Lewis: Cunniffe Atkinson Croston Walker: Davies Adams: McManus Haley Taylor Smith Crossley Sadler:
Tries - Cunniffe Croston Smith: Goals - Lewis(2) Walker(2):
DEWSBURY - Chester: Hardacre Killingbeck Jayne Davies: Britton France: Morgan Osborne McTiffin Pearson Jenkins Sankey: Tries - Morgan Sankey: Goals - Chester(2):
Referee F Peel (Bradford) Att -   H.T. 10 - 10

Sat 14 Dec 1935 HUNSLET away lost 6 - 7
HUNSLET - Walkington: Atkinson Morrell Winter A.N.Other: Todd Thornton: Tolson(S/O) White Dawson Stansfield Plenderleith Beverley:
Try - Thornton: Goals - Tolson(2):
CASTLEFORD - Lewis: Cunniffe Atkinson Croston Walker: Davies Adams: McManus Haley Taylor Smith A.Askin Crossley: Goals - Lewis(3):
Referee J F Armstrong (Hud'field) Att - 9500 H.T. 4 - 5

Sat 21 Dec 1935 BRADFORD NORTHERN home won 23 - 5
CASTLEFORD - Lewis: Cunniffe Atkinson Croston Walker: Davies Adams: McManus Haley Taylor Smith A.Askin Crossley: Tries - Walker(2) Cunniffe Atkinson Croston: Goals - Lewis(4):
BRADFORD N - Carmichael: Gray Hutchinson Smith Jackson: Billington Spillane: Higson Thorpe Morgan Chadwick Collins Moore:
Try - Hutchinson: Goal - Carmichael:
Referee W Hemmings (Halifax) Att -   H.T. 13 - nil

Thu 26 Dec 1935 YORK home won 17 - 7
CASTLEFORD - Lewis: Cunniffe Atkinson Croston Walker: Davies(S/O) Adams: McManus Haley Taylor Smith Crossley Sadler:
Tries - Atkinson Walker Crossley: Goals - Lewis(4):
YORK - Dingsdale: Western Rosser Hunt Elias: Kelleher Thomas: Sharpe Myers Prosser Banks Fender Welsh: Try - Western: Goals - Dingsdale(2):
Referee J F Armstrong (Hud'field) Att - 8000 H.T. 12 - 5

Sat 28 Dec 1935 HULL away lost 2 - 15
HULL - Miller: Gouldstone Wilson Fifield Corner: Courtney Herbert: L.Barlow G.Barlow Carmichael Booth Dawson Ellerington:
Tries - Gouldstone Courtney Ellerington: Goals - Miller(3)
CASTLEFORD - Lewis: Cunniffe Atkinson Croston Walker: Davies Adams: McManus Haley Taylor Smith Crossley Sadler: Goal - Lewis:
Referee B Laughlin (Batley) Att - 9000 H.T. nil - 12

Sat 4 Jan 1936 HUDDERSFIELD home won 15 - 14
CASTLEFORD - Lewis: Cunniffe Atkinson Croston Walker: Davies Adams: McManus Haley Taylor Smith A.Askin Sadler: Tries - Haley Smith A.Askin: Goals - Lewis(3):
HUDDERSFIELD - Lockwood: Johnson Mountain Fiddes Markham: Madden Pepperell: Fuller Watson Evans Prosser Senior Aspinall:
Tries - Johnson Fiddes: Goals - Pepperell(4):
Referee J E Taylor (Wakefield) Att - 7500 H.T. 10 - 5

Sat 11 Jan 1936 SWINTON away lost nil - 8
SWINTON - Scott: Kenny Hickman H.Evans Buckingham: Green Holland: Wright Armitt Hughes Hodgson Spruce Butters: Goals - Hodgson(2) Scott(1)(DG):
CASTLEFORD - Lewis: England Atkinson Croston Walker: Cunniffe Adams: McManus Haley Taylor Smith A.Askin Sadler:
Referee A Hill (Leeds) Att - 19000 H.T. nil - 6

SEASON 1935-36

Sat 18 Jan 1936 BRAMLEY home won 32 - nil
CASTLEFORD - Lewis: Don Craven Atkinson Croston
Walker: Cunniffe Adams: McManus Haley Taylor Smith
Crossley A.Askin:
Tries - Croston(3) Atkinson(2) Cunniffe: Goals - Lewis(7):
BRAMLEY - Rees: Hodgkiss Duke Abram Ellingham:
Gowarth Bardy: Kirk Bowden Graham Pearson Maudsley
Ballantyne:
Referee W Hemmings (Halifax) Att-4000 H.T. 14 - nil

Sat 1 Feb 1936 WIGAN home lost 10 - 20
CASTLEFORD - Lewis: Cunniffe Walker Croston F.Smith:
Davies Huggett: McManus Haley Taylor THOMAS
BANKS(150) A.Askin Crossley:
Tries - Walker Crossley: Goals - Lewis(2):
WIGAN - Newey: Ellaby Innes G.Davies O'Sullivan:
Banheld H.Gee: Edwards Golby A.Davies Hathway Thomas
Seeling:
Tries - Ellaby(3) Innes Davies Gee: Goal - Gee:
Referee J W Webb (Manchester) Att–7000 H.T. nil - 2

Sat 8 Feb 1936 ROCHDALE HORNETS home
won 16 - 3 CHALLENGE CUP ROUND 1
CASTLEFORD - Lewis: HAROLD THOMAS(151) Atkinson
Croston Walker: Davies Adams: McManus Haley Taylor
Smith A.Askin Crossley:
Tries - Thomas(2) Atkinson Croston: Goals - Lewis(2):
ROCHDALE H - Sayer: Williams Davies Downey Tolan:
Matthews Helme: Thompson Dean Moore Knapman
Gaunt Logan: Try - Matthews:
Referee P Cowell (Warrington) Att-11220 H.T. 8 - 3

Sat 15 Feb 1936 ST HELENS RECS away lost 8 - 24
ST HELENS R - Lythgoe: Bailey Atherton Frodsham Large:
Hampson Prescott: Highcock Dolan Kilnshaw Randolph
Parr Jennion:
Tries - Large(2) Hampson(2) Bailey Frodsham:
Goals - Hampson(2) Atherton:
CASTLEFORD - Lewis: Harold Thomas Walker Croston
Cunniffe: Davies Adams: Banks(S/O) Haley Taylor Smith
A.Askin Crossley:
Tries - Walker Croston: Goal - Lewis:
Referee B Laughlin (Batley) Att - 1186 H.T. nil - 8

Sat 22 Feb 1936 LEIGH home won 8 - nil
CHALLENGE CUP ROUND 2
CAASTLEFORD - Lewis: Cunniffe Atkinson Croston Walker:
Davies Adams: McManus Haley Taylor Smith A.Askin
Crossley:
Goals - Lewis(2) Atkinson(2):
LEIGH - Farrington: Stringman Spensley Critchley Squires:
Pitcher McHugh: Montford Richardson Morley Prescott
Greenhalgh Hutchinson:
Referee B Timility (Manchester) Att - 9558 H.T. 4 - nil

Wed 26 Feb 1936 KEIGHLEY home won 22 - 6
CASTLEFORD - Lewis: Cunniffe Davies Croston Walker:
Hardy Adams: McManus Haley Taylor Smith STANLEY
ALLEN(152) Crossley:
Tries - Lewis Croston Hardy Adams: Goals - Lewis(5):

KEIGHLEY - Taylor: Sherburn Rainton Foster Orchard:
Davies Hockey Traill Halliday Jones Dixon McGoun Sykes:
Tries - Hockey Jones:
Referee F Peel (Bradford) Att - 3000 H.T. 10 - nil

Sat 29 Feb 1936 WAKEFIELD TRINITY away won 9 -3
WAKEFIELD T - Bonner: Batten Whittaker Pollard Ryan:
Herbert Carr: Wilkinson Nicholson Hobson Horton
Watson Rowan: Try - Batten:
CASTLEFORD - Lewis: Cunniffe Davies Croston Walker:
Hardy Adams: McManus Haley Taylor Smith A.Askin
Sadler: Tries - Cunniffe(2) Walker:
Referee J W Webb (Broughton Att - 3000 H.T. 6 - 3

Sat 7 Mar 1936 SALFORD away lost 4 - 5
CHALLENGE CUP ROUND 3
SALFORD - Osbaldestin: Hudson Brown Risman Edwards:
Jenkins Watkins: Williams Day Bradbury Middleton Harris
Feetham:
Try - Edwards: Goal - Risman:
CASTLEFORD - Lewis: Cunniffe Atkinson Croston Walker:
Davies Adams: McManus Haley Taylor Smith A.Askin
Crossley:
Goals - Lewis(2):
Referee A Brown (Wakefield) Att - 24000 H.T. 4 - 5

Wed 11 Mar 1936 BATLEY home won 14 - 7
CASTLEFORD - Atkinson: Cunniffe Davies Croston Walker:
Hardy Adams: McManus Haley Taylor Smith A.Askin
Crossley:
Tries - Cunniffe Hardy Adams Crossley: Goal - Walker:
BATLEY - Goldie: Brydon Pollard Kitson Smith: Shirley
Swift: Dyson Myers Squire Hudson Midgeley Farrar:
Try - Hudson: Goals - Pollard(2):
Referee J E Taylor (Wakefield) Att - 2000 H.T. 8 - nil

Sat 14 Mar 1936 WARRINGTON home won 10 - 9
CASTLEFORD - Lewis: Cunniffe Atkinson Croston Walker:
Davies Adams: McManus Haley Banks Smith A.Askin
Taylor:
Tries - Cunniffe Smith: Goals - Lewis(2):
WARRINGTON - Haslehurst: Garrett Rutledge Halson
Hewitt: Heeson Rollins: Hardman Cotton Miller Flannery
Chadwick Chapman:
Try - Hardman: Goals - Flannery(3):
Referee B Timilty (Manchester) Att - 4000 H.T. 7 - 7

Wed 18 Mar 1936 BRADFORD NORTHERN away
lost 5 - 11
BRADFORD N - Carmichael: Gray Winnard Wilson
Grainge: Jackson Spillane: Morgan Dilorenzo Jones Smith
Chadwick Moore:
Tries - Winnard Grainge Jackson: Goal - Winnard:
CASTLEFORD - Lewis: Cunniffe Davies Atkinson Croston:
Hardy Adams: McManus Haley Allen Smith A.Askin Taylor:
Try - Smith: Goa - Lewis:
Referee - Att - 4000 H.T. 2 - 5

Sat 28 Mar 1936 SALFORD home lost 11 - 15
CASTLEFORD - Lewis: Cunniffe Atkinson Croston Walker:
Davies Adams: McManus Haley Banks Smith A.Askin
Taylor:
Tries - Cunniffe Adams Smith: Goal - Lewis:
SALFORD - Osbaldestin: Hudson Miller Brown Edwards:
Jenkins Watkins: Williams Day Bradbury Middleton Harris
Feetham:
Tries - Hudson Jenkins Watkins: Goals - Jenkins(2) Brown:
Referee P Cowell (Warrington) Att-10000 H.T. 3 - 8

Sat 4 Apr 1936 LEEDS away lost 3 - 5
LEEDS - Brough: E.Harris F.Harris Parker Smith: Ralph
Williams: Dyer Hall Sattherthwaite Jubb Casewell
Whitehead: Try - E.Harris: Goal - Williams:
CASTLEFORD - Lewis: Cunniffe Atkinson Croston Walker:
Hardy Adams: McManus Haley Allen Smith A.Askin Taylor:
Try - Atkinson:
Referee J E Taylor (Wakefield) Att-12000 H.T. nil - 5

Fri 10 Apr 1936 LEEDS home won 31 - 3
CASTLEFORD - Lewis: Cunniffe Atkinson Croston Walker:
Hardy Adams: McManus Haley Allen Smith A.Askin
Sadler: Tries - Cunniffe(2) Croston(2) Atkinson Walker
Smith: Goals Lewis(5)
LEEDS - Eaton: E.Harris F.Harris Brough Smith: Brogden
Richards: Dyer Hall Satterthwaite Ripley Casewell Isaac:
Try - E.Harris:
Referee A Brown (Wakefield) Att - 16000 H.T. 7 - 3

**Sat 11 Apr 1936 FEATHERSTONE ROVERS home
won 18 - 5**
CASTLEFORD - Lewis: Cunniffe Davies Croston Walker:
Hardy Adams: McManus Haley A.N.OTHER(153) Crossley
Taylor Sadler:
Tries - Lewis(2) Hardy Walker: Goals - Lewis(3):
FEATHERSTONE R - Dennis: Asquith Brogden Naylor
Lingard: Evans Ward: Coulson Morris Hemingway Taylor
Dixon Sherwood: Try - Lingard: Goal - Sherwood:
Referee J F Armstrong (Hud'field) Att - 4000 H.T. 5 – nil

Mon 13 Apr 1936 YORK away lost 5 - 14
YORK - Dingsdale: Haigh Rosser Sullivan Hardgrave: Rees
Thomas: Prosser Field Sharpe Fender Coldrick Welsh:
Tries - Welsh(2) Fender Coldrick: Goal - Dingsdale:
CASTLEFORD - Lewis: Cunniffe Atkinson Croston Walker:
Hardy Adams: McManus Haley Allen Smith A.Askin
Sadler: Try - Hardy: Goal - Lewis:
Referee E Willis (Hull) Att - 10000 H.T. 5 - 3

**Tue 14 Apr 1936 FEATHERSTONE ROVERS away
won 16 - nil**
FEATHERSTONE R - Crummack: Lingard Brogden(S/O)
Naylor: Evans Ward: Coulson Morris Lomas Hemingway
Dyson Darlison:
CASTLEFORD - Lewis: Cunniffe Atkinson Croston Walker:
Hardy Adams: Taylor Haley Allen Smith A.Askin Crossley:
Tries - Croston Walker Hardy Crossley:
Goals - Atkinson(2):
Referee A Hill (Leeds) Att -   H.T. 16 - nil

Sat 25 Apr 1936 DEWSBURY away won 10 - 6
DEWSBURY - Chester: Hobson Turner Whitehead
Hardacre: Britton Werrett: Morgan Pearson McTiffin
Wormald Evans Sankey: Goals - Chester(3):
CASTLEFORD - Lewis: Cunniffe Davies Croston Walker:
Hardy Adams: McManus Haley Taylor Smith Allen JACK
CHEETHAM(154):
Tries - Croston(2): Goals - Lewis Walker:
Referee F Peel (Bradford) Att - 2000 H.T. 5 - 6

Sat 2 May 1936 WARRINGTON away lost 8 - 28
WARRINGTON - Baxter: Jarrett Rutledge Dingsdale
Hewitt: Hawker Goodall: Cotton Hardman Rankin
Flannery Chadwick Chapman:
Tries - Dingsdale(2) Hawker(2) Jarrett Rutledge:
Goals - Rankin(5):
CASTLEFORD - Lewis: WILFRED(BUCK)BOUCHER(155)
Davies Croston Walker: Hardy England: McManus Haley
Taylor Smith A.Askin Jack Cheetham:
Tries - Davies Croston: Goal - Lewis:
Referee J F Armstrong (Hud'field) Att - 5000 H.T. nil - 23

**Mon 4 May 1936 HULL KINGSTON ROVERS away
lost 7 - 27**
HULL K R - McWatt: Eastwood Whitton Spamer Wood:
McGowan Dale: Blanshard Ramsden Eddomd Tattersfield
Walshaw Saddington:
Tries - Wood(2) Dale(2) Ramsden: Goals - McWatt(5)(DG):
CASTLEFORD - Lewis: Davies Boucher Croston A.Askin:
Hardy England McManus ROBERT WHELAN(156) Allen
ALFRED GOODWIN(157) Crossley Taylor:
Try - Croston: Goals - Allen(2):
Referee B Laughlin (Batley) Att -   H.T. 2 – 9

Frank Walker
D. No 148
1935-36 to 1941-42

SEASON 1935-36

D.N	PLAYER		DEBUT	L MATCH	APP	S JB	T.AP	TRI'S	G'LS	D.G	P'TS
21	ATKINSON	ARTHUR			30	0	30	11	4	0	41
39	PLIMMER	JAMES		07/09/1935	1	0	1	0	0	0	0
79	LEWIS	GEORGE			41	0	41	5	99	0	213
98	ASKIN	THOMAS C.			13	0	13	1	0	0	3
111	DAVIES	WILLIAM H.			33	0	33	4	0	1	14
116	TAYLOR	THOMAS L.			38	0	38	0	0	0	0
117	ASKIN	AMBROSE			27	0	27	2	0	0	6
123	HALEY	HAROLD			40	0	40	2	0	0	6
124	SMITH	FRANK Snr.			40	0	40	10	2	0	34
125	KNOWLES	DONALD		16/11/1935	4	0	4	0	0	0	0
128	POLLITT	JOHN			1	0	1	0	0	0	0
130	CROSTON	ALFRED JAMES			40	0	40	22	0	0	66
131	GILL	JAMES		12/10/1935	1	0	1	0	0	0	0
133	ADAMS	LESLIE			37	0	37	5	0	0	15
134	SADLER	EDWARD L.			18	0	18	5	0	0	15
135	CUNNIFFE	BERNARD			35	0	35	14	0	0	42
136	CROSSLEY	JAMES M.			29	0	29	4	0	0	12
139	ENGLAND	ERIC			8	0	8	2	0	0	6
141	McMANUS	PATRICK B.			40	0	40	0	0	0	0
144	HUGGETT	WILLIAM E. (BILL)			3	0	3	0	0	0	0
147	HARDY	THOMAS	28/09/1935		14	0	14	5	0	0	15
148	WALKER	FRANK	19/10/1935		29	0	29	10	4	0	38
149	CRAVEN	DON	30/10/1935	18/01/1936	3	0	3	1	0	0	3
150	BANKS	THOMAS	01/02/1936		4	0	4	0	0	0	0
151	THOMAS	HAROLD	08/02/1936	15/02/1936	2	0	2	2	0	0	6
152	ALLEN	STANLEY	26/02/1936		8	0	8	0	2	0	4
153	A.N.OTHER		11/04/1936	11/04/1936	1	0	1	0	0	0	0
154	CHEETHAM	JACK	25/04/1936	02/05/1936	2	0	2	0	0	0	0
155	BOUCHER	WILFRED (BUCK)	02/05/1936		2	0	2	0	0	0	0
156	WHELAN	ROBERT	04/05/1936	04/05/1936	1	0	1	0	0	0	0
157	GOODWIN	ALFRED	04/05/1936	04/05/1936	1	0	1	0	0	0	0
	31		**11**	**9**	**546**	**0**	**546**	**105**	**111**	**1**	**539**

COMPETITION		P	W	D	L	FOR	AGT
LEAGUE	POSITION 12 OF 30	38	22	0	16	503	366
YORK'S CUP		1	0	0	1	8	11
RL CUP		3	2	0	1	28	8
PLAYERS RECORDS		**42**	**24**	**0**	**18**	**539**	**385**

Acton & Willesden and Streatham & Mitcham were admitted to the league.

The French side Lyons Villeurbanne returned the compliment of the previous season by playing a return friendly fixture at Castleford on 21 September 1935, Castleford again came out as winners 18–5.

Arthur Atkinson made his 300th appearance for the club in the 8-nil victory at home against Leigh on 22 February 1936, with Arthur celebrating the occasion with two goals.

George Lewis increased the record for most points scored in a League game to 17 against Hunslet at home on the 31 August 1935 and also increased the record for most goals in a season to 99.

**Sat 22 Aug 1936 FEATHERSTONE ROVERS away
won 27 - 3 LYON CUP -FRIENDLY**
FEATHERSTONE R - A.N.Other: Asquith Hammond Naylor
Newton: Ward Hamer: Padgett Morris Hemingay Taylor
Dyson Sherwood: Try - Hamer:
CASTLEFORD - Lewis: Cunniffe Davies Croston Walker:
Hardy Adams: Allen Haley Taylor Smith Crossley Sadler:
Tries - Cunniffe(2) Davies Croston Walker Allen Crossley:
Goals - Lewis(3):
Referee A S Dobson (Pontefract) Att - 3000 H.T. 8 - nil

Sat 29 Aug 1936 HUNSLET away won 22 - 5
HUNSLET - Walkington: Bennett Yates Winter Dennis:
Booth Thornton: Tolson White Rhodes Dawson
Plenderleith Morrell: Try - Winter: Goal - Rhodes:
CASTLEFORD - Lewis: Cunniffe Davies Walker Croston:
Hardy Adams: Taylor Haley Allen Smith Crossley Sadler:
Tries - Walker(2) Croston(2) Davies Haley:
Goals - Lewis(2):
Referee B Laughlin (Batley) Att - 6000 H.T. 8 - nil

Wed 2 Sep 1936 DEWSBURY away won 17 - 3
DEWSBURY - McNamara: Hobson Whitehead Killingbeck
Copley: Hill Werrett: Pearson Bowden McTiffin Swift
Morgan Sankey: Try - Hill:
CASTLEFORD - Lewis: Cunniffe Davies Walker Croston:
Hardy Adams: Taylor Haley Allen Smith Crossley Sadler:
Tries - Adams(2) Sadler(2) Walker: Goal - Lewis:
Referee F Peel (Bradford) Att - 3000 H.T. 8 - nil

**Sat 5 Sep 1936 HULL KINGSTON ROVERS home
won 21 - 4**
CASTLEFORD - Lewis: Walker Croston Davies Cunniffe:
Hardy Adams: Allen Haley Taylor Smith Crossley Sadler:
Tries - Lewis Walker Croston Crossley Sadler:
Goals - Lewis(3):
HULL K R - McWatt: Wood Mcgowan Whitton Stoke:
Young Phillips: Maskill Ramsden Beaumont Eddoms
Tattersfield Cayser: Goals - McWatt(2):
Referee A Hill (Leeds) Att - 6000 H.T. 8 - 2

**Sat 12 Sep 1936 HALIFAX away lost nil - 7
YORKSHIRE CUP ROUND 1**
HALIFAX - Lockwood: Watson Brook Treen Thomas: Todd
Bowden: Baynham Meek Irving Childe Cox Thornber:
Try - Bowden: Goals - Lockwood(2):
CASTLEFORD - Lewis: Walker Croston Davies Cunniffe:
Hardy Adams: McManus Haley Allen Smith Crossley
Sadler:
Referee B Timilty (Manchester) Att - 9750 H.T. nil - 5

Wed 16 Sep 1936 SALFORD home won 11 - 7
CASTLEFORD - Lewis: Cunniffe Davies Croston Walker:
Hardy Adams: McManus(S/O) Banks Taylor Smith
Crossley Sadler:
Tries - Cunniffe(2) Croston: Goal - Lewis:
SALFORD - Osbaldestin: Turner Miller Brown Pearson:
Evans Schofield: Williams Day Bradbury Dalton Harris
Feetham: Try - Pearson: Goals - Schofield(2):
Referee L Greenwood (Rochdale) Att - 6500 H.T. 5 - 2

**Sat 19 Sep 1936 BROUGHTON RANGERS away
lost 2 - 18**
BROUGHTON R - Howells: Kenny Stott Abbott Smith:
Garvey Thompson: Whitcombe Jones Morgan Bunter
Mills Manning:
Tries - Kenny Stott Smith Mills: Goals - Stott(3):
CASTLEFORD Lewis: Cunniffe Davies Croston GILBERT
ROBINSON(158): Hardy Adams: McManus Banks Taylor
Smith Crossley Sadler: Goal - Smith:
Referee J E Taylor (Wakefield) Att - 5000 H.T. nil - 10

**Sat 26 Sep 1936 WAKEFIELD TRINITY home
won 33 - 13**
CASTLEFORD - Lewis: Cunniffe Atkinson Croston Davies:
Hardy Adams: Banks Haley Taylor Smith Crossley Sadler:
Tries - Cunniffe(2) Atkinson(2) Smith(2) Sadler: Goals -
Lewis(6):
WAKEFIELD T - Knowles: Ryan Malpass Exley Hughes:
Herbert Goodfellow: Wilkinson Carter Hobson Horton
Flowers Watson:
Tries: Malpass Exley Herbert: Goals Knowles (2):
Referee A Hill (Leeds) Att - 10200 H.T. 10 - 10

Sat 3 Oct 1936 BATLEY away won 12 - 9
BATLEY - Goldie: Nunn Pollard Kitson Smith: Brydon
Dooler: Earnshaw Fallon Darlison Foley Hudson Brown:
Try - Nunn: Goals - Brown(3):
CASTLEFORD - Lewis: Cunniffe Atkinson Croston Davies:
Hardy Adams: Banks Haley Taylor Smith Crossley Sadler:
Tries - Cunniffe Adams: Goals - Lewis(2)(DG):
Referee F Peel (Bradford) Att - 6000 H.T. 8 - 9

Sat 10 Oct 1936 HUNSLET home won 11 - 8
CASTLEFORD - Lewis: Davies Gilbert Robinson Croston
Walker: Hardy Huggett: Taylor Haley Banks Smith
Crossley Sadler: Try - Croston: Goals - Lewis(4):
HUNSLET - Wilson: Atkinson Morrell Abell Batten:
Johnson Harrison: Tolson White Rhodes Dawson
Plenderleith Elson: Tries - Natten(2) Goal - Rhodes:
Referee F Peel (Bradford) Att - 6500 H.T. 4 - 5

Sat 17 Oct 1936 LEEDS home won 20 - 8
CASTLEFORD - Lewis: Cunniffe Atkinson Croston Walker:
Hardy Adams: Banks Haley Taylor Smith Crossley Sadler:
Tries - Atkinson Cunniffe Croston Smith: Goals - Lewis(4):
LEEDS - Eaton: E.Harris F.Harris Pollard Smith: Brogden
Williams: Satterthwaite Hall Dyson Jubb Dyer Whitehead:
Tries - E.Harris F.Harris: Goal - Pollard:
Referee J E Taylor (Wakefield) Att - 16000 H.T. 17 - 3

Sat 24 Oct 1936 NEWCASTLE away won 10 - 7
NEWCASTLE - James: Craven Tetlow Maddock Turton:
Pickard Dale: Walton(S/O) Suddes Taylor Norcliffe Jones
Knowles:
Try - Knowles: Goals - James Knowles:
CASTLEFORD - Lewis: Walker Croston Atkinson Davies:
Hardy TOM(TOT)WALSH(159): Banks GORDON
COTTINGTON(160) Taylor Crossley A.Askin Sadler:
Tries - Walker Sadler: Goals - Lewis(2):
Referee J Armstrong (Huddersfield) Att - 2000 H.T. 5 - 5

SEASON 1936-37

Sat 31 Oct 1936 KEIGHLEY home won 4 - nil
CASTLEFORD - Lewis: Boucher Atkinson T.C.Askin Walker:
Davies Walsh: Banks Haley Taylor Cottington Crossley
Sadler: Goals - Lewis Atkinson:
KEIGHLEY - Bowkett: Sherburn Mason Bevan Orchard:
Phelps Davies: Traill Halliday McGoun Dixon Talbot Gill:
Referee S Adams (Hull) Att - 6300 H.T. 2 - nil

Sat 7 Nov 1936 SALFORD away lost nil - 2
SALFORD - Osbaldestin: Gear Brown Pearson Turner:
Miller Schofield: Williams Shaw Bradbury Dalton Harris
Feetham:
Goal - Pearson:
CASTLEFORD - Lewis: Walker Atkinson Davies Thomas
C.Askin: Hardy Walsh: Banks Cottington Taylor Smith
Crossley Sadler:
Referee L Thorpe (Wakefield) Att - 4000 H.T. nil - nil

Sat 14 Nov 1936 BRAMLEY home won 21 - 4
CASTLEFORD - Pollitt: Cunniffe Atkinson Croston
Walker(S/O): Hardy Adams: Taylor Cottington Banks
Smith Crossley Sadler:
Tries - Hardy(2) Atkinson Croston Crossley:
Goals - Pollitt(3):
BRAMLEY - Taylor: Davidson Lingard Rees Hodgkiss:
Starling Bardy: Walkington Vickers Larvin Pearson Webb
Ballantyne:
Goals - Taylor(2):
Referee W Hemmings (Halifax) Att -   H.T. 11 - nil

Sat 21 Nov 1936 LIVERPOOL STANLEY away lost 7-23
LIVERPOOL S - Belshaw: Robinson Woodcock McDonnell
Maloney: Glover Kirk: Davies Lowe Woods Smith Shaw
Stock:
Tries - Maloney(2) Woodcock Lowe Smith:
Goals - Woodcock(2) Belshaw Shaw(DG):
CASTLEFORD - Lewis: Cunniffe Atkinson Croston Walker:
Hardy Adams: Banks Haley Taylor Smith Crossley Sadler:
Try - Croston: Goals - Lewis Atkinson:
Referee F Peel (Bradford) Att - 3000 H.T. 7 - 8

Sat 28 Nov 1936 DEWSBURY home won 32 - 13
CASTLEFORD - Lewis: Cunniffe Atkinson Croston Walker:
Hardy Adams: Taylor Cottington Banks Smith Crossley
Sadler:
Tries - Cunniffe(2) Atkinson Croston Hardy Adams Smith
Crossley: Goals - Walker(3) Lewis:
DEWSBURY - McNamara: Hobson Killingbeck Whitworth
Hardacre: Jones Naylor: Pearson Sunley McTiffin Prescott
Osborne Sankey:
Tries - Killingbeck(3): Goals - Killingbeck(2):
Referee A Hill (Leeds) Att - 5000 H.T. 11 - 8

**Sat 5 Dec 1936 FEATHERSTONE ROVERS away
won 17 - 3**
FEATHERSTONE R - Dennis: Lingard Brogden Hammond
Naylor: Evans Hamer: Hemingway Morris A.N.Other
Dyson Taylor Ward:
Try - Naylor:
CASTLEFORD - Lewis: Davies Croston Atkinson Cunniffe:

Walsh Adams: Banks Cottington Taylor Smith Crossley
Sadler:
Tries - Cunniffe(2) Walsh Croston Sadler: Goal - Atkinson:
Referee L Thorpe (Wakefield) Att - 3000 H.T. 6 - 3

Sat 12 Dec 1936 NEWCASTLE home won 31 - 8
CASTLEFORD - Lewis: Cunniffe Atkinson Croston Davies:
Hardy Adams: McManus Cottington Banks Smith Crossley
Sadler: Tries - Atkinson Adams Banks Smith Sadler:
Goals Lewis(8):
NEWCASTLE - James: Turton Maddock Knowles
Williamson: Pickard Dale: Walton Suddes McAvoy Taylor
Edwards Atherton:
Tries - Knowles McAvoy: Goal - James:
Referee B Laughlin (Batley) Att - 3000 H.T. 6 - 8

Sat 19 Dec 1936 BRAMLEY away won 16 - nil
BRAMLEY - Taylor: Davidson Lingard Rees Hodgkiss:
Starling Howarth: Walkington Bowden Graham Pearson
Webb Ballantyre:
CASTLEFORD - Lewis: Cunniffe Atkinson Croston Walker:
Hardy Adams: McManus Cottington Taylor Smith Crossley
Sadler: Tries - Cunniffe Atkinson Croston Walker:
Goals - Lewis Atkinson:
Referee J E Taylor (Wakefield) Att - 2500 H.T. 16 - nil

**Fri 25 Dec 1936 FEATHERSTONE ROVERS home
won 31 - 5**
CASTLEFORD - Lewis: Cunniffe Atkinson Davies Walker:
Hardy Walsh: Allen Cottington Taylor Banks Ambrose
Askin Sadler:
Tries - Walker(3) Atkinson(2) Cunniffe Hardy Banks Sadler:
Goals - Lewis(2)
FEATHERSTONE R - Dennis: Noble Brogden Naylor
Newton: Evans Lingard: Hemingway Morris Coulson
Taylor Bratley Sherwood:
Try - Taylor: Goal - Sherwood:
Referee S Adams (Hull) Att - 5000 H.T. 10 - nil

Sat 26 Dec 1936 YORK away won 15 - 7
YORK - Dingsdale: Isaac Moores Sullivan Richards: Rees
Hunt: Sharpe Field Coldrick Elias Fender Welsh:
Try - Richards: Goals - Dingsdale(2):
CASTLEFORD - Pollitt: Cunniffe Atkinson Croston Walker:
Hardy Adams: Taylor Cottington Allen Smith Crossley
Sadler:
Tries - Cunniffe(2) Adams: Goals - Pollitt(2) Atkinson:
Referee A Hill (Leeds) Att - 3000 H.T. 10 - 2

**Fri 1 Jan 1937 BRADFORD NORTHERN away
won 10- 5**
BRADFORD N - Carmichael: Jackson Winnard Murray
Grainge: Billington Spillane: Higson Dilorenzo Targett
Smith Morgan Moore:
Try - Jackson: Goal - Winnard:
CASTLEFORD - Pollitt: Cunniffe Atkinson Croston Walker:
Hardy Adams: Taylor Cottington Allen Smith Crossley
Sadler:
Tries - Croston Allen: Goals - Pollitt Atkinson:
Referee A E Harcing (Manchester) Att - 9000 H.T. 7 - nil

SEASON 1936-37

Sat 2 Jan 1937 WIGAN home lost nil - 7
CASTLEFORD - Pollitt: Cunniffe Atkinson Croston Walker:
Hardy Adams: Taylor Cottington Allen Smith Crossley
Sadler:
WIGAN - Sullivan: Morley Innes G.Davies Ellaby: Garvey
Gee: Banks Goby Edwards Thomas A.Davies Jones:
Try - Gee: Goals - Sullivan(2):
Referee -   Att - 9000 H.T. nil - 5

Sat 9 Jan 1937 KEIGHLEY away won 10 - 7
KEIGHLEY - Herbert: Orchard Sherburn Mason Lloyd:
Richards Phelps: Halliday Traill Jones McGoun Talbot
Dixon:
Try - Lloyd: Goals - Herbert Sherburn:
CASTLEFORD - Lewis: Cunniffe Atkinson Croston Walker:
Hardy Adams: Allen Cottington Taylor Banks Crossley
Sadler:
Tries - Cunniffe(2): Goals - Lewis(2):
Referee F Peel (Bradford) Att - 6000 H.T. 7 - 5

**Sat l6 Jan 1937 BRADFORD NORTHERN home
lost 11 - 12**
CASTLEFORD - Lewis: Cunniffe Atkinson Croston Walker:
Hardy Adams: Banks Cottington Allen Smith Crossley
Sadler:
Tries - Atkinson Walker Hardy: Goal - Atkinson:
BRADFORD N - Winnard: Jackson Hutchinson Murray
Grainge: Billington Spillane: Higson Dilorenzo Morgan
Smith Orford Moore:
Tries - Jacksonn Orford: Goals - Winnard(3):
Referee B Laughlin (Batley) Att - 7400 H.T. 5 - 3

**Sat 23 Jan 1937 HULL KINGSTON ROVERS away
lost 6 - 17**
HULL K R - White: Eastwood Foster Spamer Wood: Dale
Young: Brown Ramsden Thompson Eddoms Cayser
Tattersfield:
Tries - Wood Dale Brown: Goals - Tattersfield(3) Dale(DG):
CASTLEFORD - Lewis: Cunniffe Davies Croston Walker:
Hardy Walsh: McManus Haley Cottington Smith Crossley
Sadler:
Tries - Croston Sadler:
Referee A Hill (Leeds) Att - 2000 H.T. nil - 6

Sat 30 Jan 1937 HUDDERSFIELD home won 13 - 7
CASTLEFORD - Lewis: Cunniffe Atkinson Croston Walker:
Hardy ARTHUR GREEN(161): McManus Haley Taylor
Smith Crossley Sadler:
Tries - Cunniffe Hardy Green: Goals - Lewis(2):
HUDDERSFIELD - Scourfield: Madden Mountain Fiddes
Johnson: Pepperell Royal: Sherwood Watson Langford
Senior Tiffany Aspinall: Try - Royal: Goals - Sherwood(2):
Referee J E Taylor (Wakefield) Att - 4000 H.T. 11 - 5

Sat 6 Feb 1937 WIDNES away lost 2 - 10
WIDNES - Bradley: Evans Topping Barber Yates: Shannon
McCue: Silcock Jones Roberts McDowell Millington Hoey:
Tries - Topping Barber: Goals - Topping(2):
CASTLEFORD - John Pollitt: Cunniffe Atkinson Croston
Walker: Hardy Arthur Green: McManus Cottington Taylor

Smith Crossley Sadler:
Goal - Atkinson:
Referee B Laughlin (Batley) Att - 4000 H.T. 2 - 5

**Sat 13 Feb 1937 BATLEY away draw 2 - 2
CHALLENGE CUP ROUND 1**
BATLEY - Goldie: Nunn Pollard Kitson Farrar: Frowen
Blackburn: Oates Fallon Darlison Foley Hudson Brown:
Goal - Brown:
CASTLEFORD - Lewis: Cunniffe Atkinson Croston Walker:
Hardy Adams: McManus Cottington Taylor Smith Allen
Sadler:
Goal - Lewis:
Referee P Cowell (Warrington) Att - 10400 H.T. nil - nil

**Wed 17 Feb 1937 BATLEY home won 8 - 4
CHALLENGE CUP ROUND 1 REPLAY**
CASTLEFORD - Lewis: Cunniffe Atkinson Croston Walker:
Hardy Adams: McManus Cottington Taylor Smith Allen
Sadler:
Tries - Walker Sadler: Goal - Atkinson:
BATLEY - Goldie: Nunn Pollard Kitson Farrar: Frowen
Blackburn: Oates Fallon Darlison Foley Hudson Brown:
Goals - Brown(2):
Referee P Cowell (Warrington) Att - 10875 H.T. 3 - 2

Sat 20 Feb 1937 LIVERPOOL STANLEY home won 9 - 8
CASTLEFORD - Lewis: Hardy Atkinson Croston Walker:
William H Davies Adams: McManus Cottington Taylor
Smith Banks Sadler:
Try - Hardy: Goals - Lewis(2) Atkinson:
LIVERPOOL S - Belshaw: Robinson Howarth McDonnell
Maloney: Glover Frodsham: Davies Lowe Woods Shaw
Smith Stocks:
Tries - McDonnell Stocks: Goal - Belshaw:
Referee L Orford (St Helens) Att - 8200 H.T. 4 - nil

**Sat 27 Feb 1937 WIGAN home draw 5 - 5
CHALLENGE CUP ROUND 2**
CASTLEFORD - Lewis: Cunniffe Atkinson Croston Walker:
Hardy Adams: McManus Cottington Taylor Smith Allen
Sadler:
Try - Atkinson: Goal - Atkinson:
WIGAN - Sullivan: Holder Innes Davies Ellaby: Garvey Gee:
Banks Golby Gregory Thomas Harrison Jones:
Try - Garvey: Goals - Sullivan:
Referee A E Harding (Manchester) Att - 21000 H.T. 2 - 3

**Wed 3 Mar 1937 WIGAN away lost 6 - 13
CHALLENGE CUP ROUND 2 REPLAY**
WIGAN - Sullivan: Holder Innes Davies Morley: Garvey
Gee: Banks Golby Gregory Thomas Harrison Jones:
Tries - Gee(2) Holder: Goals - Sullivan(2):
CASTLEFORD - Lewis: Cunniffe Atkinson Croston Walker:
Hardy Adams: McManus Haley Taylor Allen Banks Sadler:
Tries - Cunniffe Walker:
Referee F Peel (Bradford) Att - 26000 H.T. 3 - 8

SEASON 1936-37

Sat 6 Mar 1937 WIDNES home won 13 - 5
CASTLEFORD - Lewis: Cunniffe Atkinson Croston Walker: Hardy Adams: GEORGE GREAVES(162) Cottington Taylor Smith Crossley Sadler:
Tries - Cunniffe Smith Crossley: Goals - Lewis Atkinson:
WIDNES - Jacks: Evans Topping Barber Yates: Shannon McCue: Silcock Jones Higgins Hoey Roberts Millington:
Try - Topping: Goal - Jacks:
Referee A E Harding (Manchester) Att - 4000 H.T. 5 - 3

Sat 20 Mar 1937 HULL home lost nil - 3
HULL - Miller: Davies Oliver Wilson Overton: Courtney Herbert: Thacker H Barlow L Barlow Dawson Booth Ellerington: Try - Davies:
CASTLEFORD - Lewis: Cunniffe Atkinson Croston Walker: Hardy Adams: T.L.Taylor Cottington Allen Smith ROBERT M.TAYLOR(163) Sadler:
Referee A Hill (Leeds) Att - 7000 H.T. nil - nil

Fri 26 Mar 1937 LEEDS away lost 2 - 9
LEEDS - Eaton: E.Harris F.Harris Pollard Brogden: Jones Jenkins: Dyer Murphy Prosser Jubb Tattersfield Whitehead: Tries - E.Harris Tattersfield Brogden:
CASTLEFORD - Lewis: Cunniffe Atkinson Croston Walker: Hardy Adams: McManus Cottington T.L.Taylor Smith R.Taylor Sadler: Goal - Lewis:
Referee J E Taylor (Wakefield) Att - 21000 H.T. nil - 6

Sat 27 Mar 1937 BROUGHTON RANGERS home draw nil - nil
CASTLEFORD - Lewis: Cunniffe Atkinson Croston Walker: Walsh Adams: McManus Cottington T.L.Taylor Smith R.Taylor Sadler:
BROUGHTON R - Howells: Briscoe Stott Abbott Cumberbatch: Kenney Thompson: Whitcombe Jones Hodgson Bunter Roughsedge Manning:
Referee P Cowell (Warrington) Att - 5000 H.T.

Mon 29 Mar 1937 YORK home won 22 - 7
CASTLEFORD - Lewis: Cunniffe Atkinson Croston Walker: Walsh Adams: T.L.Taylor Cottington Allen Smith R.Taylor Sadler: Tries - Walker(2) Atkinson Croston: Goals - Atkinson(4) Walsh(DG):
YORK - Dingsdale: Whitehead Moores Rees Sullivan: Hunt Thomas: Sharpe Field Coldrick Elias Waudby Fender:
Try - Whitehead: Goals - Dingsdale(2):
Referee J E Taylor (Wakefield) Att - 8000 H.T. 10 - 2

Sat 3 Apr 1937 HUDDERSFIELD away lost 9 - 28
HUDDERSFIELD - Scourfield: Johnson Madden Fiddes Markham: Pepperell Royal: Sherwood Whitehead Evans Tiffany Senior Aspinall:
Tries - Fiddes(2) Pepperell(2) Johnson Madden: Goals - Sherwood(5):
CASTLEFORD - Lewis: Cunniffe Atkinson Croston Hardy: Walsh Adams: McManus Cottington T.L.Taylor Allen Smith Sadler: Tries - Cunniffe Croston Cottington:
Referee S Adams (Hull) Att - 6000 H.T. 6 - 16

Sat 10 Apr 1937 BATLEY home won 34 - 17
CASTLEFORD - Lewis: England Atkinson Croston Walker: Walsh Hardy: T.L.Taylor Cottington Greaves Smith R.Taylor ANDY McMANUS(164):
Tries - Croston (4) England Atkinson Walsh Greaves: Goals - Atkinson(5)
BATLEY - Bennett: Farrar Pollard Kitson Goldie: Frower Blackburn: Oates Fallon Darlison Earnshaw Foley Brown:
Tries - Pollard(2) Brown: Goals - Brown(4):
Referee A Brown (Wakefield) Att - 3000 H.T. 18 - 7

Sat 17 Apr 1937 HULL away draw 5 - 5
HULL - Miller: Hurley Oliver Goodall Davies: Johnson Courtney: Stead G.Barlow Thacker Booth Morrell Ellerington: Try - Ellerington: Goal - Oliver:
CASTLEFORD - Lewis: Cunniffe Atkinson Walsh Walker: Hardy Adams: T.L.Taylor Cottington Greaves Smith R.Taylor Sadler: Try - Sadler: Goal - Atkinson:
Referee A Hill (Leeds) Att - 5000 H.T. 5 - 5

Mon 19 Apr 1937 WIGAN away won 13 - 10
WIGAN - Sullivan: Morley Innes Davies Holder: Garvey Gee: Banks Golby Kershaw Thomas Gregory Jones:
Tries - Innes Garvey: Goals - Sullivan(2):
CASTLEFORD - Lewis: Cunniffe Atkinson Croston Walker: Walsh Adams: Greaves Cottington T.L.Taylor R.Taylor Smith Sadler:
Tries - Croston(2) Cunniffe: Goals - Lewis Atkinson:
Referee J Armstrong (Hud'field) Att - 5000 H.T. 6 - 10

Sat 1 May 1937 WAKEFIELD TRINITY away lost nil -21
WAKEFIELD T - Teall: Milner Malpass Davies Whitworth: Goodfellow Herbert: Crossland Carter Eddom Exley Flowers Watsor:
Tries - Watson(2) Milner Malpass Davies: Goals - Milner(2)Teall(DG):
CASTLEFORD - ERNEST SCHOFIELD(165): Cunniffe Atkinson Croston Walker: Hardy Adams: Greaves Cottington T.L.Taylor Robert M.Taylor Smith Sadler:
Referee S Adams (Hull) Att - 3000 H.T. nil - 2

Thomas (Tot) Walsh
D. No 159
1936-37 to 1945-46

Gordon Cottington
D. No 160
1936-37 to 1945-46

SEASON 1936-37

D.N	PLAYER		DEBUT	L MATCH	APP	SUB	T.AP	TRI'S	G'LS	D.G	P'TS
21	ATKINSON	ARTHUR			35	0	35	13	23	0	85
79	LEWIS	GEORGE			37	0	37	1	49	1	103
98	ASKIN	THOMAS C.		07/11/1936	2	0	2	0	0	0	0
111	DAVIES	WILLIAM H.		20/02/1937	17	0	17	1	0	0	3
116	TAYLOR	THOMAS L.			39	0	39	0	0	0	0
117	ASKIN	AMBROSE		25/12/1936	2	0	2	0	0	0	0
133	HALEY	HAROLD			13	0	13	1	0	0	3
124	SMITH	FRANK Snr.			38	0	38	6	1	0	20
128	POLLITT	JOHN		06/02/1937	5	0	5	0	6	0	12
130	CROSTON	ALFRED JAMES			39	0	39	21	0	0	63
133	ADAMS	LESLIE			34	0	34	6	0	0	18
134	SADLER	EDWARD L.			42	0	42	11	0	0	33
135	CUNNIFFE	BERNARD			37	0	37	21	0	0	63
136	CROSSLEY	JAMES M.			28	0	28	4	0	0	12
139	ENGLAND	ERIC			1	0	1	1	0	0	3
141	McMANUS	PATRICK B.			16	0	16	0	0	0	0
144	HUGGETT	WILLIAM E. (BILL)			1	0	1	0	0	0	0
147	HARDY	THOMAS			38	0	38	7	0	0	21
148	WALKER	FRANK			37	0	37	14	3	0	48
150	BANKS	THOMAS			19	0	19	2	0	0	6
152	ALLEN	STANLEY			17	0	17	1	0	0	3
155	BOUCHER	WILFRED (BUCK)			1	0	1	0	0	0	0
158	ROBINSON	GILBERT	19/09/1936	10/10/1936	2	0	2	0	0	0	0
159	WALSH	THOMAS	24/10/1936		12	0	12	2	0	1	8
160	COTTINGTON	GORDON	24/10/1936		30	0	30	1	0	0	3
161	GREEN	ARTHUR	30/01/1937	06/02/1937	2	0	2	1	0	0	3
162	GREAVES	GEORGE	06/03/1937		5	0	5	1	0	0	3
163	TAYLOR	ROBERT M.	20/03/1937	01/05/1937	8	0	8	0	0	0	0
164	McMANUS	ANDY	10/04/1937	10/04/1937	1	0	1	0	0	0	0
165	SCHOFIELD	ERNEST	01/05/1937	01/05/1937	1	0	1	0	0	0	0
	30		8	9	559	0	559	115	82	2	513

	COMPETITION		P	W	D	L	FOR	AGT
RL RECORDS	LEAGUE		38	25	2	11	490	325

THESE REORDS SCORES AND SCORERS MATCH

			P	W	D	L	FOR	AGT
	LEAGUE	POSITION 6 OF 30	38	25	2	11	492	325
	YORK'S CUP		1	0	0	1	0	7
	RL CUP		4	1	2	1	21	24
	PLAYERS RECORDS		43	26	4	13	513	356

In the league Newcastle replaced Acton & Willesden and the London Club Streatham & Mitcham withdrew after playing 26 matches, their remaining 12 fixtures being counted as wins for their opponents with Castleford benefiting from this ruling by being awarded four league points.

The home game against Broughton Rangers on 27 March 1937 resulted in another of those infrequent scores nil–nil.

George Lewis became the first player to kick 200 goals in the 12–9 victory against Batley away on 3 October 1936.

Once again Arthur Atkinson was selected for the Great Britain team to tour Australasia.

This season was the most successful league campaign to date, with Castleford finishing in sixth place.

SEASON 1937-38

Sat 2l Aug 1937 FEATHERSTONE ROVERS home lost 11 - 22 LYON CUP - FRIENDLY
CASTLEFORD - Staines: Walker Croston Atkinson Hardy: Davies Adams: McManus Cottington Greaves Smith Crossley I.Williams:
Tries - Walker Croston Hardy: Goal - Staines:
FEATHERSTONE R - Pollitt: Newton Hammond Naylor Asquith: Evans Ward: Hemingway Darlison Sherwood Dyson J.Evans Taylor: Tries - Newton Asquith Ward Sherwood: Goals - Sherwood(5):
Referee A S Dobson (Pontefract) Att-2000 H.T. 8 - 10

Sat 28 Aug 1937 HULL KINGSTON ROVERS home won 15 - 14
CASTLEFORD - Lewis: Cunniffe MATTHEW KILLINGBECK(166) Croston Walker: Hardy Adams: McManus Haley Taylor Smith Greaves Crossley:
Tries - Croston(2) Hardy: Goals - Killingbeck(2) Lewis:
HULL K R - White: Edmonds McWatt Spamer Eastwood: Young Dale: Maskill Ramsden Thompson Beaumont Jordan Cayser:
Tries - Eastwood Young: Goals - McWatt(4):
Referee E Devine (Leeds) Att - 4000 H.T. 7 - 2

Wed 1 Sep 1937 HUDDERSFIELD away lost 11 - 26
HUDDERSFIELD - Scourfield: Madden Fiddes Mountain Markham: Pepperell Royal: Sherwood Whitehead Evans Shaw Aspinall McDonald: Tries - Madden Mountain Royal McDonald: Goals Fiddes(7):
CASTLEFORD - Lewis: Cunniffe Killingbeck Croston Walker: Hardy Adams: McManus Haley Taylor Smith Crossley George Greaves: Try - Walker: Goals - Lewis(4):
Referee F Peel (Bradford) Att - 6000 H.T. 4 - 21

Sat 4 Sep 1937 HUNSLET away won 13 - 3
HUNSLET - Walkington: Batten Wilson Winter Yates: Johnson Thornton: Tolson White Stansfield Bennett Wagstaff Beverley: Try - Winter:
CASTLEFORD - Lewis: Cunniffe Killingbeck Croston Walker: Hardy Adams: McManus Haley Taylor Smith Banks Crossley:
Tries - Walker Hardy Smith: Goals - Lewis(2):
Referee J E Taylor (Wakefield) Att - 5000 H.T. 3 - 3

Sat 11 Sep 1937 DEWSBURY home lost 6 - 8 YORKSHIRE CUP ROUND 1
CASTLEFORD - Lewis: Cunniffe Atkinson Croston Walker: Hardy Adams: McManus Haley Taylor Smith Banks Crossley: Goals - Lewis(2) Atkinson:
DEWSBURY - Chester: Hobson Western Hunter Veysey: Davies Werrett: Hammond Crabtree McTiffin Morgan Prescott Seeling: Tries - Hunter Werrett: Goal - Chester:
Referee G S Phillips (Widnes) Att - 8300 H.T. 4 - 3

Sat 18 Sep 1937 BRAMLEY away won 14 - 3
BRAMLEY - Taylor: Hodgkiss Rees Lingard Davidson: Phelps Adams: Dyson Graham Walkington Mason Pearson Webb: Try - Phelps:
CASTLEFORD - Lewis: Cunniffe Atkinson Killingbeck Hardy: Walsh Adams: McManus Haley Taylor Crossley

Banks FRED BRINDLE(167):
Tries - Killingbeck(2) Lewis Cunniffe: Goal - Lewis:
Referee S Adams (Hull) Att - 1500 H.T. 3 - 3

Sat 25 Sep 1937 SALFORD home won 21 - 4
CASTLEFORD - Lewis: Cunniffe Atkinson Croston Killingbeck: Hardy Adams: McManus Haley Taylor Crossley Banks Brindle:
Tries - Cunniffe Atkinson Croston: Goals - Lewis(6):
SALFORD - Osbaldestin: Brown Gear Risman Edwards: Miller Watkins: Williams Day Reeve Cambridge Davies Dalton: Goals - Risman(2):
Referee F Fairhurst (Wigan) Att - 8600 H.T. 9 - 4

Sat 2 Oct 1937 BATLEY home won 39 - 8
CASTLEFORD - Lewis: Cunniffe Atkinson Croston Killingbeck: Hardy Adams: McManus Haley Taylor Crossley Banks Brindle:
Tries - Croston(3) Cunniffe Atkinson Killingbeck Hardy Crossley Brindle: Goals - Lewis(6):
BATLEY - Bennett: Nunn Pollard Cecil Goldie: Frowen Bone: Renton Fallon Darlison Hudson Farrar Brown: Goals - Brown(3)(DG):
Referee J F Armstrong (Hud'field) Att - 6500 H.T. 18 - 6

Sat 9 Oct 1937 HULL KINGSTON ROVERS away won 23 - 10
HULL K R - McWatt: Edwards Perrett Spamer Eastwood: Dale McGowar: Thompson Shillito Maskill Greaves Middleton Beaumont(S/O):
Tries - Eastwood McGowan: Goals - Dale(2):
CASTLEFORD - Lewis: Cunniffe Atkinson Croston Killingbeck: Hardy Adams: McManus Cottington Taylor Crossley Smith Brindle: Tries - Croston(2) Killingbeck(2) Smith: Goals - Lewis(3) Atkinson:
Referee A Devine (Leeds) Att - 7500 H.T. 11 - 7

Sat 16 Oct 1937 ST HELENS RECS away lost 10 - 12
ST HELENS R - E.Dixon: Pimblett Bailey Beesley Grundy: Tracy H.Dixon: Parr Lewington Dunn Atherton Winstanley Jennion:
Tries - Pimblett Atherton: Goals - Winstanley(3):
CASTLEFORD - Lewis: Eric England Atkinson Killingbeck Walker: Hardy Adams: McManus Cottington WILLIAM STEAD(168) Smith Crossley Brindle:
Tries - Killingbeck(2): Goals - Lewis(2):
Referee A Hill (Leeds) Att - 2170 H.T. 3 - 12

Sat 23 Oct 1937 WAKEFIELD TRINITY home won 26 - 9
CASTLEFORD - Lewis: ILLTYD(TUBBY)M.WILLIAMS(169) Atkinson Croston Killingbeck: Hardy Adams: McManus Cottington Taylor Crossley Banks Brindle:
Tries - Lewis Williams Atkinson Croston Killingbeck Adams: Goals - Lewis(3) Killingbeck:
WAKEFIELD T - Teall: Whitworth Turner Malpass Stott: Herbert Goodfellow: Wilkinson Lee Eddom Exley Flowers(S/O) Watson: Try - Malpass: Goals - Lee(3):
Referee B Laughlin (Batley) Att - 5000 H.T. 15 - 2

Sat 30 Oct 1937 BRADFORD NORTHERN away lost 3 - 15

BRADFORD N - Carmichael: Jackson Winnard Pollard Grainge: Billington Spillane: Higson Dilorenzo Morgan Harrison Smith Moore:
Tries - Billington(2) Winnard: Goals - Pollard(3):
CASTLEFORD - Lewis: Williams Atkinson Croston Killingbeck: Hardy Adams: McManus Haley Taylor Crossley Thomas Banks Brindle:
Try - Atkinson:
Referee J E Taylor (Wakefield) Att - 11000 H.T. nil - 5

Sat 6 Nov 1937 ST HELENS RECS home won 15 - 6
CASTLEFORD - Lewis: Walsh Atkinson Croston Killingbeck: Hardy Adams: McManus Haley Taylor Stead Crossley Brindle:
Tries - Killingbeck(2) Walsh Hardy Haley:
ST HELENS R - Lythgoe: Grundy Bailey E.Dixon Large: Tracy H.Dixon: Parr Lewington Dunn Winstanley Rankin Moran:
Tries - Large Tracy:
Referee J W Webb (Manchester) Att-3000 H.T. 12 - 3

Sat 13 Nov 1937 WARRINGTON away won 14 - 3
WARRINGTON - Jones: Garrett Brown Shankland Davies: DeLloyd Cueto: Miller Cotton Hardman Welsby Bennett Chapman:
Try - Davies:
CASTLEFORD - Lewis: Walsh Atkinson Croston Killingbeck: Hardy Adams: McManus Haley Taylor Smith Crossley Brindle:
Tries - Croston Hardy: Goals - Lewis(4):
Referee F Peel (Bradford) Att - 7500 H.T. 2 - 3

Sat 20 Nov 1937 BRADFORD NORTHERN home won 17 - 9
CASTLEFORD - Lewis: CYRIL WILLIAMS(170) Atkinson Croston Killingbeck: Hardy Adams: Stead Haley Taylor Smith Crossley Brindle:
Tries - C.Williams Adams Stead Haley Smith:
Goal - Killingbeck:
BRADFORD N - Carmichael: Jackson Winnard Pollard Grainge: Billington Hayes: Higson Dilorenzo Edwards Harrison Smith Moore:
Try - Billington: Goals - Pollard(2) Winnard:
Referee L Thorpe (Wakefield) Att - 13000 H.T. 11 - 2

Sat 27 Nov 1937 HULL away lost nil - 7
HULL - Miller: Hurley Oliver Wilson Corner: Johnson Courtney: Thacker G.H.Barlow L.Barlow Booth Dawson Ellerington:
Try - Corner: Goals - Oliver Miller(DG):
CASTLEFORD - Lewis: C.Williams Atkinson Croston Killingbeck: Hardy Adams: McManus Haley Taylor Stead Smith Brindle:
Referee E Devine (Leeds) Att - 7000 H.T. nil - 7

Sat 4 Dec 1937 FEATHERSTONE ROVERS home won 7 - 2
CASTLEFORD - Lewis: C.Williams Atkinson Croston Killingbeck: Walsh Adams: McManus Haley Taylor Smith I.M.Williams Brindle: Try - Croston: Goals - Lewis(2):

FEATHERSTONE R - Pollitt: Asquith Naylor Dennis Newton: W.Evans Hamer: Pearson A.N.Other Hemingway Dyson Taylor Sherwood: Goal - Sherwood:
Referee P Hughes (Bramley) Att - 1000 H.T. 7 - nil

Sat 18 Dec 1937 HUNSLET home won 26 - 10
CASTLEFORD - Lewis: C.Williams Atkinson Croston Killingbeck: Hardy Adams: McManus Haley Taylor Smith Crossley Brindle:
Tries - Killingbeck(3) C.Williams Atkinson Croston:
Goals - Lewis(2) Atkinson Killingbeck:
HUNSLET - Walkington: Batten Morrell Yates Jenner: Morris Thornton: Tolson(S/O) White Thompson Tiffany Newbound Stansfield:
Tries - Jenner Morris: Goals - Walkington Thornton(DG):
Referee S Adams (Hull) Att - 9000 H.T. 13 - 2

Sat 25 Dec 1937 FEATHERSTONE ROVERS away won 17 - 4
FEATHERSTONE R - Pollitt: Asquith Davies Hammond Newton: Hughes Ward: Hemingway Mullins Pearson Evans Taylor Sherwood: Goals - Sherwood(2):
CASTLEFORD - Lewis: C.Williams Atkinson Croston Killingbeck: Hardy Adams: McManus Haley Taylor Smith Crossley Brindle:
Tries - Killingbeck(4) Taylor: Goal - Lewis:
Referee T Marley (Wakefield) Att - 6000 H.T. 11 - 2
Match Abandoned After 68 Minutes For Fog – Result Stood

Mon 27 Dec 1937 YORK home home won 25 - 5
CASTLEFORD - Lewis: C.Williams Atkinson Croston Killingbeck: Hardy Adams: McManus Haley Stead Smith Crossley Brindle:
Tries - Croston(2) Killingbeck Stead Smith:
Goals - Lewis(4) Killingbeck:
YORK - Knowles: Bainbridge Isaac Richards Bean: Hunt Ridgewell: Sharpe Williams Wheatley Fender Elias Welsh:
Try - Bainbridge: Goal - Knowles:
Referee J E Taylor (Wakefield) Att - 6500 H.T. 15 - nil

Sat 1 Jan 1938 WARRINGTON home draw 10 - 10
CASTLEFORD - Killingbeck: Cunniffe Atkinson Croston C.Williams: Hardy Adams: McManus Haley Taylor Smith(S/O) Crossley Brindle:
Tries - Croston Adams: Goals - Killingbeck(2):
WARRINGTON - Holding: Garrett Brown Dingsdale Jenkins: De Lloyd Cueto: Hardman Cotton Miller Arkwright Bennett Chapman:
Tries - Cueto Chapman: Goals - Holding(2):
Referee A E Harding (Manchester) Att-12000 H.T. 5-7

Sat 8 Jan 1938 DEWSBURY away lost 10 - 14
DEWSBURY - Chester: Wood Johnson Hunter Veysey: Nicholson Bowen: McTiffin Hammond Wormald Prescott Osborne Morgan:
Tries - Wood Veysey: Goals - Chester(4):
CASTLEFORD - Walker: Cunniffe Atkinson Croston Killingbeck: Hardy Adams: McManus Haley Taylor Crossley Allen Brindle:

SEASON 1937-38

Tries - Killingbeck Hardy: Goals - Killingbeck(2):
Referee F Peel (Bradford) Att - 5000 H.T. nil - 4

Sat 15 Jan 1938 HUDDERSFIELD home won 6 - nil
CASTLEFORD - GORDON BONNER(171): C.Williams
Atkinson Croston Killingbeck: Hardy Walsh: McManus
Haley Taylor Crossley Stead Brindle:
Tries - Croston Killingbeck:
HUDDERSFIELD - Lockwood: Johnson Bailey Fiddes
Madden: Graham Royal: Sherwood Whitehead Langford
Shaw Booth McDonald:
Referee E Devine (Leeds) Att - 4200 H.T. nil - nil

Sat 22 Jan 1938 WIGAN away lost 5 - 12
WIGAN - Sullivan: Holder Williamson Ward Moray: Garvey
H.Gee: K.Gee Golby Sharratt Kershaw Thomas Jones:
Tries - Holder Williamson: Goals - Sullivan(3):
CASTLEFORD - Lewis: C.Williams Atkinson Croston
Killingbeck: Hardy Walsh: McManus Haley Taylor Stead
Crossley Brindle: Try - Stead: Goal - Lewis:
Referee J F Armstrong (Hud'field) Att - 11000 H.T. nil - 5

Sat 29 Jan 1938 KEIGHLEY home won 3 - nil
CASTLEFORD - Lewis: C.Williams Atkinson CHARLES
STAINES(172) Killingbeck: Hardy Walsh: McManus
Cottington Taylor Crossley(S/O) Stead Brindle:
Try - Atkinson:
KEIGHLEY - Farrington: Sherburn Towill Hammond Lloyd:
Horrod Spillane: Traill Halliday Fuller Thornber Butler Gill:
Referee S Adams (Hull) Att - 5000 H.T. 3 - nil

Sat 5 Feb 1938 SALFORD away lost 5 - 8
SALFORD - Osbaldestin: Hudson Gear Brown Edwards:
Risman Watkins: Williams Day Davies Dalton Thomas
Feetham: Tries - Osbaldestin Edwards: Goal - Risman:
CASTLEFORD - Lewis: Cunniffe Atkinson GORDON
INNES(173) C.Williams: Hardy Adams: McManus Haley
Taylor Stead Crossley Brindle:
Try - Hardy: Goal - Lewis:
Referee E Devine (Leeds) Att - 12000 H.T. nil - 3

Sat 12 Feb 1938 WAKEFIELD TRINITY away won 9 - 2
WAKEFIELD T - Teall: Watson Turner Whitworth
Appleyard: Malpass Herbert: Wilkinson Lee Eddom Exley
Flowers Bratley: Goal - Lee:
CASTLEFORD - Lewis: C.Williams Atkinson Innes Walker:
Hardy Walsh: Stead Cottington Taylor Smith Crossley
I.M.Williams:
Try - Atkinson: Goals - Lewis(2) Atkinson:
Referee A Hill (Leeds) Att - 9000 H.T. 9 - nil

Sat 19 Feb 1938 NEWCASTLE home won 18 - 9 CHALLENGE CUP ROUND 1
CASTLEFORD - Lewis: Cunniffe Atkinson Croston
C.Williams: Innes Adams: Stead Cottington Taylor Smith
Crossley Brindle:
Tries - C.Williams(2) Adams(2) Goals - Lewis(3):
NEWCASTLE - Evans: Ryan Davies Tetlow Cumberbatch:
Beattie Frowen: Walton Suddes Atherton Grimshaw
Ellerington Foster:

Tries - Ryan(3):
Referee E Houghton (Warrington) Att - 8020 H.T. 5 - 4

Sat 26 Feb 1938 LIVERPOOL STANLEY home won 14 - 6
CASTLEFORD - Lewis: Cunniffe Atkinson Croston
C.Williams: Hardy Walsh: McManus Haley Taylor Stead
Smith Brindle:
Tries - Croston Stead: Goals - Lewis(4):
LIVERPOOL S - Bolland: Howarth Gutteridghe Robinson
Maloney: Jones Burkhill: Davies Lowe Nolan Smith Gray
Shaw:
Goals - Bolland(2) Shaw(DG):
Referee J Orford (St Helens) Att - 7000 H.T. 4 - 4

Sat 5 Mar 1938 BRAMLEY home won 21 - 12
CASTLEFORD - Lewis: Innes Atkinson Croston C.Williams:
Hardy Walsh: McManus Cottington Taylor Smith Stead
Brindle:
Tries - Lewis Atkinson Croston C.Williams Smith:
Goals - Lewis(3):
BRAMLEY - H.Taylor: Fletcher Murphy Smith Cowling:
Rees Phelps: Desborough Harling Graham Mason Gater
S.Taylor:
Tries - Murphy Cowling: Goals - H.Taylor(3):
Referee J F Armstrong (Hud'field) Att - 6500 H.T. 9 - 7

Sat 12 Mar 1938 ST HELENS home won 18 - 2 CHALLENGE CUP ROUND 2
CASTLEFORD - Lewis: C.Williams Atkinson Croston
Killingbeck: Hardy Walsh: McManus Haley Taylor Smith
Stead Brindle:
Tries - Killingbeck Hardy Smith Brindle: Goals - Lewis(3):
ST HELENS - Butler: Ellaby Twist Fearnley Powell: Myers
Bradbury: Hill Roberts Smith Hughes Garner Hutchinson:
Goal - Powell:
Referee J W Webb (Manchester) Att-12577 H.T. 8-nil

Sat 19 Mar 1938 DEWSBURY home lost 10 - 15
CASTLEFORD - Lewis: C.Williams Atkinson Innes
Killingbeck: Boucher Walsh: Stead Cottington Taylor
Smith Crossley Brindle:
Tries - Innes Boucher: Goals - Lewis(2):
DEWSBURY - Johnson: Wood Sullivan Western Veysey:
Nicholson Werrett: Hammond Whitham Crabtree Morgan
Osborne Seelir g:
Tries - Veysey Werrett Morgan: Goals - Western Morgan
Johnson(DG):
Referee F Fairhurst (Wigan) Att - 1300 H.T. 10 - nil

Sat 26 Mar 1938 HALIFAX home draw 7 - 7 CHALLENGE CUP ROUND 3
CASTLEFORD - Lewis: Innes Atkinson Croston C.Williams:
Hardy Walsh: McManus Haley Taylor Stead Crossley
Brindle: Try - Innes: Goals - Lewis(2):
HALIFAX - Lockwood: Hickey Treen Smith Bevan: Todd
Goodall: Baynham Field Kay Irving Cox Beverley:
Try - Irving: Goals - Lockwood(2):
Referee A Holbrook (Warrington) Att - 24355 H.T. 4 - 7

Wed 30 Mar 1938 HALIFAX away lost 7 - 11 CHALLENGE CUP ROUND 3 REPLAY
HALIFAX - Lockwood: Hickey Smith Treen Bevan: Todd Goodall: Baynham Field Irving Chadwick Cox Dixon: Tries - Hickey Treen Bevan: Goal - Lockwood: CASTLEFORD - Lewis: C.Williams Atkinson Croston Killingbeck: Hardy Walsh: McManus Haley Taylor Stead Crossley Brindle: Try - Croston: Goals - Lewis(1)(DG): Referee A Holbrook (Warrington) Att - 25214 H.T. nil - 3

Sat 2 Apr 1938 WIGAN home won 32 - 2
CASTLEFORD - Lewis: C.Williams Atkinson Croston Innes: Hardy Walsh: McManus Haley Taylor Stead Crossley Brindle: Tries - Croston(2) Hardy(2) Atkinson Innes: Goals - Lewis(3) Atkinson(4): WIGAN - Newey: Holder Williamson Ward C Davies: Jenkins H.Gee: Banks Golby K.Gee Woods A.Davies Jones: Goal - Jenkins: Referee G S Phillips (Widnes) Att - 8000 H.T. 18 - nil

Thu 7 Apr 1938 LIVERPOOL STANLEY away won 5 - 4
LIVERPOOL S - Gutteridge: Worthington Jones Robinson Maloney: Howarth Burkhill: Davies Lowe Nolan Smith Shaw Grundy: Goals - Nolan(2): CASTLEFORD - Lewis: Innes Atkinson Croston C.Williams: Hardy Walsh: McManus Haley Taylor Stead Crossley Brindle: Try - Stead: Goal - Atkinson: Referee F Peel (Bradford) Att -   H.T. 5 - 2

Sat 9 Apr 1938 KEIGHLEY away lost 2 - 7
KEIGHLEY - Farrington: Sherburn Towill Bevan Lloyd: Horrod Sowden: Traill Holiday McGoun Thormber Casewell Gill: Try - Horrod: Goals - Farrington(2): CASTLEFORD - Lewis: Innes Atkinson Croston C.Williams: Hardy Walsh: McManus Haley Taylor Smith Stead Brindle: Goal - Atkinson: Referee E Devine (Leeds) Att - 5500 H.T. 2 - 5

Mon 11 Apr 1938 HULL home won 20 - 8
CASTLEFORD - Lewis: Cunniffe Atkinson Croston Innes: Hardy I.M.Williams: McManus Cottington Taylor Crossley Stead Brindle: Tries - Croston(2) Atkinson I.M.Williams: Goals - Lewis(4): HULL - Miller: Hurley Wilson Corner Dockar: Herbert Johnson: Morrell G.H.Barlow L.Barlow Thacker Wray Booth: Tries - Dockar Wray: Goal - Miller: Referee A Hill (Leeds) Att - 5910 H.T. 5 - 5

Fri 15 Apr 1938 LEEDS home lost 4 - 19 CASTLEFORD
- Lewis: Innes Atkinson Croston Cyril Williams: Hardy I.M.Williams: McManus Haley Taylor Stead Crossley Brindle: Goals - Atkinson(2): LEEDS - Eaton: E.Harris F.Harris Brogden Smith: Hey Jenkins: Dyer Murphy Prosser Jubb Whitehead Watson: Tries - E.Harris(2) Brogden(2) Jenkins: Goals - Eaton Brogden(DG): Referee S Adams (Hull) Att - 23000 H.T. 4 - 11

Sat 16 Apr 1938 BATLEY away lost 3 - 14
BATLEY - Bennett: Nunn Pollard Kitson Brown: Cecil Ralph: Rhodes Hall Darlison Hudson Foley Oakland: Tries - Nunn Brown: Goals - Brown(4): CASTLEFORD - Lewis: Cunniffe Atkinson Innes Matthew Killingbeck E.William Huggett: I.M.Williams: McManus Cottington Taylor Stead Smith Crossley: Try - Smith: Referee T Marley (Wakefield) Att - 5000 H.T. nil - 4

Mon 18 Apr 1938 YORK away won 17 - 13
YORK - Knowles: Taylor Moores Parker Ryan: Hunt Richards: Sharpe Williams Wheatley White Welsh Wilson: Tries - Moores Parker Wheatley: Goals - Knowles(2): CASTLEFORD - Lewis: Cunniffe Innes Staines Walker: Boucher LEONARD GARBETT(174): Stead Haley Stanley Allen Smith Crossley I.M.Williams: Tries - Cunniffe(2) Smith: Goals - Lewis(2) Walker(2): Referee B Laughlin (Batley) Att - 6000 H.T. 10 - 2

Tue 19 Apr 1938 LEEDS away lost 9 - 24
LEEDS - Eaton: E.Harris Williams Lingard Brogden: Hey Jenkins: Prosser Murphy Dyer Jibb Whitehead Watson: Tries - Lingard(3) Harris(2) Brogden: Goals - Williams(2) Whitehead: CASTLEFORD - Gordon Bonner: Cunniffe Innes Staines Walker: Boucher Garbett: McManus Cottington Taylor Stead Smith Crossley: Try - Walker: Goals - Walker(3): Referee F Peel (Bradford) Att - 17000 H.T. 5 – 8

Fred Bridle
D. No 167
1937-38 to 1946-47

Charlie Staines
D .No 172
1937-38 to 1950-51

SEASON 1937-38

D.N	PLAYER		DEBUT	L MATCH	APP	SL B	T.AP	TRI'S	G'LS	D.G	P'TS
21	ATKINSON	ARTHUR			36	0	36	10	12	0	54
79	LEWIS	GEORGE			37	0	37	3	74	1	159
116	TAYLOR	THOMAS L.			38	0	38	1	0	0	3
123	HALEY	HAROLD			30	0	30	2	0	0	6
124	SMITH	FRANK Snr			24	0	24	8	0	0	24
130	CROSTON	ALFRED JAMES			32	0	32	23	0	0	69
133	ADAMS	LESLIE			23	0	23	5	0	0	15
135	CUNNIFFE	BERNARD			17	0	17	5	0	0	15
136	CROSSLEY	JAMES M.			35	0	35	1	0	0	3
139	ENGLAND	ERIC		16/10/1937	1	0	1	0	0	0	0
141	McMANUS	PATRICK B.			36	0	36	0	0	0	0
144	HUGGETT	WILLIAM E.(BILL)		16/04/1938	1	0	1	0	0	0	0
147	HARDY	THOMAS			35	0	35	10	0	0	30
148	WALKER	FRANK			9	0	9	3	5	0	19
150	BANKS	THOMAS		30/10/1937	7	0	7	0	0	0	0
152	ALLEN	STANLEY		18/04/1938	2	0	2	0	0	0	0
155	BOUCHER	WILFRED (BUCK)			3	0	3	1	0	0	3
159	WALSH	THOMAS			17	0	17	1	0	0	3
160	COTTINGTON	GORDON			11	0	11	0	0	0	0
162	GREAVES	GEORGE		01/09/1937	2	0	2	0	0	0	0
166	KILLINGBECK	MATTHEW	28/08/1937	16/04/1938	27	0	27	21	10	0	83
167	BRINDLE	FRED	18/09/1937		33	0	33	2	0	0	6
168	STEAD	WILLIAM	16/10/1937		25	0	25	5	0	0	15
169	WILLIAMS	ILLTYD (Tubby)	23/10/1937		8	0	8	2	0	0	6
170	WILLIAMS	CYRIL	20/11/1937	15/04/1938	23	0	23	5	0	0	15
171	BONNER	GORDON	15/01/1938	19/04/1938	2	0	2	0	0	0	0
172	STAINES	CHARLIE	29/01/1938		3	0	3	0	0	0	0
173	INNES	GORDON	05/02/1938		14	0	14	3	0	0	9
174	GARBETT	LEONARD	18/04/1938		2	0	2	0	0	0	0
	29		**9**	**8**	**533**	**0**	**533**	**111**	**101**	**1**	**537**

COMPETITION		P	W	D	L	FOR	AGT
LEAGUE	POSITION 7 OF 30	36	23	1	12	481	320
YORK'S CUP		1	0	0	1	6	8
RL CUP		4	2	1	1	50	29
PLAYERS RECORDS		**41**	**25**	**2**	**14**	**537**	**357**

With a great deal of attention being focused at the present time on attendances, it is interesting to note the number of spectators being attracted to games this season both at home and away.

There were 33 games were the attendance was over 5,000, 10 games where the attendance exceeded 10,000 and two games where the attendance exceeded 20,000. These two games were in the third round of the Challenge Cup. A crowd of 24,355 attended the 7–7 draw against Halifax at home on 26 March 1938 and four days later in the replay at Halifax on 30 March 1938 a crowd of 25,214 witnessed a Halifax victory by 11–7.

Sat 20 Aug 1938 FEATHERSTONE ROVERS Away won 30 - 12   LYON CUP - FRIENDLY
FEATHERSTONE R - Goldie: Asquith Kelly Blackburn Longley: Hughes Moxon: Hemingway Mullins Dyson Taylor Evans Ward:
Tries - Ward(2): Goals - Goldie(2) Ward(DG):
CASTLEFORD - Lewis: Cunniffe Innes Boucher Walker: Hardy Green: McManus Haley Stead Williams Horan Brindle:
Tries - Lewis Cunniffe Innes Boucher Walker Hardy Williams Horan: Goals - Walker(3):
Referee A S Dobson (Pontefract) Att -   H.T. 17 - 7

Sat 27 Aug 1938 SWINTON home won 12 - 9
CASTLEFORD - Lewis: Cunniffe Atkinson Croston Innes: Hardy Garbett: McManus Haley Taylor Stead JOHN HORAN(175) Brindle:
Tries - Atkinson Stead: Goals - Lewis(3):
SWINTON - Barnes: Hickman Lewis Green Warry: Evans Dempsey: Stoddart Armitt Hughes Hodgson Williams Butters:
Try - Butters: Goals - Hodgson(2) Barnes(DG):
Referee F Fairhurst (Wigan) Att - 7500 H.T. 7 - 2

Sat 3 Sept 1938 BARROW away lost 7 - 8
BARROW - French: Cumberbatch Biggin Gummer Thornburrow: McDonnell Little: Blackburn Wood Skelly Hattersley Ayres Marklew:
Tries - Cumberbatch Gummer: Goal - French(DG):
CASTLEFORD - Lewis: Walker Atkinson Croston Innes: Hardy Garbett: Stead Haley Taylor Horan Staines Brindle:
Try - Garbett: Goals - Staines(2):
Referee E Devine (Leeds) Att - 10500 H.T. nil - 5

Sat 10 Sept 1938 HULL KINGSTON ROVERS away lost nil - 12   YORKSHIRE CUP ROUND 1
HULL K R - White: Eastwood Oliver McWatt Hutchinson: Morgan Naylor: Shillito Ramsden Maskell Clarke Blanchard Cayser:
Tries - Naylor Blanchard: Goals - Oliver(3):
CASTLEFORD - Lewis: Cunniffe Atkinson Croston Innes: Hardy Garbett: McManus Cottington Taylor Stead Staines Brindle:
Referee E Houghton (Warrington) Att - 5000 H.T. nil - 5

Wed 14 Sept 1938 WIGAN home won 15 - 13
CASTLEFORD - Lewis: Cunniffe Atkinson Boucher Walker: Hardy Adams: Stead Haley Taylor Staines Smith Brindle:
Tries - Cunniffe Hardy Adams: Goals - Walker(3):
WIGAN - Sullivan: Morley Ward Williamson Holder: Garvey H.Gee: Banks Golby K.Gee Thomas Kershaw Bowen:
Tries - Ward(2) Morley: Goals - Sullivan(2):
Referee A Holbrook (Warrington) Att - 5000 H.T. 9 - 5

Sat 17 Sept 1938 HULL home won 9 - 4
CASTLEFORD - Lewis: Cunniffe Atkinson(S/O)Croston Walker: Hardy Adams: Stead Haley Taylor Staines Sadler Brindle:
Try - Croston: Goals - Walker(3):

HULL - Miller: Hurley Brogden Wilson(S/O)Overton: Herbert Johnson Thacker G.Barlow L.Barlow Booth Dawson Ellerington:
Goals - Miller(2):
Referee F Peel (Bradford) Att - 9000 H.T. 2 - nil

Sat 24 Sept 1938 FEATHERSTONE ROVERS away won 30 - 8
FEATHERSTONE R - Goldie: Asquith L.Davies Naylor Barker: Ward Moxon: Senior Mullins Dyson Pearson Taylor Aspinall:
Tries - Davies(2): Goal - Ward:
CASTLEFORD - Lewis: Cunniffe Atkinson Croston Walker: Hardy Adams: Stead Haley Taylor Staines Sadler Brindle:
Tries - Croston(2) Brindle(2) Walker Staines:
Goals - Walker(6):
Referee A Hill (Leeds) Att - 4000 H.T. 7 - 5

Wed 28 Sept 1938 DEWSBURY away won 15 - 6
DEWSBURY - Chester: Wood Moore Western Johnson: Cunliffe Sullivan: Hammond Nicholson Crabtree Ellis Prescott Morgan:
Tries - Johnson Morgan:
CASTLEFORD - Lewis: Cunniffe Atkinson Croston Walker: Boucher Adams: Stead Haley Taylor Staines Sadler Brindle:
Tries - Atkinson Croston Haley: Goals - Walker(3):
Referee S Adams (Hull) Att - 3000 H.T. 12 - nil

Sat 1 Oct 1938 WARRINGTON home won 12 - 8
CASTLEFORD - Lewis: Cunniffe Innes Croston Walker: Boucher Adams: Stead Haley Taylor Staines Sadler Brindle:
Tries - Croston Adams: Goals - Walker(2) Lewis(DG):
WARRINGTON - Brown: Peake Davies Dingsdale Jenkins: De Lloyd Parker: Edge Cotton Miller Gregory Arkwright Chapman:
Tries - Davies Jenkins: Goal - Parker(DG):
Referee G S Phillips (Widnes) Att - 8000 H.T. 7 - 2

Sat 8 Oct 1938 SALFORD away lost nil - 17
SALFORD - Osbaldestin: Hudson Gear Risman Edwards: Harrison Watkins: Davies Day Bradbury Dalton Thomas Feetham:
Tries - Osbaldestin Hudson Edwards: Goals - Risman(4):
CASTLEFORD - Lewis: Cunniffe Innes Croston Walker: Hardy Adams: Taylor Haley Stead(S/O) Sadler Staines Brindle:
Referee J F Armstrong (Hud'field) Att - 8000 H.T. nil - 5

Sat 15 Oct 1938 BRAMLEY home draw 7 - 7
CASTLEFORD - Lewis: Cunniffe Innes Croston REGINALD LLOYD(176): Hardy Adams: Stead Haley Taylor Smith Sadler Brindle:
Try - Hardy: Goals - Lewis(2):
BRAMLEY - Taylor: Hargrave Birmingham Murphy Davidson: Starling Spillane: Pearson Cooper Desborough Mason Webb Ballantyne:
Try - Spillane: Goals - Taylor(2):
Referee B Laughlin (Batley) Att -   H.T. 7 - nil

SEASON 1938-39

Sat 22 Oct 1938 BATLEY away lost 5 - 9
BATLEY - Bennett: Williams Nunn Thomas Brown:
Blackburn Frowen: Targett Fallon Rhodes Hudson Foley
Farrar:
Try - Thomas: Goals - Brown(3):
CASTLEFORD - Lewis: Cunniffe Walker Croston Lloyd:
Hardy Adams: McManus Haley Taylor Smith Sadler
Brindle: Try Smith: Goal - Walker:
Referee E Devine (Leeds) Att - 5000 H.T. 5 - 9

**Sat 29 Oct 1938 FEATHERSTONE ROVERS home
won 17 - 6**
CASTLEFORD - Lewis: Croston Atkinson Walker Lloyd:
Hardy Garbett: McManus Haley Taylor Smith Sadler
Brindle:
Tries - Walker Lloyd Hardy: Goals - Lewis(4):
FEATHERSTONE R - Goldie: Asquith Davies Askin Longley:
Hughes Moxon: Hemingway Golby Senior Naylor Butcher
Aspinall: Goals - Goldie(3):
Referee F Peel (Bradford) Att - 4000 H.T. 4 - 4

Sat 5 Nov 1938 KEIGHLEY away lost 8 - 11
KEIGHLEY - Farrington: Sherburn Towill Killingbeck
McDonald: Horrod Sowden: Traill Halliday Fuller Casewell
Harris Foster(S/O):
Tries - McDonald(2) Farrington: Goal - Farrington:
CASTLEFORD - Lewis: Walker Atkinson Innes Lloyd: Hardy
Illtyd(Tubby)M.Williams: Stead Haley Taylor Staines Sadler
Brindle:
Tries - Lloyd Stead: Goal - Lewis:
Referee A Hill (Leeds) Att - 6000 H.T. nil - 11

Sat 12 Nov 1938 SALFORD home won 12 - 5
CASTLEFORD - Lewis: Cunniffe JAMES ROBINSON(177)
Croston Lloyd: Atkinson Walsh: McManus Haley Stead
Sadler Smith Brindle:
Tries - Walsh Stead: Goals - Atkinson(2) Lewis(DG):
SALFORD - Osbaldestin: Hudson Gear Risman Edwards:
Harrison Watkins: Gardner Day Bradbury Dalton Davies
Feetham:
Try - Edwards: Goal - Risman:
Referee E Houghton (Warrington) Att - 6000 H.T. 7 - 3

Sat 19 Nov 1938 HULL away won 10 - 6
HULL - Miller: Hurley Goodall Corner Overton: Courtney
Johnson: Thacker G.Barlow L.Barlow Booth Dawson
Mathers:
Goals - Miller(3):
CASTLEFORD - Lewis: Cunniffe Robinson Brindle Lloyd:
Atkinson Walsh: McManus Haley Stead Smith Horan
Sadler:
Tries - Robinson Walsh: Goals - Atkinson(2):
Referee J F Armstrong (Hud'field) Att - 6000 H.T. 7 - 2

Sat 26 Nov 1938 BARROW home lost 2 - 12
CASTLEFORD - Lewis: Hardy Gordon Innes Robinson
Lloyd: Atkinson Walsh: McManus Haley Stead Sadler
Smith Brindle: Goal - Atkinson:
BARROW - French: Cumberbatch Higgins McDonnell
Harris: Gummer Little: Hattersley McKeating Skelly Troup

Ayres Marklew:
Tries - Higgins McDonnell: Goals - French(3):
Referee P Cowell (Warrington) Att - 6000 H.T. 2 - 4

Sat 3 Dec 1938 HUNSLET away won 10 - 3
HUNSLET - Johnson: Batten Morrell Winter Turton: Morris
Howden: Tolson Britton Bennett Newbound Stansfield
Isaac:
Try - Winter:
CASTLEFORD - Lewis: Cunniffe Atkinson Robinson Lloyd:
Hardy Adams: McManus Haley Stead Smith Horan
Brindle:
Tries - Hardy Brindle: Goals - Atkinson(2):
Referee F Peel (Bradford) Att - 8500 H.T. 7 - 3

**Sat 10 Dec 1938 WAKEFIELD TRINITY home
won 16 - 5**
CASTLEFORD - Lewis: Atkinson Robinson Croston
Cunniffe: Hardy Adams: McManus Haley Stead Smith
Sadler Brindle:
Tries - Atkinson Croston Hardy Brindle:
Goals - Atkinson(2):
WAKEFIELD T - Teall: Watson Turner Whitworth
Appleyard: Jones Goodfellow: Wilkinson Lee McTiffin
Exley Flowers Bratley:
Try - Wilkinson: Goal - Lee:
Referee A Hill (Leeds) Att - 10500 H.T. 3 - 3

Sat 17 Dec 1938 OLDHAM away draw 11 - 11
OLDHAM - Turner: Hodgkinson Lowe Downey Hall:
Matthews Smith: Reed Brooks Moore Givvons Ambler
Elson:
Tries - Matthews Brooks Givvons: Goal - Downey:
CASTLEFORD - Lewis: Atkinson Robinson Croston Lloyd:
Hardy Adams: McManus Haley Stead Smith Sadler
Brindle:
Tries - Croston Lloyd Brindle: Goal - Lewis:
Referee E Devine (Leeds) Att - 4000 H.T. 3 - 8

Sat 24 Dec 1938 HUDDERSFIELD home won 22 - nil
CASTLEFORD - Lewis: Atkinson Croston Robinson Lloyd:
Hardy Adams: McManus Haley Stead Smith Sadler
Brindle:
Tries - Hardy(2) Adams(2) Atkinson Robinson:
Goals - Lewis(2)
HUDDERSFIELD - Taylor: Johnson Madden Fiddes
Markham: Pepperell Graham: Sherwood Rowland Evans
Hughes Shaw Bailey:
Referee B Laughlin (Batley) Att - 7500 H.T. 8 - nil

Mon 26 Dec 1938 KEIGHLEY home won 6 - 2
CASTLEFORD - Lewis: Atkinson Croston Robinson Lloyd:
Hardy Adams: McManus Haley Stead Smith Sadler
Brindle:
Tries - Robinson Lloyd:
KEIGHLEY - Farrington: Sherburn Towill Jenkins
McDonald: Horrod Phelps: Traill Halliday Fuller Thornber
Casewell Harris:
Goal - Farrington:
Referee J F Armstrong (Hud'field) Att - 11000 H.T. nil -nil

Tue 27 Dec 1938 YORK away won 16 - 7
YORK - Outhwaite: Bean Taylor Parker G.Dennis: Hunt
L.Dennis: Sharpe Deighton Coldrick Elias Welsh
Carrington: Try - Taylor: Goals - Taylor(2):
CASTLEFORD - Lewis: Atkinson Croston Robinson Lloyd:
Hardy Adams: McManus Haley Taylor Smith Sadler
Brindle:
Tries - Atkinson Sadler Hardy Croston: Goals - Lewis(2):
Referee W Hemmings (Halifax) Att - 9000 H.T. 8 - 7

Sat 31 Dec 1938 SWINTON away lost 5 - 11
SWINTON - Barnes: Hopkin Lewis Warry Jenkins: Evans
Bowyer: Wright Armitt Hughes Hodgson Stoddart Butters:
Try - Hopkin: Goals - Hodgson(3)(DG):
CASTLEFORD - Lewis: Atkinson Robinson Croston Lloyd:
Hardy Adams: McManus Haley Stead Smith Sadler
Brindle: Try - Adams: Goal - Lewis:
Referee Mr A Hill (Leeds) Att - 6000 H.T. 5 - 6

Sat 7 Jan 1939 OLDHAM home won 16 - 5
CASTLEFORD - Lewis: Cunniffe Atkinson Robinson Lloyd:
Hardy Adams: McManus Haley Stead Sadler Horan
Brindle:
Tries - Lloyd(3) Adams: Goals - Lewis Atkinson:
OLDHAM - Griffiths: Hodgkinson Lowe Mitchell Turner:
Downey Schofield: Read Brooks Moore Elson Greenwood
Pugh: Try - Turner: Goal - Schofield:
Referee J Orford (St Helens) Att - 4500 H.T. 13 - 3

Sat 14 Jan 1939 WARRINGTON away won 27 - 13
WARRINGTON - Belshaw: Chapman Brown Dingsdale
Davies: De Lloyd(S/O) Parker: Edge Cotton Miller Gregory
Arkwright "Mason":
Tries - Davies(2) Arkwright: Goals - Belshaw(2):
CASTLEFORD - Lewis: Cunniffe Atkinson Robinson Lloyd:
Hardy(S/O)Adams: McManus Haley Stead Smith Sadler
Brindle:
Tries - Cunniffe Robinson Lloyd Sadler Brindle:
Goals - Lewis(5) Atkinson:
Referee - Att - H.T.

Sat 21 Jan 1939 WIDNES home won 9 - 2
CASTLEFORD - Lewis: Cunniffe Robinson Croston Lloyd:
Walsh Adams: McManus Haley Stead Smith Sadler
Brindle: Try - Croston: Goals - Lewis(3):
WIDNES - Bradley: Simcock Topping Barber Evans: Kelly
McCue: Higgins Cullen Hoey McDowell Warburton
Millington: Goal - Topping:
Referee F Fairhurst (Wigan) Att - 7000 H.T. 6 - 2

**Sat 28 Jan 1939 BRADFORD NORTHERN away
won 11 - 3**
BRADFORD N - Ward: Case Winnard Gilbert Grainge:
Bennett Burns: Higson Dilorenzo Whitcombe Harrison
Smith Moore: Try - Case:
CASTLEFORD - Lewis: Cunniffe Croston Robinson Lloyd:
Walsh Adams: McManus Haley(S/O) Stead Smith Sadler
Brindle:
Tries - Sadler(2) Walsh: Goal - Lewis:
Referee Mr J F Armstrong(H'field) Att - 10000 H.T. nil - 3

**Sat 3 Feb 1939 OLDHAM away lost 3 - 10
CHALLENGE CUP ROUND 1**
OLDHAM - Griffiths: Hall Rhydderch Stott Turner: Downey
Schofield: Read Brooks Moore Lowe Ambler Elson:
Tries - Rhydderch Turner: Goals - Griffiths Stott:
CASTLEFORD - Lewis: Lloyd Robinson Croston Cunniffe:
Hardy Adams: McManus Cottington Stead Sadler Smith
Brindle: Try - Lloyd:
Referee J E Taylor (Wakefield) Att-20000 H.T. nil - nil

Sat 10 Feb 1939 BATLEY home won 27 - 9
CASTLEFORD - Lewis: JOSEPH HOLMES(178) Croston
Robinson Lloyd: Hardy Adams: McManus Haley Stead
Sadler Smith Brindle:
Tries - Holmes Croston Robinson Sadler Brindle:
Goals - Lewis(6):
BATLEY - Bennett: Williams Lingard Nunns Thomas:
Blackburn Bone: Rhodes Hall Sparkes Brown Farrar
Hudson:
Try - Thomas: Goals Brown(3):
Referee S Adams (Hull) Att - 6500 H.T. 14 - 2

Sat 24 Feb 1939 WIGAN away lost 8 - 10
WIGAN - Sullivan: Morley O.Jones Williamson Holder:
Garvey H.Gee: Banks Davies Moxey Williams I.Jones
Bowen:
Tries - Morley Gee: Goals - Sullivan Garvey(DG):
CASTLEFORD - Lewis: Cunniffe Brindle Robinson Lloyd:
Hardy Walsh: McManus Haley Taylor Crossley Smith
Sadler:
Tries - Haley(2): Goal - Lewis:
Referee E Devine (Leeds) Att - 10000 H.T. 2 - 8

Wed 1 Mar 1939 BRAMLEY away won 23 - 8
BRAMLEY - Rees: Murphy Birmingham Sedgwick
Hodgkiss: Starling Spillane: Mason Graham Bancroft Gater
Norcliffe Cooper:
Tries - Hodgkiss Starling: Goal - Norcliffe:
CASTLEFORD - Lewis: Cunniffe Croston Robinson Lloyd:
Hardy Adams: McManus Haley Stead Smith Sadler
Brindle:
Tries - Cunniffe(2) Croston(2) Lewis Lloyd Stead:
Goal - Lewis:
Referee L Thorpe (Wakefield) Att - 2000 H.T. 6 - 3

**Sat 4 Mar 1939 HULL KINGSTON ROVERS home
won 23 - 12**
CASTLEFORD - Lewis: Cunniffe Robinson Croston Lloyd:
Hardy Adams: McManus Haley Stead Smith Sadler
Brindle:
Tries - Sadler(2) Cunniffe Hardy McManus:
Goals - Lewis(4):
HULL K R - McWatt: Beaumont Hutchinson Whitworth
Milner: Naylor Morgan: Blanchard Ramsden Brown Clarke
Bedford Cayser:
Tries - Naylor Cayser: Goals - McWatt(3):
Referee B Laughlin (Batley) Att - 5000 H.T. 15 - 5

SEASON 1938-39

Sat 18 Mar 1939 WIDNES away won 4 - nil
WIDNES - Bradley: Hughes Topping Kelly Evans: Shannon McCue: Higgins Jones McDowell Roberts Hoey Millington:
CASTLEFORD - Lewis: Cunniffe Robinson Croston Lloyd: Hardy Adams: McManus Haley Stead Smith Sadler Brindle: Goals - Lewis(2):
Referee A Hill (Leeds) Att - 4000 H.T. 4 - nil

Mon 20 Mar 1939 WAKEFIELD TRINITY away won 11 - 8
WAKEFIELD T - Teall: Watson Malpass Turner Appleyard: Goodfellow Ball: Wilkinson Lee McTiffin Orford Exley Bratley: Tries - Appleyard Goodfellow: Goal - Lee:
CASTLEFORD - Lewis: Cunniffe Robinson Croston Lloyd: Hardy Adams: McManus Haley Stead Smith Crossley Brindle: Try - Croston: Goals - Lewis(3) Haley(DG):
Referee F Peel (Bradford) Att - 6000 H.T. 9 - 3

Sat 25 Mar 1939 DEWSBURY home won 11 - 6
CASTLEFORD - Lewis: Cunniffe Robinson Croston Lloyd: Hardy Adams(S/O): McManus Cottington Stead Smith Sadler Brindle:
Tries - Cunniffe(2) Brindle: Goal - Lewis:
DEWSBURY - McNamara: Western Germaine Field Veysey: Nicholson Bowen: Hammond Lawton(S/O) Greaves Ellis Osborne McManus: Tries - Veysey(2):
Referee P Hughes (Bramley) Att - 5000 H.T. 3 - 3

Sat 1 Apr 1939 YORK home won 12 - 4
CASTLEFORD - Lewis: Cunniffe Robinson Croston Lloyd: Hardy Walsh: McManus Cottington Taylor Smith Sadler Brindle:
Tries - Croston Hardy: Goals - Lewis(3):
YORK - Knowles: Bean C.Taylor A.Taylor G.Dennis: Watkinson L.Dennis: Sharpe Deighton Dobbs Carrington Elias White: Goals - Knowles(1)(DG):
Referee W Hemmings (Halifax) Att - 7000 H.T. 7 - 2

Fri 7 Apr 1939 LEEDS away lost nil - 8
LEEDS - Eaton: E.Harris F.Harris Madden Smith: Evans Jenkins: Prosser Murphy Wheatley Jubb Tattersfield Watson:
Tries - Madden Tattersfield: Goal - Evans:
CASTLEFORD - Lewis: Cunniffe Croston Robinson Lloyd: Hardy Walsh: McManus Haley Stead Smith Sadler Brindle:
Referee L Thorpe (Wakefield) Att - 27700 H.T. nil - 6

Sat 8 Apr 1939 HULL KINGSTON ROVERS away won 11 - 8
HULL K R - McWatt: Spamer Eastwood Perrett Milner: Naylor Morgan: Bedford Ramsden Maskill Beaumont Clarke Cayser: Tries - Milner(2): Goal - Milner:
CASTLEFORD - Lewis: Cunniffe Robinson Croston Lloyd: Walsh Adams: Taylor Cottington Stead Horan Sadler Brindle: Tries - Croston(2) Lloyd: Goal - Lewis:
Referee J F Armstrong (Hud'field) Att - 7000 H.T. 8 - 3

Mon 10 Apr 1939 LEEDS home won 20 - 11
CASTLEFORD - Lewis: Cunniffe Robinson Croston Lloyd: Hardy Adams: Taylor Haley Stead Horan Sadler Brindle: Tries - Cunniffe(3) Robinson Hardy Brindle: Goal - Lewis:
LEEDS - Kelly: E.Harris F.Harris Price Eaton: Evans Madden: Wheatley Murphy Dyer Jubb Tattersfield Watson:
Tries - Evans Wheatley Price: Goal - Jubb:
Referee J E Tayor (Wakefield) Att - 20000 H.T. 8 - nil

Tue 11 Apr 1939 HUNSLET home draw 7 - 7
CASTLEFORD - NORMAN GUEST(179): Cunniffe Robinson Croston Lloyd: Hardy Adams: McManus Haley Taylor Crossley Sadler Brindle: Try - Cunniffe: Goals - Croston(2):
HUNSLET - Walkington: Batten Morrell Winter Turton: Morris Booth: Tolson White Bennett Newbound Casewell Whitehead:
Try - Morrell: Goals - Walkington Whitehead(DG):
Referee S Adams (Hull) Att - 10000 H.T. 5 - 7

Sat 15 Apr 1939 HUDDERSFIELD away won 19 - nil
HUDDERSFIELD - A.Davies: Johnson W.T.Davies Fiddes Markham: Pepperell Grahame: Sherwood Gray Taylor Shaw Roland Bailey:
CASTLEFORD - Guest: Cunniffe Robinson Croston Lloyd(S/O): Hardy Adams: Stead Haley Taylor Horan Sadler Brindle:
Tries - Cunniffe(2) Croston(2) Sadler: Goals - Croston(2):
Referee A Hill (Leeds) Att - 14500 H.T. 5 - nil

Sat 22 Apr 1939 BRADFORD NORTHERN home won 16 - 5
CASTLEFORD - Lewis: Cunniffe Robinson Croston Holmes: Hardy Adams: Taylor Haley Stead Sadler Horan Brindle: Tries - Sadler(2) Robinson Croston: Goals - Croston(2):
BRADFORD N - Carmichael: Case Billington Gilbert Freeman: Bennett Hayes: Whitcombe Dilorenzo Edwards Harrison Smith Foster: Try - Carmichael: Goal Carmichael:
Referee T Marley (Wakefield) Att - 8000 H.T. 13 - nil

Sat 29 Apr 1939 HALIFAX home won 21 - 4
CHAMPIONSHIP SEMI FINAL
CASTLEFORD - Lewis: Cunniffe Robinson Croston Holmes: Hardy Adams: Stead Haley Taylor Horan Sadler Brindle: Tries - Hardy(2) Robinson Croston Holmes:
Goals - Croston(2) Lewis:
HALIFAX - Lockwood: Smith Rule Treen Hickey: Todd Goodall: Baynham Field Irving Childs Chadwick Beverley: Goals - Lockwood(2):
Referee F Fairhurst (Wigan) Att - 15000 H.T. 13 - nil

Sat 13 May 1939 SALFORD lost 6 - 8
CHAMPIONSHIP FINAL - AT MAINE ROAD MANCHESTER
CASTLEFORD - Lewis: Cunniffe Robinson Croston Lloyd: Hardy Adams: Stead Haley Taylor Horan Sadler Brindle: Tries - Robinson Brindle:
SALFORD - Miller: Hudson Gear Risman Edwards: Kenny Watkins: Davies Day Bradbury Dalton Thomas Feetham:
Tries - Edwards Kenny: Goal Risman:
Referee S Adams (Hull) Att - 69504 H.T. 6 – 5

Reg Lloyd
D. No 176
1938-39 to 1950-51

Norman Guest
D. No 179
1938-39 to 1949-50

Jim Robinson
D. No 177
1938-39 to 1947-48

SATURDAY 7 JAN 1939 v OLDHAM HOME WON 16 - 5
Back Row.- F Brindle P McManus W Stead A Atkinson J Horan L Adams H Haley
Front Row – F Smith B Cuniffe T Hardy G Lewis R Lloyd J Robinson

SEASON 1938-39

D.N	PLAYER		DEBUT	L MATCH	APP	SUB	T.AP	TRI'S	G'LS	D.G	P'TS
21	ATKINSON	ARTHUR			21	0	21	5	11	0	37
79	LEWIS	GEORGE			42	0	42	1	50	2	107
116	TAYLOR	THOMAS L.			23	0	23	0	0	0	0
123	HALEY	HAROLD			39	0	39	3	0	1	11
124	SMITH	FRANK Snr			27	0	27	1	0	0	3
130	CROSTON	ALFRED JAMES			36	0	36	20	8	0	76
133	ADAMS	LESLIE			33	0	33	6	0	0	18
134	SADLER	EDWARD L.			38	0	38	10	0	0	30
135	CUNNIFFE	BERNARD			34	0	34	13	0	0	39
136	CROSSLEY	JAMES M.			3	0	3	0	0	0	0
141	McMANUS	PATRICK B.			29	0	29	1	0	0	3
147	HARDY	THOMAS			37	0	37	13	0	0	39
148	WALKER	FRANK			10	0	10	2	18	0	42
155	BOUCHER	WILFRED (BUCK)			3	0	3	0	0	0	0
159	WALSH	THOMAS			9	0	9	3	0	0	9
160	COTTINGTON	GORDON			5	0	5	0	0	0	0
167	BRINDLE	FRED			44	0	44	10	0	0	30
168	STEAD	WILLIAM			38	0	38	4	0	0	12
169	WILLIAMS	ILLTYD (Tubby)		05/11/1938	1	0	1	0	0	0	0
172	STAINES	CHARLIE			9	0	9	1	2	0	7
173	INNES	GORDON		26/11/1938	8	0	8	0	0	0	0
174	GARBETT	LEONARD			4	0	4	1	0	0	3
175	HORAN	JOHN	27/08/1938		11	0	11	0	0	0	0
176	LLOYD	REGINALD	15/10/1938		32	0	32	11	0	0	33
177	ROBINSON	JAMES	12/11/1938		31	0	31	9	0	0	27
178	HOLMES	JOSEPH	10/02/1939		3	0	3	2	0	0	6
179	GUEST	NORMAN	11/04/1939		2	0	2	0	0	0	0
	27		**5**	**2**	**572**	**0**	**572**	**116**	**89**	**3**	**532**

COMPETITION		P	W	D	L	FOR	AGT
LEAGUE	POSITION 2 OF 28	40	29	3	8	502	287
YORK'S CUP		1	0	0	1	0	12
RL CUP		1	0	0	1	3	10
CHAMPIONSHIP		2	1	0	1	27	12
PLAYERS RECORDS		**44**	**30**	**3**	**11**	**532**	**321**

The league was reduced to 28 clubs through the withdrawal of Newcastle.

Arthur Atkinson celebrated his 400th appearance for the Club by kicking a goal in a 16–5 victory against Oldham at home on 7 January 1939.

Whilst in both cup competitions the Club fell at the first hurdle, but in league terms it still ranks as one of the greatest in the history of the club.

Castleford finished 2nd out of 28, still the highest league position achieved, only equalled in season 1969/70 and becoming the Yorkshire League Champions in the process.

In the top four play off, as it was then, we beat Halifax at home in the semi-final 21–4, to earn a place in the final on 13 May 1939 against Salford at Manchester City's Main Road Stadium. In front of what was then a world record attendance for a rugby league game of 69,509 we were beaten by Salford 8–6, with a try scored in the last seven minutes.

In the opinion of many good judges at the time the team of 1938/39 was considered to be better than the Challenge Cup winning side of 1934/35, unfortunately the 1939/45 war intervened and the opportunity to progress to greater achievements was sadly lost.

SEASON 1939-40

Sat 19 Aug 1939 FEATHERSTONE ROVERS home lost 5 - 25 LYON CUP FRIENDLY

CASTLEFORD - Lythgoe: Cunniffe Robinson A.N.Other Lloyd: A.N.Other Adams: McManus Haley Goodwin Stead Smith Sadler: Try - A.N.Other(No6): Goal Lythgoe:
FEATHERSTONE R - Pollitt: Jackson Parkin Davies Longley: Hughes Hamer: Hemingay Golby Dyson Pearson Taylor Jacobs:
Tries - Davies(3) Hamer Dyson: Goals - Pollitt(5):
Referee A S Dobson (Pontefract) Att - H.T. nil - 10

Sat 26 Aug 1939 BRADFORD NORTHERN away lost 10 - 29

BRADFORD N - Carmichael: Lambert Bennett Gilbert Walters: Davies Hayes: Higson Dilorenzo Whitcombe Harrison Foster Moore:
Tries - Walters(3) Harrison(2) Lambert Gilbert:
Goals - Carmichael(3)(DG):
CASTLEFORD - Lewis: Holmes Croston Robinson Lloyd: Hardy Adams: Taylor Cottington Stead Smith Atkinson Sadler:
Tries - Croston Sadler: Goals - Croston(2):
Referee A Hill (Leeds) Att - 12000 H.T. 5 - 13

Sat 2 Sep 1939 HUNSLET home winning 3 - nil

CASTLEFORD - Lewis: Holmes Croston Robinson Lloyd: Hardy Adams: McManus(S/O) Cottington Taylor Atkinson Sadler Brindle: Try - Atkinson:
HUNSLET - Walkington: Batten Morrell Turton Batchelor: Thornton Booth: Bennett(S/O) White Tolson Thompson Newbound Whitehead:
Referee - Att - H.T.
Abandoned After 37 Minutes - Torrentrial Rain

LEAGUE CANCELLED DUE TO THE OUTBREAK OF WAR

Sat 16 Sep 1939 LEEDS home lost 15 - 19 FRIENDLY

CASTLEFORD - Lythgoe: Holmes Walker Robinson Lloyd: Hardy Adams: McManus Cottington Taylor Horan Atkinson Sadler:
Tries - Hardy(2) Holmes: Goals - Walker(2) Lythgoe:
LEEDS - Maltby: Dennis Price Jones Madden: Morris Phillips: Wheatley Carter Prosser Jubb Tattersfield Watson:
Tries - Madden(3) Watson(2): Goals - Morris(2):
Referee A S Dobson (Pontefract) Att-3000 H.T. 10 - 8

Sat 23 Sep 1939 YORK home lost 10 - 16 FRIENDLY

CASTLEFORD - Lythgoe: Croston Walker Robinson Lloyd: Hardy Pritchard(York): McManus Smith Taylor Horan Demaine Sadler:
Tries - Walker Sadler: Goals - Walker(2):
YORK - Knowles: Thompson Taylor Gamble G.Dennis: Bowen L.Dennis: Coldrick Deighton Goulden Barrett Carrington Welsh:
Tries - Carrington(2) Gamble G.Dennis:
Goals - Knowles(2):
Referee A Hill (Leeds) Att - 3000 H.T. 2 - 13

WAR EMERGENCY LEAGUE - YORKSHIRE SECTION

Sat 30 Sep 1939 BATLEY away lost 19 - 24

BATLEY - Bennett: Brown Kitson Thomas Lingard: Blackburn Cecil: Terry Fallon Sparkes Hudson Morgan Foley:
Tries - Lingard(3) Cecil(2) Blackburn: Goals - Brown(3):
CASTLEFORD - PETER LYTHGOE(180): CYRIL WHITHAM(181) Walker Robinson JAMES PARKER(182): Hardy ALBERT COLLINS(183): Taylor Cottington Smith Crossley HARRY SLATER(184) Sadler:
Tries - Hardy(2) Walker: Goals - Lythgoe(4) Walker:
Referee E Devine (Leeds) Att - 2000 H.T. 12 - 11

Sat 7 Oct 1939 HUNSLET Home won 15 - 8

CASTLEFORD - Lythgoe: Whitham Walker Croston Lloyd: Hardy Collins: McManus Haley Stead Taylor Crossley Sadler:
Tries - Lythgoe Walker Croston:
Goals - Croston(2) Walker:
HUNSLET - Walkington: Place Morrell Winter Longley: Turton Thornton: Grace Britton Bennett Newbound Thompson Whitehead:
Tries - Longley Thornton: Goal - Walkington:
Referee L Thorpe (Wakefield) Att - 3000 H.T. 5 - 3

Sat 14 Oct 1939 BRAMLEY away won 11 - 5

BRAMLEY - Taylor: Murphy Wilson Sedgewick Johnson: Birmingham Spillane: Desborough Bowden Bancroft Gater Pearson Cooper:
Try - Sedgewick: Goal - Spillane:
CASTLEFORD - Lythgoe: Cunniffe Croston Walker Lloyd: Boucher Collins: Mcmanus Haley Taylor Crossley Slater Sadler:
Tries - Walker(3): Goal - Croston:
Referee J E Taylor (Wakefield) Att - 9000 H.T. 3 - 5

Sat 21 Oct 1939 YORK home won 34 - 8

CASTLEFORD - Lythgoe: Cunniffe Walker Croston Lloyd: Boucher Walsh: McManus Haley Taylor Slater HARRY TOWNSLEY(185):
Tries - Walker(3) Lloyd(2) Cunniffe Boucher Walsh:
Goals - Croston(3) Boucher(2):
YORK - Knowles: Bean Taylor Bowen G.Dennis: Pritchard L.Dennis: Goulden Coldrick Thompson White Carrington Welsh:
Tries - G.Dennis Pritchard: Goal - Knowles:
Referee T Marley (Wakefield) Att - 2000 H.T. 13 - nil

Sat 28 Oct 1939 HUDDERSFIELD away lost 5 - 12

HUDDERSFIELD - G.S.Pepperell: Johnson Fiddes W.T.Davies Inglesfield: S.V.Pepperell Grahame: Sherwood Gray G.Gronow Shaw K.Gronow Bailey:
Tries - Johnson Fiddes: Goals - Davies(3):
CASTLEFORD - Lythgoe: Cunniffe Walker Croston Lloyd: Boucher Walsh: McManus Haley Taylor Slater Townsley Sadler:
Try - Boucher: Goal - Croston:
Referee L Thorpe (Wakefield) Att - 4000 H.T. 3 - 7

Sat 4 Nov 1939 BRAMLEY home won 33 - 4

CASTLEFORD - Lythgoe: Cunniffe Walker Croston Lloyd: Boucher Walsh: McManus Haley Taylor Smith Crossley Townsley:
Tries - Cunniffe(2) Lloyd(2) Croston Haley Smith:
Goals - Croston(6):
BRAMLEY - Taylor: Murphy Wilson Sedgewick Longbottom: Knott Cawood: Bancroft Bowden Desborough Pearson Webb Gater:
Goals - Taylor(2):
Referee F Peel (Bradford) Att - 890 H.T. 10 - 4

Sat 18 Nov 1939 WAKEFIELD TRINITY home won 8 - 6

CASTLEFORD - Lewis: Cunniffe Walker Croston Lloyd: J JONES(Leeds)(G)(186) Lythgoe: McManus Haley Taylor Smith Crossley Sadler:
Tries - Cunniffe Crossley: Goal Walker:
WAKEFIELD T - Oliver: Appleyard Turner Malpass Whitehead: Jones Goodfellow: Wilkinson Marson McTiffin Exley Orford Bratley:
Tries - Turner Bratley:
Referee A Hill (Leeds) Att - 3000 H.T. 5 - 6

Sat 25 Nov 1939 HULL away lost 12 - 13

HULL - Miller: Dockar Herbert Mills Bowers: Lawrence Johnson: Thacker Wilkinson Mathers Booth Dawson Comer:
Tries - Dockar Bowers Mathers: Goals - Miller(2):
CASTLEFORD - Lythgoe: Whitham Walker Croston Lloyd: TREVOR BOWEN(Dewsbury)(G)(187) Walsh: McManus Haley Taylor Slater Crossley Sadler:
Tries - Sadler(2): Goals - Croston(3):
Referee L Dalby (York) Att - H.T.

Sat 2 Dec 1939 KEIGHLEY home won 14 - 8

CASTLEFORD - Lythgoe: Atkinson Walker Croston Lloyd: Walsh Adams: McManus Haley Taylor Crossley Slater Sadler:
Tries - Atkinson Croston Lloyd Sadler: Goal - Croston:
KEIGHLEY - Farrington: Jones Bennett Towill Best: Phelps Sowden: Traill Nicholson Fuller Harris McGoun Forster:
Tries - Jones Towill: Goal - Farrington:
Referee E Devine (Leeds) Att - 2000 H.T. 8 - nil

Sat 9 Dec 1939 HUNSLET away lost 7 - 15

HUNSLET - Knowles(York)(G): Batten Morrell Winter Turton: Herbert(Hull)(G) Thornton: Bennett White Newbound Thompson Cresswell Whitehead:
Tries - Batten Herbert Whitehead: Goals - Knowles(3):
CASTLEFORD - Lythgoe: Walker Atkinson Croston Lloyd: Walsh Adams: McManus Haley Taylor Crossley Horan Sadler:
Try - Croston: Goals - Lythgoe(2):
Referee F Peel (Bradford) Att - 2250 H.T. 7 - 10

Sat 16 Dec 1939 BATLEY home won 20 - 10

CASTLEFORD - Lewis: Cunniffe Atkinson Croston Lloyd: Walsh Lythgoe: Taylor Haley Crossley Horan Slater Sadler:
Tries - Sadler(2) Croston Lloyd: Goals - Lythgoe(4):

BATLEY - Bennett: Pears Hudson Lingard Longley: Blackburn Cecil: Terry Fallon Sparkes Brown Morgan Foley: Tries - Pears Cecil: Goals - Brown(2):
Referee J E Taylor (Wakefield) Att - 950 H.T. 10 - 7

Mon 25 Dec 1939 FEATHERSTONE ROVERS away lost 13 - 16

FEATHERSTONE R - Guest(Castleford)(G): Longley Parkin Hughes Tennant: Morgan Hamer: Hemingway Golby Dyson Pearson Sherwood(S/O)Jacobs:
Tries - Longley Hamer: Goals - Sherwood(5):
CASTLEFORD - Lythgoe: Cunniffe Atkinson Croston Lloyd: Hardy Walsh: Stead(S/O) Haley Taylor Crossley Smith(S/O) Sadler:
Tries - Atkinson Croston Taylor: Goals - Croston Lythgoe:
Referee E Devine (Leeds) Att - 3000 H.T. 3 - 7

Tue 26 Dec 1939 DEWSBURY home won 13 - 2

CASTLEFORD - Lewis: Cunniffe Walker Croston Lloyd: Staines Walsh: McManus Haley Taylor Horan Crossley Sadler:
Tries - Croston Crossley Sadler: Goals - Walker(2):
DEWSBURY - Higgins: Wood Western Davies Burns: Moxon Royal: Hammond Crabtree Banks Morgan Kershaw Seeling:
Goal - Morgan:
Referee A S Dobson (Pontefract) Att- 3000 H.T. nil - 2

Sat 2 Mar 1940 WAKEFIELD TRINITY away lost nil - 31

WAKEFIELD T - Oliver: Appleyard Turner Malpass Whitehead: Jones Goodfellow: Wilkinson Nicholson Eddom Exley Orford Bratley:
Tries - Turner(3) Bratley(2) Goodfellow Wilkinson:
Goals - Whitehead(5):
CASTLEFORD - Lewis: Cunniffe Walker Croston Joseph Holmes: Hardy Walsh: McManus Haley Taylor Crossley Horan Sadler:
Referee - Att - 2700 H.T.

Sat 9 Mar 1940 HALIFAX home won 18 - 4

CASTLEFORD - Lythgoe: Walker Atkinson Robinson Lloyd: Hardy Adams: McManus Haley Taylor Horan JOSEPH ELLIS(Dewsbury) G)(188) Sadler:
Tries - Lythgoe Walker Lloyd Hardy Taylor Horan:
HALIFAX - Lockwood: Bevan Rule Treen Elias: Todd Hurcombe: Kavanagh Meek Irving Chadwick Cox Beverley: Goals - Lockwood(2):
Referee J E Taylor (Wakefield) Att - 15000 H.T .15 - 4

Sat 16 Mar 1940 HALIFAX away lost 9 - 12

HALIFAX - Lockwood: Elias Rule Treen Edwards(Salford)(G): Hurcombe Todd: Brereton Meek Irving Childs Chadwick Beverley:
Tries - Irving Childs: Goals - Lockwood(3):
CASTLEFORD - Lythgoe: Staines Atkinson Robinson Walker: Hardy Adams: McManus Haley Taylor Joseph Ellis(Dewsbury)(C) Crossley Sadler:
Tries - Staines Walker Adams:
Referee A Hill (Leeds) Att - 6000 H.T. 6 - 5

Fri 22 Mar 1940 FEATHERSTONE ROVERS home won 18 - 11
CASTLEFORD - Lythgoe: Staines Atkinson Robinson Walker: Hardy Walsh: Stead Haley Taylor Horan Smith Sadler:
Tries - Atkinson(2) Sadler Walker: Goals - Walker(3):
FEATHERSTONE R - Parkin: Longley Stott(Oldham)(G) Hughes Tennant: Moxon Hamer: Hemingway Golby Dyson Pearson Sherwood Jacobs:
Tries - Longley Moxon Tennant: Goal - Stott:
Referee -   Att - 3500 H.T. 8 - 3

Sat 23 Mar 1940 BRADFORD NORTHERN home lost 15 - 19
CASTLEFORD - Lythgoe: Walker Atkinson Robinson Lloyd: Hardy Adams: McManus Haley Taylor Horan(S/O) Smith Sadler:
Tries - Walker(2) Lloyd: Goals - Walker(3):
BRADFORD N - Ward: Case Walters Winnard Lambert: Brogden Hayes: Higson(S/O) Dilorenzo Edwards Smith Harrison Moore:
Tries - Case Harrison Moore: Goals - Ward(5):
Referee E Devine (Leeds) Att - 4800 H.T. 7 - 5

Mon 25 Mar 1940 BRADFORD NORTHERN away lost 10 - 24
BRADFORD N - Ward: Case Walters Brogden Lambert: Davies Hayes: Whitcombe Dilorenzo Higson Harrison Foster Moore:
Tries - Case Walters Davies Harrison: Goals - Ward(6):
CASTLEFORD - Lythgoe: Cunniffe Robinson Walker Staines: Hardy Walsh: Stead Haley Taylor Crossley Horan Sadler:
Tries - Cunniffe Walsh: Goals - Walker Haley(DG):
Referee S Adams (Hull) Att - 14500 H.T. 8 - 15

Tue 26 Mar 1940 LEEDS away won 10 - 4
LEEDS - Kelly: Toothill Eaton F.Harris Dennis: Evans Price: Newbound Carter Dyer Hebb McManus Watson:
Goals - Kelly(2):
CASTLEFORD - Lythgoe: Cunniffe Croston Robinson Walker: Hardy Adams: Stead Cottington Taylor Staines JOHN H.FOX(189) Horan:
Tries - Staines Croston: Goals - Walker(2):
Referee L J Dalby (York) Att - 7200 H.T. nil - 2

Sat 30 Mar 1940 LEEDS home won 10 - 9
CASTLEFORD - Lythgoe: Croston Walker Robinson Lloyd: Walsh Adams: McManus Haley Taylor Crossley Fox Horan:
Tries - Walsh(2)   Goals - Walker(2):
LEEDS - Eaton: Toothill F.Harris Evans Watson: Hey Jenkins: Newbound Murphy Dyer McManus Hebb Jubb:
Try - Jenkins: Goals - Eaton(3):
Referee J E Taylor (Wakefield) Att - 3500 H.T. 5 - nil

Sat 6 Apr 1940 YORK away lost 6 - 20
YORK - Knowles: Bean Taylor Bowen Day: Pritchard Dennis: Sharpe Deighton Dobbs Goulden Wheatley White:
Tries - Wheatley(2) Bean Taylor: Goals - Knowles(4):

CASTLEFORD - Walker: Walsh Robinson Croston Lloyd: Hardy Adams: McManus Cottington Taylor Crossley Fox Sadler:
Tries - Robinson Croston:
Referee W Hemmings (Halifax) Att - 2000 H.T.

Sat 13 Apr 1940 HULL KINGSTON ROVERS away won 11 - 5
HULL K R - McWatt: Hutchinson Carmichael Dockar Milner: Eastwood Ness: Maskill Ramsden Hodgson Blanchard Boxall Clark:
Try - Dockar: Goal - Milner:
CASTLEFORD - Lythgoe: Whitham Croston Robinson Walker: Hardy Walsh: McManus Haley Taylor Crossley Walton Sadler:
Try - Croston: Goals - Walker(4):
Referee L J Dalby (York) Att - 2000 H.T. 9 - 5

Sat 20 Apr 1940 KEIGHLEY away draw 5 - 5
KEIGHLEY - Phelps: Best Towill Foster Western(Dewsbury)(G): Bennett Davies: Traill Watson Nicholson Matthews Dibb Farrar:
Try - Davies: Goal - Matthews:
CASTLEFORD - Lythgoe: Atkinson Croston Robinson Walker: Hardy Walsh: Walton Haley Taylor Crossley Townsley Sadler:
Try - Sadler: Goal - Walker:
Referee E Devine (Leeds) Att - 2000 H.T. 5 - 3

Sat 27 Apr 1940 HULL home won 18 - 2
CASTLEFORD - Lythgoe: Lloyd Robinson Croston Walker: Hardy Walsh: McManus Haley Taylor Walton W Sherwood(Featherstone R)(G)(26)Sadler(S/O):
Tries - Lloyd Croston Walsh Sherwood: Goals - Walker(3):
HULL - Miller: Dockar Allan Hogg Bowers: Lawrence Bilton: Thacker Barlow Vinder Booth Mathers Courtney:
Goal - Miller:
Referee A Hill (Leeds) Att - 2500 H.T. 10 - 2

Sat 4 May 1940 HUDDERSFIELD home won 13 - 3
CASTLEFORD - Lythgoe: Walker Robinson Atkinson Lloyd: Hardy Walsh: GEORGE BANKS(Wigan)(G)(190) Haley Taylor Crossley McManus Sadler:
Tries - Walker Hardy Sadler: Goals - Walker(2):
HUDDERSFIELD - Inglesfield: Swallow Davies Towill Pimblett: Pepperell Grahame: Sherwood Gray Townend Booth Gronow Bailey: Try - Towill:
Referee E Devine (Leeds) Att - 3000 H.T. 13 - 3

Sat 11 May 1940 HULL KINGSTON ROVERS home won 12 - 7
CASTLEFORD - Lythgoe: Hardy Walker Robinson Croston: ALBERT ASTBURY(191) Walsh: Banks(Wigan)(G) Haley Taylor Atkinson Walton Sadler:
Tries - Walker Atkinson: Goals - Walker(2) Astbury:
HULL K R - McWatt: Spamer Dockar Tattersfield Blanchard: Carmichael Daddy: Hodgson Ramsden Maskill Eddoms Mountain Sharpe:
Try - Daddy: Goals - Carmichael(2):
Referee J E Taylor (Wakefield) Att - 1000 H.T. 10 - nil

SEASON 1939-40

Sat 18 May 1940 DEWSBURY away lost 5 - 13
DEWSBURY - Higgins: Batten(Hunslet)(G)
Morrell(Hunslet(G) A.N.Other Elias: Nicholson Royal:
Hammond White Pearson Kershaw A.N.Other McManus:
Tries - Batten Morrell Elias: Goals - Higgins(2):
CASTLEFORD - Lythgoe: Whitham Croston Robinson
Walker: Hardy Walsh: Banks(Wigan)(G) Haley Taylor
Walton Atkinson Sherwood(Featherstone R)(G)
Try Walsh: Goal - Walker:
Referee A S Dobson (Pontefract) Att -   H.T. nil - nil

Sat 1 Jun 1940 HUNSLET home won 17 - 10
YORKSHIRE CUP ROUND 1
CASTLEFORD - Lythgoe: Whitham Robinson Croston
Walker: Hardy Walsh: Walton Haley Taylor
Banks(Wigan)(G) Atkinson ERIC JONES(192):
Tries - Whitham Hardy Walsh: Goals - Walker(4):

HUNSLET - Walkington: Batten Morrell Rookes Turton:
Yates Booth: To son White Stansfield Burnell Thompson
Whitehead:
Tries - Morrell Booth: Goals - Whitehead(1)(DG):
Referee J E Taylor (Wakefield) Att - 2000 H.T. 5 - 3

Sat 8 Jun 1940 HULL KINGSTON ROVERS home
lost 6 - 12 YORKSHIRE CUP ROUND 2
CASTLEFORD - Lythgoe: Walker Robinson Croston
Whitham: Hardy Walsh: Richard Walton Haley Taylor
Banks(Wigan)(G) Atkinson Edward L Sadler:
Goals - Walker(3):
HULL K R - McWatt: Spamer Eastwood Dockar Milner:
Ness Daddy: Maskill Ramsden Blanchard Clarke Boxall
Hodgson:
Tries - Ness(2):   Goals - McWatt(2)(DG):
Referee E Devine (Leeds) Att - 1000 H.T. 4 – 2

Harry Slater
D. No 184
1939-40 to 1946-47

Eric Jones
D. No 192
1939-40 to 1946-47

SEASON 1939-40

D.N		PLAYER		DEBUT	L MATCH	APP	SUB	T.AP	TRI'S	G'LS	D.G	P'TS
21		ATKINSON	ARTHUR			16	0	16	6	0	0	3
23		WALTON	RICHARD		08/06/1940	7	0	7	0	0	0	2
59	G	SHERWOOD	WILLIAM (F'STONE R.)			2	0	2	1	0	0	117
79		LEWIS	GEORGE			6	0	6	0	0	0	18
116		TAYLOR	THOMAS L.			32	0	32	2	0	0	0
123		HALEY	HAROLD			27	0	27	1	0	1	10
124		SMITH	FRANK Snr			7	0	7	1	0	0	0
130		CROSTON	ALFRED JAMES			25	0	25	12	20	0	0
133		ADAMS	LESLIE			10	0	10	1	0	0	0
134		SADLER	EDWARD L.		08/06/1940	27	0	27	10	0	0	0
135		CUNNIFFE	BERNARD			11	0	11	5	0	0	6
136		CROSSLEY	JAMES M.			19	0	19	2	0	0	76
141		McMANUS	PATRICK B.			20	0	20	0	0	0	15
147		HARDY	THOMAS			21	0	21	5	0	0	0
148		WALKER	FRANK			28	0	28	15	36	0	0
155		BOUCHER	WILFRED (BUCK)			4	0	4	2	2	0	5
159		WALSH	THOMAS			22	0	22	7	0	0	15
160		COTTINGTON	GORDON			5	0	5	0	0	0	0
167		BRINDLE	FRED			1	0	1	0	0	0	3
168		STEAD	WILLIAM			6	0	6	0	0	0	0
172		STAINES	CHARLES			5	0	5	2	0	0	0
175		HORAN	JOHN			10	0	10	1	0	0	0
176		LLOYD	REGINALD			20	0	20	9	0	0	27
177		ROBINSON	JAMES			19	0	19	1	0	0	28
178		HOLMES	JOSEPH		02/03/1940	3	0	3	0	0	0	0
180		LYTHGOE	PETER	30/09/1939		27	0	27	2	11	0	6
181		WHITHAM	CYRIL	30/09/1939		7	0	7	1	0	0	3
182		PARKER	JAMES	30/09/1939		1	0	1	0	0	0	0
183		COLLINS	ALBERT	30/09/1939		3	0	3	0	0	0	3
184		SLATER	HARRY	30/09/1939		7	0	7	0	0	0	21
185		TOWNSLEY	HARRY	21/10/1939		4	0	4	0	0	0	0
186	G	JONES	J (LEEDS)	18/11/1939	18/11/1939	1	0	1	0	0	0	0
187	G	BOWEN	TREVOR (DEWSBURY)	25/11/1939	25/11/1939	1	0	1	0	0	0	30
188	G	ELLIS	JOSEPH (DEWSBURY)	09/03/1940	16/03/1940	2	0	2	0	0	0	0
189		FOX	JOHN H.	26/03/1940		3	0	3	0	0	0	3
190	G	BANKS	GEORGE (WIGAN)	04/05/1940		5	0	5	0	0	0	3
191		ASTBURY	ALBERT	11/05/1940	11/05/1940	1	0	1	0	1	0	0
192		JONES	ERIC	01/06/1940		1	0	1	0	0	0	6
5		38		13	7	416	0	416	86	70	1	400

COMPETITION		P	W	D	L	FOR	AGT
WAR LEAGUE	POSITION 6 OF 15	28	16	1	11	364	300
YORK'S CUP		2	1	0	1	23	22
VIOD PRE W.L. GAMES		2	1	0	1	13	29
PLAYERS RECORDS		32	18	1	13	400	351

The 1939/40 season was interrupted by the outbreak of war. After only two league games the league fixtures were cancelled.

Two friendly matches were played, and then a War Emergency League was introduced with the Club playing in the Yorkshire Section consisting of the 15 Yorkshire Clubs which played in the League the previous season. The Lancashire Section only consisted of 12 clubs, St Helens Recs being the club who had dropped out of the competition. The Championship was decided by the teams heading each league playing off

This was the first season when 'Guest' players were allowed due to the outbreak of the Second World War (which resulted in several players being called up for war service), these are identified in the statistics with their normal club after their name and the letter (G) in brackets. we had five such players

The Challenge Cup competition was cancelled.

SEASON 1940-41

WAR EMERGENCY LEAGUE YORKSHIRE SECTION

Sat 31 Aug 1940 FEATHERSTONE ROVERS away lost 11 – 23 LYON CUP - FRIENDLY
FEATHERSTONE R - R Parkin: Longley Tennant Hughes Blackburn: Hamer Moxon: Hemingway Bowden Dyson Pearson R.Taylor C.Taylor:
Tries - Longley Tennant Hughes Hamer Pearson:
Goals - Blackburn(4):
CASTLEFORD - Brookes: Whitham Atkinson Walker Lane: Hardy Carr: Wagstaff Bolton Carrington Street Pennington Jones:
Tries - Hardy(2) Brookes: Goals - Walker:
Referee A S Dotson (Pontefract) Att - H.T. 7 - 8

Sat 7 Sept 1940 WAKEFIELD TRINITY away lost 2 - 8
WAKEFIELD T - Harraclough: Milner Whitworth Turner Jenkinson: Goodfellow Taylor: Wilkinson Marson Nicholson Orford Flowers Murphy:
Tries - Marson Flowers: Goal - Milner:
CASTLEFORD - Lythgoe: Whitham Atkinson Walker JACK LANE(193): Hardy Walsh: FRANK WAGSTAFF(194) EDWARD BOLTON(195) GEORGE CARRINGTON (York)(G)(196) JACK STREET(197) ERIC PENNINGTON(198) Jones: Goal - Walker:
Referee - Att - 1250 H.T. 2 - nil

Sat 14 Sept 1940 FEATHERSTONE ROVERS home lost 9 - 20
CASTLEFORD - KENNETH BROOKES(199): Cunniffe Atkinson Walker Lane: Hardy Walsh: Taylor Cottington Wagstaff Street Pennington Brindle:
Try - Cunniffe: Goals - Atkinson(3):
FEATHERSTONE R - Parkin: Longley Tennant Hughes Blackburn: Hamer Moxon: Hemingway Bowden Dyson Pearson Taylor Sherwood:
Tries - Longley Tennant: Goals - Sherwood(7):
Referee F Peel (Bradford) Att - H.T. 9 - 4

Sat 21 Sept 1940 HUNSLET away lost 2 - 18
HUNSLET - Walkington: Turton Rookes Batten Morrell(S/O): Booth Watson: Bennett White Britton(Hull K R) Casewell Thompson Whitehead:
Tries - Batten(2) Turton 1Try scorer unknown:
Goals - Thompson(2) Walkington:
CASTLEFORD - Lythgoe: Cunniffe Atkinson(S/O) Walker Lane: HERBERT KEAR(200) Walsh: George.Banks (Wigan)(G) Cottington Wagstaff ALBERT CADDICK(201) Pennington Brindle: Goal - Atkinson:
Referee J F Thorpe (Wakefield) Att - 1500 H.T.

Sat 28 Sept 1940 KEIGHLEY away won 16 - 3
KEIGHLEY - Phelps: Thirling Towill Bennett Reynolds: Davies Barrett: Powell Pickles Mason Flanagan Harris Farrar: Try - Davies:
CASTLEFORD - Lythgoe: Parker Atkinson Walker Lane: Brookes Walsh: Banks (Wigan)(G) Cottington Wagstaff Street Pennington Jones:
Tries - Walsh(3) Walker: Goals - Walker(2):
Referee J E Taylor (Wakefield) Att - 1500 H.T. 3 - 3

Sat 5 Oct 1940 HULL home lost 5 - 12
CASTLEFORD - Atkinson: Lane Walker Lloyd Whitham: RICHARD ALLMAN(Featherstone R)(G)(202) Brookes: Taylor Cottington Banks (Wigan)(G) Street Pennington Jones:
Try - Street: Goal - Walker:
HULL - Miller: Overton Allen Herbert Corner: Bilton Smailes:Pinder Hattersley Monkhouse Booth Taylor Kavanagh:
Tries - Smailes Booth: Goals - Miller(3):
Referee A Hill (Leeds) Att - 1000 H.T. 5 - 2

Sat 12 Oct 1940 BATLEY home won 18 - 6
CASTLEFORD - FRANK CARR(203): Whitham JOSEPH RENNARD(204) Walker Lloyd: Hardy Brookes: Taylor Cottington Wagstaff Pennington Street Jones:
Tries - Rennard(2): Goals - Walker(6):
BATLEY - Thewlis: Lovell Lingard Brown Williams: Nunn Bone: Rhodes Lockwood Sparkes(S/O) Terry Morgan Foley:
Goals - Brown(3)
Referee Devine (Leeds) Att - 500 H.T. 4 - 2

Sat 19 Oct 1940 BRAMLEY away won 8 - 5
BRAMLEY - Taylor: Bateson Parker G.Murphy Dennis: Rodgers Naylor: Westwood Bowden Pearson Webb D.Murphy Cooper:
Try - Naylor: Goal - Taylor:
CASTLEFORD - THOMAS HART(205): Lane Walker Rennard DENNIS BADDELEY(206): Allman (Featherstone R)(G) Brookes: Banks (Wigan)(G) Taylor Wagstaff Street Pennington Jones:
Tries - Lane Brookes: Goal - Walker:
Referee W Hemming (Halifax) Att - 500 H.T. 5 - 2

Sat 26 Oct 1940 BRAMLEY home won 10 - 6
CASTLEFORD - Hart: Lane Walker Croston Cunniffe: Hardy Brookes: Taylor Cottington Banks (Wigan)(G) Street Pennington Jones:
Tries - Walker Hardy: Goals - Walker(2):
BRAMLEY - Taylor: Bateson Parker G.Murphy Dennis: Gibbons Naylor: Trevis Pearson Westwood Copeman Webb Cooper:
Goals - Taylor(3):
Referee J E Taylor (Wakefield) Att - 1000 H.T. 5 - 2

Sat 2 Nov 1940 BRADFORD NORTHERN away lost 3 - 17
BRADFORD N - Carmichael: Best Winnard E.Ward Walters: McWatt (Hull K R)(G) D.Ward: Higson Carter (Leeds)(G) Whitcombe Foster Roberts Moore:
Tries - Best(2) Winnard(2) McWatt: Goal - E.Ward:
CASTLEFORD -Thomas Hart: Lane Walker Croston Richard Allman (Featherstone R)(G): Brookes Walsh: Taylor Cottington Wagstaff Street Pennington Jones:
Try - Walker:
Referee - J E Taylor (Wakefield) Att - 3000 H.T. 14 - nil

SEASON 1940-41

Sat 9 Nov 1940 HUNSLET home won 14 – 7
CASTLEFORD – HAWES(207): Lane Atkinson Croston
Walker: Hardy Brookes: McManus Cottington Taylor
Wagstaff Pennington Jones:
Tries - Lane Croston: Goals - Walker(4):
HUNSLET - Kelly: Place Morrell Rookes Turton: Watson
Booth: Tolson(S/O) Brttton Satterthwaite Casewell
Thompson Whitehead:
Try - Place: Goals - Whitehead(2):
Referee S Adams (Hull) Att - 1000 H.T. nil - 2

Sat 16 Nov 1940 BATLEY away won 10 - nil
BATLEY - Thewlis: Harris Walker Thomas Lovell: Farrar
Bone: Rhodes Lockwood(S/O) Sparkes Brown Morgan
Foley:
CASTLEFORD - Brookes: Lane Walker Croston Whitham:
Hardy Walsh: Banks (Wigan)(G) Cottington Wagstaff
Pennington Street Jones:
Tries - Walker Croston: Goals - Walker(2):
Referee V Devine (Leeds) Att - 1000 H.T. 5 - nil

Sat 23 Nov 1940 HALIFAX home won 9 - 3
CASTLEFORD - Atkinson: Lane Croston Walker Rennard:
Hardy Brookes: Taylor Cottington Banks (Wigan)(G)
Pennington Wagstaff Jones:
Try - Jones: Goals - Walker(3):
HALIFAX - Lockwood: Bevan Rule Dockar Irving: Todd
Hurcombe: Osborne Meek Childs Brereton Dixon
Beverley: Try - Hurcombe:
Referee F Peel (Bradford) Att - 1000 H.T. 9 - nil

Sat 7 Dec 1940 DEWSBURY away lost 13 - 17
DEWSBURY - Sullivan(Wigan): Barnes(Swinton)
Campbell(New Zealand) Bradbury(St Helens) Germaine
Sterling (New Zealand) Royal: Thomas(Broughton) Jones
(Broughton) Crabtree McManus Garner(St Helens)
Seeling:
Tries - Campbell(2) Bradbury: Goals: - Sullivan(4):
CASTLEFORD - Atkinson: Whitham Walker Croston Lane:
Hardy Walsh: Taylor Cottington Wagstaff Crossley
Pennington Jones:
Try - Croston: Goals - Walker(4) Walsh(DG):
Referee F Peel (Bradford) Att - 2500 H.T. 11 - 8

Sat 14 Dec 1940 HUDDERSFIELD home won 13 - 5
CASTLEFORD - Brookes: Whitham Walsh Croston Lane:
Hardy Garbett: McManus Cottington Taylor Wagstaff
Pennington Jones:
Tries - Walsh Croston Hardy: Goals - Croston(2):
HUDDERSFIELD - Rees: Green Parker Davies Clapham:
Walker Grahame: Sherwood Gray Chadwick Clarke Booth
Hunter: Try - Clapham: Goal - Davies:
Referee F Devine (Leeds) Att - 500 H.T. 10 – 2

Sat 21 Dec 1940 YORK away won 12 - 5
YORK - Mills: Bean Taylor Woodcock Hall: Jenkins(Salford)
Pritchard: Dobbs Stringer Goulden Maude Simmons
White: Try - Jenkins: Goal - Jenkins:

CASTLEFORD - Kear: Lane Croston Atkinson Whitham:
Hardy Brookes: McManus Cottington Wagstaff Street
Pennington Jones:
Tries - Croston Brookes: Goals - Croston(2) Atkinson:
Referee S Adams (Hull) Att - 1500 H.T. 2 - 5

**Wed 25 Dec 1940 WAKEFIELD TRINITY home
lost 4 - 11**
CASTLEFORD - Kear: Lane Walker Atkinson Lloyd: Hardy
Brookes: McManus Cottington Taylor Wagstaff
Pennington Jones: Goals - Walker(2):
WAKEFIELD T - Pollttt: Whitworth Turner Carress
Whitehead: Malpass Goodfellow: Wilkinson Darlison
Nicholson Wiby Flowers Orford:
Tries - Whitehead(2) Whtworth: Goal - Pollitt:
Referee F Peel (Bradford) Att - 1581 H.T. 4 - 5

Sat 28 Dec 1940 KEIGHLEY home won 25 - 11
CASTLEFORD - Atkinson: Lane Walker Croston Lloyd:
Jones Brookes: McManus Cottington Taylor Wagstaff
Street Pennington: Tries - Pennington(2) Walker Croston
Lloyd: Goals - Walker(5):
KEIGHLEY - Murray: Davies Towill Bennett Thurling:
Daddy Barrett: Flanagan Nicholson Pickles Harris
Thornber Foster:
Tries - Barrett Flanagan Nicholson: Goal - Davies:
Referee L Thorpe (Wakefield) Att - 500 H.T. 15 - nil

Sat 11 Jan 1941 LEEDS away lost 7 - 15
LEEDS - Kelly: Warrior Rhodes Harris Hebb: Billingtnn
Jenkins: Murphy Prosser Maskill Satterthwaite Foreman
Tattersfield: Tries - Harris Billington Prosser:
Goals Kelly(3):
CASTLEFORD - Brookes: Lane Walker Croston Lloyd:
Jones Walsh: McManus Cottington Taylor Street Wagstaff
Pennington: Try - Pennington: Goals - Walker(2):
Referee J H Taylor (Wakefield) Att - 1500 H.T. 2 - 15

**Sat 15 Feb 1941 BRADFORD NORTHERN home
lost 4 - 14**
CASTLEFORD - KELLY(Hunslet)(208): Lane Walsh Croston
Cyril Whitham(S/O): Jones Brookes: McManus Haley
Taylor Banks (Wigan)(G) Wagstaff Pennington:
Goals - Croston(2):
BRADFORD N - Carmichael: Best Winnard E Ward
Walters: McWatt D.Ward: Whitcombe Wilkinson Roberts
Foster Smith Moore
Tries - Foster(2) Whitcombe Smith: Goal - Carmichael:
Referee F Devine (Leeds) Att - 1600 H.T. 4 - nil

Sat 22 Feb 1941 HULL away lost nil - 11
HULL - Ingram: Dockar Brogden Allen Wilson: Hilton
Beales: Hattersley Monkhouse Thacker Taylor Kavanagh
A.N.Other:
Tries - Dockar Kavanagh Brogden: Goal - Allen:
CASTLEFORD - JOSEPH CARMICHAEL(Bradford
N)(G)(209): Lane Walker Croston Rennard: Hardy Walsh:
McManus VICTOR DARLISON (Wakefield T)(G)(210) Taylor
Wagstaff Pennington Jones:
Referee L Thorpe (Wakefield) Att 1200 H.T. nil - 6

94

SEASON 1940-41

Sat 1 Mar 1941 FEATHERSTONE ROVERS away lost 2 - 10
FEATHERSTONE R - Parkin: Langley Hughes W.Tennant Jackson: Darbyshire Moxon: Hemingway Golby Dyson Pearson Taylor Sherwood:
Tries - Jackson Darbyshire: Goals - Sherwood(2):
CASTLEFORD - Kelly(Hunslet)(G): Lane Atkinson Croston Walker: Hardy Walsh: McManus Darlison(Wakefield T)(G) Bank(Wigan)(G) Wagstaff B.TAYLOR(211) Jones:
Goal - Walker:
Referee F Peel (Bradford) Att - 1200 H.T. 2 - 2

Sat 8 Mar 1941 DEWSBURY home lost 8 - 14
CASTLEFORD - Kelly(Hunslet)(G): Rennard Walker Croston Lloyd: Walsh Robinson: McManus Haley Banks(Wigan)(G) Pennington Wagstaff Jones:
Tries - Rennard Walker: Goal - Croston:
DEWSBURY - Sullivan: Barnes Bradbury Kenny Germain: Tracy Royal: Crattree Jones Thomas Kershaw Garner McManus:
Tries - Bradbury(2) Kenny MacManus: Goal - Royal(DG):
Referee A S Dobson (Pontefract) Att -   H.T. 6 - 3

Sat 15 Mar 1941 HALIFAX away won 13 - 6 YORKSHIRE CUP ROUND 1
HALIFAX - Lockwood: Bevan Rule Elias Doyle: Todd Parker: Brereton Meek Irving Dixon Chiids Beverley:
Goals - Lockwood(2)(DG):
CASTLEFORD - Guest: Rennard Croston Walker Lloyd: Robinson Walsh: McManus Haley Taylor Wagstaff Pennington Jones:
Tries - Croston(2) Rennard: Goals - Walker(2):
Referee J E Taylor (Wakefield) Att -   H.T. 6 - 3

Sat 22 Mar 1941 HUDDERSFIELD away lost 3 - 8 YORKSHIRE CUP ROUND 2
HUDDERSFIELD - Belshaw: Johnson Lewis Fiddes G.Pepperell: S.Pepperell Grahame: Sherwood Cotton Gray Caley Hughes Charman:
Tries - Belshaw Johnson: Goals - Belshaw:
CASTLEFORD - Lewis: Lane Walker Croston Rennard: Robinson Walsh: McManus Cottington Taylor Crossley Smith Jones: Tries - Croston:
Referee -   Att - 3054 H.T. 3 - nil
After 80 minutes the score was 3 - 3 and the referee ordered extra time to be played. Several Castleford players refused to play owing to having to report for various war time duties, and the Castleford team walked off the field. Huddersfield kicked off against no opposition, Belshaw scored a try kicked the goal, and the Yorkehire County Committee awarded the match to Huddersfield.

Sat 29 Mar 1941 LEEDS home won 23 - 4
CASTLEFORD - Brookes: Walker Croston Robinson Rennard: HERBERT GOODFELLOW(Wakefield T)(212) (G) Walsh: McManus Victor Darlison(Featherstone R)(G) Wagstaff Crossley Pennington Jones: Tries - Croston(2) Robinson(2) Jones: Goals - Walker(3) Darlinson(DG):

LEEDS - Eaton: Toothill F.Harris Rhodes Warrior: Morris A.N.Other: Prosser Murphy Edwards Satterthwaite Tattersfield Foreman: Goals: Tattersfield(1) D/G
Referee A S Dobson (Featherstone) Att - H.T. 13 - 4

Sat 12 Apr 1941 FEATHERSTONE ROVERS away won 8 – 5 CHALLENGE CUP ROUND 1
FEATHERSTONE - Parkin: Longley Tennant Hughes Jackson: Hawes Moxon: Hemingway Golby Dyson Pearson Taylor Street:Try - Tennant: Goal - Moxon(DG):
CASTLEFORD - Lewis: Rennard Walker Croston Lloyd: Robinson Walsh: McManus Cottington Taylor Smith Stead Jones: Tries - Lloyd Croston: Goal - Croston:
Referee A E Harding (Manchester) Att 1760 H.T. 3 - nil
After 80 minutes the score was 3 -3 and the referee ordered extra time at the end of which the score was 5 - 5 and the teams were ordered to play until someone scored. Jim Croston scored a try after 17 minutes. The match had lasted 117 minutes.

Mon 14 Apr 1941 YORK away lost 5 - 17
YORK - Knowles: Bean Taylor J.Mills Howarth: Watkinson Pritchard: Dobson Stringer Goulden Maude W.Mills White:
Tries - Howarth(2) Bean Taylor J.Mills: Goal - Knowles:
CASTLEFORD - Kear: Jack Lane(S/O) DENNIS WARRIOR(Leeds)(G)(213) Jones James Parker: Brookes Walsh: McManus Taylor Stead Wagstaff Pennington Street:Try - Pennington: Goal - Walsh:
Referee S Adams (Hull) Att - 2000 H.T. nil - 5
This Was A Home Fixture But Played At York

Sat 19 Apr 1941 ST HELENS home won 21 - 13 CHALLENGE CUP ROUND 2
CASTLEFORD - Lewis: Hardy Robinson Croston Rennard: Walsh Adams: McManus Cottington Taylor Crossley Smith W Sherwood(Featherstone R):
Tries - Hardy Walsh Adams: Goals - Croston(6):
ST HELENS - Butler: Pierce Stott Waring Grundy: Tracey Dixon: Davies Fishwick(S/O) Garner Fearnley Finney Twist:
Tries - Waring(2) Garner: Goals - Grundy(2):
Referee C S Phillips (Widnes) Att - 2000 H.T. 9 – 13

Sat 26 Apr 1941 BRADFORD NORTHERN away lost 4 - 18 CHALLENGE CUP ROUND 3
BRADFORD - Carmichael: Best Winnard Ward Walters: Risman Hayes: Whitcomhe Carter Higson Foster Smith Moore:Tries - Walters(3) Higson:
Goals - Carmichael(2) Ward(DG):
CASTLEFORD - Brookes: Hardy Robinson Croston Lloyd: Walsh Adams: McManus Cottington Taylor Smith Pennington William Sherwood(Featherstone R):
Goals - Croston(2):
Referee A Holbrook (Warrington) Att 10000 H.T. 2 - 13

SEASON 1940-41

D.N		PLAYER		DEBUT	L MATCH	APP	SUB	T.AP	TRI'S	G'LS	D.G	P'TS
21		ATKINSON	ARTHUR			12	0	12	0	5	0	10
26	G	SHERWOOD	WILLIAM (F'STONE R)		26/04/1941	2	0	2	0	0	0	0
79		LEWIS	GEORGE			3	0	3	0	0	0	0
116		TAYLOR	THOMAS L.			21	0	21	0	0	0	0
123		HALEY	HAROLD			3	0	3	0	0	0	0
124		SMITH	FRANK Snr			4	0	4	0	0	0	0
130		CROSTON	ALFRED JAMES			20	0	20	12	16	0	68
133		ADAMS	LESLIE			2	0	2	1	0	0	3
135		CUNNIFFE	BERNARD			3	0	3	1	0	0	3
136		CROSSLEY	JAMES M.			4	0	4	0	0	0	0
141		McMANUS	PATRICK B.			17	0	17	0	0	0	0
147		HARDY	THOMAS			15	0	15	3	0	0	9
148		WALKER	FRANK			23	0	23	6	41	0	100
159		WALSH	THOMAS			20	0	20	5	1	1	19
160		COTTINGTON	GORDON			20	0	20	0	0	0	0
167		BRINDLE	FRED			2	0	2	0	0	0	0
168		STEAD	WILLIAM			2	0	2	0	0	0	0
174		GARBETT	LEONARD			1	0	1	0	0	0	0
176		LLOYD	REGINALD			9	0	9	2	0	0	6
177		ROBINSON	JAMES			7	0	7	2	0	0	6
179		GUEST	NORMAN			1	0	1	0	0	0	0
180		LYTHGOE	PETER			3	0	3	0	0	0	0
181		WHITHAM	CYRIL		15/02/1941	8	0	8	0	0	0	0
182		PARKER	JAMES		14/04/1941	2	0	2	0	0	0	0
190	G	BANKS	GEORGE (WIGAN)			10	0	10	0	0	0	0
192		JONES	ERIC			25	0	25	2	0	0	6
193		LANE	JACK	07/09/1940	14/04/1941	22	0	22	2	0	0	6
194		WAGSTAFF	FRANK	07/09/1940		23	0	23	0	0	0	0
195		BOLTON	EDWARD	07/09/1940	07/09/1940	1	0	1	0	0	0	0
196	G	CARRINGTON	GEORGE (YORK)	07/09/1940	07/09/1940	1	0	1	0	0	0	0
197		STREET	JACK	07/09/1940		13	0	13	1	0	0	3
198		PENNINGTON	ERIC	07/09/1940		25	0	25	4	0	0	12
199		BROOKES	KENNETH	14/09/1940		19	0	19	2	0	0	6
200		KEAR	HERBERT	21/09/1940		4	0	4	0	0	0	0
201		CADDICK	ALBERT	21/09/1940	21/09/1940	1	0	1	0	0	0	0
202	G	ALLMAN	RICHARD (F'STONE R)	05/10/1940	02/11/1940	3	0	3	0	0	0	0
203		CARR	FRANK	12/10/1940	12/10/1940	1	0	1	0	0	0	0
204		RENNARD	JOSEPH	12/10/1940		10	0	10	4	0	0	12
205		HART	THOMAS	19/10/1940	02/11/1940	3	0	3	0	0	0	0
206		BADDELEY	DENNIS	19/10/1940		1	0	1	0	0	0	0
207		HAWES		09/11/1940	09/11/1940	1	0	1	0	0	0	0
208	G	KELLY	(HUNSLET)	15/02/1941	08/03/1941	3	0	3	0	0	0	0
209	G	CARMICHAEL	JOSEPH (B'DFORD N)	22/04/1941	22/02/1941	1	0	1	0	0	0	0
210	G	DARLISON	VICTOR (W'FIELD T)	22/02/1941	29/03/1941	3	0	3	0	0	1	2
211		TAYLOR	B.	01/03/1941	01/03/1941	1	0	1	0	0	0	0
212	G	GOODFELLOW	HERBERT (W'FIELD T)	29/03/1941	29/03/1941	1	0	1	0	0	0	0
213	G	WARRIOR	DENNIS (LEEDS)	14/04/1941	14/04/1941	1	0	1	0	0	0	0
	9	47		21	17	377	0	377	47	63	2	271

		COMPETITION				P	W	D	L	FOR	AGT
	RL RECORDS	LEAGUE = WAR LEAGUE				24	11	0	13	224	239

THESE RECORDS SCORES AND SCORERS MATCH

				P	W	D	L	FOR	AGT
	WAR LEAGUE	POSITION 9 OF 14		24	11	0	13	222	239
	YORK'S CUP			2	1	0	1	16	14
	VOID PRE W.L. GAMES			3	2	0	1	33	36
	PLAYERS RECORDS			**29**	**14**	**0**	**15**	**271**	**289**

This was the second season where 'Guest' players were allowed, we had nine and twenty debutants overall.

SEASON 1941-42

WAR EMERGENCY LEAGUE

Whilst the war Emergency League was still in operation there was only one league of 17 clubs with no separate Yorkshire and Lancashire Sections. The clubs who had dropped out were Broughton Rangers, Leigh, Liverpool Stanley, Salford, Swinton and Warrington.

Sat 30 Aug 1941 FEATHERSTONE ROVERS home lost 12 - 14 LYON CUP FRIENDLY
CASTLEFORD - Guest: Baddeley Rennard Walker Lane: Hardy Walsh: McManus Haley Wagstaff Pennington Street Jones:
Tries - Rennard Walker: Goals - Rennard(2) Walker:
FEATHERSTONE R - Parkin: Longley Tennant Allman Blackburn: Higgins Moxon: Hemingway Golby Dyson Judge Taylor Sherwood:
Tries - Allman Higgins: Goals - Sherwood(3) Higgins:
Referee A Hill (Leeds) Att - 1500 H.T. 5 - 10

Sat 6 Sep 1941 BRADFORD NORTHERN away lost 21 - 29
BRADFORD N - Carmichael: Best Winnard E.Ward Walters: Billington D.Ward: Whitcombe Carter Higson Foster Smith Hutchinson: Tries - Walters(3) D.Ward(2) Hutchinson(2) Best Winnard: Goal - E.Ward:
CASTLEFORD - Walker: Lloyd Croston Robinson Rennard: Hardy Walsh: McManus Haley Wagstaff Crossley Street Pennington:
Tries - Croston Rennard Walsh Wagstaff Crossley:
Goals - Croston(3):
Referee E Devine (Leeds) Att - 7000 H.T.

Sat 13 Sep 1941 BRAMLEY home won 18 - 7
CASTLEFORD - Walker: Rennard STAN POWELL(St Helens)(G)(214) Croston Lloyd: Hardy Walsh: McManus Haley Taylor Wagstaff Pennington Jones:
Tries - Rennard(3) Pennington:
Goals - Walker Powell Walsh(DG):
BRAMLEY - Taylor: Robinson Mortimer Sedgewick Barraclough: Gibbons Naylor: Brown Pearson Moore Webb King Bartle: Try - Brown: Goals - Robinson(2):
Referee F Peel (Bradford) Att - few hundred H.T. 13 - 2

Sat 20 Sep 1941 WAKEFIELD TRINITY home won 13 -9
CASTLEFORD - Walker: Rennard(S/O) Powell(St Helens)(G)Croston Lloyd: Hardy Hayes: McManus Haley Taylor Smith Eric Pennington Jones:
Tries - Rennard Croston Lloyd: Goals - Walker Powell:
WAKEFIELD T - Turner: Taylor Carress Whitworth Milner: Rylance Goodfellow(S/O): Wilkinson Darlison Eddom Orford Blanchard Allinson:
Try - Milner: Goals - Milner(3):
Referee A Hill (Leeds) Att -   H.T. 10 - nil

Sat 27 Sep 1941 OLDHAM away lost 3 - 8
OLDHAM - Taylor: Williams Mitchell Stott Lees: Kerwick Dixon: Ambler Cunliffe(S/O) Greenwood Lowe Taylor

Cattlin: Tries - Mitchell Lees: Goal - Stott:
CASTLEFORD - Astbury: Rennard Croston Powell(St Helens)(G) Street: Crossley Brookes: McManus Haley(S/O) Taylor JAMES NICHOLLS(215) Wagstaff Jones:
Try - Brookes:
Referee G S Philips (Widnes) Att - 4000 H.T. 3 - 3

Sat 4 Oct 1941 BROUGHTON RANGERS home won 33 - 5
CASTLEFORD - Brookes: Astbury Powell(St Helens)(G) Croston Lloyd: Hardy Walsh: McManus Cottington Taylor Nicholls Jones Street:
Tries - Croston(3) Powell(2) Astbury Lloyd Walsh McManus: Goals - Powell(3):
BROUGHTON R - Rees: Murphy Pendlebury Bell Field: Hickman Blackley: Bradbury O'Donnell Cattlin Taylor Brown Billington: Try - Cattlin: Goal - Field(DG):
Referee F Sharpe (Dewsbury) Att -   H.T. 19 - nil
Match declared void when Broughton Rangers dropped out of the league

Sat 11 Oct 1941 ST HELENS away lost 2 - 16
ST HELENS - Butler: Grundy Stott Twist Bate: Jenkins Tracey: Davies Andrew Noonan(Leigh)(G) McDowell(Widnes)(G) Garner Fearnley:
Tries - Noonan(2) Grundy Stott: Goals - Grundy(2):
CASTLEFORD - Astbury: Baddeley Powell(St Helens)(G) Croston Lloyd: Walsh Hayes: McManus Cottington Taylor Nicholls Street Jones: Goal - Powell:
Referee G S Philips (Widnes) Att - 2000 H.T. nil - 3

Sat 18 Oct 1941 BATLEY home won 12 - 7
CASTLEFORD - Astbury: Rennard Powell(St Helens)(G) Walker Lloyd: Walsh Adams: McManus Haley Wagstaff Smith Nicholls Jones: Tries - Rennard(2) Walker Smith:
BATLEY - Davies: Brennan Lingard Ward Wilkinson: Downey Farrar: Ramsden Brook Bradley Hirst G.Morgan J.Morgan: Try - J.Morgan: Goals - G.Morgan(2):
Referee A S Dobson (Pontefract) Att - 1000 H.T. 3 - 7

Sat 25 Oct 1941 DEWSBURY home won 18 - 2 YORKSHIRE CUP ROUND 1 1ST LEG
CASTLEFORD - Walker: Joseph Rennard Powell(St Helens)(G) Croston Lloyd: Robinson Adams: McManus Haley Wagstaff Smith Nicholls Jones:
Tries - Croston Lloyd Robinson Smith: Goals - Walker(3):
DEWSBURY - Barnes(Swinton)(G): Higgins Towill Edwards(Salford)(G) Francis: Bradbury Miller(Salford)(G): Hammond Davies(Salford)(G) Gardiner Kershaw Thomas(Salford)(G) McManus: Goal - Hammond:
Referee L Thorpe (Wakefield) Att - 5000 H.T. 10 - 2

Sat 1 Nov 1941 DEWSBURY away lost 5 - 8 YORKSHIRE CUP ROUND 1 2ND LEG
DEWSBURY - Miller: Hudson Bradbury Williams Francis: Kenny Royal: Hammond Nicholson Gardiner Kershaw(S/O) McDowell McManus:
Tries - Miller Hudson: Goal - Hammond:
CASTLEFORD - Walker: Powell(St Helens)(G) Robinson

SEASON 1941-42

Croston Lloyd: Walsh Adams: McManus Haley Wagstaff Smith Nicholls Jones: Try - Wagstaff: Goal - Walker: Referee A S Dobson (Pontefract) Att-4000 H.T. nil - 5
CASTLEFORD won 23 - 10 on aggregate

Sat 8 Nov 1941 HUDDERSFIELD away lost 6 - 14 YORKSHIRE CUP ROUND 2 1ST LEG
HUDDERRSFIELD - Belshaw: Peake G.Pepperell Fiddes Lewis: S.Pepperell Grahame: G.Hughes Cotton(S/O) Reed Hodgson E.Hughes Chapman:
Tries - Fiddes Chapman:
Goals - Hodgson(2) Belshaw(l)(DG):
CASTLEFORD - Walker: Baddeley Robinson Croston Powell(St Helens)(G): Hardy Walsh: McManus Haley Wagstaff Smith Nicholls Jones: Tries - Croston(2):
Referee S Adams (Hull) Att - 5335 H.T. nil - 8

Sat 15 Nov 1941 HUDDERSFIELD home won 6 - 5 YORKSHIRE CUP ROUND 2 2ND LEG
CASTLEFORD - Walker: Powell(St Helens)(G) Robinson Croston Lloyd: Hardy Walsh: McManus Cottington Wagstaff Smith Nicholls Jones:
Tries - Croston Jones:
HUDDERSFIELD - Belshaw: Peake G.Pepperell Fiddes Pimblett: S.Pepperell Grahame: G.Hughes Cotton Reed Hodgson E.Hughes Chapman:
Try - S.Pepperell: Goal - S.Pepperell:
Referee L Thorpe (Wakefield) Att - 5000 H.T. nil - nil
HUDDERSFIELD won 19 - 12 on aggregate

Sat 22 Nov 1941 LEEDS away lost nil - 6
LEEDS - Taylor: Harris McKenzie Toothill Higgins: Evans Jenkins: Murphy Prosser Wensley Robert Desborough Gill:
Tries - Jenkins(2):
CASTLEFORD - Guest: Baddeley Croston Powell(St Helens)(G) Walker: Astbury Walsh: McManus Cottington Taylor Smith Horan Jones:
Referee A S Dobson (Pontefract) Att -   H.T. nil - 3

Sat 29 Nov 1941 ST HELENS home won 12 - 5
CASTLEFORD - Frank Walker: KENNETH LARGE(St Helens)(G)(216) Robinson Croston Powell(St Helens)(G): Astbury Walsh: McManus Haley Taylor Wagstaff Nicholls Jones: Tries - Walsh Taylor: Goals - Powell(3):
ST HELENS - Butler: Doyle J.Waring Stott G.Waring: Bowen Tracey: Davies Noonan Thompson Fearnley McDowell Twist: Try - Davies: Goal - Stott:
Referee F Peel (Bradford) Att -   H.T. 12 - nil

Sat 6 Dec 1941 HUDDERSFIELD home won 15 - 7
CASTLEFORD - Astbury: Baddeley Atkinson Croston Kenneth Large(St Helens)(G): Hardy Walsh: Taylor Haley Wagstaff Street Nicholls Jones:
Tries - Croston(3): Goals - Walsh(3):
HUDDERSFIELD - Belshaw: Peake Lewis Fiddes Clapham: S.Pepperell Grahame: Mallinson Booth Read Ashworth E.Hughes Chapman: Try - Fiddes: Goals - Belshaw(2):
Referee J E Taylor (Wakefield) Att -   H.T. 10 - 4
Match should have been played at Huddersfield but switched to Castleford because of the Yorkshire Cup

Final between Bradford N and Dewsbury being played at Huddersfield

Sat 13 Dec 1941 HALIFAX home lost 2 - 4
CASTLEFORD - Brookes: Astbury Walsh Croston Baddeley: Hardy HAROLD MOXON(Featherstone R)(G)(217): Taylor Haley Wagstaff Street Fox Jones: Goal - Croston:
HALIFAX - Lockwood: Elias Smith Rule Pickles: Manley Todd: Baynham Meek Irving Childs Brereton Dixon:
Goals - Lockwood Brereton(DG):
Referee L Thorpe (Wakefield) Att -   H.T. 2 - nil

Sat 20 Dec 1941 WAKEFIELD TRINITY away lost 2 -27
WAKEFIELD T - Teall: Jenkinson Hutchinson Turner Siddle: Jepson Goodfellow: Wilkinson Darlison Blanchard Orford Marson Manning:
Tries - Jepson(3) Goodfellow(2) Jenkinson Siddle:
Goals - Teall(2) Goodfellow:
CASTLEFORD - Herbert Kear: Jones Fox Croston Astbury: Baddeley Brookes: Taylor Cottington Wagstaff Nicholls Street Haley: Goal - Croston:
Referee F Peel (Bradford) Att - 1000 H.T. nil - 16

Thu 25 Dec 1941 FEATHERSTONE ROVERS home lost 4 - 11
CASTLEFORD – HOYLE(218): Astbury Walsh Jones Lloyd: Hardy Hayes: Stead Cottington McManus Smith Nicholls Fox: Goals - Walsh(2):
FEATHERSTONE R - Morgan: Lane Tennant Longley Hossack: Hamer Moxon: Hemingway Golby Lyman Major Taylor Sherwood:
Tries – Lane(2) Longley :   Goal - Sherwood:
Referee J E Taylor (Wakefield) Att - 2000 H.T. 4 - 3

Sat 27 Dec 1941 HUNSLET home lost 8 - 21
CASTLEFORD - Lewis: Baddeley Jones Walsh Brookes: Hayes Astbury: McManus Cottington Wagstaff Smith Fox Nicholls:
Tries - Baddeley Smith: Goal - Walsh:
HUNSLET - White: Batten Rookes Frewston Thurwell: Watson Thurling: Moore Britton Crossley Thompson Bartle Burnell:
Tries - Batten(3) Frewston Thurwell: Goals - Thompson(3):
Referee S Thompson (Pontefract) Att - 1000 H.T. 3 - 13

Sat 10 Jan 1942 OLDHAM home lost 16 - 31
CASTLEFORD - Lewis: BUCKLE(Dewsbury)(G)(219) Atkinson ALBAN LONGLEY(Featherstone R)(G) 220) Baddeley: Astbury Walsh: McManus Cottington Taylor Nicholls Wagstaff Jones:
Tries - Walsh(2) Buckle Baddeley: Goals - Walsh(2):
OLDHAM - Thomas: Wilkinson Stott Towill Lees: Bowyer Heywood: Ambler Dean Cattlin Taylor Pugh Givvons:
Tries - Lees(3) Wilkinson Stott Cattlin Givvons:
Goals - Stott(4) Cattlin(DG):
Referee L Thorpe (Wakefield) Att - 600 H.T. 3 - 8

Sat 14 Feb 1942 DEWSBURY away Lost 7 - 22
DEWSBURY - Sullivan(Wigan)(DP): Walters(Bradford N)(G) Miller Edwards(Salford)(G) Francis(Wigan)(G): Kenny Jenkins(Leeds)(G): Hammond Nicholson Gardner

SEASON 1941-42

McManus Kershaw Tattersfield(Leeds)(G):
Tries - Francis(2) Miller McManus: Goals Sullivan(5):
CASTLEFORD - Brookes: <u>ERIC BATTEN(Hunslet)(G)(221)</u>
<u>CYRIL MORRELL(Hunslet)(G)(222)</u> <u>RONALD</u>
<u>TURTON(Hunslet)(G)(223)</u> <u>DESMOND CASE(Bradford</u>
<u>N)(G)(224)</u>: <u>OLIVER MORRIS(Leeds)(G)(225)</u> Walsh:
McManus Cottington Taylor Nicholls Wagstaff Jones:
Try - Case: Goals - Walsh(2):
Referee -   Att - 3000 H.T. 5 - 9

Sat 14 Mar 1942 KEIGHLEY away lost nil - 13
KEIGHLEY - L.Jones: Western Higginbottom Barrett
Thurling: Davies Goodall: H.Jones Bowden Foster
Flanagan Webb Thornber: Tries - Flanagan(2) Thurling:
Goals - Higginbottom Flanagan:
CASTLEFORD - Brookes: J.WARD(Rochdale H)(G)(226):
<u>Arthur Atkinson</u> JACK BRADBURY(St Helens)(G)(227)
Lloyd: Astbury Walsh: McManus Cottington Taylor
Nicholls Wagstaff Jones:
Referee F Peel (Bradford) Att - 2000 H.T. nil - nil

Sat 21 Mar 1942 HUDDERSFIELD away won 19 - nil
HUDDERSFIELD - McGurk: Peake Lewis Davies Elias:
Grahame Todd: Hughes Cotton Read Mallinson Booth
Ashworth:
CASTLEFORD - Brookes: Astbury Bradbury(St Helens)(G)
Ward(Rochdale H)(G): <u>THOMAS</u>
<u>CLAPHAM(Huddersfield)(G)(228)</u> CHARLIE GLOVER
(Wigan)(G)(229) <u>THOMAS MCCUE(Widnes)(G)(230)</u>:
McManus Taylor Street Nicholls Wagstaff Jones:
Tries - Ward(2) Astbury McCue Wagstaff:
Goals - Astbury Glover:
Referee S Sharpe (Dewsbury) Att - 3000 H.T. 5 - nil

Sat 28 Mar 1942 BRAMLEY away won 17 - 15
BRAMLEY - Walkington(Hunslet)(G): Turton(Hunslet)(G)
Sedgewick Morrell(Hunslet)(G) Barraclough: Watson
Thornton: Desborough Pearson Moore Gater Webb
Cooper: Tries - Barraclough Thornton Desborough:
Goals - Walkington(3)
CASTLEFORD - Brookes: Baddeley Powell(St Helens)(G)
Bradbury(St Helens)(G) Ward(Rochdale H)(G): Astbury
Walsh: McManus <u>J.NICHOLSON(Dewsbury)(G)(231)</u> Taylor
Street Wagstaff Jones: Tries - Baddeley Powell Astbury:
Goals - Powell(2) Walsh(2):
Referee L Thorpe (Wakefield) Att -   H.T. 2 - 3

Sat 4 Apr 1942 LEEDS home won 24 - 10
CASTLEFORD - Lythgoe: Astbury Ward(Rochdale H)(G)
<u>Jack Bradbury(St Helens)(G)</u> Baddeley:
Glover(Wigan)(G)(233) RAY HAMER(Featherstone
R)(G)(232): McManus <u>JOSEPH GOLBY(Featherstone</u>
<u>R)(G)(233)</u> JOSEPH BRADBURY(Salford)(G)(234) Taylor
Wagstaff Jones: Tries - Astbury(2) Bradbury(St Helens)(2)
Taylor Jones: Goals - Glover(2) Astbury:
LEEDS - Taylor: Higgins Eaton Jubb Longley: Tennant
Garbutt: Satterthwaite Murphy Roberts Pearson
Desborough Tattersfield:
Tries - Longley Desborough: Goals - Taylor(2):
Referee L Thorpe (Wakefield) Att -   H.T. 16 - nil

Mon 6 Apr 1942 HALIFAX away lost nil - 5
HALIFAX - Lockwood: Bevan Smith Rule Elias: Todd
McCue: Baynham Meek Irving Millington Childs Dixon:
Try - Bevan: Goal - Lockwood:
CASTLEFORD - Brookes: Astbury <u>ALFRED</u>
<u>CHESTER(Dewsbury)(G)(235)</u> Jones <u>J.Ward(RochdaleH)(G)</u>
<u>Albert Collins</u> <u>Leonard Garbett</u>: McManus Haley
Bradbury(Salford)(G) Taylor Wagstaff Street:
Referee F Peel (Bradford) Att -   H.T. nil - 3

Sat 25 Apr 1942 OLDHAM away lost 3 - 14
CHALLENGE CUP ROUND 2 1ST LEG
OLDHAM - G.Thomas: Wilkinson Taylor Mitchell Lees:
Stott Smith: Parr Dean(Rochdale H)(G) Ogden Pugh
W.Thomas(Wigan)(G)Cattlin(Rochdale H)(G):
Tries - Mitchell Stott :   Goals - Stott(4):
CASTLEFORD - Peter Lythgoe: Brookes IDRIS
TOWILL(Huddersfield)(G)(236) Robinson Astbury:
Glover(Wigan))GP) Adams: McManus Haley <u>Joseph</u>
<u>Bradbury(Salford)(G)</u> Taylor Wagstaff Jones:
Try - Jones:
Referee W Hemmings (Halifax) Att - 3000 H.T. 3 - 8

Sat 2 May 1942 OLDHAM home lost nil - 10
CHALLENGE CUP ROUND 2 2ND LEG
CASTLEFORD - Brookes: <u>Dennis Baddeley</u> Robinson
<u>IdrisTowill(Huddersfield)(G)</u> Albert(Jack) Astbury:
<u>Glover(Wigan)(G)</u> <u>Leslie Adams</u>: Taylor Haley <u>George</u>
<u>Banks(Wigan)(G)</u> Smith Wagstaff Jones:
OLDHAM - Thomas: Wilkinson F.Taylor Mitchell Lees:
Stott Smith: Parr Dean Ogden Pugh J.Taylor Cattlin:
Tries - Wilkinson F.Taylor: Goals - Stott(2):
Referee A E Harding (Manchester) Att - 1500 H.T. nil - 2

**CASTLEFORD DID NOT FIELD A TEAM IN SEASONS
1942-43 AND 1943-44 OWING TO PLAYERS BEING
CALLED UP FOR NATIONAL SERVICE**

Stan Powell
D. No 214
Guest 1941-42 & 1944-45
Cas Player 1948-49 &
         1949-50

SEASON 1941-42

D.NO		PLAYER		DEBUT	L MATCH	APP	SUB	T.AP	TRI'S	G'LS	D.G	P'TS
21		ATKINSON	ARTHUR		14/03/1942	3	0	3	0	0	0	0
79		LEWIS	GEORGE			2	0	2	0	0	0	0
109		HAYES	WILLIAM			4	0	4	0	0	0	0
116		TAYLOR	THOMAS L.			19	0	19	2	0	0	6
123		HALEY	HAROLD			15	0	15	0	0	0	0
124		SMITH	FRANK Snr			10	0	10	3	0	0	9
130		CROSTON	ALFRED JAMES			15	0	15	12	5	0	46
133		ADAMS	LESLIE		02/05/1942	5	0	5	0	0	0	0
136		CROSSLEY	JAMES M.			2	0	2	1	0	0	3
141		McMANUS	PATRICK B.			23	0	23	1	0	0	3
147		HARDY	THOMAS			9	0	9	0	0	0	0
148		WALKER	FRANK		29/11/1941	10	0	10	1	6	0	15
159		WALSH	THOMAS			18	0	18	5	12	1	41
160		COTTINGTON	GORDON			10	0	10	0	0	0	0
168		STEAD	WILLIAM			1	0	1	0	0	0	0
174		GARBETT	LEONARD		06/04/1942	1	0	1	0	0	0	0
175		HORAN	JOHN			1	0	1	0	0	0	0
176		LLOYD	REGINALD			11	0	11	3	0	0	9
177		ROBINSON	JAMES			8	0	8	1	0	0	3
179		GUEST	NORMAN			1	0	1	0	0	0	0
180		LYTHGOE	PETER		25/04/1942	2	0	2	0	0	0	0
183		COLLINS	ALBERT		06/04/1942	1	0	1	0	0	0	0
189		FOX	JOHN H.			4	0	4	0	0	0	0
190	G	BANKS	GEORGE (WIGAN)		02/05/1942	1	0	1	0	0	0	0
191		ASTBURY	JACK		02/05/1942	19	0	19	5	2	0	19
192		JONES	ERIC			26	0	26	3	0	0	9
194		WAGSTAFF	FRANK			22	0	22	3	0	0	9
197		STREET	JACK			10	0	10	0	0	0	0
198		PENNINGTON	ERIC		20/09/1941	3	0	3	1	0	0	3
199		BROOKES	KENNETH			12	0	12	1	0	0	3
200		KEAR	HERBERT		20/12/1941	1	0	1	0	0	0	0
204		RENNARD	JOSEPH		25/10/1941	6	0	6	7	0	0	21
206		BADDELEY	DENNIS		02/05/1942	11	0	11	3	0	0	9
214	G	POWELL	STAN (St HELENS)	13/09/1941		13	0	13	3	11	0	31
215		NICHOLLS	JAMES	27/09/1941		17	0	17	0	0	0	0
216	G	LARGE	ALBANY (F'STONE R)	29/11/1941	06/12/1941	2	0	2	0	0	0	0
217	G	MOXON	HAROLD (F'RSTONE R)	13/12/1941	13/12/1941	1	0	1	0	0	0	0
218		HOYLE		26/12/1941	26/12/1941	1	0	1	0	0	0	0
219	G	BUCKLE	(DEWSBURY)	10/01/1942	10/01/1942	1	0	1	1	0	0	3
220	G	LONGLEY	ALBANY (F'STONE R)	10/01/1942		1	0	1	0	0	0	0
221	G	BATTEN	ERIC (HUNSLET)	14/02/1942	14/02/1942	1	0	1	0	0	0	0
222	G	MORRELL	CYRIL (HUNSLET)	14/02/1942	14/02/1942	1	0	1	0	0	0	0
223	G	TURTON	RONALD (HUNSLET)	14/02/1942	14/02/1942	1	0	1	0	0	0	0
224	G	CASE	DESMOND (B'FORD N.)	14/02/1942	14/02/1942	1	0	1	1	0	0	3
225	G	MORRIS	OLIVER (LEEDS)	14/02/1940	14/02/1940	1	0	1	0	0	0	0
226	G	WARD	J. (ROCHDALE H)	14/03/1942	06/04/1942	5	0	5	2	0	0	6
227	G	BRADBURY	JACK (St HELENS)	14/03/1942	04/04/1942	4	0	4	2	0	0	6
228	G	CLAPHAM	THOMAS (H'RSFIELD)	21/03/1942	21/03/1942	1	0	1	0	0	0	0
229	G	GLOVER	CHARLIE (WIGAN)	21/03/1942	02/05/1942	4	0	4	0	3	0	6
230	G	McCUE	THOMAS (WIDNES)	21/03/1942	21/03/1942	1	0	1	1	0	0	3
231	G	NICHOLSON	J. (DEWSBURY)	28/03/1942	28/03/1942	1	0	1	0	0	0	0
232	G	HAMER	RAYMOND (F'STONE)	04/04/1942		1	0	1	0	0	0	0
233	G	GOLBY	JOSEPH (F'STONE R.)	04/04/1942	04/04/1942	1	0	1	0	0	0	0
234	G	BRADBURY	JOSEPH (SALFORD)	04/04/1942	25/04/1942	3	0	3	0	0	0	0
235	G	CHESTER	ALFRED (DEWSBURY)	06/04/1942	06/04/1942	1	0	1	0	0	0	0
236	G	TOWILL	IDRIS (H'DDERSFIELD)	25/04/1942	02/05/1942	2	0	2	0	0	0	0
	22		56		23	31	351	0	351	62	39	1	266

COMPETITION		P	W	D	L	FOR	AGT
WAR LEAGUE	POSITION 14 OF 17	20	8	0	12	195	253
YORK'S CUP		4	2	0	2	35	29
R.L. CUP		2	0	0	2	3	24
VOID GAME BROUGHTON R.		1	1	0	0	33	5
PLAYERS RECORDS		**27**	**11**	**0**	**16**	**266**	**311**

SEASON 1944-45

WAR EMERGENCY LEAGUE

The club was back in business this season once again playing in the War Emergency League bringing the league back up to 17 teams – Batley Barrow Bradford N Castleford Dewsbury Featherstone R Halifax Huddersfield Hull Hunslet Keighley Leeds Oldham St Helens Wakefield T Wigan York.

Sat 2 Sep 1944 DEWSBURY home won 20 - 5
CASTLEFORD - G.Lewis: EDWARD KARLE(237) Croston Guest Longley(Featherstone R)(G): Robinson Walsh: McManus Haley Wagstaff Fox Nicholls Jones:
Tries - Croston(2) Fox Nicholls: Goals - Guest(4):
DEWSBURY - Ledgard: Dagnan Cammac Risman(Salford)(G) Withington: Hey(Leeds)(G) Herberts(Hull)(G): Hammond Day(Salford)(G) Crossland Curran(Salford)(G) Kershaw Bradbury:
Try - Dagnan: Goal - Risman:
Referee A Hill (Leeds) Att -   H.T. 10 - 3

Sat 9 Sep 1944 DEWSBURY away lost nil - 28
DEWSBURY - Ledgard: Dagnan(Oldham)(G) Risman(Salford)(G) Gear(Salford)(G) Withington: Hey(Leeds)(G) Royal: Hammond Day(Salford)(G) Pearson(Bramley)(G) Curran(Salford)(G) Kershaw Malkin:
Tries - Dagnan(4)Risman Pearson: Goals - Risman(5):
CASTLEFORD - RONALD LEWIS(238): Guest Robinson Croston Brookes: Hardy Hayes: McManus JOHN HILL(239) Wagstaff HAROLD HALE(240) Nicholls Jones:
Referee A Hill (Leeds) Att - 4000 H.T. nil - 10

Sat 16 Sep 1944 ST HELENS home won 26 - 11
CASTLEFORD - R.Lewis: LEN WARD(241) Guest Robinson LEONARD BROWN(242) GEORGE FISHER(243) Walsh: McManus Haley Wagstaff Fox Nicholls Jones:
Tries - Ward(3) Guest(2) Wagstaff:
Goals - Guest(3) Walsh(DG):
ST HELENS - Green: Gregory Waring Evans Riley: Clough French: Cotton Goodier Thompson Mills Higgins Matthews:
Tries - Riley Clough Matthews: Goal - French:
Referee A S Dobson (Pontefract) Att 2000 H.T. 11- nil

Sat 23 Sep 1944 HUDDERSFIELD away draw 8 - 8
HUDDERSFIELD - W.Davies: Peake Bardon Fiddes Lewis: McGurk Burrows: Baxter J.Davies Miller Corfield Mallinson A.N.Other: Goals - W.Davies(3) Burrows(DG):
CASTLEFORD - R.Lewis: Ward Robinson Guest F.LINGARD(Batley)(G)(244) Brookes Walsh: McManus Haley Wagstaff Nicholls Hale Jones:
Tries - Wagstaff McManus: Goal - Walsh:
Referee W Hemmings (Halifax) Att - 3500 H.T. 6 - 3

Sat 7 Oct 1944 HUNSLET home draw 6 - 6
CASTLEFORD - R.Lewis: Ward Robinson Croston Brookes: Hardy Hayes: Taylor Haley Wagstaff Hale Nicholls Jones:
Goals - Croston(3):
HUNSLET - Walkington: Thurling Morrell Winter Williamson: Watson Fletcher: Townsend Britton Billing

Plenderleith Clarkson Traill: Goals - Clarkson(3):
Referee T Marley (Wakefield) Att - 3000 H.T. 4 - 2

Sat 14 Oct 1944 BATLEY away lost 3 - 5
BATLEY - Cousins: Lingard Murphy Riches Roberts: Barrett Gee(Wigan)(G): Hammond Golby Sparkes Foley Mountain Seeling: Try - Cousins: Goal - Cousins:
CASTLEFORD - R.Lewis: Ward Robinson Croston JOSEPH BIBBY(245): Hardy Walsh: Taylor Cottington Wagstaff Nicholls Hale Jones: Try - Nicholls:
Referee L Thorpe (Wakefield) Att - 2000 H.T. 3 - nil

Sat 21 Oct 1944 HUNSLET away lost 3 - 6
YORKSHIRE CUP ROUND 1 1ST LEG
HUNSLET - Walkington: Thurling Morrell Winter Williamson: Goddard Fletcher: Plenderleith Billings Townend Stansfield Clarkson Traill:
Tries - Thurling Plenderleith:
CASTLEFORD - G.Lewis: Ward Robinson Alfred James Croston R.Lewis: Brookes Hayes: McManus Cottington Taylor Nicholls Harold Hale Jones: Try - Robinson:
Referee F Cottam (Wakefield) Att - 2000 H.T. 3 - nil

Sat 28 Oct 1944 HUNSLET home lost 2 - 8
YORKSHIRE CUP ROUND 1 2ND LEG
CASTLEFORD - George Lewis: Ward Robinson Jones R.Lewis: Hardy Walsh: McManus Cottington Taylor Wagstaff Nicholls Fox   Goal - Walsh:
HUNSLET - Walkington: Thurling Morrell Winter Williamson: Watson Goddard: Plenderleith Sweeting Billington Stansfield Clarkson Traill:
Tries - Morrell Williamson: Goal - Clarkson:
Referee L Thorpe (Wakefield) Att - 5000 H.T. 2 - nil

Sat 4 Nov 1944 LEEDS away won 3 - nil
Leeds - Cussens: Eaton Madden Lees Nicholson: A.N.Other Gee(Wigan)(G): Satterthwaite Murphy Rees Scott Flanagan Tattersfield:
CASTLEFORD - F.Lewis: Powell(St Helens)(G) ALEX FIDDES(Huddersfield)(G)(246) Guest HARGRAVE(York)(G)(247): KENNETH KENDALL(Huddersfield)(G)(248) Walsh: McManus Cottington Wagstaff Nicholls JACK EAST(249) Jones:
Try - Powell:
Referee S Adams (Hull) Att - 2000 H.T. nil - nil

Sat 11 Nov 1944 YORK home won 22 - nil
CASTLEFORD - F.Lewis: Ward WILLIAM(BILLY)STOTT (Wakefield T)(G)(250) HARRY MURPHY(Wakefield T)(G)(251) RON CARRES(Wakefield T)(G)(252): RON RYLANCE(Wakefield T)(G)(253) Hayes: McManus Haley Taylor Wagstaff Nicholls Jones:
Tries - Ward(2) Rylance(2) Stott Taylor:
Goals - Stott Rylance:
YORK - Smith: Brightmore(Featherstone R)(G) Ingham Bean Simmons: Fearn Watkinson: Shillito(Halifax)(G) Bradshaw(Featherstone R)(G)Goodman(Featherstone R)(G) Dobbs Maude Beverley:
Referee R Rawlinson (Mirfield) Att - 2000 H.T. 8 - nil

SEASON 1944-45

Sat 18 Nov 1944 BRADFORD NORTHERN away lost 2 - 14
BRADFORD N - Carmichael: Batten A.N.Other E.Ward Best: Bennett D.Ward: Whitcombe Darlison Higson Foster H.Smith Hutchinson: Tries - Best(3) Batten: Goal - E.Ward:
CASTLEFORD - R.Lewis: Ward Guest FRANK REES(Rochdale H)(G)(254) GEORGE CLINTON(255): PERCY SEARLES(Featherstone R)(G)(256) Hayes: McManus Cottington Taylor Nicholls Fox Jones: Goal - Guest:
Referee T Marley (Wakefield) Att - 3500 H.T. nil - 3

Sat 25 Nov 1944 BATLEY home won 25 - nil
CASTLEFORD - R.Lewis: Ward Robinson Guest Clinton: Brookes Walsh: McManus Cottington Taylor Wagstaff Nicholls Jones:
Tries - Ward(3) Guest Clinton Walsh McManus: Goals - Walsh(2):
BATLEY - Cousins: Gabriel France Murphy Brennan: Matterson Phillips: Sparkes Golby Morgan Brown Ferguson(Oldham) Seeling:
Referee F Cottam (Wakefield) Att - 2000 H.T. 19 - nil

Sat 9 Dec 1944 OLDHAM home won 15 - nil
CASTLEFORD - R.Lewis: Ward Robinson Guest Clinton: Brookes Walsh: McManus Cottington Taylor Wagstaff Nicholls Jones:
Tries - Robinson(2) Ward Brookes Jones:
OLDHAM - Radcliffe: Aspinall Turner Higginbottom Thomas: Rees Riley: Gardner Frost Pugh Lowe Laird Wood:
Referee A S Dobson (Pontefract) Att - 2000 H.T. 6 - nil

Sat 23 Dec 1944 OLDHAM away lost 5 - 13
OLDHAM - Radcliffe: Aspinall Higginbottom Turner Ratcliffe: Rees Schofield: Gardner Dean Rostron Pugh Laird Wood:
Tries - Aspinall Turner Laird: Goals - Radcliffe(2):
CASTLEFORD - R.Lewis: Ward Robinson Guest Clinton: Walsh Brookes: McManus Cottington Taylor Wagstaff Nicholls Jones:
Try - Clinton: Goal - Walsh:
Referee G S Phillips (Widnes) Att - 5000 H.T. nil - 8

Tue 26 Dec 1944 FEATHERSTONE ROVERS away won 8 - 3
FEATHERSTONE R - Barraclough: Place Ogden Longley Hossack: Bonas Searles: Hemingway Bowden Beal Wright Garner Street:
Try - Searles:
CASTLEFORD - R Lewis: Ward Robinson Guest Clinton: Brookes Walsh: McManus Cottington Taylor East Wagstaff Jones:
Tries - Ward Brookes: Goal - Walsh:
Referee L Thorpe (Wakefield) Att - 1400 H.T. 5 - 3

Sat 6 Jan 1945 HULL home won 35 - nil
CASTLEFORD - R.Lewis: Guest Robinson Powell(St Helens)(G) Clinton: Brookes Hayes: McManus Cottington Taylor Nicholls Wagstaff Jones:
Tries - Guest(2) Powell(2) Wagstaff(2) Robinson Clinton

Brookes Taylor Jones: Goal - Powell:
HULL - Oliver: Hogg Allan Shaw Davies: Glynn Crane: Beales Winfield Hattersley French Clark Atkinson:
Referee E Devine (Leeds) Att -   H.T. 15 - nil

Sat 13 Jan 1945 HUNSLET away won 11 - 3
HUNSLET - Eaton(Leeds)(G): Beckwith Fletcher Watson Williamson: Garside Wood: Plenderleith Britton Townend Billings Clarkson Downing(Hull K R)(G):
Try - Watson:
CASTLEFORD - R.Lewis: Ward Robinson Alex Fiddes(Huddersfield)(G) Clinton: Hayes Brookes: McManus Cottington Taylor Wagstaff Nicholls Jones:
Tries - Hayes(2) Brookes: Goal - Fiddes:
Referee W Hemmings (Halifax) Att -   H.T. 3 - nil

Sat 3 Feb 1945 WAKEFIELD TRINITY away lost 5 - 6
WAKEFIELD T - Teall: Perry Stott Townend Fletcher: Rylance Goodfellow: Wilkinson Marson Eddom Orford Moore Murphy Tries - Perry Fletcher:
CASTLEFORD - R.Lewis: Clinton Robinson Walsh ARCHER(257): Brookes Hayes: McManus Cottington Taylor Nicholls Wagstaff East:
Try - Brookes: Goal - Walsh:
Referee A Howgate (Dewsbury) Att 2000 H.T. 5 - 6

Sat 10 Feb 1945 ST HELENS away won 16 - 2
ST HELENS - King: Gregory Powell J.Waring Howarth: Bate Ball: Thompson Phillips Delves Shaw Riley Mills:
Goal - Powell:
CASTLEFORD - R.Lewis: Robinson JACK KITCHING(Bradford N)(G)(258) William(Billy)Stott(Wakefield T)(G) Clinton: Brookes Hayes: McManus Cottington Taylor Nicholls Wagstaff Jones:
Tries - Robinson Stott Clinton McManus: Goals - Stott(2):
Referee G S Phillips (Widnes) Att - 1000 H.T. 5 - 2

Sat 17 Feb 1945 LEEDS home won 10 - 4
CASTLEFORD - R.Lewis: Len Ward Guest JACK CLINTON(Wigan)(G)(259) G.Clinton: Brookes Hayes: McManus Cottington Taylor East Wagstaff Jones:
Tries - G.Clinton(2) Goals - Guest(2):
LEEDS - Eaton: Bell Dick Cornelius Staniland: Lawrence Jenkins: Satterthwaite Murphy Dyer Scott Benson Tattersfield:
Goals - Eaton(2):
Referee S Adams (Hull) Att -   H.T. 7 - nil

Sat 24 Feb 1945 YORK away won 27 - 12
YORK - Knowles: Sullivan Ingham Davies Wilson: Watkinson Sowden: Shillito Deighton Stringer Smith Dobbs Beverley:
Tries - Deighton Beverley: Goals - Davies(3):
CASTLEFORD - R.Lewis: Hardy Guest G.Clinton J.Clinton(Wigan)(G): GEORGE BENNETT(Bradford N)(G)(260) Hayes: McManus Haley Wagstaff East EDWARD LAVENDER(261) Jones:
Tries - J.Clinton(3) Bennett(2) G.Clinton Lavender:
Goals - Guest(3):
Referee -   Att -   H.T.

SEASON 1944-45

Sat 3 Mar 1945 HALIFAX home lost 5 - 8
CHALLENGE CUP PRELIMINARY ROUND 1ST LEG
CASTLEFORD - R.Lewis: Hardy J.Clinton(Wigan)(G)
Robinson G.Clinton: Brookes Hayes: McManus Haley
Lavender Nicholls East Jones:
Try - G.Clinton: Goal - G.Clinton:
HALIFAX - Taylor: Malone Rule Toss Bassett: Humphrey
McCue: Morgan Jones McDowell Millington Meek
Dixon(S/O): Tries - Rule Bassett: Goal - Taylor:
Referee F Fairhurst (Wigan) Att - 6600 H.T. 3 - nil

Sat 10 Mar 1945 HALIFAX away lost 3 - 8
CHALLENGE CUP PRELIMINARY ROUND 2ND LEG
HALIFAX - Taylor: Malone Rule Todd Bassett: Humphrey
McCue: Morgan Jones McDowell Millington Meek Dixon:
Tries - Dixon Bassett: Goal - Taylor:
CASTLEFORD - R.Lewis: Guest Jack Clinton(Wigan)(G)
Robinson G.Clinton: Brookes Hayes: McManus Haley
Taylor Fox Nicholls Jones: Try - J.Clinton:
Referee A Holbrook (Warrington) Att - 7000 H.T. 3 - 5

Sat 31 Mar 1945 HULL away lost nil - 3
HULL - Oliver: Dockar Allen Crane Ness: Lawrence
Carmichael: Beales Sweeting Beaumont Clark Atkinson
A.Dockar: Try - Crane:
CASTLEFORD - R.Lewis: Lavender Guest Robinson
G.Clinton: Brookes Hayes: Taylor Haley Wagstaff Nicholls
East Jones:
Referee F Armstrong (Hud'field) Att - 4000 H.T. nil - nil

Sat 2 Apr 1945 FEATHERSTONE ROVERS home
won 16 - 3
CASTLEFORD - R.Lewis: GORDON BOOTH(262) Robinson
WILF NESS(Hull)(G)(263) G.Clinton: Brookes Hayes: Taylor
SAM SWEETING(Hull)(G)(264) Wagstaff Nicholls East
Jones: Tries - Brookes(3) Nicholls: Goals - Brookes(2):
FEATHERSTONE R - Parkin: Place Allman Ogden Lane:
Bond Higgins: Hemingway Bowden Wood Wright
Sherwood Street: Try - Wright:
Referee J E Taylor (Wakefield) Att - 1800 H.T. 11 - 3

Sat 7 Apr 1945 HUDDERSFIELD home won 9 - 3
CASTLEFORD - R.Lewis: Guest Robinson Hardy G.Clinton:
Brookes Hayes: Taylor Cottington Wagstaff Nicholls
JAMES C.BLACK (265)East:
Try - Black: Goals - Brookes(3):
HUDDERSFIELD - Leake: Booth(Castleford)(G) Fiddes
Winkworth Brown(Castleford)(G): Todd McGurk:
Mallinson Whitehead Miller Baxter Corfield Givvons:
Try - McGurk:
Referee J E Taylor (Wakefield) Att - 2000 H.T. 4 - nil

Sat 21 Apr 1945 WAKEFIELD TRINITY home
lost 2 - 10
CASTLEFORD - R.Lewis: Guest LADIS
DAVIES(York)(G)(266) Robinson Alban
Longley(Featherstone R)(G): Brooks William Hayes: Taylor
JIM BOWDEN(Featherstone R)(G)(267) Frank Wagstaff
Nicholls Black Jones: Goal - Brookes:
WAKEFIELD T - Teall: Perry Brown Townend Copley:

Fletcher Goodfellow: Wilkinson Golby Eddom Orford
J.Brown(Batley)(G) Murphy:
Tries - Fletcher Murphy: Goals - Perry(2):
Referee A Howgate (Dewsbury) Att -   H.T.

END OF WAR EMERGENCY LEAGUE

Ronnie Lewis
D. No 238
1944-45 to 1952-53

John Hill
D. No 239
1944-45 to 1955-56

George Clinton
D. No 255
1944-45 to 1951-52

Jack Kitching
D. No 258
Guest 1944-45
Cas Player 1950-51
to 1951-52

Eddie Lavender
D. No 261
1944-45 to 1947-48

SEASON 1944-45

D.N		PLAYER		DEBUT	L MATCH	APP	SUB	T.AP	TRI'S	G'LS	D.G	P'TS
79		LEWIS	GEORGE		28/10/1944	3	0	3	0	0	0	0
109		HAYES	WILLIAM		21/04/1945	17	0	17	2	0	0	6
116		TAYLOR	THOMAS L.			20	0	20	2	0	0	6
123		HALEY	HAROLD			9	0	9	0	0	0	0
130		CROSTON	ALFRED JAMES		21/10/1944	5	0	5	2	3	0	12
141		McMANUS	PATRICK B.			21	0	21	3	0	0	9
147		HARDY	THOMAS			7	0	7	0	0	0	0
159		WALSH	THOMAS			11	0	11	1	7	1	19
160		COTTINGTON	GORDON			15	0	15	0	0	0	0
177		ROBINSON	JAMES			22	0	22	5	0	0	15
179		GUEST	NORMAN			17	0	17	5	13	0	41
189		FOX	JOHN H.			5	0	5	1	0	0	3
192		JONES	ERIC			25	0	25	2	0	0	6
194		WAGSTAFF	FRANK		21/04/1945	23	0	23	4	0	0	12
199		BROOKES	KENNETH			19	0	19	8	6	0	36
214	G	POWELL	STAN (ST HELENS)			2	0	2	3	1	0	11
215		NICHOLLS	JAMES			24	0	24	3	0	0	9
220	G	LONGLEY	ALBANY (F'STONE R)		21/04/1945	2	0	2	0	0	0	0
237		KARLE	EDDIE	02/09/1944	02/09/1944	1	0	1	0	0	0	0
238		LEWIS	RONALD	09/09/1944		26	0	26	0	0	0	0
239		HILL	JOHN	09/09/1944		1	0	1	0	0	0	0
240		HALE	HAROLD	09/09/1944	21/10/1944	5	0	5	0	0	0	0
241		WARD	LEN	16/09/1944	17/02/1945	14	0	14	10	0	0	30
242		BROWN	LEONARD	16/09/1944		1	0	1	0	0	0	0
243		FISHER	GEORGE	16/09/1944	16/09/1944	1	0	1	0	0	0	0
244	G	LINGARD	F (BATLEY)	23/09/1944	23/09/1944	1	0	1	0	0	0	0
245		BIBBY	JOSEPH	14/10/1944	14/10/1944	1	0	1	0	0	0	0
246	G	FIDDES)	ALEX (H'DERSFIELD)	04/11/1944	13/01/1945	2	0	2	0	1	0	2
247	G	HARGRAVE	(YORK)	04/11/1944	04/11/1944	1	0	1	0	0	0	0
248	G	KENDALL	KENNETH (H'DSFIELD)	04/11/1944		1	0	1	0	0	0	0
249		EAST	JACK	04/11/1944		9	0	9	0	0	0	0
250	G	STOTT	WILLIAM (BILLY) (W'D T)	11/11/1944	10/02/1945	2	0	2	2	3	0	12
251	G	MURPHY	HARRY (W'KEFIELD T)	11/11/1944	11/11/1944	1	0	1	0	0	0	0
252	G	CARRES	RON (WAKEFIELD T)	11/11/1944	11/11/1944	1	0	1	0	0	0	0
253	G	RYLANCE	RON (WAKEFIELD T)	11/11/1944	11/11/1944	1	0	1	2	1	0	8
254	G	REES	FRANK (ROCHDALE H)	18/11/1944	18/11/1944	1	0	1	0	0	0	0
255		CLINTON	GEORGE	18/11/1944		16	0	16	8	1	0	26
256	G	SEARLES	PERCY (F'STONE R)	18/11/1944	18/11/1944	1	0	1	0	0	0	0
257		ARCHER		03/02/1945	03/02/1945	1	0	1	0	0	0	0
258	G	KITCHING	JACK (BRADFORD N)	10/02/1945		1	0	1	0	0	0	0
259	G	CLINTON	JACK (WIGAN)	17/02/1945	10/03/1945	4	0	4	4	0	0	12
260	G	BENNETT	GEORGE (BR'FORD N)	24/02/1945	24/02/1945	1	0	1	2	0	0	6
261		LAVENDER	EDWARD	24/02/1945		3	0	3	1	0	0	3
262		BOOTH	GORDON	02/04/1945		1	0	1	0	0	0	0
263	G	NESS	WILF (HULL)	02/04/1945	02/04/1945	1	0	1	0	0	0	0
264	G	SWEETING	SAM (HULL)	02/04/1945	02/04/1945	1	0	1	0	0	0	0
265		BLACK	JAMES C.	07/04/1945		2	0	2	1	0	0	3
266	G	DAVIES	LADIS (YORK)	21/04/1945		1	0	1	0	0	0	0
267	G	BOWDEN	JIM (F'STONE R)	21/04/1945	21/04/1945	1	0	1	0	0	0	0
	19		49		31	25	351	0	351	71	36	1	287

	COMPETITION		P	W	D	L	FOR	AGT
	WAR LEAGUE	POSITION 6 OF 17	23	14	2	7	274	139
	YORK'S CUP		2	0	0	2	5	14
	RL CUP		2	0	0	2	8	16
	PLAYERS RECORDS		**27**	**14**	**2**	**11**	**287**	**169**

Sadly three players lost their lives in the war: Leslie Adams, who never returned from a flight over Burma with the RAF; Peter Lythgoe who last played in the 1941/42 season; and Eric England killed in an air raid, who had played his last game in the 1937/38 season. The large number of players who played their last game (12) in 1941/42, and would not play again, was another reflection of the toll the war took on this generation.

SEASON 1945-46

ONE DIVISION ONLY

The 1945/46 Season brought the return of normal league football. With Bramley, Broughton Rangers, Hull K R, Liverpool Stanley, Rochdale Hornets, Salford, Swinton, Warrington, And Widnes rejoining the league and Workington Town being admitted it brought the number of competing teams to 27 playing in the one division.

Sat 18 Aug 1945 FEATHERSTONE ROVERS away won 25 - 7   LYON CUP FRIENDLY
FEATHERSTONE R - Parkin: Place Ogden Smith Lane: Allman Moxon: Wood Raybould Goodman Wright Street Garner:
Try - Place: Goals - Wright(2):
CASTLEFORD - Lewis: Booth Hardy Robinson Clinton: Brookes Hamer: Taylor Darlison Wagstaffe Nicholls Street Jones:
Tries - Lewis Booth Robinson Hamer Brookes:
Goals - Brookes(5):
Referee A S Dobson (Pontefract)   Att -   H.T.   5 - 2

Sat 25 Aug 1945 SALFORD away lost nil - 10
SALFORD - Caulfield: Dagnan Edwards Risman Healey: Harrison Jones: Gardner Day Davies Evans Vibart Curran:
Tries - Dagnan(2):   Goals - Risman(2):
CASTLEFORD - Lewis: Booth Robinson Clinton East: Brookes Hamer: Taylor Cottington Slater Nicholls Street Jones:
Referee -   Att - 10000 H.T. nil - nil

Wed 29 Aug 1945 WARRINGTON home won 13 - 9
CASTLEFORD - Lewis: Booth Brookes Robinson Clinton: JAMES THOMAS(268) Hamer: William Stead Cottington Taylor Fox Slater Jones:
Tries - Brookes Robinson Clinton: Goals - Brookes(2):
WARRINGTON - Jones: Ratcliffe Lee Higginbottom Holland: Belshaw Helme: Miller Cotton Jones Baker Mason Chapman:
Try - Lee: Goals - Belshaw(3):
Referee L Thorpe (Wakefield) Att - 4000 H.T. 10 - 2

Sat 1 Sep 1945 HALIFAX home won 6 - 5
CASTLEFORD - Lewis: Booth GEOFFREY BRIGGS(269)Robinson Clinton: Brookes Hamer: McManus Cottington Taylor Slater East Jones:
Goals - Briggs(3):
HALIFAX - Davies: Daniles Mason Humphrey Taylor: Rule Hurcombe: Childs Pritchard Irving Smith Meek Dixon:
Try - Hurcombe: Goal - Taylor:
Referee A Hill (Leeds) Att - 4000 H.T. 4 - 5

Sat 8 Sep 1945 HUDDERSFIELD away lost 5 - 16
HUDDERSFIELD - Leake: Todd Fiddes Winkworth Bawden: Burrows Byrne: Booth Whitehead Gronow Baxter Givvons Robson:
Tries - Todd(2) Fiddes Booth: Goals - Bawden(2):
CASTLEFORD - Lewis: Booth Clinton Robinson Wilfred(Buck)Boucher: Brookes Hamer: McManus

Cottington Taylor East Slater Jones:
Try - Clinton: Goal - Boucher:
Referee R Rawlinson (Mirfield) Att - 5000 H.T. 2 - 3

Sat 15 Sep 1945 YORK home won 18 - 7
CASTLEFORD - Lewis: Brookes Briggs Robinson Clinton: James Thomas Hamer: McManus Cottington Taylor Nicholls Slater Jones:
Tries - Clinton(2) Brookes Hamer: Goals - Robinson(3):
YORK - Knowles: Brown Taylor Smith Fearn: Watkinson Benson: Crossley Deighton Dobbs Nicholls White Davies:
Try - Benson: Goals - Davies(2):
Referee F Cottam (Wakefield) Att - 2712 H.T. 11 - 5

Sat 22 Sep 1945 BRADFORD NORTHERN away lost nil - 2
BRADFORD N - Carmichael: Batten Kitching Bennett Best: Davies D.Ward: Whitcombe Darlison Higson Roberts Marklew Hutchinson:
Goal - Carmichael:
CASTLEFORD - Lewis: Booth Robinson Clinton Hardy: Brookes Hamer: Taylor Cottington Slater Nicholls East Jones:
Referee W Hemmings (Halifax)   Att -   H.T. nil - 2

Sat 29 Sep 1945 BRAMLEY home won 19 - 4
CASTLEFORD - Lewis: DAVIES(270) Robinson Clinton Hardy: Brookes Hamer: Taylor Cottington Nicholls Jack Street East Jones:
Tries - Hardy Brookes Hamer: Goals - Brookes(5):
BRAMLEY - McAndrew: Robinson Gibson Womersley Sedgewick: Lloyd Spillane: Pearson Wetherill Wilks Rawson Baxter Drabble:
Goals - Gibson(2):
Referee A Howgate (Dewsbury) Att -   H.T. 4 - 2

Sat 6 Oct 1945 LEEDS away lost 4 - 11 YORKSHIRE CUP ROUND 1 1ST LEG
LEEDS - Lockwood: Batten Cornelius Price Tate: Evans Jenkins: Satterthwaite Murphy Wheatley Jubb Scott Owens:
Try - Owens: Goals - Lockwood(4):
CASTLEFORD - Lewis: Booth Clinton Robinson Hardy: Brookes Hamer: McManus Cottington Nicholls(S/O) Smith East Jones:
Goals - Brookes 2):
Referee A Howgate (Dewsbury) Att -   H.T. 2 - 4

Sat 13 Oct 1945 LEEDS home won 11 - 10 YORKSHIRE CUP ROUND 1 2ND LEG
CASTLEFORD - Lewis: Booth Robinson Clinton Hardy: Brookes Hamer: Taylor Haley Smith Fox East Jones:
Try - East: Goals - Brookes(3) Smith:
LEEDS - Lockwood: Tate Price Cornelius Evans: Williams Jenkins: Satterthwaite Murphy Wheatley Jubb Scott Owens:
Tries - Owens(2): Goals - Lockwood(2):
Referee L Thorpe (Wakefield) Att - 6700 H.T. 4 - 2

SEASON 1945-46

Sat 20 Oct 1945 WARRINGTON away lost 8 - 19
WARRINGTON - Belshaw: Ratcliffe L.Jones Higginbottom
Johnson: Baxter Helme: Jones Cotton Miller Bennett Ryan
Taylor: Tries - Ratcliffe L.Jones Johnson Bennett
Higginbottom: Goals - Belshaw Ryan:
CASTLEFORD - Lewis: Booth Clinton Robinson WIILIAM
CHURM(271) Brookes Hamer: Taylor Cottington Smith
Lavender East Jones:
Tries - Brookes Taylor: Goal - Brookes:
Referee A Hill(Leeds) Att - 7000 H.T. 3 - 14

Sat 27 Oct 1945 SWINTON home won 20 – 10
CASTLEFORD - Lewis: Hardy Robinson Clinton Booth:
Brookes Hamer: Taylor Cottington Nicholls Lavender East
Jones: Tries - Clinton Hamer Nicholls Lavender:
Goals - Brookes(4):
SWINTON - Lowe: Crossland McGurk Schofield Shaw:
Bowyer Turner: Wright Davies Hughes Stoddart Garner
Ducker: Tries - Crossland Schofield: Goals - Lowe(2):
Referee - G S Phillips (Widnes) Att - 5000 H.T. 5 - 0

Sat 3 Nov 1945 LEEDS away lost nil - 9
LEEDS - Lockwood: Tate Price Cornelius Batten: Evans
Jenkins: Satterthwaite Murphy Wheatley Scott Walters
Owens: Try - Price: Goals - Lockwood(3):
CASTLEFORD - Lewis: Booth Robinson Clinton Hardy:
Brookes Hamer: Taylor Cottington Nicholls Smith
Lavender Jones:
Referee A Howgate (Dewsbury) Att - 4000 .T. nil - 2

Sat 10 Nov 1945 KEIGHLEY home won 7 - nil
CASTLEFORD - Lewis: Clinton Bernard Cunniffe Robinson
Booth: Brookes Hamer: Cottington Haley Smith Nicholls
Lavender Jones: Try - Cunniffe: Goals - Brookes(2):
KEIGHLEY - Mills: Coldwell Thatcher Towill Ward: Davies
Burrett: Fuller Lockwood Butterfield Harris Foster Foley:
Referee A Hill (Leeds) Att - 2000 H.T. 2 - nil

**Sat 17 Nov 1945 COTE BASQUE won 11 – 8
FRIENDLY AT BAYONNE**
COTE BASQUE team not known
CASTLEFORD - Lewis: Booth Clinton Robinson Hardy:
Brookes Hamer: Taylor Haley Cottington Smith Nicholls
East: Tries – Hardy Hamer Haley: Goal – Brookes :
Referee - Att - 5000 H.T. 8 - nil

**Sunday 18 Nov 1945 BORDEAUX away draw 8 - 8
FRIENDLY AT MUNICIPAL STADIUM BORDEAUX**
Bordeaux team not known
CASTLEFORD - Lewis: Booth Clinton Robinson Hardy:
Brookes Hamer: Taylor Haley Cottington Smith Nicholls
East: Tries - Nicholls Hardy: Goals – Brookes:
Referee - Att - 15000 H.T. 3 - 3

Sat 24 Nov 1945 SALFORD home won 15 - 5
CASTLEFORD - Lewis: East Robinson Clinton Booth:
Brookes Hamer: McManus Haley Cottington Smith
Lavender Jones:
Tries - Clinton Booth Jones: Goals - Brookes(3):
SALFORD - H.Jones: Snipe Miller R.Jones Todd: Harrison

Watkins: Brown Day Gardner Thomas Hartley Curran:
Try - Todd: Goal - Brown:
Referee F Fairhurst (Wigan) Att - 4000 H.T. 10 - 2

Sat 1 Dec 1945 BARROW away lost 6 - 18
BARROW - Jones: Lewthwaite Spooner Bowker Rice:
Horne Bowker: Troup Woods Hughes Pedley Petcher
Little: Tries - Little(2) Rice Lewthwaite 1 Try scorer
unknown: Goals - Jones(3):
CASTLEFORD - Lewis: HARRY BRUMMITT(272) Robinson
Clinton Booth: Brookes Hamer: Taylor Haley Nicholls
Lavender Fox Jones: Goals - Brookes(3):
Referee F Fairhurst (Wigan) Att - H.T. 2 - 12

**Sat 8 Dec 1945 HULL KINGSTON ROVERS home
won 14 - 5**
CASTLEFORD - Lewis: Hardy Robinson Clinton Booth:
Brookes Hamer: Taylor Haley Smith Nicholls Lavender
Jones:
Tries - Clinton Booth Hamer Lavender: Goal - Brookes:
HULL K R - McWatt: Gee Hutchins Mills Ness: Morgan
Whitworth: Wilmot Ramsden Beaumont Bedford Atkinson
Collinson: Try Morgan: Goal - McWatt:
Referee L Thorpe (Wakefield) Att - 2000 H.T. 11 - nil

**Sat 15 Dec 1945 HULL KINGSTON ROVERS away
won 14 - 11**
HULL K R - McWatt: Eastwood Goldswain Bratley
Hutchins: Ness Whitworth: Clark Ramsden Beaumont
Bedford Atkinson Collinson:
Tries - Goldswain Collinson Eastwood:
Goal - McWatt:
CASTLEFORD - Briggs: Lloyd Clinton Kendall Hardy:
Brookes Hamer: Taylor Haley Smith Nicholls Lavender
Jones:
Tries - Hardy Lavender: Goals - Briggs(4):
Referee A Hill (Leeds) Att - 5000 H.T. 7 - 8

Sat 22 Dec 1945 BATLEY home lost 4 - 13
CASTLEFORD - Briggs: Hardy Clinton Kendall Booth:
Brookes JAMES BYRNE(273): Taylor Haley Nicholls
Lavender Fox John Horan:
Goals - Brookes (2):
BATLEY - Eaton: Taylor Lingard Etty Gabriel: Phillips Gee:
Grimshaw Golby Mulcaby Jukes Brown Hudson:
Tries - Etty Gee Phillips : Goals - Brown(2):
Referee J Probert (Wakefield) Att - 2500 H.T. nil - 8

**Tue 25 Dec 1945 WAKEFIELD TRINITY away
lost 5 - 23**
WAKEFIELD T - Teall: Copley Stott Townend Baddeley:
Rylance Goodfellow: Wilkinson Marson Higgins Allinson
Moore Bratley:
Tries - Copley(3) Rylance Wilkinson: Goals - Stott(4):
CASTLEFORD - Briggs: Thomas Hardy Robinson Clinton
Booth: Brookes James Byrne: Taylor Haley Lavender
Nicholls Smith Jones:
Try - Lavender: Goal - Briggs:
Referee A Hill (Leeds) Att - H.T. 5 - 13

SEASON 1945-46

Sat 29 Dec 1945 HULL away won 14 - 6
HULL - Hogg: Jeffreys Watts Bowers Glynn: Lawrence
Craine: Thacker Sweeying Tindall Booth Wray Holt:
Goals - Watts(3):
CASTLEFORD - Briggs: East Clinton Robinson Jones:
Kendall Hamer: Taylor Haley Lavender Nicholls Smith Fox:
Tries - Nicholls Smith: Goals - Briggs(4)
Referee A Howgate (Dewsbury) Att - 6000 H.T. nil - 6

**Sat 5 Jan 1946 BRADFORD NORTHERN home
lost 2 - 6**
CASTLEFORD - Briggs: Lavender Robinson Kendall Clinton:
Brookes Hamer: Taylor Haley Cottington Smith Nicholls
Fox: Goal - Briggs:
BRADFORD N - Carmichael: Troth Kitching Billington Best:
Bennett D.Ward: A.N.Other Darlison Higson Roberts
Cording Marklew: Tries - Troth Best:
Referee A C Dodd (Hull) Att - 4000 H.T. nil - 3

Sat 12 Jan 1946 HUNSLET home lost 5 - 13
CASTLEFORD - Briggs: Brummitt Robinson Kendall Booth:
Brookes SIDNEY BARKER(274): Taylor Haley Lavender
Smith Crossley Fox: Try - Robinson: Goal - Brookes:
HUNSLET - Walkington: Williamson Morrell Rookes O'Neil:
Ruston Watson: Plenderleith White Newbound Stansfield
Whitehead Clarkson:
Tries - Rookes Ruston Stansfield: Goals - Clarkson(2):
Referee L Thorpe (Wakefield) Att - 6000 H.T. 5 - 10

Sat 26 Jan 1946 SWINTON away won 15 - 11
SWINTON - Lowe: Lewis K.Turner Yates Schofield: McGurk
C.Turner: Garner Davies Hughes Ducker Knowles Spruce:
Tries - Schofield Ducker Knowles: Goal - Lowe:
CASTLEFORD - Briggs: Booth Robinson Clinton Harry
Brummitt: Brookes Walsh: Taylor Hill Lavender Smith
Nicholls Jones:
Tries - Clinton Brookes Taylor: Goals - Briggs(3); Referee
A Holbrook (Warrington) Att -   H.T. 10 - 3

**Sat 2 Feb 1946 FEATHERSTONE ROVERS home
won 7 - 6**
CASTLEFORD - Briggs: RONALD COPLEY(275) Brookes
Clinton JAMES THORNBURROW(276): FRED
CHURCH(277) Walsh: Taylor Haley Lavender Smith
Nicholls Jones: Try - Walsh: Goals - Briggs(2):
FEATHERSTONE R - Chapman: Ward Tennant Smith
Walton: Bennett Higgins: Desborough Nash Wagstaffe
Wright Garner Jacobs: Goals - Wright(2) Higgins:
Referee F Fairhurst (Wigan) Att - 4000 H.T. 4 - 2

**Sat 9 Feb 1946 ST HELENS home won 10 - 4
CHALLENGE CUP ROUND 1 1ST LEG**
CASTLEFORD - Briggs: Copley Kendall Clinton
Thornburrow:: Brookes Hamer: Taylor Cottington Crossley
Nicholls Smith Jones:
Tries - Hamer Copley: Goals - Briggs(2):
ST HELENS - Ball: Doyle Mills Leyland Gregory: Bradbury
French: Davies Goodier Thompson Hornby Heaton Birch:
Goals - Ball(1)(DG):
Referee J W Webb (Broughton) Att - 5000 H.T. 5 - 2

**Sat 16 Feb 1946 ST HELENS away lost 5 - 14
CHALLENGE CUP ROUND 1 2ND LEG**
ST HELENS - Ball: Doyle Mills Myers Gregory: Tracey
French: Davies Hornby Litherland Heaton Leyland Birch:
Tries - Doyle(3) Mills: Goal - Ball:
CASTLEFORD - Briggs: Copley Kendall Clinton James
Thornburrow: Brookes Hamer: Taylor Cottington Crossley
Nicholls Lavender Jones: Try - Brookes: Goal - Briggs:
Referee R Kendall (Keighley) Att - 6000 H.T. 2 - 14

Sat 23 Feb 1946 YORK away won 19 - 9
YORK - Knowles: Bean Taylor Wilson Miller: Fearn Benson:
Smith Deighton McArdle Davies Nicholas Brown:
Try - Davies: Goals - Knowles(3):
CASTLEFORD - Briggs: Copley ARTHUR BASTOW(278)
Church Clinton: Brookes Thomas(Tot)Walsh: MAXWELL
ROBINSON(279)Cottington Crossley Lavender Nicholls
Jones: Tries - Cottington Walsh Jones:
Goals - Briggs(4) Walsh(DG):
Referee A C Dodd (Hull) Att -   H.T. 12 - 9

Sat 9 Mar 1946 DEWSBURY home won 6 - 5
CASTLEFORD - Briggs: Copley Kendall Bastow Lloyd:
Brookes Hamer: Taylor Cottington Crossley Smith Nicholls
Lavender: Tries - Copley Lloyd:
DEWSBURY - Ledgard: Kilgannon Hey Sullivan
Withington: Pierce Clough: Hammond McKeating Waters
Hickey Hughes McManus: Try - Pierce: Goal - Ledgard:
Referee W Hemmings (Halifax) Att - 5000 H.T. 3 - 5

Sat 16 Mar 1946 DEWSBURY away lost 2 - 7
DEWSBURY - Ledgard: Withington Sullivan Hey Clark:
Pierce Bowen: Kelly Holt Hickey Waters McKeating
Hammond: Try - Hey: Goals - Ledgard(2):
CASTLEFORD - Briggs: Copley Clinton Bastow Lloyd:
Brookes Hamer: Taylor Cottington Crossley Smith
Lavender Nicholls: Goal - Briggs:
Referee A Hill (Leeds) Att - 3000 H.T. 2 - 7

Sat 23 Mar 1946 HUDDERSFIELD home won 9 - 3
CASTLEFORD - Briggs: Copley Bastow Kendall Lloyd:
Church Hamer: Taylor Haley Crossley Nicholls Smith
Lavender: Tries - Copley Hamer Church:
HUDDERSFIELD - Leake: Anderson Fiddes Pepperell
Bawden: Grahame Morgan: Whitehead Moran Mallinson
Baxter Nicholson Givvons: Try - Fiddes:
Referee A Hill (Leeds) Att - 6000 H.T. 9 - 3

Sat 30 Mar 1946 BATLEY away won 13 - 7
BATLEY - Ingram: Evans Eaton Etty Gabriel: Phillips Gee:
Rhodes Golby Grimshaw Jukes Brown Tattersfield:
Try - Eaton: Goals - Rhodes(2):
CASTLEFORD - Briggs: Copley Bastow Clinton Lloyd:
Brookes Hamer: McManus Cottington Crossley Nicholls
Smith Lavender:
Tries - Bastow Clinton McManus: Goals - Briggs(2):
Referee T Armitage (Huddersfield) Att -   H.T. 3 - 4

SEASON 1945-46

Wed 3 Apr 1946 WAKEFIELD TRINITY home won 9 - 2
CASTLEFORD - Briggs: Copley Bastow Clinton Lloyd:
Church Hamer: McManus Haley Thomas L Taylor Nicholls
Smith Lavender: Try - McManus: Goals - Briggs(3):
WAKEFIELD T - Oliver: Perry Townsend Fletcher Baddeley:
Jones Kielty: Wilkinson Marson Higgins Exley Moore
Bratley: Goal - Oliver:
Referee A Hill (Leeds) Att - 7500 H.T. 5 - nil

Sat 6 Apr 1946 BRAMLEY away won 7 - 2
BRAMLEY - Hodgson: Ellener Gibson Womersley Bartle:
Pearce Birmingham: Marshall King Bancroft Gater Baxter
Sedgewick: Goal - Gibson(DG):
CASTLEFORD - Briggs: Copley Bastow Clinton Lloyd:
Brookes GEORGE LANGFIELD(280): McManus Cottington
Slater Smith Nicholls Lavender:
Try - Langfield: Goals - Briggs(2):
Referee W Hemmings (Halifax) Att - 3500 H.T. 7 - 2

Tue 9 Apr 1946 KEIGHLEY away won 10 - nil
KEIGHLEY - Mills: Burnett Holmes Fell Kelly: Barrett
Burnell: Ferguson Croft Foster Flanagan Farrar McManus:
CASTLEFORD - Briggs: Copley Bastow Clinton Lloyd:
Church Langfield: McManus Cottington Slater Smith
Nicholls Lavender: Tries - Bastow(2): Goals - Briggs(2):
Referee A Howgate (Dewsbury) Att - 1500 H.T. 10 - nil

Sat 13 Apr 1946 HUNSLET away won 6 - 2
HUNSLET - Lorriman: Williamson Buck Smith O'Neil:
Ruston Watson: Stansfield Britton Newbound Whitehead
Clarkson Traill: Goal - Whitehead:
CASTLEFORD - Briggs: Kendall Copley Clinton Church:
Brookes Langfield: McManus Haley Slater Smith Lavender
East: Tries - Langfield Slater:
Referee G S Phillips (Widnes) Att - 10500 H.T. 3 - 2

Fri 19 Apr 1946 FEATHERSTONE ROVERS away lost 11 - 14
FEATHERSTONE R - Chapman: Longley Barraclough Smith
Edwards: Bennett Higgins: Ramskill Garner Wagstaffe
Kent Jacobs Street:
Tries - Longley(2) Edwards Garner: Goal - Higgins:
CASTLEFORD - Briggs: Kendall Copley Clinton Church:
Brookes Langfield: McManus Cottington Slater Nicholls
Smith Crossley:
Tries - Copley Church Brookes: Goal - Briggs:
Referee J E Taylor (Wakefield) Att - 6000 H.T. 11 - 2

Sat 20 Apr 1946 HULL home won 17 - 10
CASTLEFORD - Briggs: Kendall Copley Clinton Bastow:
Brookes Langfield: McManus Haley Crossley Nicholls
Lavender East:
Tries - Copley(2) McManus: Goals - Brookes(4):
HULL - Miller: Joy Shaw Wilson Jewison: Lawrence Smales:
Thacker Sweeting Shillito Jimmison Tindall Kavanagh:
Tries - Joy Lawrence: Goals - Miller(2):
Referee A Hill (Leeds) Att - 4000 H.T. 7 - 2

Mon 22 Apr 1946 LEEDS home won 10 - nil
CASTLEFORD - Briggs: Kenneth Kendall Copley Bastow
Clinton: Church Langfield: McManus Cottington Crossley
Nicholls Smith Lavender:
Tries - Church Langfield: Goals - Briggs(2):
LEEDS - Gray: Best Price Cox Whitehead: Batten Feather:
Prosser(S/O) Horsfall Carter Wheatley Foreman Watson:
Referee R Kendall (Keighley) Att - 9000 H.T. 2 - nil

Sat 27 Apr 1946 HALIFAX away lost 3 - 17
HALIFAX - Chalkley: A.N.Other Bevan Humphreys
Pentelow: Hurcombe Gardiner: Nolan Meek Greenwood
Gronow Smith Green: Tries - Pentelow(2) Bevan:
Goals - A.N.Other(3) Chalkley(DG):
CASTLEFORD - Briggs: Lloyd Copley Bastow ROY
NORTON(281) KENNETH WAGSTAFF(282) Langfield:
McManus Gordon Cottington M.Robinson Crossley
Lavender East: Try - East:
Referee L J Dalby (York) Att - H.T. 3 - 5

Wed 1 May 1946 BARROW home lost 7 - 12
CASTLEFORD - A.N.OTHER(283): Lloyd Copley Bastow
Clinton: Kenneth Brookes Langfield: McManus Haley
Crossley Lavender Nicholls East:
Try - Langfield : Goals - Brookes(2):
BARROW - French: Boyd Bowker Higgin Spooner: Kerr
Bowyer: Grainger Woods Sorriel Ayres(S/O) Scott
Traloure:
Tries - Bowker Spooner: Goals - French(2) Bowker(DG)
Referee A Howgate (Dewsbury) Att - 3000 .T. 7 - 6

Ron Copley
D. No 275
1945-46 to 1947-48

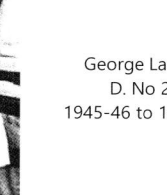

Arthur Bastow
D. No 278
1945-46 to 1951-52

George Langfield
D. No 280
1945-46 to 1951-52

SEASON 1945-46

D.N	PLAYER		DEBUT	L MATCH	APP	S JB	T.AP	TRI'S	G'LS	D.G	P'TS
116	TAYLOR	THOMAS L.		03/04/1946	27	0	27	2	0	0	6
123	HALEY	HAROLD			17	0	17	0	0	0	0
124	SMITH	FRANK Snr.			25	0	25	2	1	0	8
135	CUNNIFFE	BERNARD		10/11/1945	1	0	1	1	0	0	3
136	CROSSLEY	JAMES M.			13	0	13	0	0	0	0
141	McMANUS	PATRICK B.			15	0	15	3	0	0	9
147	HARDY	THOMAS		25/12/1945	10	0	10	2	0	0	6
155	BOUCHER	WILFRED (BUCK)		08/09/1945	1	0	1	0	1	0	2
159	WALSH	THOMAS		23/02/1946	3	0	3	2	0	1	8
160	COTTINGTON	GORDON		27/04/1946	25	0	25	1	0	0	3
168	STEAD	BILL		29/08/1945	1	0	1	0	0	0	0
175	HORAN	JOHN		22/12/1945	1	0	1	0	0	0	0
176	LLOYD	REGINALD			10	0	10	1	0	0	3
177	ROBINSON	JAMES			21	0	21	2	3	0	12
184	SLATER	HARRY			10	0	10	1	0	0	3
189	FOX	JOHN H.			7	0	7	0	0	0	0
192	JONES	ERIC			24	0	24	2	0	0	6
197	STREET	JACK		29/09/1945	2	0	2	0	0	0	0
199	BROOKES	KENNETH		01/05/1946	34	0	34	7	35	0	91
215	NICHOLLS	JAMES			31	0	31	2	0	0	6
232	HAMER	RAYMOND			26	0	26	6	0	0	18
238	LEWIS	RONALD			16	0	16	0	0	0	0
239	HILL	JOHN			1	0	1	0	0	0	0
248	KENDALL	KENNETH		22/04/1946	13	0	13	0	0	0	0
249	EAST	JACK			15	0	15	2	0	0	6
255	CLINTON	GEORGE			36	0	36	9	0	0	27
261	LAVENDER	EDWARD			29	0	29	4	0	0	12
262	BOOTH	GORDON			18	0	18	2	0	0	6
268	THOMAS	JAMES	29/08/1945	15/09/1945	2	0	2	0	0	0	0
269	BRIGGS	GEOFFREY	01/09/1945		25	0	25	0	38	0	76
270	DAVIES		29/09/1945	29/09/1945	1	0	1	0	0	0	0
271	CHURM	WILLIAM	20/10/1945	20/10/1945	1	0	1	0	0	0	0
272	BRUMMITT	HARRY	01/12/1945	26/01/1946	3	0	3	0	0	0	0
273	BYRNE	JAMES	22/12/1945	25/12/1945	2	0	2	0	0	0	0
274	BARKER	SIDNEY	12/01/1946	12/01/1946	1	0	1	0	0	0	0
275	COPLEY	RON	02/02/1946		17	0	17	6	0	0	18
276	THORNBURROW	JIM	02/02/1946	16/02/1946	3	0	3	0	0	0	0
277	CHURCH	FRED	02/02/1946		8	0	8	2	0	0	6
278	BASTOW	ARTHUR	23/02/1946		12	0	12	3	0	0	9
279	ROBINSON	MAXWELL	23/02/1946		2	0	2	0	0	0	0
280	LANGFIELD	GEORGE	06/04/1946		8	0	8	4	0	0	12
281	NORTON	ROY	27/04/1946	27/04/1946	1	0	1	0	0	0	0
282	WAGSTAFF	KENNETH	27/04/1946	27/04/1946	1	0	1	0	0	0	0
283	A N OTHER		01/05/1946	01/05/1946	1	0	1	0	0	0	0
	44		**16**	**21**	**520**	**0**	**520**	**66**	**78**	**1**	**356**

COMPETITION		P	W	D	L	FOR	AGT
LEAGUE	POSITION 11 OF 27	36	22	0	14	326	298
YORK'S CUP		2	1	0	1	15	21
RL CUP		2	1	0	1	15	18
PLAYERS RECORDS		**40**	**24**	**0**	**16**	**356**	**337**

The Club played two notable friendlies on a weekend trip to France beating Cote Basque 11–8 on Saturday 17 November 1945 in a game played at the Bayonne the following day drawing 8–8 against Bordeaux played at the Municipal Stadium Bordeaux.

George Clinton (who later in the 60s became 'A' and First Team Coach) played in the most games with 36 out of a total of 40 league and cup games, he also played in the pre-season Lyons Cup friendly against Featherstone Rovers and the two friendlies in France.

John H Fox played for a Northern Services XV against a New Zealand Army XV at Headingley on 10 November 1945 but was on the losing side 7–14.

SEASON 1946-47

Sat 24 Aug 1946 FEATHERSTONE ROVERS home won 16 - 7 LYON CUP FRIENDLY
CASTLEFORD - Briggs: Copley Guest J.Robinson Bastow: Church Langfield: McManus Haley H.Fox Nicholls Slater Lavender:
Tries - Lavender(2) Copley Church: Goals - Briggs(2):
FEATHERSTONE R - Chapman: Mahon Smith Barraclough Longley: Bennett Crabtree: Hemingway Raybould Kemp Wright Campy Garner:
Try - Smith: Goals - Wright(2):
Referee A S Dobson (Pontefract) Att -   H.T.

Sat 31 Aug 1946 BRADFORD NORTHERN home won 10 - 2
CASTLEFORD - Briggs: Copley Guest J.Robinson Bastow: Church Langfield: McManus Haley HAROLD FOX(284) Nicholls Slater Lavender:
Tries - Guest Church: Goals - Briggs(2):
BRADFORD N - Carmichael: Troth Walters Case Edwards: Barker D.Ward: Higson Darlison Hutchinson Smith Marklew Mugglestone:
Goal - Carmichael:
Referee L Thorpe (Wakefield) Att - 4300 H.T. 8 - nil

Thu 5 Sep 1946 HULL away lost 8 - 12
HULL - Miller: Bowers Sinclair Watts Jones: Lawrence Jewitt: Tindall Booth Sweeting Bedford Shakesby Jimmeson:
Tries - Lawrence Shakesby: Goals - Miller(3):
CASTLEFORD - Briggs: Copley Guest Bastow Lloyd: J.Robinson Hamer: McManus Haley Slater Lavender Nicholls John H Fox:
Tries - Copley Guest: Goal - Haley(DG):
Referee W Hemmings (Halifax) Att - 9000 H.T. 4 - 6

Sat 7 Sep 1946 HUDDERSFIELD away lost 8 - 19
HUDDERSFIELD - Leake: Pimblett G.Pepperell Madden Bawden: S.Pepperell Morgan: Bradbury J.Morgan Taylor Baxter Robson Givvons:
Tries - Pimblett(2) Bawden Morgan Givvons:
Goals - Bawden(2):
CASTLEFORD - Briggs: Copley Guest J.Robinson Lloyd: Bastow Ray Hamer: McManus Haley Nicholls Slater Lavender James C. Black:
Tries - J.Robinson Lloyd: Goal - Briggs:
Referee J E Taylor (Wakefield) Att - 10500 H.T. 5 - 13

Sat 14 Sep 1946 LEEDS away won 11 - 8 YORKSHIRE CUP ROUND 1 1ST LEG
LEEDS - Kelly: Batten Davies Price Best: Williams Evans: Newbound Carter Wheatley Foreman J.Fox Watson:
Tries - Davies Carter: Goal - Foreman:
CASTLEFORD - Briggs: Copley Guest J.Robinson Lloyd: Church Langfield: McManus Haley Harold Fox Lavender Staines Jones:
Tries - Copley Guest Church: Goal - Staines:
Referee L Thorpe (Wakefield) Att - 13000 H.T. 3 - 5

Mon 23 Sep 1946 LEEDS home won 16 - 7 YORKSHIRE CUP ROUND 1 2ND LEG
CASTLEFORD - Briggs: Copley Guest J.Robinson Lloyd: Church Langfield: McManus Haley Harold Fox Lavender Slater Fred Brindle:
Tries - Brindle(2) Guest Langfield: Goals - Briggs Church:
LEEDS - Kelly: Batten T.Williams Davies Price: R.Williams Gray: Newbound Carter Booth Wheatley Foreman Watson:
Try - R.Williams: Goals - Foreman(2):
Referee W Hemmings (Halifax) Att - 9500 H.T. 8 - 2

Sat 28 Sep 1946 HULL KINGSTON ROVERS away lost 10 - 25
HULL K R - McWatt: Gee Goldswain Ness Beaumont: Mills Richards: Hill Ramsden Clarke Bedford Atkinson Dockar:
Tries - Dockar(3) Ness Bedford:
Goals - McWatt(4) Dockar(DG):
CASTLEFORD - Briggs: Copley J.Robinson Bastow Lloyd: Church Langfield: McManus Haley Harold Fox Lavender Slater Jones:
Tries - Church Langfield: Goals - Briggs(2):
Referee L Thorpe (Wakefield) Att - 4000 H.T. 5 - 18

Thu 3 Oct 1946 WAKEFIELD TRINITY away lost 2 - 11 YORKSHIRE CUP ROUND 2
WAKEFIELD T - Teall: Perry Murphy Fletcher Robinson: Rylance S.Kielty: Wilkinson Marson Higgins Exley Moore Bratley:
Tries - Bratley(2) Perry: Goal - Perry:
CASTLEFORD - Briggs: Copley Guest J.Robinson Lloyd: Church Langfield: McManus Haley Harold Fox Harry Slater Staines Lavender:
Goal - Briggs:
Referee A Hill (Dewsbury) Att - 16000 H.T. nil - 11

Sat 5 Oct 1946 OLDHAM home won 22 - 6
CASTLEFORD - Briggs: Copley Guest J.Robinson Lloyd: Church Langfield: McManus Hill Crossley Staines Lavender Jones:
Tries - Langfield(2) Guest McManus: Goals - Briggs(5):
OLDHAM - Griffiths: Doughty Gummer Harris Large: Kerwick Rees: Ogden Frost Parr Shaw Phillips Pugh:
Tries - Large Kerwick:
Referee P Cowell (Warrington) Att - 4000 H.T. 11 - 3

Sat 12 Oct 1946 HUNSLET away won 18 - 10
HUNSLET - Walkington: Williamson Watson Metcalfe Buck: Booth Burnell: Bennett Phillips Newbound Billings Stansfield Clarkson:
Tries - Williamson Buck: Goals - Clarkson(2):
CASTLEFORD - Briggs: Copley Guest J.Robinson Bastow: Church Langfield: McManus Hill Crossley Lavender Staines Jones: Tries - Guest J.Robinson Langfield Staines:
Goals - Briggs(3):
Referee L Thorpe (Wakefield) Att -   H.T. 8 - 3

SEASON 1946-47

Sat 19 Oct 1946 HULL KINGSTON ROVERS home won 14 - 5
CASTLEFORD - Briggs: Copley Guest J.Robinson Lloyd: Church Langfield: McManus Haley Crossley Lavender Staines Jones: Tries - McManus Staines: Goals - Briggs(4):
HULL K R - W.McWatt: Gee Goldswain Sharkett Beaumont: Mills Richard: Middleton E.McWatt Clark Atkinson Wilmot Dockar:
Try - Richards: Goal - W.McWatt:
Referee L J Dale (York) Att - 6000 H.T. 7 - 5

Sat 26 Oct 1946 YORK away lost 4 - 9
YORK - Knowles: Bean Taylor L.Davies Walton: Benson Watkinson: Waudby Deighton Goulden White E.R.Davies Brown:
Try - Walton: Goals - Knowles(2)(DG):
CASTLEFORD - Geoffrey Briggs: Copley J.Robinson Guest Lloyd: Church Langfield: McManus Haley Crossley Staines Lavender Jones: Goals - Briggs(2):
Referee A Howgate (Dewsbury) Att - 4870 H.T. nil - nil

Sat 2 Nov 1946 SWINTON away won 11 - 7
SWINTON - Turner: Lewis Warry Winkworth Williams: McGurk Roper: Hughes Davies Stoddart Palin Hodgkinson Bowyer:
Try - Lewis: Goals - Turner Bowyer(DG):
CASTLEFORD - Guest: Copley J.Robinson Bastow Lloyd: THOMAS GRAHAME(285) Langfield: McManus Haley Crossley Staines Lavender Jones:
Try - Copley: Goals - Langfield(3) Guest(DG):
Referee W Hemmings (Halifax) Att - 9000 H.T. 6 - 4

Sat 9 Nov 1946 HUNSLET home won 24 - 10
CASTLEFORD - Guest: Copley Bastow J.Robinson Lloyd: Grahame Langfield: McManus Haley Crossley Lavender Staines Jones: Tries - Lloyd(2) Langfield(2) Crossley Lavender: Goals - Langfield(3):
HUNSLET - Walkington: O'Neil Aspinall Griffiths Booth: Watson Burnell: Bennett Britton Newbound Billings Clarkson Traill:
Tries - Griffiths Watson: Goals - Clarkson(2):
Referee A Hill (Dewsbury) Att - 6600 H.T. 13 - 7

Sat 16 Nov 1946 OLDHAM away lost 5 - 8
OLDHAM - Griffiths: Inglesfield Harris Large Morgan: Rees Kerwick: Ogden Brooks(S/O) Moore Shaw Pugh Ayres:
Tries - Inglesfield Large: Goal - Griffiths:
CASTLEFORD - Guest: Copley Bastow J.Robinson ARTHUR BEDFORD(286): Grahame Langfield: McManus Haley(S/O) Crossley Lavender Staines Jones:
Try - Jones: Goal - Langfield:
Referee J E Taylor (Wakefield) Att - 5500 H.T. 5 - 8

Sat 23 Nov 1946 SWINTON home won 22 - 3
CASTLEFORD - Lewis: Copley Guest Bastow Church: Grahame Langfield: McManus Haley Crossley Lavender Staines Jones:
Tries - Guest(3) Bastow Church Langfield: Goals - Langfield(2):

SWINTON - G.E.Turner: K.Turner Winkworth Taylor Williams: Warry Roper: Hughes Davies Stoddart Hodgkinson Palin Dockar: Try - Warry:
Referee F Fairhurst (Wigan) Att - 3000 H.T. 8 - 3

Sat 30 Nov 1946 LEEDS away lost 5 - 8
LEEDS - Kelly: Caldwell Price Cornelius Whitehead: Williams Jenkins: Prosser Murphy Brereton Watson Wheatley Owens: Tries - Price Williams: Goal - Kelly:
CASTLEFORD - Lewis: Copley Guest J.Robinson Bastow: Grahame Langfield: McManus Haley Crossley Lavender Staines Jones: Try - Bastow: Goal - Langfield:
Referee W Hemmings (Halifax) Att – 13500 H.T. 5 - 3

Sat 7 Dec 1946 FEATHERSTONE ROVERS home won 7 - nil
CASTLEFORD - Lewis: Copley Guest J.Robinson Bastow: Grahame Langfield: McManus Hill Crossley Lavender East Jones:
Try - Langfield: Goals - Langfields(2):
FEATHERSTONE R - Barraclough: Stephenson Allman Quick Smith: Crabtree Herbert: Hemingway King Wood Atherton Garner Richardson:
Referee A Hill (Dewsbury) Att - 2700 H.T. 2 - nil

Sat 14 Dec 1946 BELLE VUE RANGERS away won 8 - 6
BELLE V R - Harris: Barr Powell Waring McCormick: Kenny W.Watkins: Thomas Jones Gwyther Fearnley E.Watkins Brown:
Tries - Waring Fearnley:
CASTLEFORD - Lewis: Bastow Guest J.Robinson Lloyd: Grahame Langfield: McManus Hill Crossley Lavender Staines Jones
Tries - Guest Grahame: Goal - Langfield:
Referee T Armitage (Huddersfield) Att – 4000 H.T. 5 - 6

Wed 25 Dec 1946 WAKEFIELD TRINITY home won 6 - nil
CASTLEFORD Lewis: Copley Guest J.Robinson Lloyd: Grahame Langfield: McManus Hill Crossley Lavender Staines Jones:
Tries - Copley Lavender:
WAKEFIELD T - Teall: Perry Stott Baddeley Longley: Brookes Banks: Wilkinson Marson Higgins Exley Murphy Bratley:
Referee W Hemmings (Halifax) Att - 9100 .T. 3 - nil

Thu 26 Dec 1946 FEATHERSTONE ROVERS away won 12 - 4
FEATHERSTONE R - Barraclough: Smith Allman Quick Blackburn: Bennett Herbert: Wood King Stephenson Taylor Garner Richardson:
Goals - Quick(2):
CASTLEFORD - Lewis: Copley J.Robinson Guest Bastow: Grahame Langfield: McManus Hill Crossley Lavender Staines Jones:
Tries - Copley Grahame: Goals - Langfield(3):
Referee W Hemmings (Halifax) Att - 5400 .T. 7 - nil

SEASON 1946-47

Sat 28 Dec 1946 BELLE VUE RANGERS home won 12- 5
CASTLEFORD - Lewis: Copley Bastow J.Robinson Lloyd: Grahame Langfield: McManus Haley Crossley Lavender Staines East:
Tries - Grahame Langfield: Goals - Langfield(3):
BELLE V R - Tierney: Harris Waring Powell McCormick: Kenny Watkins: Thomas Jones Glendinning Fearnley Gwyther Brown: Try – McCormick: Goal - Watkins(DG):
Referee F Smith (Barrow) Att - 8000 H.T. 12 - 5

Wed 1 Jan 1947 WARRINGTON away lost 9 - 10
WARRINGTON - Les.Jones: Bevan Williams Higginbottom Johnson: De Lloyd Helme: Hal.Jones Cotton O'Toole Featherstone Ryan Chapman: Tries - Bevan Williams: Goals - Higginbottom Les.Jones(DG):
CASTLEFORD - Lewis: Copley Bastow J.Robinson Lloyd: Grahame Langfield: McManus Hill Crossley Staines Lavender Jones: Try - Staines: Goals - Langfield(3):
Referee T Hemmings (Halifax) Att - 13000 H.T. 9 - 8

Sat 4 Jan 1947 BRADFORD NORTHERN away lost 5 - 22
BRADFORD N - Carmichael: Edwards Kitching E.Ward Walters: Davies D.Ward: Whitcombe Darlison Higson Tyler Smith Foster:
Tries - E.Ward Walters D.Ward Whitcombe:
Goals - E.Ward(5):
CASTLEFORD - Lewis: Copley Bastow J.Robinson Lloyd: Grahame Langfield: McManus Hill Crossley Lavender Staines Jones: Try - Bastow: Goal - Langfield:
Referee A Hill (Dewsbury) Att - 12000 H.T. 5 - 3

Sat 11 Jan 1947 BATLEY home won 5 - 3
CASTLEFORD - Lewis: Bastow J.Robinson Guest Lloyd: Grahame Langfield: McManus Hill Smith Staines Lavender Eric Jones: Try - Guest: Goal - Langfield:
BATLEY - Eaton: A.N.Other Riches Etty Gabriel: Hesketh Gee: Rhodes Golby Morgan Hargreaves Whitehead Hudson: Try - Gabriel:
Referee W Hemmings (Halifax) Att - 3000 H.T. 3 - 3

Sat 18 Jan 1947 KEIGHLEY away draw 3 - 3
KEIGHLEY - Mills: Wilson Thatcher Elias Barrett: Horrod Burnell: Childs Stringer Fuller Farrar Flanagan Marklew: Try - Elias:
CASTLEFORD - Lewis: Bastow J.Robinson Guest Copley: Grahame Langfield: McManus Haley M.Robinson Smith Lavender Staines: Try - Copley:
Referee F Seed (Halifax) Att - 3000 H.T. 3 - 3

Sat 25 Jan 1947 WARRINGTON home won 12 - nil
CASTLEFORD - Lewis: Copley J.Robinson Guest Lloyd: Grahame Langfield: McManus Haley M.Robinson Lavender Smith Staines:
Tries - McManus Smith: Goals - Langfield(2)(DG):
WARRINGTON - L.Jones: Bevan Williams Higginbottom Johnson: De Lloyd Davies: H.Jones Cotton O'Toole Featherstone Ryan Shuttleworth:
Referee G S Phillips (Widnes) Att -   H.T. 7 - nil

Sat 22 Feb 1947 SWINTON home won 19 - 2 CHALLENGE CUP ROUND 1 1ST LEG
CASTLEFORD - Lewis: Copley J.Robinson Guest Lloyd: Bastow Langfield: McManus Haley M.Robinson Lavender Smith Staines:
Tries - Guest(2) Lloyd Langfield Staines:
Goals - Langfield(2):
SWINTON - Morgan: K.Turner Lewis E.G.Turner Warry: Winkworth Roper: Stoddart Osmond Garner Palin Hodgkinson Syddal:
Goal - Morgan:
Referee F Fairhurst (Wigan) Att - 6000 H.T. 5 - nil

Sat 1 Mar 1947 SWINTON away lost 7 - 8 CHALLENGE CUP ROUND 1 2ND LEG
SWINTON - Morgan: K.Turner Lewis E.G.Turner Williams: Winkworth Roper: Stoddart Davies Garner Palin Hodgkinson Duckar:
Tries - Williams Turner: Goal - Morgan:
CASTLEFORD - Lewis: Copley J.Robinson Guest Lloyd: Grahame Langfield: McManus Haley M.Robinson Lavender Smith Staines:
Try - Langfield: Goals - Langfield(2):
Referee - 1st Half - Mr W Ainscough (Touch Judge):
         2nd Half - Mr A Hill (Leeds): Att - 9500 H.T. 2 - 5

Sat 22 Mar 1947 BATLEY away won 13 - 2 CHALLENGE CUP ROUND 2
BATLEY - Eaton: Hesketh Riches Etty Gabriel: Stokes Gee: Rhodes Golby Morgan Hargreaves Waters Hudson:
Goal - Rhodes:
CASTLEFORD - Lewis: Copley J.Robinson Guest Lloyd: Grahame Langfield: McManus Haley M.Robinson Lavender Smith Staines:
Tries - J.Robinson Guest Grahame: Goals - Langfield(2):
Referee F Fairhurst (Wigan) Att - 8000 H.T. 2 - 2

Sat 29 Mar 1947 WARRINGTON away lost nil - 5 CHALLENGE CUP ROUND 3
WARRINGTON - L.Jones: Bevan Higginbottom Fleming Johnson: De Lloyd Davies: H.Jones Cotton O'Toole Featherstone Day Ryan:
Try - Bevan: Goal - Higginbottom:
CASTLEFORD - Lewis: Copley J.Robinson Guest Lloyd: Grahame Langfield: McManus Haley M.Robinson Lavender Smith Staines:
Referee A S Dobson (Pontefract) Att - 18125 H.T. nil - 2

Fri 4 Apr 1947 WAKEFIELD TRINITY away lost 5 - 24
WAKEFIELD T - Teall: Perry Stott Fletcher Longley: Jones Banks: Wilkinson Marson Higgins Moore Booth Bratley:
Tries - Stott Perry Longley Banks: Goals - Stott(6):
CASTLEFORD - Lewis: Copley J.Robinson Guest Lloyd: Grahame Langfield: McManus Haley M.Robinson Lavender Smith Staines:
Try - Staines: Goal - Langfield:
Referee R Kendall (Keighley) Att - 14000 H.T. 5 - 14
BENEFIT MATCH FOR HARRY WILKINSON (WAKEFIELD TRINITY)

SEASON 1946-47

Sat 5 Apr 1947 DEWSBURY home lost 4 - 12
CASTLEFORD - Lewis: Bastow J.Robinson Guest Lloyd:
Grahame Langfield: McManus Haley M.Robinson
Lavender Crossley Staines: Goals - Guest(2):
DEWSBURY - Ledgard: Armitage Clark Sheehy
Withington: Davies Royal: Hammond McKeating
Plenderleith Cox Holt Street:
Tries - Clark Street: Goals - Ledgard(3):
Referee W Hemmings (Halifax) Att - 4000 H.T. 4 - nil

Mon 7 Apr 1947 LEEDS home lost 2 - 10
CASTLEFORD - Guest: Copley J.Robinson Bastow Lloyd:
Church Langfield: McManus Haley Crossley Nicholls
Smith Staines: Goal - Guest:
LEEDS - Cook: Best Cornelius Price Batten: Williams
Jenkins: Brereton Murphy Jubb Gheatley Watson Owens:
Tries - Jenkins Jubb: Goals - Cook(2):
Referee A S Dobson (Pontefract) Att -   H.T. 2 - 5

Sat 12 Apr 1947 HULL home won 18 - 5
CASTLEFORD - Lewis: Arthur Bedford J.Robinson Guest
Bastow: Grahame Langfield: Nicholls Haley Crossley
Lavender Smith Staines: Tries - J.Robinson Langfield
Bastow Lavender: Goals - Guest Langfield(1)(DG):
HULL - Miller: Sanders Sinclair Sullivan Bowers: Lawrence
Smales: Fallon Noble Desborough Hattersley Tindall
Kavanagh: Try - Lawrence: Goal - Miller:
Referee T Armitage (Huddersfield) Att - 5000 H.T. 8 - 2

Sat 19 Apr 1947 BRAMLEY home won 33 - 5
CASTLEFORD - Guest: Clinton J.Robinson Bastow Lloyd:
Grahame Langfield: Crossley Haley M.Robinson Nicholls
Lavender Staines: Tries - Staines(3) Langfield(2) Clinton
Lloyd: Goals - Guest(6):
BRAMLEY - Longbottom: Lorriman Gibson Sowden
Sedgewick: Robinson Bennett: Moon Tibbett Marsden
Gater Moran Murphy: Try - Bennett: Goal - Moran:
Referee W Hemmings (Halifax) Att - 3000 H.T. 20 - nil

Sat 26 Apr 1947 HUDDERSFIELD home lost 4 - 21
CASTLEFORD - Lewis: Bastow J.Robinson Guest Lloyd:
Grahame Langfield: M.Robinson Haley Crossley Nicholls
Lavender Staines: Goals - Guest Langfield:
HUDDERSFIELD - Leake: Anderson Hunter Madden
Bawden: S.Pepperell W.Morgan: Taylor Whitehead
Thomas Givvons Foley H.Morgan:
Tries - Madden(2) Hunter Bawden Givvons:
Goals - Bawden(3):
Referee A S Dobson (Pontefract) Att - 6000 H.T. 2 - 8

Tue 29 Apr 1947 DEWSBURY away lost 7 - 17
DEWSBURY - Ledgard: Armitage Clark Sheehy
Withington: Davies Royal: Hammond McKeating
Plenderleith Cox Holt Street:
Tries - Royal Davies Armitage: Goals - Ledgard(4):
CASTLEFORD - Guest: SIDNEY WARD(287) J.Robinson
Bastow Lloyd: Clinton Langfield: McManus Hill Crossley
Lavender LEONARD TAYLOR(288) Staines:
Try - Lloyd: Goals - Langfield(2):
Referee R Rawlinson (Mirfield) Att - 4500 H.T. nil - 14

**Wed 7 May 1947 WORKINGTON TOWN home
lost 12 - 19**
CASTLEFORD - Lewis: Bastow J.Robinson Guest Lloyd:
Thomas Grahame Langfield: Patrick B.McManus Haley
Crossley Lavender Leonard Taylor Staines:
Tries - Bastow Staines: Goals - Langfield(2) Guest:
WORKINGTON T - Hagan: Askew Carr Jackson Rogers:
Risman Pepperell: Miller Ackerley Hayton Park Shearman
Ivison:
Tries - Jackson(2) Askew Risman Pepperell:
Goals - Risman(2):
Referee F Smith (Barrow) Att - 3500 H.T. 5 - 8

**Sat 10 May 1947 WORKINGTON TOWN away
lost 13 - 26**
WORKINGTON T - Hagan: Askew Carr Jackson Burnyeat:
Risman Pepperell: Miller Ackerley Hayton Shearman Park
Ivison:
Tries - Jackson Burnyeat Pepperell plus 3 tries with
scorers not known:
Goals - Risman(2) plus 2 goals scorer not known:
CASTLEFORD - Lewis: Clinton Bastow Guest Lloyd: Church
Langfield: Nicholls Haley Crossley Lavender Staines East:
Tries - Clinton(2) Lloyd : Goals - Langfield(2):
Referee G S Phillips (Widnes) Att - 12000 H.T. 8 - 13

Sat 17 May 1947 BRAMLEY away won 19 - 11
BRAMLEY - (Team from Programme)- Longbottom:
Lorriman Gibson Sowden A.N.Other: Robinson Bennett:
Moon Tebbutt Harrison Moran or A.N.Other Murphy
Sedgewick:
Tries - Moon Tebbutt Gibson: Goal - Moon:
CASTLEFORD - Lewis: Booth J.Robinson Guest Lloyd:
Bastow Langfield: Nicholls Haley Crossley Lavender
Staines East:
Tries - East(2) Booth Guest Langfield: Goals - Guest(2):
Referee S Adams (Hull) Att - 3200 H.T. 13 - nil

Tue 20 May 1947 BATLEY away lost nil - 12
BATLEY - Eaton: Baddeley Etty Butcher Gabriel: Stokes
Laycock: Rhodes Golby Morgan Waters Whitehead
Hudson:
Tries - Laycock Hudson: Goals - Rhodes(2) Laycock(DG):
CASTLEFORD - Lewis: Booth J.Robinson Guest Lloyd:
Bastow Langfield: Nicholls COLIN RIPLEY(289) Crossley
Lavender Frank Smith Snr Staines:
Referee L Thorpe (Wakefield) Att - 3000 H.T. nil - 10

Sat 24 May 1947 YORK home won 19 - 4
CASTLEFORD - Lewis: Lloyd Guest J.Robinson Booth:
Bastow Langfield: DYL HARRIS(290) Haley Crossley
Lavender Nicholls Staines:
Tries - Lloyd Langfield Staines:
Goals - Guest(3)(DG) Langfield:
YORK - Knowles: Howarth Taylor L.Davies Walton: Benson
Watkinson: Waudby Deighton E.R.Davies Brown
Carrington Goulden:
Goals - Knowles(2):
Referee B Lester (Leeds) Att - 3000 H.T. 6 - 4

SEASON 1946-47

Mon 26 May 1947 KEIGHLEY home won 22 - 11
CASTLEFORD - Lewis: Booth Guest J.Robinson Lloyd:
Bastow Langfield: Harris Haley Crossley Lavender Nicholls
Staines:
Tries - Staines(2) Booth Nicholls: Goals - Guest(5):
KEIGHLEY - Mills: Clapham Rule Ward Elias: Barrett
Burnell: Childs Winterbottom Fuller Flanagan Fell
Marklew: Tries - Clapham(2) Burnell: Goal - Mills
Referee S Adams (Hull) Att - 3000 H.T. 10 – 8

Harold Fox
D. No 284
1946-47 to 1949-50

Dyl Harris
D. No 290
1946-47 to 1950-51

SAT 14 SEPTEMBER 1946 YORKSHIRE CUP ROUND 1 1ST LEG LEEDS AWAY WON 11 – 8
Back Row – Pat McManus Harold Fox Harold Haley Eddie Lavender Geoff Briggs Ron Copley Charlie Staines
Fron Row – Eric Jones Fred Church Jim Robinson George Langfield Reg Lloyd Norman Guest

114

SEASON 1946-47

D.N	SEASON	PLAYER		DEBUT	L MATCH	APP	SUB	T.AP	TRI'S	G'LS	D.G	P'TS
123		HALEY	HAROLD			32	0	32	0	0	1	2
124		SMITH	FRANK Snr.		20/05/1947	11	0	11	1	0	0	3
136		CROSSLEY	JAMES M.			28	0	28	1	0	0	3
141		McMANUS	PATRICK B.		07/05/1947	35	0	35	3	0	0	9
167		BRINDLE	FRED		23/09/1946	1	0	1	2	0	0	6
172		STAINES	CHARLES			37	0	37	12	1	0	38
176		LLOYD	REGINALD			34	0	34	8	0	0	24
177		ROBINSON	JAMES			41	0	41	4	0	0	12
179		GUEST	NORMAN			39	0	39	15	22	2	93
184		SLATER	HARRY		03/10/1946	6	0	6	0	0	0	0
189		FOX	JOHN H.		05/09/1946	1	0	1	0	0	0	0
192		JONES	ERIC		11/01/1947	18	0	18	1	0	0	3
215		NICHOLLS	JAMES			12	0	12	1	0	0	3
232		HAMER	RAYMOND		07/09/1946	2	0	2	0	0	0	0
238		LEWIS	RONALD			26	0	26	0	0	0	0
239		HILL	JOHN			10	0	10	0	0	0	0
249		EAST	JACK			4	0	4	2	0	0	6
255		CLINTON	GEORGE			3	0	3	3	0	0	9
261		LAVENDER	EDWARD			42	0	42	3	0	0	9
262		BOOTH	GORDON			4	0	4	2	0	0	6
265		BLACK	JAMES C.		07/09/1946	1	0	1	0	0	0	0
269		BRIGGS	GEOFFREY		26/10/1946	11	0	11	0	21	0	42
275		COPLEY	RON			30	0	30	6	0	0	18
277		CHURCH	FRED			12	0	12	4	1	0	14
278		BASTOW	ARTHUR			31	0	31	5	0	0	15
279		ROBINSON	MAXWELL			10	0	10	0	0	0	0
280		LANGFIELD	GEORGE			41	0	41	17	42	2	139
284		FOX	HAROLD	31/08/1946		5	0	5	0	0	0	0
285		GRAHAME	THOMAS	02/11/1946	07/05/1947	24	0	24	4	0	0	12
286		BEDFORD	ARTHUR	16/11/1946	12/04/1947	2	0	2	0	0	0	0
287		WARD	SIDNEY	29/04/1947		1	0	1	0	0	0	0
288		TAYLOR	LEONARD	29/04/1947	07/05/1947	2	0	2	0	0	0	0
289		RIPLEY	COLIN	20/05/1947	20/05/1947	1	0	1	0	0	0	0
290		HARRIS	DYL	25/04/1947		2	0	2	0	0	0	0
	34			7	13	559	0	559	94	87	5	466

COMPETITION		P	W	D	L	FOR	AGT
LEAGUE	POSITION 13 OF 28	36	19	1	16	398	354
YORK'S CUP		3	2	0	1	29	26
RL CUP		4	2	0	2	39	17
PLAYERS RECORDS		43	23	1	19	466	397

Leigh returned to the League, for the first time since 1939-40, bringing the total to 28 teams.

Broughton Rangers changed their name to Belle Vue Rangers, having moved from Broughton in Salford to the Belle Vue Stadium Manchester in 1933.

Sat 23 Aug 1947 HULL away lost 15 - 27
HULL - Miller: Ryan Sullivan Sinclair Bowers: Jackson Lawrence: Shillitoe Hand Jimmison Booth A.Bedford E.Bedford: Tries - Sullivan Bowers Ryan Lawrence Shillitoe: Goals - Miller(5)(DG):
CASTLEFORD - Lewis: Lloyd Guest Bastow Booth: Church Langfield: M.Robinson Haley Nicholls Staines Lavender East:
Tries - Langfield Church Guest: Goals - Langfield(3):
Referee A Hill (Leeds) Att - 14000 H.T. 10 - 14

Sat 30 Aug 1947 WAKEFIELD TRINITY home lost 13 - 14
CASTLEFORD - Lewis: Copley Bastow Guest Lloyd: Church Langfield: Harris Hill Nicholls Staines Lavender FRANK MUGGLESTONE(291):
Tries - Copley Guest Mugglestone: Goals - Langfield Guest:
WAKEFIELD T - Teall: Perry Jenkinson Fletcher Baddeley: Rylance Goodfellow: Wilkinson Marson Taylor Hughes Howes Bratley:
Tries - Baddeley Howes: Goals - Rylance(4):
Referee T Armitage (Huddersfield) Att - 7000 H.T. 5 - 7

Wed 3 Sep 1947 FEATHERSTONE ROVERS away lost 8 - 11
FEATHERSTONE R - Barraclough: Crabtree Quick Tennant(S/O) Darlison: Allman Higgins: Palmer Garner Pawson Allinson Taylor Richardson:
Try - Palmer: Goals - Barraclough(4):
CASTLEFORD - Lewis: Booth Bastow Guest(S/O) Lloyd: Church Langfield: Harris Hill Nicholls Lavender Staines Mugglestone:
Tries - Guest Nicholls: Goal - Guest:
Referee A Hill (Dewsbury) Att - 4800 H.T.

Sat 6 Sep 1947 BRADFORD NORTHERN home won 18 -8
CASTLEFORD - Lewis: Booth Copley Guest Lloyd: Church Clinton: Harris Nicholls Crossley Staines Lavender Mugglestone:
Tries - Nicholls(2) Guest Church: Goals - Staines(2) Clinton:
BRADFORD N - Carmichael: Batten Kitching E.Ward Walters: Davies Jones: Greaves Darlison Smith Foster Tyler Traill:
Tries - Batten(2): Goal - Carmichael:
Referee F Cottam (WAkefield) Att - 6000 H.T. 10 - 3

Wed 10 Sep 1947 BRADFORD NORTHERN away won 19 - 11
BRADFORD N - Carmichael: Batten Kitching E.Ward Walters: Davies Jones: Greaves Darlison Smith Foster Tyler Traill:
Tries - Kitching(2) Batten: Goal - Carmichael:
CASTLEFORD - Lewis: Booth Copley J.Robinson Lloyd: Church Clinton: Harris Nicholls Crossley Staines Lavender Mugglestone:
Tries - Copley Staines Robinson: Goals - Staines(5):
Referee A S Dobson (Pontefract) Att - 7000 H.T. 14 - 2

Sat 13 Sep 1947 FEATHERSTONE ROVERS away won 9 - 5 YORKSHIRE CUP ROUND 1 1ST LEG
FEATHERSTONE R - Barraclough: Smith Luckman Allman Edwards: Gunn Herbert: Palmer Garner Maiden Allinson Stephenson Richardson:
Try - Edwards: Goal - Barraclough:
CASTLEFORD - Lewis: Bastow Copley J.Robinson Lloyd: Church Clinton: Harris Nicholls Crossley Staines Lavender Mugglestone: Try - Bastow: Goals - Staines(3):
Referee S Adams (Hull) Att - 5000 H.T.

Wed 17 Sep 1947 FEATHERSTONE ROVERS home won 6 - 3 YORKSHIRE CUP ROUND 1 2ND LEG
CASTLEFORD - Lewis: Bastow Copley Guest Lloyd: Church Clinton: Harris Haley Crossley Staines Nicholls Mugglestone:
Tries - Harris Mugglestone:
FEATHERSTONE R - Barraclough: Smith Luckman J.Stephenson P.Stephenson: Russell Allman: Palmer Garner Maiden Pawson Taylor Richardson:
Try - Pawson:
Referee T Armitage (Huddersfield) Att - 6000 H.T. 3 - nil

Sat 27 Sep 1947 BRAMLEY home won 16 - 11
CASTLEFORD - Lewis(S/O): Clinton Guest Bastow Lloyd: ALFRED FISHER(292) Langfield: Harris Haley Crossley Staines Nicholls Mugglestone:
Tries - Lewis Bastow Lloyd Langfield:
Goals - Staines Langfield(DG):
BRAMLEY - Oliver: Baxter Gibson Bartlett Richards: Robinson Bennett: Roberts White Moon Whitehead(S/O) Webb Murphy:
Tries - Murphy(2) Richards: Goal - Gibson:
Referee T Armitage (Huddersfield) Att – 4000 H.T. 11 - 8

Tue 30 Sep 1947 KEIGHLEY away won 9 - 2 YORKSHIRE CUP ROUND 2
KEIGHLEY - Mills: Elias Rule Ward Hoyle: Barrett Hudson: Childs Winterbottom Gibson Farrar Marklew McManus:
Goal - Mills:
CASTLEFORD - Lewis: Copley J.Robinson Bastow Lloyd: Church Langfield: Nicholls Haley Crossley Lavender Staines Mugglestone:
Try - Church: Goals - Langfield(1)(2DG):
Referee W Hemmings (Halifax) Att - 5190 H.T. 2 - 2

Sat 4 Oct 1947 ROCHDALE HORNETS away lost 7 - 8
ROCHDALE H - Robinson: Hearthman Winstanley Gummer Thompson: Lowrey Lamb: Wagstaff Dean Ayres Ellison Booth Oxley:
Tries - Thompson Lamb: Goal - Winstanley:
CASTLEFORD - Guest: Copley J.Robinson Bastow Lloyd: Church Langfield: Crossley Haley Nicholls Staines Lavender Mugglestone:
Try - Langfield: Goals - Langfield(2):
Referee R Rawlinson (Mirfield) Att - 5000 H.T. 5 - 6

Wed 8 Oct 1947 NEW ZEALAND lost 3 - 17
CASTLEFORD - Guest: Copley Clinton Bastow Lloyd:

SEASON 1947-48

Church Langfield: Nicholls Haley Crossley Lavender
Staines Mugglestone: Try - Clinton:
NEW ZEALAND - R.Nuttall: R.G.McGregor H.D.Anderson
M.W.Robertson A.J.McInnarney: D.A.Barchard
R.Cunningham: J.J.Johnson P.A.Smith L.R.Pye
A.E.C.Gillman C.McBride T.H.Hardwick:
Tries - Robertson Gillman McBride: Goals - Nuttall(4):
Referee L Thorpe (Wakefield) Att - 11000 H.T. 3 - 7

Wed 11 Oct 1947 HUDDERSFIELD away lost 5 - 50
HUDDERSFIELD - Pepperell: Oughton Madden Bawden
Cooper: Devery Morgan: Taylor Whitehead Nicholson
Thomas Baxter Givvon:
Tries - Cooper(4) Nicholson(3) Oughton Madden Bawden
Devery Baxter: Goals - Devery(6) Bawden:
CASTLEFORD - Guest: Copley Bastow J.Robinson Church:
Lewis Clinton: Harris Nicholls Crossley Lavender GEORGE
STOREY(293) Staines
Try - Lewis: Goal - Staines
Referee S Adams (Hull) Att - 13000 H.T. 5 - 14

Wed 15 Oct 1947 LEEDS away lost 4 - 19
YORKSHIRE CUP SEMI FINAL
LEEDS - Cook: Batten Price Cornelius Whitehead: Williams
Jenkins: Prosser Carter Wheatley Foreman Flanagan
Owens:
Tries - Cook Owens Williams:
Goals - Whitehead(4) Foreman:
CASTLEFORD - Lewis: Guest Bastow J.Robinson Lloyd:
Fred Church Langfield: Harris Haley Nicholls Staines
Lavender Mugglestone:
Goal - Langfield(2):
Referee A Howgate (Dewsbury) Att - 16000 H.T. 2 - 6

Sat 18 Oct 1947 OLDHAM home won 7 - 5
CASTLEFORD - Lewis: Ward Bastow Guest Clinton:
Alf.Fisher JOEY DUDLEY(294): M.Robinson Haley Crossley
Staines Lavender Mugglestone:
Try - Fisher: Goals - Staines Crossley(DG):
OLDHAM - Griffiths: Inglesfield Mitchell Mahoney Large:
Kenny Smith: Ogden Frost Thompson Rostron Pugh
Ayres:
Try - Inglesfield: Goal - Griffiths:
Referee G S Phillips (Widnes) Att - 6000 H.T. 5 - nil

Sat 25 Oct 1947 BATLEY away lost 13 - 15
BATLEY - Eaton: Riches Etty A.N.Other A.N.Other: Hesketh
Laycock: Jessop Lightfoot Morgan Terry "Johnson"
Waters:
Tries - Eaton Riches Jessop: Goals - Eaton(3):
CASTLEFORD - Lewis: Clinton J.Robinson Guest Lloyd:
Alf.Fisher Langfield: M.Robinson Haley Crossley Nicholls
Staines Mugglestone:
Tries - Guest Lloyd Staines: Goals - Langfield(2):
Referee S Adams (Hull) Att - 4000 H.T. 8 - 5

Sat 8 Nov 1947 YORK away won 30 - 15
YORK - Knowles: Tate Taylor Dennis Cole: Pearson
Thomas: Brown Waddington Davies Billings Hodgson
Wileman:

Try - Waddington: Goals - Knowles(6):
CASTLEFORD - Lewis: Lloyd Guest Bastow Booth:
Alf.Fisher Langfield: Harris Haley M.Robinson Edward
Lavender Crossley Mugglestone:
Tries - Lloyd Bastow Fisher Langfield Harris Mugglestone:
Goals - Langfield(6):
Referee L Thorpe (Wakefield) Att - 2310 H.T. 10 - 13

Sat 15 Nov 1947 HULL KINGSTON ROVERS home
won 19 - nil
CASTLEFORD - Lewis: Guest Bastow LEONARD
SKIDMORE(295) Lloyd: Alf.Fisher Langfield: Harris Haley
M.Robinson Crossley Staines Mugglestone:
Tries - Staines(2) Guest Lloyd Fisher: Goals - Guest(2):
HULL K R - McWatt: Richards Dockar Jackson McBain:
Steele Daddy: Senior Ramsden Hartley Wilmot Scholes
Goldswain:
Referee R Rawlinson (Mirfield) Att - 5000 H.T. 3 - nil

Sat 22 Nov 1947 OLDHAM away lost 3 - 7
OLDHAM - Barraclough: Inglesfield Mitchell Mahoney
Large: Kenny Smith: Moore Munday Taylor Pugh Ambler
Ayres:
Try - Taylor: Goals - Barraclough Smith(DG):
CASTLEFORD - Lewis: Guest Bastow Skidmore Booth:
Alf.Fisher Langfield: Harris Haley Nicholls Staines Crossley
Mugglestone:
Try - Lewis:
Referee F Cottam (Wakefield) Att - 5000 H.T. 3 - 7

Sat 29 Nov 1947 YORK home won 25 - 4
CASTLEFORD - Lewis: Bastow Guest Skidmore Lloyd:
Alf.Fisher Langfield: Harris Haley M.Robinson Crossley
Staines Mugglestone:
Tries - Bastow(2) Staines Langfield Mugglestone:
Goals - Guest(5):
YORK - Knowles: Cole Taylor Kitchingman Walton:
Pearson Dennis Simpson Hutchinson Waddington Brown
Goulden Wileman:
Goals - Knowles(2):
Referee W Hemmings (Halifax) Att - 4000 H.T. 12 - 4

Sat 6 Dec 1947 HULL KINGSTON ROVERS away
won 2 - nil
HULL K R - McWatt: Dodd Smith Jackson Richards: Daddy
Steele: Hill Ramsden Wilmot Scholes Downing Dockar:
CASTLEFORD - Lewis: Copley Skidmore Guest Bastow:
Alf.Fisher Langfield: Harris Harold Haley Crossley Nicholls
Staines Mugglestone:
Goal - Guest:
Referee A Hill (Dewsbury) Att - 5000 H.T. nil - nil

Sat 13 Dec 1947 BATLEY home won 18 - 12
CASTLEFORD - Lewis: Bastow Guest Skidmore Lloyd:
Alf.Fisher Langfield: Harris THOMAS WHITTLESTONE(296)
Crossley DESMOND FOREMAN(297) Nicholls
Mugglestone:
Tries - Lloyd(2) Langfield Crossley: Goals - Guest(3):
BATLEY - Eaton Butcher Riches Stokes Etty: Hesketh
Laycock: Jessop Golby Terry Hargreaves Williams

Backhouse:
Tries - Hesketh Jessop: Goals - Eaton(3):
Referee R Kendall (Keighley) Att - 6000 H.T. 12 - 5

Sat 20 Dec 1947 SWINTON away lost 9 - 12
SWINTON - E.G.Turner: Winkworth Warham Myers
Williams: Warry Riley: Stoddart Osmand Garner Jones
Armitt Roughley:
Tries - Jones Armitt: Goals - Jones(2) Armitt:
CASTLEFORD - Lewis: Bastow Guest Skidmore Lloyd:
Alf.Fisher Langfield: Harris Whittlestone Crossley Foreman
Staines Mugglestone:
Try - Mugglestone: Goals - Guest(3):
Referee W Hemmings (Halifax) Att - 4000 H.T. 7 - 7

**Thu 25 Dec 1947 WAKEFIELD TRINITY away
lost 4 - 13**
WAKEFIELD T - Gray: Jenkinson Stott Boocker Baddeley:
Fletcher Goodfellow: Wilkinson Marson Higgins Booth
Murphy Bratley:
Tries - Fletcher Stott Higgins: Goals - Stott
Fletcher(DG):
CASTLEFORD - Guest: Ward Bastow Skidmore Lloyd:
Alf.Fisher Langfield: Harris Whittlestone Crossley Staines
Foreman Mugglestone:
Goals - Guest(2):
Referee S Adams (Hull) Att - 9000 H.T. 2 - 10

**Fri 26 Dec 1947 FEATHERSTONE ROVERS home
won 13 - 11**
CASTLEFORD - Langfield: Bastow Alf.Fisher Guest Lloyd:
ARTHUR(DIAMOND)FISHER(298) Dudley: Crossley
Whittlestone Staines Foreman Nicholls Mugglestone:
Tries - Art.Fisher: Goals - Guest Foreman:
FEATHERSTONE R - Blackburn: Gunn Crabtree Davies
Waring: Allman Russell: Palmer Mogg Pawson Allinson
Kent Richardson:
Tries - Waring(2) Allinson: Goal - Blackburn:
Referee B Lester (Leeds) Att - 6000 H.T. 6 - 3

Sat 27 Dec 1947 HULL home won 10 - 7
CASTLEFORD - Lewis: Bastow Guest Skidmore Copley:
Art.Fisher Langfield: Nicholls Whittlestone Crossley
Foreman Staines Mugglestone:
Tries - Copley Langfield: Goals - Guest(2):
HULL - Miller: Bowers Ingram Ryan Watts: Lawrence
Jewitt: Booth Watt Shillito A.Bedford Tindall E.Bedford: Try
- Ryan: Goals - Miller(2):
Referee L J Dalby (York) Att - 6000 H.T. 5 - 7

Sat 3 Jan 1948 DEWSBURY home won 13 - 3
CASTLEFORD - Lewis: Bastow Guest Skidmore Lloyd:
Art.Fisher Dudley: Nicholls Whittlestone Crossley Foreman
Staines Mugglestone:
Tries - Guest Fisher Dudley: Goals Foreman(2):
DEWSBURY - J.Kelly: Withington B.Kelly Quick Gilbertson:
Evans Robinson: Hammond McKeating Plenderleith Cox
Sewell Murray:
Try - Cox:
Referee W Hemmings (Hull) Att - 6000 H.T. 8 - nil

Sat 10 Jan 1948 HUNSLET away draw 8 - 8
HUNSLET - Griffiths: Williamson Watson Graham Carroll:
Rushton A.Burnell: Bennett Britton Gronow Metcalfe
W.Burnell Clarkson:
Tries - Carroll(2):   Goal - Clarkson:
CASTLEFORD - Lewis: Bastow Guest Skidmore Lloyd:
Art.Fisher Langfield: Harris Whittlestone Crossley Foreman
Staines Mugglestone:
Tries - Bastow Fisher: Goal - Guest:
Referee T Armitage (Huddersfield) Att - 12000 H.T. 8 - 8

Sat 17 Jan 1948 WARRINGTON away lost 2 - 9
WARRINGTON - Jones: Bevan Pimblett Knowelden
Johnson: Fleming Helme: Derbyshire Cotton Riley
Featherstone Ryan Palin: Try - Bevan: Goals - Palin(3):
CASTLEFORD - Lewis: Bastow Guest Skidmore Lloyd:
Art.Fisher Langfield: Harris Whittlestone Nicholls Foreman
FRED BENNETT(299) Mugglestone:
Goal - Guest:
Referee A Howgate (Dewsbury) Att - 6000 H.T.
Abandoned after 70 minutes Result Stood

Sat 24 Jan 1948 HUNSLET home won 21 - 8
CASTLEFORD - Lewis: Bastow Guest Skidmore Lloyd:
Art.Fisher Langfield: Harris JAMES JONES(300) Crossley
Foreman Staines Mugglestone:
Tries - Langfield(2) Crossley(2) Staines:
Goals - Langfield(2)Guest:
HUNSLET - Smith: Williamson Rushton Carroll Rookes:
Graham Watson: Bennett Britton Newbound Metcalfe
W.Burnell Clarkson:
Tries - Rookes Burnell: Goal - Clarkson:
Referee A S Dobson (Pontefract) Att - 8000 H.T. 8 - 2

**Sat 31 Jan 1948 ROCHDALE HORNETS home
won 10 - 5**
CASTLEFORD - Lewis: Bastow Guest Skidmore Lloyd:
Art.Fisher Langfield: Harris Jones Crossley Foreman
Nicholls Staines: Tries - Langfield(2) Goals - Guest(2):
ROCHDALE H - Griffiths: Thompson Winstanley Gummer
Nicholson: Kerr Lamb: Booth Dean Rothwell Butler Oxley
Fearnley:
Try - Kerr: Goal - Griffiths:
Referee W Stockley (Leigh) Att - 6500 H.T. 5 - nil

**Sat 7 Feb 1948 WIGAN away lost nil - 27
CHALLENGE CUP ROUND 1 1ST LEG**
WIGAN - Ryan: Ratcliffe Ward Ashcroft Hilton: Mountford
Bradshaw: Gee Egan Barton White Blan Hudson:
Tries - Ratcliffe(2) Hilton(2) Ashcroft Mountford Gee:
Goals - Ward(3):
CASTLEFORD - Lewis: Bastow Guest Skidmore Lloyd:
Art.Fisher Langfield: Harris Jones Crossley Foreman
Staines Mugglestone:
Referee S Adams (Hull) Att - 22000 H.T. nil - 8

**Sat 14 Feb 1948 WIGAN home lost 7 - 19
CHALLENGE CUP ROUND 1 2ND LEG**
CASTLEFORD - Lewis: Bastow Guest Skidmore Lloyd:
Art.Fisher Langfield: Harris Jones Crossley Foreman

Staines Mugglestone:
Try - Guest: Goals - Foreman Guest:
WIGAN - Ryan: Ratcliffe Lawrenson Ashcroft Hilton:
Mountford Bradshaw: Gee Egan Banks White Blan
Hudson:
Tries - Ratcliffe(2) Hilton Lawrenson Ashcroft:
Goals - Lawrenson Gee:
Referee G S Phillips (Widnes) Att - 14000 H.T. 5 - 11

Sat 21 Feb 1948 WIGAN away lost 13 - 34
WIGAN - Ryan: Ratcliffe Lawrenson Ashcroft Hilton:
Mountford Bradshaw: Gee Egan Banks Barton Blan
Hudson:
Tries - Hilton(4)Lawrenson(2) Hudson(2): Goals - Gee(5):
CASTLEFORD - Lewis: Ronald Copley Skidmore James
Robinson Lloyd: Art.Fisher Langfield: Harris Jones Fox
Foreman Staines Mugglestone:
Try - Foreman: Goals - Langfield(4)(DG):
Referee L Thorpe (Wakefield) Att - 10500 H.T. 4 - 18

**Sat 13 Mar 1948 FEATHERSTONE ROVERS home
won 20 - 5   LYON CUP FRIENDLY**
CASTLEFORD - Lewis: Ward Skidmore Alf.Fisher Lloyd:
Langfield Dudley: Harris Whittlestone Nicholls Staines
Foreman Mugglestone:
Tries - Foreman(2) Ward Harris: Goals - Langfield(4):
FEATHERSTONE R - Luckman: Best Davies Tennant
Crabtree: Gilbertson Russell: Bramley Garner Palmer
Allinson Payne Duffy:
Try - Russell: Goal - Luckmam:
Referee H Norton (Pontefract) Att - 3000 H.T. 10 - 5

Sat 20 Mar 1948 KEIGHLEY away lost 7 - 8
KEIGHLEY - Mills: Ward Thatcher Greeny Elias: Barratt
Davies: Thornton Pritchard Childs Sykes Craven Clarkson:
Tries - Greeny Davies: Goal - Mills:
CASTLEFORD - Lewis: Ward Alf.Fisher Skidmore Lloyd:
Dudley Langfield: Harris Jones Nicholls Staines Foreman
Mugglestone:
Try - Skidmore: Goals - Langfield(2):
Referee E Thomas (Halifax) Att - 2300 H.T. 5 - 8

Fri 26 Mar 1948 LEEDS home won 18 - 5
CASTLEFORD - Lewis: Ward Guest Skidmore Clinton:
Alf.Fisher Langfield: Harris Jones Nicholls Foreman Staines
Mugglestone:
Tries - Lewis Langfield Nicholls Staines: Goals -
Guest(3):
LEEDS - Cook: Kenny Warrior T.L.Williams Whitehead:
R.Williams Jenkins: Prosser Ogden Wheatley Clues
Flanagan Owens:
Try - Whitehead: Goal - Cook:
Referee A Hill (Dewsbury) Att - 12000 H.T.

Sat 27 Mar 1948 HUDDERSFIELD home lost 7 - 20
CASTLEFORD - Lewis: Ward Guest Skidmore Lloyd:
Alf.Fisher Langfield: Harris Jones Nicholls Foreman Staines
Mugglestone:
Try - Skidmore: Goals - Guest(2):
HUDDERSFIELD - Pepperell: Anderson Bawden Devery

Cooper: Neil Walsh: Meek Whitehead Thomas Robson
Baxter Valentine:
Tries - Devery Cooper Meek Thomas:
Goals - Bawder (2) Devery(2):
Referee R Kendall (Keighley) Att - 10000 H.T. 2 - 10

Mon 29 Mar 1948 LEEDS away lost nil - 9
LEEDS - Cook: Warrior T.L.Williams Price Kenny:
Verrenkamp Jenkins: Prosser Davies Wheatley Clues
Pansegrouw Owens:
Try - Clues: Goals - Cook(3):
CASTLEFORD - Lewis: Ward Guest Skidmore Lloyd:
Art.Fisher Langfield: Harris Jones Nicholls Foreman
Staines Mugglestone:
Referee A S Dotson (Pontefract) Att - 13500 H.T. nil - 2

Sat 3 Apr 1948 BRAMLEY away lost 3 - 9
BRAMLEY - Longbottom: Hart Bartlett Lazenby Lorriman:
Dinnen Bennett: Rhodes White Cluderay Hebb Whitehead
Sedgewick:
Try - Bennett: Goals - Whitehead(3):
CASTLEFORD - Lewis: Sidney Ward Guest Skidmore
Lloyd: Art.Fisher Langfield: Harris Jones Nicholls Foreman
Staines Mugglestone:
Try - Lloyd:
Referee L J Dalby (York) Att - 3000 H.T. 3 - nil

Sat 10 Apr 1948 WARRINGTON home won 12 - 2
CASTLEFORD - Lewis: Clinton Guest Skidmore Lloyd:
Art.Fisher Langfield: Harris Jones Nicholls Staines
Foreman Mugglestone:
Tries - Staines Foreman: Goals - Langfield(2) Guest:
WARRINGTON - Jones: Bevan Pimblett Powell Williams:
Knowelden Helme: Derbyshire Cotton Riley Bath Ryan
Palin:
Goal - Jones(DG):
Referee N T Railton (Wigan) Att - 7000 H.T. 7 - 2

Tue 13 Apr 1948 DEWSBURY away won 13 - nil
DEWSBURY - J.Kelly: Townsend B.Kelly James Armitage:
Evans Royal: Hammond McKeating Shakesby Plenderleith
Holt Murray:
CASTLEFORD - Lewis: Clinton Guest Skidmore Lloyd:
Art.Fisher Dudley: Harris Jones Nicholls Staines Foreman
Mugglestone:
Tries - Fisher Clinton Foreman: Goals - Guest(2):
Referee S Adams (Hull) Att - 6000 H.T. 8 - nil

Sat 17 Apr 1948 KEIGHLEY home won 37 - 5
CASTLEFORD - Guest: Bastow Alf.Fisher Skidmore Lloyd:
Art.Fisher Clinton: Harris Jones Crossley Staines Foreman
Mugglestone:
Tries - Mugglestone(4) Bastow Lloyd Clinton Staines
Foreman: Goals - Staines(4) Foreman:
KEIGHLEY - Mills: Thurling Clarkson Lambert Elias: Barrett
Davies: Fuller Pritchard Gibson Farrar Fell McManus:
Try - Lambert: Goal - Mills:
Referee F Cottam (Wakefield) Att - 4000 H.T.

SEASON 1947-48

Mon 19 Apr 1948 WIGAN home lost 6 - 14
CASTLEFORD - Guest: Bastow Alf.Fisher Skidmore Lloyd:
Art.Fisher Clinton: Harris Jones Nicholls Staines Foreman
Mugglestone: Goals - Staines(3):
WIGAN - Ryan: Nordgren Ward Lawrenson Hilton:
Cunliffe Bradshaw: Gee Egan Banks White Barton Hudson:
Tries - Nordgren Bradshaw: Goals - Ward(4):
Referee H Holland (St Helens) Att - 12000 H.T. 4 - 5

Sat 24 Apr 1948 SWINTON home won 32 - 3
CASTLEFORD - Guest: Bastow Skidmore Alf.Fisher Lloyd:
Clinton Dudley: Harris Jones Crossley Foreman Staines
Mugglestone:
Tries - Foreman(3) Fisher(2) Bastow: Goals - Staines(7):
SWINTON - Winkworth: Warham Tucker Myers Turner:
Warry Riley: Stoddart Osmond Rudge Garner Jones
Armitt:
Try - Riley:
Referee G S Phillips (Widnes) Att - 3700 H.T. 12 - nil

**Wed 28 Apr 1948 COLONIALS home won 31 - 26
FRIENDLY BENEFIT MATCH - JAMES CROSSLEY,
HAROLD HALEY, PATRICK B.MCMANUS, FRANK
SMITH**
CASTLEFORD - Guest: Bastow Alf.Fisher Skidmore Lloyd:
Clinton Dudley: Harris Haley Crossley Foreman Staines
Mugglestone: Tries - Fisher(2) Foreman Staines Clinton
Dudley Guest: Goals - Staines(5)
COLONIALS - Cook(Leeds): Anderson(Huddersfield)
J.McDonald(Halifax) E.McDonald(Halifax) Rika(Halifax):
Brookes(Wakefield T) Kielty(Halifax): McManus(Castleford)
Brereton(Leed) Pansegrouw(Leeds) Clues(Leeds)
Robson(Huddersfield) Valentine(Huddersfield)
Smith(Halifax): (7 forwards used)
Tries - Clues(2) J.McDonald(2) Cook Robson: Goals -
Rika(4):
Referee A S Dobson (Pontefract) Att - H.T. 18 – 15

Joey Dudley
D. No 294
1947-48 to 1952-53

Des Foreman
D. No 297
1947-48 to 1948-49

Arthur (Diamond) Fisher
D. No 298
1947-48 to 1951-52

James Jones
D. No 300
1947-48 to 1950-51

Frank Mugglestone
D. No 291
1947-48 to 1951-52

Alf Fisher
D. No 292
1947-48 to 1951-52

SEASON 1947-48

D.N	PLAYER		DEBUT	L MATCH	APP	SUB	T.AP	TRI'S	G'LS	D.G	P'TS
123	HALEY	HAROLD		06/12/1947	14	0	14	0	0	0	0
136	CROSSLEY	JAMES M.			29	0	29	3	0	1	11
172	STAINES	CHARLES			40	0	40	9	27	0	81
176	LLOYD	REGINALD			37	0	37	8	0	0	24
177	ROBINSON	JAMES		21/02/1948	8	0	8	1	0	0	3
179	GUEST	NORMAN			38	0	38	8	35	0	94
215	NICHOLLS	JAMES			30	0	30	4	0	0	12
238	LEWIS	RONALD			36	0	36	4	0	0	12
239	HILL	JOHN			2	0	2	0	0	0	0
249	EAST	JACK			1	0	1	0	0	0	0
255	CLINTON	GEORGE			15	0	15	3	1	0	11
261	LAVENDER	EDWARD		08/11/1947	13	0	13	0	0	0	0
262	BOOTH	GORDON			6	0	6	0	0	0	0
275	COPLEY	RON		21/02/1948	12	0	12	3	0	0	9
277	CHURCH	FRED		15/10/1947	12	0	12	3	0	0	9
278	BASTOW	ARTHUR			32	0	32	9	0	0	27
279	ROBINSON	MAXWELL			6	0	6	0	0	0	0
280	LANGFIELD	GEORGE			32	0	32	12	27	4	98
284	FOX	HAROLD			1	0	1	0	0	0	0
287	WARD	SIDNEY		03/04/1948	7	0	7	0	0	0	0
290	HARRIS	DYL			34	0	34	2	0	0	6
291	MUGGLESTONE	FRANK	30/08/1947			40	0	40	9	0	0	27
292	FISHER	ALFRED	27/09/1947			18	0	18	5	0	0	15
293	STOREY	GEORGE	11/10/1947			1	0	1	0	0	0	0
294	DUDLEY	JOEY	18/10/1947			6	0	6	1	0	0	3
295	SKIDMORE	LEONARD	15/11/1947			26	0	26	2	0	0	6
296	WHITTLESTONE	THOMAS	13/12/1947			8	0	8	0	0	0	0
297	FOREMAN	DESMOND	13/12/1947			23	0	23	7	5	0	31
298	FISHER	ARTHUR (DIAMOND)	26/12/1947			16	0	16	5	0	0	15
299	BENNETT	FRED	17/01/1948			1	0	1	0	0	0	0
300	JONES	JAMES	24/01/1948			15	0	15	0	0	0	0
	31		**10**	**6**	**559**	**0**	**559**	**98**	**95**	**5**	**494**

COMPETITION		P	W	D	L	FOR	AGT
LEAGUE	POSITION 13 OF 28	36	13	1	16	456	383
YORK'S CUP		4	3	0	1	28	29
RL CUP		2	0	0	2	7	46
NEW ZEALAND		1	0	0	1	3	17
PLAYERS RECORDS		**43**	**22**	**1**	**20**	**494**	**475**

This season heralded the first visit to Castleford of the New Zealand touring side on 8 October 1947, with the tourists registering a 17–3 victory.

The Challenge Cup Final between Wigan and Bradford Northern was the first final to be attended by a reigning Monarch, King George VI, the first to be televised and the first to be all ticket.

SEASON 1948-49

Sat 21 Aug 1948 BRADFORD NORTHERN away lost 2 - 9
BRADFORD N - Leake: Batten Jenkins E.Ward Edwards: Davies D.Ward: Whitcombe Darlison Smith Foster Tyler Traill: Try - E.Ward: Goal - E.Ward(3):
CASTLEFORD - Lewis: Bastow Alf.Fisher Skidmore Lloyd: Clinton Langfield: Harris Jones Robinson Foreman Staines Mugglestone:
Goal - Staines:
Referee T Armitage (Huddersfield) Att - 7500 H.T. nil - 6

Sat 28 Aug 1948 DEWSBURY home won 33 - 3
CASTLEFORD - Lewis: Bastow Guest Skidmore Lloyd: Alf.Fisher Langfield: Harris Jones Crossley Foreman Staines Mugglestone:
Tries - Staines(2) Guest Skidmore Lloyd Fisher Mugglestone   Goals - Staines(6):
DEWSBURY - Kelly: Withington Sheehy Bevan Clark: Clough Williams: Hammond Bradshaw Plenderleith Thomas Shakesby Murray:
Try - Clough:
Referee S Adams (Hull) Att - 8000 H.T. 12 - 3

Sat 4 Sep 1948 HUDDERSFIELD away lost 15 - 23
HUDDERSFIELD - Hunter: G.R.Pepperell Bawden Reid Cooper: Devery Walsh: Maiden Meek Davies Robson Nicholson Valentine:
Tries - Hunter(2) Cooper:
Goals - Bawden(4) Devery Reid(DG 2):
CASTLEFORD - Lewis: Bastow Guest Skidmore Lloyd: Alf.Fisher Langfield: Harris Jones Crossley Foreman Staines Mugglestone:
Try - Langfield:
Goals - Foreman(2) Staines(2) Crossley(DG) Langfield(DG):
Referee L Thorpe (Wakefield) Att - 15875 H.T. 13 - 6

Wed 8 Sep 1948 HULL home won 17 - 3
CASTLEFORD - Lewis: Bastow Guest Skidmore Lloyd: Alf.Fisher Langfield: Harris Jones Crossley Foreman Staines Mugglestone:
Tries - Guest Fisher Mugglestone:
Goals - Langfield(2) Foreman Staines:
HULL - Ingram: Madden Jewitt Shaw Ruan: Lawrence Jackson: Tindall Watt Booth Hattersley Poole Evans:
Try - Ryan:
Referee A Howgate (Dewsbury) Att - 6000 H.T. 9 - nil

**Sat 11 Sep 1948 BRAMLEY home away won 37 - 7
YORKSHIRE CUP ROUND 1 1ST LEG**
CASTLEFORD - Lewis: Bastow Skidmore Guest Lloyd: Alf.Fisher Langfield: Harris Jones Crossley Foreman Staines Mugglestone:
Tries - Foreman(2) Skidmore Fisher Langfield Staines Lloyd:
Goals - Staines(7) Langfield(DG):
BRAMLEY - Oliver: Bedford Bartlett Gibson Lazenby: Cawood Bennett: Cluderay McKinnell Rhodes Whitehead Hebb Mullins:
Try - Cluderay: Goals - Whitehead(2):
Referee A S Dobson (Pontefract) Att - 7500 H.T.

**Wed 15 Sep 1948 BRAMLEY away won 12 - 10
YORKSHIRE CUP ROUND 1 2ND LEG**
BRAMLEY - Longbottom: Brogden Gibson Lazenby Hart: Pickering Bennett: Cluderay McKinnell Rhodes Whitehead Birkin Hebb:
Tries - Gibson Whitehead: Goals - Hebb(2):
CASTLEFORD - Lewis: Bastow Guest Skidmore Lloyd: Alf.Fisher Langfield: Harris Jones Crossley Foreman Staines Mugglestone:
Tries - Lewis Guest: Goals - Staines(3):
Referee L Thorpe (Wakefield) Att - 3500 H.T. 7 - 5

Sat 18 Sep 1948 WIDNES home won 7 - 3
CASTLEFORD - Lewis: Bastow Guest Skidmore Lloyd: Alf.Fisher Langfield: Harris Jones Crossley Foreman Staines Mugglestone:
Try - Harris: Goals - Staines(2):
WIDNES - Hutton: Kenny Bradley A.Naughton Jolly: Twigg Anderson: Warburton Reynolds D.Naughton Higgins Leigh McCue:
Try - D.Naughton:
Referee F Smith (Barrow) Att - 8200 H.T. 2 - 3

Sat 25 Sep 1948 HULL KINGSTON ROVERS away won 14 - 7
HULL K R - Lufford: Schofield Smith Barraclough Richards: Daddy Keen: Hartley Ramsden Senior Welsby Goldswain Dockar:
Try - Welsby: Goals - Dockar(2):
CASTLEFORD - Lewis: Bastow Alf.Fisher Guest Lloyd: Art.Fisher Langfield: Harris Jones Crossley Foreman Staines Mugglestone:
Tries - Art.Fisher(2):   Goals - Staines(4):
Referee L J Dalby (York) Att - 5000 H.T. 2 - 7

**Tue 28 Sep 1948 HULL home won 11 - nil
YORKSHIRE CUP ROUND 2**
CASTLEFORD - Lewis: Bastow Skidmore Guest Lloyd: Alf.Fisher Langfield: Harris Jones Robinson Foreman Crossley Staines:
Tries - Skidmore Staines Langfield: Goal - Staines:
HULL - Miller: Bowers Sinclair Madden Ryan: Lawrence Jackson: Fallon Watt Booth Poole Kavanagh Evans:
Referee T Armitage (Hudd'field) Att - 10368 H.T. 5 - nil

Sat 2 Oct 1948 WORKINGTON TOWN home won 10 - 7
CASTLEFORD - Lewis: Bastow Guest Skidmore Lloyd: Alf.Fisher Langfield: Harris Jones Crossley Foreman Staines Mugglestone:
Tries - Bastow Lloyd: Goals - Staines(2):
WORKINGTON T - McGilvray: Graham Carr Paskins Large: Risman Pepperell: Miller McKeating Hayton Mudge Telford Ivison:
Try - Mudge :   Goals - Risman(2):
Referee C F Appleton (Warrington) Att - 7300 H.T. 5 -nil

SEASON 1948-49

Wed 6 Oct 1948 AUSTRALIA lost 8 - 10
CASTLEFORD - Lewis: Booth Skidmore Guest Lloyd(S/O):
Alf.Fisher Langfield: Harris Jones Crossley(S/O) Foreman
Staines Mugglestone:
Tries - Booth Mugglestone: Goal - Staines:
AUSTRALIA - Bulgin: Dimond Pegg Horrigan Graves:
Thompson Hopkins: Brosnan Benton Hand Gibbs Hall
Cowie:
Tries - Graves(2):   Goals - Graves(2):
Referee L Thorpe (Wakefield) Att - 14004 H.T. 5 - 2

Sat 9 Oct 1948 SWINTON away lost 5 - 12
SWINTON - Morgan: E.G.Turner Winkworth Taylor Daley:
Warry G.Turner: Stoddart Osmond Atherton Garner
Armitt Tucker:
Goals - Morgan(5) (DG):
CASTLEFORD - Lewis: Booth Skidmore Guest Lloyd:
Alf.Fisher Langfield: Harris Jones Crossley Foreman
Staines Mugglestone:
Try - Booth: Goal - Staines:
Referee A Hill (Dewsbury) Att - 7000 H.T. 3 - 2

**Wed 13 Oct 1948 WAKEFIELD TRINITY home won 6 -
5 YORKSHIRE CUP SEMI FINAL**
CASTLEFORD - Lewis: Booth Skidmore Guest Bastow:
Alf.Fisher Langfield: Harris Jones Robinson Foreman
Staines Mugglestone:
Goals - Staines(3):
WAKEFIELD T - Luckman: Duggan Ivill Fletcher Boocker:
Rylance Goodfellow: Wilkinson Marson Higgins Murphy
Howes Bratley:
Try - Duggan: Goal - Rylance:
Referee A S Dobson (Pontefract) Att -18500 H.T. 4 - 2

Sat 16 Oct 1948 SWINTON home lost 8 - 10
CASTLEFORD - Lewis: Bastow Skidmore Guest Lloyd:
Alf.Fisher Langfield: Harris Jones Robinson Foreman
Staines IKE OWENS(301):
Tries - Skidmore Foreman: Goal - Staines:
SWINTON - Morgan: E.G.Turner Winkworth Taylor Daley:
Warry G.Turner: Garner Osmond Atherton Knowles
Aemitt Tucker:
Tries - E.G.Turner Daley: Goals - Morgan(2):
Referee H Holland (Liverpool) Att - 10713 H.T. 5 - nil

**Sat 23 Oct 1948 WORKINGTON TOWN away
lost 4 - 14**
WORKINGTON T - Risman: Graham Carr Paskins Large:
Gibson Pepperell: Miller McKeating Hayton Wareing
Mudge Ivison:
Tries - Graham Wareing Pepperell Mudge: Goal - Risman:
CASTLEFORD - Lewis: Gordon Booth Bastow Guest Lloyd:
Alf.Fisher Langfield: Robinson Jones Crossley
GEORGE(CHARLIE)HOWARD(302) Foreman Staines:
Goals - Staines (2):
Referee T Armitage (Hud'field) Att - 11000 H.T. nil - 3

**Sat 30 Oct 1943 BRADFORD NORTHERN lost 9 - 18
YORKSHIRE CUP FINAL - AT HEADINGLEY**
CASTLEFORD - Lewis: Bastow Guest Skidmore Lloyd:
Alf.Fisher Langfield: Harris Jones Crossley Staines
Foreman Mugglestone:
Try - Foreman: Goals - Foreman Staines Langfield(DG):
BRADFORD N - Carmichael: Batten E.Ward Leake
Edwards: Davies D.Ward: Whitcombe Darlison Greaves
Foster Tyler Trai l:
Tries - Edwards(2) Leake Foster: Goals - Edwards(3):
Referee G S Phil ips (Widnes) Att - 31393 H.T. 4 - 2

Sat 6 Nov 1948 WIDNES away lost nil - 8
WIDNES - Hutton: Kenny Reynolds Hughes Bradley:
Twigg Anderson: Warburton Hayes D.Naughton
Whittaker Leigh J.Naughton:
Tries - Reynolds Whittaker: Goal - Anderson(DG):
CASTLEFORD - Lewis: Bastow Clinton Guest Lloyd:
Alf.Fisher Langfield: Harris Jones Crossley Foreman
Staines Mugglestone:
Referee A Hill (Dewsbury) Att - 9000 H.T. nil - 3

**Sat 13 Nov 1948 BRADFORD NORTHERN home
lost 5 - 11**
CASTLEFORD - Lewis: Bastow Skidmore JEFF WARD(303)
Clinton: Alf.Fisher Langfield: Robinson Jones Crossley
Mugglestone Staines Owens:
Try - Clinton: Goal - Langfield:
BRADFORD N - Carmichael: Batten Leake Jenkins Walters:
Davies D.Ward: Whitcombe Darlison Greaves Smith Tyler
Traill:
Tries - Batten Leake Walters: Goal - Carmichael:
Referee L J Dalby (York) Att - 4981 H.T. 5 - 2

Sat 20 Nov 1943 OLDHAM away lost 5 - 11
OLDHAM - Barraclough: Batten Mitchell Harris Mahoney:
Chalmers Jones: Ogden Brooks Tomlinson Pilkington
Denegan Leyland:
Try - Harris: Goals - Barraclough(4):
CASTLEFORD - Lewis: Bastow Skidmore Ward Lloyd:
Clinton Langfield: Robinson Jones Nicholls Staines
Crossley Mugglestone:
Try - Clinton: Goal - Langfield:
Referee W Hemmings (Halifax) Att – 9690 H.T. nil - 2

Sat 4 Dec 1948 HUNSLET away lost 7 - 8
HUNSLET - Griffiths: Bowman Evans Watson Carroll:
Rushton A.Burnell: Bennett Whitehead Fogharty Metcalfe
W.Burnell Rookes:
Tries - Evans A.Burnell: Goal - Griffiths:
CASTLEFORD - Lewis: Ward Skidmore Guest Lloyd:
Alf.Fisher Langfield: Harris LISTER MOGG(304) Robinson
Staines Foreman Owens:
Try - Foreman: Goals - Staines Guest(DG):
Referee A Howgate (Dewsbury) Att - 8000 H.T. 2 - 5

SEASON 1948-49

Sat 11 Dec 1948 BRAMLEY home won 20 - 5
CASTLEFORD - Lewis: Bastow Skidmore Ward Lloyd:
Alf.Fisher Langfield: Harris Mogg Crossley Foreman
Staines Mugglestone:
Tries - Lloyd Langfield Crossley Staines:
Goals - Langfield(2)Staines(2):
BRAMLEY - Gibson: Rock Bartlett Lazenby Lorriman:
Pickering Cawood: Rhodes McKinnell Cluderay
Whitehead Murphy Mullins:
Try - Unknown   Goal - Whitehead:
Referee E Thomas (Halifax) Att - 3700 H.T. 13 - nil

Sat 18 Dec 1948 BATLEY away lost 3 - 17
BATLEY - Eaton Perry Stokes Riches Etty Hesketh Burnell
Pickersgill Lawton Hartley Lavender Moore Flitcroft
Tries - Stokes(2) Etty(2) Riches: Goal - Perry:
CASTLEFORD - Lewis Bastow Skidmore Ward Lloyd
Alf.Fisher Langfield Harris Mogg Crossley Foreman
Staines Mugglestone   Try - Langfield:
Referee M Coates (Pudsey) Att - 5000 H.T. 3 - 11

Sat 25 Dec 1948 WAKEFIELD TRINITY home won 13 - 7
CASTLEFORD - Alf.Fisher: Bastow Skidmore
Ward(S/O)Lloyd: HARRY PARKER(305) Langfield: Harris
Jones JOSEPH ANDERSON(306) Crossley Staines
Mugglestone:
Tries - Skidmore Ward Lloyd: Goals - Langfield(2):
WAKEFIELD T - Luckman: Duggan Rylance Davies
Armitage: Fletcher Goodfellow: Taylor Marson Higgins
Murphy Booth Bratley:
Try - Rylance: Goals - Murphy (2):
Referee A Howgate (Dewsbury) Att - 12000 H.T. 10 - 5

Mon 27 Dec 1948 FEATHERSTONE ROVERS away won 15 - 10
FEATHERSTONE R - Lorriman: Crabtree Ogden Tennant
A.N.Other:Allman Derry: Welburn Allinson Bolton Kent
Pawson Richardson: Tries - A.N.Other Richardson:
Goals - Lorriman Allman(DG):
CASTLEFORD - Alf.Fisher: Bastow Skidmore Ward Lloyd:
Parker Langfield: Harris Mogg Anderson Crossley Staines
Mugglestone:
Tries - Bastow Ward Staines: Goals - Langfield(2) (DG):
Referee L Thorpe (Wakefield) Att - 5200 H.T. 10 - 2

Tue 28 Dec 1948 OLDHAM home won 9 - 7
CASTLEFORD - Lewis: Skidmore DANNY SHEEHY(307)
Ward Lloyd: Parker Langfield: Harris Jones Nicholls
Crossley Staines Owens:
Try - Owens: Goals - Langfield(2) (DG):
OLDHAM - Barraclough: Tate Platt Harris Inglesfield:
Batten Jones: O'Brien Brooks H.Tomlinson Donegan
A.Tomlinson Leyland: Try - Platt: Goals - Barraclough(2):
Referee W Stockley (Leigh) Att - 6000 H.T. 2 - 7

Sat 1 Jan 1949 KEIGHLEY home lost 5 - 7
CASTLEFORD - Lewis: Bastow Skidmore Sheehy Lloyd:
Parker Langfield: Harris Mogg James Nicholls Staines
Mugglestone Owens:

Try - Owens: Goal - Langfield:
KEIGHLEY - Mills: Ward Pierce Barrett Elias: De Lloyd
Davies: Thornton A.N.Other Gibson Farrar Sykes Mullhall:
Try - Elias: Goals - Mills(2):
Referee T Armitage (Huddersfield) Att - 6800 H.T. nil - 4

Sat 8 Jan 1949 FEATHERSTONE ROVERS home lost 14 - 15
CASTLEFORD - Alf.Fisher: Bastow Skidmore
A.N.OTHER(308) Lloyd: Sheehy Langfield: Maxwell
Robinson Jones Crossley Desmond Foreman
Mugglestone Owens:
Tries - A.N.Other Foreman: Goals - Langfield(4):
FEATHERSTONE R - Townsend: A.Tennant W.Tennant
Allman Ogden: Church Russell: Welburn Allinson Bolton
Kent Payne Gant:
Tries - Allman Church Payne: Goals - Townshend(3):
Referee W Hemmings (Halifax) Att – 5000 H.T. 4 - 10

Sat 15 Jan 1949 WAKEFIELD TRINITY away lost 9 - 15
WAKEFIELD T - Luckman: Duggan Rylance Davies
Boocker: Fletcher Ogden: Pilkington Marson Higgins
Murphy Foreman Bratley:
Tries - Boocker Fletcher Foreman: Goals - Murphy(3):
CASTLEFORD - Lewis: Bastow Skidmore Guest Lloyd:
Danny Sheehy Langfield: Harris Jones Anderson Crossley
Mugglestone Ike Owens:
Try - Sheehy: Goals - Langfield(3):
Referee S Adams (Hull) Att - 8500 H.T. nil - 7

Sat 22 Jan 1949 HULL away lost 7 - 12
HULL - Hart: Madden Sinclair Sullivan Ryan: Lawrence
Jackson: Danter Watt Poole Baxter Bedford Downing:
Tries - Sinclair Ryan: Goals - Hart(3):
CASTLEFORD - Lewis: Skidmore Alf.Fisher Ward Lloyd:
Art.Fisher Langfield: ARTHUR SENIOR(309) Jones
Anderson Crossley Howard Mugglestone:
Try - Skidmore: Goals - Langfield(2):
Referee A Howgate (Dewsbury) Att - 10000 H.T. 3 - 5

Sat 29 Jan 1949 HUNSLET home won 4 - 3
CASTLEFORD - Guest: Skidmore Powell Ward Lloyd:
Art.Fisher Langfield: Senior Jones Anderson Crossley
Howard Mugglestone: Goals - Langfield(2):
HUNSLET - Griffiths: Bowman Graham Evans Williams:
Gray Watson: Bennett Whitehead Fogharty W.Burnell
Carroll Davies: Try - Watson:
Referee T Armitage (Huddersfield) Att - 9571 H.T. 2 - nil

Sat 12 Feb 1949 BRAMLEY home won 10 - 2
CHALLENGE CUP ROUND 1 1ST LEG
CASTLEFORD - Lewis: Art.Fisher Skidmore Guest Lloyd:
Powell Langfield: Harris Jones Crossley Howard Staines
Mugglestone:
Tries - Guest Mugglestone: Goals - Langfield(2):
BRAMLEY - Oliver: Lorriman Gibson Warrior Rock:
Pickering Jewitt: Rhodes White Hulme Meggan Baldwin
Rawson: Goal - Rhodes:
Referee C F Appleton (War' ton) Att - 7900 H.T. nil - 2

124

Sat 19 Feb 1949 BRAMLEY away won 10 - 2
CHALLENGE CUP ROUND 1 2ND LEG
BRAMLEY - Oliver: Rock Warrior Gibson Lorriman:
Pickering Jewitt: Rhodes McKinnell Hulme Baldwin
Whitehead Mullins: Goal - Whitehead:
CASTLEFORD - Lewis: Skidmore Powell Guest Lloyd:
Alf.Fisher Langfield: Harris Jones Anderson Crossley
Howard Mugglestone:
Tries - Guest Fisher: Goals - Langfield(2):
Referee P Cowell (Warrington) Att - 10500 H.T. 2 - 2

Sat 26 Feb 1949 YORK home won 8 - 2
CASTLEFORD - Guest: Skidmore Ward Powell Lloyd:
A.N.Other Langfield: Harris Jones Anderson Crossley
Staines Storey:
Tries - Guest Crossley: Goal - Langfield:
YORK - Kitchingham: McLennan Thornton Bassett
Inglesfield: Hurcombe Benson: Banks Pinder Flowers
Waddington Goulden Hodgson:
Goal - Kitchingham:
Referee F Cottam (Wakefield) Att - 5785 H.T. 5 - 2

Sat 5 Mar 1949 BRADFORD NORTHERN away
lost 5 - 11 CHALLENGE CUP ROUND 2
BRADFORD N - Carmichael: Batten Kitching E.Ward
Edwards: Davies D.Ward: Tyler Darlison Greaves(S/O)
Foster Radford Traill:
Tries - Edwards(2) E.Ward: Goal - Carmichael:
CASTLEFORD - Guest: Ward Skidmore Powell Lloyd:
Art.Fisher Langfield: Harris Jones Anderson Staines
Howard Storey(S/O):
Try - Langfield: Goal - Langfield:
Referee F Smith (Barrow) Att - 14000 H.T. nil - nil

Sat 12 Mar 1949 HUDDERSFIELD home lost 13 - 14
CASTLEFORD - Lewis: Skidmore Guest Powell Lloyd:
Alf.Fisher Langfield: Harris Jones Anderson Howard
Staines Townsley
Try - Langfield: Goals - Langfield(3) (DG) Guest(DG):
HUDDERSFIELD - Hunter: Anderson Bawden Devery
Cooper: Ferguson Walsh: Meek Lightfoot Davies Owens
Hughes Valentine:
Tries - Devery Cooper: Goals - Bawden(4):
Referee S Adams (Hull) Att - 11789 H.T. 7 - 5

Sat 19 Mar 1949 YORK away won 5 - 3
YORK - Kitchingham: McLennan Thornton Bassett Dennis:
Hurcombe Benson: Banks Jenkins Hollingsworth Hodgson
Goulden Taylor: Try - Thornton:
CASTLEFORD - Lewis: Skidmore Guest Powell Lloyd:
Alf.Fisher Langfield: Harris Whittlestone Anderson Staines
Townsley Mugglestone: Try - Staines: Goal - Langfield:
Referee L Thorpe (Wakefield) Att - 5000 H.T. 5 - 3

Sat 26 Mar 1949 WHITEHAVEN away won 12 - nil
WHITEHAVEN - McKeown: Coirnelius Fearon Harris Varty:
Whitwell Keen: Smith Frost Holbrow Petcher Lewis Davies:
CASTLEFORD - Lewis: Skidmore Guest Ward Lloyd:
Alf.Fisher Langfield: Harris Jones Anderson Storey
Townsley Mugglestone:

Tries - Ward Mugglestone: Goals - Langfield(2) Guest:
Referee L J Dalby (York) Att - 7000 H.T. 7 - nil

Sat 2 Apr 1949 WHITEHAVEN home won 30 - 3
CASTLEFORD - Lewis: Skidmore Guest Ward Lloyd:
Alf.Fisher Langfield: Harris Whittlestone Anderson Storey
Townsley Mugglestone:
Tries - Lloyd(2) Fisher(2) Guest Ward Skidmore Langfield:
Goals - Langfield(3):
WHITEHAVEN - Proud: Cornelius Jackson Harris Godfrey:
Whitwell Keen: Hargreaves Frost Dover Petcher Lewis
James: Try - Jackson:
Referee F Smith (Barrow) Att - 5579 H.T. 19 - nil

Sat 9 Apr 1949 BRAMLEY away won 6 - 5
BRAMLEY - Oliver: Rock Warrior Gray Lorriman: Pickering
Jewitt: Hulme Britton Mullins Rawson Hebb Baldwin:
Try - Rawson: Goal - Oliver:
CASTLEFORD - Lewis: Skidmore Guest Ward Lloyd:
Alf.Fisher Langfield: Harris Jones Crossley Storey Townsley
Mugglestone:
Goals - Langfield(3):
Referee T Armitage (Huddersfield) Att - 3000 H.T. 2 - 5

Fri 15 Apr 1949 LEEDS home lost 16 - 17
CASTLEFORD - Lewis: Skidmore Guest Powell Lloyd:
Alf.Fisher Langfield: Harris Jones Anderson Townsley
Staines Mugglestone:
Tries - Powell Lloyd: Goals - Langfield(4) Staines:
LEEDS - Cox: Turnbull Bartlett Proctor Verrenkamp:
Williams Jenkins: McMaster Kearney Gronow Clues
Clarkson Murphy
Tries - Verrenkamp(2) Jenkins: Goals - Cox(2) Clarkson(2):
Referee P Cowell (Warrington) Att - 14000 H.T. 11 - 10

Sat 16 Apr 1949 HULL KINGSTON ROVERS home
won 35 - 15
CASTLEFORD - Lewis: Skidmore Ward Alf.Fisher Lloyd:
RICHARD CLAUGHTON(310) Langfield: Harris Jones
Crossley Staines Townsley Mugglestone:
Tries - Ward(3) Fisher(3) Townsley:
Goals - Langfield(6) Claughton:
HULL K R - McWatt: Richards Smith H.Mills Chapman:
Steele R.Mills: Wilmot Bradshaw Welsby Barraclough
Scholes Dockar:
Tries - Smith(2) Dockar: Goals - McWatt(3):
Referee F Cottam (Wakefield) Att - 6250 H.T. 10 - 5

Mon 18 Apr 1949 LEEDS away lost 4 - 30
LEEDS - Cook: Verrenkamp Bartlett Proctor Staniland:
Williams Jenkins: Gronow Kearney Prosser Clues Clarkson
Murphy: Tries - Verrenkamp(3) Murphy(2) Bartlett
Staniland Prosser Goals - Clarkson(3):
CASTLEFORD - Lewis: Skidmore Ward Alf.Fisher Lloyd:
Claughton Langfield: Harris Jones Crossley Staines Harry
Townsley Mugglestone:
Goals - Claughton(2):
Referee S Adams (Hull) Att - 17000 H.T. 4 - 17

SEASON 1948-49

Tue 19 Apr 1949 BATLEY home lost 8 - 12
CASTLEFORD - Lewis: Bastow <u>Leonard Skidmore</u> Ward
Lloyd: Parker Langfield: Harris Jones Crossley Storey
Staines Mugglestone:
Tries - Bastow Harris: Goal - Langfield:
BATLEY - Eaton: Etty Stokes Templeton Westbury:
Hesketh Burnell: Pickersgill Lawton Hartley Lavender
Moore Hattersley:
Tries - Lavender Moore: Goals - Eaton(3):
Referee E Thomas (Halifax) Att - 8200 H.T. 5 - 5

Sat 23 Apr 1949 DEWSBURY away lost 9 - 22
DEWSBURY - Pearson: Pollard Mahoney Bevan Clark:
Constance Williams: Hammond Bradshaw Shakesby
A.Street Thompson H.Street:
Tries - Pollard(3) A.Street(2) Bevan:
Goals - Pollard Constance:
CASTLEFORD - Lewis: Bastow Powell Ward Parker:
Alf.Fisher Langfield: Harris Jones <u>James M Crossley</u>
Staines Storey Mugglestone:
Try - Fisher: Goals - Langfield(3):
Referee T Armitage (Huddersfield) Att - 6000 H.T. 4 - 8

Sat 30 Apr 1949 KEIGHLEY away lost 5 - 6
KEIGHLEY - Mills: Ward Pierce Creeney Buckley: De Lloyd
Davies: Thornton Pritchard Gibson Bedford Flanagan
Sykes:
Tries - Ward Creeney:
CASTLEFORD - Lewis: Bastow Powell Alf.Fisher Lloyd:
Langfield Dudley: <u>Arthur Senior</u> <u>Thomas Whittlestone</u> Fox
<u>Fred Bennett</u> Staines Mugglestone:
Try - Lloyd: Goal - Langfield:
Referee M Coates (Pudsey) Att - 4000 H.T. 5 – 3

Ike Owens
D. No 301
1948-49

George (Charlie) Howard
D. No 302
1948-49 to 1958-59

Jeff Ward
D. No 303
1948-49 to 1949-50

Harry Parker
D. No 305
1948-49 to 1952-53

Joe Anderson
D. No 306
1948-49 to 1954-55

Richard Claughton
D. No 310
1948-49 to 1953-54

SEASON 1948-49

D.N	PLAYER		DEBUT	L MATCH	APP	SUB	T.AP	TRI'S	G'LS	D.G	P'TS
136	CROSSLEY	JAMES M.		23/04/1949	33	C	33	2	0	1	8
172	STAINES	CHARLES			37	C	37	7	42	0	105
176	LLOYD	REGINALD			42	C	42	9	0	0	27
179	GUEST	NORMAN			29	C	29	7	1	2	27
185	TOWNSLEY	HARRY		18/04/1949	8	C	8	1	0	0	3
214	POWELL	STAN			10	0	10	1	0	0	3
215	NICHOLLS	JAMES		01/01/1949	3	0	3	0	0	0	0
238	LEWIS	RONALD			39	0	39	1	0	0	3
255	CLINTON	GEORGE			4	0	4	2	0	0	6
262	BOOTH	GORDON		23/10/1948	4	0	4	2	0	0	6
278	BASTOW	ARTHUR			27	0	27	3	0	0	9
279	ROBINSON	MAXWELL		08/01/1949	9	0	9	0	0	0	0
280	LANGFIELD	GEORGE			45	0	45	8	57	6	150
284	FOX	HAROLD			1	0	1	0	0	0	0
290	HARRIS	DYL			38	0	38	2	0	0	6
291	MUGGLESTONE	FRANK			37	0	37	5	0	0	15
292	FISHER	ALFRED			36	0	36	10	0	0	30
293	STOREY	GEORGE			7	0	7	0	0	0	0
294	DUDLEY	JOEY			1	0	1	0	0	0	0
295	SKIDMORE	LEONARD		19/04/1949	40	0	40	7	0	0	21
296	WHITTLESTONE	THOMAS		30/04/1949	3	0	3	0	0	0	0
297	FOREMAN	DESMOND		08/01/1949	21	0	21	6	4	0	26
298	FISHER	ARTHUR (DIAMOND)			5	0	5	2	0	0	6
299	BENNETT	FRED		30/04/1949	1	0	1	0	0	0	0
300	JONES	JAMES			37	0	37	0	0	0	0
301	OWENS	IKE	16/10/1948	15/01/1949	7	0	7	2	0	0	6
302	HOWARD	GEORGE (CHARLIE)	23/10/1948		7	0	7	0	0	0	0
303	WARD	JEFF	13/11/1948		19	0	19	7	0	0	21
304	MOGG	LISTER	04/12/1948		5	0	5	0	0	0	0
305	PARKER	HARRY	25/12/1948		6	0	6	0	0	0	0
306	ANDERSON	JOSEPH	25/12/1948		13	0	13	0	0	0	0
307	SHEEHY	DANNY	28/12/1948	15/01/1949	4	0	4	1	0	0	3
308	A N OTHER		08/01/1949	26/02/1949	2	0	2	1	0	0	3
309	SENIOR	ARTHUR	22/01/1949	30/04/1949	3	0	3	0	0	0	0
310	CLAUGHTON	RICHARD	16/04/1949		2	0	2	0	3	0	6
	35		**10**	**13**	**585**	**0**	**585**	**86**	**107**	**9**	**490**

COMPETITION		P	W	D	L	FOR	AGT
LEAGUE	POSITION 19 OF 29	36	16	0	20	382	356
YORK'S CUP		5	4	0	1	75	40
RL CUP		3	2	0	1	25	15
AUSTRALIA		1	0	0	1	8	10
PLAYERS RECORDS		**45**	**22**	**0**	**23**	**490**	**421**

Whitehaven were admitted to the League to bring the total to 29.

This season saw the Club reach the final of the Yorkshire Cup for the first t me. Unfortunately we lost to Bradford Northern 18–9.

The Club created history by paying its highest transfer fee at that time - £2,750 to Leeds for their Welsh International loose forward Ike Owens. However, after he had played in only seven games he was transferred to Huddersfield for the same fee.

6 October 1948 saw the Australian touring team at Wheldon Road. Australia won 10-8 in a match in which four players were sent off – Jim Crossley and Reg Lloyd for Castleford, and the Australians E Brosnan and D Hall, the game being watched by over 14,000 spectators.

Charlie Staines increased the record for most points scored in a League game to 18 against Dewsbury at home on 28 August 1948 and on the 11 September 1948 against Bramley at home increased the record for most points in a Cup game to 17.

SEASON 1949-50

Sat 13 Aug 1949 FEATHERSTONE ROVERS home won 11 - 5 LYON CUP FRIENDLY
CASTLEFORD - Lewis: Bastow Powell Ward Mugglestone: Alf Fisher Parker: Fox Hill Anderson Howard Staines Storey:
Tries - Mugglestone Staines Storey: Goal - Staines:
FEATHERSTONE R - Townsend: Crabtree Jones Ogden Altass: Church Russell: Bolton Wood Lavin Kent Lambert Richardson: Try - Crabtree: Goal - Townsend:
Referee A S Dobson (Pontefract) Att - 4000 H.T. 8 - nil

Sat 20 Aug 1949 HULL KINGSTON ROVERS home won 24 - 12
CASTLEFORD - Lewis: Bastow Guest Ward Lloyd: Alf.Fisher Langfield: Harris Jones Anderson Howard Staines Mugglestone: Tries - Guest Langfield Ward Mugglestone: Goals - Langfield(4) Guest(2)
HULL K R - McWatt: Scholes A N Other Chapman Tullock: Brown Nichol: Wilmot Ramsden Bradshaw Barraclough Welsby Dockar:
Tries - Scholes Brown: Goals - McWatt(3):
Referee M Coates (Pudsey) Att - 5000 H.T. 10 - 2

Wed 24 Aug 1949 YORK away won 12 - 9
YORK - Kelly: Inglesfield Bower Thornton Hanshaw: Bilton Benson: Hollingsworth Jenkins Moon Goulden Hodgson Taylor:
Try - Taylor: Goals - Kelly(3):
CASTLEFORD - Lewis: Bastow Guest Ward Lloyd: Alf.Fisher Langfield: Anderson Staines Harris Howard Storey Mugglestone:
Tries - Langfield Mugglestone: Goals - Langfield(3):
Referee A Hill (Dewsbury) Att - 5000 H.T. 2 - 2

Sat 27 Aug 1949 KEIGHLEY home won 28 - 5
CASTLEFORD - Lewis: Bastow Guest Ward Lloyd: Alf.Fisher Langfield: Harris Jones Anderson Howard Staines Mugglestone:
Tries - Bastow(2) Ward(2) Fisher Langfield:
Goals - Langfield(4) Guest(DG):
KEIGHLEY - Mills: Ward Sheehy Barrett Redman: De Lloyd Davies: Brereton Britton Thornton Flanagan Farrar Mulhall:
Try - Mulhall: Goal - Mills:
Referee T Armitage (Hud'field) Att - 5500 H.T. 18 - nil

Wed 31 Aug 1949 HUDDERSFIELD away lost 5 - 29
HUDDERSFIELD - Hunter: Anderson Bawden Ferguson Cooper: G R Pepperell Banks: Leake Pritchard Daley Owens Nicholson Valentine:
Tries - Cooper(3) Anderson(2) Pepperell Hunter:
Goals - Bawden(4):
CASTLEFORD - Lewis: Bastow Art.Fisher Ward Lloyd: Alf.Fisher Langfield: Harris Jones Anderson Howard Staines Mugglestone:
Try - Alf.Fisher: Goal - Langfield:
Referee F Cottam (Wakefield) Att - 16400 H.T. nil - 10

Sat 3 Sep 1949 SWINTON away lost 5 - 18
SWINTON - Morgan: Myers Winkworth Welsh Coburn:

Moran Riley: Stoddart Osmond Atherton Knowles Wood Holder:
Tries - Winkworth(3) Welsh: Goals - Morgan(3):
CASTLEFORD - Lewis: Bastow Art.Fisher Ward Lloyd: Alf.Fisher Langfield: Harris Jones Anderson Howard Storey Mugglestone: Try - Alf.Fisher: Goal - Langfield:
Referee L J Dalby (York) Att - 6000 H.T. 5 - 10

Mon 5 Sep 1949 WORKINGTOWN TOWN home won 18 - 7
CASTLEFORD - Lewis: Claughton Bastow Ward Lloyd: Art.Fisher Langfield: Harris Jones Anderson Staines Howard Mugglestone:
Tries - Bastow Lloyd Staines Fisher: Goals - Langfield(3):
WORKINGTON T - Risman: Lawrenson Paskins Telford Carr: Gibson Reilly: Telford McKeating Hayton Mudge Wareing Iveson: Try - Carr: Goals - Risman(2):
Referee P Cowell (Warrington) Att - 7512 H.T. 8 - 4

Sat 10 Sep 1949 HULL home won 12 - 8 YORKSHIRE CUP ROUND 1 1ST LEG
CASTLEFORD - Lewis: Art.Fisher(S/O) Bastow Guest Lloyd: Alf.Fisher Langfield: Harris Jones Anderson Howard Staines Mugglestone: Goals - Guest(3) Langfield(3):
HULL - Hart: Watts Sinclair Turner Ryan: Lawrence Burnell: Danter Watt Tindall Bedford Poole Evans(S/O):
Tries - Ryan Tindall: Goal - Hart:
Referee W Hemmings (Halifax) Att - 11000 H.T. 8 - 8

Wed 14 Sep 1949 HULL away draw 13 - 13 YORKSHIRE CUP ROUND 1 2ND LEG
HULL - Hart: Watts Sinclair Turner Ryan: Lawrence Burnell: Danter Watt Tindall Bedford Poole Downing:
Tries - Turner(2) Ryan: Goals - Hart(2):
CASTLEFORD - Guest: Bastow Alf.Fisher Ward Lloyd: Art.Fisher Langfield: Harris Jones Anderson Howard Staines Mugglestone: Try - Howard:
Goals - Langfield(3)(DG) Mugglestone(DG):
Referee L Thorpe (Wakefield) Att - 12000 H.T.

Sat 17 Sep 1949 YORK home won 15 - 8
CASTLEFORD - Guest: Bastow Ward Alf.Fisher Lloyd: Art.Fisher Langfield: Harris Jones Anderson Howard Staines Mugglestone:
Tries - Bastow Staines Langfield: Goals - Langfield(3):
YORK - Kelly: Dennis Taylor Kitchingham Inglesfield: Turner Bilton: Moon Jenkins Waddington Goulden Hollingsworth Hodgson:
Tries - Taylor Goulden: Goals - Kelly(DG):
Referee A S Dobson (Pontefract) Att - 5370 H.T. 2 - 3

Wed 21 Sep 1949 BRADFORD NORTHERN away lost 6 - 13 YORKSHIRE CUP ROUND 2
BRADFORD N - Carmichael: Batten Leake E Ward Walters: Davies D Ward: Day Darlison Greaves Foster Tyler Moore:
Tries - Batten(2) Walters: Goals - E Ward(2):
CASTLEFORD - Guest: Bastow Ward Alf.Fisher Lloyd: Art.Fisher Langfield: Harris Jones Anderson Howard Staines Mugglestone: Goals - Langfield(3):
Referee S Adams (Hull) Att - 14550 H.T. 2 - 3

SEASON 1949-50

Sat 1 Oct 1949 BATLEY away won 29 - 5
BATLEY - Chapman: Perry Stokes Templeton Burrows:
Hesketh Harrison: Pickersgill Lawton Fallon Hargreaves
Moore Palmer: Try - Burrows: Goal - Perry:
CASTLEFORD - Lewis: Parker Guest Alf.Fisher Lloyd:
Art.Fisher Langfield: Harris Jones Anderson Howard
Staines Mugglestone:
Tries - Guest(3) Langfield(2):   Goals - Langfield(6) Staines:
Referee L J Dalby (York) Att - 4000 H.T. 17 - 2

Sat 8 Oct 1949 BATLEY home lost 9 - 20
CASTLEFORD - Lewis: Parker Guest Alf.Fisher Lloyd:
Art.Fisher Langfield: Harris Jones Anderson Howard
Staines Mugglestone:
Try - Art.Fisher: Goals - Langfield(3):
BATLEY - Chapman: Perry Stokes Riches Etty: Hesketh
Laycock: Pickersgill Carter Hartley Palmer Moore
Hattersley:
Tries - Riches Etty Laycock Moore: Goals - Perry(4):
Referee W Hemmings (Halifax) Att - 6500 H.T. 6 - 10

Sat 15 Oct 1949 WAKEFIELD TRINITY home lost 7 - 8
CASTLEFORD - Lewis: Stan Powell Guest Jeff Ward Lloyd:
Art.Fisher Langfield: Harris Jones Anderson Howard
Staines Mugglestone:
Try - Guest: Goals - Langfield Staines:
WAKEFIELD T - Luckman: Duggan Froggett Boocker
Jenkinson: Rylance Fletcher: Booth Marson Higgins
Murphy Howes Hughes:
Tries - Froggett Hughes: Goal - Rylance:
Referee S Adams (Hull) Att - 10961 H.T. 5 - nil

Sat 22 Oct 1949 HULL away lost 4 - 8
HULL - Hart: Watts Turner Evans Ryan: Shaw Burnell:
Poole Wilkinson Tindall Baxter Bedford Scott:
Tries - Ryan(2):   Goal - Hart:
CASTLEFORD - Lewis: Brown Guest REG THORNTON(311)
Alf.Fisher: Art.Fisher Langfield: Harris Jones Anderson
Staines Howard Mugglestone   Goals - Langfield(2):
Referee F Cottam (Huddersfield) Att - 8000 H.T. 4 - 3

Sat 5 Nov 1949 FEATHERSTONE ROVERS away won 11 - 4
FEATHERSTONE R - Blackburn: Crabtree Tennant Watts
Altass: Church Russell: Hemingway Wood Lavin Kent
Ogden Gant: Goals - Blackburn(2):
CASTLEFORD - Lewis: PERCY ALDRED(312) Art.Fisher
Bastow Lloyd: Parker Langfield: Harris Jones Anderson
Howard Staines Mugglestone:
Tries - Lewis Bastow Art.Fisher: Goal - Langfield:
Referee A Howgate (Dewsbury) Att - 3800 H.T. 2 - 4

Sat 12 Nov 1949 BRAMLEY home won 4 - 2
CASTLEFORD - Lewis: Aldred Art.Fisher Bastow Lloyd:
Parker Langfield: Harris Jones Anderson Howard
Mugglestone Clinton: Goals - Langfield(2):
BRAMLEY - Ingram: Rock Warrior Silverwood Bagshaw:
Gibson Jewitt: Rhodes White Hebb Rawson Longley
Davidson: Goal - Gibson:
Referee R Gelder (Wakefield) Att - 2700 H.T. 2 - 2

Sat 19 Nov 1949 OLDHAM away draw 5 - 5
OLDHAM - Glanville: Baxter Ward Mitchell Spencer: Heyes
Gilmore: Ogden Keith Brooks Fearnley Leyland Goldswain:
Try - Fearnley: Goal - Glanville:
CASTLEFORD - Lewis: Aldred Art.Fisher Bastow Lloyd:
Parker Langfield: Harris Jones Anderson Howard Staines
Mugglestone: Try - Bastow: Goal - Langfield:
Referee M Coates (Pudsey) Att - 8519 H.T. 5 - nil
**Abandoned for fog after 55 minutes –
Replayed 25 mar 1950**

Sat 26 Nov 1949 HUDDERSFIELD home lost 11 - 15
CASTLEFORD - Lewis: Aldred Art.Fisher Bastow Lloyd:
Parker Langfield: Harris Jones Anderson Howard Staines
Mugglestone: Try - Howard: Goals - Langfield(4):
HUDDERSFIELD - Hunter: Anderson Bawden Devery
Cooper: Pepperell Banks: Wilmot Pritchard Bairstow
Owens Robson Valentine:
Tries - Anderson Devery Cooper:
Goals - Devery(2) Bawden:
Referee A Howgate (Dewsbury) Att - 8000 H.T. 9 - 8

Sat 3 Dec 1949 HUNSLET away won 10 - 2
HUNSLET - Griffiths: Bowman Sinclair Williams
Williamson: Evans Ellenor: Newbound Rees W Burnell
Jones Thompson Carroll:
Goal - Griffiths:
CASTLEFORD - Lewis: Aldred Art.Fisher Bastow Lloyd:
Parker Langfield Harris Jones Anderson Howard Staines
Mugglestone:
Tries - Lloyd Fisher: Goals - Langfield(2):
Referee L Thorpe (Wakefield) Att - 7000 H.T. 3 - 2

Sat 10 Dec 1949 SWINTON home lost 5 - 8
CASTLEFORD - Lewis: Aldred Art.Fisher Bastow Lloyd:
Parker Langfield Harris Jones Anderson Howard Staines
Mugglestone:
Try - Langfield: Goal - Langfield:
SWINTON - Morgan: Turner Winkworth Kenny Welsh:
Moran Riley: Stoddart Osmond Atherton Knowles Woods
Holder:
Tries - Winkworth Knowles: Goal - Morgan:
Referee C F Appleton (War'ton) Att - 4500 H.T. nil - nil

Sat 17 Dec 1949 LIVERPOOL STANLEY home won 31 - 2
CASTLEFORD - Lewis: CYRIL WOOLFORD(313) Bastow
Art.Fisher Lloyd: Parker Langfield: Harris Jones Anderson
Howard LEO FLEMING(314) LESLIE ROWLEY(315):
Tries - Parker(2) Bastow Lloyd Langfield Howard Rowley:
Goals - Langfield(5):
LIVERPOOL S - Forsyth: Todd Cox Clare Jackson: Cockram
Molyneux: Derbyshire Kennedy Beasley Sparks Leyland
Preston:
Goal - Forsyth:
Referee N T Railton (Wigan) Att - 4000 H.T. 6 - nil

Sat 24 Dec 1949 WAKEFIELD TRINITY away lost 10 - 33
WAKEFIELD T - Luckman: Baddeley Froggett Davies

Boocker: Rylance Fletcher: Booth Marson Higgins Murphy Howes Hughes:
Tries - Fletcher(2) Luckman Baddeley Rylance Hughes Higgins: Goals - Rylance(5) Hughes(DG):
CASTLEFORD - Lewis: Woolford Norman Guest Bastow Lloyd: Parker Langfield: Harris Jones Anderson Howard Clinton Mugglestone:
Tries - Parker Guest: Goals - Langfield(2):
Referee A S Dobson (Pontefract) Att - 10135 H.T. 5 - 25

Mon 26 Dec 1949 FEATHERSTONE ROVERS home won 23 - 15
CASTLEFORD - Lewis: Woolford Aldred Bastow Lloyd: Art.Fisher Langfield: Fox Jones Anderson Howard Fleming Rowley: Tries - Fisher(2) Woolford Aldred Fleming:
Goals - Langfield(4):
FEATHERSTONE R - Davies: Tennant Church Graham Altass: Gilbertson Russell: Hemimgway Wood Major Kent Ogden Payne:
Tries - Church Russell Major: Goals - Davies(3):
Referee S Adams (Hull) Att - 6500 H.T. 14 - 8

Tue 27 Dec 1949 HUNSLET home won 16 - 9
CASTLEFORD - Lewis: Woolford Aldred Bastow Parker: Art.Fisher Langfield: Fox Jones Anderson Howard Staines Mugglestone:
Tries - Parker Langfield Mugglestone Staines:
Goals - Staines Langfield:
HUNSLET - Griffiths: Bowman Sinclair Evans Williamson: D James Talbot: Bennett Doyle Jones Metcalf W Burnell C James: Try - Bowman: Goals - Talbot(2) Griffiths:
Referee A Howgate (Dewsbury) Att - 11000 H.T. 8 - 2

Sat 31 Dec 1949 HALIFAX away lost nil - 13
HALIFAX - Chalkley: Daniels Price E McDonald O'Connor: Dean Kielty: Hatfield Ackerley Olsen Greenwood Cox Birkin:
Tries - Daniels Price Greenwood: Goals - Chalkley(2):
CASTLEFORD - Lewis: Woolford Aldred Bastow Parker: Art.Fisher Langfield: Fox Jones Anderson Howard Staines Mugglestone:
Referee M Coates (Pudsey) Att - 11500 H.T. nil - 2

Sat 7 Jan 1950 BRADFORD NORTHERN away won 19 - nil
BRADFORD N - Leake: Johnson E Ward Jenkins Walters: Davies Jones: Day Darlison Bedford Foster Sharpe Traill:
CASTLEFORD - Lewis: Woolford Bastow Aldred Lloyd: Art.Fisher Langfield: Fox Jones Anderson Howard Mugglestone:
Tries - Bastow Aldred Fisher: Goals - Langfield(5):
Referee H Squires (Ossett) Att - 9000 H.T. 2 - nil

Sat 14 Jan 1950 HULL home won 17 - 11
CASTLEFORD - Lewis: Woolford Bastow Aldred Lloyd: Art.Fisher Langfield: Fox Jones Anderson Howard Staines Mugglestone:
Tries - Woolford Fisher Aldred: Goals - Langfield(4):
HULL - Hart: Gittoes Shaw Rushton Ryan: Conway Northern: Danter Watts Jimmieson Bedford Scott Evans:

Tries - Ryan(2) Rushton: Goal - Hart:
Referee L Thorpe (Wakefield) Att - 6000 H.T. 2 - 3

Sat 21 Jan 1950 BRAMLEY away won 9 - 5
BRAMLEY - Ingram: Rock Lazenby Warrior Gibson: Gray Jewitt: Rhodes Silverwood Cluderay Hebb Hulme Baldwin:
Try - Hulme: Goal - Rhodes:
CASTLEFORD - Lewis: Woolford Bastow Aldred Lloyd: Art.Fisher Langfield: Fox Jones Anderson Staines Howard Mugglestone:
Try - Aldred: Goals - Langfield(2) Mugglestone(DG):
Referee S Adams (Hull) Att - 3900 H.T. 2 - nil

Sat 4 Feb 1950 BATLEY away lost 9 - 10 CHALLENGE CUP ROUNDd 1 1ST LEG
BATLEY - Chapman: Perry Etty Stokes Harrison: Riches Laycock: Hartley Carter Pickersgill McAvoy Moore Westbury:
Tries - Harrison Carter: Goals - Perry(2):
CASTLEFORD - Lewis: Woolford Aldred Bastow Lloyd: Art.Fisher Langfield: Fox Jones Anderson Howard Staines Mugglestone:
Try - Anderson: Goals - Langfield(3):
Referee C F Appleton (Warrington) Att - 8500 H.T. 4 - 8

Sat 11 Feb 1950 BATLEY home draw 6 - 6 CHALLENGE CUP ROUND 1 2ND LEG
CASTLEFORD - Lewis: Woolford Aldred Bastow Lloyd: Art.Fisher Langfield: Fox Jones Anderson Howard Staines Mugglestone: Goals - Langfield(3):
BATLEY - Eaton: Perry Etty Stokes Harrison: Riches Laycock: Hartley Carter Pickersgill McAvoy Moore Westbury: Tries - Perry Harrison:
Referee G S Phillips (Widnes) Att - 9500 H.T. 6 - 6

Sat 18 Feb 1950 KEIGHLEY away lost 9 - 16
KEIGHLEY - Mills: Ward Barrett Creeney Ivill: De Lloyd Jenkins: Brereton Britton Callaghan Mulhall Bedford Davies:
Tries - Ivill Brereton: Goals - Mills(5):
CASTLEFORD - Lewis: Woolford Aldred Bastow Lloyd: C A ADAMS(316) Langfield: Harold Fox WILLIAM T PRITCHARD(317) Anderson Howard JOHN COWES(318) Staines:
Try - Aldred: Goals - Langfield(3):
Referee R Gelder (Wakefield) Att - 6000 H.T. 4 - 7

Sat 4 Mar 1950 LIVERPOOL STANLEY away lost 3 - 13
LIVERPOOL S - Cox: Hertzman Todd Clare Cockram: Forsyth Lea: Beesley Wilson Riley Sparke Leyland Preston:
Tries - Preston(2) Lea: Goals - Forsyth(2):
CASTLEFORD - Lewis: Bastow Aldred GEORGE BROUGHTON(319) Lloyd: C A Adams Langfield: Harris Jones Anderson Cowes PETER GRONOW(320) Howard:
Try - Lewis
Referee A Hill (Dewsbury) Att 359 H.T. 3 - 10

Sat 11 Mar 1950 DEWSBURY home won 13 - 5
CASTLEFORD - Lewis: Lloyd Aldred ARCHIE FERGUSON(321) Broughton: Art.Fisher Langfield: Harris

Jones Anderson Howard Staines Mugglestone:
Try - Aldred: Goals - Langfield(4)(DG):
DEWSBURY - Pearson: Pollard Mahoney Lewis Cowling:
Rylance Williams: Wood Bradshaw Harter Holt A Street H
Street: Try - Pollard: Goal - Rylance:
Referee N T Railton (Liverpool) Att - 7500 H.T. 6 - 5

Sat 18 Mar 1950 HALIFAX home lost 8 - 15
CASTLEFORD - Lewis: Parker Aldred Ferguson Broughton:
Art.Fisher Langfield: Harris Jones Anderson Howard
Staines Mugglestone: Goals - Langfield(4):
HALIFAX - Chalkley: Daniels McDonald Stokes Falcon:
Dean Kielty: Hatfield Hanley Olson Greenwood White
Birkin:
Tries - McDonald Dean Birkin: Goals - Chalkley(3):
Referee P Cowell (Warrington) Att - 6000 H.T. 2 - 3

Sat 25 Mar 1950 OLDHAM away lost 9 - 21
OLDHAM - Platt: Warham Ward Mitchell Batten: Heyes
Silva: Ogden Dean Anthony Fearnley Leyland Goldswain:
Tries - Warham(2) Heyes(2) Silva: Goals - Goldswain(3):
CASTLEFORD - Lewis: Art.Fisher Aldred Broughton Lloyd:
Ferguson Langfield: Harris Jones Anderson Staines
Howard Mugglestone:
Try - Staines: Goals - Langfield(3):
Referee S Adams (Hull) Att - 6891 H.T. 2 - 10

**Mon 27 Mar 1950 BRADFORD NORTHERN home
won 27 - 9**
CASTLEFORD - Lewis: Aldred Ferguson Broughton Lloyd:
Art.Fisher Parker: Harris Jones Anderson Howard Staines
Mugglestone: Tries - Ferguson Broughton Fisher Parker
Mugglestone: Goals - Staines(5) Aldred:
BRADFORD N - Carmichael: Johnson Leake Jenkins Smith:
Heritage Jones: Day Haley Greaves Foster Bedford Moore:
Try - Bedford: Goals - Carmichael(3):
Referee F Cottam (Wakefield) Att - 6000 H.T. 15 - 7

Sat 1 Apr 1950 WORKINGTON TOWN away lost 4 - 16
WORKINGTON T - Risman: Graham Paskins Gibson
Wilson: Lawrenson Thomas: Cavanagh McKeating Hayton
Telford Mudge Ivison:
Tries - Paskins Wilson: Goals - Risman(5):
CASTLEFORD - Lewis: Aldred Ferguson Broughton Lloyd:
Art.Fisher Parker: Harris Jones Anderson Howard Staines
Mugglestone: Goals - Staines(2):
Referee T W Watkinson (Pend'bury) Att 8404 H.T. nil - 6

Fri 7 Apr 1950 LEEDS away lost 10 - 12
LEEDS - Cook: Staniland Bartlett Proctor Verrenkamp:
Williams Watson: Prosser Kearney Hopper Clues Murphy
Clarkson: Tries - Staniland Bartlett: Goals - Cook(3):
CASTLEFORD - Lewis: Aldred Broughton Ferguson Parker:
Art.Fisher Langfield: Harris Jones Anderson(S/O) Staines
Howard Mugglestone:
Tries - Ferguson Langfield: Goals - Langfield(2):
Referee A S Dobson (Pontefract) Att - 18000 H.T. 10 - 4

Sat 8 Apr 1950 DEWSBURY away lost nil - 18
DEWSBURY - Thompson: Pollard Mahoney Rylance
Cowling: Constance Butler: Hammond Bradshaw Harter

Cartey A Street H Street:
Tries - Cowling(3) Butler: Goals - Rylance(3):
CASTLEFORD - Lewis: Broughton Aldred Ferguson LEWIS
O'CONNOR(322): Art.Fisher Langfield: Harris Jones
Anderson LESLIE HAUGHEY(323) Howard Mugglestone
Referee C F Appleton (War'gton) Att - 5000 H.T. nil - 10

Mon 10 Apr 1950 LEEDS home won 7 - 2
CASTLEFORD - Lewis: Broughton Aldred Ferguson
O'Connor: Art.Fisher Langfield: Harris Jones Anderson
Haughey Staines Mugglestone:
Try - Aldred: Goals - Langfield Mugglestone(DG):
LEEDS - Cox: Staniland Wright Proctor Verrenkamp:
Williams Feather: McMaster Battersby Prosser Clues
Murphy Clarkson: Goal - Clarkson:
Referee J W Jackson (Barrow) Att - 7000 H.T. 4 - nil

**Sat 15 Apr 1950 HULL KINGSTON ROVERS away
won 10 - 6**
HULL K R - J Lewis: Tulloch H Lewis Austin A.N.Other:
A.N.Other Mills: Palframan Smith Barker Barraclough
Scholes Dockar:
Goals - Barker(2) J Lewis:
CASTLEFORD - R Lewis: Lewis O'Connor Aldred Ferguson
Lloyd: Art.Fisher Langfield: Harris Jones Fleming Staines
Haughey Mugg estone:
Tries - O'Connor Aldred: Goals - Langfield(2):
Referee A Howcate (Dewsbury) Att – 4263 H.T. 10 - 2

Wed 19 Apr 1950 OLDHAM home won 7 - 5
CASTLEFORD - Lewis: Parker Ferguson Aldred Lloyd:
Art.Fisher Langfield: Harris Jones Anderson Staines
Haughey Mugglestone:
Try - Ferguson: Goals - Langfield Staines:
OLDHAM - Barraclough: Warham Ward Mitchell Williams:
Daley Rea: Jackson Keith Anthony Leyland Fearnley
Goldswain:
Try - Warham: Goal - Barraclough:
Referee W S Sm th (Dewsbury) Att - 5500 H.T. 5 - nil

**Sat 22 Apr 1950 A WELSH XIII home won 19 - 11
FRIENDLY**
CASTLEFORD - Lewis: Broughton Aldred Ferguson Lloyd:
Art.Fisher Langfield: Anderson Jones Hoare Fleming
Haughey Staines:
Tries - Langfield(2) Broughton Ferguson Lloyd:
Goals Langfield(2)
WELSH X111 - R Durston(Bridgend): M Rosser(Cardiff)
Alexander(Ystradgynlais) R Thomas(Bridgend) D
Hier(Ystradgynlais): Griffiths(Ystradgynlais) W
Lewis(Ystradgyn ais): Lloyd(Ystradgynlais) J Gore(Blaina) J
Gibson(Cardiff) J Warham(Cardiff) B McNally(Cardiff)
James(Ystradgyn ais):
Tries - Rosser Thomas Warham: Goal - Durston:
Referee F R Jones (Rawdon) Att - 4500 H.T. 8 – 6

Percy Aldred
D. No 312
1949-50 to 1950-51

Cyril Woolford
D. No 313
1949-50 to 1953-54

Leo Fleming
D. No 314
1949-50 to 1954-55

John Cowes
D. No 318
1949-50 to 1951-52

George Broughton
D. No 319
1949-50 to 1952-53

Archie Feguson
D. No 321
1949-50 to 1951-52

Les Haughy
D. No 323
1949-50 to 1956-57

SEASON 1949-50

D.N	PLAYER		DEBUT	L MATCH	APP	SL B	T.AP	TRI'S	G'LS	D.G	P'TS
172	STAINES	CHARLES			35	0	35	4	11	0	34
176	LLOYD	REGINALD			35	0	35	3	0	0	9
178	GUEST	NORMAN		24/12/1949	12	0	12	6	5	1	30
214	POWELL	STAN		15/10/1949	1	0	1	0	0	0	0
238	LEWIS	RONALD			39	0	39	2	0	0	6
242	BROWN	LEONARD			1	0	1	0	0	0	0
255	CLINTON	GEORGE			2	0	2	0	0	0	0
278	BASTOW	ARTHUR			28	0	28	8	0	0	24
280	LANGFIELD	GEORGE			40	0	40	10	100	2	234
284	FOX	HAROLD		18/02/1950	9	0	9	0	0	0	0
290	HARRIS	DYL			33	0	33	0	0	0	0
291	MUGGLESTONE	FRANK			38	0	38	4	0	3	18
292	FISHER	ALFRED			12	0	12	3	0	0	9
293	STOREY	GEORGE			2	0	2	0	0	0	0
298	FISHER	ARTHUR (DIAMOND)			36	0	36	9	0	0	27
300	JONES	JAMES			40	0	40	0	0	0	0
302	HOWARD	GEORGE (CHARLIE)			39	0	39	3	0	0	9
303	WARD	JEFF		15/10/1949	10	0	10	3	0	0	9
305	PARKER	HARRY			17	0	17	5	0	0	15
306	ANDERSON	JOSEPH			41	0	41	1	0	0	3
310	CLAUGHTON	RICHARD			1	0	1	0	0	0	0
311	THORNTON	REG	27/01/1951	09/04/1951	1	0	1	0	0	0	0
312	ALDRED	PERCY	05/11/1949		26	0	26	8	1	0	26
313	WOOLFORD	CYRIL	17/12/1949		11	0	11	2	0	0	6
314	FLEMING	LEO	17/12/1949		3	0	3	1	0	0	3
315	ROWLEY	LESLIE	17/12/1949		2	0	2	1	0	0	3
316	ADAMS	C A	18/02/1950	04/03/1950	2	0	2	0	0	0	0
317	PRITCHARD	WILLIAM T.	18/02/1950	18/02/1950	1	0	1	0	0	0	0
318	COWES	JOHN	04/03/1950		2	0	2	0	0	0	0
319	BROUGHTON	GEORGE	04/03/1950		9	0	9	1	0	0	3
320	GRONOW	PETER	04/03/1950	04/03/1950	1	0	1	0	0	0	0
321	FERGUSON	ARCHIE	11/03/1950		10	0	10	3	0	0	9
322	O'CONNOR	LEWIS	08/04/1950	15/04/1950	3	0	3	1	0	0	3
323	HAUGHEY	LESLIE	08/04/1950		4	0	4	0	0	0	0
	34		**13**	**9**	**546**	**0**	**546**	**78**	**117**	**6**	**480**

COMPETITION		P	W	D	L	FOR	AGT
LEAGUE	POSITION 12 OF 29	36	20	0	16	429	386
YORK'S CUP		3	1	1	1	31	34
RL CUP		2	0	1	1	15	16
VOID - OLDHAM		1	0	1	0	5	5
PLAYERS RECORDS		**42**	**21**	**3**	**18**	**480**	**441**

At the end of the season on 22 April 1950 a Welsh team visited Wheldon Road in a friendly game with Castleford emerging winners 19-11.

George Langfield improved the record for goals in a season to 100.

SEASON 1950-51

Sat 12 Aug 1950 FEATHERSTONE ROVERS home won 15 - 12 LYON CUP FREINDLY
CASTLEFORD - Lewis: Broughton Aldred Claughton C.Anderson: Parker Langfield: Fleming Hill Staines Haughey Rowley Mugglestone
Tries - Claughton(2) Mugglestone: Goals - Langfield(3)
FEATHERSTONE R - Blackburn: Church Kelly Tennant Altass: Jarvis Derry: Welburn Wood Lavin Kent Richardson Payne
Tries - Kelly Lavin: Goals - Blackburn(2) (DG):
Referee.R Gelder (Wakefield) Att -   H.T. 7 - 10

Tue 22 Aug 1950 BATLEY away lost 6 - 8
BATLEY - Chapman: Harrison Etty Riches Perry: Kenny Royal: Pilkington Hattersley Hartley Palmer Briggs Mawson:
Goals - Perry(4):
CASTLEFORD - Lewis: Parker Aldred Broughton Lloyd: Art.Fisher Langfield: Fleming Hill J.Anderson Haughey Howard Mugglestone:
Goals - Langfield(3):
Referee H Squires (Ossett) Att - 6000 H.T. 6 - 2

Sat 26 Aug 1950 BELLE VUE RANGERS home won 16 - 10
CASTLEFORD - Lewis: Broughton Aldred Ferguson Lloyd: Art.Fisher Langfield: J.Anderson Hill Staines Howard Haughey Mugglestone:
Tries - Aldred Fisher: Goals - Langfield(5)
BELLE V R - Gregory: Cope Price Morgan Smith: Thatcher Rees: Ayles Hunt K.Ogden Tonge Fawcett Pimblett:
Tries - Rees Ogden: Goals - Gregory(2):
Referee P Cowell (Warrington) Att - 5500 H.T. 7 - 5

Mon 28 Aug 1950 BRADFORD NORTHERN home won 15 - 8
CASTLEFORD - Lewis: Woolford Broughton Ferguson Aldred: Art.Fisher Langfield: J.Anderson Hill Staines Howard Haughey Mugglestone
Tries - Broughton Fisher Staines: Goals - Langfield (3):
BRADFORD N - Leake: Batten Kitching Mageen Walters: Davies D.Ward: Day Haley Greaves Jones Tyler Radford
Tries - Ward Greaves: Goal - Ward
Referee S Adams (Hull) Att - 6000 H.T. 10 - nil

Sat 2 Sep 1950 KEIGHLEY away won 14 - 9 YORKSHIRE CUP ROUND 1 1st LEG
KEIGHLEY - Mills: Ward Barrett Creeney Redman: De Lloyd Jenkins: Thornton Britten Callaghan Mulhall Bedford I.Davies:
Tries - Redman Mulhall Davies:
CASTLEFORD - Lewis: Woolford Aldred Ferguson Broughton: Art.Fisher Langfield: J.Anderson Hill Staines Howard Haughey Mugglestone:
Tries - Woolford Broughton: Goals - Langfield(3) (DG):
Referee A Hill (Dewsbury) Att - 7500 H.T. 14 - 3

Wed 6 Sep 1950 KEIGHLEY home lost 2 - 4 YORKSHIRE CUP ROUND 1 2nd LEG
CASTLEFORD - Lewis: Woolford Aldred Ferguson

Broughton: Art.Fisher Langfield: J.Anderson Hill Charles Staines Howard Haughey Mugglestone:
Goal - Langfield:
KEIGHLEY - Mills: Ward Redman Creeney Ivill: De Lloyd Jenkins: Thornton Britten Callaghan Mulhall Bedford Davies: Goals - Mills(2):
Referee L Thorpe (Wakefield) Att - 4000 H.T. nil - 4

Sat 9 Sep 1950 BRAMLEY away won 9 - 5
BRAMLEY - Silverwood: Lazenby Gibson Warrior Humphries: Pickering Bennett: Rhodes Baxter Meegan Baldwin Eddison Davison:
Try - Humphries: Goal - Gibson:
CASTLEFORD - Lewis: Woolford Aldred Ferguson(S/O) Broughton: Art.Fisher Langfield: J.Anderson Jones Fleming Haughey Howard Mugglestone:
Try - Broughton: Goals - Langfield(3):
Referee T Armitage (Huddersfield) Att -   H.T. 9 - nil

Sat 16 Sep 1950 KEIGHLEY home lost 14 - 15
CASTLEFORD - Lewis: Lloyd Aldred Ferguson Broughton: Art.Fisher Langfield: Harris Jones J.Anderson Howard Haughey Mugglestone:
Tries - Langfield Howard: Goals - Langfield(4):
KEIGHLEY - Mills: A.N.Other Prescott Creeney Redman: De Lloyd Davies: Callaghan Winterbottom Mulhall Flanagan Bedford I.Davies:
Tries - A.N.Other Flanagan Bedford: Goals - Mills(3):
Referee L J Dalby (York) Att - 5600 H.T. 7 - 15

Wed 20 Sep 1950 BRADFORD NORTHERN away won 4 - nil YORKSHIRE CUP ROUND 2
BRADFORD N - Leake: Batten Kitching Mageen Walters: Jones D.Ward: Day Haley Greaves Radford Tyler Moore:
CASTLEFORD - Lewis: Broughton Bastow Aldred Woolford: Art.Fisher Langfield: J.Anderson Jones Fleming Howard Haughey Mugglestone:
Goals - Langfield(1) (DG):
Referee A Hill (Dewsbury) Att -113000 H.T. 2 - nil

Sat 23 Sep 1950 SALFORD away won 11 - 9
SALFORD - G.Moses: Aspinall Pimblett Danby Stirrup: Davies Chadderton: Hawkins Curran Alder Jones D.Moses Kenny: Try - Danby: Goals - Davies(3):
CASTLEFORD - Lewis: Bastow Aldred Ferguson Broughton: Art.Fisher Langfield: J.Anderson Jones Fleming Howard Haughey Mugglestone:
Tries - Mugglestone: Goals - Langfield(4):
Referee F Cottam (Wakefield) Att - 6000 H.T. 2 - 9

Sat 30 Sep l950 HULL home won 15 - 3
CASTLEFORD - Lewis: Lloyd Aldred Bastow Broughton: Art.Fisher Langfield: J.Anderson Jones Fleming Haughey Howard Mugglestone:
Tries - Lloyd(2) Broughton: Goals - Langfield(3):
HULL - Hart: Gittoes Shaw Turner Francis: Lawrence Burnell: Danter Harris Foreman Baxter Bedford Evans:
Try - Foreman:
Referee A Howgate (Dewsbury) Att - 4000 H.T. 15 - 3

SEASON 1950-51

Sat 7 Oct 1950 WIGAN away lost 5 - 43
WIGAN - Cunliffe: Silcock Broome Roughley Nordgren:
Ashcroft Bradshaw: Gee Curran Woosey Slevin Ward
Large:
Tries - Nordgren(2) Cunliffe Broome Roughley Ashcroft
Curran Woosey Ward: Goals - Ward(8):
CASTLEFORD - Lewis: Woolford Aldred Bastow
Broughton: Art.Fisher Langfield: J.Anderson Jones Fleming
Haughey Howard Mugglestone:
Try - Broughton: Goal - Langfield:
Referee A Hill (Dewsbury) Att - 20000 H.T. 3 - 19

Tue 10 Oct 1950 BATLEY away draw 2 - 2
YORKSHIRE CUP SEMI FINAL
BATLEY - Chapman: Perry Riches Etty Harrison: Kenny
Royal: Pilkimgton Carter Pickersgill Palmer Sewell
Mawson: Goal - Perry:
CASTLEFORD - Lewis: Lloyd Aldred Bastow Broughton:
Art.Fisher Langfield: J.Anderson Jones Fleming Howard
Haughey Mugglestone: Goal - Langfield:
Referee L J Dalby (York) Att - 12700 H.T. nil - 2

Fri 13 Oct 1950 BATLEY home won 13 - 9
YORKSHIRE CUP SEMI FINAL REPLAY
CASTLEFORD - Aldred: Lloyd Brown Bastow Broughton:
Art.Fisher Langfield: J.Anderson Jones Fleming Howard
Haughey Mugglestone:
Tries - Lloyd: Goals - Langfield(4) (DG):
BATLEY - Eaton: Perry Templeton Etty Harrison: Riches
Royal: Pilkimgton Carter Sewell Palmer Lavender Mawson:
Try - Harrison: Goals - Perry(3):
Referee M Coates (Pudsey) Att - 12000 H.T. 11 - 4

Sat 14 Oct 1950 HUDDERSFIELD home draw 13 - 13
CASTLEFORD - Lloyd: Brown Aldred Ferguson Woolford:
Parker Langfield: Harris Jones Fleming Howard Haughey
Mugglestone:
Try - Aldred: Goals - Langfield(4) Mugglestone(DG):
HUDDERSFIELD - Hunter: Cracknell Bawden Henderson
Cooper: Pepperell Thomas: Wagstaffe Mundy Wilmot
Nicholson Owens Valentine:
Tries - Hunter Henderson Nicholson: Goals - Bawden(2):
Referee L Thorpe (Wakefield) Att - 9000 H.T. 8 - nil

Sat 21 Oct 1950 WIDNES away won 4 - 3
WIDNES - Hutton: Townend Shaw Fleming H.Hill:
Rawlinson Anderson: Rowbottom Frost Wilcox Leigh F.Hill
Reynolds: Try - H.Hill:
CASTLEFORD - Lloyd: Brown Ferguson Aldred Woolford:
Parker Langfield: J.Anderson Jones(S/O) Fleming Haughey
Howard Mugglestone: Goals - Langfield(1) (DG):
Referee A Howgate (Dewsbury) Att – 7658 H.T. nil - 3

Sat 28 Oct 1950 WIGAN home lost 12 - 15
CASTLEFORD - Lloyd: Brown Aldred Ferguson Broughton:
Art.Fisher Langfield: J.Anderson Jones Fleming Howard
Haughey Mugglestone:
Tries - Fisher Langfield: Goals - Langfield(3):
WIGAN - Ward: Ratcliffe Broome Roughley Nordgren:
Cunliffe Alty: Gee Mather Curran Barton Slevin Blan:

Tries - Alty(2) Roughley: Goals - Gee(2) Ward:
Referee C Appleton (Warrington) Att - 13007 H.T. 6 - 8

Sat 4 Nov 1950 HUDDERSFIELD lost 3 - 16
YORKSHIRE CUP FINAL - at Headingley, Leeds
CASTLEFORD - Lewis: Brown Aldred Broughton Lloyd:
Art.Fisher Langfield: J.Anderson Jones Fleming Howard
Haughey Mugglestone: Try - Lloyd:
HUDDERSFIELD - Hunter: Cracknell Bawden Clark Cooper:
Pepperell Banks: Wagstaffe Mundy Wilmot Nicholson
Ewens Valentine:
Tries - Pepperell(2):   Goals - Bawden(5):
Referee R Gelder (Wakefield) Att - 28610 H.T. 3 - 7

Sat 11 Nov 1950 FEATHERSTONE ROVERS home
lost 15 - 16
CASTLEFORD - Lloyd: Brown Aldred Kitching Broughton:
Art.Fisher Langfield: Harris Jones J.Anderson Howard
Haughey Mugglestone:
Tries - Broughton(2) Langfield: Goals - Langfield(3):
FEATHERSTONE R - Miller: Blackburn Lambert Naylor
Kelly: Church Russell: Welburn Wood Ogden Payne
Bolton Gant:
Tries - Lambert Russell: Goals - Miller(3) (DG2):
Referee A Hill (Dewsbury) Att - 7000 H.T. 6 - 11

Sat 18 Nov 1950 HULL KINGSTON ROVERS away
lost 10 - 20
HULL K R - Ingram: Tullock O'Connor H.Mills Scholes:
Spencer R.Mills: Lavin Smith Pafreyman Barraclough
Annets Moore:
Tries - Tullock(4) Ingram O'Connor: Goal - R.Mills:
CASTLEFORD - Lloyd: COLIN ANDERSON(324) Aldred
Kitching Broughton: Ferguson Langfield: Harris Jones
J.Anderson Howard Haughey Brown:
Tries - C.Anderson Ferguson: Goals - Langfield(2):
Referee W Hemmings (Halifax) Att - 5000 H.T. 7 - 11

Sat 25 Nov 1950 DEWSBURY home lost 12 - 15
CASTLEFORD - Lewis: Brown Aldred Kitching Broughton:
Parker Langfield: Harris Jones J.Anderson Howard
Haughey Mugglestone:
Tries - Brown Aldred: Goals - Langfield(3):
DEWSBURY - Clark: Pollard Mahoney Rylance Lambert:
Constance Butler: Hammond Bradshaw Carty Holt Tate
H.Street:
Tries - Pollard Mahoney Lambert: Goals - Rylance(3):
Referee R Gelder (Wakefield) Att - 6000 H.T. 7 - 10

Sat 2 Dec 1950 HUNSLET away lost 5 - 10
HUNSLET - Evans: Snowden Sinclair Quarmby
Williamson(S/O): Talbot A.Burnell: Bennett Hartley
W.Burnell Metcalfe Carroll James:
Tries - Snowden Carroll: Goals - Talbot(2):
CASTLEFORD - Lewis: Aldred Brown Kitching Broughton:
Parker Langfield: Cowes Jones J.Anderson(S/O) Haughey
Howard Mugglestone:
Try - Aldred: Goal - Langfield:
Referee Mr T Armitage (Huddersfield) Att -6000 H.T. 2- 6

Sat 9 Dec 1950 HALIFAX home lost 13 - 24
CASTLEFORD - Aldred: Brown Bastow Kitching Broughton:
Claughton Langfield: Harris Jones J.Anderson Howard
Haughey Mugglestone:
Tries - Broughton(2) Langfield: Goals - Claughton(2):
HALIFAX - Chalkley: Daniels Price Todd Cook: Mather
Kielty: Condon Ackerley Olson White H.Greenwood
Fearnley:
Tries - Cook(3) Daniels(2) White: Goals - Chalkley(3):
Referee L J Dalby (York) Att - 5000 H.T. 5 - 13

**Mon 25 Dec 1950 WAKEFIELD TRINITY home
lost 9 - 21**
CASTLEFORD - Aldred: Woolford Brown Kitching
Broughton: Art.Fisher Langfield: Harris Jones J.Anderson
Fleming Haughey Mugglestone:
Try - Broughton: Goals - Langfield(3):
WAKEFIELD T - Luckman: Baddeley Varley Froggett
Boocker: Meredith Ogden: Booth Marson Robinson
Hudson Murphy Hughes: Tries - Baddeley Ogden Booth
Robinson Hughes: Goals - Meredith(3):
Referee Mr T Armitage (Huddersfield) Att 7100 H.T. 4- 8

Sat 13 Jan 1951 HULL away won 8 - 5
HULL - Hart: Tyrner Watts Lawrence Frabcis: Cox
Northern: Danter Harris Foreman Clark Scott Whiteley:
Try - Francis: Goal - Hart:
CASTLEFORD - Ferguson: Woolford Aldred Kitching
Broughton: Art.Fisher Langfield(S/O): Harris Jones
Fleming Haughey Howard Mugglestone:
Tries - Kitching Broughton: Goal - Langfield:
Referee A Howgate (Dewsbury) Att - 5000 H.T. nil - nil

Sat 20 Jan 1951 WIDNES home won 22 - 13
CASTLEFORD - Ferguson: Woolford Aldred Kitching
Broughton: Claughton Dudley: Harris Jones Fleming
Howard Haughey Mugglestone:
Tries - Woolford Aldred Broughton Claughton:
Goals - Claughton(5):
WIDNES - Hutton: Townend Shaw Fleming Hill: Twigg
Davies: Rowbottom Hayes Leigh Woodward Higgins
Reynolds:
Tries - Hill(2) Woodward: Goals - Hutton(2):
Referee C Appleton (Warrington) Att - 4000 H.T. 10 - 5

Sat 27 Jan 1951 HALIFAX away lost nil - 31
HALIFAX - Chalkley: Daniels Price Todd Cook: Mather
Kielty: Condon Ackerley Olson White H.Greenwood
Fearnley:
Tries - Todd(3) Cook(3) Daniels: Goals - Chalkley(5):
CASTLEFORD - Claughton: Woolford Aldred Broughton
Lloyd: Parker Langfield: DENNIS THORNTON(325) Jones
Fleming Mugglestone East RONALD WALTER(326):
Referee H Squires (Ossett) Att - 8000 H.T. nil - 13

**Sat 3 Feb 1951 WAKEFIELD TRINITY away
lost 10 - 14**
WAKEFIELD T - Davis: Duggan Davies Froggett Boocker:
Meredith Ogden: Booth Marson Robinson Murphy
Hudson Hughes:

Tries - Boocker(3) Duggan: Goal - Booth:
CASTLEFORD - IRVING BARRACLOUGH(327): Broughton
Kitching Aldred Lloyd: Art.Fisher Langfield: Harris Jones
Thornton Haughey Howard East:
Tries - Langfield Howard: Goals - Langfield(2):
Referee M Coates (Pudsey) Att - 7173 H.T. nil - 3

**Sat 10 Feb 1951 BELLE VUE RANGERS away lost 5 - 8
CHALLENGE CUP ROUND 1 1st LEG**
BELLE V R - Gregory: Bevan Morgan A.Jones Pimblett:
Price Rees: Ayles Hunt Gwyther Tonge Phillips Tierney:
Tries - Bevan(2)   Goal - Gregory:
CASTLEFORD - Barraclough: Broughton Kitching Aldred
Lloyd: Art.Fisher Langfield: Harris Jones Thornton
Haughey Howard East:
Try - Lloyd: Goal - Barraclough(DG)
Referee L J Dalby (York) Att - 5000 H.T. nil - nil

**Sat 17 Feb 1951 BELLE VUE RANGERS home
lost 2 - 5 CHALLENGE CUP ROUND 1 2nd LEG**
CASTLEFORD - Barraclough: Broughton Kitching Aldred
Woolford: Art.Fisher Langfield: Harris Jones Thornton
Haughey Howard East Goal - Langfield:
BELLE V R - Gregory: Bevan Morgan A.Jones Pimblett:
Thatcher Rees: Ayles Hunt Gwyther Tonge Phillips
Tierney: Try - Jones: Goal - Rees(DG)
Referee F Smith (Barrow) Att - 5000 H.T. nil - 3

**Sat 24 Feb 1951 HULL KINGSTON ROVERS home
won 27 - 12**
CASTLEFORD - Barraclough: Lloyd Kitching Brown
Broughton: Parker Langfield: Harris Jones Thornton
Howard Haughey East: Tries - Kitching(2) Broughton(2)
Brown: Goals - Langfield(5) Barraclough(DG):
HULL K R - Lewis: Tullock Annetts Warters Cornforth:
Spence Millar: Young Tonge Moore Barraclough Scholes
Dockar: Tries - Annetts(2):   Goals - Dockar(3):
Referee G Battersby (Barrow) Att - 2500 H.T. 19 - 9

Sat 3 Mar 1951 YORK home won 27 - 5
CASTLEFORD - Barraclough: Broughton C.Anderson
Kitching Lloyd: Parker Langfield: Harris Jones Thornton
Haughey Howard East:
Tries - Broughton(2) Kitching(2) Anderson:
Goals - Langfield(4) Barraclough(2):
YORK - Cox: Cowling McLennan Jenkinson Tate:
Lockwood Williams: Prosser Dolan Hollongworth
Wheatley Harker Inglesfield:
Try - Cox: Goal - Jenkinson:
Referee H Harrison (Ossett) Att - 3500 H.T. 7 - 5

Sat 10 Mar 1951 HUNSLET home lost 8 - 17
CASTLEFORD - Barraclough: Aldred Kitching Brown
Broughton: Parker Langfield: Harris James Jones Thornton
Howard Haughey Mugglestone: Goals - Langfield(4):
HUNSLET - Evans: Williams Thornton Anson Williamson:
Talbot A.Burnell: Bennett Rees Harter Carroll Thompson
James: Tries - Thornton Williamson Carroll Thompson
James: Goal - Talbot:
Referee J Hebblethwaite (York) Att - 5000 H.T. 6 - 6

SEASON 1950-51

Sat 17 Mar 1951 FEATHERSTONE ROVERS away won 13 - 7
FEATHERSTONE R - Miller: W.Tennant A.Tennant Golding Cording: Jarvis Russell: Welburn Wood Ogden Bolton Hulme Lambert: Try - A.Tennant: Goals - Miller(2):
CASTLEFORD - Barraclough: Reginald Lloyd Kitching Brown Broughton: Parker Langfield: Harris Hill J.Anderson Howard Haughey Rowley:
Tries - Broughton(2) Kitching: Goals - Langfield(2):
Refgree - Mr H Squires (Ossett) Att - 3200 H.T. 3 - nil

Fri 23 Mar 1951 LEEDS away lost 4 - 27
LEEDS - Cook: Turnbull Staniland Proctor Ryan: Feather Watson: McMaster Kearney Kendrick Poole Clues Clarkson: Tries - Turnbull Ryan Feather Watson Kendrick: Goals - Cook(6):
CASTLEFORD - Barraclough: Broughton Brown Aldred Parker: Art.Fisher Langfield: Harris Hill J.Anderson Howard Haughey Rowley: Goals - Langfield(2):
Referee J Jackson (Barrow) Att - 17679 H.T. nil - 12

Sat 24 Mar 1951 SALFORD home lost 9 - 12
CASTLEFORD - Barraclough: Broughton Brown Aldred Parker: Art.Fisher Langfield: Harris Hill J.Anderson East Howard Rowley: Try - Aldred: Goals - Langfield(3):
SALFORD - G.Moses: Danby Finnan Aspinall S.Williams: J.Davies Harrison: D.M.Davies McKinney Grainger Brown Rogers Kenny:
Tries - Williams Brown: Goals - J.Davies(3):
Referee S Abram (Wigan) Att - 3000 H.T. 7 - 8

Mon 26 Mar 1951 LEEDS home lost 5 - 22
CASTLEFORD - Aldred: Woolford Art.Fisher Broughton WILLIAM GUNBY(328): Claughton Langfield: Harris Hill J.Anderson Haughey Howard Rowley:
Try - Harris: Goal - Langfield:
LEEDS - Cook: Turnbull Ryan Proctor Staniland: Bartlett Watson: McMaster Kearney Kendrick Poole Clues Clarkson:
Tries - Turnbull Poole Clues Clarkson: Goals - Cook(5):
Referee T W Watkinson (Man'ster) Att 7700 H.T. 5 - 14
Match Abandoned After 74 Minutes, Result Stood

Sat 31 Mar 1951 BRADFORD NORTHERN away lost nil - 5
BRADFORD N - Phillips: Batten E.Ward Mageen McLean: Hastings D.Ward: Day Haley Greaves Jones Tyler Moore: Try - Moore: Goal - Phillips:
CASTLEFORD - Aldred: C.Anderson Kitching Art.Fisher Broughton: Claughton Langfield: Thornton Hill J.Anderson Howard Haughey East:
Referee W Stockley (Swinton) Att - 5000 H.T. nil - 5

Tue 3 Apr 1951 DEWSBURY away lost 5 - 16
DEWSBURY - Thompson: Pollard Rylance Clark Lambert: Constance Butler: Danter Bradshaw Welsby Evans A.Street H.Street:
Tries - Pollard(2) Rylance Clark: Goals - Rylance(2):
CASTLEFORD - Aldred: C.Anderson Kitching Art.Fisher Broughton: Claughton Langfield: Harris Hill Thornton

J.Anderson Haughey Howard:
Try - Harris: Goal - Langfield:
Referee F Smith (Barrow) Att - 5000 H.T. nil - 10

Sat 7 Apr 1951 BATLEY home lost 10 - 11
CASTLEFORD - Aldred: Woolford Kitching C.Anderson Broughton: Art.Fisher Langfield: Harris JACK TAYLOR(329) J.Anderson Fleming Haughey Howard:
Goals - Langfield(5):
BATLEY - Leake: Perry Riches Kenny Etty: Steele Laycock: Pilkington McIntyre Kavanagh Palmer Pickersgill Mawson:
Try - Steele: Goals - Perry(4):
Referee E Hopkins (Leeds) Att - 3500 H.T. 6 - 6

Mon 9 Apr 1951 YORK away lost 9 - 18
YORK - Cox: Cowling Jenkinson Lindley Tate: Benson Williams: Waddington Matthews Wheatley Watts Golden Inglesfield: Tries - Cowling Jenkinson Lindley Tate:
Goals - Jenkinson(3):
CASTLEFORD - Percy Aldred: Gunby C.Anderson Kitching Broughton: Art.Fisher Langfield: Harris Hill Dennis Thornton J.Anderson Haughey Howard:
Tries - Gunby(2) Kitching:
Referee B Lester (Leeds) Att - 4000 H.T. 3 - 18

Sat 14 Apr 1951 BRAMLEY home won 19 - 13
CASTLEFORD - Barraclough: Gunby Kitching C.Anderson Broughton: Claughton Parker: Harris Hill J.Anderson Howard Haughey:
Tries - Kitching C.Anderson Parker: Goals - Claughton(5):
BRAMLEY - Pickering: Whitehouse Gibson Warrior Humphries: Lazenby Rushton: Hebb Sutcliffe Cludersy Clarkson Eddison Thompson:
Tries - Gibson(2) Humphries: Goals - Gibson(2):
Referee H Holland (St Helens) Att - 2500 H.T. 19 - 2

Mon 16 Apr 1951 HUDDERSFIELD away lost 9 - 21
HUDDERSFIELD - Hunter: Cracknell Clark Devery Cooper: G.R.Pepperell Thomas: Wagstaffe Lightfoot Wilmot Morrison "NEWMAN" Valentine: Tries - Thomas(2) Hunter Cracknell Morrison: Goals - Cooper(3)
CASTLEFORD - Barraclough: Brown Claughton C.Anderson Gunby: Parker Langfield: Harris Hill J.Anderson Haughey Howard Leslie Rowley:
Try - Langfield: Goals - Langfield(3):
Referee J Jackson (Barrow) Att - 5894 H.T. 9 - 3

Sat 21 Apr 1951 BELLE VUE RANGERS away lost 5 - 39
BELLE V R - Gregory: Bevan Morgan Thatcher Pimblett: Price Rees: Ayles Fawcett Gwyther Tonge Phillips Tierney:
Tries - Price(3) Bevan(2) Morgan(2) Gregory Fawcett:
Goals - Gregory (6)
CASTLEFORD - Barraclough: Woolford Kitching C.Anderson Art.Fisher: Langfield KENNETH PYE(330): Harris Hill J.Anderson Fleming Haughey Howard:
Try - Woolford: Goal - Langfield:
Referee L J Dalby (York) Att - 4000 H.T. nil - 13

SEASON 1950-51

Tue 24 Apr 1951 KEIGHLEY away lost 2 - 22
KEIGHLEY - Lewis: Ward Taylor Creeney Buckley: Redman
Barrett: Brereton Britton Ferguson Mulhall Kelly I.Davies:
Tries - Redman(2) Taylor Brereton: Goals - Lewis(5):
CASTLEFORD - Barraclough: Woolford DERRICK
HANSELL(331) C.Anderson Art.Fisher: Claughton Parker:
Dyl Harris Hill J.Anderson Howard Haughey Fleming:
Goal - Claughton
Referee F Smith (Barrow) Att - 4000 H.T. nil - 10

Colin Anderson
D. No 324
1950-51 to 1955-56

Ron Walter
D. No 326
1950-51 to 1957-58

Bill Gunby
D. No 328
1950-51 to 1952-53

Ken Pye
D. No 330
1950-51 to 1962-63

YORKSHIRE CUP SEMI FINAL REPLAY FRIDAY 13 OCTOBER 1950 BATLEY HOME WON 13 – 9
Back Row – Les Haughy Len Brown Arthur Bastow Charlie Howard Frank Mugglestone Leo Fleming Jimmy Jones
Joe Anderson
Front Row – Arthur Fisher Percy Aldred George Langfield Reg Lloyd George Broughton

SEASON 1950-51

D.N	PLAYER		DEBUT	L MATCH	APP	SUB	T.AP	TRI'S	G'LS	D.G	P'TS
172	STAINES	CHARLIE		06/09/1950	4	0	4	1	0	0	3
176	LLOYD	REGINALD		17/03/1951	18	0	18	5	0	0	15
238	LEWIS	RONALD			15	0	15	0	0	0	0
239	HILL	JOHN			16	0	16	0	0	0	0
242	BROWN	LEONARD			17	0	17	2	0	0	6
249	EAST	JACK			9	0	9	0	0	0	0
258	KITCHING	JACK			21	0	21	8	0	0	24
278	BASTOW	ARTHUR			7	0	7	0	0	0	0
280	LANGFIELD	GEORGE			41	0	41	6	91	4	208
290	HARRIS	DYL		24/04/1951	26	0	26	2	0	0	6
291	MUGGLESTONE	FRANK			26	0	26	1	0	1	5
294	DUDLEY	JOEY			1	0	1	0	0	0	0
298	FISHER	ARTHUR (DIAMOND)			30	0	30	3	0	0	9
300	JONES	JAMES		10/03/1951	27	0	27	0	0	0	0
302	HOWARD	GEORGE (CHARLIE)			42	0	42	2	0	0	6
305	PARKER	HARRY			15	0	15	1	0	0	3
306	ANDERSON	JOSEPH			34	0	34	0	0	0	0
310	CLAUGHTON	RICHARD			9	0	9	1	13	0	29
312	ALDRED	PERCY		09/04/1951	37	0	37	6	0	0	18
313	WOOLFORD	CYRIL			17	0	17	3	0	0	9
314	FLEMING	LEO			19	0	19	0	0	0	0
315	ROWLEY	LESLIE		16/04/1951	5	0	5	0	0	0	0
318	COWES	JOHN			1	0	1	0	0	0	0
319	BROUGHTON	GEORGE			39	0	39	18	0	0	54
321	FERGUSON	ARCHIE			13	0	13	1	0	0	3
323	HAUGHEY	LESLIE			42	0	42	0	0	0	0
324	ANDERSON	COLIN	18/11/1950		10	0	10	3	0	0	9
325	THORNTON	DENNIS	27/01/1951	09/04/1951	10	0	10	0	0	0	0
326	WALTER	RONALD	27/01/1951		1	0	1	0	0	0	0
327	BARRACLOUGH	IRVING	03/02/1951		13	0	13	0	2	2	8
328	GUNBY	WILLIAM	26/03/1951		4	0	4	2	0	0	6
329	TAYLOR	JACK	07/04/1951		1	0	1	0	0	0	0
330	PYE	KENNETH	21/04/1951		1	0	1	0	0	0	0
331	HANSELL	DERRICK	24/04/1951	24/04/1951	1	0	1	0	0	0	0
	34		**8**	**8**	**572**	**8**	**572**	**65**	**106**	**7**	**421**

	COMPETITION		P	W	D	L	FOR	AGT
	LEAGUE	POSITION 25 OF 29	36	12	1	23	376	548
	YORK'S CUP		6	3	1	2	38	40
	RL CUP		2	0	0	2	7	13
	PLAYERS RECORDS		**44**	**15**	**2**	**27**	**421**	**601**

For the second time in the Club's history Castleford reached the Yorkshire Cup final, but had to play five games to do so. However, we again lost the final this time against Huddersfield at Headingley 16–3.

The season ended on a low note with only one win out of the last eleven games. Which heralded the 1950s and the poorest decade in performance terms in the Clubs history

One of the debutantes was Ken Pye, who in a career of 344 matches played at scrum half, loose forward and blind side prop and also captained the side.

SEASON 1951-52

Sat 11 Aug 1951 FEATHERSTONE ROVERS away lost 11 - 19 LYON CUP FRIENDLY
FEATHERSTONE R - Miller: Cording Golding A.Tennant A.N.Other: Church Evans: Kent Fawley Bolton Longley Payne Lambert:
Tries - Cording(2) Evans Fawley Lambert: Goals - Miller(2):
CASTLEFORD - C.Anderson: Woolford Kitching K.Pye Gunby: R.Batten Langfield: J.Anderson Hill Cowes Walter Howard Mugglestone:
Try - Woolford: Goals - Langfield(4):
Referee H Moxon (Featherstone) Att -

Sat 18 Aug 1951 BRAMLEY away Lost 12 - 18
BRAMLEY - Pickering: Hemingway Gibson Warrior Humphries: Lazenby Rushton: Hebb Sutcliffe Cluderay Baldwin Eddison Thompson:
Tries - Humphries Sutcliffe Eddison Thompson:
Goals - Gibson(3):
CASTLEFORD - Lewis: Gunby Kitching C.Anderson Broughton: ROBERT BATTEN(332) Langfield: Cowes Hill Fleming Howard Haughey Mugglestone:
Tries - Anderson Langfield: Goals - Langfield(3):
Referee S Abram (Wigan) Att - 2000 H.T. 4 - 10

Wed 22 Aug 1951 BRADFORD NORTHERN away lost 6 - 34
BRADFORD N - Phillips: Hawes Hastings E.Ward McLean: Dickson Goddard: Day Haley Greaves Radford Tyler Traill:
Tries - McLean(4) Dickson Day Radford Hawes:
Goals - Phillips(5):
CASTLEFORD - Lewis: Woolford Ferguson C.Anderson Broughton: Claughton Langfield: Cowes Hill Fleming Howard Haughey Mugglestone:
Goals - Langfield(3):
Referee N T Railton (Wigan) Att - 10000 H.T. 2 - 15

Wed 25 Aug 1951 HUDDERSFIELD home lost 18 - 22
CASTLEFORD - Lewis: Woolford Ferguson C.Anderson Broughton: Claughton Langfield: J.Anderson Hill Haughey Howard ARTHUR KITSON(333) East:
Tries - C.Anderson East: Goals - Langfield(5) (DG):
HUDDERSFIELD - Hunter: Cracknell Wainwright Devery Cooper: Thomas Banks: Cavanagh Mundy Pyatt Griffin Owens Valentine:
Tries - Cooper(4) Hunter Cracknell:
Goals - Wainwright Devery:
Referee D Halliday   Att - 5351 H.T. 9 - 11

Wed 29 Aug 1951 BARROW home lost 10 - 25
CASTLEFORD - Lewis: Woolford Ferguson C.Anderson Broughton: Claughton Langfield: J.Anderson Jack Taylor Haughey Howard Kitson Mugglestone:
Tries - C.Anderson Langfield: Goals - Kitson Langfield(DG):
BARROW - Stretch: Lewthwaite Jackson Goodwin Castle: Horne Toohey: Pearson McKinnell Webster Grundy Hartley Ayres:
Tries - Ayres(2) Jackson Castle Grundy: Goals - Stretch(5):
Referee T W Watkinson (Man'ster) Att - 3916 H.T. 5 - 10

Sat 1 Sep 1951 KEIGHLEY home won 14 - 11 YORKSHIRE CUP ROUND 1 1ST LEG
CASTLEFORD - Lewis: Woolford Kitching C.Anderson Broughton: Claughton Langfield: Cowes Mogg Fleming Howard Haughey East:
Tries - Kitching(2): Goals - Claughton(3) Langfield:
KEIGHLEY - Lewis: Ward Prescott Creeney Ivill: Redman Jenkins: Brereton Britton L.Davies Mulhall Flanagan Sanderson:
Try - Ward: Goals - Lewis(4):
Referee H Squires (Ossett) Att - 3597 H.T. 2 - 7

Mon 4 Sep 1951 KEIGHLEY away lost nil - 9 YORKSHIRE CUP ROUND 1 2ND LEG
KEIGHLEY - Lewis: Ward Prescott Creeney Taylor: Redman Barrett: Brereton Britton Ramsden Mulhall Kelly Sanderson:
Try - Prescott: Goals - Lewis(3):
CASTLEFORD - Lewis: Woolford Kitching C.Anderson Broughton: Claughton Langfield: Cowes Lister Mogg Fleming Howard Haughey East:
Referee A Hill (Dewsbury) Att - 5600 H.T. nil - nil

Mon 10 Sep 1951 WAKEFIELD TRINITY home lost 20 - 21
CASTLEFORD - Lewis: Woolford C.Anderson Kitching Gunby: Batten Langfield: HAROLD WELSBY(334) FRED WINTERBOTTOM(335) Fleming Howard John Cowes East
Tries - Woolford C.Anderson: Goals - Langfield(6) (DG):
WAKEFIELD T - Luckman: Reynolds Hirst Froggett Boocker: Meredith Evans: Booth Horner Higgins Robinson Howes Hughes:
Tries - Reynolds Froggett Boocker Booth Robinson: Goals - Hirst(2) Meredith(DG):
Referee J W Jackson (Barrow) Att - 6700 H.T. 11 - 12

Sat 15 Sep 1951 BATLEY home lost 17 - 22
CASTLEFORD - Barraclough: Woolford C.Anderson Kitching Gunby: Claughton Langfield: Welsby Winterbottom Fleming Haughey Walter East:
Tries - Kitching Claughton Langfield: Goals - Langfield(4):
BATLEY - Leake: Harrison Riches Kenny Calvert: Popplewell Laycock: Pilkington Pinder Palmer Briggs Lavender Mawson:
Tries - Harrison(2) Calvert Popplewell: Goals - Laycock(5):
Referee C F Appleton (Warrington) Att - 3100 H.T. 8 - 8

Sat 22 Sep 1951 KEIGHLEY away lost 7 - 23
KEIGHLEY - Lewis: Ward Lockwood Creeney Prescott: Redman Barrett: Brereton Ramsden Mulhall Bedford Kelly Sanderson:
Tries - Ward Mulhall Bedford: Goals - Lewis(7):
CASTLEFORD - Barraclough: Woolford Leonard Brown Ferguson Gunby: Claughton Langfield: Welsby Winterbottom Haughey East Fleming Clinton:
Try - Woolford: Goals - Barraclough(2):
Referee N T Railton (Wigan) Att - 5000 H.T. 3 - 7

SEASON 1951-52

Sat 29 Sep 1951 WIDNES home lost 10 - 23
CASTLEFORD - Lewis: Woolford C.Anderson Archie
Ferguson Broughton: Batten Langfield: Welsby
Winterbottom Haughey Clinton Fleming Frank
Mugglestone:
Tries - Woolford Anderson: Goals - Langfield(2):
WIDNES - Bradley: Owen Shaw Jolley Hill: Sale Davies:
Naughton Hayes Wilcox Higgins Lamb Kemel:
Tries - Hill(2) Sale(2) Shaw: Goals - Jolley(4):
Referee T W Watkinson (Man'ster) Att - 3784 H.T. 3 - 11

Wed 3 Oct 1951 NEW ZEALAND Lost 9 - 10
CASTLEFORD - Lewis: Woolford Kitching C.Anderson
Broughton: Batten Langfield: Welsby Winterbottom
Fleming Haughey Walter Clinton:
Try - Walter: Goals - Langfield(3):
NEW ZEALAND - D.White: J.R.Edwards W.Sorenson
C.A.Eastlake B.E.Robertson: J.F.Dodd D.A.Barchard:
R.J.Cranch K.English J.J.Curtain G.J.Burgoyne F.G.Mulcare
W.G.Davidson:
Tries - Burgoyne Mulcare: Goals - White(2):
Referee R Gelder (Wakefield) Att - 6643 H.T. 9 - 8

Sat 6 Oct 1951 BATLEY away lost 3 - 39
BATLEY - Walshaw: Harrison Riches Kenny Calvert:
Popplewell Laycock: Pilkington Fryer Tindall Palmer
Lavender Mawson:
Tries - Harrison(3) Kenny(2) Calvert(2) Popplewell
Lavender:
Goals - Laycock(5) Walshaw:
CASTLEFORD - Lewis: Woolford Jack Kitching C.Anderson
Broughton: Batten Langfield: Welsby Winterbottom
Haughey Fleming Walter Clinton:
Try - Fleming:
Referee S Abram (Wigan) Att - 5000 H.T. nil - 18

Sat 13 Oct 1951 CARDIFF away won 26 - 5
CARDIFF - Bennett: Hunt Moses Russell Rosser: Pugh
Richards: Douglas Gibson Campbell McNally Warman
Hughes:
Try - McNally: Goal - Russell:
CASTLEFORD - Lewis: Woolford Batten C.Anderson
Broughton: Art.Fisher Pye: J.Anderson Winterbottom
Welsby East Howard Clinton:
Tries - Woolford(2) Broughton(2) C.Anderson Fisher:
Goals - Fisher(2) Clinton(2):
Referee W Stockley (Leigh) Att - 1500 H.T. 19 - nil

**Sat 20 Oct 1951 BELLE VUE RANGERS home
won 12 - 2**
CASTLEFORD - Lewis: Gunby Batten C.Anderson
Broughton: Art.Fisher Langfield: Welsby Winterbottom
J.Anderson Fleming Howard Clinton:
Tries - Gunby(2):   Goals - Langfield(3):
BELLE V R - Gregory: Bevan Morgan Pimblett Jones:
Thatcher Ogden: Ayles Hunt Gwyther Faucitt Phillips
Tierney:
Goal - Tierney:
Referee F Smith (Barrow) Att - 3000 H.T. 6 - 2

Sat 27 Oct 1951 WIDNES away lost 14 - 20
WIDNES - Bradley: Owen Shaw Bremend Hill:
Fleming(S/O) Davies: Naughton Heyes Smith Lamb De
Witt Kemel:
Tries - Hill(2) Shaw Davies: Goals - Bradley(4):
CASTLEFORD - Lewis: Gunby Batten C.Anderson
Broughton: Art.Fisher(S/O) Langfield: Welsby
Winterbottom ..Anderson(S/O) TREVOR PETCHER(336)
Howard Clinton:
Tries - Gunby Batten: Goals - Langfield(4):
Referee J W Jowett (Leeds) Att - 6173 H.T. 2 - 12

Sat 3 Nov 1951 DONCASTER home won 13 - 7
CASTLEFORD - Lewis: Gunby Bastow C.Anderson
Woolford: Batten Langfield: Welsby Winterbottom
Fleming Howard Petcher Clinton:
Try - Langfield: Goals - Langfield(4) (DG):
DONCASTER - Griffiths: Cooper Price Williams Norbury:
Clough Tynan: Gronow Doyle Jones Street Carty Davies:
Try - Cooper: Goals - Griffiths(2):
Referee R Gelder (Wakefield) Att - 1941 H.T. 9 - nil

Sat 10 Nov 1951 DEWSBURY away lost 10 - 21
DEWSBURY - Thompson: Pollard Mahoney Frain Lambert:
Withington Thomas: Hatfield Bradshaw Wilmot Holt Fox
Payne:
Tries - Pollard Mahoney Frain Lambert Thomas:
Goals - Thompson(3):
CASTLEFORD - Lewis: Gunby Bastow C.Anderson
Woolford: Batten Langfield: Welsby Winterbottom
Fleming Howard Petcher Clinton:
Tries - Gunby(2):   Goals - Langfield(2):
Referee C F Appleton (Warr'gton) Att - 4000 H.T. 2 - 11

Sat 17 Nov 1951 HUNSLET home lost 12 - 24
CASTLEFORD - Lewis: Gunby Arthur Bastow Alfred Fisher
Woolford: Batten Langfield: Welsby Winterbottom
J.Anderson Howard Trevor Petcher Clinton:
Tries - Woolford Anderson: Goals - Langfield(3):
HUNSLET - Evans: Bowman Williams Waite Potter: Talbot
Robinson: Bennett Rees W.Burnell Gunney Metcalfe
Carroll:
Tries - Bowman(2) Waite Potter Talbot Gunney:
Goals - Talbot(3):
Referee G S Phillips (Widnes) Att - 5500 H.T. 2 - 12

Sat 24 Nov 1951 HULL away lost 9 - 20
HULL - Hart: Gittoes Francis Hutton Watts: Conway
Burnell: Hopkins Harris Coverdale Scott Bedford Whiteley:
Tries - Francis Hutton Watts Whiteley: Goals - Hart(4):
CASTLEFORD - Barraclough: Gunby Batten C.Anderson
HERBERT COATES(337): Arthur(Diamond)Fisher Pye:
Welsby Winterbottom J.Anderson Howard Fleming
Clinton:
Try - C.Anderson: Goals - Barraclough(3):
Referee S Abram (Wigan) Att - 5000 H.T. 2 - 20

SEASON 1951-52

Sat 1 Dec 1951 CARDIFF home won 16 - 8
CASTLEFORD - Lewis: Gunby C.Anderson Coates
Broughton: Batten Pye: Welsby Hill J.Anderson Howard
TERRY DOLAN(338) Clinton:
Tries - Gunby(2) Broughton Pye: Goals - C.Anderson(2):
CARDIFF - Bowen: Rosser W.Thomas O'Brien Evans:
Russell Smith: Harris Carter Gibson Hughes Douglas
L.Thomas:
Tries - W.Thomas Carter: Goal - Russell:
Referee N T Railton (Wigan) Att - 2092 H.T. 6 - 5

Sat 8 Dec 1951 DONCASTER away lost 5 - 18
DONCASTER - Griffiths: Cooper Heritage Williams
Norbury: Clough Tynan: Belshaw Doyle Jones Street Carty
Davies:
Tries - Cooper(2) Heritage Norbury: Goals - Griffiths (3):
CASTLEFORD - Lewis: Gunby C.Anderson Batten
Woolford: Pye Langfield: Welsby Hill J.Anderson Howard
Haughey Clinton:
Try - Batten: Goal - Langfield:
Referee T W Watkinson (Man'ster) Att - 2500 H.T. 5 - 11

Sat 15 Dec 1951 YORK home draw 8 - 8
CASTLEFORD - Lewis: C.Anderson HARRY JONES(339)
Batten Broughton: Pye Langfield: Welsby Hill J.Anderson
Howard Haughey Jack East:
Goals - Langfield(4):
YORK - McLennan: Tate Stokes Dawson Baddeley:
Lockwood Wilson: Hollingworth Jenkins Harker Briggs
Watts Inglesfield:
Tries - Dawson Baddeley: Goals - Lockwood
Referee F Smith (Barrow) Att - 2000 H.T. 6 - 3

**Sat 22 Dec 1951 FEATHERSTONE ROVERS away
lost 10 - 15**
FEATHERSTONE R - Miller: Blackburn Golding Tennant
Mitchell: Shaw Russell: Daly Fawley Hulme J.Ogden Gant
Sinclair:
Tries - Tennant(2) Mitchell: Goals - Miller(3):
CASTLEFORD - Barraclough: Gunby C Anderson Jones
Broughton: Pye Langfield: Welsby Fred Winterbottom
J Anderson Haughey Howard George Storey:
Tries - C Anderson Howard: Goals - Langfield(2):
Referee L Thorpe (Wakefield) Att - 2600 H.T. 5 - 13

**Mon 25 Dec 1951 WAKEFIELD TRINITY away
lost 10 - 29**
WAKEFIELD T - Hirst: Duggan Mortimer Froggett Davies:
Meredith Fletcher: Higgins Horner Hudson Murphy
Robinson Storey:
Tries - Duggan(4) Mortimer Froggett Davies:
Goals - Hirst(4):
CASTLEFORD - Lewis: Gunby C.Anderson Jones
Broughton: Pye George Langfield: Welsby Clinton
J.Anderson Howard Haughey DAVID HUGHES(340):
Tries - Jones Langfield: Goals - Langfield(2):
Referee G S Phillips (Widnes) Att - 7000 H.T. nil - 21

**Wed 26 Dec 1951 FEATHERSTONE ROVERS home
lost 11 - 15**
CASTLEFORD - Lewis: Gunby C.Anderson Jones Woolford:
Claughton Pye: Welsby Hill J.Anderson Haughey Terry
Dolan Hughes:
Try - Woolford: Goals - Claughton(4):
FEATHERSTONE R - Miller: Batten Golding Tennant
Mitchell: Shaw Russell: Daley Fawley Hulme M.Ogden
Gant Sinclair:
Tries - Batten(3): Goals - Miller(3):
Referee H Harrison (Horbury) Att - 4500 H.T. 6 - 15

Sat 29 Dec 1951 YORK away lost 5 - 12
YORK - McLennan: Tate Stokes Dawson Baddeley: Wilson
Lockwood: Hollingworth Jenkins Harker Briggs Watts
Inglesfield:
Tries - Tate Baddeley: Goals - Harker(2) Baddeley:
CASTLEFORD - Lewis: Gunby Batten Jones Coates:
Claughton Pye: Welsby Hill J.Anderson Haughey Clinton
Hughes:
Try - Claughton: Goal - Claughton:
Referee S Abram (Wigan) Att - 6598 H.T. 5 - 5

Sat 5 Jan 1952 DEWSBURY home won 12 - nil
CASTLEFORD - Lewis: Gunby Batten Jones Coates:
Claughton Pye: Welsby Hill J.Anderson Haughey Clinton
Hughes:
Tries - Gunby Batten: Goals - Claughton(3):
DEWSBURY - Thompson: Pollard Bevan Waring
Withington: Thomas Butler: Hadfield Bradshaw Wilmot
Holt Ormerod Evans:
Referee W Stockley (Leigh) Att - 4000 H.T. 9 - nil

**Sat 12 Jan 1952 HULL KINGSTON ROVERS home
won 13 - 3**
CASTLEFORD - Lewis: Gunby Batten Jones Coates:
Claughton Pye: Welsby Hill J.Anderson Haughey Clinton
Hughes:
Tries - Gunby Coates Claughton: Goals - Claughton(2):
HULL K R - Lewis: Tullock Mills Rushton Briggs: McAvoy
Armitage: Grice Brookfield Dockar Bowering Barraclough
Turner:
Try - Tullock:
Referee G Battersby (Barrow) Att - 3000 H.T. 5 - nil

**Sat 19 Jan 1952 HULL KINGSTON ROVERS away
lost nil - 3**
HULL K R - H.Lewis: Tullock McAvoy Mills Rushton:
Knoweldon Armitage: Grice Brookfield Young
Barraclough Dockar Turner:
Try - Rushton:
CASTLEFORD - R.Lewis: Gunby Batten Jones Coates:
Claughton Pye: Welsby Hill J.Anderson Haughey Clinton
Hughes:
Referee J Jackson (Barrow) Att - 5000 H.T. nil - nil

Sat 2 Feb 1952 HUDDERSFIELD away lost 7 - 24
HUDDERSFIELD - Dyson: Cracknell Pepperell Henderson
Cooper: Rylance Banks: Pyatt Curran Griffin Brown Slevin
Valentine:

SEASON 1951-52

Tries - Cooper(3) Henderson(2) Valentine:
Goals - Rylance(3):
CASTLEFORD - Lewis: Gunby Jones Batten Broughton:
Parker Pye: Welsby Hill J Anderson Haughey Howard
Hughes:
Try - Parker: Goals - Lewis(2):
Referee W Stockley (Leigh) Att - 8210 H.T. 2 - 16

Sat 9 Feb 1952 SWINTON home lost 4 - 5
CHALLENGE CUP ROUND 1 1ST LEG
CASTLEFORD - Lewis: Woolford Batten Jones Broughton:
Claughton Pye: Welsby Hill J Anderson Howard Haughey
Clinton:
Goals - Claughton(2):
SWINTON - Blan: Burn Welsh Winkworth Jevons: Moran
Thomas: Billington Osmond Scott Price Woods Armitt:
Try - Blan: Goal - Blan:
Referee N T Railton (Wigan) Att - 4260 H.T. 4 - nil

Sat 16 Feb 1952 SWINTON away won 9 - 2
CHALLENGE CUP ROUND 1 2ND LEG
SWINTON - Blan: Burn Winkworth Senior Jevons: Moran
Thomas: Billington Osmond Scott Knowles Price Armitt:
Goal - Blan:
CASTLEFORD - Lewis: Woolford Batten Jones Broughton:
Claughton Pye: Welsby Hill J Anderson Haughey Howard
Clinton:
Try - Broughton: Goals - Claughton(3):
Regferee - Mr R Gelder (Wakefield) Att - 10000 H.T. 5 - 2

Sat 23 Feb 1952 BRADFORD NORTHERN home
lost 3 - 12
CASTLEFORD - Lewis: Woolford Batten Jones Broughton:
Claughton Pye: Welsby Hill J Anderson Howard Haughey
Clinton:
Try - Broughton:
BRADFORD N - Phillips: Smith Mageen E.Ward McLean:
L.Haley G.Jones: Shreeve N.Haley W.Jones Foster Tyler
Traill:
Tries - McLean(3) Mageen:
Referee G S Phillips (Widnes) Att - 12000 H.T. 3 - 6

Sat 1 Mar 1952 LEIGH home lost 6 - 7
CHALLENGE CUP ROUND 2
CASTLEFORD - Lewis: Woolford Batten Jones Broughton:
Claughton Pye: Welsby Hill Fleming Howard Haughey
Clinton:
Tries - Broughton Claughton:
LEIGH - Ledgard: Kindon Hayes Harris Bevan: Baxter
Bradshaw: Wright Egan Burke Pawsey Mossop
Foster(S/O):
Try - Hayes: Goals - Ledgard(2):
Referee G S Phillips (Widnes) Att - 12500 H.T. nil - 5

Sat 8 Mar 1952 BARROW away lost 8 - 19
BARROW - Jones: Castle Jackson Lewthwaite Marshall:
Horne Toohey: Longman McKinnell Pearson Grundy
Parker McGregor:
Tries - Lewthwaite(2) Castle Marshall McKinnell:
Goals - Horne(2):

CASTLEFORD - Lewis: Woolford Batten Jones Broughton:
Claughton Pye: Welsby Hill Fleming Haughey Howard
Clinton:
Tries - Broughton(2):   Goal - Claughton:
Referee R Gelder (Wakefield) Att - 9286 H.T. 3 - 19

Sat 15 Mar 1952 BRAMLEY home won 17 - 11
CASTLEFORD – Lewis: Woolford Batten Jones Broughton:
Claughton Pye: Welsby Hill J Anderson Howard Haughey
Clinton:
Tries - Jones Broughton Pye: Goals - Claughton(4):
BRAMLEY - Powell: Varley Gibson Rushton Uttley: Harding
Jenkins: Newbound Sutcliffe Cluderay Baldwin Flanagan
Eddison:
Tries - Uttley(3 :   Goal - Powell:
Referee T W Watkinson (Man'ester) Att - 2500 H.T. 7 - 8

Sat 22 Mar 1952 BELLE VUE RANGERS away
lost 6 - 10
BELLE V R - Gregory: Bevan Morgan Williams Lloyd: Price
Rees: Ayles Fawcitt Gwyther Tierney Phillips Pimblett:
Tries - Williams Pimblett: Goals - Tierney Price(DG):
CASTLEFORD - Lewis: Woolford ALBERT LUNN(341) Jones
Broughton: Claughton Pye: Welsby Hill J Anderson
Howard Haughey Clinton:
Goals - Claughton(3):
Referee H Squires (Ossett) Att - 1219 H.T. 4 - 8

Sat 29 Mar 1952 HULL home lost 2 - 8
CASTLEFORD - Lewis: Woolford Batten Jones Herbert
Coates: Claughton Pye: Welsby Hill J.Anderson Haughey
Clinton Fleming: Goal - Claughton:
HULL - Hart: Gittoes Whiteley Francis Watts: Conway
Burnell: Scott Harris Coverdale Bedford Markham Hutton:
Tries - Hart Whiteley: Goal - Hart:
Referee N T Railton (Wigan) Att - 960 H.T. 2 - 3

Sat 5 Apr 1952 HUNSLET away lost 3 - 16
HUNSLET - Talbot: Snowden Artis Thornton Potter:
Robinson A.Burnell: Bennett Rees W.Burnell Thompson
Shaw Carroll:
Tries - Snowder (2):   Goals - Talbot(5):
CASTLEFORD - Lewis: Woolford Claughton Jones
Broughton: Batten Pye: Welsby Hill J.Anderson Howard
Haughey George Clinton:
Try - Woolford:
Referee W Stockley (Leigh) Att - 3000 H.T. nil - 9

Fri 11 Apr 1952 LEEDS away lost 9 - 12
LEEDS - Murphy: Turnbull Brown McLellan Staniland:
Ward Stevenson : McMaster Wood Horsfall Poole Clues
Scholes:
Tries - Staniland(2):   Goals - Murphy(2) Stevenson(DG):
CASTLEFORD - Barraclough: Woolford Batten Jones
Broughton: JOSHUA J.PYE(342) K.Pye: Welsby Hill
J.Anderson Howard Haughey C.Anderson:
Try - Hill: Goals - Barraclough(3):
Referee S Abram (Wigan) Att - 13000 H.T.

SEASON 1951-52

Mon 14 Apr 1952 LEEDS home lost 7 - 18
CASTLEFORD - Barraclough: Woolford Batten Jones
Broughton: J.J.Pye Dudley: Welsby Hill J.Anderson
Howard Haughey C.Anderson:
Try - Dudley: Goals - Barraclough(2):
LEEDS - Murphy: Turnbull Ward McLellan Staniland:
Feather Pratt: McMaster Wood Hopper Kendrew Poole
Moore:
Tries - Staniland(3) Turnbull: Goals - Murphy(3):
Referee J W Jackson (Barrow) Att - 6220 H.T. 7 - 12

Mon 15 Apr 1952 KEIGHLEY home won 19 - 12
CASTLEFORD - Lewis: Jones Batten Lunn Broughton:
J.J.Pye Claughton: Welsby Hill J.Anderson Howard
Fleming C.Anderson:
Tries - Jones(2) Broughton: Goals - Lunn(5):
KEIGHLEY - Plowman: Ward Anson Clark O'Hara: Barrett
Riley: Callighan Britton I.Davies Mulhall Saxton James:
Tries - Riley Davies: Goals - Plowman(3):
Referee S Abram (Wigan) Att - 2500 H.T. 9 – 7

Bob Batten
D. No 332
1951-52 to 1954-55

Harold Welsby
D.No 334
1951-52 to 1955- 56

Harry Jones
D. No 339
1951-52 to 1952-53

David Hughes
D. No 340
1951-52 to 1958-59

Albert Lunn
D. No 341
1951-52 to 1962-63

Jos J Pye
D. No 342
1951-52 to 1956-57

SEASON 1951-52

D.N	PLAYER		DEBUT	L MATCH	APP	SUB	T.AP	TRI'S	G'LS	D.G	P'TS
238	LEWIS	RONALD			36	0	36	0	2	0	4
239	HILL	JOHN			24	0	24	1	0	0	3
242	BROWN	LEONARD		22/09/1951	1	0	1	0	0	0	0
249	EAST	JACK		15/12/1951	8	0	8	1	0	0	3
255	CLINTON	GEORGE		05/04/1952	27	0	27	0	2	0	4
258	KITCHING	JACK		06/10/1951	7	0	7	3	0	0	9
278	BASTOW	ARTHUR		17/11/1951	3	0	3	0	0	0	0
280	LANGFIELD	GEORGE		25/12/1951	21	0	21	5	52	4	127
291	MUGGLESTONE	FRANK		29/09/1951	4	0	4	0	0	0	0
292	FISHER	ALFRED		17/11/1951	1	0	1	0	0	0	0
293	STOREY	GEORGE		22/12/1951	1	0	1	0	0	0	0
294	DUDLEY	JOEY			1	0	1	1	0	0	3
298	FISHER	ARTHUR (DIAMOND)		24/11/1951	4	0	4	1	2	0	7
302	HOWARD	GEORGE (CHARLIE)			31	0	31	1	0	0	3
304	MOGG	LISTER		04/09/1951	2	0	2	0	0	0	0
305	PARKER	HARRY			1	0	1	1	0	0	3
306	ANDERSON	JOSEPH			28	0	28	1	0	0	3
310	CLAUGHTON	RICHARD			22	0	22	4	27	0	66
313	WOOLFORD	CYRIL			28	0	28	8	0	0	24
314	FLEMING	LEO			18	0	18	1	0	0	3
318	COWES	JOHN		10/09/1951	5	0	5	0	0	0	0
319	BROUGHTON	GEORGE			28	0	28	10	0	0	30
321	FERGUSON	ARCHIE		29/09/1951	5	0	5	0	0	0	0
323	HAUGHEY	LESLIE			32	0	32	0	0	0	0
324	ANDERSON	COLIN			26	0	26	8	2	0	28
326	WALTER	RONALD			3	0	3	1	0	0	3
327	BARRACLOUGH	IRVING			6	0	6	0	10	0	20
328	GUNBY	WILLIAM			20	0	20	9	0	0	27
329	TAYLOR	JACK		29/08/1951	1	0	1	0	0	0	0
330	PYE	KENNETH			23	0	23	2	0	0	6
332	BATTEN	ROBERT	18/08/1951		31	0	31	3	0	0	9
333	KITSON	ARTHUR	25/08/1951		2	0	2	0	1	0	2
334	WELSBY	HAROLD	10/09/1951		36	0	36	0	0	0	0
335	WINTERBOTTOM	FRED	10/09/1951	22/12/1951	14	0	14	0	0	0	0
336	PETCHER	TREVOR	27/10/1951	17/11/1951	4	0	4	0	0	0	0
337	COATES	HERBERT	24/11/1951	29/03/1952	7	0	7	1	0	0	3
338	DOLAN	TERRY	01/12/1951	26/12/1951	2	0	2	0	0	0	0
339	JONES	HARRY	15/12/1951		21	0	21	4	0	0	12
340	HUGHES	DAVID	25/12/1951		7	0	7	0	0	0	0
341	LUNN	ALBERT	22/03/1952		2	0	2	0	5	0	10
342	PYE	JOSHUA J.	11/04/1952		3	0	3	0	0	0	0
	41		11	18	546	0	546	66	103	4	412

	COMPETITION		P	W	D	L	FOR	AGT
	LEAGUE	POSITION 28 OF 31	36	8	1	27	370	579
	YORK'S CUP		2	1	0	1	14	20
	RL CUP		3	1	0	2	19	14
	NEW ZEALAND		1	0	0	1	9	10
	PLAYERS RECORDS		42	10	1	31	412	623

In the League Liverpool Stanley became Liverpool City, and Cardiff and Doncaster were admitted, bringing the number of teams up to 31.

Jack Kitching took over as Player/Coach from Billy Rhodes who had held the Trainer's duties since 1932/33 season.

We also played the New Zealand tourists but again we lost, by only the narrowest of margins 9 - 10

A notable debutante was Albert Lunn who went on to make 363 appearances and set Club career records of 875 goals and 1870 points.

SEASON 1952-53

Sat 16 Aug 1952 FEATHERSTONE ROVERS home won 29 - 14 LYON CUP FRIENDLY
CASTLEFORD - Lewis: Broughton Jones Lunn Gunby:
Hague K.Pye: Welsby Hill J.Anderson Howard Simpson
C.Anderson: Tries - Jones(3) Broughton Gunby Pye
Simpson: Goals - Lunn(3) C.Anderson:
FEATHERSTONE R - Naylor: Mitchell Metcalfe Tennant
Blackburn: Shaw Amales: Reynolds M.Ogden Gant
J.Ogden Longley Lambert:
Tries - Mitchell Lambert: Goals - Mitchell(4):
Referee A S Dobson (Pontefract) Att - 3500 H.T. 7 - 9

Sat 23 Aug 1952 HUNSLET home won 16 - 7
CASTLEFORD - Lewis: Woolford Lunn Jones Broughton:
Batten K.Pye: Welsby Hill Fleming Howard Haughey
C.Anderson: Tries - Jones Anderson: Goals - Lunn(5):
HUNSLET - Evans: Bowman Thornton Williams Potter:
Talbot A.Burnell: Bennett Rees Shaw Thompson Gunney
Carroll: Try - Bowman: Goals - Talbot Gunney:
Referee N T Railton (Wigan) Att - 5600 H.T. 2 - 5

Tue 26 Aug 1952 DEWSBURY away won 18 - 7
DEWSBURY - Thompson: Frain Callighan Waring
Hemingway: Pollard Thomas: Hatfield Bradshaw Ellis Holt
Tate Payne: Try - Waring: Goals - Thompson(2):
CASTLEFORD - Lewis: Woolford Lunn Jones Broughton:
Batten K.Pye: Welsby Hill J.Anderson Howard PETER
SIMPSON(343) C.Anderson:
Tries - Broughton(2) Hill C.Anderson: Goals - Lunn(3):
Referee G S Phillips (Widnes) Att - 5500 H.T. 12 - 4

**Sat 30 Aug 1952 KEIGHLEY away lost 7 - 16
YORKSHIRE CUP ROUND 1 1ST LEG**
KEIGHLEY - Lockwood: Rock Ivill Anson Ward: Prescott
Riley: Ramsden Traill Davies Mulhall Raines Holdbrook:
Tries - Ivill(2) Ward Prescott: Goals - Prescott(2):
CASTLEFORD - Lewis: Gunby Lunn Jones Broughton:
Batten K.Pye: Welsby Hill J.Anderson Howard Simpson
C.Anderson: Try - Broughton: Goals - Lunn C.Anderson:
Referee F Smith (Barrow) Att - 6000 H.T. 3 - 13

**Wed 3 Sep 1952 KEIGHLEY home won 8 - 6
YORKSHIRE CUP ROUND 1 2ND LEG**
CASTLEFORD - Lewis: Batten Lunn Jones Broughton:
Claughton K.Pye: Welsby Hill J.Anderson Howard
Haughey C.Anderson: Goals - Lunn(4):
KEIGHLEY - Lockwood: Rock Clark Anson Ward: Prescott
Riley: Ramsden Traill Davies Mulhall James Holdbrook:
Goals - Lockwood(2) Ward:
Referee F Smith (Barrow) Att - 6700 H.T. 4 - 2

Sat 6 Sep 1952 WHITEHAVEN away lost 5 - 18
WHITEHAVEN - Fearon: W.Nicholson Carr Emery
Harrison: Garrett Keen: McAlone Richardson Maxwell
R.Nicholson James Tomlinson:
Tries - W.Nicholson(3) Harrison: Goals - Harrison(3):
CASTLEFORD - Lewis: Batten Lunn Jones Broughton:
K.Pye Joey Dudley: Welsby Hill J.Anderson Howard
Haughey C.Anderson: Try - Lunn: Goal - Lunn:
Referee T W Watkinson (Man'ster) Att - 5000 H.T. 2 - 10

146

Wed 10 Sep 1952 FEATHERSTONE ROVERS home won 13 - 5
CASTLEFORD - Lewis: R.Batten Lunn Jones Broughton:
ROY HAGUE(344) K.Pye: Welsby Hill J.Anderson Howard
Simpson C.Anderson:
Try - Broughton: Goals - Lunn(5):
FEATHERSTONE R - J.Blackburn: E.Batten Tennant
A.Blackburn Hoyle: Cording Evans: M.Ogden Whitemore
Daley Gant J.Ogden Lambert:
Try - Batten: Goal - Cording:
Referee C F Appleton (Warrington) Att - 4300 H.T. 6 - 3

Sat 13 Sep 1952 HALIFAX home lost 12 - 20
CASTLEFORD - Lewis: Batten Lunn Jones Broughton:
Hague K.Pye: Welsby Hill J.Anderson Howard Walter
C.Anderson: Tries - Broughton(2): Goals - Lunn(3):
HALIFAX - Palin: Daniels Lynch Creeney Cook: Dean Kielty:
Condon Ackerley Hopkins White Fearnley Clarkson:
Tries - Daniels Lynch Cook White: Goals - Palin(4):
Referee W Stockley (Leigh) Att - 5000 H.T. 5 - 15

Sat 20 Sep 1952 WIDNES away lost 11 - 12
WIDNES - Sale: Hill Kinsey Ratcliffe Hazlehurst: Oster
Davies: Rowbottom Hayes Lamb Higgins De Witt Todd:
Tries - Ratcliffe De Witt: Goals - Sale(3):
CASTLEFORD - Lewis: Batten Lunn Jones Broughton:
STANLEY BEAUMONT(345) K.Pye: Welsby Hill J.Anderson
Howard Haughey C.Anderson:
Try - J.Anderson: Goals - Lunn(4):
Referee H Harrison (Ossett) Att - 5040 H.T. 2 - 8

Sat 27 Sep 1952 KEIGHLEY home lost 11 - 17
CASTLEFORD - Irving Barraclough: Batten Jones Lunn
Broughton: Beaumont K.Pye: Welsby Hill J.Anderson
Haughey Howard C.Anderson:
Try - Jones: Goals - Barraclough(4):
KEIGHLEY - Palin: Rock Anson Ivill Bleasby: Clark
Gallagher: Ramsden Harden Davies Devanney Raines
Holdbrook: Tries - Rock Bleasby Clark: Goals - Palin(4):
Referee R Gelder (Wakefield) Att - 3500 H.T. 11 - 5

Sat 4 Oct 1952 ST HELENS away lost 17 - 18
ST HELENS - Lowe: Dickinson Roach Gullick McCormick:
Honey Langfield: Parr Blakemore Whittaker Parsons
Bretherton Cale:
Tries - Honey(2) Dickinson Whittaker: Goals - Langfield(3):
CASTLEFORD - Lewis: Walter Lunn C.Anderson
Broughton: Parker K.Pye: J.Anderson Hill Fleming Howard
Haughey Hughes: Try - Parker: Goals - Lunn(7):
Referee H Squires (Ossett) Att - 10852 H.T. 6 - 10

Sat 11 Oct 1952 HUDDERSFIELD home lost 10 - 28
CASTLEFORD - Lewis: Jones Lunn C.Anderson Broughton:
Parker K.Pye: J.Anderson Hill Fleming Howard Haughey
Hughes: Tries - Jones(2): Goals - Lunn(2):
HUDDERSFIELD - Hunter: Henderson Rylance Devery
Cooper: Pepperell Banks: Slevin Curran Griffin Brown
Large Valentine: Tries - Henderson(3) Hunter Cooper
Large: Goals - Devery(4) Rylance:
Referee M Coates (Pudsey) Att - 8400 H.T. 8 - 12

SEASON 1952-53

Sat 18 Oct 1952 ROCHDALE HORNETS away lost 14 - 15
ROCHDALE H - Cahill: W.S.Jones Stanford R.Jones
McGilvray: Taylor Vallett: Mitchell Cunliffe Hawkins Fisher
McNally Ellean Tries - Taylor Elleann one scorer not
known: Goals - Stanford(2) R.Jones:
CASTLEFORD - Lewis: H.Jones Lunn C.Anderson
Broughton: Parker K.Pye: J.Anderson Hill Fleming Howard
Haughey Hughes: Tries - Lunn Parker: Goals - Lunn(4):
Referee L J Dalby (York) Att - 4377 H.T. 2 - 10

Sat 25 Oct 1952 DONCASTER home won 28 - 8
CASTLEFORD - Lewis: Jones Lunn C.Anderson Broughton:
Parker K.Pye: J.Anderson Hill Fleming Howard Haughey
Hughes: Tries - Broughton(2) Lunn Pye Howard Hughes:
Goals - Lunn(5):
DONCASTER - Griffiths: Norbury Grace Badger Hanshaw:
Clough Heritage: Hammond Croft Belshaw Bates Street
Guest: Tries - Norbury Hanshaw: Goal - Griffiths
Referee G S Phillips (Widnes) Att - 3500 H.T. 5 - 3

Sat 8 Nov 1952 BRADFORD NORTHERN away lost 9 - 16
BRADFORD N - Phillips: Hawes Seddon Hastings McLean:
L.Haley Goddard: Tyler N.Haley Greaves Hambling
W.Jones Griffett: Tries - Hawes McLean Greaves
Hambling: Goals - Phillips(2):
CASTLEFORD - Lewis: Woolford Lunn C.Anderson
Broughton: Parker K.Pye: J.Anderson Hill Fleming Howard
Haughey Hughes: Try - Woolford: Goals - Lunn(3):
Referee N T Railton (Wigan) Att - 10500 H.T. 5 - 7

Sat 15 Nov 1952 HULL home won 10 - 3
CASTLEFORD - Lewis: Woolford Lunn C.Anderson
Broughton: Parker K.Pye: J.Anderson Hill Fleming Howard
Haughey Hughes:
Tries - C.Anderson Hughes: Goals - Lunn(2):
HULL - Hart: Cox Turner Francis Watts: Conway Tripp:
Hopkins Harris Coverdale Markham Scott Hutton:
Try - Cox:
Referee J Jackson (Barrow) Att - 1790 H.T. nil - 3

Sat 22 Nov 1952 BATLEY away lost 3 - 8
BATLEY - Walshaw: Harrison Riches Kenny Etty: Riley
Laycock: Wagstaffe McIntyre Jones Palmer Briggs
Shirtcliffe: Tries - Harrison(2): Goal - Jones:
CASTLEFORD - Lewis: Woolford Lunn C.Anderson George
Broughton: Harry Parker K.Pye: J.Anderson Hill Fleming
Howard Haughey Hughes Try - Lunn:
Referee W E Stockley (Leigh) Att - 4000 H.T. 3 - 2

Sat 13 Dec 1952 HULL KINGSTON ROVERS home won 22 - 2
CASTLEFORD - Lewis: Beaumont Lunn HAROLD
ODDY(346) ARTHUR STANILAND(347): Batten K.Pye:
J.Anderson Hill Fleming Howard Haughey Hughes:
Tries - Lunn(2) Oddy Staniland: Goals - Lunn(5):
HULL K R - Edwards: Egan Mills Knowelden J.Moore:
Armitage Daddy: Palfryman Smith F.Moore Turner Young
Dockar: Goal - Dockar:

Referee C F Appleton (Warrington) Att - 2500 H.T. 7 - 2

Sat 20 Dec 1952 DONCASTER away won 7 - 6
DONCASTER - Grace: Cooper Heritage Williams Norbury:
Flanshaw Tynan Belshaw Croft Street Bates Davies Guest:
Tries - Cooper Williams:
CASTLEFORD - Lewis: Beaumont Lunn Oddy Staniland:
Batten K.Pye: Welsby Hill Fleming Howard Haughey
C.Anderson: Try - Batten: Goals - Lunn(2):
Referee S Abram (Wigan) Att - 400 H.T. 2 - 3

Thu 25 Dec 1952 WAKEFIELD TRINITY home won 17 - 14
CASTLEFORD - Lewis: Beaumont Lunn Oddy Staniland:
Batten K.Pye: J.Anderson Hill Fleming Howard Haughey
C.Anderson: Try - C.Anderson: Goals - Lunn(7):
WAKEFIELD T - Luckman: Fewster Mortimer Froggett
Boocker: Constance Evans: Booth Horner Higgins
Robinson Kelly Storey:
Tries - Boocker Constance: Goals - Mortimer(4):
Referee G S Phillips (Widnes) Att - 6616 H.T. 6 - 4

Fri 26 Dec 1952 FEATHERSTONE ROVERS away won 11 - 8
FEATHERSTONE R - Davies: E.Batten Metcalfe Kelly
Cording: Fennel Evans: Welburn Fawley Daley M.Ogden
Hulme Sinclair: Tries - Fawley Sinclair: Goal - Fennell:
CASTLEFORD - Lewis: Beaumont Lunn Oddy Staniland:
R.Batten K.Pye: J.Anderson Hill Fleming Howard Haughey
C.Anderson:
Tries - Beaumont Pye C.Anderson: Goal - Lunn:
Referee W Stockley (Swinton) Att - 5800 H.T. 5 - 5

Sat 27 Dec 1952 WIDNES home won 20 - 5
CASTLEFORD - Lewis: Jones Oddy Lunn Staniland: Batten
K.Pye: J.Anderson Hill Fleming Howard Haughey
C.Anderson:
Tries - Pye(2) Jones C.Anderson: Goals - Lunn(4):
WIDNES - Sale: Dawson Owen Kinsey Hazlehurst: Davies
Rawlinson: Rowbottom Hayes Wilcox Johnson Todd
Kemel: Try - Dawson: Goal - Sale:
Referee S Abram (Wigan) Att - 8000 H.T. 12 - 3

Sat 3 Jan 1953 YORK home won 15 - 9
CASTLEFORD - Lewis: Jones Lunn Oddy Staniland: Batten
K.Pye: J.Anderson Hill Fleming Haughey Howard
C.Anderson
Tries - Jones Staniland J.Anderson: Goals - Lunn(3):
YORK - Hargreaves: Tate Thornton Robinson Taylor:
Lockwood Denris: Waddington Jenkins Simpson Watts
Dolan BriggsTry - Tate: Goals - Hargreaves(2) Dolan:
Referee N T Railton (Wigan) Att -1000 H.T. 7 - 2

Sat 17 Jan 1953 BRADFORD NORTHERN home won 8 - 7
CASTLEFORD - Lewis: Jones Lunn Oddy Staniland: Batten
K.Pye: J.Anderson Hill Fleming Haughey Howard
C.Anderson: Goals - Lunn(4):
BRADFORD N - Phillips: Hawes Mageen Hastings McLean:
L.Haley G.Jones Shreeve N.Haley Greaves Hambling Tyler

Traill: Try - Hastings: Goals - Phillips(2):
Referee F Smith (Barrow) Att -10096 H.T. 6 - 3

Sat 24 Jan 1953 WAKEFIELD TRINITY away lost 4 - 5
WAKEFIELD T - Luckman: Froggett Burton Mortimer
Boocker: Holliday Evans: Booth Shaw Robinson Kelly
Storey Howes: Try - Froggett: Goal - Mortimer:
CASTLEFORD - Lewis: Woolford Oddy Lunn JACK
HAYNES(348): Batten K.Pye: J.Anderson Hill Fleming
Howard Haughey C.Anderson: Goals - Lunn(2):
Referee J W Jackson (Barrow) Att - 8133 H.T. 2 - 3

Sat 31 Jan 1953 ST HELENS home lost nil - 8
CASTLEFORD - Lewis: Walter Lunn Oddy Woolford: Batten
K.Pye: J.Anderson Hill Fleming Simpson Haughey
C.Anderson:
ST HELENS - Moses: Llewellyn Greenall Gullick
McCormick: Dickinson Langfield: Prescott Blakemore Parr
Parsons Bretherton Karalius:
Tries - Llewellyn Dickinson: Goal - Langfield:
Referee W Stockley (Leigh) Att - 7000 H.T. nil - nil

**Sat 7 Feb 1953 HUDDERSFIELD away lost 14 - 36
CHALLENGE CUP ROUND 1 1ST LEG**
HUDDERSFIELD - Hunter: Henderson Devery Pepperell
Cooper: Ramsden Banks: Slevin Curran Bowden Brown
Large Valentine:
Tries - Cooper(4) Henderson(3) Devery: Goals - Devery(6):
CASTLEFORD - Lunn: Beaumont Jones Oddy Woolford:
Batten K.Pye: J.Anderson Hill Fleming Haughey Simpson
Hughes: Tries - Oddy Batten: Goals - Lunn(4):
Referee C F Appleton (Warrgton) Att - 14988 H.T. 9 - 15

**Sat 14 Feb 1953 HUDDERSFIELD home lost 2 - 6
CHALLENGE CUP ROUND 1 2ND LEG**
CASTLEFORD - Lunn: Beaumont C.Anderson Oddy Gunby:
Batten K.Pye: J.Anderson Hill Fleming Haughey Simpson
FRED WARD(349): Goal - Lunn:
HUDDERSFIELD - Hunter: Henderson Devery Pepperell
L.Cooper: Ramsden Banks: Slevin Curran Bowden Brown
J.Cooper Valentine: Tries - L.Cooper(2):
Referee N T Railton (Wigan) Att - 7500 H.T. 2 - 6

Sat 21 Feb 1953 HALIFAX away lost 14 - 32
HALIFAX - Griffiths: Cook Lynch Creeney Bradley: Dean
Kielty: Condon Ackerley Wilkinson White Fearnley
Clarkson:
Tries - White(3) Clarkson(2) Cook Creeney Bradley
Goals - Griffiths(4):
CASTLEFORD - Lewis: Beaumont Lunn Oddy Gunby:
Batten K.Pye: J.Anderson Hill Fleming Haughey Simpson
C.Anderson: Tries - Pye(2): Goals - Lunn(4):
Referee G S Phillips (Widnes) Att - 8000 H.T. 4 - 19

Sat 28 Feb 1953 YORK away won 13 - 5
YORK - Hargreaves: Tate Wilson Dawson Priestley:
Robinson Riley: Judge Jenkins Hollingworth Watts Dolan
Taylor: Try - Robinson: Goal - Hargreaves:
CASTLEFORD - Lewis: Gunby Lunn Oddy ROY
LAMBERT(350): Batten K.Pye: J.Anderson Hill Fleming

Haughey Simpson Hughes:
Tries - Lunn Lambert Batten: Goals - Lunn(2):
Referee S Abram (Wigan) Att - 4078 H.T. 6 - nil

Sat 7 Mar 1953 WHITEHAVEN home lost 8 - 14
CASTLEFORD - Ronald Lewis: Harry Jones Lunn Oddy
Lambert: Batten K.Pye: J.Anderson Hill RONALD
LYLES(351) Haughey Simpson Hughes:
Tries - Lambert(2): Goal - Lunn:
WHITEHAVEN - Varty: W.Nicholson Garrett Smith Fearon:
Reid Keen: McAlone Graham Killen R.Nicholson
Tomlinson Rodgers:
Tries - W.Nicholson(2) Smith Fearon: Goal - Reid:
Referee C F Appleton (Warrington) Att - 5060 H.T. 8 - 6

Sat 14 Mar 1953 KEIGHLEY away lost 4 - 15
KEIGHLEY - Lockwood: Prescott Taylor Ivill Ward: Black
Rowland: Woosey Harden Davies Murphy Palin
Holdbrook: Tries - Ward(2) Ivill: Goals - Palin(3):
CASTLEFORD - J.J.Pye: DENZIL WEBSTER(352) Lunn
C.Anderson Lambert: Batten K.Pye: Fleming Hill
J.Anderson Haughey Simpson Walter:
Goals - Lunn Lambert(DG):
Referee J W Jackson (Barrow) Att - 3200 H.T. nil - 4

**Sat 21 Mar 1953 ROCHDALE HORNETS home
won 21 - 15**
CASTLEFORD - J.J.Pye: Webster Lunn Oddy Lambert:
Batten K.Pye: Fleming Hill J.Anderson Haughey Walter
C.Anderson:
Tries - Webster(2) Lambert(2) Haughey: Goals - Lunn(3):
ROCHDALE H - Cahill: Oldroyd R.Jones Harris W.Jones:
Stanford Vallett: Livesey Ellean Hawkins Fisher Schofield
McNally:
Tries - Cahill Oldroyd Vallett: Goals - Schofield(3):
Referee G S Phillips (Widnes) Att - 4300 H.T. 18 - 3

Fri 3 Apr 1953 LEEDS away lost 10 - 22
LEEDS - Cook: Turnbull Ward Moores Broughton:
Williams Watson: Nutting Wood Gwyther Clues Poole
Scholes:
Tries - Turnbull Ward Broughton Scholes: Goals - Cook(5):
CASTLEFORD - J.J.Pye: Woolford Lunn Oddy Lambert:
Batten K.Pye: J.Anderson HARRY THORNLEY(353) Fleming
Haughey Simpson C.Anderson:
Tries - Lambert(2): Goals - Lunn(2):
Referee C F Appleton (Warr'ton) Att - 13500 H.T. 7 - 13

Sat 4 Apr 1953 HUNSLET away lost 6 - 19
HUNSLET - Evans: Snowden Williams Waite Williamson:
Ormondroyd Talbot: Harter Rees Grant Shaw Thompson
James:
Tries - Snowden Waite Shaw: Goals - Talbot(5):
CASTLEFORD - J.J.Pye: JACKSON APPLEYARD(354) Lunn
Oddy Lambert: Batten K.Pye: Fleming Thornley J.Anderson
Haughey Simpson C.Anderson:
Goals - Lunn(3):
Referee A Howgate (Dewsbury) Att - H.T. 4 - 7

SEASON 1952-53

Mon 6 Apr 1953 LEEDS home lost 2 - 23
CASTLEFORD - J.J.Pye: Walter Lunn Oddy Lambert:
Claughton ARNOLD GRACE(355): J.Anderson Hughes
Fleming Haughey Simpson C.Anderson:
Goal - Lunn:
LEEDS - Morgan: Turnbull Moores Broughton Garbutt:
Watson Stevenson: Kendrick Wood Gwyther Hopper
Poole Scholes:
Tries - Turnbull(2) Stevenson(2)Garbutt:
Goals - Morgan(4):
Referee S Abram (Wigan) Att - 6379 H.T. nil - 8

Mon 13 Apr 1953 HULL away lost 12 - 31
HULL - Watkinson: Drake Francis Turner Cox: Moat Tripp:
Scott Lawson Foreman Markham Hockley Whiteley:
Tries - Whiteley(2) Turner Cox Moat Markham Hockley:
Goals - Whiteley(5)
CASTLEFORD - J.J.Pye: Webster Lunn Oddy Lambert:
Batten Claughton: J.Anderson Hill Lyles Walter Simpson
C.Anderson:
Tries - Batten Claughton: Goals - Lunn(3)
Referee T Armitage (Huddersfield) Att - 5000 H.T. 7 - 8

**Wed 15 Apr 1953 HULL KINGSTON ROVERS away
lost 7 - 13**
HULL K R - D.Chalkley: Tullock Knowelden Rushton
Briggs: Key Kirby: Palfryman Smith Moore Evans
Barraclough R.Chalkley:
Tries - Tullock Knowelden Barraclough:
Goals - D.Chalkley(2):
CASTLEFORD - J.J.Pye: Lunn C.Anderson Webster Oddy:
Batten Claughton: J.Anderson Hill MAURICE
PERRETT(356) Simpson Walter Hughes:
Try - Batten: Goals - Lunn(2):
Referee W Stockley (Manchester) Att - 2000 H.T. 7 - 10

Sat 18 Apr 1953 DEWSBURY home lost 2 - 24
CASTLEFORD - J.J.Pye: Woolford Walter Oddy TERENCE
WHITEHEAD(357): Batten Claughton: J.Anderson Hill
Perrett Haughey Fleming C.Anderson:
Goal - Pye:
DEWSBURY - Thompson: Pollard Callighan Price
Hemingway: Wilson Lea: Danter Bradshaw Wilmot Holt
Evans Withington:
Tries - Pollard(4) Thompson Callighan:
Goals - Thompson(3):
Referee M Coates (Pudsey) Att - 3029 H.T. nil - 10

Mon 20 Apr 1953 BATLEY home won 7 - 5
CASTLEFORD - J.J.Pye: William Gunby Oddy C.Anderson
Thornley: Batten Hague: J.Anderson Hill J ROBINSON(358)
Fleming Haughey Hughes:
Try - Batten: Goals - C.Anderson(2):
BATLEY - Walshaw: Harrison Etty Kenny Walford:
Popplewell Laycock: Wagstaff Fryer Pickersgill Palmer
Jones Westbury:
Try - Harrison: Goal - Laycock:
Referee J W Jackson (Barrow) Att - 1867 H.T. 5 - 5

Tue 28 Apr 1953 HUDDERSFIELD away lost 5 - 38
HUDDERSFIELD - Hunter: Henderson Pepperell Cooper
Sullivan: Rylance Banks: Slevin Curran Bowden Brown
Large Valentine
Tries - Henderson(5)Sullivan(2) Pepperell Cooper Large
Goals - Rylance 2) Bowden(2):
CASTLEFORD - . J.Pye: Stanley Beaumont Lunn Oddy
Thornley: Batten Hague: J Robinson Hill Fleming Ward
Haughey C.Anderson:
Try - Ward: Goal - Lunn:
Referee J W Jackson (Barrow) Att - 9915 H.T. 5 - 19

Haold Oddy
D. No 346
1952-53 to 1955-56

Athur Staniland
D. No 347
1952-53 to 1955-56

Fred Ward
D. No 349
1952-53 to 1957-58

Denzil Webster
D. No 352
1952-53 to 1956-57

SEASON 1952-53

D.N	PLAYER		DEBUT	L MATCH	APP	SUB	T.AP	TRI'S	G'LS	D.G	P'TS
238	LEWIS	RONALD		07/03/1953	27	0	27	0	0	0	0
239	HILL	JOHN			37	0	37	1	0	0	3
294	DUDLEY	JOEY		06/09/1952	1	0	1	0	0	0	0
302	HOWARD	GEORGE (CHARLIE)			24	0	24	1	0	0	3
305	PARKER	HARRY		22/11/1952	7	0	7	2	0	0	6
306	ANDERSON	JOSEPH			37	0	37	2	0	0	6
310	CLAUGHTON	RICHARD			5	0	5	1	0	0	3
313	WOOLFORD	CYRIL			10	0	10	1	0	0	3
314	FLEMING	LEO			29	0	29	0	0	0	0
319	BROUGHTON	GEORGE		22/11/1952	16	0	16	8	0	0	24
323	HAUGHEY	LESLIE			34	0	34	1	0	0	3
324	ANDERSON	COLIN			36	0	36	6	3	0	24
326	WALTER	RONALD			9	0	9	0	0	0	0
327	BARRACLOUGH	IRVING		27/09/1952	1	0	1	0	4	0	8
328	GUNBY	WILLIAM		20/04/1953	5	0	5	0	0	0	0
330	PYE	KENNETH			34	0	34	6	0	0	18
332	BATTEN	ROBERT			32	0	32	6	0	0	18
334	WELSBY	HAROLD			10	0	10	0	0	0	0
339	JONES	HARRY		07/03/1953	17	0	17	6	0	0	18
340	HUGHES	DAVID			14	0	14	2	0	0	6
341	LUNN	ALBERT			38	0	38	7	105	0	231
342	PYE	JOSHUA J.			10	0	10	0	1	0	2
343	SIMPSON	PETER	26/08/1952		15	0	15	0	0	0	0
344	HAGUE	ROY	10/09/1952		4	0	4	0	0	0	0
345	BEAUMONT	STANLEY	20/09/1952	28/04/1953	10	0	10	1	0	0	3
346	ODDY	HAROLD	13/12/1952		23	0	23	2	0	0	6
347	STANILAND	ARTHUR	13/12/1952		7	0	7	2	0	0	6
348	HAYNES	JACK	24/01/1953	24/01/1953	1	0	1	0	0	0	0
349	WARD	FRED	14/02/1953		2	0	2	1	0	0	3
350	LAMBERT	ROY	28/02/1952		8	0	8	7	0	1	23
351	LYLES	RONALD	07/03/1953		2	0	2	0	0	0	0
352	WEBSTER	DENZIL	14/03/1953		4	0	4	2	0	0	6
353	THORNLEY	HARRY	03/04/1953		4	0	4	0	0	0	0
354	APPLEYARD	JACKSON	04/04/1953		1	0	1	0	0	0	0
355	GRACE	ARNOLD	06/04/1953		1	0	1	0	0	0	0
356	PERRETT	MAURICE	15/04/1953		2	0	2	0	0	0	0
357	WHITEHEAD	TERENCE	18/04/1953	18/04/1953	1	0	1	0	0	0	0
358	ROBINSON	J.	20/04/1953	28/04/1953	2	0	2	0	0	0	0
	38		**16**	**11**	**520**	**0**	**520**	**65**	**113**	**1**	**423**

COMPETITION		P	W	D	L	FOR	AGT
LEAGUE	POSITION 20 OF 30	36	15	0	21	392	502
YORK'S CUP		2	1	0	1	15	22
RL CUP		2	0	0	2	16	42
PLAYERS RECORDS		**40**	**16**	**0**	**24**	**423**	**566**

After only one season in the League Cardiff dropped out, reducing the number of teams to 30.

Billy Rhodes once more took over the Trainer's duties from player/coach Jack Kitching.

Albert Lunn in only his second season whilst playing in 38 out of a total of 40 league and cup games, improved the record for goals in a season to 105.

One of the debutantes was Denzil Webster, whilst he only made 98 appearances before his transfer to York he did have a strike rate of 63 tries, which was remarkable considering the teams performances and also earned him representative honours with Yorkshire.

SEASON 1953-54

Sat 15 Aug 1953 BATLEY home won 22 - 9
CASTLEFORD - Lunn: Staniland Oddy BRIAN HALE(359)
Lambert: Batten K.Pye: Fleming Hill J.Anderson Howard
Simpson F Ward:
Tries - Lambert Batten Simpson F Ward: Goals - Lunn(5):
BATLEY - Bateson: Perry Etty Kenny Harrison: Laycock
Graham: Wagstaff Battersby Palmer Westbury Shirtcliffe
Briggs: Try - Perry: Goals - Perry(3):
Referee S Abram (Wigan) Att - 4859 H.T. 10 - 4

Wed 19 Aug 1953 DEWSBURY away lost 2 - 18
DEWSBURY - Thompson: Pollard Callighan Price
Hemingway: G.Waring Laycock: Hatfield D.Waring Danter
Stephenson Holt T.Briggs:
Tries - Pollard(2) Price Hemingway: Goals - Thompson(3):
CASTLEFORD - Lunn: Staniland Oddy Brian Hale Lambert:
Batten K.Pye: Fleming Hughes J.Anderson Howard
C.Anderson F Ward: Goal - Lunn:
Referee L Thorpe (Wakefield) Att - 4000 H.T. 2 - 7

**Sat 22 Aug 1953 WORKINGTON TOWN away
lost 8 - 58**
WORKINGTON T - Risman: Southward Hill Gibson Wilson:
Dawson Thomas: Hayton Eden Price Mudge Thompson
Ivison: Tries - Southward(4) Gibson(3) Wilson(3) Price(3)
Risman   Goals - Risman(8):
CASTLEFORD - J.J.Pye: ALAN METCALFE(360) Claughton
Lambert LEONARD EXLEY(361): Hague Grace: Perrett
Thornley Ronald Lyles Haughey Kitson Walter:
Tries - Lambert Grace: Goal - Kitson:
Referee F Smith (Barrow) Att - 7000 H.T. 3 - 22

**Sat 29 Aug 1953 LIVERPOOL CITY home
won 12 - nil**
CASTLEFORD - J.J.Pye: Staniland Oddy Lambert ALAN
MARCHANT(362): Hague Grace: Perrett WILLIAM
BRADSHAW(363) J.Anderson Simpson Haughey F Ward:
Tries - Staniland Marchant Haughey F Ward:
LIVERPOOL C - Tobin: Bennett Cox White Adair: Ogden
Parkes: Reilly O'Mara Hill Curran Richards Davies:
Referee J W Jackson (Barrow) Att - 925 H.T. 6 - nil

Tue 1 Sep 1953 KEIGHLEY away won 12 - 8
KEIGHLEY - Wilman: Rock Holgate Anson Ward: Black
Rowlands: Woosey Traill Palin Murphy Raines Holdbrook
Goals - Palin(4):
CASTLEFORD - J.J.Pye: Staniland Oddy Lunn Lambert:
Batten K.Pye: J.Anderson Bradshaw Fleming Howard
Haughey F Ward: Tries - Lunn Batten: Goals - Lunn(3):
Referee N T Railton (Wigan) Att - 5000 H.T. 5 - 4

**Sat 5 Sep 1953 HALIFAX home lost nil - 11
YORKSHIRE CUP ROUND 1 1ST LEG**
CASTLEFORD - J.J.Pye: Staniland Oddy Lunn Lambert:
Batten K.Pye: Simpson Bradshaw Fleming Haughey
Howard F Ward:
HALIFAX - Griffiths: Daniels Todd Creeney Bradley: Dean
Kielty: Thorley Ackerley Wilkinson Clarkson Fearnley
Callighan: Tries - Daniels(2) Kielty: Goal - Kielty:
Referee C F Appleton (Warr'ton) Att - 7660 H.T. nil - 5

**Mon 7 Sep 1953 HALIFAX away lost 3 - 9
YORKSHIRE CUP ROUND 1 2ND LEG**
HALIFAX - Knopf: Daniels Sykes Creeney Bradley: Dean
Kielty: Thorley Ackerley Wilkinson Clarkson Fearnley
Callighan: Tries - Daniels Sykes Bradley:
CASTLEFORD - J.J.Pye: Staniland Oddy Lunn Lambert:
Hague K.Pye: Simpson Bradshaw Fleming Haughey
Howard F Ward: Try - K.Pye:
Referee F Smith (Barrow) Att - 10537 H.T. nil - 6

**Sat 12 Sep 1953 HULL KINGSTON ROVERS away
won 28 - 7**
HULL K R - Buckle: Tullock Barraclough Rushton Knapp:
Cornforth A.N.Other: Moore Smith Young Tonge Sutton
Edwards: Try - Barraclough: Goals - Buckle(2)
CASTLEFORD - J.J.Pye: Staniland Oddy Lunn Lambert:
Batten K.Pye: Simpson Bradshaw Fleming Howard
Haughey F Ward:
Tries - K.Pye(3) Lunn Lambert Batten: Goals - Lunn(5):
Referee A Hill (Dewsbury) Att - 3000 H.T. 10 - 4

Sat 19 Sep 1953 KEIGHLEY home won 21 - 13
CASTLEFORD - J.J.Pye: Staniland Oddy Lunn Lambert:
Batten K.Pye: Simpson Bradshaw J.Anderson Howard
Haughey F Ward:
Tries - Lunn Batten K.Pye: Goals - Lunn(6):
KEIGHLEY - Johnson: Rock Holgate Prescott Ward: Black
Rowlands: Woosey Traill Raines Murphy James
Holdbrook:
Tries - Holgate Prescott Murphy: Goals - Johnson(2):
Referee C F Appleton (Warr'ton) Att - 5000 H.T. 16 - 5

Sat 26 Sep 1953 LIVERPOOL CITY away won 26 - 12
LIVERPOOL C - Cox: Cockram Ogden Hayes Adair: Hand
Smith: Wright O'Mara Reilly Whittaker Curran Doneghan:
Tries - Cockram(2) Goals - Reilly(3):
CASTLEFORD - J.J.Pye: Staniland Oddy Lunn Lambert:
Batten K.Pye: Simpson William Bradshaw Fleming Howard
Haughey F Ward: Tries - Lambert(2) Staniland Lunn
K.Pye Howard: Goals - Lunn(4):
Referee S Adams (Hull) Att - 500 H.T. 8 - 4

Sat 3 Oct 1953 HALIFAX away lost 12 - 17
HALIFAX - Griffiths: Daniels Lynch Todd Knopf: Dean
Broadhurst: Thorley Ackerley Wilkinson Fearnley Schofield
Callighan: Try - Daniels: Goals - Griffiths(6) Lynch(DG):
CASTLEFORD - J.J.Pye: Staniland Webster Lunn Lambert:
Batten K.Pye: Simpson Hill J.Anderson Howard
C.Anderson F Ward:
Tries - Webster C.Anderson: Goals - Lunn(3):
Referee E P Wilmot (Rochdale) Att - 10300 H.T. 7 - 11

Sat 10 Oct 1953 WARRINGTON home lost 13 - 28
CASTLEFORD - J.J.Pye: Staniland Webster Lunn Lambert:
Batten K.Pye: Simpson Hill J.Anderson Howard
C.Anderson F Ward:
Tries - K.Pye(2) Lambert: Goals - Lunn(2):
WARRINGTON - Frodsham: Bevan A.Naughton
Humphries Challinor: Ryder Helme: D.Naughton F.Wright
G.Wright Bath Phillips Ryan:

SEASON 1953-54

Tries - Challinor(3) Bevan(3): Goals - Bath(5):
Referee J W Jackson (Barrow) Att - 6414 H.T. 6 - 20

Sat 17 Oct 1953 ST HELENS away lost 9 - 35
ST HELENS - Moses: Llewellyn Greenall Gullick
McCormick: Metcalfe Honey: Ayles Blakemore Parr
Parsons Bretherton Prescott: Tries - Llewellyn(3)
McCormick(3) Honey(2) Parr: Goals - Metcalfe(4):
CASTLEFORD - J.J.Pye: DEREK SMART(364) Lunn Oddy
Staniland: Batten K.Pye: J.Anderson Hill Simpson Howard
C.Anderson F Ward: Try - Oddy: Goals - Lunn(3):
Referee H Squires (Ossett) Att - 19000 H.T. 2 - 22

Sat 31 Oct 1953 YORK home won 8 - 7
CASTLEFORD - J.J.Pye: Smart Lunn Oddy Staniland: Batten
K.Pye: J.Anderson Hill Fleming Howard F Ward
C.Anderson: Tries - Staniland Batten: Goal - Lunn:
YORK - Hargreaves: Hamblett Dawson G.Smith B.Smith:
Robinson Coulson: Waddington Jenkins Taylor Watts
Harher Harlow: Try - B.Smith: Goals - Harker(2):
Referee C F Appleton (Warrington) Att-4000 H.T.5 - 5

Sat 7 Nov 1953 BATLEY away lost 12 - 17
BATLEY - Bateson: Perry Kilroy Etty Frain: Cox Foley:
Pickersgill Fryer Greenwood Palmer Jones Mawson:
Tries - Perry Kilroy Frain: Goals - Perry(3) Bateson(DG):
CASTLEFORD - Oddy: Lambert Webster Lunn Staniland:
Batten K.Pye: J.Anderson Hill Fleming Howard Simpson
C.Anderson: Tries - Webster Batten: Goals - Lunn(3):
Referee R L Thomas (Oldham) Att - 2500 H.T. 7 - 3

Wed 11 Nov 1953 ST HELENS home lost 14 - 31
CASTLEFORD - J.J.Pye: BRIAN GILL(365) C.Anderson Lunn
Staniland: Batten K.Pye: J.Anderson Hill Fleming Howard
Simpson F Ward: Tries - Gill F Ward: Goals - Lunn(4):
ST HELENS - Moses: Llewellyn Greenall Honey
McCormick: Metcalfe Ball: Prescott Ayles Parr Parsons
Bretherton Karalius:
Tries - Honey(2) Parsons(2) Greenall: Goals - Metcalfe(8):
Referee F Smith (Barrow) Att - 3073 H.T. 4 - 17

Sat 14 Nov 1953 DONCASTER home won 14 - 10
CASTLEFORD - J.J.Pye: C.Anderson Lambert Lunn
Staniland: Batten K.Pye: J.Anderson Hill Perrett Howard
Simpson F Ward:
Tries - Staniland F Ward: Goals - Lunn(4):
DONCASTER - Barraclough: Gunn Wilkinson Bates
Cranswick: Woolford Tynan: Belshaw Doyle Davies Dooler
Bowers Guest: Goals - Barraclough(5):
Referee S Abrams (Wigan) Att - 2878 H.T. 7 - 6

Sat 21 Nov 1953 LEEDS away lost 14 - 48
LEEDS - Morgan: Verrankamp McLellan Jones Broughton:
Brown Stevenson: Shillito Wood Hopper Clues Poole Blan:
Tries - Broughton(3) Verrankamp(2) McLellan(2) Jones
Brown Blan: Goals - Jones(9):
CASTLEFORD - J.J.Pye: Lambert C.Anderson Lunn
Staniland: Hague K.Pye: J.Anderson Hill Fleming Howard
Simpson F Ward: Tries - Staniland(2): Goals - Lunn(4):
Referee W Stockley (Leigh) Att - 12500 H.T. 2 - 26

**Sat 28 Nov 1953 WORKINGTON TOWN home
lost 14 - 18**
CASTLEFORD - ERNEST WARD(366): Smart Webster
Lambert Staniland: Lunn K.Pye: Simpson Hill Fleming
Howard Kitson F.Ward:
Tries - Smart Lambert: Goals - Lunn(2) Kitson(2):
WORKINGTON T - Risman: Southward Kerwick Ivill
Wilson: Archer Thomas: Hayton Lymer Henderson Key
Thompson Ivison:
Tries - Wilson(2) Thomas Hayton: Goals - Risman(3):
Referee N T Railton (Wigan) Att - 5600 H.T. 2 - 10

Sat 5 Dec 1953 WARRINGTON away lost 12 - 36
WARRINGTON - Frodsham: Bevan Ryder A.Naughton
Challinor: Price Helme: Bath Wright Lowe White Phillips
Ryan:
Tries - Bevan(2) Naughton(2) Helme(2) Phillips Ryan:
Goals - Bath(6):
CASTLEFORD - E.Ward: Lambert Lunn Oddy Staniland:
Claughton K.Pye: Simpson Hill J.Anderson Kitson Howard
F.Ward: Tries - K.Pye(2): Goals - Lunn(3):
Referee E Hopkins (Leeds) Att - 9479 H.T. 7 - 16

Sat 12 Dec 1953 DEWSBURY home lost 2 - 14
CASTLEFORD - J.J.Pye: Roy Lambert E.Ward Lunn
Staniland: Oddy K.Pye: Fleming Hill J.Anderson Simpson
Kitson F.Ward: Goal - Kitson:
DEWSBURY - Thompson: Pollard Price Waring
Hemingway: Ormandroyd LaycocK: Flannery Moyser
Danter Payne Metcalfe Withington:
Tries - Pollard Hemingway Laycock Withington:
Goal - Thompson:
Referee E P Wilmot (Rochdale) Att - 3790 H.T. 2 - 8

**Sat 19 Dec 1953 FEATHERSTONE ROVERS away
lost 4 - 25**
FEATHERSTONE R - Goulding: E.Batten Metcalfe Tennant
Marchant: Mullaney Fox: Welburn Bradshaw Hulme
Howes Sinclair Lambert:
Tries - Fox(2) Lambert(2) Batten Metcalfe Marchant:
Goals - Fox(2):
CASTLEFORD - Oddy: Webster Lunn E.Ward C.Anderson:
R.Batten K.Pye: Simpson Hill Fleming Howard Kitson
F.Ward: Goals - Kitson(2):
Referee M Coates (Pudsey) Att - 3800 H.T. 4 - 6

**Fri 25 Dec 1953 WAKEFIELD TRINITY away
lost 4 - 21**
WAKEFIELD T - Hirst: Cooper Holliday Froggett Boocker:
Lockwood Fletcher: Booth Shaw Lindley Kelly Robinson
Clifft:
Tries - Cooper(2) Boocker Booth Kelly: Goals - Hirst(3):
CASTLEFORD - J.J.Pye: Smart E.Ward Webster Lunn:
Batten K.Pye: Fleming Hill J.Anderson Howard Simpson
C.Anderson: Goals - Lunn(2):
Referee A Howgate (Dewsbury) Att - 4600 H.T. 2 - 14

SEASON 1953-54

Sat 26 Dec 1953 FEATHERSTONE ROVERS   home won 18 - 13
CASTLEFORD - J.J.Pye: Smart E.Ward Webster Lunn:
R.Batten K.Pye: Fleming Hill J.Anderson Kitson Simpson
C.Anderson:
Tries - Smart(2) Webster Lunn: Goals - Kitson(2) Lunn:
FEATHERSTONE R - Goulding: Marchant Tennant Kelly
E.Batten: Mullaney D.Fox: Welburn Bradshaw M.Ogden
Howes Sinclair Lambert:
Try - Lambert: Goals - Fox(3) (2DG):
Referee H Squires (Ossett) Att - 5340 H.T. 3 - 8

Sat 2 Jan 1954 BRADFORD NORTHERN away lost 8 -18
BRADFORD N - Phillips: Hawes Jenkins Seddon McLean:
L.Haley Goddard: Tyler N.Haley Jones Foster Storey Traill:
Tries - McLean(2) Seddon Foster: Goals - Phillips(3):
CASTLEFORD - Lunn: Smart E.Ward Webster Staniland:
Batten K.Pye: ALAN KENDRICK(367) Hill J.Anderson(S/O)
Simpson Kitson C.Anderson:
Tries - Webster Hill: Goal - Kitson:
Referee A Hill (Dewsbury) Att - 10500 H.T. nil - 8

Sat 9 Jan 1954 HULL KINGSTON ROVERS home lost 5 - 12
CASTLEFORD - E.Ward: Smart Webster Lunn Staniland:
Hague K.Pye: Kendrick Hill Simpson F.Ward Kitson
C.Anderson(S/O):   Try - F.Ward: Goal - Kitson:
HULL K R - Rushton: Egan Sutton Beck Austin: Spence
Kirby: Palfryman Smith Harbour Holt M.Anderson
A.N.Other: Tries - Austin(2) Sutton Anderson:
Referee R Gelder (Wakefield) Att - 2609 H.T. 2 - 6

Sat 16 Jan 1954 BRADFORD NORTHERN home lost 6 - 45
CASTLEFORD - J.J.Pye: Smart E.Ward Webster Staniland:
Cyril Woolford Claughton: Kendrick Hill Fleming Simpson
Kitson C.Anderson: Goals - Kitson(3):
BRADFORD N - Phillips: Knopf McLean Jenkins Mageen:
L.Haley Goddard: Tyler N.Haley Jones Foster Storey Traill:
Tries - McLean(5) Knopf(3) Jenkins Mageen L.Haley:
Goals - Phillips(6):
Referee S Adams (Hull) Att - 3491 H.T. 2 - 18

Sat 23 Jan 1954 HULL away lost 5 - 15
HULL - Hutton: Bowman Riches Turner Watts: Conway
Tripp: Scott Harris Coverdale Markham Hockley Whiteley:
Tries - Bowman(2) Watts: Goals - Hutton(2) Scott(DG):
CASTLEFORD - J.J.Pye: Webster E.Ward Oddy Staniland:
Batten Claughton: Kendrick Hill Perrett Howard GEORGE
DOOLER(368) F.Ward: Try - Oddy: Goal - E.Ward:
Referee M Coates (Pudsey) Att - 9000 H.T. 5 - 10

Sat 13 Feb 1954 DONCASTER home won 8 - 5
CHALLENGE CUP ROUND 1 1ST LEG
CASTLEFORD - E.Ward: Smart Webster Staniland Lunn:
Batten K.Pye: Kendrick Hill J.Anderson Howard
C.Anderson F.Ward:
Tries - Smart C.Anderson: Goal - E.Ward:
DONCASTER - Barraclough: Wilkinson Woolford Anson

Hayter: Gunn Tynan: Davies Doyle Pacey Bowers Freeman
Guest: Try - Wilkinson: Goal - Barraclough:
Referee J W Jackson (Barrow) Att - 4000 H.T. 2 - 5

Thu 18 Feb 1954 DONCASTER away lost 2 - 7
CHALLENGE CUP ROUND 1 2ND LEG
DONCASTER - Barraclough: Wilkinson Woolford Anson
Hayter: Gunn Tynan: Davies Doyle Pacey Bowers Freeman
Guest: Try - Anson: Goals - Barraclough(2):
CASTLEFORD - E.Ward: Smart Webster Staniland Lunn:
Batten K.Pye: Kendrick Hill J.Anderson Howard
C.Anderson F.Ward: Goal - E.Ward:
Referee C F Appleton (Warrington) Att - 1500 H.T. 2 - 2

Sat 20 Feb 1954 HUNSLET home lost 11 - 18
CASTLEFORD - E Ward: Smart Webster Oddy Staniland:
Claughton K.Pye Kendrick Hill J.Anderson Howard
C.Anderson F.Ward:
Try - Staniland: Goals - E.Ward(4):
HUNSLET - Evans: Snowden Bradshaw Waite Willams:
Talbot A.Burnell: Hatfield Smith W.Burnell Carroll Gunney
James:
Tries - Bradshaw Waite Williams A.Burnell:
Goals - Gunney(2) Talbot:
Referee R Gelder (Wakefield) Att - 4500 H.T. 9 - 10

Sat 27 Feb 1954 WAKEFIELD TRINITY home Lost 9 - 28
CASTLEFORD - E Ward: Smart Webster GEORGE
NORBURY(369) Staniland: Richard Claughton K.Pye: Alan
Kendrick Hughes J.Anderson Howard C.Anderson F.Ward:
Try - Smart: Goals - E.Ward(3):
WAKEFIELD T - T.Hirst: Cooper Bell Holliday Boocker:
Fewster Fletcher: Booth Shaw Adams Haigh Robinson
Kelly:
Tries - Boocker(2) Bell Booth Haigh Robinson:
Goals - Hirst(5):
Referee A Hill (Dewsbury) Att - 4231 H.T. 7 - 12

Sat 13 Mar 1954 YORK away lost 3 - 9
YORK - Hargreaves: Lord Dawson G.Smith B.Smith:
Robinson Riley: Waddington Milner Harlow Watts Dooler
Owens:
Try - Robinson: Goals - Harlow(2) Riley(DG):
CASTLEFORD - E Ward: Smart Webster Lunn Norbury:
Batten K.Pye: Perrett Hughes J.Anderson Howard Walter
F.Ward: Try - Webster:
Referee S Adams (Hull) Att - 6398 H.T. 3 - 7

Sat 20 Mar 1954 DONCASTER away draw 14 - 14
DONCASTER - Barraclough: Watson Wilkinson Anson
Bates: Gunn Tynan: Davies Doyle Pacey Carnill Freeman
Bowers:
Tries - Bates Bowers: Goals - Barraclough(4):
CASTLEFORD - E.Ward: Smart Webster Lunn Norbury:
Batten K.Pye: Perrett Hughes J.Anderson Howard Walter
F.Ward:
Tries - Norbury(3) Webster: Goal - Lunn:
Referee E Clay (Rothwell) Att - 1100 H.T. 8 - 9

Sat 27 Mar 1954 HALIFAX home lost 11 - 17
CASTLEFORD - E.Ward: Smart Webster Lunn Norbury:
Batten K.Pye: J.Anderson Hughes Perrett Howard Walter
F.Ward: Try - Lunn: Goals - Lunn(4):
HALIFAX - Griffiths: Daniels Lynch Todd Bevan: Dean
Kielty: Thorley Ackerley Illingworth Pearce Schofield
Clarkson:
Tries - Daniels Lynch Todd: Goals - Griffiths(4):
Referee H Squires (Ossett) Att - 4900 H.T. 9 - 9

Sat 3 Apr 1954 HUDDERSFIELD away won 25 - 20
HUDDERSFIELD - Dyson: Henderson Rose Grace Cooper:
Ramsden Quinn: Slevin Bradshaw Bowden Fairbank
Briggs Valentine:
Tries - Henderson(2) Grace Cooper: Goals - Dyson(4):
CASTLEFORD - E.Ward: Smart Webster Lunn Norbury:
Batten K.Pye: J.Anderson Hughes Perrett Howard Walter
F.Ward: Tries - Pye(2) Webster Lunn F.Ward:
Goals - Lunn(3) E.Ward(2):
Referee A Hill (Dewsbury) Att - 4769 H.T. 13 - 10

Sat 10 Apr 1954 HULL home lost 11 - 21
CASTLEFORD - E.Ward: Smart Webster Lunn Staniland:
Batten K.Pye: J.Anderson Hughes Perrett Howard Walter
F.Ward:
Try - F.Ward: Goals - Lunn(4):
HULL - Hutton: Bowman Riches Francis Watts: Drake
Tripp: Scott Harris Coverdale Markham Hockley Whiteley:
Tries - Watts(2) Bowman Scott Markham:
Goals - Hutton(2) Bowman:
Referee T Armitage (Huddersfield) Att - 4572 H.T. 7 – 8

Mon 12 Apr 1954 HUDDERSFIELD home won 23 - 17
CASTLEFORD - E.Ward: Smart Webster Lunn Staniland:
Batten K.Pye: J.Anderson Hill Perrett Howard Walter
F.Ward:
Tries - Webster Pye Anderson: Goals - E.Ward(7):
HUDDERSFIELD - Hunter: Henderson Pepperell Rose
Cooper: Rylance Banks: Slevin Bradshaw Bowden Fairbank
Griffin Valentine:
Tries - Henderson Pepperell Valentine: Goals - Rylance(4):
Referee A Hill (Dewsbury) Att - 5350 H.T. 11 - 12

Sat 17 Apr 1954 HUNSLET away lost 12 - 27
HUNSLET - Evans: Snowden Williams Waite Williamson:
Gabbitas Tate: Hatfield Smith W.Burnell Carroll Gunney
James: Tries - Williams(3) Snowden Williamson:
Goals - Gunney(6):
CASTLEFORD - E.Ward: Smart Webster Lunn Staniland:
Batten K.Pye: J.Anderson Hill Perrett Howard Walter
F.Ward:
Tries - Webster Anderson: Goals - E.Ward(2) Lunn:
Referee M Bizot (France) Att - 5000 H.T. 5 - 12

Mon 19 Apr 1954 LEEDS home lost 13 - 22
CASTLEFORD - Lunn: Smart Webster E.Ward Staniland:
Batten K.Pye: J.Anderson Hughes Perrett Howard Walter
F.Ward:
Try - Smart: Goals - E.Ward(5):
LEEDS - Dunn: Bartlett Moore Scholes Turnbull: Parker
Pratt: Skelton Power Horsfall Poole Clues Blan:
Tries - Turnbull(2) Bartlett Blan: Goals - Dunn(5):
Referee R Gelder (Wakefield) Att - 6318 H.T. 6 – 7

Len Exley
D. No 361
1953-54

Alan Marchant
D. No 362
1953-54

Derek Smart
D. No 364
1953-54 to 1959-60

Ernest Ward
D. No 366
1953-54 to 1955-56

SEASON 1953-54

D.N	PLAYER		DEBUT	L MATCH	APP	SUB	T.AP	TRI'S	G'LS	D.G	P'TS
239	HILL	JOHN			24	0	24	1	0	0	3
302	HOWARD	GEORGE (CHARLIE)			33	0	33	1	0	0	3
306	ANDERSON	JOSEPH			30	0	30	2	0	0	6
310	CLAUGHTON	RICHARD		27/02/1954	6	0	6	0	0	0	0
313	WOOLFORD	CYRIL		16/01/1954	1	0	1	0	0	0	0
314	FLEMING	LEO			17	0	17	0	0	0	0
323	HAUGHEY	LESLIE			8	0	8	1	0	0	3
324	ANDERSON	COLIN			19	0	19	2	0	0	6
326	WALTER	RONALD			9	0	9	0	0	0	0
330	PYE	KENNETH			36	0	36	13	0	0	39
332	BATTEN	ROBERT			29	0	29	6	0	0	18
333	KITSON	ARTHUR			9	0	9	0	13	0	26
340	HUGHES	DAVID			8	0	8	0	0	0	0
341	LUNN	ALBERT			34	0	34	7	69	0	159
342	PYE	JOSHUA J.			20	0	20	0	0	0	0
343	SIMPSON	PETER			23	0	23	1	0	0	3
344	HAGUE	ROY			5	0	5	0	0	0	0
346	ODDY	HAROLD			17	0	17	2	0	0	6
347	STANILAND	ARTHUR			32	0	32	7	0	0	21
349	WARD	FRED			34	0	34	7	0	0	21
350	LAMBERT	ROY		12/12/1953	18	0	18	7	0	0	21
351	LYLES	RONALD		22/08/1953	1	0	1	0	0	0	0
352	WEBSTER	DENZIL			23	0	23	9	0	0	27
353	THORNLEY	HARRY			1	0	1	0	0	0	0
355	GRACE	ARNOLD			2	0	2	1	0	0	3
356	PERRETT	MAURICE			12	0	12	0	0	0	0
359	HALE	BRIAN	15/08/1953	19/08/1953	2	0	2	0	0	0	0
360	METCALFE	ALLAN	22/08/1953	22/08/1953	1	0	1	0	0	0	0
361	EXLEY	LEN	22/08/1953	22/08/1953	1	0	1	0	0	0	0
362	MARCHANT	ALAN	29/08/1953	29/08/1953	1	0	1	1	0	0	3
363	BRADSHAW	WILLIAM	29/08/1953	26/09/1953	7	0	7	0	0	0	0
364	SMART	DEREK	17/10/1953		20	0	20	6	0	0	18
365	GILL	BRIAN	11/11/1953	11/11/1953	1	0	1	1	0	0	3
366	WARD	ERNEST	28/11/1953		22	0	22	0	26	0	52
367	KENDRICK	ALAN	02/01/1954		8	0	8	0	0	0	0
368	DOOLER	GEORGE	23/01/1954	23/01/1954	1	0	1	0	0	0	0
369	NORBURY	GEORGE	27/02/1954		5	0	5	3	0	0	9
	37		11	12	520	0	520	78	108	0	450

COMPETITION		P	W	D	L	FOR	AGT
LEAGUE	POSITION 26 OF 30	36	11	1	24	437	728
YORK'S CUP		2	0	0	2	3	20
RL CUP		2	1	0	1	10	12
PLAYERS RECORDS		**40**	**12**	**1**	**27**	**450**	**760**

Ernest Ward the Great Britain and former Bradford Northern star made his debut on Saturday, 28 November 1953, at full back versus Workington Town at home, he also took over as Coach from Billy Rhodes.

**Sat 7 Aug 1954 WAKEFIELD TRINITY away
lost nil - 3 CHARITY MATCH FRIENDLY**
WAKEFIELD T - Team not known
CASTLEFORD - J.J.Pye: Norbury East E.Ward Staniland:
Parker K.Pye: Fleming Hill Kitson Haughey C.Anderson
F.Ward:

Sat 14 Aug 1954 HUDDERSFIELD away lost 17 - 43
HUDDERSFIELD - Hunter: Henderson Rose Sullivan
Cooper: Ramsden Banks: Slevin Bradshaw Flint Fairbank
Griffin Large:
Tries - Cooper(4) Henderson(3) Rose(2) Sullivan Ramsden:
Goals - Flint(3) Hunter Cooper:
CASTLEFORD - J.J.Pye: Smart Lunn Oddy Staniland:
KENNETH PEASE(370) K.Pye: J.Anderson Hill Perrett
Haughey C.Anderson F.Ward:
Tries - K.Pye(2) Lunn: Goals - Lunn(4):
Referee A Hill (Dewsbury) Att - 6331 H.T. 10 - 8

**Wed 18 Aug 1954 BRADFORD NORTHERN home
lost 4 - 8**
CASTLEFORD - J.J.Pye: FRANK EAST(371) Lunn E.Ward
Staniland: Kenneth Pease K.Pye: J.Anderson JACK
BOOT(372) Simpson Haughey C.Anderson F.Ward:
Goals - Lunn E.Ward:
BRADFORD N - Phillips: Knopf Mageen Jenkins Smith:
L.Haley Goddard: Carter N.Haley Jones Foster Griffett
Storey: Goals - Phillips(4):
Referee J W Jowett (Leeds) Att - 2500 H.T. 2 - 6

Sat 21 Aug 1954 SALFORD home won 19 - nil
CASTLEFORD - J.J.Pye: Smart Lunn E.Ward Staniland:
Oddy K.Pye: J.Anderson Hill Simpson Haughey
C.Anderson F.Ward: Tries - Smart Lunn K.Pye Simpson
F.Ward: Goals - E.Ward(2):
SALFORD - Smith: Hartley Cartwright Roughley Baines:
Houghton Harrison: Marston Boardman Alder Grainger
Greenwood Rogers:
Referee G Battersby (Barrow) Att - 2350 H.T. 13 - nil

Sat 28 Aug 1954 BATLEY away won 17 - 8
BATLEY - Walshaw: Westbury Etty Riley McDonald: Smith
Northern: Pickersgill Battersby Redfearn Palmer Payne
Briggs: Goals - Walshaw(4):
CASTLEFORD - J.J.Pye: Webster Lunn E.Ward Staniland:
Oddy K.Pye: J.Anderson Hill Simpson Haughey
C.Anderson F.Ward:
Tries - Webster(2) K.Pye: Goals - Lunn(4):
Referee H Harrison (Wakefield) Att - 3200 H.T. 5 - 8

Sat 4 Sep 1954 BELLE VUE RANGERS home won 33 - 7
CASTLEFORD - J.J.Pye: Webster E.Ward Lunn Staniland:
Oddy K.Pye: J.Anderson Hill Simpson Haughey
C.Anderson F.Ward: Tries - Lunn(2) Webster E.Ward
Staniland Haughey F.Ward: Goals - Lunn(6):
BELLE V R - Gregory: Dagnan Morgan Jones Day: Brown
Cleworth: Pugsley Lannon Atherton Tierney Jennings
Pimblett: Try - Jennings: Goals - Tierney(2):
Referee W Rigby (Leigh) Att - 3752 H.T. 17 - 2

**Sat 11 Sep 1954 BRADFORD NORTHERN home lost
10 - 13 YORKSHIRE CUP ROUND 1**
CASTLEFORD - J.J.Pye: Webster Lunn E.Ward Staniland:
Oddy K.Pye: J.Anderson Hill Fleming Haughey C.Anderson
F.Ward: Tries - Webster K.Pye: Goals - Lunn(2):
BRADFORD N - Phillips: Knopf Mageen Jenkins Wilson:
Sharrock Hamilton: Tyler N.Haley Jones Foster Griffett
Storey: Try - Griffett: Goals - Phillips(4)(DG):
Referee J Jackson (Barrow) Att - 8200 H.T. 5 - 9

**Sat 18 Sep 1954 BLACKPOOL BOROUGH away
won 45 - 12**
BLACKPOOL B - Peace: Emmett Reece Hockenhull Perkins:
Ryder Fleming: Wright McPartland Fisher Barraclough
Rike Armitt: Tries - Perkins Fisher: Goals - Peace(3):
CASTLEFORD - J.J.Pye: Webster Lunn E.Ward Staniland:
Oddy K.Pye: J.Anderson Hill ANDREW KETT(373) Haughey
C.Anderson F.Ward: Tries - Oddy(3) K.Pye(2)
Staniland(2) Webster E.Ward: Goals - Lunn(9):
Referee T Armitage (Huddersfield) Att - 3301 H.T.

Sat 25 Sep 1954 SALFORD away lost nil - 23
SALFORD - Smith: Hartley Fairhurst Roughley Baron:
Davies Harrison: Marston McKinney Grainger Moses
Greenwood Rogers: Tries - Hartley(2) Harrison(2)
Roughley Baron Rogers: Goal - Davies:
CASTLEFORD - J.J.Pye: Webster Lunn E.Ward Staniland:
Oddy K.Pye: J.Anderson Boot Kett Haughey C.Anderson
F.Ward:
Referee M Coates (Pudsey) Att - 2903 H.T.

Sat 2 Oct 1954 HULL home lost 13 - 18
CASTLEFORD - J.J.Pye: Webster Lunn E.Ward Smart: Oddy
K.Pye: J.Anderson Hill Simpson Haughey TONY
HARDCASTLE(374) F.Ward:
Tries - Smart(3): Goals - Lunn E.Ward:
HULL - Hutton: Bowman Watkinson Turner Moat: Conway
Tripp: Scott Harris Coverdale Clark Hockley W.Drake:
Tries - Bowman Watkinson Conway Hockley:
Goals - Hutton(3):
Referee H Squires (Ossett) Att - 4908 H.T. 5 - 15

**Sat 9 Oct 1954 BELLE VUE RANGERS away
won 18 - nil**
BELLE V R - R.Morgan: Cleworth D.Morgan Jones Day:
R.Brown Rees: Pugsley Welsby J.Brown Tierney Jennings
Pimblett:
CASTLEFORD - J.J.Pye: Webster Lunn E.Ward Staniland:
Oddy K.Pye: J.Anderson Hill Haughey Hardcastle
C.Anderson F.Ward:
Tries - Lunn(2) J.J.Pye Staniland: Goals - Lunn(3):
Referee S Adams (Hull) Att - 944 H.T. nil - nil

Sat 16 Oct 1954 BRAMLEY home won 14 - 11
CASTLEFORD - J.J.Pye: Webster Lunn E.Ward Smart: Oddy
K.Pye: J.Anderson Hill Haughey Howard Hardcastle
F.Ward: Tries - Smart(2): Goals - E.Ward(4):
BRAMLEY - Wilson: Humphries Warrior Kelly Garbutt:
Dudley Burnell: Nutting Hanley Bell Tomlinson Baldwin
Guy: Try - Humphries: Goals - Wilson(4):

SEASON 1954-55

Referee A Howgate (Dewsbury) Att - 3830 H.T. 7 - 4

Mon 25 Oct 1954 HALIFAX away lost 9 - 18
HALIFAX - Griffiths: Bevan Lynch Fearis Todd: Dean Kielty: Olsen Ackerley Illingworth Wilkinson Pearce Callighan:
Tries - Fearis Todd Dean Callighan: Goals - Griffiths(3):
CASTLEFORD - J.J.Pye: Staniland Webster E.Ward Smart: Robert Batten K.Pye: Haughey Hill Kitson Howard Hardcastle F.Ward:
Try - Webster: Goals - Kitson(2) E.Ward(DG):
Referee C F Appleton (Warr'ton) Att - 3350 H.T. 2 - 12

Sat 30 Oct 1954 DONCASTER away lost 3 - 20
DONCASTER - Guest: Badger Woolford Hayter Cranswick: Watson Gunn: Pacey Doyle Freeman Bowers Baddeley Anson:
Tries - Cranswick(2) Guest Hayter: Goals - Guest(4):
CASTLEFORD - J.J.Pye: Norbury Webster Lunn Smart: Oddy K.Pye: Leo Fleming Boot Arthur Kitson Haughey Howard C.Anderson: Try - K.Pye:
Referee A Hill (Dewsbury) Att - 1301 H.T. nil - 9

Sat 6 Nov 1954 BATLEY home lost 11 - 13
CASTLEFORD - J.J.Pye: Staniland Webster E.Ward Smart: K.Pye Grace: J.Anderson Boot Andrew Kett Tony Hardcastle Haughey Walter:
Tries - Staniland(2)Anderson: Goal - E.Ward:
BATLEY - Risman: Perry Cox Kilroy Field: Smith Northern: Greaves Battersby Redfearn Palmer Jones Briggs:
Try - Smith: Goals - Risman(5):
Referee R Gelder (Wakefield) Att - 1735 H.T. 6 - 9

Sat 13 Nov 1954 HUNSLET away lost 7 - 15
HUNSLET - Backhouse: Snowden Evans Waite L.Williams: R.Williams A.N.Other: Hatfield Welsh Shaw Gunney Clues Carroll:
Tries - Snowden Waite L.Williams: Goals - Backhouse(3):
CASTLEFORD - J.J.Pye: Lunn Webster E.Ward Staniland: K.Pye Grace: J.Anderson Boot Haughey Howard F.Ward Hughes:
Try - Staniland: Goals - E.Ward(2):
Referee S Adams (Hull) Att - 2500 H.T. 7 - 5

Sat 20 Nov 1954 BLACKPOOL BOROUGH home won 30 - 9
CASTLEFORD - J.J.Pye: Lunn Webster E.Ward Staniland: K.Pye Grace: J.Anderson Boot Haughey Howard F.Ward Hughes: Tries - Webster(4) Staniland(2) Lunn Grace: Goals - E.Ward(2) Lunn:
BLACKPOOL B - Peace: Emmitt Ryder Walsh Higham: Bebe Kelly: Wright Lester Fisher Rika Armitt Horrocks:
Try - Higham: Goals - Peace(3):
Referee J W Jackson (Barrow) Att - 1629 H.T. 11 - 9

Sat 27 Nov 1954 HULL away draw 11 - 11
HULL - Hutton: W.Drake Riches Brindle Coulman: Conway Tripp: Scott Harris Coverdale Markham Hockley Whiteley:
Tries - W.Drake(2) Brindle: Goal - Hutton:
CASTLEFORD - J.J.Pye: Lunn Webster Oddy C.Anderson: K.Pye Grace: J.Anderson Hill Haughey Howard Walter

F.Ward: Tries - Webster(2) Lunn: Goal - Lunn:
Referee N T Railton (Wigan) Att - 3500 H.T.

Sat 11 Dec 1954 YORK home won 19 - 10
CASTLEFORD - J.J.Pye: Lunn Webster E.Ward Staniland: K.Pye Grace: J.Anderson Boot Haughey Howard Walter F.Ward:
Tries - Staniland(2) Walter: Goals - E.Ward(5):
YORK - Hargreaves: Hamblett Dawson Smith Hansell: Robinson Riley: Waddington Dolan Yorke O'Brien Dooler Taylor: Tries - Hamblett Riley: Goals - Yorke(2):
Referee T Armitage (Huddersfield) Att – 2342 H.T. 14 - 5

Sat 18 Dec 1954 DEWSBURY home won 30 - 10
CASTLEFORD - J.J.Pye: Lunn Webster E.Ward Staniland: K.Pye Grace: J.Anderson Boot Haughey Howard Walter F.Ward:
Tries - Webster(2) Staniland F.Ward: Goals - E.Ward(9):
DEWSBURY - Popplewell: Dickinson Callighan Clark Waring: Ward Morton: Wilmot Moyser Ormandroyd Dolan Stephenson Withington:
Tries - Dickinson Clark: Goals - Callighan(2):
Referee J Jowett (Leeds) Att - 2040 H.T. 21 - nil

Sat 25 Dec 1954 WAKEFIELD TRINITY home won 19 - 8
CASTLEFORD - J.J.Pye: Smart Webster E.Ward Staniland: Oddy Grace: J.Anderson Boot Haughey Howard Walter F.Ward:
Tries - Smart Staniland Oddy: Goals - E.Ward(5):
WAKEFIELD T - Mortimer: Bell Holliday Burton Froggett: Fewster Fletcher: Harrison Shaw Lindley Robinson Kelly Clifft:
Tries - Froggett(2):   Goal - Mortimer:
Referee E Hopkins (Leeds) Att - 5680 H.T. 15 - 5

Mon 27 Dec 1954 FEATHERSTONE ROVERS away draw 8 - 8
FEATHERSTONE R - Fennell: Marchant Metcalfe Clamp Cording: Hirst Fox: Welburn Fawley Shreeve Barraclough Hulme Lambert:
Tries - Hirst Lambert: Goal - Fox:
CASTLEFORD - J.J.Pye: Smart Webster Lunn Staniland: Oddy Grace: J.Anderson Boot Haughey Walter Howard F.Ward:
Tries - Smart J.Anderson: Goal - Grace(DG)
Referee S Adams (Hull) Att - 7000 H.T. -

Sat 1 Jan 1955 FEATHERSTONE ROVERS home lost 8 - 19
CASTLEFORD - J.J.Pye: Smart Lunn E.Ward Staniland: K.Pye Grace: J.Anderson Boot Haughey Howard Walter F.Ward:
Tries - E.Ward F.Ward: Goal - E.Ward:
FEATHERSTONE R - Allen: Marchant Metcalfe Clamp Cording: Fennell D.Fox: Shreeve Bradshaw Hulme Barraclough Lambert P.Fox:
Tries - D.Fox(2) Lambert: Goals - Fennell(4) D.Fox:
Referee M Coates (Pudsey) Att - 6100 H.T. 5 - 12

SEASON 1954-55

Sat 8 Jan 1955 LEEDS away lost 12 - 26
LEEDS - Dunn: Turnbull McLellan Jones Scholes: Brown
Stevenson: Horsfall Wood Hopper Poole Sewell Last:
Tries - Turnbull(3) Scholes Brown Poole: Goals - Jones(4):
CASTLEFORD - J.J.Pye: Smart E.Ward Oddy Staniland:
K.Pye Grace: <u>Joseph Anderson</u> Boot Haughey Howard
Walter F.Ward:
Tries - Smart Staniland: Goals - E.Ward(3):
Referee J P Hebblethwaite (York) Att - 12000 H.T. 7 - 11

Sat 29 Jan 1955 HUNSLET home lost 16 - 21
CASTLEFORD - EDWARD RHODES(375): Smart Webster
E.Ward BRIAN WINN(376): Oddy Grace: ALAN
HORSFALL(377) Boot Haughey Howard C.Anderson
F.Ward:
Tries - Webster(2) Smart Winn: Goals - E.Ward(2):
HUNSLET - Talbot: Snowden Evans Waite Williamson:
R.Williams A.Burnell: Hatfield Smith Shaw Gunney Clues
James:
Tries - Hatfield(2) Snowden Waite Gunney:
Goals - Talbot(3):
Referee C H Harrison (Ossett) Att - 5800 H.T. 8 - 15

Sat 5 Feb 1955 WAKEFIELD TRINITY away lost 7 - 13
WAKEFIELD T - Ripley: Cooper Bell Mortimer Sweeney:
Fewster Evans: Harrison Bridges Adams Robinson Kelly
Clifft:
Tries - Cooper Mortimer Fewster: Goals - Ripley(2):
CASTLEFORD - J.J.Pye: Smart Webster E.Ward Staniland:
Oddy K.Pye: Welsby Boot Haughey Howard C.Anderson
F.Ward:
Try - Webster: Goals - E.Ward(2):
Referee A Hill (Dewsbury) Att - 4073 H.T. 2 - 10

Sat 12 Feb 1955 SALFORD away lost 5 - 13
CHALLENGE CUP ROUND I
SALFORD - Smith: Lambert Hartley Fairhurst Wilson:
Jones Keavney: Marston Boardman Moses Greenwood
Council Todd:
Tries - Hartley(2) Lambert: Goals - Keavney(2):
CASTLEFORD - J.J.Pye: Smart Webster E.Ward Staniland:
C.Anderson K.Pye: Horsfall Boot Haughey Howard F.Ward
FRANK BIRKIN(S/O)(378):
Try - Webster: Goal - E.Ward:
Referee M Coates (Pudsey) Att - 5296 H.T. 3 - 10

Sat 5 Mar 1955 WHITEHAVEN home lost 5 - 11
CASTLEFORD - J.J.Pye: Smart Oddy E.Ward Staniland:
Grace K.Pye: Horsfall Boot Haughey Howard Walter
F.Ward:
Try - Smart: Goal - E.Ward:
WHITEHAVEN - Byers: Smith Dawson Lowden Harrison:
Garratt Keen: McAlone Crewdson Cavanagh NcCourt
Stamper Farr:
Tries - Byers Smith Lowden: Goal - Lowden:
Referee R L Thomas (Oldham) Att - 1647 H.T. 5 - 3

**Sat 12 Mar 1955 BRADFORD NORTHERN away
draw 23 - 23**
BRADFORD N - Phillips: Smith Jenkins Seddon McLean:
Sutton Haley: Tyler Collins Jones Foster Radford Traill:
Tries - McLean(3) Smith Radford: Goals - Phillips(4):
CASTLEFORD - J.J.Pye: Smart Webster E.Ward Staniland:
Oddy K.Pye: Horsfall Boot Welsby Haughey Howard
F.Ward:
Tries - Smart E.Ward Howard: Goals - E.Ward(7):
Referee R Welsby (Warrington) Att - 3437 H.T.

Sat 19 Mar 1955 HALIFAX home lost 9 - 29
CASTLEFORD - J.J.Pye: Smart Webster E.Ward Norbury:
Oddy K.Pye: Welsby Horsfall Haughey Howard Walter
F.Ward: Try - Webster: Goals - E.Ward(3):
HALIFAX - Lockwood: Daniels Lynch Todd Bevan: Dean
Kielty: Thorley Ackerley Wilkinson Henderson Schofield
Fearnley:
Tries - Lynch(2) Bevan(2) Daniels: Goals - Lockwood(7):
Referee A Hill (Dewsbury) Att - 3544 H.T. 9 - 18

Sat 2 Apr 1955 HUDDERSFIELD home won 9 - 5
CASTLEFORD - E.Ward: Norbury Webster East <u>Brian Winn</u>:
JOHN WINN(379) K.Pye: Horsfall Boot Welsby Howard
Haughey F.Ward: Try - F.Ward: Goals - E.Ward(3):
HUDDERSFIELD - Dyson: Henderson Roughley Hunter
Cooper: Rylance Ramsden: Slevin Bradshaw Bowden
Briggs Large Valentine:
Try - Henderson: Goal - Dyson:
Referee J W Jowett (Leeds) Att - 3083 H.T. 7 - 5

Sat 9 Apr 1955 WHITEHAVEN away lost 9 - 20
WHITEHAVEN - Byers: Smith Dawson Lowdon Harrison:
Garratt Keen: McAlone Crewdson Cavanagh McCourt
Donaldson Parr:
Tries - Harrison(2) Smith Parr: Goals - Lowdon(4):
CASTLEFORD - E.Ward: Norbury Webster East Lunn:
J.Winn K.Pye: Horsfall Boot Welsby Haughey Howard
Walter: Try - Lunn: Goals - E.Ward(3):
Referee R Gelder (Wakefield) Att - 4211 H.T. 9 - 7

Mon 11 Apr 1955 LEEDS home draw 13 - 13
CASTLEFORD - E.Ward: Norbury Webster East Lunn:
J.Winn K.Pye: Horsfall Boot Welsby Haughey Howard
Birkin: Try - K.Pye: Goals - E.Ward(5):
LEEDS - Dunn: Turnbull Brown Jones Broughton:
Stevenson Pratt: Shelton Wood Anderson Poole Hanson
Last: Try - Jones: Goals - Jones(5):
Referee A E Durkin (Dewsbury) Att - 8000 H.T. 7 - 9

Tue 12 Apr 1955 BRAMLEY away lost 12 - 22
BRAMLEY - Wilson: Humphries Garbutt Ogden Guy:
Dudley Langfield: Young Hanley Huggins Sykes
Tomlinson Baldwin: Tries - Wilson Garbutt Young Sykes:
Goals - Wilson(4) Langfield:
CASTLEFORD - E.Ward: Norbury Webster East Lunn:
J.Winn K.Pye: Horsfall Boot Welsby Haughey Howard
Birkin: Tries - Webster K.Pye: Goals - E.Ward(3):
Referee A Hill (Dewsbury) Att - 3254 H.T. 8 - 4

SEASON 1954-55

Sat 16 Apr 1955 KEIGHLEY home won 28 - 16
CASTLEFORD - J.J.Pye: Lunn Webster E.Ward Oddy:
J.Winn K.Pye: Horsfall Hill Welsby Haughey Walter Birkin:
Tries - Webster(3) E.Ward K.Pye Birkin: Goals E.Ward(5):
KEIGHLEY - Cook: Hopkins L.Ward Hallas Bleasby:
Verrenkamp Rowlands: Woosey Traill James Murphy
Ratcliffe Raines: Tries - L.Ward Bleasby Verrenkamp
Rowlands: Goals - Cook(2):
Referee Mr N T Railton (Liverpool) Att - 2696 H.T. 20 -3

Tue 19 Apr 1955 YORK away lost 7 - 19
YORK - Hargreaves: Hamblett Parkin G.Smith B.Smith:
Foster Riley: Waddington Nerry Harker Taylor O'Brien
Dawson:
Tries - Hamblett Foster Taylor: Goals - Harker(5):
CASTLEFORD - J.J.Pye: Lunn Webster E.Ward CLIFFORD
BURTON(380): J.Winn K.Pye: Welsby Hill Perrett Walter
Haughey Birkin: Try - Birkin: Goals - Lunn Ward:
Referee H Harrison (Ossett) Att - 3307 H.T. nil - 12

Fri 22 Apr 1955 DEWSBURY away lost 7 - 10
DEWSBURY - Clark: Wilson Broadhead Thomas Dickinson:
Kilner Waterson: Danter Moyser Ormanroyd Ellis Leonard
Field: Tries - Wilson Ellis: Goals - Broadhead(2):
CASTLEFORD - E.Ward: J.J.Pye Webster Burton George
Norbury: J.Winn K.Pye: Horsfall Hill Perrett Howard
Haughey Birkin:
Try - Norbury: Goals - E.Ward(2):
Referee J P Hebblethwaite (York) Att - 980 H.T. 5 - 8

Wed 27 Apr 1955 DONCASTER home won 19 - 9
CASTLEFORD - E.Ward: Hague Webster Rhodes J.J.Pye:
K.Pye Grace: Perrett Hill DENNIS NORTON(381) Howard
Haughey Birkin:
Tries - Rhodes J.J.Pye K.Pye: Goals - E.Ward(5):
DONCASTER - Barraclough: Raynor Blackburn Ratcliffe
Fairhurst: Ward Guest: Doyle Croft Freeman Oxby
A.N.Other Bowers:
Try - Croft: Goals - Barraclough(3):
Referee A Howgate (Dewsbury) Att - 1500 H.T. 6 - 7

Tue 3 May 1955 KEIGHLEY away lost 7 - 8
KEIGHLEY - L.Ward: Hollindrake O'Hara Smith Holgate:
Verrenkamp Rowlands: Woosey Traill Hopkins Murphy
Curnow Raines:
Tries - Smith Holgate: Goal - L.Ward:
CASTLEFORD - E.Ward: Hague Burton Rhodes J.J.Pye:
Grace K.Pye: Welsby Hill Norton Howard Haughey Birkin:
Try - Grace: Goals - E.Ward(2):
Referee M Coates (Pudsey) Att - 1685 H.T. nil – 8

Ken Pease
D. No 370
1954-55

Frank East
D. No 371
1954-55 to 1958-59

Jack Boot
D. No 372
1954-55 to 1957-58

Alan Horsfall
D. No 377
1954-55 to 1957-58

John Winn
D. No 379
1954-55 to 1956-57

Cliff Burton
D. No 380
1954-55 to 1958-59

D.N	PLAYER		DEBUT	L MATCH	APP	SUB	T.AP	TRI'S	G'LS	D.G	P'TS
239	HILL	JOHN			16	0	16	0	0	0	0
302	HOWARD	GEORGE (CHARLIE)			25	0	25	1	0	0	3
306	ANDERSON	JOSEPH		08/01/1955	21	0	21	2	0	0	6
314	FLEMING	LEO		30/10/1954	2	0	2	0	0	0	0
323	HAUGHEY	LESLIE			38	0	38	1	0	0	3
324	ANDERSON	COLIN			14	0	14	0	0	0	0
326	WALTER	RONALD			13	0	13	1	0	0	3
330	PYE	KENNETH			35	0	35	12	0	0	36
332	BATTEN	ROBERT		25/10/1954	1	0	1	0	0	0	0
333	KITSON	ARTHUR		30/10/1954	2	0	2	0	2	0	4
334	WELSBY	HAROLD			10	0	10	0	0	0	0
340	HUGHES	DAVID			2	0	2	0	0	0	0
341	LUNN	ALBERT			24	0	24	9	33	0	93
342	PYE	JOSHUA J.			33	0	33	2	0	0	6
343	SIMPSON	PETER			5	0	5	1	0	0	3
344	HAGUE	ROY			2	0	2	0	0	0	0
346	ODDY	HAROLD			21	0	21	4	0	0	12
347	STANILAND	ARTHUR			23	0	23	14	0	0	42
349	WARD	FRED			28	0	28	5	0	0	15
352	WEBSTER	DENZIL			31	0	31	23	0	0	69
355	GRACE	ARNOLD			14	0	14	2	0	1	8
356	PERRETT	MAURICE			4	0	4	0	0	0	0
364	SMART	DEREK			17	0	17	12	0	0	36
366	WARD	ERNEST			34	0	34	5	81	1	179
369	NORBURY	GEORGE		22/04/1955	7	0	7	1	0	0	3
370	PEASE	KENNETH	14/08/1954	18/08/1954	2	0	2	0	0	0	0
371	EAST	FRANK	18/08/1954		5	0	5	0	0	0	0
372	BOOT	JACK	18/08/1954		21	0	21	0	0	0	0
373	KETT	ANDREW	18/09/1954	06/11/1954	3	0	3	0	0	0	0
374	HARDCASTLE	TONY	02/10/1954	06/11/1954	5	0	5	0	0	0	0
375	RHODES	EDWARD	29/01/1955		3	0	3	1	0	0	3
376	WINN	BRIAN	29/01/1955	12/04/1955	2	0	2	1	0	0	3
377	HORSFALL	ALAN	29/01/1955		11	0	11	0	0	0	0
378	BIRKIN	FRANK	12/02/1955		8	0	8	2	0	0	6
379	WINN	JOHN	02/04/1955		7	0	7	0	0	0	0
380	BURTON	CLIFFORD	19/04/1955		3	0	3	0	0	0	0
381	NORTON	DENNIS	27/04/1955		2	0	2	0	0	0	0
	37		**12**	**9**	**494**	**0**	**494**	**99**	**116**	**2**	**533**

COMPETITION			P	W	D	L	FOR	AGT
LEAGUE	POSITION 21 OF 31		36	13	4	19	518	516
YORK'S CUP			1	0	0	1	10	13
RL CUP			1	0	0	1	5	13
PLAYERS RECORDS			**38**	**13**	**4**	**21**	**533**	**542**

Blackpool Borough were admitted to the League increasing the number of teams to 31.

Castleford opened the season with the half back pairing of Pye and Pease. However, it was neither a successful or long lasting "dish" as Kenneth Pease only appearances for the Club were the first two matches of the season and both were lost.

Another debutante, loose forward Francis (Frank) Birkin, was signed from Salford and made an inauspicious debut against his former club in the first round Challenge Cup defeat, when he was sent off by referee Mr Matt Coates and missed the next five matches.

During the season the Castleford and Yorkshire prop forward, Joe Anderson, was transferred to Leeds.

The first World Cup was played in France during October and November 1954. Whilst we did not have any players selected, the Great Britain Team Manager was the Castleford Chairman and Director, Gideon Shaw.

Albert Lunn increased the record for most points scored in a League game to 18 against Belle Vue Rangers on the 4 September 1954 and Ernest Ward equalled it against Dewsbury at home on the 18 December 1954.

SEASON 1955-56

Sat 20 Aug 1955 WORKINGTOWN TOWN home lost 11 - 20
CASTLEFORD - J.J.Pye: Lunn JOHN SHERIDAN(382) E.Ward Staniland: Hague K.Pye: Welsby Hill Perrett Anderson Haughey Birkin: Try - Sheridan: Goals - E.Ward(4):
WORKINGTON T - S.Thompson: Southward Wookey Gibson Ivill: Faulder Roper: Hayton Lymer Key Herbert C.Thompson Edgar: Tries - Wookey Faulder C.Thompson Edgar:
Goals - Southward(4):
Referee G S Phillips (Widnes) Att - 3300 H.T. 9 - 5

Mon 22 Aug 1955 HUDDERSFIELD away lost 6 - 30
HUDDERSFIELD - Dyson: Henderson Waitwright Sullivan Hunter: Ramsden Banks: Slevin Bradshaw Bowden Briggs Large Valentine: Tries - Wainwright(2) Dyson Henderson Ramsden Valentine: Goals - Dyson(5) Bowden:
CASTLEFORD - J.J.Pye: Lunn Sheridan E.Ward Smart: Hague K.Pye: Harold Welsby Hill Horsfall Haughey Anderson Birkin:
Tries - Smart Anderson:
Referee A Howgate (Dewsbury) Att - 5576 H.T. 3 - 12

Fri 26 Aug 1955 DEWSBURY home won 29 - 8
YORKSHIRE CUP ROUND 1
CASTLEFORD - J.J.Pye: Smart Webster E.Ward Lunn: Hague K.Pye: Horsfall Hill Haughey Howard F.Ward Birkin: Tries - Smart(3) Webster(2): Goals - E.Ward(7):
DEWSBURY - Bosworth: Waring Callighan Popplewell Wilson: Rees Lea: Danter Moyser Wilmot Dolan Ormondroyd Withington: Tries - Waring Wilson: Goal - Waring:
Refefee T W Watkinson (Man'ster) Att - 4608 H.T. 19 - 2

Wed 31 Aug 1955 HALIFAX home lost 7 - 17
CASTLEFORD - J.J.Pye: Smart Webster E.Ward Lunn: Hague K.Pye: Horsfall Hill Haughey Howard F.Ward Anderson:
Try - Smart: Goals - Lunn(2):
HALIFAX - Griffiths: Daniels Todd Palmer Bevan: Dean Kielty: Thorley Ackerley Wilkinson Henderson Schofield Fearnley:
Tries - Daniels Bevan Fearnley: Goals - Griffiths(4):
Referee T Armitage (Huddersfield) Att - 5419 H.T. 7 - 9

Sat 3 Sep 1955 WIDNES away lost 8 - 31
WIDNES - Sale: Williamson Kinsey Dawson Ratcliffe: Butler Davies: Rowbottom Kemel Tomlinson V.Smith T.Smith Worth: Tries - Kinsey(2) Williamson Dawson Ratcliffe Butler Rowbottom: Goals - Sale(5):
CASTLEFORD - E.Ward: Smart Oddy Rhodes Lunn: Hague Grace: Horsfall Hill Haughey Howard F.Ward Anderson:
Tries - Lunn Howard: Goal - Lunn:
Referee M Coates (Pudsey) Att -   H.T. nil - 8

Sat 10 Sep 1955 HUNSLET home lost 13 - 17
CASTLEFORD - E.Ward: Smart Oddy Sheridan Lunn: Hague K.Pye: Horsfall Hill Haughey Howard Anderson F.Ward:
Tries - E.Ward Smart F.Ward: Goals - E.Ward(2):
HUNSLET - Langton: Williams Evans Harrison Williamson: Gabbitas A.Burnell: Hatfield Smith Shaw Carroll Clues James:
Tries - Williams 2) Williamson(2) Harrison: Goal - Evans:
Referee S Adams (Hull) Att - 5422 H.T. nil - 6

Mon 12 Sep 1955 HULL KINGSTON ROVERS away lost 7 - 13
HULL K R - Buckle: Hartley Goulding Thornton Garry: Key Parker: Grice Tong Evans Thompson Smith Shires:
Try - Grice: Goals - Buckle(5):
CASTLEFORD - J.J.Pye: Smart Sheridan Oddy Lunn: Hague K.Pye: Norton Boot Haughey Howard Anderson F.Ward:
Try - F.Ward: Goals - Lunn(2):
Referee C Whiteley (Ossett) Att - 4819 H.T. 3 - 6

Wed 14 Sep 1955 HULL KINGSTON ROVERS home won 17 - nil YORKSHIRE CUP ROUND 2
CASTLEFORD - E.Ward: Smart Oddy Sheridan Lunn: Hague K.Pye: Horsfall Hill Haughey Howard F.Ward Birkin: Tries - E.Ward Smart Sheridan Howard F.Ward: Goal - E.Ward:
HULL K R - Buckle: Golder Goulding Thornton Garry: Key Ellener: Hall Tong Grice Evans Sutton Smith:
Referee C F Appleton (Warrington) Att - 4570 H.T. 3 - nil

Sat l7 Sep 1955 WAKEFIELD TRINITY away lost 15 - 22
WAKEFIELD T - Mortimer: Smith Burton Bell Cooper: Houlden Kielty: Harrison Shaw Ashall Robinson Firth Armstead: Tries - Smith(3) Shaw: Goals - Houlden(5):
CASTLEFORD - E.Ward: Smart Oddy Sheridan Lunn: Hague K.Pye: Horsfall Hill Haughey Howard Anderson F.Ward:
Tries - Oddy Lunn F.Ward: Goals - E.Ward(3):
Referee A Howgate (Dewsbury) Att - 3029 H.T. 2 - 15

Sat 24 Sep 1955 WIDNES home won 12 - 10
CASTLEFORD - E.Ward: Smart Webster Sheridan TONY FRETWELL(383): Hague K.Pye: Horsfall Hill Haughey Howard F.Ward Birkin: Tries - Webster Birkin: Goals - E.Ward(3):
WIDNES - Sale: Williamson Kinsey Callighan Greenough: Butler Davies: Rowbottom Hayes Tomlinson Lamb Smith Simpson: Tries - Callighan Simpson: Goals - Sale(2):
Referee W Stockley (Leigh) Att - 3660 H.T. 7 - 10

Wed 28 Sep 1955 HALIFAX home lost 8 - 24
YORKSHIRE CUP SEMI-FINAL
CASTLEFORD - J.J.Pye: Smart Webster E.Ward Lunn: Oddy K.Pye: Horsfall Hill Norton Howard Anderson Birkin: Goals - Lunn(3) E.Ward:
HALIFAX - Griffiths: Daniels Lynch Palmer Bevan: Dean Kielty: Thorley Ackerley Wilkinson Henderson Schofield Fearnley:
Tries - Daniels Lynch Palmer Bevan Kielty Thorley: Goals - Griffiths(3):

SEASON 1955-56

Referee R Welsby (Warrington) Att - 8135 H.T. 6 - 8

Sat 1 Oct 1955 HALIFAX away lost 7 - 44
HALIFAX - Todd: Daniels Freeman Palmer Bevan: Dean
Kielty: Thorley Ackerley Henderson Schofield Pearce
Fearnley: Tries - Bevan(3) Freeman(2) Todd Daniels
Palmer Dean Schofield: Goals - Freeman(4) Dean(3):
CASTLEFORD - E.Ward: Smart Rhodes Lunn Burton: Oddy
K.Pye: Horsfall Hill Norton Howard Anderson Hughes:
Try - Lunn: Goals - E.Ward(2):
Referee T Armitage (Huddersfield) Att -   H.T. 7 - 26

Sat 8 Oct 1955 BATLEY home won 32 - 18
CASTLEFORD - J.J.Pye: Smart Webster Lunn Oddy: Hague
K.Pye: Horsfall Hill Norton Haughey F.Ward Birkin:
Tries - Smart(2) J.J.Pye Webster K.Pye Norton:
Goals - Lunn(7):
BATLEY - Bateson: Clark Fawcett Riley Field: Smith
Ackroyd: Palmer Westbury Jones Etty Jackson Naylor:
Tries - Clark Smith: Goals - Bateson(6):
Referee E Clay (Rothwell) Att - 2322 H.T. 9 - 13

**Sat 15 Oct 1955 BLACKPOOL BOROUGH home
won 32 - 7**
CASTLEFORD - E.Ward: Smart Webster Lunn Sheridan:
Hague K.Pye: Horsfall Hill Norton Haughey F.Ward Birkin:
Tries - Smart(3) Webster(2) E.Ward Lunn Sheridan:
Goals - E.Ward(4)
BLACKPOOL B - Bebe: Emmitt Ryder Peace McArthur:
Wilkinson Dunn: Wright Mundy Collier Armitt Fisher
Thornley: Try - Emmitt: Goals - McArthur(2):
Referee T E Rees (Oldham) Att - 2237 H.T. 14 - nil

**Sat 22 Oct 1955 BRADFORD NORTHERN away
lost 20 -34**
BRADFORD N. - Phillips: Smith Mageen Seddon McLean:
Jenkins Hamilton: Jones Mackie Radford Griffett Carter
Traill:
Tries - Seddon(2) Phillips Smith Mageen McLean Jenkins
Carter: Goals - Phillips(5):
CASTLEFORD - E.Ward: Anderson Webster Lunn Harold
Oddy: Hague K.Pye: Horsfall Hill Norton Howard F.Ward
Birkin: Tries - Webster Oddy K.Pye Birkin: Goals -
E.Ward(4):
Referee -   Att -   H.T. -

Sat 29 Oct 1955 DEWSBURY home lost 13 - 18
CASTLEFORD - E.Ward: BRIAN CASWELL(384) Webster
Lunn Staniland: Hague Grace: Howard Hill Norton F.Ward
Anderson Birkin: Try - Howard: Goals - E.Ward(4) Grace:
DEWSBURY - Bosworth: Pollard Cox Taylor Dickinson:
Popplewell Lea: Danter Waring Wilmot Dolan
Ormandroyd Withington:
Tries - Waring(2) Pollard Dickinson: Goals - Bosworth(3):
Referee R Gelder (Wakefield) Att - 2613 H.T. 4 - 10

Sat 5 Nov 1955 HULL away lost 11 - 44
HULL - Watkinson: Bowman Francis Turner Watts: Moat
Finn: Scott Holdstock Coverdale Markham W.Drake
Whiteley: Tries - Bowman(3) Moat(3) Francis(2) Watts

162

Markham: Goals - Watkinson(7):
CASTLEFORD - E.Ward: Smart Sheridan Lunn Staniland:
Hague K.Pye: Horsfall Hill Norton Howard Walter F.Ward:
Try - K.Pye: Goals - E.Ward(4):
Referee A Hill (Dewsbury) Att - 7000 H.T. 11 - 21

**Sat 12 Nov 1955 WORKINGTON TOWN away
lost 5 - 23**
WORKINGTON T - S.Thompson: Metherell Wookey
Gibson Marshall: Archer Ralph: Hayton Richardson Lymer
C.Thompson Edgar Herbert: Tries - Wookey(2) Gibson
C.Thompson Herbert: Goals - S.Thompson(4):
CASTLEFORD - E.Ward: Smart Sheridan Lunn Staniland:
Roy Hague K.Pye: Horsfall Hill Norton Howard F.Ward
Hughes:
Try - F.Ward: Goal - E.Ward:
Referee G S Phillips (Widnes) Att - 3797 H.T. nil - 7

Wed 16 Nov 1955 NEW ZEALAND lost 7 - 31
CASTLEFORD - E.Ward: Smart Webster Lunn Sheridan:
RAYMOND FEWSTER(385) K.Pye: Horsfall Hill Dennis
Norton Howard F.Ward Hughes: Try - Smart: Goals -
E.Ward(2):
NEW ZEALAND - R.L.Moore: V.Bakalich R.J.McKay
W.Sorenson L.J.McNicol: N.K.Roberts P.Creedy:
B.McLennan J.R.Butterfield M.D.Maxwell G.S.McDonald
R.W.Percy I.N.Grey: Tries - McKay(2) Percy(2) Bakalich
Sorenson McNicol: Goals - Moore(5):
Referee S Adams (Hull) Att - 2500 H.T. 2 - 16
**Dennis Norton Collapsed On The Field During The
Game, And Died Later In Hospital.**

**Sat 19 Nov 1955 BRADFORD NORTHERN home
lost 17 - 19**
CASTLEFORD - E.Ward: Webster Sheridan Lunn Smart:
Fewster K.Pye: Horsfall Hill Perrett Howard F.Ward Birkin:
Tries - Webster Sheridan F.Ward: Goals - E.Ward(4)
BRADFORD N - Phillips: Jenkins Haley Seddon McLean:
Sutton Oddy: Belshaw Mackey Hambling Jones Carter
Glyn:
Tries - Jenkins Haley McLean: Goals - Phillips(5):
Referee T Armitage (Huddersfield) Att – 3266 H.T. 12 -
12

Sat 26 Nov 1955 DEWSBURY away lost 3 - 12
DEWSBURY - Popplewell: G.Waring Thomas Todd Clark:
Ripley Lea: Danter M.Waring Shillito Dolan Jennings
Callighan: Tries - G.Waring Thomas: Goals - Clark(3):
CASTLEFORD - E.Ward: Smart Sheridan Lunn Staniland:
Fewster K.Pye: LEONARD OLSEN(386) Horsfall Perrett
Howard F.Ward Birkin: Try - F.Ward:
Referee J W Jowett (Leeds) Att - 3000 H.T. nil - 7

Sat 3 Dec 1955 YORK home won 25 - 19
CASTLEFORD - Rhodes: Smart Sheridan Lunn Staniland:
Fewster K.Pye: Horsfall Hill Olsen F.Ward Howard Birkin:
Tries - Sheridan Fewster Birkin: Goals - Lunn(8):
YORK - Hargreaves: Hamblett Parkin Robinson Smith:
Foster Riley: Moore Illingworth Priestley Watts Harlow
Deighton:

Tries - Hamblett(3) Smith Illingworth: Goals - Harlow(2):
Referee R Gelder (Wakefield) Att - 2551 H.T. 19 - 2

Sat 10 Dec 1955 WAKEFIELD TRINITY home lost 11 - 13
CASTLEFORD - E.Ward: Webster Sheridan Lunn Smart:
Fewster K.Pye: Perrett Hill Leonard Olsen Howard F.Ward
Birkin: Try - Webster: Goals - Lunn(4):
WAKEFIELD T - Mortimer: Smith Bell Holliday Cooper:
Lockwood Fletcher: Harrison Shaw Hague Kelly Jacques
Clifft: Tries - Bell Cooper Fletcher: Goals - Mortimer(2):
Referee G Wilson (Dewsbury) Att - 2331 H.T. 9 - 3

Mon 12 Dec 1955 RUGBY LEAGUE X111 - 15 NEW ZEALAND – 28 Specially Arranged Friendly Match For The DENNIS NORTON MEMORIAL FUND.
R.L.X111 - E.Ward(Castleford): Smart(Castleford)
Haggie(New Zealand Sheridan(Castleford)
Snowden(Hunslet): Fletcher(Wakefield
T.)K.Pye(Castleford): Hulme(Featherstone
R.)Fawley(Featherstone R.) Anderson(Leeds)
Lambert(Featherstone R.) F.Ward(Castleford)
H.Street(Leeds)
Tries - Fawley Lambert F.Ward: Goals - E.Ward(3):
NEW ZEALAND - Moore: Hawes Baxter Lynch McNicol:
Seddon Creedy: Bond Butterfield McLellan Kilkelly Riddell
Grey: Tries - McNicol(2) Hawes Baxter Lynch Creedy:
Goals - Moore(2) McLellan(2) Creedy:
Referee R Gelder (Wakefield) Att - 1000 H.T. 10 - 12

Sat 24 Dec 1955 DONCASTER home won 19 - 11
CASTLEFORD - E.Ward: Webster Sheridan Lunn Smart:
Winn Grace: Horsfall Hill Perrett F.Ward RAYMOND
BURTON(387) Birkin(S/O): Tries - E.Ward Sheridan Birkin:
Goals - Lunn(5)
DONCASTER - Hayter: Badger Winnard Ratcliffe Fairhurst:
Woolford Gunn: Tyler Doyle Bradley Baddeley Davies
Bowers: Try - Woolford: Goals - Winnard(4):
Referee C Whiteley (Ossett) Att - 2300 H.T. 10 - 4

Mon 26 Dec 1955 DONCASTER away lost 2 - 10
DONCASTER - Hayter: Fairhurst Ratcliffe Winnard Watson:
Woolford Gunn: Tyler Doyle Croft Baddeley Bradley
Bowers:
Tries - Fairhurst(2): Goals - Winnard(2):
CASTLEFORD - Ernest Ward: Smart Webster Lunn
Staniland: Winn Grace: Horsfall(S/O) Hill Perrett F.Ward
Howard Frank Birkin: Goal - Lunn:
Referee G Philpott (Leeds) Att - 1076 H.T. 2 - nil

Tue 27 Dec 1955 FEATHERSTONE ROVERS home won 18 - 9
CASTLEFORD - Rhodes: Webster Sheridan Lunn Smart:
Winn Grace: Simpson Hill RAYMOND RAYNOR(388)
Howard Anderson East: Tries - Smart(2) Winn East: Goals
- Lunn(3):
FEATHERSTONE R - Fennell: Elford Metcalfe Clamp
Tennant: Mullaney D.Fox: Welburn Fawley Berry
Barraclough Hulme Lambert: Try - Metcalfe: Goals -
Fennell(3):

Referee M Coates (Pudsey) Att - 5772 H.T. 15 - 6

Sat 31 Dec 1955 YORK away lost 13 - 36
YORK - Holmes Hamblett Parkin Robinson B.Smith:
Foster Riley: Moore Illingworth Harker Watts Dooler
Deighton:
Tries - Hamblett(3) Parkin Smith Foster Moore Harker:
Goals - Harker(6):
CASTLEFORD - Lunn: Webster Sheridan Burton Smart:
Fewster Grace: Simpson(S/O) Hill Raynor F.Ward East
Anderson: Tries - Smart(2) Burton: Goals - Lunn(2):
Referee E Clay (Rothwell) Att - 5858 H.T. nil - 22

Sat 7 Jan 1956 BLACKPOOL BOROUGH away lost 10 - 26
BLACKPOOL B - Hilton: Emmitt Wood Fearis Ryder:
Brennan Dunn: Wright Lester Collier Armitt Walsh
Lennon:
Tries - Emmitt(2) Wood Armitt: Goals - Hilton(6)Ryder:
CASTLEFORD - JACK BARNES(389): Webster Sheridan
Lunn Smart: Fewster K.Pye: Maurice Perrett Hill Raynor
Howard F.Ward East: Tries - Webster(2): Goals -
Lunn(2):
Referee G Wilson (Dewsbury) Att - 1512 H.T. 5 - 5

Sat 14 Jan 1956 BRAMLEY home lost 7 - 25
CASTLEFORD - Jackson Appleyard: Webster Sheridan
Lunn Smart: Winn K.Pye: Raynor John Hill FRED
RICHARDSON(390) Howard F.Ward Anderson:
Try - Webster: Goals - Lunn(2):
BRAMLEY - Wilson: Riley Dudley Garbutt Nepia: Armitage
Langfield: Smith Kennedy Young Hammill Sykes Baldwin:
Tries - Dudley(2) Garbutt(2) Riley:
Goals - Langfield(3) Wilson(2):
Referee S Abram (Wigan) Att - 1278 H.T. 7 - 17

Sat 21 Jan 1956 FEATHERSTONEROVERS away lost 8 - 23
FEATHERSTONE R - Fennell: Johnson Metcalfe Clamp
Marsden: Mullarey D.Fox: Welburn Bradshaw Hulme
Binks Lambert P.Fox: Tries - Metcalfe(2) D.Fox(2) Johnson:
Goals - Fennell(3) P.Fox:
CASTLEFORD - J J.Pye: Webster Sheridan Lunn Smart:
Fewster K.Pye: Simpson Boot Raynor Howard F.Ward
Anderson: Tries - Lunn Fewster: Goal - Lunn:
Referee J P Hebblethwaite (York) Att - 5000 H.T. 3 - 10

Sat 28 Jan 1956 KEIGHLEY away lost 9 - 35
KEIGHLEY - Black: Hollindrake Taylor Hallas Smith:
Verrenkamp Barron: Clarkson Traill Raines Murphy
Hopkin Holbrook: Tries - Smith(4) Hollindrake(2)
Hallas(2) Barron:
Goals - Hollindrake(2) Clarkson(2)
CASTLEFORD - Rhodes: Webster Sheridan Lunn Smart:
Fewster K.Pye: Simpson Horsfall Raynor East Howard
Colin Anderson: Tries - Webster Sheridan Howard:
Referee E Clay (Rothwell) Att - 3115 H.T. 6 - 19

Sat 11 Feb 1956 BLACKPOOL BOROUGH home won 12 -9 CHALLENGE CUP ROUND 1

SEASON 1955-56

CASTLEFORD - Rhodes: Smart Webster Lunn Staniland: Fewster K.Pye: Peter Simpson Boot Horsfall Howard Richardson F.Ward: Tries - Smart(2): Goals - Lunn(3): BLACKPOOL B - Hilton: Emmitt Fearis Wood Ryder: Brennan Dunn: Wright Mundy Collier Armitt Walsh Lannon:
Try - Mundy: Goals - Hilton(3):
Referee T W Watkinson(Manchester) Att - 2600 H.T. 5 - 5

Sat 18 Feb 1956 LEEDS away lost 7 - 17
LEEDS - Dunn: Turnbull McLennan Lendil Broughton: Brown Stevenson: Anderson Wood Hopper Robinson Poole Street:
Tries - Turnbull McLennan Broughton:
Goals - Dunn(3) Brown:
CASTLEFORD - Rhodes: Smart Webster Lunn J.J.Pye: Fewster K.Pye: Horsfall Boot Richardson Howard Walter F.Ward:
Try - Richardson: Goals - Lunn(2):
Referee A E Durkin (Dewsbury) Att - 10000 H.T. 7 - 7

Sat 25 Feb 1956 KEIGHLEY home lost 3 - 13
CASTLEFORD - Rhodes: Smart Webster Lunn Staniland: Fewster K.Pye: Horsfall Boot Richardson Howard JACK WOOLLEY(391) F.Ward: Try - K.Pye:
KEIGHLEY - Frain: Hollindrake Taylor Hallas Smith: Verrenkamp Barron: Clarkson Traill Hopkins Murphy James Holbrook: Tries - Hallas(2) Smith: Goals - Clarkson(2):
Referee G Philpott (Leeds) Att - 2590 H.T. nil - 6

Sat 3 Mar 1956 ST HELENS away lost 5 - 48
CHALLENGE CUP ROUND 2
ST HELENS - Moses: Llewellyn Greenall Senior Carlton: Dickinson Rhodes: Prescott McCabe Terry Parsons Silcock Karalius: Tries - Llewellyn(6) Carlton(2) Dickinson(2) Rhodes McCabe: Goals - Rhodes(6):
CASTLEFORD - Rhodes: Smart Webster Lunn Arthur Staniland: Fewster K.Pye: Horsfall Boot Fred Richardson Howard Jack Woolley F.Ward: Try - Webster:
Goal - Lunn:
Referee H Harrison (Ossett) Att - 15500 H.T. nil - 23

Sat 10 Mar 1956 BRAMLEY away lost 10 - 31
BRAMLEY - Wilson: Riley Dudley Garbutt Kelly: Rushton Langfield: Smith Heath Young Sykes Hammill Baldwin: Tries - Riley Dudley Garbutt Rushton Sykes:
Goals - Wilson(8):
CASTLEFORD - Rhodes: Smart Webster Sheridan Lunn: Fewster Grace: Horsfall Boot Raymond Raynor Walter Howard F.Ward: Tries - Smart Webster: Goals - Lunn(2):
Referee T Armitage(Huddersfield) Att - 2557 H.T. 10 - 18

Sat 17 Mar 1956 HUDDERSFIELD home lost 5 - 41
CASTLEFORD - Rhodes: Burton Webster Sheridan Lunn: Fewster K.Pye: Horsfall Boot RONALD BICKERDYKE(392) Howard RONALD BRADLEY(393) F.Ward:
Try - Horsfall: Goal - Lunn:

HUDDERSFIELD - Dyson: Henderson Barrow Ramsden Sullivan: Banks Smales: Slevin Bradshaw Fairbank Briggs Large Valentine: Tries - Barrow(2) Sullivan(2) Dyson Henderson Bradshaw Fairbank Large: Goals - Dyson(7):
Referee G Scott (Wakefield) Att - 3327 H.T. nil - 23

Sat 24 Mar 1956 HULL home lost 7 - 12
CASTLEFORD - Sheridan: Smart Webster Lunn Burton: Fewster K.Pye: Horsfall Boot ROWLAND BERRY(394) Howard Ronald Bradley Hughes: Try - Smart: Goals - Lunn(2):
HULL - Hutton: Cowan Turner Cooper Bowman: Moat Finn: Scott Harris Coverdale Drake Markham Whiteley: Tries - Cowan Bowman Drake Markham:
Referee J H Chadwick (Batley) Att - 1206 H.T. 7 - 12

Sat 31 Mar 1956 HULL KINGSTON ROVERS home won 32 - 12
CASTLEFORD - Rhodes: Smart Webster Lunn Burton: Fewster K.Pye: Horsfall ANTHONY CLOUGH(395) Berry Howard HARRY WILLIAMS(396) F.Ward: Tries - Smart(3) Webster(3) Burton Ward: Goals - Lunn(2)Williams(2):
HULL K R - Buckle: Goulder Thornton Hancock Garry: Parker Marsden: Grice Brookfield Croft Burton Walters Smith:
Tries - Goulder(2): Goals - Buckle(3):
Referee J Manley (Warrington) Att - 1645 H.T.

Mon 2 Apr 1956 LEEDS home won 26 - 15
CASTLEFORD - Rhodes: Smart Webster Lunn Burton: Fewster K.Pye: Horsfall Boot Berry Howard F.Ward Hughes:
Tries - Burton(2) Smart Webster Pye Ward: Goals - Lunn(4):
LEEDS - Lendill: Hodgkinson Brown Wilkinson Scholes: Stevenson Pratt: Anderson Wood Tomlinson Robinson Sewell Street: Tries - Scholes Robinson - plus 1 try: Goals - Lendill(3)
Referee C Whiteley (Ossett) Att - 5759 H.T. 11 - 7

Tue 3 Apr 1956 BATLEY away won 16 - 6
BATLEY - Walshaw: Clark Riley Gardener Field: Ackroyd P.Bates: Palmer Battersby Westbury Bates Wright Briggs: Tries - Clark Field:
CASTLEFORD - Rhodes: Smart Webster Lunn Burton: Sheridan K.Pye: Horsfall Boot Berry Williams F.Ward Hughes:
Tries - Burton(2) Smart Webster: Goals - Lunn(2):
Referee - Att - 2750 H.T. 13 - nil

Sat 7 Apr 1956 HUNSLET away lost 15 - 18
HUNSLET - Evans: Snowden Byrom Sutcliffe Potter: Gabbitas Moore: Hadfield Smith Shaw Poole Gunney James:
Tries - James Gunney: Goals - Gunney(4) Evans(2):
CASTLEFORD - Rhodes: Smart Webster Lunn Burton: Fewster K.Pye: Horsfall Boot Howard F.F.Ward Williams Hughes:
Tries - Webster(3): Goals - Lunn(3):
Referee J Flanagan (Keighley) Att - 3500 H.T. 5 – 4

John Sheridan
D. No 382
1955-56 to 1965-66

Raymond Fewster
D. No 385
1955-56 to 1956-57

Jack Barnes
D. No 389
1955-56 to 1964-65

Rowland Berry
D. No 394
1955-56 to 1957-58

Harry Williams
D. No 396
1955-56 to 1957-58

SEASON 1955-56

D.N	PLAYER		DEBUT	L MATCH	APP	SUB	T.AP	TRI'S	G'LS	D.G	P'TS
239	HILL	JOHN		14/01/1956	27	0	27	0	0	0	0
302	HOWARD	GEORGE (CHARLIE)			35	0	35	4	0	0	12
323	HAUGHEY	LESLIE			12	0	12	0	0	0	0
324	ANDERSON	COLIN		28/01/1956	16	0	16	1	0	0	3
326	WALTER	RONALD			3	0	3	0	0	0	0
330	PYE	KENNETH			35	0	35	5	0	0	15
334	WELSBY	HAROLD		22/08/1955	2	0	2	0	0	0	0
340	HUGHES	DAVID			7	0	7	0	0	0	0
341	LUNN	ALBERT			41	0	41	5	65	0	145
342	PYE	JOSHUA J.			9	0	9	1	0	0	3
343	SIMPSON	PETER		11/02/1956	5	0	5	0	0	0	0
344	HAGUE	ROY		12/11/1955	16	0	16	0	0	0	0
346	ODDY	HAROLD		22/10/1955	9	0	9	2	0	0	6
347	STANILAND	ARTHUR		03/03/1956	10	0	10	0	0	0	0
349	WARD	FRED			35	0	35	9	0	0	27
352	WEBSTER	DENZIL			30	0	30	23	0	0	69
354	APPLEYARD	JACKSON		14/01/1956	1	0	1	0	0	0	0
355	GRACE	ARNOLD			7	0	7	0	1	0	2
356	PERRETT	MAURICE		07/01/1956	7	0	7	0	0	0	0
364	SMART	DEREK			38	0	38	26	0	0	78
366	WARD	ERNEST		26/12/1955	22	0	22	4	46	0	104
371	EAST	FRANK			4	0	4	1	0	0	3
372	BOOT	JACK			12	0	12	0	0	0	0
375	RHODES	EDWARD			15	0	15	0	0	0	0
377	HORSFALL	ALAN			33	0	33	1	0	0	3
378	BIRKIN	FRANK		26/12/1955	16	0	16	4	0	0	12
379	WINN	JOHN			4	0	4	1	0	0	3
380	BURTON	CLIFFORD			8	0	8	6	0	0	18
381	NORTON	DENNIS		16/11/1955	10	0	10	1	0	0	3
382	SHERIDAN	JOHN	20/08/1955		26	0	26	7	0	0	21
383	FRETWELL	TONY	24/09/1955	24/09/1955	1	0	1	0	0	0	0
384	CASWELL	BRIAN	29/10/1955	29/10/1955	1	0	1	0	0	0	0
385	FEWSTER	RAYMOND	16/11/1955		19	0	19	2	0	0	6
386	OLSON	LEN	26/11/1955	10/12/1955	3	0	3	0	0	0	0
387	BURTON	RAYMOND	24/12/1955	24/12/1955	1	0	1	0	0	0	0
388	RAYNOR	RAYMOND	27/12/1955	10/03/1956	7	0	7	0	0	0	0
389	BARNES	JACK	07/01/1956		1	0	1	0	0	0	0
390	RICHARDSON	FRED	14/01/1956	03/03/1956	5	0	5	1	0	0	3
391	WOOLLEY	JACK	25/02/1956	03/03/1956	2	0	2	0	0	0	0
392	BICKERDYKE	RONALD	17/03/1956		1	0	1	0	0	0	0
393	BRADLEY	RONALD	17/03/1956	24/03/1956	2	0	2	0	0	0	0
394	BERRY	ROWLAND	24/03/1956		4	0	4	0	0	0	0
395	CLOUGH	ANTHONY	31/03/1956		1	0	1	0	0	0	0
396	WILLIAMS	HARRY	31/03/1956		3	0	3	0	2	0	4
	44		15	20	546	0	546	104	114	0	540

COMPETITION		P	W	D	L	FOR	AGT
LEAGUE	POSITION 27 OF 30	36	9	0	27	462	751
YORK'S CUP		3	2	0	1	54	32
RL CUP		2	1	0	1	17	57
NEW ZEALAND		1	0	0	1	7	31
PLAYERS RECORDS		42	12	0	30	540	871

In the League with the Manchester based club Belle Vue Rangers dropping out before the start of the season the League was reduced to 30 teams, and the final positions were decided on a percentage basis.

The first game of the season saw the debut of a young centre John Sheridan, who went on to play 300 games for the club at centre, loose forward and prop, he also captained the team before coaching both 'A' Team and First Team.

In light of the team's overall performance Derek Smart finished with a very creditable 26 tries from 38 appearances.

SEASON 1956-57

Sat 11 Aug 1956 WAKEFIELD TRINITY home lost 6 - 36 CHARITY MATCH FRIENDLY
CASTLEFORD - Lunn: Smart Webster Sheridan Hindley: Fewster K.Pye: Perrett Boot Haughey Howard Richardson Hughes: Goals - Lunn(3):
WAKEFIELD T - Mortimer: Smith Bell Froggett Cooper: Holliday Rollin: Harrson Shaw Lindley Kelly Armstead Clifft: Tries - Smith(3) Holliday(3) Froggett Rollin: Goals - Mortimer(6):
Referee R Gelder (Wakefield) Att - 2150 H.T.

Sat 18 Aug 1956 HUDDERSFIELD away lost 6 - 24
HUDDERSFIELD - Dyson: Hendeson Barrow Sullivan Waihwright: Barrett Smales: Slevin Bradshaw Griffin Briggs Large Bowman:
Tries - Sullivan(2) Wainwright Large: Goals - Dyson(6):
CASTLEFORD - Lunn: Smart Webster Sheridan Burton: Fewster K.Pye: Haughey Clough Howard FRED BARRETT(397) Ward Hughes: Tries - Sheridan Fewster:
Referee A Howgate (Dewsbury) Att - 2274 H.T. 6 - 15

Wed 22 Aug 1956 BLACKPOOL BOROUGH home lost 12 - 30
CASTLEFORD - Lunn: KENNETH HINDLEY(398) Webster Barnes Burton: Fewster K.Pye: DESMOND CLARKSON(399) Clough Horsfall Fred Barrett Williams Ward:
Tries - Webster Fewster: Goals - Clarkson(3):
BLACKPOOL B - Hilton: Emmitt Ryder Fearis McArthur: Dunn Brennan: Collier Mundy Wright Armitt Walsh Duffy:
Tries - Emmitt(2) McArthur(2) Ryder Fearis Dunn Duffy: Goals - Hilton(3):
Referee J W Jackson (Barrow) Att - 3142 H.T. 7 - 6

Sat 25 Aug 1956 YORK home lost 10 - 18
CASTLEFORD - Rhodes: Hindley Webster Lunn Burton: Fewster Arnold Grace: Horsfall Boot Berry Haughey Williams K.Pye: Tries - Webster Burton: Goals - Lunn(2):
YORK - Hargreaves: Hamblett Robinson Holmes B.Smith: Flannery Riley: Moore Illingworth Yorke Watts Dooler E.Dawson: Tries - Illingworth Watts: Goals - Yorke(6):
Referee E Clay (Rothwell) Att - 1883 H.T. nil - 2

Mon 27 Aug 1956 HULL away lost 6 - 39
HULL - Watkinson: Darlington Cooper Turner Watts: Moat Tripp: Hopkins Harris Coverdale J.Drake W.Drake Whiteley: Tries - Watts(2) Moat(2) Darlington Cooper Turner Tripp Whiteley: Goals - W.Drake(6):
CASTLEFORD - Rhodes: JAMES HUNT(400) Webster Lunn Burton: Fewster Winn: Horsfall Boot Berry Leslie Haughey Williams K.Pye: Goals - Lunn(3):
Referee A E Durkin (Dewsbury) Att - 8000 H.T. 4 - 23

Sat 1 Sep 1956 BRADFORD NORTHERN home won 23 - 17 YORKSHIRE CUP ROUND 1
CASTLEFORD - Rhodes: Hindley Webster Lunn Burton: Fewster Winn: Horsfall Boot Berry Howard Ward K.Pye: Tries - Webster(2) Lunn Burton Ward: Goals - Lunn(4):
BRADFORD N - Jenkins: Todd Sutton Seddon M.Davies: D.Davies Lee: Jones Mackie Radford Griffett Scroby Glynn: Tries - M.Davies(4) Seddon: Goal - Seddon:

Referee J C Clapham (Wigan) Att - 3037 H.T. 8 - 9

Mon 3 Sep 1956 ROCHDALE HORNETS home lost 15 - 29
CASTLEFORD - Rhodes: JOHN CROSSLEY(401) Webster Lunn Burton: Fewster Winn: Howard Clough Bickerdyke Ward Williams K.Pye: Try - Pye: Goals - Lunn(6):
ROCHDALE H - Cahill: Short Jones Smith Chisnall: Birchall Evans: Gallagher Gill Hanson Kelly Tierney Horrocks: Tries - Chisnall(2) Evans(2) Hanson: Goals - Jones(7):
Referee R Welsby (Warrington) Att - 2628 H.T. 4 - 15

Sat 8 Sep 1956 SALFORD away lost 15 - 22
SALFORD - Smith: Walker Cheshire Hanley Dodd: Gregory Keavney: Lomas Hemmings Alder Duffy Fieldhouse Parr: Tries - Dodd Keavney Lomas Parr: Goals - Smith(5):
CASTLEFORD - Rhodes: Crossley Webster Lunn Burton: Hindley Winn: Horsfall Boot Ronald Bickerdyke Williams Ward K.Pye:
Tries - Webster Horsfall Ward: Goals - Lunn(3):
Referee E Clay (Rothwell) Att - 4498 H.T. 2 - 12

Tue 11 Sep 1956 HUNSLET home lost 9 - 26 YORKSHIRE CUP ROUND 2
CASTLEFORD - Rhodes: Crossley Webster Lunn Burton: Hindley Winn: Horsfall Boot Ward Williams Hughes K.Pye: Try - Webster: Goals - Lunn(3):
HUNSLET - Talbot: Snowden Stockdill Langton Preece: Gabbitas Burne l: Hatfield Smith Shaw Poole Clues Gunney: Tries - Snowden(2) Stockdill Langton Burnell Shaw: Goals - Talbot(4):
Referee C F Appleton (Warr'ton) Att - 4839 H.T. 5 - 13

Sat 15 Sep 1956 FEATHERSTONE ROVERS home lost 9 - 30
CASTLEFORD - Edward Rhodes: East Burton Lunn John Crossley: Hindley John Winn: RONALD GUTHRIE(402) Boot Walter Wi liams Ward K.Pye:
Try - Burton: Goals - Lunn(3):
FEATHERSTONE R - Fennell: Scholes Metcalfe Woolford Clamp: Hirst D.Fox: Kirk W.Ward Fearnley Hockley Barraclough Lambert: Tries - Fennell(2) Clamp(2) Scholes Hirst: Goals - Fennell(6):
Referee R Gelder (Wakefield) Att - 5452 H.T. 5 - 15

Sat 22 Sep 1956 YORK away lost 9 - 30
YORK - Hargreaves: Hamblett Parkin G.Smith B.Smith: Flannery Riley: Moore Illingworth Yorke Deighton Dooler Dawson: Tries - Hamblett B.Smith Moore Illingworth: Goals - Yorke(9):
CASTLEFORD - J.J.Pye: East Burton Lunn Fewster: Hindley KEITH HARRISON(403): Guthrie Boot Walter Williams Ward K.Pye: Try - Ward: Goals - Lunn(3):
Referee A E Du kin (Dewsbury) Att – 5852 H.T. 4 - 13

Sat 29 Sep 1956 HUDDERSFIELD home lost 17 - 32
CASTLEFORD - J.J.Pye: Burton Webster Lunn Fewster: Hindley RONALD EVANS(404): Ronald Guthrie Boot ARTHUR WILMOT(405) Williams Anthony Clough Hughes: Try - Lunn: Goals - Lunn(7):

SEASON 1956-57

HUDDERSFIELD - Dyson: Henderson Hunter Sullivan Barrow: Ramsden Smales: Slevin Bradshaw Bowden Briggs Large Bowman: Tries - Barrow(3) Briggs(2) Henderson Sullivan Large: Goals - Dyson(4):
Referee J H Chadwick (Batley) Att - 3358 H.T. 8 - 16

Sat 6 Oct 1956 ROCHDALE HORNETS away lost 4 - 11
ROCHDALE H - Cahill: Short Jones Smith Ralph: Chisnall Evans: Livesey Bowden Hanson Kelly Tierney Horrocks: scorers not known
CASTLEFORD - J.J.Pye: East Denzil Webster Lunn COLIN TAYLOR(406): Fewster Evans: Wilmot Boot Howard Williams Ward K.Pye: Goals - Lunn(2):
Referee C Whiteley (Ossett) Att - 4581 H.T. 4 - 6

Sat 13 Oct 1956 KEIGHLEY home lost 8 - 17
CASTLEFORD - Joshua J.Pye: East Lunn Burton Taylor: Hindley Evans: Wilmot Boot Horsfall Howard Ward Pye: Tries - Burton Horsfall: Goal - Lunn:
KEIGHLEY - Frain: Hollindrake Taylor Hallas Jackson: Verrenkamp Brown: Marston Harden Bardgett Murphy Lowe Hopkins:
Tries - Hollindrake(2) Hallas: Goals - Hollindrake(4):
Referee M Coates (Pudsey) Att - 2000 H.T. 6 - 5

Sat 20 Oct 1956 LIVERPOOL CITY away won 18 - 3
LIVERPOOL C - Wood: Barton Hunt Boycott Walsh: Brown Parkes: Pearson Fishwick Thornett Hockenhull Teggin Rigby: Try - Barton:
CASTLEFORD - Lunn: East Sheridan Burton TERENCE SMITH(407): Fewster Evans: Wilmot Boot Berry Howard Ward Pye:
Tries - East Ward Pye Burton: Goals - Lunn(3):
Referee H Harrison (Ossett) Att - 991 H.T. 8 - nil

Sat 27 Oct 1956 WIDNES home lost 11 - 18
CASTLEFORD - Lunn: East Burton Sheridan Smith: Fewster Evans: Wilmot Boot Berry Howard Ward Pye:
Try - Smith: Goals - Lunn(4):
WIDNES - Parker: Ratcliffe Thompson Dawson Owen: Myler Butler: Smith Hayes Tomlinson Simpson Lamb Tobin: Tries - Ratcliffe Butler Tomlinson Tobin: Goals - Dawson(3):
Referee C F Appleton (Widnes) Att - 2224 H.T. 9 - 5

Sat 3 Nov 1956 WIDNES away lost 2 - 12
WIDNES - Prescott: Williamson Kinsey Dawson Owen: Myler Butler: Smith Hayes Tomlinson Simpson Lamb Tobin: Tries - Owen Myler: Goals - Dawson(3):
CASTLEFORD - Barnes: East Lunn Sheridan Terence Smith: Fewster Evans: Wilmot WILLIAM FLANAGAN(408) Berry Howard Ward Pye: Goal - Lunn:
Referee G Scott (Wakefield) Att - 2767 H.T. nil - 9

Sat 10 Nov 1956 LIVERPOOL CITY home won 22 - 14
CASTLEFORD - Barnes: Fewster Sheridan Lunn Hunt: Hindley Evans: Wilmot Flanagan Berry Howard Ward Pye: Tries - Fewster(2) Sheridan Pye: Goals - Barnes(4) Lunn:

LIVERPOOL C - Wood: Barton Boycott Ashby Whyment: Hunt Kelly: Skelhorn Cartledge Pearson Bamber Hockenhull Davies:
Tries - Barton Boycott: Goals - Wood(4):
Referee D T H Davies (Pendlebury) Att - 1149 H.T. 12 - 9

Sat 17 Nov 1956 DONCASTER home won 26 - 15
CASTLEFORD - Barnes: Fewster Sheridan Burton East: Hindley Evans: Wilmot Flanagan Berry Howard Ward Pye: Tries - East(2) Hindley(2) Flanagan Howard:
Goals - Barnes(4):
DONCASTER - Gunn: Fairhurst Wrigglesworth Wilkinson Cranswick: Northern Pycroft: Jukes Larkin Binnersley Winnard Watson Matthews: Tries - Fairhurst Wrigglesworth Cranswick: Goals - Winnard(3):
Referee G Wilson (Dewsbury) Att - 1500 H.T. 15 - 12

Sat 24 Nov 1956 BRADFORD NORTHERN away lost 14 - 24
BRADFORD N - Seddon: Rodwell Winnard Smith Davies: Haley Lancaster: Belshaw Hanley Carter Jones Radford Scroby:
Tries - Davies(3) Jones(2) Scroby: Goals - Seddon(3):
CASTLEFORD - Barnes: East Sheridan Burton Fewster: Hindley Evans: Wilmot Flanagan Berry Howard DERRICK SCHOFIELD(409) Pye:
Tries - East Schofield: Goals - Barnes(3) Schofield:
Referee J H Chadwick (Batley) Att - 3747 H.T. 9 - 7

Sat 1 Dec 1956 DONCASTER away won 14 - 5
DONCASTER - Hayter: Reyner Wrigglesworth Wilkinson Cranswick: Northern Pollard: Jukes Freeman Baddeley Taylor Winnard Matthews:
Try - Cranswick: Goal - Winnard:
CASTLEFORD - Barnes: East Sheridan Burton Fewster: Hindley Evans: Berry Flanagan Howard Schofield Ward Pye: Tries - East Sheridan: Goals - Barnes(4):
Referee J Manley (Warrington) Att - 700 H.T. 4 - 2

Sat 8 Dec 1956 HULL home lost 12 - 33
CASTLEFORD - Barnes: East Sheridan Burton Raymond Fewster: Hindley Evans: Berry Flanagan Howard Schofield Ward Pye: Tries - East Fewster: Goals - Barnes(3):
HULL - Hutton: Gittoes Turner Cowan Watts: Moat Finn: Scott Harris J.Drake Markham W.Drake Whiteley:
Tries - W.Drake(2) Whiteley(2) Watts Markham Moat: Goals - Hutton(6):
Referee J C Clapham (Wigan) Att - 2675 H.T. 4 - 10

Sat 15 Dec 1956 HULL KINGSTON ROVERS away lost 5 - 21
HULL K R - Buckle: Garry Hancock B.Coulson Shaw: Key G.Coulson: Pickersgill Tong Evans Croft Hall Harper: Tries - Garry B.Coulson Shaw: Goals - Buckle(6):
CASTLEFORD - Barnes: East Sheridan Burton EDWARD BRYANT(410): Hindley Evans: Wilmot Flanagan Berry Howard Ward Schofield:
Try - East: Goal - Barnes:
Referee R Welsby (Warrington) Att – 2090 H.T. 3 - 14

SEASON 1956-57

Tue 25 Dec 1956 WAKEFIELD TRINITY home draw 14 - 14
CASTLEFORD - Barnes: East Sheridan Burton Bryant: Hindley Evans: Wilmot Flanagan Thornley Howard Schofield Pye: Tries - East Pye: Goals - Barnes(4):
WAKEFIELD T - Lockwood: Smith N.Fox Holliday Houlden: Rollin Bullock: Harrison Bridges Haigh Kelly Armstead Lamming: Tries - Lockwood Smith: Goals - Fox(4):
Referee E Clay (Rothwell) Att - 2559 H.T. 7 - 7

Wed 26 Dec 1956 FEATHERSTONE ROVERS away lost 5 - 31
FEATHERSTONE R - Fennell: Scholes Metcalfe Woolford Clamp: Mullaney D.Fox: Welburn Fawley Kirk Hockley Fearnley Lambert: Tries - Clamp(2) Fennell Metcalfe Woolford Fearnley Lambert: Goals - Fennell(5):
CASTLEFORD - Barnes: East Sheridan Burton Bryant: Hindley Evans: Wilmot Flanagan Howard Schofield Ward Pye: Try - East: Goal - Barnes:
Referee R L Thomas (Oldham) Att - 2400 H.T. 5 - 15

Sat 29 Dec 1956 HUNSLET away lost 6 - 10
HUNSLET - Langton: Snowden Stockdill Sutcliffe Child: Gabbitas Tate: Hatfield Smith Shaw Poole Gunney Watts: Tries - Tate Gunney: Goals - Langton(2):
CASTLEFORD - Barnes: East Lunn Burton Bryant: Hindley Evans: Wilmot Flanagan Thornley Schofield Howard Ward: Tries - Lunn Ward:
Referee A Howgate (Dewsbury) Att - 5000 H.T. nil - 5

Sat 5 Jan 1957 BATLEY away lost 12 - 16
BATLEY - Walshaw: O'Hara Gardner Field Smith: Riley Halloran: Palmer Battersby Etty Westbury Binks Naylor: Tries - Smith(2) O'Hara Field: Goals - Walshaw(2):
CASTLEFORD - Barnes: East Lunn Burton Bryant: Hindley Evans: Wilmot Flanagan Thornley Schofield Howard Ward: Tries - Evans Schofield: Goals - Barnes(3):
Referee J W Jackson (Barrow) Att - 2300 H.T. nil - 14

Sat 12 Jan 1957 BRADFORD NORTHERN home won 13 - nil
CASTLEFORD - Lunn: East Sheridan Burton Bryant: Hindley Evans: Berry Flanagan Thornley Schofield Howard Ward: Try - East: Goals - Lunn(5):
BRADFORD N - Seddon: Rodwell Winnard Smith Jenkins: Hayley Lancaster: Carter Hanley Hambling Radford Jones Scroby:
Referee J Manley (Warrington) Att - 2600 H.T. 4 - nil

Sat 19 Jan 1957 WAKEFIELD TRINITY away lost 13 - 39
WAKEFIELD T - Lockwood: Smith Fox Bell Cooper: Houlden Rollin: : Harrison Shaw Lumb Kelly Firth Armstead:
Tries - Bell(2) Cooper(2) Smith Fox Rollin Harrison Firth: Goals - Fox(6):
CASTLEFORD - Lunn: East Sheridan Burton SIDNEY GREATBATCH(411): Hindley Evans: Berry Flanagan Thornley Schofield Ward Pye:
Tries - Pye(2) Burton: Goals - Lunn(2):
Referee J W Jowett (Leeds) Att - 3134 H.T. 10 - 16

Sat 26 Jan 1957 BATLEY home won 19 - 14
CASTLEFORD - Barnes: East Sheridan Lunn Burton: BARRY WALSH(412) Evans: Berry Flanagan Thornley Schofield Howard Pye:
Tries - Walsh Schofield Evans: Goals - Lunn(5):
BATLEY - Fox: Clark Gardner Ireland O'Hara: Halloran Ross: Palmer Battersby Etty Cawthra Naylor Briggs:
Tries - O'Hara Briggs: Goals - Fox(4):
Referee G Scott (Wakefield) Att - 1760 H.T. 9 - 9

Sat 2 Feb 1957 BLACKPOOL BOROUGH away lost 7 - 18
BLACKPOOL B - Dutton: Emmitt Sowden Fearis Morgan: Brennan McGrath: Wright Lester Fisher Grundy Walsh Thornley:
Tries - Emmitt Fearis Walsh Thornley: Goals - McGrath(3):
CASTLEFORD - Lunn: East CHARLES NAYLOR(413) GEOFFREY G.WARD(414) Burton: Walsh Evans: Berry Flanagan Thorney Schofield Howard Pye:
Try - Pye: Goals - Lunn(2):
Referee A Howgate (Dewsbury) Att - 1073 H.T. 2 - 12

Sat 9 Feb 1957 DONCASTER away won 15 - 5 CHALLENGE CUP ROUND 1
DONCASTER - Winnard: Williamson Wrigglesworth Wilkinson Altass: Northern Pollard: Jukes Larkin Davies Baddeley Field Bowers: Try - Field: Goal - Winnard:
CASTLEFORD - Barnes: East Sheridan Lunn G.G.Ward: Walsh Evans: Berry Flanagan Howard Schofield F.Ward Pye: Tries - Sheridan(3): Goals - Lunn(3):
Referee D T H Davies (Manchester) Att - 1800 H.T. 5 - 5

Sat 16 Feb 1957 HUNSLET home lost 7 - 27
CASTLEFORD - Barnes: East Sheridan Lunn G.G.Ward: Walsh Evans: Berry Flanagan Howard Schofield F.Ward Pye: Try - Walsh: Goals - Lunn(2):
HUNSLET - Langton: Snowden Stockdill Sutcliffe Preece: Gabbitas Burnell: Hatfield Kelly Shaw Gunney Clues Waite: Tries - Snowden(3) Preece(2) Stockdill Waite: Goals - Stockdill(2) Gunney:
Referee C H Harrison (Horbury) Att - 4969 H.T. 7 - 17

Sat 23 Feb 1957 BARROW home lost 2 - 9 CHALLENGE CUP ROUND 2
CASTLEFORD - Lunn: East Sheridan Burton G.G.Ward: Walsh Evans: Berry Flanagan Thornley Schofield Howard F.Ward: Goal - Lunn:
BARROW - Ball: Lewthwaite Jackson Rea Castle: Horne Harris: Woosey Redhead Barton Wilson Goodwin Grundy: Try - Grundy: Goals - Ball(3):
Referee T W Watkinson (Man'ster) Att - 2725 H.T. nil - 2

Wed 27 Feb 1957 LEEDS away lost 9 - 24
LEEDS - Quinn: Hodgkinson McLellan Jones Broughton: Lendill Stevenson: Anderson Prior Hopper Poole Robinson Street: Tries - Jones Broughton Lendill Prior: Goals - Jones(4 Quinn(2):
CASTLEFORD - Lunn: East Sheridan Burton G.G.Ward: Walsh Evans: Berry Flanagan Thornley Howard F.Ward Pye: Tries - East Walsh Pye:

SEASON 1956-57

Referee H Squires (Ossett) Att - 5842 H.T. 3 - 14

Sat 2 Mar 1957 SALFORD home draw 9 - 9
CASTLEFORD - Lunn: East Sheridan Burton G.G.Ward:
Walsh Evans: Wilmot Flanagan Thornley Schofield
Howard F.Ward:
Try - East: Goals - Lunn(3):
SALFORD - Smith: Baines Walker Cheshire Gregory: Jones
Keavney: Ayles Dutton Alder Council Duffy Parr:
Try - Baines: Goals - Smith(3);
Referee R Welsby (Warrington) Att - 2700 H.T. 7 - 4

Sat 9 Mar 1957 DEWSBURY home won 46 - 13
CASTLEFORD - Lunn: East Sheridan G.G.Ward Burton:
Walsh Evans: Berry Flanagan Pye Thornley Schofield
F.Ward:
Tries - East(4) G.G.Ward(2) Burton Walsh Evans Lunn:
Goals - Lunn(8):
DEWSBURY - Cox: Grainger Wilson Pollard Clark: Brown
O'Donnell: Pickersgill Waring Smith Farrar Farnell Carroll:
Tries - O'Donnell(2) Clark: Goals - Cox(2):
Referee J Flanagan (Keighley) Att – 2677 H.T. 20 - 10

**Sat 23 Mar 1957 HULL KINGSTON ROVERS home
won 15 - 11**
CASTLEFORD - Lunn: East(S/O) Sheridan G.G.Ward
Burton: Walsh Evans: Berry William Flanagan Pye Thornley
Schofield F.Ward:
Try - Sheridan: Goals - Lunn(6):
HULL K R - Ellerby: Garry Fishwick B.Coulson Stark: Beck
G.Coulson: Grice Brookfield Hall Matthews Harper
Bedford:
Try - Fishwick: Goals - Beck(4):
Referee H Squires (Ossett) Att - 2606 H.T. 9 - 4

Sat 30 Mar 1957 DEWSBURY away won 22 - 5
DEWSBURY - Cox: Grainger Wilson Taylor Pollard:
Harding O'Donnell: Pickering Waring Smith Barnford
Withington Carroll:
Try - Carroll: Goal - Harding:
CASTLEFORD - Lunn: East Sheridan G.G.Ward Naylor:
Walsh Evans: Berry Boot Pye Schofield Howard F.Ward:
Tries - East G.G.Ward Howard F.Ward: Goals - Lunn(5):
Referee J Flanagan (Keighley) Att - 1020 H.T. 10 - nil

Sat 6 Apr 1957 BRAMLEY home won 17 - 10
CASTLEFORD - Lunn: Burton Sheridan G.G.Ward Naylor:
Walsh Evans: Berry Boot Pye Thornley Schofield F.Ward:
Tries - Sheridan Naylor F.Ward: Goals - Lunn(4):
BRAMLEY - Dudley: Noble Kelly Rushton Humphreys:
Armitage Langfield: Smith Heath Young Baldwin Hammill
Garbutt:
Tries - Rushton Humphreys: Goals - Langfield(2):
Referee C Harrison (Ossett) Att - 2927 H.T. 7 - 7

Sat 20 Apr 1957 BRAMLEY away lost 12 - 33
BRAMLEY - Wilson: Noble Kelly Rushton Cranswick:
Armitage Langfield: Smith Heath Young Baldwin Hammill
Garbutt:
Tries - Rushton(2) Garbutt(2) Wilson Noble Cranswick:
Goals - Langfield(6):
CASTLEFORD - Lunn: Burton Sheridan G.G.Ward Naylor:
Walsh Evans: Berry Boot Pye Schofield Howard F.Ward:
Tries - Burton Pye: Goals - Lunn(3):
Referee J Manley (Warrington) Att - 2501H.T. nil - 20

Mon 22 Apr 1957 LEEDS home won 16 - 9
CASTLEFORD - ARTHUR HATTEE(415): Burton Sheridan
Lunn G.G.Ward: Walsh Evans: Berry Boot Pye Thornley
Schofield F.Ward:
Tries - Burton G.G.Ward Pye Thornley: Goals - Hattee(2):
LEEDS - Quinn: Davies McLellan Jones Broughton: Lendill
Pratt: Belshaw Prior Tomlinson Poole Robinson Last:
Try - Quinn: Goals - Jones(2) Quinn(DG):
Referee T W Watkinson (Man'ster) Att - 9176 H.T. 3 - 6

Tue 23 Apr 1957 KEIGHLEY away lost 11 - 29
KEIGHLEY - Phillips: Smith Hallas Hollindrake Bleasby:
Verrenkamp Black: Marston Daniels Grice Bennett
Crewdson Glynn:
Tries - Hollindrake(2) Black(2) Phillips Smith Hallas:
Goals - Hollindrake(4):
CASTLEFORD - Hattee: Burton Bryant Lunn G.G.Ward:
Walsh Evans: Thornley Boot Pye A.N.OTHER(416) Howard
Williams:
Tries - Burton Bryant Pye: Goal - Lunn:
Referee R Gelder (Wakefield) Att - 3529 H.T. 2 – 18

Ken Hindley   Ron (Curly) Evans
D. No 398   D. No 404
1956 -57 to 1957-58   1956-57 to 1960-61

SEASON 1956-57

Colin Taylor
D. No 406
1956-57 to 1963-64

Eddie Bryant
D. No 410
1956-57 to 1962-63

Barry (Taffy) Walsh
D. No 412
1956-57 to 1961-62

Geoff G Ward
D. No 414
1956-57 to 1965-66

SEASON 1957-58

Ian Corban
D. No 417
1957-58 to 1959-60

Keith Bridges
D. No 419
1957-58 to 1962-63

Albert Tonk nson
D. No 420
1957-58 to 1363-64

Jack Hirst
D. No 424
1957-58 to 1964-65

Bill Bryant
D. No 426
1957-58 to 1969-70

Colin Battye
D. No 427
1957-58- to 1965-66

John Berry
D. No 421
1957-58 to ˉ962-63

Charlie Wright
D. No 423
1957-58 to 1958-59

SEASON 1956-57

D.N	PLAYER		DEBUT	L MATCH	APP	SUB	T.AP	TRI'S	G'LS	D.G	P'TS
302	HOWARD	GEORGE (CHARLIE)			29	0	29	2	0	0	6
323	HAUGHEY	LESLIE		27/08/1956	3	0	3	0	0	0	0
326	WALTER	RONALD			2	0	2	0	0	0	0
330	PYE	KENNETH			35	0	35	11	0	0	33
340	HUGHES	DAVID			3	0	3	0	0	0	0
341	LUNN	ALBERT			35	0	35	4	96	0	204
342	PYE	JOSHUA J.		13/10/1956	4	0	4	0	0	0	0
349	WARD	FRED			34	0	34	7	0	0	21
352	WEBSTER	DENZIL		06/10/1956	10	0	10	6	0	0	18
353	THORNLEY	HARRY			15	0	15	1	0	0	3
355	GRACE	ARNOLD		25/08/1956	1	0	1	0	0	0	0
364	SMART	DEREK			1	0	1	0	0	0	0
371	EAST	FRANK			28	0	28	17	0	0	51
372	BOOT	JACK			17	0	17	0	0	0	0
375	RHODES	EDWARD		15/09/1956	7	0	7	0	0	0	0
377	HORSFALL	ALAN			7	0	7	2	0	0	6
379	WINN	JOHN		15/09/1956	6	0	6	0	0	0	0
380	BURTON	CLIFFORD			36	0	36	10	0	0	30
382	SHERIDAN	JOHN			26	0	26	8	0	0	24
385	FEWSTER	RAYMOND		08/12/1956	17	0	17	5	0	0	15
389	BARNES	JACK			15	0	15	0	27	0	54
392	BICKERDYKE	RONALD		08/09/1956	2	0	2	0	0	0	0
394	BERRY	ROWLAND			26	0	26	0	0	0	0
395	CLOUGH	ANTHONY		29/09/1956	4	0	4	0	0	0	0
396	WILLIAMS	HARRY			11	0	11	0	0	0	0
397	BARRETT	FRED	18/08/1956	22/08/1956	2	0	2	0	0	0	0
398	HINDLEY	KENNETH	22/08/1956		21	0	21	2	0	0	6
399	CLARKSON	DESMOND	22/08/1956	22/08/1956	1	0	1	0	3	0	6
400	HUNT	JAMES	27/08/1956		2	0	2	0	0	0	0
401	CROSSLEY	JOHN Snr.	03/09/1956	15/09/1956	4	0	4	0	0	0	0
402	GUTHRIE	RONALD	15/09/1956	29/09/1956	3	0	3	0	0	0	0
403	HARRISON	KEITH	22/09/1956	22/09/1956	1	0	1	0	0	0	0
404	EVANS	RONALD	29/09/1956		32	0	32	3	0	0	9
405	WILMOT	ARTHUR	29/09/1956		15	0	15	0	0	0	0
406	TAYLOR	COLIN	06/10/1956		2	0	2	0	0	0	0
407	SMITH	TERENCE	20/10/1956	03/11/1956	3	0	3	1	0	0	3
408	FLANAGAN	WILLIAM	03/11/1956	23/03/1957	22	0	22	1	0	0	3
409	SCHOFIELD	DERRICK	24/11/1956		22	0	22	3	1	0	11
410	BRYANT	EDWARD	15/12/1956		7	0	7	1	0	0	3
411	GREATBATCH	SIDNEY	19/01/1957	19/01/1957	1	0	1	0	0	0	0
412	WALSH	BARRY	26/01/1957		14	0	14	4	0	0	12
413	NAYLOR	CHARLES	02/02/1957		4	0	4	1	0	0	3
414	WARD	GEOFFREY G.	02/02/1957		13	0	13	4	0	0	12
415	HATTEE	ARTHUR	22/04/1957		2	0	2	0	2	0	4
416	A N OTHER		23/04/1957	23/04/1957	1	0	1	0	0	0	0
	45				**546**	**0**	**546**	**93**	**129**	**0**	**537**
			20	**18**							

COMPETITION		P	W	D	L	FOR	AGT
LEAGUE	POSITION 25 OF 30	38	11	2	25	488	739
YORK'S CUP		2	1	0	1	32	47
RL CUP		2	1	0	1	17	14
PLAYERS RECORDS		**42**	**13**	**2**	**27**	**537**	**800**

This season saw Len Garbett being promoted from 'A' Team Coach to First Team Coach, taking over from Ernest Ward, but this was not an instant success, losing the first eleven league games before winning away at Liverpool City.

Albert Lunn increased the record for most points scored in a League game to 19 against Dewsbury at home on the 9 March 1957.

SEASON 1957-58

Sat 10 Aug 1957 WHITES - 16 STRIPES - 20
PRACTICE MATCH FRIENDLY
WHITES - Hattee: East Sheridan Lunn Smart: Walsh Evans:
Berry Horsfall Shaw-Trialist(Howard) Schofield Thornley
F.Ward Tries - Lunn Walsh Berry Ward: Goals - Lunn(2):
STRIPES - Barnes: Naylor Burton G.G.Ward Hunt: Hague
White: Wilmot Corban Howard(Shaw)
Hughes(Walter)Tonkinson Taylor:
Tries - Burton(3) Hunt Taylor Tonkinson: Goal - Barnes:

Sat 17 Aug 1957 SALFORD home won 21 - 8
CASTLEFORD - Barnes: G.G.Ward Sheridan Lunn Burton:
Walsh Evans: R.Berry IAN CORBAN(417) Howard Schofield
Taylor F.Ward: Tries - Sheridan(2) Lunn: Goals - Lunn(6):
SALFORD - Walker: Jones Preece Cheshire McArthur:
Bettinson Keavney: Ayles Openshaw Hancock Alder
Fieldhouse Duffy: Tries - Walker Jones: Goal - McArthur:
Referee R L Thomas (Oldham) Att - 2000 H.T. 16 - 3

Wed 21 Aug 1957 HALIFAX away lost 17 - 22
HALIFAX - Owen: Dean Mather Palmer Freeman: Riley
Broadhurst: Thorley Moyser Helliwell Holmes Clifft Traill:
Tries - Freeman(2) Palmer Traill: Goals - Owen(5):
CASTLEFORD - Barnes: G.G.Ward Sheridan Lunn Burton:
Walsh Evans: R.Berry Corban Howard Schofield Taylor
F.Ward: Tries - Sheridan Berry Howard: Goals - Lunn(4):
Referee J H Chadwick (Dewsbury) Att - 7697 H.T. 5 - 8

Sat 24 Aug 1957 ROCHDALE HORNETS away
lost 9 -18
ROCHDALE H - Cahill: Ralph Short Jones Buxton: Chisnall
Fishwick: Gill Dagnall Scholes Kelly Bailey Trumble:
Tries - Short(2): Goals - Jones(6):
CASTLEFORD - Barnes: G.G.Ward Sheridan Lunn East:
Walsh Evans: Arthur Wilmot Boot Howard Schofield
Thornley F.Ward: Try - Walsh: Goals - Lunn(3):
Referee H Squires (Ossett) Att - 3749 H.T. 7 - 5

Mon 26 Aug 1957 BRADFORD NORTHERN home
lost 5 - 19
CASTLEFORD - Lunn: East Sheridan G.G.Ward Burton:
Walsh Evans: Thornley Boot Pye Howard Taylor F.Ward:
Try - Howard: Goal - Lunn:
BRADFORD N - Beevers: Jenkins Winnard Smith Rodwell:
Davies Oddy: Carter Kosanovic Hambling Hemingway
Griffett Scroby:
Tries - Jenkins(2) Rodwell(2) Carter: Goals - Beevers(2):
Referee J Flanagan (Keighley) Att - 4282 H.T. 5 - 6

Sat 31 Aug 1957 DONCASTER away won 29 - 9
YORKSHIRE CUP ROUND 1
DONCASTER - Peace: Williamson Burrows Ratcliffe
Worsley: Northern Fennell: Jukes Larkin Field Gilbert
Winnard Matthews:
Try - Matthews: Goals - Peace(2) Ratcliffe:
CASTLEFORD - Barnes: East Sheridan Lunn Burton: Walsh
Evans: R.Berry Horsfall Pye Schofield Howard F.Ward:
Tries - F.Ward(3) Sheridan Walsh Pye East:
Goals - Barnes(3):
Referee J C Clapham (Wigan) Att - 650 H.T. 13 - 2

Wed 4 Sep 1957 WAKEFIELD TRINITY home
lost 9 - 28
CASTLEFORD - Barnes: East Sheridan Lunn Burton: Walsh
Evans: R.Berry Alan Horsfall Pye(S/O) Williams Howard
Schofield: Try - Walsh: Goals - Barnes(3):
WAKEFIELD T - Lockwood: Houlden Mortimer Fox
Cooper: Holliday Rollin: Harrison Shaw Coverdale Kelly
Haigh Chamberlain:
Tries - Mortimer(3) Houlden(2) Harrison: Goals - Fox(5):
Referee M Coates (Pudsey) Att - 6631 H.T. 7 - 13

Sat 7 Sep 1957 LIVERPOOL CITY away won 32 - 18
LIVERPOOL C - Palin: Halton Ashby Hunt Silley: Belshaw
Walker: Pearson Fishwick Cartledge Hockenhull Tegin
Davies:
Tries - Halton Hunt Belshaw Fishwick: Goals - Belshaw(3):
CASTLEFORD - Barnes: East Sheridan Lunn Burton: Walsh
Evans: R.Berry GORDON GRAHAM(418) Pye Howard
Williams Hughes: Tries - Sheridan(3) Burton Walsh Evans
Hughes Pye: Goals - Barnes(3) Lunn:
Referee H Harrison (Ossett) Att - 1200 H.T. 16 - 2

Tue 10 Sep 1957 LEEDS home lost 6 - 19
YORKSHIRE CUP ROUND 2
CASTLEFORD - Hattee: East Sheridan Lunn Burton: Walsh
Evans: R.Berry Jack Boot Pye Howard Harry Williams
F.Ward: Goals - Hattee(3):
LEEDS - Quinn: Dunn Lendil Jones Broughton: Brown
Stevenson: Shelton Prior Anderson Tomlinson Robinson
Street: Tries - Tomlinson(2) Quinn: Goals - Jones(5):
Referee T W Watkinson (Man'ster) Att - 9963 H.T. 2 - 7

Sat 14 Sep 1957 FEATHERSTONE ROVERS home
won 16 - 5
CASTLEFORD - Barnes: East Sheridan Lunn Burton: Walsh
Evans: R.Berry KEITH BRIDGES(419) Howard Schofield
Thornley F.Ward:
Tries - East(2)Sheridan Walsh: Goals - Barnes(2):
FEATHERSTONE R - Fennell: Lancaster Evans Woolford
Field: Mullaney Fox: Welburn Fawley Jones Fearnley
Clamp Lambert: Try - Mullaney: Goal - Fennell:
Referee G Scott (Wakefield) Att - 6195 H.T. 11 - nil

Sat 21 Sep 1957 HUDDERSFIELD away lost 7 - 23
HUDDERSFIELD - Dyson: Wainwright Kilroy Cecil Sullivan:
Ramsden Smales: Slevin Wood Flint Bowman Thompson
Valentine: Tries - Sullivan(4) Kilroy: Goals - Dyson(4):
CASTLEFORD - Barnes: East Sheridan Hunt Smart: Walsh
Evans: Thornley Bridges Howard Schofield Taylor F.Ward:
Try - Sheridan: Goals - Barnes(2):
Referee A E Durkin (Dewsbury) Att - 4600 H.T. 4 - 14

Sat 28 Sep 1957 ROCHDALE HORNETS home
lost 15 - 26
CASTLEFORD - Lunn: East Sheridan E.Bryant Smart: Walsh
Evans R.Berry Bridges Thornley Schofield ALBERT
TONKINSON(420) F.Ward:
Tries - Smart Walsh Tonkinson: Goals - Schofield(2) Lunn:
ROCHDALE H - Cahill: Ralph Short Smith Buxton: Taylor
Fishwick: Livesey Bowden Scholes Appleton McNally

173

Baxter: Tries - Ralph(2) Smith Buxton Taylor Fishwick:
Goals - Smith(4):
Referee R Welsby (Warrington) Att - 3000 H.T. 8 - 11

Sat 5 Oct 1957 BATLEY away lost 8 - 24
BATLEY - Walshaw: O'Hara Sutton Gardner Smith:
Lockwood Glover: Palmer Battersby Etty Hainsworth
Anson Fox: Tries - O'Hara Sutton Palmer Hainsworth:
Goals - Walshaw(6):
CASTLEFORD - Barnes: East Sheridan Lunn Smart: Walsh
Evans: Walter Bridges Pye Schofield Tonkinson F.Ward:
Tries - Sheridan Ward: Goal - Schofield:
Referee - Att - H.T.

Sat 12 Oct 1957 DONCASTER home won 34 - nil
CASTLEFORD - Barnes: East Sheridan Lunn Burton: Naylor
Evans: R.Berry Bridges Pye Schofield Walter F.Ward:
Tries - Walter(2) East Sheridan Lunn Burton Naylor Ward:
Goals - Barnes(5):
DONCASTER - Peace: Williamson Wrigglesworth Oldroyd
Mitchell: Marant Pollard: Belshaw Larkin Nock Baddeley
Field Matthews:
Referee G Battersby (Barrow) Att - 1900 H.T. 18 - nil

**Sat 19 Oct 1957 FEATHERSTONE ROVERS away
lost 21 - 35**
FEATHERSTONE R - Fennell: Kinsey Tennant Evans
Woolford: Mullaney Fox: Jones Fawley Hockley Fearnley
Clamp Lambert: Tries - Woolford(2) Clamp(2) Evans
Mullaney Fox: Goals - Fennell(4) Fox(3):
CASTLEFORD - Barnes: East Sheridan Lunn Burton: Walsh
Evans: R.Berry Corban Pye Schofield Walter F.Ward:
Tries: Ward(2) East Lunn Pye: Goals - Barnes(2) Lunn:
Referee H Squires (Ossett) Att - 4700 H.T. 8 - 20

Sat 26 Oct 1957 WIDNES away lost 7 - 26
WIDNES - Wright: Ratcliffe Broom Dawson Owen: Myler
J.Smith: T.Smith Kemel Bate D.Smith Hill Callighan:
Tries - Owen(2) Myler(2) Dawson D.Smith:
Goals - Dawson(4):
CASTLEFORD - Barnes: East Sheridan Burton G.G.Ward:
Walsh Evans: R.Berry Bridges Pye Schofield Tonkinson
F.Ward: Try - East: Goals - Barnes(2):
Referee A E Durkin (Dewsbury) Att – 3000 H.T. 2 - 18

Sat 2 Nov 1957 BRAMLEY home draw 19 - 19
CASTLEFORD - Barnes: East Sheridan Burton G.G.Ward:
Walsh Evans: R.Berry Bridges Howard Taylor Ronald
Walter F.Ward: Tries - East(2) Evans: Goals - Barnes(5):
BRAMLEY - Wilson: Noble Kelly Garbutt Starling: Dudley
Harding: Nutting Wood Smith Hammill Dooler Baldwin:
Tries - Kelly Garbutt Harding: Goals - Wilson(5):
Referee D T H Davies (Manchester) Att - 2290 H.T. 9 - 10

Sat 9 Nov 1957 KEIGHLEY away lost 7 - 23
KEIGHLEY - J.Phillips: Bleasby Hallas Taylor Hollindrake:
Verrenkamp Barron: Marston Traill Bardgett Lowe
S.Phillips Glyn: Tries - Bleasby(2) Hollindrake(2) Barron:
Goals - J.Phillips(2) Hollindrake(2):
CASTLEFORD - Barnes: East Sheridan Lunn Burton: Walsh

Evans: JOHN BERRY(421) Bridges Howard Schofield Taylor
F.Ward: Try - Taylor: Goals - Barnes(2):
Referee G Scott (Wakefield) Att - 4000 H.T. 7 - 10

**Sat 16 Nov 1957 BLACKPOOL BOROUGH home
lost 15 - 26**
CASTLEFORD - Barnes: East Sheridan Naylor Smart: Walsh
Evans: J.Berry Bridges Pye Thornley F.Ward Taylor:
Tries - Smart Pye Ward: Goals - Barnes(3):
BLACKPOOL B - Lowe: Emmett Wood Fearis Morgan:
Foden Brennan: Wright Mundy Maughan Grundy
Standish Knowles: Tries - Emmett(2) Wood(2)
Standish(2): Goals - Fearis(3) (DG):
Referee J C Clapham (Wigan) Att - 1340 H.T. 10 - 10

**Sat 23 Nov 1957 WAKEFIELD TRINITY away
Lost 10 -27**
WAKEFIELD T - Lockwood: Hirst Fox Metcalfe Cooper:
Houlden Rollin: Harrison Shaw Coverdale Haigh Kelly
Chamberlain: Tries - Hirst(3) Cooper(2): Goals - Fox(6):
CASTLEFORD - Taylor: G.G.Ward Sheridan Lunn Hunt:
JEFFREY PYE(422) Hindley: J.Berry Bridges K.Pye Howard
Harry Thornley F.Ward:
Tries - G.G.Ward Hunt: Goals - Lunn(2):
Referee G Wilson (Dewsbury) Att - 6000 H.T. 8 - 6

Sat 30 Nov 1957 HALIFAX home lost 11 - 22
CASTLEFORD - Barnes: G.G.Ward Sheridan Lunn James
Hunt: J.Pye Hindley: J.Berry Bridges K.Pye Howard
CHARLES WRIGHT(423) F.Ward:
Try - Wright: Goals - Barnes(4):
HALIFAX - Briers: Williams Burnett Palmer Fremman: Dean
Kielty: Thorley Ackerley Wilkinson Henderon Clifft Traill:
Tries - Palmer(2) Freeman(2) Williams Burnett:
Goals - Williams(2):
Referee E Clay (Rothwell) Att - 2700 H.T. 6 - 5

Sat 7 Dec 1957 DEWSBURY home lost 13 - 17
CASTLEFORD - Barnes: East Sheridan Lunn G.G.Ward:
J.Pye Hindley: J.Berry Bridges K.Pye Howard Wright Fred
Ward: Tries - Sheridan J.Pye K.Pye: Goals - Barnes(2):
DEWSBURY - Bosworth: Grainger J.Callighan Taylor
Ripley: Foley O'Donnell: Pickersgill Bradshaw Judge Poole
Bamford E.Callighan:
Tries - J.Callighan Foley Judge: Goals - Bosworth(4):
Referee Mr C F Appleton(Warrington) Att -1007 H.T. 13 -7

Sat 14 Dec 1957 DONCASTER away lost 5 - 8
DONCASTER - Ratcliffe: Williamson Peace Wilkinson
Hayter: Fennell Wrigglesworth: Belshaw Doyle Hartley
Baddeley Rothery Matthews: Goals - Peace(4):
CASTLEFORD - Barnes: East Sheridan Lunn Naylor: J.Pye
Evans: Rowland Berry Bridges K.Pye Howard Taylor
Wright: Try - Sheridan: Goal - Barnes:
Referee T W Watkinson (Man'ster) Att - 485 H.T. nil - 2

**Sat 21 Dec 1957 HULL KINGSTON ROVERS home
lost 20 - 21**
CASTLEFORD - Barnes: East Sheridan G.G.Ward Naylor:
Walsh Evans: J.Berry Bridges K.Pye Howard Wright Taylor:

Tries - East(2) Sheridan Naylor: Goals - Barnes(4):
HULL K R - Ellerby: Shaw Kellett Wilson Stark: Riley Evans:
Hall Brookfield Sims Matthews Griffett Bangs:
Tries - Kellett(2) Stark Evans Matthews: Goals - Kellett(3):
Referee J Manley (Warrington) Att - 1053 H.T. 12 - 13

Wed 25 Dec 1957 BRAMLEY away lost 2 - 21
BRAMLEY - Wilson: Noble Kelly Rushton CranswicK:
Dudley Pollard: Smith Wood Shaw Dooler Hammill
Garbutt: Tries - Cranswick(2) Dudley: Goals - Wilson(6):
CASTLEFORD - Barnes: East Sheridan G.G.Ward Burton:
Walsh Evans: JACK HIRST(424) Corban K.Pye Howard
Wright Taylor: Goal - Barnes:
Referee H Harrison (Ossett) Att - 2754 H.T. 2 - 7

Thu 26 Dec 1957 HUNSLET home won 16 - 10
CASTLEFORD - Barnes: East Sheridan Lunn Burton: J.Pye
Evans: Hirst Corban K.Pye Howard Wright Taylor:
Tries - Sheridan(3) Burton: Goals - Barnes(2):
HUNSLET - Langton: Snowden Stockdill Sutcliffe Colin:
Gabbitas Burnell: Hatfield Smith Cooper Boland Platt
Gunney: Tries - Snowden Hatfield: Goals - Langton(2):
Referee R Gelder (Wakefield) Att - 3091 H.T. 10 - 2

**Sat 28 Dec 1957 BRADFORD NORTHERN away
lost 12 - 35**
BRADFORD N - Beevers: Hemingway Jenkins Smith
Davies: L.Haley G.Haley: McLean Kosanovic Radford Jones
Feather Scroby: Tries - Davies(5) Jenkins(2) Radford(2)
Hemingway L.Haley: Goal - Jenkins:
CASTLEFORD - Barnes: East Sheridan Lunn Burton: J.Pye
Evans: Hirst Corban K.Pye Howard Tonkinson E.Bryant:
Tries - East Sheridan: Goals - Barnes(3):
Referee H Squires (Ossett) Att - 3075 H.T. 7 - 11

Sat 11 Jan 1958 SALFORD away lost 2 - 8
SALFORD - Gregory: Jones Cheshire Lowdon McArthur:
Hanley Keavney: Hancock Boardman Ayles Clarke Connell
Duffy: Tries - Jones McArthur: Goal - Lowdon:
CASTLEFORD - Barnes: East Sheridan G.G.Ward Lunn:
Walsh Evans: Hirst Corban K.Pye Howard Wright Taylor:
Goal - Barnes:
Referee C Whiteley (Ossett) Att - 4000 H.T. nil - 8

Sat 18 Jan 1958 HUDDERSFIELD home lost 7 - 46
CASTLEFORD - Barnes: East Sheridan G.G.Ward Lunn:
Walsh Evans: Hirst Corban K.Pye Howard Wright Taylor:
Try - Walsh: Goals - Barnes(2):
HUDDERSFIELD - Dyson: Plunkett Kilroy Barrow
Needham: Cecil Smales: Slevin Wood Killen Bowman
Clarke Thornley: Tries - Kilroy(4) Needham(2) Barrow
Smales Bowman Clarke: Goals - Dyson(8):
Referee G Wilson (Dewsbury) Att - 1876 H.T. 2 - 18

Sat 1 Feb 1958 BATLEY home won 19 - 7
CASTLEFORD - Barnes: East Sheridan G.G.Ward Lunn:
Walsh Evans: Hirst Corban J.Berry Howard Wright
E.Bryant:
Tries - Sheridan(3) G.G.Ward Walsh: Goals - Barnes Lunn:
BATLEY - Walshaw: Clark Sutton Lockwood Smith: Hirst

Foley: Palmer Whitehead Etty Hainsworth Armstead
Thompson: Try - Hirst: Goals - Walshaw(2):
Referee J Manley (Warrington) Att - 1140 H.T. 13 - 7

**Sat 8 Feb 1958 LEEDS away lost 6 - 31
CHALLENGE CUP ROUND 1**
LEEDS - Quinn: Hemingway McLennan Jones Hodgkinson:
Brown Stevenson: Skelton Prior Robinson Tomlinson Dick
Whitehead: Tries - Hemingway(4) Jones Brown
Stevenson Quinn Robinson: Goals - Jones(2):
CASTLEFORD - Barnes: East Sheridan G.G.Ward Lunn:
Walsh Evans: Hirst Corban J.Berry Howard Wright
E.Bryant: Tries - East Sheridan:
Referee F Smith (Barrow) Att - 12000 H.T. 3 - 16

Sat 15 Feb 1958 HULL away lost 2 - 45
HULL - Kershaw: Watts A.N.Other Dannatt Harrison:
Broadhurst Finn: Hambling Harris J.Drake Sykes W.Drake
Whiteley: Tries - W.Drake(3) Watts(2) Dannatt(2)
Broadhurst(2) A.N.Other Harris: Goals - Sykes(6):
CASTLEFORD - Lunn: East Sheridan G.G.Ward Burton:
Walsh Evans: Hirst Corban J.Berry Howard Wright K.Pye:
Goal - Lunn:
Referee J Jowett (Leeds) Att - 9020 H.T. 2 - 23

**Sat 22 Feb 1958 HULL KINGSTON ROVERS away
lost 5 - 34**
HULL K R - Kellett: Coulson Eiley Mageen Shaw: Key
Evans: Grice Brookfield Coverdale Holland Sims Griffett:
Tries - Coulson(2) Riley(2) Mageen Shaw Brookfield Sims:
Goals - Kellett(5):
CASTLEFORD - Lunn: East Sheridan G.G.Ward Naylor:
Walsh Evans: Hirst Corban J.Berry Howard Schofield
Wright: Try - Sheridan: Goal - Lunn:
Referee G Philpott (Leeds) Att - 3000 H.T. nil - 18

Sat 1 Mar 1958 LIVERPOOL CITY home won 12 - 11
CASTLEFORD - Lunn: East Sheridan G.G.Ward Burton:
Charlie Naylor Evans: Hirst Bridges Howard Derrick
Schofield Wright K.Pye:
Tries - East Wright: Goals - Lunn(3):
LIVERPOOL C - Ashby: Barton Belshaw Morris Halton:
Hunt Walker: Pearson Fishwick Cartledge Simpson Lyons
Hockenhull: Tries - Barton(2) Halton: Goal - Hunt:
Referee C F Appleton (Warrington) Att - 1159 H.T. 2 - 8

Sat 8 Mar 1958 KEIGHLEY home lost 5 - 21
CASTLEFORD - Lunn: East Sheridan G.G.Ward Burton:
BRIAN BECK(425) Evans: J.Berry Bridges Howard Taylor
E.Bryant WILLIAM BRYANT(426):
Try - Sheridan: Goal - Lunn:
KEIGHLEY - J.Phillips: Smith Hallas Bleasby Hollindrake:
Redman Barron: Shreeve Heath Bardgett G.Phillips
Spillane Lowe: Tries - Redman(2) Smith Bleasby Shreeve:
Goals - Phillips(3):
Referee Mr A Howgate (Dewsbury) Att – 684 H.T. nil - 10

Sat 22 Mar 1958 HUNLSET away lost 13 - 45
HUNSLET - Langton: Byrom Walker Stockdill Colin:
Gabbitas Tate: Cooper Smith Auckland Shaw Gunney

SEASON 1957-58

Poole: Tries - Langton(2) Walker(2) Gabbitas(2) Byrom Stockdill Colin Tate Gunney: Goals - Langton(6):
CASTLEFORD - Lunn: East Sheridan G.G.Ward Hindley: COLIN BATTYE(427) Evans: Hirst Bridges Howard NORMAN ASHALL(428) K.Pye Wright:
Tries - Sheridan G.G.Ward Bridges: Goals - Lunn(2):
Referee R Gelder (Wakefield) Att - 2500 H.T. nil - 20

Sat 29 Mar 1958 WIDNES home lost 11 - 30
CASTLEFORD - Lunn: East Sheridan G.G.Ward Hindley: Walsh Evans: Hirst Bridges MICHAEL LUMB(429) Tonkinson Ashall W.Bryant: Try - East: Goals - Lunn(4):
WIDNES - Wright: Owen Broom Dawson Ratcliffe: Myler Walker: Smith Kemel Bate D.Smith De Witt Major:
Tries - Owen(3) Broom(2) Dawson: Goals - Dawson(6):
Referee D T H Davies (Manchester) Att - 574 H.T. 6 - 18

Fri 4 Apr 1958 YORK away lost 5 - 35
YORK - Hargreaves: B.Smith Swift Flannery Foster: Robinson Jackson: Yorke Milner Henderson O'Brien Poole Dawson: Tries - Foster(3) Flannery Robinson Yorke Dawson: Goals - Yorke(7):
CASTLEFORD - Hattee: East Sheridan Burton Hindley: Beck Evans: Hirst Bridges Ashall Wright Tonkinson W.Bryant: Try - Hirst: Goal - Hattee:
Referee A E Durkin (Dewsbury) Att - 6000 H.T. 5 - 18

Sat 5 Apr 1958 DEWSBURY away lost 15 - 18
DEWSBURY - Cook: Grainger J.T.Callighan Todd Taylor: Bosworth Lea: Judge Lockwood Hopper Cox Bamford E.Callighan:
Tries - Cox(2) J.T.Callighan Lea: Goals - Bosworth(3):
CASTLEFORD - Hattee: East Sheridan Burton Hindley: Beck Evans: Hirst Bridges Michael Lumb Tonkinson

Wright W.Bryant: Try - Hindley:
Goals - Hattee(5) Beck(DG):
Referee E Clay (Leeds) Att - 1000 H.T. 11 - 13

Mon 7 Apr 1958 HULL away lost 2 - 52
CASTLEFORD - Hattee: East Sheridan Burton Hindley: Brian Beck Evans: Hirst Bridges Ashall Tonkinson Wright W.Bryant: Goal - Hattee:
HULL - Bateson: Watts Cooper Saville Dannatt: Broadhurst Finn: Scott Harris Hambling Sykes W.Drake Whiteley: Tries - Finn(4) Watts(2) Sykes(2) Saville Scott Harris Hambling: Goals - Bateson(8):
Referee C F Appleton (Warrington) Att – 3000 H.T. 2 - 21

Sat 12 Apr 1958 BLACKPOOL BOROUGH away lost 3 - 37
BLACKPOOL B - Dutton: Emmitt Ryder Fearis Knowles: Brennan Down: Grundy Lester Fisher Clayton Maughan Healey: Tries - Brennan(2) Emmitt Ryder Fearis Fisher Maughan: Goals - Fearis(8):
CASTLEFORD - Hattee: G.G.Ward Sheridan Battye Burton: J.Pye Kenneth Hindley: Hirst Corban Norman Ashall Tonkinson Wright W.Bryant: Try - Sheridan:
Referee A Howgate(Dewsbury) Att - 2000 H.T. 3 - 22

Wed 23 Apr 1958 YORK home lost 13 - 23
CASTLEFORD - Taylor: East Sheridan Battye G.G.Ward: Burton Evans: Hirst Bridges MAURICE ASKIN(430) Tonkinson Wright W.Bryant:
Tries - East Sheridan Askin: Goals - Hirst(2):
YORK - Hargreaves: B.Smith Drake G.Smith Foster: Robinson Jackson: Yorke Milner Watts O'Brien Poole Dawson: Tries - G.Smith Robinson Watts Poole Dawson: Goals - Yorke(4):
Referee G Scott (Wakefield) Att - 1527 H.T. 13 – 2

1957-58 SQUAD
Standing – Ken Holmes (Secretary) Frank East Cliff Burton Geoff Ward Eddie Bryant Albert Tonkinson
Rowland Berry Len Garbett (Coach)
Sitting – David Smart John Sheridan Harry Thornley Albert Lunn Jim Hunt Ken Pye
Kneeling – Ron Evans Barry Walsh

SEASON 1957-58

D.N	PLAYER		DEBUT	L MATCH	APP	SUB	T.AP	TRI'S	G'LS	D.G	P'TS
302	HOWARD	GEORGE (CHARLIE)			29	0	29	2	0	0	6
326	WALTER	RONALD		02/11/1957	4	0	4	2	0	0	6
330	PYE	KENNETH			23	0	23	5	0	0	15
340	HUGHES	DAVID			1	0	1	1	0	0	3
341	LUNN	ALBERT			30	0	30	3	32	0	73
349	WARD	FRED		07/12/1957	19	0	19	8	0	0	24
353	THORNLEY	HARRY		23/11/1957	7	0	7	0	0	0	0
364	SMART	DEREK			4	0	4	2	0	0	6
371	EAST	FRANK			36	0	36	15	0	0	45
372	BOOT	JACK		10/09/1957	3	0	3	0	0	0	0
377	HORSFALL	ALAN		04/09/1957	2	0	2	0	0	0	0
380	BURTON	CLIFFORD			24	0	24	3	0	0	9
382	SHERIDAN	JOHN			41	0	41	27	0	0	81
389	BARNES	JACK			26	0	26	0	54	0	108
394	BERRY	ROWLAND		14/12/1957	13	0	13	1	0	0	3
396	WILLIAMS	HARRY		10/09/1957	3	0	3	0	0	0	0
398	HINDLEY	KENNETH		12/04/1958	9	0	9	1	0	0	3
400	HUNT	JAMES		30/11/1957	3	0	3	1	0	0	3
404	EVANS	RONALD			37	0	37	2	0	0	6
405	WILMOT	ARTHUR		24/08/1957	1	0	1	0	0	0	0
406	TAYLOR	COLIN			16	0	16	1	0	0	3
409	SCHOFIELD	DERRICK		01/03/1958	15	0	15	0	3	0	6
410	BRYANT	EDWARD			5	0	5	0	0	0	0
412	WALSH	BARRY			26	0	26	8	0	0	24
413	NAYLOR	CHARLES		01/03/1958	6	0	6	2	0	0	6
414	WARD	GEOFFREY G			23	0	23	3	0	0	9
415	HATTEE	ARTHUR			5	0	5	0	10	0	20
417	CORBAN	IAN	17/08/1957		13	0	13	0	0	0	0
418	GRAHAM	GORDON	07/09/1957	07/09/1957	1	0	1	0	0	0	0
419	BRIDGES	KEITH	14/09/1957		22	0	22	1	0	0	3
420	TONKINSON	ALBERT	28/09/1957		10	0	10	1	0	0	3
421	BERRY	JOHN	09/11/1957		11	0	11	0	0	0	0
422	PYE	JEFFREY	23/11/1957		7	0	7	1	0	0	3
423	WRIGHT	CHARLIE	30/11/1957		19	0	19	2	0	0	6
424	HIRST	JACK	25/12/1957		17	0	17	1	2	0	7
425	BECK	BRIAN	08/03/1958	07/04/1958	4	0	4	0	0	1	2
426	BRYANT	WILLIAM	08/03/1958		7	0	7	0	0	0	0
427	BATTYE	COLIN	22/03/1958		3	0	3	0	0	0	0
428	ASHALL	NORMAN	22/03/1958	12/04/1958	5	0	5	0	0	0	0
429	LUMB	MICHAEL	29/03/1958	05/04/1958	2	0	2	0	0	0	0
430	ASKIN	MAURICE	23/04/1958		1	0	1	1	0	0	3
	41		**14**	**16**	**533**	**0**	**533**	**94**	**101**	**1**	**486**

COMPETITION		P	W	D	L	FOR	AGT
LEAGUE	POSITION 29 OF 30	38	7	1	30	445	893
YORK'S CUP		2	1	0	1	35	28
RL CUP		1	0	0	1	6	31
PLAYERS RECORDS		**41**	**3**	**1**	**32**	**486**	**952**

For the Boxing Day fixture against Hunslet Len Garbett swapped the position of First Team Coach for that of Company Secretary. Billy Rhodes took over as Trainer for his fourth spell and celebrated with a 16–10 victory. Billy's spell was a short one lasting only a few weeks before former international loose forward and Castleford born Harry Street took over and is acknowledged as the architect of "Classy Cas ".

Saturday, 22 March 1958 saw Albert Lunn become the first player to kick 400 goals for the club in the 45–13 away defeat at Hunslet.

John Sheridan played in all 41 league and cup games. John also narrowly failed to improve the try scoring record with 27 and was carried off injured in the last game of the season against York at home after attempting to "bust" his way under the posts looking to notch one of those vital touchdowns.

A notable debutante was William (Bill) Bryant

SEASON 1958-59

Sat 9 Aug 1958 DONCASTER home won 17 - 5
CHARITY MATCH FRIENDLY
CASTLEFORD - Lunn: G.G.Ward Sheridan Burton East:
J.Pye(C.Battye)K.Pye(Evans): J.Berry Corban Thornley
Howard(Taylor) Wright(W.Bryant) Tonkinson:
Tries - Ward(2) Sheridan Burton Tonkinson: Goal - Lunn:
DONCASTER - Appleyard: Hinchcliffe Ratcliffe Rotheray
Askin: Milner Northern: Belshaw Stokes Hartley Burt
Yemm Shoebottom: Try - Hinchcliffe: Goal - Appleyard:
Referee H Pickersgill (Castleford) Att - 600 .T. nil - 3

Sat 16 Aug 1958 ROCHDALE HORNETS home
won 15 - 14
CASTLEFORD - Lunn: East Sheridan Burton Battye: Walsh
Evans: Hirst Corban K.Pye Howard Wright Tonkinson:
Try - Battye: Goals - Lunn(6):
ROCHDALE H. - Cahill: Buxton Jones Short Ralph: Smith
Fishwick: Scholes Dagnall Hanson Bailey Parsons Parr:
Tries - Short Ralph Smith Parsons: Goal - Jones:
Referee D T H Davies (Manchester) Att - 2093 H.T. 10 - 8

Tue 19 Aug 1958 BATLEY away won 21 - 18
BATLEY - S.Thompson: Clark Sutton Cox O'Hara: Hirst
Talbot: Palmer Moyser Fearnley Armstead R.Thompson
Briggs: Tries - Clark Cox: Goals - S.Thompson(6):
CASTLEFORD - Lunn: Ward Sheridan Burton Battye: Walsh
Evans: Hirst Corban K.Pye Howard Wright Tonkinson:
Tries - Ward(2) Walsh: Goals - Lunn(6):
Referee G Davies (Wakefield) Att - 3000 H.T. 10 - 10

Sat 23 Aug 1958 HULL KINGSTON ROVERS away
won 26 - 16
HULL K R - Fishwick: Wilson Mageen Mortimer Coulson:
Riley Elliott: Grice Walters Coverdale Griffett Taylor
Scholes: Tries - Grice Griffett: Goals - Fishwick(5):
CASTLEFORD - Lunn: Ward Sheridan Barnes Battye:
Burton Evans: Berry JAMES LAWSON(431) K.Pye Howard
Taylor Tonkinson:
Tries - Sheridan(3) Battye Evans Pye: Goals - Lunn(4):
Referee J Jowett (Leeds) Att - 5300 H.T. 15 - 6

Tue 26 Aug 1958 DONCASTER home won 20 - 4
CASTLEFORD - Lunn: Ward Barnes Battye East: Burton
Evans: Berry Corban K.Pye Wright Taylor Tonkinson:
Tries - Battye East: Goals - Lunn(5) Barnes(2):
DONCASTER - Appleyard: Hinchcliffe Ratcliffe Hayter
Williamson: Wrigglesworth Northern: Belshaw Larkin Burt
Barrett Baddeley Shoebottom: Goals - Appleyard(2):
Referee J H Chadwick (Batley) Att - 3149 H.T. 8 - 4

Sat 30 Aug 1958 HULL KINGSTON ROVERS home
lost 5 - 33   YORKSHIRE CUP ROUND 1
CASTLEFORD - Lunn: Ward Sheridan Barnes Battye:
Burton Evans: Berry PETER UMPLEBY(432) K.Pye Howard
Wright Tonkinson: Try - Wright: Goal - Barnes:
HULL K R - Kellett: Wilson Riley Mageen Shaw: Key Elliott:
Grice Keegan Sims Holland Scholes Taylor:
Tries - Riley(2) Kellett Wilson Shaw Key Elliott:
Goals - Kellett(6):
Referee C F Appleton (Warrington) Att - 4369 H.T. 2 - 8

Sat 6 Sep 1958 SWINTON away lost 3 - 37
SWINTON - Gowers: Berry Mather Blan Doughty:
Parkinson Cartwright: Thompson Roberts Lamb Moses
Smith Haynes: Tries - Berry(3) Doughty(3) Parkinson
Lamb Smith: Goals - Gowers(5):
CASTLEFORD - Lunn: Ward Sheridan Hattee East: Walsh
Evans: Hirst Peter Umpleby Berry Howard Taylor
Tonkinson: Try - Taylor:
Referee J Flanagan (Keighley) Att - 6350 H.T. nil - 17

Sat 13 Sep 1958 BRAMLEY home won 10 - 9
CASTLEFORD - Lunn: Ward Sheridan(S/O) Battye East:
Burton Evans: Berry Bridges K.Pye Howard E.Bryant Taylor:
Goals - Lunn(5):
BRAMLEY - Wilson: Noble Kelly Rushton Humphries:
Dudley Bunting: Hammill Kennedy Baldwin Shaw Sykes
Garbutt: Try - Humphries: Goals - Wilson(3):
Referee J Senior (Bradford) Att - 2000 H.T. 6 - 7

Sat 20 Sep 1958 LIVERPOOL CITY away lost 7 - 16
LIVERPOOL C - Ashby: Halton Speakman Hunt
Donaldson: Twiss Woodrow: Payne Fishwick Simpson
Shiels Cartledge Teggin:
Tries - Donaldson Fishwick: Goals - Twiss(5):
CASTLEFORD - Lunn: Ward Sheridan Battye Walsh: Burton
Evans: Wright Bridges K.Pye Tonkinson E.Bryant Taylor:
Try - Burton: Goals - Lunn(2):
Referee R Gelder (Wakefield) Att - 800 H.T. 4 - 7

Sat 27 Sep 1958 KEIGHLEY away lost 7 - 21
KEIGHLEY - J.Phillips: Hollindrake Ellerby Hallas Bleasby:
Sabine Hebden: Shreeve Hemmings Bardgett S.Phillips
Glynn Crewdson: Tries - Hollindrake Hallas Bleasby
Sabine Hemmings: Goals - J.Phillips(3)
CASTLEFORD - Lunn: Ward Hattee Burton Battye: ALAN
HARDISTY(433) Evans: Wright Bridges K.Pye Howard
E.Bryant Taylor: Try - Taylor: Goals - Lunn Hattee:
Referee C F Appleton (Warri'ton) Att - 4000 H.T. 2 - 10

Sat 4 Oct 1958 BARROW home lost 15 - 21
CASTLEFORD - Barnes: Sheridan Hattee Burton Battye:
Hardisty Evans: Wright Bridges K.Pye Howard Tonkinson
Taylor: Tries - Burton Battye Evans: Goals - Barnes(3):
BARROW - Dawes: Lowther Woolveridge Skeels Castle:
Horne Harris: Hubbold McIntyre Suart Grundy Ducie
Goodwin: Tries - Castle(2) Lowther McIntyre Grundy:
Goals - Dawes(3):
Referee J Manley (Warrington) Att - 2500 H.T. 5 - 11

Sat 11 Oct 1958 HULL KINGSTON ROVERS home
Lost 5 - 12
CASTLEFORD - Lunn: Burton Hattee Sheridan HOWARD
CARTWRIGHT(434): Hardisty Evans: Wright Bridges K.Pye
Howard Tonkinson Taylor:
Try - Tonkinson: Goal - Lunn:
HULL K R - Kellett: Coulson Riley Mortimer Wilson: Key
Elliott: Grice Brookfield Rogers Keegan Taylor Jacques:
Tries - Coulson(2):   Goals - Kellett(3):
Referee J P Hebblethwaite (York) Att - 2145 H.T. 5 - 3

SEASON 1958-59

Sat 18 Oct 1958 DEWSBURY away won 12 - 10
DEWSBURY - Cox: Taylor Callighan Broadhead Clark:
Foley Halloran: Kirk Harden Lumb Popplewell Anson
Marchant: Tries - Broadhead Foley: Goals - Cox(2):
CASTLEFORD - Lunn: PENI LATU(435) Hattee Sheridan
Battye: Burton Evans: Hirst Bridges K.Pye E.Bryant
Tonkinson W.Bryant: Tries - Burton(2): Goals - Lunn(3):
Referee G Philpott (Leeds) Att - 2000 H.T. 9 - nil

**Sat 25 Oct 1958 BLACKPOOL BOROUGH home
won 10 - 8**
CASTLEFORD - Lunn: Battye Burton Sheridan Ward:
Hardisty Evans: Askin Bridges K.Pye Tonkinson Howard
E.Bryant: Tries - Ward Pye: Goals - Lunn(2):
BLACKPOOL B - Lowe: Emmitt Ryder O'Brien Foden:
Brennan Dunn: Fisher Lannon Maughan Parker Standish
Knowles: Tries - Emmitt(2): Goal - Lowe:
Referee D T H Davies (Manchester) Att - 2250 H.T. 4 - 5

Sat 1 Nov 1958 HUNSLET away lost 12 - 35
HUNSLET - Langton: Preece Stockdill Walker Byrom:
Gabbitas Doyle: Cooper Smith Platt Brumfield Gunney
Shaw: Tries - Preece(3) Walker(2) Byrom Shaw:
Goals - Langton(7):
CASTLEFORD - Lunn: East Hattee Sheridan Ward: Burton
Evans: Askin Bridges K.Pye Howard E.Bryant Taylor:
Tries - Sheridan Pye: Goals - Lunn(3):
Referee N T Railton (Wigan) Att - 4500 H.T. 7 - 15

Sat 8 Nov 1958 HUDDERSFIELD home lost 14 - 19
CASTLEFORD - Lunn: East Burton Sheridan Ward: Hardisty
Evans: Askin Bridges K.Pye Howard Taylor Tonkinson:
Tries - Burton Taylor: Goals - Lunn(4):
HUDDERSFIELD - Dyson: Iredale Barrow Ashcroft Breen:
Balmforth Quinn: Slevin Wood Killern Fairbank Colburn
Clarke: Tries - Iredale Barrow Breen: Goals - Dyson(5):
Referee J H Chadwick (Batley) Att - 3000 H.T. 12 - 9

**Sat 22 Nov 1958 FEATHERSTONE ROVERS home
won 27 - 14**
CASTLEFORD - Lunn: East Sheridan Burton Ward: Hardisty
GEORGE BROWN(436): Hirst Bridges K.Pye Howard
Wright Tonkinson: Tries - Ward(2) Burton Hardisty
Tonkinson: Goals - Lunn(6):
FEATHERSTONE R - Cooper: Kinsey Evans Hunt Woolford:
Mullaney Marchant: Moore Ward Hockley Ellis Lambert
Clawson: Tries - Kinsey Mullaney: Goals - Clawson(4):
Referee J P Hebblethwaite(York) Att - 4420 H.T. 9 -12

Sat 29 Nov 1958 DONCASTER away lost 14 - 18
DONCASTER - Swales: Worsley Naylor Halifihi Williamson:
Wrigglesworth Northern: Belshaw Larkin Burt Hepworth
Matthews Sykes:
Tries - Wrigglesworth(2): Goals - Swales(6):
CASTLEFORD - Lunn: East Sheridan Burton Ward: Hardisty
Brown: Hirst Bridges K.Pye Howard Wright Tonkinson:
Tries - Pye Wright: Goals - Lunn(4):
Referee A E Durkin (Dewsbury) Att – 1000 H.T. 8 - 12

Sat 6 Dec 1958 YORK home won 18 - 7
CASTLEFORD - Lunn: East Sheridan Burton Ward: Hardisty
Brown: Hirst Bridges K.Pye Howard Wright Tonkinson:
Tries - Sheridan Brown Pye Wright: Goals - Lunn(3):
YORK - Hargreaves: B.Smith G.Smith Drake Todd:
Flannery Jackson: Yorke Milner Henderson Watts Dawson
Deighton: Try - Hargreaves: Goals - Yorke(2):
Referee J Senior (Bradford) Att - 2665 H.T. 16 - 4

**Sat 13 Dec 1958 BLACKPOOL BOROUGH away
lost 10 - 23**
BLACKPOOL B - Dutton: Emmitt Wood Lowe Hutson:
Brennan Dunn: Parker Standish Healey Fisher Weir Lomas:
Tries - Emmitt(3) Lowe Brennan: Goals - Weir(3) Lowe:
CASTLEFORD - Lunn: East Hattee Burton Ward: Hardisty
Brown: Hirst Bridges K.Pye Howard Wright Tonkinson:
Tries - Hardisty Brown: Goals - Lunn(2):
Referee G Scott (Wakefield) Att - 1500 H.T. nil - 3

Sat 20 Dec 1958 HALIFAX home lost 15 - 40
CASTLEFORD - Lunn: East Sheridan Burton Ward: Hattee
Brown: Hirst Bridges K.Pye Wright WILLIAM
BROWNLEY(437) Tonkinson:
Tries - Burton Hattee Pye: Goals - Lunn (3):
HALIFAX - Briers: Snowden Dean Palmer Freeman:
Williams Pratt: Thorley Shaw Fairbank Wilkinson Sparks
Clifft: Tries - Snowden(2) Palmer(2) Williams(2) Briers
Dean Freeman Wilkinson: Goals - Williams(5):
Referee K R Rathbone (St Helens) Att - 2600 H.T. 5 - 19

Thu 25 Dec 1958 WAKEFIELD TRINITY home lost 7 -19
CASTLEFORD - Lunn: Battye Sheridan Burton Ward:
Hardisty Brown: Hirst Bridges K.Pye Howard Wright
Tonkinson: Try - Battye: Goals - Lunn(2):
WAKEFIELD T - Mortimer: Smith Skene Fox Lotriet: Rollin
Holliday: Adams Oakes Evans Vines Lindley Lamming:
Tries - Fox(2) Lotriet Adams Lamming:
Goals - Mortimer Fox:
Referee E Clay (Rothwell) Att - 5700 H.T. 5 - 5

**Fri 26 Dec 1958 FEATHERSTONE ROVERS away
lost 12 - 27**
FEATHERSTONE R - Fennell: Smith Greatorex Hunt
Woolford: Mullaney Marchant: Moore Fawley Anderson
Clamp Jones Clawson: Tries - Smith(2) Woolford(2)
Greatorex Hunt Clawson: Goals - Clawson(3):
CASTLEFORD - Lunn: PETER E.SMALL(438) Sheridan
Burton East: Battye Evans: Hirst Bridges JOHN
CLARK(439) Howard W.Bryant Tonkinson:
Tries - Burton(2): Goals - Lunn(3):
Referee H Harrison (Horbury) Att - 3700 H.T. 5 - 13

Sat 27 Dec 1958 YORK away lost 7 - 16
YORK - Hargreaves: Swift Smith Thompson Foster:
Flannery Hunter: Henderson Crosby Watts O'Brien Kidd
Dawson: Tries - Swift Dawson: Goals - Hunter(5):
CASTLEFORD - Lunn: Frank East Small Burton Ward:
Hardisty Evans: Hirst David Hughes K.Pye Howard Wright
Tonkinson: Try - Evans: Goals - Lunn(2):
Referee T W Watkinson (Man'ster) Att - 4008 H.T. 4 - 12

179

SEASON 1958-59

Sat 3 Jan 1959 DEWSBURY home won 29 - nil
CASTLEFORD - Lunn: Battye Small Burton Ward: Hardisty
Brown: Hirst Bridges K.Pye Wright Tonkinson Sheridan:
Tries - Sheridan(2) Battye Small Hardisty: Goals - Lunn(7):
DEWSBURY - Popplewell: Taylor Callighan M.Clark J.Clark:
Bousted Foley: Kirk Waring Lumb Pratt Withington
Marchant:
Referee J Flanagan (Keighley) Att - 1789 H.T. 9 - nil

Sat 24 Jan 1959 HULL home lost 10 - 22
CASTLEFORD - Lunn: Battye Small Burton Ward: Hardisty
Brown: Hirst Bridges K.Pye Howard Wright Sheridan:
Tries - Small Ward: Goals - Lunn(2):
HULL - Keegan: Gill Ali Cowan Watts: Matthews Finn:
Scott Harris J.Drake Sykes P.Whiteley J.Whiteley:
Tries - Finn(2) Cowan P.Whiteley: Goals - Keegan(5):
Referee K Rathbone (St Helens) Att - 2736 H.T. 5 - 2

Sat 31 Jan 1959 KEIGHLEY home lost 15 - 28
CASTLEFORD - Lunn: ROBERT TAYLOR(440) Small Burton
Ward: Battye Brown: Hirst Bridges K.Pye W.Bryant
Tonkinson Sheridan:
Tries - Brown Pye Sheridan: Goals - Lunn(3):
KEIGHLEY - J.Phillips: Hollindrake Jackson Mortimer
Bleasby: Smith Hebden: Shreeve Waring Bardgett Lowe
S.Phillips Glynn: Tries - S.Phillips(2) Hollindrake Mortimer
Smith Glynn: Goals - J.Phillips(5):
Referee G Scott (Wakefield) Att - 2510 H.T. 12 - 15

Sat 7 Feb 1959 BARROW away lost nil - 26
BARROW - Ball: Barker Skeels Rea Castle: Horne Black:
Suart McIntyre Ducie Grundy Delves Goodwin:
Tries Barker(2) Skeels McIntyre Ducie Grundy:
Goals - Ball(4):
CASTLEFORD - Lunn: Battye Burton Small Ward: Hardisty
Brown: Hirst Bridges Askin Clark Tonkinson Sheridan:
Referee A E Durkin (Dewsbury) Att - 3726 H.T. nil - 15

Sat 14 Feb 1959 LIVERPOOL CITY home won 22 - 12
CASTLEFORD - Lunn: Battye R.Taylor Small Ward: Hardisty
Brown: Hirst Bridges K.Pye Howard Tonkinson Sheridan:
Tries - Taylor Hardisty Brown Sheridan: Goals - Lunn(5):
LIVERPOOL C - Hardman: Barton Wright Speakman
Halton: Hunt Walker: Payne Fishwick Simpson Cartlidge
Lyons Hockenhull:
Tries - Hardman Wright: Goals - Hunt(2) Walker(DG):
Referee J Manley (Warrington) Att - 1650 H.T. 17 - 7

Sat 21 Feb 1959 BRAMLEY away won 11 - 8
CHALLENGE CUP ROUND 1
BRAMLEY - Wilson: Noble Dudley Rushton Kershaw:
Wrigglesworth Bunting: Baldwin Wood Marker Baddeley
Hammill Barker: Goals - Wilson(4):
CASTLEFORD - Lunn: Battye R.Taylor Small Burton:
Hardisty Brown: Hirst Bridges K.Pye Howard Tonkinson
Sheridan: Try - Burton: Goals - Lunn(4):
Referee D T H Davies (Manchester) Att - 2680 H.T. 5 - 6

Sat 7 Mar 1959 HULL KINGSTON ROVERS away
lost nil - 20   CHALLENGE CUP ROUND 2
HULL K R - Kellett: Coulson Riley Key Moat: Paul Elliott:
Grice Ackerley Holland Jenkins Jacques Taylor:
Tries - Coulson Moat Jacques Taylor: Goals - Kellett(4):
CASTLEFORD - Lunn: Battye R.Taylor Small Ward: Hardisty
Brown: Hirst Bridges K.Pye Howard Tonkinson Sheridan:
Referee N T Railton (Wigan) Att - 7000 H.T. nil - 4

Wed 11 Mar 1959 BRADFORD NORTHERN away
won 23 - 9
BRADFORD N - Seddon: Daniels Penketh Winnard
Jenkins: McLean Higgins: McLean Kosanovic Radford
Jones Walton Hey: Tries - Daniels Winnard Hey:
CASTLEFORD - Lunn: Burton R.Taylor Small Ward:
Hardisty Brown: Hirst Bridges K.Pye Howard Tonkinson
Sheridan:
Tries - Brown(2) Taylor Ward Pye: Goals - Lunn(4):
Referee R Gelder (Wakefield) Att - 2000 H.T. 12 - 6

Sat 14 Mar 1959 BRADFORD NORTHERN home
lost 11 - 12
CASTLEFORD - Lunn: Battye R.Taylor Small Ward: Hardisty
Brown: Hirst Bridges K.Pye Askin Tonkinson Sheridan:
Try - Battye: Goals - Lunn(4):
BRADFORD N - Beevers: Doran Jenkins Seddon Daniels:
Penketh Higgins: Mclean Kosanovic Radford Jones
Walton Hey: Tries - Seddon Daniels: Goals - Seddon(3):
Referee H Chadwick (Batley) Att - 1993 H.T. 7 - 10

Sat 21 Mar 1959 BRAMLEY away lost 10 - 11
BRAMLEY - Winnard: Murthick Wrigglesworth Jackson
Humphries: Rushton Pollard: Hammill Wood Marker
Baddeley Shaw Dudley: Try - Marker: Goals - Winnard(4):
CASTLEFORD - Lunn: Battye Burton Small Ward: Hardisty
Brown: Hirst Bridges K.Pye Howard Tonkinson Sheridan:
Goals - Lunn(4) Sheridan(DG):
Referee J Senior (Bradford) Att - 1300 H.T. 6 - 9

Sat 28 Mar 1959 HULL away lost 13 - 31
HULL - Keegan: Cowan Boustead Turner Waters:
Broadhurst Smith: Scott Holdstock Hambling P.Whiteley
Sykes J.Whiteley: Tries - Smith(2) Cowan(2) Boustead
Scott Sykes: Goals - Keegan(5):
CASTLEFORD - Lunn: Burton R.Taylor Small Ward:
Hardisty Brown: Hirst Bridges Howard Wright Tonkinson
Sheridan: Tries - Small(3):   Goals - Lunn(2):
Referee G Davies (Wakefield) Att - 8000 H.T. 5 - 23

Tue 30 Mar 1959 HUNSLET home lost 14 - 23
CASTLEFORD - Lunn: Battye R.Taylor Small Burton:
Hardisty Brown: Hirst Bridges Howard Tonkinson Charles
Wright E.Bryant:
Tries - Taylor Tonkinson: Goals - Lunn(4):
HUNSLET - Langton: Colin Preece Walker Griffiths:
Gabbitas Doyle: Hatfield Tate Rhodes Poole Gunney
Shaw:
Tries - Preece Walker Hatfield Tate Shaw:
Goals - Langton(4);
Referee A E Durkin (Dewsbury) Att - 4270 H.T. 9 - 8

SEASON 1958-59

**Tue 31 Mar 1959 WAKEFIELD TRINITY away
lost 14 - 47**
WAKEFIELD T - Metcalfe: Smith Skene Fox Round: Rollin
Holliday: Harrison Haigh Vines Firth Lamming Turner:
Tries - Smith(3) Round(2) Lamming(2) Harrison Haigh
Firth Turner: Goals - Fox(7):
CASTLEFORD - Lunn: Battye R.Taylor Small TREVOR
DALE(441): Burton Brown: Hirst Bridges Askin Howard
Tonkinson E.Bryant:
Tries - Battye Burton: Goals - Lunn(4):
Referee C F Appleton (Warr'ton) Att - 7000 H.T. 7 - 24

Sat 4 Apr 1959 HUDDERSFIELD away lost 23 - 27
HUDDERSFIELD - Dyson: Barrow Plunkett Ashcroft Breen:
Cecil Lockwood: Slevin Wood Killen Fairbank Colburn
Driver: Tries - Breen(3) Barrow Ashcroft :
Goals Dyson(3) Colburn(3):
CASTLEFORD - Barnes: Brown R.Taylor Small Burton:
Hardisty KEITH HEPWORTH(442): Hirst Corban Askin
Howard Tonkinson Sheridan:
Tries - Taylor Burton Hardisty Hepworth Sheridan:
Goals - Barnes(4):
Referee H Pearce (Leeds) Att - 2530 H.T. 13 - 12

Wed 8 Apr 1959 BATLEY home won 39 - 3
CASTLEFORD - Lunn: Battye R.Taylor Small Burton:
Hardisty Brown: Hirst Bridges Askin C.Taylor Sheridan
THOMAS SMALES(443):
Tries - Hardisty(2) Sheridan(2) Battye R.Taylor Brown:
Goals - Lunn(9):
BATLEY - Shuttleworth: Brook Sutcliffe Field Sutton:
Lawson Geldard: Palmer Harewood McDermott Priestley
Briggs Armstead:
Try - Briggs:
Referee H Harrison (Horbury) Att - 1707 H.T. 15 - nil

Sat 18 Apr 1959 HALIFAX away lost 2 - 27
HALIFAX - Owen: Snowden Burnett Palmer Freeman:
Dean Pratt: Thorley T.Taylor Fairbank Turnbull Sparks
Clifft:
Tries - Turnbull(3) Snowden(2) Freeman Sparks:
Goals - Owen(3):
CASTLEFORD - Hattee: Battye R.Taylor Small Burton:
Hardisty Brown: Hirst Bridges K.Pye C.Taylor Sheridan
Smales: Goal - Hattee:
Referee R Gelder (Wakefield) Att - 3800 H.T. 2 - 19

**Tue 21 Apr 1959 ROCHDALE HORNETS away
lost 10 - 16**
ROCHDALE H - Cahill: Buxton Trumble Lawrenson Ralph:
Chisnall Fishwick: Grundy Dagnall Hanson Bailey Thomas
Parr: Tries - Lawrenson Ralph: Goals - Cahill(5):
CASTLEFORD - Barnes: Walsh Clifford Burton Small Ward:
Hardisty J.Pye: Hirst Bridges Askin Howard Sheridan
Smales: Tries - Small Ward: Goals - Barnes(2):
Referee G Wilson (Dewsbury) Att - 2641 H.T. 8 - 4

Sat 25 Apr 1959 SWINTON home lost 5 - 34
CASTLEFORD - Lunn: Battye Small Barnes Walsh: Hardisty
J.Pye: Hirst Bridges K.Pye George(Charlie)Howard

Sheridan Thomas Smales: Try - Battye: Goal - Barnes:
SWINTON - Gowers: McMahon Smethurst Critchley
Stopford: Parkinson Cartwright: Thompson Roberts Leese
Lamb Norburn Blan: Tries - Stopford(3) McMahon(3)
Cartwright Norburn: Goals - Gowers(5):
Referee F J Howker (Rochdale) Att - 1110 H.T. 2 - 10

**Thu 7 May 1959 CASTLEFORD - 37 HARRY STREET"S
XIII – 42 TESTIMONIAL MATCH for CHARLIE HOWARD
FRIENDLY**
CASTLEFORD - Hattee: Small Ward Burton Walsh: Hardisty
K.Pye: Hirst Bridges Howard Tonkinson Sheridan H.Street:
Tries - Howard(2) Small Ward Burton Walsh Hardisty
Sheridan Street: Goals - Hattee(2) Howard(2) Bridges:
HARRY STREET'S XIII - Mullaney(Featherstone R):
Smith(Featherstone R) Brownley(Castleford)
Woolford(Featherstone R) Marchant(Featherstone R):
Fennell(Featherstone R) D.Fox(Featherstone
R)Anderson(Featherstone R) Corban(Castleford)
Berry(Castleford) Robinson(Leeds) Sewell(Leeds)
F.Ward(Leeds):
Tries - Woolford(3) Robinson(2) Ward(2) Brownley Corban
Berry: Goals - Fennell(4) Mullaney Sewell:
Referee H Pickersgill (Castleford)

Alan Hardisty
D. No 433
1958-59 to1970-71
Double R.L. Cup Winning Captain
Most tries in a Career 206

Howard Cartwright
D. No 434
1958-59 to 1963-64

George Brown
D. No 436
1958-59 to 1962-63

Peter Small
D. No 438
1958-59 to 1968-69

Keith Hepworth
D. No 442
1958-59 to 1971 72

John Clark
D. No 439
1958-59 to 1964-65

CHALLENGE CUP ROUND 2 SATURDAY 7 MARCH1959 HULL KINGSTON ROVERS AWAY LOST NIL - 20
Back Row – Charlie Howard Geoff Ward Jack Hirst Albert Tonkinson Peter Small Keith Bridges Robert Taylor
Front Row – Alan Hardisty George Brown John Sheridan Ken Pye Albert Lunn Colin Battye

SEASON 1958-59

D.N	PLAYER		DEBUT	L MATCH	APP	SU3	T.AP	TRI'S	G'LS	D.G	P'TS
302	HOWARD	GEORGE (CHARLIE)		25/04/1959	31	Ɔ	31	0	0	0	0
330	PYE	KENNETH			32	Ɔ	32	8	0	0	24
340	HUGHES	DAVID		27/12/1958	1	Ɔ	1	0	0	0	0
341	LUNN	ALBERT			37	Ɔ	37	0	119	0	238
371	EAST	FRANK		27/12/1958	12	Ɔ	12	1	0	0	3
380	BURTON	CLIFFORD		21/04/1959	36	Ɔ	36	12	0	0	36
382	SHERIDAN	JOHN			35	Ɔ	35	12	0	1	38
389	BARNES	JACK			7	Ɔ	7	0	13	0	26
404	EVANS	RONALD			17	Ɔ	17	3	0	0	9
406	TAYLOR	COLIN			12	Ɔ	12	3	0	0	9
410	BRYANT	EDWARD			8	Ɔ	8	0	0	0	0
412	WALSH	BARRY			6	Ɔ	6	1	0	0	3
414	WARD	GEOFFREY G			30	Ɔ	30	8	0	0	24
415	HATTEE	ARTHUR			9	Ɔ	9	1	2	0	7
417	CORBAN	IAN			4	Ɔ	4	0	0	0	0
419	BRIDGES	KEITH			33	Ɔ	33	0	0	0	0
420	TONKINSON	ALBERT			33	Ɔ	33	3	0	0	9
421	BERRY	JOHN			5	Ɔ	5	0	0	0	0
422	PYE	JEFFREY			2	Ɔ	2	0	0	0	0
423	WRIGHT	CHARLIE		30/03/1959	19	Ɔ	19	3	0	0	9
424	HIRST	JACK			30	Ɔ	30	0	0	0	0
426	BRYANT	WILLIAM			3	Ɔ	3	0	0	0	0
427	BATTYE	COLIN			27	Ɔ	27	10	0	0	30
430	ASKIN	MAURICE			9	Ɔ	9	0	0	0	0
431	LAWSON	JAMES	23/08/1958	23/08/1958	1	Ɔ	1	0	0	0	0
432	UMPLEBY	PETER	30/08/1958	06/09/1958	2	Ɔ	2	0	0	0	0
433	HARDISTY	ALAN	27/09/1958		27	Ɔ	27	7	0	0	21
434	CARTWRIGHT	HOWARD	11/10/1958		1	Ɔ	1	0	0	0	0
435	LATU	PENI	18/10/1958	18/10/1958	1	Ɔ	1	0	0	0	0
436	BROWN	GEORGE	22/11/1958		22	Ɔ	22	7	0	0	21
437	BROWNLEY	WILLIAM	20/12/1958		1	Ɔ	1	0	0	0	0
438	SMALL	PETER	26/12/1958		20	Ɔ	20	6	0	0	18
439	CLARK	JOHN	26/12/1958		2	Ɔ	2	0	0	0	0
440	TAYLOR	ROBERT	31/01/1959		12	Ɔ	12	5	0	0	15
441	DALE	TREVOR	31/03/1959		1	Ɔ	1	0	0	0	0
442	HEPWORTH	KEITH	04/04/1959		1	Ɔ	1	1	0	0	3
443	SMALES	THOMAS	08/04/1959	25/04/1959	4	Ɔ	4	0	0	0	0
	37		**13**	**9**	**533**	**Ɔ**	**533**	**91**	**134**	**1**	**543**

COMPETITION		P	W	D	L	FOR	AGT
LEAGUE	POSITION 25 OF 30	38	13	0	25	527	732
YORK'S CUP		1	0	0	1	5	33
RL CUP		2	1	0	1	11	28
PLAYERS RECORDS		**41**	**14**	**0**	**27**	**543**	**793**

Albert Lunn scored his 1,000th point for Castleford in the home game versus Featherstone Rovers on 22 November 1958 playing at full back; he kicked 6 goals in a 27-4 win. Albert then became the first player to score 500 goals for the club in the 12-11 defeat at home to Bradford Northern on 14 March 1959. He went on to improve his own club record for the most goals in a season to 119.

Three notable Debutantes were Alan Hardisty, Peter Small and Keith Hepworth

SEASON 1959-60

Sat 8 Aug 1959 DONCASTER away lost 25 - 29
CHARITY MATCH FRIENDLY
DONCASTER - Stokes: Hinchcliffe(Worsley)
Halifihi(Faleteau) Frost(Naylor)Williamson: Devaney
Downs(Northern): Hartley Larkin Field Sykes Burt(Yemm)
Scholes: Tries - Faleteau Devaney Northern Hartley
Scholes: Goals - Stokes(7):
CASTLEFORD - Lunn: Battye R.Taylor Dale Smart: Walsh
Evans: Hirst Corban K.Pye(Askin) Tonkinson C.Taylor
Sheridan:
Tries - Smart(2) Sheridan(2) Battye: Goals - Lunn(5):
Referee -   Att -   H.T.

Sat 15 Aug 1959 LIVERPOOL CITY away won 25 - 13
LIVERPOOL C - Ashby: Halton Hockenhull Hunt
Speakman: McGrath Toohey: Payne Dutton Cartledge
Winstanley Davies Dibble:
Tries - Halton Hockenhull McGrath: Goals - Hunt(2):
CASTLEFORD - Lunn: Battye R.Taylor Small Smart:
Hardisty Hepworth: Hirst Corban K.Pye Tonkinson
C.Taylor Sheridan:
Tries - R.Taylor(2) Small Smart Hardisty: Goals - Lunn(5):
Referee A E Durkin (Dewsbury) Att - 1000 H.T.13 - 7

Wed 19 Aug 1959 BATLEY home won 22 - 16
CASTLEFORD - Lunn: Battye R.Taylor Small Smart:
Hardisty Hepworth: Hirst Corban K.Pye Tonkinson
C.Taylor Sheridan:
Tries - Battye Smart Hardisty Hepworth: Goals - Lunn(5):
BATLEY - Thompson: Brook Sutcliffe A.N.Other Clark:
Lawton Foster: Redfearn Whitehead Helliwell Kelly
Langhorne Briggs:
Tries - Sutcliffe Briggs: Goals - Thompson(3) Lawton(2):
Referee J Senior (Bradford) Att - 2583 H.T. 14 - 9

Sat 22 Aug 1959 HUNSLET home lost 14 - 29
CASTLEFORD - Lunn: Battye R.Taylor Small DOUGLAS
IREDALE(444): Hardisty Hepworth: Hirst Corban K.Pye
Tonkinson C.Taylor Sheridan:
Tries - Battye Small Iredale Tonkinson: Goal - Lunn:
HUNSLET - Langton: Colin Stockdill Preece Walker:
Gabbitas Doyle: Hatfield Smith Eyre Poole Gunney Shaw:
Tries - Gabbitas(2) Shaw(2) Stockdill Walker Poole:
Goals - Langton(4):
Referee A Fairbotham (Hull) Att - 4486 H.T. 8 - 10

Thur 27 Aug 1959 BARROW away won 20 - 13
BARROW - Dawes: Woolveridge Goodwin Rea Castle:
Sharpe Black: Hubbold Wilson Whitehead Grundy
Robinson Delves:
Tries - Sharpe Hubbold Wilson: Goals - Dawes(2):
CASTLEFORD - Lunn: Smart R.Taylor Small Iredale:
Hardisty Brown: Hirst Corban K.Pye Tonkinson C.Taylor
Sheridan:
Tries - R.Taylor Iredale Hardisty Brown: Goals - Lunn(4):
Referee G Philpott (Leeds) Att - 3670 H.T. 12 - 3

Sat 29 Aug 1959 DEWSBURY away lost 14 - 27
YORKSHIRE CUP ROUND 1
DEWSBURY - Ledgard: Laycock Calligan Bosworth Clark:

Moore O'Donnell: Kirk Lockwood Bamford Fisher Farrar
Sayer: Tries - Clark(2) O'Donnell Kirk Lockwood:
Goals - Ledgard(6):
CASTLEFORD - Lunn: Derek Smart R.Taylor Small Iredale:
Hardisty Brown: Hirst Corban K.Pye Tonkinson C.Taylor
Sheridan: Tries - Smart(2) Brown Tonkinson: Goal - Lunn:
Referee N T Railton (Wigan) Att - 2000 H.T. 11 - 7

Sat 5 Sep 1959 BLACKPOOL BOROUGH home
won 44 - 3
CASTLEFORD - Lunn: Ward R.Taylor Barnes Iredale: Brown
Hepworth: Hirst Bridges K.Pye Tonkinson C.Taylor
Sheridan: Tries - R.Taylor(3) Ward(2) Pye(2) Iredale
Brown C.Taylor Sheridan Lunn: Goals - Lunn(4):
BLACKPOOL B - Gregson: Ratcliffe Wood Foden
Meadows: Wilkinson Dunn: Wright Hall Walsh Maughan
Nrophy Knowles: Try - Wright:
Referee F Howker (Rochdale) Att - 2162 H.T. 14 - 3

Sat 12 Sep 1959 KEIGHLEY away lost 12 - 26
KEIGHLEY - Mortimer: Hollindrake Sabine Dudley Bleasby:
Birchall Parr: Bloomfield Waring Narey Glynn Crewdson
Ward: Tries - Sabine(2) Narey(2) Bleasby Ward:
Goals - Mortimer(4):
CASTLEFORD - Lunn: Battye R.Taylor Small Iredale: Brown
Hepworth: Hirst Bridges K.Pye Tonkinson C.Taylor
Sheridan: Tries - Iredale Pye: Goals - Lunn(3):
Referee H Harrison (Horbury) Att - 3000 H.T. 7 - 12

Sat 19 Sep 1959 HUDDERSFIELD home won 32 - 7
CASTLEFORD - Lunn: R.Taylor Barnes Small Iredale: J.Pye
Brown: Hirst Bridges K.Pye Tonkinson C.Taylor Sheridan:
Tries - Brown(3) J.Pye Hirst Sheridan:
Goals - Lunn(6) Barnes:
HUDDERSFIELD - Dyson: Breen Curry Ashcroft Wicks:
Lockwood Smales: Slevin Wood Flint Fairbank Devereux
Redfearn: Try - Fairbank: Goals - Dyson(2):
Referee J Manley (Warrington) Att - 3414 H.T. 17 - 7

Sat 26 Sep 1959 BRAMLEY away lost 10 - 14
BRAMLEY - Winnard: Noble Wrigglesworth Rushton
Humphries: Kelly Pollard: Hainsworth Kennedy Tindale
Baddeley Marker Wilson:
Tries - Humphries Kelly: Goals - Wilson(4):
CASTLEFORD - Lunn: R.Taylor Barnes Small Iredale: J.Pye
Brown: Hirst Bridges K.Pye Tonkinson C.Taylor Sheridan:
Tries - Barnes Iredale: Goals - Lunn(2):
Referee A E Durkin (Dewsbury) Att - 2600 H.T.10 - 4

Sat 3 Oct 1959 HULL KINGSTON ROVERS home
lost 8 - 14
CASTLEFORD - Lunn: Battye R.Taylor Small Iredale: J.Pye
Brown: Hirst Bridges Maurice Askin Tonkinson C.Taylor
Sheridan:
Tries - R.Taylor Small: Goal - Lunn:
HULL K R - Kellett: Coulson Wilson Burwell Paul: Moat
Bunting: Rowbottom Ackerley Coverdale Jenkins Farnhill
Jacques:
Tries - Burwell Paul: Goals - Kellett(4):
Referee D S Brown (Dewsbury) Att - 3268 H.T. 8 - 9

SEASON 1959-60

Sat 10 Oct 1959 YORK away lost 12 - 34
YORK - Hargreaves: Gillespie Smith Drake Todd: Flannery
Stevenson: Yorke Milner Dickinson Howden O'Brien
Dawson: Tries - Gillespie(2) Flannery(2) Dickinson(2)
Stevenson O'Brien: Goals - Yorke(5):
CASTLEFORD - Arthur Hattee: Battye R.Taylor Small
Iredale: J.Pye Brown: Hirst Bridges K.Pye Tonkinson
C.Taylor Sheridan: Tries - R.Taylor(2) Iredale(2):
Referee K Rathbone (St Helens) Att - 4000 H.T. 3 - 19

Sat 17 Oct 1959 DONCASTER home won 38 - 13
CASTLEFORD - Lunn: Battye R.Taylor Small Iredale: JOHN
WILSON(445) Brown: Hirst Bridges K.Pye Clark C.Taylor
Sheridan: Tries - Battye(4) R.Taylor Small Iredale Wilson
Clark Sheridan: Goals - Lunn (4):
DONCASTER - Smalley: Hinchcliffe Halifihi Wilkinson
Naylor: Devaney Northern: Hartley Heath Vessey Swales
Strawbridge Goldswain:
Tries - Halifihi Northern Heath: Goals - Swales(2):
Referee G Philpott (Leeds) Att - 1919 H.T. 20 - 3

Sat 24 Oct 1959 BATLEY away lost 13 - 18
BATLEY - Taylor: Clark Sutcliffe Field Ireland: Lawton
Foley: Harrison Moyser Fox Kelly Armstead Platt:
Tries - Clark(2) Lawton Moyser: Goals - Lawton(3):
CASTLEFORD - Lunn: Battye Dale Small Iredale: Wilson
Brown: Hirst Corban K.Pye Tonkinson C.Taylor Sheridan:
Tries - Battye Iredale C Taylor: Goals - Lunn(2):
Referee E Clay (Rothwell) Att - 2500 H.T. 10 - 5

**Sat 31 Oct 1959 ROCHDALE HORNETS home
won 21 - 13**
CASTLEFORD - Lunn: Battye Dale Ward Iredale: Wilson
Brown: Hirst JOSEPH HAMPTON(446) K.Pye Clark C.Taylor
Sheridan:
Tries - Iredale Brown Sheridan: Goals - Lunn(6):
ROCHDALE H - Cahill: Unsworth Jones Shortt Ledger:
Chisnall Fishwick: Scholes Dagnall Williams Thomas Parr
Horrocks: Tries - Shortt(2) Fishwick: Goals - Jones(2):
Referee K Rathbone (St Helens) Att - 2028 H.T. 6 - 8

Sat 7 Nov 1959 SALFORD away lost 12 - 25
SALFORD - Cheshire: Walker Preece E.Jones G.Jones:
Brennan Banks: Adamson McGuiness Donoghue Alder
Council Duffy: Tries - Cheshire Preece Brennan Banks
McGuiness: Goals - Walker(5):
CASTLEFORD - Lunn: Battye R.Taylor Small Iredale: Wilson
Brown: Hirst Bridges K.Pye Clark C.Taylor Sheridan:
Tries - Brown Bridges: Goals - Lunn(3):
Referee A E Durkin (Dewsbury) Att - 3000 H.T.7 - 20

Sat 14 Nov 1959 HULL away lost 10 - 46
HULL - Bateson: Cowan Saville Kershaw Wanklyn:
Matthews Finn: Evans Harris J.Drake Sykes W.Drake
Whiteley: Tries - Bateson(2) Matthews(2) Saville Kershaw
Wanklyn Finn J.Drake Sykes: Goals - Bateson(8):
CASTLEFORD - Lunn: Battye Ward Small Iredale: Wilson
Brown: Hirst Bridges K.Pye KENNETH RHODES(447)
W.Bryant C.Taylor: Tries - Iredale Hirst: Goals - Lunn(2):
Referee H Pearce (Leeds) Att - 5000 H.T. 5 - 20

**Sat 21 Nov 1959 LIVERPOOL CITY home
won 22 - 12**
CASTLEFORD - Lunn: Battye Ward Wilson Iredale:
Hardisty Hepworth: J.Berry Bridges K.Pye W.Bryant Clark
Sheridan:
Tries - Sheridan(2) Hardisty Hepworth: Goals - Lunn(5):
LIVERPOOL C - Ashby: Halton Hockenhull Hunt Pye:
Walker Woodrow: Payne Fishwick Simpson Cartledge
Davies McGrath: Tries - Halton Hunt: Goals - Payne(3):
Referee C F Appleton (Warr'ton) Att - 600 H.T. 12 - nil

**Sat 28 Nov 1959 BRADFORD NORTHERN away
lost 8 - 19**
BRADFORD N - Seddon: Doran Brook Winnard Smith:
Davies Lancaster: Marston Kosanovic Radford
Hemmingway Feather Jones:
Tries - Doran Lancaster Marston: Goals - Seddon(5):
CASTLEFORD - Lunn: Ward Dale Wilson Iredale: Hardisty
Hepworth: Hirst Bridges K.Pye C.Taylor Clark Sheridan:
Tries - Ward Bridges: Goal - Lunn:
Referee F J Howker (Rochdale) Att - 1700 H.T. 3 - 5

Sat 5 Dec 1959 SALFORD home lost 10 - 23
CASTLEFORD - Lunn: Ward R.Taylor Wilson Walsh:
Hardisty Brown: Hirst Bridges K.Pye Clark C.Taylor
Sheridan: Tries - R.Taylor(2): Goals - Lunn(2):
SALFORD - Gregory: G.Jones Preece Cheshire E.Jones:
Brennan Banks: Alder Boardman Donoghue Parsons
Hartley Duffy: Tries - G.Jones(2) Alder(2) Cheshire:
Goals - Cheshire(3) Preece:
Referee K.Rathbone (St Helens) Att - 1687 H.T. 5 - nil

Sat 12 Dec 1959 LEEDS away lost 15 - 29
LEEDS - Quinn: Hodgkinson Hallas Rosenberg Johnson:
Jones Horsman: Skelton Prior Jubb Fairbank Whitehead
Goodwin: Tries - Rosenberg(2) Horsman(2) Hodgkinson
Jones Skelton: Goals - Jones (4):
CASTLEFORD - Lunn: Ward R.Taylor COLIN
BUTTERFIELD(448) Dale: Wilson Brown: Hirst Bridges K
Pye E.Bryant C.Taylor Sheridan:
Tries - R.Taylor Brown Pye: Goals - Lunn(3):
Referee N T Railton (Wigan) Att - 2513 H.T. 5 - 16

Sat 19 Dec 1959 KEIGHLEY home won 11 - 10
CASTLEFORD - Lunn: Ward Wilson Barnes Trevor Dale:
Hardisty Brown: Hirst Bridges K.Pye C.Taylor E.Bryant
Sheridan: Tries - Wilson Hardisty Brown: Goal - Lunn:
KEIGHLEY - Hollindrake: Smith Cecil Jackson Bleasby:
Birchall Dudley: Bloomfield Waring Narey Glynn Holmes
F.Ward: Tries - Cecil Birchall: Goals - Hollindrake(2):
Referee F J Howker (Rochdale) Att - 1200 H.T. 5 - 5

**Fri 25 Dec 1959 WAKEFIELD TRINITY away
lost 2 - 20**
WAKEFIELD T - Round: F.Smith Skene Fox Thomas:
Poynton Holliday: Wilkinson Oakes J Smith Vines
Sampson Turner:
Tries - F.Smith Thomas J.Smith Turner: Goals - Fox(4):
CASTLEFORD - Lunn: Ward Barnes Wilson Small: Hardisty
Evans: Hirst Bridges K.Pye C.Taylor E.Bryant Sheridan:

SEASON 1959-60

Goal - Lunn:
Referee D T H Davies (Manchester) Att - 5370 H.T. 2 - 5

Sat 26 Dec 1959 FEATHERSTONE ROVERS home lost 5 - 24
CASTLEFORD - Lunn: Ward Barnes Wilson Small: Hardisty Brown: Hirst Corban K.Pye C.Taylor W.Bryant Sheridan:
Try - Wilson: Goal - Lunn:
FEATHERSTONE R - Fennell: Smith Greatorex Hunt Woolford: Mullaney Fox: Moore Fawley Anderson Lambert Hockley Clifft:
Tries - Clifft(2) Smith Mullaney: Goals - Fennell(6):
Referee E Clay (Rothwell) Att - 4800 H.T. nil - 14

Sat 2 Jan 1960 DONCASTER away won 15 - 11
DONCASTER - Hindley: Smith Wilkinson Strawbridge Askin: Redman Northern: Belshaw Heath Hartley Yemm Swales Hepworth:
Tries - Smith(2) Askin: Goal - Swales:
CASTLEFORD - Lunn: Butterfield Barnes Small Jeffrey Pye: Wilson Brown: Hirst Bridges K.Pye C.Taylor E.Bryant Sheridan:
Tries - Small(2) Brown: Goals - Lunn(3):
Referee C Whiteley (Ossett) Att - 1000 H.T. 8 - nil

Sat 9 Jan 1960 BRAMLEY home won 16 - 5
CASTLEFORD - Lunn: FRANK GREEN(449) Small Barnes Clark: Wilson Brown: Hirst Bridges K.Pye C.Taylor JOHN LINDLEY(450) Sheridan:
Tries - Small(2) Clark Wilson: Goals - Lunn(2):
BRAMLEY - Noble: Murthick Kelly Wrigglesworth Davies: Rushton Quinn: Chase Jenkins Hainsworth Marker Rogers Croll:
Try - Wrigglesworth: Goal - Rogers:
Referee A E Durkin (Dewsbury) Att - 2113 H.T. 7 - 5

Sat 23 Jan 1960 HULL KINGSTON ROVERS away lost 10 - 14
HULL K R - Kellett: Paul Wilson Riley Coulman: Moat Bunting: Rowbottom Ackerley Coverdale Jenkin Farnhill Last:
Tries - Moat Last: Goals - Kellett(4):
CASTLEFORD - Lunn: Green Small Barnes Clark: Wilson Brown: Hirst Bridges K.Pye C.Taylor Lindley Sheridan:
Tries - Green Clark: Goals - Lunn(2):
Referee L Gant (Featherstone) Att - 2800 H.T. 2 - 14

Sat 6 Feb 1960 YORK home won 5 - 4
CASTLEFORD - Lunn: Green Barnes Small Iredale: Wilson Brown: Hirst Bridges K.Pye BERT SAYER(S/O)(451) Lindley Sheridan:
Try - Green: Goal - Lunn:
YORK - Hargreaves: Gillespie Hunter Houlden Foster: Flannert Stevenson: Yorke Milner Watts O'Brien Dickinson Dawson: Goals - Yorke(2):
Referee J Senior (Bradford) Att - 2959 H.T. 5 - 2

Sat 13 Feb 1960 BRADFORD NORTHERN home lost 4 - 8 CHALLENGE CUP ROUND 1
CASTLEFORD - Lunn: Green R.Taylor Small Iredale: Wilson Brown: Hirst Bridges K.Pye Lindley C.Taylor Sayer:
Goals - Lunn(2):
BRADFORD N - Seddon: Doran Penketh Winnard Smith: D.Davies Higgins: Marston Kosanovic Feather Hemingway Jones A.Davies Tries - Smith(2):   Goal - Seddon:
Referee F J Howker (Rochdale) Att - 3725 H.T. nil - 8

Sat 20 Feb 1960 HUNSLET away lost 3 - 8
HUNSLET - Langton: Griffiths Shelton Walker Colin: Tate Newall: Hatfield Gomersall Eyre Poole Gunney Shaw:
Tries - Langton Griffiths: Goal - Langton:
CASTLEFORD - Lunn: R.Taylor Barnes Small Iredale: Wilson Brown: Hirst Bridges K.Pye E.Bryant C.Taylor Sheridan: Try - Bryant:
Referee R Gelder (Wakefield) Att - 4000 H.T. 3 - 3

Sat 27 Feb 1960 BARROW home won 17 - 8
CASTLEFORD - Lunn: Battye Barnes Small R.Taylor: Wilson Hepworth: Hirst Bridges Lindley E.Bryant C.Taylor Sayer:
Tries - Battye(2) Small: Goals - Lunn(4):
BARROW - Dawes: Glasson Rea Skeels Woolveridge: Ball Black: Dinaldson(S/O) J.Wilson Campbell Walters Delves D.Wilson(S/O):
Tries - Skeels D.Wilson: Goal - Dawes:
Referee R L Thomas (Oldham) Att - 1500 H.T. 9 - nil

Sat 5 Mar 1960 HUDDERSFIELD away won 12 - 7
HUDDERSFIELD - Dyson: Brown Stocks Ashcroft Wicks: Lockwood Smales: Killeen Close Flint Noble Shacklady Ramsden: Try - Smales: Goals - Dyson(2):
CASTLEFORD - Lunn: Battye Barnes Small Iredale: Wilson Hepworth: Hirst Corban K.Pye E.Bryant Lindley C.Taylor:
Tries - Barnes Iredale: Goals - Lunn(3):
Referee G Davies (Wakefield) Att - 5485 H.T. 5 - 5

Sat 12 Mar 1960 HULL home lost 11 - 19
CASTLEFORD - Lunn: R.Taylor Barnes Small Iredale: Wilson Brown: Hirst Bridges K.Pye Lindley C.Taylor Sheridan:
Try - Brown: Goals - Lunn(4):
HULL - Bateson: Saville Halifihi Kershaw Johnson: Broadhurst Finn: Scott Lawson J.Drake Sykes P.Whiteley J.Whiteley:
Tries - Halifihi Broadhurst J.Whiteley:
Goals - Bateson(4) (DG)
Referee A E Durkin (Dewsbury) Att - 4060 H.T. 7 - 14

Sat 19 Mar 1960 ROCHDALE HORNETS away lost 4 - 17
ROCHDALE H - Buxton: Unsworth Atherton Short Simms: Hilton Fishwick: Scholes Sivill McFarlane Allander Parr McGurrin:
Tries - Atherton Short Fishwick: Goals - McGurrin(4):
CASTLEFORD - Lunn: Battye Barnes Small Iredale: Wilson Hepworth: Hirst Bridges K.Pye Lindley C.Taylor Sheridan:
Goals - Lunn(2):
Referee D S Brown (Dewsbury) Att - 1685 H.T. 4 - 5

SEASON 1959-60

Sat 26 Mar 1960 WAKEFIELD TRINITY home lost 2 - 10
CASTLEFORD - Lunn: Battye Butterfield Barnes Small:
Wilson Brown: Hirst Bridges K.Pye Lindley C.Taylor Sayer:
Goal - Lunn:
WAKEFIELD T - Metcalfe: Hirst Skene Etty(S/O)Thomas:
Poynton Holliday: Smith Wakefield Sampson Vines Firth
Lamming: Tries - Skene Poynton: Goals - Sampson(2):
Referee M Coates (Pudsey) Att - 8376 H.T. 2 - nil

Sat 2 April 1960 BLACKPOOL BOROUGH away
won 17 - 10
BLACKPOOL B - Dutton: Wilkshire Lowe Gee Meadows:
Foden Bishop: Lomas Keegan Hopwood Stazicker
Maughan Normington:
Tries - Bishop Stazicker: Goals - Maughan(2):
CASTLEFORD - Lunn: Battye Barnes Butterfield Small:
Hardisty Hepworth: Hirst Bridges K.Pye Lindley C.Taylor
Sheridan:
Tries - Battye(2) Small: Goals - Lunn(4):
Referee L Gant (Wakefield) Att - 750 H.T. 7 - 7

Fri 8 April 1960 HALIFAX away lost 5 - 42
HALIFAX - Owen: Snowden Burnett Palmer Freeman:
Williams Marchant: Fox Shaw Crabtree Scroby Sparks
Renilson:
Tries - Freeman(4) Burnett(2) Palmer(2) Snowden Sparks:
Goals - Owen(6):
CASTLEFORD - Lunn: Battye Butterfield Barnes Small:
Hardisty Hepworth: Hirst Ian Corban J.Berry Sayer(S/O)
C.Taylor Sheridan:
Try - Battye: Goal - Lunn:
Referee R Oliver (Wakefield) Att - 2571 H.T. 5 - 18

Mon 18 April 1960 LEEDS home won 19 - 17
CASTLEFORD - Lunn: Wilson Butterfield Ward Small:
Hardisty Hepworth: Hirst Bridges Lindley Sayer W.Bryant
C.Taylor:
Tries - Butterfield Small Hepworth: Goals - Lunn(5):
LEEDS - Thornett: Rosenberg Hallas Pickup Hodgkinson:
Jones Evans: Skelton Umpleby Tomlinson Sewell
Robinson Goodwin:
Tries - Hodgkinson Evans Robinson:
Goals - Jones(3) Thornett(DG):
Referee A E Durkin (Dewsbury) Att - 5507 H.T. 11 - 6

Tue 19 April 1960 FEATHERSTONE ROVERS away
lost 13 - 14
FEATHERSTONE R - Cooper: Greatorex Evans Bell
Woolford: Mullaney Dunning: Moore Fawley Dixon Jones
Clamp Hockley:
Tries - Greatorex Woolford Mullaney Fawley:
Goal - Fawley:
CASTLEFORD - Lunn: Wilson Barnes Ward Small: Hardisty
Evans: Hirst Bridges John Lindley Sayer E.Bryant C.Taylor:
Tries - Ward(2) Bryant: Goals - Lunn(2):
Referee G Wilson (Dewsbury) Att - 7100 H.T. 5 - 9

Wed 27 April 1960 HALIFAX home won 20 - 14
CASTLEFORD - Lunn: Battye Butterfield Ward Iredale:
Hardisty Hepworth: Hirst Bridges Clark Sheridan Barnes
C.Taylor:
Tries - Battye Butterfield Ward Sheridan: Goals - Lunn(4):
HALIFAX - Owen: Snowden Burnett Palmer Jackson:
Critchley Marchant: Fox Shaw Crabtree Jarman Scroby
Renilson: Tries - Jackson(2):   Goals - Owen(4):
Referee H Pearce (Leeds) Att - 2785 H.T. 9 - 9

Sat 30 April 1960 BRADFORD NORTHERN home
won 26 - 9
CASTLEFORD - Lunn: Wilson Butterfield Robert Taylor
Douglas Iredale: Hardisty Hepworth: Hirst Hampton Clark
Sheridan Barnes C.Taylor:
Tries - Butterfield Iredale Hepworth Hirst: Goals - Lunn(7):
BRADFORD N - Walshaw: Doran Penketh Brook Smith:
Higgins Lancaster: Walton Kosanovic Feather Hemingway
Robbins Winnard: Try - Lancaster: Goals - Walshaw(3):
Referee G Philpott (Leeds) Att - 2607 H.T. 4 – 9

Bert Sayer
D. No 451
1959-60 to 1960-61

John Wilson
D. No 445
1959-60 to 1960-61

Colin Butterfield
D. No 448
1959-60 to 1962-63

Frank Green
D. No 449
1959-60 to 1963-64

SEASON 1959-60

D.N	PLAYER		DEBUT	L MATCH	APP	SUB	T.AP	TRI'S	G'LS	D.G	P'TS
330	PYE	KENNETH			33	0	33	4	0	0	12
341	LUNN	ALBERT			39	0	39	1	110	0	223
364	SMART	DEREK		29/08/1959	4	0	4	4	0	0	12
382	SHERIDAN	JOHN			33	0	33	7	0	0	21
389	BARNES	JACK			21	0	21	2	1	0	8
404	EVANS	RONALD			2	0	2	0	0	0	0
406	TAYLOR	COLIN			38	0	38	2	0	0	6
410	BRYANT	EDWARD			8	0	8	2	0	0	6
412	WALSH	BARRY			1	0	1	0	0	0	0
414	WARD	GEOFFREY G.			13	0	13	6	0	0	18
415	HATTEE	ARTHUR		10/10/1959	1	0	1	0	0	0	0
417	CORBAN	IAN		08/04/1960	9	0	9	0	0	0	0
419	BRIDGES	KEITH			29	0	29	2	0	0	6
420	TONKINSON	ALBERT			12	0	12	2	0	0	6
421	BERRY	JOHN			2	0	2	0	0	0	0
422	PYE	JEFFREY		02/01/1960	5	0	5	1	0	0	3
424	HIRST	JACK			39	0	39	3	0	0	9
426	BRYANT	WILLIAM			4	0	4	0	0	0	0
427	BATTYE	COLIN			19	0	19	13	0	0	39
430	ASKIN	MAURICE		03/10/1959	1	0	1	0	0	0	0
433	HARDISTY	ALAN			17	0	17	5	0	0	15
436	BROWN	GEORGE			25	0	25	12	0	0	36
438	SMALL	PETER			31	0	31	11	0	0	33
439	CLARK	JONN			10	0	10	3	0	0	9
440	TAYLOR	ROBERT		30/04/1960	20	0	20	13	0	0	39
441	DALE	TREVOR		19/12/1959	5	0	5	0	0	0	0
442	HEPWORTH	KEITH			15	0	15	4	0	0	12
444	IREDALE	DOUGLAS	22/08/1959	30/04/1960	24	0	24	13	0	0	39
445	WILSON	JOHN	17/10/1959		26	0	26	4	0	0	12
446	HAMPTON	JOE	31/10/1959		2	0	2	0	0	0	0
447	RHODES	KENNETH	14/11/1959	14/11/1959	1	0	1	0	0	0	0
448	BUTTERFIELD	COLIN	12/12/1959		8	0	8	3	0	0	9
449	GREEN	FRANK	09/01/1960		4	0	4	2	0	0	6
450	LINDLEY	JOHN	09/01/1960	19/04/1960	12	0	12	0	0	0	0
451	SAYER	BERT	06/02/1960		7	0	7	0	0	0	0
	35			**8**	**10**	**520**	**0**	**520**	**119**	**111**	**0**	**579**

COMPETITION		P	W	D	L	FOR	AGT
LEAGUE	POSITION 18 OF 30	38	18	0	20	561	630
YORK'S CUP		1	0	0	1	14	27
RL CUP		1	0	0	1	4	8
PLAYERS RECORDS		**40**	**18**	**0**	**22**	**579**	**665**

A significant debutante this season was Frank Green. Whilst only making 15 appearances in total over four seasons, he was the first ever signing from the Club's recently formed Under 17s Junior Amateur Section later to be joined by an Under 19s team. The two junior teams would become a rich source of talent for the Club over the next few years before a change in Amateur Rugby League policy brought about their demise.

Albert Lunn was still in the record setting groove when he became the first player to kick 600 goals for the club in the 17–8 home victory against Barrow on 27 February 1960.

Sat 13 Aug 1960 LIVERPOOL CITY away won 21 - 7
LIVERPOOL C - Ashby: Halton Hockenhull Cookson
Donaldson: Jeffries Walker: Crosby Fishwick Cox
Cartledge Highcock McGrath: Try - Cox: Goals - Jeffries(2):
CASTLEFORD - Lunn: Battye Butterfield G.G.Ward BRIAN
MARSDEN(452):Hardisty Hepworth: Hirst Hampton Pye
Sayer Barnes C.Taylor:
Tries - Battye(2) Ward Marsden Hardisty: Goals - Lunn(3):
Referee M Coates (Pudsey) Att – 1000 H.T. 15 - nil

Wed 17 Aug 1960 WAKEFIELD TRINITY home lost 9 - 26
CASTLEFORD - Lunn: Battye Butterfield G.G.Ward
Marsden: Hardisty Hepworth: Hirst Hampton Pye
Sheridan Barnes Taylor: Try - Hardisty: Goals - Lunn(3):
WAKEFIELD T - Round: Smith Skene Fox Etty: Poynton
Holliday: Wilkinson Oakes Chamberlain Briggs Lamming
Turner:
Tries - Smith(2) Round Fox Etty Poynton: Goals - Fox(4):
Referee J P Hebblethwaite (York) Att - 10907 H.T. 9 -7

Sat 20 Aug 1960 SALFORD home lost 14 - 16
CASTLEFORD - Lunn: Battye Butterfield Ward Small:
Hardisty Evans: Hirst Hampton Pye Sayer Barnes Sheridan:
Tries - Battye Small: Goals - Lunn(4):
SALFORD - Gregory: Jones Cheshire Bettison Walker:
Lendill Dunn: Hancock Boardman Alder Hartley Council
Duffy:
Tries - Hartley(2) Cheshire Council: Goals - Cheshire(2):
Referee N T Railton (Wigan) Att -3464 H.T. 8 - 16

Tue 23 Aug 1960 BATLEY away lost 6 - 12
BATLEY - Lawton: B.Pratt Shuttleworth Sutcliffe Ireland:
Geldard W.Pratt: Harrison Whitehead Fox Kelly Langhorne
Dick: Tries - B.Pratt W.Pratt: Goals - Lawton(3):
CASTLEFORD - Lunn: Battye Butterfield G.G.Ward
Marsden: Hardisty Ronald Evans: J.Berry JOHNNY WARD
(453) Pye W.Bryant Sheridan E.Bryant:
Tries - Butterfield E.Bryant:
Referee L Gant (Wakefield) Att - 2400 H.T.

Sat 27 Aug 1960 BRADFORD NORTHERN away won 25 - 7 YORKSHIRE CUP ROUND 1
BRADFORD N - Walshaw: Doran Greenall Brook Smith:
Davies Broadbent: Marston Kosanovic Walton Robbins
Hemingway Jones: Try - Davies: Goals - Walshaw(2):
CASTLEFORD - Lunn: Battye Butterfield Small Marsden:
Hardisty Brown: Hirst Bridges Pye Sheridan Barnes
E.Bryant: Tries - Battye(3) Brown Sheridan: Goals -Lunn(5):
Referee T W Watkinson (Man'ster) Att - 1774 H.T. 10 - 4

Sat 3 Sep 1960 LEIGH home won 19 - 11
CASTLEFORD - Lunn: Battye Butterfield G.G.Ward
Marsden: Hardisty Brown: Hirst Bridges Pye Sheridan
Tonkinson E.Bryant:
Tries - Battye Hardisty Pye: Goals - Lunn(5):
LEIGH - Hosking: Hutson Howard Lewis Fisher: Chadwick
Fallon: Brophy Tabern Hurt Platt Higgs Sanderson:
Tries - Fallon(2) Hurt: Goal - Fallon:
Referee D T H Davies (Manchester) Att - 3036 H.T. 9 - 3

Wed 7 Sep 1960 HUDDERSFIELD away lost 3 - 15 YORKSHIRE CUP ROUND 2
HUDDERSFIELD - Dyson: Brown Booth Ashcroft Breen:
Lockwood Smales: Slevin Wood Noble Devereux Bowman
Thornley: Tries - Brown Ashcroft Breen: Goals - Dyson(3):
CASTLEFORD - Lunn: Battye Butterfield G.G.Ward
Marsden: Hardisty Brown: Hirst Bridges Pye Sheridan
Tonkinson E.Bryant: Try - Ward:
Referee J Manley (Warrington) Att - 3656 H.T. 3 - 4

Sat 10 Sep 1960 BRAMLEY home won 46 - 20
CASTLEFORD - Lunn: Battye Small G.G.Ward Marsden:
Hardisty Brown Hirst Bridges Tonkinson W.Bryant
Sheridan E.Bryant:
Tries - Marsden(2) Hardisty(2) Brown(2) Small Bridges
Tonkinson Sheridan: Goals - Lunn(8):
BRAMLEY - Pinder: Noble Kershaw Firth Garside:
Wrigglesworth Pollard: Smith Kennedy Hainsworth
Rogers Baddeley Winnard:
Tries - Garside(2) Firth Wrigglesworth: Goals Winnard(4):
Referee J Senior (Bradford) Att - 2082 H.T. 18 - 3

Sat 17 Sep 1960 HULL away lost 15 - 27
HULL - Donnat:: Harrison Cowan Saville Johnson:
Matthews Finn: Scott Harris J.Drake Sykes W.Drake
J.Whiteley: Tries - Sykes(2) Johnson Matthews W.Drake:
Goals - W.Drake(6):
CASTLEFORD - Lunn: Battye Small G.G.Ward Marsden:
Hardisty Brown: Hirst Bridges Pye Sheridan Tonkinson
E.Bryant: Tries - Battye Ward Brown: Goals - Lunn(3):
Referee E Clay (Rothwell) Att - 4749 H.T. 13 - 15

Mon 19 Sep 1960 YORK home won 19 - 8
CASTLEFORD – PETER BRIERS(454): Battye Butterfield
G.G.Ward Marsden: Hardisty Brown: Hirst Bridges Pye
Tonkinson Sheridan E.Bryant:
Tries - Marsden Hardisty Sheridan: Goals - Briers(5):
YORK - Hargreaves: Swift Hunter Foster Snelling: Flannery
Jackson: Yorke Milner Bowes Watts O'Brien Kidd:
Tries - Swift Snelling: Goal - Yorke:
Referee A E Durkin (Dewsbury) Att - 1748 H.T. 11 - 3

Wed 28 Sep 1960 BRADFORD NORTHERN away won 18 - 17
BRADFORD N - Walshaw: Doran Brook Trumble Nunns:
Davies Broadbent: Marston Kosanovic Walton Robbins
Hemingway Jones(S/O):
Tries - Marston(2) Broadbent: Goals - Walshaw(4):
CASTLEFORD - Briers: Battye Small G.G.Ward Marsden:
Hardisty Brown: Hirst Bridges Pye Tonkinson Sayer(S/O)
E.Bryant:
Tries - Hardisty(2) Ward Marsden: Goals - Briers(3):
Referee H Pearce (Leeds) Att - 1500 H.T. 13 - 9

Sat 15 Oct 1960 WORKINGTON TOWN home lost 6 - 15
CASTLEFORD - Lunn: Battye Small G.G.Ward Marsden:
Hardisty Brown: Hirst J.Ward Pye Tonkinson Sheridan
E.Bryant: Tries - G.G.Ward(2):
WORKINGTON T - Faulder: Foord O'Neil Brennan Ryan:

Lowdon Roper: Martin Sandham McLeod Edgar Herbert McCall: Tries - O'Neil(2) Brennan: Goals - Lowdon(3): Referee F J Howker (Rochdale) Att - 2656 H.T.

Sat 22 Oct 1960 KEIGHLEY away won 15 - 12
KEIGHLEY - Frain: Smith Plunkett Eyre Bleasby: Sabine Barron: Bloomfield Waring Crewdson Priestley Phillips Jackson: Tries - Smith(2): Goals - Bloomfield(2) Frain: CASTLEFORD - Barnes: Battye Small G.G.Ward Butterfield: Hardisty Brown: Tonkinson J.Ward Pye Sayer Sheridan E.Bryant:
Tries - Small Hardisty Sheridan: Goals - Barnes(3): Referee C Whiteley (Ossett) Att -   H.T. 10 - 7

Sat 29 Oct 1960 SALFORD away won 19 - 7
SALFORD - A.N.Other: Baines Cheshire Bettison A.N.Other: Lendill Dunn: Hancock Kilgannon Donoghue Parsons Stott Duffy: Try - Stott: Goals - Cheshire(2): CASTLEFORD - John Wilson: Battye Small G.G.Ward Butterfield: Hardisty Brown: Tonkinson J.Ward Pye Sayer Sheridan E.Bryant: Tries - Hardisty(2) Small Butterfield Pye: Goals - Hardisty Sheridan:
Referee G Scott (Wakefield) Att -1998 H.T. 8 - nil

Sat 5 Nov 1960 DONCASTER home won 16 - 10
CASTLEFORD - Lunn: Battye Small G.G.Ward Butterfield: Hardisty Brown: Tonkinson J.Ward(S/O) Pye Barnes(S/O) Sheridan Sayer: Tries - Butterfield Sayer: Goals - Lunn(5): DONCASTER - Price: Clark Mills Reed Precious: Dalby Doyle(S/O): Field Heath(S/O) Yemm Hartley Matthews(S/O) Strawbridge:
Tries - Precious Strawbridge: Goals - Dalby(2): Referee G Davies (Wakefield) Att - 1875 H.T. 13 - 3

Sat 12 Nov 1960 HUDDERSFIELD away lost nil - 22
HUDDERSFIELD - Dyson: Brown Booth Ashcroft Breen: Lockwood Smales: Slevin Close Noble Devereux Bowman Valentine: Tries - Breen(2) Bowman(2) Dyson Noble: Goals - Dyson(2): CASTLEFORD - Lunn: Battye Small G.G.Ward Butterfield: Hardisty Hepworth: Tonkinson J.Ward Pye Sheridan Barnes E.Bryant:
Referee A E Durkin (Dewsbury) Att - 3279 H.T. nil - 8

Sat 19 Nov 1960 DEWSBURY home won 14 - 9
CASTLEFORD - Lunn: Green Small G.G.Ward Butterfield: Hardisty Brown: Tonkinson Hampton Pye Sayer Sheridan JOHN WALKER(455):
Tries - Hardisty(2): Goals - Lunn(4): DEWSBURY - Ledgard: France Callighan Sutton Laycock: Davies Bullock: Thorley Lockwood Lumb Pearce Schofield Marchant: Try - Bullock: Goals - Ledgard(3): Referee G Philpott (Leeds) Att - 1500 H.T. -

Sat 26 Nov 1960 LEIGH away lost 10 - 36
LEIGH - Hewitt: Leadbetter Fisher Howard Humble: Chadwick Fallon: Brophy Tabern Owen Hurt Martin Platt: Tries - Leadbetter(2) Martin(2) Humble Tabern Hurt Platt: Goals - Fallon(6): CASTLEFORD - Lunn: Green Butterfield G.G.Ward Small:

Hardisty Brown: Tonkinson Hampton Pye Sayer Sheridan Walker: Tries - Hardisty(2): Goals - Lunn(2): Referee E Clay (Rothwell) Att - 3000 H.T. 3 - 21

Sat 3 Dec 1960 BRADFORD NORTHERN home draw 7 - 7
CASTLEFORD - Barnes: Green Butterfield G.G.Ward Small: Hardisty Brown: Tonkinson Hampton Pye Sayer W.Bryant Walker: Try - Hardisty: Goals - Barnes(2): BRADFORD N - Seddon: De Klerk Penketh Nunns Smith: Davies Higgins: McLean Kosanovic Holland G.Robbins T.Robbins Jones: Try - Nunns:
Goals - Seddon Higgins(DG): Referee D T H Davies (Manchester) Att - 934 H.T. 2 - 5

Sat 10 Dec 1960 LEEDS away lost 8 - 22
LEEDS - Thornett: Rosenberg Hallas Pickup Hodgkinson: Jones Evans: Skelton Simms Jubb Fairbank Tomlinson Goodwin:
Tries - Thornett Hallas Jones Evans: Goals - Jones(5): CASTLEFORD - Lunn: Battye Butterfield G.G.Ward Small: Hardisty Brown: Tonkinson Bridges Pye Sheridan Barnes Sayer: Tries - Ward Hardisty: Goal - Lunn: Referee G Wilson (Dewsbury) Att - 7836 H.T. 8 - 9

Sat 17 Dec 1960 LIVERPOOL CITY home won 24 - 14
CASTLEFORD - Lunn: Battye Small G.G.Ward Green: Hardisty Brown: MALCOLM KIRK(456) Bridges Pye Tonkinson Sheridan Sayer:
Tries - Battye(2) Small(2): Goals - Lunn(6): LIVERPOOL C. - Jeffries: Halton Ollier Ashby Donaldson: Twiss Walker: Cox Dutton Highcock Upton Hockenhull McGrath:
Tries - Halton(2) Ollier Donaldson: Goal - Jeffries: Referee N T Railton (Wigan) Att - 1585 H.T. 9 - 2

Sat 24 Dec 1960 HULL home lost 17 - 23
CASTLEFORD - Lunn: Battye Small G.G.Ward Green: Hardisty Hepworth: Malcolm Kirk Bridges(S/O) Pye Tonkinson Sheridan Sayer:
Tries - Green Tonkinson Sheridan: Goals - Lunn(4): HULL - Bateson: Kershaw Cowan Saville Hollindrake: Broadhurst Smith: Scott Harris(S/O) J.Drake Sykes W.Drake J.Whiteley:
Tries - Cowan(2) Saville Hollindrake Whiteley: Goals - Bateson(4): Referee J Manley (Warrington) Att – 3216 H.T. 12 - 6

Mon 26 Dec 1960 FEATHERSTONE ROVERS away lost 7 - 26
FEATHERSTONE R. - Fennell: Charlesworth Greatorex Hunt Woolford: Mullaney Fox: Hammill Fawley Dixon Lambert Clawson Clifft:
Tries - Greatorex Woolford Mullaney Fox Clawson Clifft: Goals - Fennell(4): CASTLEFORD - Lunn: Battye Butterfield G.G.Ward Small: Hardisty Hepworth: Tonkinson Bridges Pye Brownley Sheridan Sayer: Try - Small: Goals - Lunn(2): Referee G Philpott (Leeds) Att - 4500 H.T. -

SEASON 1960-61

Sat 31 Dec 1960 WAKEFIELD TRINITY away lost 7 - 21
WAKEFIELD T - Metcalfe: Hirst Nunn Fox Firth: Poynton
Rollin: Smith Oakes Chamberlain Briggs Lamming Turner:
Tries - Hirst Fox Firth Poynton Briggs: Goals - Fox(3):
CASTLEFORD - Lunn: E.Bryant G.G.Ward Small Butterfield:
Hardisty Hepworth: Tonkinson Bridges Clark Sheridan
Sayer Brownley: Try - Ward: Goals - Lunn(2):
Referee D T H Davies (Manchester) Att - 9818 H.T. 7 - 7

Sat 7 Jan 1961 BATLEY home won 13 - 11
CASTLEFORD - Lunn: E.Bryant Small G.G.Ward Butterfield:
Hardisty Brown: BRIAN ROWE(457) J.Ward Tonkinson
Sayer Sheridan Brownley:
Tries - J.Ward(2) G.G.Ward: Goals - Lunn(2):
BATLEY - A.N.Other: B.Pratt Shuttleworth Ireland Mitchell:
Geldard W.Pratt: Harrison Fryer Fox Kelly McVeigh Dick:
Tries - B.Pratt Fox Dick: Goal - Fox:
Referee C F Appleton (Warrington) Att - 1680 H.T. 8 - 8

**Sat 14 Jan 196l WORKINGTON TOWN away
lost 5 - 13**
WORKINGTON T - Lowdon: Foord O'Neill Bell Crosby:
Archer Roper: Herbert Moss Martin Gardiner Mcleod
McCall:
Tries - Foord(2) Lowdon: Goals - Gardiner Archer(DG):
CASTLEFORD - Lunn: E.Bryant Small Butterfield Clark:
Brown Hepworth: Tonkinson J.Ward Rowe Brownley
Sheridan Walker: Try - Small: Goal - Lunn:
Referee N T Railton(Wigan) Att –1850 H.T. nil - 3

Sat 21 Jan 1961 HUDDERSFIELD home draw nil - nil
CASTLEFORD - Lunn: E.Bryant Small G.G.Ward Battye:
Hardisty Hepworth: Tonkinson Bridges Pye Sheridan
Barnes Sayer:
HUDDERSFIELD - Dyson: Breen Booth Haywood Wicks:
Lockwood Smales: Slevin Close Noble Shacklady Bowman
Valentine:
Referee L Gant (Wakefield) Att - 1479 H.T.

Sat 4 Feb 1961 HUNSLET home won 10 - 5
CASTLEFORD - Briers: Battye Small G.G.Ward E.Bryant:
Hardisty Hepworth: Tonkinson Bridges Pye Sheridan
Barnes Sayer:
Tries - Ward Bryant: Goals - Briers(2):
HUNSLET - Langton: Walker Shelton Preece Stockdill:
Gabbitas Newall: Adams Gomersall Hartley Gunney Eyre
Moyser: Try - Walker: Goal - Langton:
Referee G Davies (Wakefield) Att - 2700 H.T. nil - 5

**Sat 11 Feb 1961 DEWSBURY CELTIC won 32 - nil
CHALLENGE CUP ROUND 1 - at Crown Flatt Dewsbury**
Dewsbury C. - Bragg: Schofield Newsome Keegan Varley:
Jones Walton: Porritt Speight Wallace Gibson Kendle
Noble:
CASTLEFORD - Lunn: Battye Small G.G.Ward Walsh:
Hardisty Hepworth: Tonkinson Bridges Pye Sheridan
Barnes Sayer:
Tries - Battye(3) Lunn Small Ward Walsh Hardisty:
Goals - Lunn(4):
Referee F J Howker (Rochdale) Att - 1750 H.T. 21 - nil

Sat 18 Feb 1961 DONCASTER away won 8 - 4
DONCASTER - Frice: Hinchcliffe Mills Holt Precious: Dalby
Doyle: Burt Heath Yemm Rose Platt Asquith:
Goals - Dalby(2):
CASTLEFORD - Lunn: Battye Small G.G.Ward Walsh:
DEREK EDWARDS(458) Brown: Tonkinson Brownley Pye
Barnes Sheridan Walker:
Tries - Battye Small: Goal - Lunn:
Referee H Pearce (Leeds) Att - 1000 H.T. 6 - 2

**Sat 25 Feb 1961 ST HELENS home lost 10 - 18
CHALLENGE CUP ROUND 2**
CASTLEFORD - Lunn: Battye Small G.G.Ward Walsh:
Hardisty Hepworth: Tonkinson Bridges Pye Rowe
Sheridan Sayer:
Tries - Hardisty Sheridan: Goals - Lunn(2):
ST HELENS - Rhodes: Vollenhoven Large McGinn Sullivan:
Smith Murphy: Terry Dagnall Measures Vines Huddart
Karalius:
Tries - Vollenhoven(2) Sullivan Murphy:
Goals - Rhodes(3):
Referee C F Appleton (Warrington) Att - 13000 H.T.10 - 5

Sat 4 Mar 1961 YORK away lost 9 - 10
YORK - Hargreaves: Foster little Houlden Sullivan:
Flannery Jackson: Yorke Milner Dawson Coglan Kidd
Ward: Tries - Houlden Coglan: Goals - Yorke(2):
CASTLEFORD - Lunn: Battye Small G.G.Ward Walsh:
Hardisty Hepworth: Clark J.Ward Pye Rowe Sheridan
Sayer:
Try - Small: Goals - Lunn(3):
Referee T W Watkinson (Manchester) Att 3033 H.T. 4 - nil

Sat 11 Mar 1961 KEIGHLEY home won 22 - 10
CASTLEFORD - Lunn: Battye Small G.G.Ward Walsh:
Hardisty Hepworth: Hirst Bridges Pye Rowe Sheridan
Sayer:
Tries - Walsh(2) Small Hardisty: Goals - Lunn(5):
KEIGHLEY - Brown: Taylor Plunkett Todd Sharpe: Sabine
Barron: Haigh Waring Phillips Fall Crewdson Wright:
Tries - Todd Sabine: Goals - Brown(2):
Referee G Wilson (Dewsbury) Att - 2200 H.T. 10 - 5

**Sat 18 Mar 1961 HULL KINGSTON ROVERS home
won 22 - 14**
CASTLEFORD - Lunn: Battye Small G.G.Ward Walsh:
Hardisty Brown: Hirst Joseph Hampton Pye Rowe
Sheridan Sayer:
Tries - Battye Small Walsh Hardisty:
Goals - Lunn(4)Hardisty(DG):
HULL K R - Kellett: Mullins Major Riley Harris: Paul
Bunting: Coverdale Ackerley Tyson Trowell Taylor Poole:
Tries - Kellett Taylor: Goals - Kellett(4):
Referee L Gant (Wakefield) Att - 2374 H.T. 12 - 5

**Sat 1 Apr 1961 HULL KINGSTON ROVERS away
lost 10 - 16**
HULL K R - Kellett: Paul Matthews Mullins Riley: Elliott
Bunting: Coverdale Ackerley Kingsbury Trowell Taylor
Poole: Tries - Bunting Ackerley: Goals - Kellett(5):

SEASON 1960-61

CASTLEFORD - Lunn: Battye Small G.G.Ward Walsh:
Hardisty Brown: PETER MARSTON(459) Bridges Pye(S/O)
Rowe Sheridan C.Taylor:
Tries - Hardisty Sheridan: Goals - Lunn(2):
Referee G Davies (Wakefield) Att -5050 H.T. 5 - 2

Mon 3 Apr 1961 LEEDS home lost 12 - 16
CASTLEFORD - Lunn: Walsh Small G.G.Ward Marsden:
Hardisty Edwards: Peter Marston Bridges Tonkinson Rowe
Sheridan Bert Sayer:
Tries - Small Edwards: Goals - Lunn(3):
LEEDS - Thornett: Hodgkinson Hallas Jones Ratcliffe:
Oldroyd Evans: Robinson Umpleby Whitehead Fairbank
Goodwin Stacey: Tries - Hodgkinson Jones Ratcliffe
Fairbank: Goals - Hallas(2):
Referee R Oliver (Wakefield) Att - 9000 H.T. 2 - 5

Sat 8 Apr 1961 BRAMLEY away lost 5 - 13
BRAMLEY - Wilson: Murthick Stone Larkin Garside:
Wrigglesworth Quinn: Hainsworth Kennedy Cooper
Marker Shaw Kelly: Try - Murthick: Goals - Wilson(5):
CASTLEFORD - Lunn: Battye Small G.G.Ward Walsh:
Hardisty Edwards: Tonkinson Bridges Pye Sheridan Rowe
Taylor: Try - Small: Goal - Lunn:
Referee C Whiteley (Ossett) Att - 2100 H.T. 2 - 7

Mon 17 Apr 1961 HUNSLET away lost 10 - 14
HUNSLET - Langton: Walker Preece Stockdill Raynor:
Astbury Tate: Adam Prior Moyser Burton Gunney
Baldwinson:
Tries - Walker Gunney: Goals - Langton(4):
CASTLEFORD - Lunn: Battye Small G.G.Ward Walsh:
Hardisty Brown: Tonkinson Bridges Pye Rowe Walker
Sheridan:
Tries - Walsh Walker: Goals - Lunn(2):
Referee R L Thomas (Oldham) Att - 2500 H.T. 7 - 8

Sat 22 Apr 1961 DEWSBURY away won 20 - 3
DEWSBURY - Ripley: Pratt Callighan Hinchcliffe Laycock:
Balmforth Bullock: Thorley Lockwood Walker Pearce
Schofield Bosworth:
Try - not known:
CASTLEFORD - Barnes: Battye Small G.G.Ward Walsh:
Hardisty Brown: Tonkinson Bridges KEITH SLATTER(460)
Rowe Walker Sheridan:
Tries - Battye(2) Small Ward Hardisty Sheridan:
Goal - Hardisty:
Referee E Clay (Rothwell) Att - 1400 H.T. 11 - nil

**Mon 1 May 1961 FEATHERSTONE ROVERS home
lost 2 - 5**
CASTLEFORD - Lunn: Battye Small E.Bryant Walsh:
Hardisty Brown: Tonkinson Bridges Slatter Brian Rowe
Walker Sheridan: Goal - Lunn:
FEATHERSTONE R - Andersonn: Reynolds Greatorex Hunt
Evans: Mullaney Fox: Hammill Fawley Hockley Lambert
Clawson Clifft: Try - Greatorex: Goal - Clawson:
Referee E Clay (Rothwell) Att - 4342 H.T. nil – 3

Brian Marsden
D. No 452
1960-61 to 1962-63

Johnny Ward
D. No 453
1960-61 to 1969-70

Johnny Walker
D. No 455
1960-61 to 1967-68

Brian Rowe
D. No 457
1960-61

Derek Edwards
D. No 458
1960-61 to 1971-72

SEASON 1960-61

D.N	PLAYER		DEBUT	L MATCH	APP	S JB	T.AP	TRI'S	G'LS	D.G	P'TS
330	PYE	KENNETH			33	0	33	2	0	0	6
341	LUNN	ALBERT			33	0	33	1	88	0	179
382	SHERIDAN	JOHN			37	0	37	8	1	0	26
389	BARNES	JACK			14	0	14	0	5	0	10
404	EVANS	RONALD	23/08/1960		2	0	2	0	0	0	0
406	TAYLOR	COLIN			4	0	4	0	0	0	0
410	BRYANT	EDWARD			18	0	18	2	0	0	6
412	WALSH	BARRY			12	0	12	5	0	0	15
414	WARD	GEOFFREY G.			37	0	37	12	0	0	36
419	BRIDGES	KEITH			23	0	23	1	0	0	3
420	TONKINSON	ALBERT			31	0	31	2	0	0	6
421	BERRY	JOHN			1	0	1	0	0	0	0
424	HIRST	JACK			13	0	13	0	0	0	0
426	BRYANT	WILLIAM			3	0	3	0	0	0	0
427	BATTYE	COLIN			33	0	33	17	0	0	51
433	HARDISTY	ALAN			38	0	38	23	2	1	75
436	BROWN	GEORGE			24	0	24	4	0	0	12
437	BROWNLEY	WILLIAM			5	0	5	0	0	0	0
438	SMALL	PETER			34	0	34	16	0	0	48
439	CLARK	JOHN			3	0	3	0	0	0	0
442	HEPWORTH	KEITH			13	0	13	0	0	0	0
445	WILSON	JOHN		29/10/1960	1	0	1	0	0	0	0
446	HAMPTON	JOE		18/03/1961	7	0	7	0	0	0	0
448	BUTTERFIELD	COLIN			20	0	20	3	0	0	9
449	GREEN	FRANK			5	0	5	1	0	0	3
451	SAYER	BERT		03/04/1961	23	0	23	1	0	0	3
452	MARSDEN	BRIAN	13/08/1960		12	0	12	5	0	0	15
453	WARD	JOHNNY	23/08/1960		9	0	9	2	0	0	6
454	BRIERS	PETER	19/09/1960		3	0	3	0	10	0	20
455	WALKER	JOHN	19/11/1960		8	0	8	1	0	0	3
456	KIRK	MALCOLM	17/12/1960	24/12/1960	2	0	2	0	0	0	0
457	ROWE	BRIAN	07/01/1961	01/05/1961	12	0	12	0	0	0	0
458	EDWARDS	DEREK	18/02/1961		3	0	3	1	0	0	3
459	MARSTON	PETER	01/04/1961	03/04/1961	2	0	2	0	0	0	0
460	SLATTER	KEITH	22/04/1961		2	0	2	0	0	0	0
	35		9	7	520	0	520	107	106	1	535

COMPETITION		P	W	D	L	FOR	AGT
LEAGUE	POSITION 17 OF 30	36	16	2	18	465	502
YORK'S CUP		2	1	0	1	28	22
RL CUP		2	1	0	1	42	18
PLAYERS RECORDS		40	18	2	20	535	542

The result of the first round draw of the Challenge Cup was a fixture against the amateur side Dewsbury Celtic, the game being played at Dewsbury's Crown Flatt ground. It also spurned 'one of them tales' - towards the end of the game in the midst of a scrum in the Castleford half, one of the Dewsbury players said, "Kenny (to Kenny Pye the Captain) we are on bonus if we score". Kenny, taking pity on them said to Keith Bridges Cas's Hooker "Keith shove thee feet across". Keith duly obliged and the Referee awarded the penalty.

Unfortunately, the story had an unhappy ending for the Dewsbury team because the goal kick was missed and the final score was a 32–nil Castleford victory.

In the same game, Albert Lunn became the first player to kick 700 goals for the club.

The Club was also on the receiving end of a rare piece of generosity from our near neighbours and arch rivals Featherstone Rovers when we signed Johnny Ward from them on a free transfer; Johnny joining his former school mates from Ashton Road, Alan Hardisty and Keith Hepworth.

The home league fixture against Huddersfield on 21 January 1961 featured one of those rare Rugby League results a nil-nil draw.

Another notable debutante was Derek Edwards, another product from the Club's Junior Section.

Sat 19 Aug 1961 WAKEFIELD TRINITY home lost 7 - 42
CASTLEFORD - Lunn: Walsh Small G.G.Ward Marsden:
Hardisty Hepworth: Tonkinson Bridges Pye Taylor Barnes
Sheridan: Try - Hepworth: Goals - Lunn(2):
WAKEFIELD T - Round: Smith Skene Fox Prinsloo: Poynton
Holliday: Wilkinson Kosanovic Firth Steele Payne
Lamming:
Tries - Prinsloo(2) Firth(2) Smith Skene Fox Poynton
Payne Lamming: Goals - Fox(5) Round:
Referee C F Appleton (War'gton) Att - 8850 H.T. nil - 15

Tue 22 Aug 1961 BATLEY away lost 8 - 9
BATLEY - Lawton: Mitchell Render Sutcliffe Ireland:
Astbury Pratt: Harrison Whiteford Fox McVeigh Westbury
Dick: Try - Pratt: Goals - Lawton(3):
CASTLEFORD - Lunn: Battye G.G.Ward Small Marsden:
Hardisty Hepworth: Tonkinson Bridges Pye Taylor Walker
Sheridan: Tries - Pye Taylor: Goal - Lunn:
Referee H Hunt (Guiseley) Att - 3000 H.T. 3 - 5

Sat 26 Aug 1961 CASTLEFORD & FEATHERSTONE ROVERS 20 NEW ZEALAND 31
AT WHELDON ROAD CASTLEFORD
CASTLEFORD & FEATHERSTONE R - Lunn(C):
Greatorex(FR) Hunt(FR) G.G.Ward(C) C.Battye(C):
Hardisty(C) Fox(FR): Hammill(FR) Fawley(FR) Dixon(FR)
Clawson(FR) Hockley(FR) Sheridan(C):
Tries - Ward(2) Hunt Hammill: Goals - Clawson(4):
NEW ZEALAND - W.R.Harrison: B.T.Reidy K.R.McCracken
R.S.Cooke J.P.Ford: J.A.Bond G.S.Farrar: S.K.Edwards
J.R.Butterfield R.W.Harrison R.H.G.Duffy R.D.Hammond
B.E.Castle: Tries - Castle(2) Reidy Cooke Bond Butterfield
Hammond: Goals - Cooke(5):
Referee E Clay (Rothwell) Att - 5797 H.T. 2 - 23

Mon 28 Aug 1961 WORKINGTON TOWN away lost 12 - 33
WORKINGTON T - Lowdon: Southward O'Neill Fereira
Pretorious: Archer Roper: Herbert McLeod Martin Edgar
Gardiner Eve: Tries - Edgar(2) O'Neill Archer Roper
McLeod Eve: Goals - Fereira(6):
CASTLEFORD - Lunn: Walsh G.G.Ward Small Battye:
Hardisty Brown: Hirst J.Ward Pye Taylor Walker Sheridan:
Tries - Small Brown: Goals - Lunn(3):
Referee G Wilson (Dewsbury) Att - 3470 H.T. 3 - 13

Fri 1 Sep 1961 HALIFAX home won 37 - 8
YORKSHIRE CUP ROUND 1
CASTLEFORD - Lunn: Walsh G.G.Ward Small Marsden:
Hardisty Brown: Hirst J.Ward Pye Tonkinson Walker
Sheridan: Tries - Hardisty(3) Small Brown Hirst J.Ward:
Goals - Lunn(8):
HALIFAX - James: Snowden Williams Dixon Freeman:
Critchley Marchant: Fox Shaw Kelly Scroby Fogerty
Broadbent: Tries - Williams Freeman: Goal - James:
Referee N T Railton (Wigan) Att - 4404 H.T. 15 - 5

Tue 5 Sep 1961 KEIGHLEY home won 14 - 10
CASTLEFORD - Lunn: Walsh G.G.Ward Small Marsden:

Hardisty Brown: Hirst J.Ward Pye Tonkinson Walker
Sheridan: Tries - Small Pye: Goals - Lunn(4):
KEIGHLEY - Brown: Smith Eyre Todd Bleasby: Edwards
Barron: Kingsbury Waring Bloomfield Sewell Crewdson
Wright: Tries - Smith Bleasby: Goals - Brown(2):
Referee L Gant (Wakefield) Att - 1958 H.T. 6 - 2

Fri 8 Sep 1961 BRADFORD NORTHERN away lost nil - 8
BRADFORD N - Hattee: Brook Sutcliffe Haley Penketh:
Davies Broadbent: McLean Wigglesworth Marston
Hemingway Jones Winnard: Goals - Hattee(4):
CASTLEFORD - Lunn: Walsh G.G.Ward Small Marsden:
Edwards Brown: Hirst J.Ward Pye Tonkinson Walker
Sheridan:
Referee H Pearce (Leeds) Att - 1470 H.T. nil - 4

Wed 13 Sep 1961 LEEDS away lost 12 - 20
YORKSHIRE CUP ROUND 2
LEEDS - Thornett: Ratcliffe Hallas Hattee Wrigglesworth:
Jones Evans: Robinson Simms Whitehead Fairbank
Goodwin Shaw:
Tries - Ratcliffe(3) Hattee: Goals - Jones(4):
CASTLEFORD - Lunn: Walsh G.G.Ward Small Marsden:
Hardisty Brown: Hirst J.Ward Pye Tonkinson Walker
Sheridan: Tries - J.Ward(2): Goals - Lunn(3):
Referee D T H Davies (Man'ster) Att - 11451 H.T. nil - 7

Sat 16 Sep 1961 SALFORD home won 53 - 8
CASTLEFORD - Lunn: Walsh G.G.Ward Small Marsden:
Hardisty Brown: Hirst(S/O)J.Ward Pye Tonkinson Walker
Sheridan: Tries - Walsh(4) Small(2) G.G.Ward Marsden
Hardisty Brown J.Ward: Goals - Lunn(10):
SALFORD - Gregory: Jones Bettinson Richards Brant:
Brennan Dunn: Council(S/O) Kilgannon Hardman Rees
Parkinson Duffy:
Tries - Gregory Richards: Goal - Richards:
Referee C F Appleton (Warr'ton) Att - 2500 H.T. 22 - 3

Mon 18 Sep 1961 YORK home won 21 - 12
CASTLEFORD - Lunn: Walsh G.G.Ward Small Marsden:
Hardisty Brown: Hirst J.Ward Pye Tonkinson Walker
Sheridan:
Tries - Hardisty(2) Small Walker Walsh: Goals - Lunn(3):
YORK - Hargreaves: Foster Hunter Houlden Coglan:
Flannery Stevenson: Yorke Crosby Pratt Dawson Kidd
Ward: Tries - Ward(2): Goals - Yorke(3):
Referee J Senior (Bradford) Att - 3788 H.T. 13 - 5

Sat 23 Sep 1961 BRAMLEY away lost 7 - 24
BRAMLEY - Wilson: Smith Stone Larkin Murthick:
Wrigglesworth Quinn: Hainsworth Kennedy Cooper Horn
Baddeley(S/O) Chamberlain:
Tries - Larkin Murthick Wrigglesworth Stone:
Goals - Wilson(6):
CASTLEFORD - Lunn: Walsh G.G.Ward Small Marsden:
Hardisty Brown: Slatter J.Ward Pye Tonkinson Walker
Sheridan: Try - Marsden: Goals - Lunn(2):
Referee C Whiteley (Ossett) Att - 2600 H.T. 5 - 6

SEASON 1961-62

Sat 7 Oct 1961 HULL KINGSTON ROVERS home won 19 - 9
CASTLEFORD - Briers: Walsh G.G.Ward Small Marsden: Hardisty Brown: GEOFFREY BLOOMFIELD(461) J.Ward Brownley W.Bryant Walker Sheridan:
Tries - Walsh Small J.Ward: Goals - Briers(5):
HULL K R - Kellett: Stocks Major Burwell Mullins: Elliott Bunting: Coverdale Holdstock Tyson Murphy Taylor Poole: Try - Mullins: Goals - Kellett(3):
Referee D T H Davies (Manchester) Att - 2911 H.T.

Sat 14 Oct 1961 HUNSLET away won 18 - 4
HUNSLET - Langton: Marshall Shelton Newall Preece: Gabbitas Tate: Hartley Prior Eyre Sayer Gunney Baldwinson: Goals - Langton(2):
CASTLEFORD - Briers: Walsh G.G.Ward Small Cartwright: Hardisty Brown: Hirst J.Ward Pye W.Bryant Walker Sheridan:
Tries - Walsh G.G.Ward J.Ward Bryant: Goals - Briers(3)
Referee G Wilson (Dewsbury) Att - 4000 H.T. 10 - 2

Sat 28 Oct 1961 DEWSBURY away won 10 - 5
DEWSBURY - Bedford: Foley Evans Firth Pratt: Balmforth Bullock: Thorley Lockwood Walker Schofield Rushworth Bosworth: Try - Bullock: Goal - Schofield:
CASTLEFORD - Briers: Walsh G.G.Ward Small Cartwright: Hardisty Brown: Tonkinson(S/O) J.Ward Pye W.Bryant Walker Sheridan:
Tries - G.G.Ward Small: Goals - Briers(2):
Referee H Pearce (Leeds) Att - 1300 H.T. 2 - nil

Sat 4 Nov 1961 DONCASTER home won 22 - 5
CASTLEFORD - Briers: Walsh G.G.Ward Small Cartwright: Hardisty Brown: Tonkinson J.Ward Pye W.Bryant Walker Sheridan: Tries - Walsh G.G.Ward Small Cartwright:
Goals - Briers(5):
DONCASTER - Price(S/O): Smith Davies Mortimer Precious: Reed Doyle: Yemm Wakefield Hepworth Swales Rose Cole: Try - Swales: Goal - Swales:
Referee G Davies (Wakefield) Att - 1750 H.T. 17 - nil

Sat 11 Nov 1961 HULL away won 21 - 10
HULL - Bateson: Kershaw Gemmell Hollindrake Barnwell: Matthews Finn: W.Drake Harris Storey Sykes Smith J.Whiteley: Tries - Kershaw Gemmell: Goals - Bateson(2):
CASTLEFORD - Briers: Walsh G.G.Ward Small Cartwright: Hardisty Brown: Tonkinson J.Ward Pye W.Bryant Taylor Sheridan: Tries - Brown(2) Cartwright Hardisty Sheridan:
Goals - Briers(3):
Referee C Whiteley (Ossett) Att - 3000 H.T. 16 - 2

Sat 18 Nov 1961 HALIFAX away lost 4 - 9
HALIFAX - James: Williams Burnett Dixon Freeman: Robinson Marchant: Scott Shaw Crabtree Turnbull Phillips McFarlane: Tries - Williams Dixon Phillips:
CASTLEFORD - Peter Briers: Walsh G.G.Ward Small Cartwright: Hardisty Brown: Tonkinson J.Ward Pye W.Bryant Taylor Sheridan: Goals - Briers(2):
Referee L Thompson (Batley) Att - 4931 H.T. 4 - 6

Sat 25 Nov 1961 WIDNES home won 5 - 2
CASTLEFORD - Lunn: Walsh G.G.Ward Small Hepworth: Hardisty Brown: Tonkinson Brownley Pye W.Bryant Walker Sheridan: Try - Hepworth: Goal - Lunn:
WIDNES - Randall: Chisnall Bright F.Myler Gaydon: Lowe Heyes: Hurstfield Kemel E.Bate R.Bate Gallighan Hughes:
Goal - Randall
Referee D T H Davies (Man'ster) Att - 4049 H.T. 5 - nil

Sat 2 Dec 1961 WIDNES away lost 10 - 18
WIDNES - Randall: Chisnall Bright Lowe Gaydon: Myler Heyes: Hurstfield Kemel R.Bate Winstanley Gallighan Hughes:
Tries - Gaydon(2) Chisnall Lowe: Goals - Randall(3):
CASTLEFORD - Lunn: Walsh G.G.Ward Small Hepworth: Hardisty Brown: Tonkinson Brownley Pye W.Bryant Walker Sheridan: Tries - Ward Small: Goals - Lunn(2):
Referee E Clay (Rothwell) Att - 4000 H.T. 2 - 8

Sat 16 Dec 1961 SALFORD away lost 3 - 8
SALFORD - Gregory: Jones Hindley Cheshire Dorning: Richards Dunn: Council Harwood Hardman Loughlin Simcox Rees: Tries - Hindley Richards: Goal - Richards:
CASTLEFORD - Lunn: Walsh G.G.Ward Small Hepworth: Hardisty Brown: Hirst J.Ward Pye W.Bryant Walker Sheridan: Try - Small:
Referee B Hall (Wakefield) Att - 2300 H.T. 3 - 3

Sat 23 Dec 1961 BRADFORD NORTHERN home won 34 - 10
CASTLEFORD - Lunn: Walsh G.G.Ward Small Battye: Hardisty Hepworth: Hirst J.Ward Tonkinson W.Bryant Walker Sheridan: Tries - Hardisty(2) Walsh J.Ward Bryant Sheridan: Goals - Lunn(8):
BRADFORD N - Seddon: Grainger Davies Nunns Doran: Whitaker Broadbent: Hatfield Wigglesworth Hardcastle Hemingway Robbins Winnard:
Tries - Doran(2):   Goals - Seddon(2):
Referee H Hunt (Culcheth) Att - 2056 H.T. 15 - 5

Sat 6 Jan 1962 DEWSBURY home won 21 - nil
CASTLEFORD - Lunn: Walsh G.G.Ward Small Battye: Hardisty Brown: Tonkinson J.Ward Pye W.Bryant Walker(S/O) Sheridan:
Tries - Walsh G.G.Ward Small Battye Walker:
Goals - Lunn(3):
DEWSBURY - Bedford: Foley Evans Firth Osborne: D.Lockwood Bullock: Thorley A.Lockwood Connelly Schofield Rushworth Harwood:
Referee C F Appleton (War'gton) Att - 2335 H.T. 15 - nil

Sat 13 Jan 1962 KEIGHLEY away won 16 - 6
KEIGHLEY - Owen: Smith Brown Todd G.Jackson: Edwards Hebden: Bloomfield Anderson Fall Phillips Haigh V.Jackson: Goals - Owen(3):
CASTLEFORD - Lunn: Walsh G.G.Ward Small Battye: Hardisty Brown: Tonkinson J.Ward Pye W.Bryant Walker Sheridan: Tries - J.Ward Bryant: Goals - Lunn(5):
Referee L Wingfield (Normanton) Att -1500 H.T. 5 - 6

SEASON 1961-62

Sat 27 Jan 1962 BATLEY home won 23 - 3
CASTLEFORD - Lunn: Walsh G.G.Ward Small Battye:
Hardisty Brown: J.Berry J.Ward Pye W.Bryant Walker
Sheridan:
Tries - Battye(2) Brown Berry Walker: Goals - Lunn(4):
BATLEY - Astbury: Illingworth Ward Hammond Field:
Shuttleworth Pratt: Fairbank Whiteford Etty McVeigh Dick
Johnstone: Try - Field:
Referee F J Howker (Rochdale) Att - 3360 H.T. 13 - 3

Sat 3 Feb 1962 HULL KINGSTON ROVERS away
lost 5 - 15
HULL K R - Kellett: Harris Clark Major Paul: Elliott Bunting:
Coverdale Ackerley Tyson Taylor(S/O) Bonner Poole:
Tries - Kellett Paul Elliott: Goals - Kellett(3):
CASTLEFORD - Lunn: Walsh G.G.Ward Small Battye:
Hardisty Brown: Tonkinson J.Ward Pye W.Bryant Walker
Sheridan:
Try - G.G.Ward: Goal - Lunn:
Referee B Hall (Wakefield) Att - 7150 H.T. 5 - 5

Sat 10 Feb 1962 BRADFORD NORTHERN home
won 12 - nil CHALLENGE CUP ROUND 1
CASTLEFORD - Lunn: Walsh G.G.Ward Small Battye:
Hardisty Brown: Tonkinson J.Ward Brownley W.Bryant
Walker Sheridan:
Tries - G.G.Ward Small: Goals - Lunn(3):
BRADFORD N - Seddon: Grainger Nunns Davies Coggle:
Schofield Tate: Hatfield Wigglesworth Hardcastle Marker
Doran Taylor:
Referee C F Appleton (Warr'ton) Att - 4250 H.T. 2 - nil

Sat 17 Feb 1962 WORKINGTON TOWN home
won 21 - 3
CASTLEFORD - Lunn: Walsh G.G.Ward Small Marsden:
Hardisty Hepworth: Berry J.Ward Tonkinson W.Bryant
Walker Sheridan:
Tries - Walsh Hardisty Hepworth: Goals - Lunn(6):
WORKINGTON T - Lowdon: Southward Bell O'Neill
Pretorious: Archer Roper: Edgar Ackerley Martin Garrick
McLeod Eve Try - Southward:
Referee K Rathbone (St Helens) Att - 3700 H.T. 16 - nil

Sat 24 Feb 1962 HULL home lost 9 - 18
CASTLEFORD - Lunn: Barry Walsh G.G.Ward Small
Marsden: Hardisty Hepworth: Berry J.Ward Tonkinson
W.Bryant Walker Sheridan:
Try - Hardisty: Goals - Lunn(3):
HULL - Keegan: Rosenberg Gemmell Hollindrake Sullivan:
Davidson Finn: Scott Corban J.Drake Smith Booth
Whiteley:
Tries - Gemmell(2) Rosenberg Hollindrake:
Goals - Hollindrake(3):
Referee T W Watkinson (Man'ster) Att - 4537 H.T. 2 - 5

Sat 3 Mar 1962 HUNSLET home won 27 - 14
CHALLENGE CUP ROUND 2
CASTLEFORD - Lunn: Battye G.G.Ward Small Marsden:
Hardisty Hepworth: Hirst J.Ward Tonkinson W.Bryant
Walker Sheridan:

Tries - Marsden(2) Small Bryant Sheridan: Goals - Lunn(6):
HUNSLET - Langton: Smith Shelton Render Lee: Preece
Newall: Adams Prior Hartley Eyre Gunney Baldwinson:
Tries - Shelton Render: Goals - Langton(4):
Referee D T H Davies (Man'ster) Att - 9033 H.T. 17 - 7

Sat 10 Mar 1962 DONCASTER away won 13 - 5
DONCASTER - Price: Goodchild Lockwood Saville Davies:
Dean Doyle: Kirk Wakefield Hepworth Asquith Swales
Heath:
Try - Dean: Goal - Swales:
CASTLEFORD - Lunn: Battye G.G.Ward Small Marsden:
Hardisty Hepworth: Berry J.Ward Tonkinson(S/O)
W.Bryant E.Bryant Sheridan:
Tries - Battye(2) Small: Goals - Lunn(2):
Referee C F Appleton (Warrington) Att - 1400 H.T. 5 - 5

Sat 17 Mar 1962 LEEDS home won 15 - 3
CASTLEFORD - Lunn: Battye G.G.Ward Small Marsden:
Hardisty Hepworth: Berry J.Ward Brownley W.Bryant
Walker Sheridan:
Tries - Battye G.G.Ward Small: Goals - Lunn(3):
LEEDS - Thornett: Ratcliffe Hattee Hallas Cadywold:
Davies Evans: Terry Simms Robinson Fairbank Pickup
Shaw:
Try - Cadywold:
Referee S Shepherd (Oldham) Att - 9813 H.T. 8 - nil

Sat 24 Mar 1962 HUDDERSFIELD home draw 4 - 4
CHALLENGE CUP ROUND 3
CASTLEFORD - Lunn: Battye G.G.Ward Small Marsden:
Hardisty Hepworth: Berry J.Ward Brownley W.Bryant
Walker Sheridan: Goals - Lunn(2):
HUDDERSFIELD - Dyson: Breen Stocks Deighton Wicks:
Davies Smales: Slevin Close Noble Clark Bowman Kilroy:
Goals - Dyson(2):
Referee T W Watkinson (Man'ster) Att - 16150 H.T. 4 - 4

Wed 28 Mar 1962 HUDDERSFIELD away lost 4 - 10
CHALLENGE CUP ROUND 3 REPLAY
HUDDERSFIELD - Dyson: Breen Stocks Deighton Wicks:
Davies Smales: Slevin Close Noble Clark Bowman Strong:
Tries - Wicks Davies: Goals - Dyson(2):
CASTLEFORD - Lunn: Battye G.G.Ward Small Marsden:
Hardisty Hepworth: Clark J.Ward Brownley W.Bryant
Walker Sheridan: Goals - Lunn(2):
Referee C F Appleton (War'gton) Att - 21398 H.T. 2 - nil

Tue 3 Apr 1962 YORK away won 8 - 2
YORK - Hargreaves: Foster Hunter Sheehan Francis:
Flannery Smith: Goodwin Milner Kidd Ward Walker
Jackson: Goal - Hunter:
CASTLEFORD - Lunn: Battye G.G.Ward Small Marsden:
Hardisty Hepworth: Hirst J.Ward Tonkinson W.Bryant
Walker Sheridan:
Tries - Small Walker: Goal - Lunn:
Referee H Pearce (Leeds) Att - 3798 H.T. 5 - 2

Sat 7 Apr 1962 HALIFAX home won 11 - 8
CASTLEFORD - Lunn: C.Battye MALCOLM BATTYE(462)

SEASON 1961-62

Butterfield Marsden: Hardisty Hepworth: Hirst J.Ward
Tonkinson Brownley Walker Sheridan:
Try - Hardisty: Goals - Lunn(4):
HALIFAX - James: Jackson Burnett Rhodes Freeman:
Williams Marchant: Fox Shaw Crabtree Phillips Turnbull
Broadbent:
Tries - Jackson Phillips: Goal - James:
Referee G Philpott (Leeds) Att - 3952 H.T. 4 - 5

Tue 10 Apr 1962 HUNSLET home won 26 - 6
CASTLEFORD - Lunn: C.Battye M.Battye Butterfield
Marsden: Hardisty Hepworth: Hirst J.Ward Brownley
Tonkinson W.Bryant Walker:
Tries - Walker(2) Lunn C.Battye Butterfield J.Ward:
Goals - Lunn(3) Hardisty(DG):
HUNSLET - Langton: White Newall Render Lee: Gabbitas
Watts: Adams Smith Eyre Baldwinson Whitehead Gunney:
Tries - Watts Gunney:
Referee A E Durkin (Dewsbury) Att - 4345 H.T. 15 - nil

Thu 12 Apr 1962 LEEDS away lost 9 - 10
LEEDS - Thornett: Wrigglesworth Hallas Hattee Ratcliffe:
Jones Evans: Robinson Simms Shaw Sykes Neumann
Pickup:
Tries - Thornett(2):   Goals - Jones(2):
CASTLEFORD - Lunn: C.Battye Butterfield Small ERIC
NOWELL(463): Hardisty Hepworth: Tonkinson J.Ward
Brownley W.Bryant Walker Sheridan:
Try - Sheridan: Goals - Lunn(3):
Referee K Rathbone (St Helens) Att - 8575 H.T. 5 - 10

Sat 14 Apr 1962 WAKEFIELD TRINITY away
lost 3 - 23
WAKEFIELD T - Round: Greenwood Skene Fox Hirst: Rollin
Holliday: Williamson Kosanovic Smith Vines Payne Turner:
Tries - Greenwood Hirst Rollin Payne Turner:
Goals - Fox(4):
CASTLEFORD - Lunn: C.Battye Butterfield Small M.Battye:
Hardisty Edwards: Berry J.Ward Brownley W.Bryant
Tonkinson Walker:
Try - J.Ward:
Referee J P Hebblethwaite(York) Att - 11888 H.T. nil - 11

Wed 18 Apr 1962 FEATHERSTONE ROVERS home
lost 4 - 11
CASTLEFORD - Lunn: C.Battye G.G.Ward Small Cartwright:
Hardisty Hepworth: Berry J.Ward Sheridan W.Bryant
Walker E.Bryant:
Goals - Lunn(2):
FEATHERSTONE R - Anderson: Greatorex Cooper Hunt
Jordan: Lingard Fox: Hammill W.Ward Lambert Ramshaw
Clawson Lamming:
Try - Fox: Goals - Clawson(4):
Referee R Appleyard (Leeds) Att - 6101 H.T. -

Sat 21 Apr 1962 HUDDERSFIELD home lost 5 - 9
CASTLEFORD - Lunn: C.Battye G.G.Ward Small Cartwright:
Hepworth Brown: Berry J.Ward Slatter W.Bryant Walker
Sheridan:

Try - Cartwright: Goal - Lunn:
HUDDERSFIELD - Dyson: Breen Deighton Heywood Wicks:
Davies Smales: Slevin Close Rowe Clark Bowman
Ramsden:
Try - Breen: Goals - Dyson(3):
Referee D S Brown (Dewsbury) Att - 3000 H.T. 2 - 5

Mon 23 Apr 1962 FEATHERSTONE ROVERS away
won 26 - 8
FEATHERSTONE R. - Anderson: Greatorex Cooper Hunt
Jordan: Lingard Fox: Hammill Ward Lambert Ramshaw
Clawson Lamming:
Tries - Greatorex Cooper: Goal - Clawson:
CASTLEFORD - Lunn: C.Battye G.G.Ward Butterfield
Cartwright: Hardisty Hepworth: Berry J.Ward Slatter
W.Bryant Walker Sheridan:
Tries - Cartwright Hardisty Hepworth Bryant:
Goals - Lunn(6) Hepworth(DG):
Referee R Gelder (Wilmslow) Att - 6714 H.T. 10 - nil

Sat 28 Apr 1962 HUDDERSFIELD away lost 2 - 6
HUDDERSFIELD - Dyson: Breen Booth Heywood Wicks:
Smales Lancaster: Slevin Close Rowe Clark Bowman Kilroy:
Tries - Breen Wicks:
CASTLEFORD - Lunn: Small G.G.Ward Butterfield
Cartwright: Hardisty Hepworth: Berry J.Ward Walker
W.Bryant MAURICE WILLIAMS(464) Sheridan:
Goal - Lunn:
Referee M Coates (Pudsey) Att - 8472 H.T. 2 - 6

Mon 30 Apr 1962 BRAMLEY home won 16 - 7
CASTLEFORD - Lunn: Nowell G.G.Ward Butterfield
Cartwright: Hardisty Hepworth: Berry J.Ward Walker
W.Bryant Williams Sheridan:
Tries - Butterfield Cartwright: Goals - Lunn(5):
BRAMLEY - Wilson: Smith Strafford Rushton Murthick:
Wrigglesworth Quinn: Hainsworth Clough Cooper
Robbins Baddeley Chamberlain:
Try - Strafford: Goals - Wilson(2):
Referee P Geraghty (York) Att - 4207 H.T. 7 – 7

Malcolm Battye
D. No 462
1961-62-1966-67

197

SEASON 1961-62

Eric Nowell
D. No 463
1961-62 to 1963-64

Maurice Williams
D. No 464
1961-62 to 1964-65

SEASON 1962-63

Jack Gamble
D. No 465
1962-63 to 1966-67

Frank Dickinson
D. No 467
1962-63 to 1963-64

Frank Smith Jnr
D. No 468
1962-63 to 1964-65

Dougie Walton
D. No 469
1962-63 to 1971-72

Denis Jones
D. No 470
1962-63 to 1963-64

Kenny Foulkes
D. No 471
1962-63 to 1964-65

Keith Howe
D. No 473
1962-63 to 1969-70

Trevor Bedford
D. No 474
1962-63 to 1970-71

SEASON 1961-62

D.N	PLAYER		DEBUT	L MATCH	APP	SUB	T.AP	TRI'S	G'LS	D.G	P'TS
330	PYE	KENNETH			22	0	22	2	0	0	6
341	LUNN	ALBERT			36	0	36	1	113	0	229
382	SHERIDAN	JOHN			40	0	40	4	0	0	12
389	BARNES	JACK			1	0	1	0	0	0	0
406	TAYLOR	COLIN			5	0	5	1	0	0	3
410	BRYANT	EDWARD			2	0	2	0	0	0	0
412	WALSH	BARRY		24/02/1962	26	0	26	11	0	0	33
414	WARD	GEOFFREY G.			38	0	38	9	0	0	27
419	BRIDGES	KEITH			2	0	2	0	0	0	0
420	TONKINSON	ALBERT			29	0	29	0	0	0	0
421	BERRY	JOHN			12	0	12	1	0	0	3
424	HIRST	JACK			14	0	14	1	0	0	3
426	BRYANT	WILLIAM			31	0	31	5	0	0	15
427	BATTYE	COLIN			21	0	21	7	0	0	21
433	HARDISTY	ALAN			40	0	40	13	0	1	41
434	CARTWRIGHT	HOWARD			10	0	10	5	0	0	15
436	BROWN	GEORGE			23	0	23	6	0	0	18
437	BROWNLEY	WILLIAM			11	0	11	0	0	0	0
438	SMALL	PETER			38	0	38	17	0	0	51
439	CLARK	JOHN			1	0	1	0	0	0	0
442	HEPWORTH	KEITH			22	0	22	4	0	1	14
448	BUTTERFIELD	COLIN			7	0	7	2	0	0	6
452	MARSDEN	BRIAN			20	0	20	4	0	0	12
453	WARD	JOHNNY			38	0	38	10	0	0	30
454	BRIERS	PETER		18/11/1961	6	0	6	0	20	0	40
455	WALKER	JOHN			38	0	38	6	0	0	18
458	EDWARDS	DEREK			2	0	2	0	0	0	0
460	SLATTER	KEITH			3	0	3	0	0	0	0
461	BLOOMFIELD	GEOFFREY	07/10/1961	07/10/1961	1	0	1	0	0	0	0
462	BATTYE	MALCOLM	07/04/1962		3	0	3	0	0	0	0
463	NOWELL	ERIC	12/04/1962		2	0	2	0	0	0	0
464	WILLIAMS	MAURICE	28/04/1962		2	0	2	0	0	0	0
	32			**4**	**3**	**546**	**0**	**546**	**109**	**133**	**2**	**597**

COMPETITION		P	W	D	L	FOR	AGT
LEAGUE	POSITION 12 OF 30	36	21	0	15	501	369
YORK'S CUP		2	1	0	1	49	28
RL CUP		4	2	1	1	47	28
PLAYERS RECORDS		**42**	**24**	**1**	**17**	**597**	**425**

This season got off to a disastrous start and not just by losing the first two league games beaten at Wheldon Road 7-42 by Wakefield Trinity, and losing at Mount Pleasant 8-9 to Batley. The game at Batley also saw hooker Keith Bridges breaking his leg. This was a bitter disappointment for Keith as he had been selected to represent a combined Castleford and Featherstone team to play the New Zealand tourists the following week and was replaced by Willis Fawley of Featherstone.

However, true to the saying "one man's loss is another man's gain" Keith's absence presented an opportunity for Johnny Ward who played in 38 of the remaining 40 games.

Albert Lunn increased the record for most points scored in a League game to 20 against Salford on the 16 September 1961 and became the first Castleford player to kick 800 goals for the club on 3 March 1962 in the 27–14 home victory against Hunslet.

At the end of the season Peter Small became only the second Castleford player to tour Australasia following Arthur Atkinson in 1929. Peter earned high praise as a stand-in scrum half on the New Zealand leg of the tour, and was rewarded with his test debut on the wing against the Kiwis at Auckland on 11 August 1962 scoring a try in a 8-27 defeat.

SEASON 1962-63

TWO DIVISIONS

The League was split into two divisions for the first time since 1904/05 with 16 teams in Division 1 and 14 teams in Division 2. As each team played each other home and away, the Championship play off system was abandoned and the team at the top of the table was declared champions.

Division 1 consisted of Bramley, Castleford, Featherstone Rovers, Halifax, Huddersfield, Hull, Hull K R, Leeds, Oldham, St Helens, Swinton, Wakefield, Warrington, Widnes Wigan And Workington Town.

Division 2 consisted of Barrow, Batley, Blackpool Borough, Bradford Northern, Dewsbury, Doncaster, Hunslet, Keighley, Leigh, Liverpool City, Rochdale Hornets, Salford, Whitehaven and York.

However the season started with a new competition – the Eastern and Western Divisions,

Sat 18 Aug 1962 YORK away lost 7 – 26
EASTERN DIVISION
YORK - Hargreaves: G.Smith Houlden Hunter Foster: Flannery J.Smith: Howden Crosby Pratt Kidd Parkin Coglan: Tries - Hargreaves G.Smith J.Smith Coglan: Goals - Hunter(6) Hargreaves:
CASTLEFORD - Lunn: Cartwright Butterfield G.G.Ward Marsden: Hardisty Brown: John Berry Keith Bridges Pye Tonkinson W.Bryant Walker: Try - Ward: Goals - Lunn(2): Referee T W Watkinson (Man'ster) Att - 2082 H.T. 5 - 17

Wed 22 Aug 1962 HUNSLET home won 23 - 18
EASTERN DIVISION
CASTLEFORD - Lunn: JACK GAMBLE(465) Butterfield G.G.Ward Marsden: Hardisty Geo.Brown: Tonkinson GILBERT BROWN(466) Slatter Williams Walker Sheridan: Tries - Gamble(2)Marsden: Goals - Lunn(6) Hardisty(DG): HUNSLET - Langton: Smith Shelton Preece Walker: Gabbitas Stevenson: Dodds Prior Eyre Lambert Whitehead Gunney: Tries - Walker Eyre: Goals - Langton(5) Stevenson(DG): Referee P Geraghty (York) Att - 4297 H.T. 9 - 14

Sat 25 Aug 1962 KEIGHLEY home won 26 - 15
EASTERN DIVISION
CASTLEFORD - Lunn: Gamble Butterfield G.G.Ward Marsden: Hardisty Geo.Brown: Tonkinson J.Ward Slatter W.Bryant Williams Sheridan: Tries - Butterfield G.G.Ward Hardisty Slatter Sheridan Gamble: Goals - Lunn(4): KEIGHLEY - Owen: Smith Jackson Todd Taylor: Sabine Reilly: Worthy Waring Phillips Crewdson Bloomfield Eyre: Tries - Smith(2) Reilly: Goals - Owen(3): Referee C F Appleton (War'gton) Att 3600 H.T. 10 - 10

Mon 27 Aug 1962 HULL away lost 5 - 11
EASTERN DIVISION
HULL - Keegan: Rosenberg Gemmell Hollindrake Sullivan: Devonshire McGowan: Whitehead Corban Drake Storey Booth Clixby: Tries - Devonshire(2) Rosenberg: Goal - Keegan:

CASTLEFORD - Lunn: Gamble Butterfield G.G.Ward Marsden: Hardisty Geo.Brown: Tonkinson J.Ward Slatter W.Bryant Walker Sheridan: Try - Butterfield: Goal - Lunn: Referee C Whiteley (Ossett) Att - 6600 H.T. 5 - 3

Sat 1 Sep 1962 HUNSLET away lost 12 - 22
EASTERN DIVISION
HUNSLET - Langton: Smith Shelton Preece Lee: Garforth Stevenson: Hartley Prior Eyre Gunney Ward Ramsey: Tries - Preece(2) Shelton Gunney: Goals - Langton(5): CASTLEFORD - Lunn: Gamble Butterfield G.G.Ward Marsden: Hardisty Geo.Brown: Tonkinson J.Ward Kenneth Pye W.Bryant Walker Sheridan: Tries - Butterfield Marsden: Goals - Lunn(3): Referee N T Railton (Wigan) Att - 4000 H.T. 3 - 2

Fri 7 Sep 1962 BATLEY home won 28 - 2
YORKSHIRE CUP ROUND 1
CASTLEFORD - Lunn: Gamble G.G.Ward Small Marsden: Hardisty Hepworth: Tonkinson J.Ward Slatter W.Bryant Walker Sheridan: Tries - Gamble(2) Small Hardisty J.Ward Sheridan: Goals - Lunn(5): BATLEY - Lawton: Boustead Astbury Shuttleworth Hammond: Geldard Foster: Fairbank Fryer Nixon Kennedy Briggs Dick: Goal - Lawton: Referee T W Watkinson (Man'ster) Att - 4732 H.T. 5 - 2

Sat 15 Sep 1962 YORK home won 20 - 13
EASTERN DIVISION
CASTLEFORD - Lunn: Gamble G.G.Ward Small Marsden: Hardisty Hepworth: Slatter J.Ward Brownley W.Bryant Walker Sheridan: Tries - Lunn Gamble Small Bryant: Goals - Lunn(4): YORK - Hargreaves: Smith Quinn Sullivan Foster: Sheehan Hunter: Yorke Milner Crosby Kidd Pratt Parkin: Tries - Smith Sheehan Milner: Goals - Yorke(2): Referee K Rathbone (St Helens) Att - 4344 H.T. 5 - 5

Mon 17 Sep 1962 HULL KINGSTON ROVERS away lost 12 - 28 YORKSHIRE CUP ROUND 2
HULL K R - Kellett: Paul Major Blackmore Harris: Elliott Hatch: Grice Flanagan Drake Tyson Taylor Poole: Tries - Paul(3) Major(2) Poole: Goals - Kellett(5): CASTLEFORD - Lunn: C.Battye Gamble Butterfield Marsden: Hardisty Hepworth: Slatter J.Ward Brownley W.Bryant Walker Sheridan: Tries - Butterfield Hardisty: Goals - Lunn(3): Referee D T H Davies (Man'ster) Att - 10650 H.T. 4 - 13

Sat 22 Sep 1962 KEIGHLEY away lost 8 - 26
EASTERN DIVISION
KEIGHLEY - Owen: Plunkett Jackson Frain Bleasby: Sabine Reilly: Haigh Redman Phillips Crewdson Bloomfield Eyre: Tries - Plunkett Bleasby Reilly Eyre: Goals - Owen(7): CASTLEFORD - Lunn: Gamble C.Battye Butterfield Marsden: Hardisty Geo.Brown: Slatter J.Ward William Brownley W.Bryant Walker Sheridan: Goals - Lunn(4): Referee G Philpott (Leeds) Att - 1750 H.T. 2 - 9

SEASON 1962-63

Sat 29 Sep 1962 HULL home won 16 - 6
EASTERN DIVISION
CASTLEFORD - FRANK DICKINSON(467): Gamble
G.G.Ward Green FRANK SMITH Jnr(468): Hardisty
Hepworth: Tonkinson J.Ward Slatter W.Bryant Walker
E.Bryant:
Tries - Smith(2) Gamble J.Ward: Goals - Dickinson(2):
HULL - Keegan: Devonshire Gemmell Hollindrake
Matthews: Doyle-Davidson Finn: Whitehead Clixby
W.Drake Macklin(SO) Story Sykes:
Goals - Keegan(3):
Referee J Manley (Warrington) Att - 4434 H.T. 6 - 6

Sat 6 Oct 1962 HALIFAX home won 21 - 15
CASTLEFORD - Dickinson: Gamble G.G.Ward Butterfield
Smith: Hardisty Hepworth: Tonkinson J.Ward Slatter
W.Bryant Walker E.Bryant:
Tries - G.G.Ward Hardisty J.Ward Slatter W.Bryant:
Goals - Dickinson(3):
HALIFAX - James: Jackson Burnett Williams Freeman:
Robinson A.N.Other: Crabtree Taylor Scroby Renilson
Turnbull Duffy:
Tries - Jackson(2) Robinson: Goals - James(3):
Referee L Gant (Wakefield) Att - 5003 H.T. 11 - nil

Sat 13 Oct 1962 ST HELENS away draw 10 - 10
ST HELENS - Coslett: Vollenhoven Briers Sullivan Killeen:
Northey Smith: Arkwright Dagnall Watson Temby
Huddart Major:
Tries - Huddart Major: Goals - Coslett(2):
CASTLEFORD - Dickinson: Gamble G.G.Ward Small
Marsden: Hardisty Hepworth: Tonkinson J.Ward Slatter
W.Bryant Walker E.Bryant:
Tries - Marsden Hardisty: Goals - Dickinson(2):
Referee M.Coates (Pudsey) Att - 9000 H.T. 2 - 3

Sat 20 Oct 1962 SWINTON home won 18 - 14
CASTLEFORD - Dickinson: Gamble G.G.Ward Small
Marsden: Hardisty Hepworth: Tonkinson J.Ward Slatter
W.Bryant Walker E.Bryant:
Tries - Gamble Marsden: Goals - Dickinson(6):
SWINTON - Gowers: McMahon Halliwell Robinson Speed:
Parkinson Cartwright: Roberts Clarke Morgan Norburn
Bonser Blan:
Tries - Cartwright Norburn: Goals - Gowers(4):
Referee K Rathbone (St.Helens) Att - 6601 H.T. 11 - 7

Sat 27 Oct 1962 FEATHERSTONE ROVERS away
lost 11 - 15
FEATHERSTONE R - Fennell: Waterworth Cooper
Greatorex Jordan: Hunt Fox(S/O): Hammill Ward
Nicholson Ramshaw Clawson Clifft:
Tries - Hunt(2) Fox: Goals - Clawson(3):
CASTLEFORD - Dickinson: Gamble G.G.Ward Small
Marsden: Hardisty Hepworth: Tonkinson J.Ward Slatter
W.Bryant Walker E.Bryant(S/O):
Tries - Gamble(3): Goal - Dickinson:
Referee N T Railton (Wigan) Att - 8308 H.T. 8 - 7

Sat 3 Nov 1962 HULL home won 21 - 14
CASTLEFORD - Lunn: Gamble G.G.Ward Small Marsden:
Hardisty Hepworth: Tonkinson J.Ward Sheridan DOUGLAS
WALTON(469) Walker E.Bryant:
Tries - Small(3) G.G.Ward Sheridan: Goals - Lunn(3):
HULL - Keegan: Rosenberg Hollindrake Kershaw
Devonshire: Nimb Finn: Drake Walters Whitehead Storey
Booth Clixby:
Tries - Hollindrake Devonshire: Goals - Keegan(4):
Referee C Whiteley (Ossett) Att - 5594 H.T. 3 - 7

Sat 10 Nov 1962 HALIFAX away won 10 - 5
HALIFAX - James: Jackson Burnett Dixon Freeman:
Robinson Marchant: Scott Shaw Scroby Turnbull Duffy
Renilson:
Try - Burnett: Goal - James:
CASTLEFORD - Lunn: Gamble G.G.Ward Small Marsden:
Hardisty Hepworth: Tonkinson J.Ward Walton DENIS
JONES(470) Walker Sheridan:
Tries - Lunn J.Ward: Goals - Lunn(2):
Referee S Shepherd (Oldham) Att - 4960 H.T. 3 - 5

Sat 17 Nov 1962 ST HELENS home lost 7 - 8
CASTLEFORD - Dickinson: Gamble G.G.Ward Small
Marsden: Hardisty Hepworth: Tonkinson J.Ward Walker
W.Bryant Jones E.Bryant:
Try - Walker: Goals - Dickinson(2):
ST HELENS - Coslett: Vollenhoven Donovan Northey
Killeen: Sm th Heaton: Knowles Dagnall Watson Tembey
French Major: Tries - Killeen(2):   Goal - Coslett:
Referee D H Davies (Manchester) Att – 8007 H.T. 5 - 5

Sat 24 Nov 1962 SWINTON away lost 8 - 17
SWINTON - Gowers: Speed Fleet Buckley Stopford:
Parkinson Cartwright: Bretherton T.Roberts K.Roberts
Norburn Bonser Blan:
Tries - Fleet Buckley Stopford: Goals - Gowers(4):
CASTLEFORD - Dickinson: Gamble G.G.Ward Small
Marsden: Hardisty George Brown: Tonkinson J.Ward
Jones W.Bryant Walker E.Bryant:
Tries - Gamble Small: Goal - Dickinson:
Referee M Coates (Pudsey) Att - 6000 H.T. 3 - 9

Sat 1 Dec 1962 FEATHERSTONE ROVERS home
won 8 - 6
CASTLEFORD - Lunn: Gamble G.G.Ward Small Marsden:
Hardisty Hepworth: Hirst J.Ward Tonkinson W.Bryant
Walker E.Bryant:
Tries - Gamble G.G.Ward: Goal - Lunn:
FEATHERSTONE R - Fennell: Waterworth Cooper
Greatorex Jordan: Lingard Dooler: Hammill Fawley
Hockley Ramshaw Clawson Clifft:
Goals - Clawson(3):
Referee E Clay (Rothwell) Att - 9193 H.T. 5 - 6

Sat 8 Dec 1962 HULL away won 11 - 10
HULL - Keegan: Devonshire Gemmell Mountain
Matthews: Nimb Finn: W.Drake Puckering Macklin Booth
Sykes P.Whiteley:
Tries - Devonshire Matthews: Goals - Nimb Sykes:

SEASON 1962-63

CASTLEFORD - Lunn: Gamble G.G.Ward Small Marsden: Hardisty Hepworth: Hirst J.Ward Tonkinson W.Bryant Walker E.Bryant:
Tries - Gamble Hardisty Walker: Goal - Lunn:
Referee R Gelder (Wilmslow) Att - 4000 H.T. 8 - 8

Sat 15 Dec 1962 OLDHAM away won 10 - 2
OLDHAM - Patterson: Elliott Holden Fisher Noon: Nestor Pycroft: Mumberson Wood Robinson Ogden Smethurst Platt: Goal - Platt:
CASTLEFORD - Dickinson: Gamble G.G.Ward Small Marsden: Hardisty Hepworth(S/O): Hirst J.Ward Tonkinson(S/O) W.Bryant Walker E.Bryant:
Tries - G.G.Ward Hardisty: Goals - Dickinson(2):
Referee J Senior (Bradford) Att - 3059 H.T. 7 - nil

Wed 30 Jan 1963 WARRINGTON home lost 9 - 12
CASTLEFORD - Dickinson: Gamble G.G.Ward Small Marsden: Hardisty Edwards: Hirst J.Ward Walton W.Bryant Walker E.Bryant:
Try - Small: Goals - Dickinson(2) (DG)
WARRINGTON - Fraser: Challinor Holden Pickavance Glover: Greenough Edwards: Payne Brindle Winslade Fisher Gilfedder Delooze: Tries - Glover Greenough:
Goals - Gilfedder(2) Challinor(DG):
Referee K Rathbone (St Helens) Att - 4400 H.T. 4 - 10

Sat 9 Feb 1963 LEEDS home lost 8 - 10
CHALLENGE CUP ROUND 1
CASTLEFORD - Albert Lunn: Gamble G.G.Ward Small Marsden: Hardisty Hepworth: Hirst J.Ward Jones W.Bryant Walker E.Bryant:
Tries - Hardisty Walker: Goal - Lunn:
LEEDS - Thornett: Wriglesworth Pickup Jones Cowan: Rees Evans: Robinson Simms Walker Sykes Neumann Shaw:
Tries - Pickup Jones: Goals - Jones(2):
Referee R Gelder (Wilmslow) Att - 11000 H.T. 4 - nil

Sat 9 Mar 1963 HUDDERSFIELD home lost 4 - 7
CASTLEFORD - Dickinson: Gamble G.G.Ward Butterfield Marsden: Hardisty Hepworth: Hirst J.Ward Tonkinson W.Bryant Walker Sheridan:
Goals - Dickinson(2):
HUDDERSFIELD - Dyson: Hollands Ford Haywood Senior: Halsey Bullock: Kilkenny Close Noble Kilroy Bowman Ogden:
Try - Senior: Goals - Dyson(2):
Referee P Geraghty (York) Att - 3291 H.T. 4 - nil

Sat 16 Mar 1963 HUDDERSFIELD away won 15 - 7
HUDDERSFIELD - Dyson: Senior Ford Haywood Booth: Halsey Smales: Rowe Close Kilroy Bowman Cherrington Redfearn:
Try - Booth: Goals - Dyson(2):
CASTLEFORD - Dickinson: Gamble G.G.Ward Butterfield Marsden: Hardisty KENNETH FOULKES(471): Tonkinson J.Ward Jones Sheridan Walker Edward Bryant:
Tries - Foulkes(2) Walker: Goals - Dickinson(3):
Referee G Wilson (Pudsey) Att - 3347 H.T. 8 - nil

Sat 23 Mar 1963 WIDNES away lost 7 - 8
WIDNES - Randall: Chisnall Lowe Mort Gaydon: Heyes G.Smith: T.Smith Kemel Bate Hughes Measures Karalius:
Tries - Chisnall Gaydon: Goals - Randall:
CASTLEFORD - Dickinson: Gamble G.G.Ward Butterfield Small: Hardisty Foulkes: Tonkinson J.Ward Jones Sheridan Walker W.Bryant: Try - Hardisty: Goals - Dickinson(2):
Referee C Whiteley (Ossett) Att - 8100 H.T. 2 - 5

Sat 30 Mar 1963 HULL KINGSTON ROVERS home draw 7 - 7
CASTLEFORD - Dickinson: Gamble G.G.Ward Green Marsden: Hardisty Hepworth: Tonkinson J.Ward Jones Sheridan Walker W.Bryant:
Try - Gamble: Goals - Dickinson(2):
HULL K R - Kellett: Paul Major Blackmore Harris: Elliott Bunting: Coverdale Lockwood Tyson Murphy Taylor Chamberlain:
Try - Harris: Goals - Kellett(2):
Referee M Coates (Pudsey) Att - 3347 H.T. 2 - 5

Sat 6 Apr 1963 LEEDS away lost 3 - 10
LEEDS - Thornett: Cowan Pickup Hattee Davies: Rees Evans: Robinson Umpleby Walker Shaw Tomlinson Neumann: Tries - Cowan Rees: Goals - Hattee(2):
CASTLEFORD - Dickinson: Gamble G.G.Ward Green Brian Marsden: Hardisty Hepworth: Tonkinson J.Ward Jones Sheridan Walker W.Bryant:
Try – W Bryant:
Referee W Hemingway (Dewsbury) Att – 9843 H.T. 3 - 7

Mon 15 Apr 1963 WIGAN home won 18 - 7
CASTLEFORD - Dickinson: Gamble G.G.Ward Colin Butterfield Smith: Hardisty Hepworth: Tonkinson J.Ward Slatter W.Bryant Walker Walton:
Tries - G.G.Ward(2) Smith Hardisty: Goals - Dickinson(3):
WIGAN - Winton: Bootle McCormack Davies Lake: McLeod Parr: Belshaw Clark Larkin Collier Stephens Gregory: Try - McCormack: Goals - Winton(2):
Referee C F Appleton (Warrington) Att – 5524 H.T. 8 - 2

Mon 16 Apr 1963 BRAMLEY away won 17 - 10
BRAMLEY - Heap: Smith Rogers Larkin Elliott: Rushton Wrigglesworth: Hainsworth Clough Cooper Horn Jubb Robbins: Tries - Smith Rushton: Goals - Elliott(2):
CASTLEFORD - Dickinson: Gamble G.G.Ward M.Battye Smith: Hardisty Hepworth: Hirst J.Ward Slatter Tonkinson Walton Walker:
Tries - Hardisty(2) Hepworth: Goals - Dickinson(4):
Referee G Davies (Wakefield) Att - 4650 H.T. 9 - 4

Sat 20 Apr 1963 WIDNES home lost 7 - 10
CASTLEFORD - Dickinson: Gamble G.G.Ward M.Battye Cartwright: Hardisty Hepworth: Hirst J.Ward Slatter Tonkinson Walton Walker:
Try - Gamble: Goals - Dickinson(2):
WIDNES - Randall: Gaydon Briers Thompson Mort: Lowe Heyes: Hurstfield Kemel E.Bate R.Bate Measures Karalius:
Tries - Thompson: Goals - Randall(2):
Referee T W Watkinson (Man'ster) Att - 3851 H.T. 7 - 5

SEASON 1962-63

Sat 27 Apr 1963 OLDHAM home won 23 - 4
CASTLEFORD - Dickinson: Gamble G.G.Ward M.Battye
Cartwright: Hardisty Hepworth: Tonkinson J.Ward DAVID
GRACE(472) W.Bryant Walker Sheridan:
Tries - Bryant(2) Gamble Cartwright Sheridan:
Goals - Dickinson(4):
OLDHAM - Noon: Elliott Donovan Nestor Simms: Kellett
Fallon: Mumberson Taylor McIntyre Johnson Rae Parker:
Goals - Noon(2):
Referee K Rathbone (St Helens) Att - 4160 H.T. 11 - 2

Wed 1 May 1963 WAKEFIELD TRINITY away lost 8 - 23
WAKEFIELD T - Round: Hirst Greenwood Fox Coetzer:
Thomas Holliday: Wilkinson Kosanovic Sampson Vines
Turner Pearman:
Tries - Hirst Coetzer Holliday Kosanovic Pearman:
Goals - Fox(4):
CASTLEFORD - Dickinson: Gamble G.G.Ward M.Battye
Cartwright: Hardisty Foulkes: Hirst J.Ward Slatter
Tonkinson W.Bryant Walker:
Tries - Gamble Foulkes: Goal - Dickinson:
Referee L Thompson (Batley) Att - 11762 H.T. 3 - 12

Sat 4 May 1963 WORKINGTON TOWN home won 18 - 7
CASTLEFORD - Dickinson: KEITH HOWE(473) Green Small
Smith: Nowell Hepworth: Hirst J.Ward Slatter W.Bryant
Tonkinson Walker:
Tries - Howe(2) Bryant(2): Goals - Dickinson(3):
WORKINGTON T - Lowdon: Glastonbury O'Neill
McDowell Bell: Archer Roper: Martin Tabern McLeod
Foster Gardner McFarlane:
Try - Roper: Goals - Foster(2):
Referee J Manley (Warrington) Att - 4577 H.T. 8 - 7

Mon 6 May 1963 HULL KINGSTON ROVERS away lost 18 - 32
HULL K R - Mullins: Paul Major Blackmore Harris: Elliott
Bunting: Grice Flanagan Fox Tyson Bonner Clark:
Tries - Harris(2) Major Blackmore Bunting Grice:
Goals - Clark(7):
CASTLEFORD - TREVOR BEDFORD(474): Howe Nowell
M.Battye Smith: Hardisty Foulkes: Hirst J.Ward Slatter
Clark Walker Sheridan:
Tries - Howe Nowell Clark Sheridan:
Goals - Hardisty(2) Hirst:
Referee E Clay (Rothwell) Att - 6900 H.T. 2 - 22

Mon 14 May 1963 WARRINGTON away lost 3 - 23
WARRINGTON - Conroy: Thomas Challinor Pickavance
Glover: Greenough Edwards: Payne Dickens Brindle
Winslade Hicks Gilfedder: Tries - Greenough(2) Challinor
Glover Gilfedder: Goals - Hicks(2) Gilfedder(2):
CASTLEFORD - Bedford: Howe Nowell Small Green:
Hardisty Hepworth: Hirst J.Ward Slatter W.Bryant Walker
Sheridan: Try - Green:
Referee M Coates (Pudsey) Att - 7436 H.T. 3 - 13

Sat 18 May 1963 LEEDS home won 13 - 4
CASTLEFORD - Bedford: Howe Smith Small Cartwright:
Hardisty Foulkes: Hirst J.Ward Tonkinson W.Bryant Walker
Sheridan:
Tries - Howe Small Hardisty: Goals - Hardisty(2):
LEEDS - Simpson: Cowan Pickup Jones Wriglesworth:
Shoebottom Evans: Joyce Simms Walker Robinson
Tomlinson Shaw: Goals - Jones (2):
Referee N T Railton (Wigan) Att - 5839 H.T. 3 - 4

Wed 22 May 1963 WAKEFIELD TRINITY home won 21 - 8
CASTLEFORD - Bedford: Gamble Smith Small Howe:
Hardisty Hepworth: Hirst J.Ward Tonkinson W.Bryant
Walker Sheridan: Tries - Smith(2) Hardisty Bryant
Sheridan: Goals - Hardisty(3):
WAKEFIELD T - Round: Smith Brooks Greenwood Coetzer:
Rollin Holliday: Wilkinson Kosanovic Bloomfield Briggs
Blakeley Turner:
Tries - Smith Greenwood: Goal - Bloomfield:
Referee G Philpott (Leeds) Att - 9330 H.T. 6 - nil

Sat 25 May 1963 WORKINGTON TOWN away won 18 - 8
WORKINGTON T - Lowdon: Glastonbury Bell Brennan
Southward: Archer Roper: Edgar Tabern Gardner McLeod
Foster Eve: Tries - Glastonbury Bell: Goal - Foster:
CASTLEFORD - Bedford: Gamble Smith Small Howe:
Hardisty Hepworth: Hirst J.Ward Tonkinson W.Bryant
Walker Sheridan:
Tries - Hardisty(2) Hepworth Walker: Goals - Hardisty(3):
Referee N T Railton (Wigan) Att - 3496 H.T. nil - 3

Mon 27 May 1963 WIGAN away draw 18 - 18
WIGAN - Winton: Lake Ashton Davies Carlton: McLeod
Shillinglaw: Barton Clarke Collier Stephens Lyon Evans:
Tries - Lake(2) Carlton Collier: Goals - Winton(3):
CASTLEFORD - Bedford: Gamble Nowell Small Howe:
Hardisty Hepworth: Hirst J.Ward Tonkinson W.Bryant
Walker Sheridan:
Tries - Gamble Small Howe Bryant: Goals - Hardisty(3):
Referee R Oliver (Wakefield) Att - 7523 H.T. 13 - 3

Wed 29 May 1963 BRAMLEY home won 8 - nil
CASTLEFORD - Bedford: Gamble Nowell Small Howe:
Hardisty Hepworth: Hirst J.Ward Slatter W.Bryant Walker
Sheridan: Tries - Small Walker: Goal - Hardisty:
BRAMLEY - Wilson: Smith Rogers Butterfield Elliott:
Wrigglesworth Brown: Hainsworth Clough Jubb Horn
Carling E.Bryant:
Referee H Hunt (Warrington) Att - 4900 H.T. 5 - nil

SEASON 1962-63

D.N	PLAYER		DEBUT	L MATCH	APP	SUB	T.AP	TRI'S	G'LS	D.G	P'TS
330	PYE	KENNETH		01/09/1962	2	0	2	0	0	0	0
341	LUNN	ALBERT		09/02/1963	14	0	14	2	40	0	86
382	SHERIDAN	JOHN			23	0	23	6	0	0	18
410	BRYANT	EDWARD		16/03/1963	14	0	14	0	0	0	0
414	WARD	GEOFFREY G.			31	0	31	8	0	0	24
419	BRIDGES	KEITH		18/08/1962	1	0	1	0	0	0	0
420	TONKINSON	ALBERT			33	0	33	0	0	0	0
421	BERRY	JOHN		18/08/1962	1	0	1	0	0	0	0
424	HIRST	JACK			17	0	17	0	1	0	2
426	BRYANT	WILLIAM			34	0	34	9	0	0	27
427	BATTYE	COLIN			2	0	2	0	0	0	0
433	HARDISTY	ALAN			40	0	40	16	14	1	78
434	CARTWRIGHT	HOWARD			5	0	5	1	0	0	3
436	BROWN	GEORGE		24/11/1962	7	0	7	0	0	0	0
437	BROWNLEY	WILLIAM		22/09/1962	3	0	3	0	0	0	0
438	SMALL	PETER			22	0	22	10	0	0	30
439	CLARK	JOHN			1	0	1	1	0	0	3
442	HEPWORTH	KEITH			28	0	28	2	0	0	6
448	BUTTERFIELD	COLIN		15/04/1963	12	0	12	4	0	0	12
449	GREEN	FRANK			5	0	5	1	0	0	3
452	MARSDEN	BRIAN		06/04/1963	25	0	25	4	0	0	12
453	WARD	JOHNNY			39	0	39	4	0	0	12
455	WALKER	JOHN			40	0	40	6	0	0	18
458	EDWARDS	DEREK			1	0	1	0	0	0	0
460	SLATTER	KEITH			20	0	20	2	0	0	6
462	BATTYE	MALCOLM			5	0	5	0	0	0	0
463	NOWELL	ERIC			5	0	5	1	0	0	3
464	WILLIAMS	MAURICE			2	0	2	0	0	0	0
465	GAMBLE	JACK	22/08/1962		36	0	36	19	0	0	57
466	BROWN	GILBERT	22/08/1962		1	0	1	0	0	0	0
467	DICKINSON	FRANK	29/09/1962		20	0	20	0	47	1	96
468	SMITH	FRANK Jnr.	29/09/1962		9	0	9	5	0	0	15
469	WALTON	DOUGLAS	03/11/1962		6	0	6	0	0	0	0
470	JONES	DENIS	10/11/1962		8	0	8	0	0	0	0
471	FOULKES	KENNY	16/03/1963		5	0	5	3	0	0	9
472	GRACE	DAVID	27/04/1963		1	0	1	0	0	0	0
473	HOWE	KEITH	04/05/1963		8	0	8	5	0	0	15
474	BEDFORD	TREVOR	06/05/1963		7	0	7	0	0	0	0
	38		10	9	533	0	533	109	102	2	535

COMPETITION		P	W	D	L	FOR	AGT
LEAGUE D 1	POSITION 4 OF 16	30	16	3	11	370	321
EASTERN DIDVISION		8	4	0	4	117	137
YORK'S CUP		2	1	0	1	40	30
RL CUP		1	0	0	1	8	10
PLAYERS RECORDS		41	21	3	17	535	498

The weather, however, was the talking point of the season, for after winning 10-2 at Oldham on 15 December 1962 frozen grounds prevented further matches from being played until the visit of Warrington on 30 January 1963. This game only took place after a massive operation involving a special 'Swedish' mechanical snow sweeper, followed by dozens of coke burning braziers to thaw the frozen ground. In playing terms the "beat the freeze" effort to fulfil fixtures was not a success. As well as losing to Warrington 12–9, but also ten days later on 9 February 1963 losing to Leeds in the first round of the Challenge Cup 10–8.

It was a disappointing day all round for full back, goal kicker and groundsman Albert Lunn. Albert, who had led his many helpers in their task to ensure the game took place, was then in the match itself on the receiving end of two pieces if bad luck. A vital goal kick rebounding off the backs of the Leeds players, then a fly kick by Lewis Jones rebounding off Albert back into his arms with Jones scoring under the posts. Albert was then forced to announce his retirement following the game due to ill health.

A notable debutante was Douglas (Duggie) Walton aged 16, "capped" by Great Britain at 18, and an undoubted brilliant future was later tragically blighted by a serious knee injury.

SEASON 1963-64

TWO DIVISIONS

In Division 1 Hunslet and Keighley had been promoted from Division 2 to replace relegated Oldham and Bramley. In Division 2 Bradford N were disbanded after playing only 13 games, with these results being deleted from the table.

Sat 24 Aug 1963 WAKEFIELD TRINITY home won 33 -7
CASTLEFORD - Bedford: Gamble Smith G.G.Ward Howe: Hardisty Hepworth: Hirst J.Ward Tonkinson Bryant Walker Sheridan: Tries - Gamble(2) Smith(2) Howe Hardisty Hepworth: Goals Hardisty(6):
WAKEFIELD T - Round: Hirst Brooke Fox Greenwood: Poynton Holliday: Wilkinson Kosanovic Campbell Turner Vines Pearman: Try - Holliday: Goals - Fox(2):
Referee N T Railton (Wigan) Att - 9800 H.T. 10 - 5

Wed 28 Aug 1963 ST HELENS away lost 11 - 20
ST HELENS - Coslett: Vollenhoven Williams Northey Killeen: Harvey Smith: Temby Dagnall Watson Goddard French Huddart:
Tries - Northey(2) Smith Temby: Goals - Coslett(4):
CASTLEFORD - Bedford: Gamble G.G.Ward Smith Howe: Edwards Hepworth: Hirst J.Ward Jones Bryant Walker Sheridan: Tries - Smith J.Ward Walker: Goal - Jones:
Referee G Philpott (Leeds) Att - 10882 H.T. 5 - 10

Sat 31 Aug 1963 HULL KINGSTON ROVERS away lost 8 - 47
HULL K R - Clark: Paul Moore B.Burwell Blackmore: A.Burwell Elliott: Tyson Flanagan Drake Taylor Chamberlain Poole: Tries - Paul(4) A.Burwell(2) Moore Taylor Poole: Goals - Clark(10):
CASTLEFORD - Bedford: Gamble Smith G.G.Ward Howe: Edwards Hepworth: Hirst J.Ward Tonkinson Bryant Barnes Sheridan: Tries - Smith Hepworth: Goal - Barnes:
Referee R L Thomas (Oldham) Att - 8050 H.T. 3 - 14

Wed 4 Sep 1963 WIDNES home lost 8 - 19
CASTLEFORD - Dickinson: C.Battye Smith G.G.Ward Small: Hardisty Hepworth: Hirst J.Ward Tonkinson Bryant Walker Sheridan: Tries - G.G.Ward Hepworth: Goal - Dickinson:
WIDNES - Randall: Chisnall Briers Mort Thompson: Myler Smith: Hurstfield Kemel E.Bate R.Bate Measures Karalius: Tries - Chisnall Briers Mort Thompson Measures: Goals Randall(2):
Referee G T Scholefield (Salford) Att - 6238 H.T.8 - 11

Sat 7 Sep 1963 LEEDS away lost 3 - 20
YORKSHIRE CUP ROUND 1
LEEDS - Simpson: Cowan Broatch Pickup Wriglesworth: Jones Evans: Robinson Umpleby Joyce Tomlinson Neumann Shaw:
Tries - Cowan Broatch Pickup Robinson: Goals - Jones(4):
CASTLEFORD - Bedford: Howe G.G.Ward Small Cartwright: Hardisty Hepworth: Hirst J.Ward Tonkinson Bryant Walker Sheridan: Try - Bryant:
Referee J Manley (Warrington) Att - 9959 H.T. nil - 7

Sat 14 Sep 1963 SWINTON away lost 8 - 19
SWINTON - Gowers: McGregor Fleet F.Halliwell Stopford: Parkinson Williams: K.Halliwell Clarke Morgan Norburn Cummings Bonser:
Tries - F.Halliwell Norburn Cummings: Goals - Gowers(5):
CASTLEFORD - Barnes: Howe Smith G.G.Ward Howard Cartwright: Small Hepworth: Hirst J.Ward Tonkinson Bryant Walker Sheridan:
Tries - Howe Hepworth: Goal - Barnes:
Referee Mr L Wingfield(Norm'ton) Att - 7000 .T. nil - 15

Sat 21 Sep 1963 WARRINGTON home won 11 - 10
CASTLEFORD - Barnes: Howe Smith Small G.G.Ward: Edwards Hepworth: Hirst J.Ward Walton Bryant Walker Sheridan: Tries - Bryant(2) Edwards: Goal - Sheridan:
WARRINGTON - Conroy: Thomas Holden Fraser Catterall: Greenough Edwards: Payne Dickens Brindle Winslade Fisher Hayes: Tries - Holden Fraser: Goals - Fraser(2):
Referee S Shepherd (Oldham) Att - 4707 H.T. 6 - 7

Sat 28 Sep 1963 HUDDERSFIELD away lost 3 - 5
HUDDERSFIELD - Curry: Stocks Ford Haywood Breen: Blackett Deighton: Rowe Strong Noble Ogden(S/O) Kilroy Ramsden: Try - Ogden: Goal - Curry:
CASTLEFORD - Barnes: Howe Smith G.G.Ward Nowell: Edwards Foulkes: Hirst J.Ward Jones Bryant Walker Sheridan: Try - Smith:
Referee B Hall (Lupset) Att - 5912 H.T. 3 - 5

Sat 5 Oct 1963 DEWSBURY home won 25 - 19
EASTERN DIVISION
CASTLEFORD - Frank Dickinson: Howe DENNIS BAKER(475) Smith Nowell: Hardisty Foulkes: Hirst J.Ward Tonkinson Bryant Walton Sheridan:
Tries - Howe(2) Bryant(2) Sheridan: Goals - Dickinson(5):
DEWSBURY - Mortimore: Osborne Harvey Hutchinson Firth: Davies Hirst: Rushworth Smith Taylor Lowe Turnbull Jones: Tries - Osborne Firth Hirst: Goals - Jones(5)
Referee E Clay (Rothwell) Att - 4103 H.T. 15 - 9

Sat 12 Oct 1963 WORKINGTON TOWN home lost 11 - 22
CASTLEFORD - Eric Nowell: Gamble Baker Smith Howe: Hardisty Hepworth: Hirst J.Ward Clark Bryant Walker Sheridan: Try - Hepworth: Goals - Clark(4):
WORKINGTON T - Charlton: Glastonbury Lowdon Bell Hughes: Archer Newall: Edgar Tabern Martin McCleod Gardiner Eve:
Tries - Lowdon Bell Archer Eve: Goals - Lowdon(5):
Referee T W Watkinson Man'ster) Att - 4867 H.T. 11 -12

Sat 19 Oct 1963 KEIGHLEY home won 28 - 4
CASTLEFORD - Edwards: Howe Small Smith M.Battye: Hardisty Hepworth: Clark J.Ward Tonkinson Bryant Walker Sheridan:
Tries - Howe(3) Battye Hardisty J.Ward: Goals - Clark(5):
KEIGHLEY - Owen: Smith Aspinall Jackson Sharpe: Edwards Barron: Phillips Anderson Pye Crewdson Gaines Eyre: Goals - Owen(2):
Referee M Coates (Pudsey) Att - 3320 H.T. 3 - 4

SEASON 1963-64

Sat 26 Oct 1963 DEWSBURY away won 13 - 5
EASTERN DIVISION
DEWSBURY - Hirst: Osborne Harvey Hutchinson Firth:
Davies Newsome: Walker Ashcroft Taylor Lowe Turnbull
Jones: Try - Davies: Goal - Jones:
CASTLEFORD - Edwards: Howe Small M.Battye Smith:
Hardisty Hepworth: Clark J.Ward Tonkinson Bryant Walker
Sheridan: Tries - Smith Clark Bryant: Goals - Clark(2):
Referee H Cook (Beverley) Att - 2700 H.T. 6 - 2

Sat 9 Nov 1963 WIGAN away won 18 - 12
WIGAN - Boston: Carlton McLeod Davies Lake: Bolton
Carr: Collier Sayer Barton Lyon McTigue Gilfedder:
Tries - Lake(2) Boston Bolton
CASTLEFORD - Edwards: Howe Small ROY BELL(476)
Smith: Hardisty Hepworth: Hirst J.Ward Clark Bryant Jones
Walker:
Tries - Howe Small Smith Hardisty: Goals - Clark(3):
Referee M Coates (Pudsey) Att - 8691 H.T. 10 - 9

Wed 13 Nov 1963 AUSTRALIA won 13 - 12
CASTLEFORD - Edwards: Howe Bell Small Smith: Hardisty
Hepworth: Hirst J.Ward Clark Bryant Jones Walker:
Tries - Ward(2) Smith: Goals - Clark(2):
AUSTRALIA - Johns: Irvine Langlands Rushworth Dimond:
Gleeson Stanton: J.Cleary Walsh Quinn Day Wilson Raper:
Tries - Irvine Langlands: Goals - Langlands(2) Johns(DG):
Referee G Davies (Wakefield) Att - 7887 H.T. 10 - 5

Sat 16 Nov 1963 HULL home won 18 - 5
CASTLEFORD - Edwards: Howe Bell Small Smith: Hardisty
Hepworth: Hirst J.Ward Clark Jones Walton Walker:
Tries - Hardisty(2) Howe Smith: Goals - Clark(3):
HULL - Keegan: Rosenberg Gemmell Hollindrake Sullivan:
Carmichael Finn: Drake McGlone Macklin C.Booth R.Booth
P.Whiteley: Try - Sullivan: Goal - Keegan:
Referee D T H Davies (Man'ster) Att - 4902 H.T. 10 - nil

Sat 23 Nov 1963 LEEDS home won 28 - 2
CASTLEFORD - Edwards: Howe Small Bell Smith: Hardisty
Hepworth: Hirst J.Ward Clark Bryant Walker Sheridan:
Tries - Sheridan(2) Howe Small Smith Ward:
Goals - Clark(5):
LEEDS - Dewhirst: Davies Broatch Shoebottom
Wrigglesworth: Oldroyd Evans: Joyce Lockwood Walker
Thomas Clark Neuman: Goal - Dewhirst:
Referee C F Appleton (Warr'ton) Att - 4097 H.T. 7 - nil

Sat 30 Nov 1963 DONCASTER away won 22 - nil
EASTERN DIVISION
DONCASTER - Price: Goodchild Rushton Stocks Tasker:
Horsman Doyle: Goodyear Heath Kirk Hepworth Pell
Redfearn:
CASTLEFORD - Edwards: Howe Small Bell Smith: Hardisty
Hepworth: Hirst Brown Clark Bryant Walker Sheridan:
Tries - Hardisty(3) Smith Clark Bryant: Goals - Clark(2):
Referee G Philpott (Leeds) Att - 1400 H.T. 13 - nil

Sat 7 Dec 1963 HUDDERSFIELD home won 13 - 2
CASTLEFORD - Edwards: Howe Small Bell Smith: Hardisty
Hepworth: Hirst J.Ward Clark Bryant Walker Sheridan:
Tries - Howe Hepworth Sheridan: Goals - Hardisty(2):
HUDDERSFIELD - Curry: Booth Stocks Haywood Senior:
Blackett Smales: Rowe Close Anderson Ogden Bowman
Ramsden(S/O):   Goal - Curry:
Referee F K Howker (Rochdale) Att - 4839 H.T. 9 - 2

Sat 14 Dec 1963 LEEDS away lost 3 - 5
LEEDS - Dewhurst: Cowan Broatch Jones Wriglesworth:
Rees Shoebottom: Robinson Lockwood Chamberlain
McVeigh Davis Neumann: Try - Jones: Goal - Jones:
CASTLEFORD - Edwards: Howe Small Bell Smith: Hardisty
Hepworth: Hirst Brown Clark Bryant ANDREW
JOHNSON(477) Walker: Try - Bryant:
Referee L Gant (Wakefield) Att - 5890 H.T. 3 - 5

Sat 28 Dec 1963 WARRINGTON away won 16 - nil
WARRINGTON - Fraser: Conroy Holden Melling Glover:
Aspinall Smith: Brindle Dickens Davies Cherrington Hicks
Thomas:
CASTLEFORD - Edwards: Howe Small Bell Gamble:
Hardisty Hepworth: Hirst J.Ward David Grace Bryant
Walker Sheridan:
Tries - Howe(2) Hardisty(2):   Goals - Grace(2):
Referee G Wilson (Dewsbury) Att - 6875 H.T. 10 - nil

Wed 1 Jan 1964 HUNSLET home lost 5 - 13
CASTLEFORD - Edwards: Howe Small Bell Gamble:
Hardisty Hepworth: Hirst J.Ward HAROLD
McCARTNEY(478) Bryant Johnson Walker:
Try - Howe: Goal - Hardisty:
HUNSLET - Langton: Griffiths Shelton Preece Thompson:
Gabbitas Watts: Hartley Prior Eyre Baldwinson Gunney
Ward: Tries - Griffiths(2) Thompson: Goals - Langton(2):
Referee L Gant (Wakefield) Att - 8103 H.T. 2 - 2

Sat 11 Jan 1964 WAKEFIELD TRINITY away lost 8 - 9
WAKEFIELD T - Wraith: Smith Metcalfe Pearman Mann:
Rollin Holliday: Vines Oakes(S/O) Plumstead Payne
Turnbull Turner: Try - Turner: Goals - Payne(3):
CASTLEFORD - Edwards: Howe Small Bell Gamble:
Hardisty Hepworth: Hirst J.Ward(S/O) Albert Tonkinson
Bryant Johnson Walker:
Tries - Howe Hepworth: Goal - Hardisty:
Referee E Lawrinson (Warrington) Att - 8646 H.T. 8 - 4

Sat 25 Jan 1964 HULL KINGSTON ROVERS home
won 14 - 6
CASTLEFORD - Edwards: Howe Bell Gamble Smith:
Hardisty Hepworth: Hirst CLIVE DICKINSON(479) Clark
Bryant Johnson Colin Taylor:
Tries - Smith(2) Howe Clark: Goal - Clark:
HULL K R - Kellett: Paul Major Moore Harris: Elliott
Bunting: F.Fox Flanagan P.Fox Tyson Palmer Taylor:
Tries - Moore Harris:
Referee E Clay (Rothwell) Att - 4247 H.T. 8 - 3

SEASON 1963-64

Sat 1 Feb 1964 WIDNES away lost 10 - 16
WIDNES - Whitfield: Gaydon Briers Thompson Randall:
Myler Owen: Bate Kemel Walsh Collier Measures Hughes:
Tries - Briers Hughes: Goals - Randall(4) Whitfield:
CASTLEFORD - Edwards: Howe G.G.Ward Gamble Smith:
Hardisty Foulkes: Hirst J.Ward Clark Bryant Walker Bell:
Tries - Howe Hardisty: Goals - Clark(2)
Referee L Gant (Wakefield) Att - 4760 H.T. 7 - 9

Sat 8 Feb 1964 ST HELENS away won 13 - 6
CHALLENGE CUP ROUND 1
ST HELENS - Northey: Vollenhoven Todd Mooney Harvey:
Murphy Smith: Major Burdell French Warlow Huddart
Ashcroft: Tries - Vollenhoven Todd:
CASTLEFORD - Edwards: Howe Bell G.G.Ward Gamble:
Hardisty Hepworth: Hirst J.Ward Clark Bryant Walton
Sheridan:
Tries - Howe(2) Hardisty: Goals - Clark Hardisty(DG):
Referee M Coates (Pudsey) Att - 15977 H.T. 8 - 3

Sat 15 Feb 1964 BATLEY away won 27 - 7
EASTERN DIVISION
BATLEY - Bateson: Smith Ward Shuttleworth Hammond:
Geldard Oliver: Sharp Fryer Kennedy Dick Noble Foster:
Try - Hammond: Goals - Bateson(2):
CASTLEFORD - Edwards: Howe Bell G.G.Ward Gamble:
Hardisty Hepworth: Hirst J.Ward Clark Bryant Walton
Sheridan: Tries - Howe(3) Hardisty(2) J.Ward Sheridan:
Goals - Clark(3):
Referee R Welsby (Warrington) Att - 3070 H.T. 11 - 5

Sat 22 Feb 1964 HALIFAX home won 13 - 12
CASTLEFORD - Bedford: Howe Bell G.G.Ward Gamble:
Hardisty Hepworth: Hirst J.Ward Clark Bryant Johnson
Walton:
Tries - Bedford Gamble Hepworth: Goals - Hardisty(2):
HALIFAX - Rhodes: Jackson Jones Dixon Freeman: Kellett
Daley: Roberts Shaw Duffy Hardcastle Fogerty Renilson:
Tries - Dixon(2) Jackson Hardcastle:
Referee G Philpott (Leeds) Att - 5863 H.T. 5 - 3

Sat 29 Feb 1964 WHITEHAVEN away won 29 - 5
CHALLENGE CUP ROUND 2
WHITEHAVEN - Baker: Lowther Powe Wren Colloby:
Barnes Hazeldon: Williamson Lynch Moss Moore Lill
Holliday: Try - Wren: Goal - Holliday:
CASTLEFORD - Edwards: Howe Bell G.G.Ward Gamble:
Hardisty Hepworth: Hirst J.Ward Clark Bryant Walton
Sheridan: Tries - Howe(2) Hardisty(2) Gamble Bryant
Walton: Goals - Hardisty(4):
Referee R Gelder (Wilmslow) Att - 6634 H.T. 16 - nil

Sat 14 Mar 1964 BLACKPOOL BOROUGH away
won 25 - 4 CHALLENGE CUP ROUND 3
BLACKPOOL B - McCarrick: Wiseman Phillips Maltby
Bagshaw: Fairhurst Bishop: Hopwood Hall Whitworth
Payne Normington Leatherbarrow:
Goals - McCarrick(2):
CASTLEFORD - Edwards: Howe Bell G.G.Ward Smith:
Hardisty Hepworth: Hirst J.Ward Clark Bryant Walton

Sheridan: Tries - Smith(2) Hardisty(2) Howe Bell Bryant:
Goals - Clark(2):
Referee E Clay (Rothwell) Att - 7206 H.T. 12 - 4

Sat 21 Mar 1964 DONCASTER home won 23 - 8
EASTERN DIVISION
CASTLEFORD - Edwards: Howe Bell G.G.Ward Smith:
Hardisty Foulkes: Hirst J.Ward Clark Johnson Walton
Sheridan: Tries - Howe(2) Foulkes Johnson Sheridan:
Goals - Clark(4):
DONCASTER - Astbury: Goodchild Stocks Saville Bonson:
Horsman Doyle: Goodyear Widdop Brownley Hepworth
Pell Redfearn: Tries - Goodchild Hepworth: Goal - Saville
Referee E Clay (Rothwell) Att - 3035 H.T. 8 - 5

**Wed 25 Mar 1964 FEATHERSTONE ROVERS away
won 19 - 5**
FEATHERSTONE R - Cooper: Greatorex Penketh Jordan
Thomas: Bel Dooler: Terry Kosanovic Dixon Morgan
Loxton D.Fox: Try - Jordan: Goal - Fox:
CASTLEFORD - Edwards: Howe Bell Small Smith: Hardisty
Hepworth: Hirst J.Ward Clark Bryant Walton Sheridan:
Tries - Howe Smith Hardisty Hirst Walton:
Goals - Clark(2):
Referee D S Brown (Dewsbury) Att - 7809 H.T. 3 - nil

Sat 28 Mar 1964 KEIGHLEY away won 28 - nil
KEIGHLEY - Owen: Plunkett Frain O'Brien Daniel: Edwards
Reilly: Crewdson Anderson Pye Wright Diambulo Eyre:
CASTLEFORD - Edwards: Howe Small G.G.Ward Smith: Bell
Hepworth: Hirst Dickinson Clark Bryant Walton Sheridan:
Tries - Smith(2) Ward Hepworth Clark Bryant:
Goals - Clark(4)Walton:
Referee D S Brown (Dewsbury) Att - 2200 H.T. 15 - nil

**Mon 30 Mar 1964 FEATHERSTONE ROVERS home
won 14 - 5**
CASTLEFORD - Edwards: Howe Bell G.G.Ward Smith:
Hardisty Hepworth: Hirst J.Ward Denis Jones Bryant
Walton Sheridan:
Tries - Howe(2)   Goals - Hardisty(2) (DG) Walton:
FEATHERSTONE R - Cooper: Greatorex Penketh Jordan
Thomas: Bell Dooler: Terry Kosanovic Tonks Dixon Loxton
Fox: Try - Thomas: Goal - Fox:
Referee J Manley (Warrington) Att - 10439 H.T. 4 - 5

Tue 31 Mar 1964 HALIFAX away won 9 - 4
HALIFAX - James: Jackson Burnett Jones Freeman: Kellett
Marchant: Scroby Shaw Duffy Roberts Dixon Renilson
Goals - James(2):
CASTLEFORD - Edwards: Howe G.G.Ward Small Smith:
Hardisty Foulkes: Hirst J.Ward Slatter Bryant Walker
Walton: Tries - Howe Smith Hardisty:
Referee R Appleyard (Leeds) Att - 8309 H.T. 3 - 4

Sat 4 Apr 1964 SWINTON home won 17 - 2
CASTLEFORD - Edwards: Howe G.G.Ward Small Smith: Bell
Hepworth: Hirst J.Ward Clark Bryant Walton Sheridan:
Tries - Bryant(2) Howe: Goals - Clark(4):
SWINTON - Gowers: McGregor Eckersley Speed Stopford:

SEASON 1963-64

Parkinson Williams: Halliwell Clarke Simpson Morgan Cummings Blan: Goal - Blan:
Referee F J Howker (Rochdale) Att - 8387 H.T. 3 - 2

Mon 6 Apr 1964 WORKINGTON TOWN away lost 9 - 43
WORKINGTON T - Charlton: Glastonbury Bell Hughes Colloby: Archer Newall: Gardiner M.McFarlane Martin Smith Foster J.McFarlane:
Tries - Glastonbury(2) Bell(2) Hughes Colloby Newall Smith J.McFarlane: Goals - Foster(8):
CASTLEFORD - Edwards: Gamble G.G.Ward Small Smith: Bell Foulkes: Williams J.Ward Slatter Johnson Walker Sheridan: Try - Smith: Goals - Johnson(3):
Referee J Manley (Warrington) Att - 3832 H.T.

Fri 10 Apr 1964 WIGAN home won 24 - 14
CASTLEFORD - Bedford: How Bell G.G.Ward Smith: Hardisty Foulkes: Hirst Dickinson Clark Bryant Walker Walton:
Tries - Clark(2) Hardisty Foulkes: Goals - Clark(5) Hardisty(DG):
WIGAN - Winton: Boston Ashton Davies Lake: Hesketh Shillinglaw: Barton Sayer McTigue Stephens Gilfedder Evans:
Tries - Lake(2) Boston Shillinglaw: Goal - Winton:
Referee C F Appleton (War'gton) Att - 11496 H.T. 17 - nil

Sat 18 Apr 1964 WIDNES draw 7 - 7
CHALLENGE CUP SEMI FINAL - AT STATION ROAD SWINTON
CASTLEFORD - Edwards: Howe Bell G.G.Ward Smith: Hardisty Hepworth: Hirst J.Ward Clark Bryant Walton Sheridan:
Try - Howe: Goals - Clark(2):
WIDNES - Randall: Gaydon Briers Myler Chisnall: Lowe Owen Hurstfield Kemel E.Bate Collier Measures Karalius:
Try - Myler: Goals - Randall(2):
Referee E Clay (Rothwell) Att - 25603 H.T. 7 - 5

Wed 22 Apr 1964 WIDNES lost 5 - 7
CHALLENGE CUP SEMI FINAL REPLAY - AT BELLE VUE WAKEFIELD
CASTLEFORD - Edwards: Gamble Bell G.G.Ward Smith: Hardisty Hepworth: Hirst J.Ward Clark Bryant Walton Sheridan: Try - Hardisty: Goal - Clark:
WIDNES - Randall: Chisnall Briers Myler Thompson: Lowe Owen Hurstfield Kemel Collier Measures Hughes Karalius:
Try - Thompson: Goals - Randall(2):
Referee E Clay (Rothwell) Att - 28736 H.T. 5 - 2

Sat 25 Apr 1964 HUNSLET away lost 11 - 12
HUNSLET - Langton: Griffiths Shelton Preece Thompson: Abbey Watts: Robinson Prior Fox Eyre Gunney Taylor:
Tries - Griffiths Taylor: Goals - Langton(3):
CASTLEFORD - Edwards: Gamble Bell Small Frank Green: Hardisty Hepworth: Hirst Dickinson Clark Bryant Johnson Walker:
Tries - Hardisty(3): Goal - Clark: :
Referee L Gant (Wakefield) Att - 2600 H.T. 8 - 12

Wed 29 Apr 1964 BATLEY home won 35 - 5
EASTERN DIVISION
CASTLEFORD - Edwards: Gamble G.G.Ward Small M.Battye: Hardisty Hepworth: Hirst J.Ward Clark Bryant Walker Baker:
Tries - Gamble(2) G.G.Ward(2) Hardisty(2) Bryant(2) Baker: Goals - Clark(4):
BATLEY - Smith: Ward Vickers Molloy Noble: Butterfield Oliver: Sharp Fryer Hinchcliffe Briggs Kennedy Barlow:
Try - Ward: Goal - Kennedy:
Referee H Morgan (Oldham) Att - 4300 H.T. 16 - nil

Fri 1 May 1964 BRAMLEY home won 11 - 2
EASTERN DIVISION SEMI FINAL
CASTLEFORD - Edwards: Gamble Bell Small M.Battye: Hardisty Hepworth: Hirst J.Ward Clark Bryant Walker Walton:
Tries - Small Hardisty Hepworth: Goal - Clark:
BRAMLEY - Rogers: Smith Kelly Wrigglesworth Hollindrake: Woolford Barron: Jubb Morgan Horne Parker Bastian E.Bryant:
Goal - Rogers:
Referee R Gelder (Wilmslow) Att - 7384 H.T. 8 - 2

Tue 12 May 1964 HULL away won 27 - 8
HULL - Keegan: Devonshire Stocks Carmichael Sullivan: Davidson Finn: Rowe McGlone R.Booth Neale Broom Sykes:
Tries - Devonshire Sykes: Goal - Broom:
CASTLEFORD - Edwards: Gamble G.G.Ward Small M.Battye: Hardisty Hepworth: Hirst J.Ward Clark Bryant Walker Walton:
Tries - Walton(2) Hardisty Hepworth J.Ward :
Goals - Clark(6):
Referee J Manley (Warrington) Att - 6000 H.T. 12 - nil

Sat 23 May 1964 HALIFAX home lost 12 - 20
EASTERN DIVISION FINAL - AT FARTOWN HUDDERSFIELD
CASTLEFORD - Edwards: Howe G.G.Ward Small Gamble: Hardisty Hepworth: Hirst Dickinson Clark Bryant Walker Walton:
Tries - Howe Dickinson: Goals - Clark(3):
HALIFAX - James: Jackson Burnett Kellett Freeman: Robinson Marchant: Roberts Shaw Scott Dixon Fogerty Renilson:
Tries - Jackson(2) Robinson Dixon: Goals - James(4):
Referee R L Thomas (Oldham) Att - 10798 H.T. 8 - 10

Wed 27 May 1964 ST HELENS home won 11 - 10
CASTLEFORD - Bedford: Howe Gamble Bell Small: Hardisty ROY WARD(480): Hirst Brown Clark Bryant Walker Walton:
Tries - Howe(2) Hardisty: Goal - Clark:
ST HELENS - Coslett: Pimblett Williams Todd Benyon: Harvey Murphy: Tembey Burdell Owen Warlow Hicks Laughton:
Tries - Pimblett Murphy: Goals - Coslett(2):
Referee D T H Davies (Manchester) Att - 38412 H.T.

In the Challenge Cup we had our most successful campaign since the Cup Final victory of 1934/35. A magnificent victory over St Helens away in the first round 13 – 6, which "allegedly" saw Referee Mat Coates jumping with delight after the final whistle, was followed by a 29 – 5 victory at Whitehaven away in round two. The third round tie away at Blackpool Borough saw Derek Edwards (now settled at full back) being married on the morning of the match before being whisked away by Director George Gregory to take part in the 25 – 4 victory.

The semi-final draw paired us against Widnes at Station Road Swindon with the game finishing in a 7 – 7 draw. The replay was four days later on the Wednesday evening at Bell Vue Wakefield before a (difficult to imagine now) packed ground of nearly 29,000 spectators. With only seconds left on the watch we heeled a scrum just in our own half, Alan Hardisty made the initial break putting Geoff Ward through the gap, with Roy Bell and Jack Gamble on his outside. However, as he approached the Widnes full back Randall he was tackled from behind by Jim Measures the speedy Widnes second rower, the opportunity had gone the whistle went for time and we had lost 7 – 5, so near but so far.

Dennis Baker
D. No 475
1963-64 to 1967-68

Andrew (Fl;ash) Johnson
D. No 477
1963-64 to 191964-65

Harold McCartney
D. No 478
1963-64 to 1967-68

Clive Dickinson
D. No 479
1963-64 to 1974-75

CHALLENGE CUP SEMI FINAL SAT 18 APRIL 1964 V WIDNES DREW 7 - 7 - AT STATION ROAD SWINTON
Back Row – Jack Hirst John Clark Doug Walton Geoff Ward Bill Bryant Frank Smith Jnr John Sheridan
Front Row – Derek Edwards Johnny Ward Keith Hepwo th Alan Hardisty Roy Bell Keith Howe

SEASON 1963-64

D.N	PLAYER		DEBUT	L MATCH	APP	SUB	T.AP	TRI'S	G'LS	D.G	P'TS
382	SHERIDAN	JOHN			28	0	28	6	1	0	20
389	BARNES	JACK			4	0	4	0	2	0	4
406	TAYLOR	COLIN		25/01/1964	1	0	1	0	0	0	0
414	WARD	GEOFFREY G.			26	0	26	4	0	0	12
420	TONKINSON	ALBERT		11/01/1964	9	0	9	0	0	0	0
424	HIRST	JACK			42	0	42	1	0	0	3
426	BRYANT	WILLIAM			42	0	42	15	0	0	45
427	BATTYE	COLIN			1	0	1	0	0	0	0
433	HARDISTY	ALAN			37	0	37	30	18	3	132
434	CARTWRIGHT	HOWARD		14/09/1963	2	0	2	0	0	0	0
438	SMALL	PETER			26	0	26	3	0	0	9
439	CLARK	JOHN			30	0	30	6	73	0	164
442	HEPWORTH	KEITH			37	0	37	11	0	0	33
449	GREEN	FRANK		25/04/1964	1	0	1	0	0	0	0
453	WARD	JOHNNY			37	0	37	7	0	0	21
455	WALKER	JOHN			30	0	30	1	0	0	3
458	EDWARDS	DEREK			36	0	36	1	0	0	3
460	SLATTER	KEITH			2	0	2	0	0	0	0
462	BATTYE	MALCOLM			5	0	5	1	0	0	3
463	NOWELL	ERIC		12/10/1963	3	0	3	0	0	0	0
464	WILLIAMS	MAURICE			1	0	1	0	0	0	0
465	GAMBLE	JACK			21	0	21	6	0	0	18
466	BROWN	GILBERT			3	0	3	0	0	0	0
467	DICKINSON	FRANK		05/10/1963	2	0	2	0	6	0	12
468	SMITH	FRANK Jnr.			32	0	32	20	0	0	60
469	WALTON	DOUGLAS			21	0	21	4	2	0	16
470	JONES	DENIS		30/03/1964	6	0	6	0	1	0	2
471	FOULKES	KENNY			7	0	7	2	0	0	6
472	GRACE	DAVID		28/12/1963	1	0	1	0	2	0	4
473	HOWE	KEITH			38	0	38	36	0	0	108
474	BEDFORD	TREVOR			7	0	7	1	0	0	3
475	BAKER	DENNIS	05/10/1963		3	0	3	1	0	0	3
476	BELL	ROY	09/11/1963		29	0	29	1	0	0	3
477	JOHNSON	ANDREW	14/12/1963		8	0	8	1	3	0	9
478	McCARTNEY	HAROLD	01/01/1964		1	0	1	0	0	0	0
479	DICKINSON	CLIVE	25/01/1964		5	0	5	1	0	0	3
480	WARD	ROY	27/05/1964		1	0	1	0	0	0	0
	37		6	8	585	0	585	159	108	3	699

COMPETITION		P	W	D	L	FOR	AGT
LEAGUE D 1	POSITION 6 OF 16	30	18	0	12	436	338
EASTERN DIDVISION		8	7	0	1	168	66
YORK'S CUP		1	0	0	1	3	20
RL CUP		5	3	1	1	79	29
AUSTRALIA		1	1	0	0	13	12
PLAYERS RECORDS		45	29	1	15	699	465

Fate was once again to play a major part in shaping a player's career. Early season injuries to recognised full backs Trevor Bedford, Jack Barnes and Frank Dickinson, saw three-quarter or halfback and copy book tackler Eric Nowell drafted in at full-back at home to Workington Town (12 October 1963). Although on the losing side 11–23 he had an impressive game. However the following week Eric was to be married and another half-back, Derek Edwards, was drafted in at full back. Eric never played for the first team again and the rest, as they say, is history.

On Wednesday, 13 November 1963 we entertained the Australian tourists. Frank Smith managed to bend from his great height to pick up a long ball out wide off his toes (the Aussies dared to suggest he had knocked on!!) and raced 40 yards to score and clinch victory by 13–12. Johnny Ward's two try performance earned him a place in the Great Britain team for the third test against the Australians at Headingley on 30 November 1963. Great Britain won a highly charged game 16–5, Johnny scoring a try on his test debut.

Alan Hardisty and Bill Bryant made their Great Britain debuts alongside Johnny Ward in the international against France at Perpignan on 8 March 1964, Great Britain winning 11–5. In the return fixture on 18 March at Leigh our three lads were again in the Great Britain side with Alan scoring two tries in a 39–0 victory.

SEASON 1964-65

ONE DIVISION

The League system reverted to one Division with Bradford Nnorthern being reformed and re-entering the league and consequently the Eastern and Western Division competitions were abandoned.

Substitutes for injuries allowed but only up to and including half time

Sat 22 Aug 1964 WAKEFIELD TRINITY home draw 7 - 7
CASTLEFORD - Edwards(Bell): Howe G.G.Ward Small Smith: Hardisty Hepworth: Williams(Clark) Brown Walker Bryant Walton Baker: Try - Hardisty: Goals - Hardisty(2):
WAKEFIELD T - Metcalfe: Coetzer Rushton Fox Jones: Poynton(S/O) Holliday: Campbell Hawksley Sampson Plumstead Turnbull Haigh: Try - Rushton: Goals - Fox(2):
Referee F J Howker (Rochdale) Att - 10618 H.T. 4 - 5

Tue 25 Aug 1964 BATLEY away won 32 - 7
BATLEY - Bateson: Smith A.N.Other Vickers Raynor: Mountain Butterfield: Sharp Fryer Kennedy Briggs Mulloy Noble: Try - Butterfield: Goals - Bateson(2):
CASTLEFORD - Bell(Edwards): Howe G.G.Ward Small Smith: Hardisty Hepworth: McCartney Brown Clark Johnson Bryant Walton: Tries - Edwards(2) Walton(2) Howe G.G.Ward Brown Clark: Goals - Clark(4):
Referee J Manley (Warrington) Att - 3000 H.T. 11 - 2

Sat 29 Aug 1964 WORKINGTON TOWN away lost 8 - 29
WORKINGTON T - Charlton: Glastonbury Bell Hughes Colloby: Archer Roper(Lowdon): Gardiner Tabern Martin Foster Edgar McFarlane: Tries - Glastonbury(2) Bell Hughes Roper Gardiner McFarlane: Goals - Foster(4):
CASTLEFORD - Edwards: Howe Smith Gamble C.Battye: Bell(Foulkes) Hepworth: McCartney Brown Clark Bryant Johnson Walton: Tries - Clark Walton: Goal - Clark:
Referee E Lawrinson (Warrington) Att - 5303 H.T. 3 - 17

Mon 31 Aug 1964 HUNSLET home won 27 - nil
CASTLEFORD - Bedford: Howe G.G.Ward Gamble C.Battye: Hardisty Foulkes: Slatter Brown Clark Bryant Walker Walton: Tries - Howe(2) Ward Battye Hardisty Foulkes Bryant: Goals Clark(3):
HUNSLET - Langton: Griffiths Shelton Preece Goodman: Hood Stevenson: Hartley Prior Taylor Ward Gunney Ramsey:
Referee S Shepherd (Oldham) Att - 6536 H.T. 21 - nil

Sat 5 Sep 1964 HULL KINGSTON ROVERS home lost 8 - 16 YORKSHIRE CUP ROUND 1
CASTLEFORD - Bedford: Howe G.G.Ward Gamble C.Battye: Hardisty Hepworth: Hirst Brown Clark Bryant Walker Walton: Goals - Hardisty(2) Clark(2):
HULL K R - Kellett: Young Moore Blackmore Harris: Elliott Bunting: Bath Holdstock Tyson Palmer Taylor Poole: Tries - Palmer Poole: Goals - Kellett(5):
Referee S Shepherd (Oldham) Att - 7747 H.T. 4 - 14

Sat 12 Sep 1964 SWINTON away lost 9 - 24
SWINTON - Gowers: Speed(Robinson) Fleet Buckley Stopford: Parkinson Williams: Bate Clarke Halliwell Rees Cummings Hurt: Tries - Stopford(2): Goals - Gowers(9):
CASTLEFORD - Edwards: Howe G.G.Ward Gamble(Bedford) C.Battye: Hardisty Hepworth: Hirst Gilbert Brown: Slatter Bryant Clark Walton:
Try - Bryant: Goals - Clark(3):
Referee G Scott (Wakefield) Att - 8000 H.T. 4 - 8

Sat 19 Sep 1964 DONCASTER home won 22 - 3
CASTLEFORD - Bedford: Howe G.G.Ward Bell C.Battye: Edwards Kenneth Foulkes: Hirst Dickinson Slatter Bryant Walker Walton:
Tries - Howe(3) Battye Edwards Dickinson: Goals - Bell(2):
DONCASTER - Astbury: Goodchild Saville Stocks Tomlinson: Horsman Goodyear: Robinson Widdop Holt Hepworth Morris Smith: Try - Smith:
Referee H Pearce (Leeds) Att - 3000 H.T. 9 - 3

Sat 26 Sep 1964 WIGAN away lost 13 - 33
WIGAN - Ashby: Boston Ashton A.Davies Lake: Hill Parr: Barton Clarke Stephens P.Davies Lyons Evans:
Tries - Ashton(2) Lake(2) Boston Hill Lyons: Goals - Ashton(6):
CASTLEFORD - Bedford: Howe R.Ward(M.Battye) Bell Frank Smith Jnr: C.Battye Hepworth: Hirst Dickinson Slatter Clark Bryant Walton:
Try - Walton: Goals - Clark(5):
Referee P Geraghty (York) Att - 11946 H.T. 7 - 22

Sat 3 Oct 1964 DEWSBURY away won 15 - 9
DEWSBURY - Hirst: Harris Osborne Wiltshire Marsh: Harvey Newall: Walker Mullins Taylor Lowe Turnbull Jones: Try - Wiltshire: Goals - Jones(3):
CASTLEFORD - Bedford: DAVID APPLEYARD(481) Bell TREVOR WARING(482) C.Battye: ROGER MILLWARD(483) Hepworth: ABE TERRY(484)(Hirst) Dickinson Williams Bryant Clark Walton(M.Battye):
Tries - Bell C.Battye Walton: Goals - Clark(3):
Referee R Percival (Warrington) Att - 3400 H.T. 5 - 7

Sat 10 Oct 1964 YORK home won 20 - 5
CASTLEFORD - Bedford: C.Battye G.G.Ward M.Battye PETER BARTON(485): Hardisty Hepworth: Terry Dickinson McCartney Clark Barnes Bell:
Tries - C.Battye Barton Hepworth Barnes: Goals - Clark(4):
YORK - Duck(Sheehan): Smith Hunter Rippon Foster: Flannery Evans: Yorke Milner Pratt Steel Walker Ramsden:
Try - Steel: Goal - Yorke:
Referee B Baker (Bolton) Att - 4085 H.T. 12 - 5

Sat 17 Oct 1964 BRADFORD NORTHERN away won 7 - 5
BRADFORD N - Todd: Walker Lord Brooke Levula: Whittaker Jones: Tonkinson Ackerley Wilkinson Fisher Ashcroft Rae:
Try - Rae: Goal - Todd:

CASTLEFORD - Bedford: C.Battye G.G.Ward M.Battye
Barton: Hardisty Millward: Terry Dickinson
Williams(McCartney) Bryant Clark Barnes:
Try - Ward: Goals - Clark(2):
Referee S Shepherd (Oldham) Att - 5844 H.T. 2 - nil

Sat 24 Oct 1964 LEEDS home won 13 - 6
CASTLEFORD - Bedford: Howe G.G.Ward M.Battye
C.Battye: Hardisty Hepworth: Terry Dickinson Williams
Bryant Walton Barnes: Tries - Howe M.Battye Hepworth:
Goals - Hardisty Hepworth(DG):
LEEDS - Dewhurst: Cowan Broatch Gemmell
Wriglesworth: Shoebottom Oldroyd: Drake Lockwood
Chamberlain Clark Neumann Sykes(Firth):
Goals - Dewhurst(3):
Referee H Hunt (Warrington) Att - 5500 H.T. 5 - 4

Sat 31 Oct 1964 HULL home won 6 - 4
CASTLEFORD - Bedford: Howe G.G.Ward RONALD
WILLETT(486) C.Battye: Hardisty Hepworth: Terry
Dickinson Williams Bryant Walton Jack Barnes:
Goals - Willett(3):
HULL - Keegan: Sulllivan Doyle-Davidson Rosenberg
Barnwell: Huxley Foulkes: Macklin McGlone Broom Neale
Sykes(Edson) J.Whiteley: Goals - Broom(2):
Referee T Keane (Oldham) Att - 4489 H.T. nil - 4

Sat 7 Nov 1964 DONCASTER away won 27 - 7
DONCASTER - Astbury: Goodchild Saville Horsman
Dewsbury: Woodfield Doyle: Goodyesr Heeley Trowell
Oxenham(Morris) Hepworth Smith:
Try - Goodchild: Goals - Dewsbury(2):
CASTLEFORD - Bedford: Howe G.G.Ward Willett C.Battye:
Hardisty Hepworth: Hirst Dickinson Williams Bryant
Walker Clark: Tries - C.Battye(2) Clark(2) Ward Willett
Hepworth: Goals - Willett(3):
Referee R Appleyard (Leeds) Att - 2000 H.T. 16 - 2

Sat 14 Nov 1964 SWINTON home lost 2 - 3
CASTLEFORD - Bedford: Howe G.G.Ward Willett C.Battye:
Hardisty Hepworth: Hirst Dickinson Williams Bryant
Walker Clark: Goal - Willett:
SWINTON - Gowers: Harris Fleet Buckley Speed:
Parkinson Cartwright: Bate Clarke Halliwell Bonner Rees
Bpnser: Try - Harris:
Referee B Baker (Wigan) Att - 5000 H.T. 2 - nil

Sat 21 Nov 1964 HULL away won 10 - 2
HULL - Keegan: B.Sullivan Doyle-Davidson Rosenberg
C.Sullivan: Huxley Foulkes: Booth Coverley Broom Neale
Edson J.Whiteley: Goal - Broom:
CASTLEFORD - Bedford: Howe G.G.Ward Willett C.Battye:
Hardisty Hepworth: Terry Dickinson Williams Bryant
Walker JOHN TAYLOR(487):
Tries - Howe Hardisty: Goals - Willett(2):
Referee H Morgan (Oldham) Att - 6500 H.T. 7 - 2

Sat 28 Nov 1964 BRAMLEY home won 25 - 9
CASTLEFORD - Bedford: Edwards G.G.Ward Willett
C.Battye: Hardisty(Howe) Hepworth: Terry Dickinson

Williams(Walker) Bryant Taylor Sheridan:
Tries - Battye(2) Hardisty Bryant Taylor: Goals - Willett(5):
BRAMLEY - Rogers: Smith Wriglesworth Butterfield
Hollindrake: Wolford Barron: Jubb Morgan
Horne(Hainsworth) Robbins(Elliott)Parker E.Bryant:
Try - Wrigglesworth: Goals - Hollindrake(3):
Referee G Wilson (Dewsbury) Att - 3771 H.T. 18 - 2

Sat 5 Dec 1964 WIGAN home won 17 - nil
CASTLEFORD - Bedford: Edwards G.G.Ward Willett
C.Battye: Millward Hepworth: Terry Dickinson Williams
Bryant Taylor Sheridan(Walker):   Tries - Ward Millward
Dickinson Taylor Walker: Goal - Willett:
WIGAN - Ashby: Carlton Ashton Davies Lake: Hill Parr:
McTigue Clarke Stephens Lyons Evans Gilfedder:
Referee H Hunt (Lowton) Att - 5765 H.T. 3 - nil

Sat 12 Dec 1964 YORK away won 9 - 8
YORK - Hargreaves: Smith Hunter Houlden Rippon:
Sheehan Evans: Kidd Milner Crosby Payne Elmer
Ramsden: Tries - Elmer(2):   Goal - Payne:
CASTLEFORD - Bedford: Barton Edwards(Millward) Willett
C.Battye: Hardisty Hepworth: Terry Dickinson
McCartney(Sheridan) Taylor Walker Walton:
Try - Barton: Goals - Willett(3):
Referee D T H Davies (Pendlebury) Att – 3082 H.T. nil - 5

Sat 19 Dec 1964 BATLEY home won 31 - 4
CASTLEFORD - Bedford: C.Battye M.Battye Willett
Barton(Gamble): Hardisty Hepworth: Terry Dickinson
Sheridan Bryant(Walker) Taylor Walton:
Tries - Gamble(2) C.Battye Willett Barton Dickinson Bryant
Taylor Walton: Goals - Willett(2):
BATLEY - Warner: G.Smith Holdsworth(Ward)
Shuttleworth Raynor: Geldard Butterfield: Sharpe Fryer
Fox B.Smith Briggs Foster: Goals - Warner(2):
Referee E Clay (Rothwell) Att - 3600 H.T. 17 - 4

Mon 28 Dec 1964 HULL KINGSTON ROVERS away lost 3 - 10
HULL K R - Kellett: Burwell Major Moore Blackmore: Elliott
Gillard: Bath Flanagan Drake(Pollard) Tyson Mennell
Poole: Tries - Blackmore(2):   Goals - Kellett(2):
CASTLEFORD - Bedford: C.Battye Gamble Willett Barton:
Hardisty Hepworth: Terry Dickinson Walker
Walton(Johnson) Taylor Sheridan:
Try - C.Battye:
Referee T Keane (Oldham) Att - 9650 H.T. 3 - nil

Sat 2 Jan 1965 LEEDS away lost 5 - 7
LEEDS - Hick: Cowan Landers(Broatch) Gemmell
Wriglesworth: Shoebottom Batten: Clark Lockwood
Walker(Morgan) Sykes Neumann Chamberlain:
Try - Hick: Goals - Shoebottom(2):
CASTLEFORD - Bedford: C.Battye(Millward) G.G.Ward
Willett Barton: Gamble Hepworth: Terry Dickinson
Maurice Williams(Clark) Taylor Walker Sheridan:
Try - Hepworth: Goal – Willett:
Referee B Baker (Norwich) Att - 6949 H.T. 5 - 3

SEASON 1964-65

Sat 9 Jan 1965 DEWSBURY home won 24 - nil
CASTLEFORD - Bedford: Howe G.G.Ward Small C.Battye:
Willett Hepworth: Terry Dickinson Slatter Walker Taylor
Walton: Tries - Howe(2) Battye(2) Ward Small:
Goals - Willett(2) Ward:
DEWSBURY - Hirst: Osborne Newall Hutchinson Marsh:
Firth Newsome: Naylor Mullins Taylor Blackburn(Laycock)
Rushworth Lowe:
Referee E Lawrinson (Warr'ton) Att - 3012 H.T. 12 - nil

Sat 16 Jan 1965 HALIFAX away lost 3 - 23
HALIFAX - James: Williamson Burnett Todd Freeman:
Robinson Baker: Roberts Harrison Scott Fogerty Dixon
Renilson:
Tries - Freeman(3) James Robinson: Goals - James(4):
CASTLEFORD - Bedford: Howe G.G.Ward Small Gamble:
Willett Hepworth: Terry Dickinson Slatter Taylor Walker
Walton(John Clark): Try - Gamble:
Referee P Geraghty (York) Att - 3986 H.T. nil - 23

Sat 30 Jan 1965 HUNSLET away won 20 - 5
HUNSLET - Langton: Griffiths Shelton Render Lee: Preece
Marchant(S/O): Hartley(S/O) Whitaker Eyre Ramsey
Gunney Ward(Taylor): Try - Gunney: Goal - Langton:
CASTLEFORD - RONALD HILL(488): Gamble G.G.Ward
Small C.Battye: Hardisty Hepworth: Terry Dickinson Slatter
Bryant(S/O) Taylor Walton: Tries - Hardisty(2) Small
Hepworth: Goals - Hardisty(3) Hill:
Referee T Keane (Oldham) Att - 5000 H.T. 8 - nil

**Sat 6 Feb 1965 ST HELENS away lost 9 - 22
CHALLENGE CUP ROUND 1**
ST HELENS - Coslett: Vollenhoven Northern Barrow
Killeen: Benyon Murphy: Temby Dagnall Watson Warlow
Hicks Laughton: Tries - Barrow Killeen Murphy Temby:
Goals - Coslett(4)Murphy:
CASTLEFORD - Bedford: Gamble G.G.Ward Willett
C.Battye: Hardisty Hepworth: Terry Dickinson Slatter
Bryant Taylor Walton(Walker):
Try - Hardisty: Goals - Willett(3):
Referee G Wilson (Dewsbury) Att - 20000 H.T. 4 - 12

Sat 20 Feb 1965 HALIFAX home won 10 - 5
CASTLEFORD - Bedford: Howe G.G.Ward Willett C.Battye:
Hardisty Hepworth: Terry Dickinson BARRY
CHARLESWORTH(489) Bryant Walton Taylor:
Goals - Willett(5):
HALIFAX - James: Jackson Kellett Todd Freeman:
Robinson Daley: Roberts Harrison Scroby Fogerty Dixon
Renilson: Try - Kellett: Goal - James:
Referee F J Howker (Rochdale) Att - 4338 H.T. 4 - 5

Sat 27 Feb 1965 KEIGHLEY home won 29 - 10
CASTLEFORD - Bedford: Howe G.G.Ward Willett C.Battye:
Hardisty Hepworth: Terry Dickinson Charlesworth Bryant
Walker Taylor(Hirst): Tries - Howe(2) Willett Battye
Charlesworth Bryant Hirst: Goals - Willett(4):
KEIGHLEY - Owen: Aspinall O'Brien Thomas(Chapman)
Edwards: Sabine Jones: Fall Anderson Walsh(Haigh)
Crewdson Eyre Blakeley:

Tries - O'Brien Thomas: Goals - Owen(2):
Referee D S Brown (Dewsbury) Att - 3012 H.T. 19 - 5

Sat 6 Mar 1965 KEIGHLEY away won 18 - 2
KEIGHLEY - Owen: Aspinall O'Brien Chapman Edwards:
Sabine Jones: Fall Anderson(Haigh) Walsh Crewdson
Gaines Eyre: Goal - Owen:
CASTLEFORD - Bedford: Howe M.Battye Willett C.Battye:
Hardisty Hepworth: Terry Dickinson Charlesworth Bryant
Walton Small
Tries - Howe Willett Battye Hardisty: Goals - Willett(3):
Referee H Hunt (Warrington) Att - 1300 H.T. 8 - nil

Sat 13 Mar 1965 BRAMLEY away won 21 - 9
BRAMLEY - Fogers: A.Smith Larkin Heap Hollindrake:
Wolford Barron: Hainsworth Morgan Jubb Robbins Parker
E.Bryant: Try - Hillindrake: Goals Hollindrake(3):
CASTLEFORD - Edwards: Howe M.Battye Willett C.Battye:
Hardisty Hepworth: Terry Dickinson Charlesworth Bryant
Walton Taylor: Tries - Hardisty(2) M.Battye Hepworth
Bryant: Goals - Willett(3):
Referee G Wilson (Dewsbury) Att - 2550 H.T. 8 - 7

**Sat 20 Mar 1965 WORKINGTON TOWN home
won 32 - nil**
CASTLEFORD - Edwards: Howe Small Willett C.Battye:
Hardisty Hepworth: Terry Dickinson Charlesworth Bryant
Walton Taylor:
Tries - Small(3) Hardisty(3) Hepworth(2): Goals - Willett(4):
WORKINGTON T - Charlton: Southward Colloby Bell
Glastonbury: Archer Roper: Edgar Allan Martin
Gardiner(Kirkbride) Smith J.McFarlane:
Referee S Shepherd (Oldham) Att - 1751 H.T. 16 - nil

**Sat 27 Mar 1965 BRADFORD NORTHERN home
won 22 - 10**
CASTLEFORD - Edwards: DENNIS HARRIS(490) Small
Willett C.Battye: Hardisty Hepworth: Terry(Walker)
Dickinson Charlesworth Bryant Walton Taylor:
Tries - Edwards Harris Hardisty Hepworth:
Goals - Willett(5):
BRADFORD N - Stock: Brown Brooke Lord
Walker(Metcalfe): Budge Smales: Hardcastle Ackerley
Tonkinson Hepworth Clawson Rae:
Tries - Brooke Rae: Goals - Clawson(2):
Referee T Keane (Oldham) Att - 6260 H.T. 22 - 10

Sat 3 Apr 1965 WAKEFIELD TRINITY away lost 7 - 27
WAKEFIELD T - Metcalfe: Jones Thomas Fox Coetzer:
Poynton Hopwood: Dolton Shepherd Campbell Haigh
Sampson Holliday:
Tries - Coetzer(5) Jones(2): Goals - Fox(3):
CASTLEFORD - Edwards: Howe Small Willett
C.Battye(M.Battye): Hardisty Hepworth: Terry Dickinson
Charlesworth Bryant Walton Taylor:
Try - Willett: Goals - Willett(2):
Referee D S Brown (Dewsbury) Att - 15314 H.T. 2 - 15

SEASON 1964-65

Wed 7 Apr 1965 FEATHERSTONE ROVERS home won 29 - 7
CASTLEFORD - Edwards: C.Battye M.Battye Willett Barton:
Hardisty Hepworth: Terry Dickinson Charlesworth
Walton(Millward)Taylor(RICHARD PARKER(491)) Small:
Tries - C.Battye(2) Willett Hardisty Hepworth:
Goals - Willett(7):
FEATHERSTONE R. - Dawson: Thomas Cotton Lynch Bell:
Smith Fox: Tonks Kosanovic Dixon Ramshaw Morgan
Nicholson: Try - Lynch: Goals - Fox(2):
Referee R Appleyard (Leeds) Att - 7581 H.T. 9 - 7

Sat 17 Apr 1965 HULL KINGSTON ROVERS home won 17 - 12
CASTLEFORD - Edwards: C.Battye M.Battye Willett Barton:
Hardisty Hepworth: Terry Dickinson Charlesworth Andrew
Johnson Walton(Jack Hirst) Small:
Tries - Barton Willett Hardisty: Goal - Willett(4):
HULL K R - Kellett: Mullins Burwell Moore Blackmore:
Gillard Cooper(Elliott): Bath Walker Tyson Holliday Foster
Poole: Tries - Holliday Poole: Goals - Kellett(3):
Referee P Geraghty (York) Att - 6629 H.T. 12 - 2

Mon 19 Apr 1965 FEATHERSTONE ROVERS away won 15 - 2
FEATHERSTONE R - Darbyshire: Smith Rawes Bell Jordan:
Bennett Dooler: Tonks Kosanovic Dixon Eastwood
Morgan Fox: Goal - Darbyshire:
CASTLEFORD - Edwards: C.Battye M.Battye Willett Barton:
Hardisty Hepworth(G.G.Ward): Terry Dickinson
Charlesworth Walton Walker Small:
Tries - C.Battye Barton Walker: Goals - Willett(3):
Referee H Pearce (Leeds) Att - 6930 H.T. 7 - nil

Sat 24 Apr 1965 HUNSLET home won 18 - 7 CHAMPIONSHIP ROUND 1
CASTLEFORD - Bedford: C.Battye M.Battye G.G.Ward
Barton: Hardisty Edwards: Terry Dickinson Charlesworth
Taylor Walker Small:
Tries - Hardisty(3) Barton: Goals - Hardisty(2) Edwards

Trevor Waring
D. No 482
1964-65 to 1966-67

HUNSLET - Langton: Griffiths Shelton Preece Render:
Gabbitas(Ward) Marchant: Hartley Dunn Eyre Ramsey
Baldwinson Taylor(Gunney):
Try - Griffiths: Goals - Langton(2):
Referee S Shepherd (Oldham) Att - 6100 H.T. 8 - 2

Sat 1 May 1965 WORKINGTON TOWN home won 11 - 3 CHAMPIONSHIP ROUND 2
CASTLEFORD - Edwards: Howe M.Battye Willett(Bedford)
Barton: Hardisty Hepworth: Terry Dickinson Charlesworth
Bryant Walton(Taylor) Small:
Tries - Barton Hardisty Hepworth: Goal - Willett:
WORKINGTON T - Charlton: Glastonbury O'Neill Bell
Colby: Archer Roper: Edgar Allen Martin Kirkbride Smith
McFarlane: Try - O'Neill:
Referee J Manley (Warrington) Att - 8084 H.T. 11 - nil

Sat 15 May 1965 HALIFAX home lost 18 - 26 CHAMPIONSHIP SEMI FINAL
CASTLEFORD - Bedford: C.Battye M.Battye Willett Barton:
Gamble Edwards: Terry Dickinson Charlesworth Bryant
Walton Small: Tries - Willett Barton Charlesworth Bryant:
Goals - Willett(3):
HALIFAX - James: Jackson Burnett Kellett Freeman:
Robinson Daley: Roberts Kelley(Duffy) Scroby Fogerty
Dixon Renilson: Tries - Fogerty(2) Burnett Robinson
Daley Renilson: Goals - James(4):
Referee J Manley (Warrington) Att - 10765 H.T. 15 - 3

With the league structure returning to one division the Championship play off was extended to the top sixteen clubs, and with victories over Hunslet at home in round one 18 – 7, and Workington at home in round two 11 – 3, we had progressed to a semi-final tie against Halifax at home. The morning of the match brought withdrawals through injury of Alan Hardisty and Keith Hepworth. However the weakened team took the first half by storm going in at the break with a 15 – 3 lead to the chants of "Easy" "Easy" by the home supporters ringing round the ground. Unfortunately the chants were rather premature and a powerful second half performance by Halifax brought them a 26 – 18 victory, who went on to beat St Helens 15 – 7 in the final.

Roger Millward
D. No 483
1964-65 to 1965-66

SEASON 1964-65

Abe Terry
D. No 484
1964-64 to 1965-66

Peter Barton
D. No 485
1964-65 to 1965-66

Ronnie Willett
D. No 486
1964-65 to 1968-69

John Taylor
D. No 487
1964-65 to 1966-67

SEASON 1964-65

SEASON 1965-66

Ron Hill
D. No 488
1964-65 to 1968-69

Dennis Harris
D. No 490
1964-65 to 1970-71

Ian Stenton
D. No 492
1965-66 to 1972-73

Trevor Briggs
D. No to 493
1965-66 to 1977-78

SEASON 1965-66

Mike Redfearn
D. No 494
1965-66 to 1976-77

Tony Miller
D. No 495
1965-66 to 1973-74

John Hinchcliffe
D. No 496
1965-66 to 1966-67

Brian Lockwood
D. No 497
1965-66 to 1974-75

SEASON 1964-65

D.N	PLAYER		DEBUT	L MATCH	APP	SUB	T.AP	TRI'S	G'LS	D.G	P'TS
382	SHERIDAN	JOHN			5	1	6	0	0	0	0
389	BARNES	JACK		31/10/1964	4	0	4	1	0	0	3
414	WARD	GEOFFREY G.			23	1	24	6	1	0	20
424	HIRST	JACK		17/04/1965	6	3	9	1	0	0	3
426	BRYANT	WILLIAM			29	0	29	7	0	0	21
427	BATTYE	COLIN			35	0	35	17	0	0	51
433	HARDISTY	ALAN			30	0	30	20	10	0	80
438	SMALL	PETER			15	0	15	5	0	0	15
439	CLARK	JOHN		16/01/1965	11	3	14	4	27	0	66
442	HEPWORTH	KEITH			34	0	34	11	0	1	35
455	WALKER	JOHN			15	5	20	2	0	0	6
458	EDWARDS	DEREK			17	1	18	4	1	0	14
460	SLATTER	KEITH			8	0	8	0	0	0	0
462	BATTYE	MALCOLM			12	3	15	2	0	0	6
464	WILLIAMS	MAURICE		02/01/1965	11	0	11	0	0	0	0
465	GAMBLE	JACK			10	1	11	3	0	0	9
466	BROWN	GILBERT		12/09/1964	6	0	6	1	0	0	3
468	SMITH	FRANK Jnr.		26/09/1964	4	0	4	0	0	0	0
469	WALTON	DOUGLAS			29	0	29	6	0	0	18
471	FOULKES	KENNY		19/09/1964	2	1	3	1	0	0	3
473	HOWE	KEITH			22	1	23	13	0	0	39
474	BEDFORD	TREVOR			26	2	28	0	0	0	0
475	BAKER	DENNIS			1	0	1	0	0	0	0
476	BELL	ROY			6	1	7	1	2	0	7
477	JOHNSON	ANDREW		17/04/1965	3	1	4	0	0	0	0
478	McCARTNEY	HAROLD			4	1	5	0	0	0	0
479	DICKINSON	CLIVE			33	0	33	3	0	0	9
480	WARD	ROY			1	0	1	0	0	0	0
481	APPLEYARD	DAVID	03/10/1964		1	0	1	0	0	0	0
482	WARING	TREVOR	03/10/1964		1	0	1	0	0	0	0
483	MILLWARD	ROGER	03/10/1964		3	3	6	1	0	0	3
484	TERRY	ABE	03/10/1964		29	0	29	0	0	0	0
485	BARTON	PETER	10/10/1964		12	0	12	8	0	0	24
486	WILLETT	RONALD	31/10/1964		25	0	25	8	70	0	164
487	TAYLOR	JOHN	21/11/1964		19	1	20	3	0	0	9
488	HILL	RONALD	30/01/1965		1	0	1	0	1	0	2
489	CHARLESWORTH	BARRY	20/02/1965		13	0	13	2	0	0	6
490	HARRIS	DENNIS	27/03/1965		1	0	1	1	0	0	3
491	PARKER	RICHARD	07/04/1965		0	1	1	0	0	0	0
	39			**11**	**8**	**507**	**30**	**537**	**131**	**112**	**1**

Total: **619**

COMPETITION		P	W	D	L	FOR	AGT
LEAGUE ONE D	POSITION 3 OF 30	34	25	1	8	555	294
YORK'S CUP		1	0	0	1	8	16
RL CUP		1	0	0	1	9	22
CHAMPIONSHIP		3	2	0	1	47	36
PLAYERS RECORDS		**39**	**27**	**1**	**11**	**619**	**368**

Coach Harry Street left the Club at the end of December with 'A' Team Coach George Clinton stepping up to take charge of the 1st Team.

We were much more successful in our league campaign finishing third - our best position since 1938/39.

The Club were again represented at international level with Alan Hardisty playing for Great Britain against France at Perpignan and scoring a try in a 18–8 defeat, and in the return fixture at Swinton, Alan Hardisty and debutante Duggie Walton played in the 17–7 victory.

A notable debutante was Roger Millward who according to some was discovered by "television" through its Sunday lunchtime screening of Under 17's junior games. However, for those of us who had followed his progress from being a 10 year old schoolboy playing for Wheldon Lane Junior School, we already new he was a star of the future.

Another debutante was Ron Hill who broke his jaw in his debut game at Hunslet.

SEASON 1965-66

Substitutes allowed for any reason up to and including half time

Sat 21 Aug 1965 WAKEFIELD TRINITY away won 24 - 5
WAKEFIELD T - Round: Jones Davies Thomas Coetzer: Poynton Hopwood: Steel Milner Campbell Ravouvou Haigh Holliday(Plumstead): Try - Jones: Goal - Round:
CASTLEFORD - Edwards: M.Battye Gamble Willett Barton: Hardisty Hepworth: Terry J.Ward(Dickinson)Charlesworth Bryant Walker Small:
Tries - Hardisty(2) Willett Hepworth: Goals - Willett(6):
Referee H Pearce (Leeds) Att - 10414 H.T. 8 - 3

Sat 28 Aug 1965 ST HELENS home lost 15 - 19
CASTLEFORD - Edwards: M.Battye Gamble Willett Barton: Hardist Hepworth(C.Battye): Terry(Dickinson) J.Ward Charlesworth Bryant Walker Small:
Tries - Gamble Willett Bryant: Goals - Willett(3):
ST HELENS - Coslett: Vollenhoven Wood Smith Pimblett: Harvey Murphy: Temby Dagnall(Markey) Watson Warlow Mantle(Benyon) Hicks:
Tries - Coslett Wood Harvey: Goals - Coslett(5):
Referee H Morgan (Oldham) Att - 8940 H.T. 13 - 7

Mon 30 Aug 1965 DONCASTER away won 35 - 9
DONCASTER - Astbury: Roberts Goodchild(Price)Arrand Dewsbury: Williams Charlton: Robinson Trowell Holt Saville Oxenham Jackson:
Try - Williams: Goals - Dewsbury(3):
CASTLEFORD - Hill: C.Battye Gamble Willett M.Battye: Hardisty Edwards: Taylor J.Ward(Dickinson) Charlesworth Bryant Walker Small:
Tries - Hardisty(2) Gamble Willett M.Battye Edwards Small: Goals - Hill(6) Willett:
Referee R L Thomas (Oldham) Att - 2050 H.T. 16 - 7

Sat 4 Sep 1965 FEATHERSTONE ROVERS home won 22 - 8 YORKSHIRE CUP ROUND 1
CASTLEFORD - Edwards: C.Battye Gamble Willett(Hill) M.Battye: Hardisty Hepworth: Charlesworth J.Ward Dickinson Bryant Walker Small:
Tries - C.Battye Gamble M.Battye Hardisty: Goals - Willett(3) Hill(2):
FEATHERSTONE R - Darbyshire: Greatorex Northern(Cotten) Lynch Thomas: Smith Dooler: Tonks(S/O) Farrar Tucker Ramshaw Agar Nicholson: Goals - Darbyshire(4):
Referee E Lawrinson(Warrington) Att - 6556 H.T. 9 - 2

Sat 11 Sep 1965 HULL home won 15 - 3
CASTLEFORD - Hill: C.Battye Gamble Small Peter Barton: Millward Hepworth: Terry J.Ward Charlesworth Bryant Walker Taylor: Tries - Ward Bryant Walker: Goals - Hill(3):
HULL - Keegan: Oliver Huxley Doyle-Davidson Sullivan: Devonshire Foulkes: Macklin(C.Booth) McGlone Broom Neale Harrison Johnson: Try - Sullivan:
Referee D T H Davies (Manchester) Att - 5570 H.T. 11 - 3

Tue 14 Sep 1965 HALIFAX home won 25 - 8 YORKSHIRE CUP ROUND 2
CASTLEFORD - Hill: C.Battye Gamble Small Millward: Edwards Hepworth: Terry J.Ward Charlesworth Bryant Walker Taylor:
Tries - Gamble(2) C.Battye Small Bryant: Goals - Hill(5):
HALIFAX - James: Todd Burnett Kellett Freeman: Robinson Daley: Roberts Harrison Scroby Fogerty Hardcastle Renilson: Goals - James(4):
Referee D T H Davies (Man'ster) Att - 9194 H.T. 12 - 4

Sat 18 Sep 1965 ST HELENS away lost 6 - 21
ST HELENS - Coslett: Vollenhoven Wood Williams Killeen: Murphy Prosser: Watson Dagnall Warlow Hicks Mantle Laughton: Tries - Vollenhoven Murphy Watson Hicks Laughton: Goals - Coslett(3):
CASTLEFORD - Hill: C.Battye Gamble Small M.Battye: Edwards Hepworth: Terry Dickinson Charlesworth(J.Ward) Bryant Walker Taylor: Goals - Hill(3):
Referee E Clay (Rothwell) Att - 12000 H.T. 4 - 13

Fri 24 Sep 1965 WIGAN home lost 9 - 12
CASTLEFORD - Edwards: C.Battye Geoffrey G.Ward Small M.Battye: M llward Hepworth: Terry Dickinson Charlesworth Bryant Walker Taylor:
Try - Millward: Goals - Millward(3):
WIGAN - Ashby: Carlton Holden Ashton Lake: Hesketh Parr: McTigue Sayer Woosey Lyon A.Stephens Major:
Tries - Lake Hesketh: Goals - Ashton(3):
Referee T Keane (Oldham) Att - 9203 H.T. 4 - 5

Mon 27 Sep 1965 HUNSLET away lost 10 - 17 YORKSHIRE CUP SEMI FINAL
HUNSLET - Langton: Lee Shelton Render Thompson: Preece Marchant: Hartley Prior Eyre Ramsey Gunney Ward: Tries - Lee(2) Eyre: Goals - Langton(4):
CASTLEFORD - Bedford: Howe C.Battye M.Battye Millward: Edwards Hepworth: Terry J.Ward Barry Charlesworth Walker Bryant Taylor:
Tries - Millward(2): Goals - Millward(2):
Referee R L Thomas (Oldham) Att - 9753 H.T. nil - 7

Sat 2 Oct 1965 WIGAN away won 10 - 8
WIGAN - Ashby: Boston Holden Ashton Carlton(O'Loughlin): Hesketh Parr: Gardner Sayer Woosey Lyons Stephens Evans: Goals - Ashton(4):
CASTLEFORD - Edwards: Howe IAN STENTON(492) M.Battye Gamble: Hardisty Millward: Walton Dickinson Sheridan(McCartney) Small Walker Taylor:
Tries - Hardisty Taylor: Goals - Millward(2):
Referee R Appleyard (Leeds) Att - 7890 H.T. 8 - 8

Wed 6 Oct 1965 NEW ZEALAND lost 6 - 7
CASTLEFORD - Edwards: Willett Gamble Stenton(Hepworth) M.Battye: Hardisty Millward: Walton Dickinson Sheridan Small Walker Taylor: Goals - Millward(3):

217

SEASON 1965-66

NEW ZEALAND - Tait: Reidy Strong Bailey Langton: Walshe(Brown) Irvine: Edwards C.O'Neil(Mattson) Scholefield Deacon Orchard White:
Try - Bailey: Goals - Tait(2):
Referee H Pearce (Leeds) Att - 5600 H.T. 2 - 5
Floodlights were installed at Wheldon Road, the only ones in Yorkshire at that time. Officially switched on by Mr Denis Howell MP, the Minister Of Sport, for this game.

Mon 11 Oct 1965 YORK home won 20 - 5
CASTLEFORD - Edwards: C.Battye Gamble Willett M.Battye: Hardisty Millward: Terry Dickinson Walton Bryant Walker Taylor:
Tries - C.Battye(2) M.Battye Walker: Goals - Millward(4):
YORK - Duck: Meillan Hunter(Tees) Flannery Rippon: Houlden Evans: Yorke Crosby Walker(Storey) Fowler Drake Payne: Try - Evans: Goal - Yorke:
Referee R Jackson (Elland) Att - 6650 H.T. 11 - nil

Sat 16 Oct 1965 WARRINGTON away won 15 - 7
WARRINGTON - Conroy: Fisher Melling Pickavance Glover: Aspinall Smith: Payne Dickens Hill Winslade Robinson Hayes: Try - Glover: Goals - Hayes(2):
CASTLEFORD - Edwards: C.Battye M.Battye Willett TREVOR BRIGGS(493): Hardisty Millward: Terry(S/O) Dickinson Walker Bryant Small Taylor:
Tries - Millward(2) M.Battye: Goals - Millward(3):
Referee E Clay (Rothwell) Att - 5870 H.T. 15 - 2

Fri 22 Oct 1965 DEWSBURY home won 15 - nil
CASTLEFORD - Bedford: C.Battye M.Battye Willett Briggs: Edwards Hepworth: Terry(Slatter) Dickinson Walker Bryant Small Taylor:
Tries - Briggs Walker Small: Goals - Willett(3):
DEWSBURY - Hirst: Marsh Sullivan Osborne Harris: Ward Newall: Walker Mullins Taylor Lowe Blackburn Robinson:
Referee R Appleyard (Leeds) Att - 4455 H.T. 4 - nil

Tue 26 Oct 1965 LEEDS home draw 7 - 7
BBC 2 FLOODLIT COMPETITION ROUND 1
CASTLEFORD - Edwards: C.Battye M.Battye Willett(Millward) Briggs: Hardisty Hepworth: Slatter Dickinson Walker Bryant Small Taylor:
Try - Hepworth: Goals - Willett Millward:
LEEDS - Thornett: Cowan Shoebottom Gemmell Wriglesworth: Broatch Rollin: Clark Lockwood Firth Sykes Neumann Poole: Try - Thornett: Goals - Shoebottom(2):
Referee G Wilson (Dewsbury) Att - 7500 H.T. 2 - 5

Sat 30 Oct 1965 YORK away won 26 - 9
YORK - Duck: Meillan Flannery Tees Rippon: Houlden Evans: Yorke Crosby Walker Fowler Drake Payne:
Try - Walker: Goals - Yorke(3):
CASTLEFORD - Bedford: C.Battye M.Battye Willett Briggs: Millward Hepworth: Terry J.Ward Walker(Taylor) Bryant Small Sheridan: Tries - Willett(2) Hepworth Walker: Goals - Millward(5) Willett(2):
Referee G Philpott (Leeds) Att - 3010 H.T. 12 -9

Sat 6 Nov 1965 BATLEY away won 21 - 6
BATLEY - Warner: Levula Smith Ward Rayner: Geldard Hobson: Hinchcliffe A.N.Other Parratt Hopwood Robinson Noble: Goals - Levula(3):
CASTLEFORD - Bedford: C.Battye M.Battye Willett Briggs: Hardisty Hepworth: Terry J.Ward Taylor Small(Slatter) Walker Sheridan: Tries - Willett Briggs Hardisty Small Sheridan: Goals - Willett(3):
Referee G T Schofield (Salford) Att - 2000 H.T. 14 - 4

Fri 12 Nov 1965 BRAMLEY home won 32 - nil
CASTLEFORD - Edwards: C.Battye(Hepworth) Gamble Willett Briggs: Hardisty Millward: Terry J.Ward Taylor Bryant Walker Sheridan: Tries - Millward(2) Bryant(2) Gamble Willett Briggs Hardisty: Goals - Willett(4):
BRAMLEY - Rogers: Mann Toohey Heap Taylor: Wolford Barron: Hainsworth Groves Horn Robbins Parker Humble:
Referee P Geraghty (York) Att - 4387 H.T. 13 - nil

Sat 20 Nov 1965 HUNSLET away draw 8 - 8
HUNSLET - Langton: Lee Shelton Preece Thompson: Pickles Marchant: Hartley Prior Baldwinson Ramsey Gunney Ward:
Tries - Shelton Thompson: Goal - Langton:
CASTLEFORD - Edwards: C.Battye Gamble Willett Briggs: Hardisty Hepworth: Terry J.Ward Taylor Small Walker John Sheridan: Goals - Willett(4):
Referee J Manley (Warrington) Att - 3100 H.T. 4 - 5

Thu 25 Nov 1965 OLDHAM away won 6 - 4
BBC 2 FLOODLIT COMPETITION ROUND 2
OLDHAM - Tomlinson: G.Simms McCormack Crowther T.Simms: Warburton Canning: Mumberson Taylor Wilson Ogden Burns Parker(Fletcher): Goals - Tomlinson(2):
CASTLEFORD - Edwards: C.Battye Gamble Willett Briggs: Hardisty Hepworth: Terry J.Ward Dickinson(Taylor) Bryant Walker Small: Tries - Battye Small:
Referee E Clay (Rothwell) Att - 853 H.T. 3 - 2

Sat 27 Nov 1965 BRADFORD NORTHERN home won 21 - 2
CASTLEFORD - Edwards: C.Battye Gamble Willett Briggs: Millward Hepworth: Terry(Slatter) J.Ward Dickinson Taylor Walker MICHAEL REDFEARN(494): Tries - Battye Gamble Briggs Millward Taylor: Goals - Redfearn(3):
BRADFORD N - Rhodes: Williamson Breakspeare Walker Lord: Stockwell Sutcliffe: Tonkinson Ackerley Hill Ashton Clawson Rae: Goal - Clawson:
Referee D S Brown (Dewsbury) Att - 4320 H.T. 3 - nil

Tue 30 Nov 1965 WIDNES away won 12 - 9
BBC 2 FLOODLIT COMPETITION SEMI FINAL
WIDNES - Whitfield: Hare Aspey Briers Gaydon: Lowe Ward: Hurstfield Karalius Walsh Collier Larkin(Carden) Winstanley: Tries - Hare: Goals - Whitfield(3):
CASTLEFORD - Edwards: C.Battye Gamble Willett Briggs: Millward Hepworth: Slatter J.Ward Dickinson Taylor Walker Redfearn:
Tries - Gamble Taylor: Goals - Willett(3):
Referee G Philpott (Leeds) Att - 4776 H.T. 10 - 4

SEASON 1965-66

Sat 4 Dec 1965 BRAMLEY away won 13 - 10
BRAMLEY - Simpson: Mann Davies Rogers Elliott: Wolford Barron: Hainsworth Groves Jubb Robbins Brook(Parker) Bryant: Goals - Simpson(5):
CASTLEFORD - Edwards: C.Battye Gamble Willett Briggs: Hardisty Millward: <u>Keith Slatter</u> Dickinson Walker Taylor Small Redfearn:
Tries - Briggs Hardisty Small: Goals - Willett(2):
Referee F Leach (St Helens) Att - 3200 H.T. 2 - 4

Sat 11 Dec 1965 HALIFAX home lost 4 - 8
CASTLEFORD - Edwards: C.Battye M.Battye Willett Briggs: Hardisty Hepworth(Millward): Terry Dickinson Walker Bryant Small Taylor: Goals - Willett Millward:
HALIFAX - James: Stevenson Burnett Todd Freeman: Kellett Daley: Roberts Harrison Scroby Mills Ramshaw Renilson: Tries - Stevenson Harrison: Goal - James:
Referee J P Hebblethwaite (York) Att - 5326 H.T. 2 - 3

Tue 14 Dec 1965 ST HELENS away won 4 - nil
BBC 2 FLOODLIT COMPETITION FINAL
ST HELENS - Barrow: Vollenhoven Wood Benyon Killeen: Murphy Prosser: French Dagnall Watson Hicks Mantle Laughton:
CASTLEFORD - Edwards: C.Battye M.Battye Willett Briggs: Hardisty Millward: Terry J.Ward Dickinson Bryant Taylor Small: Goals - Willett(2):
Referee L Gant (Wakefield) Att - 11510 H.T. 2 - nil

Sat 18 Dec 1965 HULL away won 6 - 3
HULL - Keegan: Stocks Davidson Maloney Sullivan: Devonshire McGowan: Pearson McGlone Brook O'Brien Harrison Neale: Try - McGowan:
CASTLEFORD - Edwards: C.Battye M.Battye Willett Briggs: Hardisty Hepworth: McCartney Dickinson Walker Bryant Taylor Small: Tries - Willett Dickinson:
Referee P Geraghty (York) Att - 5700 H.T. 3 - nil

Sat 1 Jan 1966 KEIGHLEY home won 28 - 9
CASTLEFORD - Edwards: C.Battye Hardisty(M.Battye) Willett Appleyard: Millward Hepworth: Terry J.Ward Dickinson Bryant Taylor Small(Walker):
Tries - C.Battye M.Battye Appleyard Bryant Small Edwards: Goals - Willett(5):
KEIGHLEY - Keith: Jefferson Dickinson Thomas Moulding: Sabine Hare: Worthy Anderson Bloomfield(Walsh) Gaines Garbett Blakeley: Try - Moulding: Goals - Jefferson(3):
Referee R Appleyard (Leeds) Att - 4435 H.T. 17 - 7

Sat 8 Jan 1966 LEEDS away lost 7 - 8
LEEDS - Thornett: Cowan Hynes Broatch Wriglesworth: Shoebottom Rollin: Clark Owens Firth Neumann Davies Poole: Tries - Shoebottom(2):   Goal - Shoebottom:
CASTLEFORD - Edwards: C.Battye M.Battye Willett(Bedford) Briggs: Millward Hepworth: Terry J.Ward Dickinson Bryant Taylor Small:
Try - Briggs: Goals - Millward(2):
Referee J Manley (Warrington) Att - 6439 H.T. 2 - 5

Sat 29 Jan 1966 DEWSBURY away won 9 - 2
DEWSBURY - First: Marsh Sullivan Osborne Edwards: Ward Newall: Walker Mullins Taylor Lowe Cook Smith: Goal - Lowe:
CASTLEFORD - Edwards: C.Battye Hill Willett Briggs: Millward Hepworth(S/O): Terry J.Ward Dickinson(S/O) Bryant Taylor Small: Try - Small: Goals - Millward(2) Hill:
Referee J P Hebblethwaite(York) Att - 2300 H.T. 7- nil

Sat 5 Feb 1966 DONCASTER home won 35 - 2
CASTLEFORD - Edwards: C.Battye Hill Willett(M.Battye) Briggs: Millward Hepworth: Terry J.Ward Dickinson Bryant Taylor(Redfearn)Small: Tries - C.Battye(2) Hill(2) Millward(2) Bryant(2) Ward: Goals - Hill(4):
DONCASTER - Williams: Goodchild Rushton Arrand Stocks: Woodfield Charlton(Donald): B.Robinson Trowell D.Robinson(Brownley) Hume Thomas McVeigh: Goal - Williams:
Referee H Pearce (Leeds) Att - 3062 H.T. 13 - 2

Sat 12 Feb 1966 HUNSLET home won 18 - 2
CASTLEFORD - Edwards: C.Battye Hill Willett Briggs: Millward R.Ward: Terry J.Ward McCartney Bryant Taylor Small:
Tries - C.Battye Hill Willett J.Ward: Goals - Hill(3):
HUNSLET - Langton: Lee Shelton Preece Thompson: Chamberlain Abbey: Hartley Prior(Whitehead) Eyre Larkin Wilson Ward: Goal - Langton:
Referee D T H Davies (Man'ster) Att - 4196 H.T. 10 - 2

Sat 19 Feb 1966 HULL KINGSTON ROVERS away lost 9 - 14
HULL K.R. - Kellett: C.Young Elliott Moore Blackmore: Stephenson Bunting: Pollard Flanagan(S/O) Tyson Holliday G.Young(Murphy) Mullins:
Tries - Stephenson Holliday: Goals - Kellett(4):
CASTLEFORD - Edwards: C.Battye Hill Willett Appleyard(Briggs): Millward Hepworth: Terry(Dickinson) J.Ward(S/O) McCartney Taylor Walker Small:
Try - Willett: Goals - Hill(3):
Referee R Appleyard (Leeds) Att - 7000 H.T. 4 - 9

Sat 26 Feb 1966 WARRINGTON away lost 7 - 15
CHALLENGE CUP ROUND 1
WARRINGTON - Bootle: Fisher McDougall(Conroy) Pickavance Glover: Aspinall Gordon: Tembey Woolvine Winslade Clark(Payne)Robinson Hayes:
Tries - McDougall Glover Gordon: Goals - Bootle(3):
CASTLEFORD - Edwards: C.Battye M.Battye(Bedford) Hill Briggs: Willett Millward: McCartney TONY MILLER(495) Dickinson Redfearn Walker Small:
Try - Small: Goals - Hill(2):
Referee P Geraghty (York) Att - 8955 H.T. 5 - 12

Sat 12 Mar 1966 BRADFORD NORTHERN away draw 3 - 3
BRADFORD N - Rhodes: Smith Brooke Walker Williamson(Budge): Stockwell Smales: Goddard Ackerlewy Morgan Hill Clawson Rae: Try - Smales:
CASTLEFORD - Bedford: C.Battye Hill Willett Howe:

Millward Hepworth: Terry J.Ward McCartney Taylor
Walker Small(Dickinson): Try - C.Battye:
Referee D S Brown (Dewsbury Att - 9816 H.T. nil - nil

Sat 19 Mar 1966 HALIFAX away lost 10 - 17
HALIFAX - James: Jones Burnett Kellett Freeman:
Robinson Daley: Roberts Harrison Scroby Fogerty Dixon
Renilson:
Tries - Jones Freeman Fogerty: Goals - James(4):
CASTLEFORD - Edwards: C.Battye Hill Willett
Howe(Millward): Hardisty Hepworth: Terry J.Ward
McCartney Taylor Walker Small(Dickinson):
Tries - Small(2): Goals - Hill(2):
Referee G Philpott (Leeds) Att - 6265 H.T. 8 - 8

**Fri 25 Mar 1966 HULL KINGSTON ROVERS home
won 19 - 5**
CASTLEFORD - Bedford(R.Ward): Colin Battye Hepworth
Willett Howe: Millward Edwards: Terry J.Ward Dickinson
Bryant Taylor Small:
Tries - Willett Edwards Small: Goals - Millward(5):
HULL K R - Kellett: C.Young Wrigglesworth(S/O) Moore
Blackmore: Elliott Bunting: Pollard Flanagan Tyson
Holliday Foster Mullins: Try - Bunting: Goal - Holliday:
Referee H Hunt (Lowton) Att - 5800 H.T. 6 - 5

Wed 30 Mar 1966 WARRINGTON home won 9 - 4
CASTLEFORD - Edwards: Howe Waring Willett Millward:
Hardisty R.Ward (Hepworth): Terry J.Ward Taylor Bryant
Walker Small: Tries - Willett(3):
WARRINGTON - Affleck: Hutchinson Fisher(Leigh) Briggs
Clarke: Scahill Owen: Davies Wolvine Brady Jones
Marsden Churm: Goals - Affleck(2):
Referee T Keane (Oldham) Att - 5800 H.T. 3 - nil

Fri 1 Apr 1966 BATLEY home won 39 - nil
CASTLEFORD - Edwards: Howe Waring Willett Millward:
Hardisty Hepworth: Abe Terry J.Ward McCartney
Dickinson Walker Small: Tries - Waring(3) Millward(3)
Howe(2) Dickinson(2) Edwards: Goals - Willett(3):
BATLEY - Smith: A.N.Other Ward Shuttleworth Raynor:
Oldroyd Doyle: Hinchcliffe Scott Parrott Johnson
Else(Cullen) Hopwood:
Referee J P Hebblethwaite (York) Att - 1688 H.T. 9 - nil

**Fri 8 Apr 1966 WAKEFIELD TRINITY home
draw 6 - 6**
CASTLEFORD - Edwards: Howe Waring Willett Millward:
Hardisty Hepworth: McCartney J.Ward Dickinson Bryant
Parker Small: Goals - Willett(2) Millward:
WAKEFIELD T - Metcalfe: Jones Garthwaite N.Fox Coetzer:
Poynton Owen: Bath Shepherd Turner Plumstead Haigh
D.Fox: Tries - Jones N.Fox:
Referee H Pearce (Leeds) Att - 9068 H.T. 2 - 3

**Mon 11 Apr 1966 FEATHERSTONE ROVERS home
won 8 - 5**
CASTLEFORD - Edwards: Howe Waring Willett Millward:
Hardisty Hepworth: McCartney J.Ward Dickinson Bryant
Parker Walker: Tries - Howe Millward: Goal - Willett:
FEATHERSTONE R - Cooper: Thomas Hartley Bell
Westwood: Smith Dooler: Tonks Kosanovic Eastwood
Nicholson Brown Smales:
Try - Hartley: Goal - Smales:
Referee M Naughton (Widnes) Att - 7598 H.T. nil - 2

Tue 12 Apr 1966 KEIGHLEY away lost nil - 2
KEIGHLEY - Keith: Smart Dickinson Hebblethwaite
Moulding: Sabine Hare: Bloomfield Anderson Worthy
Crewdson(Aspinall) Eyre Garbett:
Goal - Hebblethwaite:
CASTLEFORD - Edwards: Howe Waring Willett Millward:
Hardisty(Bedford) Hepworth: McCartney J.Ward Dickinson
Parker Walker Small(Miller):
Referee E Clay (Rothwell) Att - 2715 H.T. nil - 2

Sat 16 Apr 1966 LEEDS home won 12 - 10
CASTLEFORD - Bedford: Howe Stenton Willett Millward:
Edwards Hepworth: McCartney Miller JOHN
HINCHCLIFFE(496) Parker Dickinson BRIAN
LOCKWOOD(497):
Tries - Bedford Howe: Goals - Willett(3):
LEEDS - Hick(Watson): Ratcliffe Wrigglesworth Gemmell
Atkinson: Hynes(Davies) Seabourne: Joyce Owens Morgan
Neumann Sykes Batten:
Tries - Gemmell Atkinson: Goals - Seabourne(2):
Referee G Wilson (Dewsbury) Att - 2878 H.T. 7 - 7

**Fri 22 Apr 1966 FEATHERSTONE ROVERS away
won 17 - 9**
FEATHERSTONE R - Kellett: Greatorex Hartley J.Bell
Westwood: Smith P.Bell: Tonks Kosanovic Forsythe
Morgan Tucker Smales:
Try - Smales: Goals - Smales(3):
CASTLEFORD - Edwards: Howe Stenton(M.Battye) Willett
Millward: Hardisty Hepworth: McCartney Miller Hinchcliffe
Bryant Parker Lockwood:
Tries - Millward Bryant Lockwood: Goals - Willett(4):
Referee T Keane (Oldham) Att - 4941 H.T. 7 - 7

**Sat 30 Apr 1966 HULL KINGSTON ROVERS home
lost 10 - 13 CHAMPIONSHIP ROUND 1**
CASTLEFORD - Edwards: Howe Waring Willett Roger
Millward: Hardisty Hepworth: Hinchcliffe J.Ward Dickinson
Small(Richard Parker)Walker Lockwood:
Tries - Willett Hepworth: Goals - Willett Millward:
HULL K R - Kellett: Young Wrigglesworth(Stephenson)
Moore Blackmore: Elliott Bunting: Fox Flanagan Tyson
Holliday Foster Major:
Try - Foster: Goals - Kellett(4) Foster:
Referee J.Manley (Warrington) Att - 7358 H.T. nil – 7

SEASON 1965-66

D.N	PLAYER		DEBUT	L MATCH	APP	S JB	T.AP	TRI'S	G'LS	D.G	P'TS
382	SHERIDAN	JOHN		20/11/1965	6	0	6	1	0	0	3
414	WARD	GEOFFREY G.		24/09/1965	1	0	1	0	0	0	0
426	BRYANT	WILLIAM			29	0	29	9	0	0	27
427	BATTYE	COLIN		25/03/1966	32	1	33	11	0	0	33
433	HARDISTY	ALAN			26	0	26	9	0	0	27
438	SMALL	PETER			36	0	36	12	0	0	36
442	HEPWORTH	KEITH			33	3	36	4	0	0	12
453	WARD	JOHNNY			30	1	31	3	0	0	9
455	WALKER	JOHN			34	1	35	4	0	0	12
458	EDWARDS	DEREK			40	0	40	4	0	0	12
460	SLATTER	KEITH		04/12/1965	3	3	6	0	0	0	0
462	BATTYE	MALCOLM			20	3	23	5	0	0	15
465	GAMBLE	JACK			16	0	16	8	0	0	24
469	WALTON	DOUGLAS			3	0	3	0	0	0	0
473	HOWE	KEITH			13	0	13	4	0	0	12
474	BEDFORD	TREVOR			7	3	10	1	0	0	3
478	McCARTNEY	HAROLD			12	1	13	0	0	0	0
479	DICKINSON	CLIVE			28	6	34	3	0	0	9
480	WARD	ROY			2	1	3	0	0	0	0
481	APPLEYARD	DAVID			2	0	2	1	0	0	3
482	WARING	TREVOR			6	0	6	3	0	0	9
483	MILLWARD	ROGER		30/04/1966	31	3	34	15	35	0	115
484	TERRY	ABE		01/04/1966	29	0	29	0	0	0	0
485	BARTON	PETER		11/09/1965	3	0	3	0	0	0	0
486	WILLETT	RONALD			38	0	38	15	57	0	159
487	TAYLOR	JOHN			31	2	33	3	0	0	9
488	HILL	RONALD			11	1	12	3	34	0	77
489	CHARLESWORTH	BARRY		27/09/1965	9	0	9	0	0	0	0
491	PARKER	RICHARD		30/04/1966	5	1	6	0	0	0	0
492	STENTON	IAN	02/10/1965		4	0	4	0	0	0	0
493	BRIGGS	TREVOR	16/10/1965		19	1	20	6	0	0	18
494	REDFEARN	MICHAEL	27/11/1965		4	1	5	0	3	0	6
495	MILLER	TONY	26/02/1966		3	1	4	0	0	0	0
496	HINCHCLIFFE	JOHN	16/04/1966		3	0	3	0	0	0	0
497	LOCKWOOD	BRIAN	16/04/1966		3	0	3	1	0	0	3
	35		6	9	572	33	605	125	129	0	633

COMPETITION		P	W	D	L	FOR	AGT
LEAGUE ONE D	POSITION 5 OF 30	34	23	3	8	524	233
YORK'S CUP		3	2	0	1	57	33
F. TROPHY		4	3	1	0	29	20
RL CUP		1	0	0	1	7	15
NEW ZALND		1	0	0	1	6	7
CHAMPIONSHIP		1	0	0	1	10	13
PLAYERS RECORDS		**44**	**28**	**4**	**12**	**633**	**321**

In order to promote their newly launched second television channel the BBC introduced the BBC2 Floodlit Competition played on a Tuesday evening with the second half televised live. Whilst having floodlights was supposed to be a prerequisite to entry in the competition it was not strictly adhered to as our fist ever opponents were Leeds, who did not install their lights until the end of the season. However, in those days the normal floodlights were not bright enough for the technology of the period and therefore to ensure a good picture the BBC supplemented them with additional "banks" of lights at the four corners of the ground. This competition also introduced the 'four tackle' rule which was later adopted for all competitions from December 1966.

The competition proved to be a huge success for the Club. In the final away at St Helens we produced a magnificent defensive display to win the Trophy 4–nil through two Ronnie Willett penalty goals.

Duggie Walton sustained a serious knee injury during a training session prior to the Warrington game on 16 October 1965. Whilst Duggie went on to play in a further 54 games, the injury prevented him producing the displays that earned him his International Cap in the previous season, not only a personal disaster for Duggie but the curtailment of a fantastic talent both for Club and Country.

Notable Debutants were double Challenge Cup winners Mick Redfearn and Brian Lockwood.

SEASON 1966-67

**Sat 29 Jul 1966 BRADFORD NORTHERN home
lost 13 - 20 CHARITY MATCH FRIENDLY**
CASTLEFORD - Bedford: Howe Hill Baker(Stenton)Austin:
Millward Hepworth (R.Ward): Walton Dickinson
Tucker(McCartney) Small(Lockwood)Walker Taylor:
Tries - Hepworth Dickinson Lockwood: Goals - Hill(2):
BRADFORD N - Rhodes: Smith(Larkin) Kellett Walker
Williamson(Lord): Stockwell Breakespeare: Birchall
Morgan Goddard Bowman Clawson Rae:
Tries - Larkin Williamson Lord Birchall: Goals - Clawson(4):
Referee R Sykes (Featherstone) Att - 3562 H.T. 10 - 7

**Mon 15 Aug 1966 LEIGH away won 16 - 11
BBC 2 FLOODLIT COMPETITION PRELIMINARY
ROUND 1ST LEG**
LEIGH - Tyrer: Ashcroft G.Lewis Collins Walsh: Briggs
Shillingshaw: Robinson J.Lewis Davies Welding Higgs
Carney(Wharton): Try - Tyrer: Goals - Tyrer(4):
CASTLEFORD - Bedford: Howe Hill Willett(JACK
AUSTIN)(498): Gamble Hepworth: Walton Dickinson
DAVID TUCKER(499) Small Walker Taylor:
Tries - Small(2) Howe Taylor: Goals - Hill(2):
Referee H Pearce (Leeds) Att - 4500 H.T. 8 - 6

Sat 20 Aug 1966 WAKEFIELD TRINITY home won 8 - 4
CASTLEFORD - Bedford: Howe Gamble Willett Austin:
Edwards Hepworth: Walton Dickinson Tucker(McCartney)
Small Walker Taylor:
Tries - Hepworth Walker: Goal - Willett:
WAKEFIELD T - Metcalfe: Batty Garthwaite Fox Coetzer:
Poynton Owen: Bath Clough Turner(Sampson) Haigh Bell
Hawley: Goals - Fox(2):
Referee B Baker (Wigan) Att - 6800 H.T. 6 - 2

**Mon 22 Aug 1966 WORKINGTON TOWN home
won 18 - 2**
CASTLEFORD - Hill: Howe Gamble Willett Austin: Edwards
Hepworth: Walton Dickinson McCartney Small Walker
Lockwood:
Tries - Howe Austin Hepworth Small: Goals - Hill(3):
WORKINGTON T - Charlton: Glastonbury Colloby Bell
Davies: W.Smith Newall: Curwend Moss Garratt R.Smith
J.McFarlane Pattinson: Goal - W.Smith:
Referee D S Brown (Dewsbury) Att - 4235 H.T. 7 - nil

Fri 26 Aug 1966 LEEDS away lost 2 - 23
LEEDS - Risman: Cowan Broatch Hynes Ratcliffe:
Shoebottom Rollin: Clark Moscatt Firth Neumann
Chamberlain Davies: Tries - Broatch(2) Ratcliffe
Shoebottom Rollin: Goals - Risman(4):
CASTLEFORD - Hill: Howe Gamble Willett Austin: Baker
Hepworth: Walton(McCartney) Dickinson Tucker Small
Walker Lockwood: Goal - Hill:
Referee J Manley (Warrington) Att - 7455 H.T. nil - 10

**Mon 29 Aug 1966 WORKINGTON TOWN away
lost 4 - 17**
WORKINGTON T - Charlton: Glastonbury Colloby
Bell(Southward) Davies: W.Smith Newall: Curwen
Moss(M.McFarlane) Martin R.Smith J.McFarlane Pattinson:

Tries - Newall J.McFarlane Pattinson: Goals - W.Smith(4):
CASTLEFORD - Bedford: Howe Hill Willett Austin: PETER
WADDLE(500) Hepworth: Hinchcliffe Dickinson Tucker
Small Walker(Miller) Lockwood   Goals - Willett(2):
Referee T Keane (Oldham) Att - 2500 H.T. 4 - 5

**Fri 2 Sep 1966 BATLEY home won 32 - 2
YORKSHIRE CUP ROUND 1**
CASTLEFORD - Hill: JAMES SMITH(501)(Howe) Gamble
Willett Austin: R.Ward Hepworth: Tucker Dickinson John
Hinchcliffe Small J.Ward Taylor: Tries - Austin(2) Howe
Hepworth Dickinson Small: Goals - Willett(7):
BATLEY - Warner: Pratt Smith Ward Raynor: Geldard
Pyecroft: Kennedy Scott Parrott Saville Hopwood Foster:
Goal - Saville:
Referee T Keane (Oldham) Att - 3952 H.T. 9 - 2

**Wed 7 Sep 1966 LEIGH home won 39 - 18
BBC 2 FLOODLIT COMPETITION PRELIMINARY
ROUND 2ND LEG**
CASTLEFORD - Hill: Howe Gamble Willett Austin: Hardisty
Hepworth: Walton J.Ward Tucker Bryant Small
Taylor(Dickinson):
Tries - Hardisty(4) Gamble Bryant Small: Goals - Willett(9):
LEIGH - Tyrer: Tickle Lewis Collins Walsh: Briggs Lowe:
Robinson Dickens Cotton Wharton Welding Brooks:
Tries - Briggs Cotton: Goals - Tyrer(6):
Referee E Lawrinson (Warrington) Att - 5214 H.T. 25 - 11

Sat 10 Sep 1966 BATLEY away won 32 - 8
BATLEY - Warner: Pratt Ward Smith Rayner: Butterfield
Pyecroft: Parrott(Robinson) Scott Kennedy Saville
Hopwood Foster: Tries - Pratt Smith: Goal - Kennedy:
CASTLEFORD - Hill: Howe Gamble Willett Austin: Hardisty
R.Ward: Walton Dickinson Tucker Bryant Walker(J.Ward)
Small: Tries - Howe(2) Bryant(2) Willett Hardisty:
Goals - Willett(7):
Referee S Shepherd (Oldham) Att - 1200 H.T. 7 - 8

**Wed 14 Sep 1966 HALIFAX home lost 14 - 18
YORKSHIRE CUP ROUND 2**
CASTLEFORD - Hill: Howe Gamble Willett Austin: Hardisty
R.Ward: Walton(S/O) J.Ward(S/O) Dickinson Bryant Small
Taylor: Tries - J.Ward Dickinson: Goals - Willett(4):
HALIFAX - James: Jones Dixon Todd Freeman: Robinson
Daley: Roberts(S/O) Kelley Scroby Ramshaw Renilson
Burnett: Tries - Robinson Scroby: Goals - James(6):
Referee B Baker (Wigan) Att - 6334 H.T. 14 - 2

Fri 16 Sep 1966 BRAMLEY home won 24 - 10
CASTLEFORD - HOWARD BIBB(502): Howe Gamble Hill
Austin: Hardisty R.Ward: DENNIS HARTLEY(503) J.Ward
Dickinson Bryant Small Walker:
Tries - Austin(2) Howe Ward Bryant Small: Goals - Hill(3):
BRAMLEY - Simpson: Mann Delaney Butterfield
Hollindrake: Wolford Hopwood: Horn Barlow Hirst
Jackson Baldwin(Walsh) Rogers:
Tries - Delaney Hopwood: Goals - Hollindrake(2):
Referee G T Schofield (Salford) Att - 3741 H.T. 11 - 5

SEASON 1966-67

Fri 23 Sep 1966 HUNSLET home won 27 - 9
CASTLEFORD - Bibb: Howe Gamble Hill Briggs: Hardisty
Hepworth: Hartley J.Ward Tucker Small Dickinson Walker:
Tries - Hardisty(3) Howe(2) Hill Small: Goals - Hill(3):
HUNSLET - Marshall: Goodman Evans
Chamberlain(Richmond) Thompson: Preece Williams:
Larkin(Jarvis) Dunn Wilson Mennell Gunney McNally:
Try - Gunney: Goals - Marshall(3):
Referee D S Brown (Preston) Att - 4697 H.T. 8 - 4

Fri 30 Sep 1966 HALIFAX home won 32 - 22
CASTLEFORD - Bibb: Briggs Gamble Bell Austin: Hardisty
Hepworth: Hartley Miller Tucker Small Walker Hill:
Tries - Briggs Bell Hardisty Miller Tucker Small:
Goals - Hill(7):
HALIFAX - James: Jones Dixon Todd Freeman: Robinson
Daley: Scroby Harrison Fogerty Ramshaw Renilson
Burnett(Mills):
Tries - Fogerty(2) James Daley: Goals - James(5):
Referee H Pearce (Leeds) Att - 5216 H.T. 22 - 4

**Sat 8 Oct 1966 HULL KINGSTON ROVERS away
lost 13 - 19**
HULL K R - Kellett: Young Burwell Elliott Blackmore:
Millward (Moore)Bunting: Fox Flanagan Tyson Holliday
Palmer Major:
Tries - Millward(2) Young: Goals - Kellett(5):
CASTLEFORD - Bedford: Appleyard Gamble Bell Austin:
Hardisty Hepworth: Hartley Dickinson Tucker Bryant
Walker Small:
Tries - Gamble Bell Bryant: Goals - Hardisty Dickinson:
Referee G Philpott (Leeds) Att - 8800 H.T. 5 - 15

**Tue 11 Oct 1966 LEEDS away draw 11 - 11
BBC 2 FLOODLIT COMPETITION ROUND 1**
LEEDS - Risman: Ratcliffe Broatch Gemmell Wriglesworth:
Watson Rollin: Barnard Astbury Chamberlain Neumann
Davies Batten: Try - Broatch: Goals - Risman(4):
CASTLEFORD - Bibb: Appleyard Gamble Bell Austin:
Hardisty Hepworth: Hartley J.Ward Tucker Bryant Small
Hill: Try - Hardisty: Goals - Hill(3) Hardisty(DG):
Referee J P Hebblethwaite (York) Att - 7102 H.T. 5 - 4

**Fri 14 Oct 1966 BRADFORD NORTHERN home
won 10 - 7**
CASTLEFORD - Bedford: Malcolm Battye Gamble Bell
Austin: Hardisty Hepworth: Hartley J.Ward
Tucker(Walker)Bryant Small Hill:
Tries - Gamble Bryant: Goals - Hill(2):
BRADFORD N. - Rhodes: Williamson Brooke(Larkin)
Kellett Kelly(Lord): Stockwell Breakespeare: Goddard
Mullins Crawshaw Bowman Fearnley Rae:
Try - Bowman: Goals - Rhodes(2):
Referee R Appleyard (Leeds) Att - 7268 H.T. 8 - 7

Sat 22 Oct 1966 YORK away won 20 - 10
YORK - Duck: Hindwell Rippon Sheehan Foster: Horner
Sullivan: Yorke Walton Kidd Hunter Walker Redfearn:
Tries - Foster Redfearn: Goals - Yorke(2):
CASTLEFORD - Bedford: Howe Gamble Willett Austin:

Edwards Hepworth(Bell): Hartley J.Ward Tucker Bryant
Small Hill(Walker):
Tries - Bryant(2) Howe Edwards: Goals - Willett(4):
Referee E Leach (St Helens) Att - 2876 H.T. 5 - 3

**Fri 28 Oct 1966 HULL KINGSTON ROVERS home
lost 9 - 15**
CASTLEFORD - Bedford: Howe Bell Willett Austin:
Edwards Hepworth: Hartley J.Ward Tucker Bryant Small
Hill(Walker): Try - Edwards: Goals - Willett(3):
HULL K R - Kellett: Young Burwell Moore Blackmore:
Millward Bunting: Fox Flanagan Tyson Holliday Foster
Major: Tries - Young(2) Major: Goals - Kellett(3):
Referee G Wilson (Dewsbury) Att - 7818 H.T. 7 - 4

Wed 2 Nov 1966 SWINTON away lost 5 - 25
SWINTON - Rhodes(R.Williams): Whitehead Fleet Buckley
Gomersall: Davies G.Williams: Halliwell Clarke Scott Rees
Speed Robinson: Tries - Buckley(2) Whitehead
G.Williams Robinson: Goals - Whitehead(5):
CASTLEFORD - Bedford: Howe Bell Willett Austin:
Edwards Hepworth: Hartley J.Ward McCartney Walker
Dickinson Lockwood: Try - Walker: Goal - Willett:
Referee J P Hebblethwaite (York) Att - 3000 H.T. 5 - 15

Sat 5 Nov 1966 DEWSBURY away won 22 - 15
DEWSBURY - Hirst: Osborne B.Firth Walker Marsh: Budge
Newall: Naylor R.Firth Coates Lowe Boocock Beevers:
Tries - Osborne Marsh R.Firth: Goals - Beevers(3):
CASTLEFORD - Edwards(Bedford): Howe Trevor Waring
Willett Austin: Hardisty Hepworth: Hartley J.Ward Walker
Bryant Small Lockwood:
Tries - Howe(3) Waring Austin Hartley: Goals - Willett(2):
Referee P Geraghty (York) Att - 2300 H.T. 14 - 10

**Tue 8 Nov 1966 WARRINGTON home won 31 - 10
BBC 2 FLOODLIT COMPETITION ROUND 2**
CASTLEFORD - Bedford(Edwards): Howe Stenton Willett
Austin: Hardisty Hepworth: Hartley Miller Walker Bryant
Small Lockwood: Tries - Austin(2) Hardisty(2) Bedford
Stenton Bryant: Goals - Willett(5):
WARRINGTON - Conroy: Aspey Leigh Pickavance Glover:
Scahill Gordon: Brindle Woolvine Brady Winslade Briggs
Clarke: Tries - Glover Briggs: Goals - Leigh(2):
Referee D T H Davies (Man'ster) Att - 4792 H.T. 13 - 7

Fri 11 Nov 1966 ST HELENS away lost 2 - 13
ST HELENS - Coslett: Vollenhoven Barrow Benyon
Pimblett: Douglas Bishop: WarLow Dagnall Watson
French Mantle Hayes(Halsall):
Tries - Pimblett Bishop Warlow: Goals - Coslett(2):
CASTLEFORD - Bedford: Howe Stenton Willett Austin:
Gamble R.Ward: Hartley J.Ward(Miller)Walker Bryant
Small Lockwood: Goal - Willett:
Referee R Appleyard (Leeds) Att - 9000 H.T. 2 - 8

Fri 18 Nov 1966 SWINTON home won 19 - 7
CASTLEFORD - Edwards: Howe Stenton Willett Austin:
Jack Gamble (Bedford) Hepworth: Hartley Dickinson
McCartney Walker Small Bell:

Tries - Howe(3) Edwards Austin: Goals - Willett(2):
SWINTON - Gowers: Whitehead Fleet Buckley Gomersall:
Rhodes Williams: Halliwell Cummings Scott Rees Simpson
Robinson: Try - Buckley: Goals - Gowers(1) (DG):
Referee T Keane (Oldham) Att - 3953 H.T. 6 - 7

Sat 26 Nov 1966 BRAMLEY away won 34 - 9
BRAMLEY - Delaney: Mann Toohey D.Sampson
Butterfield: Wolford Hopwood: Hirst Clough Horn Fisher
M.Sampson Holliday:
Try - Toohey: Goals - D.Sampson(2) Butterfield(DG):
CASTLEFORD - Edwards: Howe Stenton Willett Austin:
Hardisty Hepworth: Hartley Dickinson McCartney Small
Walker Bell: Tries - Howe(3) Willett Austin Hardisty
McCartney Small: Goals - Willett(5):
Referee J P.Hebblethwaite (York) Att - 1950 H.T. 20 - 7

Fri 2 Dec 1966 ST HELENS home won 25 - 7
CASTLEFORD - Edwards: Howe Stenton Willett Austin:
Hardisty Hepworth: Hartley Dickinson Walker Bryant
Small Bell: Tries - Howe Stenton Hardisty Hepworth
Small: Goals - Willett(5):
ST HELENS - F.Barrow: Vollenhoven A.Barrow Benyon
Killeen: Douglas Prosser: Halsall Dagnall Watson Warlow
Mantle Coslett: Try - Douglas: Goals - Killeen(1) (DG):
Referee J Manley (Warrington) Att - 6178 H.T. 11 - 5

Tue 6 Dec 1966 BARROW home won 21 - 5
BBC 2 FLOODLIT COMPETITION SEMI FINAL
CASTLEFORD - Edwards: Howe Stenton Willett Austin:
Hardisty Hepworth: Hartley Dickinson Walker Bryant
Small Bell: Tries - Stenton Austin Walker:
Goals - Willett(5) Hartley(DG):
BARROW - Tees: Burgess Challinor Dawes Wear: Brophy
Smith: Hopwood Wright Kelland Kirchen Backhouse
Delooze: Try - Delooze: Goal - Delooze:
Referee H G Hunt (Guiseley) Att - 6500 H.T. 6 - 2

Fri 9 Dec 1966 DEWSBURY home won 10 - 2
CASTLEFORD - Edwards: Howe Stenton Willett Austin:
Hardisty R.Ward: Hartley Dickinson Walker Bryant Small
Lockwood(Roy Bell):
Tries - Howe Hartley: Goals - Willett(2):
DEWSBURY - Hirst: Marsh B.Firth Walker Osborne: Budge
Newall: Naylor R.Firth Coates Lowe Cook Blakeley:
Goal - Blakeley(DG):
Referee R Appleyard (Leeds) Att - 3346 H.T. 7 - 2

Sat 17 Dec 1966 KEIGHLEY away won 26 - 2
KEIGHLEY - Jefferson: Smart Newton Thomas Wilmot:
Dickinson(S/O) Evans: Worthy Anderson Walsh Eyre
Gaines(Garbett)Aspinall: Goal - Jefferson(DG):
CASTLEFORD - Edwards: Howe Stenton Willett Austin:
GLYN JONES(504) Hepworth: Hartley Miller Walker Small
Bryant Hill(McCartney):   Tries - Hepworth(2) Howe Jones
Small McCartney: Goals - Willett(4):
Referee D S Brown (Preston) Att - 1665 H.T. 5 - 2

Tue 20 Dec 1966 SWINTON home won 7 - 2
BBC 2 FLOODLIT COMPETITION FINAL
CASTLEFORD - Edwards: Howe Stenton Willett Austin:
Hardisty Hepworth: Hartley Dickinson McCartney Bryant
Small Walker: Try - Austin: Goals - Willett Hepworth(DG):
SWINTON - Gowers: Whitehead GomersaLL Buckley
Davies: Fleet G.Williams: Halliwell Clarke Scott(Cummings)
Rees Simpson Robinson: Goal - Whitehead:
Referee J.Manley (Warrington) Att - 8986 H.T. 7 - 2

Sat 31 Dec 1966 DONCASTER home won 39 - nil
CASTLEFORD - Edwards: Howe Stenton Willett Austin:
Hardisty Hepworth: Hartley Miller Walker Bryant Small
Redfearn:
Tries - Austin(2) Bryant(2) Redfearn(2) Edwards Howe
Stenton Willett Hardisty: Goals - Hepworth(2) Willett:
DONCASTER - A.Goodyear: Arrand Waring Battye
Tomlinson: Brook Grainger (McCone):
Strawbridge(G.Goodyear) Hawksley Pell Brown Jeff Bell:
Referee J P Hebblethwaite (York) Att - 3438 H.T. 17 - nil

Sat 14 Jan 1967 HULL away won 32 - 12
HULL - Keegan: Oliver Huxley Maloney Sullivan:
Devonshire Foulkes(Doyle Davidson): Harrison McGlone
Broom O'Brien Trotter Sykes:
Tries - Sullivan Sykes: Goals - Maloney(3):
CASTLEFORD - Edwards: Howe Stenton Willett Austin:
Hardisty Hepworth: Hartley Miller Walker Bryant Small
Redfearn: Tries - Bryant(2) Howe Stenton Hardisty
Hartley: Goals - Willett(7):
Referee S Shepherd (Oldham) Att - 6100 H.T. 27 - 2

Sat 21 Jan 1967 YORK home won 16 - 11
CASTLEFORD - Edwards: Howe Stenton Willett Austin:
Jones RICHARD BROWN(505): Hartley J.Ward Walker
Bryant(S/O) Small Redfearn:
Tries - Howe(2) Stenton Small: Goals - Willett Brown(DG):
YORK - Hunter: Hindwell Rippon Sheehan Meillan: Horner
Sullivan: Kidd Walton Walker Storey Payne Redfearn(S/O):
Tries - Walker: Goals - Payne(4):
Referee H Pearce (Leeds) Att - 4281 H.T. 11 - 2

Sat 28 Jan 1967 DONCASTER away won 29 - 10
DONCASTER - Rushton: Arrand Battye Waring Tomlinson:
Brook P.Bell (Donald): M.Pell Hawkseley(Morris) Jeff
Brown Oxenham R.Bell:
Tries - Battye Brook: Goals - M.Pell(2):
CASTLEFORD - Edwards: Howe Stenton(Bibb) Baker
Austin: Hardisty Hepworth: Hartley J.Ward Walker Harris
Small Redfearn: Tries - Howe(3) Hepworth(3) Austin
Hardisty Small: Goal Harris:
Referee T Keane (Oldham) Att - 1900 H.T. 11 - 10

Sat 4 Feb 1967 LEIGH away won 10 - 8
CHALLENGE CUP ROUND 1
LEIGH - Tyrer: Tickle Lewis Collins Walsh: Briggs Grainey:
Davies Higgs Winslade Murphy Welding NcVay:
Goals - Tyrer(4):
CASTLEFORD - Edwards: Howe TONY THOMAS(506)
Small Austin: Hardisty Hepworth: Hartley J.Ward Tucker

1934-35 R.L. CHALLENGE CUP TEAM AND OFFICIALS
Payers Standing – Frank Smith Tommy Taylor Ted Sadler Donald Knowles(Res) Pat McManus
Players Seated – Bernard Cunniffe George Lewis Jim Croston Arthur Atkinson Tommy Askin Harold Haley Jim Crossley
Players Kneeling – Lesley Adams Billy Davies Inset Eric England(Res)
Officials Left to Right – Mr T Appleyard(Director) Billy Rhodes(Trainer) Mr H Robertshaw(Director) Mr
E Atkinson(Director) Mr J H Williams(Director) Mr F Briggs(Director) Mr S Armitage(Director) Mr A F Smith(Director)
Mr W Smith(Director) Mr S Bolderson(Director) Mr G Shaw(Chairman) Mr L Battye(Director)

Back row (left to right): Alan Shillito, Roy Southernwood, Barry Johnson, Kevin Beardmore, Keith England, Ian Fletcher, Neil Battye.
Middle row: Malcolm Reilly (Coach), Keith Jones, Dean Mountain, Gary Hyde, Phillip Payne, Neil Greatbach, Kevin Ward, Stuart Walker (Physio).
Front row: David Poulter (Chairman), Stuart Horton, David Plange, Tony Marchant, John Joyner (Captain), Bob Beardmore, David Roockley,
Jamie Sandy, David Sampson (Asst. Coach).

Left to right: Darryl Van de Velde (Coach), Bernadette Scatchard (Physio), Keith England, Neil Roebuck, David Nelson, Tony Smith, Graham Steadman, Dean Sampson, Paul Whitehead, Tawera Nikau, Richard Blackmore, Graeme Bradley, Lee Crooks (Captain), John Joyner, Martin Ketteridge, Grant Anderson, Graham Southernwood, Simon Middleton, St John Ellis, John Wray, Andy Clarke, Mike Ford, Stan Timmins (Trainer), Mick Morgan (Asst Coach).

1990 YORKSHIRE CUP WINNING SQUAD
Back Row – Lee Crooks Giles Boothroyd St John Ellis Neil Battye Grant Anderson David Plange Neil Roebuck
Middle Row – Daryl Van de Veld(Coach) Mick Morgan(Ass Coach) Kevin Beardmore Gary Atkins Dean Sampson
Keith England Ian Bragger Stan Timmins(Fitness Conditioner)
Front Row – Shaun Irwin Graham Steadman Paul Fletcher Gary French John Joyner Jeff Hardy Steve Larder

**LEE CROOKS LIFTS
THE 1990 YORKSHIRE CUP**

**CELEBRATING THE 1990 YORKSHIRE CUP WIN
OVER WAKEFIELD TRINITY 11 - 8**

CELEBRATING THE 1991 YORSHIRE CUP VICTORY OVER BRADFORD NORTHERN 28 - 6
Back Row - (Unknown) St John Ellis Richie Blackmore Neil Battye Shaun Irwin Tony Smith
Grant Anderson(Did not play) David Nelson Graeme Bracley Martin Ketteridge
Front Row - Keith England Graham Southernwood Dean Sampson Tawera Nikau Mike Ford
Missing Graham Steadman

**THE TEAM CELEBRATE THE 1994 REGAL TROPHY
FINAL VICTORY OVER WIGAN 33 - 2**
Back Row Tawera Nikau Simon Middleton Tony Kemp
Richard Russell Andy Hay
Richard Blackmore Tony Morrison Dean Sampson Mike
Ford Allan Agar(Football Co-Ordinator)
Front Row-John Joyner (Team Manager) Grant Anderson
Lee Crooks St John Ellis Martin Ketteridge Ian Smales

**LEE CROOKS AND MARTIN KETTERIDGE LIFT THE
1994 REGAL TROPHY**

**BRAD DAVIES AND ADRIAN VOWLES WITH 2005
NATIONAL LEAGUE TROPHY
AFTER THE VICTORY OVER WHITEHAVEN 36 - 8**

**TERRY MATTERSON CHRIS CHARLES AND ANDREW
HENDERSON WITH THE 2007 NATIONAL LEAGUE
TROPHY
AFTER THE VICTORY OVER WIDNES VIKINGS 42 - 10**

JACK & IAN FULTON PROUDLY LEADING THE TEAM OUT AT WEMBLEY IN 2014

CASTLEFORDS THREE MAN OF STEEL WINNERS

ADRIAN VOWLES
1999

RANGI CHASE
2011

DARYL CLARK
2014

R.L.C.C. Final v Huddersfield
1934-35 Won 11–8

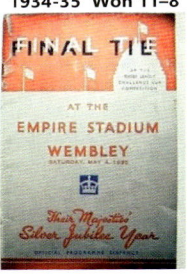

Championship Final V Salford
1938-39 Lost 6–8

Y.C. Final v Bradford
1948-49 Lost 9–18

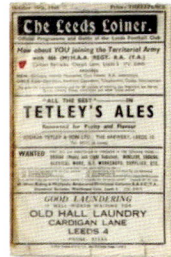

Y.C. Final v Huddersfield
1950-51 Lost 3-16

Eastern D. Final v Halifax
1963-64 Lost 12–20

Floodlit T Final v St Helens
1965-66 Won 4-0

Floodlit T Final v Swinton
1966-67 Won 7–2

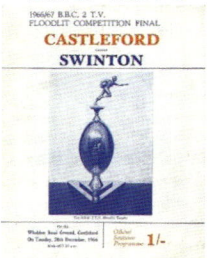

Floodlit T Final v Leigh
1967-68 Won 8–5

Y.C. Final Final v Leigh
1968-69 Lost 11-22

R.L.C.C. Final v Salford
1968-69 Won 11-6

Championsip Final v Leeds
1968-69 Lost 14-16

R.L.C.C. Final v Wigan
1669-70 Won 7-2

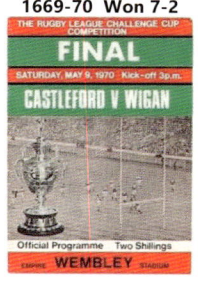

Charity Shield v St Helens
1970-71 Draw 19-19

ROLL OF HONOUR AND PROGRAMME FRONT COVERS

Y.C. Final v Hull K.R.
1971-72 Lost 7-11

Floodlit T. Final v Leigh
1976-77 Won 12-4

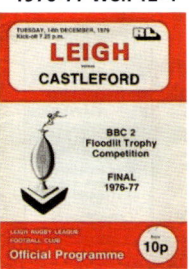

Players No6 T. Final v Blackpool B.
1976-77 Won 25-15

Y.C. Final v Featherstone R
1977-78 Won 17-7

Y.C. Final v Bradford N
1981-82 Won 10-5

Y.C. Final v Hull
1983-84 lost 2-13

Premiership Final v Hull K,R.
1983-84 Lost 10-18

Y.C. Final v Hull K.R.
1985-86 Lost 18-22

R.L.C.C. Final v Hull K.R.
1985-86 Won 15-14

C.W. Final v Halifax
1986-87 Lost 8-9

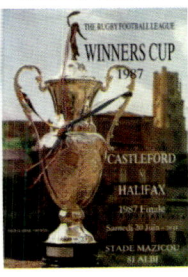

Y.C. Final v Hull F.C.
1986-87 Won 31-24

Y.C. Final v Bradford N.
1987-88 Draw 12-12

ROLL OF HONOUR AND PROGRAMME FRONT COVERS

Y.C. Final Replay v Bradford N.
1987-88 Lost 2-11

Y.C. Final v Leeds
1988-89 lost 12-33

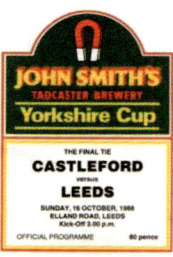

Y.C. Final v Wakefield T.
1990-91 Won 11-8

Y.C. Final v Bradford N.
1991-92 Won 28-6

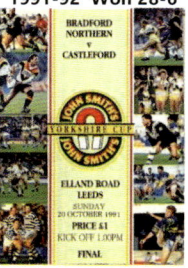

R.L.C.C. Final v Wigan
1991-92 Lost 12-28

Regal T.Final v Wigan
1993-94 Won 33-2

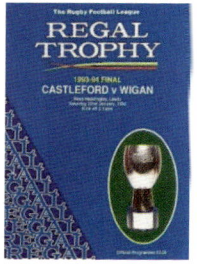

Premiership Final v Wigan
1993-94 Lost 20-24

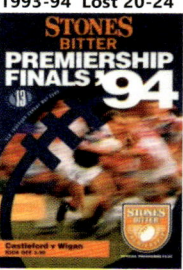

N.L Final v Whitehaven
2005 Won 36-8

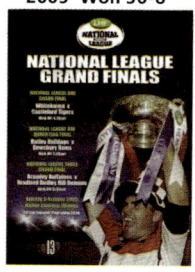

N.L Final v Widnes V.
2007 Won 42 - 10

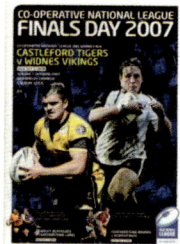

R.L.C.C Final v Leeds R.
2014 Lost 10-23

Yorkshire League Winners
1932-33, 1938-39, 1964-65.

Most Career Appearances   John Joyner   613
Most Career Tries   Alan Hardisty 206
Most Career Goals   Albert Lunn   875
Most Career Points   Albert Lunn   1870

SEASON 1966-67

Harris(Bibb) Dickinson Walker:
Tries - Austin Hepworth: Goals - Harris Hardisty(DG):
Referee G Wilson (Dewsbury) Att - 10000 H.T. 2 - 6

Sat 11 Feb 1967 LEEDS home won 19 - 15
CASTLEFORD - Bibb: Howe Thomas Willett Austin: Jones
Hepworth: Hartley J.Ward Dickinson Bryant Small Walker:
Tries - Howe(2) Thomas Willett Small:
Goals - Willett Hartley:
LEEDS - Risman: Cowan Hynes Gemmell Atkinson:
Broatch Rollin: Clark Lockwood Eyre Neumann Davies
Batten(Poole):
Tries - Risman Gemmell Poole: Goals - Risman(3):
Referee J Manley (Warrington) Att - 9156 H.T. 8 - 2

**Sat 25 Feb 1967 HULL KINGSTON ROVERS away
draw 9 - 9   CHALLENGE CUP ROUND 2**
HULL K R - Kellett: Young Burwell Moore Blackmore:
Millward Elliott: Fox Flanagan Tyson Holliday Major
Foster: Try - Blackmore: Goals - Kellett(3):
CASTLEFORD - Edwards: Howe Thomas Willett Austin:
Hardisty Hepworth: Hartley J.Ward Taylor Bryant Small
Walker: Try - Taylor: Goals - Willett Hardisty(DG2):
Referee R L Thomas (Oldham) Att - 15830 H.T. nil - 7

**Wed 1 Mar 1967 HULL KINGSTON ROVERS home
won 13 - 6 CHALLENGE CUP ROUND 2 REPLAY**
CASTLEFORD - Edwards: Howe Thomas Willett Austin:
Hardisty Hepworth: Hartley J.Ward Taylor(Dickinson)
Bryant Small Walker:
Tries - Austin Hardisty Small: Goals - Willett(2):
HULL K R - Kellett: Young Burwell Moore Blackmore:
Millward Elliott: Fox Flanagan Tyson Holliday Major
Foster: Goals - Kellett(2) Foster(DG):
Referee R.L.Thomas (Oldham) Att - 22582 H.T. 2 - 4

After a 9 – 9 draw in the second round tie against
Hull K R away. The replay was fixed for the following
Wednesday with a 4.00 pm kick off. Although we had
floodlights Hull K R refused to play under them
claiming they had lost a match in the previous season
under lights when the referee awarded their
opponents a try when the touchdown had occurred
after the ball had rebounded back into play off the
advertising hoarding. With factories, offices and
schools closing early to allow supporters to get to the
game the euphoria also inspired many "non regulars"
to attend. This resulted in a very large crowd
descending on the ground at the same time close to
kick off. When it became apparent that crowds could
not gain entry before the scheduled start attempts
were made to delay the kick off. Unfortunately Hull K
R would not co-operate and sent the team out onto
the field. The crowd inside the ground cheered and
those outside the ground forced their entry any way
they could. This resulted in perimeter fences broken
down an official attendance of 22,582 an unofficial
attendance of several thousand more witnessed a
terrific game of rugby and a Castleford victory 13 –6.

The Crowd Breaking in
(Picture from -The Grounds of Rugby League published in
1991 by Trevor Delaney)

The following Saturday we had three representative
in the Great Britain team which played France at
Wigan Alan Hardisty, Keith Hepworth and Bill Bryant
(with the 'Cas' faithful claiming we should have had a
fourth in Keith Howe), However, the clamour of the
faithful were cruelly silenced when disastrously all
three sustained injuries, the worst being Bill Bryant
with a broken leg.

Wed 8 Mar 1967 HULL home lost 3 - 10
CASTLEFORD - Edwards: Howe Thomas Willett Austin:
Jones R.Ward: Hartley Miller Tucker Small
Dickinson(R.Brown) Walker(JOHN BELL(507)):   Try - Howe:
HULL - Keegan: Oliver Doyle-Davidson Maloney Lunn:
Devonshire Foulkes : Pearson McGlone Broom Stocks
Edson Sykes: Tries - Keegan Foulkes:
Goals - Maloney(2)   Att - 7600 H.T. nil - 5
Referee B Baker (Wigan)

**Sat 18 Mar 1867 FEATHERSTONE ROVERS away
lost 7 - 8 CHALLENGE CUP ROUND 3**
FEATHERSTONE R - Wrigglesworth: Thomas Cotton
Jordan Greatorex: Smith Dooler: Tonks(Taylor) Harris
Dixon Morgan Thompson Smales:
Tries - Smith Dooler: Goal - Smales
CASTLEFORD - Edwards: Howe Thomas Willett
Austin(Brown): Hardisty R.Ward: Hartley J.Ward Taylor
Small Dickinson Walker:
Try - Hardisty: Goals - Willett(2):
Referee J Manley (Warrington) Att - 15000 H.T. 2 - 5

Only Alan Hardisty had recovered sufficiently to play
in the third round of the Challenge Cup at
Featherstone . With Rovers leading 8 – 4 near the end
of the game Alan broke through the defence but was
chased all the way to the line by Gary Jordan who
forced him out wide. We could not add the
conversion and we lost the game 8 – 7. Featherstone
progressed to the final beating Barrow 17 – 12 to lift
the Cup.

SEASON 1966-67

Mon 20 Mar 1967 HALIFAX away lost 10 - 25
HALIFAX - Cooper: Goodchild Burnett Dixon Freeman: Robinson Pycroft: Scroby Foye Kelley Ramshaw Fearnley Renilson: Tries - Dixon Freeman Robinson Scroby Renilson: Goals - Cooper(5):
CASTLEFORD - Bibb: Howe Hill Willett Appleyard: Hardisty Brown: Hartley J.Ward Taylor Small(Redfearn) Walton Walker: Tries - Hardisty(2): Goals - Hill(2):
Referee T Keane (Oldham) Att - 4209 H.T. 5 - 20

Wed 22 Mar 1967 BRADFORD NORTHERN away lost 8 - 14
BRADFORD N - Rhodes: Jones Wriglesworth Kellett Lord: Stockwell Breakspeare(Diabara): Roberts Mullins Goddard Taylor Clawson Rae:
Tries - Wriglesworth(2) Stockwell Rae: Goal - Clawson:
CASTLEFORD - Hill: Howe Lockwood Willett Appleyard: R.Ward Brown: Hartley J.Ward Taylor Redfearn Walton Walker: Tries - Appleyard Walker: Goal - Hill:
Referee R Appleyard (Leeds) Att - 7893 H.T. 5 - 5

Sat 25 Mar 1967 WAKEFIELD TRINITY away lost 10 - 35
WAKEFIELD T - Cooper: Hirst Brooke Fox Coetzer: Battye Poynton: Bath Prior Campbell Haigh Clarkson Hawley:
Tries - Hirst Fox Battye Poynton Prior Campbell Haigh: Goals Fox(7):
CASTLEFORD - Hill: Howe Lockwood Willett Appleyard: Hardisty Brown: Hartley Miller Dickinson JOSEPH KIRKBRIGHT(508)(J.Ward) Redfearn Walker:
Tries - Howe(2): Goals - Hill(2):
Referee E Lawrinson (Warr'ton) Att - 7607 H.T. nil - 19

Mon 27 Mar 1967 FEATHERSTONE ROVERS away lost 13 - 15
FEATHERSTONE R - Darbyshire: Hartley Cotton(Greatorex)Newlove Jordan: Nash Watts: Tonks Harris Dixon Morgan Thompson(Kosanovic) Lyons:
Try - Morgan: Goals - Darbyshire(3) Dixon(2DG) Harris(DG):
CASTLEFORD - Edwards(Redfearn): Howe Bibb Hill Appleyard: Hardisty Brown(R.Ward): Hartley Miller John Taylor Walton J.Ward Walker:
Try - Hardisty: Goals - Hill(5):
Referee J P Hebblethwaite (York) Att - 4695 H.T. 4 - 11

Tue 28 Mar 1967 BATLEY home won 10 - 6
CASTLEFORD - Bibb: Briggs Hill Lockwood Appleyard: Jones R.Ward: Hartley Miller Walker Walton Dickinson Redfearn: Tries - Jones Ward: Goals - Hill(2):
BATLEY - Scott: Rayner Hepworth Ward Naidole: Oldroyd Butterfield: Balow Whitehead Smith Saville Johnson Cullen: Tries - Ward Naidole:
Referee W H Thompson (Hud'field) Att - 2997 H.T. 5 - 3

Fri 31 Mar 1967 HUNSLET away lost 7 - 12
HUNSLET - Marshall: Goodman Evans Chamberlain Brown: Lee Williams: Croft Dunn Wilson Jarvis Gunney Halligan: Tries - Goodman Gunney: Goals - Marshall(3):
CASTLEFORD - Bedford: Briggs Hill Lockwood James

Smith: Thomas R.Ward: Hartley J.Ward Dickinson Small Walton(Redfearn) Walker: Try - Walker: Goals - Hill(2):
Referee P Geraghty (York) Att - 1650 H.T. 5 - 10

Mon 3 Apr 1967 FEATHERSTONE ROVERS home won 16 - 10
CASTLEFORD - Hill: Howe Thomas DEREK FOSTER(509) Briggs: Jones R.Ward: Walton(Hartley) Miller Walker Small Dickinson J.Ward:
Tries - Briggs Walker: Goals - Hill(4) (DG):
FEATHERSTONE R - Wrigglesworth: Thomas Cotton Jordan Hartley: Nash Dooler: Tonks Kosanovic Dixon Taylor Morgan Smales: Goals - Smales(4) Dooler(DG):
Referee E Lawrinson (Warrington) Att - 5493 H.T. 14 - 6

Wed 5 Apr 1967 KEIGHLEY home lost 6 - 8
CASTLEFORD - Hill: Howe Thomas Lockwood Briggs: Hardisty R.Ward: Hartley Miller Walker Small Dickinson J.Ward: Goals - Hill(2) Hardisty(DG):
KEIGHLEY - Jefferson: Newton Thomas Dickinson Moulding: Hare Evans: Worthy Pell Crewdson Eyre Aspinall Render:
Tries - Jefferson Render: Goal - Jefferson:
Referee H Pearce (Leeds) Att - 3838 H.T. 4 - 5

Fri 14 Apr 1967 HULL home won 21 - 7
CHAMPIONSHIP ROUND 1
CASTLEFORD - Bedford: Howe Hill Foster Briggs: Hardisty R.Ward(Jones): Hartley Dickinson Walker Small Redfearn J.Ward:
Tries - Briggs(2) Hardisty: Goals - Hill(5) Hardisty(DG):
HULL - Keegan: Oliver Doyle-Davidson Maloney Sullivan: Devonshire Foulkes: Harrison McGlone Broom Neale O'Brien Stocks: Try - Devonshire: Goals - Maloney(2):
Referee D T H Davies (Man'ster) Att - 6345 H.T. 17 - 7

Sat 22 Apr 1967 LEEDS away won 13 - 9
CHAMPIONSHIP ROUND 2
LEEDS - Risman: Smith Hynes Gemmell Atkinson: Broatch Seabourne: Joyce Crosby Chamberlain Sykes Hick Batten:
Try - Broatch: Goals - Risman(2) Seabourne(DG):
CASTLEFORD - Hill: Howe Thomas Foster Briggs: Hardisty Hepworth: Hartley Miller Tucker(Harris) Small Redfearn J.Ward: Tries - Howe Hardisty Hepworth: Goals - Hill(2):
Referee D T H Davies (Man'ster) Att - 10518 H.T. 5 - 7

Sat 29 Apr 1967 ST HELENS away lost 3 - 14
CHAMPIONSHIP SEMI FINAL
ST HELENS - Barrow: Vollenhoven Houghton Smith Killeen: Douglas Bishop: Warlow Sayer Watson French Mantle Robinson(Hogan):
Tries - Vollenhoven Smith: Goals - Killeen(4):
CASTLEFORD - Edwards: Howe Thomas Hill Briggs: Hardisty Hepworth: Hartley J.Ward Tucker Small Harris Redfearn: Try - Thomas:
Referee F Lindop (Wakefield) Att - 15000 H.T. nil - 9

SEASON 1966-67

Mon 8 May 1967 HULL KINGSTON ROVERS away lost 25 – 28 CYRIL KELLETT and DAVE ELLIOTT BENEFIT MATCH FRIENDLY

HULL K.R. - Kellett: Young Burwell Moore Wainwright: Millward Elliott(Bunting: Fox Flanagan Tyson Holliday Major(Lowe) Foster:
Tries - Moore(4) Young Elliott Flanagan Burwell: Goals - Kellett Millward:
CASTLEFORD - Bedford: Briggs Hill R.Ward(Cooper) Smith: Hardisty Hepworth: Hartley Miller Dickinson Small(Taylor) Redfearn Reilly:
Tries - Hardisty(3) Small Taylor: Goals - Hill(4) Taylor:
Referee H.Cook (Beverley) Att - 5000 H.T.

Mon 15 May 1967 HULL away won 28 - 24 CYRIL SYKES BENEFIT MATCH FRIENDLY

HULL - Keegan: Oliver Doyle-Davidson Maloney Devonshire: Davidson(Brown) Foulkes: Harrison Jukes Edson(McLane) Neil O'Brien Sykes:
Tries - Oliver(2) Sykes(2) Maloney Devonshire: Goals - Maloney(2)Keegan:
CASTLEFORD - Edwards: Briggs Hill Redfearn Smith: Hardisty Hepworth (A.N.Other): Hartley Dickinson J.Ward Small Taylor Reilly(Miller):
Tries - Hardisty(2) Dickinson(2) Redfearn Smith A.N.Other Taylor: Goals - Hill(2):
Referee H.Cook (Beverley) Att - H.T.

Jack Austin
D. No 498
1966-67 to 1969-70

David Tucker
D. No 499
1966-67 to 1968-69

Howard Eibb
D. No 502
1966-67 to 1969-70

Dennis Hartley
D. No 503
1966-67 t o 1974-75

Glyn Jones
D. No 504
1966-67 to 1971-72

Richard (Dickie) Brown
D. No 505
1966-67 to 1970-71

Tony Thomas
D. No 506
1966-67 tc 1970-71

Derek Foster
D. No 509
1966-67 to1973-74

SEASON 1966-67

D.N	PLAYER		DEBUT	L MATCH	APP	SUB	T.AP	TRI'S	G'LS	D.G	P'TS
426	BRYANT	WILLIAM			23	0	23	13	0	0	39
433	HARDISTY	ALAN			30	0	30	24	1	6	86
438	SMALL	PETER			44	0	44	15	0	0	45
442	HEPWORTH	KEITH			32	0	32	11	2	1	39
453	WARD	JOHNNY			28	2	30	2	0	0	6
455	WALKER	JOHN			40	3	43	6	0	0	18
458	EDWARDS	DEREK			24	1	25	4	0	0	12
462	BATTYE	MALCOLM		14/10/1966	1	0	1	0	0	0	0
465	GAMBLE	JACK		18/11/1966	17	0	17	3	0	0	9
469	WALTON	DOUGLAS			13	0	13	0	0	0	0
473	HOWE	KEITH			42	1	43	34	0	0	102
474	BEDFORD	TREVOR			12	2	14	1	0	0	3
475	BAKER	DENNIS			2	0	2	0	0	0	0
476	BELL	ROY		09/12/1966	10	2	12	2	0	0	6
478	McCARTNEY	HAROLD			5	3	8	2	0	0	6
479	DICKINSON	CLIVE			28	2	30	2	1	0	8
480	WARD	ROY			14	1	15	1	0	0	3
481	APPLEYARD	DAVID			7	0	7	1	0	0	3
482	WARING	TREVOR		05/11/1966	1	0	1	1	0	0	3
486	WILLETT	RONALD			33	0	33	4	85	0	182
487	TAYLOR	JOHN		27/03/1967	11	0	11	2	0	0	6
488	HILL	RONALD			27	0	27	1	51	1	107
490	HARRIS	DENNIS			3	1	4	0	2	0	4
492	STENTON	IAN			13	0	13	6	0	0	18
493	BRIGGS	TREVOR			9	0	9	4	0	0	12
494	REDFEARN	MICHAEL			10	3	13	2	0	0	6
495	MILLER	TONY			12	2	14	1	0	0	3
496	HINCHCLIFFE	JOHN		02/09/1966	2	0	2	0	0	0	0
497	LOCKWOOD	BRIAN			13	0	13	0	0	0	0
498	AUSTIN	JACK	15/08/1966		37	0	37	17	0	0	51
499	TUCKER	DAVID	15/08/1966		18	0	18	1	0	0	3
500	WADDLE	PETER	29/08/1966		1	0	1	0	0	0	0
501	SMITH	JAMES	02/09/1966	31/03/1967	2	0	2	0	0	0	0
502	BIBB	HOWARD	16/09/1966		8	2	10	0	0	0	0
503	HARTLEY	DENNIS	16/09/1966		39	1	40	3	1	1	13
504	JONES	GLYN	17/12/1966		6	1	7	2	0	0	6
505	BROWN	RICHARD	21/01/1967		5	2	7	0	0	1	2
506	THOMAS	TONY	04/02/1967		11	0	11	2	0	0	6
507	BELL	JOHN	08/03/1967	08/03/1967	0	1	1	0	0	0	0
508	KIRKBRIGHT	JOSEPH	25/03/1967		1	0	1	0	0	0	0
509	FOSTER	DEREK	03/04/1967		3	0	3	0	0	0	0
	41		**12**	**8**	**637**	**30**	**667**	**167**	**143**	**10**	**807**

COMPETITION		P	W	D	L	FOR	AGT
LEAGUE ONE D	POSITION 8 OF 30	34	21	0	13	560	409
F. TROPHY		6	5	1	0	125	57
YORK'S CUP		2	1	0	1	46	20
RL CUP		4	2	1	1	39	31
CHAMPIONSHIP		3	2	0	1	37	30
PLAYERS RECORDS		**49**	**31**	**2**	**16**	**807**	**547**

We again achieved success in the BBC2 Floodlit Competition, beating Swinton in the final 7–2 and retaining the trophy for the second successive year. Or to be precise we had won a second successive trophy having been allowed to keep the original trophy the previous season.

Among the debutantes were two players purchased from other clubs who would play a significant part in the future success of the Club - Dennis Hartley from Hunslet and Tony Thomas from Wakefield Trinity.

SEASON 1967-68

Fri 11 Aug 1967 BRADFORD NORTHERN home lost 5 – 35 GIDEON SHAW MEMORIAL TROPHY FRIENDLY
CASTLEFORD - Bibb: Howe Briggs(Appleyard) Foster Austin: R.Ward Brown: Hartley Miller Fox(Lockwood) Small Bryant(Walker) Walton(Reilly):
Try - Foster: Goal - Small:
BRADFORD N - Rhodes: Jones Wrigglesworth Kellett(Larkin) Lord: Stockwell Diabara: Roberts Fisher Goddard Taylor Clawson Rae: Tries - Wrigglesworth(3) Jones Fisher Taylor Rae: Goals - Clawson(7):
Referee R Appleyard (Leeds) Att - 4719 H.T. 5 - 17

Sat 19 Aug 1967 WAKEFIELD TRINITY away lost 11 - 31
WAKEFIELD T - Cooper: Hirst Brooke N.Fox Coetzer: Poynton D.Fox: Bath Shepherd Steel Clarkson Haigh Hawley: Tries - N.Fox(2) Clarkson(2) Coetzer Steel Hawley: Goals - N.Fox(5):
CASTLEFORD - Bedford: Howe Hill Baker Austin: Edwards Roy Ward (Lockwood): Hartley Miller FRANK FOX(510) Bryant Small Walton:
Tries - Bedford Austin Fox: Goal - Hill:
Referee E Clay (Rothwell) Att - 6720 H.T. nil - 13

Mon 21 Aug 1967 HULL KINGSTON ROVERS home won 20 - 19
CASTLEFORD - Bedford: Howe Hill Dennis Baker(Lockwood) Austin: Edwards Hepworth(S/O): Fox Miller Walker Small Bryant Walton (Hartley):
Tries - Howe Hill Edwards Bryant: Goals - Hill(4):
HULL K.R - Wainwright: Young Burwell Moore Ballantyne: Millward Bunting: Holliday Flanagan Tayloe Lowe Major Foster: Tries - Wainwright Moore Millward: Goals - Millward(4) Holliday(DG):
Referee G Wilson (Dewsbury) Att - 6500 H.T. 7 - 12

Fri 25 Aug 1967 SALFORD home won 21 - 14
CASTLEFORD - Bedford: Howe Stenton Hill Austin: Edwards Hepworth: Hartley Ward Fox Bryant Small Walker:
Tries - Small(2) Howe Hill Bryant: Goals - Hill(3):
SALFORD - Evans: Sims Southward Bettinson Murphy: Hesketh Brennan: Collier Burdell Bott Whitehead Henighan Hughes: Tries - Southward Brennan: Goals - Murphy(4): Referee T Keane (Oldham) Att - 6156 H.T. 6 - 7

Mon 28 Aug 1967 FEATHERSTONE ROVERS away won 18 - 9
FEATHERSTONE R - Wrigglesworth: Thomas Greatorex Jordan Hartley: Smith Watts: Tonks Harris Nicholson Morgan Thompson Smales(Forsythe):
Tries - Wrigglesworth Morgan Smales:
CASTLEFORD - Bedford: Howe(Briggs)Stenton Hill Austin: Edwards Hepworth: Hartley J.Ward Fox Small Bryant Lockwood:
Tries - Howe Stenton Bryant Lockwood: Goals - Hill(3):
Referee H Pearce (Leeds) Att - 6700 H.T. 5 - 10

Fri 1 Sept 1967 HULL home lost 7 - 13 YORKSHIRE CUP ROUND 1
CASTLEFORD - Bedford: Howe Stenton Willett Austin:
Edwards Hepworth: Hartley Brown Fox Bryant(S/O)Redfearn Hill: Try - Stenton: Goals - Willett(2):
HULL - Keegan: Oliver Doyle-Davidson Maloney Stocks: Devonshire Davidson: Harrison McGlone Neale Edson Broom Sykes:
Tries - Oliver(2) Davidson: Goals - Maloney Broom(DG):
Referee R L Thomas (Oldham) Att - 7592 H.T. 5 - 2

Wed 6 Sept 1967 HUDDERSFIELD home lost 2 - 5
CASTLEFORD - Edwards: Howe Stenton Thomas Austin: Hardisty Hepworth (Bedford): Hartley Brown Fox Bryant Harold McCartney Hill: Goal - Hill:
HUDDERSFIELD - Wallace: Holland Haywood Longstaffe Booth: Calvert (Russell) Loxton: Van Bellen Close Davies Valentine Bloomfield Tomlinson   Try - Holland: Goal Davies:
Referee G Philpott (Leeds) Att - 5070 H.T. 2 - nil

Fri 15 Sept 1967 SALFORD away won 19 - 14
SALFORD - Evans: Jackson Bettinson Critchley(Hill) Sims: Hesketh Brennan: Collier Burdell Ogden Bott Smethurst(Breen) Whitehead: Tries - Collier(2) Ogden Breen: Goal - Sims:
CASTLEFORD - Edwards: Howe Stenton Thomas Austin: Hardisty Brown: Hartley Miller Fox JOHN McKALROY(511) Redfearn Hill:
Tries - Hardisty(2) Thomas: Goals - Hill(4) Hardisty(DG):
Referee R Appleyard (Leeds) Att - 6500 H.T. 5 - 3

Fri 22 Sept 1967 LEEDS home lost 8 - 25
CASTLEFORD - Edwards: Howe Stenton Foster Austin: Thomas Hepworth: Hartley J.Ward Fox McKalroy(Miller) Small Redfearn: Tries - Austin Ward: Goal - Redfearn:
LEEDS - Risman: Langley Hynes Gemmell(Watson)Hick: Shoebottom Rollin: Clark Lockwood K.Eyre Chamberlain Barnard Joyce: Tries - Hick(2) Hynes Gemmell Chamberlain: Goals - Risman(5):
Referee P Geraghty (York) Att - 7600 H.T. nil - 15

Sat 30 Sept 1967 HUNSLET away lost 8 - 10
HUNSLET - Marshall: Hurl Evans Chamberlain Thompson: Lee Williams: Bancroft Dunn Larkin Baldwinson Jarvis White: Tries - Thompson Baldwinson: Goals - Marshall Dunn(DG):
CASTLEFORD - Edwards: Appleyard Hill Thomas MALCOLM REILLY(512) Austin: Thomas Hepworth: Hartley Ward Fox Bryant(McKalroy) Small Walker: Tries - Reilly Walker: Goal - Hill:
Referee H Hunt (Guiseley) Att 2300 H.T. 5 - 7

Sat 7 Oct 1967 HULL home won 28 - 5
CASTLEFORD - Edwards: Appleyard Stenton Reilly Austin: Thomas Hepworth: Hartley Ward Bryant Small Walker Redfearn: Tries - Appleyard(3) Reilly(2) Ward:
Goals - Redfearn(4) Hepworth(DG):
HULL - Keegan: Oliver Doyle-Davidson Maloney Stocks: Devonshire Davidson(Barnwell): Harrison McGlone Broom Edson Macklin Trotter: Try - Oliver: Goal - Maloney:
Referee D T H Davies (Manchester) Att 3229 H.T. 15 - 3

SEASON 1967-68

Fri 13 Oct 1967 BRAMLEY home lost 5 - 20
CASTLEFORD - Edwards: Appleyard Stenton Reilly Briggs:
Thomas Hepworth: Fox Dickinson Bryant Small Walker
Redfearn: Try - Stenton: Goal - Redfearn:
BRAMLEY - Hollindrake: Mann Delaney D.Sampson
Greenwood: Wolford Hopwood: Horn Barlow Jackson
Bastion Ashton M.Sampson: Tries - Hollindrake Delaney
Horn M.Sampson: Goals - Hollindrake(4):
Referee R Jackson (Halifax) Att - 3625 H.T. 2 - 15

Tue 17 Oct 1967 KEIGHLEY home won 18 - 7
BBC 2 FLOODLIT COMPETITION ROUND 1
CASTLEFORD - Edwards: Appleyard Thomas Hill Austin:
Jones Hepworth(Waddle): Hartley Dickinson Walton Bryant
Small Reilly:
Tries - Appleyard Thomas Austin Small: Goals - Hill(3):
KEIGHLEY - Hare: Moulding Dickinson Thomas O'Brien:
Newton Hartley: Pollard(Garbutt) Feather(Walker)
Hardcastle Aspinall Gaines Palmer:
Try - Thomas: Goals - Hartley(2):
Referee R Appleyard (Leeds) Att - 1170 H.T. 3 - 7

Fri 20 Oct 1967 WARRINGTON away won 17 - 11
WARRINGTON - Affleck: Coupe Cannon Pickavance
Hutchinson: Melling Owen: Ashcroft Harrison Brady Parr
Briggs Clark: Try - Melling: Goals - Affleck(4):
CASTLEFORD - Hill: Appleyard Thomas Peter Waddle
Austin: Jones DAVID(Danny)HARGRAVE(513): Hartley
Dickinson Walton Bryant Small Redfearn:
Tries - Austin(2) Small: Goals - Hill(3) Redfearn(DG):
Referee F Lindop (Wakefield) Att - 5626 H.T. 3 - 7

Fri 27 Oct 1967 YORK home won 22 - 5
CASTLEFORD - Edwards: Appleyard Hill Thomas Austin:
Hepworth Hargrave: Hartley Dickinson Walton Bryant
Redfearn Reilly: Tries - Appleyard Austin Hepworth Reilly:
Goals - Hill(5):
YORK - Kendle: Hindwell Sheehan Rippon Rothwell: Horner
Sullivan: Kidd K.Hunter Deighton Storey Walker G.Hunter:
Try - Storey: Goal - Kendle:
Referee H Pearce (Leeds) Att - 2075 H.T. 7 - 5

Sat 4 Nov 1967 DEWSBURY away won 13 - 5
DEWSBURY - Edwards: Osborne Newall Whincup Walker:
Budge Bates(Hayman): Naylor Stephenson Taylor
Lowe(Robinson) Cook Blakeley: Try - Walker: Goal - Lowe:
CASTLEFORD - Bedford: Briggs Thomas Hill Austin: Edwards
Hepworth: Hartley Dickinson Walton Bryant Redfearn Reilly:
Tries - Thomas Edwards Redfearn: Goals - Hill(2):
Referee T A Ryan (Wigan) Att - 1800 H.T. 5 - 2

Thu 9 Nov 1967 AUSTRALIA won 22 - 3
CASTLEFORD - Hill: Briggs Thomas Harris Austin: Edwards
Hepworth: Hartley Ward Walton Bryant Redfearn Reilly:
Tries - Edwards(2) Ward(2) Hepworth Bryant: Goals -
Hill(2):
AUSTRALIA - Langlands: Irvine Saddler Moore Hannigan:
Branson Junee: Sattler Walters Manteit Thomson Goldspink
Lynch: Try - Manteit:
Referee G Philpott (Leeds) Att - 5738 H.T. 14 - nil

Sat 11 Nov 1967 SWINTON away lost 6 - 7
SWINTON - Whitehead: Stopford Gomersall Buckley
Williams: Fleet Gowers: Goddard Cummings Simpson Rees
Hutton Robinson: Try - Simpson: Goals - Whitehead(2):
CASTLEFORD - Bedford: Briggs(Appleyard) Harris Hill
Austin: Thomas Hargrave: Hartley Ward Walton
McKalroy(Dickinson) Redfearn Reilly: Goals - Hill(2) (DG):
Referee P Geraghty (York) Att - 2500 H.T. 2 - 7

Fri 17 Nov 1967 WARRINGTON home won 26 - 15
CASTLEFORD - Bedford: Appleyard(Harris) Hill Thomas
Austin: Edwards Hepworth: Hartley Ward Walton Bryant
Redfearn Reilly:
Tries - Reilly(2) Appleyard Austin Bryant Redfearn:
Goals - Hill(2) (DG) Hepworth(DG):
WARRINGTON - Conroy: Coupe Melling Allen
Glover(Scahill): Harvey Gordon: Ashcroft Carrington Price
Briggs Cotton Clarke(Churm):
Tries - Coupe(2) Allen: Goals - Allen(2) Melling(DG):
Referee G T Schofield (Salford) Att - 4587 H.T. 11 - 11

Sat 25 Nov 1967 HALIFAX away draw 2 - 2
HALIFAX - James: Goodchild Jones Dixon Gamble:
Robinson Baker: Scroby Anderson Crawshaw Mills Fearnley
Renilson: Goal - James:
CASTLEFORD - Stenton: Harris Hill Thomas(Willett) Austin:
Edwards Hepworth: Hartley Ward Walton Bryant Redfearn
Reilly: Goal - Hill:
Referee R T Thomas (Oldham) Att - 2969 H.T. nil - nil

Tue 28 Nov 1967 LEEDS home won 12 - 9
BBC 2 FLOODLIT COMPETITION ROUND 2
CASTLEFORD - Stenton: Harris Hill Willett Austin: Edwards
Hepworth: Hartley Ward(Dickinson) Walton Bryant
Redfearn Reilly: Tries - Harris Willett: Goals - Willett(2)
Hepworth(DG):
LEEDS - Dewhirst: Cowan Hynes Langley Atkinson:
Shoebottom Seabourne: Clark Coverley K.Eyre(Sunderland)
Fozzard A.Eyre Batten: Try - Langley: Goals - Dewhirst(2)
Seabourne:
Referee E Lawrinson (Warrington) Att - 6357 H.T. 7 - 2

Fri 1 Dec 1967 KEIGHLEY home won 15 - 6
CASTLEFORD - Bedford: Harris Stenton Willett Austin:
Edwards Hepworth: Hartley Dickinson Walton Fox(John
Walker) Redfearn Reilly: Tries - Harris Willett Hartley:
Goals - Willett(2) Redfearn(DG):
KEIGHLEY - Rogers: O'Brien Dickinson Roberts Moulding:
Hartley Evans: Worthy Pell Crewdson Hardcastle Wilson
Palmer: Goals - Hartley(3):
Referee E Clay (Rothwell) Att - 2302 H.T. 10 - 2

Tue 12 Dec 1967 WARRINGTON   won 14 - 2
**BBC 2 FLOODLIT COMPETITION SEMI-FINAL - AT
HEADINGLEY LEEDS**
CASTLEFORD - Stenton: Harris Thomas Willett Austin:
Edwards Hepworth: Hartley Ward Walton Bryant Redfearn
Reilly: Tries - Harris(2) Edwards Bryant: Goal - Willett:
WARRINGTON - Conroy: Coupe Melling Allen Glover:
Scahill(Harvey)Gordon: Ashcroft Carrington Price Briggs

230

SEASON 1967-68

J.Clarke(Parr) R.Clarke: Goal - Melling(DG):
Referee R L Thomas (Oldham) Att 3844 H.T. 9 - 2

Fri 15 Dec 1967 BRADFORD NORTHERN home
won 7 - 3
CASTLEFORD - Hill: Harris Thomas Willett Austin: Edwards
Hepworth: Hartley Dickinson Walton(Fox) Bryant Redfearn
Reilly: Try - Harris: Goals - Willett Redfearn(DG):
BRADFORD N. - Price: Jones Wriglesworth Thomas
Ambrum: Stockwell Diabira: Roberts Fisher Hill Ramshaw
Clawson Rae: Try - Thomas:
Referee H Pearce (Leeds) Att - 8513 H.T. 5 - nil

Sat 23 Dec 1967 HULL away lost 6 - 22
HULL - Keegan: Oliver Hancock Gemmell Sullivan:
Devonshire Davidson: Harrison McGlone Trotter Edson
Macklin Neale: Tries - Keegan Devonshire Davidson
Trotter: Goals - Davidson(4) Keegan:
CASTLEFORD - Stenton: Harris Thomas Willett Austin:
Hardisty Hepworth(Edwards): Hartley Ward Walton Bryant
Redfearn Reilly: Goals - Willett(3):
Referee G Wilson (Dewsbury) Att - 6500 H.T. 6 - 12

Sat 30 Dec 1967 SWINTON home won 20 - 15
CASTLEFORD - Edwards: Harris(Austin) Thomas Stenton
Willett: Hardisty Hepworth: Hartley Ward Walton Bryant
Redfearn Reilly: Tries - Harris Willett Hardisty Bryant:
Goals - Willett(3) Hepworth(DG):
SWINTON - Gowers: Price Fleet Gomersall Williams:
Robinson Kenny: Goddard Cummings McKay Simpson
Stephens Hutton(Bate):
Try - Fleet: Goals - Gowers(5) Kenny(DG):
Referee J Elliott (Barrow) Att - 4515 H.T. 10 - 9

Mon 1 Jan 1968 DONCASTER home won 35 - 2
CASTLEFORD - Edwards: Hill Thomas Stenton Austin:
Hardisty Hepworth: Hartley Ward(Dickinson) Walton Fox
Redfearn Reilly: Tries - Austin(3) Hill Thomas Stenton
Hardisty Ward Reilly: Goals - Hill(4):
DONCASTER - Cross(Yates): James Gafney Towle Arrand:
Brook McCone: Brannan Hawksley Jeff Tomlinson
Strawbridge Townend: Goal - Towle:
Referee J.P.Hebblethwaite (York) Att - 2523 H.T. 10 -2

Fri 6 Jan 1968 HULL KINGSTON ROVERS away
lost nil - 4
HULL K R - Cooper: Young Burwell Longstaffe Moore:
Millward C.Cooper: Holliday Flanagan Mennell Lowe(Taylor)
Foster Major: Goals - Holliday(2):
CASTLEFORD - Edwards: Hill Thomas Stenton Austin:
Hardisty Hepworth: Hartley Dickinson Walton(Tucker) Fox
Redfearn Reilly:
Referee P Geraghty (York) Att - 10850 H.T. nil - nil

Tue 16 Jan 1968 LEIGH won 8 - 5
BBC 2 FLOODLIT COMPETITION FINAL - AT
HEADINGLEY LEEDS
CASTLEFORD - Edwards: Harris Thomas Stenton Willett:
Hardisty Hepworth: Hartley Ward Walton Bryant(Dickinson)
Redfearn Reilly: Goals - Willett(4):

LEIGH - Grainey: Tickle Lewis Collins Walsh: Entwistle
A.Murphy: Whitworth Ashcroft Major Welding M.Murphy
Gilfedder Try - Tickle: Goal - Gilfedder:
Referee F Lindop (Wakefield) Att - 9716 H.T. 6 - 5

Sat 20 Jan 1968 YORK away won 40 - 19
YORK - Kendle: Rippon Sheehan Horner Simpson: Elliott
Sullivan: Kidd P.Walker Bath D.Walker Storey Payne:
Tries - Rippon(2) Sheehan Horner Storey:
Goals - Kendle(2):
CASTLEFORD - Edwards: Harris Stenton Willett Hill: Hardisty
Hepworth(Thomas): Hartley Ward Fox Dickinson Redfearn
Reilly: Tries - Harris(2) Reilly(2) Edwards Stenton Hardisty
Dickinson: Goals - Willett(8):
Referee T Keane (Oldham) Att - 1896 H.T. 20 - 8

Sat 27 Jan 1968 LEEDS away lost 5 - 16
LEEDS - Risman: Smith Hynes Langley(Brown) Atkinson:
Watson Seabourne: Clark Crosby K.Eyre Ramsey A.Eyre
Batten:
Tries - Smith(2):   Goals - Risman(3) Seabourne(2DG):
CASTLEFORD - Hill: Thomas Stenton Willett Austin: Hardisty
Edwards: Hartley Ward Fox Dickinson Redfearn(Small)
Reilly: Try - Thomas: Goal - Willett:
Referee J Elliott (Barrow) Att - 7356 H.T. 3 - 7

Sat 3 Feb 1968 B O C M (HULL) home won 39 - 6
CHALLENGE CUP ROUND 1
CASTLEFORD - Edwards: DAVID STEPHENS(514) Thomas
Stenton Willett: Hardisty Hepworth: Hartley
Ward(Dickinson) Walton Bryant Redfearn Reilly: Tries -
Hardisty(2) Edwards Stephens Thomas Stenton Willett
Hartley Reilly: Goals - Willett(6):
B O C M - Dave Robson: Kilby Oaten Atkin Pollington: Hunt
Norton: Start Ahern Don Robson Wallace Colgrave Sim:
Goals - Colgrave(2) Sim(DG):
Referee H Hurt (Guiseley) Att - 4930 H.T. 11 - 6

Mon 5 Feb 1968 HUNSLET home won 19 - 3
CASTLEFORD - Hill: Stephens Thomas Willett David
Appleyard: Jones Hepworth: Hartley Ward Walton Bryant
Small Reilly(Dickinson):   Tries - Willett(2) Appleyard
Hepworth Bryant: Goals - Willett(2):
HUNSLET - Marshall: B.Lee Hurl Richmond Thompson:
Chamberlain Abbey S.Lee: Bancroft Dunn Jarvis White
Baldwinson Walker: Try - Walker:
Referee R Jackson (Halifax) Att - 2813 H.T. 16 - nil

Fri 9 Feb 1968 HALIFAX home won 25 - 6
CASTLEFORD - Hill(Thomas): Harris Stenton Willett Austin:
Jones Hepworth: McKalroy Ward Walton Bryant Small
Lockwood: Tries - Willett Hepworth Walton Bryant Small:
Goals - Willett(5):
HALIFAX - Geidsuin: Goodchild Jones Dixon Rayner:
Robinson Baker: Scroby Kelly Crawshaw Reeves(Halmshaw)
Kirkbride Fearnley: Tries - Goodchild Dixon:
Referee R Appleyard (Leeds) Att - 5040 H.T. 16 - 3

SEASON 1967-68

Sat 17 Feb 1968 BRAMLEY away won 21 - 10
BRAMLEY - Wolford: Greenwood Dewhurst D.Sampson
Hollindrake: Bollon Hopwood: Horn Barlow Holliday
Plumstead Lock M.Sampson:
Tries - Wolford D.Sampson: Goals - Dewhurst(2):
CASTLEFORD - Stenton: Stephens Thomas Willett Harris:
Hardisty Hepworth(Edwards): Hartley Ward Walton Bryant
Small Reilly:
Tries - Bryant(3) Stephens Small: Goals - Willett(3):
Referee R L Thomas (Oldham) Att - 3000 H.T. 10 - 2

Sat 24 Feb 1968 WORKINGTON TOWN away won 7 - 2 CHALLENGE CUP ROUND 2
WORKINGTON T - Charlton: Davies Bell Crellin Sewell:
Kitchen Turnbull: Martin Moss Wilson(Eve) Smith McFarlane
Pattinson: Goal - Crellin:
CASTLEFORD - Edwards: Stephens Stenton Willett Harris:
Hardisty Hepworth: Hartley Ward Walton Bryant Small
Reilly: Try - Hartley: Goals - Willett Hardisty(DG):
Referee T Keane (Oldham) Att - 6900 H.T. nil - 2

Fri 1 Mar 1968 HUDDERSFIELD away lost 5 - 14
HUDDERSFIELD - Rhodes: Major Ford Wallace Senior:
Haywood Brakespeare: Hepplestone Close Van Bellin
Valentine Dobson Redfearn:
Tries - Major Van Bellen: Goals - Rhodes(4):
CASTLEFORD - Stenton: Stephens Thomas Willett Harris:
Hardisty (Austin) Lockwood: Hartley Ward Walton Bryant
Small Reilly: Try - Small: Goal - Willett:
Referee G Philpott (Leeds) Att - 5094 H.T. nil - 9

Sat 9 Mar 1968 DONCASTER away won 33 - nil
DONCASTER - Rushton: Brook Battye Waring Sullivan:
McCone Bell: Yates Hawksley Bolus(Grainger) Jeff
Tomlinson Sykes:
CASTLEFORD - Hill: Stephens Thomas Willett Howe:
Edwards Hepworth: Hartley Ward Walton Bryant Small
Reilly: Tries - Bryant(4) Stephens Ward Reilly:
Goals - Willett(6):
Referee D S Brown (Dewsbury) Att - 2000 H.T. 23 - nil

Sat 16 Mar 1968 WAKEFIELD TRINITY away lost 5 - 18 CHALLENGE CUP ROUND 3
WAKEFIELD T - Cooper: Hirst Coetzer N.Fox Batty: Poynton
Bonnar: Jeanes Oakes D.Fox McLeod Haigh Hawley:
Tries - Batty(2) Coetzer Haigh: Goals - N.Fox(3):
CASTLEFORD - Stenton: Stephens Thomas Willett Austin:
Edwards Hepworth: Hartley Ward Walton Bryant Small
Reilly: Try - Stephens: Goal - Hepworth(DG):
Referee D T H Davies (Man'ster) Att - 19115 H.T. 2 - 7

Fri 22 Mar 1968 DEWSBURY home won 18 - 6
CASTLEFORD - Edwards(Thomas): Foster Stenton Willett
Briggs: Hardisty Hepworth: Hartley Dickinson(Miller)
McKalroy Bryant Lockwood Reilly: Tries - Briggs(2) Foster
Reilly: Goals - Willett(2) Hepworth(DG):
DEWSBURY - Hirst: Osborne Walker N.Stephenson Tolson:
Budge Newall: Naylor M.Stephenson Taylor Lowe Bates
Blakeley: Goals - N.Stephenson(2) Newall(DG):
Referee R Appleyard (Leeds) Att - 3346 H.T. 5 - 6

Thu 4 Apr 1968 BRADFORD NORTHERN away won 14 - 2
BRADFORD N - Price: Jones D.Toohey Wriglesworth
Thomas: Stockwell Daley: Roberts Ackerley(Fisher)
Clawson Ramshaw Taylor Rae: Goal - Clawson:
CASTLEFORD - Hill: Stephens Stenton Willett Foster:
Hepworth Hargrave: Hartley Miller McKalroy Bryant
Lockwood Reilly:
Tries - Stenton Reilly: Goals - Willett(3) Reilly(DG):
Referee D T H Davies (Manchester) Att - 5904 H.T. 5 - 2

Sat 6 Apr 1968 KEIGHLEY away won 7 - 6
KEIGHLEY - Jefferson: O'Brien Roberts Wilmot Moulding:
Kellett Evans: Worthy Pell Crewdson Palmer Potter
Aspinall: Tries - Wilmot Aspinall:
CASTLEFORD - Hill: Stephens Stenton Willett
Briggs(Thomas): Hepworth Hargrave: Hartley Miller
McKalroy Bryant Lockwood Reilly: Try - Stephens:
Goals - Willett(2):
Referee H Pearce (Leeds) Att - 1689 H.T. 2 - 6

Fri 12 Apr 1968 WAKEFIELD TRINITY home lost 4 - 5
CASTLEFORD - Hill: Stephens Stenton Willett Austin:
Hepworth Hargrave: Hartley Dickinson Fox Bryant Small
Reilly: Goals - Hepworth(2DG)
WAKEFIELD T - Cooper: Paley Brooke Coetzer Batty:
Poynton Bonnar: Jeanes Shepherd D.Fox Clarkson(Round)
Haigh Hawley: Try - Clarkson: Goal - Fox:
Referee T Keane (Oldham) Att - 9000 H.T. 4 - 3

Mon 15 Apr 1968 FEATHERSTONE ROVERS home won 10 - 8
CASTLEFORD - Hill: Stephens Stenton Willett Austin:
Edwards Hepworth: Hartley Dickinson Fox Bryant
Lockwood Reilly(Small):
Tries - Stephens Dickinson: Goals - Willett(2):
FEATHERSTONE R - C.Kellett: Newlove D.Kellett Jordan
Hartley: Smith(Agar) Nash: Tonks Lyman Dixon Morgan
Thompson Smales: Goals - Kellett(3) Smales(DG):
Referee E Clay (Rothwell) Att - 5295 H.T. 2 - 4

Fri 19 Apr 1968 SALFORD home won 47 - 15 CHAMPIONSHIP ROUND 1
CASTLEFORD - Hill: Stephens Stenton Willett Austin:
Edwards(Hargrave) Hepworth: Hartley Dickinson Walton
Bryant Redfearn Reilly: Tries - Stenton(3) Hill(2) Reilly(2)
Willett Dickinson Walton Bryant: Goals - Willett(6) Hill:
SALFORD - Gwilliam: Hill McInnes Hesketh Kelly: Watkins
Prosser: Bott Burdell Ogden Whitehead Smethurst
Brennan(Breen):
Tries - Watkins Prosser Whitehead: Goals - Hill(3):
Referee J Manley (Warrington) Att 5500 H.T. 23 - 9

Sat 24 Apr 1968 WAKEFIELD TRINITY away lost 14 - 17 CHAMPIONSHIP ROUND 2
WAKEFIELD T - Cooper: McDonagh(Morgan) Brooke
Coetzer Garthwaite: Batty Owen: Jeanes Shepherd
D.Fox(Campbell) Round McLeod Hawley:
Tries - Coetzer Batty Jeanes: Goals - Fox(3) Round:

SEASON 1967-68

CASTLEFORD - Hill: Stephens(Foster) Stenton Willett Austin:
Hepworth Hargrave: Hartley Dickinson Walton(Small)
Bryant Redfearn Reilly: Tries - Stenton Austin: Goals -
Willett(4):
Referee G Wilson (Dewsbury) Att - 12894 H.T. 14 – 12

Frok Fox
D. No 510
1967-68 to 1969-70

John McKalroy
D. No 511
1967-68 to 1969-70

Malcolm Reilly
D. No 512
1967-68 yo 1985-86

David (Danr y) Hargrave
D. No 513
1967-68 tc 1972-73

David Stephens
D. No 514
1967-68 to 1969-70

BBC2 FLOODLIT COMPETITION WINNERS 1965-65 1966-67 1967-68

Back Row – C Dickinson D Walton F Fox D Harley W Bryant D Stephens P Small M Redfearn M Reilly
Middle Row – G Gregory Dr I Butler L T Foster (All Directors) G Clin⁺on (Coach) Alan Hardisty(Captain) Len
Garbett (Secretary) G N Hardy F Jones (Directors) F Whitehead (Physiotherapist)
Front Row – R Simpson (V Chairman) J Austin I Stenton R Willett W E Broxup (Chairman) K Hepworth R Hill
D Edwards H H Clarkson (Director)

SEASON 1968-69

**Mon 23 Sep 1968 WAKEFIELD TRINITY home
won 18 – nil BBC 2 FLOODLIT COMPETITION
PRELIMINARY ROUND 2ND LEG**
CASTLEFORD - Edwards: Briggs Hill Thomas Austin:
Hardisty Hepworth: Hartley Dickinson Ward Lockwood
Small Reilly:
Tries - Hill Austin: Goals - Hill(3) Hardisty(3DG):
WAKEFIELD T - Wraith: Garthwaite Brooks N.Fox Batty:
Topliss Ward: Jeannes Firth Campbell Round Endersley
Hawley:
Referee W Thompson (Hud'field) Att - 6664 H.T. 7 - nil

Fri 27 Sep 1968 HUDDERSFIELD home won 11 - 7
CASTLEFORD - Edwards: Briggs Stephens Thomas Austin:
Hardisty Hepworth(Hill): Hartley Dickinson Fox Small
Redfearn(Reilly)Lockwood:
Try - Edwards: Goals Hill(2)(DG) Hardisty(DG):
HUDDERSFIELD - Walace: Major Evans Booth
Kersey-Brown: Rhodes(Loxton) Breakespeare: Hardwick
Close Van Bellen Davies Dobson Tomlinson:
Try - Booth: Goals - Davies(2):
Referee P Geraghty (York) Att - 4884 H.T. 2 - 7

**Sunday 29 Sep 1968 BRADFORD NORTHERN away
won 16 - 15 YORKSHIRE CUP SEMI FINAL**
BRADFORD N - Price: Jones D.Toohey L.Thomas
V.Thomas: Stockwell Daley : Mills Fisher Goddard
Clarkson Clawson Rogers:
Try - Clawson: Goals - Price(5) (DG):
CASTLEFORD - Edwards: Briggs Stephens Thomas Austin:
Hardisty Brown: Hartley Dickinson Ward Lockwood Small
Reilly:
Tries - Thomas Dickinson Small Reilly: Goals - Hardisty(2):
Referee E Lawrinson (Warrington) Att 12125 H.T. 13 - 8

Sat 5 Oct 1968 DEWSBURY away won 20 - 12
DEWSBURY - Hirst: Osborne Walker N.Stephenson
Marriott: Budge A.Bates: Naylor M.Stephenson Taylor
Lowe J.Bates Blakeley:
Tries - Marriott Budge: Goals - Lowe(2) (DG):
CASTLEFORD - Edwards: Stephens Hill Thomas MICHAEL
DAY(515): Hardisty Hargrave: Fox Ward Tucker
Small(Brown) Redfearn Lockwood: Tries - Stephens
Thomas Hardisty Ward: Goals - Hill(3) Hard sty(DG):
Referee D T H Davies(Manchester) Att-2500 H.T. 8 - 7

**Tue 8 Oct 1968 WIGAN away lost 7 - 10
BBC 2 FLOODLIT COMPETITION ROUND 1**
Wigan - Tyrer: Francis Ashton Ashurst(Rowe) O'Loughlin:
Hill Parr: Stephens Clarke Gardiner Fogerty(Mills) Lyon
Boyd: Try - Francis(2):   Goals - Tyrer(2):
CASTLEFORD - Edwards: Briggs(Harris) Thomas Stephens
Day: Hardisty Hargrave: Hartley Ward Fox Lockwood
Redfearn Brown: Try - Day: Goals - Hardisty(1) (DG):
Referee H Hunt (Guiseley) Att - 10809 H.T. ni - 5

**Sat 12 Oct 1968 WORKINGTON Town home
won 20 - 6**
CASTLEFORD - Edwards: Howe Hill Thomas Stephens:
Jones(Hardisty) Hargrave: Hartley Dickinson Ward

Redfearn Lockwood(Fox) Reilly:
Tries - Howe(2) Redfearn Lockwood:
Goals - Hill(2) Hardisty(DG) Ward(DG):
WORKINGTON T - Charlton: Davies Crellin Wright Tait:
Turnbull Whitaker: Wilson(Eve) Moss McCourt Smith
McFarlane Pattinson: Tries - Davies(2):
Referee E Leach (St Helens) Att - 2989 H.T. 8 - 6

**Sunday 13 Oct 1968 BRADFORD NORTHERN away
won 10 - 9**
BRADFORD N - Price: Jones Thomas Wriglesworth Litten:
Stockwell Diabara: Mills Fisher Goddard Hill(Rogers)
Clawson Sykes: Try - Litten: Goals - Price(3):
CASTLEFORD - Bibb: Stephens Hill Thomas Kirkbright:
Jones Hargrave: Fox Miller Dickinson Redfearn Lockwood
Brown: Tries - Hill Jones: Goals - Hill(2):
Referee J Manley (Warrington) Att - 7601 H.T. 10 - 4

**Sat 19 Oct 1968 LEEDS lost 11 - 22
YORKSHIRE CUP FINAL - AT BELLE VUE WAKEFIELD**
CASTLEFORD - Edwards: Howe Hill Thomas Stephens:
Hardisty Hargrave: Hartley Dickinson Ward Small
Lockwood(Redfearn) Reilly:
Try - Hill: Goals - Hill(2) Hardisty(2DG):
LEEDS - Risman: Smith Hynes Watson Atkinson:
Shoebottom Seabourne: Clark Crosby K.Eyre
Ramsey(Hick) A.Eyre Batten:
Tries - Smith Watson Atkinson Hick: Goals - Risman(5):
Referee J Manley (Warrington) Att - 12573 H.T. 8 - 10

Fri 25 Oct 1968 LEIGH home draw 2 - 2
CASTLEFORD - Edwards: Howe Hill Foster Day: Hardisty
Jones: Hartley Miller Fox(Tucker) Redfearn Small Reilly:
Goal - Hill:
LEIGH - Grainey: Hoffman Stringer Collins Walsh:
Eckersley Jones: Murphy Ashcroft Watts Welding
Middlehurst Highcock: Goal - Grainey:
Referee T Keane (Oldham) Att - 4229 H.T. nil - nil

Sat 26 Oct 1968 HUNSLET away won 16 - 11
HUNSLET - Marshall: Hurl Clark Chamberlain Thompson:
Morgan Hunt: Larkin Dunn Baldwinson Gaines(Sanderson)
Walker Preece: Try - Hurl: Goals - Marshall(4):
CASTLEFORD - Edwards: Kirkbright Ronald Hill Foster
Day: Hardisty Hargrave: Hartley Miller Tucker Redfearn
Small Reilly(Brown):
Tries - Hargrave Small: Goals - Hill(3) Hardisty(1) (DG):
Referee J Elliott (Barrow) Att - 3000 H.T. 9 - 7

Mon 4 Nov 1968 HALIFAX away won 13 - 9
HALIFAX - James: Goodchild Jones Hepworth(Eastwood)
Raynor: Robinson Baker: Dewhirst Foye Reeves Dixon
Kirkbride Renilson:
Try - Goodchild: Goals - James(2) (DG):
CASTLEFORD - Edwards: Howe Small
Stephens(Lockwood) Day: Hardisty Hargrave: Hartley
Dickinson Ward Tucker Harris Redfearn:
Try - Day: Goals - Redfearn(2) Hardisty(2DG) Ward(DG):
Referee P Geraghty (York) Att - 4305 H.T. 9 - 2

236

SEASON 1968-69

Fri 8 Nov 1968 SWINTON home won 30 - 8
CASTLEFORD - Bibb: Howe Small Stephens Day: Hardisty
Hepworth: Hartley Dickinson Ward Tucker Redfearn Reilly:
Tries - Small(2) Howe Stephens Hartley Dickinson Ward
Reilly: Goals - Hardisty(2) Redfearn:
SWINTON - Gowers: Gomersal Fleet Buckley(Kenny)
Stopford: Philbin Williams: Holliday Clarke Scott
Cummings Hutton Robinson:
Tries - Kenny Scott; Goal - Gowers
Referee R L Thomas (Oldham) Att - 4009 H.T. 19 - nil

**Fri 15 Nov 1968 HULL KINGSTON ROVERS away
lost 13 - 15**
HULL K R - Moore: Young Burwell Wriglesworth
Coupland: Millward Cooper: Hall Flanagan Mennell
Beetson Clawson Lowe:
Tries - Burwell(2) Coupland: Goals - Millward(3):
CASTLEFORD - Edwards: Howe Small Stephens Day:
Hardisty Hepworth: Hartley Dickinson Fox
Tucker(Lockwood) Redfearn Reilly:
Tries - Howe Hardisty Lockwood: Goals - Redfearn(2):
Referee R Appleyard (Leeds) Att - 8200 H.T. 4 - 10

**Fri 22 Nov 1968 BRADFORD NORTHERN home
won 17 - 14**
CASTLEFORD - Edwards: Howe(Briggs) Small Stephens
Day: Hardisty Hepworth: Hartley Dickinson Ward
Lockwood Redfearn Reilly:
Tries - Day Hepworth Hartley: Goals - Hardisty(4):
BRADFORD N - Price: V.Thomas Rhodes Stockwell
L.Thomas: Broatch Daley: Goddard Fisher Hill Clarkson
Sykes Broadbent:
Tries - Stockwell Clarkson: Goals - Price(4):
Referee E Clay (Rothwell) Att - 4998 H.T. 5 - 4

Sat 30 Nov 1968 BATLEY away won 11 - nil
BATLEY - Gittins: Hemmings Harrison Goode Hepworth:
Edwards Gorman: Thomas Brian Smith Tyson Hopwood
Bernard Smith Doyle:
CASTLEFORD - Bibb: Howe Small Stephens Austin:
Edwards Hepworth: Fox(David Tucker) Dickinson Ward
Lockwood Redfearn Reilly: Try - Bibb:
Goals - Redfearn(4):
Referee P Geraghty (York) Att - 1200 H.T. 9 - nil

Fri 6 Dec 1968 HULL away lost nil - 5
HULL - Keegan: A.Macklin Maloney Gemmell H.Firth:
Hancock Davidson: Harrison R.Firth J.Macklin Forster
Trotter Brown: Try - A.Macklin: Goal - Maloney:
CASTLEFORD - Edwards: Howe Small Stephens(Thomas)
Austin: Hardisty Hargrave: Hartley Dickinson Ward
Lockwood Redfearn Reilly:
Referee H Hunt (Guiseley) Att - 6500 H.T. nil - 5

Fri 13 Dec 1968 YORK home won 40 - 8
CASTLEFORD - Edwards: Howe Small Thomas ALAN
LOWNDES(516): Hardisty Hargrave: Hartley Dickinson Fox
Redfearn Lockwood Reilly: Tries - Howe(2) Lowndes(2)
Hardisty(2) Small Reilly: Goals - Redfearn(8):
YORK - Kendle(Peckett): Dickson Horner Sheehan Rippon:

Devonshire(Deighton) Elliott: Kidd Walton Taylor Storey
Payne Hepworth: Tries - Dickson(2): Goal - Kendle:
Referee W Thompson (Hud'field) Att - 2800 H.T. 18 - 5

Fri 20 Dec 1968 HULL home won 23 - 3
CASTLEFORD - Edwards: Howe Small Thomas Lowndes:
Hardisty Hargrave: Hartley Dickinson Fox McKalroy
Redfearn Reilly: Tries - Lowndes(2) Hardisty(2) Small:
Goals - Redfearn(3) Hardisty(DG):
HULL - Keegan: A.Macklin Maloney Gemmell Stocks:
Hancock Davidson: Harrison Firth J.Macklin Jervis(Forster)
Trotter Brown: Try - A.Macklin:
Referee F Lindop (Wakefield) Att - 3850 H.T. 5 - 3

Thu 26 Dec 1968 LEEDS away lost 5 - 14
LEEDS - Risman: Cowan Hynes Watson Smith:
Shoebottom(Langley) Seabourne: Clark Crosby K.Eyre
Ramsay A.Eyre Batten:
Tries - Cowan Hynes: Goals - Risman(3) Seabourne(DG):
CASTLEFORD - Edwards: Howe Small Thomas
Lowndes(Stephens): Hardisty Jones: Hartley Dickinson Fox
Redfearn Lockwood Reilly: Try - Howe: Goal - Redfearn:
Referee D S Brown (Preston) Att - 15675 H.T. 2 - 7

Fri 3 Jan 1969 BATLEY home won 11 - 5
CASTLEFORD - Bibb: Briggs ROY APPLEYARD(517)(Small)
Thomas Austin: Edwards Jones: Hartley Ward
McKalroy(Fox) Redfearn Lockwood Reilly:
Try - Edwards: Goals - Redfearn(4):
BATLEY - Gittins: Marsh Bell Morris Hepworth: Butterfield
Gorman: Walker Brian Smith Tyson Thomas Hopwood
Doyle: Try - Gorman: Goal - Doyle:
Referee F Lindop (Wakefiel) Att - 3032 H.T. 9 - 2

Fri 10 Jan 1969 HALIFAX home won 14 - 5
CASTLEFORD - Bibb: Howe Stephens(Small) Thomas
Briggs: Edwards ROBERT SPURR(518): Hartley Dickinson
Ward Bryant(Lockwood) Redfearn Reilly:
Tries - Howe Stephens Edwards Reilly: Goal - Redfearn:
HALIFAX - Hepworth: Kelly Jones Robinson Goodchild:
Eastwood Baker: Dewhirst Anderson Kelley Kirkbride
Michael Halmshaw: Try - Hepworth: Goal - Jones:
Referee P Geraghty (York) Att - 3437 H.T. 8 - 5

Fri 17 Jan 1969 HUDDERSFIELD away draw 7 - 7
HUDDERSFIELD - Haywood(Wallace): Booth Evans Naylor
Senior: Leek Breakespeare: Hepplestone Close Van Bellen
Dobson Taylor Mitchel: Try - Senior: Goals - Wallace(2):
CASTLEFORD - Bedford: Howe(Briggs) Peter Small
Thomas Redfearn: Edwards Hargrave: Hartley Dickinson
Ward Bryant(Fox) Lockwood Reilly:
Try - Briggs: Goals - Redfearn(2):
Referee R Appleyard (Leeds) Att - 1732 H.T. 2 - nil

Tue 21 Jan 1969 KEIGHLEY away won 12 - 10
KEIGHLEY - Jefferson: Cockcroft Wilmot O'Brien Roberts:
Kellett Evans: Worthy Whittaker Pollard Potter Larkin
Aspinall(Rogers): Goals - Jefferson(5):
CASTLEFORD - Bedford: Briggs Redfearn Thomas Day:
Edwards Hepworth: Hartley Dickinson Ward(Hargrave)

Bryant(Fox) Lockwood Reilly:
Tries - Briggs(2):   Goals - Redfearn(3):
Referee J Elliott (Barrow) Att - 1926 H.T. 5 - 6

**Sat 25 Jan 1969 HUNSLET away won 19 - 7
CHALLENGE CUP ROUND 1**
HUNSLET - Marshall: Hurl Clark Chamberlain(Simpson)
Thompson: Morgan Williams: Larkin Maskill Slatter Gaines
Gunney Walker: Try - Thompson: Goals - Marshall(2):
CASTLEFORD - Bedford: Briggs Foster Thomas Day:
Edwards Hepworth: Hartley Dickinson Fox Redfearn
Lockwood Reilly: Tries - Thomas Hepworth Redfearn:
Goals - Redfearn(3) Reilly(DG) Hepworth(DG):
Referee J Manley (Warrington) Att - 5400 H.T. 9 - nil

Fri 31 Jan 1969 LEEDS home lost 3 - 18
CASTLEFORD - Bedford: Briggs Foster Thomas Day:
Edwards Hepworth: McKalroy Dickinson(Miller) Fox
Redfearn Lockwood Reilly(Howe):   Try - Briggs:
LEEDS - Risman: Smith Hynes Lamb Langley: Watson
Seabourne: Clark Crosby K.Eyre A.Eyre Hick Ramsey:
Tries - Watson(2) Smith Ramsey: Goals - Risman(3):
Referee J P Hebblethwaite(York) Att - 10300 H.T. nil - 12

**Sat 15 Feb 1969 WIGAN home won 12 - 8
CHALLENGE CUP ROUND 2**
CASTLEFORD - Edwards: Briggs Foster Thomas Lowndes:
Hardisty Hepworth: Hartley Ward(S/O) Fox Redfearn
Lockwood Reilly:
Tries - Hardisty Ward: Goals - Redfearn(2) Hepworth(DG):
WIGAN - Ashton: Jones Ashurst Rowe Francis: D.Hill
Jackson: Gardiner Clarke Ashcroft Stephens Hogan(S/O)
Laughton: Tries - Francis(2): Goal - Ashton:
Referee R L Thomas (Oldham) Att - 8347 H.T. 5 - 5

**Sat 1 Mar 1969 LEEDS home won 9 - 5
CHALLENGE CUP ROUND 3**
CASTLEFORD - Bedford: Briggs Howe Thomas Lowndes:
Edwards Hepworth: Hartley Dickinson Ward Redfearn
Lockwood Reilly: Try - Briggs: Goals - Redfearn(3):
LEEDS - Risman: Smith Hynes Watson Cowan:
Shoebottom Seabourne: Clark Crosby K.Eyre A.Eyre
Hick(Fozzard) Batten: Try - Risman: Goal - Risman:
Referee E Lawrinson (Warrington) Att - 13180 H.T. 2 - 2

Fri 7 Mar 1969 BRAMLEY home won 25 - nil
CASTLEFORD - Bedford: Briggs Foster(Howe) Thomas
Lowndes: Edwards Hargrave: Hartley Dickinson Fox
Redfearn NORMAN BULLEN(519)(Lockwood)Reilly:
Tries - Briggs Howe Thomas Lowndes Hartley Dickinson
Lockwood: Goals - Redfearn(2):
BRAMLEY - Dewhirst: Smith D.Sampson(Wilkes)
Bollen(Jackson) Craker: Wolford Horsman: Horn Price
Higginbottom Plumstead Pearson Elliott:
Referee J P Hebblethwaite (York) Att - 3274 H.T. 2 - nil

Wed 12 Mar 1969 KEIGHLEY home won 17 - 4
CASTLEFORD - Bedford: Briggs Howe Willett Lowndes:
Edwards(Thomas) Hargrave: Fox Dickinson Ward Harris
Lockwood Reilly:

Tries - Briggs(3) Harris Lockwood: Goal - Willett:
KEIGHLEY - Kellett: Cockcroft O'Brien Roberts Pascoe:
Jefferson (Wilmot) Evans: Worthy Whittaker Pollard Larkin
Potter Garbett: Goals - Garbett Jefferson(DG):
Referee E Lawrinson (Warrington) Att - 2370 H.T. 11 - 4

Sat 22 Mar 1969 YORK away lost 8 - 12
YORK - Rippon: Horner Sheehan(D.Walker) Devonshire
Hindwell: Elliott Sullivan: Taylor P.Walker Storey Payne
Hepworth H.Deighton:
Tries - Elliott Hepworth: Goals - Payne(2) (DG):
CASTLEFORD - Bedford: Briggs Howe Thomas Lowndes:
Hardisty Hepworth: Hartley Dickinson Ward Redfearn
Lockwood Reilly: Tries - Briggs Hardisty: Goal - Redfearn:
Referee H Hunt (Guiseley) Att - 2700 H.T. nil - 12

**Sat 29 Mar 1969 WAKEFIELD TRINITY won 16 - 10
CHALLENGE CUP SEMI-FINAL AT HEADINGLEY LEEDS**
CASTLEFORD - Edwards: Briggs Howe Thomas Lowndes:
Hardisty Hepworth: Hartley Dickinson Ward Redfearn
Lockwood Reilly:
Tries - Briggs Hardisty: Goals - Redfearn(5):
WAKEFIELD T - Cooper: Slater Brooks N.Fox Hirst: Batty
Bonnar: Jeannes Hill D.Fox Ramshaw Haigh Hawley:
Tries - Hirst(2):   Goals - N.Fox(2):
Referee J Manley (Warrington) Att - 21685 H.T. 7 - 10

**Fri 4 Apr 1969 WAKEFIELD TRINITY   away
won 13 - 4**
WAKEFIELD T - Paley(Wraith): Slater Brooks Carlton Hirst:
Batty D.Ward: McLeod Hill Jeannes Ramshaw Haigh
Hawley: Goals - Carlton(2):
CASTLEFORD - Bedford: Briggs Howe Thomas
Lowndes(Willett): Edwards Hepworth: Hartley Miller Fox
Redfearn Harris Reilly:
Tries - Howe Lowndes Hepworth: Goals - Redfearn(2):
Referee E Lawrinson (Warrington) Att-8898 H.T. 8 - 4

**Mon 7 Apr 1969 FEATHERSTONE ROVERS away
lost 13 - 16**
FEATHERSTONE R - C.Kellett: Smith Newlove Jordan
Hartley: D.Kellett Hudson: Tonks Farrar Lyons Thompson
Morgan Brown:
Tries - C.Kellett Hudson: Goals - C.Kellett(5):
CASTLEFORD - Bedford: Willett Harris Thomas Lowndes:
Edwards Hepworth: Hartley Miller Fox Redfearn
Lockwood Reilly:
Tries - Harris(2) Lowndes: Goals - Redfearn(2):
Referee Mr I Meskimmon(Brighouse) Att - 5765 H.T. 5 -9

**Fri 11 Apr 1969 HULL KINGSTON ROVERS home
lost 10 - 11**
CASTLEFORD - Bedford: Harris Howe Thomas Lowndes:
Edwards Hargrave: Hartley Dickinson Ward Redfearn Fox
Reilly: Tries - Howe Ward: Goals - Redfearn(2):
HULL K R - Markham: Wainwright Moore Burwell
Stephenson: Millward Cooper: Clawson Flanagan Mennell
Hickson Lowe G.Young:
Try - Cooper: Goals - Millward(3) Clawson:
Referee J Reed (Leeds) Att - 5481 H.T. 5 - nil

Mon 14 Apr 1969 HUNSLET home lost 5 - 10

CASTLEFORD - Edwards(Bedford): Willett Howe Thomas
Lowndes: Hardisty Hargrave: Hartley Dickinson Ward
Redfearn McKalroy Harris:
Try - Hardisty: Goal - Redfearn:
HUNSLET - Marshall: Brown Clark Chamberlain Lee:
Harpin Hunt: Bancroft Dunn Larkin Hepples Gunney
Preece: Tries - Hunt(2):   Goals - Marshall Gunney(DG):
Referee D T H Davies (Man'ter) Att - 2750 H.T. nil - 5

Sunday 20 Apr 1969 BRAMLEY away won 23 - 2

BRAMLEY - A.N.Other: Wilkes(Kelly) Sampson Bollon
Craker: Wolford Horsman: Horn(Jackson) Barlow Adams
Higginbottom Pearson Cullen: Goal - Wolford:
CASTLEFORD - Edwards: Willett Howe Thomas Lowndes:
Hardisty Hepworth: Hartley Dickinson Ward Fox
Kirkbright Redfearn (GRAHAM BLAKEWAY)(520):
Tries - Willett(2) Hardisty(2) Kirkbright:
Goals - Redfearn(3) Willett:
Referee E Leach (St Helens) Att - 2000 H.T. 15 - 2

Fri 25 Apr 1969 HULL home won 14 - 10
CHAMPIONSHIP ROUND 1

CASTLEFORD - Edwards: Ronald Willett Howe Thomas
Harris: Hardisty Hepworth: Hartley Dickinson Fox
Redfearn Lockwood Reilly:
Tries - Harris Hepworth: Goals - Redfearn(3) Hardisty(DG):
HULL - Keegan: Macklin Maloney Gemmell H.Firth:
Hancock Davidson: O'Brien R.Firth Broom(Edson) Forster
Jervis Trotter: Tries - H.Firth(2): Goals - Maloney(2):
Referee J Manley (Warrington) Att - 6060 H.T. 4 - 7

Sat 3 May 1969 SWINTON home won 50 - 8
CHAMPIONSHIP ROUND 2

CASTLEFORD - Edwards: Briggs Howe Thomas Lowndes:
Hardisty Hepworth: Hartley Dickinson Ward Redfearn
Lockwood(Fox) Reilly(Bedford):
Tries - Hardisty(3) Howe(2) Lowndes(2) Hepworth(2)
Reilly(2) Edwards: Goals - Redfearn(7):
SWINTON - Gowers: Fleet Gomersall Buckley
Philbin(Whittle): Atkinson Kenny: Holliday Clarke Simpson
Smith Hutton D.Robinson:
Tries - Buckley Smith: Goal - Gowers:
Referee R L Thomas (Oldham) Att - 6450 H.T. 29 - nil

Sat 10 May 1969 ST HELENS away won 18 - 6
CHAMPIONSHIP SEMI-FINAL

ST HELENS - Walsh: Barrow Benyon Myler Jones: Whittle
Bishop: Warlow Sayer Rees Mantle Chisnall(Egan) Coslett:
Goals - Coslett(3):
CASTLEFORD - Edwards: Briggs Howe Thomas Lowndes:
Hardisty Hepworth: Hartley Dickinson(Miller) Fox
Kirkbright Harris Redfearn:
Tries - Lowndes(2) Briggs Hepworth: Goals - Redfearn(3):
Referee F Lindop (Wakefield) Att - 10734 H.T. 2 - 6

Sat 17 May 1969 SALFORD won 11 - 6
CHALLENGE CUP FINAL - AT WEMBLEY

CASTLEFORD - Edwards: Briggs Howe Thomas Lowndes:
Hardisty Hepworth: Hartley Dickinson Ward Redfearn

Lockwood Reilly:
Tries - Howe Hardisty Hepworth: Goal - Redfearn:
SALFORD - Gwilliam: Burgess Whitehead Hesketh
Jackson: Watkins Brennan: Ogden Dickens Bott Coulman
Dixon Hill: Goals - Hill(3):
Referee D S Brown (Preston) Att - 97939 H.T. 3 - 4
Lance Todd Trophy Winner - Malcolm Reilly
(Castleford) Cup Presented By Sir Denis Blundell(High
Commissioner For New Zealand)

Sat 24 May 1969 LEEDS lost 14 - 16
CHAMPIONSHIP FINAL - AT ODSAL STADIUM
BRADFORD

CASTLEFORD - Edwards: Briggs Howe Thomas Lowndes:
Hardisty Hepworth: Hartley(S/O) Dickinson Ward
Redfearn Lockwood Reilly(Fox): Tries - Hardisty
Dickinson: Goals - Redfearn(3) Hardisty(DG):
LEEDS - Risman: Cowan Hynes Watson Atkinson:
Shoebottom Seabourne(Langley): Clark(Hick) Crosby
K.Eyre Joyce Ramsey Batten:
Tries - Cowan Atkinson: Goals - Risman(4) Ramsey(DG):
Referee W Thompson (Hud'field) Att - 28400 H.T. 11 – 7

In the Challenge Cup we reached the Twin Towers of
Wembley for the first time since 1934/35. with a 19 –
7 victory in round one away to Hunslet, a tremendous
12 – 8 victory over Wigan at home in round two, and
truly epic 9 –5 victory at home to Leeds in round
three saw us reach our second semi-final of the 60's.
Wakefield Trinity were our opponents, the previous
years runners up in the 'infamous' watersplash final.
With two tries apiece it was the magnificent goal
kicking of Mick Redfearn with 5 successful kicks that
"finally" saw us through to Wembley.
The final was against big spenders Salford with David
Watkins at stand off and former Caslefordian Ron Hill
at loose forward. For the neutrals in the capacity
crowd and millions of TV viewers the game might not
have lived up to the pre match publicity. However,
with a winning margin of three tries and one goal to
only three goals against, Malcolm Reilly winning the
Lance Todd Trophy it was a well-deserved victory and
a day to be savoured by all Castleford supporters.

Between the Challenge Cup semi-final and final we
also progressed to the final of the Championship Top
16 play off. Victories in round one at home to Hull 14
– 10, round two at home to Swinton 50 – 8, and a
semi-final victory away to St Helens 18 – 6, resulted in
a final appearance against Leeds at Odsal Bradford
the week after Wembley. After leading at half time 11
– 7 we suffered the losses in the second half of
Wembley hero Malcolm Reilly through injury and
Dennis Hartley sent off and we just went down in the
closing stages 16 – 14.

Michael day
D. No 515
1968-69 to 1970-71

Alan Lowndes
D. No 516
1968-69 to 1976-77

Roy Appleyard
D. No 517
1968-69 to 1973-74

Robert Spurr
D. No 518
1968-69 to 1982-83

Norman Bullen
D. No 519
1968-69 to 1971-72

Graham Blakeway
D. No 520
1968-69 to 1971-72

Captain Alan Hardisty and Coach Derek Turner with the
Cup between them are lifted Shoulder High by the
Jubilant Players

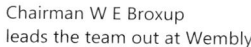

Chairman W E Broxup
leads the team out at Wembly

1968-69 R.L CHALLENGE CUP WIINING SQUAD

Back Row – (Directors) F Jones G N Hardy L T Foster Dr I Butler
Middle Row – D Turner (Coach) C Dickinson M Reilly B Lockwood D Hartley F Fox T Briggs M Redfearn D Harris
D Edwards L Garbett (Secretary)
Front Row – R Simpson (V Chairman) K Howe T Thomas A Hardisty (Captain) W.E Broxup (Chairman) K Hepworth
A Lowndes J Ward H.H. Clarkson (Director)

The Two H Bombs - Keith Hepworth and Alan Hardisty raise the Cup aloft at the homecoming on top of the Old
Castleford Boys Modern School

SEASON 1968-69

D.N	PLAYER		DEBUT	L MATCH	APP	SUB	T.AP	TRI'S	G'LS	D.G	P'TS
426	BRYANT	WILLIAM			7	0	7	0	0	0	0
433	HARDISTY	ALAN			36	1	37	20	24	19	146
438	SMALL	PETER		17/01/1969	26	2	28	7	0	0	21
442	HEPWORTH	KEITH			31	0	31	9	0	2	31
453	WARD	JOHNNY			35	0	35	5	0	2	19
458	EDWARDS	DEREK			47	0	47	4	0	0	12
473	HOWE	KEITH			27	2	29	14	0	0	42
474	BEDFORD	TREVOR			11	2	13	0	0	0	0
479	DICKINSON	CLIVE			42	0	42	5	0	0	15
486	WILLETT	RONALD		25/04/1969	5	1	6	2	2	0	10
488	HILL	RONALD		26/10/1968	11	1	12	5	30	0	75
490	HARRIS	DENNIS			12	1	13	5	0	0	15
492	STENTON	IAN			8	0	8	3	0	0	9
493	BRIGGS	TREVOR			26	3	29	14	0	0	42
494	REDFEARN	MICHAEL			38	2	40	2	74	0	154
495	MILLER	TONY			6	2	8	0	0	0	0
497	LOCKWOOD	BRIAN			35	5	40	5	0	0	15
498	AUSTIN	JACK			14	0	14	3	0	0	9
499	TUCKER	DAVID		30/11/1968	5	2	7	0	0	0	0
502	BIBB	HOWARD			5	0	5	1	0	0	3
503	HARTLEY	DENNIS			46	0	46	3	0	0	9
504	JONES	GLYN			5	0	5	1	0	0	3
505	BROWN	RICHARD			3	2	5	0	0	0	0
506	THOMAS	TONY			34	3	37	5	0	0	15
508	KIRKBRIGHT	JOSEPH			4	0	4	1	0	0	3
509	FOSTER	DEREK			7	0	7	0	0	0	0
510	FOX	FRANK			22	7	29	0	0	0	0
511	McKALROY	JOHN			4	0	4	0	0	0	0
512	REILLY	MALCOLM			41	1	42	8	1	1	28
513	HARGRAVE	DAVID (DANNY)			16	2	18	1	0	0	3
514	STEPHENS	DAVID			22	1	23	5	0	0	15
515	DAY	MICHAEL	05/10/1968		11	0	11	3	0	0	9
516	LOWNDES	ALAN	13/12/1968		18	0	18	11	0	0	33
517	APPLEYARD	ROY	03/01/1969		1	0	1	0	0	0	0
518	SPURR	ROBERT	10/01/1969		1	0	1	0	0	0	0
519	BULLEN	NORMAN	07/03/1969		1	0	1	0	0	0	0
520	BLAKEWAY	GRAHAM	20/04/1969		0	1	1	0	0	0	0
	37			6	4	663	41	704	142	131	24	736

COMPETITION		P	W	D	L	FOR	AGT
LEAGUE ONE D	POSITION 4 OF 30	34	24	2	8	462	255
YORK'S CUP		5	3	1	1	71	65
F. TROPHY		3	2	0	1	40	21
RL CUP		5	5	0	0	67	36
CHAMPIONSHIP		4	3	0	1	96	40
PLAYERS RECORDS		**51**	**37**	**3**	**11**	**736**	**417**

In the league Liverpool Stanley changed its name to Huyton.

We commenced the season with a new first team coach with former Wakefield Trinity and Great Britain International forward Derek Turner taking over from George Clinton.

Dennis Hartley played for Great Britain against France in the home victory at St Helens 34–10 and in the away defeat at Toulouse 13–9.

Notable Debutants were double Challenge Cup Winner Alan Lowndes and long serving Robert Spurr with over 300 appearances in 15 seasons.

Substitutes Allowed At Any Time

Sat 19 Jul 1969 TOMMY SMALES XIII - 17 JOHN SHERIDAN XIII – 19   FRIENDLY
SMALES XIII - Edwards(Bedford): Briggs Foster Thomas Austin: Hardisty Spurr(G.Stephens): Hartley Dickinson Ward Redfearn Lockwood Norton: Tries - Hardisty(2) Foster Stephens Dickinson: Goal - Redfearn:
SHERIDAN XIII - Bedford(Knight): Day Shaw(Brunyee) Bibb Guest: Johnson G.Stephens(Spurr): Fox Miller McKalroy(D.Ward) Bullen(Lloyd) Biscomb(Coventry) Kirkbright(Ackroyd):   Tries - Knight Bibb Spurr McKalroy Biscomb: Goals - Johnson Ackroyd:
Referee -   Att - 1260   H.T.

Fri 25 Jul 1969 HULL KINGSTON ROVERS home won 32 – 19 ALAN HARDISTY - KEITH HEPWORTH BENEFIT MATCH FRIENDLY
CASTLEFORD - Thomas: Briggs(Norton) Howe(Bibb) Foster Lowndes: Hardisty Hepworth: Fox Dickinson Ward Redfearn Miller Reilly: Tries - Thomas Foster Lowndes Hepworth Dickinson Miller: Goals - Redfearn(7):
HULL K R - Markham: Young(Coupland) Burwell Moore Longstaffe: Millward Stephenson(Brook): Hickson Flanagan Wallis Young(Collins)Lowe Small:
Tries - Flanagan(3) Millward Brook: Goals - Millward(2):
Referee A J Dobell (Mexborough) Att - 2750 H.T. 17 - 11

Sun 3 Aug 1969 DONCASTER away won 13 - 3
DONCASTER - Goodyear(Cross): Denton Battye James Towle: Brook McCone: Holt(S/O) Hawksley Fortis McLane Arrand Brown(Baker):   Try - McCone:
CASTLEFORD - Thomas: Stephens Howe Foster Briggs: Hardisty Hepworth: Fox Dickinson Miller Redfearn Lockwood(Bedford) Reilly:
Tries - Hardisty(2) Briggs: Goals - Redfearn(2):
Referee R Appleyard (Leeds) Att - 1500 H.T. 11 - nil

Sat 9 Aug 1969 HULL away lost 4 - 30 YORKSHIRE CUP ROUND 1
HULL - Keegan: Sullivan Gemmell Maloney H.Firth: Hancock Davidson: Harrison R.Firth J.Macklin Forster Kirchin Trotter: Tries - Sullivan Gemmell Hancock Davidson Macklin Trotter: Goals - Maloney(6):
CASTLEFORD - Bedford: Stephens Howe Thomas Briggs: Hardisty Jones: Fox Dickinson Ward Redfearn(McKalroy) Miller(S/O) Lockwood: Goals - Redfearn(2):
Referee T Keane (Oldham) Att - 6300 H.T. 4 - 10

Wed 13 Aug 1969 WAKEFIELD TRINITY away won 16 - nil
WAKEFIELD T - Wraith: McDonagh Brook Carlton Batty: Bonnar(Morgan)Poynton(Crook): Campbell Hill Handforth Spencer Ballantyne Cooper:
CASTLEFORD - Edwards: Stephens Bibb(Bedford) Thomas Briggs: Hardisty Hepworth: Hartley Dickinson Ward Redfearn Lockwood Reilly(Fox):
Tries - Briggs Hartley Reilly Fox: Goals - Redfearn(2):
Referee E Clay (Rothwell) Att - 5942 H.T. 8 - nil

Sat 16 Aug 1969 ST HELENS away lost 3 - 27
ST HELENS - Barrow: B.Jones Walsh Myler Wilson: Whittle Gartland: Watson Egan Wanbon Mantle Chisnall Coslett: Substitute L Jones:Tries - B.Jones Walsh Myler Gartland L.Jones: Goals - Coslett(6):
CASTLEFORD - Bibb: Day(TERRY BISCOMB(521)) Bedford Thomas Briggs: Edwards Hepworth(ALAN ACKROYD(522)): Hartley Dickinson Fox Redfearn Joseph Kirkbright Lockwood: Try - Lockwood:
Referee R Jackson (Halifax) Att - 6400 H.T. 3 - 18

Wed 20 Aug 1969 LEEDS home won 11 - 2
CASTLEFORD - Edwards: Austin Briggs Thomas Biscomb: Jones Hargrave: Hartley Dickinson Fox Redfearn Bullen Lockwood:
Tries - Briggs Biscomb Dickinson: Goal - Redfearn:
LEEDS - Holmes: Smith Hynes Langley Atkinson: Watson(S/O) Shoebottom: Clark Crosby K.Eyre Fozzard Hick Batten: Goal - Shoebottom:
Referee F Lindop (Wakefield) Att - 7000 H.T. nil - 2

Sat 23 Aug 1969 YORK away lost 4 - 12
YORK - Kendle: Hindwell Horner Devonshire Rippon(Sheehan): Elliott Sullivan: Taylor P.Walker Forsyth D.Walker(Dunham) Hepworth Deighton:
Tries - Horner P.Walker: Goals - Kendle(3):
CASTLEFORD - Edwards: Austin Briggs Thomas Biscomb: Jones(Bedford)Hargrave: Hartley Dickinson Fox Redfearn Bullen Reilly(S/O)   Goals - Redfearn(2):
Referee J E Elliott (Barrow) Att - 3227 H.T. 2 - 2

Mon 1 Sept 1969 FEATHERSTONE ROVERS away won 19 - 7
FEATHERSTONE R - C.Kellett: Cotton Newlove Smith Hartley: D.Kellett Nash: Windmill Farrar Rhodes Morgan Thompson Smales: Try - Rhodes: Goals - C.Kellett(2):
CASTLEFORD - Edwards: Lowndes Howe Thomas Briggs: Hardisty Hepworth: Hartley Dickinson Ward Redfearn Miller Lockwood: Tries - Hardisty(2) Edwards Briggs Ward: Goals Hardisty Redfearn:
Referee T Keane (Oldham) Att - 6722 H.T. 9 - 2

Sat 6 Sept 1969 BRAMLEY away lost 10 - 19
BRAMLEY - Dewhirst: Hughes Bollon(Sampson) Toohey Kelly: Wolford Gallagher: Horn Barlow Pearson Higginbottom Plumstead Ashton:
Tries - Hughes Gallagher Pearson: Goals - Dewhirst(5):
CASTLEFORD - Edwards: Lowndes(Keith Howe) Stenton Foster Briggs: Hardisty Hargrave: Hartley Miller Ward Redfearn Fox Lockwood:
Tries - Foster Hardisty: Goals - Redfearn(2):
Referee P Geraghty (York) Att - 1700 H.T. 4 - 14

Wed 10 Sept 1969 ST HELENS home won 9 - 3
CASTLEFORD - Edwards: Austin Thomas Stenton Briggs: Hardisty Hargrave: Hartley Miller Ward Redfearn Biscomb Lockwood: Try - Miller: Goals Redfearn(3):
ST HELENS - Walsh: Jones Benyon Whittle Wilson: Myler

243

Gartland: Halsall Karalius Chisnall Mantle Wanbon Coslett:
Try - Benyon:
Referee D S Brown (Preston) Att - 5856 H.T. 5 - nil

Fri 12 Sept 1969 DONCASTER home won 23 - 5
CASTLEFORD - Edwards: Austin David Stephens Thomas
Briggs: Hardisty Hargrave(Hepworth): Hartley Miller
Dickinson Redfearn Biscomb Lockwood: Tries - Briggs(2)
Thomas Dickinson Lockwood: Goals - Redfearn(4):
DONCASTER - Towle: Denton Battye Cross(Tomlinson)
Arrand: Brook McCone: Holt Hawksley(Yates) Jeff Watts
Townend McLean: Try - Jeff: Goal - Towle:
Referee H G Hunt (Guiseley) Att - 3081 H.T. 3 - 5

Sat 20 Sept 1969 HUDDERSFIELD away won 31 - 10
HUDDERSFIELD - Wallace: Major Pickup Evans
Kersey-Brown: Leek Breakespeare (Loxton): Goddyear
Muir Van Bellen Taylor(Long) Mitchell Tomlinson:
Tries - Van Bellen(2): Goals - Wallace(2):
CASTLEFORD - Edwards: Austin Stenton Thomas Briggs:
Hardisty Hepworth: Hartley Dickinson Ward Miller
WILLIAM KIRKBRIDE(523) Redfearn:
Tries - Thomas(2) Stenton Briggs Hardisty Kirkbride
Redfearn: Goals - Stenton(2) Redfearn(2) Ward(DG):
Referee R Appleyard (Leeds) Att - 2647 H.T. 14 - 10

**Tue 23 Sept 1969 HULL KINGSTON ROVERS away
draw 13 - 13**
HULL K R - Markham: Stephenson Burwell Wrigglesworth
Coupland(Moore): Millward Cooper: Clawson Flanagan
Hickson Lowe(Small) Wallis Young:
Try - Wallis: Goals - Millward(4) Flanagan(DG):
CASTLEFORD - Bedford: Jack Austin(S/O) Stenton Thomas
Briggs: Hardisty Hepworth: Hartley Miller Ward Redfearn
Kirkbride Lockwood: Try - Thomas:
Goals - Redfearn(3) Stenton(DG) Hardisty(DG):
Referee E Lawrinson(Warrington) Att - 7296 H.T. 9 - 9

Fri 26 Sept 1969 YORK home won 24 - 9
CASTLEFORD - Bedford: Lowndes Stenton Thomas Briggs:
Hardisty Hepworth(Lockwood): Hartley Dickinson Ward
Miller Kirkbride Redfearn: Tries - Bedford Lowndes
Thomas Hardisty Hepworth Ward: Goals - Redfearn(3):
YORK - Rippon: Hindwell Sheehan Horner Rothwell: Elliott
Sullivan: Taylor P.Walker Dunham Meillam Neale
Deighton(Hird): Try - Elliott: Goals - Sullivan(3):
Referee R L Thomas (Oldham) Att - 4830 H.T. 11 - 2

**Mon 29 Sept 1969 HUDDERSFIELD away won 18 - 10
BBC 2 FLOODLIT COMPETITION PRELIMINARY
ROUND 1ST LEG**
HUDDERSFIELD - Wallace: Kersey-Brown Evans Naylor
Pickup: Leek Breakespeare(Loxton): Van Bellen Close Long
Taylor Dobson Tomlinson:
Tries - Long Dobson: Goals - Wallace(2):
CASTLEFORD - Bedford: Lowndes Stenton Thomas Briggs:
Hardisty Edwards: Hartley Dickinson(Miller) Fox Redfearn
Kirkbride Lockwood: Tries - Lowndes Stenton Briggs
Hardisty: Goals - Redfearn(2)Stenton(DG):
Referee D T H Davies (Man'ster) Att - 1750 H.T. 18 - nil

Sat 4 Oct 1969 HULL away lost 7 - 15
HULL - Keegan: Sullivan Doyle-Davidson Maloney Abbey:
Hancock Davidson: Harrison McGlone J.Macklin Forster
Kirchin Trotter: Try - Davidson: Goals - Maloney(6):
CASTLEFORD - Edwards: Lowndes Stenton(Bedford)
Thomas Briggs: Hardisty Hargrave: Hartley Miller Fox
Redfearn Biscomb Lockwood:
Try - Edwards: Goals - Redfearn(2):
Referee F Lindop (Wakefield) Att - 5000 H.T. nil - 8

**Wed 8 Oct 1969 HUDDERSFIELD home won 19 - 2
BBC 2 FLOODLIT COMPETITION PRELIMINARY
ROUND 2ND LEG**
CASTLEFORD - Bedford: IAN GUEST(524) Stenton Thomas
Briggs: Hardisty Hargrave: Hartley Miller Ward Kirkbride
Lockwood Reilly:
Tries - Hardisty(2) Briggs: Goals - Stenton(5):
HUDDERSFIELD - Wallace: Major Evans Naylor Pickup:
Calvert Loxton: Van Bellen(Muir) Close Long
(Breakespeare) Dobson Davies Tomlinson: Goal - Davies:
Referee S Shepherd (Oldham) Att - 4000 H.T. 7 - 2

Fri 10 Oct 1969 BRAMLEY home won 15 - 5
CASTLEFORD - Bedford: Foster Stenton Thomas Briggs:
Hardisty(Hargrave)GARY STEPHENS(525): Hartley Spurr
Ward Kirkbride Lockwood Reilly: Tries - Foster Spurr
Lockwood: Goals - Stenton(2) Hargrave(DG):
BRAMLEY - Dewhurst: Hughes D.Toohey(Idle) D.Sampson
Kelly: Bollon Wolford: G.Pearson Barlow M.Sampson
(Horn) Plumstead T.Pearson Ashton:
Try - Kelly: Goal - Dewhurst:
Referee I Meskimmon (Hud'field) Att - 4429 H.T. 10 - nil

Fri 17 Oct 1969 DEWSBURY home won 7 - 4
CASTLEFORD - Bedford: Foster Stenton Thomas Briggs:
Edwards Appleyard: Hartley Spurr Fox Kirkbride Redfearn
Lockwood: Try - Thomas: Goals - Stenton(2):
DEWSBURY - Darbyshire: Fletcher Firth N.Stephenson
Tate: Agar(Newall) Bates: Naylor M.Stephenson Coates
Lowe Bates Robinson: Goals - Darbyshire Agar(DG):
Referee G Philpott (Leeds) Att - 4566 H.T. 2 - 4

**Tue 21 Oct 1969 SALFORD away won 16 - 12
BBC 2 FLOODLIT COMPETITION ROUND 1**
SALFORD: D.Hill: Burgess Whitehead Hesketh Richards:
McInnes(Jackson)Prosser: Ogden Burdell Bott(Henninhan)
Coulman Smethurst Dixon:
Tries - Hesketh Richards: Goals - D.Hill(3):
CASTLEFORD - Edwards: Biscomb Foster Thomas Briggs:
Hargrave Appleyard: Hartley Dickinson Ward Kirkbride
Lockwood Reilly:
Tries - Lockwood Reilly: Goals - Reilly(2) (3DG):
Referee G Wilson (Dewsbury) Att - 7583 H.T. 5 - 5

**Sat 25 Oct 1969 BRADFORD NORTHERN away
won 18 - 17**
BRADFORD N - Price: R.Reynolds Stockwell Thomas
Litten: Broatch Diabira: Mills Fisher Foster Clarkson
Oswald Fearnley:
Tries - R.Reynolds Diabira Oswald: Goals - Price(3) (DG):

CASTLEFORD - Edwards: Foster Briggs Thomas Biscomb: Hargrave Appleyard: Hartley Dickinson Bryant(Redfearn) Kirkbride Lockwood Reilly:
Tries - Kirkbride(2) Briggs Thomas: Goals - Redfearn(3):
Referee E Leach (St Helens) Att - 7026 H.T. 3 - 7

Fri 31 Oct 1969 HUNSLET home won 15 - 10
CASTLEFORD - Edwards: Biscomb Foster Thomas Briggs: PHILIP JOHNSON(526) Appleyard: Hartley Dickinson Ward Kirkbride(Redfearn) Bullen Reilly:
Tries - Foster Thomas Redfearn:
Goals - Reilly(2) Redfearn:
HUNSLET - Marshall: Lee Hudson Chamberlain Thompson: Morgan(Harpin) Hunt: Larkin Cardiss Baldwinson Hepples(Gunney) Payne Sanderson:
Tries - Cardiss Payne: Goals - Marshall(2):
Referee H Cook (Beverley) Att - 4327 H.T. 10 - 5

Fri 14 Nov 1969 HALIFAX away lost 5 - 8
HALIFAX - James: Jones Willicombe Geidziun Raynor: Hepworth Sanderson: Dewhirst Foye Kelley Fogerty Halmshaw(Reeves) Baker:
Tries - James Sanderson: Goal - James:
CASTLEFORD - Edwards: Biscomb Foster Thomas Briggs: Hardisty Appleyard(Hargrave): Hartley Dickinson Ward Kirkbride Lockwood Reilly: Try - Biscomb: Goal - Hardisty:
Referee T Keane (Oldham) Att - 2599 H.T. 3 - 5

Sat 22 Nov 1969 HULL KINGSTON ROVERS home won 14 - 7
CASTLEFORD - Edwards: Guest LESLIE SHAW(527)(Hargrave) Thomas Briggs: Hardisty Jones: Bryant Dickinson Redfearn Kirkbride Lockwood(S/O) Reilly: Goals - Redfearn(7):
HULL K R - Markham: Stephenson Moore Wriglesworth Ballantyne: Millward(Gay) Dooler: Clawson Holdstock Hossell(Rose) Wallis Small Cooper(S/O):
Try - Millward: Goals - Millward(2):
Referee E Clay (Rothwell) Att - 4032 H.T. 8 - 7

Tue 25 Nov 1969 LEEDS home won 9 - 7
BBC 2 FLOODLIT COMPETITION ROUND 2
CASTLEFORD - Edwards(Hargrave): Guest Briggs Thomas Foster: Hardisty Jones: Hartley Dickinson(S/O) Redfearn Kirkbride Lockwood Reilly:
Try - Reilly: Goals - Redfearn(3):
LEEDS - Risman: Smith Hynes(S/O) Watson(Holmes) Atkinson: Shoebottom Seabourne: Joyce Shepherd K.Eyre Barnard(Hick) Ramsey Batten:
Try - Hynes: Goals - Risman Seabourne(DG):
Referee W H Thompson (Hud'field) Att - 5760 H.T. 4 - 5

Sat 29 Nov 1969 WIGAN home won 29 - 13
CASTLEFORD - Edwards: Guest Hargrave Thomas Briggs: Hardisty Jones: Hartley Dickinson Redfearn Kirkbride Lockwood(Bedford) Reilly(Bryant):
Tries - Guest(2) Thomas(2) Dickinson: Goals - Redfearn(7):
Wigan - Tyrer: Wright Francis Rowe Eastham: C.Hill Parr(Mills): Stephens Clarke Hogan O'Loughlin Ashurst Laughton:

Tries - Ashurst Clarke Stephens: Goals - Tyrer(2):   :
Referee J Manley (Warrington) Att - 4472 H.T. 14 - 3

Tue 2 Dec 1969 LEIGH home lost 11 - 12
BBC 2 FLOODLIT COMPETITION SEMI-FINAL
CASTLEFORD - Edwards: Guest Hargrave Thomas Briggs: Hardisty Jones: Hartley Dickinson Redfearn Kirkbride(William Bryant) Lockwood Reilly:
Tries - Briggs Redfearn Reilly: Goal - Redfearn:
LEIGH - Ferguson Tickle Dorrington(Warburton) Collins Walsh: Eckersley Murphy: Chisnall Ashcroft Watts Welding Grimes Lyon: Tries - Tickle Walsh: Goals - Ferguson(3):
Referee D S Brown (Preston) Att - 5972 H.T. 5 - 7

Fri 19 Dec 1969 HUDDERSFIELD home lost 5 - 12
CASTLEFORD - Bedford: Briggs Shaw Thomas Lowndes: Hardisty(Jones) Stephens: Hartley Dickinson Ward Redfearn Lockwood Reilly:
Try - Lowndes: Goal - Redfearn:
HUDDERSFIELD - Wallace(S/O): Major Breakespeare Evans Kersey-Brown(Starkey): Leek Loxton: Van Bellen Close Davies Taylor Long Tomlinson:
Tries - Tomlinson(2):   Goals - Davies(3):
Referee H Hunt (Guiseley) Att - 1683 H.T. nil - 12

Fri 26 Dec 1969 LEEDS away lost nil - 8
LEEDS - Risman: Smith Hynes Cowan Atkinson: Shoebottom Seabourne: Burke Shepherd K.Eyre A.Eyre(Hick) Ramsey Batten:
Tries - Shoebottom Hick: Goal - Risman:
CASTLEFORD - Bedford: Foster Briggs(GLEN KNIGHT(528)) Thomas Lowndes(Fox): Hardisty Jones: Hartley Dickinson Ward Redfearn Lockwood Reilly:
Referee R Jackson (Halifax) Att - 18556 H.T. nil - 5

Sat 27 Dec 1969 KEIGHLEY home won 23 - 6
CASTLEFORD - Bedford: Foster Hepworth Thomas Lowndes: Hardisty Jones(Knight): Hartley(Fox) Dickinson Ward Redfearn Lockwood Reilly: Tries - Foster(2) Dickinson(2) Thomas: Goals – Redfearn(4):
KEIGHLEY - Jefferson(Render): Moulding Wilmot Roberts Hollindrake: Butler Evans: Worthy(Greenwood) Whittaker Clark Hepworth Dickinson Garbett:
Goals - Jefferson(2) (DG):
Referee W H Thompson(Hud'field) Att - 4000 H.T. 12 - 6

Sat 10 Jan 1970 WIGAN away won 11 - 10
WIGAN - Tyrer: O'Loughlin C.Hill D.Hill Francis: Jackson Parr: Stephens Mills Fletcher(Ashcroft) Hogan Ashurst Laughton: Tries - Tyrer Hogan: Goals - Tyrer(2):
CASTLEFORD - Bedford: Guest GARY JORDAN(529) Redfearn Lowndes: Hardisty Hepworth: Hartley Dickinson Ward Miller Lockwood(Fox) Reilly:
Tries - Guest Hardisty Miller: Goal - Redfearn:
Referee P Geraghty (York) Att - 6129 H.T. nil - 5

Fri 16 Jan 1970 SALFORD away won 12 - 7
SALFORD - Charlton: Jackson Whitehead Hesketh Richards: Watkins Prosser: Bott Burdell Smethurst

SEASON 1969-70

Coulman R.Hill Dixon:
Try - Charlton: Goals - Richards(2):
CASTLEFORD - Bedford: Knight Thomas Jordan Lowndes:
Hardisty Hargrave: Hartley Dickinson <u>Johnny Ward</u>
Redfearn Miller Reilly:
Tries - Ward Reilly: Goals - Knight(2) Hardisty(DG):
Referee G Philpott (Leeds) Att - 8630 H.T. 9 - 7

Sat 31 Jan 1970 HUNSLET away won 33 - 5
HUNSLET - Marshall: Lee Blake Simpson Thompson:
Harpin Williams: Larkin(Richardson) Dunn Crewdson
Gunney Baldwinson Sanderson:
Try - Crewdson: Goal - Marshall: :
CASTLEFORD - Edwards: Shaw Hargrave Thomas
Lowndes(Bedford): Hardisty(Redfearn) TONY DEAN(530):
Hartley Dickinson Ackroyd Kirkbride Lockwood Reilly:
Tries - Hargrave(3) Lowndes(3) Shaw Hardisty Dean:
Goals - Hardisty(3):
Referee D T H Davies (Manchester) Att - 2500 H.T. 25 -5

Sat 7 Feb 1970 HULL home won 15 - nil
CHALLENGE CUP ROUND 1
CASTLEFORD - Edwards: Briggs Hargrave Thomas
Lowndes: Hardisty Hepworth: Hartley Dickinson Redfearn
Kirkbride Lockwood Reilly:
Tries - Briggs(2) Hargrave: Goals - Redfearn(3):
HULL - Keegan: Sullivan Gemmell Maloney Firth:
Davidson Foulkes: Harrison McGlone(Forster) J.Macklin
Kirchin Trotter Ibbetson:
Referee D S Brown (Preston) Att - 9274 H.T. 10 - nil

Sat 21 Feb 1970 BARROW away won 12 - 4
CHALLENGE CUP ROUND 2
BARROW - Whitfield: Billingham Leake Jarrett Douglas:
Brophy Jones: Harrison Evans(Crayston) Sanderson Foster
McFarlane Robinson: Goals - Jarrett(2):
CASTLEFORD - Edwards: Briggs Hargrave Thomas
Lowndes: Hardisty Hepworth: Hartley Dickinson Redfearn
Kirkbride Miller Reilly:
Tries - Hardisty Hepworth: Goals - Redfearn(3):
Referee F Lindop (Wakefield) Att - 10600 H.T. 5 - 2

Sat 28 Feb 1970 DEWSBURY away won 12 - 11
DEWSBURY - Newall: Childe Clark N.Stephenson Tate:
Budge A.Bates: Naylor M.Stephenson Taylor
Whittington(Robinson) J.Bates Lowe:
Try - J.Bates: Goals - N.Stephenson(4):
CASTLEFORD - Edwards: Briggs Hargrave(Bedford)
Thomas Lowndes: Jones Hepworth: Hartley Dickinson
Ackroyd(Fox) Kirkbride Miller Redfearn:
Tries - Edwards Bedford: Goals - Redfearn(2) (DG):
Referee E Lawrinson (Warrington) Att - 2500 H.T. 5 - 6

Sat 7 Mar 1970 SALFORD home won 15 - nil
CHALLENGE CUP ROUND 3
CASTLEFORD - Edwards: Briggs Hargrave Thomas
Lowndes: Hardisty Hepworth: Hartley Dickinson Redfearn
Kirkbride Lockwood Reilly:
Tries - Hardisty(3): Goals - Redfearn(3)
SALFORD - Charlton: Henighan Whitehead Hesketh

Richards: Watkins Prosser: Roberts Ward Bott Coulman
Smethurst Dixon:
Referee D S Brown (Preston) Att - 15000 H.T. 10 - nil

Tue 10 Mar 1970 BRADFORD NORTHERN home won 10 - 4
CASTLEFORD - Edwards: Briggs Hargrave(Stenton)
Thomas Lowndes: Hardisty Hepworth: Hartley(S/O)
Dickinson Redfearn Kirkbride Lockwood Reilly:
Tries - Briggs Lowndes: Goals - Redfearn Hepworth(DG):
BRADFORD N - Rhodes: Beaumont Lamb Fox Croft:
Stockwell Daley: Mills Fisher Hill(Oswald) Clarkson
Macklin Joyce: Goals - Fox(2):
Referee R Jackson (Halifax) Att - 6000 H.T. 7 - 4

Fri 13 Mar 1970 HALIFAX home won 15 - 7
CASTLEFORD - Edwards: Briggs Thomas Stenton
Lowndes: Hardisty Hepworth(Knight): Hartley Dickinson
Redfearn Kirkbride Miller(Bullen)
STEVE(Knocker)NORTON(531):
Tries - Briggs(2) Edwards: Goals - Redfearn(3):
HALIFAX - James: Kelly Jones Willicombe Hepworth:
Burton Baker: Dewhirst Foye Ferguson Fogerty Reeves
Halmshaw: Try - Fogerty: Goals - James(1) (DG):
Referee R Appleyard (Leeds) Att - 4476 H.T. nil - 4

Fri 20 Mar 1970 SALFORD home won 20 - 5
CASTLEFOD - Edwards: Briggs Hargrave Stenton Lowndes:
Hardisty Hepworth: Hartley Dickinson Redfearn Kirkbride
Lockwood Reilly(Fox): Tries - Hardisty(2) Briggs Lowndes:
Goals - Redfearn(3) Hardisty(DG):
SALFORD - Charlton: Henighan Jackson(Crank)
Whitehead Richards: Hesketh Brennan: Roberts Snell
Ward Coulman Smethurst Dixon: Try - Richards:
Goal - Richards:
Referee R L Thomas (Oldham) Att - 6002 H.T. 10 - 5

Fri 27 Mar 1970 WAKEFIELD TRINITY home won 28 - 2
CASTLEFORD - Edwards(Stenton): Briggs Thomas
Hargrave Lowndes: Hardisty Jones: Fox Dickinson Ackroyd
Kirkbride Lockwood(Miller)Norton:
Tries - Thomas(2) Stenton Hargrave Lowndes Norton:
Goals - Hardisty(4) (DG):
WAKEFIELD T - Wraith: Slater Brooke Marston(Crook)
Carlton: Topliss Ward: Jeannes Hill Handforth Ramshaw
Ballantynr Haigh: Goal - Hill:
Referee J Manley (Warrington) Att - 7350 H.T. 7 - 2

Mon 30 Mar 1970 FEATHERSTONE ROVERS home lost 14 - 22
CASTLEFORD - Stenton: Briggs Hargrave Thomas
Lowndes: Knight Jones: Fox Dickinson
Redfearn(GEOFFREY(Sammy)LLOYD(532)) Kirkbride
Ackroyd Norton:
Tries - Dickinson Norton: Goals - Knight(3) Stenton(DG):
FEATHERSTONE R - Box: Bailey-Lee(Newlove) D.Kellett
Smith Hartley: Harding Nash: Dixon D.Morgan Lyons
Rhodes(A.Morgan) Thompson Farrar:
Tries - Nash(2) Dixon Thompson: Goals - Box(5):

SEASON 1969-70

Tue 31 Mar 1970 HULL home won 9 - 3
CASTLEFORD - Stenton: Briggs Hargrave Thomas Shaw:
Johnson Jones: Hartley Spurr Frank Fox(Ackroyd) John
McKalroy Lloyd Biscomb:
Try - Biscomb: Goals - Stenton(2) Jones(DG):
HULL - Keegan: Sullivan Gemmell Maloney Firth: Huxley
Davidson: Harrison McGlone Forster Kirchem Boxhall
Ibbetson: Try - Firth:
Referee J Manley (Warrington) Att - 4500 H.T. 4 - 3

Sat 4 Apr 1970 ST HELENS home won 6 - 3
CHALLENGE CUP SEMI FINAL - AT STATION ROAD
SWINTON
CASTLEFORD - Edwards: Briggs Hargrave(Stenton)
Thomas Lowndes: Hardisty Hepworth: Hartley Dickinson
Ackroyd Kirkbride Norton Reilly:
Goals - Hardisty(DG) Kirkbride(DG) Reilly(DG):
ST HELENS - Barrow: Jones Walsh Whittle Wilson: Myler
Heaton: Halsall(Rees) Sayer Watson Mantle
Chisnall(Prescott) Coslett: Try - Jones:
Referee W Thompson (Hud'field) Att - 18916 H.T. 2 - 3

Fri 10 Apr 1970 KEIGHLEY away won 15 - 7
KEIGHLEY - Jefferson: Wilmot Newton(Garbett)
Hollindrake Pascoe: Smith Cryer: Bryant Feather Brosnan
Hepworth Searle Butler:
Try - Hepworth: Goals - Jefferson(2):
CASTLEFORD - Edwards: Briggs Thomas Stenton
Lowndes: Hardisty Hepworth: Hartley Spurr Ackroyd
Kirkbride Miller Reilly(Dickinson):
Tries - Briggs Thomas Reilly: Goals - Ackroyd(3):
Referee J Elliott (Barrow) Att - 2000 H.T. 2 - 2

Fri 17 Apr 1970 HUDDERSFIELD home won 17 - 7
CHAMPIONSHIP ROUND 1
CASTLEFORD - Edwards: Guest Thomas Stenton
Lowndes(Hargrave): Hardisty Hepworth: Hartley Dickinson
Redfearn Kirkbride Ackroyd Reilly:
Tries - Thomas Stenton Hargrave: Goals - Redfearn(4):
HUDDERSFIELD - Wallace: Major Naylor(Leese) Evans
Pickup: Leek Loxton: Van Bellen Close Davies Valentine
Dobson Breakespeare: Try - Leek: Goals - Wallace Davies:
Referee R L Thomas (Oldham) Att - 6084 H.T. 12 - 5

Sat 25 Apr 1970 FEATHERSTONE ROVERS home
won 15 - 3   CHAMPIONSHIP ROUND 2
CASTLEFORD - Edwards: Guest Thomas Stenton Lowndes:
Hardisty Hepworth (Hargrave): Hartley Miller Redfearn
Kirkbride(Norton) Ackroyd Reilly:
Tries - Stenton Hardisty Miller: Goals - Redfearn(3):
FEATHERSTONE R - Box: Bailey-Lee Hay Smith Hartley:
Kellett Nash: Dixon D.Morgan(A.Morgan) Lyons Rhodes
Thompson Farrar: Try - Rhodes:
Referee D T H Davies (Man'ster) Att - 8525 H.T. 3 - nil

Sat 2 May 1970 ST HELENS home draw 9 - 9
CHAMPIONSHIP SEMI FINAL
CASTLEFORD - Edwards(Hargrave): Briggs Thomas

Stenton Lowndes(Ackroyd): Hardisty Hepworth: Hartley
Dickinson Redfearn Kirkbride Norton Reilly:
Try - Reilly: Goals - Redfearn(3):
ST HELENS - Barrow: Jones Benyon Walsh Wilson: Myler
Heaton: Halsall Sayer Watson Mantle Chisnall Coslett:
Try - Benyon: Goals - Coslett(2) Walsh:
Referee E Lawrinson (Warrington) Att - 9108 H.T. 7 - 5

Mon 4 May 1970 ST HELENS away lost 12 - 21
CHAMPIONSHIP SEMI FINAL REPLAY
ST HELENS - Barrow: Jones Benyon Walsh Wilson:
Myler(Whittle) Heaton: Rees(Prescott) Sayer Watson
Mantle Chisnall Coslett:
Tries - Wilson(3) Fees Prescott: Goals - Coslett(3):
CASTLEFORD - Howard Bibb: Guest Shaw Foster Day:
Johnson Jones: DENIS WARD(533) Miller Ackroyd Bullen
Blakeway Spurr: Tries - Guest Spurr: Goals - Ackroyd(3):
Referee G Wilson (Dewsbury) Att - 12000 H.T. 10 - 8

Sat 9 May 1970 WIGAN won 7 - 2
CHALLENGE CUP FINAL - AT WEMBLEY STADIUM
LONDON
CASTLEFORD - Edwards: Briggs Thomas Stenton
Lowndes: Hardisty(Hargrave) Hepworth: Hartley Dickinson
Redfearn Kirkbride Lockwood Reilly:
Try - Lowndes: Goals - Redfearn(2):
WIGAN - Tyrer(Hill): Jones Francis Rowe O'Loughlin: Hill
Parr: Ashcroft Burdell Hogan Ashurst Robinson Laughton:
Goal - Tyrer:
Referee G F Lindop (Wakefield) Att - 95255 H.T. 5 - 2
Lance Todd Trophy Winner - William Kirkbride
(Castleford) Cup Presented By The Earl Of Derby

As the holders of the Challenge Cup we went all out
to retain the trophy. Victories over Hull at home 15 –
nil in round one, was followed by a second round
victory away at Barrow 12 – 4. In round three we were
again to beat our last years final opponents Salford,
who included in their line-up a member of our
previous seasons victorious cup side Johnny Ward, at
home 15 – nil. The semi-final against St Helens at
Swinton was won in unusual fashion, with drop goals
from three different players Alan Hardisty, Bill
Kirkbride (his only drop goal for the club) and Mal
Reilly, to one try by the Saints we had earned our
second successive final appearance by 6 – 3.
Our final opponents were Wigan, whom we had
beaten in round two the previous year. The game
itself was disappointing in that we again failed to play
the "Classy" football that had become our hallmark.
With Castleford winning 5 – 2 the Wigan full back and
goal kicker Colin Tyrer was substituted following an
incident with Keith Hepworth. The incident, which
every Wigan supporter claimed changed the course of
the game also probably, cost "Heppy" the chance of
winning the Lance Todd Trophy despite a typical all
action display, the trophy being awarded to
Castleford's Bill Kirkbride for another outstanding
performance.

SEASON 1969-70

The week before Wembley brought controversy of a different kind. Having finished second in the league we won through to the semi-final of the Championship Top 16 play off with victories against Huddersfield at home in round one 17 – 7 and Featherstone Rovers at home in round two 15 –3. The semi-final against St Helens at home on the previous Saturday to the Wembley final ended in a 9 – 9 draw. Despite protests by the club we were ordered to play the replay on the Monday five days before the Cup Final by the Rugby Football League. We fielded fifteen reserves, after a magnificent performance and leading 10 – 8 until the last ten minutes our 'reserves' eventually lost 21 – 12. It was significant that no action was taken against the club for fielding a reserve side.

Terry Biscomb
D. No 521
1969-70 to 1975-76

Alan Ackroyd
D. No 522
1969-70 to 1975-76

Gary Stephens
D. No 525
1969-70 to 1980-81

Phil Johnson
D. No 526
1969-70 to 1980-81

Leslie Shaw
D. No 527
1969-70 to 1973-74

Glen Knight
D. No 528
1969-70 to 1973-74

Tony Dean
D. No 530
1969-70 to 1972-73

Steve (Knocker) Norton
D. No 531
1969-70 to 1976-77

Geoff(Sammy) Lloyd
D. No 532
1969-70 to 1977-78

Bill Kirkbride Trevor Briggs Ian Stenton & Alan Lowndes
Running Round Wembly with The Cup

The Players Lift the Coach Tommy Smales Shoulder
High with The Cup

THE 1969-70 R.L CHALLENGE CUP WINNING SQUAD

Back Row – S Bolstridge(Physiotherapist) G Gregory Dr   Butler(Directors)
Middle Row – T Smales(Coach) T Briggs C Dickinson M Redfearn D Hartley W Kirkbride M Reilly B Lockwood S Norton
D Hargrave L Garbett(Secretary)
Front Row W E Broxup(Vice Chairman) I Stenton T Thomas A Hardisty(Captain) R Simpson(Chairman) K Hepworth
D Edward A Lowndes F Jones(Director

D.N	PLAYER		DEBUT	L MATCH	APP	SUB	T.AP	TRI'S	G'LS	D.G	P'TS
426	BRYANT	WILLIAM		02/12/1969	2	2	4	0	0	0	0
433	HARDISTY	ALAN			38	0	38	19	9	5	85
442	HEPWORTH	KEITH			22	1	23	2	0	1	8
453	WARD	JOHNNY		16/01/1970	18	0	18	3	0	1	11
458	EDWARDS	DEREK			35	0	35	4	0	0	12
473	HOWE	KEITH		06/09/1969	3	1	4	0	0	0	0
474	BEDFORD	TREVOR			13	7	20	2	0	0	6
479	DICKINSON	CLIVE			38	1	39	6	0	0	18
492	STENTON	IAN			19	3	22	5	13	3	47
493	BRIGGS	TREVOR			42	0	42	18	0	0	54
494	REDFEARN	MICHAEL			37	3	40	3	89	1	189
495	MILLER	TONY			19	2	21	3	0	0	9
497	LOCKWOOD	BRIAN			33	1	34	4	0	0	12
498	AUSTIN	JACK		23/09/1969	6	0	6	0	0	0	0
502	BIBB	HOWARD		04/05/1970	3	0	3	0	0	0	0
503	HARTLEY	DENNIS			43	0	43	1	0	0	3
504	JONES	GLYN			14	1	15	0	0	1	2
506	THOMAS	TONY			45	0	45	15	0	0	45
508	KIRKBRIGHT	JOSEPH		16/08/1969	1	0	1	0	0	0	0
509	FOSTER	DEREK			12	0	12	5	0	0	15
510	FOX	FRANK		31/03/1970	12	6	18	1	0	0	3
511	McKALROY	JOHN		31/03/1970	1	1	2	0	0	0	0
512	REILLY	MALCOLM			30	0	30	7	4	4	37
513	HARGRAVE	DAVID (DANNY)			23	8	31	6	0	1	20
514	STEPHENS	DAVID		12/09/1969	4	0	4	0	0	0	0
515	DAY	MICHAEL			2	0	2	0	0	0	0
516	LOWNDES	ALAN			26	0	26	10	0	0	30
517	APPLEYARD	ROY			5	0	5	0	0	0	0
518	SPURR	ROBERT			5	0	5	2	0	0	6
519	BULLEN	NORMAN			4	1	5	0	0	0	0
520	BLAKEWAY	GRAHAM			1	1	2	0	0	0	0
521	BISCOMB	TERRY	16/08/1969		10	1	11	3	0	0	9
522	ACKROYD	ALAN	16/08/1969		9	3	12	0	6	0	12
523	KIRKBRIDE	WILLIAM	20/09/1969		31	0	31	3	0	1	11
524	GUEST	IAN	08/10/1969		9	0	9	4	0	0	12
525	STEPHENS	GARY	10/10/1969		2	0	2	0	0	0	0
526	JOHNSON	PHILIP	31/10/1969		3	0	3	0	0	0	0
527	SHAW	LESLIE	22/11/1969		5	0	5	1	0	0	3
528	KNIGHT	GLEN	26/12/1969		2	3	5	0	5	0	10
529	JORDAN	GARY	10/01/1970		2	0	2	0	0	0	0
530	DEAN	TONY	31/01/1970		1	0	1	1	0	0	3
531	NORTON	STEVE(KNOCKER)	13/03/1970		5	1	6	2	0	0	6
532	LLOYD	GEOFFREY(SAMMY)	30/03/1970		1	1	2	0	0	0	0
533	WARD	DENIS	04/05/1970	04/05/1970	1	0	1	0	0	0	0
	44				637	48	685	130	126	18	678
			13	**10**							

COMPETITION		P	W	D	L	FOR	AGT
LEAGUE ONE D	POSITION 2 OF 30	34	25	1	8	493	298
YORK'S CUP		1	0	0	1	4	30
F. TROPHY		5	4	0	1	73	43
RL CUP		5	5	0	0	55	9
CHAMPIONSHIP		4	2	1	1	53	40
PLAYERS RECORDS		**49**	**36**	**2**	**11**	**678**	**420**

For the second successive season we started with a new Coach, with Derek Turner leaving to take over at Leeds and former Huddersfield and Great Britain scrum half Tommy Smales taking his place.

Bill Kirkbride became the first Castleford player to play for Cumberland in their 42–3 victory over Yorkshire at Craven Park Hull, the Yorkshire side also contained Castleford team mates Alan Lowndes, Johnny Ward and Derek Edwards.

The summer tour to Australasia contained a record number of Castleford and former Castleford players – Derek Edwards, Alan Hardisty, Dennis Hartley, Keith Hepworth, Malcolm Reilly (Castleford), Roger Millward (Hull K R) and Johnny Ward (Salford).
Four notable Debutants were Gary Stephens Philip Johnson Steve (Knocker) Norton and Geoffrey (Sammy) Lloyd.

SEASON 1970-71

A substituted player allowed to come back on as a substitute

Fri 7 Aug 1970 HULL KINGSTON ROVERS away won 37 – 3 BENEFIT MATCH FOR BUNTING MAJOR MULLINS (HULL KINGSTON ROVERS) FRIENDLY
HULL K R - Markham: Sullivan Wainwright Rooms Collins: Brook Cooper (Ottoway): Clawson(Maxwell) Woolford Wiley Mennell(Palmer) Young (Flanagan) Wallis:
Try - Wainwright:
CASTLEFORD - Stenton(Dean): Briggs(Walsh) Thomas Hargrave Foster: Jones Smales: Hartley(C.Taylor) Dickinson Redfearn(Spurr) Kirkbride Lockwood Reilly:
Tries - Stenton(2) Foster(2) Jones(2) Thomas Hargrave Taylor: Goals - Lockwood(3) Reilly(2):
Referee H Cook (Beverley) Att -   H.T. 24 - 3

Sat 15 Aug 1970 ST HELENS home draw 19 - 19 CHALLENGE MATCH - CUP HOLDERS V LEAGUE CHAMPIONS
CASTLEFORD - Bedford(Johnson): Briggs Hargrave Stenton Lowndes: Hardisty Jones: Hartley Dickinson Redfearn Kirkbride Lockwood(Norton) Reilly:
Tries - Briggs Stenton Redfearn: Goals - Redfearn(5):
ST HELENS - Barrow: Jones Benyon Walsh Wilson: Myler Heaton: Rees Karalius Watson Mantle Sheffield Coslett:
Tries - Jones Watson Sheffield:
Goals - Coslett(4) Walsh(DG):
Referee M Naughton (Widnes) Att - 5226 H.T. 4 - 14

Sat 22 Aug 1970 HUDDERSFIELD away won 24 -10
HUDDERSFIELD - Wallace: Leese Pickup Naylor Senior(Evans): Leek Loxton: Van Bellen Hepplestone Davies Valentine Dobson Taylor(S/O): Goals - Davies(5):
CASTLEFORD - Edwards: Briggs Hargrave Stenton Foster: Hardisty Jones(Johnson): Hartley Dickinson Redfearn Kirkbride(S/O) Lockwood Reilly:
Tries - Hardisty(2) Stenton Foster: Goals - Redfearn(6):
Referee G Wilson (Dewsbury) Att - 2800 H.T. 7 - 10

Thu 27 Aug 1970 HALIFAX away won 22 - 12
HALIFAX - James: Kelly Jones Willicombe Hepworth: Raynor Baker: Ferguson Foye Manning(Dewhirst) Fogerty Martin Reeves: Tries - Baker Reeves: Goals - James(3):
CASTLEFORD - Edwards: Briggs Johnson Stenton Foster: Hardisty Hargrave: Hartley Dickinson Redfearn Kirkbride Lockwood(Norton)Reilly: Tries - Hardisty(3) Foster:
Goals - Redfearn(4) Hardisty(DG):
Referee E Clay (Rothwell) Att - 2910 H.T. 8 - 7

Sat 29 Aug 1970 HALIFAX home won 29 - 4 YORKSHIRE CUP ROUND 1
CASTLEFORD - Edwards: Briggs Hargrave(Johnson) Stenton Foster: Hardisty Hepworth: Hartley Dickinson Redfearn Norton Lockwood Reilly:
Tries - Hardisty(2) Briggs Foster Hartley Dickinson Reilly:
Goals - Redfearn(4):
HALIFAX - James: Kelly Willicombe Jones Hepworth: Rayner(Michael)Baker(Davies): Ferguson Foye Manning

Fogerty Martin Reeves: Goals - James(2):
Referee J Elliott (Barrow) Att - 5226 H.T. 8 - 4

Mon 31 Aug 1970 FEATHERSTONE ROVERS home won 24 - 13
CASTLEFORD - Edwards: Briggs Johnson(Hargrave) Stenton Foster: Hardisty Hepworth: Hartley Dickinson Redfearn Kirkbride Lockwood Reilly(Norton):
Tries - Hardisty(2) Hargrave Foster Hepworth Redfearn:
Goals - Redfearn(3):
FEATHERSTONE R - C.Kellett: Bailey-Lee(Smith) Hay Newlove Hartley: Harding Hudson: Tonks(Cotter) Bridges Windmill Rhodes(Bailey-Lee)Thompson Farrar:
Tries - Hartley(2) Cotton: Goals - Kellett(2):
Referee G Kershaw (York) Att - 6619 H.T. 13 - 13

Sat 5 Sept 1970 SWINTON away won 15 - nil
SWINTON - Gowers: Preston Gomersall Davies Pratt: Kenny M.Philbin (Price): Bate Clarke Holliday Smith Whittle(Hoyle) B.Philbin:
CASTLEFORD - Edwards: Briggs Shaw Stenton Foster: Hardisty Hargrave: Hartley Spurr Redfearn Kirkbride Lockwood Reilly(Norton): Tries - Edwards Foster Hargrave: Goals - Redfearn(2) Hargrave(DG):
Referee R Jackson (Halifax) Att - 3600 H.T. nil - nil

Mon 7 Sept 1970 LEEDS home lost 7 - 14 YORKSHIRE CUP ROUND 2
CASTLEFORD - Edwards: Briggs Thomas Stenton Foster: Hardisty Hargrave: Hartley Dickinson Redfearn Kirkbride(Ackroyd) Ackroyd(Norton) Lockwood:
Try - Hargrave: Goals - Redfearn Hardisty(DG):
LEEDS - Holmes: Langley Hynes Cowan Atkinson: Shoebottom Fawdington: Pitchford Dunn(Handscombe) Bence Hick (Watson)Haigh Batten:
Tries - Shoebottom Dunn: Goals - Holmes(3) Hynes(DG):
Referee E Lawrinson (Warrington) Att - 12479 H.T. 2 - 2

Wed 9 Sept 1970 SALFORD away won 13 - 11
SALFORD - Charlton: Jackson Whitehead Hesketh Richards: Watkins Prosser: Ward Egan Bott Coulman Smethurst Dixon:
Tries - Jackson(2) Ward: Goal - Egan(DG):
CASTLEFORD - Edwards: Briggs Thomas Stenton Foster: Hardisty Hargrave: Hartley Dickinson(Spurr) Redfearn Kirkbride Ackroyd(Appleyard) Norton:
Tries - Stenton(2) Briggs: Goals - Redfearn(2):
Referee D G Kershaw (York) Att - 7806 H.T. 10 - 8

Fri 11 Sept 1970 WIGAN home lost 16 - 17
CASTLEFORD - Edwards: Briggs Thomas Stenton Foster: Hardisty Hargrave: Hartley Spurr Redfearn Kirkbride Lloyd(Dickinson)Lockwood:
Tries - Foster Redfearn: Goals - Redfearn(4) Hardisty(DG):
WIGAN - Tyrer: Wright Whittle(Gandy) (Hogan) Francis Cunningham: D.Hill Parr: Stephens Clarke Fletcher Robinson Ashurst Laughton:

251

Tries - Francis Hill Parr: Goals - Tyrer(2) Ashurst(2DG):
Referee E Leach (St Helens) Att – 7031 H.T. 7- 13

Wed 16 Sept 1970 SALFORD home lost 6 - 36
CASTLEFORD - Edwards(Shaw): Briggs Gary Jordan
Stenton Foster: Thomas Appleyard: Hartley Dickinson
Ackroyd Kirkbride Lockwood Norton:
Tries - Briggs Appleyard:
SALFORD - Charlton: Jackson Whitehead Hesketh
Richards: Watkins Prosser: Bott Egan Ward(sub) Coulman
Smethurst(sub) Dixon: Tries - Hesketh(2) Prosser(2)
Charlton Richards: Goals - Watkins(7) (2DG):
Referee S Shepherd (Oldham) Att - 5482 H.T. 3 - 22

Fri 18 Sept 1970 WIDNES away lost 10 - 23
WIDNES - Dutton: Brown Thompson(McLoughlin) Aspey
Hughes: Boylan Bowden: Larkin(Macko) Foran French
Macko(Newton) Walsh Nicholls:
Tries - Newton(2) Macko: Goals - Dutton(6) Boylan(DG):
CASTLEFORD - Trevor Bedford: Lowndes Harris Stenton
Foster Thomas Appleyard: Ackroyd(Norton) Dickinson
Redfearn Lockwood Norton (Hartley) Spurr:
Tries - Stenton(2):   Goals - Redfearn(2):
Referee G Wilson (Dewsbury) Att - 5700 H.T. 5 - 9

Fri 25 Sept 1970 BRAMLEY home won 40 - 5
CASTLEFORD - Edwards: Lowndes Norton Stenton Foster:
Hargrave Appleyard: Hartley Dickinson Redfearn Biscomb
Lockwood Spurr: Tries - Spurr(3) Norton(2) Edwards
Lowndes Stenton Foster Hartley:
Goals - Lockwood(3) Stenton Redfearn:
BRAMLEY - Dewhurst: Goodchild D.Sampson Idle Craker:
Hughes Gallagher: Horn Price M.Sampson Higginbottom
Pearson(Branfoot) Ashton(Plumstead):
Try - Goodchild: Goal - Dewhurst:
Referee E Hill (Bradford) Att - 3896 H.T. 24 - 2

Tue 29 Sept 1970 ST HELENS away lost 7 - 14
BBC 2 FLOODLIT COMPETITION ROUND 1
ST HELENS - Barrow: Jones Benyon Walsh Wilson: Myler
Kelly: Halsall(Turner) Karalius Rees Mantle Sheffield
Coslett:
Tries - Walsh Halsall: Goals - Coslett(3) Walsh(DG):
CASTLEFORD - Edwards: Foster(Norton) Thomas Stenton
Lowndes: Hargrave Appleyard: Hartley Dickinson IAN
VAN BELLEN(534) Kirkbride Redfearn Spurr:
Try - Van Bellen: Goals - Redfearn(2):
Referee G Wilson (Dewsbury) Att – 7000 H.T. 2 - 7

**Fri 2 Oct 1970 HULL KINGSTON ROVERS away
lost 5 - 7**
HULL K R - Coupland: Stephenson Moore Willett Rooms:
Brook Cooper: Clawson Flanagan Wiley Lines Palmer
Wallis: Try - Rooms: Goals - Clawson Cooper(DG):
CASTLEFORD - Edwards(Biscomb): JOHN WALSH(535)
Hargrave Stenton Dennis Harris: Johnson Appleyard:
Hartley Dickinson Van Bellen(Norton) (Van Bellen)
Kirkbride Lockwood Spurr:
Try - Hargrave: Goal - Lockwood:
Referee T Keane (Oldham) Att - 4734 H.T. 3 - 2

Fri 9 Oct 1970 HUDDERSFIELD home won 23 - 6
CASTLEFORD - Edwards: Walsh Hargrave Stenton Day:
Johnson Hepworth: Hartley Dickinson Van Bellen Norton
Lockwood Reilly(Spurr): Tries - Hargrave Stenton Johnson
Norton Reilly: Goals - Lockwood(4):
HUDDERSFIELD - Bedford: Hoosen Evans Mullaney
Senior: Leek Branch(Leese): Hepplestone Close Davies
Dobson Hinchcliffe(Scroby)Tomlinson: Goals - Davies(3):
Referee P Geraghty (York) Att - 4867 H.T. 16 - 4

Wed 11 Nov 1970 BATLEY home won 16 - 7
CASTLEFORD - Edwards(Hargrave): Foster Briggs Stenton
Walsh: Hardisty Hepworth: Van Bellen Spurr(Bullen) Miller
Lockwood Norton Reilly:
Tries - Hardisty(2) Hargrave Stenton: Goals - Hepworth(2):
BATLEY - Gittins: Marsh Toohey Holmes Hemmings:
Watts Oldroyd: Walker(Barlow) O'Hara Tyson Brooke
Martin Standedge: Try - Marsh: Goals - Toohey(2):
Referee H Hunt (Prestbury) Att - 2801 H.T. 6 - 2

Sat 14 Nov 1970 HULL away lost 3 - 14
HULL - Owbridge: Huxley(Devonshire) Sullivan Maloney
Macklin: Hancock Davidson: Harrison McGlone Broom
Kirchin Forster Ibbertson (Boxhall):
Tries - Owbridge Huxley: Goals - Maloney(4):
CASTLEFORD - Knight: Walsh Hargrave Stenton(Thomas)
Briggs: Hardisty Hepworth: Van Bellen Miller Ackroyd
Lockwood Norton(Richard Brown) Spurr: Try - Walsh:
Referee J Naughton (Widnes) Att - 2000 H.T. nil - 5

Sat 21 Nov 1970 WARRINGTON home won 22 - 7
CASTLEFORD - Knight: Briggs Thomas Stenton Day:
Hargrave Hepworth: Van Bellen Miller Redfearn Ackroyd
JOHN COVENTRY(536)(Spurr) Norton:
Tries - Briggs Stenton Day Hargrave Hepworth Ackroyd:
Goals - Knight(2):
WARRINGTON - Whitehead(Jones) (Whitehead): Barton
Cracknell(Highton) Melling Heritage: Aspinall Brady:
Halliwell Price Brady Parr Western Gregory:
Try - Aspinall: Goals - Whitehead Aspinall:
Referee T Keane (Oldham) Att - 2196 H.T. 8 - 2

Sat 28 Nov 1970 WHITEHAVEN away lost 3 - 7
WHITEHAVEN - Donnelly: Buchanan Powe Rose Morris:
Shimmings Smith: McLeod McFarlane Martin McCracken
Gainford(Messanger)Hunter:
Try - McLeod: Goals - Donnelly(2):
CASTLEFORD - Knight(Spurr): Briggs RAY NEWTON(537)
Stenton Day: Thomas Hepworth: Hartley Miller Van Bellen
Lockwood Ackroyd Norton: Try - Stenton:
Referee S Shepherd (Oldham) Att - 1981 H.T.

Fri 4 Dec 1970 HULL home won 18 - 9
CASTLEFORD - Stenton: Foster Newton Hargrave Briggs:
Johnson Hepworth: Van Bellen (Hartley) Dickinson
Redfearn William Kirkbride(Norton)Lockwood Reilly(S/O):
Tries - Stenton Hargrave Johnson Lockwood:
Goals - Redfearn(3):
HULL - Owbridge: Sullivan Crane Maloney Devonshire:
Hancock Davidson: Harrison McGlone O'Brien Kirchin

Boxall(Robson) Ibbertson:
Try - Ibbertson: Goals - Maloney(3):
Referee J Elliott (Barrow) Att - 3013 H.T. 8 - 9

Sat 12 Dec 1970 ST HELENS away lost 5 - 9

ST HELENS - Houghton: Jones Myler Glover Wilson:
Whittle Heaton: Rees(Wanbon) Sayer Woodyer Prescott
Sheffield Coslett: Try - Whittle: Goals - Coslett(2) (DG):
CASTLEFORD - Stenton: Foster Newton Hargrave Briggs:
Johnson Dean: Hartley Dickinson Van Bellen
Redfearn(Norton) Lockwood Reilly:
Try - Johnson: Goal - Van Bellen(DG):
Referee E Clay (Rothwell) Att - 4300 H.T. 3 - 4

Sat 19 Dec 1970 SWINTON home lost 13 - 21

CASTLEFORD - Stenton: Foster Newton Thomas Briggs:
Johnson(Jones)Hargrave: Hartley Dickinson Van Bellen
Ackroyd Lockwood Norton:
Tries - Foster Briggs Hargrave: Goals - Ackroyd(2):
SWINTON - Cadman: Fleay Gomersall Buckley M.Philbin:
Davies Kenny: McKay B.Philbin Simpson Smith Cramant
Pattinson: Tries - Fleay M.Philbin Davies:
Goals - Cadman(4) Kenny(DG) Pattinson(DG):
Referee J Naughton (Widnes) Att - 3100 H.T. 5 - 9

Sat 26 Dec 1970 LEEDS away lost 9 - 14

LEEDS - Holmes: Smith(Langley) Hynes Cowan Atkinson:
Wainwright Shoebottom: Burke Fisher Cookson(Eccles)
Ramsey Haigh Batten:
Tries - Hynes Wainwright: Goals - Holmes(3) (DG):
CASTLEFORD - Stenton: Foster Briggs Hargrave Guest:
Hardisty Jones: Hartley Dickinson Van Bellen Redfearn
Lockwood Norton: Try - Hardisty: Goals - Redfearn(3):
Referee D G Kershaw (York) Att - 10043 H.T. 5 - 7

Fri 8 Jan 1971 BRADFORD NORTHERN home
won 12 - 7

CASTLEFORD - Edwards: Foster Stenton Newton Briggs:
Hardisty Hepworth: Hartley Dickinson Van Bellen
Lockwood(Spurr) Redfearn Norton:
Tries - Foster Briggs: Goals - Redfearn(2) Van Bellen(DG):
BRADFORD N - Price: Redfearn Lamb Watson Thompson:
Stockwell Diabira (Thomas): McCorley Walker Hill
Sykes(Diabira) Small Fearnley:
Try - Fearnley: Goals - Price(1) (DG):
Referee W Greenhalgh (Ashton in Makerfield) Att - 4150
H.T. 6 - 7

Sat 16 Jan 1971 WHITEHAVEN home won 32 - 3

CASTLEFORD - Edwards: Foster(Walsh) Stenton(Spurr)
Hargrave Briggs: Jones Hepworth: Hartley Dickinson Van
Bellen Lockwood Redfearn Norton:
Tries - Van Bellen(2) Edwards Briggs Jones Lockwood
Norton Walsh: Goals - Redfearn(4):
WHITEHAVEN - Gallagher: Cassie Powe Charlton
(Shimmings) Morris: Mather Smith: McLeod(McLean)
McFarlane Glaister Davidson Gainford Hunter:
Try - Morris:
Referee H G Hunt (Preston) Att - 3947 H.T. 13 - nil

Sat 23 Jan 1971 WHITEHAVEN away won 15 - nil
CHALLENGE CUP ROUND 1

WHITEHAVEN - Gallagher: Cassie Powe Shimmings
Morris: Kitching Smith: McLeod(Davidson) McFarlane
Martin Huddart(Gainford) McCracken Hunter:
CASTLEFORD - Edwards: Foster Newton(Norton) Hargrave
Briggs: Jones Hepworth: Hartley Dickinson Van Bellen
Lockwood(Spurr) Redfearn Reilly:
Tries - Foster Hargrave Briggs: Goals - Redfearn(3):
Referee M Naughton (Widnes) Att - 3432 H.T. 2 - nil

Sat 30 Jan 1971 LEIGH away lost 3 - 12

LEIGH - Ferguson: Collins Eckersley L.Chisnall Walsh:
Murphy Canning D.Chisnall Ashcroft(Fiddler) (Ashcroft)
Watts Clarkson Grimes Smethurst:
Tries - Collins Walsh: Goals - Ferguson(2) Murphy(DG):
CASTLEFORD - Edwards: Walsh Newton Tony Thomas
Briggs: Jones Hepworth: Hartley Dickinson Van Bellen
Coventry(Spurr) Redfearn Norton: Try - Hepworth:
Referee E Clay (Rothwell) Att - 5858 H.T. nil - 6

Sat 6 Feb 1971 WARRINGTON away lost 16 - 17

WARRINGTON - Conroy: Henighan Fleet McInnes
Heritage: Aspinall Leatherbarrow (J.Brady): Larkin Harrison
B.Brady Jones Lightfoot Parr: Tries - McInnes(2) Henighan
Heritage Larkin: Goal - Aspinall:
CASTLEFORD - Edwards: Newton Stenton PAUL
HIGGINS(538) Briggs: Hardisty Hepworth: Hartley
Dickinson Van Bellen Redfearn Lockwood Norton:
Tries - Redfearn Norton: Goals - Redfearn(5):
Referee G F Lindop (Wakefield) Att - 2896 H.T. 11 - 11

Sat 13 Feb 1971 ST HELENS home won 12 - 6

CASTLEFORD - Edwards: Walsh(Hargrave) Stenton Foster
Briggs: Hardisty Hepworth: Van Bellen Dickinson Redfearn
Lockwood Spurr Norton(Hartley):
Tries - Briggs Spurr: Goals - Redfearn(2) Hardisty(DG):
ST HELENS - Wils: Jones Glover Walsh Wilson: Whittle
Heaton: Stephers Karalius Watson Mantle
Chisnall(Prescott) Coslett: Tries - Jones Walsh:
Referee T Keane (Oldham) Att 4929 H.T. nil - 3

Fri 19 Feb 1971 KEIGHLEY home won 9 - 6
CHALLENGE CUP ROUND 2

CASTLEFORD - Edwards: Foster Stenton Hargrave Briggs:
Hardisty Hepworth: Hartley Dickinson Van Bellen
Lockwood Redfearn Spurr:
Try - Hardisty: Goals - Redfearn(3):
KEIGHLEY - Jefferson: O'Brien Wilmot Aspinall Pascoe:
Smith Evans: Clark Whittaker A.Eyre Dickinson Garbett
Butler: Goals - Jefferson(3):
Referee A Givvons (Oldham) Att - 9875 H.T. 4 - 2

Fri 26 Feb 1971 LEIGH home won 6 - 5

CASTLEFORD - Edwards: Foster Stenton LESLIE
SHEARD(539) Briggs: Hardisty Hepworth: Hartley
Spurr(Dickinson) Van Bellen Coventry Redfearn
Lockwood: Goals - Redfearn(2) Van Bellen(DG):
LEIGH - Eckersley: Ferguson Collins A.Barrow Walsh:
Murphy Canning: Chisnall W.Barrow Watts Fiddler Lester

Smethurst: Try - Ferguson: Goal - Ferguson:
Referee J Elliott (Barrow) Att - 5817 H.T. 6 - 3

**Sat 6 Mar 1971 SALFORD home won 9 - 8
CHALLENGE CUP ROUND 3**
CASTLEFORD - Edwards: Foster Sheard Hargrave
(Stenton) Briggs: Hardisty Hepworth: Hartley Dickinson
Van Bellen Coventry Redfearn Lockwood(Spurr):
Try - Redfearn: Goals - Redfearn(3):
SALFORD - Charlton(Jackson): Colloby Watkins Hesketh
Richards: Gill Prosser(Charlton): Bott Devlin
Ward(Hardacre)Coulman Kirkbride Dixon:
Tries - Watkins Coulman: Goal - Watkins:
Referee D S Brown (Preston) Att - 8357 H.T. 2 - nil

Sat 13 Mar 1971 BRAMLEY away won 20 - 17
BRAMLEY - Dewhurst: Goodchild D.Sampson Briggs
Austin: Hughes Astbury: Horn Price M.Sampson Payne
Jackson(Idle) Wolford:
Tries - Briggs Payne Wolford: Goals - Dewhurst(4):
CASTLEFORD - Stenton: Foster Sheard(Briggs) Hargrave
Lowndes: Jones Stephens: Hartley Spurr(Dickinson) Van
Bellen Coventry(Spurr)Redfearn Lockwood:
Tries - Lowndes Van Bellen Redfearn Lockwood:
Goals - Redfearn(4):
Referee W Thompson (Hud'field) Att - 2000 H.T. 5 - 12

**Tue 16 Mar 1971 HULL KINGSTON ROVERS home
won 24 - 13**
CASTLEFORD - Edwards: Foster Hargrave Briggs Lowndes:
Jones Stephens: Van Bellen Dickinson Ackroyd(Hartley)
Redfearn Lockwood Spurr: Tries - Foster Briggs Hartley
Lockwood: Goals - Redfearn(6):
HULL K.R. - Markham: Wainwright Moore Longstaffe
Rooms: Druery Daley: Clawson Flanagan(Palmer)
(Flanagan) Hickson Wallis Young(Palmer)Cooper:
Tries - Cooper(2) Wallis: Goals - Clawson(2):
Referee E Lawrinson (Warrington) Att - 4329 H.T. 6 - 8

Fri 19 Mar 1971 WIDNES home won 10 - 5
CASTLEFORD - Edwards: Foster Hargrave Briggs Lowndes:
Hardisty Stephens: Van Bellen Dickinson Redfearn
Coventry(Hartley) Lockwood (Jones) Spurr:
Tries - Hargrave Spurr: Goals - Redfearn(2):
WIDNES - McLaughlin: Brown Bowden Aspey Hughes:
O'Neill Boylan: Newton McIntyre Barnes(Warlow)
Fitzpatrick Sheridan Foran: Try - Bowden: Goal - Aspey:
Referee H Hunt (Prestbury) Att - 4453 H.T. 10 - 5

**Sat 27 Mar 1971 LEEDS lost 8 - 19 CHALLENGE CUP
SEMI FINAL - AT ODSAL STADIUM BRADFORD**
CASTLEFORD - Stenton: Foster Hargrave Newton Briggs:
Hardisty Stephens: Hartley Dickinson Van Bellen Coventry
Redfearn Lockwood: Goals - Redfearn(3) (DG):
LEEDS - Holmes: Smith Hynes Cowan Atkinson:
Wainwright Shoebottom: Burke Fisher(Hick) Barnard
Ramsey Haigh Batten:
Tries - Cowan(2) Hynes: Goals - Holmes(4) Hynes(DG):
Referee E Lawrinson (Warr'ton) Att - 25500 H.T. 2 - 12

Fri 2 Apr 1971 LEEDS home lost 2 - 15
CASTLEFORD - Sheard: Walsh Hargrave Stenton Day:
Hardisty Stephens: Van Bellen Dickinson(S/O) Redfearn
Coventry Lockwood Spurr: Goal - Sheard:
LEEDS - Holmes: Langley Hynes(S/O) Dyl Atkinson:
Wainwright Shoebottom: Burke Handscombe(Hick) Bence
Ramsey Haigh Batten:
Tries - Atkinson Handscombe Batten: Goals - Holmes(3):
Referee G Wilson (Dewsbury) Att - 6917 H.T. 2 - 7

Tue 6 Apr 1971 BATLEY away won 14 - 11
BATLEY - Gittins: Marsh Toohey Holmes Hemmings:
Watts Oldroyd: Grinhaff Hudson Tyson Brooke Martyn
Doyle. Subs Edwards J.Fox:
Try - Marsh: Goals - Toohey(3) Oldroyd(DG):
CASTLEFORD - Sheard: Walsh Hardisty Shaw Foster: Jones
Stephens(Hargrave): Van Bellen Dickinson Redfearn
Coventry(Hartley)Lloyd Lockwood(Coventry):
Tries - Hargrave Redfearn: Goals - Lloyd(4):
Referee K Allatt (Huddersfield) Att - 1578 H.T. 4 - 4

Fri 9 Apr 1971 HALIFAX home lost 9 - 11
CASTLEFORD - Stenton: Walsh(Lloyd) Hargrave Newton
Foster: Hardisty Jones: Hartley Dickinson Van Bellen
Coventry Redfearn Spurr:
Try - Jones: Goals - Redfearn(2) (DG):
HALIFAX - James: Burton Jones Willicombe Hepworth:
Kellett Baker: Fogerty Borthwick Dewhirst Reeves Michael
Halmshaw:
Try - James: Goals - James(1) (DG) Kellett(2DG):
Referee D G Kershaw (York) Att - 3655 H.T. 7 - 7

**Mon 12 Apr 1971 FEATHERSTONE ROVERS away
lost 5 - 12**
FEATHERSTONE R. - C.Kellett: Hartley Coventry
Newlove(Rhodes) K.Kellett: Mason Hudson: Tonks Bridges
Farrar Hollis Thompson Rhodes (Nash):
Tries - Tonks Hollis: Goals - C.Kellett(3):
CASTLEFORD - Sheard: Walsh Newton Foster Day:
Hardisty(Hargrave) Stephens: Hartley Dickinson Van
Bellen Coventry Redfearn Spurr: .
Try - Van Bellen: Goal - Redfearn:
Referee E Clay (Rothwell) Att - 2972 H.T. 2 - 5

Fri 16 Apr 1971 WIGAN away lost 4 - 16
WIGAN - Tyrer: Fuller Francis(Gandy) Rowe Wright: Hill
Ayres: Ashcroft Clarke Fletcher Ashurst O'Loughlin
Laughton:
Tries - Rowe Ayres Clarke O'Loughlin: Goals - Tyrer(2):
CASTLEFORD - Hardisty: Walsh Foster Newton Day:
Hargrave(Johnson) Appleyard: Hartley Spurr Van Bellen
Coventry Redfearn(Lloyd) Biscomb:
Goals - Redfearn(1) (DG):
Referee F Lindop (Wakefield) Att - 12009 H.T. 4 - 16

**Sun 18 Apr 1971 BRADFORD NORTHERN away
lost 11 - 25**
BRADFORD N - Carlton: Lamb Thomas(Vans) Watson
Redfearn: Treasure Diabira: Butler Walker(Wilson)
McCurly Galagher Small Joyce:

SEASON 1970-71

Tries - Thomas Evans Watson Diabira – 1 Try Scorer
unknown: Goals - Carlton(5)
CASTLEFORD - Hardisty: Day Walsh Appleyard Ian Guest:
Johnson Jones: Hartley Dickinson Van Bellen
Coventry(Lloyd) DENNIS FOWLER(540)(Spurr) Biscomb:
Tries - Day Appleyard Van Bellen: Goal - Van Bellen:
Referee D G Kershaw (York) Att - 4662 H.T. 6 - 15

**Fri 23 Apr 1971 WAKEFIELD TRINITY away
lost 4 – 10 CHAMPIONSHIP ROUND 1**
WAKEFIELD T - Cooper: Slater Hegarty Wraith
McDonagh(Fox): Marston Harkin: Jeannes Hill Valentine
Ramshaw Morgan Hawley:
Tries - Slater(2):   Goals - Slater Fox:
CASTLEFORD - Stenton(Newton): Michael Day Hargrave
Johnson Foster: Alan Hardisty Jones: Van Bellen(Hartley)
Dickinson Ackroyd Coventry Redfearn Biscomb:
Goals - Redfearn(2):
Referee T.Keane (Oldham) Att - 2786 H.T. 2 - 5

In the Challenge Cup we made a determined effort to reach Wembley for the third successive season. Victories in round one away at Whitehaven 15 – nil, which was Malcolm Reilly's last game in his first spell for the club before leaving to play for Manly in Australia, at home to Keighley 9 – 6 in round two and at home to Salford 9 – 8 in round three. Our semi-final opponents for the game at Odsal Bradford were Leeds, a Castleford side which only included 5 players and a substitute from the pervious years final team, could not make it three in a row losing 19 – 8.

Ian Van Bellen
D. No 534
1970-71 to 1972-73

John Walsh
D. No 535
1970-71 to 1971-72

John Coventry
D. No 536
1970-70 to 1972-73

Ray Newton
D. No 537
1970-71 to 1977-78

Paul Higgins
D. No 538
1970-71 to 1974-75

Les Sheard
D, No 539
1970-71 to 1971-72

SEASON 1970-71

D.N	PLAYER		DEBUT	L MATCH	APP	SUB	T.AP	TRI'S	G'LS	D.G	P'TS
433	HARDISTY	ALAN		23/04/1971	27	0	27	13	0	4	47
442	HEPWORTH	KEITH			17	0	17	3	2	0	13
458	EDWARDS	DEREK			25	0	25	3	0	0	9
474	BEDFORD	TREVOR		18/09/1970	2	0	2	0	0	0	0
479	DICKINSON	CLIVE			34	3	37	1	0	0	3
490	HARRIS	DENNIS		02/10/1970	2	0	2	0	0	0	0
492	STENTON	IAN			34	1	35	12	1	0	38
493	BRIGGS	TREVOR			30	1	31	11	0	0	33
494	REDFEARN	MICHAEL			35	0	35	7	87	3	201
495	MILLER	TONY			4	0	4	0	0	0	0
497	LOCKWOOD	BRIAN			34	0	34	4	8	0	28
503	HARTLEY	DENNIS			32	7	39	3	0	0	9
504	JONES	GLYN			12	2	14	2	0	0	6
505	BROWN	RICHARD		14/11/1970	0	1	1	0	0	0	0
506	THOMAS	TONY		30/01/1971	10	1	11	0	0	0	0
509	FOSTER	DEREK			33	0	33	11	0	0	33
512	REILLY	MALCOLM			11	0	11	2	0	0	6
513	HARGRAVE	DAVID (DANNY)			30	5	35	12	0	1	38
515	DAY	MICHAEL		23/04/1971	8	0	8	2	0	0	6
516	LOWNDES	ALAN			7	0	7	2	0	0	6
517	APPLEYARD	ROY			7	1	8	2	0	0	6
518	SPURR	ROBERT			18	10	28	5	0	0	15
519	BULLEN	NORMAN			0	1	1	0	0	0	0
521	BISCOMB	TERRY			4	1	5	0	0	0	0
522	ACKROYD	ALAN			10	0	10	1	2	0	7
523	KIRKBRIDE	WILLIAM		04/12/1970	12	0	12	0	0	0	0
524	GUEST	IAN		18/04/1971	2	0	2	0	0	0	0
525	STEPHENS	GARY			7	0	7	0	0	0	0
526	JOHNSON	PHILIP			9	4	13	3	0	0	9
527	SHAW	LESLIE			2	1	3	0	0	0	0
528	KNIGHT	GLEN			3	0	3	0	2	0	4
529	JORDAN	GARY		16/09/1970	1	0	1	0	0	0	0
530	DEAN	TONY			1	0	1	0	0	0	0
531	NORTON	STEVE (KNOCKER)			17	10	27	5	0	0	15
532	LLOYD	GEOFFREY (SAMMY)			2	3	5	0	4	0	8
534	VAN BELLEN	IAN	29/09/1970		31	0	31	6	1	3	26
535	WALSH	JOHN	02/10/1970		12	1	13	2	0	0	6
536	COVENTRY	JOHN	21/11/1970		14	0	14	0	0	0	0
537	NEWTON	RAY	28/11/1970		12	1	13	0	0	0	0
538	HIGGINS	PAUL	06/02/1971		1	0	1	0	0	0	0
539	SHEARD	LESLIE	26/02/1971		6	0	6	0	1	0	2
540	FOWLER	DENNIS	18/04/1971		1	0	1	0	0	0	0
	42		**7**	**9**	**559**	**54**	**613**	**112**	**108**	**11**	**574**

	COMPETITION			P	W	D	L	FOR	AGT
	LEAGUE ONE D	POSITION 12 OF 30		34	18	0	16	467	403
	YORK'S CUP			2	1	0	1	36	18
	F. TROPHY			1	0	0	1	7	14
	RL CUP			4	3	0	1	41	33
	CHAMPIONSHIP			1	0	0	1	4	10
	ST HELENS Cup W v Champ			1	0	0	1	19	19
	PLAYERS RECORDS			**43**	**22**	**1**	**20**	**574**	**497**

Sunday Rugby was sanctioned by the RFL. However, they also disbanded the County Leagues' arrangements.

There was also another change of Coach midway through the season with Alan Hardisty being appointed Player/Coach from December, taking over from Tommy Smales.

On 29 August 1970, Alan Hardisty became the first Castleford player to score 200 tries for the club in the 29–4 home victory over Halifax.
After the last game of the season an away defeat 10-4 at Wakefield Trinity in the Championship Top 16 play-off, Alan announced his retirement as a player to concentrate on his coaching duties.,

256

SEASON 1971-72

Sun 24 JUL 1971 BRADFORD NORTHERN away lost 8 - 17 CHARITY MATCH - JOE PHILLIPS MEMORIAL TROPHY FRIENDLY
BRADFORD N - Carlton: Lamb Tees Watson Redfearn: Treasure Diabara: McCurley Walker Hill Small Gallagher Fearnley: Subs - Stockwell Wilson Sykes Thompson
Tries -Tees(2) Fearnley: Goals - Tees(4):
CASTLEFORD - Edwards: Briggs Worsley Foster Walsh: Hargrave Jones: Hartley Miller Van Bellen Redfearn A.Dickinson Lockwood: Subs - Dean Coventry Achroyd Stenton :Tries - Briggs Foster: Goal - Van Bellen:
Referee J Senior (Bradford) Att - 1783 H.T. 6 - 3

Fri 30 Jul 1971 BATLEY home won 24 - 5 YORKSHIRE CUP ROUND 1
CASTLEFORD - Edwards: Foster Stenton(Briggs) KEITH WORSLEY(541) Lowndes: Hargrave Stephens: Hartley Miller Van Bellen ALAN DICKINSON(542)(Blakeway) Lockwood Blakeway(Ackroyd): Tries - Edwards Foster Worsley Lowndes Dickinson Van Bellen:
Goals - Van Bellen(3):
BATLEY - Gittins: Marsh Toohey Holmes Secker: Watts Oldroyd: Grinnhoff Hudson(Piwinski) Hall Brooke Chalkley Doyle: Try - Marsh: Goal - Gittins(DG):
Referee A Givvons (Oldham) Att - 2944 H.T. 13 - 5

Fri 6 Aug 1971 WAKEFIELD TRINITY home won 13 - 10 YORKSHIRE CUP ROUND 2
CASTLEFORD - Edwards: Foster Norton Worsley Lowndes: Hargrave Jones: Hartley(S/O)Miller Van Bellen(S/O) A.Dickinson(S/O) Lockwood Blakeway(Ackroyd):
Tries - Foster Hargrave Ackroyd:
Goals - Blakeway Ackroyd:
WAKEFIELD T - Crook: Slater(S/O) Wraith(S/O) Fox Backhouse: Topliss Harkin(Barends): Jeanes(S/O) Hill(Valentine) Valentine(Ballantyne) Harrison Ramshaw Morgan: Goals - Fox(3) (2DG):
Referee E Lawrinson (War'ton) Att - 4655 H.T. 2 - 10

Fri 13 Aug 1971 KEIGHLEY home won 12 - 7 YORKSHIRE CUP SEMI FINAL
CASTLEFORD - Edwards: Foster Norton Worsley Lowndes: Hargrave Jones (Stephens): Hartley Miller Van Bellen A.Dickinson(Lockwood) Ackroyd Blakeway:
Tries - Foster(2): Goals - Blakeway(2) Van Bellen:
KEIGHLEY - Jefferson: Simpson Wilmot Harrison(Smith) Moulding: Fawdington Hartley: Clark Whittaker A Eyre Brosnan O'Brien Garbett:
Tries - Wilmot: Goals - Jefferson(2):
Referee D S Brown (Preston) Att - 4814 H.T. 2 - nil

Sat 21 Aug 1971 HULL KINGSTON ROVERS lost 7 - 11 YORKSHIRE CUP FINAL AT BELLE VUE WAKEFIELD
CASTLEFORD - Edwards: Foster Norton Worsley Lowndes: Hargrave Stephens: Hartley Miller Van Bellen(Ackroyd) A.Dickinson Lockwood Blakeway:
Tries - Foster: Goals - Ackroyd(2):
HULL K R - Markham: Stevenson Coupland Kirkpatrick Longstaff: Millward Daley: Wiley Flanagan Millington

Wallis Palmer(Cooper)Brown:
Try - Longstaff: Goals - Millward(4):
Referee A Givvons (Oldham) Att - 5536 H.T.3 - 7
White Rose Trophy won by Markham Hull K R

Tue 24 Aug 1971 HULL away won 16 - 2
HULL - Owbridge Sullivan Devonshire(Doyle-Davidson) Huxley Macklin: Hancock Foulkes: M.Harrison Firth J.Harrison Kirchin Boxall Casey (Trotter):   Goal - Boxall:
CASTLEFORD - Edwards: Briggs Norton Worsley Lowndes: Hargrave Stephens(Jones): Hartley Miller Van Bellen Ackroyd A.Dickinson Blakeway:
Tries - Blakeway Van Bellen: Goals - Ackroyd(5):
Referee J Jackson (Halifax) Att - 2200 H.T. 9 - 2

Sat 28 Aug 1971 ROCHDALE HORNETS away won 15 - 5
ROCHDALE H - Chamberlain: Ratu Crellin Hillman(Machen) Brelsford: Myler Cartland: Watson Clarke Brown Welding Flanagan Delooze:
Try - Cartland: Goals - Chamberlain:
CASTLEFORD - Edwards: Foster Briggs Norton(Worsley) Lowndes: Hargrave Jones: Walton Miller Redfearn Biscomb(Ackroyd) Ackroyd(Spurr) Blakeway:
Tries - Edwards Norton Blakeway:
Goals - Redfearn 2) Blakeway(DG):
Referee R Appleyard (Leeds) Att - 1680 H.T. 10 - 5

Mon 30 Aug 1971 KEIGHLEY home won 18 - 9
CASTLEFORD - Edwards: Foster Norton Worsley Lowndes: Jones Appleyard: Walton Miller Redfearn Biscomb Blakeway(GEOFFREY WRIGHT(543)) Spurr:
Tries - Norton Worsley Biscomb Spurr:
Goals - Appleyard(2) Redfearn:
KEIGHLEY - Jicke ls: Simpson Smith Harrison Aspinall: Jefferson(Hartley) Evans: Naylor Whittaker Clarke Clarkson Garbett Butler(Brosnan):
Try - Jefferson: Goals - Garbett(2) Jefferson:
Referee D G Kershaw (York) Att - 3021 H.T. 9 - 5

Fri 3 Sep 1971 HALIFAX home won 24 - 12
CASTLEFORD - Edwards: Foster Norton Worsley Lowndes: Jones(Briggs)Appleyard: Walton Miller Redfearn A.Dickinson(Spurr) Biscomb Blakeway(A.Dickinson):
Tries - Foster(2) Norton Lowndes Appleyard Dickinson:
Goals - Redfearn(3):
HALIFAX - James: Rayner Davies Willicombe Tudball: Hepworth(Robinson)Sanderson: Ferguson Scanlon Jackson(Callon) Reeves Martin Halmshaw:
Tries - Reeves Martin: Goals - James(3):
Referee J W Ditchfield (Barrow) Att - 3552 H.T. 10 - 2

Wed .8 Sep 1971 ST HELENS home won 22 - 13
CASTLEFORD - Edwards: Foster Norton Worsley Lowndes: Johnson Appleyard: Walton Miller Van Bellen(A.Dickinson) Ackroyd A.Dickinson (Redfearn) Blakeway: Tries - Foster Norton Edwards Dickinson:
Goals - Ackroyd(4) Blakeway:
ST HELENS - Pimblett: Taylor Glover Houghton Wilson(Brown): Kelly Heaton: Rees Karalius

Helliwell(Stephens) Stillwell Chisnall Coslett:
Tries - Kelly(2) Houghton: Goals - Coslet:(2):
Referee R Wood(Dalton in Furness) Att 5247
H.T. 11 - nil

Sun 12 Sep 1971 BRADFORD NORTHERN away lost 15 - 36

BRADFORD N - Tees: Lamb Stockwell Watson Redfearn:
Treasure Diabira (Jackson): Butler(Hill) Walker Hinchcliffe
Gallagher Jackson (Blacker) Joyce Tries - Treasure(2)
Gallagher(2) Joyce(2) Lamb Walker: Goals - Tees(5) (DG):
CASTLEFORD - Edwards: Briggs(Walsh) Norton Worsley
Lowndes: Johnson(Briggs) Appleyard: Walton(Redfearn)
Miller Van Bellen A.Dickinson Ackroyd Blakeway:
Tries - Briggs Miller Van Bellen: Goals - Ackroyd(3):
Referee G F Lindop (Wakefield) Att - 632ˊ H.T. 5 - 18

Wed .15 Sep 1971 NEW ZEALAND won 25 - 8

CASTLEFORD - Edwards: Briggs Norton Worsley Walsh:
Johnson Appleyard: Hartley Miller Van Bellen Ackroyd
Redfearn(A.Dickinson)Blakeway(Newton):
Tries - Edwards Briggs Worsley Johnson Miller:
Goals - Ackroyd(5):
NEW ZEALAND - McLennan: Whittaker O'Sullivan Lowther
Brereton: Williams (Woolard) Cooksley: Tatanah Fisher
Orchard Eade Greengrass Kriletich:
Tries - Brereton Kriletich: Goal - Tatanah:
Referee E Clay (Rothwell) Att - 5825 H.T. 5 - 8

Sat 18 Sep 1971 ROCHDALE HORNETS home won 25 - 16

CASTLEFORD - Edwards: Foster Norton Worsley(Briggs)
Lowndes: Johnson Appleyard: Hartley C.Dickinson Van
Bellen Ackroyd(A.Dickinson) Redfearn Blakeway:
Tries - Foster(2) Norton(2) Johnson Van Bellen
A.Dickinson: Goals - Appleyard Ackroyd:
ROCHDALE H - Chamberlain: Machen Crellin Aspinall
Brelsford: Myler Cartland(Worrall): Birchall Clarke Brown
Flanagan(DeLooze)Sheffield Hodgkinson: Tries - Crellin
Aspinall Brelsford Myler: Goals - Chamberlain(2):
Referee W J Greenhalgh (A in M) Att - 3463 H.T. 14 - 5

Sat 25 Sep 1971 HALIFAX away won 14 - 8

HALIFAX - James: Rayner Davies Willicombe Tudball:
Baker Sanderson (Hepworth): Dewhirst Hawksley Jackson
Reeves Martin Halmshaw:
Tries - Rayner Sanderson: Goal - James:
CASTLEFORD - Sheard: Briggs Norton Worsley
Lowndes(Hargrave): Johnson Appleyard: Walton
C.Dickinson Van Bellen Ackroyd(Blakeway)(Ackroyd)
Redfearn A.Dickinson:
Tries - Briggs Worsley: Goals - Ackroyd(3); Redfearn:
Referee H G Hunt (Prestbury) Att - 2003 H.T. 4 - 8

Fri 1 Oct 1971 LEEDS home draw 12 - 12

CASTLEFORD - Edwards: Briggs Norton Worsley Walsh:
Hargrave Appleyard: Walton C.Dickinson Van Bellen
Ackroyd A.Dickinson Blakeway(Spurr):
Tries - Worsley Van Bellen: Goals - Ackroyd(3):
LEEDS - Hick: Claughton Holmes Dyl Parkeˊ: Hardisty

Barham: Pitchford Handscombe Cookson(Pickup)
Eccles(Goodwin) Haigh Batten:
Tries - Holmes Barham: Goals - Holmes(3):
Referee A Givvons (Oldhham) Att - 9080 H.T. 7 - 5

Tue 5 Oct 1971 HUDDERSFILED home lost 7 - 8 BBC 2 FLOODLIT COMPETITION ROUND 1

CASTLEFORD - Edwards: Foster Briggs Worsley John
Walsh: Johnson Keith Hepworth: Hartley A.Dickinson Van
Bellen(Spurr) Redfearn Ackroyd Hargrave:
Try - Foster: Goals - Ackroyd(2):
HUDDERSFIELD - Bedford: Hooson Evans Pickup
McDonagh: Chamberlain Loxton: Hepplestone Appleyard
Weavil Davies Naylor Tomlinson(Forster):
Goals - Davies(2) (DG2):
Referee E Clay (Rothwell) Att - 2915 H.T. 5 - 2

Sat 9 Oct 1971 KEIGHLEY away won 24 - 5

KEIGHLEY - Jickles: Smith Wilmot Fawdington Cockcroft:
Hartley Evans(Harrison): Cotton Whitaker
Clarkson(Brosnan) O'Brien Hepworth Garbett:
Try - Cockcroft: Goal - Hartley:
CASTLEFORD - Edwards: Foster Sheard Worsley Briggs:
Johnson(Hargrave) Appleyard: Hartley Miller Redfearn
A.Dickinson Coventry(Bullen) Fowler:
Tries - Johnson(2) Briggs Redfearn: Goals - Redfearn(6):
Referee J F Jones (Widnes) Att - 1659 H.T. 14 - 3

Sun 17 Oct 1971 BATLEY away won 9 - 2

BATLEY - Secker: Hemmings Edwards Holmes Hepworth:
Watts Oldroyd (Taylor): Tyson O'Hara Standidge(Grinhaff)
Brooke Fox Doyle: Goal - Brooke:
CASTLEFORD - Edwards: Foster Norton(S/O) Worsley
Briggs(Hargrave): Johnson Appleyard: Van Bellen Miller
Redfearn Coventry Bullen A.Dickinson:
Try - Norton: Goals - Redfearn(3):
Referee A Givvons (Oldham) Att - 1300 H.T. nil - nil

Fri 22 Oct 1971 BATLEY home won 22 - 13

CASTLEFORD - Edwards: Foster Norton Worsley Lowndes:
Johnson Dean: Van Bellen Miller Redfearn Coventry
Lockwood A.Dickinson:
Tries - Norton Dean Miller Redfearn: Goals - Redfearn(5):
BATLEY - Esckar: Hemmings Holmes(Edwards) Chalkley
Hepworth: Watts Taylor: Grinhoff Smith Standidge(Tyson)
Brooke Fox Doyle:
Try - Standidge: Goals - Brooke(4) Esckar(DG):
Referee R Wood (Barrow) Att - 3030 H.T. 15 - nil

Sat 30 Oct 1971 WORKINGTON TOWN away won 4 - nil

WORKINGTON T - Thompson: McQuire Tait Marland
Thornwaite: Nicholson(Walker) Newall: Moore Allen
McCourt Curwen Bowman(Shepherd) Branthwaite:
CASTLEFORD - Edwards: Foster Leslie Sheard(Hargrave)
Worsley Lowndes: Johnson Dean: Van Bellen C.Dickinson
Redfearn Coventry Lockwood A.Dickinson:
Goals - Redfearn(2):
Referee A Givvons (Oldham) Att – 817 H.T. 4 - nil

258

SEASON 1971-72

Wed 3 Nov 1971 WAKEFIELD TRINITY home won 12 - 5
CASTLEFORD - Hargrave: Foster Norton Worsley Lowndes: Johnson(Jones) Dean(Johnson): Hartley(Van Bellen) (Hartley) C.Dickinson Redfearn Coventry Lockwood A.Dickinson:
Tries - Hargrave Foster: Goals - Redfearn(2) Dean(DG):
WAKEFIELD T - Cooper: Smith Wraith Hegarty Backhouse: Bell(Crook) Harkin: Valentine Handforth(Hawley) Ballantyne Harrison Fox Morgan:
Try - Hegarty: Goal - Fox:
Referee P Hegarty (York) Att - 4167 H.T. 9 - nil

Sat 6 Nov 1971 BLACKPOOL BOROUGH home won 19 - 4
CASTLEFORD - Hargrave: Foster Norton Worsley Lowndes: Johnson Dean (Jones): Hartley C.Dickinson Redfearn Coventry(Van Bellen) Ackroyd A.Dickinson:
Tries - Norton Johnson Dean:
Goals - Redfearn(3) Ackroyd(2):
BLACKPOOL B - Pickup: Cantillon(Warburton) Hill Jackson Aspey: Cassidy Bishop: Loughlin Egan Walker Crank Cooke Hall: Goals - Hill(2):
Referee R Dennett (Warrington) Att - 1957 H.T. 9 - 2

Sun 14 Nov 1971 HUNSLET away draw 7 - 7
PLAYERS No.6 COMPETITION ROUND 1
HUNSLET - Marshall: Lee Clark Blake Jack.Richardson: Barron Rycroft: Crewdson Maskill Jim.Richardson Sykes Williams(Sanderson)Griffiths:
Try - Lee: Goals - Marshall(2):
CASTLEFORD - Edwards: Foster Norton Worsley(Hargrave) Lowndes: Jones Dean: Hartley C.Dickinson Van Bellen Ackroyd Redfearn A.Dickinson (Blakeway): Try - Dean: Goals - Redfearn(2):
Referee S Shepherd (Oldham) Att - 2300 H.T. 2 - 2

Wed 17 NOV 1971 HUNSLET home won 9 - 8
PLAYERS No.6 COMPETITION ROUND 1 REPLAY
CASTLEFORD - Edwards: Foster Stenton Worsley Briggs: Glyn Jones (Hargrave) Dean: Van Bellen C.Dickinson Redfearn Ackroyd A.Dickinson Spurr:
Try - Dean: Goals - Redfearn(3):
HUNSLET - Marshall: Lee Clark Blake Jack.Richardson: Barrow Rycroft(Watson): Crewdson Maskill Jim.Richardson Sykes Williams Griffiths:
Goals - Marshall(3) (DG):
Referee S Shepherd (Oldham) Att - 2203 H.T. 2 - 6

Sat 20 Nov 1971 ST HELENS away lost 2 - 14
ST HELENS - Pimblett: Jones Benton Walsh Wilson: Kelly Heaton: Rees Greenall Chisnall Prescott Mantle Coslett:
Tries - Kelly(2): Goals - Coslett(4):
CASTLEFORD - Edwards: Foster Stenton Norton Briggs: Worsley(Hargrave) Stephens: Van Bellen C.Dickinson Redfearn Ackroyd A.Dickinson Spurr: Goal - Redfearn:
Referee G Wilson (Dewsbury) Att - 2000 H.T. 2 - 14

Fri 26 NOV 1971 LEEDS home lost 11 - 13
PLAYERS No.6 COMPETITION ROUND 2
CASTLEFORD - Edwards(Stenton): Foster Norton Worsley Briggs: Hargrave Appleyard: Walton C.Dickinson Van Bellen Redfearn Ackroyd A.Dickinson:
Try - Worsley: Goals - Redfearn(4):
LEEDS - Holmes: Cowan Langley Dyl Atkinson: Hardisty Hepworth: Burke Ward Bence Ramsey Eccles(Hick) Preece:
Tries - Holmes Cowan Burke: Goals - Holmes(2):
Referee D S Brown (Dewsbury) Att - 7253 H.T. 4 - 2

Fri 10 Dec 1971 SALFORD away lost 9 - 25
SALFORD - Charlton: McCorquodale Watkins Hesketh(Prosser) Richards: Gill Banner: Ramshaw Clarke Ward Coulman Whitehead Davies: Tries - Richards(2) Charlton Gill Whitehead: Goals - Watkins(4) (DG):
CASTLEFORD - Edwards: Foster Norton Worsley Lowndes: Johnson Appleyard: Walton C.Dickinson(Ackroyd) Redfearn A.Dickinson Lockwood Blakeway:
Try - Foster: Goals - Redfearn(3):
Referee D G Kershaw (York) Att - 6600 H.T. 4 - 15

Fri 17 Dec 1971 HUDDERSFIELD home won 17 - 2
CASTLEFORD - Edwards: Foster Norton Worsley Lowndes: Johnson(Stentor)Appleyard: Walton C.Dickinson Redfearn A.Dickinson Lockwood Blakeway(Ackroyd):
Tries - Edwards Foster Lowndes: Goals - Redfearn(4):
HUDDERSFIELD - Bedford: Hooson Evans Pickup McDonagh: Leek Loxton: Hepplestone Wilson Weaver Forster Naylor(Taylor) Tomlinson: Goal - Loxton(DG):
Referee J F Jones (Widnes) Att - 2665 H.T. 9 - 2

Mon 27 Dec 1971 BLACKPOOL BOROUGH away won 18 - 2
BLACKPOOL B - Pickup: Johnson Warburton Jackson(Crann) Aspey: Marsh Bishop(S/O): Walker Martland Egan Hall Cooke Farrell: Goal - Marsh(DG):
CASTLEFORD - Edwards: Foster(GEORGE CLAUGHTON(544)) Briggs Worsley Lowndes: Stenton Appleyard: Walton C.Dickinson Redfearn A.Dickinson(S/O) Lockwood Blakeway(Ackroyd):
Tries - Briggs(2) Lowndes Ackroyd: Goals - Redfearn(3):
Referee R Jackson (Halifax) Att - 1500 H.T. 3 - 2

Fri 31 Dec 1971 BRADFORD NORTHERN home lost 5 - 6
CASTLEFORD - Edwards: Foster Briggs Worsley(Stenton) Lowndes: Claughton Appleyard: Douglas Walton Spurr Redfearn A.Dickinson Lockwood(Ackroyd) CLIFFORD WALLIS(545): Try - Claughton: Goal - Redfearn:
BRADFORD N. - Tees: Lamb Stockwell Carlton Redfearn: Treasure Blacker: Hill Walker Long Gallagher Jackson(Small) Joyce: Goals - Tees(2) (DG):
Referee R Wood (Dalton in Furness) Att - 3086 H.T. 2 - 6

Sat 8 Jan 1972 DEWSBURY away lost 7 - 11
DEWSBURY - Smith: Ashcroft Fletcher N.Stephenson Childe: Agar A.Eates: Beverley M.Stephenson Lowe Grayshon Whittington J.Bates: Tries - Agar M.Stephenson Whittington: Goal - N.Stephenson:
CASTLEFORD - Edwards: Foster Briggs(S/O) Stenton Lowndes: Hargrave Stephens(Biscomb): Hartley

Spurr(Worsley) Redfearn Ackroyd Lockwood Wallis:
Try - Lowndes: Goals - Redfearn(2):
Referee L Gaskell (Wigan) Att - 2000 H.T. 2 - 6

Sat 15 Jan 1972 WIGAN home lost 3 - 8
CASTLEFORD - Edwards: Foster Worsley Stenton
Lowndes: Hargrave Stephens: Hartley C.Dickinson
Redfearn A.Dickinson Lockwood(Ackroyd) Wallis:
Try - Worsley:
WIGAN - Tyrer: Francis D.Hill Kevin O'Loughlin Fuller:
Davies Parr: Ashcroft(Cramant) Clarke Fletcher Ashurst
Cunningham Robinson: Goals - Ashurst(3DG) Parr(DG):
Referee J W Ditchfield (Barrow) Att - 3354 H.T. 3 - 2

Sun 23 Jan 1972 HUDDERSFIELD away lost 5 - 9
HUDDERSFIELD - Bedford: Hooson Pickup Evans Senior:
Calvert Doyle: Weavill Wilson Davies Forster Chawner
Tomlinson: Try - Calvert: Goals - Davies(3):
CASTLEFORD - STEVEN BRUNYEE(546): Foster Worsley
Stenton Lowndes: Claughton(Hargrave) Stephens: Hartley
Miller Redfearn Ackroyd Lockwood Wallis:
Try - Foster: Goal - Redfearn:
Referee T Keane (Oldham) Att - 3183 H.T 3 - 2

**Sat 29 Jan 1972 WHITEHAVEN away won 17 - nil
CHALLENGE CUP ROUND 1**
WHITEHAVEN - Donnelly: Morris Gracey Rose Sewell:
Cassie Madison: D.Martin McCracken Pringle Gainford
McFarlane R.Martin(Hunter):
CASTLEFORD - Stenton: Foster Worsley Newton Lowndes:
Hargrave(Dean)Stephens: Hartley Miller Redfearn
Ackroyd(Lockwood) Lockwood (CHARLES BIRDSALL(547))
Wallis: Tries - Lowndes(2) Hargrave:
Goals - Redfearn(3) Ackroyd(DG):
Referee S Shepherd (Oldham) Att - 2675 H.T. 15 - nil

Sun 6 Feb 1972 LEIGH away lost 11 - 21
LEIGH - Eckersley: Ferguson A.Barrow Fleet(Collins) Walsh:
Boylan Canning: Ogden W.Barrow Simpson Grimes
Martin Smethurst: Tries - Ferguson Walsh Canning:
Goals - Ferguson(5) Eakersley(DG):
CASTLEFORD - Stenton(Dean): Foster Worsley Newton
Lowndes(Bullen): Shaw Stephens: Bullen(Birdsall) Miller
Redfearn Ackroyd Lockwood Wallis:
Tries - Foster Stephens Wallis: Goal - Redfearn:
Referee G F Lindop (Wakefield) Att - 6000 H.T. 2 - 11

**Sat 12 Feb 1972 WORKINGTON TOWN home
won 27 - 2**
CASTLEFORD - Edwards: Foster(Birdsall) Worsley Newton
Briggs: Hargrave(Brunyee) Stephens: Hartley Miller
Redfearn A.Dickinson Ackroyd Wallis:
Tries - Worsley(2) Foster Newton Briggs Stephens
Redfearn: Goals - Birdsall(3):
WORKINGTON T - Thompson: Risman Marland
Nicholson(Calvin) Thornwaite: McQuire Newall: Hogan
Banks McCourt Morton(Curwen) Gorley Branthwaite:
Goal - McCourt(DG):
Referee S Shepherd (Oldham) Att - 2131 H.T. 12 - nil

**Sat 19 Feb 1972 WARRINGTON home draw 8 - 8
CHALLENGE CUP ROUND 2**
CASTLEFORD - Edwards(Briggs): Foster Worsley Newton
Lowndes: Hargrave Stephens: Hartley Miller(Ackroyd)
Redfearn A.Dickinson Lockwood Wallis:
Tries - Newton A.Dickinson: Goal - Redfearn:
WARRINGTON - Whitehead: Barton Cunliffe(Noonan)
Briggs Du-Toit: Murphy(S/O) Gordon: Wanbon Heard
Brady Clarkson Gregory Henighan:
Goals - Whitehead(3) (DG):
Referee R Wood (Dalton in Furness) Att - 5222 H.T. 3 - 2

**Wed .23 Feb WARRINGTON away lost 5 - 11
CHALLENGE CUP ROUND 2 REPLAY**
WARRINGTON - Whitehead: Barton Cunliffe Briggs
Du-Toit: Murphy(Cannon) Gordon: Wanbon Heard Brady
Gregory Clarkson Henighan:
Try - Brady: Goals - Whitehead(3) Briggs(DG):
CASTLEFORD - Edwards: Foster(Briggs) Worsley Norton
Lowndes: HargraveStephens: Hartley Miller(C.Dickinson)
Lockwood A.Dickinson Ackroyd Wallis:
Try - Ackroyd: Goal - Ackroyd:
Referee G F Lindop (Wakefield) Att - 12131 H.T. 5 - 9

Sun 27 Feb 1972 DEWSBURY home won 24 - 10
CASTLEFORD - Edwards: Briggs Worsley Newton
Lowndes: Claughton(Hargrave) Dean: DEREK
WOODALL(548)(Ackroyd) Miller Birdsall A.Dickinson
Lockwood Wallis(S/O): Tries - Briggs(2) Newton(2)
A.Dickinson(2):   Goals - Birdsall(3):
DEWSBURY - Rushton: Ashcroft Fletcher N.Stephenson
Childe(Yoward): Lee A.Bates: Beverley Hepworth Lowe
Grayshon J.Bates Robinson(Taylor):
Tries - N.Stephenson Grayshon:
Goals - N.Stephenson(1) (DG):
Referee E Lawrinson (Warrington) Att - 3074 H.T. 11 - 2

**Fri 10 Mar 1972 HULL KINGSTON ROVERS away
lost 6 - 7**
HULL K R - Markham: Stephenson Longstaff Kirkpatrick
Dunn: Millward(Moore) Hudson: Dawson(Millington)
Heslop Neale Wiley Hickson Rose:
Try - Longstaff: Goals - Millward(2):
CASTLEFORD - Brunyee: Briggs Worsley Hargrave(Shaw)
Lowndes: Johnson Dean(S/O): Redfearn Miller
Birdsall(Ackroyd) A.Dickinson Lockwood Wallis:
Tries - Briggs Dickinson:
Referee D S Brown (Preston) Att - 2630 H.T. 3 - 7

Tue 14 Mar 1972 LEEDS away lost 14 - 15
LEEDS - Hick: Parker Holmes Dyl Atkinson: Wainwright
Hepworth: Clawson Ward Pitchford(Cookson) Ramsey
Pickup Batten:
Tries - Hepworth(2) Holmes: Goals - Clawson(3):
CASTLEFORD - Edwards: Briggs Worsley Newton
Lowndes: Johnson Dean: Redfearn Miller Lockwood
A.Dickinson Lloyd Wallis:
Tries - Newton Wallis: Goals - Lloyd(4):
Referee G F Lindop (Wakefield) Att - 7289 H.T. 7 - 12

Fri 17 Mar 1972 SALFORD home won 19 - 12
CASTLEFORD - Edwards: Briggs Worsley Newton
Lowndes: Johnson(Brunyee) Dean: Redfearn Miller
Lockwood A.Dickinson Lloyd Wallis:
Tries - Briggs Lloyd Wallis: Goals - Lloyd(5):
SALFORD - Charlton: Jackson Watkins Hesketh Richards:
Prosser Banner: Coulman Clarke Grice
Whitehead(Kirkbride) Dixon Davies:
Tries - Jackson Watkins: Goals - Watkins(2) (DG):
Referee J Naughton (Widnes) Att - 3358 H.T. 7 - 12

**Fri 24 Mar 1972 HULL KINGSTON ROVERS home
won 30 - 6**
CASTLEFORD - Edwards: Briggs Worsley Newton
Lowndes: Johnson (RICHARD JAMES(549)) Dean
(Johnson): Redfearn Miller Lockwood
A.Dickinson(Ackroyd) (A.Dickinson) Lloyd Wallis:
Tries - Lockwood(3) Lowndes(2) Dean: Goals - Lloyd(6):
HULL K R - Markham: Longstaff Coupland Kirkpatrick
Dunn: Hartley Hudson: Dawson Heslop Neale Hossell
Millington Lowe(Palmer): Tries - Hartley(2):
Referee T Keane (Oldham) Att - 3288 H.T. 22 - nil

**Fri 31 Mar 1972 WAKEFIELD TRINITY away
lost 9 - 12**
WAKEFIELD T - Wraith: Major Marston Smith(Bell)
Backhouse: Topliss Ward: Jeannes Handforth
Spencer(Valentine)Harrison Morgan Fox:
Tries - Major Handforth: Goals - Ward(3):
CASTLEFORD - Edwards: Briggs Worsley(Brunyee) Newton
Lowndes: Johnson Knight: Redfearn Miller Lockwood
C.Dickinson Lloyd Blakeway: Try - Knight: Goals - Lloyd(3):
Referee R Wood (Dalton in Furness) Att - 4396 H.T. 9 - 6

Mon 3 Apr 1972 LEIGH home lost 7 - 14
CASTLEFORD - Edwards(Johnson): Foster Briggs Newton
Lowndes: Knight(Graham Blakeway) Dean: Redfearn Miller
Lockwood C.Dickinson Lloyd(Knight) Wallis:
Try - Lockwood: Goals - Lloyd(2):
LEIGH - Eckersley: Ferguson A.Barrow Collins Houghton:
Boylan Canning: Ashcroft W.Barrow Smethurst
Peters(Melling) Highcock Martyn:
Tries - Eckersley Boylan: Goals - Ferguson(4):
Referee E Leach (St Helens) Att - 2852 H.T. 2 - 2

Fri 7 Apr 1972 WIGAN away lost nil - 37
WIGAN - Francis: Whittle Hill Kevin O'Loughlin
Kieron.O'Loughlin: Davies Parr: Ashcroft Clarke Cramant
Cunningham Robinson Laughton:
Tries - Cunningham(4) Parr(2) Hill Kevin.O'Loughlin
Cramant: Goals - Francis(5):
CASTLEFORD - Edwards: Briggs Shaw Newton
Lowndes(Johnson): Knight Dean: Redfearn Miller(Birdsall)
Lockwood C.Dickinson Lloyd(Miller)Wallis:
Referee P Geraghty (York) Att - 4121 H.T. nil - 13

Wed 12 Apr 1972 HULL home won 24 - 13
CASTLEFORD - Edwards: Lloyd Shaw Newton Briggs:
Knight Dean: Redfearn Miller C.Dickinson Birdsall(Norman
Bullen) Lockwood Wallis: Tries - Edwards Lloyd Newton

Miller: Goals - Lloyd(5) Wallis(DG):
HULL - Kendle: Sullivan Devonshire Portz Firth:
Doyle-Davidson Foulkes: Harrison McGlone McLane
Boxall Crane Kirchin:
Tries - Sullivan Foulkes Crane: Goals - Kendle(2):
Referee S Shepherd (Oldham) Att - 1781 H.T. 10 - nil

**Sun 23 Apr 1972 FEATHERSTONE ROVERS away
won 18 - 14 CHAMPIONSHIP ROUND 1**
FEATHERSTONE R - Box: Bailey-Lee M.Smith(Hartley)
Newlove K.Kellett: Mason Nash: Tonks Bell Farrar Hollis
Rhodes Stone(C.Smith):
Tries - Hollis(2): Goals - Box(2) Nash(DG) Hollis(DG):
CASTLEFORD - Edwards: Lloyd Briggs Newton Lowndes:
Knight Dean: Hartley C.Dickinson(Miller) Lockwood
Birdsall Fowler Wallis:
Tries - Lloyd Lowndes Knight Wallis: Goals - Lloyd(3):
Referee M J Naughton (Widnes) Att - 4737 H.T. 5 - 7

**Sun 30 Apr 1972 BRADFORD NORTHERN away
lost 12 - 22 CHAMPIONSHIP ROUND 2**
BRADFORD N - Tees: Lamb Stockwell Watson Redfearn:
Blacker Seabourne: Butler(Hill) Cardiss Long(Butler)
Gallagher Jackson Fearnley:
Tries - Redfearn(3) Lamb: Goals - Tees(4) (DG):
CASTLEFORD - Derek Edwards(Johnson): Lloyd Briggs
Newton Lowndes: Knight Dean: Hartley C.Dickinson
Lockwood(Miller) (Lockwood)Birdsall Fowler Wallis:
Tries - Newton Knight: Goals - Lloyd(3):
Referee R Wood(Dalton in Furness) Att 10010 H.T. 8 - 12

**Mon 1 May 1972 HULL & HULL KINGSTON ROVERS
home won 28 - 27
DEREK EDWARDS BENEFIT MATCH FRIENDLY**
CASTLEFORD - Brunyee: Johnson Newton Briggs
Lowndes: Knight Dean: Hartley C.Dickinson Lockwood
Ackroyd Lloyd Wallis: Subs - Joyner Miller Van Bellen
C.Taylor Redfearn : Tries - Knight(3) Johnson Lockwood
Taylor: Goals - Lloyd(4) Hartley:
HULL & HULL K R - Wainwright(HKR): Sullivan(H)
Kirkpatrick(HKR) Moore(H) Longstaff(HKR): Hancock(H)
Foulkes(H): Harrison(H) Flanagan(HKR) Dawson(HKR)
Millington(HKR) Hossell(HKR) Markham(HKR):
Subs - Davidson (H) Millward(HKR):
Tries - Wainwright Kirkpatrick Longstaff Flanagan
Markham Millward Lindop(Referee):
Goals - Kirkpatrick Flanagan Lindop(Referee):
Referee F Lindop (Wakefield) Att -   H.T. 13 - 11

**Mon 8 May 1972 HULL away won 33 - 27
DOYLE-DAVIDSON BENEFIT MATCH FRIENDLY**
Hull - Kendle(Keegan): Sullivan Devonshire(Gemmell)
Doyle-Davidson Firth: Hancock Foulkes: Harrison Duke
Boxall(Broom) Kirchin Crane Trotter:
Tries - Sullivan(2) Keegan Doyle-Davidson Foulkes
Harrison Kirchin Goals - Broom(2) Crane:
CASTLEFORD - Brunyee: Briggs A.N.Other Higgins
Claughton: Knight Dean: C.Taylor(Poole) C.Dickinson
(Woodall) Lockwood Ackroyd(Miller)Lloyd Wallis: Tries -
Knight(3) Wallis 2) Higgins Lloyd: Goals - Lloyd(6):

SEASON 1971-72

Referee -   Att -   H.T.

Keith Worsley	Alan Dickinson	George Claughton	Cliff Wallis
D. No 541	D. No 542	D. No 544	D. No 545
1971-72 to 1979-80	1971-72 to 1978-79	1971-72 to 1982-83	1971-72 to 1973-74

Derek Woodall
D. No 548
1971-72 to 1979-80

Steve Brunyee   Charlie Birdsall
D. No 546   D. No 547
1971-72 to 1975-76   1971-72 to 1975-76

THE SQUAD THAT DEFEATED WAKEFIELD TRINITY IN ROUND 2 OF THE YORKSHIRE CUP 13 – 10

Back Row – Brian Lockwood Graham Blakeway Ian Van Bellen Alan Ackroyd Derek Foster Keith Worsley Tony Miller Alan Dickinson
Front Row Gary Stephens Derek Edwards Glyn Jones Dennis Hartley Alan Lowndes Steve Norton Danny Hargrave

SEASON 1971-72

D.N	PLAYER		DEBUT	L MATCH	APP	SUB	T.AP	TRI'S	G'LS	D.G	P'TS
442	HEPWORTH	KEITH		05/10/1971	1	0	1	0	0	0	0
458	EDWARDS	DEREK		30/04/1972	41	0	41	6	0	0	18
469	WALTON	DOUGLAS		31/12/1971	12	0	12	0	0	0	0
479	DICKINSON	CLIVE			20	1	21	0	0	0	0
492	STENTON	IAN			9	3	12	0	0	0	0
493	BRIGGS	TREVOR			27	5	32	11	0	0	33
494	REDFEARN	MICHAEL			36	2	38	3	57	0	123
495	MILLER	TONY			29	2	31	4	0	0	12
497	LOCKWOOD	BRIAN			28	1	29	4	0	0	12
503	HARTLEY	DENNIS			21	0	21	0	0	0	0
504	JONES	GLYN		17/11/1971	7	3	10	0	0	0	0
509	FOSTER	DEREK			33	0	33	17	0	0	51
513	HARGRAVE	DAVID (DANNY)			18	9	27	3	0	0	9
516	LOWNDES	ALAN			38	0	38	10	0	0	30
517	APPLEYARD	ROY			15	0	15	1	3	0	9
518	SPURR	ROBERT			5	4	9	1	0	0	3
519	BULLEN	NORMAN		12/04/1972	2	2	4	0	0	0	0
520	BLAKEWAY	GRAHAM		03/04/1972	17	3	20	2	4	1	16
521	BISCOMB	TERRY			3	1	4	1	0	0	3
522	ACKROYD	ALAN			21	12	33	3	32	1	75
525	STEPHENS	GARY			12	1	13	2	0	0	6
526	JOHNSON	PHILIP			19	3	22	5	0	0	15
527	SHAW	LESLIE			3	1	4	0	0	0	0
528	KNIGHT	GLEN			6	0	6	3	0	0	9
530	DEAN	TONY			16	2	18	5	0	1	17
531	NORTON	STEVE (KNOCKER)			23	0	23	9	0	0	27
532	LLOYD	GEOFFREY (SAMMY)			9	0	9	3	31	0	71
534	VAN BELLEN	IAN			19	2	21	5	4	0	23
535	WALSH	JOHN		05/10/1971	3	1	4	0	0	0	0
536	COVENTRY	JOHN			6	0	6	0	0	0	0
537	NEWTON	RAY			14	1	15	7	0	0	21
539	SHEARD	LESLIE		30/10/1971	3	0	3	0	0	0	0
540	FOWLER	DENNIS			3	0	3	0	0	0	0
541	WORSLEY	KEITH	30/07/1971		41	2	43	9	0	0	27
542	DICKINSON	ALAN	30/07/1971		34	2	36	8	0	0	24
543	WRIGHT	GEOFF	30/08/1971	30/08/1971	0	1	1	0	0	0	0
544	CLAUGHTON	GEORGE	27/12/1971		3	1	4	1	0	0	3
545	WALLIS	CLIFFORD	31/12/1971		19	0	19	4	0	1	14
546	BRUNYEE	STEVEN	23/01/1972		2	3	5	0	0	0	0
547	BIRDSALL	CHARLES	29/01/1972		5	4	9	0	6	0	12
548	WOODALL	DEREK	27/02/1972		1	0	1	0	0	0	0
549	JAMES	RICHARD	24/03/1972	24/03/1972	0	1	1	0	0	0	0
	42		**9**	**10**	**624**	**73**	**697**	**127**	**137**	**4**	**663**

COMPETITION		P	W	D	L	FOR	AGT
LEAGUE ONE D	POSITION 10 OF 30	34	20	1	13	488	368
YORK'S CUP		4	3	0	1	56	33
F. TROPHY		1	0	0	1	7	8
PLAYERS NO6		3	1	1	1	27	28
RL CUP		3	1	1	1	30	19
CHAMPIONSHIP		2	1	0	1	30	36
NEW ZEALAND		1	0	0	1	25	8
PLAYERS RECORDS		**48**	**26**	**3**	**19**	**663**	**500**

Alan Hardisty's announcement at the end of the previous season was to prove to be premature as he was not retained as Coach for this season being replaced by former Hunslet, Hull KR and Great Britain Captain, Harry Poole.

The RFL introduced a League Cup Competition but due to sponsorship it became known firstly as the Player's No 6 competition and then as the Regal Trophy.

We lost in the final of the Yorkshire Cup against Hull KR at Belle Vue Wakefield 11–7.

We again entertained the New Zealand tourists on 15 September, beating them 25–8.

SEASON 1972-73

**Sun 6 Aug 1972 BRADFORD NORTHERN home
won 26 – 19 THE JOE PHILLIPS MEMORIAL TROPHY -
CHARITY MATCH FRIENDLY**
CASTLEFORD - Brunyee: Foster Worsley Higgins Walsh:
Hargrave Dean: Van Bellen C.Dickinson Redfearn
Lockwood Coventry Wallis: Subs - Joyner Downham
Stephens Huddlestone :   Tries - Worsley Walsh Hargrave
Dean Lockwood Joyner: Goals - Brunyee(2) Dean(2):
BRADFORD N - Tees: Francis Treasure Watson Gobey:
Blacker Seabourne: Butler Cardiss Hinchcliffe Jackson
Joyce Fearnley: Subs - Evans Redfearn Gallacher Small
Dunn: Tries - Gobey(2) Francis Watson Redfearn:
Goals - Tees(2):
Referee P A Massey   Att -   H.T. 8 - 8

**Fri 18 Aug 1972 WAKEFIELD TRINITY away
lost 10 - 35**
WAKEFIELD T - Wraith: Major Marston Fox(Smith)
Barends: Topliss Bonnar: Jeannes Handforth
Lyons(Oswald) Valentine(Lyons)Ballantyne Morgan:
Tries - Topliss(4) Fox(2) Jeannes: Goals - Fox(6) Oswald:
CASTLEFORD - Brunyee: Briggs Worsley Newton
Lowndes: GARY BROOK(550) Dean (Stenton): Van
Bellen(Redfearn) Spurr Lockwood A.Dickinson Lloyd
Wallis: Tries - Worsley(2):   Goals - Lloyd(2):
Referee S Shepherd (Oldham) Att - 3964 H.T. 5 - 15

**Tue 22 Aug 1972 ROCHDALE HORNETS home
lost 10 - 11**
CASTLEFORD - Stenton: Foster Worsley Briggs
Lowndes(Newton): Brook Knight: Hartley C.Dickinson
Lockwood Redfearn A.Dickinson(Birdsall)Wallis:
Tries - Brook Redfearn: Goals - Knight(2):
ROCHDALE H - Holt(Hammond): Brelsford Pimblett
Machin Crellin: Brophy Gartland(Brown): Birchall(S/O)
Harris Hodgkinson Welding Sheffield Delooze:
Tries - Hammond Pimblett Welding: Goal - Delooze:
Referee A Givvons (Oldham) Att - 2106 H.T. 10 - 5

**Sun 27 Aug 1972 DEWSBURY away lost 5 - 19
YORKSHIRE CUP ROUND 1**
DEWSBURY - Rushton: Ashcroft Childe N.Stephenson
Yoward: Agar A.Bates: Bell M.Stephenson Lowe Grayshon
J.Bates(Robinson) Hankins: Tries - N.Stephenson A.Bates
Lowe: Goals - N.Stephenson(3) (DG2):
CASTLEFORD - Stenton: Foster Worsley Briggs(S/O)
Lowndes(Newton): Brook Knight: Hartley C.Dickinson
Lockwood Redfearn(S/O) A.Dickinson Wallis(Birdsall):
Try - Foster: Goal - Birdsall:
Referee E Lawrinson (Warrington) Att - 2470 H.T. nil - 4

Wed 30 Aug 1972 HALIFAX away lost 4 - 25
HALIFAX - Hepworth: Kelly Davies Willicombe Tudball:
Burton Sanderson: Fogerty Hawkesley(Reeves) Callon
Michael Martin Halmshaw: Tries - Hepworth Tudball
Burton Fogerty Callon: Goals - Burton(5):
CASTLEFORD - Stenton(Knight) (Stenton): Foster Worsley
Newton Briggs: Brook Dean: Hartley A.Dickinson Redfearn
Birdsall(Lloyd) Ackroyd Norton: Goals - Lloyd Ackroyd:
Referee D S Brown (Preston) Att - 2012 H.T. 4 - 10

Fri 1 Sep 1972 BRAMLEY home won 18 - nil
CASTLEFORD - Stenton(Knight): Lloyd Worsley Newton
JOHN JOYNER(551): Brook(Biscomb) Dean: Hartley
C.Dickinson(Brook) A.Dickinson Ackroyd Lockwood
Norton:
Tries - Ackroyd(2) Dean Lockwood: Goals - Lloyd(3):
BRAMLEY - Dewhurst: Goodchild Briggs Keegan Austin:
Hughes(Clegg) Astbury: Jarvis Price(Sampson) McCurley
Cheshire Idle Woolford:
Referee W Greenalgh (Ashton in Makerfield) Att - 1345
H.T. 13 - nil

Sun 10 Sep 1972 SWINTON away won 22 - 12
SWINTON - Gittins: Fleay Cooke Buckley
Gomersall(Hoyle): Kenny M.Philbin(Gomersall): Halsall
Evans Holliday Pattinson Smith Hutton (Atkinson):
Tries - Buckley Hutton: Goals - Cooke(3):
CASTLEFORD - Stenton(Knight): Foster Worsley Newton
Lloyd: Brook Dean: Redfearn C.Dickinson
A.Dickinson(Coventry) Ackroyd Lockwood Norton:
Tries - Brook Dean Ackroyd Lockwood: Goals - Lloyd(5):
Referee K Allatt (Huddersfiel) Att - 1969 H.T. 12 - 7

Fri 15 Sep 1972 WIDNES home won 15 - 8
CASTLEFORD - Stenton: Foster Worsley
Newton(Briggs)Lloyd: Brook Dean: Redfearn C.Dickinson
A.Dickinson Ackroyd(John Coventry) Lockwood Norton:
Tries - Worsley Dean Norton: Goals - Lloyd(3):
WIDNES - Dutton: Prescott Hughes Lowe Aspey:
Bowden(McLaughlin) Ashton: Warlow Elwell Sheridan
Foran Blackwood(Adams) Nicholls:
Tries - Hughes(2):   Goal - Dutton:
Referee D S Brown (Preston) Att - 1723 H.T. 15 - 2

**Fri 22 Sep 1972 HULL KINGSTON ROVERS away
lost 10 - 20 PLAYERS No.6 COMPETITION ROUND 1**
HULL K R - Coupland(Wainwright): Dunn Longstaff
Kirkpatrick Rooms: Hartley Daley: Windmill Flanagan
Neale Millington(Hick) Hossell Brown:
Tries - Dunn Longstaff Hick Brown: Goals - Brown(4):
CASTLEFORD - Stenton: Foster Worsley Newton Lloyd:
Brook(Briggs)Dean(Brook): Redfearn C.Dickinson
A.Dickinson Ackroyd(Biscomb)Lockwood
Norton(Ackroyd):   Goals - Lloyd(3) Dean(DG2):
Referee E Lawrinson (Warrington) Att - 2647 H.T. 8 - 8

**Sun 1 Oct 1972 BRADFORD NORTHERN away
won 32 - 20**
BRADFORD N - Tees: Lamb Stockwell Shaw Redfearn:
Blacker Seabourne: Butler Dunn Hinchcliffe Gallacher
Long(Jackson)Joyce:
Tries - Hinchcliffe Gallacher: Goals - Tees(7):
CASTLEFORD - Stenton: Foster Briggs(Johnson) Newton
Lloyd: Brook Dean: Hartley C.Dickinson A.Dickinson
Redfearn(Miller) Lockwood Norton(S/O):
Tries - Norton(3) Foster A.Dickinson Lockwood:
Goals - Lloyd(7):
Referee H G Hunt (Prestbury) Att - 5832 H.T. 15 - 6

SEASON 1972-73

Fri 6 Oct 1972 BATLEY home won 14 - 9
CASTLEFORD - Stenton: Foster Worsley Newton Lloyd:
Johnson Dean: Hartley(Miller) C.Dickinson A.Dickinson
Redfearn Lockwood Norton:
Tries - Worsley Norton: Goals - Lloyd(4):
BATLEY - Maskill: Seckar(Holmes) Toohey Lingard Marsh:
Watts Williams: Naylor Hudson Standedge J.S.Bell Brooke
J.N.Bell(Fox): Try - Brooke: Goals - Toohey(3):
Referee D S Brown (Preston) Att - 1850 H.T. 10 - 2

Sun 15 Oct 1972 DONCASTER away won 21 - 10
DONCASTER - Lawrence: Pflaster Worsley Elliott Lester:
James Stocks (Banks): Holt Moody Yates Bradley(Jeff)
Shipley Halliwell(Bradley):
Tries - Worsley Yates: Goals - Lawrence(2):
CASTLEFORD - Stenton: Foster Worsley Newton(Briggs)
Lloyd: Johnson Dean: Hartley
(JAMES(Sid)HUDDLESTONE(552)) C.Dickinson A.Dickinson
Redfearn Lockwood Norton: Tries - Foster Worsley Lloyd
Lockwood Norton: Goals - Lloyd(3):
Referee A Fryer (Warrington) Att - 1020 H.T. 10 - 10

Tue 17 Oct 1972 HUDDERSFIELD away won 15 - 9
BBC 2 FLOODLIT COMPETITION ROUND 1
HUDDERSFIELD - Bedford: Hooson Bennett Pickup Senior:
Chamberlain(Evans) Loxton: Chawner Appleyard Weavill
Tomlinson Branch(Wild) Clark:
Try - Senior: Goals - Bennett(3):
CASTLEFORD - Ian Stenton: (Briggs): Foster Worsley
Newton Lloyd: Johnson Tony Dean: Hartley C.Dickinson
A.Dickinson(Redfearn) Wallis Lockwood Norton:
Tries - Foster Worsley Lockwood:
Goals - Lloyd(2) Redfearn(DG):
Referee A Givvons (Oldham) Att - 1291 H.T. 8 - 5

Fri 20 Oct 1972 HULL KINGSTON ROVERS home won 30 - 9
CASTLEFORD - Briggs: Foster Worsley(Knight) Newton
Lloyd: Johnson Stephens: Hartley C.Dickinson
A.Dickinson(Ackroyd) Redfearn Lockwood Wallis:
Tries - Wallis(2) Worsley Knight Newton A.Dickinson:
Goals - Lloyd(6):
HULL K R - Coupland: Brook(Kirkpatrick) Hick Leighton
Dunn: Hartley Hudson: Windmill Heslop(Flanagan)
Barnard Millington Rose Hall:
Try - Hick: Goals - Hall Hudson(DG) Windmill(DG):
Referee H G Hunt (Prestbury) Att - 1683 H.T. 11 - 9

Sun 29 Oct 1972 ROCHDALE HORNETS away lost 4 -11
ROCHDALE H - Hammond(Wood): Brelsford Brophy
Hillman Pimblett: Miller Gartland: Brown Harris Courley
Cooke(Crocker) Hodgkinson Robinson:
Tries - Brophy(2) Hillman: Goal - Brophy:
CASTLEFORD - Briggs: Foster Worsley Newton Lloyd:
Johnson Stephens(Knight): Hartley C.Dickinson
A.Dickinson Ackroyd(Huddlestone)Redfearn Wallis:
Goals - Lloyd(2):
Referee G F Lindop (Wakefield) Att - 1861 H.T. 4 - 2

Fri 3 Nov 1972 KEIGHLEY home won 29 - 13
CASTLEFORD - Briggs: Foster Worsley Newton Lowndes:
Johnson Stephens(Hargrave): Hartley C.Dickinson(Miller)
A.Dickinson Redfearn Lloyd Wallis: Tries - Newton(2)
Lowndes(2) Worsey Miller Lloyd: Goals - Lloyd(4):
KEIGHLEY - Jefferson: Johnson Wilmot Cowan(O'Brien)
Simpson: Smith Hartley: Ayre Whittaker Clarkson Reeves
Garbett Butler:
Tries - Wilmot Smith Whittaker: Goals - Jefferson(2):
Referee S Shepherd (Oldham) Att - 1611 H.T. 3 - 5

Tue 7 Nov 1972 OLDHAM away lost 7 - 9
BBC 2 FLOODLIT COMPETITION ROUND 2
OLDHAM - Murphy: Elliott Larder Wainwright
Hodgkinson: Hill Gorman: Wilson Taylor Foster Daly
Ashcroft Reynolds:
Try - Elliott: Goals - Larder Gorman(DG) Foster)DG:
CASTLEFORD - Briggs: Foster Newton Worsley Lowndes:
Johnson Hargrave: Hartley C.Dickinson(Miller) A.Dickinson
Wallis Lloyd Norton: Try - Johnson: Goals - Lloyd(2):
Referee R Jackson (Halifax) Att - 2012 H.T. 7 - 2

Fri 10 Nov 1972 HUNSLET home won 43 - 10
CASTLEFORD - Briggs(Higgins): Foster Worsley Newton
Lowndes: Johnson Hargrave: Hartley Miller A.Dickinson
Wallis Lloyd Norton: Tries - Foster(5) Newton(3)
Worsley(2) Lowndes: Goals - Lloyd(5):
HUNSLET - Marshall: Taylor G.Clarke Barron
Charlton(Watson): Gaitley Horrocks(Williams): Mason
J.Clarke Dobson Sanderson Gunney Griffiths:
Tries - Gunney Griffiths: Goals - Marshall(2):
Referee R Wood (Dalton in Furness) Att 1028 H.T. 11 - 7

Sat 18 Nov 1972 LEEDS away lost 5 - 20
LEEDS - Holmes Parker Hynes Dyl Atkinson: Hardisty
Hepworth(Langley): Clawson Fisher Jeanes(Eccles) Ramsey
Cookson Batten Tries - Hardisty(2) Cookson(2):
Goals - Clawson(3) Holmes:
CASTLEFORD - Briggs: Foster Worsley Newton Lowndes:
Johnson Hargrave(Appleyard): Hartley Miller Lockwood
Wallis Lloyd(C.Dickinson) Norton:
Try - Norton: Goal - Appleyard:
Referee T Keane (Oldham) Att - 6686 H.T. nil - 13

Sun 3 Dec 1972 HUNSLET away won 41 - 8
HUNSLET - Marshall: Charlton Clark(Watson) Taylor
Richardson: Barron Rycroft: Watson Dobson Mason
Sanderson Williams Griffiths(Sykes):
Tries - Clark Barron: Goal - Marshall:
CASTLEFORD - Briggs(Lockwood): Foster Worsley Newton
Lowndes: Johnson Appleyard: Hartley Miller C.Dickinson
Wallis Lockwood(Lloyd) Norton(David(Danny)Hargrave):
Tries - Johnson(3) Worsley(2) Briggs Appleyard Wallis
Lockwood: Goals - Lloyd(4) Appleyard(3):
Referee P Geraghty (York) Att - 1000 H.T. 21 - 5

Wed 13 Dec 1972 BRADFORD NORTHERN home won 58 - 12
CASTLEFORD - Briggs: Foster Worsley Newton
Lowndes(Joyner): Johnson Appleyard: Hartley Miller

C.Dickinson(A.Dickinson) Lockwood Wallis Norton:
Tries - Appleyard(3) Briggs(2) Johnson(2) Lockwood(2)
Foster Worsley Newton A.Dickinson Norton:
Goals - Appleyard(8):
BRADFORD N. - Tees: Lamb Carlton Blacker Francis:
Treasure Seabourne: Butler Cardiss Earl Gallagher
Joyce(Hogan) Fearnley:
Tries - Earl(2): Goals - Tees(2) Treasure(DG):
Referee G F Lindop (Wakefield) Att - 1479 H.T. 24 - 7

Fri 22 Dec 1972 HULL home won 19 - 9
CASTLEFORD - Briggs: Foster Worsley Joyner Lloyd:
Johnson Appleyard: Hartley Miller C.Dickinson Lockwood
Wallis Norton(STEPHEN PINCHER(553)): Tries - Worsley
Joyner Lloyd Miller Norton: Goals - Lloyd(2):
HULL - Owbridge: Tommerup(Drew) Portz Maloney
Macklin: Geraghty Williams: Boxall Firth Walker Shaw
Crane Trotter: Try - Boxall: Goals - Maloney(3):
Referee A Fryer (Warrington) Att - 1252 H.T. 16 - 9

Tue 26 Dec 1972 FEATHERSTONE ROVERS home won 13 - 8
CASTLEFORD - Briggs: Foster Worsley Joyner(Knight)
Lloyd: Johnson Appleyard: Hartley Miller A.Dickinson
Lockwood Wallis Norton:
Tries - Foster Joyner Wallis: Goals - Lloyd(2):
FEATHERSTONE R - Box: Wilson Hartley Busfield(C.Kellett)
K.Kellett: Smith Nash: Tonks Bridges Harris Thompson
Kear(Stone) Hollis: Goals - Box(4):
Referee E Lawrinson (Warrington) Att - 3111 H.T. 5 - 6

Mon 1 Jan 1973 HUDDERSFIELD away won 17 - 8
HUDDERSFIELD - Bennett: Hooson Leese Pickup Senior:
Shaw Loxton: Hepplestone Wroe(Hall) Weavill Veivers
Naylor Tomlinson: Tries - Hooson Senior: Goal - Bennett:
CASTLEFORD - Briggs: Foster Worsley Newton(Joyner)
Lowndes: Johnson Appleyard: Hartley Miller A.Dickinson
Wallis Lloyd(Birdsall) Norton: Tries - Foster Lowndes
Norton: Goals - Appleyard(2) Lloyd(2):
Referee P A Massey   Att - 1524 H.T. 4 - 5

Sun 7 Jan 1973 WIDNES away won 20 - 8
WIDNES - Dutton: Prescott Aspey Lowe(Dearden)
Hughes: McLoughlin Ashton: Mills Elwell Walsh
Foran(George) Newton Nicholls: Goals - Dutton(4):
CASTLEFORD - Briggs: Foster Worsley Joyner
Lowndes(Higgins): Johnson Appleyard: Hartley Miller
C.Dickinson(Birdsall) Wallis A.Dickinson Norton:
Tries - Briggs Worsley Miller A.Dickinson:
Goals - Appleyard(4):
Referee R Moore (Wakefield) Att - 3037 H.T. 5 - 6

Fri 12 Jan 1973 HUDDERSFIELD home lost 20 - 22
CASTLEFORD - Briggs: Foster Worsley Newton Lowndes:
Johnson Appleyard: Hartley Miller A.Dickinson
Wallis(Joyner) Lockwood(Birdsall) Norton:
Tries - Foster Johnson Appleyard Hartley:
Goals - Birdsall(3) Appleyard
HUDDERSFIELD - Bedford: Hooson Leese Pickup
Senior(Loxton): Shaw Doyle: Hepplestone Wroe Weavill

Veivers Naylor Branch(Tomlinson):
Tries - Leese Loxton Veivers Naylor: Goals - Hooson(5):
Referee H Mason (Halifax) Att - 1719 H.T. 8 - 7

Sat 27 Jan 1973 SWINTON home won 13 - 9 CHALLENGE CUP ROUND 1
CASTLEFORD - Briggs: Foster Worsley(Joyner) Newton
Lowndes: Johnson Appleyard: Hartley Miller
A.Dickinson(C.Dickinson) Wallis Lockwood Norton:
Tries - Norton(2) Lowndes: Goals - Appleyard(2):
SWINTON - Gowers: Fleay Buckley C.Evans Jackson:
Houghton Atkinson: Bate D.Evans Young Smith Henighan
Philbin: Try - C.Evans: Goals - Gowers(3):
Referee W Greenhalgh (Ashton in Makerfield)
Att - 3736 H.T. 5 - 2

Sat 3 Feb 1973 LEEDS home won 22 - 16
CASTLEFORD - Briggs: Foster Worsley Newton Lowndes:
Johnson Appleyard: Hartley C.Dickinson
A.Dickinson(Redfearn) Wallis Lockwood Norton:
Tries - Lowndes(2) Worsley C.Dickinson:
Goals - Appleyard(4) Wallis(DG):
LEEDS - Holmes: Langley Hynes Dyl Atkinson:
Hardisty(Hay)Barham: Jeanes Fisher Pitchford(Clarkson)
(S/O) Cookson Haigh Eccles:
Tries - Barham Haigh: Goals - Hynes(4) Barham(DG):
Referee M J Naughton (Widnes) Att - 5531 H.T. 7 - 6

Sun 11 Feb 1973 HULL KINGSTON ROVERS away won 11 - 10
HULL K R - Hick: Stephenson Dunn Coupland Kirkpatrick:
Longstaff Hudson: Windmill Heslop Neale(Barnard) Lowe
Kirchin(Millington) Moore:
Tries - Kirkpatrick(2): Goals - Coupland Windmill(DG):
CASTLEFORD - Briggs(Brook): Foster Worsley Newton
Lowndes: Johnson Appleyard: Hartley(Redfearn) Miller
C.Dickinson A.Dickinson Lockwood Norton:
Tries - Johnson(2) Foster: Goal - Redfearn:
Referee S Shepherd (Oldham) Att - 4454 H.T. 6 - 8

Sun 18 Feb 1973 HUNSLET away won 39 - nil CHALLENGE CUP ROUND 2
HUNSLET - Marshall: C.Watson Clark
Barron(Taylor)Richardson: Gaitley Horrocks: Mason
Maskill D.Watson Sykes(Dobson) Sanderson Griffiths:
CASTLEFORD - Briggs: Foster Worsley(Brook) Newton
Lowndes: Johnson Appleyard: Redfearn
Miller(A.Dickinson) C.Dickinson Wallis Lockwood Norton:
Tries - Lockwood(2) Norton(2) Newton Lowndes Johnson
Appleyard C.Dickinson: Goals - Redfearn(6):
Referee H G Hunt (Prestbury) Att - 4700 H.T. 15 - nil

Fri 12 Jan 1973 HUDDERSFIELD home lost 20 - 22
BATLEY - Dewhurst: Lingard Toohey Holmes Maskill:
Watts Williams: Naylor Fox(N.Bell)(Hepworth) Grinhaff
Thomas Chalkley J.Bell:
Tries - Naylor Grinhaff Chalkley: Goals - Toohey(3):
CASTLEFORD - Briggs: Foster Newton Joyner Higgins:
Brook Appleyard(Johnson): Ian Van Bellen C.Dickinson
Redfearn(Birdsall) A.Dickinson Lockwood Wallis:

Tries - Brook(3) Foster Appleyard Birdsall Lockwood:
Goals - Appleyard(2) Redfearn(2) Birdsall:
Referee J Wall (Leigh) Att - 2028 H.T. 20 - nil

Sat 3 Mar 1973 OLDHAM home won 25 - 11
CHALLENGE CUP ROUND 3
CASTLEFORD - Briggs: Foster Worsley Newton Lowndes:
Johnson(Brook) Appleyard: Redfearn Miller C.Dickinson
Wallis Lockwood(Birdsall) Norton:
Tries - Johnson Brook Miller:
Goals - Redfearn(6) (DG) Norton(DG):
OLDHAM - Davies: Elliott Larder Wainwright Hodgkinson:
Hill McCone: Wilson Taylor Foster Irving Hall Farrell:
Try - Farrell: Goals - Larder(4):
Referee E Lawrenson (Warrington) Att - 6600 H.T. 16 - 4

Fri 9 Mar 1973 HALIFAX home won 17 - 5
CASTLEFORD - Briggs: Foster Worsley Newton Lowndes:
Johnson(Brook)Appleyard: Redfearn(A.Dickinson) Miller
C.Dickinson Wallis Birdsall Norton: Tries - Lowndes(2)
Worsley Appleyard Norton: Goal - Appleyard:
HALIFAX - Tudball: Brown Davis Willicombe Pitchforth:
Sanderson Baker: Booth Hawksley Callon Fogerty(Frain)
Martin Halmshaw: Try - Willicombe: Goal - Willicombe:
Referee R Wood (Dalton in Furness) Att - 2320 H.T. 8 - 5

Sun 18 Mar 1973 BRAMLEY away won 35 - 6
BRAMLEY - Keegan: Clegg Smith(Briggs) Bollon Austin:
Briggs(Hughes)Ward: Worthy Price Jarvis Cheshire
Ashman(Johnson) Idle: Goals - Ward(3):
CASTLEFORD - Briggs: Foster Worsley Newton Lowndes:
Brook(Johnson) Appleyard: Ackroyd Miller C.Dickinson
Wallis Lockwood Norton(A.Dickinson):
Tries - Foster(2) Newton Lowndes Johnson Norton
A.Dickinson: Goals - Ackroyd(4) Appleyard(3):
Referee A Givvons (Oldham) Att - 1500 H.T. 15 - 4

Wed 21 Mar 1973 SWINTON home won 31 - 3
CASTLEFORD - Briggs: Foster Worsley Newton Lowndes:
Johnson Appleyard: Ackroyd Miller C.Dickinson Wallis
A.Dickinson(Redfearn) Norton(A.Dickinson):
Tries - Worsley Lowndes Appleyard Ackroyd Wallis:
Goals - Appleyard(8):
SWINTON - Gittins: Fleay Cook(Atkinson) G.Evans
Jackson: Houghton Gowers: Butler D.Evans Young Whittle
Hennigan B.Philbin: Try - Houghton:
Referee M J Naughton (Widnes) Att - 2350 H.T. 14 - 3

Sun 25 Mar 1973 YORK away won 18 - 10
YORK - Wallace(Blake): Hill Clancy Quinn Meillam: Smith
Dooler: Dixon Payne(Hunter) Forsyth Dunham Edson
Sheehan: Tries - Clancy Forsyth: Goals - Quinn(2):
CASTLEFORD - Briggs(Worsley): Foster Higgins Newton
Lowndes: Johnson Appleyard: Redfearn Miller C.Dickinson
Ackroyd(Norton) A.Dickinson Wallis:
Tries - Norton(2) Briggs Foster: Goals - Appleyard(3):
Referee R Wood (Dalton in Furness) Att 3269 H.T. 7 - 10

Wed 28 Mar 1973 DONCASTER home won 37 - 8
CASTLEFORD - Higgins: Joyner Worsley Newton Lowndes:
Johnson Stephens: Redfearn Miller C.Dickinson Wallis
Lockwood Norton(A.Dickinson):
Tries - Lowndes(3) Newton(2) Stephens(2) Johnson
Lockwood: Goals - Redfearn(5):
DONCASTER - Tomlinson: Downing(Banks) Denton
Lawrence Arrand Rushton Spibey: Carlin Moody
Richardson(Crabtree) Shipley Waltham Goodyear:
Tries - Lawrence Waltham: Goal - Waltham:
Referee D G Kershaw (York) Att - 1674 H.T. 18 - 5

Fri 30 Mar 1973 YORK home won 30 - 11
CASTLEFORD - Briggs: Joyner Worsley Higgins
Lowndes(Lloyd): Johnson Appleyard: Redfearn Miller
C.Dickinson A.Dickinson Lockwood Wallis (Stephens):
Tries - Appleyard(2) Joyner Redfearn Lockwood Wallis:
Goals - Redfearn(5) (DG):
YORK - Wallace: Hill Clancy(Horner) Quinn Meillan: Blake
Smith: Forsyth Payne(Hunter) Hunter(Young) Dunham
Edson Sheehan:
Tries - Hill Dunham Sheehan: Goal - Quinn:
Referee K Allatt (Huddersfield) Att - 2457 H.T. 13 - 8

Sun 8 Apr 1973 HULL away won 12 - 11
HULL - Geraghty(Cooper): Sullivan Stenton Portz Macklin:
Devonshire Davidson: M.Harrison Boxall J.Harrison
Robson Tindall(Wardell) Casey:
Tries - Sullivan Portz Devonshire: Goal - Boxall:
CASTLEFORD - Briggs: Higgins Worsley Newton Lowndes:
Johnson(Brook) Stephens: Hartley Miller Redfearn Wallis
Lockwood(C.Dickinson) Norton:
Tries - Lowndes Stephens: Goals - Redfearn(2) (DG):
Referee R Jackson (Halifax) Att - 1500 H.T. 8 - 5

Sat 14 Apr 1973 FEATHERSTONE ROVERS lost 3 - 17
CHALLENGE CUP SEMI FINAL - AT HEADINGLEY
LEEDS
CASTLEFORD - Briggs: Foster Worsley Newton Lowndes:
Johnson(Brook) Appleyard: Hartley(Miller) C.Dickinson
Redfearn Wallis Lockwood Norton: Try - Brook:
FEATHERSTONE R - C.Kellett: Coventry Smith Newlove
K.Kellett: Mason Nash: Tonks Bridges Farrar Rhodes
Thompson Stone: Tries - Coventry Nash Thompson:
Goals - C.Kellett(3) Nash(DG):
Referee H G Hunt (Prestbury) Att - 15369 H.T. nil - 7

Tue 17 Apr 1973 KEIGHLEY away lost 10 - 13
KEIGHLEY - Jefferson: Wilkes Jickells Clayton Simpson:
Leek Sutcliffe: Burke Raistrick Illingworth Brosnan(Smith)
Clarkson Garbett(Stenton):
Try - Illingworth: Goals - Jefferson(3) (2DG):
CASTLEFORD - Briggs: Foster(Johnson) Worsley Newton
Lowndes: Brook Appleyard: Hartley(Ackroyd) Miller
C.Dickinson Wallis Lockwood Norton:
Tries - Wallis Norton: Goals - Appleyard(2):
Referee A Fryer (Warrington) Att - 1215 H.T. 8 - 7

Sat 21 Apr 1973 WAKEFIELD TRINITY hom lost 5 - 13
CASTLEFORD - Briggs(Biscomb): Shaw Worsley Higgins
Lowndes: Brook(Johnson)(Brook) Appleyard: Redfearn
Miller Ackroyd Wallis Huddlestone Lloyd:
Try - Lowndes: Goal - Lloyd:
WAKEFIELD T - Wraith: Smith Crook Wrigglesworth
Barends: Hegarty (Layton): Harkin: Campbell(Valentine)
Handforth Lyons Endersby Ballantyne Morgan:
Tries - Smith Lyons Morgan: Goals - Crook(1) (DG):
Referee T Keane (Oldham) Att - 1923 H.T. 2 - 5

**Mon 23 Apr 1973 FEATHERSTONE ROVERS away
lost nil - 15**
FEATHERSTONE R - C.Kellett: Coventry Smith Newlove
K.Kellett: Mason(Busfield) Jamieson: Tonks Bridges(Harris)
Farrar Hollis Thompson Stone:
Tries - Coventry Smith Newlove: Goals - C.Kellett(3):
CASTLEFORD - Higgins: Joyner Newton Shaw Biscomb:
Brook Appleyard: TREVOR CHAWNER(554) Miller
A.Dickinson Lockwood Wallis Norton:
Referee A Givvons (Oldham) Att - 3975 H.T. nil - 13

**Sun 29 Apr 1973 HULL KINGSTON ROVERS home
won 24 - 12 CHAMPIONSHIP ROUND 1**
CASTLEFORD - Briggs: Higgins Shaw Newton Lowndes:
Johnson Appleyard(Stephens): Redfearn C.Dickinson
Birdsall(Lloyd) A.Dickinson Lockwood(Birdsall) Wallis:
Tries - Higgins Newton Lowndes Johnson Stephens
Birdsall: Goals - Redfearn Lloyd Wallis(DG):
HULL K R - Coupland: Stephenson Dunn Longstaff
Kirkpatrick: Millward Hudson(Leighton): Windmill
Flanagan Neale Lowe Holdstock(Hall) Moore:
Tries - Coupland Stephenson: Goals - Millward(3):
Referee H G Hunt (Prestbury) Att - 3210 H.T. 9 - 10

**Wed 2 May 1973 LEEDS away lost 5 - 30
CHAMPIONSHIP ROUND 2**
LEEDS - Holmes: Smith(Edwards) Hynes Dyl Atkinson:
Hardisty Hepworth: Clawson Ward Jeanes Eccles(Hughes)
Cookson Haigh: Tries - Holmes(2) Smith(2) Atkinson
Hardisty Hepworth Haigh: Goals - Hynes(3):
CASTLEFORD - Briggs: Higgins Shaw Newton Lowndes:
Johnson Appleyard(Stephens): Redfearn C.Dickinson
Birdsall A.Dickinson(Lloyd) Ackroyd Wallis:
Try - Newton: Goal - Redfearn:
Referee S Shepherd (Oldham) Att - 5953 H.T. 5 - 19

John Joyner
D. No 551
1972-73 to 1991-92

Holds the Record for most Appearances at 613:
585 Starts plus 28 Substitutes
And Scored 185 Tries
Captain RL Chalenge Cup Winners 1986

James (Syd) Huddlestone
D. No 552
1972-73 to 1979-80

Trevor Chawner
D. No 554
1972-73 to 1973-74

SEASON 1972-73

D.N	PLAYER		DEBUT	L MATCH	APP	SU3	T.AP	TRI'S	G'LS	D.G	P'TS
479	DICKINSON	CLIVE			33	3	36	2	0	0	6
492	STENTON	IAN		17/10/1972	11	1	12	0	0	0	0
493	BRIGGS	TREVOR			35	4	39	5	0	0	15
494	REDFEARN	MICHAEL			24	5	29	2	29	4	72
495	MILLER	TONY			23	5	28	4	0	0	12
497	LOCKWOOD	BRIAN			32	0	32	13	0	0	39
503	HARTLEY	DENNIS			27	0	27	1	0	0	3
509	FOSTER	DEREK			35	0	35	18	0	0	54
513	HARGRAVE	DAVID (DANNY)		03/12/1972	3	2	5	0	0	0	0
516	LOWNDES	ALAN			29	0	29	18	0	0	54
517	APPLEYARD	ROY			24	1	25	11	44	0	121
518	SPURR	ROBERT			1	0	1	0	0	0	0
521	BISCOMB	TERRY			1	3	4	0	0	0	0
522	ACKROYD	ALAN			11	2	13	4	5	0	22
525	STEPHENS	GARY			5	3	8	4	0	0	12
526	JOHNSON	PHILIP			30	5	35	14	0	0	42
527	SHAW	LESLIE			4	0	4	0	0	0	0
528	KNIGHT	GLEN			2	6	8	1	2	0	7
530	DEAN	TONY		17/10/1972	10	0	10	3	0	2	13
531	NORTON	STEVE (KNOCKER)			32	1	33	19	0	1	59
532	LLOYD	SAMMY			19	5	24	3	64	0	137
534	VAN BELLEN	IAN		25/02/1973	2	0	2	0	0	0	0
536	COVENTRY	JOHN		15/09/1972	0	2	2	0	0	0	0
537	NEWTON	RAY			37	2	39	13	0	0	39
538	HIGGINS	PAUL			9	2	11	1	0	0	3
541	WORSLEY	KEITH			38	1	39	18	0	0	54
542	DICKINSON	ALAN			31	5	36	5	0	0	15
545	WALLIS	CLIFFORD			35	0	35	7	0	2	25
546	BRUNYEE	STEVEN			1	0	1	0	0	0	0
547	BIRDSALL	CHARLES			4	7	11	2	5	0	16
550	BROOK	GARY	18/08/1972		14	6	20	7	0	0	21
551	JOYNER	JOHN	01/09/1972		8	4	12	3	0	0	9
552	HUDDLESTONE	JAMES (SID)	15/10/1972		1	2	3	0	0	0	0
553	PINCHER	STEPHEN	22/12/1972	22/12/1972	0	1	1	0	0	0	0
554	CHAWNER	TREVOR	23/04/1973		1	0	1	0	0	0	0
	35										
			5	**6**	**572**	**78**	**650**	**178**	**149**	**9**	**850**

COMPETITION		P	W	D	L	FOR	AGT
LEAGUE ONE D	POSITION 7 OF 30	34	25	0	9	704	404
YORK'S CUP		1	0	0	1	5	19
F. TROPHY		2	1	0	1	22	18
PLAYERS NO6		1	0	0	1	10	20
RL CUP		4	3	0	1	80	37
CHAMPIONSHIP		2	1	0	1	29	42
PLAYERS RECORDS		**44**	**30**	**0**	**14**	**850**	**540**

The four tackle rule was changed to the six tackle rule.

We again started the season with a new Coach with former player and 'A' Team Coach, John Sheridan taking over from Harry Poole.

We once more made it to the semi-final stage in the Challenge Cup. Victories at home to Swinton 13–9 in round one, away at Hunslet 39–nil in round two and at home to Oldham 25-11 in round three. Our semi-final opponents at Headingley were Featherstone Rovers, who won 17–3 and then went on to beat Bradford Northern in the final.

On 10 November 1972, Derek Foster became the first Castleford player to score five tries in a game in the 43–10 victory over Hunslet at home.

Roy Appleyard increased the record for most points scored in a League game to 25 against Bradford N at home on the 13 December 1972.

A significant debutant was John Joyner

SEASON 1973-74

The League structure once again reverted to two Divisions.

In Division 1 - Bramley, Castleford, Dewsbury, Featherstone Rovers, Hull K R, Leeds, Leigh, Oldham, Rochdale, St Helens, Salford, Wakefield Trinity, Warrington, Whitehaven, Widnes, Wigan,

In Division 2 - Barrow, Batley, Blackpool Borough, Bradford Northern, Doncaster, Halifax, Huddersfield, Hull, Huyton, Keighley, New Hunslet(Formerly Hunslet), Swinton, Workington Town, York.

Sun. 12 Aug 1973 BRADFORD NORTHERN away lost 21 - 28 CHARITY MATCH FRIENDLY
BRADFORD N - Tees: Lamb Stockwell Watson Marston: Francis Redfearn: Kelly Blacker Diabira Hogan Cardiss Long: Subs - Hill Gallagher Jackson Joyce Fearnley : Tries - Watson Redfearn Kelly Fearnley: Goals - Tees(8): CASTLEFORD - Briggs: Joyner Worsley Newton Higgins: Knight Stephens: Oswald Miller Birdsall Wallis Ackroyd Lloyd: Subs - Brook Johnson Shaw Huddlestone - : Tries - Birdsall(2) Briggs Joyner Wallis: Goals - Lloyd(3): Referee - Att - 2099 H.T. 18 - 14

Fri 17 Aug 1973 WAKEFIELD TRINITY home lost 14- 21
CASTLEFORD - Briggs: Shaw Worsley Joyner Lowndes: Knight Stephens: Ackroyd Miller Birdsall Redfearn Wallis Lloyd: Tries - Worsley Lowndes Stephens Miller: Goal - Redfearn: WAKEFIELD T - Crook: Smith Hegarty(Layton) Wrigglesworth Parker: Topliss Harkin: Ballantyne Morgan Lyons Knowles Endersby Fox: Tries - Morgan(2) Crook Parker Endersby: Goals - Fox(3): Referee S Shepherd (Oldham) Att - 2883 H.T. 8 - 11

Tue 21 Aug 1973 HUDDERSFIELD home won 32 - 10 BBC 2 FLOODLIT COMPETITION PRELIMINARY ROUND 1ST LEG
CASTLEFORD - Briggs: Higgins Worsley Joyner Lowndes: Knight(Johnson) Stephens: Chawner(Birdsall) Miller Ackroyd Redfearn Wallis Lloyd: Tries - Ackroyd(2) Higgins Joyner Knight Stephens Miller Lloyd: Goals - Ackroyd(2) Lloyd(2): HUDDERSFIELD - Bedford: Hooson(Shaw) Leese Maloney Senior: Calvert Loxton: Hepplestone(Weavi l) Wroe Van Bellin Davies Branch Clark: Tries - Senior Davies: Goals - Hooson Van Bellen(DG): Referee A Givvons (Oldham) Att - 1195 H.T. 10 - 7

Fri 24 Aug 1973 WIDNES away lost 9 - 27
WIDNES - Dutton: Prescott Aspey Lowe Hughes: Bowden Ashton: Warlow(Sheridan) Elwell Mills Newton Walsh Laughton: Tries - Prescott Aspey Hughes Bowden Warlow: Goal – Dutton(5) Elwell(DG): CASTLEFORD - Briggs: Higgins Worsley Newton Lowndes(Joyner): Knight Stephens(Lowndes): Chawner(Birdsall) Miller Ackroyd Redfearn Wallis Lloyd: Try - Joyner: Goals - Lloyd(2) Redfearn(DG): Referee K Allatt (Huddersfield) Att - 3000 H.T. 9 - 12

Fri 31 Aug 1973 YORK home won 32 - 8 YORKSHIRE CUP ROUND 1
CASTLEFORD - Briggs: Joyner Worsley Newton Lowndes(Higgins): Knight Stephens: Chawner Miller Ackroyd Redfearn Wallis Lloyd(Birdsall): Tries - Joyner Newton Higgins Stephens Lloyd Lowndes: Goals - Lloyd(6) Redfearn(DG): YORK - Wallace: Meillam Broatch Quinn Clancy: Smith Dooler: Dixon Payne Forsyth Morgan(Whittaker) Edson Hawley(Sheehan): Goals - Quinn(2) Dooler(DG2): Referee T Keene (Oldham) Att - 1697 H.T. 14 - 4

Fri 7 Sept 1973 HUDDERSFIELD home won 29 - 8 YORKSHIRE CUP ROUND 2
CASTLEFORD - Briggs(Chawner): Joyner Worsley Newton Lowndes: Knight (Higgins) Stephens(Knight): Chawner(Wallis) Miller Ackroyd Redfearn Lockwood Lloyd: Tries - Worsley(2) Lowndes(2) Stephens(2) Lloyd: Goals - Lloyd(4): HUDDERSFIELD - Bedford: Leese Mullaney Doyle(S/O) Senior: Chamberlain Shepherd: Hepplestone(Weavill) Wroe Van Bellen Forster Weavill(Cane) (Druery) Davies: Goals - Davies(2) (DG2): Referee M J Naughton (Widnes) Att - 1700 H.T. 8 - 6

Sun. 9 Sept 1973 ROCHDALE HORNETS home won 21 - 19
CASTLEFORD - Briggs: Joyner Worsley Newton(Higgins) Lowndes: Knight Stephens: Redfearn(Chawner) Miller Ackroyd Wallis Lockwood(Redfearn) Lloyd: Tries - Joyner Stephens Lloyd: Goals - Lloyd(5) Redfearn(DG): ROCHDALE H - Crellin: Tickle Brophy Aspinall Brelsford(Butler): Hammond Cartland: Birchall Clarke Holliday Welding(Hodgkinson) Sheffield Whitehead: Tries - Aspinall Cartland Whitehead: Goals - Holliday(5): Referee D S Brown(Poulton de Fylde) Att - 2257 H.T. 14 - 10

Sun. 16 Sept 1973 MILLOM home won 88 - 5 PLAYERS No.6 COMPETITION ROUND 1
CASTLEFORD - Briggs: Joyner Worsley Higgins Lowndes: Knight Stephens: JAMES NAYLOR(555) Miller Redfearn(Ackroyd) Wallis(Chawner) Lockwood Lloyd: Tries - Joyner(5) Lloyd(3) Briggs(2) Knight(2) Worsley Higgins:Lowndes Naylor Miller Lockwood: Goals - Lloyd(17): MILLOM - Cummings: Gow(Hambley) Bawden Andrews James: Dawson Date: Clark Middleton Vamplew(Casson) Jackson Lupton Mawson: Try - Middleton: Goal - Gow: Referee A Givvons (Oldham) Att - 1031 H.T. 30 - 5

Wed 19 Sept 1973 HUDDERSFIELD away won 18 - nil BBC 2 FLOODLIT COMPETITION PRELIMINARY ROUND 2ND LEG
HUDDERSFIELD - Bedford: Ellis A.N.Other Leese(Mullaney) Senior: Thornton Shaw: Van Bellen Wroe Kane C.Forster

SEASON 1973-74

A.Forster Johnson:
CASTLEFORD - Briggs(Brook): Joyner Worsley Higgins
Lowndes: Johnson Knight: Naylor Spurr Ackroyd Redfearn
Lloyd(Fowler) Norton: Tries - Johnson Knight Spurr
Ackroyd: Goals - Redfearn(2) Lloyd:
Referee P Geraghty (York) Att - 696 H.T. 5 - nil

Sun. 23 Sept 1973 WARRINGTON away lost 5 - 22
WARRINGTON - Whitehead: Curling Pickup Noonan
Bevan(Philbin): Murphy(S.O) Gordon: Price(S/O) Ashcroft
Brady(Wanbon) Gregory Nicholls Briggs:
Tries - Whitehead Bevan Philbin Price:
Goals - Whitehead(4) Ashcroft(DG):
CASTLEFORD - Brook: Joyner Worsley Higgins Lowndes:
Johnson(Knight) Stephens: Naylor Miller Ackroyd(S/O)
Redfearn Lockwood(Norton) Norton(Wallis):
Try - Norton: Goal - Redfearn:
Referee G F Lindop (Wakefield) Att - 8253 H.T. nil - 8

**Wed 26 Sept 1973 WAKEFIELD TRINITY away
lost 18 - 19 YORKSHIRE CUP SEMI FINAL**
WAKEFIELD T - Wraith: Smith Crook Hegarty Parker:
Topliss Bonnar: Ballantyne(Bratt) Morgan Lyons Valentine
Endersby Ellis:
Tries - Wraith Hegarty Topliss: Goals - Crook(5):
CASTLEFORD - Briggs: Joyner Worsley Higgins Lowndes:
Knight Stephens: Chawner(S.O) Miller Ackroyd Redfearn
Lloyd Norton:
Tries - Briggs Lowndes Knight Stephens: Goals - Lloyd(3):
Referee S Shepherd (Oldham) Att - 4642 H.T. 5 - 7

Sun. 30 Sept 1973 LEIGH home won 24 - 9
CASTLEFORD - Briggs(Chawner): Joyner Worsley(Lloyd)
Higgins Lowndes: Knight Stephens: Naylor Miller
Redfearn Wallis(Briggs) Lockwood Norton:
Tries - Lowndes(2) Stephens Norton: Goals - Lloyd(6):
LEIGH - Melling: Davis Kelly Collins Randall:
McAtee(Sayer) Boylan: Fiddler Clarke Fletcher Barrow
Grimes Boyd: Try - Melling: Goals - Fiddler(3):
Referee A Moss (Manchester) Att - 2186 H.T. 9 - 4

Fri 5 Oct 1973 SALFORD away lost 5 - 16
SALFORD - Charlton: Fielding Watkins Hesketh Holland:
Gill Banner: Kear Walker Grice Davies(S/O) Dixon Prescott:
Tries - Fielding(2) Watkins Dixon: Goals - Watkins(2):
CASTLEFORD - Briggs: Leslie Shaw Joyner Higgins
Lowndes: Knight(Brook) Stephens: Naylor Miller Redfearn
Lloyd(Chawner) Lockwood Norton:
Try - Knight: Goal - Redfearn:
Referee R Jackson (Halifax) Att - 6606 H.T. nil - 10

Wed 10 Oct 1973 AUSTRALIA lost 10 - 18
CASTLEFORD - Briggs(Brook): Foster Worsley Higgins
Joyner: Knight Stephens: James Naylor(Chawner) Miller
Redfearn Lloyd Lockwood(S/O)Norton: Goals - Lloyd(5):
AUSTRALIA - Eadie: Orr Cronin Starling(Waite)
Williamson: Branighan Raudonikis: Hamilton Walters
Beetson Stevens(S.O)Maddison Pierce:
Tries - Eadie Cronin Branighan Maddison: Goals -Eadie(3):
Referee K Allatt (Huddersfield) Att - 2424 H.T. 6 - 6

Wed 17 Oct 1973 WIDNES home draw 15 - 15
CASTLEFORD - Claughton: Foster Worsley Higgins
Lowndes: Brook Stephens(Knight): Chawner Miller
Ackroyd Lloyd Lockwood Norton(Redfearn):
Tries - Brook Ackroyd Lockwood: Goals - Lloyd(3):
WIDNES - Dutton: George Warburton Lowe Allan: O'Neill
Bowden: Mills Doherty Sheridan Macko Blackwood
Adams: Try - Adams: Goals - Dutton(4) O'Neill(DG2):
Referee T Keane (Oldham) Att - 1357 H.T. 10 - 5

Wed 24 Oct 1973 OLDHAM away lost 13 - 14
OLDHAM - Murphy: Munro Elliott Wainwright O'Brien:
Blair Astbury: Clawson Taylor Hughes McCracken Hall
Reynolds: Tries - Wainwright Hall: Goals - Clawson(4):
CASTLEFORD - Briggs: Foster Worsley Higgins Lowndes:
Brook(Newton) Knight: Ackroyd(Chawner) Miller
Lockwood Lloyd Wallis Norton:
Tries - Higgins Lloyd Norton: Goals - Lloyd(2):
Referee H Mason (Halifax) Att - 1436 H.T. nil - 2

Sun. 28 Oct 1973 ST HELENS home lost 7 - 17
CASTLEFORD - Briggs: Worsley Newton Higgins Lowndes:
Knight(Joyner) Stephens: Redfearn Miller
Lockwood(Fowler) Ackroyd Lloyd Norton:
Try - Ackroyd: Goals - Lloyd(2):
ST HELENS - Pimblett: Jones Benyon(S/O) Wilson Mathias:
Eckersley(Wills) Gwilliam: Stephens(Hull) Waller James
Mantle Nicholls Coslett:
Tries - Jones Wills James: Goals - Pimblett(4):
Referee R Wood (Dalton in Furness) Att - 3303 H.T. nil - 5

**Tue 30 Oct 1973 HALIFAX home won 26 - 10
BBC 2 FLOODLIT COMPETITION ROUND 1**
CASTLEFORD - Briggs: Worsley Joyner Newton Lowndes:
Knight Stephens Redfearn Miller(C.Dickinson)
Lockwood(Higgins) Ackroyd Lloyd Norton:
Tries - Lloyd(3) Lowndes(2) Briggs: Goals - Lloyd(4):
HALIFAX - Lewis Kelly Willicombe Davies Pitchforth:
Burton Baker: Dewhirst Kawksley Frain(Watson) Callon
Martin Wood: Tries - Lewis Kelly: Goals - Burton(2):
Referee H G Hurt (Prestbury) Att - 831 H.T. 5 - 2

**Wed 7 Nov 1973 HUDDERSFIELD home won 32 - 7
CAPTAIN MORGAN TROPHY ROUND 1**
CASTLEFORD - Briggs: Joyner Worsley Newton
Lowndes(Higgins): Knight Stephens: Redfearn C.Dickinson
Lockwood Ackroyd Lloyd Norton(Birdsall):
Tries - Newton(2) Briggs Worsley Knight Lockwood:
Goals - Lloyd(7):
HUDDERSFIELD - Bedford: Ellis Leathley T.Doyle
(Chamberlain) Senior: B.Doyle Hartley: Hepplestone
Hobson Weavill Davies Branch Johnson(Van Bellen):
Try - Hartley: Goals - Davies(1) (DG):
Referee E Lawrinson (Warrington) Att - 886 H.T. 9 - 5

Sun. 11 Nov 1973 WIGAN home won 31 - 7
CASTLEFORD - Briggs: Joyner Higgins Newton Johnson:
Knight(Brook) Stephens: Redfearn C.Dickinson(Spurr)
Lockwood(S/O) Ackroyd Lloyd Norton:
Tries - Joyner(2) Ackroyd Norton Spurr Lloyd Knight:

Goals - Lloyd(4) Redfearn(DG):
WIGAN - Highton: Wright Vigo Kieron O'Loughlin
Hornby: Ayres Nulty: Farrington Gray Watts(Karalius)
Robinson Rowe(Kevin O'Loughlin)Cunningham(S.O):
Try - Vigo: Goals - Gray(2):
Referee T Keane (Oldham) Att - 2603 H.T. 20 - 2

Tue 13 Nov 1973 BRAMLEY away lost 2 - 13
BBC 2 FLOODLIT COMPETITION ROUND 2
BRAMLEY - Keegan: Goodchild Smith Hughes Austin:
T.Briggs(Bollon) Ward: D.Briggs(Ashman) Firth Cheshire
Sampson Idle Wolford:
Tries - Goodchild Austin T.Briggs: Goals - Ward(2):
CASTLEFORD - Briggs: Joyner Higgins Newton Johnson:
Knight Stephens(Brook): Redfearn Spurr Ackroyd(S/O)
Fowler(Biscomb) Lloyd Norton: Goal - Lloyd:
Referee M J Naughton (Widnes) Att -1110 H.T. 2 - nil

Sun. 18 Nov 1973 WARRINGTON away lost 7 - 15
CAPTAIN MORGAN TROPHY ROUND 2
WARRINGTON - Whitehead: Bevan Noohan Cunliffe
Pickup: Murphy(Curling) Gordon: Chisnall Ashcroft Brady
Nicholas(Wanbon) Gaskell Conroy:
Tries - Cunliffe Brady Conroy: Goals - Whitehead(3):
CASTLEFORD - Briggs: Joyner Newton Brook Higgins:
Knight Stephens: Redfearn Spurr Lockwood
Ackroyd(Fowler) Lloyd(Wallis) Wallis(Appleyard):
Try - Briggs: Goals - Lloyd(2):
Referee D G Kershaw (York) Att - 5246 H.T. 2 - 10

Sun. 25 Nov 1973 BRAMLEY home lost 10 - 14
CASTLEFORD - Briggs: Higgins(Spurr) Newton Brook
Joyner: Knight Stephens(Appleyard): Redfearn
Spurr(Biscomb) C.Dickinson Lloyd Fowler Wallis:
Tries - Newton Biscomb: Goals - Lloyd(2):
BRAMLEY - Keegan: Goodchild Smith(Bollon) Hughes
Austin: T.Briggs Ward: D.Briggs Firth Cheshire Sampson
Idle Wolford:
Tries - Austin(2) Smith Hughes: Goal - Ward:
Referee S Shepherd (Oldham) Att - 1781 H.T. 5 - 6

Sun. 9 Dec 1973 DEWSBURY home won 19 - 13
CASTLEFORD - Briggs: Derek Foster Johnson Brook
Brunyee: Appleyard(Claughton) Stephens: Redfearn Miller
C.Dickinson Lloyd Fowler Wallis(Spurr): Tries - Briggs
Foster Appleyard: Goals - Lloyd(3) Redfearn(DG2):
DEWSBURY - Rushton: Ashcroft Maloney Stephenson
Mitchell: Agar A.Bates: Beverley Voyce Lowe Grayshon
J.Bates Chalkley: Tries - Maloney Stephenson Lowe:
Goals - Stephenson(2):
Referee J V Moss (Manchester) Att - 2234 H.T. 13 - 5

Sat 15 Dec 1973 WARRINGTON away lost 9 - 18
PLAYERS No.6 COMPETITION ROUND 2
WARRINGTON - Whitehead: Bevan Noonan Reynolds
Pickup: Whittle Gordon: Chisnall Ashcroft Brady Nicholas
Wright(Gaskell) Mather: Tries - Gordon Nicholas:
Goals - Whitehead(5) Ashcroft(DG):
CASTLEFORD - Briggs(Claughton): TERRY
RICHARDSON(556) Johnson Brook Brunyee Appleyard

Stephens: Redfearn Tony Miller(Birdsall) C.Dickinson
Lloyd Fowler Wallis: Try - Lloyd: Goals - Lloyd(3):
Referee D G Kershaw (York) Att - 2208 H.T. 4 - 7

Sun. 23 Dec 1973 HULL KINGSTON ROVERS away
won 22 - 15
HULL K R - Longstaff(Pinkney): Hall Dunn Coupland
Leighton: Millward Hudson: Millington Flanagan Rose
Wiley(Holdstock) Fitzgibbon Moore:
Try - Wiley: Goals - Millward(6):
CASTLEFORD - Briggs: Claughton Newton Brook Brunyee:
Appleyard Stephens: Redfearn Spurr C.Dickinson Lloyd
Fowler Wallis: Tries - Newton(2):
Goals - Lloyd(6) Stephens(DG) Redfearn(DG):
Referee K Allatt (Huddersfield) Att - 2228 H.T. 18 - 7

Wed 26 Dec 1973 FEATHERSTONE ROVERS away
lost 6 - 10
FEATHERSTONE R - Box: Coventry Busfield Newlove
Bray(Hartley): Wilson Wood: Tonks Bridges Harris
Hollis(Rhodes) Rhodes(Gibbins)Stone:
Tries - Bray Rhodes: Goals - Box(2):
CASTLEFORD - Briggs: Claughton Newton Brook Brunyee:
Appleyard Stephens(Johnson): Trevor Chawner
Spurr(Birdsall) C.Dickinson Lloyd Fowler Wallis:
Goals - Lloyd(2) Stephens(DG):
Referee A Wood (Barrow) Att - 2771 H.T. 4 - 5

Sun. 30 Dec 1973 HULL KINGSTON ROVERS home
won 45 - 5
CASTLEFORD - Briggs(Knight): Claughton Newton
Johnson Brunyee: Brook Appleyard: Redfearn Spurr
C.Dickinson Fowler(Birdsall) Lloyd Wallis:
Tries - Johnson(2) Appleyard(2) Brunyee Spurr Dickinson
Lloyd Wallis: Goals - Lloyd(9):
HULL K R - Coupland: Stephenson Dunn Hall Leighton:
Nuttall Hudson (Holdstock): Windmill Flanagan
Barraclough Holbrook(Spivey) Fitzgibbon Moore:
Try - Fitzgibbon: Goal - Hall:
Referee M J Naughton (Widnes) Att - 2004 H.T.25 - 2

Tue 1 Jan 1974 LEIGH away won 9 - 5
LEIGH - T.Davies: J.Davies Stacey Melling Riding: McAtee
Sayer: Fiddler Walton Rowley(Bilsbury) Hicks Fletcher
Platt(Rowley): Try - Stacey: Goal - Fiddler:
CASTLEFORD - Briggs: Claughton Newton Johnson
Brunyee: Brook Appleyard: Redfearn(Ackroyd) Spurr
CHRIS FORSTER(557) Lloyd Birdsall Wallis:
Try - Forster: Goals - Lloyd Redfearn(DG) Wallis(DG):
Referee R Jackson (Halifax) Att - 1500 H.T. 7 - 2

Sun. 8 Jan 1974 SALFORD home lost 11 - 16
CASTLEFORD - Briggs: Claughton Johnson Newton
Brunyee: Brook Appleyard: Redfearn Spurr Forster
Ackroyd Lloyd Wallis: Try - Newton: Goals - Lloyd(4):
SALFORD - Charlton: Fielding Watkins Hesketh Richards:
Gill Banner(Prosser): McKay Walker Davies Dixon
Coulman Knighton:
Tries - Fielding Watkins: Goals - Watkins(4) (DG):
Referee E Lawrinson (Warrington) Att - 3515 H.T. 4 - 9

Sun. 13 Jan 1974 DEWSBURY away lost 12 - 14
DEWSBURY - Rushton: Day Maloney Stephenson Mitchell:
Agar A.Bates: Beverley Voyce Hankins Grayshon(Taylor)
J.Bates Chalkley: Tries - Stephenson Grayshon:
Goals - Stephenson(3) (DG):
CASTLEFORD - Briggs: Worsley Johnson Newton
Lowndes: Brook Appleyard: Redfearn(Lockwood) Spurr
Forster Ackroyd Lloyd Wallis(Redfearn):
Tries - Newton Brook: Goals - Lloyd(2) Redfearn(DG):
Referee A Allan (York) Att - 2495 H.T. 12 - 7

Sun. 20 Jan 1974 LEEDS home lost 12 - 20
CASTLEFORD - Briggs: Brunyee Worsley Newton
Lowndes: Brook Appleyard: Redfearn Spurr
Forster(C.Dickinson) Ackroyd Fowler Lloyd(Johnson):
Tries - Briggs Brook: Goals - Redfearn(2) Lloyd:
LEEDS - Marshall: Murrell Langley Dyl Hay: Hynes
Hepworth: Ramsey(Jeanes) Ward Clarkson(Fisher)
Cookson Eccles Batten:
Tries - Ward(2) Langley Batten: Goals - Marshall(3) (DG):
Referee S Shepherd (Oldham) Att - 5191 H.T. 2 - 10

Sat 26 Jan 1974 WIGAN away draw nil - nil
WIGAN - Tyrer: Wright Francis Kieron O'Loughlin Keven
O'Loughlin: Cassidy (D.Hill) Ayres: Bence(Grauy) Clarke
Fletcher Irving Robinson Cunningham:
CASTLEFORD - Briggs: Brunyee Worsley Newton
Lowndes: Brook Appleyard: Redfearn Spurr
Lockwood(Forster) Ackroyd Lloyd Wallis:
Referee R Moore (Wakefield) Att - 3471 H.T. nil - nil

**Sun. 3 Feb 1974 BRADFORD NORTHERN home
lost 4 - 15 CHALLENGE CUP ROUND 1**
CASTLEFORD - Briggs: Brunyee Worsley Newton
Lowndes: Brook Roy Appleyard(Johnson): Redfearn Spurr
Forster Ackroyd Lloyd Clifford Wallis(C.Dickinson):
Goals - Lloyd(2):
BRADFORD N - Mumby: Lamb Stockwell Watson
Redfearn: Kelly Seabourne: Ramsay Dunn(Jackson) Long
Gallagher Pattinson Joyve: Tries - Seabourne Gallagher
Watson: Goals - Mumby(2) Seabourne(DG):
Referee H Hunt (Cheshire) Att - 7116 H.T. 4 - 5

Sun. 17 Feb 1974 WHITEHAVEN home won 36 - 12
CASTLEFORD - Briggs(Newton): Worsley Joyner Johnson
Lowndes: Brook Stephens: Redfearn Spurr Forster
Lockwood Fowler(Ackroyd) Norton: Tries - Worsley(3)
Lowndes(2) Johnson Stephens Spurr: Goals - Redfearn(6):
WHITEHAVEN - Rose: Morris Tate Eilbeck(Barwise) Sewell:
Mather Smith: Pringle Sirkett Irving McFarlane
Glaister(McAlone) Cottier:
Tries - Pringle Sirkett: Goals - Mather(2) (DG):
Referee M J Naughton (Widnes) Att - 1643 H.T. 15 - 4

**Sun. 24 Feb 1974 WAKEFIELD TRINITY away
won 15 - 14**
WAKEFIELD T - Crook: Lumb Sheard Davies
Archer(Layton): Topliss Langton(Ellis): Valentine
Handforth Campbell Goodwin Endersby Morgan:
Tries - Topliss Endersby: Goals - Crook(4):

CASTLEFORD - Briggs: Worsley Joyner Johnson Lowndes:
Brook(Newton)Stephens: Redfearn Spurr Forster(Lloyd)
Lockwood Fowler Norton: Tries - Brook Newton
Lockwood: Goals - Redfearn(2) Lloyd:
Referee K L Gaskil (Wigan) Att - 3575 H.T. 7 - 9

Sun. 3 March 1974 ST HELENS away lost 5 - 25
ST HELENS - Eckersley: Jones Benyon Wilson Mathias:
Atherton(Pimblett) Heaton: Mantle Karalius Murphy
Nicholls Chisnall Coslett: Tries - Mathias(3) Wilson
Heaton Karalius Nicholls: Goals - Coslett(2):
CASTLEFORD - Briggs: Worsley Joyner(Knight) Newton
Brunyee: Johnson Stephens: Redfearn Spurr
A.Dickinson(Lloyd) Lockwood Fowler (A.Dickinsom)
Norton: Try - Knight: Goal - Redfearn:
Referee K Allatt (Huddersfield) Att - 5783 H.T. 2 - 5

Sun. 10 March 1974 BRAMLEY away draw 8 - 8
BRAMLEY - Keegan: Goodchild Bollon Hughes Austin:
Briggs(Tennant) Astbury: Jarvis Firth Ashman(McGurley)
Craker Idle Wolford:
Tries - Bollon McGurley: Goal - Keegan:
CASTLEFORD - Briggs: Worsley Joyner Newton Brunyee:
Johnson(Knight) Stephens: Redfearn Spurr
Lockwood(Forster) Fowler Lloyd Norton:
Tries - Johnson Spurr: Goal - Lloyd:
Referee P Geraghty (York) Att - 2010 H.T. 3 - 5

**Sun. 17 March 1974 WARRINGTON home
lost 6 - 14**
CASTLEFORD - Briggs: Brunyee Worsley Joyner Lowndes:
Glyn Knight(Johnson) Stephens: Redfearn Spurr
Lockwood(Forster) Fowler Lloyd Norton:
Tries - Worsley Lowndes:
WARRINGTON - Finnigan: Curling Cinliffe Pickup Sutton:
Briggs Lowe: Chisnall Middlehurst Brady(Jones) Wright
Wanbon Conroy. Sub Clarke
Tries - Pickup Briggs: Goals - Briggs Middlehurst(1) (2DG):
Referee T Keane (Oldham) Att - 2918 H.T. nil - 7

Sat 23 March 1974 WHITEHAVEN away won 11 - 9
WHITEHAVEN - Mather: Eilbeck Tait Rose Sewell: Evans
Smith: Vaughan Thompson Irving Sirkett McAlone(Morris)
McFarlane:
Try - Mather: Goals - Mather(2) McFarlane(DG):
CASTLEFORD - Briggs: Brunyee Worsley Joyner Lowndes:
Johnson Stephens: Redfearn Spurr C.Dickinson Forster
Fowler Norton:
Tries - Briggs Lowndes Stephens: Goal - Redfearn:
Referee M J Naughton (Widnes) Att - 500 H.T. 3 - 2

**Sun. 31 March 1974 ROCHDALE HORNETS away
won 16 - 10**
ROCHDALE H - Crellin: Brelsford Brophy McGiffen Pratt:
Butler Gartland: Brown Harris Holliday Gourley(Delooze)
Hodgkinson Halmshaw(Gourley):
Tries - Brelsford Pratt: Goals - Holliday(2):
CASTLEFORD - Briggs: Brunyee Worsley Joyner Lowndes:
Brook Stephens(Johnson): Forster Spurr
C.Dickinson(Ackroyd) Fowler Lloyd Norton:

SEASON 1973-74

Tries - Joyner Ackroyd: Goals - Lloyd(5):
Referee T Beaumont (Huddersfield) Att -   H.T.

Sun. 7 Apr 1974 OLDHAM home lost 12 - 25
CASTLEFORD - Briggs: Brunyee Worsley(Claughton)
Joyner Lowndes: Johnson Brook: Ackroyd
C.Dickinson(Spurr) Forster Fowler(S/O)Lloyd Norton(S/O):
Tries - Lowndes Lloyd: Goals - Lloyd(3):
OLDHAM - Murphy: Barton Larder Wainwright Holland:
Treaure McCone: Ashcroft Brown(S/O)Maye(Peters)
Gregory Hall Farrell(S/O):   Tries - Hall(2) Murphy Larder
Peters: Goals - Holland(3) Treasure(DG) McCone(DG):
Referee R Wood (Barrow) Att - 2029 H.T. 4 - 11

Sat 13 Apr 1974 LEEDS away won 17 - 11
LEEDS - Marshall: Sanderson Langley Hay Atkinson:
Fletcher Hepworth: Jeanes Ward Hicks Clarkson(Fisher)
Adams Batten:
Tries - Marshall Atkinson Hicks: Goal - Marshall:
CASTLEFORD - Briggs: Joyner PAUL LONGSTAFF(558)
Johnson Lowndes: Brook(Newton)Stephens: Forster Spurr
C.Dickinson(Brunyee) Ackroyd Fowler Norton
(C.Dickinson):
Tries - Stephens Spurr Ackroyd: Goals - Ackroyd(4):
Referee H Hunt (Prestbury) Att - 3193 H.T. 10 - 5

**Mon 15 Apr 1974 FEATHERSTONE ROVERS home
draw 4 - 4**
CASTLEFORD - Briggs: Joyner Longstaff Johnson
Lowndes: Brook Stephens: Forster Spurr
C.Dickinson(A.Dickinson) Ackroyd Fowler Brunyee
Goals - Ackroyd(2):
FEATHERSTONE R - Kellett: Dyas Box(Toohey) Hartley
Bray: Mason Wood: Sayer(Smith) Bell Harris Stone
Gibbins Smith(Busfield):   Goals - Kellett(2):
Referee A Givvons (Oldham) Att - 3445 H.T. 2 - 2

**Sun. 21 Apr 1974 BRAMLEY away won 14 - nil
CLUB CHAMPIONSHIP ROUND 1**
BRAMLEY - Keegan: Goodchild Tennant Hughes Waites:
Briggs Astbury: Jarvis(Greenwood) Price Ashman(Jarvis)
Idle Weston Wolford:
CASTLEFORD - Briggs(Longstaff): Joyner Longstaff
(Newton) Johnson Lowndes: Brook Stephens: Forster
Spurr C.Dickinson Ackroyd Fowler(Brunyee) Norton:
Tries - Joyner Lowndes: Goals - Ackroyd Norton(3DG):
Referee E Lawrinson (Warrington) Att - 1950 H.T. 4 - nil

**Sun. 28 Apr 1974 ST HELENS away lost 9 - 25
CLUB CHAMPIONSHIP ROUND 2**
ST HELENS - Pimblett: Jones Benyon Wilson Mathias:
Eckersley Heaton: Stephens Liptrot Murphy Mantle
Nicholls(Chisnall) Coslett: Tries - Jones Eckersley Heaton
Mantle Coslett: Goals - Coslett(5):
CASTLEFORD - Briggs(S/O): Joyner Longstaff Johnson
Lowndes(Newton): Brook Stephens: Forster Spurr
C.Dickinson Ackroyd A.Dickinson Brunyee(BRIAN
GARBETT(559)):
Try - Johnson: Goals - Ackroyd(2) Brunyee(DG):
Referee W Thompson (Hud'field) Att - 2500 H.T. 13 – 4

Terry Richardson
D. No 556
1973-74 to 1982-83

Chris Forster
D . No 557
1973-74 to 1974-75

Steve Fenton
D. No 560
1973-74 to 1986-87

D.N	PLAYER		DEBUT	L MATCH	APP	SUB	T.AP	TRI'S	G'LS	D.G	P'TS
479	DICKINSON	CLIVE			15	3	18	1	0	0	3
493	BRIGGS	TREVOR			43	0	43	9	0	0	27
494	REDFEARN	MICHAEL			36	1	37	0	17	9	52
495	MILLER	TONY		15/12/1973	18	0	18	3	0	0	9
497	LOCKWOOD	BRIAN			20	1	21	4	0	0	12
509	FOSTER	DEREK		09/12/1973	4	0	4	1	0	0	3
516	LOWNDES	ALAN			31	0	31	16	0	0	48
517	APPLEYARD	ROY		03/02/1974	11	2	13	3	0	0	9
518	SPURR	ROBERT			24	3	27	6	0	0	18
521	BISCOMB	TERRY			0	2	2	1	0	0	3
522	ACKROYD	ALAN			27	4	31	8	11	0	46
525	STEPHENS	GARY			35	0	35	11	0	2	37
526	JOHNSON	PHILIP			20	6	26	6	0	0	18
527	SHAW	LESLIE		05/10/1973	2	0	2	0	0	0	0
528	KNIGHT	GLEN		17/03/1974	21	5	26	9	0	0	27
531	NORTON	STEVE (KNOCKER)			23	0	23	4	0	3	18
532	LLOYD	GEOFFREY (SAMMY)			35	3	38	15	121	0	287
537	NEWTON	RAY			22	6	28	9	0	0	27
538	HIGGINS	PAUL			16	5	21	4	0	0	12
540	FOWLER	DENNIS			19	3	22	0	0	0	0
541	WORSLEY	KEITH			29	0	29	9	0	0	27
542	DICKINSON	ALAN			2	1	3	0	0	0	0
544	CLAUGHTON	GEORGE			6	3	9	0	0	0	0
545	WALLIS	CLIFFORD		03/02/1974	20	2	22	1	0	1	5
546	BRUNYEE	STEVEN			18	2	20	1	0	1	5
547	BIRDSALL	CHARLIE			2	7	9	0	0	0	0
550	BROOK	GARY			24	5	29	4	0	0	12
551	JOYNER	JOHN			30	2	32	13	0	0	39
554	CHAWNER	TREVOR		26/12/1973	7	6	13	0	0	0	0
555	NAYLOR	JAMES	16/09/1973	10/10/1973	6	0	6	1	0	0	3
556	RICHARDSON	TERRY	15/12/1973		1	0	1	0	0	0	0
557	FORSTER	CHRIS	01/01/1974		14	3	17	1	0	0	3
558	LONGSTAFF	PAUL	13/04/1974		4	0	4	0	0	0	0
559	GARBETT	BRIAN	28/04/1974		0	1	1	0	0	0	0
	34		**5**	**8**	**585**	**76**	**661**	**140**	**149**	**16**	**750**

COMPETITION		P	W	D	L	FOR	AGT
LEAGUE D 1	POSITION 9 OF 16	30	12	4	14	420	411
YORK'S CUP		3	2	0	1	79	35
F. TROPHY		4	3	0	1	78	33
RL CUP		1	0	0	1	4	15
CAPTAIN MORGAN		2	1	0	1	39	22
PLAYERS NO6		2	1	0	1	97	23
CHAMPIONSHIP		2	1	0	1	23	25
AUSTRALIA		1	0	0	1	10	18
PLAYERS RECORDS		**45**	**20**	**4**	**21**	**750**	**582**

Once more we started the season with a new Coach, Dave Cox taking over from John Sheridan.

With the introduction of two divisions the League Leaders were crowned as champions and another new knockout competition was launched - the Captain Morgan Trophy,

We once more entertained the Australian tourists but could not manage a third successive victory losing 18–10.

In the Players No 6 Competition we beat the amateur side Millom winning with a score of 88–5 with Geoffrey (Sammy) Lloyd kicking 17 goals out of 18 attempts and scoring 3 tries he increased the records for most goals and points 43, in a cup game , with John Joyner scoring five tries he became the second Castleford player to score five in one game.

'Sammy' Lloyd also became the record holder for the most goals in a season with 121, surpassing Albert Lunn's 1958/59 figure of 119.

In the Club Championship play-off (contested by the top 12 of Division 1 and the top 4 of Division 2) a second round defeat, away at St Helens 25–9, Steve Brunyee became the last Castleford player to score a two point drop goal.

SEASON 1974-75

Drop Kick Reduced To 1 Point

Under the Two Division League structure a "four up and four down" system of relegation and promotion between the Divisions was in operation. Therefore Bradford Northern, York, Keighley and Halifax were promoted to Division 1. Oldham, Hull K R, Leigh, Whitehaven relegated to Division 2.

Sun 25 Aug 1974 WAKEFIELD TRINITY away draw 12 - 12
WAKEFIELD T - Sheard: Smith Crook Layton Lumb: Topliss Bonnar: Ballantyne Ingham Campbell Knowles(Sherrett) Tonks Morgan: Tries - Smith Topliss: Goals - Crook(3):
CASTLEFORD - Longstaff: Joyner Johnson Newton Lowndes: Brook Stephens: Forster Spurr C.Dickinson(Brunyee) Fowler Ackroyd Lloyd:
Tries - Joyner Johnson: Goals - Lloyd(3):
Referee S Wall (Leigh) Att - 3725 H.T. 2 - 12

**Fri 30 Aug 1974 YORK home lost 13 - 19
YORKSHIRE CUP ROUND 1**
CASTLEFORD - Longstaff: Joyner Johnson Newton Lowndes: Brook Stephens: Forster Spurr C.Dickinson(Fowler) Lloyd Ackroyd(Brunyee) Norton:
Tries - Joyner Lowndes Ackroyd: Goals - Lloyd(2):
YORK - Wallace: Barends Horner Quinn Clancy: Smith(Broatch) Sullivan: Dixon Payne Hill(Cookland) Hillman Cookland(Wileman) Sheehan:
Tries - Barends Clancy Wileman:
Goals - Quinn(4) Wallace(DG) Sullivan(DG):
Referee H Hunt (Cheshire) Att - 1778 H.T. 7 - 12

Fri 6 Sept 1974 ROCHDALE HORNETS home won 24 - 16
CASTLEFORD - Briggs: Richardson Joyner Newton Lowndes: Brook Stephens: Forster Spurr C.Dickinson Fowler Lloyd Norton:
Tries - Lloyd(2) Richardson Norton: Goals - Lloyd(6):
ROCHDALE H - Crellin: Green Brophy(Simpkins) Taylor Pratt: Butcher Cartland: Birchall Clarke Whitehead Fogerty(Gourley) Cooke Halmshaw:
Tries - Brophy Taylor: Goals - Green(5):
Referee J Moss (Manchester) Att - 1700 H.T. 10 - 16

**Wed 11 Sept 1974 HUDDERSFIELD away lost 4 – 12
BBC2 FLOODLIT COMPETITION PRELIMINARY**
HUDDERSFIELD - Leathley: Hooson T.Doyle Chamberlain Senior: Knight Hartley: Van Bellen Miller Weavill Tomlonson Welsh J.Doyle:
Tries - T.Doyle Tomlinson: Goals - Hartley(3):
CASTLEFORD - Brunyee: Richardson Joyner Newton Lowndes: Brook (STEVE FENTON(560)) Stephens: Forster PETER DOWNHAM(561) Birdsall Fowler Lloyd Garbett(Woodall): Goals - Lloyd(2):
Referee P Massey (Salford) Att - 656 H.T. 2 - 7

Sun 15 Sept 1974 KEIGHLEY away lost 14 - 15
KEIGHLEY - Jickells: Stephenson Roe Simpson Wilkes: Edwards Loxton: Valentine Raistrick(Brosnan) (Raistrick)

Illingworth Garbett Orr(O'Brien) Sutcliffe:
Tries - Roe Valentine Sutcliffe: Goals - Sutcliffe(3):
CASTLEFORD - Brunyee: Richardson Joyner Newton(Fenton) Lowndes: Brook Stephens: Forster Spurr(C.Dickinson) C.Dickinson(Redfearn)Fowler Lloyd Norton: Tries - Joyner Brook: Goals - Lloyd(4):
Referee P Geraghty (York) Att - 1038 H.T. 9 - 10

Sat 21 Sept 1974 WIGAN home won 22 - 12
CASTLEFORD - Briggs: Richardson Joyner Fenton Lowndes: Brook Stephens: Redfearn C.Dickinson Forster Brunyee Lloyd Norton:
Tries - Joyner Dickinson Brunyee Norton: Goals - Lloyd(5):
WIGAN - Kevin O'Loughlin: Wright Willicombe Vigo Kieron O'Loughlin: Taylor Coyle: Fletcher Gray Bailey(Smethurst) Irving Robinson Karalius:
Tries - Coyle Irving: Goals - Gray(3):
Referee M Naughton (Widnes) Att - 1598 H.T. 12 - 6

**Fri 27 Sept 1974 SALFORD away lost 5 - 36
PLAYERS No.6 ROUND 1**
SALFORD - Charlton: Fielding Hesketh Graham Richards: Gill(Taylor)Banner: McKay Devlin Grice Knighton Dixon Corcoran: Tries - Hesketh(2) Charlton Graham Richards Banner Knighton Corcoran: Goals - Fielding(6):
CASTLEFORD - Briggs: Richardson Joyner Fenton Lowndes: Brook Stephens: Redfearn C.Dickinson Forster Lockwood Lloyd Brunyee: Try - Richardson: Goal - Lloyd:
Referee R Jackson (Halifax) Att - 4755 H.T. 2 - 13

Sun 6 Oct 1974 DEWSBURY away won 23 - 12
DEWSBURY - Gray: Mitchell Day Stephenson Simpson: Agar(Clarke) A.Bates: Bell Voyce Hankin Grayshon J.Bates(Taylor) Chalkley:
Tries - Day Agar: Goals - Stephenson(3):
CASTLEFORD - Briggs: Richardson Joyner Newton Lowndes: Brook Stephens: Redfearn C.Dickinson Lockwood(Forster) Brunyee Lloyd Norton:
Tries - Lloyd(2) Richardson Brook Stephens: Goals - Lloyd(4):
Referee R Wood (Barrow) Att - 1900 H.T. 8 - 7

Fri 11 Oct 1974 WIDNES home lost 7 - 12
CASTLEFORD - Briggs: Richardson Joyner Newton(ROY HEPTON(562)) Lowndes: Brook Stephens: Redfearn C.Dickinson Forster(Birdsall) Brunyee Lloyd Norton:
Try - Richardson: Goals - Lloyd(2):
WIDNES - Dutton: George D.O'Neill Aspey J.O'Neill: Hughes Bowden: Nelson Elwell Sheridan Allen Blackwood(Charnock) Adams:
Tries - Bowden Adams: Goals - Dutton(3):
Referee A Givvons (Oldham) Att - 1813 H.T. 2 - 2

Sun 20 Oct 1974 YORK away lost 12 - 17
YORK - Wallace: Barends Andrews Quinn Clancy: Broatch Smith(Sullivan): Dixon(Windmill) Wileman Hawley Cookland Hillman Sheehan:
Try - Cookland: Goals - Quinn(7):
CASTLEFORD - Briggs: Richardson Joyner Newton Lowndes: Brook(Fenton) Stephens: Redfearn C.Dickinson

SEASON 1974-75

Forster Lloyd Birdsall Norton:
Tries - Richardson Lowndes: Goals - Lloyd(3):
Referee S Wall (Leigh) Att - 2781 H.T. nil - nil

Fri 25 Oct 1974 HALIFAX home won 35 - 10
CASTLEFORD - Briggs: Richardson Joyner Paul Longstaff
Lowndes: Fenton Stephens: Redfearn C.Dickinson
Lockwood Lloyd Reilly Norton: Tries - Joyner Lowndes
Fenton Dickinson Lloyd Reilly Norton: Goals - Lloyd(7):
HALIFAX - Dawson: Raynor Davies Gurr Pitchforth: Burton
Sanderson: Briggs Dyson(Walton) Hoyle Martin Scott
Baker: Tries - Davies Baker: Goals - Burton(2):
Referee R Haigh (Bradford) Att - 2591 H.T. 20 - nil

Fri 8 Nov 1974 DEWSBURY home won 24 - 12
CASTLEFORD - Briggs(Birdsall): Richardson Joyner
Newton Lowndes: Fenton (Hepton) Stephens: Redfearn
C.Dickinson Lockwood Lloyd Reilly Norton:
Tries - Lowndes(2) Briggs Richardson Hepton Norton:
Goals Lloyd(3):
DEWSBURY - Rushton: Mitchell Clark Stephenson Day:
Russell A.Bates: Bell(Taylor) Voyce Hankin Grayshon
J.Bates Chalkley: Tries - Day Chalkley:
Goals - Stephenson(3):
Referee R Jackson (Halifax) Att - 2926 H.T. 3 - 5

Fri 15 Nov 1974 SALFORD away lost 10 - 13
SALFORD - Charlton: Fielding Hesketh Graham Richards:
Brophy Banner: McKay Devlin Grice Dixon Coulman
Knighton(Turnbull):
Tries - Fielding Richards Dixon: Goals - Fielding(2):
CASTLEFORD - Briggs: Richardson Joyner Newton
Lowndes: Brook Stephens: Redfearn Clive Dickinson(S/O)
Lockwood(Birdsall) Lloyd Reilly Norton:
Tries - Joyner(2):   Goals - Lloyd(2):
Referee W H Thompson (Hud'field) Att - 6470 H.T. nil -5
**MATCH DECLARED VOID - SPECTATORS INVADED
PITCH REPLAYED FRI 24 JAN 1975**

Fri 22 Nov 1974 BRAMLEY home won 15 - 11
CASTLEFORD - Briggs: Richardson Joyner Roy Hepton
Lowndes: Brook Stephens: Redfearn Spurr Lockwood
Lloyd Reilly Norton(Birdsall): Try - Spurr: Goals - Lloyd(6):
BRAMLEY - Keegan: Rowett Bollon Huxley Parker: Briggs
Astbury: Cheshire Price Standidge Idle(M.Sampson)
Weston Wolford: Tries - Keegan: Goals - Rowett(4):
Referee H Mason (Halifax) Att - 1822 H.T. 8 - 9

Fri 29 Nov 1974 ST HELENS away lost 5 - 17
ST HELENS - Pimblett: Campbell Benyon Hull Mathias:
Eckersley Heaton(Gwilliam): Warlow Karalius Charles
Mantle Chisnall Coslett:
Tries - Heaton(2) Mathias: Goals - Coslett(4):
CASTLEFORD - Briggs: Richardson Joyner Newton
Lowndes: Brook(JAMIE WALSH(563))Stephens: Redfearn
Spurr Forster(TONY JEFF(564)) Lloyd Birdsall Norton:
Try - Richardson: Goal - Lloyd:
Referee K Allatt (Huddersfield) Att - 3000 H.T. 2 - 7

**Fri 6 Dec 1974 WAKEFIELD TRINITY home
won 35 - 8**
CASTLEFORD - Briggs: Claughton Joyner Newton
Lowndes: Brook Stephens: Redfearn Spurr Birdsall Lloyd
Reilly Norton: Tries - Joyner(2) Birdsall(2) Newton
Lowndes Lloyd: Goals - Lloyd(7):
WAKEFIELD T - Oulton: Smith Layton Butterfield Archer:
Topliss Langton: Tonks Handscombe Ballantyne(Skerrett)
Morgan Ellis Hetherington:
Tries - Archer Langton: Goal - Oulton:
Referee A E Fryer (Warrington) Att - 2861 H.T. 15 - 3

**Sun 15 Dec 1974 ROCHDALE HORNETS away
won 15 - 6**
ROCHDALE H - Farrow: Brelsford Taylor McGiffen Marson:
Butler Hammond(Hillman): Birchall Clarke(S/O) Woodyer
Hodgkinson Cooke Whitehead:
Tries - Butler: Goals - Farrow Butler(DG):
CASTLEFORD - Briggs(Fenton): Richardson Joyner Newton
GEOFFREY MORRS(565): Brook Stephens: Redfearn
Spurr(S/O) Birdsall Lloyd(Forster) Reilly Norton:
Tries - Richardson Morris Redfearn:
Goals - Lloyd(2) Redfearn:
Referee D G Kershaw (York) Att - 2183 H.T. nil - 5

Sat 21 Dec 1974 ST HELENS home draw 10 - 10
CASTLEFORD - Briggs: Richardson Joyner Newton Morris:
Fenton Stephens: Redfearn(A.Dickinson) Spurr Forster
Lloyd Birdsall Reilly:
Tries - Newton Spurr: Goals - Lloyd(2):
ST HELENS - Pimblett(Hull): Campbell Benyon(Gwilliam)
Wilson Matthias: Eckersley Heaton: Charles Karalius
Murphy Nicholls Chisnall Coslett:
Tries - Campbell Eckersley: Goals - Coslett(2):
Referee P A Massey (Salford) Att - 2188 H.T. 10 - 5

**Fri 27 Dec 1974 FEATHERSTONE ROVERS home
won 23 - 5**
CASTLEFORD - Briggs(Brook): Richardson Joyner Newton
Lowndes: Fenton Stephens: Redfearn Spurr Lockwood
Lloyd Birdsall Reilly(A.Dickinson): Tries - Richardson
Joyner Newton Lowndes Spurr: Goals - Lloyd(4):
FEATHERSTONE R - Box: Dyas M.Smith(Tuffs) Hartley
K.Kellett: Newlove Butler: Dixon Noon Gibbins Rhodes
Busfield(P.Smith) Stone: Try - P.Smith: Goal - Box:
Referee K Spencer (Warrington) Att - 3960 H.T. 13 - nil

**Wed 1 Jan 1975 BRADFORD NORTHERN home
won 20 - 18**
CASTLEFORD - Briggs: Richardson Joyner Newton
Lowndes: Fenton Stephens: Redfearn Spurr Lockwood
A.Dickinson(Ackroyd) Birdsall Lloyd:
Tries - Richardson Joyner Stephens Lockwood:
Goals - Lloyd(4):
BRADFORD N - Mumby: Lamb Ward Gant Francis: Blacker
Seabourne(Kelly) Mordue Jarvis Forsyth
Gallagher(Trotter) Joyce Fearnley:
Tries - Kelly Forsyth: Goals - Mumby(6):
Referee A Givvons (Oldham) Att - 5851 H.T. 10 - 6

SEASON 1974-75

Sat 4 Jan 1975 WIGAN away lost 2 - 34
WIGAN - Fairbairn: Vigo Willicombe Hill(Francis) Hornby:
Kieron O'Loughlin Nulty: Hogan Clarke(Ashcroft) Gray
Irving Gregory Karalius: Tries - Vigo(2) O'Loughlin(2)
Willicombe Hornby Hogan Clarke: Goals - Gray(5):
CASTLEFORD - Briggs: Richardson Joyner Newton
Lowndes: Fenton(Brook) Stephens: Redfearn Spurr
A.Dickinson ALAN RHODES(566) Ackroyd Lloyd:
Goal - Lloyd:
Referee R Jackson (Halifax) Att - 5209 H.T. nil - 18

Fri 10 Jan 1975 WARRINGTON home won 20 - 8
CASTLEFORD - Briggs(Brook): Richardson Joyner Newton
Lowndes: Fenton Stephens: Hartley(Ackroyd) Spurr
Redfearn Rhodes A.Dickinson Lloyd:
Tries - Ackroyd(2) Richardson Lloyd: Goals - Lloyd(4):
WARRINGTON - Cunliffe(Lowe): Wharton Fitzpatrick
Pickup Bevan: Briggs Gordon: Chisnall Ashcroft Price
Gaskell(Jewitt) Martyn Conroy:
Tries - Wharton Gordon: Goal - Wharton:
Referee T Keane (Oldham) Att - 3035 H.T. 7 - 5

**Sun 19 Jan 1975 BRADFORD NORTHERN away
lost 12 - 17**
BRADFORD N - Carlton: Lamb Ward Gant(Kelly) Francis:
Blacker Seabourne: Earl Jarvis Jackson(Pattinson) Joyce
Trotter Fearnley:
Tries - Gant Blacker Trotter: Goals - Seabourne(4):
CASTLEFORD - Briggs: Richardson Joyner Newton
Lowndes: Brook Stephens: Hartley Spurr Lockwood
Redfearn A.Dickinson(Ackroyd) Rhodes:
Tries - Stephens Redfearn: Goals - Redfearn(3):
Referee R Campbell (Widnes) Att - 4987 H.T. 2 - 8

Fri 24 Jan 1975 SALFORD away draw 11 - 11
SALFORD - Stead: Fielding Watkins Hesketh Richards: Gill
Taylor(Brophy): Coulman Walker Fiddler Knighton
Corcoran Prescott:
Tries - Stead Richards Knighton: Goal - Watkins:
CASTLEFORD - Briggs: Richardson(Johnson) Joyner
Newton Lowndes: Brook Stephens: Hartley Spurr
Lockwood Lloyd A.Dickinson Norton:
Tries - Joyner Stephens: Goals - Lloyd(2) Norton(DG):
Referee W H Thompson (Hud'field) Att - 5251 H.T. 5 - 6

Fri 31 Jan 1975 LEEDS home won 22 - 16
CASTLEFORD - Briggs: Johnson Joyner Newton Lowndes:
Brook Stephens(Walsh): Hartley Spurr(Rhodes) Lockwood
Lloyd A.Dickinson Norton: Tries - Briggs Newton
Lowndes Brook Hartley Lockwood: Goals - Lloyd(2):
LEEDS - Holmes: Murrell Hynes Dyl Atkinson: Mason
Hepworth: Harrison Fisher Pitchford Haigh
Cookson(Ward) Batten:
Tries - Dyl Fisher Haigh Ward: Goals - Holmes(2):
Referee J V Moss (Manchester) Att - 4394 H.T. 10 - 5

**Sat 8 Feb 1975 BRADFORD NORTHERN home draw
13 - 13 CHALLENGE CUP ROUND 1**
CASTLEFORD - Briggs: Johnson Joyner Newton Lowndes:
Brook Stephens: Hartley Spurr(Reilly) Lockwood

A.Dickinson Lloyd Norton:
Tries - Brook(2) Lowndes: Goals - Lloyd(2):
BRADFORD N - Mumby: Francis Ward Gant Redfearn:
Blacker Seabourne(Kelly): Murphy Wilson Jackson Trotter
Joyce Fearnley:
Tries - Blacker(2): Goals - Mumby(3) Seabourne(DG):
Referee P Massey (Salford) Att - 6500 H.T. 3 - 8

**Sun 9 Feb 1975 BRADFORD NORTHERN away
lost 7 - 10 CHALLENGE CUP ROUND 1 REPLAY**
BRADFORD N - Mumby: Francis Ward(Kelly) Gant
Redfearn: Blacker Seabourne: Murphy Wilson(Pattinson)
Jackson Trotter Joyce Fearnley:
Tries - Jackson Joyce: Goals - Mumby(2):
CASTLEFORD - Briggs: Johnson Joyner Newton Lowndes:
Brook Stephens: Hartley A.Dickinson Lockwood Reilly
Lloyd Norton: Try - Joyner: Goals - Lloyd(2):
Referee P Massey (Salford) Att - 10076 H.T. 7 - 5

Sat 15 Feb 1975 BRAMLEY away lost 14 - 15
BRAMLEY - Keegan: Hay Huxley Bollon(Rowett) Parker:
Briggs Astbury: Jarvis Wright Standidge(Cheshire)
Greenwood Sampson Wolford:
Tries - Hay Bollon Astbury: Goals - Hay(3):
CASTLEFORD - Briggs: Johnson Joyner Newton Lowndes:
Brook Walsh: Forster GRAHAM TYREMAN(567) Lockwood
Lloyd Rhodes Norton(Redfearn):
Tries - Brook Rhodes: Goals - Lloyd(4):
Referee S Walls (Leigh) Att - 1500 H.T. 7 - 8

Sun 2 Mar 1975 HALIFAX away won 28 - 7
HALIFAX - Hepworth: Brown Davies Burton
Pitchforth(Scott): FinnerySanderson: Briggs
Hawksley(Dyson) Thomson Hoyle Martin Baker:
Try - Hoyle: Goals - Burton(2):
CASTLEFORD - Briggs: Johnson Joyner Newton(Walsh)
Lowndes: Brook Stephens: Forster(Redfearn) Spurr
Lockwood A.Dickinson Rhodes Lloyd:
Tries - Brook(2) Briggs Johnson Forster Spurr:
Goals - Lloyd(5):
Referee M Naughton (Widnes) Att - 1926 H.T. 18 - 7

Fri 7 Mar 1975 SALFORD home lost 12 - 15
CASTLEFORD - Briggs: Johnson Joyner Worsley Lowndes:
Brook Stephens: Forster Spurr Brian Lockwood
A.Dickinson Lloyd Norton:
Tries - Stephens(2): Goals - Lloyd(3):
SALFORD - Charlton: Rawlinson Graham Hesketh
Richards: Gill Banner: Coulman(Turnbull) Walker Fiddler
Knighton Mackay Prescott:
Tries - Graham Hesketh Coulman: Goals - Fiddler(3):
Referee T Keane (Oldham) Att - 2730 H.T. 5 - 15

Fri 14 Mar 1975 KEIGHLEY home won 13 - 8
CASTLEFORD - Briggs: Morris(Fenton) Joyner Worsley
Lowndes: Brook Stephens: Forster(ALAN HARDY(568))
Spurr Redfearn Rhodes Lloyd Norton:
Tries - Joyner Stephens Rhodes: Goals - Lloyd(2):
KEIGHLEY - Jickells: Johnson Roe Wilkes Stephenson:
Sabine Loxton: Burke Woolford Garforth Gallagher

Garbett Valentine:
Tries - Johnson Garbett: Goal - Garbett:
Referee J Jackson (Pudsey) Att - 1832 H.T. 6 - 2

Fri 21 Mar 1975 WIDNES away lost 9 - 19
WIDNES - Dutton: Prescott Karalius Aspey A.N.Other:
Davies Bowden: Mills Hammond Nelson Wood Foran
Adams: Tries - Davies(2) Nelson: Goals - Dutton(5):
CASTLEFORD - Briggs: Johnson Joyner Worsley Lowndes:
Brook(Higgins) Stephens: Hartley Spurr Redfearn
Rhodes(Lloyd) Birdsall Norton:
Tries - Johnson Stephens: Goals - Redfearn Stephens(DG):
Referee P Geraghty (York) Att - 3500 H.T. 4 - 12

Mon 31 Mar 1975 FEATHERSTONE ROVERS away
lost 8 - 17
FEATHERSTONE R - Box: Hill M.Smith Coventry(Marsden)
Kellett: Newlove Butler: Harris Farrar Gibbins
P.Smith(Tune) Stone Bell:
Tries - M.Smith Newlove P.Smith: Goals - Box(4):
CASTLEFORD - Briggs: Higgins Joyner Worsley(Newton)
Lowndes: Johnson Stephens: Hartley(Lloyd) Spurr
Redfearn Rhodes Birdsall Norton:
Tries - Lowndes Norton: Goal - Lloyd:
Referee A Givvons (Oldham) Att - 2478 H.T. 3 - 4

Fri 4 Apr 1975 YORK home lost 4 - 9
CASTLEFORD - Briggs: Higgins Worsley Newton Lowndes:
Johnson(Morris)Walsh: Dennis Hartley(Rhodes) Spurr
Redfearn Lloyd Birdsall Norton: Goals - Lloyd(2):
YORK - Wallace: Barends Day Wilson Quinn: Smith
Sullivan: Clawson Handforth(Dunkerley) Hetherington
Clarkson Dunkerley(Godfrey) Sheehan:
Tries - Wilson Clarkson: Goals - Quinn Wallace(DG):
Referee K Spencer (Warrington) Att - 1852 H.T. 2 - 4

Sun 6 Apr 1975 WARRINGTON away lost 16 - 25
WARRINGTON - Whitehead(Briggs): Philbin Noonan
Reynolds(Nicholas)Bevan: Whittle Gordon: Chisnall
Ashcroft Wanbon Nicholas(Brady)Martin Conroy:
Tries - Briggs Philbin Noonan Bevan Martin:
Goals - Briggs(3) Bevan(2):
CASTLEFORD - Briggs(Walsh): Lloyd Worsley Newton
Johnson: Morris Stephens: ALAN BENCE(569)(Redfearn)
Spurr Forster Rhodes Birdsall Norton:
Tries - Lloyd(2):   Goals - Lloyd(5):
Referee H Mason (Halifax) Att - 6620 H.T. 5 - 10

Sat 12 Apr 1975 LEEDS away lost 13 - 33
LEEDS - Marshall(Barham): Smith Holmes Dyl Atkinson:
Mason Hepworth: Dickinson Fisher Pitchford Dickens
Eccles Batten: Tries - Dyl(3) Smith Atkinson Mason
Batten: Goals - Marshall(6):
CASTLEFORD - Briggs: Paul Higgins Joyner Newton Lloyd:
Morris Stephens: Bence Spurr Chris Forster(Redfearn)
Birdsall Rhodes(Walsh) Norton:
Tries - Briggs Joyner Morris: Goals - Lloyd(2):
Referee P Geraghty (York) Att - 5010 H.T. 8 - 20

Fri 25 Apr 1975 WAKEFIELD TRINITY home
won 37 - 7 PREMIERSHIP ROUND 1
CASTLEFORD - Briggs: Richardson Worsley Newton
Lowndes: Morris Stephens: Bence Spurr Redfearn Birdsall
Alan Rhodes(Tyreman) Lloyd(Joyner): Tries - Worsley(3)
Lloyd(3) Briggs Newton Redfearn: Goals - Lloyd(5):
WAKEFIELD T - Oulton: Smith Crook Butterfield(Knowles)
Lumb(Morgan): Topliss Bonner: Evans Ingham Campbell
Skerrett Chester Morgan(Cooper):
Tries - Lumb Cooper: Goal – Crook(DG):
Referee T Keane (Oldham) Att - 2915 H.T. 17 - 2

Tue 29 Apr 1975 LEEDS away lost 8 - 28
PREMIERSHIP ROUND 2
Leeds - Holmes: Smith Hynes Dyl Atkinson: Mason
Hepworth(Sanderson): Dickinson Ward Pitchford
Cookson(Eccles) Batten Haigh: Tries - Smith(2) Hynes
Atkinson Pitchford Haigh: Goals - Holmes(5):
CASTLEFORD - Briggs: Richardson(Joyner) Worsley
Newton Lowndes: Morris Stephens: Bence Spurr Redfearn
Birdsall Lloyd(Tyreman) Norton:
Tries - Richardson Morris: Goal - Redfearn:
Referee M Naughton (Widnes) Att - 4514 H.T nil – 15

Jamie Walsh
D. No 563
1974-75 to 1981-82

Geoff Morris
D. No 565
1974-75 to 1981-82

Graham Tyreman
D. No 567
1974-75 to 1978-79

Alan Hardy
D. No 568
1974-75 to 1983-84

Alan Bence
D.No 569
1974-75 to 1976-77

D.N	PLAYER		DEBUT	L MATCH	APP	SUB	T.AP	TRI'S	G'LS	D.G	P'TS
479	DICKINSON	CLIVE		15/11/1974	12	0	12	2	0	0	6
493	BRIGGS	TREVOR			34	0	34	5	0	0	15
494	REDFEARN	MICHAEL			24	5	29	3	6	0	21
497	LOCKWOOD	BRIAN		07/03/1975	16	0	16	2	0	0	6
503	HARTLEY	DENNIS		04/04/1975	9	0	9	1	0	0	3
512	REILLY	MALCOLM			9	1	10	1	0	0	3
516	LOWNDES	ALAN			34	0	34	10	0	0	30
518	SPURR	ROBERT			27	0	27	4	0	0	12
522	ACKROYD	ALAN			3	3	6	3	0	0	9
525	STEPHENS	GARY			36	0	36	8	0	1	25
526	JOHNSON	PHILIP			12	1	13	3	0	0	9
531	NORTON	STEVE (KNOCKER)			27	0	27	5	0	1	16
532	LLOYD	GEOFFREY (SAMMY)			35	2	37	12	112	0	260
537	NEWTON	RAY			30	1	31	5	0	0	15
538	HIGGINS	PAUL		12/04/1975	3	1	4	0	0	0	0
540	FOWLER	DENNIS			4	1	5	0	0	0	0
541	WORSLEY	KEITH			8	0	8	3	0	0	9
542	DICKINSON	ALAN			10	2	12	0	0	0	0
544	CLAUGHTON	GEORGE			1	0	1	0	0	0	0
546	BRUNYEE	STEVEN			6	2	8	1	0	0	3
547	BIRDSALL	CHARLES			15	4	19	2	0	0	6
548	WOODALL	DEREK			0	1	1	0	0	0	0
550	BROOK	GARY			25	3	28	8	0	0	24
551	JOYNER	JOHN			34	2	36	15	0	0	45
556	RICHARDSON	TERRY			23	0	23	12	0	0	36
557	FORSTER	CHRIS		12/04/1975	17	2	19	1	0	0	3
558	LONGSTAFF	PAUL		25/10/1974	3	0	3	0	0	0	0
559	GARBETT	BRIAN			1	0	1	0	0	0	0
560	FENTON	STEVE	11/09/1974		9	5	14	1	0	0	3
561	DOWNHAM	PETER	11/09/1974	11/09/1974	1	0	1	0	0	0	0
562	HEPTON	ROY	11/10/1974	22/11/1974	1	2	3	1	0	0	3
563	WALSH	JAMIE	29/11/1974		2	5	7	0	0	0	0
564	JEFF	TONY	29/11/1974	29/11/1974	0	1	1	0	0	0	0
565	MORRIS	GEOFF	15/12/1974		7	1	8	3	0	0	9
566	RHODES	ALAN	04/01/1975	25/04/1975	11	2	13	2	0	0	6
567	TYREMAN	GRAHAM	15/02/1975		1	2	3	0	0	0	0
568	HARDY	ALAN	14/03/1975		0	1	1	0	0	0	0
569	BENCE	ALAN	06/04/1975		4	0	4	0	0	0	0
	38										
			10	10	494	50	544	113	118	2	577

COMPETITION		P	W	D	L	FOR	AGT
LEAGUE D 1	POSITION 8 OF 16	30	14	3	13	480	427
YORK'S CUP		1	0	0	1	13	19
F. TROPHY		1	0	0	1	4	12
RL CUP		2	0	1	1	20	23
PLAYERS NO6		1	0	0	1	5	36
CHAMPIONSHIP		2	1	0	1	45	35
VOID- SALFORD		1	0	0	1	10	13
PLAYERS RECORDS		**38**	**15**	**4**	**19**	**577**	**565**

The first Castleford player to score a "one pointer" drop goal was Steve Norton in the 17 all draw away at Salford on 24 January 1975.

Midway through the season saw another coaching change with Malcolm Reilly returning from Australia to become Player/Coach from December, taking over from Dave Cox.

The Captain Morgan Trophy introduced the previous season became a bit of a 'Rum Do' as it was not contested this season.

The Club Championship was changed to the Premiership which was contested between the top 8 teams of Division 1.

SEASON 1975-76

In The League Huddersfield, Hull K R, Oldham Swinton were Promoted To Division 1. York Bramley, Rochdale H Halifax Relegated To Division 2.

Fri 15 Aug 1975 WAKEFIELD TRINITY home lost 14 - 18
CASTLEFORD - Brunyee: Richardson Joyner Johnson Lowndes: Brook Stephens: Bence Spurr Birdsall Lloyd(Ackroyd) Fowler Norton:
Tries - Richardson Joyner: Goals - Lloyd(4):
WAKEFIELD T - Sheard: Smith Sutcliffe Butterfield Lumb: Topliss Hudson: Ballantyne Handscombe Campbell Idle Goodwin Morgan:
Tries - Sutcliffe(2) Smith Hudson: Goals - Lumb(3):
Referee R Haigh (Bradford) Att - 2586 H.T. 12 - 10

Fri 22 Aug 1975 WIDNES away lost 9 - 11
WIDNES - Dutton: Prescott George Hughes Jenkins: D.O'Neill Bowden: Nelson(Aspey) Elwell Walsh Hammond Allan(Doherty) Dearden: Try - Hughes: Goals - Dutton(4):
CASTLEFORD - Steven Brunyee(Morris): Richardson Worsley Newton Lowndes: Brook Stephens: Bence Spurr Ackroyd Birdsall Lloyd Norton:
Try - Ackroyd: Goals - Lloyd(3):
Referee B Shooman (Leeds) Att - 3800 H.T. 4 - 9

Fri 29 Aug 1975 HULL home draw 16 - 16 YORKSHIRE CUP ROUND 1
CASTLEFORD - Worsley: Richardson Joyner Newton Lowndes: Brook(Morris) Stephens: Bence Spurr Ackroyd(Fowler) Birdsall Lloyd Norton:
Tries - Lowndes Stephens: Goals - Lloyd(5):
HULL - Hunter: Lane Clark Portz Barr: Hancock Foulkes: Ramsey Duke Robson(Waltham) Walker(Trotter) Boxall Casey:
Tries - Barr Hancock: Goals - Boxall(4) Hancock(DG2):
Referee S Wall (Leigh) Att - 1436 H.T. 6 - 5

Tue 2 Sept 1975 HULL away won 16 - 15 YORKSHIRE CUP ROUND 1 REPLAY
HULL - Hunter: Lane Clark Crane Barr: Hancock Foulkes: Ramsey Duke Robson Trotter(Tindall) Boxall Casey:
Tries - Clark Duke Boxall: Goal - Boxall(3):
CASTLEFORD - Briggs: Richardson Joyner Newton Lowndes: Fenton Stephens: Bence(Redfearn) Spurr Ackroyd(S/O) Birdsall Lloyd Norton: Tries - Newton Redfearn Ackroyd: Goals - Lloyd(3) Birdsall(DG):
Referee M Naughton (Widnes) Att - 5000 H.T. 5 - 5

Fri 5 Sept 1975 WARRINGTON home won 24 - 14
CASTLEFORD - Briggs(Worsley): Richardson(Briggs) Joyner Newton Lowndes: Fenton Stephens: Ackroyd Spurr Redfearn Birdsall PETER COOKLAND(570)(Norton) Norton(Lloyd): Tries - Joyner(2) Lowndes Ackroyd:
Goals - Redfearn(3) Lloyd(3):
WARRINGTON - Whitehead: Curling Noonan Whittle Bevan: Briggs Gordon: Chisnall Price(Clark) Wanbon Jewitt Conroy Lyons(Peers):
Tries - Bevan(2) Briggs Jewitt: Goal - Whitehead:
Referee J McDonald (Wigan) Att - 1984 H.T. 15 - nil

Sun 14 Sept 1975 FEATHERSTONE ROVERS away lost 5 - 8 YORKSHIRE CUP ROUND 2
FEATHERSTONE R - Box: Hill(Holden) Coventry M.Smith (Hartley) Kellett: Newlove Fennell: Thompson Bridges Gibbins P.Smith Bell Stone:
Tries - Coventry Fennell: Goal - Box:
CASTLEFORD - Briggs: Richardson Joyner Newton Lowndes: Fenton Worsley) Stephens: Ackroyd Spurr(Bence) Redfearn Birdsall Fowler Norton:
Try - Newton: Goal - Redfearn:
Referee H Hunt (Cheshire) Att - 3203 H.T. nil - 8

Sun 21 Sept 1975 WAKEFIELD TRINITY away lost 12 - 21
WAKEFIELD T - Oulton: D.Smith Sheard Sutcliffe A.Smith: Topliss Hudson: Tonks Handscombe Ballantyne Idle Skerrett(Ellis) Morgan:
Tries - Handscombe(2) D.Smith: Goals - Oulton(6):
CASTLEFORD - Briggs: Richardson Joyner Newton Lowndes(Worsley): Fenton Stephens: Ackroyd TONY FISHER(571) Redfearn Birdsall Cookland Norton(Bence):
Tries - Richardson Fenton: Goals - Redfearn(3):
Referee P Oliver (Bolton) Att - 3095 H.T. 14 - 2

Wed 24 Sept 1975 LEEDS away lost 10 - 21 BBC 2 FLOODLIT COMPETITION PRELIMINARY ROUND
LEEDS - Marshall: Smith Hynes Hague Atkinson: Fletcher Hepworth(Murrell): Harrison(Dickinson) Ward Pitchford Dickens Batten Haigh: Tries - Hague(2) Hynes Dickinson Haigh: Goals - Marshall(3):
CASTLEFORD - GEOFFREY WRAITH(572): Richardson Joyner Worsley(Brook) Briggs: Fenton Stephens: Bence Redfearn Ackroyd Birdsall Cookland(Fowler) Lloyd:
Goals - Lloyd(5):
Referee A E Fryer (Warrington) Att - 3014 H.T. 4 - 5

Fri 26 Sept 1975 YORK home won 26 - 15 PLAYERS No.6 TROPHY ROUND 1
CASTLEFORD - Wraith: Richardson Joyner Worsley Briggs: Fenton Stephens Bence Fisher Redfearn Birdsall(RONALD COOMBS(573)) Fowler Lloyd: Tries - Stephens(3) Wraith Worsley Fenton: Goals - Lloyd(4):
YORK - Clancey: Barrends Day Bickley(Rushton) Wilson: Smith Harkin: Clawson Wileman Endersby(Handforth) (Endersby) Dunkerley Cooper Hetherington:
Tries - Clancey Day Smith: Goals - Hetherington(3):
Referee H G Hunt (Cheshire) Att - 1819 H.T. 15 - 7

Fri 3 Oct 1975 HULL KINGSTON ROVERS home lost 13 - 24
CASTLEFORD - Wraith: Briggs Joyner Worsley Richardson: Fenton Stephens Bence Fisher Redfearn Birdsall(Dennis Fowler) Lloyd Norton:
Tries - Worsley Bence Fowler: Goals - Lloyd(2):
HULL K R - Wallace: Dunn Turner Watson Sullivan: Burwell Millward(Hall): Millington Dickinson Lyons(Hughes) Holdstock Rose Casey: Tries - Sullivan(2) Watson Dunn Lyons Casey: Goals - Millward(3):
Referee J V Moss (Manchester) Att - 2770 H.T. 5 - 15

SEASON 1975-76

Sun 12 Oct 1975 DEWSBURY away lost 12 - 20
DEWSBURY - Langley: Simpson Hegarty(Artis)
Stephenson Pickup: Lingard(Frain) Bates: Beverley Price
Hankins Vodden Bell Clark:
Tries - Stephenson(2) Pickup Clark: Goals - Stephenson(4):
CASTLEFORD - Wraith: Briggs Joyner Worsley Richardson:
Fenton(Brook) Stephens: Bence Fisher Redfearn Cookland
Lloyd Reilly: Tries - Joyner Lloyd: Goals - Lloyd(3):
Referee M Naughton (Widnes) Att - 2600 H.T. 7 - 15

Fri 17 Oct 1975 SALFORD away lost 10 - 18
SALFORD - Stead: Fielding(Graham) Butler Hesketh
Richards: Gill Nash: Coulman(Grice) Hawksley Fiddler
Knighton Turnbull Prescott:
Tries - Hesketh(2) Richards Knighton: Goals - Fiddler(3):
CASTLEFORD - Wraith: Worsley Joyner Briggs
Richardson(CLIVE PICKERILL(574)): Brook Stephens: Bence
Birdsall Reilly Cookland(Redfearn) Lloyd Norton:
Tries - Wraith Briggs: Goals - Lloyd(2):
Referee R Jackson (Halifax) Att - 5217 H.T. 2 - 12

Fri 24 Oct 1975 HUDDERSFIELD home won 26 - 14
CASTLEFORD - Wraith: Worsley Briggs Joyner(Morris)
Newton: Brook Stephens: Bence Fisher DOUGLAS
LUCAS(575) Cookland Lloyd Reilly:
Tries - Briggs Newton Brook Lloyd: Goals - Lloyd(7):
HUDDERSFIELD - Bedford: Hoosen Clegg Doyle Cyrus:
Knight(Leathley)Hartley: Hepplestone Nelmes Weavill(Van
Bellin) Tomlinson Forster Welsh:
Tries - Hoosen Tomlinson: Goals - Hartley(4):
Referee J Percival (New Zealand) Att - 2447 H.T. 7 - 9

Sun 2 Nov 1975 KEIGHLEY away won 27 - 9
KEIGHLEY - Jickells: Stephenson Simpson Roe Parker:
Moncrieff Nicholson: Burke Raistrick Hinchcliffe Clarkson
Garbett Loxton (Pieniazek): Try - Clarkson:
Goals - Moncrieff(3):
CASTLEFORD - Wraith: Briggs Joyner Newton
Worsley(Morris): Brook Stephens: Bence Spurr Douglas
Lucas Reilly Lloyd Norton(Cookland): Tries - Wraith(2)
Briggs Worsley Stephens: Goals - Lloyd(5):
Referee J W Mean (Leyland) Att - 2014 H.T. 12 - 9

**Sun 9 Nov 1975 WAKEFIELD TRINITY away
won 24 - 14 PLAYERS No.6 TROPHY ROUND 2**
WAKEFIELD T - Crook(Oulton): D.Smith Sheard Sutcliffe
Stephens: Topliss Hudson: Tonks Handscombe Evans
Ellis(Kevin Rayne) Skerrett Morgan:
Tries - Smith Morgan: Goals - Crook(3) Culton :
CASTLEFORD - Wraith: Briggs Joyner Newton Lowndes:
Brook(Worsley) Stephens: Bence Spurr(Cookland) Fisher
Reilly Lloyd Norton:
Tries - Brook(2) Joyner Bence: Goals - Lloyd(6):
Referee A Givvons (Oldham) Att - 4070 H.T. 12 - 12

Sun 16 Nov 1975 ST HELENS away lost 9 - 22
ST HELENS - Pimblett: L.Jones Benyon Wilson Mathias:
Eckersley Heaton: C.Jones Karalius James Cunningham
Chisnall Hull:
Tries - Wilson(2) Pimblett Chisnall: Goals - Pimblett(5):

CASTLEFORD - Wraith: Briggs Joyner Newton
Lowndes(Worsley): Brook Stephens: Bence
Spurr(Cookland) Fisher Reilly Lloyd Norton:
Try - Reilly: Goals - Lloyd(3):
Referee T Beaumont (Huddersfield) Att - 3130 H.T. 4 - 7

**Sun 23 Nov 1975 HUDDERSFIELD away won 19 - 10
PLAYERS No.6 TROPHY ROUND 3**
HUDDERSFIELD - Bedford: Hooson Knight Leathley Leese:
Clegg Appleyard: Van Bellen Hepplestone Weavill Branch
Forster Welsh:
Tries - Appleyard Weavill: Goals - Clegg(2):
CASTLEFORD - Wraith: Briggs Joyner Newton
Lowndes(Worsley): Brook Stephens: Bence Spurr
Fisher(Cookland) Reilly Lloyd Norton:
Tries - Briggs Lowndes Worsley: Goals - Lloyd(5):
Referee S Wall (Leigh) Att - 3031 H.T. 16 - 8

**Sat 29 Nov 1975 WIDNES home lost 9 - 17
PLAYERS No.6 TROPHY SEMI FINAL**
CASTLEFORD - Wraith: Worsley Briggs(Cookland) Newton
Lowndes (TOM SHEPPARD(576)): Brook Stephens: Bence
Spurr Fisher Lloyd Reilly Norton:
Try - Worsley: Goals - Lloyd(3):
WIDNES - Dutton: Prescott George Aspey Tilley: Hughes
Bowden: Nelson Elwell Wood Sheridan Foran(Fitzpatrick)
Adams: Tries - Prescott Aspey: Goals - Dutton(5) (DG):
Referee A Givvons (Oldham) Att - 3416 H.T. 7 - 2

Sat 13 Dec 1975 WIGAN away lost 10 - 15
WIGAN - Francis: Vigo Kieron O'Loughlin Willicombe
Fairbairn: Whittle(Hill) Coyle: Bailey Aspinall Ashcroft
Irving Blackwood(Dootson) Melling:
Tries - Vigo O'Loughlin Willicombe: Goals - Fairbairn(3):
CASTLEFORD - Wraith: Briggs Joyner Newton Terry
Biscomb(Sheppard): Brook Stephens: Bence Spurr Fisher
Reilly Lloyd Norton: Tries - Joyner Norton:
Goals - Lloyd(2):
Referee W H Thompson (Hud'field) Att - 2127 H.T. 8 - 5

Fri 19 Dec 1975 KEIGHLEY home won 23 - 7
CASTLEFORD - Wraith: Worsley Joyner Newton Walsh:
Sheppard Pickerill: Bence Spurr Fisher(Birdsall) Cookland
Lloyd Reilly: Tries - Worsley Joyner Sheppard Spurr Reilly:
Goals - Lloyd(4):
KEIGHLEY - Jickells(Wilkes): Stephenson Pieniazech Roe
Parker: Moncrieff(Sharpe) Sutcliffe: Burke Woolford
Hinchcliffe Garforth Clarkson Garbett:
Try - Sutcliffe: Goals - Moncrieff Garbett:
Referee T J Court (Bradford) Att - 1526 H.T. nil - 2

**Fri 26 Dec 1975 FEATHERSTONE ROVERS away
draw 18 - 18**
FEATHERSTONE R - Box: Hill Coventry Tuffs Kellett:
Newlove Banner: Thompson Bridges Farrar P.Smith Bell
Stone: Tries - Kellett(3) Hill: Goals - Tuffs(3):
CASTLEFORD - Wraith: Worsley Joyner(Brook) Newton
Walsh: Sheppard(Birdsall) Stephens: Bence Spurr Fisher
Reilly Lloyd Norton:
Tries - Worsley Joyner Newton Reilly: Goals - Lloyd(3):

Referee M Naughton (Widnes) Att - 3696 H.T. 13 - 8

Thur 1 Jan 1976 BRADFORD NORTHERN away won 33 - nil
BRADFORD N - Mumby: Francis Ward Roe Redfearn: Blackburn(Slater) Seabourne: Mordue Jarvis Teasdale(Farrell) Sellers Spencer Joyce:
CASTLEFORD - Wraith(Briggs): Worsley Johnson Newton Walsh: Gary Brook (Birdsall) Stephens: Bence Spurr Fisher Cookland Lloyd Norton: Tries - Norton(3) Johnson Walsh Stephens Spurr: Goals - Lloyd(6):
Referee T Keane (Oldham) Att - 5750 H.T. 15 - nil

Sun 4 Jan 1976 OLDHAM away won 8 - 6
OLDHAM - Blair: Elliott Barton Bottom O'Brien: Wainwright McCone: Ramshaw Taylor Kear Hall Flanagan Brown: Goals - Blair(3):
CASTLEFORD - Briggs: Morris Newton Walsh Worsley: Johnson Stephens: Bence Spurr Fisher Cookland(Redfearn) Charles Birdsall Reilly:
Tries - Spurr Reilly: Goal - Walsh:
Referee F Lindop (Wakefield) Att - 1578 H.T. 8 - 4

Fri 9 Jan 1976 SWINTON home won 19 - 5
CASTLEFORD - Briggs: Worsley Joyner Newton(Morris) Walsh: Johnson Stephens: Bence Spurr Fisher(Cookland) Reilly Lloyd Norton:
Tries - Joyner Johnson Lloyd: Goals - Lloyd(5):
SWINTON - Bolton(Johns): Fleay Cooke Bruen Wardle: Dainty Atkinson: Chisnall Evans Young Heaton Dickman (Pattison) Henighan: Try - Young: Goal - Wardle:
Referee K Spencer (Warrington) Att - 1917 H.T. 12 - 5

Sun 18 Jan 1976 HULL KINGSTON ROVERS away lost 14 - 18
HULL K R - Wallace: Dunn Kirkpatrick(Turner) Robinson Sullivan: Hartley Millward: Millington(Madley) Heslop Lyons Jones Holdstock Casey:
Tries - Dunn(2): Goals - Millward(6):
CASTLEFORD - Wraith: Briggs Johnson Joyner Worsley: BRUCE BURTON(577) Stephens: Bence Spurr Fisher Reilly Lloyd(Cookland) Norton:
Tries - Worsley(2) Burton Spurr: Goal - Lloyd:
Referee P Geraghty (York) Att - 4822 H.T. 8 - 6

Fri 23 Jan 1976 BRADFORD NORTHERN home won 24 - 7
CASTLEFORD - Wraith: Briggs Johnson Joyner Worsley: Burton Stephens: Bence Spurr(Alan Ackroyd) Redfearn Reilly Cookland Norton(Walsh): Tries - Wraith(2) Johnson Joyner Stephens Ackroyd: Goals - Burton(3):
BRADFORD N. - Mumby: Pritchard Roe Ward D.Redfearn: Slater A.Redfearn: Clawson Jarvis Sellers Trotter(Teasdale) Joyce Woolford: Try - Jarvis: Goals - Mumby(2):
Referee P Massey (Salford) Att - 2791 H.T. 12 - 2

Fri 6 Feb 1976 SALFORD home lost 16 - 19
CASTLEFORD - Briggs(Wraith): Joyner Newton Johnson Worsley: Burton Stephens: Bence Fisher Dickinson(Reilly) PAUL ORR(578) Cookland Lloyd;

Tries - Stephens Orr: Goals - Lloyd(5):
SALFORD - Watkins: Fielding Butler Hesketh Richards(Graham): Gill Nash: Coulman Raistrick Grice Knighton Dixon Prescott:
Tries - Fielding Butler Richards: Goals - Watkins(5):
Referee J McDonald (Wigan) Att - 2851 H.T. 11 - 8

Sat 14 Feb 1976 SALFORD home lost 3 - 25
CHALLENGE CUP ROUND 1
CASTLEFORD - Wraith: Worsley Johnson Newton Joyner: Burton Stephens: Bence Spurr(Lloyd) Fisher Reilly Orr Norton: Try - Johnson:
SALFORD - Watkins: Fielding Butler Hesketh Richards: Gill Nash: Coulman Raistrick Grice(Corcoran) Knighton Dixon Prescott: Tries - Fielding Butler Richards Coulman Knighton: Goals - Watkins(5):
Referee M Naughton (Widnes) Att - 4872 H.T. 3 - 12

Fri 20 Feb 1976 ST HELENS home won 26 - 10
CASTLEFORD - Briggs: Worsley Walsh Sheppard Fenton: Burton Stephens (Pickerill): Redfearn Spurr Dickinson Reilly(Orr) Lloyd Norton:
Tries - Reilly(2) Burton Spurr: Goals - Lloyd(7):
ST HELENS - Pimblett: Jones Noonan Wilson(Glynn) Mathias: Benyon Heaton: Mantle Karalius Coslett Cunningham(James) Chisnall Hull:
Tries - Mathias Benyon: Goals - Pimblett(2):
Referee S Wall (Leigh) Att - 2136 H.T. 16 - 7

Fri 27 Feb 1976 DEWSBURY home won 45 - 2
CASTLEFORD - Wraith: Worsley Walsh Sheppard Briggs: (Fenton): Burton Stephens: Bence Spurr Redfearn Reilly Lloyd(Cookland) Norton: Tries - Sheppard(3) Walsh(2) Spurr(2) Briggs Burton Lloyd Norton: Goals - Lloyd(6):
DEWSBURY - Lee A.N.Other Artis Stephenson Mitchell: Lingard Bates: Beverley R.Price Frain Grayshon Bell(T.Price) Welsn: Goal - Stephenson:
Referee H Hunt (Cheshire) Att - 2279 H.T. 21 - 2

Sat 6 Mar 1976 HUDDERSFIELD away won 42 - nil
HUDDERSFIELD - Bedford: Leathley Clegg Mullaney Senior: Calvert Shepherd: Van Bellen Schofield (Hepplestone) Weavill Cramp Sheehan Rowe(T.Doyle):
CASTLEFORD - Wraith: Worsley(Cookland) Walsh Sheppard Briggs: Fenton (Joyner) Stephens: Bence Spurr Redfearn Reilly Lloyd Norton:
Tries - Norton(2) Wraith Worsley Briggs Stephens Redfearn Reilly: Goals - Lloyd(9):
Referee A E Fryer (Warrington) Att - 1388 H.T. 22 - nil

Sun 14 Mar 1976 SWINTON away won 9 - 2
SWINTON - John(Atkinson): Fleay Cooke Ward Holland: Bolton Bruen(Menigan): Chisnall Evans Earl Heaton Henighan(Lowe) Robinson: Goal - Cooke:
CASTLEFORD - Wraith: Walsh Joyner Johnson Briggs: Tom Sheppard Stephens: Bence Spurr Redfearn Reilly Lloyd Norton: Try - Lloyd: Goals - Lloyd(3):
Referee G Burton (Wakefield) Att - 1633 H.T. 4 - nil

Sat 20 Mar 1976 LEEDS away won 18 - 13
LEEDS - Marshall Smith Holmes Dyl(S/O) Atkinson:

Sanderson(Fletcher)Dick: Harrison(Eccles) Payne(Harrison) Pitchford Dickinson Ward Adams:
Try - Fletcher: Goals - Marshall(5):
CASTLEFORD - Wraith: Walsh Joyner Ph.Johnson Briggs: Burton Pickerill: Bence Spurr Fisher(PETER JOHNSON(579)) Orr Lloyd Reilly(Redfearn):
Tries - Ph.Johnson(2) Briggs Orr: Goals - Lloyd(3):
Referee R Moore (Wakefield) Att - 5510 H.T. 10 - 4

Fri 26 Mar 1976 WIGAN home won 28 - 10
CASTLEFORD - Wraith: Walsh Joyner Ph.Johnson Briggs: Burton Pickerill: Bence Spurr(Pe.Johnson) Fisher Redfearn Orr Lloyd Tries - Pickerill(2) Joyner Burton Bence Orr:
Goals - Lloyd(5):
WIGAN - Fairbairn: Wright Hill Francis Vigo: Kieron O'Loughlin Nulty: Hogan Martland Bailey(Melling) Gregory Ashcroft Irving:
Tries - Wright Gregory: Goals - Fairbairn(2):
Referee M Naughton (Widnes) Att - 2640 H.T. 10 - 10

Fri 2 Apr 1976 OLDHAM home won 31 - 18
CASTLEFORD - Wraith(Morris) (Wraith): Walsh Joyner Ph.Johnson Briggs: Burton Pickerill: Bence(Dickinson) Spurr Fisher Redfearn(Bence) Orr Lloyd:
Tries - Walsh Johnson Burton Bence Orr: Goals - Lloyd(8):
OLDHAM - Murphy: Elliott Barton Larder Lund: Treasure Patterson: Hughes Taylor Owen Kear Flanagan Brown (Herbert):
Tries - Murphy(2) Elliott Patterson: Goals - Larder(3):
Referee P Oliver (Bolton) Att - 2239 H.T. 19 - nil

Wed 7 Apr 1976 WIDNES home won 17 - 12
CASTLEFORD - Wraith: Walsh Joyner Ph.Johnson Newton: Burton Pickerill: Bence Spurr Fisher(Dickinson) Redfearn Orr Lloyd: Tries - Wraith Walsh Joyner: Goals - Lloyd(4):
WIDNES - Dutton: Prescott George Aspey Tilly: Eckersley Bowden: Stephens Hammond(Kelly) Wood Adams Kelly(Deardon) Laughton:
Tries - Eckersley Laughton: Goals - Dutton(3):
Referee S Wall (Leigh) Att - 2942 H.T. 10 - 2

Sun 11 Apr 1976 WARRINGTON away lost 19 - 23
WARRINGTON - Turley: Curling Bevan Hesford Sutton: Finnegan Gwilliam: B.Butler(Peers) Miller Wanbon Martyn Nicholas Potter(Price):
Tries - Turley(3) Bevan Potter: Goals - Hesford(4):
CASTLEFORD - Wraith: Walsh(Morris) Joyner Ph.Johnson Newton: Burton Pickerill: Bence Spurr(Dickinson) Fisher Redfearn Orr Lloyd:
Tries - Burton(2) Walsh: Goals - Lloyd(5):
Referee D G Kershaw (York) Att - 3884 H.T. 4 - 13

Thur 15 Apr 1976 LEEDS home lost 18 - 24
CASTLEFORD - Wraith: Walsh Joyner Ph.Johnson Newton: Burton Pickerill: Bence Spurr Redfearn Dickinson Orr Lloyd: Tries - Wraith Newton: Goals - Lloyd(6):
LEEDS - Marshall: Smith Fletcher Hynes Murrell: Holmes Hepworth: Harrison Payne Pitchford Eccles Dickinson Adams: Tries - Holmes Pitchford Eccles Adams:
Goals - Marshall(5) Hynes(DG) Holmes(DG):

Referee J McDonald (Wigan) Att - 4104 H.T. 9 - 13

Mon 19 Apr 1976 FEATHERSTONE ROVERS home lost 15 - 18
CASTLEFORD - Wraith: Walsh(Morris) Joyner Ph.Johnson Newton: Burton Pickerill: Redfearn Spurr Fisher(Dickinson) Orr Reilly Lloyd:
Tries - Morris Burton Lloyd: Goals - Lloyd(3):
FEATHERSTONE R - Box: Dyas Coventry Tuffs Kellett: Newlove Banner: Townend Bridges Farrar P.Smith Stone Bell: Tries - Box Tuffs Kellett Newlove: Goals - Box(3):
Referee W H Thompson (Hud'field) Att - 4876 H.T. 5 – 3

Tony Fisher
D. No 571
1975-76 to 1977-78

Geoff Wraith
D. No 572
1975-76 to 1982-83

Clive Pickerill
D. No 574
1975-76 to 1977-78

Bruce Burton
D. No 577
1975-76 to 1979-80

Paul Orr
D. No 578
1975-76 to 1981-82

SEASON 1975-76

D.N	PLAYER		DEBUT	L MATCH	APP	SUB	T.AP	TRI'S	G'LS	D.G	P'TS
493	BRIGGS	TREVOR			28	1	29	7	0	0	21
494	REDFEARN	MICHAEL			18	4	22	2	7	0	20
512	REILLY	MALCOLM			22	1	23	7	0	0	21
516	LOWNDES	ALAN			11	0	11	3	0	0	9
518	SPURR	ROBERT			31	0	31	7	0	0	21
521	BISCOMB	TERRY		13/12/1975	1	0	1	0	0	0	0
522	ACKROYD	ALAN		23/01/1976	7	2	9	4	0	0	12
525	STEPHENS	GARY			31	0	31	9	0	0	27
526	JOHNSON	PHILIP			16	0	16	7	0	0	21
531	NORTON	STEVE (KNOCKER)			25	0	25	7	0	0	21
532	LLOYD	GEOFFREY (SAMMY)			33	2	35	6	149	0	316
537	NEWTON	RAY			24	0	24	5	0	0	15
540	FOWLER	DENNIS		03/10/1975	3	3	6	1	0	0	3
541	WORSLEY	KEITH			22	6	28	10	0	0	30
542	DICKINSON	ALAN			3	4	7	0	0	0	0
546	BRUNYEE	STEVEN		22/08/1975	2	0	2	0	0	0	0
547	BIRDSALL	CHARLES		04/01/1976	12	3	15	0	0	1	1
550	BROOK	GARY		01/01/1976	12	3	15	3	0	0	9
551	JOYNER	JOHN			32	1	33	12	0	0	36
556	RICHARDSON	TERRY			12	0	12	2	0	0	6
560	FENTON	STEVE			10	1	11	2	0	0	6
563	WALSH	JAMIE			16	1	17	6	1	0	20
565	MORRIS	GEOFF			1	8	9	1	0	0	3
569	BENCE	ALAN			34	2	36	4	0	0	12
570	COOKLAND	PETER	05/09/1975		11	9	20	0	0	0	0
571	FISHER	TONY	21/09/1975		24	0	24	0	0	0	0
572	WRAITH	GEOFFREY	24/09/1975		28	1	29	9	0	0	27
573	COOMBS	RONALD	26/09/1975		0	1	1	0	0	0	0
574	PICKERILL	CLIVE	17/10/1975		8	2	10	2	0	0	6
575	LUCAS	DOUG	24/10/1975	02/11/1975	2	0	2	0	0	0	0
576	SHEPPARD	TOM	29/11/1975	14/03/1976	6	2	8	4	0	0	12
577	BURTON	BRUCE	18/01/1976		13	0	13	8	3	0	30
578	ORR	PAUL	06/02/1976		9	1	10	4	0	0	12
579	JOHNSON	PETER	20/03/1976		0	2	2	0	0	0	0
	34		**10**	**8**	**507**	**60**	**567**	**132**	**160**	**1**	**717**

	COMPETITION			P	W	D	L	FOR	AGT
	LEAGUE D 1	POSITION 9 OF 16		30	16	1	13	589	398
	YORK'S CUP			3	1	1	1	37	39
	F. TROPHY			1	0	0	1	10	21
	RL CUP			1	0	0	1	3	25
	PLAYERS NO6			4	3	0	1	78	56
	PLAYERS RECORDS			**39**	**20**	**2**	**17**	**717**	**539**

Scrum half Tom Shepherd became the first Castleford player to play for the Other Nationalities team in their 36–7 defeat against Lancashire at St Helens on 25 November 1975.

On 6 March 1976 'Sammy' Lloyd scored his 1000th point for the club in 42–ni victory over Huddersfield away and then went on to improve his own record of goals in a season set in 1973/74 from 121 to 149.

In The League Barrow, Rochdale H, Workington T, Leigh were Promoted To Division 1. Dewsbury, Keighley, Huddersfield, Swinton Relegated To Division 2.

Sat 1 Aug 1976 FEATHERSTONE ROVERS away lost 12 - 19 CHARITY MATCH FRIENDLY
FEATHERSTONE R - Box: Bray Coventry Tuffs(Quinn) Kellett: M.Smith: Butler: Townend Norris Farrar Thompson P.Smith Bell: Tries - P.Smith(2) Bray Farrar Goals - Quinn(2) Box Butler(DG):
CASTLEFORD - Wraith: Briggs(Morris) Joyner Ph.Johnson(Newton)Fenton: Burton Walsh: Bence(Woodall) Spurr(Maskill) Redfearn Orr Reilly Lloyd: Tries - Joyner Fenton: Goals - Lloyd(3):
Referee W H Thompson (Hudd'field) Att - 571 H.T. 7 - 9

Fri 6 Aug 1976 LEEDS away lost 23 - 33 TESTIMONIAL MATCH FOR JOHN ATKINSON(LEEDS) TREVOR BRIGGS(CASTLEFORD) & MICHAEL REDFEARN(CASTLEFORD) FRIENDLY
LEEDS - Marshall: Fletcher Holmes Dyl Howard: Hague Sanderson: Harrison Ward Pitchford McHugh Eccles Cookson: Subs - Mason Dickinson: Tries - Fletcher Howard Hague Sanderson Pitchford Mason Dickinson: Goals - Marshall(6):
CASTLEFORD - Wraith: Briggs Joyner Ph.Johnson Walsh: Burton Pickerill: Bence Spurr Redfearn Orr Reilly Lloyd: Subs - Tyreman Oulton: Tries - Reilly(2) Briggs Walsh Tyreman: Goals - Lloyd(2) Oulton(2): Referee - Att - 1080 H.T. 10 - 15

Sat 15 Aug 1976 HULL away lost 22 - 26 BENEFIT MATCH FOR DAVIDSON AND FOULKES (HULL) FRIENDLY
HULL - Robinson: Macklin Clark Portz Gibbons(Waltham): Hancock Davidson(Foulkes): Tindall(Salmon) Duke Wardell Boxhall Crampton Walker(Trotter): Tries - Robinson Macklin Hancock Davidson Boxall Crampton: Goals - Robinson(3) Boxall:
CASTLEFORD - Wraith: Briggs Joyner Fenton Walsh: Burton(Richardson) Pickerill(Morris): Redfearn Spurr Woodall(Hardy) Orr Cookland Lloyd: Tries - Wraith Joyner Burton Orr: Goals - Lloyd(5):
Referee Att - 2000 H.T. 12 - 23

Sat 22 Aug 1976 HULL KINGSTON ROVERS away won 18 - 12 YORKSHIRE CUP ROUND 1
HULL K R - Wallace: Dunn Smith Watson(Hall) Sullivan: Hartley Millward: Millington(S/O) Heslop Holdstock(S/O) Rose Ackroyd Casey(Hughes): Tries - Watson Hartley: Goals - Millward(3):
CASTLEFORD - Wraith: Briggs Joyner Ph.Johnson Walsh: Burton(Fenton) Pickerill: Bence(S/O) Spurr Cookland Orr Reilly(Coombs) Lloyd: Tries - Joyner Johnson Burton Orr: Goals - Lloyd(3): Referee P Massey (Salford) Att - 4772 H.T. 10 - 7

Fri 27 Aug 1976 LEEDS home draw 12 - 12 YORKSHIRE CUP ROUND 2
CASTLEFORD - Wraith: Briggs Joyner Ph.Johnson Walsh: Burton Pickerill: Redfearn(Orr) Spurr Cookland Orr(Coombs) Reilly Lloyd: Tries - Johnson Burton: Goals - Lloyd(3):
LEEDS - Marshall: A.Smith Hague Dyl D.Smith: Holmes Banner: Harrison Ward Pitchford Eccles Adams(McHugh) Cookson: Tries – D Smith Holmes: Goals - Marshall(3): Referee A Givvons (Oldham) Att - 4140 H.T. 5 - 5

Tue 31 Aug 1976 LEEDS away lost 20 - 21 YORKSHIRE CUP ROUND 2 REPLAY
LEEDS - Marshall: A.Smith Hague Dyl D.Smith: Holmes Banner: Harrison Ward Pitchford Eccles Adams(McHugh) Cookson: Tries - Dyl(2) Holmes Cookson: Goals - Marshall(4) Holmes(DG):
CASTLEFORD - Wraith: Briggs Joyner Ph.Johnson Walsh(Fenton): Burton Pickerill: Bence Spurr Redfearn Cookland(Coombs) Orr Lloyd: Tries - Joyner Burton Orr Lloyd: Goals - Lloyd(4): Referee M Naughton (Widnes) Att -6000 H.T. 13 - 15

Sun 5 Sep 1976 WAKEFIELD TRINITY away won 25 - 14
WAKEFIELD T - Sheard: Finch Crook Wriglesworth Noble: Topliss Hudson: Ballantyne Handsconbe(Ingham) Goodwin Morgan Skerrett Idle: Tries - Morgan(2) Finch Crook: Goal - Crook:
CASTLEFORD - Wraith: Fenton Briggs(Morris) Joyner Richardson: Ph.Johnson Burton: Bence(Ronald Coombs) Spurr Redfearn Cookland Orr Lloyd: Tries - Burton(2) Joyner Cookland Lloyd: Goals - Lloyd(5): Referee M Naughton (Widnes) Att - 3314 H.T. 17 - 3

Fri 10 Sep 1976 LEIGH home won 28 - 12
CASTLEFORD - Wraith: Richardson Joyner Fenton Morris(Newton): Ph.Johnson Burton: Bence Tyreman Cookland Orr(Peter Johnson) Reilly Lloyd: Tries - Cookland(2) Reilly(2) Newton Burton: Goals - Lloyd(5):
LEIGH - Watmore(McAtee) (Watmore): Davis Stacey Walsh Woods: Taylor (Rathbone) Sayer: Chisnall Ashcroft Fletcher Jones Lester Clark: Tries - Walsh Woods: Goals - Stacey(3): Referee A E Fryer (Warrington) Att - 2058 H.T. 20 - 7

Sun 19 Sep 1976 WIGAN away won 29 - 19
WIGAN - Fairbairn: Hornby Kieron O'Loughlin Francis Davies: Nulty Coyle: Ashcroft Aspinall Irving Melling(Gregory) Blackwood Hollingsworth: Tries - O'Loughlin Francis Coyle: Goals - Fairbairn(5):
CASTLEFORD - Wraith: Fenton Joyner Johnson Newton: Burton Walsh(Morris): Bence Spurr Cookland Orr(Redfearn) Reilly Lloyd: Tries - Burton(2) Joyner Orr Reilly: Goals - Lloyd(7): Referee F Lindop (Wakefield) Att - 4871 H.T. 9 - 11

Fri 24 Sep 1976 ST HELENS away lost 15 - 17
ST HELENS - Pimblett: Jones Benyon Noonan Mathias: Glynn Gwilliam: Charles(Liptrot) Karalius James Hull

Chisnall Pinner:
Tries - Glynn Pinner: Goals - Pimblett(5) (DG):
CASTLEFORD - Wraith: Fenton Joyner Johnson Newton:
Burton Walsh: Bence Spurr Dickinson Cookland Reilly
Lloyd: Tries - Wraith Joyner Burton: Goals - Lloyd(3):
Referee K Allatt (Huddersfield) Att - 4220 H.T. 10 - 11

Fri 1 Oct 1976 ROCHDALE HORNETS home won 37 -13

CASTLEFORD - Wraith: Fenton Joyner Johnson(Walsh)
Newton: Burton Stephens: Bence Spurr(Reilly) PAUL
KAHN(580) Cookland Reilly(Huddlestone) Lloyd:
Tries - Walsh(2) Wraith Joyner Johnson Reilly Lloyd:
Goals - Lloyd(8):
ROCHDALE H - Storey: Rawlinson Simpkins Burke Marsh:
Ayres Baker(De Looze): Hodgkinson Handforth Kurtianyk
Fogerty(Middlehurst) Hartley Duffy:
Tries - Marsh(2) Ayres: Goals - Storey(2):
Referee J McDonald (Wigan) Att - 2600 H.T. 19 - 5

Tue 5 Oct 1976 HULL KINGSTON ROVERS home won 16 - 8 BBC 2 FLOODLIT COMPETITION ROUND 1

CASTLEFORD - Wraith: Fenton Joyner Newton Walsh:
Burton Stephens (Morris): Bence Spurr Kahn
Cookland(Dickinson) Reilly Lloyd:
Tries - Newton Burton: Goals - Lloyd(5):
HULL K R - Wallace(Hartley): Dunn Smith Robinson
Sullivan: Hall Millward: Ackroyd Heslop Lyons Lowe
Holdstock(Rose) Casey(Holdstock):
Tries - Dunn Rose: Goal - Millward:
Referee M Naughton (Widnes) Att – 2053 H.T. 12 - nil

Sun 12 Oct 1976 WARRINGTON away won 18 - 11

WARRINGTON - Turley: Sutton Finnigan Whitehead
Hudson: Knight Hart(M.Philbin): Butler Miller Weavill
Martyn Nicholson(Dalzell)B.Philbin   Tries - Finnigan
Whitehead: Goals - Whitehead(2) Miller(DG):
CASTLEFORD - Wraith: Fenton Joyner Newton Morris:
Burton Walsh: Kahn Spurr Dickinson Cookland Reilly
Lloyd:
Tries - Fenton Walsh Kahn Lloyd: Goals - Lloyd(3):
Referee T Beaumont (Huddersfield) Att - 4874 H.T. 5 - 8

Fri 15 Oct 1976 OLDHAM home won 11 - 5

CASTLEFORD - Wraith: Fenton(Richardson) Joyner
Newton Morris: Burton Walsh: Bence Spurr Kahn
Cookland Dickinson Lloyd:
Tries - Joyner Dickinson: Goals - Lloyd(2) Burton(DG):
OLDHAM - Murphy: Elliott Jackson(Barton) Wainwright
Lund: Blair Treasure: Owen K.Taylor I.Taylor Welding
Herbert Reynolds: Try - Treasure: Goal - Blair:
Referee R Campbell (Widnes) Att - 3175 H.T. 2 - 5

Sun 24 Oct 1976 NEW HUNSLET away won 24 - 10 PLAYERS No 6 ROUND 1

NEW HUNSLET - Foster: Muscroft Broatch Kirkpatrick
Barron: Gaitley Agar: Hill(Windmill) Martin Standidge Hall
Long(Hill) Griffiths:
Tries - Muscroft Agar: Goals - Gaitley(2):
CASTLEFORD - Wraith: Fenton Joyner Newton Walsh:
Burton Stephens: Bence(Cookland) Spurr Dickinson

Cookland(Kahn) Reilly Lloyd:
Tries - Wraith(2) Burton(2):   Goals - Lloyd(6):
Referee H Hunt (Cheshire) Att - 3000 H.T. 7 - 5

Sun 31 Oct 1976 HULL KINGSTON ROVERS away lost 8 - 16

HULL K R - Hall: Dunn Smith Watson Sullivan: Hartley
Millward: Millington Heslop Holdstock Lowe Rose Casey:
Tries - Dunn Smith Watson Sullivan: Goals - Millward(2):
CASTLEFORD - Wraith: Fenton Joyner Newton Walsh:
Burton Stephens Pickerill): Kahn Spurr(Orr)
Dickinson(S/O) Orr(Reilly) Cookland Lloyd
Tries - Walsh Burton: Goal - Lloyd:
Referee J Jackson (Pudsey) Att - 4387 H.T. 3 - 3

Sat 6 Nov 1976 ST HELENS away won 22 - 18 PLAYERS No.6 ROUND 2

ST HELENS - Pimblett: Jones Benyon Noonan(Pinner)
Mathias: Glynn Gwilliam: Charles Karalius James Nicholls
Chisnall Cunningham:
Tries - Nicholls(2) James Cunningham: Goals - Pimblett(3):
CASTLEFORD - Wraith: Fenton Joyner Walsh Lowndes:
Burton Pickerill (Stephens): Kahn Spurr Dickinson
Cookland(Orr) Reilly Lloyd:
Tries - Joyner(2) Burton(2):   Goals - Lloyd(5):
Referee W H Thompson (Hud'field) Att - 3000 H.T. 5 - 18

Tue 9 Nov 1976 LEEDS away won 17 - 2 BBC 2 FLOODLIT COMPETITION ROUND 2

LEEDS - Marshall: A.Smith Holmes Dyl D.Smith: Hague
Dick: Harrison Ward Pitchford(Dickins) Eccles Dickinson
Cookson: Goal - Marshall:
CASTLEFORD - Wraith: Fenton Joyner Walsh(Pickerill)
Lowndes: Burton Stephens: Kahn Spurr Dickinson Orr
Reilly Lloyd: Tries - Burton(3):   Goals - Lloyd(4):
Referee J V Moss (Manchester) Att - 4750 H.T. 2 - 2

Fri 12 Nov 1976 SALFORD home lost 9 - 14

CASTLEFORD - Wraith: Fenton Joyner Briggs Lowndes:
Johnson Pickerill(Stephens): Bence(Redfearn) Dickinson
Kahn Orr Reilly Lloyd: Try - Joyner: Goals - Lloyd(3):
SALFORD - Watkins: Fielding Butler Graham Richards: Gill
Nash: Coulman Clarke Mantle Corcoran Dixon Knighton:
Tries - Watkins Richards: Goals - Watkins(4):
Referee R Campbell (Widnes) Att - 4160 H.T. 4 - 14

Sat 20 Nov 1976 LEEDS away won 20 - 14 PLAYERS No.6 ROUND 3

LEEDS - Holmes: A.Smith Hynes Dyl D.Smith: Hague Dick:
Harrison Ward Pitchford Eccles(Burton) White Cookson:
Tries - A.Smith Hynes D.Smith Cookson: Goal - Dick:
CASTLEFORD - Wraith: Fenton Joyner Johnson(Pickerill)
Walsh: Burton Stephens: Kahn Spurr(Huddlestone)
Dickinson Orr Reilly Lloyd:
Tries - Burton(2) Johnson Stephens: Goals - Lloyd(4):
Referee H Hunt (Prestbury) Att - 6325 H.T. 15 - 3

Sat 27 Nov 1976 WIDNES home won 15 - 10 PLAYERS No.6 SEMI FINAL

CASTLEFORD - Briggs(Pickerill): Fenton Joyner Johnson

SEASON 1976-77

Walsh: Burton Stephens: Kahn Spurr Reilly Orr Norton
Lloyd: Tries - Fenton(2) Walsh: Goals - Lloyd(3):
WIDNES - Dutton: Wright Aspey George(Knight) Jenkins:
Eckersley Bowden: Ramsey Elwell Sheridan(Wood) Foran
Dearden Laughton:
Tries - Wright Eckersley: Goals - Dutton(2):
Referee P Massey (Salford) Att - 5700 H.T. 2 - 5

Tue 7 Dec l976 HULL away won 15 - 8
BBC 2 FLOODLIT COMPETITION SEMI FINAL
HULL - Robinson: Macklin Hunter Portz Lazenby: Hancock
Hepworth: Tindall Duke Walker(Ibbertson) Boxall
Crampton(Salmon) Crane:
Tries - Hunter Boxall: Goal - Macklin:
CASTLEFORD - Wraith: Fenton Joyner Johnson Walsh:
Burton Stephens: Kahn Spurr Reilly Orr Lloyd Norton:
Tries - Fenton Burton Kahn: Goals - Lloyd (3):
Referee M Naughton (Widnes) Att - 5474 H.T. 10 - 2

Fri 10 Dec 1976 HULL KINGSTON ROVERS home
lost 12 - 23
CASTLEFORD - Wraith: Fenton Joyner Johnson(Stephens)
Walsh: Burton Pickerill: Kahn Spurr Dickinson
Huddlestone Lloyd Norton:
Tries - Fenton Spurr: Goals - Lloyd(3):
HULL K R - Leighton: Dunn Smith Watson Sullivan:
Millward(Hartley) Agar: Millington Heslop Rose(Andres)
Lowe Madeley Hughes: Tries - Lowe(2) Dunn Smith Agar
Andrews: Goals - Millward(2) (DG):
Referee T J Court (Leeds) Att - 2705 H.T. 7 - 6

Tue 14 Dec 1976 LEIGH away won 12 - 4
BBC 2 FLOODLIT COMPETITION FINAL
LEIGH - Hogan: Prescott Stacey Woods Walsh: Taylor
Sayer: Chisnall Ashcroft Fletcher Macko Grimes Boyd:
Try - Walsh: Goal - Ashcroft(DG):
CASTLEFORD - Wraith: Fenton Joyner Johnson Walsh:
Burton Stephens: Kahn Spurr Dickinson Reilly Lloyd
Norton(S/O): Tries - Walsh Burton: Goals - Lloyd(3):
Referee J R Jackson (Pudsey) Att - 5714 H.T. Nil - 1

Fri 17 Dec 1976 BARROW home won 23 - 10
CASTLEFORD - Wraith: Fenton Joyner Walsh(PETER
BRADY(581)) Lowndes: Burton Pickerill: Kahn Spurr
Dickinson Orr(Huddlestone) Lloyd Norton:
Tries - Lowndes Burton Norton: Goals - Lloyd(7):
BARROW - Thompson: Clegg Nicholson P.Hogan Holland:
Mason Dean: S.Hogan Syzmala McFarlane Kavanagh
Flynn Secker(Knight): Goals - Hogan(4) Holland:
Referee S Wall (Leigh) Att - 2266 H.T. 13 - 4

Mon 27 Dec 1976 FEATHERSTONE ROVERS away
draw 8 - 8
FEATHERSTONE R - Box: Coventry Evans Quinn Kellett:
Newlove Fennell: Thompson Bridges Farrar Stone P.Smith
Bell: Try - Newlove: Goals - Quinn(2) Bell(DG):
CASTLEFORD - Wraith: Fenton Joyner Johnson Lowndes:
Burton Stephens: Kahn Spurr Dickinson Reilly Lloyd
Norton: Tries - Reilly Norton: Goal - Lloyd:
Referee A Givvons (Oldham) Att - 6505 H.T. 3 - 6

Sat 1 Jan 1977 BRADFORD NORTHERN home
won 30 - 5
CASTLEFORD - Wraith: Fenton Joyner Johnson Lowndes:
Burton Stephens(Pickerill): Kahn Spurr Dickinson(Reilly)
Reilly(Huddlestone) Orr Lloyd: Tries - Lowndes(2)
Johnson Burton Pickerill: Goals - Lloyd(7) Burton(DG):
BRADFORD N. - Pritchard: Francis Carlton Evans Redfearn:
Blacker Seabourne(Slater): Murphy(Sellers) Astbury
Forsythe Joyce Fearnley Woolford:
Try - Francis: Goal - Seabourne:
Referee R Moore (Wakefield) Att - 4089 H.T. 12 - 2

Sun 9 Jan 1977 LEIGH away won 12 - 2
LEIGH - Woods: Prescott Stacey Grimshaw Walsh: Taylor
Sayer: Fletcher (Chisnall) Ashcroft Wilkinson Macko
Grimes Boyd(Jones): Goal - Woods:
CASTLEFORD - Wraith: Fenton Joyner Johnson Alan
Lowndes(Pickerill): Burton Stephens: Kahn Spurr Reilly Orr
Lloyd Norton (Huddlestone):
Tries - Fenton Burton: Goals - Lloyd(3):
Referee P Geraghty (York) Att - 3000 H.T. 5 - nil

Sat 22 Jan 1977 BLACKPOOL BOROUGH
won 25 – 15 PLAYERS No.6 FINAL - at SALFORD
BLACKPOOL B - Reynolds: Heritage Machen Pitman
Robinson(Lamb): Marsh Newall: Hamilton Allen Egan
Gamble Groves(Hurst) Pattinson:
Tries - Machen Allen Egan: Goals - Egan(3):
CASTLEFORD - Wraith: Fenton Joyner Johnson Briggs:
Burton Stephens: Kahn Spurr Dickinson Reilly Lloyd
Norton: Tries - Wraith Joyner Johnson Burton Stephens:
Goals - Lloyd(5):
Referee M Naughton (Widnes) Att - 4512 H.T. 15 - 10

Tue 25 Jan 1977 WIDNES away lost 3 - 13
WIDNES - Dutton: Wright Aspey George(Woods) O'Neill:
Eckersley Bowden: Ramsey Elwell Sheridan Ward(Adams)
Dearden Foran:
Tries - Wright Aspey Woods: Goals - Dutton(2)
CASTLEFORD - Wraith: Newton Joyner Johnson Briggs:
Burton Stephens: Kahn Fisher(Michael Redfearn)
Dickinson Orr Reilly Lloyd: Try - Burton:
Referee J Jackson (Pudsey) Att - 5871 H.T. 3 - 7

Fri 4 Feb 1977 ST HELENS home won 16 - 12
CASTLEFORD - Wraith: Fenton Joyner(Newton) Johnson
Briggs: Burton Stephens: Kahn Spurr Dickinson
Reilly(Norton) Orr Lloyd:
Tries - Burton Orr: Goals - Lloyd(5):
ST HELENS - Pimblett(Ashton): Jones Benyon
Cunningham Campbell: Glynn Gwilliam: D.Chisnall(Hope)
Liptrot Courtney Hull E.Chisnall Pinner:
Tries - Glynn D.Chisnall: Goals - Pinner(3):
Referee H Hunt (Cheshire) Att - 4328 H.T. 9 - 3

Sun 13 Feb 1977 NEW HUNSLET home won 27 - 6
CHALLENGE CUP ROUND 1
CASTLEFORD - Wraith: Fenton Joyner Newton Briggs:
Johnson Stephens: Kahn Spurr Dickinson Reilly(Orr) Lloyd
Norton: Tries - Johnson(2) Wraith Fenton Newton

Stephens Kahn: Goals - Lloyd(3):
NEW HUNSLET - Broatch: Muscroft Briers Kirkpatrick
Barron: Layton(Foster) Diabira: Windmill Payne Hawley
Endersby(Hall) Davies Griffiths: Tries - Muscroft Griffiths:
Referee P Massey (Salford) Att - 6800 H.T. 13 - nil

Fri 18 Feb 1977 LEEDS home lost 12 - 13

CASTLEFORD - Briggs(JOHN KAIN(582)): Fenton Johnson
Newton Richardson: Pickerill Stephens: Bence Spurr
Kahn(Brady) Orr Lloyd Norton:
Tries - Johnson Stephens: Goals - Lloyd(3):
LEEDS - Murrell: D.Smith Holmes Fletcher Wilby: Hague
Banner: Dickinson Ward Pitchford Heron(Harrison) Eccles
Fearnley:
Tries - Murrell Pitchford Heron: Goals - Holmes(2):
Referee W H Thompson (Hud'field) Att - 4217 H.T. 7 - 10

Sun 27 Feb 1977 ROCHDALE HORNETS away won 10 - 2 CHALLENGE CUP ROUND 2

ROCHDALE H - Maloney: Hartley Longstaff Wainwright
Rawlinson: Ayres Heaton: Hodkinson Clarke Gourley
Jones Cooke Coslett: Goal - Maloney:
CASTLEFORD - Wraith: Fenton Joyner Johnson Newton:
Burton Stephens: Bence Spurr Dickinson Reilly Lloyd
Norton: Tries - Fenton Burton: Goals - Lloyd(2):
Referee G F Lindop (Wakefield) Att - 5853 H.T. 3 - 2

Fri 4 Mar 1977 WORKINGTON TOWN home won 25 - 6

CASTLEFORD - Wraith(Kain): Fenton Joyner Johnson
Newton: Burton Stephens: Bence Fisher Dickinson Reilly
Orr Lloyd(Spurr): Tries - Fenton(2) Wraith Johnson
Newton: Goals - Burton(3) Lloyd(2):
WORKINGTON T - Charlton: Risman Marland Wright
McCorquodale: Wilkins(Lauder) McMillan: Fletcher Banks
Bowman L.Gorley P.Gorley Pattinson (Henney):
Try - L.Gorley: Goals - McCorquodale(1) (DG)
Referee A Givvons (Oldham) Att - 3724 H.T. 7 - 1

Sun 6 Mar 1977 WORKINGTON TOWN away won 20 - 17

WORKINGTON T - Charlton: Risman Marland Wright
Wilkins: McMillan Lauder: Fletcher Banks Bowman
L.Gorley Henney(S/O) Pattinson:
Tries - Pattinson(2) McMillan: Goals - Lauder(4):
CASTLEFORD - Claughton: Fenton Newton Kain
Richardson: JohnsonARTHUR OULTON(583): Bence
(Dickinson) Spurr Fisher Hardy Cookland(S/O) Brady: Tries
- Kain Johnson Brady: Goals - Oulton(5) Hardy(DG):
Referee J Entwistle (Salford) Att - 3050 H.T. 2 - 2

Sat 12 Mar 1977 HULL KINGSTON ROVERS home lost 15 - 25 CHALLENGE CUP ROUND 3 CASTLEFORD -

Wraith: Fenton Joyner Johnson Newton: Burton(Kain)
Stephens: Bence Spurr Dickinson(Orr) Reilly Lloyd Norton:
Tries - Fenton Stephens Reilly: Goals - Lloyd(3):
HULL K R - Tyrer: Dunn Hall Watson Sullivan: Hartley
Millward(Agar): Millington(Watkinson) Heslop Rose Lowe
Hughes(Millington) Casey:

Tries - Hartley(2) Sullivan(2) Lowe: Goals Tyrer(5):
Referee M Naughton (Widnes) Att - 10300 H.T. 5 - 15

Tue 15 Mar 1977 BARROW away lost 8 - 9

BARROW - Thompson: Clegg Nicholson Hill Holland:
McConnell Jones S.Hogan Allen Flynn Davies(Szymala)
Hadley P.Hogan: Tries - Clegg Jones Davies:
CASTLEFORD - Wraith(Claughton): Fenton Joyner Newton
Richardson: Johnson Stephens: Bence (Paul Kahn) Spurr
Dickinson Orr Lloyd Norton:
Tries - Richardson Stephens: Goal - Lloyd:
Referee J McDonald (Wigan) Att - 1918 H.T. 8 - 6

Sun 20 Mar 1977 OLDHAM away won 18 - 5

OLDHAM - O'Brien: Lund Hill Whittle Barton:
Treasure(Munro) Paterson: Owen O'Mahoney Hicks
Taylor(Ashcroft) Herbert Pollard(Taylor)
Try - Barton: Goal - O'Brien:
CASTLEFORD - Claughton: Fenton Joyner(Kain) Newton
Richardson: Johnson Stephens: Bence Fisher Dickinson
Reilly(Spurr) Orr Lloyd:
Tries - Kain Johnson Stephens Reilly: Goals - Lloyd(2) Orr:
Referee A Parker (York) Att - 1298 H.T. 5 - nil

Fri 27 Mar 1977 WIDNES home won 11 - 9

CASTLEFORD - Claughton: Kain Fenton Newton
Richardson: Johnson Stephens: Bence Spurr Dickinson
Reilly Orr Norton:
Tries - Kain Newton Norton: Goal - Claughton:
WIDNES - Dutton: Wright Aspey Tilley Woods: Hughes
Bowden: Ramsey Elwell Mills Adams Foran Laughton:
Try - Adams: Goals - Dutton(3):
Referee S Wall (Leigh) Att - 3692 H.T. 3 - 5

Fri 1 Apr 1977 WARRINGTON home won 15 - 13

CASTLEFORD - Claughton: Kain(Brady) Fenton Newton
Richardson: Johnson Stephens: Bence Fisher Dickinson
Reilly Orr Norton:
Tries - Kain Johnson Norton: Goals - Orr(3):
WARRINGTON - Turley: Curling Cunliffe Hesford Kelly:
Whitehead Gwill am: Weavill Price Case Lester Martin
B.Philbin:
Tries - Curling Hesford Kelly: Goals - Hesford(2):
Referee J V Moss (Manchester) Att - 3322 H.T. 6 - 10

Sun 3 Apr 1977 BRADFORD NORTHERN away won 29 - 13

BRADFORD N - Mumby: Pritchard Roe(Trotter) Evans
D.Redfearn(Bullock): Slater A.Redfearn: Murphy Astbury
Sellers Jackson Haigh Woolford:
Tries - Pritchard Evans Bullock: Goals - Mumby(2):
CASTLEFORD - Wraith: Fenton Brady Newton Kain:
Johnson Stephens: Bence Spurr Dickinson Reilly(Orr)
Lloyd Norton
Tries - Johnson(2) Kain Stephens Norton: Goals - Lloyd(7):
Referee M Naughton (Widnes) Att - 4523 H.T. 5 - 18

Sat 9 Apr 1977 LEEDS away Lost 20 - 25

LEEDS - Murrell: A.Smith(D.Smith) Hague Dyl Atkinson:
Holmes Sanderson: Harrison Ward(Heron) Pitchford

Eccles White Cookson: Tries - A.Smith D.Smith Atkinson Sanderson White: Goals - Cookson(4) Murrell:
CASTLEFORD - Wraith: Fenton Newton Johnson Kain: Burton Stephens: Bence Spurr Dickinson Brady Orr Lloyd: Tries - Wraith Fenton Johnson Bence: Goals - Lloyd(4): Referee J V Moss (Manchester) Att - 5586 H.T. 6 - 5

Mon 11 Apr 1977 FEATHERSTONE ROVERS home won 16 - 14
CASTLEFORD - Wraith: Fenton Newton Johnson Kain: Burton(Claughton) Stephens: JOHN BURKE(584) Fisher Dickinson Reilly Orr Lloyd:
Tries - Burke Fisher: Goals - Lloyd(5):
FEATHERSTONE R - Marsden: Dyas Gilbert Quinn Kellett: Tuffs Butler: Thompson Bridges Farrar(Sharp) Gibbins P.Smith Limb:
Tries - Gilbert(2) P.Smith: Goals - Quinn(2) Butler(DG): Referee H G Hunt (Cheshire) Att - 7768 H.T. 4 - 9

Fri 15 Apr 1977 SALFORD away lost 7 - 12 SALFORD - Watkins: Fielding Graham Hesketh(Knighton) (Hesketh)Richards(Knighton): Gill Nash: Coulman Evans Grice Mantle Dixon Prescott:
Tries - Coulman Dixon: Goals - Watkins(3): CASTLEFORD - Wraith: Claughton Fenton Newton Kain: Johnson Stephens: Burke Spurr Dickinson Reilly Lloyd Norton: Try - Johnson: Goals - Lloyd(2): Referee T J Court (Bradford) Att - 5613 H T. 7 - 5

Sun 17 Apr 1977 ROCHDALE HORNETS away lost 10 - 14
ROCHDALE H - Maloney: Longstaff Hartley Wainwright Marsh: Ayres Sanderson: Hodkinson O'Neill Gourley Coslett Cooke(Jones) Halmshaw:
Tries - Marsh Sanderson: Goals - Maloney(4): CASTLEFORD - Wraith: Claughton Fenton Newton Kain: Johnson Stephens: Bence Spurr Dickinson Reilly Lloyd(Brady) Steven(Knocker)Norton(Burke):
Tries - Wraith Kain: Goals - Lloyd(2): Referee A Allen (York) Att - 1973 H.T. 10 - 9

Fri 22 Apr 1977 WIGAN home won 18 - 3
CASTLEFORD - Wraith(Bence): Fenton Newton Kain(Richardson) Claughton: Brady Stephens: Burke Spurr Dickinson Orr Lloyd Reilly:
Tries - Wraith Richardson Spurr Lloyd: Goals - Lloyd(3): WIGAN - Burke: Vigo Greenall(Swan) Francis Hornby: Walsh Nulty Bailey Marland Ashcroft Dootson O'Neil Hollingsworth: Try - Hornby: Referee P A Massey (Salford) Att - 3262 H.T. 8 - 3

Sun 24 Apr 1977 WAKEFIELD TRINITY home won 26 -3
CASTLEFORD - Claughton: Richardson Kain Newton Briggs: Brady Stephens: Bence Spurr(Burke) Dickinson Reilly Orr Lloyd(ALFRED WESTON(585)):
Tries - Stephens(2) Claughton Richardson Bence Weston: Goals - Lloyd(3) Orr:
WAKEFIELD T - Rushton: Rigg Hale Banks(Endersby) Brown: Langton Lampkowski: Murray Handscombe Bratt

Kevin Rayne(Stringer) Skerrett Ellis: Try - Rushton: Referee W H Thompson (Hud'field) Att - 4790 H.T. 5 -nil

Sun 1 May 1977 SALFORD home won 25 - 17 PREMIERSHIP ROUND 1
CASTLEFORD - Wraith(Brady): Richardson Newton Kain Claughton: Johnson Stephens: Burke Fisher Dickinson Reilly Orr Lloyd:
Tries - Richardson(2) Stephens(2) Reilly: Goals - Lloyd(5): SALFORD - Watkins: Fielding Graham Hesketh Mayor: Butler Nash: Coulman Evans Mantle Dixon Corcoran(Frodsham) Knighton:
Tries - Fielding Hesketh Mayor: Goals - Watkins(4): Referee S Wall (Leigh) Att - 5391 H.T. 10 - 10

Tue 10 May 1977 ST HELENS home lost 12 - 36 PREMIERSHIP SEMI FINAL IST LEG
CASTLEFORD - Claughton: Richardson Newton Johnson Kain(Briggs): Burton Stephens: Burke Spurr Dickinson(Alan Bence) Reilly Orr Brady:
Tries - Richardson Stephens: Goals - Orr(3): ST HELENS - Pimblett: Jones Benyon Cunningham Mathias: Glynn Gwilliam(Ashton): D.Chisnall Liptrot James Nicholls(Karalius) E.Chisnall Pinner:
Tries - Cunningham(3) Jones Mathias Gwilliam Ashton E.Chisnall: Goals – Pimblett(6) Referee M Naughton (Widnes) Att - 6265 H.T. 2 - 23

Sat 14 May 1977 ST HELENS away lost 13 - 25 PREMIERSHIP SEMI FINAL 2ND LEG
ST HELENS - Pimblett(Pinner): Jones Benyon Cunningham Mathias: Glynn Gwilliam: D.Chisnall(Karalius) Liptrot James Hope E.Chisnall Pinner (Ashton):
Tries - Cunningham Mathias Hope E.Chisnall Ashton: Goals - Pimblett(4) Pinner:
CASTLEFORD - Claughton: Richardson Newton Johnson Kain: Burton Stephens: Burke Spurr Fisher Reilly Orr Peter Brady: Tries - Richardson Newton Orr: Goals - Orr(2): Referee J Jackson (Halifax) Att - 3800 H.T. 11 – 12

Alf Weston
D. No 585
975-76 to 1977-78

SEASON 1976-77

D.N	PLAYER		DEBUT	L MATCH	APP	SUB	T.AP	TRI'S	G'LS	D.G	P'TS
493	BRIGGS	TREVOR			12	1	13	0	0	0	0
494	REDFEARN	MICHAEL		25/01/1977	3	3	6	0	0	0	0
512	REILLY	MALCOLM			38	1	39	8	0	0	24
516	LOWNDES	ALAN		09/01/1977	7	0	7	3	0	0	9
518	SPURR	ROBERT			40	2	42	2	0	0	6
525	STEPHENS	GARY			34	3	37	13	0	0	39
526	JOHNSON	PHILIP			38	0	38	17	0	0	51
531	NORTON	STEVE (KNOCKER)		17/04/1977	18	1	19	5	0	0	15
532	LLOYD	GEOFFREY (SAMMY)			43	0	43	5	158	0	331
537	NEWTON	RAY			29	2	31	6	0	0	18
542	DICKINSON	ALAN			34	2	36	1	0	0	3
544	CLAUGHTON	GEORGE			11	2	13	1	1	0	5
551	JOYNER	JOHN			34	0	34	11	0	0	33
552	HUDDLESTONE	JAMES (SID)			1	5	6	0	0	0	0
556	RICHARDSON	TERRY			12	2	14	7	0	0	21
560	FENTON	STEVE			40	2	42	12	0	0	36
563	WALSH	JAMIE			18	1	19	6	0	0	18
565	MORRIS	GEOFF			3	3	6	0	0	0	0
567	TYREMAN	GRAHAM			1	0	1	0	0	0	0
568	HARDY	ALAN			1	0	1	0	0	1	1
569	BENCE	ALAN		10/05/1977	24	2	26	2	0	0	6
570	COOKLAND	PETER			15	0	15	3	0	0	9
571	FISHER	TONY			8	0	8	1	0	0	3
572	WRAITH	GEOFFREY			39	0	39	10	0	0	30
573	COOMBS	RONALD		05/09/1977	0	4	4	0	0	0	0
574	PICKERILL	CLIVE			8	6	14	1	0	0	3
577	BURTON	BRUCE			34	0	34	29	3	2	95
578	ORR	PAUL			30	4	34	5	10	0	35
579	JOHNSON	PETER			0	1	1	0	0	0	0
580	KAHN	PAUL	01/10/1976	15/03/1977	22	2	24	3	0	0	9
581	BRADY	PETER	17/12/1976	14/05/1977	7	5	12	1	0	0	3
582	KAIN	JOHN	18/02/1977		13	4	17	6	0	0	18
583	OULTON	ARTHUR	06/03/1977		1	0	1	0	5	0	10
584	BURKE	JOHN	11/04/1977		6	2	8	1	0	0	3
585	WESTON	ALF	24/04/1977		0	1	1	1	0	0	3
	35		6	7	624	61	685	160	177	3	837

COMPETITION		P	W	D	L	FOR	AGT
LEAGUE D 1	POSITION 3 OF 16	30	19	1	10	519	350
YORK'S CUP		3	1	1	1	50	45
F. TROPHY		4	4	0	0	60	22
RL CUP		3	2	0	1	52	33
PLAYERS NO6		5	5	0	0	106	67
CHAMPIONSHIP		3	1	0	2	50	78
PLAYERS RECORDS		48	32	2	14	837	595

The BBC2 Floodlit Competition once more brought us success. In the final away to Leigh we lifted the trophy for the fourth time after a 12 – 4 victory after an half time score of nil - 1 !!.

We also achieved success in the Players No 6 Trophy. Victories in round one away at New Hunslet 24 –10, St Helens away 22 – 18 in round two and away at Leeds 20 – 14 in round three, and in the semi-final away at Hull 15 – 8. The final played at the Willows Salford was against Blackpool Borough and although firm favourites we were made to struggle all the way before finishing winners 25 – 15 and lifting this Trophy for the first time.

Sammy' Lloyd kicked his 600th goal for the club in the home victory 18 – 3 against Wigan on 22 April 1977, and Sammy' went on for the second successive season to improve his own record of goals in a season from 149 to 158.

Malcolm Reilly was named 1st Division player of the year.

SEASON 1977-78

In the league Hull, Dewsbury, Bramley, New Hunslet were promoted to Division 1. Rochdale Hornets, Leigh, Barrow, Oldham being relegated to Division 2.

Sun 7 Aug 1977 HULL KINGSTON ROVERS away lost 12 – 23 HARRY POOLE MEMORIAL MATCH FRIENDLY
HULL K R - Leighton: Dunn Hall Watson Youngman: Hartley Agar: Millington Heslop Holdstock Lowe Cunningham Hughes: Subs - Robinson Wallace Watkinson Nuttall Hossell Moore Madley:
Tries - Hartley(2) Youngman Agar Lowe: Goals - Hall(4):
CASTLEFORD - Briggs: Fenton Ph.Johnson Newton Richardson: Burton Oulton: Burke Tyreman Dickinson Weston Pe.Johnson Reilly: Subs – J Kear D Hartley Robbins Joyner Woodall A.N.Other:
Tries - Reilly(2): Goals - Oulton(3):
Referee A Allen (York) Att - 1600 H.T. 7 - 15

Sun 14 Aug 1977 FEATHERSTONE ROVERS home won 15 – 14 CHARITY MATCH FRIENDLY
CASTLEFORD - Wraith: Richardson Joyner Ph.Johnson Newton: Burton Oulton: Bence Tyreman Woodall Pe.Johnson Weston Orr: Subs - Kear Briggs A.N.Other Hardy Dickinson Lloyd Pye :
Tries - Orr(2) Wraith: Goals - Orr(2) Lloyd:
FEATHERSTONE R - Marsden: Dyas Evans Quinn Edginton: Coventry Fennell: Townend Tingle Farrar Gibbins Busfield Vickers: Subs - Box Hobbs R.Tuffs N.Tuffs Butler Thompson Anderson S.Smith :
Tries - Edginton Coventry Hobbs R.Tuffs: Goal - N.Tuffs:
Referee   Att   H.T.

Sun 21 Aug 1977 DEWSBURY away won 12 - 5 YORKSHIRE CUP ROUND 1
DEWSBURY - Richardson: Agar Simpson Clark Mitchell: Stephenson Lee(Thornton): Beverley(Craven) Price Hankins Wood Fowler Whittington:
Goals - Stephenson(2) (DG):
CASTLEFORD - Wraith: Richardson Joyner Ph.Johnson Newton: Burton Arthur Oulton(Briggs): Burke Tyreman Dickinson Orr Reilly Lloyd:
Tries - Richardson Johnson: Goals - Lloyd(3):
Referee J V Moss (Manchester) Att - 2600 H.T. 7 - 3

Sun 28 Aug 1977 YORK home won 23 - 17 YORKSHIRE CUP ROUND 2
CASTLEFORD - Wraith: Richardson Joyner(Briggs) Newton Fenton: Ph.Johnson Burton(Reilly): Burke Tyreman Dickinson Orr Reilly(Weston) Lloyd: Tries - Joyner(2) Richardson Fenton Johnson: Goals - Lloyd(4):
YORK - Banks: Smith Day Marston Marshall: Crossley(Ferres) Harkin: Hollis Heatherington Morgan Rhodes Bennett(Clancy) Cooper: Tries - Day Heatherington Rhodes: Goals - Heatherington(4):
Referee A Givvons (Oldham) Att - 4630 H.T. 13 - 7

Fri 2 Sept 1977 WAKEFIELD TRINITY home won 33 - 21
CASTLEFORD - Wraith: Richardson Joyner Newton(Briggs) Fenton: Ph.Johnson Burton: Burke Tyreman Dickinson

Reilly Orr Lloyd: Tries - Fenton(2) Richardson Joyner Newton Burke Orr: Goals - Lloyd(5) Orr:
WAKEFIELD T - Sheard(Crook): Brown Crook(Langton) Sutcliffe Riggs: Sanderson Lampkowski: Ballantyne Handscombe Kirkbride Skerrett Idle Hudson(Kevin Rayne): Tries - Riggs(3) Sanderson Skerrett: Goals - Crook(2) Sheard:
Referee H G Hunt (Cheshire) Att - 4186 H.T. 15 - 8

Sun 11 Sept 1977 ST HELENS away lost 17 - 39
ST HELENS - Pimblett: Jones Noonan Cunningham Mathias: Glynn(Ashton) Gwilliam: D.Chisnall Liptrot James(Karalius) Nicholls E.Chisnall Pinner:
Tries - Gwilliam(3) Pimblett(2) Cunningham Mathias: Goals - Pimblett(9):
CASTLEFORD - Wraith: Richardson Joyner Briggs Fenton: Ph.Johnson Burton: John Burke(S/O) Tyreman Dickinson(Weston) Orr Reilly Lloyd:
Tries - Joyner Weston Reilly: Goals - Lloyd(4):
Referee B Shooman (Leeds) Att - 5000 H.T. 9 - 14

Wed 14 Sept 1977 NEW HUNSLET home lost 10 - 13
CASTLEFORD - Wraith: Richardson Joyner Ph.Johnson Fenton: Burton Pickerill: Weston Tyreman Dickinson Huddlestone(Reilly) Orr Lloyd:
Tries - Fenton Pickerill: Goals - Lloyd(2):
NEW HUNSLET - Foster: Francis Appleyard Hudson Barrons: Gaitley Brown: Windmill Payne Standidge Rowe Wright(Martin) Griffiths(Briers):
Tries - Brown(2) Appleyard: Goals - Gaitley(2):
Referee G Burton (Wakefield) Att - 3160 H.T. 7 - 8

Sat 17 Sept 1977 KEIGHLEY away won 14 - 4 YORKSHIRE CUP SEMI FINAL
KEIGHLEY - Jefferson(Leek): Morgan Waterhouse Leek(Pieniazek) Hedges: Bardgett Holden: Ackroyd(Wood) Woolford Garforth Clarkson Garbett Loxton: Goals - Jefferson(2):
CASTLEFORD - Wraith: Richardson Joyner Ph.Johnson Fenton: Burton Pickerill: Fisher(Orr) Tyreman Dickinson Weston Reilly Lloyd:
Tries - Richardson Fenton: Goals - Lloyd(4):
Referee M Naughton (Widnes) Att - 2594 H.T. 9 - 2

Sun 25 Sept 1977 HULL away lost 19 - 26
HULL - Hunter: Bray Clark Marshall Macklin: Hancock Lynn(Hall): Tindall Duke Sutton Salmon Boxall Crane(Ibbertson): Tries - Macklin Hancock Sutton Salmon Boxall: Goals - Marshall(5) Crane(DG):
CASTLEFORD - Wraith: Briggs Joyner(Kain) Ph.Johnson Fenton: Burton Pickerill: Fisher(Tyreman) Spurr Dickinson Weston Orr Lloyd:
Tries - Johnson(2) Fenton: Goals - Lloyd(5):
Referee M Naughton (Widnes) Att - 4406 H.T. 14 - 11

Fri 30 Sept 1977 BRAMLEY home won 26 - 2
CASTLEFORD - Wraith: Richardson Briggs Ph.Johnson Fenton: Burton Pickerill: Fisher(IAN D.(JOE) BATTYE(586)) Spurr Weston Huddlestone Orr(Fisher) Reilly:
Tries - Richardson(2) Fenton(2) Burton Huddlestone:

SEASON 1977-78

Goals - Orr(3) Burton:
BRAMLEY - Hay: Goodchild Belford Parker Rowett: Briggs
Harland: Boldy(Roberts) Tennant Lyons Clarkson Fiddler
Bond: Goal - Hay:
Referee D W Fox (Stanley) Att - 2171 H.T. 10 - 2

Wed 5 Oct 1977 BRADFORD NORTHERN home lost 5 - 15
CASTLEFORD - Wraith: Richardson Briggs(Ray Newton)
Ph.Johnson Fenton: Burton Pickerill: Fisher Spurr
Weston(Battye) Huddlestone Reilly Lloyd:
Try - Reilly: Goal - Lloyd:
BRADFORD N - Mumby: Austin Roe Evans
D.Redfearn(Blacker): Woolford A.Redfearn: Thompson
Dyson Forsythe(Mordue) Trotter Jarvis Haigh:
Tries - Thompson Trotter Jarvis: Goals - Mumby(3):
Referee T M Beaumont (Hud'field) Att - 5037 H.T. nil - 8

Sun 9 Oct 1977 WORKINGTON TOWN away lost 15-30
WORKINGTON T - Charlton: Collister Wilkins
Wright(Smith) McCorquodale: Lauder Walker: Watts
Banks Bowman L.Gorley Groves(Pattinson) P.Gorley:
Tries - Walker(2) L.Gorley(2) Wilkins P.Gorley:
Goals - McCorquodale(6):
CASTLEFORD - Wraith: Richardson Joyner Ph.Johnson
Fenton: Burton Pickerill(Claughton): Battye(Tyreman)
Spurr Fisher(Battye) Huddlestone Reilly Lloyd:
Tries - Joyner(2) Johnson: Goals - Lloyd(3):
Referee T J Court (Bradford) Att - 2800 H.T. 10 - 7

Sat 15 Oct 1977 FEATHERSTONE ROVERS won - 17 - 7
YORKSHIRE CUP FINAL - AT HEADINGLEY LEEDS
CASTLEFORD - Wraith: Richardson Joyner Ph.Johnson
Fenton: Burton Pickerill(Stephens): Fisher(Woodall) Spurr
Weston Huddlestone Reilly Lloyd:
Tries - Burton(2):   Goals - Lloyd(5) Burton(DG):
FEATHERSTONE R. - Marsden: Evans Gilbert Quinn(Tuffs)
Kellett: Newlove Butler: Townend Bridges Farrar Gibbins
Stone(Smith) Bell: Try - Smith: Goals - Quinn Townend:
Referee M Naughton (Widnes) Att - 6318 H.T. 4 - 2
WHITE ROSE TROPHY WINNER - BRUCE BURTON (CASTLEFORD)

Sun 23 Oct 1977 DEWSBURY away won 13 - nil
JOHN PLAYER ROUND 1
DEWSBURY - Richardson: Hunte Agar Pickup
Lund(Simpson): Russell Thornton: Beverley Price Hankins
Whittington Wood(Fowler) Clark:
CASTLEFORD - Wraith: Richardson Joyner Ph.Johnson
Fenton: Burton Stephens: Fisher Spurr Weston
Huddlestone Reilly Lloyd(Woodall) :
Tries - Burton Stephens: Goals - Lloyd(3) (DG):
Referee P A Massey (Salford) Att - 1700 H.T. 7 - nil

Wed 26 Oct 1977 HULL away won 10 - 7
BBC 2 FLOODLIT COMPETITION ROUND 1
HULL - Hunter: Bray Clark Marshall Macklin: Hancock
Lynn: Boxall (Wardle) Maskill Sutton Salmon Crampton
Crane: Try - Crane: Goals - Marshall(2):
CASTLEFORD - Wraith: Richardson Joyner(Briggs)

Ph.Johnson Fenton: Burton Stephens: Fisher Spurr
Weston Huddlestone(Woodall) Reilly Lloyd:
Tries - Johnson Reilly: Goals - Lloyd(2):
Referee J V Moss (Manchester) Att - 4074 H.T. 5 - nil

Sun 30 Oct 1977 WIDNES away lost 11 - 21
WIDNES - Eckersley: Wright Aspey George Woods:
Hughes Bowden: Ramsey(O'Neill) Elwell Sheridan Dutton
Hull Lasughton: Tries - Wright(2) Aspey Woods Hughes :
Goals - Woods(3):
CASTLEFORD - Wraith(Briggs): Richardson Joyner
Ph.Johnson Fenton: Burton Stephens: Fisher Spurr
Woodall Weston Reilly(Battye) Lloyd:
Try - Richardson   Goals - Lloyd(4):
Referee D Kershaw (Easingwold) Att - 7145 H.T.5 - 11

Sat 5 Nov 1977 WIDNES away lost 19 - 26
JOHN PLAYER ROUND 2
WIDNES - Eckersley: Wright Aspey George Woods:
Hughes Bowden: Ramsey Elwell Sheridan
Adams(Dearden) Hull Laughton: Tries - Elwell(2) George
Woods Hull Laughton: Goals - Woods(4):
CASTLEFORD - Wraith: Richardson Joyner Ph.Johnson
Fenton: Burton Stephens: Fisher Spurr Weston
Huddlestone Reilly Lloyd:
Tries - Joyner Fenton Burton: Goals - Lloyd(5):
Referee G F Lindop (Wakefield) Att - 5986 H.T.11 - 11

Fri 11 Nov 1977 HULL home draw 14 - 14
CASTLEFORD - Wraith: Richardson Trevor Briggs
Ph.Johnson Kain: Burton Stephens: Fisher Spurr
Weston(Woodall) Huddlestone Orr Lloyd:
Tries - Richardson Stephens: Goals - Lloyd(4):
HULL - Robinson: Bray Noble Marshall Macklin: Hancock
Lynn(Hunter): Bancroft(Lazenby) Maskill Wardell Salmon
Sutton Crane:
Try - Hancock: Goals - Marshall(5) Hancock(DG):
Referee J W Mean (Leyland) Att - 3039 H.T. 7 - 4

Tue 15 Nov 1977 LEEDS home won 14 - 10
BBC 2 FLOODLIT COMPETITION ROUND 2
CASTLEFORD - Wraith: Richardson Joyner Ph.Johnson
Fenton: Burton Stephens: Fisher Spurr Weston Orr Lloyd
Reilly(Huddlestone):
Tries - Johnson Burton: Goals - Lloyd(4):
LEEDS - Oulton: A.Smith Hague Dyl D.Smith:
Holmes(Dick) Sanderson: Harrison Ward Pitchford Eccles
Cookson Fearnley: Tries - Dyl D.Smith: Goals - Oulton(2):
Referee A Givvons (Oldham) Att - 3824 H.T. nil - 8

Sat 19 Nov 1977 LEEDS away won 28 - 16
LEEDS - Oulton(Fletcher): A.Smith Hague Dyl D.Smith:
Treasure Dick: Harrison Ward Pitchford Eccles Cookson
Fearnley(White):
Tries - Dyl Treasure Pitchford Eccles: Goals - Oulton Dick:
CASTLEFORD - Wraith: Richardson Joyner Ph.Johnson
Fenton: Burton Stephens: Fisher(Hardy) Spurr Weston Orr
Huddlestone Lloyd: Tries - Fenton(2) Johnson Burton
Spurr Weston: Goals - Lloyd(5):
Referee W H Thompson(Hud'field) Att - 3441 H.T. 18 - 8

293

SEASON 1977-78

Tue 29 Nov 1977 HULL KINGSTON ROVERS home lost 5 – 23 BBC 2 FLOODLIT COMP SEMI FINAL
CASTLEFORD - Wraith: Richardson Joyner Ph.Johnson Fenton: Burton Stephens: Fisher Spurr Weston(Hardy) Huddlestone Orr Reilly: Try - Reilly: Goal - Orr:
HULL K.R. - Hall: Dunn Smith Watson Sullivan: Hartley Millward: Millington(Hughes) Watkinson Cunningham Lowe Rose Casey: Tries - Dunn Hartley Millward Cunningham: Goals - Hall(5) Watkinson(DG):
Referee S Wall (Leigh) Att - 4902 H.T. 5 - 19

Sun 4 Dec 1977 SALFORD away lost 8 - 37
SALFORD - Watkins: Fielding Butler Hesketh Richards: Gill Nash: Grice Evans Dixon Irving Henney Prescott:
Tries - Richards(3) Gill(2) Watkins Fielding Grice Irving: Goals - Watkins(5):
CASTLEFORD - Wraith(Kain): Richardson Joyner Ph.Johnson Fenton: Burton Pickerill: DAVID BRIGGS(587) Spurr Woodall Weston Hardy (PAUL NORTON(588)) Reilly: Tries - Burton Reilly: Goal - Burton:
Referee G Burton (Wakefield) Att - 4461 H.T. 3 - 13

Sun 11 Dec 1977 WORKINGTON TOWN home won 21 - 14
CASTLEFORD - Claughton: Richardson Joyner Ph.Johnson Fenton: Burton Stephens: Tony Fisher(Kain) Tyreman Alfred Weston(D.Briggs) Huddlestone Lloyd Reilly:
Tries - Richardson(2) Joyner Burton Huddlestone: Goals - Lloyd(3):
WORKINGTON T - Charlton: Collister Risman Wright McCorquodale: Wilkins(D.Smith) Walker: Watts Banks Hirst(McCarron) Groves P.Gorley Hartley:
Tries - Collister Walker: Goals - McCorquodale(4):
Referee M Naughton (Widnes) Att - 3284 H.T. 7 - 4

Sun 18 Dec 1977 NEW HUNSLET away lost 1 - 5
NEW HUNSLET - Kemble: Francis Briers Smith Barron: Gaitley Appleyard: Windmill Netzier Standidge Proctor Griffiths Halmshaw: Try - Griffiths: Goal - Gaitley:
CASTLEFORD - Claughton: Richardson Kain Ph.Johnson NIGEL SMITH(589): Burton Stephens: D.Briggs Spurr Woodall Huddlestone(Tyreman) Lloyd Reilly:
Goal - Lloyd(DG):
Referee J Entwistle (Whitley Bay) Att – 2100 H.T. 1 - 5

Mon 26 Dec 1977 FEATHERSTONE ROVERS home won 17 - 7
CASTLEFORD - Claughton: Richardson Joyner Ph.Johnson Fenton: Burton Stephens: D.Briggs Spurr Woodall Cookland(Tyreman) Lloyd Reilly:
Tries - Richardson Joyner Burton: Goals - Lloyd(4):
FEATHERSTONE R - Box: N.Tuffs Evans Gilbert(Limb) Coventry: Newlove(Robinson) Fennell: Townend Noon Stone Gibbins Smith Bell:
Try - Newlove: Goals - Townend(2):
Referee H G Hunt (Cheshire) Att - 6234 H.T. nil - 2

Sun 1 Jan 1978 BRADFORD NORTHERN away won 20 - 18
BRADFORD N - Mumby: Barends Austin Evans Roe: Blacker(Slater) Wolford: Van Bellen Dyson(Howard) Mordue Trotter Jarvis Joyce:
Tries - Mumby Austin Evans Roe: Goals - Mumby(3):
CASTLEFORD - Claughton: Richardson Joyner Ph.Johnson Fenton: Burton Stephens: D.Briggs Spurr Woodall Cookland Lloyd Reilly:
Tries - Burton(2) Richardson Reilly: Goals - Lloyd(4):
Referee J Jackson (Pudsey) Att - 9237 H.T. 17 - 5

Sun 8 JAN 1978 WAKEFIELD TRINITY away winning 7 - 5 – Match abandoned at H.T. owing to fog. Replayed Sun 23 Apr 1978
WAKEFIELD T - Sheard: Riggs Midgley Brown Fletcher: Smith Lampkowski: Ballantyne Astbury Handscombe Lockwood Skerrett Idle: Try - Riggs: Goal - Smith:
CASTLEFORD - Claughton: Richardson Joyner Kain Fenton: Burton Stephens: Battye Spurr Woodall Cookland Lloyd Reilly: Try - Richardson: Goals - Lloyd(2):
Referee A Givvons (Oldham) Att - 4772 H.T. 7 - 5

Fri 13 Jan 1978 HULL KINGSTON ROVERS home draw 21 - 21
CASTLEFORD - Claughton: Richardson Joyner Ph.Johnson Fenton: Burton Stephens: Battye(Hardy) Tyreman Woodall Cookland(Wraith) Lloyd Reilly:
Tries - Burton Battye Tyreman: Goals - Lloyd(6):
HULL K.R. - Leighton: Dunn Smith Watson Youngman: Hartley Millward: Millington Watkinson Cunningham Lowe Rose Hughes: Tries - Dunn Watson Hartley Cunninghamn Lowe: Goals - Millward(3):
Referee M Naughton (Widnes) Att - 3655 H.T. 19 - 11

Sun 22 Jan 1978 WIGAN away lost 15 - 21
WIGAN - Fairbairn: Vigo Willicombe Swann Hornby: Kieron O'Loughlin Foster: Hogan Clarke(O'Neill) Bailey Ashurst Wood Hollingsworth: Tries - Vigo(2) Willicombe Swann Ashurst: Goals - Fairbairn(3):
CASTLEFORD - Claughton: Richardson(Wraith) Joyner Ph.Johnson Fenton: Burton Stephens: DAVID SAMPSON(590) Spurr Woodall Cookland Lloyd Reilly(Hardy):
Tries - Joyner Burton Cookland: Goals - Lloyd(3):
Referee T Beaumont (Hud'field) Att - 5200 H.T. 13 - 11

Fri 27 Jan 1978 DEWSBURY home won 32 - 7
CASTLEFORD - Wraith: Claughton Kain(Morris) Ph.Johnson Fenton: Burton Stephens: Sampson Hardy Cookland JAMES CRAMPTON(591) Lloyd(S/O) Reilly(Woodall): Tries - Fenton(5) Claughton(2) Johnson: Goals - Burton(2) Lloyd:
DEWSBURY - Richardson: Brunt Agar(Lee) Simpson Mitchell: Hegarty Russell: Beverley Price Hankins(S/O) Craven Fowler Welsh: Try - Russell: Goals - Simpson(2):
Referee R Dennett (Warrington) Att - 3402 H.T. 14 - nil

SEASON 1977-78

Wed 1 Feb 1978 WARRINGTON home won 17 - 12
CASTLEFORD - Wraith: Claughton Joyner Ph.Johnson
Fenton: Burton Stephens: Sampson Hardy Woodall
Cookland Crampton(Huddlestone) Orr:
Tries - Fenton(2) Orr: Goals - Burton(4):
WARRINGTON - Finnegan: Hesford Benyon
Wilson(Whitehead) Bevan: Kelly Gordon: Wanbon(Eccles)
Dalgreen Nicholas Martyn Philbin Potter:
Tries - Dalgreen Martyn: Goals - Hesford(3):
Referee R Campbell (Widnes) Att - 3401 H.T. 10 - 4

Sun 5 Feb 1978 BRAMLEY away won 20 - 10
BRAMLEY - Hay: Waites Sampson Crook Rowett: Langton
Sayer: Johnstone Tennant Higginbottom Knowles
Roberts(S/O) Bond: Tries - Crook Sayer: Goals - Hay(2):
CASTLEFORD - Wraith: Claughton Joyner(Morris)
Ph.Johnson Fenton: Burton Stephens: Sampson Hardy
Woodall Cookland Crampton(Huddlestone) Orr:
Tries - Fenton(2) Joyner Stephens: Goals - Burton(4):
Referee J McDonald (Wigan) Att - 2250 H.T. 8 - 7

**Sun 26 Feb 1978 PILKINGTON RECS away
won 23 – 22 CHALLENGE CUP ROUND 1 - At
KNOWSLEY ROAD ST HELENS**
PILKINGTON R - Glover: Casey Hill Shea Hull: McCabe
Simmons: Forster(Highcock) Gormley Cross Smith
Highcock(Finney) Wright:
Tries - Gormley(2) Hull Wright: Goals - Glover(5):
CASTLEFORD - Wraith: Claughton Nigel Smith(Morris)
Ph.Johnson Fenton: Burton Stephens: Sampson
Hardy(Tyreman) Cookland Orr Reilly Crampton:
Tries - Johnson Fenton Burton Stephens Cookland:
Goals - Burton(4):
Referee W H Thompson(Hud'field) Att - 7750 H.T. 13 -20

Wed 1 Mar 1978 ST HELENS home lost 12 - 29
CASTLEFORD - Wraith: Claughton Walsh Ph.Johnson
Fenton(Morris): Burton Stephens: D.Briggs Tyreman
Cookland Crampton(Hardy) Reilly Lloyd:
Tries - Claughton Johnson: Goals - Lloyd(3):
ST HELENS - Pimblett: Jones Glynn Cunningham Mathias:
Francis Gwilliam(Ashton): D.Chisnall Liptrot James
Nicholls Karalius Pinner(Courtney):
Tries - Pimblett Jones Cunningham Mathias Liptrot
Pinner: Goals - Pimblett(5) (DG):
Referee R Campbell (Widnes) Att - 4154 H.T. 7 - 10

**Sun 12 Mar 1978 WORKINGTON TOWN away
draw 8 - 8 CHALLENGE CUP ROUND 2**
WORKINGTON T - Charlton: Roper Wilkins Wright
McCorquodale: Burke McMillan: Calvin Banks
Watts(Hartley) P.Gorley L.Gorley Pattinson:
Try - McMillan: Goals - McCorquodale(2) (DG):
CASTLEFORD - Wraith: Claughton Joyner Ph.Johnson
Fenton: Burton Stephens: D.Briggs Tyreman Reilly(S/O)
Norton Orr Lloyd: Tries - Claughton Burton: Goal - Lloyd:
Referee D Kershaw (York) Att - 5422 H.T. 3 - 6

**Tue 14 Mar 1978 WORKINGTON TOWN home
draw 8 - 8 CHALLENGE CUP ROUND 2 REPLAY**
CASTLEFORD - Wraith: Claughton Joyner Ph.Johnson
Fenton: Burton Stephens: D.Briggs Tyreman Reilly Norton
Orr Lloyd: Tries - Claughton Joyner: Goal - Lloyd:
WORKINGTON T - Charlton(Roper): Risman Wilkins
Wright McCorquodale: Burke McMillan: Calvin Banks
Watts P.Gorley L Gorley Blackwood (Hartley):
Try - L.Gorley: Goals - McCorquodale(2) (DG):
Referee - J V Moss (Manchester) Att - 6055 H.T. 0 - 7

**Thu 16 Mar 1978 WORKINGTON TOWN won 20 - 13
CHALLENGE CUP ROUND 2 2ND REPLAY - AT
CENTRAL PARK WIGAN**
WORKINGTON T - Wilkins: Roper Risman
Wright(Atkinson McCorquodale: Burke McMillan:
Calvin(Martin) Banks Watts L.Gorley P.Gorley Pattinson:
Tries - McMillan(2) P.Gorley: Goals - McCorquodale(2):
CASTLEFORD - Wraith: Claughton Joyner(Morris)
Ph.Johnson Fenton: Burton Stephens: D.Briggs(Sampson)
Tyreman Reilly Norton Orr Lloyd:
Tries - Claughton Tyreman Reilly Orr: Goals - Lloyd(4):
Referee W H Thompson (Hud'field) Att - 3250 H.T. 7 - 5

**Sun 19 Mar 1978 FEATHERSTONE ROVERS away lost
15 - 25 CHALLENGE CUP ROUND 3**
FEATHERSTONE R - Box: Coventry Evans Quinn Kellett:
Newlove Fennell Clawson Bridges Gibbins Stone Smith
Bell: Tries - Smith(2) Evans Newlove Bell: Goals - Box(5):
CASTLEFORD - Wraith(Morris): Claughton Joyner
Ph.Johnson Fenton: Burton Stephens: Sampson Tyreman
Reilly(Cookland) Norton Orr Lloyd:
Tries - Wraith Morris Johnson: Goals - Lloyd(3):
Referee S Wall (Leigh) Att - 9998 H.T. 5 - 5
**THE MATCH WAS CASTLEFORD'S FOURTH
CHALLENGE CUP TIE IN EIGHT DAYS**

Fri 24 Mar 1978 DEWSBURY away lost 5 - 23
DEWSBURY- Richardson: Mitchell Brunyee Simpson Agar:
Ferres Thornton Artis Price Hankins Grayshon
Whittington(Craven) Welsh: Tries - Mitchell Agar Artis
Hankins: Goals - Ferres(4) (DG) Artis:
CASTLEFORD - Claughton: Morris Burton Johnson(Kain)
Fenton: Pickerill Stephens: Sampson Tyreman Cookland
Orr Lloyd(D.Briggs) Norton: Try - Burton: Goal - Burton:
Referee P A Massey (Salford) Att - 1400 H.T. nil - 18

**Mon 27 Mar FEATHERSTONE ROVERS away
won 32 - 15**
FEATHERSTONE R - Robinson: Tune Busfield Hobbs
Tennant: R.Tuffs(Barker) Butler: Townend Noon(Tingle)
Sharpe Anderson Spells Limb:
Tries - Busfield Hobbs Tuffs: Goals - Hobbs(3):
CASTLEFORD - Claughton(Reilly): Richardson Burton(Kain)
Fenton Morris: Pickerill Stephens: D.Briggs Hardy
Sampson Orr Reilly(Cookland) Norton:
Tries - Richardson(3) Fenton(3) Burton Kain:
Goals - Orr(3) Burton:
Referee J V Moss (Manchester) Att - 4128 H.T. 19 - 5

SEASON 1977-78

Thu 30 Mar 1978 WARRINGTON away lost nil - 39
WARRINGTON - Finnigan: Hesford Benyon Wilson Bevan:
Kelly Gordon: Lester Dalgreen(Case) Whittaker Nartyn
Philbin Potter(Gwilliam): Tries - Wilson(2) Kelly(2)
Finnigan Benyon Bevan: Goals - Hesford(9):
CASTLEFORD - Morris: Richardson Burton Ph.Johnson
Kain: <u>Clive Pickerill</u> Stephens: D.Briggs Tyreman Sampson
Orr Reilly Norton (Hardy):
Referee G Kershaw (Easingwold) Att - 3771 H.T. nil - 17

Sun 2 Apr 1978 SALFORD home lost 14 - 22
CASTLEFORD - Wraith: Claughton Fenton Ph.Johnson
Morris: Burton Stephens: D.Briggs Tyreman Sampson
<u>Peter Cookland</u>(Norton) Norton(Huddlestone)
<u>Geoffrey(Sammy)Lloyd</u>:
Tries - Burton Stephens: Goals - Lloyd(4):
SALFORD - Bailey: Fielding Watkins
Turnbull(Mayor)Richards: Butler Harris: Grice Evans
Henney Irving Dixon Knighton: Tries - Richards(2)
Fielding Watkins Knighton: Goals - Watkins(3) (DG):
Referee A E Fryer (Warrington) Att - 3728 H.T. 7 - 13

Wed 5 Apr 1978 WIDNES home lost 9 - 27
CASTLEFORD - Wraith: Claughton Morris Ph.Johnson
Fenton: Burton Stephens: D.Briggs Tyreman
Sampson(Woodall) Norton Huddlestone Reilly:
Tries - Claughton Fenton Tyreman:
WIDNES - Eckersley: Wright Aspey George(Moran)
O'Neill: Gill Bowden: Ramset(Dearden) Elwell Mills Shaw
Hull Adams: Tries - Adams(3) Wright George O'Neill
Shaw: Goals - Eckersley(3):
Referee S Wall (Leigh) Att - 4468 H.T. 3 - 14

Fri 14 Apr 1978 WIGAN home won 34 - 10
CASTLEFORD - Wraith: Claughton Joyner(Morris)
Ph.Johnson Fenton: Burton Stephens: D.Briggs
Tyreman(Woodall) Sampson Huddlestone Norton Reilly:
Tries - Burton(4) Wraith Morris Johnson Stephens:
Goals Burton(5):
WIGAN - Fairbairn: Vigo Willicombe Hornby(Swann)
Ramsdale: Kieron.O'Loughlin Walsh: Woods
Clarke(O'Neill) Reagan Foran Melling Hollingsworth:
Tries - O'Neill Reagan: Goals - Fairbairn(2):
Referee P A Massey (Salford) Att - 3633 H.T. 24 - nil

Mon 17 Apr 1978 LEEDS home won 36 - 25
CASTLEFORD - Wraith: Claughton(Woodall) Joyner
Ph.Johnson(Morris) Fenton: Burton Stephens: D.Briggs
Hardy Sampson Huddlestone Norton Reilly:
Tries - Joyner(2) Burton(2) Huddlestone(2) Stephens
Norton: Goals - Burton(5) Norton:
LEEDS - Oulton: D.Smith Gibson Dyl(Wilby) Murrell:
Holmes Sanderson: Harrison Ward Pitchford
Eccles(Heron) Fearnley Crane:
Tries - Holmes Ward Pitchford Heron Crane:
Goals - Gibson(4) Oulton:
Referee H G Hunt (Cheshire) Att - 5393 H.T. 20 - 5

Wed 19 Apr 1978 HULL KINGSTON ROVERS away lost 3 - 27
HULL K R - Tyrer(Agar): Youngman Smith Watson
Sullivan: Hartley Millward: Millington Watkinson(Heslop)
Lockwood Hughes Rose Casey:
Tries - Hartley(2) Sullivan Millward Casey:
Goals - Tyrer(4) Millward(2):
CASTLEFORD - Wraith: Morris Joyner Ph.Johnson Fenton:
Burton(Kain) Stephens: D.Briggs Hardy Sampson
Huddlestone(Woodall) Norton Reilly: Try - Burton:
Referee B Shooman (Leeds) Att - 3621 H.T. 3 - 11

Sun 23 Apr 1978 WAKEFIELD TRINITY away won 20 - 17
WAKEFIELD T - Sheard(A.N.Other): Riggs Brown Hughes
Fletcher: Smith Hudson(Kirkbride): Burke Handscombe
Clarkson Keith Rayne Skerrett Idle:
Tries - Riggs Fletcher Rayne: Goals - Smith(4):
CASTLEFORD - Wraith: <u>John Kain</u> Joyner Morris Fenton:
Burton Stephens: D.Briggs Hardy Woodall(GARY
ROBBINS(592)) Huddlestone Sampson Norton:
Tries - Fenton(4) Joyner Burton: Goal - Burton:
Referee A Givvons (Oldham) Att - 5326 H.T. 11 – 10

Paul Norton
D. No 588
1977-78 to 1982-83

David Sampson
D. No 590
1977-78 to 1980-81

Jimmy Crampton
D. No 591
1977-78 to 1983-84

SEASON 1977-78

D.N	PLAYER		DEBUT	L MATCH	APP	SUB	T.AP	TRI'S	G'LS	D.G	P'TS
493	BRIGGS	TREVOR		11/11/1977	5	5	10	0	0	0	0
512	REILLY	MALCOLM			36	1	37	7	0	0	21
518	SPURR	ROBERT			19	0	19	1	0	0	3
525	STEPHENS	GARY			33	1	34	7	0	0	21
526	JOHNSON	PHILIP			42	0	42	13	0	0	39
532	LLOYD	GEOFFREY (SAMMY)		02/04/1978	32	0	32	0	102	2	206
537	NEWTON	RAY		05/10/1977	3	1	4	1	0	0	3
542	DICKINSON	ALAN			7	0	7	0	0	0	0
544	CLAUGHTON	GEORGE			22	1	23	7	0	0	21
548	WOODALL	DEREK			11	9	20	0	0	0	0
551	JOYNER	JOHN			33	0	33	15	0	0	45
552	HUDDLESTONE	JAMES (SID)			18	4	22	4	0	0	12
556	RICHARDSON	TERRY			28	0	28	16	0	0	48
560	FENTON	STEVE			41	0	41	29	0	0	87
563	WALSH	JAMIE			1	0	1	0	0	0	0
565	MORRIS	GEOFF			7	8	15	2	0	0	6
567	TYREMAN	GRAHAM			18	5	23	3	0	0	9
568	HARDY	ALAN			9	6	15	0	0	0	0
570	COOKLAND	PETER		02/04/1978	12	2	14	2	0	0	6
571	FISHER	TONY		11/12/1977	15	0	15	0	0	0	0
572	WRAITH	GEOFFREY			35	2	37	2	0	0	6
574	PICKERILL	CLIVE		30/03/1978	11	0	11	1	0	0	3
577	BURTON	BRUCE			45	0	45	27	30	1	142
578	ORR	PAUL			21	1	22	3	8	0	25
582	KAIN	JOHN		23/04/1978	6	6	12	1	0	0	3
583	OULTON	ARTHUR		21/08/1977	1	0	1	0	0	0	0
584	BURKE	JOHN		11/09/1977	4	0	4	1	0	0	3
585	WESTON	ALF		11/12/1977	16	2	18	2	0	0	6
586	BATTYE	IAN D.(JOE)	30/09/1977		3	3	6	1	0	0	3
587	BRIGGS	DAVID	04/12/1977		16	2	18	0	0	0	0
588	NORTON	PAUL	04/12/1977		13	1	14	1	1	0	5
589	SMITH	NIGEL	18/12/1977	26/02/1978	2	0	2	0	0	0	0
590	SAMPSON	DAVID	22/01/1978		15	1	16	0	0	0	0
591	CRAMPTON	JAMES	27/01/1978		5	0	5	0	0	0	0
592	ROBBINS	GARY	23/04/1978		0	1	1	0	0	0	0
	35		7	11	585	62	647	146	141	3	723

COMPETITION		P	W	D	L	FOR	AGT
LEAGUE D 1	POSITION 10 OF 16	30	13	2	15	515	583
YORK'S CUP		4	4	0	0	66	33
F. TROPHY		3	2	0	1	29	40
RL CUP		5	2	2	1	74	76
PLAYERS NO6		2	1	0	1	32	26
VOID - WAKEFIELD		1	1	0	0	7	5
PLAYERS RECORDS		45	23	4	18	723	763

The season commenced with Hull KR and Castleford playing a memorial match for Harry Poole a former player and coach of the respective clubs.

Having previously been beaten in four Yorkshire Cup finals, this was the season when we lifted the Cup for the first time. Victories in round one away at Dewsbury 12–5; at home to York 23–17 in round two; and away at Keighley 14–4 in the semi-final. The final at Headingley against Featherstone Rovers finished in a 17–7 victory, with Bruce Burton being awarded the White Rose Man of the Match trophy.

The Challenge Cup campaign was very eventful and unique. Our first round opponent was the St Helens amateur side Pilkington Recs with the game played at Knowsley Road we just scraped a victory 23–22. The second round tie was away at Workington Town and finished in an 8 all draw, the replay at home also finished in an 8 all draw. The second replay at Central Park Wigan finished 20–13 in our favour. The third round tie at Featherstone Rovers, our fourth Challenge Cup-tie in eight days proved to be a 'match too far' ending in a 25–15 defeat.

Steve Fenton became the third Castleford player to score five tries in a match verses Dewsbury on 27 January 1978.

SEASON 1978-79

In the League Leigh, Barrow Rochdale Hornets Huddersfield were promoted to Division 1. Hull New Hunslet Bramley Dewsbury were relegated to Division 2.

Sun 13 Aug 1978 FEATHERSTONE ROVERS home draw 26 - 26 CHARITY MATCH FRIENDLY
CASTLEFORD - Wraith: Richardson Kain Ph.Johnson Fenton: Burton Walsh: Briggs Tyreman Sampson Huddlestone Crampton Norton:
Subs used - Claughton Morris J.Battye Spurr Woodall Orr Cookland Beardmore C.Battye:
Tries - Richardson Burton Claughton Orr Beardmore:
Goals - Norton(4) Orr Sampson(DG):
FEATHERSTONE R - Box: Coventry R.Tuffs Gilbert Quinn: N.Tuffs Fennell: Townend Tingle Spells Jarvis Bell Smith: Subs used - Robinson Marsden Hobbs Barker Anderson Clawson Noon Vickers Tennant Limb Tune:
Tries - R.Tuffs Quinn N.Tuffs Smith Robinson Noon:
Goals - Quinn(4):
Referee R Moore (Wakefield) Att - 1670 H.T. 11 - 15

Sun 20 Aug 1978 DEWSBURY home won 18 - 11 YORKSHIRE CUP ROUND 1
CASTLEFORD - Wraith: Claughton Joyner Ph.Johnson Fenton: Burton Stephens: Briggs Tyreman(Spurr) Hardy Crampton Huddlestone Norton: Tries - Wraith Johnson Burton Crampton: Goals - Norton(3):
DEWSBURY - Brunyee: Mitchell Simpson Stephenson Brunt: Ferres Richardson(Clarke): Weavill Price Whittington Fowler Grayshon Welsh:
Try - Ferres Goals - Stephenson(4):
Referee S Wall (Leigh) Att - 3016 H.T. 10 - 2

Sun 27 Aug 1978 HALIFAX away lost 8 - 20 YORKSHIRE CUP ROUND 2
HALIFAX - Birts: Howard Snee Garrod Cholmondeley: Blacker Langton: Grinhaff P.Martin Wood Scott(Davies) J.Martin Loxton:
Tries - Langton Scott Loxton: Goals - Birts(5) Scott(DG):
CASTLEFORD - Wraith: Richardson Joyner Ph.Johnson Fenton: Burton Stephens: David Briggs(S/O) Tyreman Hardy Crampton Orr(Huddlestone)Norton:
Tries - Richardson Burton: Goal - Norton:
Referee M Naughton (Widnes) Att - 2289 H.T. 5 - 15

Sun 3 Sep 1978 WAKEFIELD TRINITY away lost 11 - 20
WAKEFIELD T - Midgeley: A.N.Other Smith S.O.Else Juliff: Topliss Hudson(Sutcliffe): Ballantyne Handscombe Kirkbride(Keith Rayne)Ashurst Skerrett Idle:
Tries - Juliff(2) Hudson S.O.Else: Goals - Smith(4):
CASTLEFORD - Wraith: Richardson Joyner Ph.Johnson(Claughton)Fenton: Burton Stephens: Battye(Kear) Spurr BARRY KEAR(593)(Woodall) Huddlestone Norton TONY HALMSHAW(594):
Tries - Wraith Richardson Joyner: Goal - Norton:
Referee J McDonald (Wigan) Att - 5154 H.T. 5 - 7

Sun 10 Sep 1978 WORKINGTON TOWN home won 12 - 7
CASTLEFORD - Wraith: Richardson Joyner Ph.Johnson Fenton: Burton Stephens: Battye(Claughton) Spurr Kear(Halmshaw) Huddlestone Norton Halmshaw(Crampton):
Tries - Joyner Stephens: Goals - Norton(3):
WORKINGTON T - Charlton: Collister Wilkins Risman McCorquodale: McMillan Walker: Beverley Banks Bowman Hartley(Blackwood) P.Gorley Pattinson:
Try - Collister: Goals - McCorquodale(2):
Referee R Campbell (Widnes) Att - 2947 H.T. 10 - 3

Sun 17 Sep 1978 BRADFORD NORTHERN away won 31 - 19
BRADFORD N - Mumby: Barends D.Redfearn Parker Gant: Wolford A.Redfearn (Slater): Van Bellen Fisher Fox Starbuck(Dyson) Trotter Haigh: Tries - Haigh(2) D.Redfearn Wolford: Goals - Fox(3) A.Redfearn(DG):
CASTLEFORD - Wraith: Richardson Joyner Ph.Johnson Fenton: Burton Stephens: GEORGE BALLANTYNE(595) Spurr Kear Crampton Norton Halmshaw:
Tries - Joyner(2) Richardson Fenton Burton Stephens Crampton: Goals - Norton(5):
Referee M Naughton (Widnes) Att - 5871 H.T. 7 - 11

Fri 22 Sep 1978 SWINTON home won 18 - 10 JOHN PLAYER COMPETITION ROUND 1
CASTLEFORD - Wraith: Richardson Joyner Ph.Johnson Fenton (Claughton): Burton(Huddlestone) Stephens: Ballantyne Spurr Kear Crampton Norton Halmshaw:
Tries - Stephens(2) Joyner Johnson: Goals - Norton(3):
SWINTON - Johns(Gorton): Potts Cooke Kevin.O'Loughlin Davies: Crehan Bolton: Ashcroft(Phythian) Jolly Doran Earl Highton Peters:
Tries - O'Loughlin Crehan: Goals - Johns(2):
Referee K Spencer (Warrington) Att - 3221 H.T. 8 - 10

Tue 26 Sep 1978 WAKEFIELD TRINITY home won 20 - 11 BBC 2 FLOODLIT COMPETITION ROUND 1
CASTLEFORD - Wraith: Richardson Joyner(Walsh) Norton Claughton: Ph.Johnson Stephens: Ballantyne Spurr Kear Crampton Huddlestone Halmshaw(Orr):
Tries - Joyner(2) Wraith Richardson: Goals - Norton(4):
WAKEFIELD T - McDermott: Barwood Smith Hughes Juliffe: Topliss Lampkowski(Midgeley): Burke McCurrie Bratt(Kirkbride) Keith Rayne Skerrett Idle:
Tries - Juliffe(2): Goals - Smith(2) Topliss(DG):
Referee J Jackson (Pudsey) Att - 5046 H.T. 7 - 9

Sun 1 Oct 1978 ST HELENS away lost 14 - 48
ST HELENS - Pimblett: Jones Glynn Cunningham Mathias: Francis (Holding) Gwilliam: D.Chisnall Liptrot James Karalius Knighton(Noonan) Pinner:
Tries - Glynn(3) Noonan(2) Cunningham Holding James Knighton Pinner: Goals - Pimblett(9):
CASTLEFORD - Wraith(JOHN KEAR(596)): Richardson Walsh Ph.Johnson Claughton (PETER TAYLOR(597)): Morris Stephens: Ballantyne Spurr B.Kear(Wraith) Crampton Huddlestone Norton:

298

Tries - Richardson(2) Taylor:
Goals - Norton(2) Stephens(DG):
Referee T J Court (Leeds) Att - 6016 H.T. 6 - 15

Fri 6 Oct 1978 HUDDERSFIELD home won 17 - 9
CASTLEFORD - Claughton: Richardson Joyner Ph.Johnson
Walsh(BARRY HIGGINS(598)): Morris Stephens: Ballantyne
Spurr Woodall Crampton Huddleston(Taylor) Norton:
Tries - Johnson Higgins Ballantyne: Goals - Norton(4):
HUDDERSFIELD - Rushton: Cramp Leathley Mullaney
Senior: Knight Shepherd: Hepplestone Wroe Lyons Burton
Johnson(Hobson) Branch: Tries - Cramp(2) Knight:
Referee A E Fryer (Warrington) Att - 3407 H.T. 7 - 6

Sat 14 Oct 1978 LEEDS away lost 12 - 19
LEEDS - Oulton: A.Smith Hague Holmes Atkinson:
Sanderson Dick: Dickinson Ward Pitchford Adams
Cookson(Eccles) Crane: Tries - Smith Hague Holmes
Adams: Goals - Oulton(3) Ward(DG):
CASTLEFORD - Wraith: Higgins Joyner Ph.Johnson
Claughton: Burton Stephens: Ballantyne Spurr Woodall
Crampton Norton Halmshaw(Huddleston):
Tries - Wraith Stephens: Goals - Norton(3):
Referee J V Moss (Manchester) Att - 6360 H.T.12 - 13

Fri 20 Oct 1978 WIDNES home won 15 - 12
CASTLEFORD - Wraith: Richardson Joyner Ph.Johnson
Claughton: Burton Stephens: Battye Spurr Woodall
Crampton(Huddleston)Huddleston(Taylor) Norton:
Tries - Joyner Spurr Crampton: Goals - Norton(3):
WIDNES - Eckersley: Bentley Aspey George Burke: Moran
Bowden: Mills(Shaw) Elwell(Burke) Hogan(Mills) Adams
Hull Laughton: Tries - Burke Mills: Goals - Burke(3):
Referee P A Massey (Salford) Att - 3670 H.T. 10 - 7

Sun 29 Oct 1978 WARRINGTON away lost 13 - 24
WARRINGTON - Ganley: Kelly Hesford Benyon Benan:
Clarke(Gwilliam)Gordon: Lester Cunningham Whittaker
Martin Case(Hunter) Potter: Tries - Bevan(3) Ganley
Whittaker: Goals - Hesford(4) (DG):
CASTLEFORD - Wraith: Richardson Joyner Ph.Johnson
Claughton: Burton(Higgins) Stephens: Battye(Ballantyne)
Spurr Woodall Huddleston Taylor Norton:
Tries - Richardson Johnson Stephens: Goals - Norton(2):
Referee W H Thompson(Hud'field) Att - 5726 H.T. 3 - 14

Fri 3 Nov 1978 ROCHDALE HORNETS home
won 15 - 14
CASTLEFORD - Wraith: Richardson Higgins Ph.Johnson
Claughton: Morris Stephens: Battye(Huddleston) Spurr
Woodall Orr Crampton Norton:
Tries - Richardson Claughton Morris: Goals - Norton(3):
ROCHDALE H - Prime: Holland McGiffen Wainwright
Marsh(McLoughlin): Ayres Woods: Hodkinson Langan
Cook Jones(Gourley) Coslett Birdsall:
Tries - Holland(2) Ayres: Goals - Woods(2) (DG):
Referee G Hartley (Australia) Att - 3269 H.T. 5 - 9

Tuesday 7 Nov 1978 ST HELENS away lost 5 – 47
BBC 2 FLOODLIT COMPETITION ROUND 2
ST HELENS - Pimblett: Jones Glynn Francis Mathias:
Holding Gwilliam James Liptrot Hope(Smith)
Nicholls(Arkwright) Knighton Pinner:
Tries - Glynn(3) Francis(3) Jones Mathias Gwilliam James
Hope: Goals - Pimblett(7):
CASTLEFORD - Wraith: Richardson Joyner Ph.Johnson
(Higgins) Claughton: Morris Stephens: Ballantyne
Spurr(Tyreman) Woodall Orr Huddleston Norton:
Try - Ballantyne: Goal - Norton:
Referee T Beaumont (Hud'field) Att - 4247 H.T. nil - 23

Sun 12 Nov 1978 LEIGH away lost 11 - 15
LEIGH - Hogan: Stacey Prescott(Brown) Woods Garrity:
Donlan McAtee: Wilkinson Taylor Fiddler Rowley Daley
Platt: Tries - Garrity Donlan Taylor:
Goals - Woods(2)Donlan(DG) Platt(DG):
CASTLEFORD - Wraith: Richardson Joyner Ph.Johnson
DAVID FINCH(599): Morris Stephens: GARY PYE(600)
(Pe.Johnson) Spurr Woodall Orr(Claughton) Reilly Norton:
Tries - Richardson(2) Ph.Johnson: Goal - Norton:
Referee R Moore (Wakefield) Att - 2500 H.T. 8 - 9

Sun 19 Nov 1978 HUDDERSFIELD away won 22 - 10
HUDDERSFIELD - Rushton: Hooson Leathley Pritchard
Senior: Knight(Ward) Bates: Wilson Schofield Hepplestone
Hobson(Johnson) Rowe Branch:
Tries - Hooson Branch: Goals - Wilson(2):
CASTLEFORD - Wraith: Richardson GARY HYDE(601)
Ph.Johnson Claughton: Morris Stephens: BRIAN
HUGHES(602) Spurr Woodall(Pe.Johnson) Finch
Reilly(Walsh) Norton: Tries - Hyde Ph.Johnson Morris
Stephens: Goals - Norton(5): :
Referee B Shooman (Leeds) Att - 2517 H.T. 9 - 2

Fri 24 Nov 1978 SALFORD home won 34 - 10
CASTLEFORD - Claughton: Richardson Joyner Ph.Johnson
Hyde: Burton Stephens: Hughes Spurr Woodall(Dickinson)
Finch Orr Norton: Tries - Hyde(2) Joyner Burton Stephens
Finch Orr: Goals - Norton(6) Burton(DG):
SALFORD - Steed: Fielding Butler Hesketh(Turnbull)
Richards: Rule Nash: Sheffield(McGreel) Ashcroft Dixon
Irving Philbin Prescott:
Tries - Fielding Richards: Goals - Rule(2):
Referee A E Fryer (Warrington) Att - 3429 H.T. 14 - 10

Sun 3 Dec 1978 WORKINGTON TOWN home
won 20 - 9 JOHN PLAYER COMPETITION ROUND 2
CASTLEFORD - Wraith: Richardson Joyner Ph.Johnson
Hyde: Burton Stephens: Alan Dickinson Spurr Woodall
Finch(Huddleston) Orr Norton:
Tries - Johnson(2) Richardson Burton: Goals - Norton(4):
WORKINGTON T - Charlton: Wright Thompson
Wilkins(Risman) McCorquodale: McMillan Walker:
Beverley P.Gorley McCarron(Verty) L.Gorley Hartley
Pattinson: Try - Wright: Goals - McCorquodale(3):
Referee P A Massey (Salford) Att - 2976 H.T. 13 - 2

Sun 10 Dec 1978 WIDNES away lost 13 - 16
WIDNES - Eckersley: Wright Hughes Aspey P.Shaw: Burke
Myler: Hogan Elwell Mills G.Shaw Dearden Adams:
Try - Wright: Goals - Burke(6) Adams(DG):
CASTLEFORD - Wraith: Richardson Joyner Ph.Johnson
Hyde: Burton Stephens: Hughes Spurr Woodall
Huddlestone(Pe.Johnson) Orr Norton:
Tries - Richardson(2) Stephens: Goals - Norton(2):
Referee T J Court (Leeds) Att - 6526 H.T. 13 - 9

**Sun 17 Dec 1978 HULL KINGSTON ROVERS away
lost 10 - 23 JOHN PLAYER COMPETITION ROUND 3**
HULL K R - Hall: Youngman Smith Hartley Sullivan:
Millward Agar: Millington Watkinson Lockwood Lowe
Rose Hughes: Tries - Sullivan Millward Agar Watkinson
Lockwood: Goals - Millward(4):
CASTLEFORD - Wraith: Richardson Joyner Ph.Johnson
Hyde: Burton Stephens: Hughes Spurr Woodall
Finch(Claughton) Orr Norton(Huddlestone):
Tries - Hyde Finch: Goals - Orr(2):
Referee R Campbell (Widnes) Att - 6586 H.T. 10 - 7

**Tue 26 Dec 1978 FEATHERSTONE ROVERS away
won 14 - 10**
FEATHERSTONE R - Box: Gilbert Coventry Marsden
Kellett(S/O): Evans Fennell(R.Tuffs): Anderson
Handscombe Morgan Vickers Jarvis(N.Tuffs) Bell:
Tries - Evans Bell: Goals - Box(2):
CASTLEFORD - Wraith: Richardson Joyner Hyde(Walsh)
Claughton: Burton Stephens: Hughes Spurr(Peter
Johnson) Woodall Finch Reilly(S/O) Orr:
Tries - Finch(2) Stephens Pe.Johnson: Goal - Finch:
Referee J McDonald (Wigan) Att - 4409 H.T. 6 - nil

Tue 23 Jan 1979 WIGAN away won 13 - nil
WIGAN - Fairbairn: Ramsdale Butler Greenall Hornby:
O'Loughlin Bolton: Breheny(Regan) Karalius O'Neill
Melling Foran Boyd:
CASTLEFORD - Wraith: Richardson Joyner(Claughton)
Johnson Fenton(Halmshaw): Burton Stephens: Hughes
Spurr Woodall Finch Reilly Orr:
Tries - Finch(2) Burton: Goals - Orr(2):
Referee G F Lindop (Wakefield) Att - 3300 H.T. 13 - nil

**Sun 11 Feb 1979 WARRINGTON away won 15 - 9
CHALLENGE CUP ROUND 1**
WARRINGTON - Finnegan: Clarke Hesford Benyon Bevan:
Kelly Gordon: Lester Cunningham Eccles Martyn Case
Peers(Hunter): Try - Benyon: Goals - Hesford(3):
CASTLEFORD - Wraith: Claughton Joyner Johnson Fenton:
Burton Stephens: Hughes Spurr Woodall Finch Reilly Orr:
Tries - Wraith(2) Claughton: Goals - Orr(3):
Referee W H Thompson (Hud'field) Att - 6500 H.T. nil -4

**Sun 18 Feb 1979 HULL KINGSTON ROVERS away
lost 13 - 19**
HULL K R - Hall: Youngman Smith Hartley Sullivan:
Millward Agar(Harkin): Clarkson Watkinson Lockwood
Lowe Rose Hogan: Tries - Hogan(2) Hall Sullivan
Millward: Goals - Millward(2):

CASTLEFORD - Wraith: Richardson Joyner Johnson
Fenton: Burton Stephens: Ballantyne Hughes Woodall
Finch Reilly(Halmshaw) Orr:
Tries - Joyner Fenton Stephens: Goals - Orr(2):
Referee D G Kershaw (York) Att - 6400 H.T. 3 - 10

Fri 23 Feb 1979 ST HELENS home draw 13 - 13
CASTLEFORD - Wraith: Richardson Joyner Hyde Fenton:
Johnson Stephens: Hughes Tyreman Woodall Crampton
Halmshaw Orr:
Tries - Hyde Stephens Crampton: Goals - Orr(2):
ST HELENS - Pimblett: Jones Noonan Cunningham
Mathias: Glynn(Parkes) Gwilliam: Hope Liptrot James
Pickavance(Arkwright) Knighton Pinner:
Tries - Cunningham Parkes: Goals - Pimblett(3) (DG):
Referee K Allatt (Southport) Att - 3642 H.T. nil - 3

**Sun 4 Mar 1979 DEWSBURY home won 31 - 15
CHALLENGE CUP ROUND 2**
CASTLEFORD - Wraith: Richardson Joyner(Claughton)
Johnson Fenton: Burton Stephens: Hughes Spurr Woodall
Finch Reilly(Crampton) Orr: Tries - Wraith Richardson
Fenton Burton Stephens Spurr Finch: Goals - Orr(5):
DEWSBURY - Richardson: Agar Austin Simpson Mitchell:
Hegerty(S/O) Lee: Weavill Roberts Johnson(S/O) Hankin
Craven(Wood) Artis(Fowler):
Tries - Austin Fowler: Goals - Agar(2) Artis(2) (DG):
Referee H G Hunt (Cheshire) Att - 5573 H.T. 15 - 10

**Sat 10 Mar 1979 ST HELENS home lost 6 - 10
CHALLENGE CUP ROUND 3**
CASTLEFORD - Wraith: Richardson Joyner Johnson
Fenton: Burton Stephens: Hughes Spurr Woodall
Crampton(Finch) Halmshaw Orr: Goals - Orr(3):
ST HELENS - Pimblett: Parkes Glynn Cunningham Mathias:
Francis Gwilliam: D.Chisnall Liptrot James Nicholls
E.Chisnall Pinner:
Tries - Chisnall: Goals - Pimblett(3) (DG):   :
Referee J V Moss (Manchester) Att - 7272 H.T. 2 - 10

Wed 14 Mar 1979 SALFORD away lost 5 - 16
SALFORD - Stead(McCreal): Fielding Whitfield Turnbull
Hey: Nash Harris: Lang O'Neill Grice Dixon(Coulman)
Williams Prescott:
Tries - Hey Harris O'Neill: Goals - Fielding(3) Nash(DG):
CASTLEFORD - Wraith: Claughton Joyner Hyde Fenton:
Johnson Burton: Hughes Spurr Woodall Norton
Halmshaw(KEVIN WARD(603)) Orr: Try-Joyner: Goal-Orr:
Referee J Smith (Halifax) Att - 2668 H.T. 3 - 10

Sun 25 Mar 1979 BARROW away lost 18 - 21
BARROW - Tickle: Clegg Ball French McConnell: Mason
Nulty: McCourt Allen Mantle(Flynn) Hadley Irving
Gainford:
Tries - Tickle Ball McConnell Nulty Allen: Goals - Ball(3):
CASTLEFORD - Wraith: Richardson Joyner Johnson
Fenton: Burton Walsh: Gary Robbins Tyreman(Reilly)
Woodall(Spurr) Ward Huddlestone Norton:
Tries - Johnson(2) Richardson Walsh: Goals - Norton(3):
Referee G F Lindop (Wakefield) Att - 2787 H.T. 10 - 5

SEASON 1978-79

Fri 30 Mar 1979 LEEDS home lost 10 - 34
CASTLEFORD - Wraith(S/O): Richardson(Claughton) Hyde Johnson Fenton: Burton Walsh: Battye Spurr Hughes(GARY CONNELL(604)) Finch Reilly Norton: Tries - Walsh Reilly: Goals - Norton(2): LEEDS - Hague: A.Smith Holmes Dyl(D.Smith) Atkinson: Sanderson Dick: Dickinson Ward Pitchford Joyce(Cookson) Eccles Crane: Tries - Holmes Atkinson Sanderson Dick Ward Eccles: Goals Dick(8): Referee K Allatt (Southport) Att - 4254 H.T. 10 - 7

Wed 4 Apr 1979 LEIGH home lost 13 - 26
CASTLEFORD - Wraith: Richardson Hyde Johnson Fenton: Burton Stephens (Claughton): Ian D.(Joe)Battye Tyreman Connell Finch Norton Orr: Tries - Hyde Johnson Fenton: Goals - Norton(2): LEIGH - Swann: Drummond Bilsbury Donlan(Worgan) Brown: Woods J.Taylor: Yates K.Taylor Rowley Macko Daley Platt(Bowman): Tries - Daley(2) Bilsbury Brown Platt: Goals - Woods(5) (DG): Referee J McDonald (Wigan) Att - 2645 H.T. 10 - 10

Sun 15 Apr 1979 BRADFORD NORTHERN home won 28 - 12
CASTLEFORD - Wraith: Hyde Joyner Johnson Fenton: Burton Walsh: Ballantyne Tyreman Connell Finch Reilly(Halmshaw) Norton(Claughton): Tries - Fenton(2) Burton(2) Wraith Hyde: Goals - Norton(4) Burton: BRADFORD N - Mumby: Gill Roe Gant(Okulicz) Redfearn: Ferres Roberts: Van Bellen Dyson(Casey) Thompson Grayshon Mordue Casey(Forsyth): Tries - Redfearn Forsyth: Goals - Mumby(3): Referee J V Moss (Manchester) Att - 4690 H.T. 15 - 2

Tue 17 Apr 1979 FEATHERSTONE ROVERS home won 20 - 7
CASTLEFORD - Wraith(Claughton): Hyde Joyner Johnson Fenton: Burton Walsh: Ballantyne Spurr(Tyreman) Connell Finch Reilly Norton: Tries - Reilly(2) Joyner Connell: Goals - Norton(4): FEATHERSTONE R - Box: N.Tuffs Marsden Coventry Kellett: Evans Barker (Fennell): Bence Handscombe Anderson Hobbs Smith Bell: Try - Marsden: Goals - Hobbs(2): Referee T J Court (Leeds) Att - 4688 H.T. 13 - 2

Fri 20 Apr 1979 WAKEFIELD TRINITY home won 32 - 10
CASTLEFORD - Wraith(Claughton): Hyde Joyner Johnson Fenton: Burton Walsh: Ballantyne Tyreman Connell(Spurr) Finch Reilly Norton: Tries - Finch(3) Hyde(2) Burton(2) Fenton: Goals - Norton(4): WAKEFIELD T - Plummer: Barwood Butterfield Flynn Reed: Needham Tinker: Clawson Stringer Murray Robinson Bratt Thompson(Rose): Tries - Reed Robinson: Goals - Murray(2): Referee H G Hunt (Cheshire) Att - 4003 H.T. 21 - 8

Fri 27 Apr 1979 HULL KINGSTON ROVERS home lost 20 - 34
CASTLEFORD - Claughton: Hyde Joyner Johnson Fenton(JOHN CROSSLEY Jnr(605)): Burton Walsh: Ballantyne Spurr Woodall(Tyreman) Finch Ward Norton: Tries - Burton(3) Spurr: Goals - Norton(4): HULL K R - Robinson: Hubbard Smith Hartley Sullivan: Millward(Watson)Agar: Holdstock Watkinson Lockwood Lowe Clarkson Hogan: Tries - Hartley(2) Hubbard Sullivan Agar Lockwood Lowe: Goals - Hubbard(6) Agar(DG): Referee J V Moss (Manchester) Att - 4647 H.T. 8 - 16

Tue 1 May 1979 BARROW home won 18 - 11
CASTLEFORD - Wraith: Hyde Joyner(Crossley) Johnson Fenton: Burton Walsh: Ballantyne Spurr Connell Finch(Tyreman) Orr Norton: Tries - Joyner Crossley Burton Norton: Goals - Norton(3): BARROW - Tickle Leadbetter French Ball Barton: McConnell Nulty Lupton Allen(Szymala) Flynn Hadleigh Irving Gainford: Tries - Tickle Irving: Goals - Ball(2) Allen(DG): Referee S Wall (Leigh) Att - 2695 H.T. 10 - 1

Tue 3 May 1979 ROCHDALE HORNETS away won 16 - 10
ROCHDALE H - McLoughlin: Holland McGriffin(Ayres) Fletcher Johnson: Wainwright Woods: Cooke Langan Burns Rathbone(Hodgkinson) Garside(Rathbone) Birdsall: Tries - Fletcher Cooke: Goals - Woods(2): CASTLEFORD - Claughton: Crossley Hyde Johnson(Walsh) Fenton: Burton Walsh(Stephens): Woodall Tyreman Connell Orr(Spurr) Reilly Norton(Orr): Tries - Hyde(2) Fenton Connell: Goals - Norton(2): Referee W Allen (Huddersfield) Att - 710 H.T. 13 - 5

Mon 7 May 1979 WARRINGTON home won 11 - 2
CASTLEFORD - Claughton: Crossley Hyde Johnson Fenton: Burton Stephens: Hughes Spurr Connell Huddlestone Finch Reilly(Tyreman): Tries - Crossley(2) Hughes: Goal - Burton: WARRINGTON - Finnigan: M.Kelly Hesford(Hunter) Benyon Sutton: K.Kelly Fairhurst: Hogan(Lester) Waller Eccles Case Martyn Gwilliam: Goal - Eccles: Referee M Naughton (Widnes) Att - 3611 H.T. 8 - 2

Fri 11 May 1979 WIGAN home won 21 - 7
CASTLEFORD - Wraith: Hyde Joyner Johnson Fenton: Burton Stephens(S/O): Ballantyne Spurr(Tyreman) Woodall Finch Connell(Crossley)Huddlestone: Tries - Joyner(3) Burton Huddlestone: Goals - Hyde(3): WIGAN - Dickinson: Bowden Foy Bolton Bates: Walsh A.N.Other: Gaskell Kiss(Lloyd) Martland(S/O) Grundy S.O.Else A.N.Extra: Try - A.N.Extra: Goals - Walsh(1) (DG) A.N.Extra(DG): Referee J V Moss (Manchester) Att - 3399 H.T. 6 - nil

301

Sun 13 May 1979 WORKINGTON TOWN away lost 13 - 14
WORKINGTON T - Charlton: Collister Thompson
Wright(Risman) McCorquodale: Rudd Walker: McCarron
Banks P.Gorley Hartley(R.Pattinson) Varty W.Pattinson:
Tries - McCarron(2):   Goals - McQuordale(4):
CASTLEFORD - Claughton: Fenton Hyde Finch Crossley:
Burton Walsh(Stephens): Ballantyne Graham Tyreman
Woodall Hardy Huddlestone(Wraith) B.Garbett:
Try - Walsh: Goals - Hyde(4) Hardy(2DG):
Referee G F Lindop (Wakefield) Att - 3226 H.T. 7 - 12

**Tue 15 May 1979 WARRINGTON away lost 10 - 17
PREMIERSHIP ROUND 1**
WARRINGTON - Finnegan(Eccles): M.Kelly Hesford
Benyon(Fairhurst) Sutton: Gwilliam Gordon: Hogan
Cunningham Nicholas Case Martyn Hunter:
Tries - Benyon Sutton Gordon: Goals - Hesford(3) (2DG):
CASTLEFORD - Wraith: Claughton John Crossley Jnr
Johnson(Walsh) Fenton: Burton Stephens: Ballantyne
Spurr Connell Finch Huddlestone (Hardy) Reilly:
Tries - Burton Ballantyne: Goals - Burton(2):
Referee W H Thompson (Hud'field) Att - 3955 H.T. 2 – 9

Barry Kear
D. No 593
1978-79 to 1981-82

George Ballantyne
D. No 595
1978-79 to 1979-80

John Kear
D. No 596
1978-79 to 1987-88

David Finch
D. No 599
1978-79 to 1984-85

Gary Hyde
D, No 601
1978-79 to 1987-88

Brian Hughes
D. No 602
1978-79 to 1980-81

Kevin Ward
D. No 603
1978-79 to 1989-90

Garry Connell
D. No 604
1978-79 to 1984-85

SEASON 1978-79

D.N	PLAYER		DEBUT	L MATCH	APP	SUB	T.AP	TRI'S	G'LS	D.G	P'TS
512	REILLY	MALCOLM			14	1	15	3	0	0	9
518	SPURR	ROBERT			31	4	35	3	0	0	9
525	STEPHENS	GARY			31	2	33	13	0	1	40
526	JOHNSON	PHILIP			39	0	39	11	0	0	33
542	DICKINSON	ALAN	03/12/1978		1	1	2	0	0	0	0
544	CLAUGHTON	GEORGE			19	12	31	2	0	0	6
548	WOODALL	DEREK			25	1	26	0	0	0	0
551	JOYNER	JOHN			32	0	32	16	0	0	48
552	HUDDLESTONE	JAMES (SID)			15	6	21	1	0	0	3
556	RICHARDSON	TERRY			27	0	27	15	0	0	45
559	GARBETT	BRIAN			1	0	1	0	0	0	0
560	FENTON	STEVE			26	0	26	8	0	0	24
563	WALSH	JAMIE			11	4	15	3	0	0	9
565	MORRIS	GEOFF			6	0	6	2	0	0	6
567	TYREMAN	GRAHAM		13/05/1979	9	6	15	0	0	0	0
568	HARDY	ALAN			3	1	4	0	0	2	2
572	WRAITH	GEOFFREY			35	1	36	8	0	0	24
577	BURTON	BRUCE			33	0	33	17	4	1	60
578	ORR	PAUL			19	1	20	1	20	0	43
579	JOHNSON	PETER		26/12/1978	0	4	4	1	0	0	3
586	BATTYE	IAN D.(JOE)		04/04/1979	7	0	7	0	0	0	0
587	BRIGGS	DAVID		27/08/1978	2	0	2	0	0	0	0
588	NORTON	PAUL			30	0	30	1	84	0	171
591	CRAMPTON	JAMES			12	2	14	4	0	0	12
592	ROBBINS	GARY		25/03/1979	1	0	1	0	0	0	0
593	KEAR	BARRY	03/09/1978		6	0	6	0	0	0	0
594	HALMSHAW	TONY	03/09/1978		9	3	12	0	0	0	0
595	BALLANTYNE	GEORGE	17/09/1978		16	1	17	3	0	0	9
596	KEAR	JOHN	01/10/1978		0	1	1	0	0	0	0
597	TAYLOR	PETER	01/10/1978		1	3	4	1	0	0	3
598	HIGGINS	BARRY	06/10/1978		2	3	5	1	0	0	3
599	FINCH	DAVID	12/11/1978		21	1	22	10	1	0	32
600	PYE	GARY	12/11/1978	12/11/1978	1	0	1	0	0	0	0
601	HYDE	GARY	19/11/1978		19	0	19	11	7	0	47
602	HUGHES	BRIAN	19/11/1978		14	0	14	1	0	0	3
603	WARD	KEVIN	14/03/1979		2	1	3	0	0	0	0
604	CONNELL	GARY	30/03/1979		9	1	10	2	0	0	6
605	CROSSLEY	JOHN Jnr.	27/04/1979	15/05/1979	4	3	7	3	0	0	9
	38			**8**	**533**	**63**	**596**	**141**	**116**	**4**	**659**

COMPETITION		P	W	D	L	FOR	AGT
LEAGUE D 1	POSITION 7 OF 16	30	16	1	13	498	469
YORK'S CUP		2		0	1	26	31
F. TROPHY		2		0	1	25	58
RL CUP		3	2	0	1	52	34
PLAYERS NO6		3	2	0	1	48	42
CHAMPIONSHIP		1	0	0	1	10	17
PLAYERS RECORDS		**41**	**22**	**1**	**18**	**659**	**651**

n The Yorkshire Cup, Floodlit Trophy and John Player Trophy, we lost in Round two. In the Challenge Cup we lost in Round three, and in the Premiership play off we lost in Round one.

A notable Debutant was Kevin Ward

In the League we finished 7th of 16.

SEASON 1979-80

In the League Hull, Hunslet (who from this season changed their name from New Hunslet) York Blackpool Borough were promoted to Division 1, Barrow, Featherstone Rovers, Rochdale Hornets and Huddersfield were relegated to Division 2.

Sun 19 Aug 1979 LEEDS away lost 14 - 26 YORKSHIRE CUP ROUND 1
LEEDS - Hague: A.Smith D.Smith Holmes(Fletcher) Atkinson: Dick Sanderson: Harrison Ward Pitchford Adams Heron(Hetherington) Cookson:
Tries D.Smith(2) A.Smith Pitchford Adams Heron: Goals - Dick(4):
CASTLEFORD - Wraith: Richardson Johnson Fenton Claughton: Burton Walsh: Ballantyne Spurr(Ward) Connell(Finch) Orr(Spurr) Reilly Norton:
Tries - Burton(2) Richardson Spurr: Goal - Norton: Referee H G Hunt (Cheshire) Att - 5780 H.T. 3 - 13

Sun 2 Sep 1979 HULL away won 20 - 11
HULL - Robinson: Bray Coupland Turner Prendiville: Newlove Pickerill: Tindall(Salmon) Wileman Farrar Lazenby Boxall Birdsall:
Tries - Prendiville Tindall Farrar: Goal - Lazenby: CASTLEFORD - Wraith: Richardson Joyner Johnson Fenton: Burton Stephens: Ballantyne Spurr Reilly Ward Orr Norton:
Tries - Joyner Fenton Burton Ward: Goals - Norton(4): Referee D G Kershaw (York) Att - 8006 H.T. 15 - 5

Wed 5 Sep 1979 WAKEFIELD TRINITY home won 22 - 12 BBC 2 FLOODLIT COMPETITION PRELIMINARY ROUND
CASTLEFORD - Wraith: Richardson Joyner Johnson Fenton: Burton Stephens(Reilly): Ballantyne Spurr Connell Ward(Finch) Orr Norton: Tries - Joyner(2) Burton(2) Richardson Spurr: Goals - Norton(2):
WAKEFIELD T - Plummer(Kelly): Sutcliffe Diamond Brown Juliffe: Needham(Flynn) Tinker: Robinson McCurrie Rose Thompson Crook McDermott:
Tries - Juliffe McCurrie: Goals - Diamond(3): Referee K Allatt (Southport) Att - 3649 H.T. 16 - nil

Fri 7 Sep 1979 BLACKPOOL BOROUGH home won 41 - 16
CASTLEFORD - Wraith: Richardson Joyner Johnson Fenton(Claughton): Burton Stephens: Ballantyne Spurr(Norton) Connell Orr Reilly Norton(Huddleston):
Tries - Joyner(2) Fenton(2) Orr(2) Claughton Connell Norton: Goals - Norton(7):
BLACKPOOL B - Morrison: Wills Holmes Heritage Oxley: Mayor Chester: Earle(Lomax) Parry Gamble Corcoran Molyneux(Bailey) Bristow:
Tries - Heritage(2) Mayor: Goals - Oxley(3) Chester(DG): Referee R Whitfield (Widnes) Att - 2543 H.T. 15 - 8

Sun 16 Sep 1979 DEWSBURY home won 15 - 12 JOHN PLAYER COMPETITION ROUND 1
CASTLEFORD - Wraith: Richardson Claughton Johnson(Huddleston) Fenton: Burton Walsh: Ballantyne

Spurr Connell Ward(Orr) Reilly Norton:
Tries - Johnson Fenton Reilly: Goals - Norton(3):
DEWSBURY - Richardson: Eastwood Austin Agar Mitchell: Woolford Lee: Rangeley Roberts Johnston(Craven) Wood Hankins Haigh:
Tries - Austin(3): Goals - Agar Woolford(DG): Referee H G Hunt (Cheshire) Att - 3310 H.T. 13 - 1

Sun 23 Sep 1979 LEIGH away lost 12 - 17
LEIGH - Grimshaw: Drummond Bilsbury Swann Bullough: Woods J.Taylor: Yates K.Taylor Cooke(Wilkinson) (Green) Daley Bowman Rathbone(S/O):
Tries - Bilsbury(2) Woods: Goals - Woods(4): CASTLEFORD - Wraith: Richardson Claughton(Orr) Hyde Fenton: Burton IAN BIRKBY(606): Ballantyne Spurr Connell Ward Reilly Norton(Huddlestone):
Tries - Burton Ward: Goals - Norton(3): Referee M Beaumont (Hud'field) Att - 3247 H.T. 12 - 2

Sat 29 Sep 1979 WIGAN home won 24 - 10 JOHN PLAYER COMPETITION ROUND 2
CASTLEFORD - Wraith: Claughton Joyner Hyde Finch: Fenton Birkby: Ballantyne Spurr Connell Ward Crampton Orr(Huddleston): Tries - Claughton Joyner Spurr Ward: Goals - Finch(5) Hyde:
WIGAN - Stockley: Farnworth Coyle Ramsdale Hornby: O'Loughlin Bolton: O'Neill Pendlebury Campbell(Clough) Woods Melling Hollingsworth (Rennox):
Tries - Hornby(2) Goals - Farnworth(2): Referee S Wall (Leigh) Att - 2503 H.T. 13 - 7

Sun 7 Oct 1979 WIDNES away lost 15 - 30
WIDNES - Burke: Wright Hughes Aspey Bentley: Moran Bowden: Hogan(Mills) Elwell Shaw(Hull) Gorley Dearden Adams:
Tries - Burke(2) Aspey(2) Hughes Adams: Goals - Burke(6): CASTLEFORD - Wraith: Claughton Joyner Hyde(Worsley) Finch: Birkby Stephens: Ballantyne Spurr Woodall Connell ANDREW TIMSON(607) Crampton:
Tries - Finch Stephens Spurr: Goals - Finch(3): Referee D W Fox (Wakefield) Att - 6758 H.T. 2 - 15

Fri 12 Oct 1979 WARRINGTON home lost 5 - 15
CASTLEFORD - Wraith: Claughton Joyner Hyde Worsley: Fenton Stephens(Birkby): Woodall Spurr Connell Finch Reilly(Ballantyne) Huddlestone: Try - Fenton: Goal - Finch:
WARRINGTON - Finnegan: Sutton Hesford Bevan M.Kelly(Fairhurst): K.Kelly Gordon: Eccles Cunningham Courtney Gwilliam Hunter Potter(Worrall):
Tries - Bevan(2) Finnegan: Goals - Hesford(3): Referee H G Hunt (Cheshire) Att - 3536 H.T. 5 - 5

Tue 16 Oct 1979 HULL KINGSTON ROVERS away lost 12 - 25 BBC 2 FLOODLIT COMPETITION ROUND 1
HULL K R - Leighton: Hubbard Hartley Watson Sullivan: Hall Agar(Millward): Holdstock(Millington) Heslop Lockwood Lowe Clarkson Hogan:
Tries - Hall(2) Lowe(2) Hubbard: Goals - Hubbard(5): CASTLEFORD - Wraith: Worsley Joyner Johnson Hyde:

Fenton(J.Kear)Birkby: Woodall Spurr Connell Finch Huddlestone(Ballantyne) Crampton:
Tries - Spurr(2): Goals - Finch(3):
Referee J V Moss (Manchester) Att - 6456 H.T. 4 - 10

Sun 21 Oct 1979 SALFORD home lost 6 - 13
JOHN PLAYER COMPETITION ROUND 3
CASTLEFORD - Wraith: Richardson Joyner Johnson Finch: Fenton(Worsley) Birkby: Woodall(Huddlestone) Spurr Connell Crampton Huddlestone(Orr) Norton:
Tres - Joyner Crampton:
SALFORD - Rule: Fielding Stephenson Wilson Richards: Gill Harris: Coulman Ashcroft Dixon(Turnbull) Williams McGreal Prescott:
Tres - Wilson Ashcroft: Goals - Rule(3) (DG):
Referee M Naughton (Widnes) Att - 5240 H.T. 3 - 3

Sun 4 Nov 1979 HULL KINGSTON ROVERS away lost 13 - 18
HULL K R - Leighton(Watson): Hubbard Smith Hartley Sullivan: Hall Agar: Holdstock Tyreman Clarkson(Millington) Lowe Lockwood Hogan: Tries - Hubbard Sullivan Agar: Goals - Hubbard(4) Agar(DG):
CASTLEFORD - Wraith(Hyde): Finch Joyner Johnson Worsley: Fenton Birkby: Hughes Spurr Reilly(Woodall) Crampton Ward Norton:
Tries - Hyde Joyner Norton: Goals - Norton(2):
Referee P A Massey (Salford) Att - 6085 H.T. 5 - 6

Fri 9 Nov 1979 HUNSLET home won 26 - 10
CASTLEFORD - Keith Worsley: Finch Joyner Johnson Hyde: Fenton Birkby: Hughes(Woodall) Spurr Reilly(Higgins) Crampton Ward Norton:
Tries - Hyde(2) Johnson Fenton Spurr Crampton:
Goals - Norton(4):
HUNSLET - Murrell: Muscroft Parrish(James) Jordan Barron: Lane(Hooker) Dean: Windmill Handforth Standidge Wright Rowe Hughes:
Tries - Lane Dean: Goals - Murrell Parrish:
Referee H G Hunt (Cheshire) Att - 2821 H.T. 15 - 5

Sun 11 Nov 1979 WIGAN away draw 10 - 10
WIGAN - Fairbairn: Clough O'Loughlin Ramsdale Hornby: Foy Bolton: Breheny Smith Campbell Melling(Greenall) O'Neill Boyd(Hollingsworth)(S/O)
Tries - Foy Bolton: Goals - Fairbairn(2):
CASTLEFORD - Claughton: Finch Joyner Johnson Hyde: Fenton Birkby: Sampson Spurr Reilly Crampton(S/O) Ward Norton: Tries - Birkby(2): Goals - Finch Norton:
Referee G F Lindop (Wakefield) Att – 3036 H.T. 10 - nil

Sun 18 Nov 1979 WORKINGTON TOWN away lost 8 - 10
WORKINGTON T - Charlton: McCorquodale Thompson Rudd Beck: Canipa Walker: Beverley Banks Rowley McCarron Bill Pattinson Dobie:
Tries - Rowley Pattinson: Goals - McCorquodale(2):
CASTLEFORD - Claughton(Hyde): Richardson Joyner Johnson Finch: Fenton ROBERT BEARDMORE(608): Sampson(Connell) Spurr Reilly Orr Ward Norton:

Tries - Fenton Orr: Goal - Norton:
Referee R Campbell (Widnes) Att - 3193 H.T. 5 - 5

Sun 25 Nov 1979 BRADFORD NORTHERN home won 11 - 6
CASTLEFORD - Claughton: Finch Joyner(Richardson) Johnson Hyde: Fenton IAN ORUM(609): Hughes Spurr Reilly Orr(Halmshaw) Ward Norton:
Tries - Joyner Ward: Goals - Norton(2) Orum(DG):
BRADFORD N - Mumby: Barends Roe(Ferres) D.Redfearn Gant(Roe): Stephenson A.Redfearn: Thompson Bridges Forsythe Grayshon Van Bellen Hale(Trotter):
Tries - Barends(2)
Referee A Givvons (Oldham) Att - 5379 H.T. 10 - nil

Sun 2 Dec 1979 ST HELENS away lost 21 - 39
ST HELENS - Griffiths: Jones Peters Arkewright(Litherland) Mathias: Glynn Holding: James(Pickavance) Liptrot D.Chisnall E.Chisnall Gorley Pinner:
Tries - Holding(3) Mathias(2) Glynn(2) Griffiths E.Chisnall: Goals - Griffiths(6):
CASTLEFORD - Claughton: Finch Joyner Johnson(Richardson) Hyde: Fenton Orum: Hughes Spurr Reilly Halmshaw(Connell) Ward Norton:
Tries - Reilly(2) Finch Hyde Orum: Goals - Norton(3):
Referee D G Kershaw (York) Att - 5613 H.T. 2 - 21

Fri 7 Dec 1979 LEIGH home won 14 - 4
CASTLEFORD - Claughton: Richardson Joyner Hyde(Higgins) Finch: Johnson Orum: Hughes Spurr Connell Ward Reilly(Norton) Norton(Crampton):
Tries - Ward(2): Goals - Norton(4):
LEIGH - Grimshaw: Drummond Bilsbury Donlan Bullough: J.Taylor Green: Yates K.Taylor Cook Daley Bowman Gittins(Tabern): Goals - Yates(2):
Referee J McDonald (Wigan) Att - 3132 H.T. 12 - 2

Sun 16 Dec 1979 YORK away won 5 - nil
YORK - G.Smith: Nicholson P.Smith Banks Lindley: Day Harkin: Wardell(Cooper) Maskill Harris White Price Adams:
CASTLEFORD - Claughton: Finch Joyner Johnson Hyde: Fenton Stephens Hughes Spurr Connell Crampton (Ballantyne) Ward Norton: Try - Finch: Goal - Norton:
Referee K Spencer (Warrington) Att - 3760 H.T. nil - nil

Fri 21 Dec 1979 WIDNES home lost 6 - 15
CASTLEFORD - Claughton: Richardson Joyner(R.Beardmore) Johnson Hyde: Fenton Stephens: Ballantyne Spurr Hughes Finch(Halmshaw) Ward Norton: Goals - Norton(3):
WIDNES - Eckersley: Wright Moran(Tyler) George Burke: Taylor Bowden: Hogan Elwell Shaw Gorley Dearden Hull(O'Neill): Tres - George Gorley:
Goals - Burke(3) Elwell(DG2) Eckersley(DG):
Referee S Wall (Leigh) Att - 3006 H.T. 4 - 8

Wed 26 Dec 1979 WAKEFIELD TRINITY home lost 13 - 26
CASTLEFORD - Claughton: Richardson Hyde Johnson

Finch: Fenton Stephens: Ballantyne Spurr Hughes(Hardy) Halmshaw Connell Norton:
Tries - Hyde Finch Hughes: Goals - Norton(2):
WAKEFIELD T - Midgley: Fletcher Smith(Guest) Diamond Juliff: Topliss Lampkowski: Bratt McCurrie Skerrett Idle(Rose) Keith Rayne McDermott:
Tries - McCurrie(2) Rayne(2):   Goals - Diamond(7):
Referee R Campbell (Wigan) Att - 5385 H.T. nil - 16

Fri 4 Jan 1980 ST HELENS home lost 7 - 23
CASTLEFORD - Wraith: Richardson J.Kear Hyde STEVEN GILL(610): Claughton Stephens: Ballantyne Spurr(R.Beardmore) Hughes Tony Halmshaw (Connell) Ward(Halmshaw) Norton:
Try - Stephens: Goals - Norton(2):
ST HELENS - Parkes: Jones(Griffiths) Peters Noonan Mathias: Glynn Holding(Seldon): James Liptrot E.Chisnall Nicholls Gorley Pinner: Tries - Griffiths(2) James(2) Parkes Jones Mathias: Goal - Pinner:
Referee J McDonald (Wigan) Att - 2815 H.T. 2 - 11

Fri 18 Jan 1980 YORK home won 33 - 23
CASTLEFORD - Wraith: Claughton Joyner Hyde Finch: Fenton(Johnson) Stephens: Ballantyne KEVIN BEARDMORE(611) Hughes(Hardy) Connell Ward Norton:
Tries - Connell(2) Joyner Fenton Stephens Ballantyne Norton: Goals - Norton(6):
YORK - Banks(Harkin): Horner P.Smith G.Smith Lindley: Day Inns: Dunkerley Maskill Harris(Price) White Rhodes Adams:
Tries - Harkin Day Maskill Price Adams: Goals - Horner(4):
Referee T Beaumont (Hud'field) Att - 3087 H.T. 21 - 5

Fri 25 Jan 1980 HULL home lost 10 - 14
CASTLEFORD - Wraith: Finch Joyner Hyde Claughton: Fenton Stephens: Ballantyne K.Beardmore Hughes Connell Ward Norton:
Tries - Joyner K Beardmore: Goals - Norton(2):
HULL - Coupland(Hepworth): Prendiville Walters Evans Bray: Newlove Pickerill: Tindall Wileman Stone Birdsall Lloyd Norton: Tries - Birdsall Lloyd: Goals - Lloyd(4):
Referee R Whitfield (Widnes) Att - 5806 H.T. 7 - 7

Fri 1 Feb 1980 SALFORD away lost 12 - 22
SALFORD - Rule: Fielding Stephenson Wh tfield(Wilson) Richards: Gill Harris: Coulman Ashcroft Gourley Dixon Williams(McGreal) Prescott:
Tries - Fielding Dixon Prescott Gourley: Goals - Rule(5):
CASTLEFORD - Wraith: J.Kear Joyner Higgins(PAUL MARTIN(612)) Claughton: Johnson Stephens: Ballantyne K.Beardmore Woodall Connell Hardy Norton:
Tries - Joyner Stephens: Goals - Norton(3):
Referee G F Lindop (Wakefield) Att - 2985 H.T. 7 - 15

Sun 10 Feb 1980 KEIGHLEY away won 21 - 5 CHALLENGE CUP ROUND 1
KEIGHLEY - Jickells: Moll Waterhouse Greenwood Rowett: Bardgett(Nicholson) Diabira: Mantle Raistrick Davies(Ellis)Farrell Clarkson Ellis(Robinson):
Try - Davies: Goal - Davies:

CASTLEFORD - Wraith: Finch Joyner Hyde Fenton: Johnson Stephens: Ballantyne Spurr Hughes(Hardy) Connell Ward Norton:
Tries - Hyde(2) Finch Fenton Ward: Goals - Norton(3):
Referee P A Massey (Salford) Att - 3600 H.T. 10 - nil

Wed 13 Feb 1980 LEEDS home won 24 - 16
CASTLEFORD - Wraith: Finch Joyner Hyde Higgins(Claughton): Fenton Stephens: Ballantyne Spurr(K.Beardmore) Hardy Connell Ward Norton:
Tries - Hyde(2) Stephens Ward: Goals - Norton(6):
LEEDS - Oulton(Hetherington): A.Smith Hague Dyl D.Smith: Holmes Sanderson: Dickinson Ward Pitchford Eccles Carroll Heron: Tries - Hague Dyl D.Smith Heron: Goals - Hetherington(2):
Referee A Givvons (Oldham) Att - 4983 H.T. 17 - 3

Sun 17 Feb 1980 WORKINGTON TOWN home won 22 - 11
CASTLEFORD - Wraith: Finch Joyner Hyde(Claughton) Fenton Johnson(Hughes) Stephens: Ballantyne Spurr Hardy Connell Ward Norton:
Tries - Finch Joyner Fenton Ward: Goals - Norton(5):
WORKINGTON T - Charlton: McCorquodale Maughan Thompson Beck: O'Loughlin Wright (Rudd): Hurst Banks McCarron(Pattinson) Hartley Pattinson(Beverley) Dobie(Wright):   Tries - Charlton Beck:
Goals - McCorquodale(2) (DG):
Referee J V Moss (Manchester) Att - 3655 H.T. 15 - 3

Sun 24 Feb 1980 HULL KINGSTON ROVERS away lost 3 – 28 CHALLENGE CUP ROUND 2
HULL K R - Leighton: Hubbard Smith Hall(Lowe) Sullivan: Hartlet Agar: Holdstock Price Lockwood(Millington) Lowe(Hogan) (S/O) Rose Casey: Tries - Hubbard(2) Leighton Hartley Holdstock Lowe: Goals - Hubbard(5):
CASTLEFORD - Wraith: Finch Joyner Hyde Higgins: Fenton(Claughton) Stephens: Ballantyne Spurr Hardy(Sampson) Connell(S/O) Ward Norton:
Try - Finch:
Referee M Naughton (Widnes) Att - 9137 H.T. nil - 5

Wed 27 Feb 1980 BRADFORD NORTHERN away lost 3 - 12
BRADFORD N - Mumby(Ferres): Barends Gant D.Redfearn Parker: Stephenson A.Redfearn: I.Van Bellen Bridges Thompson Clarkson (Proctor) G.Van Bellen Okulicz:
Tries - Gant D.Redfearn: Goals - Stephenson(3):
CASTLEFORD - Wraith: Finch(K.Beardmore) Higgins Hyde Claughton: Burton Stephens: Hughes(Orum) Spurr Sampson Connell Taylor Ward: Try - Wraith:
Referee W H Thompson (Hud'field) Att - 5486 H.T. 3 - 9

Sat 1 Mar 1980 LEEDS away lost 21 - 33
LEEDS - Hague(Sanderson): A.Smith(Fletcher) D.Smith Dyl Atkinson: Holmes Dick: Lean Hetherington Cookson Carroll Cunningham Heron:
Tries - Atkinson(3) Heron(2) Dyl Dick: Goals - Dick(6):
CASTLEFORD - Wraith: Finch Higgins(Claughton) Hyde Richardson: Burton Stephens: Derek

SEASON 1979-80

Woodall(Huddlestone) Spurr Hardy Peter Taylor Ward
Norton(Higgins):   Tries - Stephens(2) Richardson Burton
Huddlestone: Goals - Norton(2) Burton:
Referee A Givvons (Oldham) Att - 6636 H.T. 5 - 20

Sun 9 Mar 1980 HUNSLET away won 14 - 12
HUNSLET - Murrell: Muscroft Parrish Smith Siulepa: Lane
Dean: Windmill Handforth(Marsden) Sykes(James)
Griffiths Rowe Hughes:
Tries - Lane Hughes: Goals - Parrish(3):
CASTLEFORD - Wraith(Orum): Richardson Joyner Hyde
Higgins: Claughton Stephens: Ballantyne Spurr
Hardy(Sampson) Connell Finch Huddlestone:
Tries - Richardson Hardy: Goals - Finch(4):
Referee C Hodgson (Maryport) Att - 1426 H.T. 2 - 10

Fri 14 Mar 1980 SALFORD home lost 8 - 20
CASTLEFORD - Claughton: Gill Higgins Finch J.Kear: Orum
Stephens(R.Beardmore): Ballantyne Spurr
Sampson(BARRY JOHNSON(613)) Connell Hardy Ward:
Tries - Gill Ward: Goal - Finch:
SALFORD - Rule: Fielding Stephenson Wilson Richards:
Gill Nash: Coulman(Latham) Ashcroft Gourley McGreal
Henney Prescott:
Tries - Rule Richards Henney Prescott: Goals - Rule(4):
Referee J E Smith (Halifax) Att - 3069 H.T. nil - 18

Sun 23 Mar 1980 WARRINGTON away draw 14 - 14
WARRINGTON - Finnegan: M.Kelly Hesford Bevan Sutton:
K.Kelly Gordon: Courtney Waller Whittaker Case Martyn
Hunter(Eccles): Try - K Kelly: Goals - Hesford(5) (DG):
CASTLEFORD - Claughton: Gill Finch Higgins J.Kear:
Joyner Stephens: Ballantyne Spurr Hardy Connell Ward
(Sampson) Reilly: Tries - Higgins Ward: Goals - Finch(4):
Referee D G Kershaw (York) Att - 3871 H.T. 9 - 9

**Wed 26 Mar 1980 HULL KINGSTON ROVERS home
lost 9 - 23**
CASTLEFORD - Claughton(Orum): Orum(Burton) Higgins
Finch Gill: Joyner Stephens: Ballantyne Spurr Sampson
Hardy NEIL JAMES(614) Connell (Brian Garbett):
Try - Orum: Goals - Finch(3):

HULL K R - Hall: Hubbard Smith Hartley Sullivan: Millward
Agar: Holdstock Price Millington Casey Rose(Lowe)
Hogan: Tries - Hubbard Smith Hartley Sullivan Millward:
Goals - Hubbard(4):
Referee P A Massey (Salford) Att - 3238 H.T. 4 - 8

**Sun 30 Mar 1980 BLACKPOOL BOROUGH away
won 13 - nil**
BLACKPOOL B - Risman: Saunders Mayor
Redford(Heritage) York: Fairhurst Chester:
Gamble(Bristow) Farry Lomax Milyneux Holmes Corcoran:
CASTLEFORD - Wraith: Finch Joyner Higgins Claughton:
Bruce Burton(Orum) Stephens: Ballantyne Spurr Hardy
Connell Reilly Huddlestone:
Tries - Joyner Burton Reilly: Goals - Finch(2):
Referee A Allen (York) Att - 1050 H.T. 13 - nil

**Sat 5 Apr 1980 WAKEFIELD TRINITY away
won 35 - 12**
WAKEFIELD T - Midgley: Diamond Morrell Brown(Guest)
Juliff: Tinker Lampkowski: Skerrett McCurrie Rose
Keith.Rayne(McDermott) Kevin.Rayne Idle(Keith.Rayne):
Tries - Skerrett Keith.Rayne: Goals - Diamond(3):
CASTLEFORD - Wraith: Richardson Claughton Finch
Fenton: Joyner Stephens: Ballantyne Spurr Hardy Connell
Reilly(Sampson) James(Sid)Huddlestone (Orum):
Tries - Wraith(2) Ballantyne(2) Joyner Spurr Hardy:
Goals - Finch(7):
Referee H G Hunt (Prestbury) Att - 3165 H.T. 23 - 7

Fri 11 Apr 1980 WIGAN home won 21 - 13
CASTLEFORD - Wraith: Richardson Joyner(Claughton)
Higgins Fenton: Crum Stephens: George Ballantyne Spurr
Hardy Finch Timson(James) Connell:
Tries - Wraith Stephens Finch: Goals - Finch(6):
WIGAN - Fairbairn: Williams Greenhall Ramsdale Hornby:
Foy Bolton: Breheny Kiss O'Neill Melling Campbell(
Clough) Hollingsworth: Tries - Foy: Goals - Faitbairn(5):
Referee M Naughton (Widnes) Att - 3242 H.T. 2 - 9

Ian Birkby
D. No 606
1979-80 to 1982-83

Andy Timpson
D. No 607
1979-80 to 1984-85

307

Robert Beardmore
D. No 608
1979-80 to 1988-89

Ian Orum
D. No 609
1979-80 to 1985-86

Steven Gill
D. No 610
1979-80 to 1987- 88

Kevin Beardmore
D. No 611
1979-80 to 1991-92

Barry Johnson
D, No 613
1979-80 to 1988-89

Neil James
D. No 614
1979-80 to 1984-85

SEPTRMBER 1979 JOHN PLAYER COMPETITION ROUND 2 v WIGAN HOME WON 24 – 10
Back Row - Sid Huddlestone George Ballantine Gary Connel Geoff Wraith David Finch Kevin Ward Paul Orr
Keith Worsley
Front Row – Jimmy Crampton Ian Birkby Gary Hyde John Joyner Bob Spurr Geaorge Claughton Steve Fenton

SEASON 1979-80

D.N	PLAYER		DEBUT	L MATCH	APP	SUB	T.AP	TRI'S	G'LS	D.G	P'TS
512	REILLY	MALCOLM			16	1	17	4	0	0	12
518	SPURR	ROBERT			35	0	35	8	0	0	24
525	STEPHENS	GARY			25	0	25	8	0	0	24
526	JOHNSON	PHILIP			20	1	21	2	0	0	6
541	WORSLEY	KEITH		09/11/1979	4	2	6	0	0	0	0
544	CLAUGHTON	GEORGE			25	6	31	2	0	0	6
548	WOODALL	DEREK		01/03/1980	6	2	8	0	0	0	0
551	JOYNER	JOHN			30	0	30	15	0	0	45
552	HUDDLESTONE	JAMES (SID)		05/04/1980	6	5	11	1	0	0	3
556	RICHARDSON	TERRY			16	2	18	4	0	0	12
559	GARBETT	BRIAN		26/03/1980	0	1	1	0	0	0	0
560	FENTON	STEVE			27	0	27	10	0	0	30
563	WALSH	JAMIE			2	0	2	0	0	0	0
568	HARDY	ALAN			12	3	15	2	0	0	6
572	WRAITH	GEOFFREY			26	0	26	4	0	0	12
577	BURTON	BRUCE		30/03/1980	9	1	10	8	1	0	26
578	ORR	PAUL			7	3	10	3	0	0	9
588	NORTON	PAUL			26	0	26	3	72	0	153
590	SAMPSON	DAVID			5	4	9	0	0	0	0
591	CRAMPTON	JAMES			8	1	9	2	0	0	6
594	HALMSHAW	TONY		04/01/1980	3	2	5	0	0	0	0
595	BALLANTYNE	GEORGE		11/04/1980	25	3	28	3	0	0	9
596	KEAR	JOHN			4	1	5	0	0	0	0
597	TAYLOR	PETER		01/03/1980	2	0	2	0	0	0	0
598	HIGGINS	BARRY			11	2	13	1	0	0	3
599	FINCH	DAVID			30	2	32	8	40	0	104
601	HYDE	GARY			23	2	25	9	1	0	29
602	HUGHES	BRIAN			13	1	14	1	0	0	3
603	WARD	KEVIN			25	1	26	11	0	0	33
604	CONNELL	GARY			28	3	31	3	0	0	9
606	BIRKBY	IAN	23/09/1979		8	1	9	2	0	0	6
607	TIMSON	ANDY	07/10/1979		2	0	2	0	0	0	0
608	BEARDMORE	ROBERT	18/11/1979		1	3	4	0	0	0	0
609	ORUM	IAN	25/11/1979		6	4	10	2	0	1	7
610	GILL	STEVEN	04/01/1980		4	0	4	1	0	0	3
611	BEARDMORE	KEVIN	18/01/1980		3	2	5	1	0	0	3
612	MARTIN	PAUL	01/02/1980		0	1	1	0	0	0	0
613	JOHNSON	BARRY	14/03/1980		0	1	1	0	0	0	0
614	JAMES	NEIL	26/03/1980		1	1	2	0	0	0	0
	39		**9**	**8**	**494**	**62**	**556**	**118**	**114**	**1**	**583**

COMPETITION		P	W	D	L	FOR	AGT
LEAGUE D 1	POSITION 11 OF 16	30	13	2	15	466	475
YORK'S CUP		1	0	0	1	14	26
F. TROPHY		2	1	0	1	34	37
RL CUP		2	1	0	1	24	33
PLAYERS NO6		3	2	0	1	45	35
PLAYERS RECORDS		**38**	**17**	**2**	**19**	**583**	**606**

In the Yorkshire Cup, Floodlit Trophy and the Challenge Cup we lost in Round two. We made it through to Round three in the John Player but did not qualify for the Premiership play-off.

Three notable Debutantes were the Beardmore twins Robert (Bob) and Kevin, and Barry Johnson

SEASON 1980-81

In the League Featherstone Rovers, Halifax, Oldham and Barrow were promoted to Division 1. Wigan, Hunslet, York Blackpool Borough were relegated to Division 2. A new London based club Fulham was admitted to Division 2.

Sun 17 August 1980 HALIFAX away won 18 - 8 YORKSHIRE CUP ROUND 1
HALIFAX - Birts: O'Byrne Conway Cholmondeley Waites: Blacker Langton: Laws O'Hara Garforth Sharpe Callon Scott(Halloran): Try - Langton: Goals - Birts(2) (DG):
CASTLEFORD - Wraith: Richardson Joyner Hyde Fenton: P.Johnson Stephens: Hughes(S/O) Spurr Connell Crampton Reilly Orr(James): Tries - Richardson Fenton Johnson Reilly: Goals - Hyde(2) Reilly:
Referee J V Moss (Manchester) Att - 2926 H.T. 3 - 1

Sun 24 August 1980 BRAMLEY home won 26 - 25 YORKSHIRE CUP ROUND 2
CASTLEFORD - Wraith: Richardson Joyner Hyde Fenton P.Johnson Stephens: Hughes Spurr Connell Ward Reilly Crampton: Tries - Stephens(2) Wraith Richardson Johnson Reilly: Goals Hyde(4):
BRAMLEY - Bibb: Dyas Nicholson Olbison Pieniazek: Ayres Langton(Winterbottom): Grinoff Sowden Bowman(Sampson) Knowles Ackroyd Bond:
Tries - Bibb Nicholson Ayres Bowman Ackroyd:
Goals - Bibb(5):
Referee J McDonald (Wigan) Att - 2173 H.T. 13 - 8

Sun 31 August 1980 OLDHAM away draw 14 - 14
OLDHAM - Murphy: Munro Hunter(Blackwood) Francis Sullivan: Ashton Gwilliam: Alexander(Herbert) O'Mahoney Lockwood Worrall Blackwood (Mordell) Flanagan:
Tries - Munro Hunter: Goals - Worrall(4):
CASTLEFORD - Wraith: Richardson Joyner Hyde(Orum) Fenton: P.JohnsonR.Beardmore: Sampson Spurr Connell James(Finch) Reilly Crampton: Tries - Richardson Connell Finch: Goals - Beardmore(2) Reilly(DG):
Referee A W Allen (York) Att - 3010 H.T. 8 - 7

Sun 7 September 1980 ST HELENS home won 22 - 21
CASTLEFORD - Wraith: Richardson Joyner Hyde Fenton(R.Beardmore): Orum Stephens: Hughes Spurr Hardy James Reilly Crampton:
Tries - Wraith Richardson Joyner Hughes: Goals - Hyde(5):
ST HELENS - Parkes: Jones Bayliss Peters Mathias: Glynn Holding: Bolton Liptrot Hope(Pinner) Pickavance Gorley Nicholls: Tries - Peters Glynn Holding: Goals - Holding(6):
Referee R Whitfield (Widnes) Att - 3268 H.T. 9 - 12

Wed 10 September 1980 HULL KINGSTON ROVERS home lost 7 – 11 YORKSHIRE CUP SEMI FINAL
CASTLEFORD - Wraith: Richardson Joyner Hyde Fenton: Orum Stephens: Sampson Spurr Hughes Hardy Connell(Timson) Crampton: Try - Spurr: Goals - Hyde(2):
HULL K R - Hall: McHugh Lowe Hogan Youngman: Hartley Harkin: Holdstock Watkinson Crooks(Robinson) Casey Rose(Millington) Crane:

Tries - Lowe Crane: Goals - Hogan(2) Harkin(DG):
Referee P A Massey (Salford) Att - 7336 H.T. 5 - 10

Sun 14 September 1980 SALFORD home won 37 - 8
CASTLEFORD - Wraith(Hyde): Richardson Joyner Hyde(R.Beardmore) Fenton: Orum Stephens: Hughes Spurr Hardy James Reilly(B.Johnson)Crampton:
Tries - Richardson(2) Beardmore(2) Wraith Joyner Hyde Fenton Crampton: Goals - Hyde(5):
SALFORD - Stead: Fielding Stephenson Whitfield Richards: Wilson Nash: Coulman O'Neill Henney Turmbull(Ashcroft) Major(Johns) Prescott:
Tries - Fielding Wilson: Goal - Whitfield:
Referee K Allatt (Southport) Att - 3063 H.T. 14 - 8

Sun 21 September 1980 WARRINGTON away lost 13 - 26
WARRINGTON - Finnegan: Thackray Duane Bevan Hesford: Kelly Gwilliam (Worrall): Courtney Waller Case Martyn Eccles)Whittaker) Hunter: Tries - Thackray(2) Bevan Hesford Eccles Hunter: oals - Hesford(4):
CASTLEFORD - Wraith: Richardson Joyner Hyde Fenton: Orum Stephens: Hughes Spurr Hardy James Reilly Crampton(Timson):
Tries - Joyner Stephens Crampton: Goals - Hyde(2):
Referee T Beaumont (Hud'field) Att - 3800 H.T. 5 - 11

Sun 28 September 1980 LEIGH away lost 18 - 22
LEIGH - Hogan: Fox Bullough(Swann) Donlan Scott: Woods Fairhurst: Cooke Tabern Hobson Daley Platt(McTighe) Gittins: Tries - Fox Woods Hobson: Goals - Fairhurst(4) Woods(DG):
CASTLEFORD - Orum: Richardson Higgins Hyde Fenton: R.Beardmore Stephens: Hughes Spurr Hardy James Ward Reilly(Finch):
Tries - Orum Fenton Spurr Ward: Goals - Hyde(3):
Referee T J Court (Leeds) Att - 3100 H.T. 13 - 9

Sun 5 October 1980 BARROW home won 23 - 18
CASTLEFORD - Wraith: Richardson(R.Beardmore) Fenton Hyde Gill: Orum Stephens: Hughes Spurr David Sampson(B.Johnson) James Finch Ward:
Tries - Hyde(3) Wraith Finch: Goals - Hyde(4):
BARROW - Tickle: Moore French Ball Camilleri: A.N.Other(Mason) Cairns(A.N.Other): Chisnall Allan Lupton Irving Flynn Mossop(Szymala):
Tries - Tickle Ball Mason Chisnall: Goals - Ball(3):
Referee S Wall (Leigh) Att - 2431 H.T. 12 - 5

Wed 8 October 1980 LEEDS away won 34 - 9
LEEDS - Oulton: A.Smith Hague Dyl D.Smith: Holmes Dick(Massa): Harrison Hetherington Rayne(Fletcher) Heron Lucas Carroll: Tries - A.Smith Hague Lucas:
CASTLEFORD - Wraith: Orum Joyner Hyde(Morris) Fenton: R.Beardmore Stephens: Hughes Spurr Reilly(B.Johnson) James Finch Ward:
Tries - Joyner Hyde Reilly James Finch Ward:
Goals - Hyde(7) Beardmore:
Referee R Campbell (Widnes) Att - 4287 H.T. 6 – 9

Sun 12 October 1980 FEATHERSTONE ROVERS away won 27 - 26

FEATHERSTONE R - Marsden: Quinn Coventry Gilbert Kellett: Evans(Hobbs) Hudson: Anderson Handscombe Morgan(Bell)Hankins Smith Hobbs(Jarvis):
Tries - Smith(2) Marsden Kellett: Goals - Quinn(7):
CASTLEFORD - Wraith: Richardson Joyner Hyde Fenton: R.Beardmore Stephens: Hughes Spurr Reilly James Finch Ward: Tries – R Beardmore Reilly James Finch Ward:
Goals - Hyde(3) R Beardmore(3):
Referee G F Lindop (Wakefield) Att - 4369 H.T. 17 - 9

Sun 19 October 1980 HALIFAX home won 23 - 9

CASTLEFORD - Wraith: Richardson Fenton Hyde Orum: R.Beardmore Gary Stephens(Joyner): Hughes Spurr B..ohnson(Reilly) James Finch Ward:
Tries - Fenton(2) Richardson Hyde R Beardmore:
Goals - Hyde(4):
HALIFAX - Birts: Snee Hirst Waites Potts: Blacker Langton: Callon(Blair) Whitehouse Standidge Walton Scott(Beevers) Loxton: Try - Langton: Goals - Birts(3):
Referee J McDonald (Wigan) Att - 3221 H.T. 15 - 9

Sun 26 October 1980 ST HELENS away won 8 - 5

ST HELENS - Griffiths: Jones Bayliss Litherland(Hegerty) Mathias: Canning J.Smith: James Nulty(Liptrot) Owen Chisnall Hope Pinner Try - Griffiths: Goal - Griffiths
CASTLEFORD - Wraith(James): Richardson Joyner Hyde Finch: Orum R.Beardmore: Hughes Spurr Reilly A N.OTHER(615)(B.Johnson) Ward Crampton:
Tries - Hyde R Beardmore: Goal - Hyde:
Referee K Steele (New Zealand) Att - 4754 H.T. nil - 5

Sun 16 November 1980 HULL home won 30 - 15

CASTLEFORD - Wraith: Richardson Joyner Hyde Fenton: Crum R.Beardmore: Hughes Spurr Reilly Finch Ward Crampton: Tries - Hyde(2) Richardson Joyner Fenton Finch: Goals - Hyde(6):
HULL - Woods: Peacham Banks Wilby(Evans) Prendiville: Gaitley Pickerill: Skerrett Crowther Stone Lloyd Birdsall(Boxall) Norton:
Tries - Skerrett Birdsall: Goals Lloyd(4) Gaitley(DG):
Referee J V Moss (Manchester) Att - 8407 H.T. 17 - 6

Sun 23 November 1980 PILKINGTON RECS home won 30 – 17 JOHN PLAYER COMPETITION ROUND 1

CASTLEFORD - Wraith: Richardson Joyner Hyde Fenton: Orum R.Beardmore: Hughes(S/O) Spurr B.Johnson Finch Ward Crampton(James) (Reilly):   Tries – R Beardmore(2) Ward(2) Hyde Finch: Goals - Hyde(6):
PILKINGTON R - Glover: Casey Hill Fairhurst Hull: McCabe(Bolan) Simmons: Cross Gormley Lea(Williams) Whittle Manning (S/O) Wright:
Tries - McCabe Lea Whittle: Goals - Glover(4):
Referee H G Hunt (Cheshire) Att - 2682 H.T. 12 - 12

Sun 30 November 1980 WIDNES away won 15 - 13

WIDNES - Burke: Wright Foy(Taylor) George Bentley: Hughes Myler: Hogan(O'Neill) Elwell Shaw Gorley Prescott Adams:

Tries - Bentley O'Neill Adams: Goals - Burke(2):
CASTLEFORD - P.Johnson: Richardson Joyner Hyde Fenton: Orum R.Beardmore: Reilly Spurr B.Johnson James Finch(Timson) Ward:
Tries - P.Johnson Finch Ward: Goals - Hyde(3):
Referee A Givvons (Oldham) Att - 5057 H.T. 15 - 3

Sun 7 December 1980 SALFORD away won 15 - 8 JOHN PLAYER COMPETITION ROUND 2

SALFORD - Whitfield: Driver Stephenson Wilson Richards: Nash Fletcher: Coulman(Ashcroft) O'Neill Yates Henney Williams Major(Smith):
Tries - Richards O Neill: Goal - Whitfield:
CASTLEFORD - Wraith: Richardson Joyner Hyde Fenton: Orum R.Beardmore: Reilly Spurr Hardy Finch Ward Crampton: Tries - Hyde(2) Orum(2) Richardson:
Referee R Campbell (Widnes) Att - 3452 H.T. 3 - 5

Sat 13 December 1980 WIDNES home won 18 - 10 JOHN PLAYER COMPETITION ROUND 3

CASTLEFORD - Wraith(P.Johnson): Richardson Joyner Hyde Fenton: Orum R.Beardmore: Brian Hughes Spurr Reilly(B.Johnson) Finch Ward Crampton:
Tries - Richardson (2) Finch Ward: Goals - Hyde(3):
WIDNES - Burke: Wright Hughes George Bentley: Myler Gregory: Hogan(S/O) Elwell Shaw O'Neill Prescott(Smith) Adams: Tries - Wright Myler: Goals – Burke(2):
Referee W H Thompson (Hud'field) Att - 3541 H.T. 2 - 2

Sat 20 December 1980 WARRINGTON draw 5 - 5 JOHN PLAYER COMPETITION SEMI FINAL - AT CENTRAL PARK WIGAN

CASTLEFORD - Morris: Richardson Joyner P.Johnson Fenton: Orum R.Beardmore: Hardy Spurr B.Johnson Finch James(Timson) Ward: Try - B.Johnson: Goal - Finch:
WARRINGTON - Finnigan(Fairhurst): Thackray Duane Bevan Hesford: Kelly Gwilliam: Courtney Waller Case Martyn Potter Hunter(Eccles):
Try - Martyn: Goal - Hesford:
Referee G F Lindop (Wakefield) Att - 4632 H.T. nil - nil

Fri 26 December 1980 WAKEFIELD TRINITY away won 23 - 8

WAKEFIELD T - Diamond: Fletcher Day Morrell Juliff: Topliss Agar (Barwood): Bratt McCurrie Forsyth Thompson Rayne(Kelly) Lampkowski:
Tries - Juliff Topliss: Goal - Diamond:
CASTLEFORD - F.Johnson: Richardson Joyner(Morris) Hyde Fenton: Orum R.Beardmore: Hardy Spurr(K.Beardmore) B.Johnson Timson James Ward:
Tries - Richardson Hyde R.Beardmore Spurr Timson:
Goals - Hyde(4):
Referee S Wall (Leigh) Att - 6000 H.T. 15 - 5

Sun 28 December 1980 WARRINGTON lost 10 - 22 JOHN PLAYER COMPETITION SEMI FINAL REPLAY - AT HEADINGLEY LEEDS

CASTLEFORD - P.Johnson: Richardson Joyner Hyde Fenton: Orum R Beardmore: Hardy(Connell) Spurr B.Johnson James Timson Ward(Hardy):

Tries - Richardson Fenton: Goals - Hyde(2):
WARRINGTON - Hesford: Thackray Duane Bevan M.Kelly:
K.Kelly Gwilliam: Courtney Waller Case Martyn Potter
Hunter(Eccles):
Tries - K.Kelly(2) Bevan Hunter: Goals - Hesford(5):
Referee R Campbell (Widnes) Att - 9249 H.T. nil - 10

Thu 1 January 1981 BRADFORD NORTHERN home won 19 - 18

CASTLEFORD - Morris: Richardson Joyner Hyde Fenton:
Orum R.Beardmore: Hardy Spurr B.Johnson Timson
James(Orr)Crampton(Connell): Tries - Morris Richardson
Joyner Timson Crampton: Goals - Hyde(2):
BRADFORD N - Mumby: Barends Hale(Carroll) Parker
McLean: Stephenson Ferres: Thompson Noble Fiddler
Grayshon Jackson Idle:
Tries - Parker(2) Mimby Stephenson: Goals - Ferres(3):
Referee H G Hunt (Cheshire) Att - 6734 H.T. 6 - 11

Sun 4 January 1981 HALIFAX away lost 5 - 11

HALIFAX - Birts: O'Byrne Garrod Cholmondeley Waites:
Blacker Langton: Askroyd Maskill Standidge
Callon(Garbett) Walton Loxton:
Try - Waites: Goals - Birts(4):
CASTLEFORD - Morris: Richardson Joyner P.Johnson
Fenton: Orum R.Beardmore: Hardy Spurr(James)
B.Johnson Timson Orr Ward:
Try - P.Johnson: Goal - Beardmore:
Referee B Robinson (Leeds) Att - 4088 H.T. 2 - 3

Sun 11 January 1981 WORKINGTON TOWN away lost 8 - 15

WORKINGTON T - Hogg: Roper Thompson O'Loughlin
Beck: McMillan Todd: Rowley Banks McCarron
Hartley(Wallbank) Varty(Hartley) Lewis:
Tries - O'Loughlin(2) McMillan: Goals - Hogg(3):
CASTLEFORD - Morris: Richardson Joyner P.Johnson
Claughton: Orum R.Beardmore: Hardy (Timson)
K.Beardmore B.Johnson Finch Connell Orr:
Try - Richardson: Goals - R.Beardmore(2) (DG):
Referee J V Moss (Manchester) Att - 2479 H.T. 7 - 10

Sun 18 January 1981 OLDHAM home won 20 - 11

CASTLEFORD - P.Johnson: Richardson(Morris) Joyner
Hyde Fenton: Orum R.Beardmore: Hardy K.Beardmore
B.Johnson Finch Connell Ward(Orr): Tries - R.Beardmore
B.Johnson Finch Ward: Goals - Hyde(4):
OLDHAM - Murphy: Munro Parrish Caffery Sullivan:
O'Neill Ashton: Alexander O'Mahoney Owen Clarkson
Herbert(Platt) Flanagan: Tries - Munro: Goals - Parrish(4):
Referee M Beaumont (Hud'field) Att - 3988 H.T. 10 - 6

Sun 25 January 1981 WORKINGTON TOWN home draw 14 - 14

CASTLEFORD - P.Johnson: Richardson Joyner(Orr) Hyde
Fenton: Orum R.Beardmore: Hardy Spurr
B.Johnson(B.Kear) Finch Connell Ward:
Tries - Richardson(2):   Goals - Hyde(4):
WORKINGTON T - Marland: Roper Thompson O'Loughlin
Hopkins: McMillan Todd: Wallbanks Banks McCarron

Hartley Pattinson Lewis:
Try - Wallbanks Pattinson: Goals - Hopkins(4):
Referee F Robinson (Leeds) Att - 3659 H.T. 4 - 5

Sun 1 February 1981 HULL KINGSTON ROVERS home lost 8 - 14

CASTLEFORD - Morris: Richardson Joyner Hyde
Fenton(Finch): Orum R.Beardmore: B.Kear Spurr Reilly
Ward Connell Crampton:
Tries - Orum R.Beardmore: Goal - Hyde:
HULL K R - Robinson: Hubbard(Laws) Proctor Hogan
McHugh: Smith Harkin: Holdstock Watkinson Crooks
Watson Casey Hall:
Tries - Hogan Smith: Goals - Hogan(4):
Referee W H Thompson (Hud'field) Att - 7689 H.T. 2 - 9

Sun 8 February 1981 WIDNES home lost 9 - 31

CASTLEFORD - Wraith: Richardson Joyner Hyde Orum:
P.Johnson R.Beardmore: B.Kear(Timson) Spurr Reilly
Connell Ward Crampton:
Try - Johnson: Goals - Hyde(3):
WIDNES - J.Myler: Wright George Cunningham Burke:
Hughes Gregory: O'Neill Elwell(Smith) Lockwood Gorley
Prescott Adams: Tries - Wright Lockwood Prescott
Adams Gregory: Goals - Burke(8):
Referee D W Fox (Wakefield) Att - 4314 H.T. 9 - 7

Sun 15 February 1981 HUYTON home won 42 - 7 CHALLENGE CUP ROUND 1

CASTLEFORD - Wraith: Richardson Joyner(Orum) (Finch)
Hyde Fenton: P.Johnson R.Beardmore: B.Kear Spurr
B.Johnson Finch(Connell) Ward Crampton:
Tries - Richardson(3) R Beardmore(2) Ward(2) Hyde
Fenton Finch: Goals - Hyde(5) Finch:
HUYTON - Tabern: Fitzsimmons Jackson Hartley Grady:
Corwell Prescott: Fletcher Andrews Banham(O'Toole)
Middlehurst Cooper Coop(Smith):
Try - Banham: Goals - Tabern(2):
Referee J W Mean (Leyland) Att - 3015 H.T. 21 - 7

Sun 22 February 1981 SALFORD away lost 15 - 17

SALFORD - Rule: Richards Whitfield Major Rogers: Francis
Nash: Yates(Coulman) O'Neill Henney McGreal
Cross(Smith) Williams:
Tries - Richards O'Neill: Goals - Rule(5) Nash(DG):
CASTLEFORD - Wraith: Richardson P.Johnson Hyde
Morris: Orum(J.Kear)R.Beardmore: B.Kear Spurr Reilly
Finch Ward Crampton: Tries - Richardson Hyde
R.Beardmore: Goals - Hyde(2) Finch:
Referee C Hodgson (Maryport) Att - 2660 H.T. 5 - 9

Sun 1 March 1981 WIDNES away lost 5 - 7 CHALLENGE CUP ROUND 2

WIDNES - Myler: Wright George Cunningham
Burke(Bentley): Hughes(Smith) Gregory: O'Neill Elwell
Lockwood Gorley Prescott Adams:
Try - Cunningham: Goals - Myler Burke:
CASTLEFORD - Wraith: Richardson Joyner Hyde Fenton:
P.Johnson R.Beardmore: Hardy Spurr Reilly Finch Ward
Crampton:

Try - Finch: Goal - Finch:
Referee G F Lindop (Wakefield) Att - 7436 H.T. 5 - 5

Sun 8 March 1981 BARROW away won 28 - 5
BARROW - French: McConnell Ball Wainewright Camilleri:
Mason Cairns (Moore): Chisnall Allen Flynn James Kirhby
Hadley: Try - James: Goal - Ball:
CASTLEFORD - Wraith: Richardson Joyner Hyde(Morris)
Fenton: P.Johnson R.Beardmore: B.Kear Spurr B.Johnson
Finch Ward Crampton: Tries - Wraith(2) Richardson(2)
Finch Ward: Goals - Finch(5):
Referee S S Haigh (Ossett) Att - 4300 H.T. 5 - 15

Sun 15 March 1981 BRADFORD NORTHERN away lost 3 - 13
BRADFORD N - Mumby: Barends D.Redfearn Parker Gant:
Stephenson A.Redfearn: Thompson(Fiddler) Handfortyh
Jackson Grayshon Idle Hale (Trotter):
Tries - Stephenson(2) Mumby D.Redfearn:
Goal - A.Redfearn(DG):
CASTLEFORD - Wraith: Richardson Joyner Fenton Morris:
P Johnson(Orum) R.Beardmore: B.Kear(Connell) Spurr
B.Johnson Finch Ward Crampton: Try - Orum:
Referee W H Thompson (Hud'field) Att - 6254 H.T. nil -3

Sun 22 March 1981 FEATHERSTONE ROVERS home won 26 - 6
CASTLEFORD - Wraith: Richardson Joyner Hyde Fenton:
P.Johnson R.Beardmore: B.Kear Spurr B.Johnson(Hardy)
Finch Ward Crampton:
Tries - Hyde(2) Joyner R Beardmore: Goals - Finch(7):
FEATHERTSONE R - Quinn: Reed Coventry Gilbert Kellett:
Evans Hudson: (Marsden): Gibbins Handscombe
Morgan(Hobbs) Vickers Smith Bell: Goals - Quinn(3):
Referee R Whitfield (Widnes) Att - 5113 H.T. 19 - 6

Wed 25 March 1981 LEIGH home won 18 - 13
CASTLEFORD - Wraith: Richardson Joyner Hyde Fenton:
Philip Johnson R.Beardmore: B.Kear Spurr Hardy Finch
Ward(Timson) Crampton:
Tries - Joyner Hyde Spurr Finch: Goals - Finch(3):
LEIGH - Hogan: Garrity Woods Donlan Fox: Dunn
Fairhurst: Wilkinson Aspinall Cooke Daley Howarth
McTighe(Pike): Try - Donlan: Goals - Woods(5):
Referee J W Mean (Leyland) Att - 3424 H.T. 13 - 11

Sun 29 March 1981 HULL away won 23 - 16
HULL - Robinson: Scruton Walters(S/O) Banks Peacham:
Chester(Gaitley)Dean(Chester): Tindall Duke
Stone(Birdsall) Crane Lloyd Norton:
Tries - Robinson Scruton Dean Crane: Goals - Lloyd(2):
CASTLEFORD - Wraith: Richardson Joyner Hyde(S/O)
Fenton:Morris R.Beardmore: B.Kear Spurr Reilly Finch
Ward Crampton: Tries - Wraith Richardson Fenton Finch:
Goals - Finch(5) (DG):
Referee J McDonald (Wigan) Att - 11705 H.T. 5 - 11

Fri 10 April 1981 HULL KINGSTON ROVERS away lost nil - 34
HULL K R - Robinson: Hubbard Smith Hogan Muscroft:
Hartley Harkin: Millington Watkinson Crooks Lowe(Dixon)
Watson Casey(Proctor): Tries - Hubbard(3) Smith Hartley
Lowe: Goals - Hubbard(7)Harkin(DG2):
CASTLEFORD - Wraith: Richardson Joyner Finch Gill:
Morris R.Beardmore: Hardy(B.Kear) Spurr Reilly Connell
Ward Crampton:
Referee J V Moss (Manchester) Att - 8220 H.T. nil - 10

Sun 12 April 1981 LEEDS home lost 10 - 21
CASTLEFORD - Wraith: Richardson Joyner(Connell) Morris
Gill: Birkby R.Beardmore: B.Kear(Hardy) Spurr B.Johnson
Finch Ward Crampton:
Tries - Birkby R Beardmore: Goals - Finch(2):
LEEDS - Wilkinson: Naylor Hague Dyl Atkinson:
A.Mackintosh (I.Mackintosh) Dick: Harrison Ward
Cookson Eccles(Townend) Holmes Heron
Tries - Wilkinson(2) Dyl(2) Holmes:
Goals - Dick(2) I.Mackintosh:
Referee P A Massey (Salford) Att - 4655 H.T. 5 - 8

Wed 15 April 1981 WARRINGTON home won 18 - 13
CASTLEFORD - Wraith: Richardson J.Kear Morris Gill:
Birkby R.Beardmore: Hardy Spurr Connell Ward Reilly
Crampton:
Tries - Ward(2) Richardson Beardmore: Goals - Birkby(3):
WARRINGTON - Paul Ford: Phil Ford Benyon Worrell
M.Kelly: K.Kelly Gwilliam (Fairhurst): Courtney(Whittaker)
Waller Case Martyn Eccles Potter:
Tries - Phil Ford(2) Eccles: Goals - Paul Ford(2):
Referee J E Smith (Halifax) Att - 3490 H.T. 10 - 5

Mon 20 April 1981 WAKEFIELD TRINITY home won 15 - 13
CASTLEFORD - Wraith: Richardson Joyner Hyde Morris:
Birkby R.Beardmore: Hardy Spurr Connell Ward
Reilly(B.Johnson) Crampton:
Tries - Richardson Hyde Morris: Goals - Birkby(3):
WAKEFIELD T - Guest: Barwood Smith(Morrell) Diamond
Buckley: Topliss Agar: Dickinson McCurrie Cocks Rayne
Kelly Hughes:
Tries - Diamond Topliss Rayne: Goals - Diamond(2):
Referee R Campbell (Widnes) Att - 5247 H.T. 8 - 8

Sun 26 April 1981 WAKEFIELD TRINITY away won 25 - 8 PREMIERSHIP ROUND 1
WAKEFIELD T - Box: Diamond Smith Day Guest: Topliss
Agar: Bratt McCurrie Forsyth(Dickinson) Kelly Rayne
Hughes: Tries - Day Kelly: Goal - Diamond:
CASTLEFORD - Wraith: Richardson Joyner Hyde Morris:
Birkby R.Beardmore: Hardy Spurr B.Johnson Finch
Ward(Connell) Crampton: Tries - Richardson(2) Birkby R
Beardmore Finch: Goals - Finch(5):
Referee S Wall (Leigh) Att - 4403 H.T. 12 - 3

SEASON 1980-81

Sun 10 May 1981 HULL home lost 11 - 12
PREMIERSHIP SEMI FINAL
CASTLEFORD - Wraith: Richardson Joyner Morris J.Kear:
Birkby R.Beardmore: Hardy Spurr Reilly(B.Johnson) Finch
Ward Crampton:
Tries - Wraith Kear Crampton: Goal - Finch:
HULL - Woods: Peacham Elliott Wilby Prendiville: Banks
Dean(Pickerill): Tindall Wileman Stone(Birdsall) Skerrett
Crane Norton:
Tries - Elliott Banks Dean: Goals - Woods Dean(DG):
Referee W.H.Thompson (Huddersfield) Att -10400
H.T. 11 – 1

SUN 17 AUGUST 1980 YORKSHIRE CUP ROUND 1 v HALIFAX AWAY WON 18 - 8
Back Row – Jimmy Crampton Malc Reilly Geoff Wraith Brian Hughes Paul Orr Gary Connell John Joyner
Front Row – Phil Johnson Terry Richardson Gary Stephens Robert Spurr Steve Fenton Gary Hyde

SEASON 1980-81

D.N	PLAYER		DEBUT	L MATCH	APP	SUB	T.AP	TRI'S	G'LS	D.G	P'TS
512	REILLY	MALCOLM			23	2	25	4	1	1	15
518	SPURR	ROBERT			40	0	40	4	0	0	12
525	STEPHENS	GARY		19/10/1980	11	0	11	3	0	0	9
526	JOHNSON	PHILIP		25/03/1981	19	1	20	5	0	0	15
544	CLAUGHTON	GEORGE			1	0	1	0	0	0	0
551	JOYNER	JOHN			37	1	38	8	0	0	24
556	RICHARDSON	TERRY			41	0	41	28	0	0	84
560	FENTON	STEVE			32	0	32	9	0	0	27
565	MORRIS	GEOFF			14	4	18	2	0	0	6
568	HARDY	ALAN			21	2	23	0	0	0	0
572	WRAITH	GEOFFREY			31	0	31	8	0	0	24
578	ORR	PAUL			3	3	6	0	0	0	0
590	SAMPSON	DAVID		05/10/1980	3	0	3	0	0	0	0
591	CRAMPTON	JAMES			29	0	29	4	0	0	12
593	KEAR	BARRY			10	2	12	0	0	0	0
596	KEAR	JOHN			2	1	3	1	0	0	3
598	HIGGINS	BARRY			1	0	1	0	0	0	0
599	FINCH	DAVID			26	3	29	15	32	1	110
601	HYDE	GARY			34	0	34	19	87	0	231
602	HUGHES	BRIAN		13/12/1980	15	0	15	1	0	0	3
603	WARD	KEVIN			34	0	34	13	0	0	39
604	CONNELL	GARY			12	6	18	1	0	0	3
606	BIRKBY	IAN			5	0	5	2	6	0	18
607	TIMSON	ANDY			4	7	11	2	0	0	6
608	BEARDMORE	ROBERT			35	3	38	17	9	1	70
609	ORUM	IAN			25	3	28	5	0	0	15
610	GILL	STEVEN			4	0	4	0	0	0	0
611	BEARDMORE	KEVIN			2	1	3	0	0	0	0
613	JOHNSON	BARRY			17	7	24	2	0	0	6
614	JAMES	NEIL			14	4	18	2	0	0	6
615	A.N.OTHER		26/10/1980	26/10/1980	1	0	1	0	0	0	0
	31		**1**	**5**	**546**	**50**	**596**	**155**	**135**	**3**	**738**

COMPETITION		P	W	D	L	FOR	AGT
LEAGUE D 1	POSITION 5 OF 16	30	18	2	10	526	459
YORK'S CUP		3	2	0	1	51	44
RL CUP		2	1	0	1	47	14
PLAYERS NO6		5	3	1	1	78	62
CHAMPIONSHIP		2	1	0	1	36	20
PLAYERS RECORDS		**42**	**25**	**3**	**14**	**738**	**599**

In The Yorkshire Cup, John Players Trophy and the Premiership playoff we reached the semi final. However, in the Challenge Cup we were beaten in Round two.

There was only one debutant this season but this was an unknown player in the away fixture at St Helens

In he League York, Wigan, Fulham Whitehaven Were promoted to Division 1. Halifax, Salford, Workington Town Oldham Were Relegated to Division 2. Carlisle and Cardiff City being admitted to Division 2.

Sun 2 Aug 1981 HULL home lost 23 - 24
CHARITY MATCH FRIENDLY
CASTLEFORD - Wraith: Richardson Hyde Morris J.Kear: Birkby R.Beardmore: B.Kear Spurr Johnson Finch Orr Crampton: Subs used- Timson Gill Norton Williams Orum Higgins - Tries - Finch(2) Birkby Norton Higgins: Goals - Finch(3) Beardmore:
HULL - Robinson: Smith Lloyd Penrose Edwards: Prenedeville Pickerill: Tindall Duke Stone Crooks Sutton Madley: Subs used- Wileman Norton Ma linson Suddaby Waltham Tries - Lloyd(2) Smith Edwards Prendeville Pickerill: Goals - Lloyd(3):
Referee D G Kershaw (Easingwold) Att - 500 H.T. 10 - 19

Sun 9 Aug 1981 HULL KINGSTON ROVERS away lost 18 – 23 CHARITY MATCH FRIENDLY
HULL K R - Fairbairn: Dunn Smith Hogan Muscroft: Hartley Hickman: Holdstock Watkinson Crooks Watson Burton Hall: Subs used- Proctor Laws Bennett Millington Price Douglas Parker
Tries - Proctor(2) Smith Hall Laws: Goals - Fairbairn(4):
CASTLEFORD - Morris: Richardson England J.Kear Gill: Birkby R.Beardmore: B.Kear Spurr Johnson Finch Orr Crampton: Subs used - Orum Simpkin Higgins James K.Beardmore Timson Norton Tries - Gill R.Beardmore Johnson: Goals - R.Beardmore(2) Finch(2)(DG):
Referee - Att - H.T. 5 - 8

Sun 16 Aug 1981 FEATHERSTONE ROVERS home won 18 – 16 YORKSHIRE CUP ROUND 1
CASTLEFORD - Wraith(Orr): Richardson Morris Hyde J.Kear: Birkby R.Beardmore: B.Kear Spurr Johnson Finch Crampton Reilly(Timson):
Tries - Birkby(2) Richardson J.Kear: Goals - Finch(3):
FEATHERSTONE R - Barker: Reed Gilbert Quinn Kellett: Evans Butler: Siddall(Hankins) Handscombe Gibbins Smith Hobbs Bell:
Tries - Quinn Gibbins: Goals - Quinn(4) Bell(DG2):
Referee J McDonald (Wigan) Att - 3041 H.T. 8 - 8

Sun 23 Aug 1981 YORK home won 42 - 30 YORKSHIRE CUP ROUND 2
CASTLEFORD - Morris(Orum): Richardson Joyner Hyde Fenton: Birkby R.Beardmore: B.Kear Spurr Johnson Timson Ward Crampton(Reilly): Tries - Tim son(3) Hyde Fenton Birkby Spurr Ward: Goals - Birkby(9):
YORK - Midgley: Pryce Brown Foster Gibson: Smith Harkin: White K.McGuire Dunkerley(Kirkbride) Hughes Price McDermott: Tries - Pryce(2) Midgley Foster Smith McDermott: Goals - Gibson(6):
Referee R Whitfield (Widnes) Att - 3453 H.T. 14 - 9

Sun 30 Aug 1981 FEATHERSTONE ROVERS away won 21 - 18
FEATHERSTONE R - Barker: Marsh Quinn G lbert Kellett:

Hayden Butler: Siddall Handscombe Gibbins(K.Hobbs) (Hudson) D.Hobbs Smith Bell: Tries - Hayden K.Hobbs D.Hobbs: Goals - Quinn(4) Butler(DG):
CASTLEFORD - Morris: Richardson Joyner Hyde Fenton: Birkby R.Beardmore: B.Kear Spurr Johnson(Timson) Finch Ward Timson(Reilly):
Tries - Birkby Johnson Ward: Goals - Birkby(6):
Referee J McDonald (Wigan) Att - 2846 H.T. 17 - 9

Wed 2 Sep 1981 BATLEY home won 40 - 3 YORKSHIRE CUP SEMI FINAL
CASTLEFORD - Morris(Orum): Richardson Joyner Hyde Fenton: Birkby Orum(R.Beardmore): B.Kear Spurr Johnson Finch Ward(Reilly) Timson: Tries - Morris(2) Fenton(2) Richardson Joyner Hyde Birkby R Beardmore Finch: Goals - Birkby(5):
BATLEY - Storey: Tingle Shaw Presley Oulton: Briggs Pickerill: Frain Cummings Woodall Vodden(Whelan) Watts Finn: Try - Shaw:
Referee A Givvons (Oldham) Att - 3003 H.T. 18 - nil

Sun 6 Sep 1981 ST HELENS home lost 17 - 32
CASTLEFORD - Morris: Richardson Joyner Hyde(Orum) Fenton: Birkby R.Beardmore: B.Kear Spurr Johnson Finch Ward(Timson) Reilly:
Tries - Spurr Finch Timson: Goals - Birkby(2) Finch(2):
ST HELENS - Canning: Jones Bayliss(Bottell) Hagerty Meadows: Arkwright Peters: James Liptrot Owen Chisnall Gorley(Hope) Pinner: Tries - Bayliss(3) Hagerty Arkwright Peters Gorley: Goals - Pinner(4)(DG3):
Referee K Allatt (Southport) Att - 3378 H.T. 7 - 21

Sun 13 Sep 1981 WARRINGTON away lost 7 - 14
WARRINGTON - Hesford: Thackray Duane Paul Ford Phil Ford: K.Kelly Gordon: Eccles Waller(S/O) Case Hunter Holbrook(Fieldhouse) Potter:
Tries - Eccles Hunter: Goals - Hesford(4):
CASTLEFORD - Claughton: Morris Joyner Hyde Fenton: Birkby R.Beardmore: Barry Kear Spurr(S/O) Johnson Orr Timson Reilly: Try – R Beardmore: Goals - Birkby(2):
Referee R Campbell (Widnes) Att - 3188 H.T. 7 - 9

Wed 16 Sep 1981 LEEDS away lost 5 - 18
LEEDS - Binder(Wilkinson): D.Smith Hague Heselwood Atkinson: Holmes Dick: Dickinson Miller(S/O) Townend Rayne W.Heron(S/O) D.Heron:
Tries - Wilkinson Dick Dickinson: Goals - Dick(4)(DG):
CASTLEFORD - Claughton(Birkby): Richardson Joyner Hyde Fenton(Orr): Orum(S/O) R.Beardmore: Hardy Spurr(S/O) Johnson Finch Norton Timson:
Try - Joyner: Goal - Finch:
Referee J E Smith (Halifax) Att - 4264 H.T. nil - 2

Sun 20 Sep 1981 BARROW home won 12 - 7
CASTLEFORD - Claughton: Richardson Joyner Hyde(Birkby) Finch: Orum R.Beardmore: Hardy(Norton) Spurr Johnson Norton(Orr) Ward Timson:
Tries - Hyde R Beardmore: Goals - Finch(3):
BARROW - Tickle: Fawkes McConnell Wainwright M.James: Mason Cairns: Gee(Lupton) Wall Flynn K.James

SEASON 1981-82

Syzmala Hadley: . Try - Wall: Goals - Tickle(2):
Referee K Spencer (Warrington) Att - 2414 H.T. 5 - 7

Sun 27 Sep 1981 HULL away lost 24 - 42
HULL - Kemble: O'Hara(Sullivan) Leuluai Harrison
Prendiville: Banks Dean: Skerrett Duke Stone
Crane(Crooks) Crooks(Lloyd) Norton:
Tries - Skerrett(2) Sullivan Harrison Prendiville Banks
Crane Crooks: Goals - Crooks(6) Lloyd(3):
CASTLEFORD - Claughton: J.Kear Richardson(Walsh)
Morris Higgins: Birkby R.Beardmore: Hardy(Orr) Spurr
Johnson Norton Ward Timson:
Tries - Higgins Johnson Ward Timson: Goals - Birkby(6):
Referee S Wall (Leigh) Att - 16150 H.T. 9 - 17

Sat 3 Oct 1981 BRADFORD NORTHERN won 10 - 5
YORKSHIRE CUP FINAL - at HEADINGLEY LEEDS
CASTLEFORD - Claughton: Richardson Fenton Hyde
Morris: Joyner R.Beardmore: Hardy(Norton) Spurr
Johnson Finch Ward Timson:
Tries - Hyde Joyner: Goals - Finch(2):
BRADFORD N - Mumby: Barends Hale Parker Gant:
Hanley A.Redfearn: Grayshon Noble
Sanderson(D.Redfearn) Van Bellen(Jasiewicz) Idle
Robinson: Try - Parker: Goal - Hanley:
Referee R Whitfield (Widnes) Att - 5852 H.T. 5 - 2
WHITE ROSE TROPHY WINNER - BARRY JOHNSON -
CASTLEFORD

Sun 11 Oct 1981 LEIGH away lost 15 - 18
LEIGH - Hogan: Drummond Bilsbury Donlan Worgan:
Woods Green: Wilkinson(Clarkson) Tabern Cooke Martyn
McTighe Potter:
Tries - Woods McTighe: Goals - Woods(6):
CASTLEFORD - Claughton: Richardson Fenton Hyde
Morris: Joyner R.Beardmore: Hardy(Paul Orr) Spurr
Johnson Finch Ward Timson(S/O):
Try - Finch: Goals - Finch(6):
Referee J W Mean (Leyland) Att - 4500 H.T. 4 - 12

Sun 18 Oct 1981 LEIGH home won 21 - 7
JOHN PLAYER COMPETITION ROUND I
CASTLEFORD - Claughton: Richardson Fenton Hyde
Morris: Joyner R.Beardmore(Birkby): Hardy(Norton) Spurr
Johnson Finch Ward Timson:
Tries - Fenton(2) Ward(2) Timson: Goals - Finch(3):
LEIGH - Hogan: Drummond Stacey Donlan Worgan:
Woods Green: Wilkinson Tabern Cooke(Clarkson) Martyn
McTighe Potter: Try - Cooke: Goals - Woods(2):
Referee J McDonald (Wigan) Att - 5116 H.T. 11 - 7

Sun 25 Oct 1981 YORK home won 40 - 4
CASTLEFORD - Claughton: Richardson Fenton Hyde
Morris: Joyner(Birkby) R.Beardmore: Hardy Spurr Johnson
Norton Ward(Connell) Timson: Tries – R Beardmore(2)
Timson(2) Fenton Hyde Hardy Ward: Goals - Hyde(8):
YORK - Smith: G.Pryce Brown Roe Gibson: Midgley
B.Hughes: Dunkerley Piwinski Kirkbride(D.Pryce)
M.Hughes White McDermott: Goals - Gibson(2):
Referee R Moore (Wakefield) Att - 3163 H.T. 19 - 4

Sun 1 Nov 1981 HULL home lost 5 - 23
JOHN PLAYER COMPETITION ROUND 2
CASTLEFORD - Claughton: Richardson Fenton
Hyde(Orum) Morris: Joyner R.Beardmore(PAUL
SPEDDING(616)): Hardy Spurr(S/O) Johnson Norton Ward
Crampton: Try - Johnson: Goal - Norton:
HULL - Kemble: Sullivan(Chester) O'Hara Harrison
Prendiville: Leuluai Dean(Lloyd): Skerrett Wileman(S/O)
Stone Crane Crooks Norton: Tries - Kemble Chrster
O'Hara Harrison Norton: Goals - Crooks(4):
Referee R Campbell (Widnes) Att - 13414 H.T. 5 - 3

Sun 8 Nov 1981 WIDNES away lost 7 - 24
WIDNES - Burke: Basnett George(J.Myler) Cunningham
Bentley: O'Loughlin Hulme: M.O'Neill(S.O'Neill) Elwell
Lockwood Whitfield Prescott Adams:
Tries - Bentley(3) Basnett(2) George: Goals - Burke(3):
CASTLEFORD - Claughton: JOHN HARRISON(617)
Fenton(Birkby) Richardson Higgins: Morris Orum: Hardy
Spurr Johnson Crampton(Spedding) Norton Timson:
Goals - Norton(3) Hardy(DG):
Referee K Allatt (Southport) Att - 5300 H.T. 7 - 5

Sun 15 Nov 1981 LEIGH home lost 17 - 20
CASTLEFORD - Claughton: Richardson J.Kear Higgins
Harrison: Morris Orum: Hardy K.Beardmore Johnson
Norton Ward Timson:
Tries - K Beardmore Norton Ward: Goals - Norton(4):
LEIGH - Hogan: Drummond Bilsbury Donlan Fox: Woods
Green: Wilkinson (Clarkson) Tabern Cooke Martyn McTigue
Potter: Tries - Hogan Bilsbury Green:
Goals - Woods(5) Donlan(DG):
Referee W H Thompson(Hud'field) Att - 3356 H.T. 8 - 14

**Sun 22 Nov 1981 HULL KINGSTON ROVERS home
lost 11 - 16**
CASTLEFORD - Claughton: Richardson J.Kear Morris Paul
Martin: Orum(Birkby) Jamie Walsh: Hardy K.Beardmore
Johnson Norton Ward(Spedding) Timson:
Try - Walsh: Goals - Norton(4):
HULL K R - Lydiatt: Hubbard Smith Proctor Muscroft:
Hartley Harkin: Millington(Laws) Watkinson Crooks Lowe
Rose(Burton) Hall:
Tries - Hartley(2) Muscroft Harkin: Goals - Hubbard(2):
Referee R Campbell (Widnes) Att - 5643 H.T. 7 - 5

Sun 29 Nov 1981 YORK away draw 15 - 15
YORK - Smith: G.Ptyce Roe Brown Gibson: Wilson
Sanderson: Townend Piwinski Dunkerley Price
Phillipo(Holdstock) Hughes:
Try - Sanderson: Goals - Gibson(6):
CASTLEFORD - Claughton: Richardson J.Kear Hyde Morris:
Orum R.Beardmore: Hardy K.Beardmore Johnson Norton
Ward Timson:
Tries - Ward(2) R.Beardmore: Goals - Norton(3):
Referee J Smith (Halifax) Att - 3994 H.T. 10 - 9

Sun 6 Dec 1981 FULHAM away won 19 - 7
FULHAM - Ganley: M'Barki Aspey Diamond Cambrian:
Crossley Bowden: Beverley Dalgreen Gourley(Doherty)

317

Herdman Wood Allen: Try - Allen: Goals - Diamond(2):
CASTLEFORD - Claughton: Richardson Fenton Hyde
Morris: Orum R.Beardmore: Hardy K.Beardmore
Johnson(Connell) Norton Ward Timson:
Tries - Timson(2) Richardson: Goals - Hyde(5):
Referee T J Court (Oldham) Att - 4675 H.T. 12 - 2

Sun 3 Jan 1982 WARRINGTON home won 34 - 13
CASTLEFORD - Claughton(Wraith): Richardson Hyde
J.Kear Morris: Birkby R.Beardmore: Hardy K.Beardmore
Johnson Crampton(Connell)Ward Timson:
Tries - Hyde(4) Birkby(2): Goals - Hyde(8):
WARRINGTON - Hesford: Fellows(R.Duane) J.Duane
Bevan(S/O) Phil Ford: Paul Ford K.Kelly: Chisnall
Cunningham(S/O) Courtney(Hunter)Eccles Case Gittins:
Tries - Fellows Cunningham Eccles: Goals - Hesford(2):
Referee J McDonald (Wigan) Att - 2744 H.T. 14 - 3

Wed 20 Jan 1982 ST HELENS away won 40 - 10
ST HELENS - Glynn: Meadows Arkwright Bayliss(Haggerty)
Litherland: Butler Holding: Chisnall Liptrot
Brownbill(Mathias) Gorley Moorby Bottell:
Tries - Mathias Gorley: Goals - Holding(2):
CASTLEFORD - Claughton: Richardson Hyde J.Kear Morris:
Birkby R.Beardmore: Hardy K.Beardmore Johnson
Spedding Ward(Wraith)Timson(Spurr):
Tries - K.Beardmore(3) R.Beardmore(2) Hyde Kear
Johnson Timson: Goals - Hyde(6) Hardy(DG):
Referee K Spencer (Warrington) Att - 3759 H.T. 31 - nil

**Tue 26 Jan 1982 HULL KINGSTON ROVERS away
lost 12 - 26**
HULL K R - Fairbairn: Hubbard Smith Hogan Muscroft:
Hartley Walsh: Holdstock Watkinson Crooks Lowe Casey
Hall(Burton): Tries - Hartley(2) Fairbairn Walsh Lowe:
Goals - Fairbairn(5) Smith(DG):
CASTLEFORD - Claughton: Richardson(Wraith) Hyde
J.Kear Morris: Birkby R.Beardmore: Hardy K.Beardmore
Johnson(Spedding) Finch Ward Timson:
Tries - Ward(2): Goals - Hyde(2) Finch:
Referee R Moore (Wakefield) Att - 7939 H.T. 7 - 11

Sun 31 Jan 1982 FULHAM home won 26 - 14
CASTLEFORD - Claughton: J.Kear Joyner Hyde Morris:
Birkby R.Beardmore: Hardy(Spedding)(Finch) K.Beardmore
Johnson Finch(Wraith) Ward Timson:
Tries - Kear Birkby K.Beardmore Finch Ward:
Goals - Hyde(5) R.Beardmore(DG):
FULHAM - Diamond: Cambriani(Radbone) Stringer
N.Tuffs M'Barki: Crossley Kinsey: Beverley Dalgreen
Gourley(Souto) Herdman Hoare Doherty:
Tries - Crossley Kinsey: Goals - Diamond(4):
Referee A Givvons (Oldham) Att - 3239 H.T. 9 - 2

Sun 7 Feb 1982 WIGAN away lost 8 - 17
WIGAN - Whitfield: Ramsdale Nicholson Aspey Gill:
Foy(Wood) Stephens: Hodkinson Jones Cunliffe Campbell
Shaw Scott:
Tries - Stephens(2) Gill: Goals - Whitfield(4):
CASTLEFORD - Claughton(Wraith): Richardson Hyde

J.Kear Morris: Birkby R.Beardmore: Hardy(Connell)
K.Beardmore Johnson Norton Ward Timson:
Try - Hyde: Goals - Hyde(2) Birkby(DG):
Referee K Allatt (Southport) Att - 4723 H.T. 4 - 5

**Sun 14 Feb 1982 CARLISLE away won 17 - 2
CHALLENGE CUP ROUND 1**
CARLISLE - Birts: Youngman Evans Davies Bardgett:
Stephenson Agar: K.Robinson Crowther Morgan
Hollingsworth(Limb) Birdsall Boyd: Goal - Birts:
CASTLEFORD - Claughton: Richardson Joyner Hyde
Fenton(J.Kear): Birkby R.Beardmore: Hardy K.Beardmore
Johnson Crampton Ward(Norton)Timson:
Tries - R.Beardmore K.Beardmore Timson:
Goals - Hyde(4):
Referee D W Fox (Wakefield) Att - 5452 H.T. 10 - 2

**Sun 21 Feb 1982 FEATHERSTONE ROVERS home
lost 5 - 21**
CASTLEFORD - Claughton: Richardson Joyner J.Kear
Morris: Birkby(Wraith) R.Beardmore: Hardy Spurr
Reilly(S/O) Norton(Connell) Ward Crampton:
Try - Richardson: Goal - Birkby:
FEATHERSTONE R - Barker: Reed Quinn Gilbert Kellett:
Hayden Hudson: Siddall Handscombe Gibbons(S/O)
Hankins Smith Bell:
Try - Gilbert Hudson Hankins: Goals - Quinn(6):
Referee S Haigh (Ossett) Att - 4343 H.T. nil - 7

**Sun 28 Feb 1982 BATLEY away won 31 - 6
CHALLENGE CUP ROUND 2**
BATLEY - Storey: Presley Shaw(Jones)Hodgson Oulton:
Parker Wilson: Woodall(Pitts) Cummings Pitts(Tonks)
Vodden Watts Douglas: Goals - Oulton(3):
CASTLEFORD - Claughton(Wraith)(S/O): Richardson
Joyner Hyde J.Kear: Birkby R.Beardmore: Connell Hardy
Johnson Crampton Ward Norton(Reilly):
Tries - Joyner(2) Hyde(2) Richardson Johnson Ward:
Goals - Hyde(5):
Referee J W Mean (Leyland) Att - 4200 H.T. 15 - 4

**Thu 4 Mar 1982 BRADFORD NORTHERN away
lost 5 - 10**
BRADFORD N - Mumby: Smith Whiteman D.Redfearn
Gant: Carroll R.A.Redfearn: Grayshon Noble
Atherton(Hale) Van Bellen Idle Rathbone:
Tries - D.Redfearn Van Bellen: Goals - Carroll(2):
CASTLEFORD - Wraith: Richardson Joyner Hyde J.Kear:
Birkby R.Beardmore: Hardy(Reilly) Spurr Johnson
Crampton Ward Norton: Try - Crampton: Goal - Hyde:
Referee W H Thompson (Hud'field) Att - 5400 H.T. 5 - 5

**Sun 14 Mar 1982 LEIGH away won 8 - 3
CHALLENGE CUP ROUND 3**
LEIGH - Hogan: Drummond Bilsbury Donlan Fox: Woods
Green: Wilkinson Tabern Cooke Martyn
Clarkson(McTigue) Potter: Try - Donlan:
CASTLEFORD - Claughton: Richardson J.Kear Hyde Morris:
Joyner R.Beardmore: Hardy Spurr(Wraith) Johnson
Reilly(Norton) Ward Crampton:

Tries - Hyde R.Beardmore: Goal - Hyde:
Referee W H Thompson(Hud'field) Att - 11791 H.T. 8 - 3

Wed 17 Mar 1982 HULL home lost 7 - 25
CASTLEFORD - Wraith: Richardson J.Kear(Birkby) TONY
MARCHANT(618) Morris: Joyner R.Beardmore: Connell
Hardy Johnson Norton Crampton Timson (Spedding):
Try – R Beardmore: Goals - Birkby R.Beardmore:
HULL - Kemble: O'Hara Day Evans Prendiville:
Topliss(Crooks) Harkin: Tindall Duke Stone
Skerrett(Busfield) Lloyd Norton: Tries - Kemble O'Hara
Topliss Harkin Norton: Goals - Lloyd(5):
Referee D G Kershaw (Easingwold) Att - 6013 H.T. 2 - 5

Sun 21 Mar 1982 WIGAN home lost 14 - 17
CASTLEFORD - Claughton: Richardson Hyde Marchant
Morris: Joyner R.Beardmore: Connell Spurr(Reilly) Johnson
Norton Crampton Timson:
Tries - Richardson Hyde: Goals - Hyde(4):
WIGAN - Whitfield: Hornby Nicholson Ramsdale Gill:
Aspey Stephens: Hodkinson Kiss Johnson
Shaw(Pendlebury)Campbell Scott:
Tries - Whitfield(2) Scott: Goals - Whitfield(4):
Referee S Wall (Leigh) Att - 3522 H.T. 7 - 7

Sat 27 Matrch 1982 HULL lost 11 - 15
CHALLENGE CUP SEMi FINAL - AT HEADINGLEY
LEEDS
CASTLEFORD - Claughton: Richardson Hyde J.Kear Morris:
Joyner R.Beardmore: Connell Hardy Johnson
Reilly(Norton) Crampton Timson:
Try - Reilly: Goals - Hyde(4):
HULL - Kemble: O'Hara Day Evans Prendiville: Topliss
Harkin: Tindall(Crane) Wileman Stone Skerrett(Lloyd)
Crooks Norton: Tries - Kemble O'Hara Prendiville Norton:
Goals - Crooks Topliss(DG):
Referee W H Thompson(Hud'field) Att - 21207 H.T. 4 -11

Wed 31 Mar 1982 BRADFORD NORTHERN home
lost 18 - 19
CASTLEFORD - Wraith(Norton): Richardson J.Kear
Hyde(Marchant) Morris: Joyner R.Beardmore: Connell
STUART HORTON(619) Johnson Crampton James Timson:
Tries - Kear Hyde Johnson Timson: Goals - Beardmore(3):
BRADFORD N - Mumby: D.Smith Hanley D.Redfearn
Parker: Carroll A.Redfearn(Hale): Van Bellen Noble
Atherton Parrott Jasiewicz Rathbone:
Tries - D.Smith(2) Van Bellen Jasiewicz:
Goals - Carroll(3)(DG):
Referee R Whitfield (Widnes) Att - 3626 H.T. 3 - 13

Sun 4 Apr 1982 WHITEHAVEN home won 36 - 8
CASTLEFORD - Claughton: Richardson Marchant J.Kear
Morris(Birkby): Joyner R.Beardmore: Connell Horton
Reilly(Norton) Crampton James Timson:
Tries - Kear(2) Connell(2) Beardmore Richardson
Marchant Timson: Goals - R Beardmore(6):
WHITREHAVEN - Stoddart: Mackie Larder(Stewart) Fisher
Bulman: Lane Hall: Grimes Barwise Rae(Simpson)
Simpson(Litt) Martyn McCullen:

Tries - Bulman Litt: Goal - Larder:
Referee R Moore (Wakefield) Att - 2495 H.T. 23 - 2

Mon 12 Apr 1982 WAKEFIELD TRINITY away lost 5 -14
WAKEFIELD T - Box: Guest(Pieniazek) Walters Parker
Moore: Winterbottom Pickerill: Bratt Wright Harris Kelly
Thompson McDermott (Clarkson):
Tries - Walters Parker: Goals - Box(3)(DG) Pickerill(DG):
CASTLEFORD - Wraith: Richardson Hyde Marchant J.Kear:
Joyner R.Beardmore: Connell Hardy(James) Johnson
Crampton Reilly Timson: Try - Joyner: Goal - Hyde:
Referee A Givvons (Oldham) Att - 4915 H.T. 5 - 8

Wed 14 Apr 1932 LEEDS home lost 9 - 18
CASTLEFORD - Wraith: Richardson J.Kear
Marchant(Morris) Finch: Birkby R.Beardmore: Connell
Horton Johnson Crampton James Norton:
Try - Marchant: Goals - Finch(3):
LEEDS - Hague: Binder Wilkinson Heselwood A.Smith:
Mackintosh Dick: Harrison McNeil(W.Heron) Burke
Keith.Rayne Kevin.Rayne D.Heron:
Tries – Keith.Rayne(2) Hague W.Heron: Goals - Dick(3):
Referee G F Lindop (Wakefield) Att - 3567 H.T. 7 - 8

Sun 18 Apr 1932 WIDNES home lost 13 - 21
CASTLEFORD - Wraith: (Morris): Richardson J.Kear
Marchant Finch: Birkby R.Beardmore: Connell(Spedding)
Horton Johnson Crampton James Timson:
Tries - Richardson Crampton James: Goals - Finch(2):
WIDNES - Burke: Wright O'Loughlin J.Myler(Foy) Basnett:
Hughes Hulme- M.O'Neill Elwell S.O'Neill(Lockwood)
Gorley Prescot- Adams: Tries - Wright Foy Hughes
Hulme Prescot:: Goals - Burke(3):
Referee J McDonald (Wigan) Att - 3618 H.T. 8 - 8

Wed 21 Apr 1982 WHITEHAVEN away won 11 - 4
WHITEHAVEN – Stoddart: Mackie Stewart Rose McClure:
Lane Walker: Rhythian Elliott Grimes Martin Taylor
Cottier(Huddart): Goals - Walker(2):
CASTLEFORD - Morris: Richardson J.Kear Marchant Finch:
Joyner R.Beardmore: Connell Horton Johnson Crampton
Spedding(Higgins)Norton:
Tries - Richardson(2) Norton: Goal - Finch:
Referee G Berry (Batley) Att - 1570 H.T. 5 - 2

Sun 25 Apr 1982 WAKEFIELD TRINITY home
won 15 -7
CASTLEFORD - Wraith: Richardson J.Kear Marchant Finch:
Joyner R.Beardmore: Connell(James) Horton Johnson
Crampton Ward Norton:
Tries - Wraith Joyner Horton: Goals - Finch(3):
WAKEFIELD T - Box: Fletcher Walters(Guest) Parker
Moore: Winterbottom Pickerill: Bratt(Clarkson) Wright
Harris Kelly Eccles McDermott:
Try - McDermott: Goals - Box(2):
Referee R Whitfield (Widnes) Att - 5649 H.T. 7 - 7

SEASON 1981-82

Wed 28 Apr 1982 BARROW away lost 18 - 26
BARROW - Tickle: Moore Thompson McConnell M.James:
Mason Cairns: Gee Fitzgerald Lupton Flynn Herbert Kirby:
Tries - Tickle(2): Moore James Cairns Fitzgerald:
Goals - Tickle(4):

CASTLEFORD - Wraith: <u>Geoffrey Morris</u> J.Kear Marchant
Higgins: JoynerR.Beardmore: Ward(Connell) Horton
Johnson Crampton James Norton:
Tries - Kear Joyner R Beardmore Johnson:
Goals - Norton(2) R Beardmore:
Referee D W Fox (Wakefield) Att - 3255 H.T. 3 – 11

Stuart Horton
D. No 619
1981-82 to 1986-87

Paull Spedding
D. No 616
1981-82 to 1983-84

Tony Marchant
D. No 618
1981-82 to 1995-96

SATURDAY 3 OCTOBER 1981 YORKSHIRE CUP FINAL v BRADFORD NORTHERN WON 10 - 5
Players And Fans Celebrate The Win
Back Row – Terry Richardson Barry Johnson Alan Hardy Paul Norton Gary Hyde Kevin Ward David Finch
Front Row – Ian Birkby Robert Beardmore Steve Fenton Geoff Morris John Joyner (Captain) Robert Spurr Andy Timpson
Missing from Photograph George Claughton

D.N	PLAYER		DEBUT	L MATCH	APP	SUB	T.AP	TRI'S	G'LS	D.G	P'TS
512	REILLY	MALCOLM			8	6	14	1	0	0	3
518	SPURR	ROBERT			19	1	20	2	0	0	6
544	CLAUGHTON	GEORGE			26	0	26	0	0	0	0
551	JOYNER	JOHN			27	0	27	8	0	0	24
556	RICHARDSON	TERRY			37	0	37	10	0	0	30
560	FENTON	STEVE			14	0	14	6	0	0	18
563	WALSH	JAMIE		22/11/1981	1	1	2	1	0	0	3
565	MORRIS	GEOFF		28/04/1982	31	2	33	2	0	0	6
568	HARDY	ALAN			26	0	26	1	0	2	5
572	WRAITH	GEOFFREY			9	8	17	1	0	0	3
578	ORR	PAUL		11/10/1981	1	5	6	0	0	0	0
588	NORTON	PAUL			20	7	27	2	17	0	40
591	CRAMPTON	JAMES			21	0	21	2	0	0	6
593	KEAR	BARRY		13/09/1981	6	0	6	0	0	0	0
596	KEAR	JOHN			24	1	25	7	0	0	21
598	HIGGINS	BARRY			4	1	5	1	0	0	3
599	FINCH	DAVID			15	0	15	4	30	0	72
601	HYDE	GARY			28	0	28	16	56	0	160
603	WARD	KEVIN			27	0	27	13	0	0	39
604	CONNELL	GARY			11	5	17	2	0	0	6
606	BIRKBY	IAN			18	8	26	8	32	1	89
607	TIMSON	ANDY			29	2	31	14	0	0	42
608	BEARDMORE	ROBERT			36	1	37	13	11	1	62
609	ORUM	IAN			8	3	11	0	0	0	0
611	BEARDMORE	KEVIN			10	0	10	6	0	0	18
612	MARTIN	PAUL		22/11/1981	1	0	1	0	0	0	0
613	JOHNSON	BARRY			38	0	38	7	0	0	21
614	JAMES	NEIL			5	2	7	1	0	0	3
616	SPEDDING	PAUL	01/11/1981		2	7	9	0	0	0	0
617	HARRISON	JOHN	08/11/1981		2	0	2	0	0	0	0
618	MARCHANT	TONY	17/03/1982		9	1	10	2	0	0	6
619	HORTON	STUART	31/03/1982		7	0	7	1	0	0	3
	32		4	5	520	52	582	131	146	4	689

COMPETITION		P	W	D	L	FOR	AGT
LEAGUE D 1	POSITION 12 OF 16	30	10	1	19	486	505
YORK'S CUP		4	4	0	0	110	54
RL CUP		4	3	0	1	67	26
PLAYERS NO6		2	1	0	1	26	30
PLAYERS RECORDS		**40**	**18**	**1**	**21**	**689**	**615**

The Yorkshire Cup yielded another trophy success, only the second in the clubs history in this competition. In the final, played at Headingley against Bradford Northern, we ran out winners 10–5, with Barry Johnson winning the White Rose Trophy for the Man of the Match.

In the Challenge Cup we reached the semi-final, our opponent at Headingley was Hull, and included former Castleford favourites Sammy Lloyd, Steve 'Knocker' Norton and a Castleford favourite of the future Lee Crooks in their line up, they edged us out of a Final appearance 15–11 (and subsequently the Humberside teams would become our cup bogie sides of the eighties).

A notable Debutant was Tony Marchant

SEASON 1982-83

In the League Oldham, Carlisle, Workington Town Halifax were promoted to Division 1. Fulham Wakefield Trinity York Whitehaven were relegated to Division 2.

Sun 22 Aug 1982 BRADFORD NORTHERN away lost 10 - 16

BRADFORD N - Mumby: Smith(Sanderson) Whiteman(Green) Davies A.N.Other: Hale A.Redfearn: Van Bellen Noble Okulicz Jackson Jasiewicz Idle
Tries - Smith Redfearn Jasiewicz:
Goals - Mumby(3)Redfearn(DG):
CASTLEFORD - Claughton: Richardson Joyner Marchant(Hyde) Kear: R.Beardmore Orum: KEVIN ANDERSON(620)(James) Hardy Johnson Finch Ward
Timson: Tries - Hyde R Beardmore: Goals - Finch(2):
Referee W H Thompson (Hud'field) Att - 4627 H.T. 5 - 10

Wed 25 Aug 1982 CARLISLE home won 20 - 18

CASTLEFORD - Claughton: Richardson(Hyde) Joyner Marchant Kear: R.Beardmore Orum: Anderson(James) Hardy(Anderson) Johnson Finch(S/O)Ward Timson:
Tries - Joyner R Beardmore Finch Timson:
Goals - Finch(4):
CARLISLE - Birts: Youngman Evans D.Bell Newton: Bardgett(Friend) Sanderson: Birdsall Crowther(S/O) Morgan Robinson(Raybould) J.Bell Boyd:
Tries - D.Bell Newton: Goals - Newton(6):
Referee R Whitefield (Widnes) Att - 2233 H.T. 14 - 16

Sun 29 Aug 1982 WARRINGTON away won 20 - 15

WARRINGTON - Hesford: Fellows R.Duane Bevan Phil Ford: Cullen Kelly: Courtney Webb(Chisnall) Cooke Eccles Fieldhouse Worrall(Finnegan):
Tries - Bevan(2) Ford: Goals - Hesford(3):
CASTLEFORD - George Claughton: Richardson Joyner Hyde Kear: R.Beardmore Orum: Anderson(Marchant) Horton Johnson Finch(James) Ward Timson:
Tries - Richardson Hyde Finch Ward: Goals - Finch(4):
Referee G F Lindop (Wakefield) Att - 3847 H.T.17 - 10

Sun 5 Sep 1982 LEEDS home lost 10 - 33
YORKSHIRE CUP ROUND 1

CASTLEFORD - Kear: Richardson Joyner Marchant Fenton: R.Beardmore Orum(Hyde): Anderson(Norton) Horton Johnson James Ward Timson:
Tries - Joyner Fenton: Goals - Beardmore(2):
LEEDS - Hague: Naylor Heselwood Wilkinson A.Smith: Holmes(Conway) Dick: Dickinson Ward(Burke) Pitchford Keith.Rayne Kevin.Rayne D.Heron: Tries - Heron(2) Naylor(2)Heselwood Wilkinson Dick: Goals - Dick(6):
Referee S Wall (Leigh) Att - 4855 H.T. nil - 23

Sun 12 Sep 1982 HULL away lost 20 - 36

HULL - Banks: Evans Day(Norton) Leuluai Prendiville: Topliss Dean: Sutton Bridges Stone Rose Crooks(Harkin) Crane: Tries - Dean(2) Evans Norton Leuluai Prendiville Crooks Topliss: Goals - Prendiville(3) Crooks(3):
CASTLEFORD - Kear: Richardson Joyner Hyde Marchant: Fenton R.Beardmore: Anderson(Crampton) (Higgins)

Horton Johnson James Connell Timson: Tries - Hyde(2) Richardson Connell: Goals - Beardmore(4):
Referee D W Fox (Wakefield) Att - 11434 H.T. 2 - 18

Sun 19 Sep 1982 HALIFAX home won 12 - 11

CASTLEFORD - Kear: Richardson Joyner(Higgins) Hyde Marchant: Fenton(Joyner) R.Beardmore: Anderson(James) Horton Johnson James(Connell) Timson Norton:
Tries - Richardson Hyde: Goals - Beardmore(3):
HALIFAX - Gorton(Marshall): O'Byrne Agar Garrod Waites: Cawood Langton: Van Bellen Whitehouse Goodwin(Sharpe) Greenwood Jarvis Bond:
Tries - Langton Bond: Goals - Agar(2) Bond(DG):
Referee R Moore (Wakefield) Att - 2416 H.T. 7 - 6

Sun 26 Sep 1982 HULL KINGSTON ROVERS home won 10 - 8

CASTLEFORD - Kear: Richardson Marchant Hyde Higgins: Joyner R.Beardmore: Hardy Horton Johnson James(Connell) Timson Norton:
Tries - Hyde Joyner Timson: Goal - Hardy(DG):
HULL K R - Fairbairn: Clark Smith Prohm Hubbard: Hartley(Hogan)Walsh: Holdstock Watkinson Crooks Lowe Casey(Kelly) Hall: Tries - Walsh Kelly: Goal - Fairbairn:
Referee R Whitfield (Widnes) Att - 4456 H.T. 9 - 8

Sun 3 Oct 1982 LEIGH away lost 16 - 32

LEIGH - Tomlinson: Drummond Henderson Donlan Fox: Woods Green: Wilkinson Tabern Clarkson(Dunn) Chisnall Hunter(Ainsworth) Potter: Tries - Drummond(2) Green(2) Donlan Tabern: Goals - Tomlinson(7):
CASTLEFORD - Kear: Richardson Marchant Hyde(Orum) Higgins: Joyner R.Beardmore: Hardy Horton Johnson James Timson(Connell) Norton:
Tries - Kear Hyde Joyner Timson: Goals - Beardmore(2):
Referee J Rascagneres (France) Att - 4128 H.T. 3 - 19

Sun 10 Oct 1982 FEATHERSTONE ROVERS home won 30 - 13

CASTLEFORD - Kear: Richardson Marchant Hyde Higgins: Joyner R.Beardmore: Ward K.Beardmore Johnson James Connell Timson: Tries - James(2) Hyde R.Beardmore K.Beardmore Timson: Goals - R.Beardmore(6):
FEATHERSTONE R - Barker: Gilbert(Marsden) Coventry Quinn Kellett: Hayden Pickerill: Siddal(Gibbins) Shaw Hankins D.Hobbs Smith Hudson:
Tries - Gilbert Kellett Hudson: Goals - Quinn(2):
Referee J McDonald (Wigan) Att - 3531 H.T. 15 - 8

Wed 13 Oct 1982 WARRINGTON home won 14 - 10

CASTLEFORD - Kear: Richardson Marchant Hyde Higgins: Joyner(Orum) R.Beardmore: Ward K.Beardmore(Spedding) Johnson James Norton Timson:
Tries - Ward Johnson: Goals - R.Beardmore(4):
WARRINGTON - Hesford: Muller Bevan R.Duane M.Kelly: Cullen K.Kelly: Courtney Webb Chisnall Eccles Fieldhouse Gregory(Cooke): Tries - Bevan Eccles: Goals - Hesford(2):
Referee T J Court (Leeds) Att - 2439 H.T. 7 - 5

SEASON 1982-83

Sun 17 Oct 1982 BARROW away lost 20 - 30
BARROW - Tickle: Bentley O'Reagan McConnell James:
Mason Cairns (Whittle): Herbert Wall Gee Flynn
Gillespie(Lupton))Hadley: Tries - Bentley O'Reagan
McConnell Mason Whittle Hadley: Goals - Tickle(6):
CASTLEFORD - Kear: Richardson Marchant Hyde Higgins:
Orum(Birkby) R.Beardmore: Ward(Orum) Horton Johnson
James(Spedding) Norton Timson:
Tries - Hyde Orum Birkby Ward: Goals - R.Beardmore(4):
Referee F Robinson (Leeds) Att - 3100 H.T. 5 - 12

Sun 24 Oct 1982 OLDHAM home lost 12 - 14
CASTLEFORD - Kear: Richardson Marchant Hyde Higgins:
Orum R.Beardmore: Ward K.Beardmore Johnson Norton
Reilly Timson:
Tries - Kear Timson: Goals - R.Beardmore(3):
OLDHAM - Taylor: Vigo Foy Hawkyard(Willis) Caffery:
Parrish Ashton: Hogan McCurrie Goodway(Platt) Coombs
Worrell Flanagan: Tries - Taylor Willis: Goals - Parrish(4):
Referee K Allatt (Southport) Att - 3861 H.T. 7 - nil

Sun 31 Oct 1982 WORKINGTON TOWN away won 23 - 10
WORKINGTON T - Hopkins: Munro Hutchinson(Wilkins)
Beattie Beck: Todd Burns: Stokes Lightfoot
Rowley(R.Pattinson) Hartley McCarron W.Pattinson:
Tries - Hopkins Munro: Goals - Hopkins(2):
CASTLEFORD - Kear: Richardson Marchant Hyde Higgins:
Orum R.Beardmore(Birkby): Ward K.Beardmore Johnson
Spedding Paul Norton (KEITH ENGLAND(621)) Timson:
Tries - Marchant(3) Richardson Orum:
Goals - R.Beardmore(4):
Referee K Spencer (Warrington) Att - 1234 H.T. 12 - 5

Sun 14 Nov 1982 LEEDS home won 32 - 5
CASTLEFORD - Kear(Orum): Richardson Marchant Hyde
Higgins: Joyner R.Beardmore(Hardy): Ward K.Beardmore
Johnson England Spedding Timson:
Tries - Timson(2) Marchant R.Beardmore Ward
K.Beardmore: Goals - R.Beardmore(7):
LEEDS - Haigh: Alan Smith Heselwood Massa Andrew
Smith(A.McIntosh): Holmes Dick: Dickinson Sowden Burke
Keith.Rayne Kevin.Rayne D.Heron:
Try - Heselwood: Goal - Dick:
Referee T M Beaumont (Hud'field) Att - 4448 H.T. 20 -nil

Sun 21 Nov 1982 ST HELENS away won 24 - 23
ST HELENS - Parkes: Ledger Arkwright Haggerty
Litherland: Peters Holding: James(Moorby) Bottell Grimes
Mathias Gorley Pinner: Tries - Parkes Ledger Haggerty
Peters Gorley: Goals - Holding(4):
CASTLEFORD - DARREN COEN(622): Richardson
Marchant Hyde Orum: Joyner R.Beardmore: Ward(Birkby)
K.Beardmore Johnson England Spedding(James) Timson:
Tries - Richardson Marchant R.Beardmore Ward:
Goals - R.Beardmore(5) Hyde:
Referee B F Walker (Barrow) Att - 3500 H.T. 9 - 8

Sun 5 Dec 1982 WIGAN home lost 10 - 16
JOHN PLAYER COMPETITION ROUND 1
CASTLEFORD - Coen: Richardson Marchant Hyde Higgins:
Joyner R.Beardmore: Ward K.Beardmore
Johnson(England) (Johnson) Spedding James Timson:
Tries - Richardson Higgins: Goals - Hyde(2):
WIGAN - Williams: Ramsdale Stephenson Whitfield
Gill(Juliff): Foy Fairhurst: Shaw Kiss Campbell West Scott
Pendlebury: Tries - Williams Whitfield Campbell West:
Goals - Whitfield(2):
Referee R Campbell (Widnes) Att - 6068 H.T. nil - 13

Sun 19 Dec 1982 LEIGH home won 21 - 7
CASTLEFORD - Coen: MARK ROACHE(623)(Orum)
Marchant Hyde Kear: Joyner R.Beardmore: Ward
K.Beardmore Spedding James Reilly(England)
Timson(S/O): Tries - Marchant Joyner R.Beardmore
K.Beardmore James: Goals - Beardmore(3):
LEIGH - Hogan: Drummond Tomlinson(Henderson)
Donlan Fox: Woods Green: Wilkinson(Hunter) Tabern
Pyke Chisnall Martyn Potter:
Try - Hogan: Goals - Woods(2):
Referee J McDonald (Wigan) Att - 2558 H.T. 11 - 2

Sun 2 Jan 1983 BRADFORD NORTHERN home lost 13 - 15
CASTLEFORD - Coen: Richardson Marchant Hyde(S/O)
Kear: Joyner R.Beardmore: Ward K.Beardmore(Connell)
Connell(Higgins) James Spedding Timson(Orum):
Tries - Marchant Joyner Higgins: Goals - R.Beardmore(2):
BRADFORD N - Green: Smith Mumby Davies Pullen:
Carroll(McLean) Fennell: Grayshon Noble Van Bellen
Jasiewicz Parrott(Sanderson) Idle:
Tries - Jasiewicz(2) Smith: Goals - Mumby(3):
Referee S Wal (Leigh) Att - 4826 H.T. 5 - 10

Sun 9 Jan 1983 WIGAN away lost 8 - 20
WIGAN - Whitfield: Ramsdale Stephenson Clare(Juliff) Gill:
Foy Fairhurst: Shaw Kiss Campbell West Scott
Pendlebury(Dunn):
Tries - Gill Foy Fairhurst Scott: Goals - Whitfield(4):
CASTLEFORD - Coen: Richardson Marchant Hyde Kear:
Joyner R.Beardmore (Orum): Ward Horton Connell
(Higgins) Spedding James England:
Tries - Coen Ward: Goal - Hyde:
Referee W H Thompson(Hud'field) Att - 7149 H.T. 3 - 10

Sun 16 Jan 1983 ST HELENS home won 31 - 10
CASTLEFORD - Coen: Richardson Marchant Kear Orum:
Joyner R.Beardmore: Ward Spurr Connell(Hardy)
James(Higgins) Spedding(James) Timson:
Tries - Marchant Kear Joyner R.Beardmore Timson:
Goals - R.Beardmore(8):
ST HELENS - Griffiths: Ledger Parkes Litherland Meadows:
Glynn Holding: James Bottell Grimes Moorby Gorley
Haggerty(Round):
Tries - Griffiths Litherland: Goals - Griffiths(2):
Referee P Massey (Salford) Att - 2915 H.T. 9 - 10

SEASON 1982-83

Sun 23 Jan 1983 WIDNES away lost 7 - 18
WIDNES - Burke: Lydon O'Loughlin Cunningham Basnett: Hughes Gregory: Hogan Gormley Tamati M.O'Neill Prescott(S.O'Neill) Adams:
Tries - Lydon Hughes Gregory Tamati   Goals - Burke(3):
CASTLEFORD - Coen: Richardson Marchant(Timson) Hyde Kear: Joyner R.Beardmore: Connell(James) K.Beardmore James(Johnson) Ward England Higgins:
Try - Hyde: Goals - R.Beardmore(2):
Referee J McDonald (Wigan) Att - 4008 H.T. 2 - 5

Sun 6 Feb 1983 BARROW home won 30 - 16
CASTLEFORD - Coen: Richardson Marchant Kear Higgins: Joyner R.Beardmore: Connell K.Beardmore Johnson(Orum) James(England) Ward Timson:
Tries - Ward(2) R.Beardmore K.Beardmore Johnson James: Goals - R.Beardmore(6):
BARROW - Tickle: Moore Ball Whittle M.James: McConnell Cairns: Hodgkinson Fitzgerald Gee(Herbert) K.James Syzmala O'Regan:
Tries - Ball(2) M.James Cairns: Goals - Ball(2):
Referee T M Beaumont(Hud'field) Att - 2528 H.T. 22 -11

Wed 16 Feb 1983 WIGAN away won 17 - 7
CHALLENGE CUP ROUND 1
WIGAN - Williams: Ramsdale(Wane) Stephenson Whitfield Juliff: Foy(Stephens) Fairhurst: Shaw Kiss Campbell Case(S/O) Scott Pendlebury:
Try - Pendlebury: Goals - Whitfield(2):
CASTLEFORD - Coen: Richardson Marchant Hyde Kear: Joyner R.Beardmore: Connell K.Beardmore(Higgins) Johnson James(S/O) Ward Timson:
Tries - Marchant(2) Ward: Goals - R.Beardmore(4):
Referee D G Kershaw(Easingwold) Att - 10737 H.T. 12 - 2

Sun 20 Feb 1983 FEATHERSTONE ROVERS away draw 17 - 17
FEATHERSTONE R - N.Barker: Marsden Quinn Marsh Kellett: Banks Pickerill: Gibbins Handscombe Hankins D.Hobbs Slatter Hudson(Siddall):
Tries - Marsh Pickerill Hankins: Goals - Quinn(4):
CASTLEFORD - Coen: Richardson Marchant Kear Higgins: Orum(Birkby) R.Beardmore: Connell Spurr Johnson James(England) Ward Timson:
Tries - Kear Higgins Timson: Goals - R.Beardmore(4):
Referee – Mr G F Lindop (Wakefield) Att - 3974 H.T. 5 - 12

Sun 27 Feb 1983 BARROW away won 14 - 9
CHALLENGE CUP ROUND 2
BARROW - Tickle: Moore Ball Whittle M.James: Mason Cairns (McConnell): Herbert Fitzgerald Gee K.James Syzmala O'Regan: Try - Ball Whittle: Goals - Ball(1) (DG):
CASTLEFORD - Coen: Richardson Marchant Hyde Kear: Joyner R.Beardmore: Connell K.Beardmore Johnson James Ward Timson(Higgins):
Tries - Marchant Hyde: Goals - R.Beardmore(3) Hyde:
Referee W H Thompson (Hud'field) Att - 7100 H.T. 9 - 9

Sun 6 Mar 1983 WIGAN home lost 6 - 14
CASTLEFORD - Coen: Richardson Marchant Hyde Kear: Orum R.Beardmore (Birkby): Hardy Robert Spurr NEIL KELLETT(624)(Geoffrey Wraith) England Connell Higgins:
Tries - Richardson England:
WIGAN - Williams: Wood(Pendlebury) Stephenson Whitfield Gill: Foy Fairhurst: Shaw(Campbell) Kiss Case Juliff Scott Wane(Shaw):
Tries - Foy Case: Goals - Whitfield(4):
Referee S Wall (Leigh) Att - 4569 Hallf time 3 - 2

Sun 13 Mar 1983 HUNSLET away won 13 - 8
CHALLENGE CUP ROUND 3
HUNSLET - Briers: Foley Murrell Roe Fitzsimmons: Townsend King: Lean Gibson Burgess(Wright) Smith(Booth) Ackland Woolford:
Try - Smith: Goals - Fitzsimmons(2) (DG):
CASTLEFORD - Coen: Richardson Marchant Hyde Kear: Joyner R.Beardmore: Connell K.Beardmore Johnson James(Higgins) Ward Timson(England):
Tries - Marchant Hyde Timson: Goals - R.Beardmore(2):
Referee R Whitfield (Widnes) Att - 14004 H.T. 5 - 5

Wed 16 Mar 1983 LEEDS away won 15 - 5
LEEDS - Wilkinson: Campbell Heselwood Dyl Andrew Smith(Conway): Hague Dick: Sykes Ward Pitchford(Squire) Keith Rayne Burke Kevin Rayne:
Try - Wilkinson: Goal - Dick:
CASTLEFORD - Coen: Richardson Marchant Hyde Kear: Joyner Orum(R.Beardmore): Connell(Timson) K.Beardmore Johnson James England Higgins:
Tries - Hyde Kear Joyner: Goals - Hyde(3):
Referee W H Thompson (Hud'field) Att - 5871 H.T. 10-5

Sun 20 Mar 1983 WIDNES home lost 13 - 31
CASTLEFORD - Coen: Richardson Marchant(Higgins) Hyde Kear: Orum R.Beardmore: Hardy K.Beardmore Johnson James England Timson(John Harrison): Tries - Marchant Hyde R.Beardmore: Goals - R.Beardmore(2):
WIDNES - Burke: Linton Hughes Kieron O'Laughlin (Tamati) Basnett: T.Myler Gregory: Hogan Elwell M.O'Neill Whitfield Prescott Adams:
Tries - Linton(2) Whitfield(2) Basnett Gregory Elwell M.O'Neill: Goals - Burke(3) (DG):
Referee J McDonald (Wigan) Att - 3511 H.T. 8 - 18

Sun 27 Mar 1983 HULL KINGSTON ROVERS away lost 17 - 23
HULL K R - Lydiat(Hartley): Clark Fairbairn Robinson Prohm: M.Smith G.Smith: Holdstock Watkinson Millington(Hall) Kelly Hogan Lazenby: Tries - Prohm(2) Hogan(2) Lydiat: Goals - Lydiat(2) Fairbairn(2):
CASTLEFORD - Coen: Richardson Kear Hyde Higgins: Ian Birkby R.Beardmore: Connell K.Beardmore Johnson James(Orum) England Reilly(Timson):
Tries - K.Beardmore(3)   Goals - R.Beardmore(3) Hyde:
Referee D W Fox (Wakefield) Att - 7134 H.T. 10 - 14

SEASON 1982-83

Sat 2 Apr 1983 HULL lost 7 - 14
CHALLENGE CUP SEMI FINAL - AT ELLAND ROAD LEEDS
CASTLEFORD - Coen: Richardson Marchant Hyde Kear: Joyner R.Beardmore (Orum): Connell K.Beardmore Johnson England Ward Higgins(James) (Higgins): Try - England: Goals - Hyde(2):
HULL - Kemble: O'Hara Evans Leuluai Prendiville: Topliss(Day) Harkin: Skerrett Bridges Stone Rose Crooks(Crane) Norton:
Tries - O'Hara Evans Leuluai Day: Goal - Crooks:
Referee W H Thompson(Hud'field) Att - 26031 H.T. 2 - 6

Mon 4 Apr 1983 HULL home won 21 - 16
CASTLEFORD Coen: Richardson Marchant Hyde Kear: Joyner Orum: Connell(Hardy) K.Beardmore Johnson James(Reilly) Ward England: Tries - Richardson Marchant Hyde Joyner Ward: Goals - Hyde(3):
HULL - Banks: O'Hara Wilby Leuluai Prendiville: Evans(Kemble) Dean: Skerrett(Crooks) Duke Stone Proctor Crooks(Norton) Crane:
Tries - O'Hara(2): Goals - Crooks(4) Prendiville:
Referee D G Kershaw(Easingwold) Att 6223 H.T. 10 - 10

Fri 8 Apr 1983 CARLISLE away won 66 - 8
AT BELLE VUE WAKEFIELD
CARLISLE - A.N.Other(1): Youngman Newton(A.N.Other 14) Evans Bardgett: Ferres Miller: Birdsall Warburton Vickers A.N.Other(11) A.N.Other(12) (A.N.Other 15)Limb:
Tries - Bardgett A.N.Other(15): Goal - A.N.Other(14):
CASTLEFORD - Coen: Richardson Marchant Hyde Roache: Joyner(Kear) R.Beardmore: Hardy K.Beardmore Johnson Ward Connell(Reilly) England:
Tries - K.Beardmore(4) Coen(3) Hyde(3) Marchant Roache R.Beardmore Johnson: Goals - R.Beardmore(12):
Referee D G Kershaw (Easingwold) Att - 1086 H.T. 38 -nil

Keith England
D. No 621
1982-83 to 1993-94

Darren Coen
D. No 622
1982-83 to 1984-85

Sun 10 Apr 1983 WORKINGTON TOWN home won 32 - 5
CASTLEFORD - DAVID ROOCKLEY(625): Richardson Marchant Hyde Kear: Joyner R.Beardmore(Orum): Connell K.Beardmore Johnson James Ward(Reilly)England:
Tries - R.Beardmore(2) Hyde Kear Johnson James:
Goals - R.Beardmore(6) Hyde:
WORKINGTON T - Smith: Roper Maughan Beattie Beck: Rudd(McQuire) Todd: Varty Lightfoot(Nixon) Falcon W.Pattinson Lewis Dobie: Try - Beck: Goal - Beattie:
Referee A Givvons (Oldham) Att - 2238 H.T. 17 - 5

Thu 14 Apr 1983 HALIFAX away won 47 - 2
HALIFAX - Smith: Priestly Agar Garrod Martin: Cawood Moses(Wilson): Van Bellen Whitehouse Sharp Bond Jarvis Langton(Greenwood): Goal - Agar:
CASTLEFORD - Coen: Richardson Marchant Hyde Kear: Joyner R.Beardmore: Hardy K.Beardmore Johnson James Connell England: Tries - K.Beardmore(3) Hyde(2) Coen R.Beardmore Hardy Connell: Goals - R.Beardmore(10): :
Referee S Wall (Leigh) Att - 984 H.T. 17 - 2

Sun 17 Apr 1983 OLDHAM away won 22 - 10
OLDHAM - Caffrey: Vigo Parrish Hawkyard Taylor: Willis Ashton: Coombes McCurrie Goodway Chadwick(McEwan) Worrall Boyd(Jones):
Tries - Hawkyard McEwan: Goals - Parrish(2):
CASTLEFORD - Coen: Richardson Marchant Hyde Kear: Joyner R.Beardmore(Orum): Hardy K.Beardmore Johnson James(Ward) Connell England: Tries - K.Beardmore(2) Marchant Joyner: Goals R.Beardmore(5):
Referee W H Thompson(Hud'field) Att - 3536 H.T. 10 - 4

Sun 24 Apr 1983 HULL KINGSTON ROVERS away lost 14 - 35 PREMIERSHIP ROUND 1
HULL K R - Fairburn: Clark M.Smith(Burton) Hall Prohm: Hartley G.Smith: Holdstock(Crooks) Watkinson White Kelly Hogan Lazenby: Tries - Hall(4) Fairbairn Hartley Hogan: Goals - Fairbairn(7):
CASTLEFORD - Coen: Terry Richardson Marchant Hyde Kear: Joyner Orum) R.Beardmore: Hardy K.Beardmore Johnson Connell(James) Ward(Connell) England:
Tries - Kear(2) Hyde R.Beardmore: Goal - R.Beardmore:
Referee J McDonald (Wigan) Att - 7664 H.T. 5 - 22

Mark Roach
D No 623
1982-83 to 1984-85

David Roockley
D. No 625
1982-83 to 1988-89

SEASON 1982-83

D.N	PLAYER		DEBUT	L MATCH	APP	SUB	T.AP	TRI'S	G'LS	D.G	P'TS
512	REILLY	MALCOLM			3	3	6	0	0	0	0
518	SPURR	ROBERT		06/03/1983	3	0	3	0	0	0	0
544	CLAUGHTON	GEORGE		29/08/1982	3	0	3	0	0	0	0
551	JOYNER	JOHN			30	0	30	10	0	0	30
556	RICHARDSON	TERRY		24/04/1983	36	0	36	8	0	0	24
560	FENTON	STEVE			3	0	3	1	0	0	3
568	HARDY	ALAN			10	3	13	1	0	1	4
572	WRAITH	GEOFFREY		06/03/1983	0	1	1	0	0	0	0
588	NORTON	PAUL		31/10/1982	7	1	8	0	0	0	0
591	CRAMPTON	JAMES			0	1	1	0	0	0	0
596	KEAR	JOHN			34	1	35	8	0	0	24
598	HIGGINS	BARRY			16	9	25	3	0	0	9
599	FINCH	DAVID			3	0	3	2	10	0	26
601	HYDE	GARY			31	3	34	22	15	0	96
603	WARD	KEVIN			27	1	28	10	0	0	30
604	CONNELL	GARY			21	3	24	2	0	0	6
606	BIRKBY	IAN		27/03/1983	1	5	6	1	0	0	3
607	TIMSON	ANDY			25	3	28	10	0	0	30
608	BEARDMORE	ROBERT			35	1	36	14	117	0	276
609	ORUM	IAN			14	13	27	2	0	0	6
611	BEARDMORE	KEVIN			24	0	24	16	0	0	48
613	JOHNSON	BARRY			31	1	32	4	0	0	12
614	JAMES	NEIL			26	6	32	5	0	0	15
616	SPEDDING	PAUL			8	2	10	0	0	0	0
617	HARRISON	JOHN		20/03/1983	0	1	1	0	0	0	0
618	MARCHANT	TONY			35	1	36	16	0	0	48
619	HORTON	STUART			8	0	8	0	0	0	0
620	ANDERSON	KEVIN	22/08/1982		6	0	6	0	0	0	0
621	ENGLAND	KEITH	31/10/1982		15	6	21	2	0	0	6
622	COEN	DARREN	21/11/1982		22	0	22	5	0	0	15
623	ROACHE	MARK	19/12/1982		2	0	2	1	0	0	3
624	KELLETT	NEIL	06/03/1983	06/03/1983	1	0	1	0	0	0	0
625	ROOCKLEY	DAVID	10/04/1983		1	0	1	0	0	0	0
	33			**6**	**8**	**481**	**65**	**546**	**143**	**142**	**1**	**714**

COMPETITION		P	W	D	L	FOR	AGT
LEAGUE D 1	POSITION 7 OF 16	30	18	1	11	629	458
YORK'S CUP		1	0	0	1	10	33
RL CUP		4	3	0	1	51	38
PLAYERS NO6		1	0	0	1	10	16
CHAMPIONSHIP		1	0	0	1	14	35
PLAYERS RECORDS		**37**	**21**	**1**	**15**	**714**	**580**

The 'Sin Bin' rule was introduced from 1 January 1983 and on 20 February 1983 Gary Connell became the first Castleford player to be 'sin binned' in the 11 all away draw at Featherstone Rovers.

Robert (Bob) Beardmore increased the record for the points scored in a League game to 27 against Carlisle played at Belle Vue Wakefield on the 8 April 1983.

A notable Debutant was Keith England

SEASON 1983-84

In the League Fulham, Wakefield Trinity Salford Whitehaven were promoted to Division 1. Barrow, Workington Town, Halifax Carlisle were relegated to Division 2, A new club, Kent Invicta being admitted to Division 2.

The value of a try was increased to four points.

Sun 7 Aug 1983 YORK away lost 32 - 35
GARY NICHOLSON BENEFIT FRIENDLY
YORK - team not known:
CASTLEFORD - Coen: Gill Harrison Howes Roache: Jones R.Beardmore: Mountain Horton Johnson Crampton Timson Battye:
Subs used- Orum Roockley I.Hartley Fletcher A.N.Other
Scorers etc. not known:

Sun 14 Aug 1983 HULL home won 32 - 20
EVA HARDAKER TROPHY FRIENDLY
CASTLEFORD - Coen: Spears Kear Hyde Roache: Jones R.Beardmore: Connell Horton Johnson Crampton England Higgins: Subs used - Orum Fletcher Roockley Mountain Wraith
Tries - Roache Jones Beardmore Connell Johnson:
Goals - Beardmore(6):
HULL - Prendiville: Scruton Leuluai Schofield Elliott: Day Collinson: Sutton Puckering Stone Rose Proctor Crane:
Subs used - Topliss Harkin Skerrett Madley DeVorde
Tries - Schofield(2) Leuluai Topliss:
Goals - Prendiville DeVorde:
Referee W H Thompson (Hud'field) Att - 853 H.T. 26 - 6

Sun 21 Aug 1983 FEATHERSTONE ROVERS away won 46 - 22
FEATHERSTONE R - Quinn: Marsh Johnson Gilbert Bardgett: Banks Pickerill (S.Barker): Siddall(Slatter) Spurr Hankins D.Hobbs Lyman Hudson:
Tries - Marsh Banks Pickerill: Goals - Quinn(5):
CASTLEFORD - Coen: Marchant Joyner Hyde Kear: KEVIN JONES(626) R.Beardmore: Connell K.Beardmore Johnson(Orum) James(NEIL BATTYE(627)) England Higgins:
Tries - Hyde(2) Marchant Joyner R.Beardmore Connell K.Beardmore Higgins: Goals - R.Beardmore(7):
Referee S Haigh (Ossett) Att - 4538 H.T. 22 - 6

Wed 24 Aug 1983 HULL KINGSTON ROVERS away won 26 - 14
HULL K R - Lydiat: Clark P.Proctor Robinson Laws: Hartley Harkin: Holdstock(Burton) Watkinson Watson Lazenby Hogan(Kelly) Hall:
Tries - Robinson Watson: Goals - Hogan(2) Lydiat:
CASTLEFORD - Coen: Kear Joyner Hyde Marchant: Jones R.Beardmore: Ward K.Beardmore Reilly James England Higgins(Battye): Tries - R.Beardmore(2) Joyner Higgins: Goals - R.Beardmore(5):
Referee D W Fox (Wakefield) Att - 6115 H.T. 14 - 12

Sun 28 Aug 1983 HULL home lost 18 - 40
CASTLEFORD - Coen: Marchant Joyner Hyde(S/O) Kear:

Jones R.Beardmore: Hardy K.Beardmore(Orum) Connell(James) Ward England Higgins:
Tries - Jones Connell James: Goals - R.Beardmore(3):
HULL - Leuluai: Solal Evans(W.Proctor) Banks Prendiville: Topliss Harkin: Edmonds Patrick Skerrett Rose(Divorty) Norton Crane: Tries - Leuluai Solal Topliss Harkin Edmonds Skerrett: Goals - Prendiville(8):
Referee R Whitfeld (Widnes) Att - 6620 H.T. 6 - 12

Sun 4 September 1983 HUDDERSFIELD home won 36 - 20 YORKSHIRE CUP ROUND 1
CASTLEFORD - Coen: Fenton Joyner Marchant Kear: Jones(Reilly) R.Beardmore: Hardy Horton Connell James England Higgins: Tries - Higgins(2) Coen Fenton Reilly England: Goals - R.Beardmore(6):
HUDDERSFIELD - Barton: Cramp Leathley Senior Thomas: Knight Greenwood: Johnson Wroe Rose Davis A.N.Other Wilson(McHugh):
Tries - Leathley Senior Johnson: Goals - Thomas(4):
Referee G Berry (Batley) Att - 2506 H.T. 8 - 14

Sun 11 September 1983 ST HELENS away won 22 - 10
ST HELENS - Rule: Ledger Allen Haggerty Meadows: Peters(Smith) Holding: Bottell Liptrot Grimes Platt Gorley Pinner: Try - Holding: Goals - Rule(3):
CASTLEFORD - Coen: Fenton Marchant Hyde Kear: Joyner R.Beardmore: Connell Hardy Spedding James England Higgins: Tries - Marchant Hyde Connell James:
Goals - R.Beardmore(3):
Referee S Wall (Leigh) Att - 4459 H.T. 10 - 2

Wed 14 September 1983 BRADFORD NORTHERN away won 12 - 8 YORKSHIRE CUP ROUND 2
BRADFORD N - Green: D.Smith Parrish Carroll Davies: Hanley Fennell: (Pennant): Van Bellen(Fleming) Noble Atherton Jasiewicz Sheldon Rathbone: Goals - Parrish(4):
CASTLEFORD - Coen: Fenton Marchant Hyde Kear: Joyner R.Beardmore: Connell K.Beardmore Hardy Ward England(James) Higgins:
Try - Connell: Goals - R.Beardmore(4):
Referee D W Fox (Wakefield) Att - 4684 H.T. 2 - 6

Sun 18 September 1983 LEIGH home won 28 - 18
CASTLEFORD - Coen: Fenton Marchant Hyde Kear: Joyner R.Beardmore: Connell(Orum) K.Beardmore Hardy Ward England Higgins(James): Tries - Hyde Joyner K.Beardmore Ward: Goals - R.Beardmore(6):
LEIGH - Hogan(Stradins): Drummond Donlan Henderson Fox: Woods Varley: Pyke Ainsworth Manfredi(Green) Howarth Fitzmartin Westhead:
Tries - Fox(2) Woods: Goals - Woods(3):
Referee T J Court (Leeds) Att - 4029 H.T. 16 - 12

Fri 23 September 1983 WAKEFIELD TRINITY away won 34 - 12 YORKSHIRE CUP SEMI FINAL
WAKEFIELD T - Box: Jones Harrison Lyons Fletcher: Stephenson Pickerill(Eden): Bratt(Harris) Maskill Thompson Hughes Geary Williams:
Tries - Fletcher Maskill: Goals - Maskill(2):

327

SEASON 1983-84

CASTLEFORD - Coen: Fenton Marchant Hyde Kear: Joyner R.Beardmore: Hardy K.Beardmore(Crampton) Connell Ward England Higgins(James):
Tries - Coen Fenton Marchant Hyde Kear Connell:
Goals - R.Beardmore(4) Hyde:
Referee D G Kershaw (Easingwold) Att - 5592 H.T. 18 -nil

Sun 25 September 1983 SALFORD away won 34 - 14
SALFORD - Shuttleworth: Driver(Bloor) Bentley Glynn Twist: Fletcher Nash: Blackwood Groves Wood Williams Turnbull McTigue: Tries - Williams(2): Goals - Twist(3):
CASTLEFORD - Coen: Fenton Marchant Hyde Kear: Joyner R.Beardmore: Connell Horton Hardy Crampton(James) Ward(Orum) England: Tries - Marchant Kear R.Beardmore Crampton Ward England: Goals - R.Beardmore(5):
Referee B F Walker (Barrow) Att - 2395 H.T. 6 - 8

Sun 2 Oct 1983 LEEDS home won 54 - 4
CASTLEFORD - Coen: Gill Marchant Fenton Kear: Joyner(Orum) R.Beardmore: Hardy Horton Reilly(Timson) James(S/O) Battye England: Tries - R.Beardmore(3) James(2) Marchant Fenton Kear: Goals - R.Beardmore(11):
LEEDS - Healey: Mitchell Creasser Wilkinson Massa: Holmes Dick: Keith.Rayne Ward Pitchford Heselwood (Squire) Carroll(W.Heron) D.Heron: Try - D.Heron
Referee K Allatt (Southport) Att - 5336 H.T. 20 - nil

Sun 9 Oct 1983 WHITEHAVEN away won 26 - 2
WHITEHAVEN - D'Leny: Gribbins Fisher(Ratcliffe) Thompson Mackie: Tomlinson Hall: Pythian Banks(Barnes) Cottier Simpson McCarron Kirkby: Goal - Gribbins:
CASTLEFORD - Coen: Gill Kear Marchant Orum: Fenton(Roockley) R.Beardmore: Connell Horton Hardy(Reilly) James Timson England:
Tries - Marchant(2) Gill Kear R.Beardmore:
Goals - R.Beardmore(2) Roockley:
Referee J McDonald (Wigan) Att - 1860 H.T. 6 - 2

Sat 15 Oct 1983 HULL lost 2 - 13
YORKSHIRE CUP FINAL - AT ELLAND ROAD LEEDS
CASTLEFORD - Coen: Fenton Marchant Hyde(Orum) Kear: Joyner R.Beardmore: Connell Horton Reilly Timson James England: Goal - R.Beardmore:
HULL - Kemble: Solal Schofield Leuluai O'Hara: Topliss Dean: Edmonds Wileman Skerrett Proctor Crooks Crane: Tries - O'Hara Procter Crane: Goals - Crane(DG):
Referee W H Thompson (Hud'field) Att - 14049 H.T. 2 - 4
WHITE ROSE TROPHY - MICK CRANE (HULL)

Wed 19 Oct 1983 OLDHAM home lost 16 - 18
CASTLEFORD - Coen: Fenton Marchant Hyde Gill(Orum): Joyner R.Beardmore: Connell(Reilly) Horton Hardy James England Higgins:
Tries - Marchant(2) Fenton: Goals - R.Beardmore(2):
OLDHAM - Littler: Hawkyard Parrish Foy(S/O) Hornby: Willis(Birkby)Ashton: Jones McCurrie Morgan Naidole(Sinclair) Lowndes Worrall:
Tries - Foy(2): Goals - Parrish(5):
Referee D G Kershaw(Easingwold) Att - 3913 H.T. 10 - 10

Sun 30 Oct 1983 HULL KINGSTON ROVERS home lost 8 - 18
CASTLEFORD - Coen: Fenton Marchant(Kear) Hyde Gill: Joyner R.Beardmore: Hardy Horton Reilly Spedding Connell England: Goals - R.Beardmore(4):
HULL K R - Fairbairn: Clark M.Smith Prohm Laws: Dorahy G.Smith: Broadhurst Rudd Casey(Kelly) Burton Hogan Hall: Tries - M.Smith Dorahy Hogan: Goals - Fairbairn(3):
Referee G F Lindop (Wakefield) Att - 5950 H.T. 2 - 12

Sun 6 Nov 1983 HULL home lost 4 - 8
JOHN PLAYER TROPHY ROUNND 1
CASTLEFORD - Coen: Fenton Marchant Hyde Gill(Roockley): Joyner(Spedding) R.Beardmore: Connell(S/O) Horton Hardy Ward England Higgins:
Goals - R.Beardmore(2):
HULL - Kemble: Evans Schofield Leuluia O'Hara: Ah Kuoi Harkin: Skerrett(S/O) Wileman(S/O) Rose Divorty (W.Proctor) Crooks Crane: Try - Evans: Goals - Crooks(2):
Referee R Campbell (Widnes) Att - 8023 H.T. 4 - 6

Sun 13 Nov 1983 LEEDS away won 28 - 10
LEEDS - Wilkinson: Massa Creasser Heselwood Prendiville: Holmes Dick: Keith.Rayne Ward Kevin.Rayne Moorby W.Heron D.Heron(Squire):
Tries - Holmes Ward: Goal - Creasser:
CASTLEFORD - Coen: Fenton(Roockley) Marchant Hyde Kear: Joyner R.Beardmore: Connell Horton Hardy Ward England Higgins(Spedding): Tries - Marchant Hyde Joyner R.Beardmore: Goals - R.Beardmore(6):
Referee W H Thompson (Hud'field) Att - 6316 H.T. 4 - 4

Sun 20 Nov 1983 WHITEHAVEN home won 50 - 2
CASTLEFORD - Coen: Fenton(Kear) Joyner Hyde Marchant: GARY FREEMAN(628)R.Beardmore: Connell Horton Alan Hardy(Spedding) Ward Timson England: Tries - Kear(2) Timson(2) Coen Joyner Hyde Ward: Goals - R.Beardmore(9):
WHITEHAVEN - D'Leny: Dalton Huddart Thompson A.N.Other: Wright Tomlinson: Phythian Banks Simpson McCarron Fraser Cottier: Goal - Thompson:
Referee J E Smith (Halifax) Att - 2776 H.T. 24 - 2

Sun 27 Nov 1983 WARRINGTON away lost 14 - 16
WARRINGTON - Hesford: Forster Day R.Duane Phil.Ford: Blacker(Scott) Kelly: Yates O'Mahoney Worrall Eccles Fieldhouse Gregory:
Tries - Ford(2) Eccles: Goals - Hesford(2):
CASTLEFORD - Coen: Marchant Joyner Hyde Kear: Freeman R.Beardmore: Spedding Horton Crampton(James) Ward Timson England:
Try - England: Goals - R.Beardmore(5):
Referee P Volanye (Batley) Att - 2843 H.T. 8 - 10

Sun 4 Dec 1983 FULHAM away draw 6 - 6
FULHAM - Ganley: Cambriani Stockley Diamond M'Barki: Eckersley(Allen) Bowden: Beverley Doherty Gourley Hull Dearden Kinsey: Try - Diamond: Goal - M'Barki:
CASTLEFORD - Coen: Fenton Joyner Hyde Marchant: Freeman R.Beardmore(Kear): Spedding Horton Crampton

SEASON 1983-84

Ward(James) Timson England: Goals - R.Beardmore(3):
Referee K Spencer (Warrington) Att - 2515 H.T. 6 - 4

Sun 11 Dec 1983 SALFORD home won 40 - 12
CASTLEFORD - Coen: Roockley(Jones) Marchant Hyde
Kear: Joyner Freeman: Ward K.Beardmore Johnson James
Crampton England: Tries - Joyner(4) Hyde Crampton
England: Goals - Hyde(6):
SALFORD - Shuttleworth: Bentley Byrne Bloor(Lamb)
Glynn: Fletcher Nash: Major Groves Smith
Dickens(Turnbull) Williams McTigue:
Tries - Byrne Nash: Goals - Shuttleworth(2):
Referee T M Beaumont (Hud'field) Att - 2872 H.T. 20 - 6

Mon 26 Dec 1983 WAKEFIELD TRINITY home won 24 - 8
CASTLEFORD - Coen: Fenton(Orum) Marchant Hyde Kear:
Joyner Freeman: Connell(James) K.Beardmore Johnson
Crampton Ward England: Tries - Freeman(2) Marchant
Hyde Johnson: Goals - Hyde(2):
WAKEFIELD T - Kelly: Fletcher S.Lewis Coventry Jones:
W.Lewis Pickerill: Hughes Maskill Bratt Geary
Burns(Williams) Stephenson:
Try - W.Lewis: Goals - Maskill(2)
Referee W H Thompson (Hud'field) Att - 8860 H.T. 14 - 2

Sun 1 Jan 1984 BRADFORD NORTHERN away draw 2 - 2
BRADFORD N - Mumby: Jackson Pennant(Carroll) Davies
Parrish: Hanley Robinson: Atherton Noble Van Bellen
Jasiewicz Sheldon(Fleming) Rathbone:
Goal - Parrish:
CASTLEFORD - Coen: Marchant Joyner Hyde Kear:
Freeman R.Beardmore: Connell K.Beardmore
Johnson(James) Ward(Orum) Crampton England:
Goal - R.Beardmore:
Referee G Berry (Batley) Att - 7167 H.T. nil - 2

Sun 8 Jan 1984 WIGAN away lost 6 - 32
WIGAN - Hampson: Ramsdale Stephenson Whitfield Juliff:
Edwards Stephens: Hemsley Tamati Case Cannon(Scott)
West Elvin:
Tries - West(2) Edwards Case: Goals - Whitfield(8):
CASTLEFORD - Coen: Marchant Joyner Hyde Kear:
Freeman R.Beardmore (Jones): Connell
K.Beardmore(Timson) Paul Spedding James Crampton
England: Try - Crampton: Goal - R.Beardmore:
Referee S Wall (Leigh) Att - 7430 H.T. nil - 10

Wed 1 Feb 1984 WIDNES away lost 8 - 14
WIDNES - Burke: Wright Hughes Linton Basnett: Gregory
Hulme: Blackwood(Haughton) Elwell Wood Adams
Whitfield J.Myler:
Tries - Wright Hughes Gregory: Goal - Gregory:
CASTLEFORD - Roockley: Gill Joyner STEVEN
ROBINSON(629) Hyde: Freeman R.Beardmore: Connell
K.Beardmore Reilly Crampton(BRETT ATKINS(630)) Ward
England: Try - England: Goals - R.Beardmore(2):
Referee C Hodgson (Maryport) Att - 3911 H.T. 2 - 14

Sun 5 Feb 1984 FULHAM home won 26 - 7
CASTLEFORD - Roockley: Marchant Joyner Freeman
Gill(Hyde): Robinson R.Beardmore: Connell K Beardmore
Crampton Ward Atkins)Reilly England:
Tries - Roockley Joyner Freeman Hyde Robinson:
Goals - R.Beardmore(3):
FULHAM - Mills Bayliss Allen Diamond Jones: Stockley
Bowden: Beverley Doherty Gourley(Hoare) Jackson
Dearden Kinsey: Goals - Diamond(3) Kinsey(DG):
Referee J Gocher (Australia) Att - 3131 H.T. 8 - 5

Sat 11 Feb 1984 KENT INVICTA away won 42 - 20 CHALLENGE CUP ROUND 1
KENT I - Penola: Richardson Elia Harding Feighan: Lane
Thaler: Van Bellen Bishop Cooper(Norton) Mordell O'Shea
Hetherington: Tries - Feighan(2) Elia: Goals - O'Shea(4):
CASTLEFORD - Roockley: Gill(Hyde) Joyner Freeman
Marchant: Robinson R.Beardmore: Connell K.Beardmore
Ward James(Battye) Atkins England: Tries - Atkins(2)
Ward(2) Hyde England: Goals - R.Beardmore(9):
Referee R Campbell (Widnes) Att - 1643 H.T. 14 - 8

Sun 19 Feb 1984 BRADFORD NORTHERN home won 29 - 6
CASTLEFORD - Roockley: Marchant Joyner Hyde Gill:
Robinson R.Beardmore: Ward K.Beardmore(S/O)
Connell(Freeman) Atkins James England(Battye):
Tries - Joyner(2) Hyde Gill R.Beardmore:
Goals - R.Beardmore(4) (DG):
BRADFORD N - Green: Parrish(Hale) Pennant Davies
Whiteman: Carroll Robinson: Grayshon Noble Van Bellen
Jasiewicz(Rathbone) Idle Fleming:
Try - Flemming: Goals - Carroll:
Referee R Whitfield (Widnes) Att - 5300 H.T. 23 - nil

Sun 26 Feb 1984 WARRINGTON home won 23 - 16 CHALLENGE CUP ROUND 2
CASTLEFORD - Roockley: Marchant Hyde Freeman Gill:
Robinson R.Beardmore: Ward K.Beardmore James Atkins
Timson Joyner:
Tries - Robinson(2) Hyde: Goals - R.Beardmore(5) (DG):
WARRINGTON - Hesford: Forster Peters R.Duane Phil
Ford: Blacker Kelly(Scott): Eccles O'Mahoney Fieldhouse
Gregory Muller Webb:
Tries - Duane Eccles Gregory: Goals - Hesford(2):
Referee J McDonald (Wigan) Att - 8071 H.T. 6 - 12

Sun 4 Mar 1984 WARRINGTON home lost 10 - 21
CASTLEFORD - Roockley: Marchant Freeman Hyde Gill:
Robinson Orum(R.Beardmore): Anderson(Atkins) Horton
England Atkins(Joyner)Timson Higgins:
Try - Horton: Goals - Hyde(3):
WARRINGTON - Paul.Ford: Forster Muller R.Duane
Phil.Ford: Blacker(Peters) Kelly: Eccles O'Mahoney Poasa
Gregory Chisnall) Fieldhouse Webb:
Tries - Paul.Ford Muller Poasa: Goals - Paul.Ford(4) (DG):
Referee K Allatt (Southport) Att - 3777 H.T. 10 - 12

329

SEASON 1983-84

Sun 11 Mar 1984 YORK away lost 12 - 14
CHALLENGE CUP ROUND 3
YORK - Midgley: G.Pryce Harrison Morrell Kain: Steadman
Wilson(Blackburn): Hooper Phillippo B.Hughes Price
M.Hughes Smith:
Tries - Steadman(2): Goals - Steadman(3):
CASTLEFORD - Roockley: Marchant Joyner Hyde Gill:
Robinson(Freeman) R.Beardmore: Ward K.Beardmore
Connell James(Higgins) Timson England:
Tries - Marchant Robinson: Goals - R.Beardmore(2):
Referee S Wall (Leigh) Att - 7362 H.T. 8 - 8

Sun 18 Mar 1984 FEATHERSTONE ROVERS home
draw 8 - 8
CASTLEFORD - Roockley: Gill Fenton Hyde Kear: Freeman
R.Beardmore: Ward K.Beardmore James England(Higgins)
Timson Joyner: Try - James: Goals - R.Beardmore(2):
FEATHERSTONE R - N.Barker: Marsh Slater Quinn Lund:
Banks Fox: Siddall Spurr Gibbins Lyman Clarkson(Hudson)
Hobbs: Goals - Quinn(3) (DG) Hobbs(DG):
Referee K Spencer (Southport) Att - 4069 H.T. 4 - 4

Sun 25 Mar 1984 ST HELENS home won 26 - 22
CASTLEFORD - Roockley: Gill(Jones) Fenton(Gill) Hyde
Kear: Freeman R.Beardmore(Anderson): Ward Horton
James Atkins Timson Joyner:
Tries - Atkins(3) Jones: Goals - Hyde(3) R.Beardmore(2):
ST HELENS - Rule: Ledger(Allen) Peters Haggerty Griffiths:
Arkwright Holding: Burke Liptrot Gorley Platt Round
Pinner: Tries - Allen Haggerty Arkwright Holding:
Goals - Griffiths(3):
Referee G F Lindop (Wakefield) Att - 2674 H.T. 18 - 6

Wed 28 Mar 1984 WIGAN home won 38 - 10
CASTLEFORD - Roockley(Coen): Gill Fenton Hyde Kear:
Gary Freeman Jones(Roockley): Ward K.Beardmore James
Atkins Timson Joyner(Anderson): Tries - Atkins(2) Gill
Fenton Kear Freeman: Goals - Hyde(7):
WIGAN - Williams: Braithwaite Stephenson Ford
Ramsdale: Edwards Stephens(S/O): Courtney(Fairhurst)
Pendlebury Case(Wane) Juliff Potter Elvin:
Tries - Braithwaite Elvin: Goal - Edwards:
Referee J Mean (Leyland) Att - 2790 H.T. 8 - nil

Sun 1 Apr 1984 LEIGH away lost 4 - 30
LEIGH - C.Johnson: Henderson Donlan Atherton Fox:
Woods P.Johnson: Wilkinson Hughes Pyke Cottrell
Howarth Westhead: Tries - Henderson Donlan Woods
Cottrell Westhead: Goals - Woods(5):
CASTLEFORD - Roockley: Gill(Coen) Fenton Hyde Kear:
Robinson R.Beardmore: Ward(Anderson) K.Beardmore
James Atkins Timson(S/O) Joyner: Try - Hyde:
Referee F Robinson (Leeds) Att - 3053 H.T. nil - 20

Sun 8 Apr 1984 HULL away lost 10 - 40
HULL - Kemble: Evans Schofield Leuluai O'Hara: Topliss
Ah Kuoi: Edmunds(Tindall) Patrick Rose Proctor Norton
(Solal) Divorty: Tries - Schofield(2) Leuluai Topliss
Edmunds Rose Norton Solal: Goals - Schofield(4):

CASTLEFORD - Roockley: Coen Fenton(Kear) Hyde
Marchant: Robinson Orum: Kevin Anderson K.Beardmore
James Atkins Crampton(Battye) Joyner:
Tries - Hyde Joyner: Goal - Anderson:
Referee S Wall (Leigh) Att - 10629 H.T. 4 - 16

Wed 11 Apr 1984 OLDHAM away won 13 - 2
OLDHAM - Hornby: Meadows Parrish Foy Bardgett:
Ashton Kirwan(Birkby): Morgan(Naidole) McCurrie
Goodway Worrall Hawkyard Flanagan: Goal - Parrish:
CASTLEFORD - Roockley: Coen Fenton Hyde Marchant:
Robinson Orum: Ward K.Beardmore Connell Atkins
Crampton Joyner:
Try - Hyde: Goals - Hyde(4) Roockley(DG):
Referee B F Ward (Barrow) Att - 2347 H.T. 1 - 2

Sun 15 Apr 1984 WIDNES home won 24 - 18
CASTLEFORD - Roockley: Coen Fenton Marchant Kear:
Robinson(James) Orum (R.Beardmore): Ward
K.Beardmore Connell Crampton Atkins Joyner:
Tries - Coen Kear Robinson Crampton Atkins:
Goals - Roockley(2):
WIDNES - Burke: Hughes Lydon(Linton) O'Loughlin
Basnett: D.Hulme Gregory: S.O'Neill(Gorley) Ruane Wood
Whitfield M.O'Neill Adams:
Tries - Basnett Hulme Whitfield: Goals - Burke(3):
Referee W H Thompson(Hud'field) Att - 3152 H.T. 12 -12

Mon 23 Apr 1984 WAKEFIELD TRINITY away
won 42 - 12
WAKEFIELD T - Rollin(Oglethorpe): Jones Eden Hendry
Hampson: A.N.Other McDermott: Hopkinson Stringer
Harris Thompson Swann Box(Wilkinson):
Tries - Jones A.N.Other: Goals - A.N.Other(2):
CASTLEFORD - Roockley: Coen Fenton Marchant Kear:
Robinson R.Beardmore: Ward(James) K.Beardmore
Connell Crampton Atkins Joyner(Orum):
Tries - Marchant(2) R.Beardmore(2) Atkins(2) Coen:
Goals - R.Beardmore(7):
Referee T M Beaumont (Hud'field) Att - 2896 H.T. 18 -12

Sun 29 Apr 1984 WIDNES home won 36 - 4
PREMIERSHIP ROUND 1
CASTLEFORD - Roockley: Coen Marchant Hyde Kear:
Robinson R.Beardmore: Ward K.Beardmore Connell(DEAN
MOUNTAIN(631)) Crampton Atkins(Orum) Joyner:
Tries - Marchant(2) R.Beardmore Atkins Joyner:
Goals - R.Beardmore(8):
WIDNES - Lyon(Lamb): Wright Hughes(Whitfield) Linton
Basnett: O'Loughlin D.Hulme: S.O'Neil Elwell Tamati
L.Gorley M.O'Neil Adams: Try - Basnett:
Referee J E Smith (Halifax) Att - 3283 H.T. 14 - nil

Mon 7 May 1984 HULL away won 22 - 12
PREMIERSHIP SEMI FINAL
HULL - Kemble: Evans Schofield Leuluai O'Hara: Topliss
Ah Kuoi: Edmunds(Crooks) Crooks(Puckering)
Rose(Dannatt) Proctor Norton Divorty:
Tries - Schofield Topliss: Goals - Schofield(2):
CASTLEFORD - Roockley: Coen Marchant Hyde Kear:

Robinson R.Beardmore: Ward K.Beardmore(Mountain)
Connell Crampton Atkins Joyner:
Tries - Hyde Ward Crampton Atkins:
Goals - R.Beardmore(3):
Referee K Allatt (Southport) Att - 12571 H.T. 16 - 6

Sat 12 May 1984 HULL KINGSTON ROVERS lost 10 -18
PREMIERSHIP FINAL - AT HEADINGLEY LEEDS
CASTLEFORD - Roockley: Coen Marchant Hyde Kear:
Steven Robinson R.Beardmore: Ward Horton Connell
James Crampton Atkins Joyner:
Try - Kear: Goals - R.Beardmore(3):
HULL K R - Fairbairn: Clark Smith Prohm Laws: Dorahy
Harkin: Holdstock Rudd Millington(Robinson) Burton
Broadhurst Hall:
Tries - Smith Prohm Laws Dorahy: Goal - Dorahy:
Referee R Campbell (Widnes) Att - 12482 H.T. 8 – nil

Kevin Jones
D. No 626
1983-84 to 1984-85

Neil Battye
D. No 627
1983-84 to 1992-93

Gary Freeman
D. No 628
1983-84

Brett Atkins
D. No 630
1983-84 to 1986-87

Dean Mountain
D. No 631
1983-84 to 1987-88

SUNDAY 18 MARCH 1984 V FEATHERSTONE ROVERS HOME DRAW 8 - 8
Back Row – John Joyner Kevin Anderson Andrew Timpson Neil James Kevin Ward John Kear
Front Row – Terry Richardson Barry Johnson (Captain) Tony Marchant Stuart Horton Ian Orum Steve Fenton

SEASON 1983-84

D.N	PLAYER		DEBUT	L MATCH	APP	SUB	T.AP	TRI'S	G'LS	D.G	P'TS
512	REILLY	MALCOLM			6	3	9	1	0	0	4
551	JOYNER	JOHN			39	1	40	14	0	0	56
560	FENTON	STEVE			24	0	24	5	0	0	20
568	HARDY	ALAN		20/11/1983	14	0	14	0	0	0	0
591	CRAMPTON	JAMES		12/05/1984	16	1	17	5	0	0	20
596	KEAR	JOHN			27	4	31	9	0	0	36
598	HIGGINS	BARRY			12	2	14	4	0	0	16
601	HYDE	GARY			34	2	36	17	26	0	120
603	WARD	KEVIN			30	0	30	6	0	0	24
604	CONNELL	GARY			29	0	29	5	0	0	20
607	TIMSON	ANDY			12	2	14	2	0	0	8
608	BEARDMORE	ROBERT			34	2	36	13	140	2	334
609	ORUM	IAN			5	12	17	0	0	0	0
610	GILL	STEVEN			16	0	16	3	0	0	12
611	BEARDMORE	KEVIN			25	0	25	2	0	0	8
613	JOHNSON	BARRY			4	0	4	1	0	0	4
614	JAMES	NEIL			19	11	30	5	0	0	20
616	SPEDDING	PAUL		08/01/1984	5	3	8	0	0	0	0
618	MARCHANT	TONY			36	0	36	16	0	0	64
619	HORTON	STUART			15	0	15	1	0	0	4
620	ANDERSON	KEVIN		08/04/1984	2	3	5	0	1	0	2
621	ENGLAND	KEITH			30	0	30	6	0	0	24
622	COEN	DARREN			30	2	32	5	0	0	20
625	ROOCKLEY	DAVID			19	3	22	1	3	1	11
626	JONES	KEVIN	21/08/1983		5	3	8	2	0	0	8
627	BATTYE	NEIL	21/08/1983		1	5	6	0	0	0	0
628	FREEMAN	GARY	20/11/1983	28/03/1984	15	2	17	4	0	0	16
629	ROBINSON	STEVEN	01/02/1984	12/05/1984	15	0	15	5	0	0	20
630	ATKINS	BRETT	01/02/1984		14	2	16	12	0	0	48
631	MOUNTAIN	DEAN	29/04/1984		0	2	2	0	0	0	0
	30		6	6	533	65	598	144	170	3	919

COMPETITION		P	W	D	L	FOR	AGT
LEAGUE D 1	POSITION 4 OF 16	30	18	3	9	686	438
YORK'S CUP		4	3	0	1	84	53
RL CUP		3	2	0	1	77	50
PLAYERS NO6		1	0	0	1	4	8
CHAMPIONSHIP		3	2	0	1	68	34
PLAYERS RECORDS		41	25	3	13	919	583

Rule Changes:
The six tackle rule was changed with a handover on the sixth tackle in place of a scrum.
At a scrum the non-offending side were given the 'Head' and fed the scrum.

For the second time in three years we reached the final of the Yorkshire Cup. Our final opponents at Elland Road Leeds were Hull and, yes, they defeated us again 13–2.

In the Challenge Cup we had victories in Round 1 and Round 2, and with Hull being knocked out in Round 2 at St Helens, our supporters were starting to dream of Wembley. However, away in the Round 3 we underestimated a York side inspired by Graham Steadman, who scored all York's points with two tries and three goals in their 14–12 victory.

Our Hull hoodoo was nearly laid in the Premiership play off. After a victory at home to Widnes in Round 1, 38–4, in the semi-final we actually managed a victory over Hull away 22–12. However, in the final at Headingley we came up against the other Hull side, Hull KR, and once more we came away empty handed with a 18–10 defeat.

Robert (Bob) Beardmore increased the record for points scored in a League Game to 31 against Leeds at home on the 2 October 1983 and also set a season's points scoring record of 334 points

A Young Gary Freeman made 15 appearances and two substitute appearances scoring four tries, and later went on to Captain New Zealand.

In the League Barrow Workington Town Hunslet Halifax were promoted to Division 1. Fulham, Wakefield Trinity Salford Whitehaven were relegated to Division 2. Three new clubs, Mansfield Marksman, Bridgend and Sheffield Eagles were admitted and Cardiff City dropped out of Division 2. Kent Invicta changed their name to Southend Invicta and Huyton changed their name to Runcorn Highfield.

Fri 10 Aug 1984 SHEFFIELD EAGLES home won 44 – 20 FRIENDLY

CASTLEFORD - Coen: Richardson Marchant Finch Fenton: Kev.Jones R.Beardmore: Connell Fletcher Johnson James Battye England:
Subs used - Orum Spears Anderson Mountain Roache Ketteridge Swift Keith Jones A.N.Other
Tries - Marchant(2) Coen Finch Kev.Jones R.Beardmore Spears Anderson: Goals - R.Beardmore(4) Finch(2):
SHEFFIELD E - Tyers: N.Cooper Davies M.Q.Campbell Aldred: Robinson A.N.Other: Harris M.Campbell Farrar S.Cooper Jowitt McDermott: Subs used - Harvey Hetherington A.N.Other Tries - Davies M.Q.Campbell M.Campbell McDermott: Goals - Aldred(2):
Referee T M Beaumont (Huddersfield) Att - H.T. 20 - 12

Fri 24 Aug 1984 HULL away lost 10 - 22 EVA HARDAKER MEMORIAL TROPHY FRIENDLY

HULL - Prendiville: Willingham Ah Kuoi Eastwood O'Hara: Evans Collinson: Lazenby Patrick Rose Dannatt Crooks Norton:
Subs used - Kemble Leuluai Topliss Skerrett Proctor Divorty - :
Tries - Ah Kuoi(2) Proctor: Goals - Divorty(3) Crooks(2):
CASTLEFORD - Roockley: Roache Marchant Fenton Finch: Kev.Jones Orum: Connell Horton Johnson Mountain James England:
Subs used - Coen Spears R.Beardmore Kear Battye Ward -
Tries - Marchant Finch: Goal - Finch:
Referee S Haigh (Ossett) Att - H.T. 10 - 6

Sun 2 Sep 1984 WIGAN home lost 12 - 20

CASTLEFORD - Roockley: Roache Marchant Fenton Finch: Joyner R.Beardmore: Connell Horton Johnson James(Mountain) Ward England(S/O):
Tries - Finch James: Goals - R.Beardmore(2):
WIGAN - Edwards: Ferguson Stephenson Whitfield Ramsdale: Cannon Fairhurst: Courtney(Dunn) O'Neil(Juliff) Case Potter West(S/O) Pendlebury(S/O):
Tries - Ferguson Cannon Case West: Goals - Whitfield(2):
Referee G Kershaw (Easingwold) Att - 4481 H.T. 8 - nil

Sun 9 Sep 1984 HALIFAX away lost 10 - 11

HALIFAX - Smith: O'Byrne Agar Dickinson(Moses) (Dickinson) Waites(Moses): Garrod Marshall: Beevers McCallion Greenwood Carroll Shillito Bond:
Try - Carroll: Goals - Agar(3) Carroll(DG):
CASTLEFORD - Coen: Roache Marchant Fenton(Orum) Hyde: Joyner R.Beardmore: Connell K.Beardmore Johnson Ward James England: Tries - Hyde(2): Goal - R.Beardmore:
Referee B F Walker (Barrow) Att - 1857 H.T. nil - 9

Sun 16 Sep 1984 LEEDS home lost 14 - 16 YORKSHIRE CUP ROUND 1

CASTLEFORD - Coen: Roache Marchant Fenton Finch: Joyner(Hyde)R.Beardmore: Connell K.Beardmore Johnson Ward(NIGEL WILSON(632)) (Ward)James England:
Tries - Finch(2): Goals - R.Beardmore(2) Finch:
LEEDS - Wilkinson: Mitchell Heselwood Creasser Smith: Hague Conway: Kevin Rayne(Owen) Ward Moorby Powell Webb D.Heron:
Tries - Heselwood Hague: Goals - Creasser(4):
Referee G F Lindop (Wakefield) Att - 4711 H.T. 2 - 8

Sun 23 Sep 1984 BRADFORD NORTHERN away lost 10 - 20

BRADFORD N - Mumby: Smith Parker Davies Tengdahl: Hanley Fennell: Crayshon Noble Stone(Van Bellen) Heron Jasiewicz Rathbone(Sheldon):
Tries - Hanley(2) Jasiewicz: Goals - Hanley(3) Mumby:
CASTLEFORD - Coen: Roache Marchant Hyde(RON SIGSWORTH(639)) Finch: Fenton Orum: James(Hyde) K.Beardmore Johnson Wilson Battye England:
Tries - Roache Hyde: Goal - Finch:
Referee K Allatt (Southport) Att - 4275 H.T. 6 - 14

Sun 30 Sep 1984 WARRINGTON home won 16 - 14

CASTLEFORD - Sigsworth: Coen Marchant(Kear) Finch Roache: Kev.Jones Orum(Marchant): Connell K.Beardmore Johnson Battye(James) Wilson England:
Tries - Coen(2) Roache: Goals - Finch(2):
WARRINGTON - Paul Ford: Garbutt I.Duane Cullen Phil Ford: Kelly Bowden: Poasa O'Mahoney Jackson Eccles(Gregory) Fieldhouse Webb(Gittins):
Tries - Garbutt Duane Poasa: Goal - Paul Ford:
Referee S Haigh (Ossett) Att - 2608 H.T. 10 - 10

Sun 7 Oct 1984 ST HELENS away lost 16 - 30

ST HELENS - Vievers: Ledger Allen Meninga Day: Arkwright Peters: Burke Liptrot Gorley Platt Round Pinner:
Tries - Meninga(2) Ledger Day Arkwright Peters: Goals - Meninga(2) Day:
CASTLEFORD - Sigsworth: Roache Marchant Fenton David Finch(Coen): Kev.Jones Orum: Connell(Wilson) K.Beardmore Johnson Battye Wilson(James) England:
Tries - Coen K.Beardmore Battye: Goals - Jones(2):
Referee J McDonald (Wigan) Att - 7366 H.T. nil - 16

Sun 14 Oct 1984 FEATHERSTONE ROVERS home won 16 - 14

CASTLEFORD - Sigsworth: Roache Marchant Coen Fenton: Kev.Jones Orum: Ward Horton Johnson Battye Wilson(Timson) Joyner:
Tries - Sigsworth Coen Wilson: Goals - Jones(2):
FEATHERSTONE R - N.Barker: Woolford(Banks) Quinn Marsden Hopkins: Slater Fox: Siddall Spurr Hankins(Gibbins) Clawson Bell Hudson:
Tries - Quinn Spurr: Goals - Quinn(3):
Referee T M Beaumont (Hud'field) Att - 3738 H.T. 14 - 2

SEASON 1984-85

Sun 21 Oct 1984 BARROW away lost 24 - 36
BARROW - Tickle: Moore(Elliott) Whittle Milby
Quirk(McJennett): McConnell Cairns: Hughes Fitzgerald
McJennett(Mossop) Clough Herbert Kirkby:
Tries - Fitzgerald(2) Whittle Milby Quirk McConnell:
Goals - Tickle(6):
CASTLEFORD - Sigsworth: Roache Marchant Coen Fenton:
Kev.Jones Orum: Ward K Beardmore Johnson
Wilson(Connell) Battye Joyner: Tries - Sigsworth Roache
K.Beardmore Joyner: Goals - Jones(4):
Referee P Volante (Batley) Att - 2100 H.T. 6 - 6

Sun 28 Oct 1984 LEIGH home won 32 - nil
CASTLEFORD - Sigsworth: Roache Coen Marchant Kear:
Kev.Jones Orum: Ward(Connell) K.Beardmore Johnson
England Battye Joyner(Higgins):
Tries - Jones(2) Sigsworth Orum Joyner: Goals - Jones(6):
LEIGH - C.Johnson: Drummond Woods Henderson Taylor:
Donlan Beazant: Wilkinson Ainsworth Van Bellen Cottrell
Howarth(Pyke) Clark:
Referee J Smith (Halifax) Att - 2900 H.T. 20 - nil

Sun 4 Nov 1984 WIDNES away lost 18 - 20
WIDNES - Lyon: Wright Burke O'Loughlin Currier: Hulme
J.Myler: M.O'Neill Middlehurst Tamati Wood Sorenson
Eyres:
Tries - Wright(2) O'Loughlin Eyres: Goals - Burke(2):
CASTLEFORD - Sigsworth(Fenton): Roache Marchant
Coen Kear: Kev.Jones Orum: Ward(Connell)
K.Beardmore(Ward) Johnson England Battye Joyner:
Tries - Sigsworth K Beardmore Joyner: Goals - Jones(3):
Referee J Mean (Leyland) Att - 3800 H.T. 12 - 14

Sun 11 Nov 1984 HUNSLET home won 22 - 20
CASTLEFORD - Sigsworth(Kear): Roache Marchant Coen
Fenton: Kev.Jones Orum: Ward K Beardmore Johnson
Timson(England) Battye Joyner:
Tries - Coen Ward Joyner: Goals - Jones(5):
HUNSLET - Kay: Rudd Tate Roe Cooper: Banks King:
Byron Gray Bateman Graham Idle(Skerrett) Woolford:
Tries - Rudd Bateman Graham: Goals - Cooper(4):
Referee F Robinson (Leeds) Att - 2996 H.T. 12 - 12

Sun 18 Nov 1984 BRIDGEND home won 42 - 4
JOHN PLAYER TROPHY ROUND 1
CASTLEFORD - Coen: Roache Marchant Fenton Kear:
Kev.Jones Orum(Wilson): Ward K.Beardmore Johnson
Timson Battye(England) Joyner: Tries - Fenton(3) Kear(2)
Marchant Ward Battye Joyner: Goals - Jones(3):
BRIDGEND - Hallett: Theaker Hindley Barwood Camilleri:
Davies(Sheehy) Flowers: Pring(Walker) Glover Bowman
Vickers Goodall Mathias: Try -
Bowman:
Referee D J Carter (Widnes) Att - 1795 H.T. 18 - 4
**MATCH SHOULD HAVE BEEN PLAYED AT BRIDGEND,
BUT PLAYED AT CASTLEFORD**

**Sun 25 Nov 1984 HULL KINGSTON ROVERS away
lost 14 - 26**
HULL K R - Fairbairn(Lydiat): Anderson Robinson Prohm

Laws: Smith Harkin: Broadhurst Watkinson Holdstock
Burton Kelly(Hall)Miller:
Tries - Lydiat Prohm Laws Smith Watkinson:
Goals - Robinson(2) Lydiat:
CASTLEFORD - Coen: Roache Marchant Fenton Kear:
Kev.Jones Orum (R.Beardmore): Ward K.Beardmore
Johnson Battye Timson(England)Joyner:
Tries - K.Beardmore Johnson: Goals - Jones(3):
Referee D J Croft (Leeds) Att - 6108 H.T. 6 - 10

Sun 2 Dec 1984 HALIFAX away lost 18 - 20
JOHN PLAYER TROPHY ROUND 2
HALIFAX - C.Anderson: O'Byrne Agar T.Anderson Hudson:
Ryan Hagan: Bella Whitehouse Neller Arnold Bond
Langmack: Tries - Hagan(2) T.Anderson Goals - Agar(4):
CASTLEFORD - Coen(Sigsworth): Roache Marchant
Fenton Kear: Kev.Jones R.Beardmore: Ward K.Beardmore
Johnson England Wilson (Timson) Joyner: Tries -
Sigsworth Kear Ward: Goals - Jones(2) R.Beardmore:
Referee S Wall (Leigh) Att - 4700 H.T. 12 - 8

Sun 9 Dec 1984 WIDNES home won 34 - 8
CASTLEFORD - Sigsworth: Roache(Higgins) Marchant
Fenton(England) Kear: Kev.Jones R.Beardmore: James
K.Beardmore Johnson England (Timson) Wilson Joyner:
Tries - Marchant(2) Sigsworth Fenton R.Beardmore:
Goals - Jones(7):
WIDNES - Burke: Wright Currier O'Loughlin Basnett:
T.Myler Hulme: M.O'Neill Middlehurst Tamati Eyres
Sorenson(Whitfield) J.Myler: Tries - Wright Currier:
Referee D W Fox (Wakefield) Att - 2597 H.T. 14 - 8

**Sun 16 Dec 1984 FEATHERSTONE ROVERS away
lost 12 - 13**
FEATHERSTONE R - N.Barker: A.N.Other Quinn Gilbert
Hopkins: Slater Hunter: Gibbins Staniforth
Hankins(Clawson) D.Hobbs Bell Lyman:
Tries - Slater(2) Quinn Goal - Bell(DG):
CASTLEFORD - Sigsworth: Roache Marchant Higgins Kear:
Kev.Jones R.Beardmore: James K.Beardmore Johnson
England(Horton) Wilson(Roockley) Joyner:
Tries - Kear James: Goals - Jones(2):
Referee R Whitfield (Widnes) Att - 3065 H.T. 2 - 8

Sun 23 Dec 1984 BARROW home lost 10 - 14
CASTLEFORD - Sigsworth: Roache Marchant Higgins Kear:
Kevin Jones (James) R.Beardmore: James(Ward)
K.Beardmore Johnson England Wilson Joyner:
Tries - Roache Marchant: Goal - R.Beardmore:
BARROW - Tickle: Rea(Elliott) Whittle Heselwood
M.James: Cannon Cairns: Hodgkinson Fitzgerald Sykes
Clough K.James Hadley(Herbert):
Tries - Cannon(2): Goals - Tickle(3):
Referee R Campbell (Widnes) Att - 2489 H.T. 4 - 6

Wed 26 Dec 1984 LEEDS away lost 14 - 20
LEEDS - Gill: Hague Creasser Lulham Hunt: Holmes
Conway: Jones Ward Hill(Clark) Patterson Powell
Fullerton-Smith:
Tries - Gill Creasser Conway: Goals - Creasser(4):

SEASON 1984-85

CASTLEFORD - Roockley: <u>Mark Roache</u> Marchant
Sigsworth Kear: Joyner R.Beardmore: Connell(Higgins)
K.Beardmore Johnson James Ward England:
Tries - Sigsworth Ward: Goals - R.Beardmore(3):
Referee G F Lindop (Wakefield) Att - 7687 H.T. 12 - 8

Tue 1 Jan 1985 BRADFORD NORTHERN home won 16 - 2
CASTLEFORD - Roockley: CHRIS CHAPMAN(634)
Marchant Sigsworth Kear: Joyner(Higgins): R.Beardmore:
Connell(Wilson) K.Beardmore Johnson James Ward
England:
Tries - Chapman K.Beardmore: Goals - R.Beardmore(4):
BRADFORD N - Mumby: Francis Parrish Davies Parker:
Hanley Robinson: Kellaway Noble Stone(Grayshon)
Sheldon Heron Fleming: Goal - Parrish:
Referee J Smith (Halifax) Att - 3465 H.T. 8 - 2

Sun 6 Jan 1985 WORKINGTON TOWN away won 24 - 6
WORKINGTON T - Stoddart: Meadows Thompson
Todd(Banks) Beck: Smith A.N.Other Grimes Lightfoot
Moffatt(Denny) Litt Hartley Maguire:
Try - Smith: Goal - Smith:
CASTLEFORD - Roockley: Kear Marchant Higgins
Chapman: Sigsworth R.Beardmore: Connell K.Beardmore
Johnson James(Joyner) Ward(Wilson) England:
Tries - Kear Marchant R.Beardmore Ward:
Goals - R.Beardmore(4):
Referee P Volante (Batley) Att - 800 H.T. 12 - nil

Wed 30 Jan 1985 ST HELENS home won 30 - 12
CASTLEFORD - Roockley: DAVID PLANGE(635) Marchant
Hyde Chapman: Joyner R.Beardmore: Connell
K.Beardmore Johnson(James) Ward Wilson(Sigsworth)
England: Tries - R.Beardmore(2) Hyde K.Beardmore
Wilson: Goals - R.Beardmore(5):
ST HELENS - Vievers(Forber): Ledger Haggerty Meninga
Day: Arkwright(Allen) Peters: Burke Bottell Gorley Platt
Round Pinner: Tries - Meninga Platt: Goals - Day(2):
Referee K Spencer (Warrington) Att - 2978 H.T. 14 - nil

Sun 3 Feb 1985 WIGAN away lost 18 - 36
WIGAN - Whitfield: Edwards Stephenson Donlan
Ferguson: Kenny Ford: Courtney(Campbell) Kiss Case
West Wane Potter: Tries - Ferguson(4) Edwards Kenny
Ford: Goals - Whitfield(4):
CASTLEFORD - Roockley: Plange Marchant
Hyde(Sigsworth) Chapman: Joyner R.Beardmore: Connell
K.Beardmore Johnson Ward Wilson(James) England:
Tries - Marchant(2) Chapman: Goals - R.Beardmore(3):
Referee T M Beaumont (Hud'field) Att - 9461 H.T. 8 - 20

Sun 17 Feb 1985 OLDHAM away won 14 - 8 CHALLENGE CUP ROUND 1
OLDHAM - A.Taylor: Vigo(Naidole) Parrish Foy M.Taylor:
Ashton P.Taylor: Jones McCurrie Phelan Goodway
Hawkyard Worrall(Flanagan):
Try - Hawkyard: Goals - Parrish(2):
CASTLEFORD - Roockley: Plange Marchant Hyde

Chapman: Sigsworth(Higgins) R.Beardmore:
Connell(MARTIN KETTERIDGE(636)) K.Beardmore Johnson
Ward England Joyner:
Tries - Plange Higgins: Goals - R.Beardmore(3):
Referee G Berry (Dewsbury) Att - 6056 H.T. 4 - 2

Sun 24 Feb 1985 WORKINGTON TOWN home won 64 – 4 CHALLENGE CUP ROUND 2
CASTLEFORD - Roockley: Plange Sigsworth(Kear) Hyde
Chapman: Joyner R.Beardmore (Higgins): Connell
K.Beardmore Johnson(Sigsworth) Ward Wilson England:
Tries - Sigsworth(3) Roockley(2) Chapman(2) Wilson(2)
Plange Hyde Joyner: Goals - Hyde(6) R.Beardmore(2):
WORKINGTON T - Tubman: Roper Thompson Jones
Beattie: Smith Burns (R.Pattinson): Nixon Banks(Falcon)
Lightfoot Litt W.Pattinson Maguire: Try - Jones:
Referee R Whitfield (Widnes) Att - 3485 H.T. 20 - 4

Wed 27 Feb 1985 OLDHAM away won 18 - 15
OLDHAM - A.Taylor: Birkby Parrish Caffrey M.Taylor:
P.Taylor Ashton: Jones McCurrie Morgan(Naidole) Phelan
Hawkyard Flanagan:
Tries - Birkby Flanagan: Goals - Parrish(3) Ashton(DG):
CASTLEFORD - Roockley: Kear Fenton Hyde Plange:
Joyner Higgins: Connell K.Beardmore Ward(Coen)
Ketteridge Wilson(Horton) England:
Tries - Kear Fenton: Goals - Hyde(5):
Referee B Gomersall (Queensland) Att - 2678 H.T. 4 - 6

Sun 3 Mar 1985 HUNSLET away lost 20 - 27
HUNSLET - Kay(Marson): Hullock Tate(Murray) Roe
Diamond: Cawood King: Byron Gray Bateman(Kay)
Bowden Idle Graham: Tries - Cawood Gray Bateman
Bowden Graham   Goals - Diamond(3) Cawood(DG):
CASTLEFORD - Roockley: Kear Marchant Hyde(Coen)
Plange: Sigsworth R.Beardmore: Connell K.Beardmore
England(Higgins Ketteridge Ward Joyner:
Tries - R.Beardmore(2) Ward: Goals - R.Beardmore(4):
Referee R.Campbell (Widnes) Att - 2400 H.T. 8 - 9

Sun 10 Mar 1985 BRAMLEY home won 58 - 18 CHALLENGE CUP ROUND 3
CASTLEFORD - Roockley: Kear(Coen) Marchant Plange
Chapman: Sigsworth R.Beardmore: Connell K.Beardmore
Johnson Ward Wilson Joyner(Higgins):
Tries - Marchant(3) K.Beardmore(3) Chapman Connell
Johnson Ward Joyner: Goals - R.Beardmore(7):
BRAMLEY - Kilner: Dyas Fletcher Mason Lund: Lister
Gascoigne(Beale): Lean(Bowman) Kelly Pitchford Harrison
Bullough Clarkson:
Tries - Lister Gascoigne Harrison: Goals - Kilner(3):
Referee D W Fox (Wakefield) Att - 4330 H.T. 34 - 6

Fri 15 Mar 1985 HULL KINGSTON ROVERS home won 22 - 12
CASTLEFORD - Roockley: Plange Coen Kear Chapman:
Sigsworth R.Beardmore(Higgins): Connell K.Beardmore
Johnson Ward Wilson England(James):
Tries - K.Beardmore(2) Plange Kear:
Goals - Roockley(2) R.Beardmore:

335

HULL K R - Fairbairn: B.Miller Robinson Prohm Lydiat:
M.Smith G.Smith: Broadhurst(Holdstock) Watkinson Ema
Hall Hogan G.Miller: Try - Prohm: Goals - Fairbairn(4):
Referee B F Walker (Barrow) Att - 4128 H.T. 12 - 6

Wed 20 Mar 1985 LEEDS home lost 6 - 16
CASTLEFORD - Roockley: Plange Coen Kear Chapman:
Sigsworth Higgins(GARY LORD(637)): Connell
K.Beardmore Johnson Ward(Ketteridge) James Joyner:
Goals - Roockley(3):
LEEDS - Hunt: Grothe Creasser Currie(S/O) Hague: Blakely
Dick: Jones Maskill(Kevin Rayne) Patterson
Fullerton-Smith Webb(Maskill) Heron:
Try - Creasser Currie: Goals - Creasser(4):
Referee D G Kershaw (Easingwold) Att - 4507 H.T. 6 - 8

Sun 24 Mar 1985 WARRINGTON away lost 14 - 16
WARRINGTON - Hesford: Carbert I.Duane Younane
Forster: Kelly A.Gregory: Shaw Moylan Worrall(Knight)
Eccles Roberts M.Gregory:
Tries - Carbert Kelly M.Gregory: Goals - Carbert(2):
CASTLEFORD - Roockley: Plange Coen(Higgins) Kear
Chapman: Sigsworth Orum: James Horton Johnson
Timson Wilson(Ketteridge) Joyner:
Tries - Chapman Sigsworth James: Goal - Roockley:
Referee G F Lindop (Wakefield) Att - 2446 H.T. 10 - 6

Tue 26 Mar 1985 HULL Home won 26 - 18
CASTLEFORD - Roockley: Plange Marchant Kear (Coen)
Chapman: Sigsworth Orum: James Horton Reilly(Johnson)
Timson Ketteridge Higgins:
Tries - Roockley(3) James: Goals - Ketteridge(5):
HULL - Kemble: K.James Schofield Leuluai O'Hara: Evans
Collinson(Sterling): Edmunds Patrick Puckering
Proctor(Dannatt) Crooks Divorty:
Tries - K.James Schofield O'Hara: Goals - Schofield(3):
Referee R Whitfield (Widnes) Att - 3820 H.T. 20 - 2

Fri 29 Mar 1985 WORKINGTON TOWN home won 36 - 8
CASTLEFORD - Roockley: Plange Marchant Hyde
Chapman: Joyner(Higgins) Orum: Connell K.Beardmore
Johnson Ward James(Timson) England:
Tries - Hyde(2) K.Beardmore(2) Marchant Chapman
Higgins: Goals - Hyde(4):
WORKINGTON T - Rae: Bower Thompson Beattie
Tubman: Smith Burns: Grimes Falcon Beverley Hartley
A.N.Other McGuire: Try - Smith: Goals - Smith McGuire:
Referee K Allatt (Southport) Att - 1992 H.T. 10 - 6

Sat 6 Apr 1985 HULL draw 10 - 10
CHALENGE CUP SEMI FINAL - at HEADINGLEY LEEDS
CASTLEFORD - Roockley: Plange Marchant Hyde
Chapman: Joyner Orum(Sigsworth) Gary Connell
K.Beardmore Johnson Ward Wilson(Timson) England:
Tries - Hyde Joyner: Goal - Hyde:
HULL - Kemble: James Schofield Leuluai O'Hara: Evans
Sterling: Skerrett Patrick Puckering(Divorty) Muggleton
Crooks Norton: Tries - O'Hara Sterling: Goal - Crooks:
Referee J McDonald (Wigan) Att - 21013 H.T. 6 - 4

Mon 8 Apr 1985 HALIFAX home lost 20 - 30
CASTLEFORD - Lord: Gill Coen Fenton Kear: IAN
HARDISTY(638) SEAN SNOWDEN(639): James Horton IAN
FLETCHER(640) Ketteridge Mountain(IAIN HARTLEY(641))
Higgins: Tries - Gill Kear Higgins: Goals - Hardisty(4):
HALIFAX - Cerchione: Brown Moll T.Anderson Agar:
Garrod Hudson: Marles Dalgreen(Isaacs) Beevers Neller
Bella Bond: Tries - Agar(2) Anderson Garrod Neller Bond:
Goals - Agar(3):
Referee G Berry (Dewsbury) Att - 2894 H.T. 6 - 20

Wed 10 Apr 1985 HULL lost 16 - 22 REPLAY
CHALLENGE CUP SEM FINAL - at HEADINGLEY LEEDS
CASTLEFORD - Roockley: Plange Marchant Hyde
Chapman: Joyner Orum (Ron Sigsworth): Ward
K.Beardmore Johnson Timson Wilson(Reilly)England:
Tries - Roockley Hyde Chapman: Goals - Hyde(2):
HULL - Kemble(Topliss): James Schofield Leuluai O'Hara:
Evans Sterling: Crooks Patrick Puckering(Edmunds)
Muggleton Norton Divorty:
Tries - James Leuluai O'Hara Sterling: Goals - Crooks(3):
Referee J McDonald (Wigan) Att - 21017 H.T. 12 - 22

Fri 12 Apr 1985 OLDHAM home lost 10 - 12
CASTLEFORD - Coen: Plange Marchant Hyde Kear: Joyner
Orum: James(Rookley) Horton Johnson England Nigel
Wilson(Fletcher) Higgins:
Tries - Plange Joyner: Goal - Hyde:
OLDHAM - Caffrey: Mitchell Parrish Foy M.Taylor: Birkby
Kirwan: Jones Lowndes Morgan Dixon Hawkyard
(Chadwick) Worrall:
Tries - Birkby Kirwan: Goals - Parrish(2):
Referee D W Fox (Wakefield) Att - 2315 H.T. 4 - 12

Sun 14 Apr 1985 HULL away lost 8 - 18
HULL - Prendiville: Eastwood Vass Elliott Welham: Portz
Windley: Dannatt Mallinson Patrick(Tomlinson) Rose
Arnett(James) Sharp:
Tries - Vass Dannatt Patrick: Goals - Prendiville(3):
CASTLEFORD - Roockley: Plange Marchant Hyde Kear:
Darren Coen Sean Snowden: Neil James Horton
Fletcher(Ketteridge) Andrew Timson England Joyner:
Try - Marchant: Goals - Plange Hyde:
Referee P Volante (Batley) Att - 6112 H.T. 8 - 6

Tue 23 Apr 1985 LEIGH away draw 24 - 24
LEIGH - P.Johnson: Taylor Henderson Fairhurst Fox:
Woods Stephens: Gelling(Ramsdale) Tabern Pyke
Hardman Howarth Westhead: Tries - Woods(2)
Henderson Westhead: Goals - Johnson(4):
CASTLEFORD - Roockley: Plange Marchant Hyde
Chapman: Ian Hardisty (Kear) Orum: Fletcher
K.Beardmore Johnson Ketteridge KEITH
JONES(642)(Horton) England:
Tries – K Beardmore(2) Hyde Ketteridge:
Goals - Hyde(3) Hardisty:
Referee J E Smith (Halifax) Att - 2117 H.T. nil – 14

Nigel Wilson
D. No 632
1984-85

Ron Sigsworth
D. No 633
1984-85

Chris Chapman
D. No 634
1984-85 to 1989-90

David Plange
D. No 635
1984-85 to 1990-91

Martin Ketteridge
D. No 636
1984-85 to 1994-95

Gary Lord
D. No 637
1984-85 to 1987-88

Ian Fletcher
D. No 640
1984-85 to 1986-87

Keith Jones
D. No 642
1984-85 to 1987-88

SUNDAY 10 MARCH 1985 CHALLENGE CUP ROUND 3 v BRAMLEY HOME WON 58 - 18
Back Row – Ron Sigsworth David Plange Nigel Wilson Kevin Ward Gary Connell Barry Johnson
Front Row – John Kear David Roockley Tony Marchant John Joyner Robert Beardmore Kevin Beardmore
Chris Chapman

SEASON 1984-85

D.N	PLAYER		DEBUT	L MATCH	APP	SUB	T.AP	TRI'S	G'LS	D.G	P'TS
512	REILLY	MALCOLM			1	1	2	0	0	0	0
551	JOYNER	JOHN			30	1	31	9	0	0	36
560	FENTON	STEVE			14	1	15	5	0	0	20
596	KEAR	JOHN			21	4	25	8	0	0	32
598	HIGGINS	BARRY			8	11	19	3	0	0	12
599	FINCH	DAVID	07/10/1984		5	0	5	3	4	0	20
601	HYDE	GARY			14	1	15	10	23	0	86
603	WARD	KEVIN			26	1	27	7	0	0	28
604	CONNELL	GARY		06/04/1985	19	3	22	1	0	0	4
607	TIMSON	ANDY		14/04/1985	7	5	12	0	0	0	0
608	BEARDMORE	ROBERT			17	1	18	6	43	0	110
609	ORUM	IAN			17	1	18	1	0	0	4
610	GILL	STEVEN			1	0	1	1	0	0	4
611	BEARDMORE	KEVIN			31	0	31	15	0	0	60
613	JOHNSON	BARRY			33	1	34	2	0	0	8
614	JAMES	NEIL		14/04/1985	17	5	22	4	0	0	16
618	MARCHANT	TONY			32	0	32	12	0	0	48
619	HORTON	STUART			7	3	10	0	0	0	0
621	ENGLAND	KEITH			28	3	31	0	0	0	0
622	COEN	DARREN		14/04/1985	18	5	23	5	0	0	20
623	ROACHE	MARK		26/12/1984	18	0	18	4	0	0	16
625	ROOCKLEY	DAVID			20	2	22	6	6	0	36
626	JONES	KEVIN		23/12/1984	13	0	13	2	39	0	86
627	BATTYE	NEIL			10	0	10	2	0	0	8
631	MOUNTAIN	DEAN			1	1	2	0	0	0	0
632	WILSON	NIGEL	16/09/1984	12/04/1985	19	4	23	4	0	0	16
633	SIGSWORTH	RON	23/09/1984	10/04/1985	21	6	27	11	0	0	44
634	CHAPMAN	CHRIS	01/01/1985		15	0	15	8	0	0	32
635	PLANGE	DAVID	30/01/1985		17	0	17	4	1	0	18
636	KETTERIDGE	MARTIN	17/02/1985		5	4	9	1	5	0	14
637	LORD	GARY	20/03/1985		1	1	2	0	0	0	0
638	HARDISTY	IAN	08/04/1985	23/04/1985	2	0	2	0	5	0	10
639	SNOWDEN	SEAN	08/04/1985	14/04/1985	2	0	2	0	0	0	0
640	FLETCHER	IAN	08/04/1985		3	1	4	0	0	0	0
641	HARTLEY	IAIN	08/04/1985		0	1	1	0	0	0	0
642	JONES	KEITH	23/04/1985		1	0	1	0	0	0	0
	36		11	11	494	67	561	134	126	0	788

COMPETITION		P	W	D	L	FOR	AGT
LEAGUE D 1	POSITION 12 OF 16	30	12	1	17	552	518
YORK'S CUP		1	0	0	1	14	16
RL CUP		5	3	1	1	162	62
PLAYERS NO6		2	1	0	1	60	24
PLAYERS RECORDS		**38**	**16**	**2**	**20**	**788**	**620**

In the Challenge Cup we again won through to the semi-final. Our opponents at Headingley were once again Hull, with the tie finishing in a 10 all draw. The replay, again played at Headingley, once more resulted in a victory for our opponents by 22–16 the hoodoo striking again.

John Joyner made his 400th appearance for the Club in the away fixture at Oldham on 27 February 1985.

A notable Debutant was Martin Ketteridge

338

n the League Swinton, Salford, York Dewsbury were promoted to Division 1. Barrow Leigh Hunslet Workington Town relegated to Division 2. Southend nvicta and Bridgend dropping out of Division 2.

Sun 1 Sep 1985 WIGAN away won 12 - 10
WIGAN - Hampson: P.Ford Stephenson Donlan Gill(Whitfield): Edwards M.Ford: Courtney Kiss Campbell West Du Toit Wane:
Tries - Hampson Edwards: Goal - Stephenson:
CASTLEFORD - Roockley(TONY SPEARS(643)): Plange Marchant Hyde Chapman: STEVE DIAMOND(644) R.Beardmore: ALAN SHILLITO(645)(Fletcher) Horton Johnson Ketteridge Ward Joyner:
Tries - Plange(2) Roockley:
Referee J Holdsworth (Kippax) Att - 11107 H.T. 8 - 4

Wed 4 Sep 1985 SHEFFIELD EAGLES home won 38 – 6 YORKSHIRE CUP PRELIMINARY ROUND
CASTLEFORD - Gill(Spears): Plange Marchant Hyde Chapman: Diamond R.Beardmore: Shillito Horton(Fletcher) Johnson(Horton) Ketteridge Ward Joyner: Tries - Plange(2) Marchant(2) Hyde R.Beardmore Joyner: Goals - R.Beardmore(5):
SHEFFIELD E - Cholmondeley: Collear Dickinson Campbell Rafferty: Powell(Welsh)Lane: Pollard(Wilders) Hetherington Farrell Bridgeman A.N.Other McDermott: Try - Wilders: Goal - Rafferty:
Referee P Volante (Batley) Att - 1699 H.T. 16 - nil

Sun 8 Sep 1985 HULL home won 22 - 14
CASTLEFORD - Roockley: Plange Marchant(Hyde) Hyde(Spears) Chapman: Diamond R.Beardmore: Ward Horton Johnson Ketteridge Ward England(Fletcher) Joyner
Tries - Marchant Diamond Horton Joyner:
Goals - R.Beardmore(3):
HULL - Kemble: James Eastwood O'Hara Prendiville: Portz Gascoigne: Crooks Patrick Skerrett Dannatt Proctor (Puckering) Divorty:
Tries - Portz Puckering: Goals - Crooks(2) Prendiville:
Referee R Campbell (Widnes) Att - 4563 H.T. 6 - 8

Sun 15 Sep 1985 HUNSLET home won 60 - 2 YORKSHIRE CUP ROUND 1
CASTLEFORD - Roockley: Plange Marchant Hyde Chapman: Diamond R.Beardmore (Spears): Ward Horton Johnson England Ketteridge Joyner(Fletcher):
Tries - Marchant(4) Chapman(4)Plange Hyde Horton:
Goals - Diamond(4) R.Beardmore(4):
HUNSLET - Kay: Olbison Tate(Milton) Murrell A.N.Other Rowse King: Wood Gray(R.Sampson) Skerrett I.Sampson Mitchell Hudson: Goal - Rowse:
Referee S Haigh (Ossett) Att - 2678 H.T. 20 - 2

Wed 18 Sep 1985 YORK home won 34 - 6
CASTLEFORD - Roockley: Plange Marchant Hyde Chapman: Diamond R.Beardmore: Ward Horton Johnson (Spears) Ketteridge England Joyner(Fletcher) :
Tries - Hyde(2) Roockley Horton Johnson Joyner:
Goals - Beardmore(5):

YORK - Smith(Rhodes): Morrell Harrison Midgley Colley: Steadman Dobson: Bowman Phillippo Hagan(A.N.Other) Price Martin Blackburn: Try - Harrison: Goal - Steadman:
Referee D W Fox (Wakefield) Att - 2755 H.T. 18 - nil

Sun 22 Sep 1985 WARRINGTON away lost 16 - 24
WARRINGTON - Ford: Carbert Peters Forster Thackray: Cullen Kelly: Eccles Webb Jackson Tamati M.Gregory Rathbone(Roberts :
Tries - Gregory(2) Kelly Tamati: Goals - Carbert(3) Ford:
CASTLEFORD - Roockley: Plange Marchant Hyde Chapman: Diamond(Spears)R.Beardmore: Ward Horton(K.Beardmore) Johnson Ketteridge England Joyner:
Tries - Plange R.Beardmore: Goals - R.Beardmore(4):
Referee D J Carter (Widnes) Att - 2850 H.T. 4 - 16

Wed 25 Sep 1985 HALIFAX away won 24 - 4 YORKSHIRE CUP ROUND 2
HALIFAX - Kilroy: St Hilaire T.Anderson(Smith) Garrod Wilson: C.Anderson Stephens: White(Robinson) McCallion Heugh James Scott Dixon: Try - C.Anderson.
CASTLEFORD - Roockley: Plange Spears Hyde Chapman(NEIL GREATBATCH(646)): Marchant R.Beardmore: Ward K.Beardmore Johnson(Fletcher) Ketteridge England(S/O) Joyner: Tries - Roockley Spears Hyde Marchant: Goals - R.Beardmore(4):
Referee G F Lindop (Wakefield) Att - 3688 H.T. 12 - 4

Sun 29 Sep 1985 SWINTON home won 28 - 16
CASTLEFORD - Roockley(Lord): Plange Spears Hyde Chapman: Marchant R.Beardmore: Ward K.Beardmore Johnson Ketteridge England(Fletcher)Joyner:
Tries - Roockley(2) Chapman Marchant K.Beardmore:
Goals - R.Beardmore(4):
SWINTON - Viller Maloney Ratcliffe Topping Bate: Wilson A.N.Other: Lomax Higgins Walsh Rowbottom Derbyshire Allen(Horrocks) (Fippon):
Tries - Bate(2) Higgins: Goals - Topping(2):
Referee G F Lindop (Wakefield) Att - 3013 H.T. 6 - nil

Wed 2 Oct 1985 LEEDS away won 14 - 10 YORKSHIRE CUP SEMI FINAL
LEEDS - Currie: Francis Creasser Wilson Smith: Lyons Conway: Hill(Webb) Maskill Keith Rayne Moorby Powell Heron: Tries - Wilson Smith: Goal - Creasser:
CASTLEFORD - Roockley: Plange Spears Hyde Chapman: Marchant(Lord) R.Beardmore: Ward K.Beardmore Johnson Ketteridge England(Fletcher) Joyner:
Tries - Spears(2) Plange: Goal - R.Beardmore:
Referee J Smith (Halifax) Att - 10334 H.T. 6 - nil

Sun 6 Oct 1985 HALIFAX away lost 8 - 14
HALIFAX - Kilroy(Smith): Wilson T.Anderson Garrod Juliff: C.Anderson Stephens: Heugh McCallion Robinson (Beevers) James Scott Dixon:
Tries - T.Anderson Heugh Dixon: Goal - Heugh:
CASTLEFORD - Lord: Plange Spears Hyde Kear(Diamond): Roockley R.Beardmore: Ward K.Beardmore Johnson Ketteridge Mountain(Fletcher) England:
Try - Ward: Goals - R.Beardmore(2):

Referee D G Kershaw(Easingwold) Att - 3117 H.T. nil -10

Sun 13 Oct 1985 ST HELENS home won 32 - 18
CASTLEFORD - Roockley: Plange(Fletcher) Marchant Hyde
Spears: Diamond(Lord) R.Beardmore: Ward K.Beardmore
Johnson Ketteridge IAN FRENCH(647) Joyner:
Tries - K.Beardmore(2) R.Beardmore French:
Goals - R.Beardmore(8):
ST HELENS - Vievers: Ledger French Conlon Day:
Arkwright Peters: Bottell Liptrot Gorley(Dwyer) Platt
Forber Pinner: Tries - French Peters: Goals - Conlon(5):
Referee J Smith (Halifax) Att - 4511 H.T. 12 - 6

Sun 20 Oct 1985 OLDHAM away lost 22 - 46
OLDHAM - Liddiard: M'Barki Foy Parrish M.Taylor: Topliss
Ashton (Kirwan): Jones Sanderson Morgan(Lowndes)
Flanagan Hobbs Warnecke: Tries - M'Barki(2) Liddiard Foy
M.Taylor Sanderson Hobbs Warnecke: Goals - Parrish(7):
CASTLEFORD - Roockley: Fenton Marchant Hyde
Spears(Lord): JAMIE SANDY(648)(Shillito) R.Beardmore:
Ward K.Beardmore Johnson Ketteridge French Joyner:
Tries - Sandy(2) Hyde: Goals - R.Beardmore(5):
Referee C Hodgson (Maryport) Att - 4210 H.T.14 - 16

**Sun 27 Oct 1985 HULL KINGSTON ROVERS lost 18 –
22 YORKSHIRE CUP FINAL - at HEADINGLEY LEEDS**
CASTLEFORD - Lord: Plange Marchant Hyde Spears:
Diamond R.Beardmore: Ward K.Beardmore Johnson
England Ketteridge Joyner: Tries - Marchant(2)
R.Beardmore: Goals - R.Beardmore(2) Diamond:
HULL K R - Fairbairn(Lydiat): Clark Dorahy Prohm Laws:
Smith Harkin: Harrison Watkinson Ema Burton Hogan
(Kelly) Miller: Tries - Miller(2) Clark: Goals - Dorahy(5):
Referee R Campbell (Widnes) Att - 12686 H.T. 6 - 10

Sun 3 Nov 1985 DEWSBURY away won 30 - 12
DEWSBURY - Richardson: Dunford Mita Collins Ramsden:
Vasey Keyworth: Mason(Broxholme) Kelly Sharp(Busfield)
Howells Jennings Stephenson:
Tries - Mita Ramsden: Goals - Vasey(2):
CASTLEFORD - Lord: Spears Marchant Hyde(Diamond)
Greatbatch: Sandy R.Beardmore: Shillito K Beardmore
Johnson French England(Ketteridge) Joyner
Tries - Lord Spears Marchant Sandy K.Beardmore:
Goals - R.Beardmore(5):
Referee R Whitfield (Widnes) Att - 1990 H.T. 12 - 8

**Sun 10 Nov 1985 WEST HULL away won 24 - 10
JOHN PLAYER TROPHY - PRELIMINARY ROUND - at
THE BOULEVARD HULL**
WEST HULL - Tock(E.Bennett): Petty Knapp Lawler Jenkins:
Allison I.Bennett: Beech Baynes Watson Elgar
Brown(Parker) Card: Try - Baynes: Goals - Petty(3):
CASTLEFORD - Lord: Greatbatch Marchant Hyde Spears:
Sandy R.Beardmore: Shillito K.Beardmore(Mountain)
Johnson Ketteridge England French:
Tries - Marchant Hyde K.Beardmore French:
Goals - R.Beardmore(4):
Referee D J Croft (Leeds) Att - 2500 H.T. 8 - 2

Thu 14 Nov 1985 WARRINGTON home lost 20 - 26
CASTLEFORD - Lord: Spears Marchant(Diamond)
Hyde(Ketteridge) Greatbatch: Sandy R.Beardmore: Ward
Horton Johnson England French Joyner: Tries - Spears
Greatbatch Horton French: Goals - Beardmore(2):
WARRINGTON - Johnson: Carbert R.Duane Blake Forster:
Kelly Gregory: Tamati Webb(Allen) Jackson(Cullen) Boyd
Gittings McGinty:
Tries - Johnson(2) Blake(2) Cullen: Goals - Carbert(3):
Referee G F Lindop (Wakefield) Att - 2653 H.T.14 - 16

**Sun 24 Nov 1985 YORK away lost 10 - 12
JOHN PLAYER TROPHY ROUND 1**
YORK - Proctor: Morrell Carter Willey Smith: Steadman
Dobson: Crooks Rhodes Marketo Price Martin Harrison:
Try - Carter: Goals - Steadman(4):
CASTLEFORD - Sandy: Greatbatch Marchant Spears
Chapman(Roockley): Diamond R.Beardmore(Chapman):
Ward Horton Johnson England Ketteridge French:
Try - Spears: Goals - R.Beardmore(2) Diamond:
Referee G F Tickle (St Helens) Att - 3765 H.T. 8 - 10

Wed 11 Dec 1985 DEWSBURY home won 16 - 12
CASTLEFORD - Roockley: Greatbatch Marchant Sandy
Spears(Plange): Diamond R.Beardmore: Ward Horton
Johnson Ketteridge England French:
Tries - Marchant Ward England: Goals - R.Beardmore(2):
DEWSBURY - Richardson: Vasey Mita Collins Ramsden:
Sefuiva Keyworth: Mason Diskin Broxholme(Howells)
Jennings(Haynes) Daley Stephenson:
Tries - Keyworth(2)   Goals - Vasey(2):
Referee D G Kershaw(Easingwold) Att - 2065 H.T. 10 - 10

Sun 15 Dec 1985 SALFORD away lost 8 - 9
SALFORD - Fletcher: Marsh O'Loughlin Byrne Glynn:
Baker(Griffiths)Bloor: Herbert(Major) Moylan Disley Blease
Battese Pendlebury:
Tries - Fletcher Baker: Goal - Baker(DG):
CASTLEFORD - Lord: Greatbatch Marchant Spears Plange:
Sandy R.Beardmore: Ward Horton Johnson Mountain
Ketteridge England: Try - England: Goals - Ketteridge(2):
Referee D W Fox (Wakefield) Att - 1888 H.T. 8 - 4

Sun 22 Dec 1985 LEEDS home lost 18 - 26
CASTLEFORD - Lord: Plange Marchant Spears Greatbatch:
Sandy R.Beardmore: Ward Horton Johnson Ketteridge
French Joyner(Mountain):
Tries - Plange(2)   Goals - Ketteridge(5):
LEEDS - Wilkinson: Smith Creasser(Moorby) Lyons Currie:
Hague Dick(S/O): Grayshon Ward Turner(Webb) Powell
Kevin Rayne Clark: Tries - Moorby Ward Powell Clark:
Goals - Creasser(3) Hague Dick:
Referee K Allatt (Southport) Att - 3971 H.T. 12 - 14

**Wed 1 Jan 1986 BRADFORD NORTHERN away
lost 18 - 26**
BRADFORD N - Potts(Moulden): Ford Donlan McGowan
Jackson: Woods Godfrey: White Noble Kellaway Mallinder
Lumby Jasewicz:
Tries - Mallinder(2) Ford Jasewiewicz: Goals - Woods(5):

SEASON 1985-86

CASTLEFORD - Lord: Greatbatch Marchant Spears Plange: Diamond R.Beardmore: Ward Horton Johnson Ketteridge French(Roockley) Joyner(Mountain):
Tries - Plange Ward Roockley: Goals - Ketteridge(3):
Referee K Spencer (Warrington) Att - 3568 H.T. 8 - 14

Sun 5 Jan 1986 SWINTON away lost 10 - 12
SWINTON - Topping: Scott Hunter Connor Bate: Jones Hewitt: Grima Melling Wright(Rowbotton) M.Holliday Derbyshire L.Holliday:
Tries - Bate Hewitt: Goals - Jones(2):
CASTLEFORD - Lord(Roockley): Plange Marchant Diamond Greatbatch: Sandy R.Beardmore: Ward Horton Johnson Ketteridge Mountain French:
Tries - Marchant French: Goal - Ketteridge:
Referee S Haigh (Ossett) Att - 1456 H.T. 6 - 4

Sun 19 Jan 1986 OLDHAM home won 28 - 4
CASTLEFORD - Roockley: Plange Marchant PHILIP PAYNE(649) Greatbatch: SandyR.Beardmore: Shillito(Mountain) Horton England(Joyner) Ketteridge Ward French: Tries - Roockley Marchant R Beardmore French: Goals - Ketteridge(6):
OLDHAM - M'Barki: G.Liddiard Foy Parrish(D.Liddiard) Taylor: Warnecke Ashton: Jones Sanderson Morgan(Kirwan) Graham Hobbs Flanagan:
Try - G.Liddiard:
Referee R Whitfield (Widnes) Att - 3736 H.T. 14 - nil

Sun 26 Jan 1986 WIDNES away lost 5 - 9
WIDNES - Burke: Basnett Currier D.Wright George: D.Hulme J.Myler: Sorenson Ruane Fieldhouse O'Neill(Newton) P.Hulme Eyres:
Try - P.Hulme: Goals - Myler(2) Eyres(DG):
CASTLEFORD - Roockley: Plange Marchant Payne Greatbatch(Kear): Steve Diamond R.Beardmore: Shillito(Mountain) Horton England Ketteridge Ward French: Try - Kear: Goal - Diamond(DG):
Referee K Spencer (Warrington) Att - 4500 H.T. 4 - 9

Wed 29 Jan 1986 YORK away lost 14 - 18
YORK - Pethybridge: Morrell Carter Proctor Willey: Steadman Dobson: Marketo Phillipo M.Hughes Price Martin C.Harrison:
Tries - Pethybridge Carter Dobson : Goal – Steadman(3):
CASTLEFORD - Roockley: Plange Marchant Payne Kear: Sandy (ROY SOUTHERNWOOD(650)) R.Beardmore: Shillito(Mountain) Horton England Ketteridge French Joyner: Tries - Plange R.Beardmore Mountain:
Goal - R.Beardmore:
Referee P N Houghton (War'gton) Att - 2162 H.T. nil - 8

Sun 2 Feb 1986 HULL away lost 12 - 34
HULL - Kemble: Eastwood Schofield(Prendiville) Leuluai O'Hara: Evans Ah Kuoi: Skerrett Mallinson Gerard Proctor(Dannatt) Crooks Norton:
Tries - Eastwood(2) Kemble Prendiville Leuluai Crooks Norton: Goals - Evans(3):
CASTLEFORD - Roockley: Plange Sandy Payne Kear: Joyner(Southernwood) R.Beardmore: Mountain Horton

England Ketteridge Ward French:
Tries - Roockley England: Goals - Ketteridge(2):
Referee G.Berry (Dewsbury) Att - 4537 H.T. 6 - 26

Sun 9 Feb 1986 HUNSLET away won 60 - 6 CHALLENGE CUP ROUND 1
HUNSLET - Kay: Rowse Bowden Kemble Warrender: Birkby King: Wood(Morgan) McCurrie Bateman Crampton Sampson(Penola) Mitchell: Try - Kay: Goal - Rowse:
CASTLEFORD - Roockley: Plange Marchant Payne Greatbatch: Sandy R.Beardmore: Ward(Southernwood) Horton England(Johnson) Ketteridge Mountain French:
Tries - French(5) Greatbatch(2) Plange Marchant R Beardmore England: Goals - Ketteridge(8):
Referee J McDonald (Wigan) Att - 2399 H.T. 34 - nil

Wed 5 Mar 1986 FEATHERSTONE ROVERS away lost 6 - 21
FEATHERSTONE F - N.Barker: Woolford Banks Heselwood Massa: Steadman Fox: Gibbins(Clarkson) Spurr Harrison Bell Smith(Clawson) Lyman:
Tries - Banks(2) Harrison: Goals - Steadman(4) Bell(DG):
CASTLEFORD - Roockley: Greatbatch Marchant(Mountain) Payne Plange: Sandy R.Beardmore(Johnson): Ward Horton England Ketteridge French Joyner:
Try - Greatbatch: Goal - Ketteridge:
Referee G F Lindop (Wakefield) Att - 2776 H.T. 2 - 8

Sun 9 Mar 1986 BARROW away won 30 - 6 CHALLENGE CUP ROUND 2
BARROW - Tickle James Williams Whittle Quirk: Smith(McConnell Cairns: Elliott(Livesey) Lightfoot D.Kendall Mossop G.Kendall Turley:
Try - Smith: Goal - Turley:
CASTLEFORD - Roockley: Greatbatch Marchant Payne Plange: Joyner R.Beardmore (Southernwood): Ward Horton Johnson Ketteridge England(Mountain) French:
Tries - Payne(2) Marchant R.Beardmore French:
Goals - Ketteridge(5):
Referee D G Kershaw (Easingwold) Att - 3800 H.T. 14 - 6

Sun 16 Mar 1986 WIGAN away won 10 - 2 CHALLENGE CUP ROUND 3
WIGAN - Hampson: Russell Stephenson Hanley Gill: Lydon Edwards: Dowling Kiss Goodway West Du Toit(Wane) Potter: Goal - Lydon:
CASTLEFORD - Roockley: Greatbatch(Sandy) Marchant Payne Plange: Joyner R.Beardmore: Ward Horton Johnson(Mountain) Ketteridge England French:
Tries - Roockley Joyner: Goal - Ketteridge:
Referee G F Lindop (Wakefield) Att - 18646 H.T. 6 - 2

Sat 22 Mar 1986 OLDHAM won 18 - 7 CHALLENGE CUP SEMI FINAL - at CENTRAL PARK WIGAN
CASTLEFORD - Roockley: Plange Marchant Payne Sandy: Joyner R.Beardmore: Ward Horton Johnson Ketteridge England(Mountain) French:
Tries - R.Beardmore(2) Marchant: Goals - Ketteridge(3):
OLDHAM - D.Liddiard: M'Barki Foy Warnecke M.Taylor:

G.Liddiard (Parrish) Ashton: Jones Sanderson Hobbs
Worrall Graham Flanagan(Nadiole):
Tries - G.Liddiard: Goal - Hobbs Ashton(DG):
Referee R Campbell (Widnes) Att - 12443 H.T. 6 - 7

Mon 24 Mar 1986 LEEDS away lost 12 - 18
LEEDS - Wilkinson: Staniland Creasser Currie Gibson:
Hague(Conway) Dick: Keith.Rayne Webb Powell
Kevin.Rayne Medley(Maskill) Heron:
Tries - Powell Kevin.Rayne Heron: Goals - Creasser(3):
CASTLEFORD - Roockley: Plange Marchant Hyde Sandy:
Joyner R.Beardmore: Shillito Horton Johnson
Ketteridge(Fletcher) Mountain(Greatbatch) England:
Tries - Roockley Johnson: Goals - Beardmore Ketteridge:
Referee T M Beaumont (Hud'field) Att - 6990 H.T. nil - 6

Fri 28 Mar 1986 HALIFAX home lost 14 - 36
CASTLEFORD - Roockley: Plange Hyde Payne Greatbatch:
Joyner Orum (Southernwood): Shillito(Fletcher)
Horton(Shillito) Johnson Jones Mountain England:
Tries - Roockley Hyde Payne: Goal - Jones:
HALIFAX - Kilroy(Crossley): Whitfield T.Anderson Wilson
George: C.Anderson Stephens: Heugh McCallion
Robinson James Scott(Bond) Dixon: Tries - McCallion(2)
Kilroy George Robinson James: Goals - Whitfield(6):
Referee G F Tickle (St Helens) Att - 6167 H.T. 10 - 24

Mon 31 Mar 1986 FEATHERSTONE ROVERS home won 24 - 16
CASTLEFORD - Roockley: Plange Marchant Payne
Greatbatch: Joyner(Hyde) R.Beardmore: Shillito(Mountain)
K.Beardmore Johnson Ketteridge Ward England:
Tries - Joyner(2) R.Beardmore Mountain:
Goals - Ketteridge(4):
FEATHERSTONE R - N.Barker: Woolford Banks Heselwood
Hopkins: Steadman Fox: Gibbins(Kelly) Spurr
Harrison(Slatter) K.Bell Smith Lyman:
Tries - Lyman(2) Barker: Goals - Steadman(2):
Referee R Whitfield (Widnes) Att - 4654 H.T. 12 - 12

Sun 6 Apr 1986 HULL KINGSTON ROVERS away lost 8 - 22
HULL K.R - Fairbairn: Stead M.Smith Lydiat(Fletcher)Laws:
G.Smith Harkin: Johnston Watkinson(Rudd) Ema Kelly
Hogan Miller:
Tries - M.Smith Ema Miller: Goals - Fairbairn(5):
CASTLEFORD - Lord: Plange Hyde Payne Greatbatch:
Marchant R.Beardmore (Roockley): Shillito Horton(S/O):
Malcolm Reilly Ketteridge Ward(Mountain) England:
Tries - Plange Greatbatch:
Referee D W Fox (Wakefield) Att - 5533 H.T. nil - 14

Wed 9 Apr 1986 BRADFORD NORTHERN home won 28 - 10
CASTLEFORD - Roockley: Plange Marchant Hyde Payne:
Joyner R.Beardmore(Lord): Ward Horton Johnson
Ketteridge Mountain(Shillito) England: Tries - Roockley
Plange Horton Mountain: Goals - Ketteridge(6):
BRADFORD N - Mumby: Ford Donlan D.Redfearn
Simpson: Woods Godfrey: White Preece Mallinder

Sharratt Lumby(Sheldon) Fleming:
Try - Ford: Goals Woods(3):
Referee K Allatt (Southport) Att - 3001 H.T. 18 - 2

Fri 11 Apr 1986 HULL KINGSTON ROVERS home won 36 - 18
CASTLEFORD - Roockley: Plange Marchant Hyde
Greatbatch: Joyner R.Beardmore(Lord): Shillito(Mountain)
K.Beardmore Johnson Ketteridge Ward Higgins:
Tries - K.Beardmore(2) Ketteridge(2) Roockley Marchant
Shillito: Goals - Ketteridge(4):
HULL K.R - Fairbairn: Stead(Fletcher) Hutchinson Lydiat
Laws: Tosnay G.Smith: Johnston Marchant Ema(Beale)
Speckman Harrison Miller:
Tries - Fletcher Marchant Miller: Goals - Fairbairn(3):
Referee R Campbell (Widnes) Att - 3398 H.T. 20 - 6

Sun 13 Apr 1986 WIGAN home lost 12 - 14
CASTLEFORD - Roockley: Plange Lord Hyde(Chapman)
Greatbatch: Southernwood Ian Orum(S/O): I.Hartley
K.Beardmore Fletcher Jones Mountain Higgins(Joyner):
Tries - K.Beardmore Chapman: Goals - Hyde Jones:
WIGAN - Hampson: Braithwaite Lydon(Berry) Russell Gill:
Hanley Edwards: Case Kiss Goodway West(S/O) Potter
Louw(Lucas): Tries - Louw(2) Russell: Goal - Lydon:
Referee P Houghton (Leigh) Att - 5384 H.T. 2 - 14

Wed 16 Apr 1986 ST HELENS away lost 12 - 62
ST HELENS - Vievers: Bailey Allen Loughlin Litherland:
Hughes Holding(Doherty): Burke(Forber) Liptrot Platt
Haggerty Round Arkwright:
Tries - Round(3) Vievers(2) Holding(2) Bailey Doherty
Liptrot Platt Haggerty: Goals - Loughlin(7):
CASTLEFORD - Roockley: Chapman Lord Plange
Greatbatch: Payne Southernwood: Iain Hartley Horton
Fletcher England Mountain (Jones) Barry Higgins
(Ketteridge):
Tries - Plange(2):   Goals - Roockley Ketteridge:
Referee D Carter (Widnes) Att - 4347 H.T. 6 - 26

Sun 20 Apr 1986 SALFORD home won 30 - 16
CASTLEFORD - Lord: Plange Marchant Hyde Chapman:
Joyner R.Beardmore: Shillito K.Beardmore Johnson Ward
Ketteridge England: Tries - Plange Hyde R.Beardmore
K.Beardmore England: Goals - Ketteridge(5):
SALFORD - Fletcher: Ford O'Loughlin Byrne(S/O)
Wiltshire: Glynn Bloor(Major): Herbert Moylan Dickens
Pendlebury Bleese McTigue:
Tries - Byrne Major Wiltshire: Goals - Pendlebury(2):
Referee C Hodgson (Maryport) Att - 2547 H.T.12 - nil

Tue 22 Apr 1986 WIDNES home draw 16 - 16
CASTLEFORD Roockley: Neil Greatbatch Philip Payne
Hyde Chapman: Marchant(Lord) Southernwood:
Mountain Horton Johnson(Fletcher) Ketteridge England
K.Beardmore:
Tries - Greatbatch Horton Johnson: Goals - Ketteridge(2):
WIDNES - Burke: S.Wright Dowd D.Wright Linton: T.Myler
J.Myler: Sorenson Elwell(Fieldhouse) M.O'Neill Gormley
P.Hulme Eyres:

SEASON 1985-86

Tries - T.Myler J.Myler O'Neill: Goals - J.Myler(2):
Referee P Volante (Batley) Att - 2264 H.T. 6 - 12

Sat 3 May 1986 HULL KINGSTON ROVERS
won 15 – 14 CHALLENGE CUP FINAL - at WEMBLEY
STADIUM LONDON
CASTLEFORD - Lord(Roockley): Plange Marchant Hyde
Jamie Sandy: Joyner R.Beardmore: Ward
K.Beardmore(Horton) Johnson England Ketteridge Ian
French: Tries - Marchant Sandy R.Beardmore:
Goals - Ketteridge R.Beardmore(DG):
HULL K R - Fairbairn: Clark Smith Prohm Laws: Dorahy
Harkin:Johnson Watkinson Ema Kelly(Smith)
Harrison(Lydiat) Miller:
Tries - Prohm(2) Lydiat: Goal - Dorahy:
Referee R Whitfield (Widnes) Att - 82134 H.T. 7 - 6
CUP PRESENTED BY PRINCESS ALEXANDRA LANCE
TODD TROPY WINNER - ROBERT BEARDMORE
(CASTLEFORD)

Tony Spears
D. No 643
1985-86 to 1986-87

Alan Shillito
D. No 645
1985-86 to 1987-88

Neil Greatbach
D. No 646
1985-86

Ian French
D. No 647
1985-86

Jamie Sandy
D. No 648
1985-86

Philip Payne
D. No 649
1985-86

Roy Southernwood
D. No 650
1985-86 to 1989-90

John Joyner Held Aloft By His Team Mates After The
15 – 14 Victory Over Hull K.R. At Wembley

SEASON 1985-86

D.N	PLAYER		DEBUT	L MATCH	APP	SUB	T.AP	TRI'S	G'LS	D.G	P'TS
512	REILLY	MALCOLM		06/04/1986	1	0	1	0	0	0	0
551	JOYNER	JOHN			29	2	31	6	0	0	24
560	FENTON	STEVE			1	0	1	0	0	0	0
596	KEAR	JOHN			3	1	4	1	0	0	4
598	HIGGINS	BARRY		16/04/1986	3	0	3	0	0	0	0
601	HYDE	GARY			25	1	26	9	1	0	38
603	WARD	KEVIN			34	0	34	3	0	0	12
608	BEARDMORE	ROBERT			38	0	38	13	64	1	181
609	ORUM	IAN		13/04/1986	2	0	2	0	0	0	0
610	GILL	STEVEN			1	0	1	0	0	0	0
611	BEARDMORE	KEVIN			15	1	16	9	0	0	36
613	JOHNSON	BARRY			33	2	35	3	0	0	12
618	MARCHANT	TONY			37	0	37	21	0	0	84
619	HORTON	STUART			28	1	29	6	0	0	24
621	ENGLAND	KEITH			33	0	33	5	0	0	20
625	ROOCKLEY	DAVID			29	5	34	13	1	0	54
631	MOUNTAIN	DEAN			11	13	24	3	0	0	12
634	CHAPMAN	CHRIS			13	1	14	6	0	0	24
635	PLANGE	DAVID			35	1	36	17	0	0	68
636	KETTERIDGE	MARTIN			37	3	40	2	61	0	130
637	LORD	GARY			14	7	21	1	0	0	4
640	FLETCHER	IAN			2	13	15	0	0	0	0
641	HARTLEY	IAIN		16/04/1986	2	0	2	0	0	0	0
642	JONES	KEITH			2	1	3	0	2	0	4
643	SPEARS	TONY	01/09/1985		15	6	21	6	0	0	24
644	DIAMOND	STEVE	01/09/1985	26/01/1986	13	3	16	1	6	1	17
645	SHILLITO	ALAN	01/09/1985		13	2	15	1	0	0	4
646	GREATBATCH	NEIL	25/09/1985	22/04/1986	22	2	24	6	0	0	24
647	FRENCH	IAN	13/10/1985	03/05/1986	20	0	20	11	0	0	44
648	SANDY	JAMIE	20/10/1985	03/05/1986	17	1	18	4	0	0	16
649	PAYNE	PHILIP	19/01/1986	22/04/1986	15	0	15	3	0	0	12
650	SOUTHERNWOOD	ROY	29/01/1986		3	5	8	0	0	0	0
	32			8	9	546	71	617	150	135	2	872

COMPETITION		P	W	D	L	FOR	AGT
LEAGUE D 1	POSITION 11 OF 16	30	12	1	17	551	585
YORK'S CUP		5	4	0	1	154	44
RL CUP		5	5	0	0	133	35
PLAYERS NO6		2	1	0	1	34	22
PLAYERS RECORDS		42	22	1	19	872	686

In the Yorkshire Cup we again reached the final It was once again at Heading against Hull KR and with the Humberside hoodoo continuing we lost 22–18.

In the Challenge Cup we earned a place in the final after three losing semi-finals in the 80's. With Hull K.R and Hull drawn against each other in Round 1 resulting in a Hull K.R victory, one of our bogey teams had been eliminated, but it was inevitable that our final opponents would be the remaining Humberside side Hull K.R, who had already beaten us in the Yorkshire Cup final and were firm favourites to repeat the performance.

However, the Humberside hoodoo was laid to rest albeit only after a last minute conversion kick by Hull K.R's John Dorahy drifted wide leaving us with a 15–14 victory. Robert (Bob) Beardmore picked up the Lance Todd Trophy after an outstanding performance which included a try and that vital one point drop goal.

Ian French became the fourth Castleford player to score five tries in a game on 9 February 1986 in the home victory against Hunslet.

SEASON 1986-87

The League Relegation and Promotion System was amended to 'three up and three down', which resulted in Leigh Barrow Wakefield Trinity being promoted to Division 1. York, Swinton Dewsbury relegated to Division 2.

Sun 24 Aug 1986 HALIFAX lost 8 - 9 OKELLS CHARITY SHIELD - AT DOUGLAS BOWL ISLE OF MAN
CASTLEFORD - Roockley: Plange Lord SHAUN IRWIN(651)(Southernwood) Spears: Joyner(Fletcher) R.Beardmore: Ward K.Beardmore Johnson Ketteridge Mountain England: Try - Lord: Goals - Ketteridge(2):
HALIFAX - Smith(Wilson): Riddlesden Whitfield Hague George: C.Anderson Stephens: Dickinson(James) McCallion Juliff Scott Bell Dixon:
Tries - Whitfield George: Goal - Hague(DG):
Referee G F Lindop (Wakefield) Att - 3276 H.T. 4 - 6

Sun 31 Aug 1986 WARRINGTON away won 26 - 20
WARRINGTON - Ford: Forster Cullen Duane Thackray: Bishop A.Gregory: Boyd(Sanderson) Tamati Worrall(Kelly) McGinty Roberts M.Gregory:
Tries - Bishop(2): Goals - Bishop(6):
CASTLEFORD - Roockley: Plange Lord Hyde Spears: Marchant R.Beardmore: Shillito(Mountain) MARTIN SLATER(652) Johnson Ketteridge Ward(Shillito) England:
Tries - Marchant R.Beardmore Ketteridge Ward: Goals - Ketteridge(5):
Referee R Whitfield (Widnes) Att - 4850 H.T. 8 - 4

Wed 3 Sept 1986 HULL home won 16 - 6
CASTLEFORD - Lord: Plange Marchant Hyde Spears: Joyner R.Beardmore(Roockley): Shillito(Fletcher) K.Beardmore Johnson Ketteridge Mountain England:
Tries - Plange Marchant Joyner: Goals - Ketteridge(2):
HULL - Hicks: James Ah Kuoi O'Hara Eastwood: Sharpe Windley: Crooks Patrick Edmonds(Proctor) Dannatt Welham Crane(Divorty): Try - Welham: Goal - Crooks:
Referee S Haigh (Ossett) Att - 4032 H.T. 6 - 6

Sun 7 Sept 1986 WAKEFIELD TRINITY home won 42 - 16
CASTLEFORD - Lord: Plange(Fletcher) Marchant(Roockley) Hyde Spears: Joyner R.Beardmore: Shillito K.Beardmore Johnson Ketteridge Mountain England:
Tries - Lord Roockley Hyde Joyner R.Beardmore Shillito Mountain: Goals - Ketteridge(7):
WAKEFIELD T - Spencer: Whiteman Eden Diamond(Bell) Jowett: Evans Hickman: Cocks Conway Gittins(Hopkinson) Brennan Lazenby Williams (Gittins):
Tries - Spencer Whiteman Brennan: Goals - Evans(2):
Referee M Beaumont (Hud'field) Att - 4673 H.T. 18 - nil

Sun 14 Sept 1986 HALIFAX home won 16 - 10 YORKSHIRE CUP ROUND 1
CASTLEFORD - Roockley: Lord CHRIS JOHNS(653) Hyde Spears: Joyner R.Beardmore: Shillito K.Beardmore Johnson Ketteridge Ward England (Atkins):
Tries - Johns K.Beardmore: Goals - Ketteridge(4):
HALIFAX - Eadie: Riddlesden Whitfield Hague George:

C.Anderson Stephens: Dickinson McCallion Fairbank(Juliff) Neller James Dixon:
Tries - Eadie Whitfield: Goal - Whitfield:
Referee G F Lindop (Wakefield) Att - 7478 H.T.12 - 10

Sun 21 Sept 1986 BARROW away won 24 - 14
BARROW - Tickle M.James McNichol Blacker Quirk: Hastings Cairn: Maskell Wilkinson Flynn Walker Mossop Turley: Tries - James Quirk Walker: Goal - Tickle:
CASTLEFORD - Roockley: Hyde Marchant Johns Spears(Plange): Joyner R.Beardmore: Ward K.Beardmore Johnson Ketteridge Atkins England:
Tries - Hyde Johns R.Beardmore K.Beardmore:
Goals - Ketteridge(3) R.Beardmore:
Referee J Mean (Leyland) Att - 3200 H.T. nil - 4

Wed 24 Sept 1986 LEEDS home won 38 - 16 YORKSHIRE CUP ROUND 2
CASTLEFORD - Roockley: Hyde Marchant Johns Plange: Joyner R.Beardmore: Ward(Shillito) K.Beardmore(Lord) Johnson Ketteridge Atkins England:
Tries - Roockley Hyde Johns Plange Joyner R.Beardmore Atkins England: Goals - Ketteridge(3):
LEEDS - Wilkinson: Francis Creasser Gibson Sharp: Holmes Conway: Smith(Gunn) Maskill Hill Kevin Rayne Medley Heron:
Tries - Creasser Gibson Rayne: Goals - Conway(2):
Referee D W Fox (Wakefield) Att - 7124 H.T. 26 - 6

Sun 28 Sept 1986 FEATHERSTONE ROVERS home won 16 - 7
CASTLEFORD - Roockley: Plange(Lord) Marchant Johns Hyde: Joyner(Plange) R.Beardmore: Ward K.Beardmore Johnson Ketteridge (Shillito) Atkins England:
Tries - Hyde(2) K.Beardmore: Goals - R.Beardmore(2):
FEATHERSTONE R - N.Barker: Marsh Banks Steadman Quinn: Langton (Hazelwood) Fox: Slatter Campbell A.Barker Clarkson (Langton) Smith Lyman (Kelly):
Goals - Quinn(3) Fox(DG):
Referee J McDonald (Wigan) Att - 5586 H.T. nil - 4

Wed 1 Oct 1986 FEATHERSTONE ROVERS away won 30 – 2 YORKSHIRE CUP SEMI FINAL
FEATHERSTONE R - N.Barker: Marsh Banks Steadman Quinn: Langton(Hazelwood) Fox: Sykes Campbell A.Barker(Harrison) Clarkson Smith Lyman:
Goal - Quinn:
CASTLEFORD - Roockley(Lord): Plange Marchant COLIN SCOTT(654) Hyde: Irwin R.Beardmore: Ward K.Beardmore Johnson Ketteridge Atkins England (Shillito):
Tries - Plange Irwin R.Beardmore Ward K.Beardmore:
Goals - R.Beardmore(3) Ketteridge(2):
Referee G F Lindop (Wakefield) Att - 5411 H.T. 6 - 2

Sun 5 Oct 1986 BRADFORD NORTHERN away lost 7 - 12
BRADFORD N - Mumby: Ford Donlan Hellewell Simpson: Redfearn Holmes: White Spurr Sherratt(Hamer) Graham Jasiewicz Bond(Moulden):
Tries - Ford(2): Goals - Mumby(2):

CASTLEFORD - Scott: Plange Marchant Lord Hyde: Joyner
R.Beardmore: Shillito(Fletcher) K.Beardmore Johnson
Ward Atkins Ketteridge:
Try - Hyde: Goals - Scott R.Beardmore(DG):
Referee P Volante (Birstall) Att - 6000 H.T. 6 - nil

Sat 11 Oct 1986 HULL won 31 - 24
YORKSHIRE CUP FINAL - AT HEADINGLEY LEEDS
CASTLEFORD - Scott: Plange Marchant Johns Hyde(Lord):
Joyner R.Beardmore: Ward K.Beardmore Johnson
Ketteridge Atkins(Shillito) England:
Tries - K.Beardmore(2) Ward Ketteridge Atkins:
Goals - Ketteridge(5) R.Beardmore(DG):
HULL - Kemble: Brand Schofield O'Hara Eastwood: Ah
Kuoi Windley: Brown(Puckering) Patrick Dannatt
Norton(Divorty) Crooks Sharp:
Tries - Brand(2) O'Hara(2):   Goals - Crooks(4):
Referee J McDonald (Wigan) Att - 11132 H.T. 12 - 18
WHITE ROSE TROPY WINNER - KEVIN BEARDMORE
CASTLEFORD

Wed 15 Oct 1986 WIDNES away lost 20 - 29
WIDNES - Burke: J.Myler D.Wright Gilbert A.Eyres: A.Myler
D.Hulme: Sorenson McKenzie Fieldhouse M.O'Neill Cleal
R.Eyres(S.O'Neill): Tries - Wright(2) A.Myler Cleal:
Goals - J.Myler(6) Burke(DG):
CASTLEFORD - Scott: Plange Irwin Johns Lord: Joyner
R.Beardmore: Ward K.Beardmore Johnson Atkins
Ketteridge England:
Tries - Plange(2) Scott Joyner: Goals - Ketteridge(2):
Referee C Hodgson (Maryport) Att - 3349 H.T. 16 - 4

Sun 26 Oct 1986 HALIFAX away won 16 - 12
HALIFAX - Eadie: Wilson Whitfield Rix George(Smith):
C.Anderson Stephens: Neller(Bell) Preece Fairbank Juliff
Dixon Hague:
Tries - Anderson Preece: Goals - Whitfield(2):
CASTLEFORD - Scott: Plange Marchant(Lord) Johns
Spears: Joyner R.Beardmore: Shillito K.Beardmore
Johnson Atkins Ketteridge England:
Tries - Scott England: Goals - Ketteridge(4):
Referee B Simpson (Manchester) Att - 4862 H.T. 4 - nil

Wed 29 Oct 1986 WIGAN home lost 6 - 12
CASTLEFORD - Scott: Plange(Spears) Irwin Johns Lord:
Joyner R.Beardmore: Ward(Shillito) K.Beardmore Johnson
Atkins Ketteridge(Fletcher) England:
Goals - Ketteridge(3):
WIGAN - Edwards: Stephenson Lydon Bell Gill: Hanley
Ford: West Dermott Case Roberts Potter Goodway(Louw):
Tries - Edwards Hanley: Goals - Gill(2):
Referee F Tickle (St Helens) Att - 6813 H.T. 6 - 4

Sun 2 Nov 1986 LEIGH home won 19 - 8
CASTLEFORD - Scott: Fenton Marchant Johns Lord: Joyner
R.Beardmore(Irwin): Shillito(Mountain) Ian Fletcher
Johnson Ward Atkins England:
Tries - Fenton Fletcher: Goals - Scott(5) (DG):
LEIGH - Collier: McCulloch Henderson Louluai
Riding(Atherton): Kerr Davis: Owen Deans Pyke(Cottrell)

Huddart Howell Westhead:
Tries - Henderson(2):
Referee J Smith (Halifax) Att - 4661 H.T. 4 - 4

Sun 16 Nov 1986 SALFORD home lost 20 - 21
CASTLEFORD - Scott: Plange Marchant(Shillito) Johns
Steve Fenton(Lord): Joyner R.Beardmore: Ward Horton
Johnson Ketteridge Atkins England: Tries - R.Beardmore
Joyner Atkins Plange: Goals - Scott(2):
SALFORD - Fletcher: Glynn O'Loughlin Byrne Wiltshire:
Austin Bloor: Herbert(Disley) Groves Major
McTigue(Blease) Selby O'Shea: Tries - Glynn O'Loughlin
Bloor: Goals - O'Shea(4) Austin(DG):
Referee A Bowman (Whitehaven) Att - 3102 H.T. 8 - 4

Sun 23 Nov 1986 FEATHERSTONE ROVERS away
won 18 - 16
FEATHERSTONE R - Bibb: Woolford Marsh Banks Kellett:
Crossley Fox: Slatter Slater Dakin Bell(Harrison)
Harrison(A.Barker) Smith:
Tries - Crossley(2):   Goals - Fox(4):
CASTLEFORD - Scott: Plange Johns Hyde Lord: Joyner
R.Beardmore: Shillito Horton(Johnson) Johnson(Ward)
Ketteridge Atkins England:
Tries - Scott(2) Hyde: Goals - Ketteridge(3):
Referee G F Lindop (Wakefield) Att - 3672 H.T.14 - 16

Sun 30 Nov 1986 FULHAM away won 34 - 24
JOHN PLAYER TROPHY ROUND 1
FULHAM - Pratt: Jones Mills Bridge Cambiani: Rees
Gibson: O'Doherty Taylor Knight Feighan(White)
Fenn(Rampling) Haggath:
Tries - Mills(2) Haggath: Goals - Fenn(4) Rees(2):
CASTLEFORD - Scott: Plange Joyner Johns Lord: Irwin
R.Beardmore: Ward Horton Johnson(Hyde) Ketteridge
Atkins(Shillito) England: Tries - Lord(3) Scott Johns
R.Beardmore: Goals - Ketteridge(5):
Referee D Carter (Widnes) Att - 1374 H.T. 12 - 12

Sat 6 Dec 1986 ST HELENS home lost 22 - 26
JOHN PLAYER TROPHY ROUND 2
CASTLEFORD - Scott: Plange(Hyde) Joyner Johns Lord:
Irwin R.Beardmore: Ward(Mountain) Horton Johnson
Ketteridge Atkins England:
Tries - Johns(2) Scott Horton: Goals - Ketteridge(3):
ST HELENS - Veivers: Ledger Allen Halliwell McCormack:
Clark Holding: Burke Harrison Jarvis Platt
Fieldhouse(Forber) Arkwright: Tries - Halliwell
McCormack Clark Holding Platt: Goals - Ledger(3):
Referee R Whitfield (Widnes) Att - 4806 H.T. 16 - nil

Sun 21 Dec 1986 WAKEFIELD TRINITY away
won 40 - 12
WAKEFIELD T - Spencer: Diamond Stanton Eden
Rotherforth: Evans(Hendry) Lyons: Hopkinson
Conway(Gittins) Thompson Gittins(Potts) Cocks Bell:
Tries - Eden Lyons: Goals - Diamond(2):
CASTLEFORD - Scott: Plange Joyner Hyde Lord: Irwin
R.Beardmore(Southernwood): Shillito Horton(Jones)
Johnson England Atkins K.Beardmore:

Tries - Atkins(2) Hyde Lord Irwin Shillito Horton:
Goals - R.Beardmore(5) Johnson:
Referee K Allatt (Southport) Att - 3178 H.T. 22 - 6

Fri 26 Dec 1986 HULL KINGSTON ROVERS home won 16 - 10

CASTLEFORD - Scott: Plange Joyner Lord Kear: Irwin
Southernwood: Shillito(Jones) K.Beardmore Johnson
Ketteridge Atkins England:
Tries - Joyner K.Beardmore: Goals - Ketteridge(4):
HULL K R - Fairbairn: Stead Lydiat M.Smith S.Smith: Parker
G.Smith(Dorahy): Broadhurst Watkinson Ema Burton
Harrison(Fletcher) Kelly: Try - Parker: Goals - Fairbairn(3):
Referee R Whitfield (Widnes) Att - 4650 H.T. 12 - 4

Thu 1 Jan 1987 BRADFORD NORTHERN home won 46 - 18

CASTLEFORD - Scott: Plange Joyner(Southernwood)
Lord(Mountain) Hyde: Irwin R.Beardmore: England
K.Beardmore Johnson Ketteridge Atkins BOB
LINDNER(655): Tries - Plange(3) R.Beardmore(2)
Southernwood Lord Lindner: Goals - Ketteridge(7):
BRADFORD N - Potts: Simpson Donlan Sidebottom Race:
Mumby Godfrey: Sherratt Noble Hamer Malinder
Fairbank Jasiewicz(Bond):
Tries - Race(2) Simpson: Goals - Mumby(3):
Referee J McDonald (Wigan) Att - 5796 H.T. 18 - 2

Sun 4 Jan 1987 LEIGH away won 12 - 6

LEIGH - C.Johnson: McCullough Riding Leuluai Bentley:
Kerr P.Johnson: Pyke Dean(Hughes) Cottrell Huddart
Collier Schubert: Try - McCullough: Goal - C.Johnson:
CASTLEFORD - Scott: Plange Joyner Hyde Kear: Irwin
R.Beardmore: England K.Beardmore Johnson Ketteridge
Atkins Lindner: Tries - Scott Joyner: Goals Ketteridge (2):
Referee K Spencer (Warrington) Att - 2500 H.T. 6 - 4

Sat 17 Jan 1987 BLACKBROOK won 74 - 6 CHALLENGE CUP PRELIMINARY ROUND - AT HEADINGLEY LEEDS

CASTLEFORD - Scott: (Roockley): Plange Marchant Hyde
Kear: Irwin R.Beardmore: England(Mountain) K.Beardmore
Johnson Ketteridge Atkins Lindner:
Tries - Plange(3) Kear(3) England(2) Atkins(2) Roockley
Marchant Johnson: Goals - Ketteridge(11):
BLACKBROOK - Woods: Tipene J.McLoughlin
D.McLoughlin Arkwright: Parkes Rodgers: Bourne
Marland O'Brien(Hill) Cooper(Irvine) Askley Winders:
Try - Bourne: Goal - Parkes:
Referee M Stone (Sydney Australia) Att - 2425 H.T. 36 -6

Sun 25 Jan 1987 WARRINGTON home lost 18 - 24

CASTLEFORD - Scott: Plange Joyner Marchant Hyde:
Irwin(Roockley) R.Beardmore: England Horton Johnson
Ketteridge Atkins Lindner:
Tries - Lindner(2) Scott Hyde: Goal - Ketteridge:
WARRINGTON - Johnson: Meadows Cullen Ropati
Forster: Kelly Bishop: Boyd Hodgson Jackson Sanderson
Roberts(R.Duane) M.Gregory(Rathbone):
Tries - Cullen(2) Johnson Meadows Kelly:

Goals - Bishop(1) DG2)
Referee P Volante (Batley) Att - 5703 H.T. 10 - 18

Sat 31 Jan 1987 WIDNES home lost 16 - 24 CHALLENGE CUP ROUND 1

CASTLEFORD - Scott: Plange Marchant Johns Hyde(Irwin):
Joyner R.Beardmore: England K.Beardmore Johnson
Ketteridge Atkins(Mountain) Lindner:
Tries - Johns Joyner Lindner: Goals - R.Beardmore(2):
WIDNES - J.Myler Thackray Wright D.Hulme Basnett:
A.Myler Sullivan: Sorenson McKenzie S.O'Neill M.O'Neill
Newton Pinner(P.Hulme): Tries - D.Hulme Basnett
A.Myler Sorenson Goals - J.Myler(4):
Referee G F Lindoo (Wakefield) Att - 4375 H.T. 4 - 6

Sun 8 Feb 1987 LEEDS home lost 12 - 14

CASTLEFORD - Scott: Plange Marchant Johns Hyde:
Joyner R.Beardmore: Mountain Horton Johnson
Ketteridge Atkins(Jones) Lindner:
Try - Lindner: Goals - R.Beardmore(4):
LEEDS - Ettingshausen: Mason Gibson McGaw Fox:
Holmes Ashton: Rayne(Moorby) Maskill Skerrett Powell
Heron Clark: Tries - Mason Ashton Powell: Goal - Maskill:
Referee P Houghton (Warrington) Att-6350 H.T. 0 - 4

Sun 15 Feb l987 WIGAN away lost 6 - 16

WIGAN - Hampson: Mordt(Stephenson) Lydon Bell Gill:
Edwards Gregory: West Kiss Case Roberts(Potter)
Goodway Hanley: Tries - Gill(2) Edwards Goodway:
CASTLEFORD - Scott: Plange(Hyde) Joyner Johns
Marchant: Irwin R.Beardmore: England K.Beardmore
Johnson Ketteridge(Mountain) Atkins Lindner:
Try - Plange: Goal - R.Beardmore:
Referee R Whitfield (Widnes) Att - 13047 H.T. 6 - 4

Fri 20 Feb 1987 SALFORD away lost 10 - 36

SALFORD - Fletcher: Austin O'Loughlin Byrne Marsh:
Glynn Wakefield: Herbert Moran Major Golby McTigue
O'Shea: Tries - O'Shea(2) Austin Marsh Herbert Golby:
Goals - O'Shea(6):
CASTLEFORD - Scott: Chapman Joyner Johns Marchant:
Irwin R.Beardmore: England(Mountain)
K.Beardmore(Roockley) Johnson Ketteridge Atkins
Lindner: Try - Atkins: Goals - R.Beardmore(3):
Referee J Smith (Halifax) Att - 2011 H.T. 8 - 18

Sun 1 Mar 1987 OLDHAM home won 22 - 18

CASTLEFORD - Scott: Marchant Joyner Chris Johns
Chapman: Irwin R.Beardmore: Shillito(Mountain) Horton
Johnson England Atkins Lindner(Hyde) (Lindner):
Tries - Marchant(2) Joyner Chapman:
Goals - R.Beardmore(3):
OLDHAM - Burke(Raper): Warnecke Foy(Hawkyard)
Bridge Taylor: Topliss Kirwan: Clarke Sanderson Waddell
Worrall Hobbs Flanagan:
Tries - Bridge Taylor Topliss: Goals - Burke(2) Hobbs:
Referee J Holdsworth (Kippax) Att - 3947 H.T. 16 - 2

SEASON 1986-87

Wed 4 Mar 1987 ST HELENS home won 12 - 10
CASTLEFORD - Scott: Plange Marchant Tony Spears
Chapman: Joyner R.Beardmore: Shillito(Ward) Horton
Johnson WAYNE THORNTON(656)(Roockley) Atkins
England: Try - Plange: Goals - R.Beardmore(4):
ST HELENS - Veivers: Ledger Allen Elia Bayliss: Clark
Holding: Burke Harrison Forber Round Haggerty(Platt)
Arkwright(Dwyer): Tries - Clark Round: Goals - Dwyer:
Referee G Berry (Dewsbury) Att - 4036 H.T. 2 - 4

Wed 18 Mar 1987 WIDNES home won 44 - 8
CASTLEFORD - Roockley: Plange Marchant Scott GRANT
ANDERSON(657): Joyner R.Beardmore: Ward
K.Beardmore Johnson Ketteridge Atkins(Shillito)England:
Tries - Anderson(2) Plange(2) Scott Joyner Roockley
Marchant: Goals - R. Beardmore(6):
WIDNES - Platt(Linton): Thackray Dowd Stockley Basnett:
Ruane Sullivan: S.O'Neill Gormley M.O'Neill Newton Eyres
Pinner(Horton): Tries - Thackray(2):
Referee B Simpson (Manchester) Att - 3250 H.T. 22 - nil

Sun 22 Mar 1987 BARROW home won 70 - 10
CASTLEFORD - Roockley: Plange Marchant Colin Scott
Anderson: Joyner(Hyde) R.Beardmore: Ward(Shillito)
K.Beardmore(Joyner) Johnson Ketteridge
Brett Atkins England:
Tries - R.Beardmore(4) Joyner(2) England(2) Plange Scott
Johnson Atkins: Goals - R.Beardmore(11):
BARROW - Tickle: Lowden Williams Kay(James) Quirk:
Blacker Cairna: Maskell Lightfoot Kendall
Walker(Morrison) Naidole McGuire:
Tries - Blacker Cairns: Goal - Lowden:
Referee A Bowman (Whitehaven) Att - 3165 H.T. 24 - nil

Sun 29 Mar 1987 OLDHAM away won 29 - 6
OLDHAM - M'Barki: Sherman Foy Warnecke Taylor:
Topliss Kirman: Hobbs Hall Waddell WorraLL(Morrison)
Clawson Raper(Jones): Try - Raper: Goal - Hobbs:
CASTLEFORD - Roockley: Plange Marchant Irwin
Anderson: Joyner R.Beardmore: Ward Horton
Johnson(Mountain) Ketteridge JOHN BLACKBURN(658)
England: Tries - Plange(2) Marchant Anderson Joyner:
Goals - R.Beardmore(4) (DG):
Referee R Whitfield (Widnes) Att - 3659 H.T. 6 - 6

Wed 1 Apr 1987 ST HELENS away won 10 - 8
ST HELENS - Parkes: Ledger Loughlin Haggerty
McCormack: Doherty Devine: Burke Harrison Hopkins
Forber Allen Dwyer:
Try - Ledger: Goals - Loughlin Ledger(DG) Doherty(DG):
CASTLEFORD - Roockley: Hyde Marchant Irwin Anderson:
Joyner R.Beardmore: Shillito(Mountain) Stuart Horton
Ward Blackburn Ketteridge England:
Try - Roockley: Goals - R.Beardmore(3):
Referee D Carter (Widnes) Att - 5570 H.T. 8 - 7

Sun 5 Apr 1987 HALIFAX home won 26 - 14
CASTLEFORD - Roockley: Plange Marchant Irwin
Anderson: Joyner R.Beardmore: Shillito(Hyde)
K.Beardmore Johnson Ketteridge(Blackburn) Ward

England: Tries - Roockley Plange Irwin K.Beardmore:
Goals - R.Beardmore(5):
HALIFAX - Eadie: Smith Wilson T.Anderson George:
Hague Simpson: Beevers McCallion Neller Juliff
Scott(James) Dixon:
Tries - Eadie Wilson Dixon: Goal - Smith:
Referee G Berry (Batley) Att - 6055 H.T. 10 - 10

Tue 7 Apr 1987 HULL away lost 6 - 18
HULL - Kemble: Eastwood Schofield O'Hara McCoid: Ah
Kuoi Dick: Dannatt Patrick S.Crooks(Divorty) L.Crooks
Elgar Norton:
Tries - Schofield Dick L.Crooks: Goals - L.Crooks(3):
CASTLEFORD - Roockley: Plange Marchant Irwin
Anderson: Joyner R.Beardmore: Ward K.Beardmore
Johnson Blackburn Ketteridge England:
Try - R.Beardmore: Goal - R.Beardmore:
Referee M Beaumont (Huddersfield) Att - 4021 H.T. 6 -6

Sun 12 Apr 1987 LEEDS away won 16 - 8
LEEDS - Healy: Mason Creasser Gibson Francis: Ashton
Conway(Holmes): Kevin.Rayne Maskill Skerrett Powell
Owen(Price) Heron Try - Gibson: Goals - Creasser(2)
CASTLEFORD - Roockley: Plange Marchant Anderson
Hyde: Joyner R.Beardmore: Shillito(Blackburn)
K.Beardmore Johnson Ward Ketteridge England:
Tries - Marchant K.Beardmore: Goals - R.Beardmore(4):
Referee S Haigh (Ossett) Att - 5853 H.T. 8 - 2

**Mon 20 Apr 1987 HULL KINGSTON ROVERS away
lost 6 - 20**
HULL K R - Fairbairn: S.Smith Thompson
Boustead(Simms)Stead: M.Smith W.Parker: Harrison Rudd
Beal Speckman Kelly G.Smith:
Tries - Parker(2) Boustead M.Smith: Goals - Fairbairn(2):
CASTLEFORD - Roockley: Plange Marchant Irwin
Anderson: Joyner Southernwood: Ward K.Beardmore
Johnson(Shillito) Ketteridge Blackburn England:
Try - Plange: Goal - Ketteridge:
Referee J McDonald (Wigan) Att - 4421 H.T. nil - 8

Sun 26 Apr 1987 HALIFAX home lost 6 - 18
PREMIERSHIP ROUND 1
CASTLEFORD - Roockley: Plange Marchant Irwin(Hyde)
Anderson: Joyner Southernwood: Shillito K.Beardmore
Ward Ketteridge Blackburn (Mountain) England:
Try - England: Goal - Ketteridge:
HALIFAX - Smith: Wilson Whitfield T.Anderson
Riddlesden: Hague Stephens: Beever(Juliff) McCallion
Neller Dixon Scott(James)Pendlebury:
Tries - Anderson(2) Wilson Riddlesden: Goal - Whitfield:
Referee G F Lindop (Wakefield) Att - 6883 H.T. 4 – nil

SEASON 1986-87

Shaun Irwin
D. No 651
1986-87 to 1992-93

Chris Johns
D. No 653
1986-87

Colin Scott
D. No 654
1986-87

Bob Lindner
D. No 655
1986-87 to 1987-88

Wayne Thornton
D. No 656
1986-87 to 1989-90

Grant Anderson
D. No 657
1986-87 to 1997

John Blackburn
D. No 658
1986-87 to 1989-90

SEASON 1987-88

1987-88 SQUAD
Back Row – Chris Chapman David Roockley Kevin Ward David Plange John Fifita Dean Sampson Bob Lindner
Kevin Beardmore Roy Southernwood
Front Row – Keith England Michael Beattie Tony Marchant John Joyne Robert Beardmore Giles Boothroyd
Wayne Thornton

SEASON 1986-87

D.N	PLAYER		DEBUT	L MATCH	APP	SUB	T.AP	TRI'S	G'LS	D.G	P'TS
551	JOYNER	JOHN			37	0	37	13	0	0	52
560	FENTON	STEVE		16/11/1986	2	0	2	1	0	0	4
596	KEAR	JOHN			3	0	3	3	0	0	12
601	HYDE	GARY			20	7	27	9	0	0	36
603	WARD	KEVIN			24	2	26	3	0	0	12
608	BEARDMORE	ROBERT			37	0	37	14	62	3	183
611	BEARDMORE	KEVIN			28	0	28	9	0	0	36
613	JOHNSON	BARRY			38	0	38	2	1	0	10
618	MARCHANT	TONY			29	0	29	8	0	0	32
619	HORTON	STUART		01/04/1987	11	0	11	2	0	0	8
621	ENGLAND	KEITH			38	0	38	7	0	0	28
625	ROOCKLEY	DAVID			16	6	22	6	0	0	24
630	ATKINS	BRETT		22/03/1987	28	1	29	9	0	0	36
631	MOUNTAIN	DEAN			4	12	16	1	0	0	4
634	CHAPMAN	CHRIS			3	0	3	1	0	0	4
635	PLANGE	DAVID			34	1	35	21	0	0	84
636	KETTERIDGE	MARTIN			36	0	36	2	80	0	168
637	LORD	GARY			15	6	21	7	0	0	28
640	FLETCHER	IAN		02/11/1986	1	5	6	1	0	0	4
642	JONES	KEITH			0	3	3	0	0	0	0
643	SPEARS	TONY		04/03/1987	8	1	9	0	0	0	0
645	SHILLITO	ALAN			16	10	26	2	0	0	8
650	SOUTHERNWOOD	ROY			3	3	6	1	0	0	4
651	IRWIN	SHAUN	24/08/1986		21	2	23	3	0	0	12
652	SLATER	MARTIN	31/08/1986	31/08/1986	1	0	1	0	0	0	0
653	JOHNS	CHRIS	14/09/1986	01/03/1987	18	0	18	7	0	0	28
654	SCOTT	COLIN	01/10/1986	22/03/1987	25	0	25	10	8	1	57
655	LINDNER	BOB	01/01/1987		9	0	9	5	0	0	20
656	THORNTON	WAYNE	04/03/1987		1	0	1	0	0	0	0
657	ANDERSON	GRANT	18/03/1987		9	0	9	3	0	0	12
658	BLACKBURN	JOHN	29/03/1987		5	2	7	0	0	0	0
	31		**8**	**8**	**520**	**61**	**581**	**150**	**151**	**4**	**906**

COMPETITION		P	W	D	L	FOR	AGT
LEAGUE D 1	POSITION 4 OF 16	30	20	0	10	631	429
CHARTY SHIELD		1	0	0	1	8	9
YORK'S CUP		4	4	0	0	115	52
RL CUP		2	1	0	1	90	30
PLAYERS NO6		2	1	0	1	56	50
CHAMPIONSHIP		1	0	0	1	6	18
PLAYERS RECORDS		**40**	**26**	**0**	**14**	**906**	**588**

The season commenced with the Okells Charity Shield between the League Champions Halifax, and the Challenge Cup Winners Castleford, at the Douglas Bowl, Isle of Man which resulted in a Halifax victory 9–8.

For the second successive season we reached the final of the Yorkshire Cup. Our opponents in the final at Headingley were our main bogey team of the eighties Hull. The hoodoo was again laid to rest with a 31–24 victory with Kevin Beardmore collecting the White Rose Man of the Match trophy.

Robert (Bob) Beardmore increased the record for points scored in a League game to 38 against Barrow at home on the 22 March 1987.

The season ended as it began with a defeat at the hands of Halifax 18–6 in Round 1 of the Premiership play off.

SEASON 1987-88

The League relegation and promotion system was again amended to 'two up and four down', which resulted in Hunslet and Swinton being promoted to Division 1. Oldham Featherstone Rovers, Barrow Wakefield Trinity relegated to Division 2. Blackpool Borough changed their name to Springfield Borough.

Sat 20 Jun 1987 HALIFAX away won 25 - 6
FRIENDLY EXHIBITION MATCH - at ALBI FRANCE

Sun 9 Aug 1987 BRAMLEY away won 26 - 16
FRIENDLY JEFF TENNANT TESTIMONIAL
CASTLEFORD - Payne: Higgins Boothroyd Hyde Plange: Southernwood R.Beardmore: Sampson Fletcher Hartley Mountain Crabtree Joyner:
Subs used - Gill Morgan - Tries - Sampson(2) Payne Boothroyd Plange Southernwood   Goals - Beardmore:

Sun 23 Aug 1987 HULL away lost 24 - 25
FRIENDLY STEVE NORTON TESTIMONIAL
CASTLEFORD - Roockley: Plange Marchant Anderson Boothroyd: Irwin Southernwood: Sampson Fletcher Mountain England Ketteridge Joyner:
Subs used - Jones Hill - Tries - Roockley Marchant Boothroyd Irwin England: Goals - Ketteridge (2):

Sun 30 Aug 1987 ST HELENS home won 20 - 10
CASTLEFORD - Roockley: Plange Marchant Anderson(Mountain)GILES BOOTHROYD(659): Irwin Southernwood: Shillito(KENNETH HILL(660)) K.Beardmore DEAN SAMPSON(661) England Ward Joyner:
Tries - Marchant Boothroyd K Beardmore Sampson: Goals - Roockley(2):
ST HELENS - Veivers: Large Loughlin Elia McCormack: Batley Holding: Burke Liptrot(Forber) Fieldhouse (Haggerty) Platt Arkwright Dwyer:
Try - Arkwright: Goals - Loughlin(3):
Referee G F Lindop (Wakefield) Att - 5419 H.T. 8 - 8

Sun 6 Sep 1987 LEIGH away lost 6 - 14
LEIGH - C.Johnson: McCullough Henderson Jeffrey Standish: Kear(P Johnson) Ford: Evans(Atherton) Dean Pyke Dunn Cottrell Menfredi:
Tries - C.Johnson Jeffrey: Goals - C.Johnson(3):
CASTLEFORD - Roockley: Plange Marchant MICHAEL BEATTIE(662) Boothroyd(Mountain): Irwin Southernwood: Shillito(Sampson) K.Beardmore JOHN FIFITA(663) England Ward Joyner: Try - Roockley: Goal - Roockley:
Referee J McDonald (Wigan) Att - 3605 H.T. 2 - 6

Sun 11 Sep 1987 HUNSLET home won 32 - 12
YORKKSHIRE CUP ROUND 1
CASTLEFORD - Roockley: Plange Marchant Beattie John Kear: Joyner Southernwood: Shillito K.Beardmore Fifita England(Sampson) Ward Lindner(Irwin): Tries - Beattie(2) Plange Marchant Joyner Ward: Goals - Plange(4):
HUNSLET - Penola: Bell Coates Wilkinson Wilson(Kay): Lowes Irvine: Sykes Sampson Bateman(Nickle) Gillespie Webb(Bateman) Platt:
Tries - Coates Irvine: Goals - Platt(2):

Referee J Smith (Halifax) Att - 4748 H.T. 16 - 2

Sun 20 Sep 1987 WIGAN away lost 18 - 44
WIGAN - Hampson: Stephenson Russell(Gill) Bell Byrne: Edwards Gregory: West(Gildart) Kiss Wane Goodway Potter Hanley: Tries - Goodway(2) Hanley(2) Stephenson Byrne Edwards: Goals - Stephenson(8):
CASTLEFORD - Roockley: Plange Hyde Beattie Boothroyd: Joyner Southernwood: Ward K.Beardmore Fifita Ketteridge(Thornton) England (Sampson) Lindner:
Tries - Roockley Hyde Beattie: Goals - Ketteridge(3):
Referee K Spencer (Warrington) Att - 13103 H.T. 12 - 28

Wed 23 Sep 1987 HALIFAX away won 10 - nil
YORKSHIRE CUP ROUND 2
HALIFAX - Eadie Taylor Longstaffe Wilkinson George: Pendlebury Stephens: Beevers McCannion Neller Dixon(Juliff) Scott(James) Hanson:
CASTLEFORD - Roockley: Plange Marchant Beattie Hyde: Joyner Southernwood (Irwin): Sampson K.Beardmore Fifita England Ketteridge Lindner:
Try - K.Beardmore: Goals - Ketteridge(3):
Referee G Kershaw (Easingwold) Att -6101 H.T. 8 - nil

Sun 27 Sep 1987 WARRINGTON home lost 30 - 40
CASTLEFORD - Roockley: Plange Marchant Beattie Hyde: Joyner Irwin(Boothroyd): Sampson K.Beardmore Fifita(Southernwood) Ketteridge Blackburn England:
Tries - Roockley Plange Marchant Hyde Fifita: Goals - Ketteridge(5):
WARRINGTON - Johnson(Thorniley): Drummond Peters McGinty Carbert: Woods Holden: Tamati Roskell Humphries Jackson Roberts(Gregory) Sanderson:
Tries - Woods(3) Drummond(2) Johnson Carbert: Goals - Woods(5):
Referee G Kershaw (Easingwold) Att -5397 H.T. 8 - 14

Wed 30 Sep 1987 FEATHERSTONE ROVERS away
won 36 - 8 YORKSHIRE CUP SEMI FINAL
FEATHERSTONE R - Bibb(Wild): Jones Crossley Quinn Marsh: Steadman Fox: Harrison Staniforth Siddall(Geary) Slatter Smith Lyman: Try - Jones: Goals - Quinn(2):
CASTLEFORD - Roockley: Plange Marchant Beattie Hyde(Boothroyd): Joyner Southernwood: Ward(Sampson) K.Beardmore Fifita Ketteridge England Lindner:
Tries - Lindner(2) Plange Marchant Beattie Southernwood Ward: Goals - Ketteridge(4):
Referee G F Lindop (Wakefield) Att - 5329 H.T. 8 - 4

Sun 4 Oct 1987 HUNSLET away won 18 - 15
HUNSLET - Irvine: Rudd Tate Bowden Wilson(Sampson): Benson King: Mason(Bateman) Webb Marson Gillespie Nickle Platt: Tries - King Gillespie: Goals - Platt(3) (DG):
CASTLEFORD - Roockley: Plange(Hyde) Marchant Beattie Boothroyd: Joyner Southernwood: Shillito(Sampson) K.Beardmore Fifita England Ketteridge Lindner:
Tries - Plange Boothroyd Sampson: Goals - Ketteridge(3):
Referee K Allatt (Southport) Att - 2601 H.T. 12 - 9

SEASON 1987-88

Sat 17 Oct 1987 BRADFORD NORTHERN draw 12 -12 YORKSHIRE CUP FINAL - at HEADINGLEY LEEDS
CASTLEFORD - Roockley: Plange Marchant Beattie Hyde: Joyner Southernwood: Shillito(R.Beardmore) K.Beardmore(Sampson) Ward Ketteridge Fifita Lindner: Tries - Plange Lindner: Goals - Ketteridge(2):
BRADFORD N - Mercer: Ford McGowan Simpson Francis: Mumby Harkin: Grayshon(Hobbs) Noble Hill Skerrett Fairbank Holmes(Roebuck):
Try - Fairbank: Goals - Mumby(2) Hobbs(2):
Referee K Allatt (Southport) Att - 10829 H.T. 10 - 4

Sun 25 Oct 1987 HULL away won 37 - 16
HULL - Fletcher: Eastwood Pearce Leuluai O'Hara: Price Windley: Dannatt Jackson Regan Brooks Sharp(Crooks) Divorty: Tries - Fletcher Price Windley: Goals - Pearce(2):
CASTLEFORD - Roockley: Plange Marchant Beattie Hyde: Southernwood(Boothroyd) R.Beardmore: Shillito(Sampson) Hill Fifita Ketteridge Ward Joyner: Tries - Fifita(3) Beattie(2) Roockley Joyner: Goals - Ketteridge(4) Beardmore(DG):
Referee D Carter (Widnes) Att - 4751 H.T. 16 - 10

Sat 31 Oct 1987 BRADFORD NORTHERN lost 2 - 11 YORKSHIRE CUP FINAL REPLAY - at ELLAND ROAD LEEDS
CASTLEFORD - Roockley: Plange Marchant Beattie Hyde: Southernwood(Fifita) R.Beardmore: Ward Hill Fifita (Sampson) Ketteridge England(Boothroyd) Joyner: Goal - Ketteridge:
BRADFORD N - Mumby: Ford McGowan Mercer Simpson: Stewart Harkin: Hobbs Noble Hill Skerrett Fairbank Heron: Tries - Hill Heron: Goals - Hobbs(1) (DG):
Referee K Allatt (Southport) Att - 8475 H.T. 2 - 4
WHITE ROSE TROPY WINNER - PAUL HARKIN (BRADFORD N)

Sun 8 Nov 1987 WIDNES away lost 12 - 31
WIDNES - Shearer: Offiah Down D.Wright Thackray: D.Ruane D.Hulme: Sorenson Mackenzie S.O'Neil M.O'Neil P.Hulme Pinner: Tries - Offiah(2) Shearer Wright Thackray: Goals - Down(5) (DG):
CASTLEFORD - Roockley: Plange Boothroyd Beattie Anderson(Steven Gill): Southernwood R.Beardmore(PAUL CRABTREE(664)): England Thornton Hill Jones Hyde Joyner: Tries - Roockley Plange: Goals - R.Beardmore(2):
Referee S Cross (Hull) Att - 4172 H.T. 8 - 19

Sun 15 Nov 1987 FEATHERSTONE ROVERS away won 34 – 12 JOHN PLAYER TROPHY ROUND 1
FEATHERSTONE R - N.Barker: Quinn Crossley(Steadman) Gilbert Marsh: Bibb Fox: Slatter(Siddall) Bell Harrison Hughes Bastion Smith:
Tries - Barker Crossley: Goals - Quinn(2):
CASTLEFORD - Roockley: Plange Marchant Beattie Boothroyd: Southernwood R.Beardmore(Hyde): Shillito(Thornton) Hill England Fifita Jones Joyner: Tries - Roockley Marchant Beattie Boothroyd Southernwood Jones: Goals - Roockley(5):
Referee K Spencer (Warrington) Att –3357 H.T. 6 - 12

352

Sat 21 Nov 1987 WIGAN away lost 16 - 26 JOHN PLAYER TROPHY ROUND 2
WIGAN - Hampson: Gill Stephenson K.Iro Lydon: Edwards Gregory: Case Dermott Wane(Gildart) Goodway Potter Hanley: Tries - Iro Edwards Wane Goodway: Goals - Stephenson(5):
CASTLEFORD - Roockley: Plange Marchant Beattie(Hyde) Boothroyd: Joyner Southernwood: Shillito(England) K.Beardmore Ward Fifita England(Jones) Lindner: Tries - Plange Fifita Lindner: Goals - Roockley(2):
Referee J Smith (Halifax) Att - 9613 H.T. nil - 18

Sun 29 Nov 1987 BRADFORD NORTHERN home won 20 - 12
CASTLEFORD - Roockley: Plange Marchant Beattie(Jones) Hyde: Joyner R.Beardmore: Shillito K.Beardmore England Fifita(Sampson) Ward Lindner: Tries - Roockley Hyde Fifita: Goals - R.Beardmore(4):
BRADFORD N - Mumby: Ford McGowan Mercer Simpson: Stewart Godfrey: Hobbs Noble Hill Skerrett Fairbank Heron(Roebuck):
Tries - Mercer Fairbank: Goals - Hobbs(2):
Referee R Whitefield (Widnes) Att - 4590 H.T. 10 - 2

Wed 2 Dec 1987 WIGAN home won 12 - 10
CASTLEFORD - Roockley: Plange Marchant Boothroyd(Anderson) Hyde: Southernwood R.Beardmore: Shillito(Sampson) K.Beardmore England Ward Jones Joyner: Try - K.Beardmore   Goals - R.Beardmore(4):
WIGAN - Hampson: Lydon K.Iro Hanley Russell: Edwards Gregory: West(Byrne) Kiss Case Gildart Potter(Lucas) Goodway: Tries - West Goodway: Goal - Lydon: Referee J Smith (Halifax) Att - 6088 H.T. 8 - 6

Sun 6 Dec 1987 LEEDS away lost nil - 44
LEEDS - Gurr: Morris Schofield Gibson Basnett: Jackson Ashton: Tunks Maskill Kevin Rayne(Fairbank) Powell Medley(Wilson) Heron: Tries - Morris(3) Schofield(2) Gibson Ashton Tunks: Goals - Maskill(6):
CASTLEFORD - Roockley: Plange Marchant Beattie Anderson: Joyner(Hyde) R.Beardmore: Alan Shillito(Jones) K.Beardmore England Fifita Ward Lindner: Referee G Kershaw (Easingwold) Att - 10619 H.T. nil - 14

Sun 13 Dec 1987 SALFORD home won 14 - nil
CASTLEFORD - Roockley: Plange Marchant Beattie Anderson: Joyner R.Beardmore: Ward K.Beardmore England Jones Fifita(Hyde) Bob Lindner(BRIAN JULIFF(665)):
Tries - Beattie Ward: Goals - R.Beardmore(3):
SALFORD - Jack: Jones Shaw O'Loughlin Gibson: Cairns Bloor: Herbert Moran Major Worrall Blease(O'Shea) McTigue:
Referee K Allatt (Southport) Att - 3381 H.T. 8 - nil

Sun 20 Dec 1987 LEIGH home lost 18 - 22
CASTLEFORD - Roockley: Plange Marchant Beattie(Jones) Anderson: Irwin R.Beardmore: Fifita(Thornton) K.Beardmore England Juliff Jones(Mountain) Joyner: Tries - Marchant Irwin: Goals - R.Beardmore(5):

LEIGH - Johnson: McCulloch(Burke) Burrill Jeffrey Horo: Kerr Ford: Owen Dean Pyke Evans Dunn Clarke(Cottrell): Tries - McCulloch Burrill Horo Kerr Dean: Goal - Johnson: Referee J Smith (Halifax) Att - 3601 H.T. 14 - 4

Sun 27 Dec 1987 HULL KINGSTON ROVERS away won 28 - 16
HULL K R - Fairbairn: Clark Fletcher Mortimer(Lydiat) S.Smith: M.Smith Parker: Taylor Rudd Beal Burton Harrison(Watkinson) Ryan: Tries - Fairbairn Burton Ryan: Goals - Fletcher(2): CASTLEFORD - Roockley: Plange Marchant Hyde Boothroyd: Irwin R.Beardmore: Ward K.Beardmore Mountain(England) Juliff(Fifita) Jones Joyner: Tries - Hyde(2) Plange Boothroyd R.Beardmore: Goals - R.Beardmore(4): Referee J McDonald (Wigan) Att - 4783 H.T. 12 - 16

Sun 3 Jan 1988 BRADFORD NORTHERN away lost 6 - 24
BRADFORD N - Mumby: Ford McGowan Mercer Simpson: Stewart Harkin: Skerrett(P.Grayshon) Noble Hill Hobbs Fairbank Roebuck(Redfearn): Tries - Mumby Ford McGowan Fairbank: Goals - Hobbs(4): CASTLEFORD - Roockley: Plange Marchant Hyde Boothroyd: Irwin R.Beardmore: Ward K.Beardmore England Fifita (Dean Mountain) Jones Joyner(Hill): Try - K.Beardmore: Goal - R.Beardmore: Referee G F Lindop (Wakefield) Att -4108 H.T. nil - 12

Sun 10 Jan 1988 HULL home won 32 - 3
CASTLEFORD - Roockley: Plange Marchant Beattie Hyde(Juliff): Irwin R.Beardmore: Ward K.Beardmore Hill England Fifita(Jones) Joyner: Tries - Plange Marchant Beattie R.Beardmore K.Beardmore: Goals - R.Beardmore(6): HULL - Fletcher: M'Barki Vass Price Brand: Pearce McCaffrey(Wilby): Puckering Jackson Carroll Brooks(Ellis) Regan Divorty: Goals - Pearce Regan(DG): Referee P Volante (Batley) Att - 3860 H.T. 14 - 3

Sun 31 Jan 1988 LEEDS away lost 14 - 22 CHALLENGE CUP ROUND 1
LEEDS - Gurr: Morris Schofield Stephenson Gibson: Creasser(Jackson) Ashton(Lyons): Tunks Maskill Fairbank Powell Medley Heron: Tries - Medley(3) Schofield: Goals - Stephenson(3): CASTLEFORD - Roockley: Plange(Hill) Marchant Beattie Juliff: Irwin R.Beardmore: Ward K.Beardmore England Fifita(Jones) Ketteridge Joyner: Tries - Roockley Beattie: Goals - R.Beardmore(3): Referee K Spencer(Warrington) Att - 14716 H.T 16 - 4

Sun 7 Feb 1988 WARRINGTON away lost 6 - 32
WARRINGTON - Johnson: Drummond Cullen Ropati Lyon: Woods Holden: Boyd Webb Jackson(Sanderson) Roberts(R.Duane) Gregory McGinty: Tries - Ropati(3) Gregory(2) Johnson: Goals - Woods(4): CASTLEFORD - Roockley: Michael Beattie Marchant Lord Hyde: Irwin R.Beardmore: Sampson(Ward) Hill Fifita

Jones(Johnson) Ketteridge England: Try - Roockley: Goal - R.Beardmore: Referee R Whitfield (Widnes) Att - 3750 H.T. 6 - 18

Fri 19 Feb 1988 SALFORD away won 28 - 12
SALFORD - Gibson: Jones Austin Shaw Bentley: Bloor Cairns(Glynn): Herbert Moran Major Blease(O'Shea) Regan McTigue: Tries - Gibson Austin: Goals - Jones(2): CASTLEFORD - Roockley: Plange Marchant Lord Hyde: Irwin R.Beardmore(Southernwood): Ward K.Beardmore Johnson England Ketteridge(Fifita) Joyner: Tries - Southernwood(2) Roockley Hyde R.Beardmore: Goals - R. Beardmore(2) Ketteridge(2): Referee A Bowman (Whitehaven) Att - 2304 H.T. 12 - 6

Sun 6 Mar 1988 SWINTON home won 76 - 16
CASTLEFORD - Roockley: Plange Marchant Hyde Anderson: Southernwood(Boothroyd) R.Beardmore: Ward(Fifita) K.Beardmore Johnson Fifita (England) Ketteridge Joyner: Tries - Plange(3) K.Beardmore(3) Hyde(2) Roockley Southernwood R.Beardmore Ward Johnson England: Goals - R.Beardmore(10): SWINTON - Topping: Ranson Scott Snape Bate: Lee Hewitt: Gelling Ainsworth Muller(Viller) Mooney(Wright) Fraser Forber: Tries - Ranson Scott Ainsworth: Goals - Topping(2): Referee R Whitfield (Widnes) Att - 3164 H.T. 28 - 12

Sun 13 Mar 1988 ST HELENS away lost 6 - 14
ST HELENS - Veivers: Ledger Loughlin Tanner Large(Dwyer): Cooper Holding: Burke(Jones) Groves Evans Forber Haggerty Platt: Tries - Large Cooper: Goals - Loughlin(3): CASTLEFORD - Roockley: Plange Marchant Hyde Anderson: Irwin (John Fifita) R.Beardmore: Ward K.Beardmore(Sampson) Johnson Ketteridge England Joyner: Try - Plange: Goal - R.Beardmore: Referee G F Lindop (Wakefield) Att - 6083 H.T. 6 - 4

Sun 20 Mar 1988 HALIFAX home lost 6 - 28
CASTLEFORD - Roockley: Plange Marchant Lord Hyde: Southernwood R.Beardmore (Hill): Ward Thornton Johnson Ketteridge(Sampson) England Joyner: Try - Marchant: Goal - R.Beardmore: HALIFAX - Eadie: Meredith Whitfield Wilkinson George: Grogan T.Anderson: James McCallion Neller Scott Bell(Beevers) Holliday(Dickinson): Tries - Wilkinson(2) Grogan Anderson Holliday: Goals - Whitfield(4): Referee J McDonald (Wigan) Att - 6970 H.T. 6 - 14

Wed 23 Mar 1988 WIDNES home lost 6 - 39
CASTLEFORD - Roockley(Southernwood): Anderson Marchant Lord Hyde: Irwin R.Beardmore: Sampson Hill Johnson(Juliff) Ketteridge Ward England: Try - Ketteridge: Goal - Beardmore: WIDNES - Platt: Thackray Currier Weight Offiah(Linton): Dowd P.Hulme Pyke McKenzie S.O'Neill(Grima) Sorenson M.O'Neill R.Eyres: Tries - Currier(4) Offiah McKenzie Eyres: Goals - Platt(5) (DG): Referee S Haigh (Ossett) Att - 3529 H.T. 2 - 19

Sun 27 Mar 1988 HUNSLET home won 26 - 14
CASTLEFORD - Lord(Roockley): Hyde Marchant Anderson
Juliff: Irwin Southernwood(R.Beardmore): Sampson Hill
Johnson Ketteridge England Joyner: Tries -
Southernwood(2) Irwin Joyner: Goals - Ketteridge(5):
HUNSLET - Lay: Senior Tate Irvine Wilson: Platt
Lulham(Coates): Mason Sampson Allan Bateman Mitchell
Webb: Tries - Irvine Wilson: Goals - Platt(3):
Referee B Simpson (Manchester) Att - 2883 H.T 8 - 2

Mon 1 Apr 1988 HALIFAX away lost 12 - 22
HALIFAX - Smith: Taylor T.Anderson Wilkinson
Riddlesden: Grogan Meredith(Robinson): Dickinson
Beevers Fairbank Bell Dixon Scott:
Tries - Fairbank(2) Grogan Scott: Goals - Smith(3):
CASTLEFORD - Lord: Hyde Marchant Irwin Anderson:
Joyner R.Beardmore: Ward(Sampson)
K.Beardmore(Southernwood) Johnson Juliff Ketteridge
England: Tries - Lord Marchant: Goals - R.Beardmore(2):
Referee K Spencer (Warrington) Att - 8364 H.T. 6 - 12

**Mon 4 Apr 1988 HULL KINGSTON ROVERS home
won 28 - 24**
CASTLEFORD - Lord: Gary Hyde Marchant Anderson
Boothroyd: Irwin (Southernwood) R.Beardmore: Sampson
Hill Johnson Ketteridge England (Roockley) Joyner:
Tries – R Beardmore(2) Anderson Boothroyd:
Goals - R.Beardmore(6):
HULL K R - Thompson: Clark Lydiat Laws Stead: M.Smith
Parker: Beall Dave Harrison Ema Burton Ryan(Des
Harrison) G.Smith(Speckman):
Tries - Laws M.Smith Parker Ryan: Goals - Clark(4):
Referee P Houghton (Warr'ton) Att - 3149 H.T. 14 - 18

Sun 10 Apr 1988 SWINTON away lost 14 - 45
SWINTON - Topping: Ranson Cassidy Snape Bate:
Frodsham Hewitt: Gelling Ainsworth Fraser(Meadows)
Sheals Forber Howarth:
Tries - Ranson(2) Ainsworth(2) Topping Cassidy Snape
Bate: Goals - Topping(6) Cassidy(DG):
CASTLEFORD - Roockley: Juliff Gary Lord Irwin Anderson:
Southernwood(Boothroyd) R.Beardmore: Sampson Hill
Johnson Blackburn(Crabtree)Ketteridge Joyner:
Tries - Juliff(2): Goals - R.Beardmore(3):
Referee R Whitfield (Widnes) Att - 1494 H.T. 8 - 15

Sun 17 Apr 1988 LEEDS home won 26 - 12
CASTLEFORD - Roockley: Boothroyd Marchant Anderson
Juliff: Irwin R.Beardmore(Southernwood): Sampson Hill
Johnson(KeithJones) Ketteridge Ward Joyner:
Tries - Irwin(2) Boothroyd Marchant Juliff:
Goals - Beardmore(2) Ketteridge:
LEEDS - Gurr: Johnson Schofield Gibson Basnett: Holmes
Ashton: Rayne Gunn(Maskill) Powell Price(Crooks)
Crooks(Medley) (Gunn) Heron:
Tries - Gurr Ashton: Goals - Maskill(2):
Referee G Berry (Batley) Att - 6979 H.T. 14 - nil

**Sun 24 Apr 1988 ST HELENS away lost 8 - 40
PREMIERSHIP ROUND 1**

ST HELENS - Loughlin: Ledger Tanner Elia Quirk:
McCormack(Allen) Devine: Burke(Fieldhouse) Groves
Evans Forber Haggerty Platt:
Tries - Groves(3) Ledger Elia Quirk Forber:
Goals - Tanner(4) Loughlin(2):
CASTLEFORD - Roockley: Plange(Boothroyd) Marchant
Anderson Brian Juliff: Irwin R.Beardmore: Sampson Hill
Johnson Ketteridge Ward Joyner(Southernwood):
Try - Irwin: Goals - R.Beardmore(2):
Referee F D Lindop (Wakefield) Att - 7209 H.T. 2 – 14

Giles Boothroyd
D. No 659
1987-88 to 1992-93

Kenny Hill
D. No 660
1987-88 to 1989-90

Dean Sampson
D. No 661
1987-88 to 2005

Michael Beattie
D. No 662
1987-88

John Fifita
D. No 663
1987-88

Paul Crabtree
D. No 664
1987-88 to 1989-90

SEASON 1987-88

G.N	PLAYER		DEBUT	L MATCH	APP	SUB	T.AP	TRI'S	G'LS	D.G	P'TS
551	JOYNER	JOHN			33	0	33	3	0	0	12
596	KEAR	JOHN		11/09/1987	1	0	1	0	0	0	0
601	HYDE	GARY		04/04/1988	22	5	27	8	0	0	32
603	WARD	KEVIN			25	1	26	4	0	0	16
608	BEARDMORE	ROBERT			24	2	26	6	63	1	151
610	GILL	STEVEN		08/11/1987	0	1	1	0	0	0	0
611	BEARDMORE	KEVIN			23	0	23	8	0	0	32
613	JOHNSON	BARRY			11	1	12	1	0	0	4
618	MARCHANT	TONY			32	0	32	10	0	0	40
621	ENGLAND	KEITH			28	2	30	1	0	0	4
625	ROOCKLEY	DAVID			32	2	34	11	10	0	64
631	MOUNTAIN	DEAN		03/01/1988	1	4	5	0	0	0	0
635	PLANGE	DAVID			28	0	28	13	4	0	60
636	KETTERIDGE	MARTIN			21	0	21	1	33	0	70
637	LORD	GARY		10/04/1998	8	0	8	1	0	0	4
642	JONES	KEITH		17/04/1988	8	6	14	1	0	0	4
645	SHILLITO	ALAN		06/12/1987	11	0	11	0	0	0	0
650	SOUTHERNWOOD	ROY			18	7	25	7	0	0	28
651	IRWIN	SHAUN			18	2	20	5	0	0	20
655	LINDNER	BOB		13/12/1987	10	0	10	4	0	0	16
656	THORNTON	WAYNE			2	3	5	0	0	0	0
657	ANDERSON	GRANT			14	1	15	1	0	0	4
658	BLACKBURN	JOHN			2	0	2	0	0	0	0
659	BOOTHROYD	GILES	30/08/1987		12	7	19	6	0	0	24
660	HILL	KENNETH	30/08/1987		12	4	16	0	0	0	0
661	SAMPSON	DEAN	30/08/1987		10	13	23	2	0	0	8
662	BEATTIE	MICHAEL	06/09/1987	07/02/1988	20	0	20	10	0	0	40
663	FIFITA	JOHN	06/09/1987	13/03/1988	21	3	24	6	0	0	24
664	CRABTREE	PAUL	08/11/1987		0	2	2	0	0	0	0
665	JULIFF	BRIAN	13/12/1987	24/04/1988	8	3	11	3	0	0	12
	30		7	11	455	69	524	112	110	1	669

COMPETITION		P	W	D	L	FOR	AGT
LEAGUE D 1	POSITION 7 OF 14	26	13	0	13	505	559
YORK'S CUP		5	3	1	1	92	43
RL CUP		1	0	0	1	14	22
PLAYERS NO6		2	1	0	1	50	38
CHAMPIONSHIP		1	0	0	1	8	40
PLAYERS RECORDS		**35**	**17**	**1**	**17**	**669**	**702**

After thirteen seasons under Coach Malcolm Reilly he was succeeded by his former Assistant David Sampson for this season.

For the third successive season we reached the Final of the Yorkshire Cup. In the Final at Headingly we drew with Bradford Northern 12-12. In the replay at Elland Road Leeds we lost 11-2 with Bradford's Paul Harkin collecting the White Rose Man of the Match trophy.

John Joyner registered his 500th appearance for the club on 19 February 1988 in the away victory, at Salford. 28–12

A notable Debutant was Dean Sampson

SEASON 1988-89

The League relegation and promotion system reverted to 'three up and three down, which resulted in Oldham, Featherstone Rovers Wakefield Trinity promoted to Division 1. Leigh, Swinton Hunslet relegated to Division 2. Springfield Borough relocated and changed their name to Chorley Borough.

Sun 14 Aug 1988 HULL home won 26 – 14 KEVIN & ROBERT BEARDMORE BENEFIT GAME FRIENDLY
CASTLEFORD – Rookly: Plange Marchant Lord Gill: Anderson R Southernwood:Sampson K Beardmore England Ketteridge Jones Joyner: Subs used – Chapman Johnson Hyde Moon Blankly G Southernwood Smith Boothroyd: Tries – Anderson(2) K Beardmore Blankly: Goals – Ketteridge(5)
HULL - Fletcher: O'Hara Wilby Gay Eastwcod: Pearce Bowers: Carroll Patrick Tomlinson Sharp Procter Divorty: Subs used – S.Crooks Jackson Dannett Welham A. N Other: Tries – Eastwood Blowers Gay: Goal – Pearce
Referee J Kendrew (Castleford) att – 1769 H.T.14 - 10

Sun 28 Aug 1988 HULL away won 18 - 8
HULL - Fletcher: Eastwood Price Wilby(Moon) O'Hara: Pearce Windley: Tomlinson(Proctor) Patrick Dannatt Boyle Sharp Divorty: Try - Dannatt: Goals - Pearce(2):
CASTLEFORD - Roockley: Plange Marchant Anderson Chapman: Irwin Southernwood: Sampson K.Beardmore England Ketteridge RON GIBBS(666) (Johnson) Joyner: Tries - Plange K.Beardmore Gibbs: Goals - Ketteridge(3):
Referee J Smith (Halifax) Att - 6562 H.T. 6 - 2

Sun 4 Sep 1988 HALIFAX home won 30 - nil
CASTLEFORD - Roockley: Plange Marchant Boothroyd Chapman: Anderson Southernwood: Ward K.Beardmore England Ketteridge(Johnson) Gibbs Joyner(R.Beardmore): Tries - Marchant(2) Roockley Anderson Ward Joyner: Goals - Ketteridge(2) Roockley:
HALIFAX - Eadie: Taylor Wilkinson(Grogan) Whitfield George: Anderson Robinson: Fairbank(Holliday) McCallion Beevers Dixon James Pendlebury:
Referee G Kershaw (Easingwold) Att - 8386 H.T. 20 - nil

Sun 11 Sep 1988 ST HELENS away draw 14 - 14
ST HELENS - Veivers: McCormack Tanner Loughlin Quirk: Cooper Bailey: Burke(Harrison) Lee Forber Allen Harrison(Jones) Dwyer:
Tries - Veivers McCormack: Goals - Loughlin(3):
CASTLEFORD - Roockley(GARY BELCHER(667)): Plange Marchant Boothroyd Chapman: Anderson Southernwood: Ward K.Beardmore England(Sampson)Ketteridge Gibbs(S/O) Joyner:
Tries - Boothroyd Anderson: Goals - Ketteridge(3):
Referee P Volante (Batley) Att - 8202 H.T. 6 - 8

Sun 18 Sep 1988 HUDDERSFIELD home won 94 - 12 YORKSHIRE CUP ROUND 1
CASTLEFORD - Belcher: Plange Marchant Boothroyd Chapman: Anderson Southernwood(S/O): Ward K.Beardmore England(Roockley) Sampson (Johnson) Ketteridge Joyner: Tries - Plange(3) Chapman(3)

K.Beardmore(3) Belcher(2) Boothroyd(2) Ketteridge(2) Sampson Joyner: Goals - Ketteridge(13):
HUDDERSFIELD - Ramsden: Taylor Bartle Farrell Lee: Sedgewick Meehan: Johnson(S/O) Cook Boothroyd Simpson(Huck) Nelson(Sewell) Kenworthy:
Tries - Taylor Bartle: Goals - Kenworthy(2):
Referee G Berry (Batley) Att - 2981 H.T. 56 - nil

Sun 25 Sep 1988 OLDHAM home won 22 - 19
CASTLEFORD - Belcher: Plange Marchant Boothroyd Chapman: Anderson R.Beardmore: Sampson K.Beardmore England Ketteridge(Irwin) Barry Johnson(Hill) Joyner:
Tries - Chapman K.Beardmore Hill Joyner: Goals - R.Beardmore(3):
OLDHAM - Round: A.N.Other Foy(Henderson) Henderson(Hawkyard) Meadows: O'Sullivan Ford: Clawson Ruane Fairbank(Gilbert) Casey Gilbert (Flanagan) Taylor:
Tries - Round Henderson Gilbert: Goals - Ruane(3) (DG):
Referee R Whitfield (Widnes) Att - 5715 H.T. 4 - 2

Wed 28 Sep 1988 YORK home won 40 - 14 YORKSHIRE CUP ROUND 2
CASTLEFORD - Belcher: Plange Marchant Irwin(Boothroyd) Chapman: Anderson R.Beardmore: Sampson(Ward) K.Beardmore Hill Ketteridge England Joyner: Tries - Chapman(2) Anderson(2) Belcher Plange Marchant Boothroyd: Goals - R.Beardmore(4):
YORK - Wigglesworth(Stephens): White Pryce Harrison St John Ellis: Atkins Dobson: Paver Horton Miles Sullivan St Hilaire Macklin-Shaw (Wheatley):
Tries - Paver St Hilaire: Goals - Sullivan(2) Macklin-Shaw:
Referee S Cross (Hull) Att - 3155 H.T. 14 - 8

Sun 2 Oct 1988 WIGAN away won 20 - 12
WIGAN - Lydon: Gill Byrne Hanley Preston: Edwards Gregory: Case(Lucas) Kiss Wane(Betts) Platt Gildart(Wane) Goodway: Tries - Hanley Preston: Goals - Lydon Gill:
CASTLEFORD - Belcher: Plange Marchant Boothroyd Chapman: Anderson R.Beardmore: Ward K.Beardmore England Ketteridge Gibbs Joyner(Hill): Tries - Plange Anderson K.Beardmore Joyner: Goals - Ketteridge(2):
Referee K Allatt (Southport) Att - 13231 H.T. 16 - 2

Wed 5 Oct 1988 HALIFAX away won 12 - 8 YORKSHIRE CUP SEMI FINAL
HALIFAX - Whitfield: Taylor Grogan Anderson Wilson: Robinson (Longstaff) Holmes: Fairbank McCallion Dickinson Dixon Scott (Ramshaw) Pendlebury:
Try - Taylor: Goals - Whitfield(2):
CASTLEFORD - Belcher(Roockley): Plange Marchant Boothroyd Chapman: Anderson R.Beardmore: Ward K.Beardmore England Ketteridge Gibbs Joyner:
Tries - Marchant Chapman: Goals - Ketteridge(2):
Referee G Berry (Batley) Att - 8432 H.T. 8 - 8

Sun 9 Oct 1988 SALFORD home won 38 - 12
CASTLEFORD - Roockley: Plange Marchant(Southernwood) Boothroyd Chapman: Anderson R.Beardmore: Sampson K.Beardmore England Ketteridge

SEASON 1988-89

Gibbs Joyner(Hill):
Tries - Chapman Anderson R.Beardmore Sampson
K.Beardmore England: Goals - Ketteridge(7):
SALFORD - Gibson: Evans Bentley Williams Hadley: Shaw
Cairns: Herbert Moran A.Worrall(Bullough)Gormley
M.Worrall Blease: Tries - Gibson Evans Bentley:
Referee F Tickle (St Helens) Att - 6151 H.T. 12 - 12

Sun 16 Oct 1988 LEEDS lost 12 - 33
YORKSHIRE CUP FINAL - at ELLAND ROAD LEEDS
CASTLEFORD - Belcher: Plange Marchant Boothroyd
Chapman(Roockley) (Sampson): Anderson R.Beardmore:
Ward K.Beardmore England Ketteridge Gibbs Joyner:
Tries - Boothroyd Joyner: Goals - Ketteridge(2):
LEEDS - Spencer: Ettingshausen Schofield Stephenson
Gibson: Lyons Ashton: Crooks Maskill Waddell(Backo)
Powell Brooke-Cowen(Medley)Heron: Tries - Schofield(2)
Gibson(2) Medley: Goals - Stephenson(6) Schofield(DG):
Referee R Whitfield (Widnes) Att - 23000 H.T. 12 - 15
WHITE ROSE TROPHY WINNER - CLIFF LYONS (LEEDS)

Sun 23 Oct 1988 WARRINGTON home won 23 - 16
CASTLEFORD - Belcher: Plange Marchant Boothroyd
SHANE HORO(668): Anderson R.Beardmore: Ward
K.Beardmore England(Sampson) Ketteridge Gibbs Joyner:
Tries - Plange Boothroyd Anderson:
Goals - Ketteridge(5) Anderson(DG):
WARRINGTON - Lyon: Drummond McGinty Thorniley
Forster: Woods Blake: Roach Tamati Humphries(Roberts)
Davidson Gregory Duane:
Tries - Thorniley Blake Davidson: Goals - Woods(2):
Referee G Kershaw (Easingwold) Att - 5220 H.T. 14 - 6

Sun 30 Oct 1988 WORKINGTON TOWN away won
28 - 2 JOHN PLAYER TROPHY PRELIMINARY ROUND
WORKINGTON T - Lowden: George Smith Mawson Beck:
Rea(Thornton) Shuttleworth: Torley(Penrice) Riley Phillips
Vannett Sullivan Higgins: Goal - Lowden:
CASTLEFORD - Roockley: Plange Marchant Boothroyd
Horo: Anderson R.Beardmore: Sampson(Ward) GRAHAM
SOUTHERNWOOD(669)(K.Beardmore) England Ketteridge
Gibbs Joyner: Tries - Roockley(2) Anderson(2) Plange:
Goals - Ketteridge(4):
Referee K Dockray (Leeds) Att - 1502 H.T. nil - nil

Sun 6 Nov 1988 FEATHERSTONE ROVERS away
won 26 - 20
FEATHERSTONE R - Bibb: Newlove Smales Banks Quinn:
Steadman Fox: Grayshon(Bastian) Bell(Clark) Harrison
Hughes Smith Lyman:
Tries - Bibb Banks Harrison: Goals - Quinn(4):
CASTLEFORD - Belcher: Plange Marchant Boothroyd
Horo: Anderson(Roockley) R.Beardmore: Ward
K.Beardmore England(Sampson) Ketteridge Gibbs Joyner:
Tries - Anderson(2) Belcher Plange Joyner:
Goals - Ketteridge(3):
Referee P Volante (Batley) Att - 5538 H.T. 12 - 8

Sat 12 Nov 1988 LEEDS away won 21 - 12
JOHN PLAYER TROPHY ROUND 1

LEEDS - Spencer: Ettingshausen Schofield Stephenson
Gibson: Lyons Ashton: Crooks(Brooke-Cowden) Maskill
Waddell Powell Medley(Price)Heron(S/O):
Tries - Gibson Lyons: Goals - Stephenson(2):
CASTLEFORD - Belcher: Plange Marchant Boothroyd
Horo: Anderson R.Beardmore: Ward(Sampson)
K.Beardmore England Ketteridge Gibbs Joyner:
Tries - Belcher Boothroyd K.Beardmore:
Goals - Ketteridge(4) Belcher(DG):
Referee- Mr B Simpson(Manchester) Att-10057 H.T. 6 - 12

Sun 20 Nov 1988 ST HELENS home won 46 - 12
CASTLEFORD - Gary Belcher(Irwin): Plange Marchant
Boothroyd Horo: Anderson(Hill) R.Beardmore: Sampson
K.Beardmore England Ketteridge Gibbs Joyner:
Tries - Anderson(3) Boothroyd(2) Horo(2) Plange
Sampson: Goals - Ketteridge(5):
ST HELENS - O'Connor: Carrington Tanner(Veivers) (Allen)
Loughlin: Quirk: Cooper Bloor: Burke Dwyer Evans Forber
Haggerty Vautin:
Tries - O'Connor Quirk: Goals - Loughlin(2):
Referee R Whitfield (Widnes) Att - 6500 H.T. 30 - 2

Sun 27 Nov 1988 BRADFORD NORTHERN home
lost 18 – 19 JOHN PLAYER TROPHY ROUND 2
CASTLEFORD - Irwin: Plange Marchant Boothroyd Horo:
Anderson R.Beardmore: Sampson K.Beardmore
England(Hill) Ketteridge Gibbs Joyner:
Tries - Boothroyd Gibbs: Goals - Ketteridge(5):
BRADFORD N - Mumby: Johnson McGowan Mercer
Simpson: Stewart Harkin: Skerrett(Ake) Noble
Hamer(Barraclough) Hobbs Fairbank Pinner:
Tries - Johnson Fairbank Pinner: Goals - Hobbs(3) (DG):
Referee S Cross Hull) Att - 8019 H.T. 8 - 6

Sun 18 Dec 1988 WARRINGTON away won 26 - 20
WARRINGTON - Woods: Bacon(Bishop) Duane Thorniley
Williamson: Turner Blake: Harman Thursfield Davidson
Sanderson Roberts Gregory(Humphries)
Tries - Bishop Thorniley Roberts: Goals - Woods(4):
CASTLEFORD - Irwin: Plange Marchant Boothroyd Horo:
Anderson R.Beardmore: Ward K.Beardmore England
Ketteridge(Sampson) Gibbs Joyner:
Tries - Irwin Marchant Boothroyd Horo Anderson:
Goals - Ketteridge(2) R.Beardmore:
Referee K Allatt (Southport) Att - 4400 H.T. 10 - 8

Mon 26 Dec 1988 HULL KINGSTON ROVERS home
won 38 - 20
CASTLEFORD - Irwin: Plange Marchant Boothroyd Horo:
Anderson R.Beardmore(Roockley): Ward K.Beardmore
England Ketteridge Gibbs (Sampson) Joyner:
Tries - Anderson(2) Boothroyd Horo England:
Goals - Ketteridge(9):
HULL K R - Fairbairn: Clarke(Laws) Fletcher Lydiat Pratt:
Smith Miller: Porter David Harrison Beall Burton Des
Harrison(Ema) Close:
Tries - Clarke Burton Close: Goals - Fletcher(4):
Referee G Berry (Batley) Att - 6282 H.T. 26 - 20

SEASON 1988-89

Sun 1 Jan 1989 BRADFORD NORTHERN home won 38 - 20
CASTLEFORD - Irwin: Plange Marchant Boothroyd Horo: Anderson R.Beardmore: Ward K.Beardmore England (Roockley) Ketteridge Gibbs(Sampson) Joyner: Tries - Horo(2) R.Beardmore(2) Irwin: Goals - Ketteridge(9): BRADFORD N - Mumby: Johnson McGowan Mercer Simpson: Stewart Harkin: Skerrett(Wilson) Noble Hamer Hobbs Fairbank Pinner:
Tries - McGowan(2) Skerrett: Goals - Hobbs(4):
Referee C Steele(Dalton in Furness) Att 7320 H.T. 18 -12

Sat 8 Jan 1989 HALIFAX away lost 12 - 21
HALIFAX - Coyne: Longstaff Hutchinson Anderson George: Grogan Lyons: Fairbank McCallion Stains(Smith) Ramshaw Wilson Holliday(Holmes): Tries - Anderson(2) George: Goals - Lyons(4) Ramshaw(DG):
CASTLEFORD - Irwin: Plange Marchant Boothroyd Horo(Chapman): Anderson R.Beardmore: Ward K.Beardmore England Ketteridge(Sampson) Gibbs(S/O) Joyner: Tries - Boothroyd Sampson:
Goals - R.Beardmore Ketteridge:
Referee - Mr K Allatt (Southport) Att - 9231 H.T. 2 - 14

Sun 22 Jan 1989 WAKEFIELD TRINITY home won 38 - 14
CASTLEFORD - Roockley: Plange(Sampson) Marchant Irwin Boothroyd: Anderson R.Beardmore: Ward(Hill) K.Beardmore England Ketteridge Gibbs Joyner:
Tries - Anderson(3) Gibbs(2) Sampson Marchant:
Goals Ketteridge(5):
WAKEFIELD T - Harcombe: Wilson Eden Hunte Fletcher: Lazenby M.Conway: Thompson B.Conway Mallinder Glancy Norton(Price) Bell:
Tries - Thompson Conway: Goals - Harcombe(3):
Referee R Whitfield (Widnes) Att - 6411 H.T. 24 - 12

Sat 28 Jan 1989 HULL away won 7 - 4
CHALLENGE CUP ROUND 1
HULL - Fletcher: Moon Blacker Price(Welham) O'Hara: Pearce Coleman: Dannatt Jackson(Crooks) Boyle Wilby Sharp Divorty: Goals - Pearce(2):
CASTLEFORD - Roockley: Horo Marchant Irwin Boothroyd(Sampson): Anderson R.Southernwood: Ward K.Beardmore England Ketteridge Gibbs Joyner:
Try - Horo: Goals - Ketteridge Roockley(DG):
Referee S Haigh (Ossett) Att - 9848 H.T. 6 - 4

Sat 11 Feb 1989 WIDNES home lost 18 - 32
CHALLENGE CUP ROUND 2
CASTLEFORD - Roockley: Horo Marchant Irwin(MARK GIBSON(670)) Chapman: Anderson R.Southernwood: Ward K.Beardmore England Ketteridge Gibbs Joyner:
Tries - Horo Southernwood: Goals - Ketteridge(5):
WIDNES - Tait: Thackray Currier Wright Offiah: D.Hulme P.Hulme: Grima McKenzie Pyke(Davies) O'Neill Koloto Eyres: Tries - Koloto(2) Tait Offiah Grima McKenzie: Goals - Currier(4):
Referee S Cross (Hull) Att - 10765 H.T. 6 - 22

Fri 17 Feb 1989 SALFORD away won 20 - 18
SALFORD - Gibson: Evans Bragger Kerry Hadley: Williams Cairns: Herbert Gormley A.Worrall Blease Brown M.Horo:
Tries - Bragger(2) Hadley: Goals - Brown(2) Kerry:
CASTLEFORD - Roockley: Horo Marchant Gibson Chapman: Anderson R.Beardmore: Ward K.Beardmore England Ketteridge(Sampson) (R.Southernwood) Gibbs Joyner: Tries - Roockley Anderson Joyner:
Goals - Roockley(3) Ketteridge:
Referee R Whitfield (Widnes) Att - 4460 H.T. 6 - 6

Wed 22 Feb 1989 BRADFORD NORTHERN away won 20 - 6
BRADFORD N - Mumby: Simpson McGowan Wilkinson(Johnson) Mercer: Stewart Godfrey(Wilson): Skerrett Noble Hamer Pendlebury Fairbank Pinner:
Try - Wilkinson: Goal - Mercer:
CASTLEFORD - Roockley: Horo Marchant Gibson Chapman: Anderson R.Beardmore: Ward K.Beardmore England Ketteridge Gibbs(Hill) Joyner:
Tries - Marchant(2) Horo: Goals - Ketteridge(4):
Referee D Carter (Widnes) Att - 4404 H.T. 12 - 6

Sun 26 Feb 1989 WAKEFIELD TRINITY away lost 8 -26
WAKEFIELD T - Harcombe(Fletcher): Eden Leuluai Mason Wilson: Lazenby M.Conway: Rayne(Mallinder) B.Conway Thompson Glancy Norton Bell: Tries - Fletcher Leuluai Mason Lazenby Bell: Goals - M.Conway(2) Harcombe:
CASTLEFORD - Roockley: Horo Marchant Gibson Chapman: Anderson R.Beardmore(R.Southernwood): Ward K.Beardmore England(Hill) Ketteridge Gibbs Joyner:
Try - Marchant: Goals - Ketteridge(2):
Referee C Steele(Dalton in Furness) Att - 5811 H.T. 8 - 12

Sun 5 Mar 1989 HULL home lost 16 - 23
CASTLEFORD - Roockley: Horo(R.Southernwood) Marchant Gibson Chapman: Anderson R.Beardmore: Ward K.Beardmore Hill(Sampson) Ketteridge England Joyner: Tries - Horo Chapmam K.Beardmore:
Goals - Ketteridge(2):
HULL - Fletcher: Moon Blacker Price(Nolan) O'Hara: Pearce Windley: Dannatt Jackson Crooks Wilby Sharp Divorty(Welham):
Tries - Blacker(2) Price O'Hara: Goals - Pearce(3) (DG):
Referee G Kershaw (Easingwold) Att - 6401 H.T. 4 - 12

Sun 19 Mar 1989 LEEDS away lost 18 - 32
LEEDS - Spencer: Ford Schofield Gibson Bentley(Lord): Creasser Ashton: Crooks Maskill Price Powell Brooke-Cowden(Waddell) Heron: Tries - Schofield Gibson Bentley Creasser Heron: Goals - Creasser(6): CASTLEFORD - Roockley: Marchant Gibson Boothroyd Chapman: Anderson Robert Beardmore (R.Southernwood): Sampson K.Beardmore Hill(PHILIP MIRFIN(671)) Ketteridge England Joyner:
Tries - Marchant Gibson Boothroyd: Goals - Ketteridge(3):
Referee R Whitfield (Widnes) Att - 12369 H.T. 10 - 18

SEASON 1988-89

Fri 24 Mar 1989 FEATHERSTONE ROVERS home draw 14 - 14

CASTLEFORD - Roockley: Marchant Anderson Boothroyd Chapman: Joyner R.Southernwood: Ward K.Beardmore Hill Sampson(Mirfin) England Ketteridge: Tries - Anderson Boothroyd: Goals - Ketteridge(2) Roockley:
FEATHERSTONE R - Bibb: Smales(Beach) (Siddall) Banks Newlove Hughes: Steadman Fox: Grayshon Clark Harrison Bastian Booth Smith:
Tries - Newlove Fox: Goals - Steadman(3):
Referee D Carter (Widnes) Att - 6895 H.T. 10 - 8

Mon 27 Mar 1989 HULL KINGSTON ROVERS away lost 30 - 32

HULL K R - Thompson: Hallas M.Fletcher Sullivan Pratt: Smith Robinson : Armstrong Richardson(Dave Harrison) Beall Des Harrison O'Brien P.Fletcher(Schultz):
Tries - Sullivan(3) Richardson:
Goals - M.Fletcher(7) Smith(DG) Armstrong(DG):
CASTLEFORD - Roockley: Marchant Anderson Boothroyd Chapman: Joyner(Horo) R.Southernwood: Ward K.Beardmore Hill(Mirfin) Sampson England Ketteridge:
Tries - Roockley Horo Mirfin Sampson:
Goals - Ketteridge(7):
Referee S Haigh (Ossett) Att - 3760 H.T. 12 - 22

Thu 30 Mar 1989 WIDNES away lost 4 - 36

WIDNES - Tait: Myers Currier Wright Offiah: Davies D.Hulme: Sorenson McKenzie(Dowd) O'Neill(Moriarty) Koloto Eyres P.Hulme:
Tries - D.Hulme(3) Offiah(2) Currier: Goals - Davies(6):
CASTLEFORD - Roockley: Shane Horo Gibson Boothroyd Chapman: Anderson R.Southernwood: Ward K.Beardmore(Thornton) England Mirfin Crabtree (DEAN BLANKLEY(672)) Ketteridge: Try - Mirfin:
Referee C Steele(Dalton in Furness) Att -11024 H.T. 4 - 14

Sun 2 Apr 1989 WIGAN home lost 4 - 17

CASTLEFORD - Roockley: Marchant Gibson Boothroyd(Thornton) Chapman: Anderson R.Southernwood: Ward Blankley England Ketteridge Crabtree (Mirfin) Joyner: Try - Roockley:
WIGAN - Hampson: Byrne Hanley Lydon Bell: Edwards Gregory(Goodway): Lucas Kiss Shelford Betts Potter Platt:
Tries - Hanley Bell: Goals - Lydon(4) (DG):
Referee F Tickle (St Helens) Att - 7289 H.T. 4 – 10

Sun 9 Apr 1989 OLDHAM away lost 18 - 34

OLDHAM - Platt: Lord Round Hyde Robinson: Henderson Ford: Clawson(Croston) Ruane Casey Allen Newton Cogger(Bates):
Tries - Cogger(2) Lord(2) Platt Hyde: Goals - Platt(5):
CASTLEFORD - David Roockley(Wayne Thornton): Marchant Gibson Battye Chapman: Anderson R.Southernwood: Ketteridge K.Beardmore England Crabtree(TERRY McALLISTER(673)) Mirfin Joyner:
Tries - Marchant Anderson Mirfin: Goals - Ketteridge(3):
Referee C Haigh (Ossett) Att - 4562 H.T. 12 - 18

Wed 12 Apr 1989 WIDNES home lost 22 - 24

CASTLEFORD - Gibson: Marchant McAllister Anderson Chapman: Joyner Blankley: Ward(Battye)K.Beardmore England Crabtree(Mirfin) Sampson Ketteridge:
Tries - Marchant Mirfin Ketteridge: Goals - Ketteridge(5):
WIDNES - Tait: Myers Currier Wright Offiah: Dowd Sullivan(Moriarty) (Smith): Sorenson Eyres Grima O'Neill Kolota P.Hulme:
Tries - Kolota(2) Currier Offiah: Goals - Currier(4):
Referee G Kershaw (Easingwold) Att - 6443 H.T. 8 - 12

Sun 16 Apr 1989 LEEDS home won 38 - 10

CASTLEFORD - Gibson: Marchant McAllister Anderson Chapman: Joyner Blankley(Battye): Ward K.Beardmore England Crabtree(Mirfin) Sampson Ketteridge:
Tries - Marchant Anderson Ward England Mirfin Sampson: Goals - Ketteridge(7):
LEEDS - Spencer:(G.Lord): Ford Schofield Gibson Bentley: Creasser M.Lord: Crooks Maskill Waddell(Price) Powell Dixon Heron: Tries - Gibson M.Lord: Goal - Creasser:
Referee S Cross (Hull) Att - 9391 H.T. 16 - 10

Sun 23 Apr 1989 HULL away lost 6 - 32
PREMIERSHIP ROUND 1

HULL - Fletcher: Eastwood Blacker Price O'Hara: Pearce(Nolan) Windley: Dannatt(Wilby) Jackson Crooks Welham Sharp Divorty: Tries - Price(2) Eastwood Pearce Nolan Windley: Goals - Nolan(3) Pearce:
CASTLEFORD - Gibson(S/O): Marchant McAllister Anderson(Battye) Chapman: Joyner R.Southernwood: Ward(Mirfin) K.Beardmore England Crabtree Sampson Ketteridge: Try - Chapman: Goal - Ketteridge:
Referee G Kershaw (Easingwold) Att - 8809 H.T. nil – 14

Ronnie Gibbs
D. No 666
1988-89 to 1989-90

Gary Belcher
D. No 667
1988-89

Graham Southernwood
D. No 669
1988-89 to 1992-93

Terry McAllister
D. No 673
1988-89 to 1994-95

SEASON 1988-89

D.N	PLAYER		DEBUT	L MATCH	APP	SUB	T.AP	TRI'S	G'LS	D.G	P'TS
551	JOYNER	JOHN			35	0	35	7	0	0	28
603	WARD	KEVIN			27	2	29	2	0	0	8
608	BEARDMORE	ROBERT		19/03/1989	22	1	23	3	9	0	30
611	BEARDMORE	KEVIN			34	1	35	9	0	0	36
613	JOHNSON	BARRY		25/09/1988	1	3	4	0	0	0	0
618	MARCHANT	TONY			35	0	35	13	0	0	52
621	ENGLAND	KEITH			36	0	36	3	0	0	12
625	ROOCKLEY	DAVID		09/04/1989	18	6	24	6	5	1	35
627	BATTYE	NEIL			1	3	4	0	0	0	0
634	CHAPMAN	CHRIS			24	1	25	10	0	0	40
635	PLANGE	DAVID			21	0	21	10	0	0	40
636	KETTERIDGE	MARTIN			36	0	36	3	129	0	270
650	SOUTHERNWOOD	ROY			12	5	17	1	0	0	4
651	IRWIN	SHAUN			10	2	12	2	0	0	8
656	THORNTON	WAYNE			0	3	3	0	0	0	0
657	ANDERSON	GRANT			36	0	36	24	0	1	97
659	BOOTHROYD	GILES			25	1	26	15	0	0	60
660	HILL	KENNETH			5	8	13	1	0	0	4
661	SAMPSON	DEAN			14	13	27	7	0	0	28
664	CRABTREE	PAUL			6	0	6	0	0	0	0
666	GIBBS	RON	28/08/1988		23	0	23	4	0	0	16
667	BELCHER	GARY	11/09/1988	20/11/1988	10	1	11	5	0	1	21
668	HORO	SHANE	23/10/1988	30/03/1989	17	1	18	11	0	0	44
669	SOUTHERNWOOD	GRAHAM	30/10/1988		1	0	1	0	0	0	0
670	GIBSON	MARK	11/02/1989		11	1	12	1	0	0	4
671	MIRFIN	PHIL	19/03/1989		2	7	9	5	0	0	20
672	BLANKLEY	DEAN	30/03/1989		3	1	4	0	0	0	0
673	McALLISTER	TERRY	09/04/1989		3	1	4	0	0	0	0
	28										
				8	**5**	**468**	**61**	**529**	**142**	**143**	**3**	**857**

COMPETITION		P	W	D	L	FOR	AGT
LEAGUE D 1	POSITION 5 OF 14	26	15	2	9	601	480
YORK'S CUP		4	3	0	1	158	67
RL CUP		2	1	0	1	25	36
PLAYERS NO6		3	2	0	1	67	33
CHAMPIONSHIP		1	0	0	1	6	32
PLAYERS RECORDS		**36**	**21**	**2**	**13**	**857**	**648**

We commenced the season with another new coach, Australian Darryl Van de Velde taking over from Dave Sampson.

For the fourth successive season we reached the Final of the Yorkshire Cup. A Club record score in Round 1 at home to Huddersfield of 94-12, including two tries and 13 Goals from Martin Ketteridge, and a hat-trick of tries by both wingers, David Plange and Chris Chapman. In Round 2 a 40-14 victory against York at home was followed by a semi-final victory away at Halifax 12-8. In the Final at Elland Road our opponents were Leeds who were inspired by White Rose man of the match Cliff Lyons and ran out victors by 33-12.

SEASON 1989-90

In the League Leigh Barrow Sheffield Eagles were promoted to Division 1. Oldham, Halifax Hull K R relegated to Division 2. also In Division 2 Springfield Borough became Trafford Borough , York changed their name to Ryedale-York and Nottingham City were admitted.

Thu 24 Aug 1989 LEEDS away lost 16 - 20 FRIENDLY JOHN HOLMES TESTIMONIAL
LEEDS - Players and sorers not known
CASTLEFORD - Gibson: Plange Irwin Anderson Marchant: Steadman R.Southernwood: Ward Beardmore England Ketteridge Battye Joyner:
Subs used - Whitehead G.Southernwood Crabtree:
Tries - Steadman Joyner Marchant: Goals Ketteridge (2):

Sun 3 Sep 1989 FEATHERSTONE ROVERS home lost 20 - 22
CASTLEFORD - STEVE LARDER(674)(Gibson): Plange Irwin Anderson Marchant: GRAHAM STEADMAN(675) R.Southernwood: Ward Beardmore England Ketteridge Gibbs Joyner(Crabtree): Tries - Plange Irwin Gibbs: Goals - Steadman(2) Ketteridge(2):
FEATHERSTONE R - Bibb: Knapper Clark P.Newlove Hughes: Banks Fox: Grayshon Staniforth(Sharp) Dakin(G.Hall) Burton Booth Fisher:
Tries - Bibb Clark Newlove Hughes: Goals - Fox(3):
Referee R Whitfield (Widnes) Att - 8649 H.T. 12 - 12

Sun 10 Sep 1989 ST HELENS away won 26 - 24
ST HELENS - Veivers: Hunte Bailey Loughlin Kay: Frodsham Griffiths: Forber Groves Harrison(Cosgrove) Jones(Haggerty) Dwyer Cooper: Tries - Veivers Griffiths Groves Harrison: Goals - Loughlin(4):
CASTLEFORD - Larder: Plange Irwin Anderson(DARREN PRICE(676)) Marchant: Steadman Dean Blankley: Ward Beardmore England Ketteridge Crabtree(ANDY CLARKE(S/O)(677)) Gibbs:
Tries - Larder Plange Irwin Gibbs: Goals - Ketteridge(5):
Referee B Galtress (Bradford) Att - 8853 H.T. 18 - 2

Sun 17 Sep 1989 HUNSLET away won 44 - Nil YORKSHIRE CUP ROUND 1
HUNSLET - Kay: Whittington Penola Wilkinson Raw: Adams Lumb: Mason Oldroyd Welsh Bateman(Wilby) Bowden(Lyons) Jackson:
CASTLEFORD - Larder: Plange Irwin Anderson(Gibson) (Crabtree) Marchant: Steadman GARY FRENCH(678): Ward Beardmore England Ketteridge Gibbs Joyner:
Tries - Plange(4) Steadman(2) Irwin Gibson French: Goals - Steadman(2) Ketteridge(2):
Referee G Kershaw (Easingwold) Att - 3383 H.T. 26 - nil

Sun 24 Sep 1989 HULL home won 18 - 10
CASTLEFORD - Larder: Plange Irwin Anderson Marchant: Steadman French: Ward(Sampson) Beardmore England(S/O) Ketteridge(Crabtree) Gibbs Joyner:
Tries - Larder(3): Goals - Steadman(3):
HULL - Fletcher(Gay): Nolan Price Wilby Liddiard: Pearce(Cleal) Doherty: Harrison(S/O) Jackson Crooks

Welham Sharp Folkes:
Try - Cleal: Goals - Pearce Nolan Doherty
Referee D Carter (Widnes) Att - 7205 H.T. 14 - 2

Wed 27 Sep 1989 HULL KINGSTON ROVERS home won 28 – 12 YORKSHIRE CUP ROUND 2
CASTLEFORD - Larder: Plange Irwin Gibson Marchant: Steadman French: Sampson Beardmore England Ketteridge(Crabtree) Gibbs(TONY SMITH(679))Joyner:
Tries - Steadman(3) Plange French: Goals - Steadman(4):
HULL K R - Fairbairn: Clark M.Fletcher Austin Pratt: M.Smith Bishop: Armstrong Rudd Niebling Botica Ema Lyman(Thompson) (Parker):
Tries - Bishop Parker: Goals - M.Fletcher(2):
Referee C Tidbal (Wakefield) Att - 6127 H.T. 4 - 6

Sun 30 Sep 1989 WARRINGTON away lost 10 - 32
WARRINGTON - Lyon: Drummond Ropati Thorniley Forster: Turner Mackie: Burke Roskell Jackson(Duane) Thomas(Molloy) Sanderson Gregory:
Tries - Lyon(2) Thorniley(2) Jackson: Goals - Turner(6):
CASTLEFORD - Larder: Plange Irwin Gibson Marchant: Steadman(Smith) French: Sampson Beardmore Crabtree Ketteridge(Clarke) Gibbs Joyner:
Try - Irwin: Goals - Steadman(2) Larder:
Referee C Steels(Dalton in Furness) Att - 4500 H.T. 4 - 12

Tue 3 Oct 1989 NEW ZEALAND lost 20 - 22
CASTLEFORD - Mark Gibson(Price): ST JOHN ELLIS(680) Irwin McAllister Marchant: Smith French: Clarke Beardmore Sampson Crabtree Ketteridge Joyner(PAUL WHITEHEAD(681)):
Tries - French Clarke Crabtree: Goals - Ellis(4):
NEW ZEALAND - Edwards: Taewa Sherlock Iro Ropati Clark(Freeman) Bancroft: Leota Wallace Todd(Goulding) Nikau Kuiti Tuuta:
Tries - Sherlock Iro Wallace: Goals - Bancroft(5):
Referee R Whitfield (Widnes) Att - 5963 H.T. 20 - 8

Tue 10 Oct 1989 FEATHERSTONE ROVERS away draw 18 – 18 YORKSHIRE CUP SEMI FINAL
FEATHERSTONE R - Bibb: Drummond Ropati Newlove Knapper: Smales Fox: Grayshon Clark Bell Burton(G.Hall) Booth P.Smith:
Tries - Bibb Newlove Knapper: Goals - Knapper(3):
CASTLEFORD - Larder: Plange Irwin Steadman Marchant: Smith French: Clarke Beardmore England(Sampson) Ketteridge Gibbs(Crabtree) Joyner:
Tries - Larder(2) Plange: Goals - Steadman(3):
Referee C Morris (Huddersfield) Att - 6250 H.T. 10 - 8

Sun 15 Oct 1989 SHEFFIELD EAGLES home won 24 -22
CASTLEFORD - Larder(Marchant): Plange Irwin Steadman Ellis: Smith French: Clarke Beardmore England Ketteridge Paul Crabtree(Sampson) Joyner:
Tries - Larder Irwin Smith Joyner: Goals - Steadman(4):
SHEFFIELD E - Mycoe(Lidbury): Nelson Dickinson Powell Gamson: Hardy Aston: Broadbent Cook Van Bellen Nickle(Grimboldby) McGuire Smiles:
Tries - Mycoe(2) Dickinson: Goals - Aston(5):

361

Referee A Bowman (Whitehaven) Att - 6602 H.T. 14 - 14

Sun 22 Oct 1989 FEATHERSTONE ROVERS home lost 26 – 28 YORKSHIRE CUP SEMI FINAL REPLAY

CASTLEFORD - Larder: Plange Irwin Smith Ellis: Steadman French (Marchant): Clarke Beardmore England Ketteridge(Sampson) Ward Joyner: Tries - Irwin(2) Plange Smith Steadman: Goals - Ellis(2) Steadman:
FEATHERSTONE R - Bibb: Drummond Ropati Newlove Knapper: Smales Fox: Grayshon Clark Glen Bell Price Booth(Whiteley) Smith:
Tries - Newlove(2) Knapper Bell Price: Goals - Knapper(4):
Referee C Morris (Huddersfield) Att - 9601 H.T. 14 - 4

Sun 29 Oct 1989 WIGAN away won 22 - 20

WIGAN - Hampson: Lydon Bell Blake Preston: Byrne(Edwards)Gregory: Davidson Dermott Lucas Gildart(Clarke)Platt Goodway: Tries - Lydon Preston Edwards Goodway: Goals - Lydon Blake:
CASTLEFORD - Larder: Plange Irwin Anderson Ellis: Steadman French: Ward G.Southernwood England Paul Mirfin(Battye) (McAllister)Sampson Joyner:
Tries - French(2)Plange Irwin: Goals - Steadman(3):
Referee G Kershaw (Easingwold) Att - 11073 H.T. 16 - 8

Wed 8 Nov 1989 BRADFORD NORTHERN home won 32 - 13

CASTLEFORD - Larder: Plange Irwin Marchant Ellis: Steadman French: Sampson G.Southernwood Ketteridge Battye(McAllister) Gibbs Joyner(WayneThornton):
Tries - Larder Ellis Sampson Southernwood Gibbs: Goals - Steadman(4) Ketteridge(2):
BRADFORD N - Johnson: Cordle McGowan Mackay Francis(Helliwell): Simpson Harkin: Richards Barraclough Fairbank Medley(Tuffs) Snee Stewart:
Tries - Mackay Simpson: Goals - McGowan(2) Harkin(DG):
Referee R Whitfield (Widnes) Att - 5153 H.T. 12 - 9

Sun 12 Nov 1989 WAKEFIELD TRINITY away lost 14 - 22

WAKEFIELD T - Perry: Eden Leuluai Mason Wilson: Jackson M.Conway: Kelly(B.Conway) Thompson Glancy Lazenby(Bell) G.Price R.Price:
Tries - Leuluai Mason Jackson: Goals - M.Conway(5):
CASTLEFORD - Larder: Plange Irwin IAN BRAGGER(682) Ellis: Steadman French: Sampson G.Southernwood England Ketteridge Gibbs(Battye) Joyner:
Tries - Plange Gibbs: Goals - Ketteridge(2) Steadman:
Referee D Asquith (York) Att - 7159 H.T. - 10 - 16

Sun 19 Nov 1989 WARRINGTON home won 40 - 6

CASTLEFORD - Larder: Plange Irwin Bragger Ellis: Steadman French: Sampson Southernwood(Beardmore) England(Ward) Ketteridge Gibbs Joyner: Tries - Larder(3) Irwin(2) Plange Steadman French: Goals - Ketteridge(4):
WARRINGTON - Myers: Drummond Rudd Thorniley Forster(Myler): Derbyshire Crompton: Molloy Roskell Muller(Harmon) Thomas Sanderson Gregory:
Tries - Crompton: Goals - Derbyshire:
Referee C Morris (Huddersfield) Att - 5267 H.T. 22 - 6

Sat 25 Nov 1989 WIDNES away lost 16 - 24

WIDNES - Davies: Kebbie Currier Devereux Offiah: D.Hulme P.Hulme: Sorenson Mackenzie Grima O'Neill Smith Eyres: Tries - Davies Currier Devereux Sorenson: Goals - Davies(4):
CASTLEFORD - Larder: Plange Irwin(Marchant) Bragger Ellis: Steadman French: Sampson(Ward) G.Southernwood England Ketteridge Gibbs Joyner: Tries - Ellis Sampson Southernwood: Goals - Ketteridge(2):
Referee G Kershaw (Easingwold) Att - 5122 H.T. 12 - 12

Sun 3 Dec 1989 CHORLEY BOROUGH away won 42 -18 REGAL TROPHY ROUND 1

CHORLEY B - Smith: Burnette Torpy Cheetham Bacon: Whittaker(Gittens) Bimson: Duffy O'Hara Bristow Knight Edwards(Meyrick) Price:
Tries - Duffy O'Hara Price: Goals - Smith(3):
CASTLEFORD - Larder: Plange Irwin Bragger Ellis: Steadman G.Southernwood: Sampson K Beardmore England Ketteridge Ward Gibbs: Tries – K Beardmore(2) Gibbs(2) Larder(2) Irwin Ellis: Goals - Ketteridge(5):
Referee B Galtress (Bradford) Att - 1496 H.T. 22 - 6

Sun 10 Dec 1989 WHITEHAVEN away won 62 - 2 REGAL TROPHY ROUND 2

WHITEHAVEN - Richardson: Dover Fisher Ackerman Howland: Shelford Ward: Howse Mounsey(Ryan) McCartney Charlton Fryer(Delaney) Petrie:
Goal - Richardson:
CASTLEFORD - Larder: Plange(Price) Irwin Bragger Ellis: Steadman(Joyner) G.Southernwood: Sampson K Beardmore England Ketteridge Ward Gibbs:
Tries - Ellis(5) Larder(3) Bragger Southernwood K Beardmore: Goals - Ketteridge(9):
Referee P Crashley (Wakefield) Att - 1753 H.T. 22 - 2

Sun 17 Dec 1989 SHEFFIELD EAGLES away won 18 -2 REGAL TROPHY ROUND 3 - at CHESTERFIELD

SHEFFIELD E - Gamson: Nelson Dickinson Powell Farrell: Hardy Aston:Kellett Cook Grimboldby(Young) Nickle(Van Bellen) McGuire Smiles: Goal - Aston:
CASTLEFORD - Larder: Ellis Irwin Bragger Price: Joyner G.Southernwood: Sampson Beardmore England(Clarke) Ketteridge Ward Gibbs:
Tries - Ellis(3) Larder: Goal Ketteridge:
Referee C Morris (Huddersfield) Att - 4500 H.T. 8 - 2

Tue 26 Dec 1989 LEEDS away lost 18 - 25

LEEDS - Lord(Delaney): Gibson Schofield Creasser Fawcett: Heron Coleman: Waddle(Gunn) Maskill Dixon Izzard Laurie Divorty: Tries - Delaney Gibson Creasser Heron: Goals - Maskill(4) Divorty(DG):
CASTLEFORD - Larder: Ellis Irwin(S/O) Bragger Anderson: Joyner G.Southernwood: Sampson Beardmore England Ketteridge(Clarke) Ward Gibbs (NEIL ROEBUCK(683)):
Tries - Ellis Ward Gibbs: Goals - Larder(2)Ketteridge:
Referee S Cross (Hull) Att - 18764 H.T. 10 - 6

Sat 30 Dec 1989 WIGAN lost 10 - 24 REGAL TROPHY SEMI-FINAL at HEADINGLEY LEEDS

SEASON 1989-90

CASTLEFORD - Larder: Ellis Irwin Bragger Anderson: Joyner French: Sampson Beardmore(G.Southernwood) England Ketteridge(Roebuck) Ward Gibbs:
Tries - Larder Ellis: Goals - Larder:
WIGAN - Lydon: Marshall Iro Bell Preston(Clarke): Edwards Gregory: Shelford Dermott Wane(Lucas) Platt Betts Hanley:
Tries - Lydon Marshall Edwards Betts: Goals - Lydon(4):
Referee R Whitfield (Widnes) Att - 10193 H.T. nil - 14

Wed 3 Jan 1990 BRADFORD NORTHERN away lost 16 - 24
BRADFORD N - Wilkinson: Cordle McGowan Marchant Mackay: Mumby Henjack: Skerrett Barraclough Hobbs Pendlebury Fairbank Stewart:
Tries - Mackay(3) Marchant: Goals - Hobbs(4):
CASTLEFORD - Larder: Boothroyd(Chapman) Irwin Bragger Anderson: Roebuck French: Sampson G.Southernwood England Ketteridge Ward Gibbs:
Tries - Roebuck Gibbs: Goals - Ketteridge(4):
Referee C Morris (Huddersfield) Att - 5556 H.T. 4 - 12

Sun 7 Jan 1990 WAKEFIELD TRINITY home lost 16 -18
CASTLEFORD - Anderson: Chapman Irwin Bragger Price: Roebuck French: Sampson G.Southernwood England(Joyner) Ketteridge Ward Ron Gibbs:
Tries - Bragger(2) Price: Goals - Ketteridge(2):
WAKEFIELD T - Leuluai: Fox Jackson Eden Wilson(Zelei): Lazenby M.Conway: Rayne W.Conway(Bell) Thompson Glancy Kelly G.Price:
Tries - Eden(2) Price: Goals – M Conway(3):
Referee J Whitelam (Hull) Att - 6978 H.T. 8 - 10

Sun 14 Jan 1990 ST HELENS away lost 12 - 39 CHALLENGE CUP PRELIMINARY ROUND
ST HELENS - Connolly: Hunte Bailey Veivers Kay: Holding Devine: Evans Groves(S/O) Bateman Forber Haggerty(Jones) Cooper: Tries - Bateman(2) Devine Evans Haggerty: Goals - Devine(9) Cooper(DG):
CASTLEFORD - Larder: Ellis(S/O) Irwin Bragger Anderson: JEFF HARDY(684) French: LEE CROOKS(685) G.Southernwood Sampson Ketteridge England Joyner(Roebuck):
Tries - Irwin Anderson: Goals - Larder Ketteridge:
Referee A Bowman (Whitehaven) Att - 8662 H.T. 6 - 9

Sat 20 Jan 1990 WIDNES home lost 22 - 30
CASTLEFORD - Larder: Price Bragger Hardy Chris Chapman(McAllister): French Roy Southernwood: Ward Beardmore Sampson Crooks England Joyner:
Tries - Larder Chapman Hardy Crooks: Goals Crooks(3):
WIDNES - Tait: Devereux Currier Wright Offiah: D.Hulme P.Hulme: Sorenson McKenzie Grima(Smith) O'Neil(Moriarti) Myler Eyres:
Tries - Offiah(4) P.Hulme Currier: Goals - Currier(3):
Referee G Kershaw (Easingwold) Att - 5135 H.T. 4 - 16

Sun 4 Feb 1990 HULL away lost 6 - 16
HULL - Gay: Eastwood Blacker Charles Turner: Mackey

Windley: Harrison Jackson(Dixon) Dannatt Cleal Walker McNamara(Welham):
Tries - Mackey Windley Dixon: Goals - Estwood(2):
CASTLEFORD - Larder: Darren Price Irwin Hardy Anderson: Steadman French: Ward(Roebuck) Beardmore(G.Southernwood) Sampson Crooks England(Ward) Joyner: Try - Steadman: Goal - Larder:
Referee D Cambell (St Helens) Att – 7494 H.T. 6 - 10

Sun 11 Feb 1990 FEATHERSTONE ROVERS away lost 6 - 12
FEATHERSTONE R - Bibb: Banks P.Newlove Manning Ropati: Sharp Fox: Grayshon Clark Dakin(Palelei) Rose Burton Smales: Tries - Ropati Palelei: Goals - Fox (2):
CASTLEFORD - Larder: Ellis Hardy Anderson Irwin: Steadman French: Ward Beardmore(G.Southernwood) Sampson Battye England Joyner(Roebuck):
Try - Larder: Goal - Steadman:
Referee R Whitfield (Widnes) Att - 6200 H.T. 2 - 2

Sun 18 Feb 1990 LEIGH home won 44 - 18
CASTLEFORD - Larder: Ellis Hardy Anderson Plange: Steadman French: Ward Beardmore Sampson Battye England(Roebuck) Joyner: Tries - Hardy(2) Ellis Steadman French Ward Joyner: Goals - Steadman(8):
LEIGH - Johnson Ledger Stephenson Moimoi Jeffrey: Ruane Beardmore: Brown Dean Cottrell Potter(Platt) Ropati Westwood(Dunn):
Tries - Jeffrey Ruane Beardmore: Goals - Johnson(3):
Referee D Asquith (York) Att - 5025 H.T. 20 - 6

Sun 25 Feb 1990 SALFORD away won 24 - 18
SALFORD - Gibson: Evans Howard Williams Kerry: Fell Brown(Lee): Whiteley(Blease) Lee(Clare) O'Neill Gormley(Burgess) Blease(Gormley) Worrall:
Tries - Howard Kerry Brown: Goals - Kerry(3):
CASTLEFORD - Larder: Ellis Hardy Anderson Plange: Steadman French: Ward Beardmore Sampson Battye(Irwin) England Joyner(Roebuck):
Tries - Larder Ellis Hardy Plange: Goals - Steadman(4):
Referee K Allatt (Southport) Att - 3178 H.T. 6 - 4

Sun 4 Mar 1990 ST HELENS home won 34 - 24
CASTLEFORD - Larder: Ellis Irwin Anderson(England) Plange: Steadman French: Ward Beardmore Sampson Battye Hardy Joyner:
Tries - Sampson(3) Larder Battye: Goals - Steadman(7):
ST HELENS - Connolly: Hunte Veivers Loughlin Quirk: Frodsham(Bailey) Devine(Bournville): Bateman Groves Mann Forber Haggerty Cooper: Tries - Quirk Frodsham Bailey Bateman   Goals - Loughlin(4):
Referee - Mr R Whitfield (Widnes) Att - 6720 H.T. 14 - 6

Sun 9 Mar 1990 SHEFFIELD EAGLES away won 18 -14 at DONCASTER
SHEFFIELD E - Gamson: Nelson Dickinson Powell Young: Mycoe Close: Broadbent(Kellett) Cook(Halifihi) Leota Nickle Nikau Aston(S/O):
Tries - Mycoe Leota: Goals - Aston(2) (DG) Close(DG):
CASTLEFORD - Larder: Ellis Irwin Anderson Plange:

SEASON 1989-90

Steadman French: Ward(Battye) Beardmore Sampson
England Hardy Joyner(Roebuck):
Tries - Larder Ellis Sampson: Goals - Steadman(3):
Referee P Crashley (Wakefield) Att - 4350 H.T. 10 - 12

Sun 18 Mar 1990 BARROW away won 42 - 14
BARROW - Thompson(Ross): James H.Tuavao Burns
Trainer: Shaw Marwood: Clayton Crarey Mossop(Rowan)
R.Tuavao Pemberton Hadley:
Tries - Burns Marwood: Goals - Marwood(3):
CASTLEFORD - Larder: Ellis Irwin Anderson Plange:
Roebuck French: Sampson G.Southernwood John
Blackburn(Hill) Battye Hardy Joyner:
Tries - Ellis Irwin Anderson Plange Southernwood Battye
Hardy: Goals - Larder(4) Ellis(3):
Referee S Cross (Hull) Att - 1170 H.T. 14 - nil

Sun 25 Mar 1990 BARROW away won 58 - 6
CASTLEFORD - Larder: Ellis Irwin Anderson Plange:
Steadman French: Sampson Beardmore England Battye
Hardy Joyner:
Tries - Irwin(3) Steadman(3) Anderson(2) Hardy(2) Larder
Ellis French: Goals - Steadman(2) French:
BARROW - Ross: James Roper Burns Trainor: Shaw
Marwood: Clayton Crarey(Cummings) B.Tuavao
Pemberton(Livesey) Rowan Hadley:
Try - Cummings: Goal - Marwood:
Referee G Kershaw (Easingwold) Att - 4030 H.T. 26 - 6

Wed 28 Mar 1990 WIGAN home won 34 - 10
CASTLEFORD - Larder: Ellis Irwin Anderson Plange:
Steadman French: Sampson Beardmore England(Ken Hill)
Battye Hardy Joyner: Tries - Ellis Anderson Steadman
French Hardy: Goals - Steadman(6) (2DG):
WIGAN - Hampson: Gilfillan Clarke Iro Preston: Edwards
Gregory: West(Byrne) Goulding(O'Donnell) Shelford
Gildart Staziker Goodway:
Tries - Clarke Goulding: Goals - Goulding:
Referee S Cross (Hull) Att - 8824 H.T. 14 - 10

Sun 1 Apr 1990 SALFORD home won 65 - nil
CASTLEFORD - Larder: Ellis Irwin(Roebuck)
Anderson(Crooks) Plange: Steadman French: Sampson
Beardmore England Battye Hardy Joyner:
Tries - Larder(4) Steadman(3) Ellis(2) Plange:
Goals - Steadman(12) French(DG):
SALFORD - Gibson: Howard Birkett Fell Kerry: Cassidy
Brown: Gill(Conroy) Lee O'Neill Gormley Blease(S/O)
Bradshaw(Walsh):
Referee D Cambell (Widnes) Att - 4749 H.T. 12 - nil

Thu 12 Apr 1990 LEIGH away won 40 - 6
LEIGH - Hill(Platt): Ledger Stephenson Burrill Round:
Jeffrey Donohue: Street(Cottrell) Ropati Potter Westhead
Collier Platt(Ruane):   Try - Ropati: Goal - Platt:
CASTLEFORD - Larder: Ellis Irwin Anderson Plange:
Steadman French(England): Crooks Beardmore(Roebuck)
England(Sampson) Battye Hardy Joyner:
Tries - Anderson(2) Plange(2) Ellis Steadman Battye
Joyner: Goals - Steadman(3) Crooks:
Referee J Smith (Halifax) Att - 4097 H.T. 14 - 2

Mon 16 Apr 1990 LEEDS home won 38 - 18
CASTLEFORD - Larder: Ellis(Boothroyd) Irwin Anderson
Plange: Hardy Roebuck: Crooks Beardmore Sampson
Battye England Joyner: Tries - Larder Anderson Hardy
Roebuck Sampson England: Goals - Crooks(7):
LEEDS - Ford: Bentley Ackerman Gibson(Butt) Fawcett:
Heron Delaney: Young(Lord) Maskill Dixon Powell Heugh
Gunn: Tries - Ford(2) Delaney: Goals - Maskill(3):
Referee C Maskill (Huddersfield) Att - 9060 H.T. 24 - 6

Sun 22 Apr 1990 LEEDS away lost 18 - 24
PREMIERSHIP ROUND 1
LEEDS - Ford: Bentley Ackerman Gibson Fawcett:
Schofield Delaney: Heugh(Gunn) Maskill Dixon
Powell(Lord) Kuiti Heron:
Tries - Schofield(2) Ford Fawcett: Goals - Maskill(4):
CASTLEFORD - Larder: Ellis Irwin Anderson Plange: Hardy
Roebuck: Crooks Beardmore Sampson Battye(Kevin
Ward) England(Boothroyd) Joyner:
Tries - Ellis Sampson England: Goals - Crooks(3):
Referee R Whitefield (Widnes) Att - 15218 H.T. 6 - 12

Steve Larder
D. No 674
1989-90 to 1990-91

Graham Steadman
D. No 675
1989-90 to 1997

Andy Clarke
D. No 677
1989-90 to 1991-92

Gary French
D. No 678
1989-90 to 1990-91

SEASON 1989-90

Tony Smith
D. No 679
1989-90 to 1997

St John Ellis
D. No 680
1989-90 to 1993-94

Ian Bragger
D. No 682
1989-90 to 1991-92

Neil Roebuck
D. No 683
1989-90 to 1992-93

Jeff Hardy
D. No 684
1989-90 to 1990-91

Lee Crooks
D. No 685
1989-90 to 1997

SEASON 1990-91

1990-91 YORKSHIRE CUP WINNING SQUAD
Back Row – Giles Boothrod St John Ellis Neil Battye Grant Anderson David Plange Neil Roebuck
Middle Row – Darryl Van de Velde (Coach) Mick Morgan (Asst. Coach) Gary Atkins Dean Sampson Keith England
Stan Timmins (Fitness Conditioner)
Front Row – Shaun Irwin Graham Steadman Lee Crooks John Joyner Jeff Hardy Steve Larder

SEASON 1989-90

D.N	PLAYER		DEBUT	L MATCH	APP	SUB	T.AP	TRI'S	G'LS	D.G	P'TS
551	JOYNER	JOHN			32	2	34	3	0	0	12
603	WARD	KEVIN		22/04/1990	20	3	23	2	0	0	8
611	BEARDMORE	KEVIN			28	1	29	3	0	0	12
618	MARCHANT	TONY			9	3	12	0	0	0	0
621	ENGLAND	KEITH			32	1	33	2	0	0	8
627	BATTYE	NEIL			12	3	15	3	0	0	12
634	CHAPMAN	CHRIS		20/01/1990	2	1	3	1	0	0	4
635	PLANGE	DAVID			27	0	27	17	0	0	68
636	KETTERIDGE	MARTIN			22	0	22	0	42	0	84
650	SOUTHERNWOOD	ROY		20/01/1990	2	0	2	0	0	0	0
651	IRWIN	SHAUN			34	1	35	16	0	0	64
656	THORNTON	WAYNE		08/11/1989	0	1	1	0	0	0	0
657	ANDERSON	GRANT			23	0	23	8	0	0	32
658	BLACKBURN	JOHN		18/03/1990	1	0	1	0	0	0	0
659	BOOTHROYD	GILES			1	2	3	0	0	0	0
660	HILL	KENNETH		28/03/1990	0	2	2	0	0	0	0
661	SAMPSON	DEAN			29	5	34	8	0	0	32
664	CRABTREE	PAUL		15/10/1989	4	5	9	1	0	0	4
666	GIBBS	RON		07/01/1990	18	0	18	8	0	0	32
669	SOUTHERNWOOD	GRAHAM			13	3	16	4	0	0	16
670	GIBSON	MARK		03/10/1989	3	2	5	1	0	0	4
671	MIRFIN	PHIL		29/10/1989	1	0	1	0	0	0	0
672	BLANKLEY	DEAN		10/09/1989	1	0	1	0	0	0	0
673	McALLISTER	TERRY			1	3	4	0	0	0	0
674	LARDER	STEVE	03/09/1989		35	0	35	29	10	0	136
675	STEADMAN	GRAHAM	03/09/1989		26	0	26	17	75	2	220
676	PRICE	DARREN	10/09/1989	04/02/1990	4	3	7	1	0	0	4
677	CLARKE	ANDY	10/09/1989		4	4	8	1	0	0	4
678	FRENCH	GARY	17/09/1989		29	0	29	9	1	1	39
679	SMITH	TONY	27/09/1989		4	2	6	2	0	0	8
680	ELLIS	ST JOHN	03/10/1989		26	0	26	23	9	0	110
681	WHITEHEAD	PAUL	03/10/1989		0	1	1	0	0	0	0
682	BRAGGER	IAN	12/11/1989		12	0	12	3	0	0	12
683	ROEBUCK	NEIL	26/12/1989		5	10	15	2	0	0	8
684	HARDY	JEFF	14/01/1990		15	0	15	9	0	0	36
685	CROOKS	LEE	14/01/1990		6	1	7	1	14	0	32
	36			**12**							
					481	**59**	**540**	**174**	**151**	**3**	**1001**

COMPETITION		P	W	D	L	FOR	AGT
LEAGUE D 1	POSITION 7 OF 14	26	16	0	10	703	448
YORK'S CUP		4	2	1	1	116	58
RL CUP		1	0	0	1	12	39
REGAL TROPHY		4	3	0	1	132	46
CHAMPIONSHIP		1	0	0	1	18	24
NEW ZEALAND		1	0	0	1	20	22
PLAYERS RECORDS		**37**	**21**	**1**	**15**	**1001**	**637**

In the Yorkshire Cup we made a great effort to make it five finals in a row. In the semi-final we drew away at Featherstone Rovers 18-18 but lost the replay at home 28-26.

We also reached the semi-final in the Regal Trophy only to be defeated at Headingley Leeds by Wigan 24-10.

St John Ellis became the fifth player to register five tries in a game at Whitehaven on 10 December 1989 in his Debut season.

Lee Crooks and Graham Steadman were both big money signings, with Lee signed for £150k from Leeds, and Graham signed for a then record fee of £170k from Featherstone Rovers.

In the League Hull K R Rochdale Hornets Oldham were promoted to Division 1. Leigh Salford Barrow relegated to Division 2.

Sun 26 Aug 1990 HULL away won 10 - 6
YORKSHIRE CUP ROUND 1
HULL - Gay: Eastwood Nolan Price Charles(Webb): Mackey Windley: Harrison Dixon Dannatt Welham(Marlowe) Walker(Welham) Jackson: Try - Webb: Goal - Eastwood:
CASTLEFORD - Larder: Ellis Irwin Anderson Boothroyd: Steadman French: Crooks(England) Southernwood England(Sampson) Battye Hardy Joyner(Crooks): Tries - Ellis Boothroyd: Goal - Crooks:
Referee J Smith (Halifax) Att - 8000 H.T. 10 - nil

Sun 2 Sep 1990 BRADFORD NORTHERN away
won 42 – 12 YORKSHIRE CUP ROUND 2 - at VALLEY PARADE BRADFORD
BRADFORD N - Simpson: Cordle Shelford McGowan Cooper(Gill): Marchant Wilson: Hobbs(Richards) Noble Hamer Medley Fairbank Pendlebury: Tries - Simpson Cordle: Goals - McGowan Cooper:
CASTLEFORD - Larder: Ellis Irwin Anderson Boothroyd: Steadman French(Battye): Crooks Southernwood Sampson England(McAllister) Hardy Roebuck: Tries - Ellis(2) Larder Steadman Southernwood Roebuck: Goals - Crooks(9):
Referee C Morris (Huddersfield) Att - 7974 H.T. 22 - 2

Sun 9 Sep 1990 WARRINGTON away lost 12 - 30
WARRINGTON - Lyon: Drummond Mercer Thorniley Rudd: Turner(Crompton) Bishop: Burke Mann Harmon Jackson Sanderson McGinty(Darbyshire): Tries - Rudd(2) Drummond Thorniley Crompton: Goals - Lyon(5):
CASTLEFORD - Larder: Ellis Irwin Anderson Boothroyd: Steadman(GARY ATKINS(686)) Roebuck: Crooks Southernwood Sampson Battye England(Ketteridge) Hardy: Tries - Irwin Battye: Goals - Crooks(2):
Referee C Morris (Huddersfield) Att - 5510 H.T. 6 - 8

Wed,12 Sep 1990 HULL KINGSTON ROVERS home
won 29 – 6 YORKSHIRE CUP SEMI FINAL
CASTLEFORD - Larder: Ellis Irwin Anderson Boothroyd: Steadman Atkins(Roebuck): Crooks Southernwood Sampson England Battye(Ketteridge) Hardy: Tries - Larder Ellis Anderson Steadman Southernwood: Goals - Crooks(4) Larder(DG):
HULL K R - Fletcher: Clark Hallas Austin Sullivan: Watson Parker: Niebling Hoe Ema Des Harrison Thompson(Irvine)Speckman(Armstrong): Try - Irvine: Goal - Hallas:
Referee P Crashley (Wakefield) Att - 7977 H.T. 6 - nil

Sun 16 Sep 1990 WIGAN home lost 18 - 38
CASTLEFORD - Larder: Ellis Irwin Anderson Boothroyd: Steadman Atkins(Roebuck): Crooks Southernwood Sampson England(Ketteridge) Ketteridge(Battye) Hardy: Tries - Steadman Crooks Battye:

Goals - Crooks(2) Steadman:
WIGAN - Hampson: Myers Iro(Gildart) Bell Botica: Edwards Gregory: Lucas Goulding(Dermott) Goodway Betts Gildart(Clarke) Hanley(Iro):   Tries - Myers(2) Botica(2) Iro Edwards Betts: Goals - Botica(4) Goulding:
Referee G Kershaw (Easingwold) Att - 9477 H.T. 12 - 10

Sun 23 Sep 1990 WAKEFIELD TRINITY won 11 - 8
YORKSHIRE CUP FINAL at ELLAND ROAD LEEDS
CASTLEFORD - Larder: Ellis Irwin Anderson Plange: Steadman Atkins(England): Crooks Southernwood Sampson Battye(Ketteridge) Hardy Roebuck: Tries - Plange Atkins: Goals - Crooks RoebuckD/G:
WAKEFIELD T - Harcombe: Jones Mason Eden Wilson: Lazenby M.Conway: Shelford B.Conway(Slater) Thompson Kelly(Perry) Price Bell: Try - Mason: Goals - Harcombe(2):
Referee J Smith (Halifax) Att - 12362 H.T. 4 - 8
WHITE ROSE TROPHY WINNER - TRACY LAZENBY WAKEFIELD TRINITY

Wed 26 Sep 1990 OLDHAM away lost 22 - 28
OLDHAM - Platt: Francis Martyn(Fairbank) Duane Lord: Clark Ford: Pyke (Donegan) Russell Fieldhouse Round McAllister Barrow: Tries - Round(2) Francis Martyn Clark: Goals - Platt(4):
CASTLEFORD - Larder: Ellis Irwin Anderson Plange: Steadman Roebuck: Crooks Southernwood Sampson Battye(Ketteridge) England Hardy: Tries - Plange(2) Larder Irwin: Goals - Crooks(3):
Referee R Whitfield (Widnes) Att - 5101 H.T. 10 - 22

Sun 30 Sep 1990 FEATHERSTONE ROVERS home
won 24 - 19
CASTLEFORD - Larder: Ellis Irwin Anderson Plange: Steadman Roebuck: Crooks(McAllister) Southernwood Sampson Battye England Hardy: Tries - Anderson(2) Larder Plange Roebuck: Goals - Crooks(2):
FEATHERSTONE R - Bibb: Butt Manning Newlove Hughes: Sharp Fox: Grayshon(Pearson) Clark Casey Burton Rose(Fisher) Smales: Tries - Fox Pearson Smales: Goals - Pearson(3) FoxD/G:
Referee J Whitelam (Hull) Att - 7637 H.T. 16 - 1

Sat 6 Oct 1990 WIDNES away lost 4 - 46
WIDNES - Davies: Devereux Currier Wright Offiah: Myler D.Hulme: Grima McKenzie Ashurst(Smith) Eyres Koloto Holliday(Spruce): Tries - Offiah(3) Hulme(2) Currier Myler McKenzie Holliday: Goals - Davies(5):
CASTLEFORD - Larder: Ellis Irwin Anderson Plange: Steadman Roebuck: Crooks Southernwood Sampson Ketteridge(Bragger) McAllister(ANDY HAY(687)) Hardy: Try - Larder:
Referee A Burke (Oldham) Att - 4185 H.T. 4 - 16

Sun 14 Oct 1990 WAKEFIELD TRINITY home
won 42 - 12
CASTLEFORD - Ellis: Larder(PAUL FLETCHER(688)) Bragger(Joynen) Anderson(Bragger) Plange: Steadman French: Crooks Beardmore Sampson Irwin Hardy Roebuck:

Tries - Plange(2) French(2) Larder Steadman Irwin Hardy:
Goals - Crooks(5):
WAKEFIELD T - Harcombe: Jones Byrne Mason
Jowett(Morris): Mortimer M.Conway: Shelford
B.Conway(Wright) Thompson Kelly Price Bell:
Tries - Byrne Kelly: Goals - Harcombe(2):
Referee R Whitfield (Widnes) Att - 7145 H.T. 28 - nil

Sun 21 Oct 1990 ST HELENS away won 29 - 16
ST HELENS - Veivers: Kay Ropati Bailey Kebbie(O'Brien):
Cooper Devine: Forber(Bateman) Groves Ward Mann
Haggerty Dwyer:
Tries - Kebbie Cooper Mann: Goals - Devine(2):
CASTLEFORD - Ellis: Larder Bragger Anderson Plange:
Steadman French: Crooks Beardmore Sampson Irwin
Hardy Joyner(Roebuck):   Tries - Steadman(3) Plange:
Goals - Steadman(5)D/G Crooks:
Referee B Galtress (Bradford) Att - 6978 H.T. 18 - 12

Sun 4 Nov 1990 AUSTRALIA lost 8 - 28
CASTLEFORD - Ellis: Larder(Fletcher) Irwin Anderson
Plange: Steadman French: Crooks(Clarke)
Beardmore(Roebuck) Sampson England Hardy
Joyner(Ketteridge):
Try - Plange: Goals - Steadman Crooks:
AUSTRALIA - Belcher: Ettingshausen Meninga
McGaw(Alexander) Shearer: Lyons Stuart(Langer):
Roach(Cartwright) Elias Lazarus(Bella) Sironen Lindner
Mackay: Tries - Ettingshausen(2) Meninga Shearer
Lindner: Goals Meninga(4):
Referee G Kershaw (Easingwold) Att - 9033 H.T. 2 - 18

**Sun 11 Nov 1990 FEATHERSTONE ROVERS away
won 22 - 6**
FEATHERSTONE R - Bibb: Butt Manning Newlove(Rose)
Simpson: Pearson Fox: Grayshon(Iti) Clark Casey Burton
Smales Tuuta: Try - Simpson: Goal - Pearson:
CASTLEFORD - Fletcher: Ellis(Larder) Irwin Anderson
Plange: Steadman French: Crooks Beardmore Sampson
England Hardy Joyner:
Tries - Anderson Plange Steadman: Goals - Crooks(5):
Referee D Carter (Widnes) Att - 5768 H.T. 10 - 2

Sun 18 Nov 1990 OLDHAM home won 28 - 10
CASTLEFORD - Fletcher: Ellis Irwin Anderson Plange:
Steadman French: Crooks(Ketteridge) Beardmore
Sampson England Hardy Joyner:
Tries - Plange(3) Anderson Steadman: Goals - Crooks(4):
OLDHAM - Hyde: Francis Martin(Irving) Anderson Lord:
Clark Ford: Fairbank Russell Round Duane(Allen)
McAlister Cogger: Tries - Hyde Lord: Goal - McAlister:
Referee J Smith (Halifax) Att - 5974 H.T. 10 - 6

Tue 27 Nov 1990 LEEDS away lost 16 - 41
LEEDS - Gallagher: Ford Irving Ackerman Bentley:
Schofield Harkin: Molloy(Powell) Gunn Wane Dixon
Heugh Kuiti(Divorty):
Tries - Kuiti(3) Molloy Schofield Irving Gallagher:
Goals - Irving(5) Schofield Harkin(DG):
CASTLEFORD - Ellis: Larder Irwin(Bragger) Anderson

Plange: Steadman French: Sampson
Beardmore(McAllister) England Ketteridge Hardy Joyner:
Tries - Plange Steadman: Goals - Steadman(4):
Referee D Campbell (St Helens) Att - 11221 H.T. 10 - 24

**Sun 2 Dec 1990 FULHAM away won 14 - 8
REGAL TROPHY ROUND 1**
FULHAM - Dwyer: Leslie Taylor Manthey M'Barki:
Cruikshank Grauf: Corcoran Rotheram McKeating(Noble)
Mellors(Winstanley) Wilkins Browning
Try - M'Barki: Goals - Dwyer(2):
CASTLEFORD - Ellis(Battye): Larder Bragger Anderson
Plange: Steadman French: Sampson(S/O) Southernwood
England Ketteridge Hardy Joyner(Roebuck):
Tries - Larder Steadman: Goals - Steadman(3):
Referee J Connolly (Wigan) Att - 810 H.T. nil - 2

**Sun 9 Dec 1990 WAKEFIELD TRINITY away won 20 -4
REGAL TROPHY ROUND 2**
WAKEFIELD T - Slater: Jones Byrne Mason Wilson:
Conway Bell: Shelford Thompson(Lazenby) Glancy Du
Toit(Kelly) Price Mortimer: Try - Shelford:
CASTLEFORD - Ellis: Larder Bragger Anderson Plange:
Steadman French: Crooks Southernwood Sampson
England(Ketteridge) Hardy Joyner (Roebuck):
Tries - Anderson Steadman Hardy Joyner:
Goals - Crooks(2):
Referee J Smith (Halifax) Att - 7030 H.T. 16 - nil

**Sun 16 Dec 1990 ROCHDALE HORNETS home lost
14 – 19 REGAL TROPHY ROUND 3**
CASTLEFORD - Ellis: Larder Bragger Anderson Plange:
Hardy French: Crooks Southernwood Sampson England
Roebuck Joyner(Ketteridge):
Tries - Larder Joyner Ketteridge: Goal - Crooks:
ROCHDALE H - Whitfield: Marriott(Holding) Abram Lord
Fox: Grogan Galbraith: Cowie M.Hall(R.Hall) Blackburn
O'Neill Humphries Nixon: Tries - Whitfield Lord Galbraith:
Goals - Whitfield(3) Holding(DG):
Referee P Gilmour (Cumbria) Att - 4043 H.T. 8 - 12

Wed 19 Dec 1990 WARRINGTON home won 22 - 18
CASTLEFORD - Fletcher: Ellis Larder(Bragger)
Anderson(Ketteridge) Plange: Steadman French: Crooks
Southernwood Sampson England Hardy Roebuck:
Tries - Fletcher Crooks England Roebuck:
Goals - Crooks(3):
WARRINGTON - Myler(Turner): Drummond Bateman
Mercer Rudd: O'Sullivan Ellis: Harmon Mann
Tees(Williamson) Thomas Phillips Cullen:
Tries - Bateman O'Sullivan Williamson: Goals - Turner(3):
Referee B Galtress (Bradford) Att – 3582 H.T. 12 - nil

Wed 26 Dec 1990 HULL away lost 6 - 22
HULL - Gay(Blacker): Eastwood Nolan Price Webb:
Mackay Entat: Harrison Dixon(Turner) Marlow Jackson
Walker Sharp: Tries - Eastwood Price Entat:
Goals - Eastwood(5):
CASTLEFORD - Fletcher(Ellis): Ellis(Atkins) Bragger
Anderson Plange: Steadman French: Sampson

Southernwood(Clarke) Ketteridge Battye Hardy Roebuck:
Try - Steadman: Goal - Steadman:
Referee I Ollerton (Wigan)   Att - 5560 H.T. 2 - 14

Tue 1 Jan 1991 BRADFORD NORTHERN home won 9 - nil

CASTLEFORD - Ellis: JONATHAN WRAY(689) Bragger
Anderson Plange: Steadman French(Ketteridge): Crooks
Roebuck(Clarke) Sampson England Hardy Joyner:
Try - Steadman: Goals - Steadman Crooks Roebuck(DG):
BRADFORD N - Moxon: Cordle Shelford Helliwell
Marchant: Simpson Summers: Hobbs(Tuffs) Noble Hamer
Medley(Richards) Fairbank Pendlebury:
Referee P Gilmour (Cumbria)   Att - 6169 H.T. 8 - nil

Sun 6 Jan 1991 WIDNES home won 20 - 10

CASTLEFORD - Ellis: Wray Bragger Anderson Plange:
Steadman Smith: Clarke(Irwin) Beardmore Sampson
England Hardy Joyner:
Tries - Anderson Plange Sampson: Goals - Steadman(4):
WIDNES - Tait: Howard Devereux Wright Offiah: Myler
D.Hulme: Grima(Moriarty) (Grima) McKenzie Faimalo
Eyres P.Hulme Holliday: Tries - Eyres(2):   Goal - Holliday:
Referee A Burke (Oldham)   Att - 6212 H.T. 10 - nil

Sun 20 Jan 1991 HULL KINGSTON ROVERS home won 30 - 2

CASTLEFORD - Ellis: Wray Bragger(Irwin) Anderson
Plange: Steadman Smith: Clarke(Crooks) Beardmore
Sampson Hardy England Joyner: Tries - Wray Bragger
Irwin Anderson Steadman Hardy: Goals - Steadman(3):
HULL K.R. - M.Fletcher: Hadi Lydiat P.Fletcher Sullivan:
Watson Parker(Des Harrison): Niebling Rudd Ema
Goulding(Vannett) Thompson Lyman:
Goal - M.Fletcher:
Referee D Asquith (York)   Att - 5561 H.T. 2 - 2

Wed 23 Jan 1991 ROCHDALE HORNETS home won 42 - nil

CASTLEFORD - Larder: Irwin Bragger(Clarke) Anderson
Plange: Steadman Smith: Crooks Beardmore Sampson
England Hardy Joyner:
Tries - Steadman(3) Smith(2) Irwin Anderson Crooks:
Goals - Steadman(4) Crooks:
ROCHDALE H - Myler: Lord Abram Whitfield Fox(Turner):
Holding Galbraith: Cowie Dean Pitt Gormley
Blackburn(Marsden) Nixon:
Referee C Morris (Huddersfield)   Att - 3850 H.T. 22 - nil

Sun 27 Jan 1991 WAKEFIELD TRINITY away won 12 - 8

WAKEFIELD T - Spencer: Jones Slater Mason
Wilson(Perry): Byrne M.Conway: Shelford B.Conway Kelly
Bell Mortimer Colbeck(Du Toit):
Try - B.Conway: Goals - M.Conway(2):
CASTLEFORD - Larder: Wray Irwin Anderson Plange:
French Smith: Crooks Southernwood Sampson(Clarke)
England Hardy Joyner(Ketteridge):
Tries - Anderson Crooks: Goals - Crooks(2):
Referee R Whitfield (Widnes)   Att - 5628 H.T. 8 - 6

Sun 3 Feb 1991 LEEDS home won 16 - 14

CASTLEFORD - Ellis: Larder Irwin Anderson Wray:
Steadman Smith: (French): Crooks Southernwood
Sampson(Clarke) England Hardy Joyner:
Tries - Ellis Irwin: Goals - Steadman(4):
LEEDS - Gallagher: Bentley Irving Gibson(Creasser)
Rombo: Schofield Harkin: Molloy Gunn Powell Lord
Dixon(Heron) Kuiti:
Tries - Rombo Schofield Kuiti: Goal - Irving:
Referee J Connolly (Wigan)   Att - 7770 H.T. 8 - 10

Tue 12 Feb 1991 WIGAN home lost 4 - 28
CHALLENGE CUP ROUND 1

CASTLEFORD - Ellis: Wray Irwin Anderson(Smith) Plange:
Steadman French: Crooks Beardmore Sampson(Clarke)
England Hardy Joyner   Try - Irwin:
WIGAN - Hampson: Myers Iro Bell Botica: Edwards
Gregory: Lucas (Clarke) Dermott Skerrett Betts
Platt(Stazicker) Hanley:
Tries - Botica(2) Myers Iro Edwards: Goals - Botica(4):
Referee J Smith (Halifax)   Att - 6644 H.T. nil - 22

Sun 24 Feb 1991 HULL KINGSTON ROVERS away won 16 - 12

HULL K R - M.Fletcher: Clark(Speckman) P.Fletcher
M.Smith Sullivan: Watson Robinson: Vannett(Goulding)
Rudd Ema Thompson Harrison Lyman:
Tries - Smith Harrison: Goals - M.Fletcher(2):
CASTLEFORD - Ellis: Wray(French) Irwin Anderson Plange:
Steadman Smith: Clarke(Battye) Beardmore Crooks
Ketteridge Hardy Joyner:
Tries - French Smith Battye: Goals - Steadman(2):
Referee C Morris (Huddersfield) Att - 4210 H.T. nil - 8

Sun 3 Mar 1991 ROCHDALE HORNETS away won 76 - 12

ROCHDALE H - Myler: Garrity Abram Lord Fox(Pitt):
Grogan(Williams) Holding: O'Neill M.Hall Humphries
Gormley Pitt(Marriott) R.Hall:
Tries - Lord(2) Abram:
CASTLEFORD - Ellis: Wray Irwin(Larder) Anderson Plange:
Steadman French: Crooks Beardmore Sampson
England(Battye) Hardy Roebuck:
Tries - Steadman(3) Ellis(2) Larder(2) French(2) Anderson
Plange Beardmore Sampson Hardy:
Goals - Steadman(10):
Referee J Connolly (Wigan)   Att - 2049 H.T. 28 - 8

Sun 10 Mar 1991 SHEFFIELD EAGLES away won 24 -20

SHEFFIELD E - Mumby: Nelson Mycoe Price Maer:
Powell(Young) Aston: Waddell(Tunks) Cook Wilby
Broadbent Bateman Farrell:
Tries - Young(2) Mycoe Aston: Goals - Aston(2):
CASTLEFORD - Ellis: Wray Irwin Anderson Plange:
Steadman(Smith) French: Crooks Beardmore Sampson
England Hardy Joyner(Roebuck):
Tries - Irwin Anderson French Roebuck:
Goals - Steadman(4):
Referee D Asquith (York)   Att - 4000 H.T. 6 - 6

SEASON 1990-91

Sun 24 Mar 1991 ST HELENS home won 28 - 4
CASTLEFORD - Ellis: Wray Irwin Anderson Plange:
Steadman French: Crooks Beardmore Sampson(Battye)
England Hardy Roebuck(Joyner):   Tries - Steadman(2)
Wray Plange Roebuck: Goals - Steadman(3) Crooks:
ST HELENS - Veivers: Hunte Ropati Loughlin Quirk:
Griffiths Bishop: Harrison(Jones) Groves Ward Dwyer
Mann Cooper (Bailey}   Try - Loughlin:
Referee D Asquith (York) Att - 6367 H.T. 6 - 4

Fri 29 Mar 1991 BRADFORD NORTHERN away lost 14 - 24
BRADFORD N - Simpson: Cordle Shelford McGowan
Gumbs: GroganIti(Summers) Iti: Hobbs(Richards) Noble
Hamer Medley Fairbank Pendlebury: Tries - Medley(3)
McGowan Gumbs: Goals - Gumbs Hobbs:
CASTLEFORD - Ellis: Wray Irwin Anderson(Larder) Plange:
Steadman(Joyner) French: Crooks Southernwood
Sampson England Hardy Roebuck:
Tries - Irwin Southernwood: Goals - Steadman(2) Crooks:
Referee A Burke (Manchester) Att - 6061 H.T. 4 - 8

Mon 31 Mar 1991 HULL home lost 14 - 16
CASTLEFORD - Fletcher: Wray Irwin Anderson Plange:
Smith French: Crooks Southernwood(Joyner) Sampson
England Hardy Roebuck:
Tries - Wray Irwin Smith: Goal - Crooks:
HULL - Gay: Eastwood Webb McGarry Turner: Entat
Mackay: Harrison Jackson Durham(Busby) Marlowe
Walker(McNamara) Sharp:
Tries - Webb McGarry Mackay: Goals - Eastwood(2):
Referee B Galtress (Bradford) Att - 6596 H.T. 10 - 6

Sun 7 Apr 1991 WIGAN away lost 4 - 24
WIGAN - Lydon: Myers Bell Goodway Botica: Clarke
Gregory: Lucas Stazicker(Goulding) West(Forshaw) (West)
Betts Gildart Hanley:
Tries - Myers(2) West Hanley: Goals - Botica(4):
CASTLEFORD - Fletcher: Wray Irwin Anderson(Steadman)
Plange: Smith(Joyner) French: Crooks Beardmore
Sampson England Hardy Roebuck: Goals - Crooks(2):
Referee G Kershaw (Easingwold) Att - 14018 H.T. 2 - 10

Sun 14 Apr 1991 SHEFFIELD EAGLES home won 28 - 10
CASTLEFORD - Fletcher: Wray Irwin(Ellis)Anderson David
Plange: Steadman(Joyner) French: Crooks Beardmore
Sampson England Hardy Roebuck:
Tries - Wray(2) Hardy(2) Fletcher: Goals - Crooks(4):
SHEFFIELD E - Mycoe: Nelson Young Price Pickdley:
Powell Aston: Broadbent(Mumby) Cook
Waddell(Grimboldy) Nickle Grimboldy(Johnson) Farrell:
Try - Young: Goals - Aston(3):
Referee R Whitfield (Widnes) Att - 4403 H.T. 6 - 8

Sun 21 Apr 1991 LEEDS home lost 20 - 24
PREMIERSHIP ROUND 1
CASTLEFORD - Fletcher: Wray(Steve Larder) Irwin
Anderson Ellis: Steadman(Battye)Gary French: Crooks
Beardmore Sampson England Jeff Hardy(S/O) Joyner:
Tries - Ellis Beardmore England Joyner: Goals - Crooks(2):
LEEDS - Gallagher: Fawcett Gibson Irving Ford: Schofield
Harkin: Powell Maskill(S/O) Wane(Lord) Heugh(Heron)
Dixon Divorty: Tries - Fawcett Schofield Heugh Dixon:
Goals - Irving(3) Schofield(2D/G):
Referee J Smith (Halifax) Att - 7058 H.T. 4 – 10

Gary Atkins
D. No 686
1990-91 to 1991-92

Andy Hay
D. No 687
1990-91 to 1994-95

Paul Fletcher
D. no 688
1990-91 to 1992-93

Jon Wray
D. No 689
1990-91 to1994-95

D.N	PLAYER		DEBUT	L MATCH	APP	SUB	T.AP	TRI'S	G'LS	D.G	P'TS
551	JOYNER	JOHN			19	6	25	3	0	0	12
611	BEARDMORE	KEVIN			17	0	17	2	0	0	8
621	ENGLAND	KEITH			30	1	31	2	0	0	8
627	BATTYE	NEIL			7	7	14	3	0	0	12
635	PLANGE	DAVID		14/04/1991	29	0	29	16	0	0	64
636	KETTERIDGE	MARTIN			6	11	17	1	0	0	4
651	IRWIN	SHAUN			28	2	30	10	0	0	40
657	ANDERSON	GRANT			36	0	36	12	0	0	48
659	BOOTHROYD	GILES			5	0	5	1	0	0	4
661	SAMPSON	DEAN			34	1	35	2	0	0	8
669	SOUTHERNWOOD	GRAHAM			18	0	18	3	0	0	12
673	McALLISTER	TERRY			1	3	4	0	0	0	0
674	LARDER	STEVE		21/04/1991	20	4	24	10	0	1	41
675	STEADMAN	GRAHAM			32	1	33	23	52	1	197
677	CLARKE	ANDY			3	7	10	0	0	0	0
678	FRENCH	GARY		21/04/1991	24	2	26	6	0	0	24
679	SMITH	TONY			8	2	10	4	0	0	16
680	ELLIS	ST JOHN			31	1	32	8	0	0	32
682	BRAGGER	IAN			10	3	13	1	0	0	4
683	ROEBUCK	NEIL			17	7	24	5	0	2	22
684	HARDY	JEFF		21/04/1991	36	0	36	6	0	0	24
685	CROOKS	LEE			31	1	32	4	61	0	138
686	ATKINS	GARY	09/09/1990		3	2	5	1	0	0	4
687	HAY	ANDY	06/10/1990		0	1	1	0	0	0	0
688	FLETCHER	PAUL	14/10/1990		8	2	10	2	0	0	8
689	WRAY	JON	01/01/1991		15	■	15	5	0	0	20
	26		4	4	468	64	532	130	113	4	750

COMPETITION		P	W	D	L	FOR	AGT
LEAGUE D 1	POSITION 4 OF 14	26	17	0	9	578	442
YORK'S CUP		4	4	0	0	92	32
RL CUP		1	0	0	1	4	28
REGAL TROPHY		3	2	0	1	48	31
CHAMPIONSHIP		1	0	0	1	20	24
AUSTRALIA		1	0	0	1	8	28
PLAYERS RECORDS		**36**	**23**	**0**	**13**	**750**	**585**

Having narrowly missed reaching the Final of the Yorkshire Cup in five successive seasons last term we did make it "five from six" this season. In Round 1 we beat old rivals Hull away 10-6, in Round 2 we beat Bradford Northern at Valley Parade 42-12, and in the semi-final we beat our other Humberside rival Hull KR at home 29-6. Our opponents in the Final played at Elland Road, were Wakefield Trinity. In a very close game which saw us behind at half time 8-4, we just managed to pull off a victory by 11-8 with the Wakefield stand off Tracy Lazenby winning the White Rose Man of the Match trophy.

The Australian tourists came to Wheldon Road once again on 4 November and ran out winners 28-8.

On 31 March 1991 in the home defeat against Hull 16-14, John Joyner made his 600th appearance for the Club when he came on as a substitute for Graham Southernwood.

Keith England, Shaun Irwin and Graham Steadman were selected for the Great Britain squad to tour Papa New Guinea, Australia and New Zealand.

SEASON 1991-92

In the League Salford Halifax Swinton were promoted to Division 1. Oldham Sheffield Eagles Rochdale Hornets relegated to Division 2.

A further change in the league structure was the formation of a Division 2 and a Division 3. Joining the previous seasons relegated teams from Division 1 in Division 2 were Carlisle Leigh London Crusaders (who had changed their name from Fulham) Ryedale-York Workington Town.

This Left Barrow Batley Bramley Chorley Borough, Dewsbury Doncaster Highfield Huddersfield, Hunslet, Nottingham, Keighley (adding Cougars to their name), Trafford Borough, Whitehaven, with Scarborough Pirates being admitted to Division 3 bringing the number to fourteen.

There was another Rule Change for this season with the "Blood Bin" Substitution introduced.

Sun 1 Sep 1991 WIGAN home won 38 - 26
CASTLEFORD - Steadman: Ellis Smith Anderson DAVID NELSON(690): Atkins(Joyner) MIKE FORD(691): Crooks Southernwood(S/O) Sampson(Fletcher) England Irwin TAWERA NIKAU(692): Tries - Ellis(2) Anderson(2) Steadman Smith Nelson: Goals - Crooks(5):
WIGAN - Hampson: Myers(Panapa) Bell Lydon Botica: Edwards Gregory: Lucas(Forshaw) Dermott Skerrett Gildart(Lucas) Platt Betts:
Tries - Betts(2) Hampson Dermott: Goals - Botica(5):
Referee C Morris (Huddersfield) Att - 8983 H.T. 12 - 18

Sun 8 Sep 1991 SALFORD away won 18 - 10
SALFORD - Gibson: Evans Fell Gilfillan Hadley: Cruikshank Kerry: Young(Birkett) Lee Stazicker Hanson(Bradshaw) Worrall Burgess: Tries - Hadley Burgess: Goal - Kerry:
CASTLEFORD - Steadman(SIMON MIDDLETON(693)): Ellis Smith Anderson Nelson: Joyner Ford: Crooks Fletcher Sampson England Irwin(Roebuck) Nikau:
Tries - Steadman Ellis: Goals - Crooks(5):
Referee G.Kershaw (Easingwold) Att - 3942 H.T. 10 - 6

Sun 15 Sep 1991 BATLEY away won 36 - 12 YORKSHIRE CUP ROUND 1
BATLEY - Hammill: Williams(S/O) Wilkinson Marshall(Bargate) Thornton: Wilson Tomlinson: Grayshon Hartley(S/O) Spendler(Kellett) Parrish Child Booth:
Tries - Wilson Booth: Goals - Parrish(2):
CASTLEFORD - Steadman: Ellis Smith Anderson(Middleton) Nelson: Joyner Ford: Crooks Fletcher England NATHAN SYKES(694) (Clarke) Irwin Nikau: Tries - Smith(2) Steadman Ford Irwin Nikau: Goals - Crooks(6):
Referee J Whitelam (Hull) Att - 3089 H.T. 24 - nil

Sun 22 Sep 1991 LEEDS home lost 8 - 13
CASTLEFORD - Steadman: Ellis Smith Anderson(Middleton) Nelson: Joyner Ford: Clarke(Ketteridge) Fletcher Crooks England Irwin Nikau:
Try - Middleton: Goals - Crooks(2):
LEEDS - Edwards: Bentley Creasser Gibson Ford: Schofield Stephens: Heugh Maskill Dixon O'Neill(Molloy) Heron(Powell) Hanley:
Tries - Creasser(2) Schofield: Goal - SchofieldD/G:
Referee R Connolly (Wigan) Att - 11546 H.T. 2 - 8

Wed 25 Sep 1991 HULL KINGSTON ROVERS home won 34 – 12 YORKSHIRE CUP ROUND 2
CASTLEFORD - Steadman: Ellis Bragger Middleton Nelson: Smith Ford: Clarke Fletcher Crooks England Irwin(Ketteridge) Nikau:
Tries - Ford(2) Steadman Nelson Nikau: Goals - Crooks(7):
HULL K R - M.Fletcher: Cook Hallas Barkworth Sodje: Crane Chatfield: Vannett Richardson(Hoe) Jackson(Anderson) P.Fletcher Des Harrison Lyman:
Try - Barkworth: Goals - M.Fletcher(4):
Referee B Galtress (Bradford) Att - 4954 H.T. 14 - 10

Sun 29 Sep 1991 ST HELENS away lost 14 - 25
ST HELENS - Tanner: Riley Connelly Bailey Quirk: Ropati Bishop: Ward Dwyer Mann Harrison(Jones) Forber Cooper: Tries - Riley Quirk Forber Cooper:
Goals - Tanner(4) Bishop(DG):
CASTLEFORD - Ellis: Ian Bragger RICHARD BLACKMORE(695)(Atkins) Middleton Nelson: Steadman Ford: Clarke Fletcher(Ketteridge) Crooks England Irwin Nikau: Tries - Steadman England Irwin: Goal - Crooks:
Referee J Smith (Halifax) Att - 6843 H.T. nil - 13

Sun 6 Oct 1991 WIDNES home lost 20 - 22
CASTLEFORD - Steadman: Ellis GRAEME BRADLEY(696) Anderson Nelson: Smith(Middleton) Ford: Crooks Kevin Beardmore England(Battye) Ketteridge Irwin Nikau:
Tries - Ellis Anderson Battye: Goals - Crooks(4):
WIDNES - Wynne: Devereux Wright Davies Currier: Dowd D.Hulme: Solomona McKenzie Faimalo Moriarty Koloto Holliday(Smith):
Tries - Devereux Wright Davies: Goals - Davies(5):
Referee G Kershaw (Easingwold) Att - 6210 H.T. 6 - 6

Wed 9 Oct 1991 FEATHERSTONE ROVERS home won 18 – 10 YORKSHIRE CUP SEMI FINAL
CASTLEFORD - Steadman: Ellis Bradley Anderson Nelson: Smith Ford: Crooks Southernwood (Roebuck) England (Ketteridge) Ketteridge (Roebuck) (Battye) Irwin Nikau:
Tries - Smith Southernwood Irwin: Goals - Crooks(3):
FEATHERSTONE R - Bibb: Butt Manning(Pearson) Newlove Simpson: Sharp Fox: Bastian(Gibbon) Clark Price Rose Fisher Tuuta: Tries - Bibb Butt: Goal - Fox:
Referee J Holdsworth (Kippax) Att - 8890 H.T. 8 - 2

Sun 13 Oct 1991 HULL KINGSTON ROVERS away won 22 - 14
HULL K R - M.Fletcher: Cook Lydiat Barkworth(Hallas) Sodje: McCarthy Chatfield: C.Harrison Chamberlain P.Fletcher Thompson(Jackson) Lyman Speckman:
Tries - M.Fletcher Lyman: Goals - M.Fletcher(3):
CASTLEFORD - Steadman: Ellis Bradley Anderson(Blackmore) Nelson: Smith Ford:

Crooks(Ketteridge) Southernwood England Battye Irwin
Nikau: Tries - Blackmore(2) Steadman Ellis Anderson:
Goal - Crooks:
Referee D Carter (Widnes) Att - 4791 H.T. 14 - 12

Sun 20 Oct 1991 BRADFORD NORTHERN won 28 – 6 YORKSHIRE CUP FINAL - at ELLAND ROAD LEEDS

CASTLEFORD - Steadman: Ellis Bradley Blackmore Nelson:
Smith Ford: Sampson(Ketteridge)Southernwood England
Battye Irwin Nikau: Tries - Steadman(2) Smith Ford
Battye: Goals - Steadman(4):
BRADFORD N - Simpson: Powell Shelford McGowan
Marchant: Anderson Iti(Croft): Hobbs Noble Hamer
Medley(Richards) Fairbank Barnett:
Try - Powell: Goal - Hobbs:
Referee J Holdsworth (Kippax) Att - 8538 H.T. 12 - 6

WHITE ROSE TROPHY WINNER - GRAHAM STEADMAN(CASTLEFORD)

Wed 23 Oct 1991 WARRINGTON away lost 6 - 23

WARRINGTON - Lyon: Drummond Rudd Thorniley
Kenyon: Shelford(Sanderson) Crompton: Burke Mann
Sumner Jackson(Harmon) Mercer Gregory:
Tries - Drummond Rudd Jackson Mercer:
Goals - Lyon(3) MannD/G:
CASTLEFORD - Steadman: Ellis Bradley Blackmore
(Middleton) Nelson: Smith Ford: Sampson Southernwood
Ketteridge Battye Irwin(Roebuck) Nikau:
Try - Nelson: Goal - Ketteridge:
Referee J Holdsworth (Kippax) Att - 4772 H.T. nil - 8

Sun 27 Oct 1991 FEATHERSTONE ROVERS home won 22 - 20

CASTLEFORD - Steadman: Ellis Bradley Middleton Nelson:
Smith Ford: Sampson Southernwood Ketteridge(Clarke)
Battye Roebuck Nikau: Tries - Smith Sampson Roebuck
Nikau: Goals - Ketteridge(3):
FEATHERSTONE R - Bibb: I.Butt Manning P.Newlove
Simpson: Pearson Fox: Burton(G.Booth) Clark
Price(Longstaff) Rose Tuuta Sharp:
Tries - Newlove(2) Booth: Goals - Fox(4):
Referee S.Cross (Hull) Att - 6790 H.T. 16 - 14

Sun 3 Nov 1991 BRADFORD NORTHERN away won 18 - 12

BRADFORD N - Wilkinson: Marchant Shelford(Simpson)
McGowan Gill: Anderson Summers: Hobbs Noble
Richards(Barnett) Croft Fairbank Pendlebury:
Tries - Gill Fairbank: Goals - Hobbs(2):
CASTLEFORD - Steadman: Ellis Bradley Middleton Nelson:
Smith(Fletcher) Ford: Clarke Southernwood Sampson
Battye Ketteridge Roebuck:
Tries - Steadman Middleton Nelson: Goals - Ketteridge(3):
Referee I Ollerton (Wigan) Att - 4153 H.T. 8 - 6

Sun 10 Nov 1991 HALIFAX home lost 16 - 22

CASTLEFORD - Steadman(S/O): Ellis Bradley Middleton
Nelson: Smith Ford: Clarke Southernwood Sampson
Battye(Nikau) Ketteridge Roebuck:
Tries - Steadman Middleton: Goals - Ketteridge(4):

HALIFAX - Wilson: Sharp Hutchinson Austin Preston:
Irvine Harkin: Harrison R.Southernwood Hill(Bell) Lord
Fogerty(Milner) Pearce: Tries - Austin Preston
Southernwood Pearce: Goals - Pearce(3):
Referee D Campbell (Widnes) Att - 7748 H.T. 14 - 6

Sun 17 Nov 1991 HULL KINGSTON ROVERS away won 22 – 10 REGAL TROPHY ROUND 1

HULL K R - M.Fletcher: Barkworth Hallas(Chatfield)
McCarthy Sodje: Crane Bishop: C.Harrison(Vannett)
Richardson Eme D.Harrison Thompson Lyman:
Tries - McCarthy Sodje: Goal - M.Fletcher:
CASTLEFORD - Ellis: Wray Bradley Middleton Nelson:
Smith(Roebuck) Ford: Clarke Southernwood(Fletcher)
Sampson Battye Ketteridge Nikau: Tries - Middleton
Smith Southernwood: Goals - Ketteridge(5):
Referee C Morris (Huddersfield) Att - 3406 H.T. 16 - 4

Mon 24 Nov 1991 DONCASTER home won 38 - 6 REGAL TROPHY ROUND 2

CASTLEFORD - Steadman: Ellis(Anderson) Bradley
Middleton Wray: Smith Ford: Clarke
Southernwood(Roebuck) Sampson Battye Ketteridge
Nikau: Tries - Steadman(3) Ellis Bradley Middleton Clarke:
Goals - Ketteridge(5):
DONCASTER - Hall(Holmes): Roache Pennant Matautia
Heptinstall: Carroll Rowse: Hermansson Evans Idle Rayne
Grimoldby Armstrong(Miller): Try - Hall: Goal - Carroll:
Referee S Cross (Hull) Att - 4146 H.T. 10 - 2

Sun 1 Dec 1991 LEEDS away lost 4 - 24 REGAL TROPHY ROUND 3

LEEDS - Edwards: Ford Creasser Irving Bentley(Gibson):
Schofield Goulding: O'Neill Gunn Molloy(James) Powell
Dixon Divorty: Tries - Dixon(2) Powell Divorty:
Goals - Irving(3) Schofield(2D/G):
CASTLEFORD - Steadman: Ellis Middleton Anderson
(Bradley) Nelson: Smith Ford: Clarke(Crooks)
Southernwood Sampson Battye Ketteridge Nikau:
Try - Nikau:
Referee D Campbell (Widnes) Att - 15409 H.T. nil - 6

Sun 15 Dec 1991 SWINTON away won 40 - 4

SWINTON - Wilkinson: Ranson Prince Pickavance(Snape)
Ratu: O'Sullivan Bellamy: Partington Garner Pucill Lowry
Clawson(Skeech) Morrison: Try - Garner:
CASTLEFORD - Steadman: Middleton Ellis Anderson
Nelson: Smith(Atkins) Ford: Crooks Southernwood
Sampson(Ketteridge) Nikau England Roebuck:
Tries - Steadman(2) Middleton Anderson Nelson Ford
Crooks: Goals - Crooks(6):
Referee S Cummings (Widnes) Att - 1524 H.T. 28 - nil

Sun 22 Dec 1991 WIGAN away lost 6 - 10

WIGAN - Hampson(Lydon): Myers Bell Miles Botica:
Panapa Edwards: Cowie (Lucas) Dermott Skerrett Betts
McGinty Clarke: Try - Lydon: Goals - Botica(3):
CASTLEFORD - Steadman: Middleton Ellis Anderson
Nelson: Smith Ford: Clarke(Bradley) Southernwood
Crooks England Nikau Roebuck(Joyner):

Try - Anderson: Goal - Crooks:
Referee A Burke (Oldham) Att - 11123 H.T. 2 - 6

Thu 26 Dec 1991 HULL home won 30 - 8
CASTLEFORD - Steadman: Middleton Ellis Anderson
Nelson: Smith Ford: Andy Clarke(Sampson)
Southernwood Crooks England Nikau Roebuck(Bradley):
Tries - Roebuck(2) Middleton Smith Crooks:
Goals - Crooks(5):
HULL - Gay: R.Nolan Blacker(Dixon) Harrison Turner:
Ronson Mackey: Spring L.Jackson Jones(G.Nolan) Marlow
Walker McNamara: Tries - Gay R.Nolan:
Referee C Morris (Huddersfield) Att - 6196 H.T. 8 - 4

Wed 1 Jan 1992 WAKEFIELD TRINITY away
draw 14 - 14
WAKEFIELD T - Spencer: Jones Mason(Perry) Eden Wilson:
Lazenby(Thompson) M.Conway: Kelly Bell Glancy Round
Jackson Price: Tries - Wilson Conway Bell: Goal - Conway:
CASTLEFORD - Steadman: Middleton Ellis Anderson
Nelson: Smith(Bradley) Ford: Crooks Southernwood
Sampson England Nikau Roebuck(Ketteridge):
Tries - Steadman Middleton Anderson: Goal - Crooks:
Referee R Whitfield (Widnes) Att - 6840 H.T. 10 - 10

Sun 5 Jan 1992 WIDNES away won 14 - 4
WIDNES - Wynne: Devereux Currier Wright Sarsfield:
Dowd P.Hulme(Atcheson): Grima(Solomona) McKenzie
Faimalo Smith Howard Holliday   Try - Wynne:
CASTLEFORD - Steadman(Smith): Middleton Ellis Bradley
Nelson: Anderson Ford: Crooks Southernwood
Sampson(Gary Atkins) Battye Ketteridge Nikau:
Tries - Nelson Anderson Battye: Goal - Crooks:
Referee J Holdsworth (Kippax) Att - 5279 H.T. 8 - 4

Sun 12 Jan 1992 SALFORD home won 26 - 12
CASTLEFORD - Steadman: Middleton Ellis
Bradley(Boothroyd) Nelson: Anderson Ford: Crooks
Southernwood Sampson(Irwin) England Ketteridge
Nikau: Tries - Steadman Middleton Ellis Crooks:
Goals - Crooks(5):
SALFORD - Gibson: Evans Reynolds Williams Birkett: Fell
Cruickshank: Young Bradshaw(Randall) Stazicker
Donegan(O'Connor) Worrall Gilfillan:
Tries - Birkett Bradshaw: Goals - Birkett(2):
Referee D Campbell (Widnes) Att - 4642 H.T. 20 - 6

Sun 19 Jan 1992 BRADFORD NORTHERN home
won 24 - 10
CASTLEFORD - Steadman: Middleton Ellis Bradley(Smith)
Nelson: Anderson Ford: Crooks Southernwood England
Irwin Ketteridge (Sampson) Nikau:
Tries - Ellis Anderson Irwin Nikau: Goals - Crooks(4):
BRADFORD N - Wilkinson: Cordle Shelford Anderson
Marchant: Simpson Summers: Hobbs Barraclough(Iti)
Hamer Medley Richards(Grayshon) Fairbank(S/O):
Tries - Marchant(2): Goal - Hobbs:
Referee J Smith (Halifax) Att - 4870 H.T. 10 - 4

Sun 26 Jan 1992 TRAFFORD BOROUGH away won
50 – nil CHALLENGE CUP ROUND 1 at HEADINGLEY
LEEDS
TRAFFORD B - Iddon(Williams): Blackman Diatlov Garnett
Hewitt: Bloor Green: Zotov(Summer) Rippon Grande
Ainsworth Meadows Johnson:
CASTLEFORD - Steadman: Middleton Ellis Blackmore
Nelson: Anderson(Roebuck) Smith: Crooks Southernwood
England(Sampson) Bradley Ketteridge Nikau:
Tries - Steadman(4) Nelson(2) Ellis Blackmore Anderson:
Goals - Crooks(7):
Referee P Volante (Birstall) Att - 1632 H.T. 22 - nil

Sun 2 Feb 1992 LEEDS away won 18 - 4
LEEDS - Edwards: Ford Irving Innes Bentley: Creasser
Goulding: Heugh Maskill Wane(Molloy) O'Neill Dixon
Divorty(Powell):   Goals - Irving(2):
CASTLEFORD - Steadman: Wray Ellis Blackmore Nelson:
Anderson Ford: Crooks Southernwood England(Smith)
Ketteridge Bradley(Sampson) Nikau:
Tries - Steadman(2) Nelson: Goals - Crooks(3):
Referee S Cummings (Widnes) Att - 14227 H.T. 6 - 2

Sun 9 Feb 1992 HUNSLET away won 28 - 12
CHALLENGE CUP ROUND 2
HUNSLET - Lay: Raw Bartliff Daniel Waites: Brooks Lowes:
McKelvie Sampson(Lumb) Bell(Precious) Coyle Mitchell
Carr: Tries - Lumb Carr: Goals - Bartliff Precious:
CASTLEFORD - Steadman: Wray(Middleton) Ellis
Blackmore Nelson: Anderson Ford(Roebuck): Crooks
Southernwood Sampson Bradley Ketteridge Nikau:
Tries - Steadman(3) Nelson: Goals - Crooks(6):
Referee D Campbell (Widnes) Att - 3100 H.T. 10 - 6

Sun 23 Feb 1992 FEATHERSTONE ROVERS home
won 19 – 12 CHALLENGE CUP ROUND 3
CASTLEFORD - Steadman: Wray Ellis Blackmore Nelson:
Anderson Ford: Crooks Southernwood England(Smith)
Bradley Ketteridge(Sampson) Nikau:
Tries - Steadman Blackmore Nelson:
Goals - Crooks(3) SteadmanD/G:
FEATHERSTONE R - Bibb: Butt Manning P.Newlove
Simpson: Pearson Fox: Casey Clark Rose(Sharp) Smales
Fisher Tuuta: Tries - Butt(2):   Goals - Fox(2):
Referee R Whitfield (Widnes) Att - 10480 H.T. 6 - 4

Sun 1 Mar 1992 WARRINGTON home won 40 - 8
CASTLEFORD - Steadman: Middleton Ellis(Smith)
Blackmore Nelson: Anderson Ford: Crooks Southernwood
Sampson(Joyner) Bradley Ketteridge Nikau:
Tries - Southernwood(2) Steadman Blackmore Nelson
Anderson Nikau: Goals - Crooks(6):
WARRINGTON - Lyon: Drummond(Forster) Rudd
Bateman Kenyon: Shelford Crompton: Harmon Mann
Sumner Jackson(Sanderson) Mercer Cullen:
Try - Shelford: Goals - Lyon(2):
Referee P Volante (Batley) Att - 5539 H.T. 16 - 8

Sun 8 Mar 1992 ST HELENS home draw 8 - 8
CASTLEFORD - Steadman: Middleton Ellis

Blackmore(Smith) Nelson: Anderson Ford: Crooks
Southernwood England(Sampson) Bradley Ketteridge
Nikau: Try - Crooks: Goals - Crooks(2):
ST HELENS - Veivers: Hunte Connolly Ropati Sullivan:
Griffiths Bishop: Ward Groves Mann Forber Nickle
Cooper: Tries - Connolly Sullivan:
Referee S Cummings (Widnes) Att - 8170 H.T. 2 - 4

Saturday 14 Mar 1992 HULL won 8 - 4
CHALLENGE CUP SEMI FINAL at HEADINGLEY LEEDS
CASTLEFORD - Steadman: Middleton Ellis Smith Nelson:
Anderson Ford: Crooks Southernwood England(Sampson)
Bradley Ketteridge Nikau: Try - Ford: Goals - Crooks(2):
HULL - Gay: Eastwood Ronson Harrison(Blacker) Turner:
McNamara Mackey: Spring Jackson Dannatt Sharp Walker
Busby(Dixon):   Try - Eastwood:
Referee C Morris (Huddersfield) Att - 14636 H.T. nil - nil

Tue 17 Mar 1992 FEATHERSTONE ROVERS away
lost 16 - 24
FEATHERSTONE R - Bibb: Butt Manning P.Newlove
Simpson: Pearson Fox: Casey Whiteley Burton Rose
Smales Fisher:
Tries - Simpson(2) Bibb Butt Newlove: Goals - Fox(2):
CASTLEFORD - Steadman(Sampson): Middleton Ellis
Smith Nelson: Anderson Ford: Crooks Southernwood
England(Paul Whitehead) Bradley Ketteridge Joyner:
Tries - Smith(2) Joyner: Goals - Crooks(2):
Referee D Campbell (Widnes) Att - 5235 H.T. nil - 6

Sun 22 Mar 1992 HULL KINGSTON ROVERS home
lost 18 - 28
CASTLEFORD - Ellis: Middleton Smith Blackmore(Joyner)
Nelson: Anderson Ford: Crooks CHRIS WATSON(697)
England(Sampson) Bradley Ketteridge Nikau:
Tries - Smith Nelson Crooks: Goals - Crooks(2) Ellis:
HULL K R - M.Fletcher: Barkworth Lyman Hallas(Cook)
Sodje: Clark Chatfield: D.Harrison Richardson Ema(Crane)
P.Fletcher Thompson Speckman: Tries - Barkworth Sodje
Clark Thompson Speckman: Goals - M.Fletcher(4):
Referee B Galtress (Bradford) Att - 5357 H.T. 6 - 10

Sun 29 Mar 1992 SWINTON home won 56 - 2
CASTLEFORD - Middleton: Wray Smith Blackmore Nelson:
Anderson(Ellis)Ford: Crooks Southernwood Sampson
Bradley Ketteridge Nikau:
Tries - Middleton(3) Blackmore(2) Wray Anderson Ellis
Ford: Goals - Crooks(8) Ketteridge(2):
SWINTON - Wilkinson: Roberts(Cooper)Irving(Roberts)
Kennett Ratu: Snape Kay: Pucill Garner Barrow Pickavance
Whitfield Longstaff(Clark):   Goal - Wilkinson:
Referee D Carter (Widnes) Att - 3552 H.T. 30 - 2

Sun 12 Apr 1992 HALIFAX away lost 8 - 24
HALIFAX - Cooper: Sharp Watson Austin Preston: Bailey
Harkin: Harrison R.Southernwood Fogerty(Hutchinson)
Milner Fieldhouse Lord:
Tries - Austin(2) Sharp Watson Bailey: Goals - Cooper(2):
CASTLEFORD - Middleton: Wray Ellis Blackmore Nelson:
Smith Ford: Crooks Southernwood(Roebuck)

Sampson(England) Bradley Ketteridge Nikau:
Try - England: Goals - Crooks(2):
Referee P Volante (Batley) Att - 6425 H.T. nil - 6

Fri 17 Apr 1992 WAKEFIELD TRINITY home
won 28 - 4
CASTLEFORD - Middleton(Steadman): Wray Ellis
Blackmore Nelson Smith Ford: Crooks Roebuck(Joyner)
England Bradley Ketteridge Nikau: Tries - Ellis(2)
Middleton Wray Smith England: Goals - Ketteridge(2):
WAKEFIELD T - Perry: Jones Mason Eden Wilson:
M.Conway Bagnall: Glancy(Slater) B.Conway Bell Round
Jackson(Lazenby) Slater(Goddard):
Goals - M.Conway(2):
Referee J Holdsworth (Kippax) Att - 6098 H.T. 4 - 4

Mon 20 Apr 1992 HULL away won 30 - 14
HULL - Gay: Eastwood R.Nolan Ronson Mighty: Stevens
Mackey: Spring(A.Jackson) L.Jackson Dannatt McNamara
Jones(Spring) Sharp(Busby):
Tries - Ronson A.Jackson: Goals - Eastwood(3):
CASTLEFORD - Steadman: Middleton Ellis Blackmore
Nelson: Smith Ford: Crooks Southernwood England(John
Joyner) Bradley Ketteridge Nikau: Tries - Steadman
Middleton Ellis Blackmore Bradley: Goals - Crooks(5):
Referee S Cummings (Widnes) Att - 5587 H.T. 10 - 2

Sun 26 Apr 1992 WAKEFIELD TRINITY home
won 28 – 18 PREMIERSHIP ROUND 1
CASTLEFORD - Steadman: Nelson Ellis Blackmore
Middleton(Smith): Anderson Ford: Crooks Roebuck
England Bradley Ketteridge(Sampson) (Ketteridge) Nikau:
Tries - Ellis(2) Bradley(2):   Goals - Crooks(6):
WAKEFIELD T - Perry: Jones Mason Goddard(Slater
)Wilson: M.Conway(Glancy) Bagnall: Kelly(Jackson)(S/O)
B.Conway Glancy(Kelly)Price Round Bell:
Tries - Wilson(2) Bagnall: Goals - M.Conway(2) Perry:
Referee C Morris (Huddersfield) Att - 6617 H.T. 8 - 6

Sat 26 May 1992 WIGAN lost 12 - 28
CHALLENGE CUP FINAL at WEMBLEY STADIUM
LONDON
CASTLEFORD - Steadman: Wray Ellis Blackmore Nelson:
Anderson(Smith) Ford: Crooks(Sampson) Southernwood
England Bradley Ketteridge Nikau:
Tries - Blackmore England: Goals - Ketteridge(2):
WIGAN - Lydon: Botica Bell Miles Offiah: Edwards
Gregory(McGinty) (Steve Hampson): Skerrett Dermott
Platt Betts McGinty(Cowie) Clarke: Tries - Offiah(2)
Edwards Hampson: Goals - Botica(5) Lydon(2DG):
Referee R Whitfield (Widnes) Att - 77286 H.T. nil - 19
LANCE TODD TROPHY WINNER - MARTIN OFFIAH
(WIGAN)

Sun 10 May 1992 ST HELENS away lost 14 - 30
PREMIERSHIP SEMI FINAL
ST HELENS - Veivers: Hunte Connolly Loughlin Sullivan:
Griffiths Bishop: Neill Dwyer(Groves) Ward(Riley) Nickle
Mann Cooper:
Tries - Loughlin Griffiths Ward Mann: Goals - Loughlin(7):

SEASON 1991-92

CASTLEFORD - Steadman(Blackmore): Wray Ellis
Anderson Middleton: Smith Ford: Sampson
Southernwood England <u>Graeme Bradley</u> Ketteridge
Nikau:
Tries - Wray Ford: Goals - Ellis(3):
Referee P Volante (Batley) Att - 9843 H.T. 8 – 12

David Nelson
D. No 690
1991-92 to 1993-94

Mike Ford
D. No 691
1991-92 to 1998

Graeme Bradley
D. No 696
1991-92

Chris Watson
D. No 697
1991-92 to 1993-94

Nathan Sykes
D. No 694
1991-92 to 2004

Richard Blackmore
D. No 695
1991-92 to 1994-95

**Tawere Nikau lifts the 1991 Yorkshire Cup after
beating Bradford Northern 28 - 6**

Tawera Nikau
D. No 692
1991-92 to 1996

Simon Middleton
D. No 693
1991-92 to 1997

D.N	PLAYER		DEBUT	L MATCH	APP	SUB	T.AP	TRI'S	G'LS	D.G	P'TS
551	JOYNER	JOHN		20/04/1992	4	6	10	1	0	0	4
611	BEARDMORE	KEVIN		06/10/1991	1	0	1	0	0	0	0
621	ENGLAND	KEITH			28	1	29	4	0	0	16
627	BATTYE	NEIL			10	2	12	3	0	0	12
636	KETTERIDGE	MARTIN			28	7	35	0	27	0	54
651	IRWIN	SHAUN			12	1	13	4	0	0	16
657	ANDERSON	GRANT			28	1	29	12	0	0	48
659	BOOTHROYD	GILES			0	1	1	0	0	0	0
661	SAMPSON	DEAN			19	11	30	1	0	0	4
669	SOUTHERNWOOD	GRAHAM			31	0	31	4	0	0	16
675	STEADMAN	GRAHAM			35	1	36	29	4	1	125
677	CLARKE	ANDY		26/12/1991	10	2	12	1	0	0	4
679	SMITH	TONY			29	8	37	12	0	0	48
680	ELLIS	ST JOHN			39	1	40	15	4	0	68
681	WHITEHEAD	PAUL		17/03/1992	0	1	1	0	0	0	0
682	BRAGGER	IAN		29/09/1991	2	0	2	0	0	0	0
683	ROEBUCK	NEIL			9	8	17	3	0	0	12
685	CROOKS	LEE			31	1	32	5	111	0	242
686	ATKINS	GARY		05/01/1992	1	3	4	0	0	0	0
688	FLETCHER	PAUL			5	3	8	0	0	0	0
689	WRAY	JON			10	0	10	3	0	0	12
690	NELSON	DAVID	01/09/1991		38	0	38	13	0	0	52
691	FORD	MIKE	01/09/1991		39	0	39	8	0	0	32
692	NIKAU	TAWERA	01/09/1991		37	-	38	6	0	0	24
693	MIDDLETON	SIMON	08/09/1991		27	6	33	14	0	0	56
694	SYKES	NATHAN	15/09/1991		1	0	1	0	0	0	0
695	BLACKMORE	RICHARD	29/09/1991		16	2	18	9	0	0	36
696	BRADLEY	GRAEME	06/10/1991	10/05/1992	29	4	33	4	0	0	16
697	WATSON	CHRIS	22/03/1992		1	0	1	0	0	0	0
	29		**8**	**7**	**520**	**71**	**591**	**151**	**146**	**1**	**897**

	COMPETITION		P	W	D	L	FOR	AGT
	LEAGUE D 1	POSITION 3 OF 14	26	15	2	9	558	365
	YORK'S CUP		4	4	0	0	116	40
	RL CUP		5	4	0	1	117	56
	REGAL TROPHY		3	2	0	1	64	40
	CHAMPIONSHIP		2	1	0	1	42	48
	PLAYERS RECORDS		**40**	**26**	**2**	**12**	**897**	**549**

We again reached the Final of the Yorkshire Cup to make it "six out of seven". In the Final again played at Elland Road, our opponents were Bradford Northern and with Graham Steadman scoring two tries and four goals to claim the White Rose Man of the Match trophy we ran out winners 28–6.

The Challenge Cup brought our second Final appearance of the season. Victories in Round 1 over Trafford Borough at Headingley, in Round 2 at Hunslet 28–12, in Round 3 we beat Featherstone Rovers at home 19-12 and in the semi-final at Headingley we beat our old semi-final hoodoo team of the 80's Hull 8–4. In the Final we played Wigan who were making their fifth successive appearance with four previous victories. Unfortunately we could not stop their run as we lost 28–12 with Martin Offiah winning the Lance Todd Trophy.

Notable Debutantes were Mike Ford, Tawara Nikau and Richard Blackmore.

SEASON 1992-93

In the League relegation and promotion in each League was amended to 'two up and two down'. This resulted in Sheffield Eagles, Leigh promoted to Division 1. Featherstone Rovers, Swinton relegated to Division 2, Huddersfield, Bramley promoted to Division 2, Ryedale-York Workington Town relegated to Division 3. Trafford Borough changed their name to Blackpool Gladiators and Scarborough Pirates dropped out of the league after only one season.

Sun 23 Aug 1992 BRADFORD NORTHERN home lost 10 – 16 YORKSHIRE CUP PRELIMINARY ROUND
CASTLEFORD - Steadman: Ellis T.Smith Blackmore Middleton: Anderson Ford: Crooks Roebuck England(Sampson) Ketteridge(Irwin) TONY MORRISON(698) Nikau:
Tries - Middleton Ford: Goal - Crooks:
BRADFORD N - Simpson: Cordle Marchant(Hamer) Shelford(McGowan) Kebbie: Anderson(Shelford) Summers: Hobbs Noble Hamer(Clark) Medley Powell Heron: Tries - Kebbie(2) Medley: Goals - Hobbs(2):
Referee P Volante (Birstall) Att - 4987 H.T. 6 - 6

Sun 30 Aug 1992 WIDNES away lost 6 - 16
WIDNES - Davies: Devereux(S/O) Currier Wright Hadley: D.Hulme Goulding: Sorenson(Howard) P.Hulme Faimalo(McCurrie) Moriarty(Eyres) Eyres(Sorenson) Holliday:
Tries - D.Hulme Goulding Eyres: Goals - Davies(2):
CASTLEFORD - Steadman: Ellis T.Smith Blackmore Middleton: Anderson(Irwin) Ford: Crooks Roebuck(Sampson) Sampson(Ketteridge) Morrison Irwin(England) (S/O) Nikau:
Try - Middleton: Goal - Crooks:
Referee C Morris (Huddersfield) Att - 6200 H.T. 2 - 4

Sun 6 Sept 1992 SALFORD home lost 20 - 24
CASTLEFORD - Steadman: Ellis Blackmore Anderson(Boothroyd) Wray: T.Smith Ford: Crooks Southernwood Sampson(Sykes)(Sampson) Morrison Irwin Nikau: Tries - Smith(2) Ford: Goals - Crooks(4):
SALFORD - Birkett: Critchley Gilfillan Williams Ford: Reid Cruikshank: Young Lee Stazicker Hansen(Donegan)(Hansen) Blease Bradshaw:
Tries - Critchley Gilfillan Ford Blease: Goals - Birkett(4):
Referee J Connolly (Wigan) Att - 4493 H.T. 8 - 18

Sun 20 Sept 1992 LEIGH away won 38 - nil
LEIGH - Platt(Fanning): Tanner Ruane Mahon Hill: Woods Donohue: Burke(Collier) Bridge Street Costello Newton(Burke) Pendlebury:
CASTLEFORD - Steadman: Ellis Boothroyd Blackmore CHRIS SMITH(699): T.Smith Ford: Sampson(Ketteridge) Roebuck England(Sampson) Morrison Irwin(Sykes) Nikau: Tries - Ford(2) Steadman Ellis England Nikau: Goals - Steadman(7):
Referee R Whitfield (Widnes) Att - 3044 H.T. 24 - nil

Sun 27 Sept 1992 HULL home won 34 - 6
CASTLEFORD - Steadman: Ellis Blackmore Boothroyd

Middleton: T.Smith Ford: Crooks Roebuck England(DEAN WILLIAMS(700)) Morrison(Ketteridge) Irwin Nikau:
Tries - Boothroyd Middleton Smith Ford Irwin:
Goals - Crooks(7):
HULL - Gay: Eastwood G.Nolan(Dearlove) Harrison Mighty: Gale R.Nolan: Marlow Dixon Jones(Wilson) Jackson Walker Busby: Try - Dearlove: Goal - Eastwood:
Referee J Smith (Halifax) Att - 5488 H.T. 26 - 2

Sun 4 Oct 1992 SHEFFIELD EAGLES away lost 16 - 20
SHEFFIELD E - Jack: Gamson Powell(Carr) Mycoe Plange: Price Aston: Broadbent(James) Cook James(Laughton) McGuire Hughes Farrell:
Tries - Carr Mycoe Farrell: Goals - Aston(4):
CASTLEFORD - Middleton: Ellis(Anderson) Blackmore T.Smith Boothroyd: PETER COYNE(701) Ford: Crooks(Sykes) Roebuck England Morrison Irwin Nikau:
Tries - Middleton Ellis Ford: Goals - Middleton Coyne:
Referee J Connolly (Wigan) Att - 4725 H.T. 10 - 6

Sun 11 Oct 1992 WIDNES home won 26 - 14
CASTLEFORD - Steadman: Ellis Blackmore T.Smith Middleton: Coyne Ford: Crooks Neil Roebuck(Anderson) Sampson Morrison Irwin(Ketteridge) Nikau:
Tries - Middleton(2) Ellis Roebuck: Goals - Crooks(5):
WIDNES - Davies: Myers Spruce(Faimalo) Devereux Hadley: D.Hulme Goulding: Sorenson(Wright) McCurrie Howard Moriarty Eyres Holliday:
Tries - Myers Holliday: Goals - Davies(3):
Referee C Steele(Dalton in Furness) Att 5998 H.T. 14 -12

Fri 16 Oct 1992 SALFORD away lost 18 - 21
SALFORD - Gibson(Williams): Evans Critchley Gilfillan Ford: Brown Coleman: Young Lee Stazicker Ackerman(Reid) Bradshaw Burgess:
Tries - Ford(2) Critchley Young: Goals - Brown(2) Lee(DG):
CASTLEFORD - Middleton: Ellis Blackmore T.Smith(Anderson) Nelson: Coyne (T.Smith)Ford: Crooks Watson Sampson Morrison Shaun Irwin(Ketteridge) Nikau:
Tries - Ellis(2) Ford: Goals - Crooks(3):
Referee J Smith (Halifax) Att - 2782 H.T. 10 - 10

Sun 1 Nov 1992 LEIGH home won 46 - 12
CASTLEFORD - Middleton: Ellis Blackmore T.Smith Nelson: Coyne (Anderson) Ford: Crooks(Morrison) Watson Sampson Morrison(Sykes) Ketteridge Nikau:
Tries - Middleton(2) Blackmore(2) Ellis Smith Coyne Anderson Ford: Goals - Crooks(3) Middleton(2):
LEIGH - Tanner: Pratt(Costello) D.Ruane Woods Hill: Blakeley Pugsley(Newton): Hansen Bridge Street A.Ruane(Pratt) Elias Pendlebury:
Tries - Woods Hansen: Goals - Blakeley(2):
Referee S Cross (Hull) Att - 3927 H.T. 24 - 6

Sun 8 Nov 1992 OLDHAM away won 40 - 22 REGAL TROPHY ROUND 1
OLDHAM - Gibson: Higgins(Tupaea) Tyrer Ropati Gumba: Warburton Kerry: Solomona(Maxwell) Russell Sheals Sherratt(Solomona) Olsen Bradbury:

Tries - Ropati Gumba Olsen: Goals - Kerry(5):
CASTLEFORD - Middleton: Ellis Blackmore T.Smith
Nelson: Coyne Ford: Crooks Watson Sampson(Anderson)
Morrison(Sykes) Ketteridge Nikau: Tries - Middleton(2)
Blackmore(2) Watson Nelson Ford: Goals - Crooks(6):
Referee I Ollerton (Wigan) Att - 4393 H.T. 16 - 4

Sun 15 Nov 1992 BRADFORD NORTHERN away won 28 - 6

BRADFORD N - Summers: Cordle McGowan Shelford
Marchant: Watson Fox: Hobbs Noble(Simpson) Hamer
Powell Fairburn Heron(Medley):   Try - Cordle: Goal - Fox:
CASTLEFORD - Middleton: Ellis Blackmore
T.Smith(Anderson) Nelson: Coyne Ford: Crooks Watson
Sampson Morrison Ketteridge Nikau: Tries - Smith(2)
Blackmore Sampson Morrison: Goals - Crooks(4):
Referee P Gilmour (Workington) Att - 6996 H.T. 18 - 6

Sun 22 Nov 1992 HULL KINGSTON ROVERS away won 8 - 2

HULL K R - M.Fletcher: Sims McKeough Hutchinson Sodje:
Goldman(Chatfield) Parker: C.Harrison Richardson
D.Harrison(Speckman) O'Brien Thompson
Speckman(P.Fletcher):   Goal - Fletcher:
CASTLEFORD - Middleton: Ellis Blackmore T.Smith Wray:
Coyne Ford: Crooks Watson Sampson Morrison
Ketteridge(England) Nikau: Try - Smith: Goals - Crooks(2):
Referee J Smith (Halifax) Att - 3172 H.T. 2 - 8

Sun 29 Nov 1992 BRADFORD NORTHERN home won 30 - 20

CASTLEFORD - Middleton: Ellis Blackmore T.Smith Wray:
Coyne Ford: Crooks(England) Watson Sampson Morrison
Ketteridge(Anderson) Nikau: Tries - Smith(2) Middleton
Ellis: Goals - Crooks(6) Middleton:
BRADFORD N - Simpson: Marchant McGowan Shelford
Anderson: Watson Summers (Noble): Hobbs(Clark)
Noble(Medley) Hamer Powell Fairbank Heron:
Tries - Shelford(2) McGowan Medley:
Goals - Marchant(2):
Referee G Kershaw (Easingwold) Att - 5852 H.T. 10 - nil

Sun 6 Dec 1992 CARLISLE home won 54 - nil
REGAL TROPHY ROUND 2

CASTLEFORD - Middleton(Wray): Ellis Blackmore T.Smith
Wray(JAMIE BLOEM(702)): Coyne Ford: Crooks Watson
Sampson(Morrison) Morrison(B/B) (England) Ketteridge
Nikau: Tries - Blackmore(3) Smith(2) Ellis Wray
Ketteridge Bloem: Goals - Crooks(9):
CARLISLE - Fox: Armstrong Clarke Pape Harris: Georgealis
Murdock(Southwell): Armstrong Thomason Brierley Knox
Lunt(A.N.Other)(Lunt) Scott:
Referee C Tidball (Wakefield) Att - 2530 H.T. 28 - nil

Fri 11 Dec 1992 ST HELENS home won 16 - 6

CASTLEFORD - Middleton: Ellis Blackmore(Anderson)
T.Smith Wray: Coyne Ford: Crooks Watson
Sampson(England) Morrison Ketteridge Nikau:
Tries - Middleton T.Smith: Goals - Crooks(4):
ST HELENS - Lyon: Casey Connolly McCracken(Loughlin)

Quirk: Ropati Cooper: Ward Dwyer Mann Harrison
Nickle(O'Donnell) Joynt: Try - Lyon: Goal - Lyon:
Referee I Ollerton (Wigan) Att - 5200 H.T. 6 - 2

Sat 19 Dec 1992 ST HELENS away won 12 - 8
REGAL TROPHY ROUND 3

ST HELENS - Lyon McCracken Connolly Laughlin Quirk:
Ropati Cooper: Neill(O'Donnell) Dwyer Ward Nickle Mann
Joynt: Try - Quirk: Goals - Lyon(2):
CASTLEFORD - Middleton(Anderson): Ellis Blackmore
T.Smith Wray: Coyne Ford: Crooks Watson Sampson
Morrison Ketteridge Nikau:
Tries - Ellis Smith: Goals - Crooks(2):
Referee C Steele (Dalton in Furness) Att - 4785 H.T. 6 - 8

Sat 26 Dec 1992 LEEDS away lost 12 - 40

LEEDS - Tait: Fallon Iro Innes Gibson(Irving): Schofield
Gregory: Molloy(O'Neill) Lowes O'Neill(Anderson) Dixon
Mercer Hanley:
Tries - Tait Fallon Iro Innes Schofield Lowes Hanley:
Goals - Irving(5) Schofield:
CASTLEFORD - Anderson: Ellis(S/O) Blackmore T.Smith
Wray: Coyne Ford(Nelson): Crooks Watson
Sampson(England) Morrison Ketteridge Nikau:
Tries - Ford Sampson: Goals - Crooks(2):
Referee D Campbell (Widnes) Att - 20258 H.T. 6 - 10

Fri 1 Jan 1993 WAKEFIELD TRINITY home draw 22 - 22

CASTLEFORD - Steadman(Fletcher): Ellis Blackmore
Anderson Wray: Coyne T.Smith: Crooks Watson
Sampson(Ketteridge) Morrison Ketteridge (England)
Nikau:
Tries - Blackmore(2) Smith(2):   Goals - Crooks(3):
WAKEFIELD T - Spencer: Jones Benson(Flynn) Eden
Wilson(Goddard): Wright Bagnall: Fritz B.Conway Webster
Round Jackson Bell:
Tries - Spencer Wilson Wright Jackson:
Goals - Benson(2) Conway:
Referee J Smith (Halifax) Att - 7903 H.T. 6 - 10

Sat 9 Jan 1993 BRADFORD NORTHERN away
lost 12 – 19 REGAL TROPHY SEMI FINAL
at VALLEY PARADE BRADFORD

BRADFORD N - Watson: Marchant McGowan Shelford
Simpson: Summers Fox: Hobbs Noble(Clark)
Hamer(Medley) Powell Fairbank Heron:
Tries - McGowan Summers Hobbs: Goals - Fox(3)
Hobbs(DG):
CASTLEFORD - Middleton: Ellis Blackmore T.Smith
Wray(Steadman): Coyne Ford: Crooks Watson
England(Sampson) Morrison Ketteridge Nikau:
Tries - Middleton Smith: Goals - Crooks(2):
Referee I Ollerton (Wigan) Att - 5602 H.T. 6 - 18

Fri 15 Jan 1993 WARRINGTON home lost 10 - 13

CASTLEFORD - Steadman: Ellis Blackmore T.Smith
Wray(Boothroyd): Coyne Ford: Crooks Watson
England(Sampson) Morrison Ketteridge Nikau:
Try - Blackmore: Goals - Crooks(3):
WARRINGTON - Penny: Rudd Bateman Thorniley Forster:

SEASON 1992-93

Ellis Mackey: Harmon(Chambers) Mann Jackson Cullen
Sanderson Shelford(Harmon):
Tries - Penny Rudd: Goals - Thorniley(2) Ellis(DG):
Referee P Gilmour (Workington) Att - 3616 H.T. nil - 8

Sun 24 Jan 1993 HULL away won 14 - 2
HULL - Gay(Dearlove): Eastwood G.Nolan Grant Sullivan:
Gale R.Nolan: Dannatt(C.Jackson) L.Jackson Jones Divet
Walker(Dannatt) McNamara (Walker): Goal - Eastwood:
CASTLEFORD - Steadman: Blackmore(Nelson) Ellis T.Smith
Middleton: Coyne Ford: Crooks Southernwood Ketteridge
Morrison ANDY FISHER(703) (Sampson) Nikau:
Tries - Steadman Middleton Coyne: Goal - Crooks:
Referee I Ollerton (Wigan) Att - 4176 H.T. 10 - 2

Sat 30 Jan 1993 WARRINGTON away won 21 - 6
CHALLENGE CUP ROUND 1
WARRINGTON - Penny: Kenyon Bateman Thorniley
Forster: Ellis Mackey: Chambers Mann Jackson
Cullen(Darbyshire) Sanderson(Harmon) Shelford:
Try - Thorniley: Goal - Thorniley:
CASTLEFORD - Steadman: Nelson Ellis T.Smith(Anderson)
Middleton: Coyne Ford: Crooks Southernwood Ketteridge
Morrison Fisher(Sampson) Nikau:
Tries - Steadman Middleton Ford:
Goals- Crooks(4) Southernwood(DG):
Referee J Connolly (Wigan) Att - 2785 H.T. 6 - 8

Sun 7 Feb 1993 SHEFFIELD EAGLES home
won 14 - 8
CASTLEFORD - Steadman: Middleton Ellis T.Smith Nelson:
Coyne(Ketteridge) Ford: Crooks(Fisher) Southernwood
Ketteridge (Anderson) Morrison Fisher(Sampson) Nikau:
Tries - Steadman Middleton Ford: Goal - Crooks:
SHEFFIELD E - Jack: Vasey Gamson Mycoe Plange: Price
Sheridan: Broadbent Cook James(Thompson)(James)
Hughes(Carr) McGuire Carr(Lumb):
Tries - Jack: Goals - Mycoe(2):
Referee D Atkin (Hull) Att - 4655 H.T. 6 - 2

Sun 14 Feb 1993 HUNSLET home won 34 - 16
CHALLENGE CUP ROUND 2
CASTLEFORD - Steadman: Middleton(Anderson) Ellis
T.Smith Nelson: Coyne Ford: Crooks Southernwood
(Sampson) Ketteridge Morrison Fisher Nikau:
Tries - Steadman Smith(2) Morrison(2):
Goals - Crooks(5):
HUNSLET - Burrow: Bartliff Lee.Sampson Beath Francis:
Brook Harkin: Rose(Wright) Roy.Sampson Mitchell
Precious Snee(Rose) Coyle:
Tries - Burrow Brook Coyle: Goals - Precious(2):
Referee S Cummings (Widnes) Att - 3719 H.T. 16 - 6

Sun 21 Feb 1993 WARRINGTON away lost 18 - 23
WARRINGTON - Penny: Kenyon Bateman(Turner) Rudd
Forster: Ellis Mackey: Chambers(Harmon) Mann
Jackson(Chambers) Sanderson Cullen Shelford: Tries -
Kenyon Bateman Ellis Jackson: Goals - Rudd(3) EllisD/G:
CASTLEFORD - Steadman: Ellis T.Smith Anderson
Nelson(Boothroyd): Coyne Ford: Crooks Southernwood

Ketteridge(Sampson) Morrison Fisher Nikau:
Tries - Anderson Boothroyd Ford: Goals - Crooks(3):
Referee P Gilmour (Workington) Att - 3790 H.T. 6 - 13

Sat 27 Feb 1993 LEEDS away lost 8 - 12
CHALLENGE CUP ROUND 3
LEEDS - Tait: Fallon Iro Innes Irving: Schofield Gregory:
Molloy Lowes O'Neill(Anderson)(Dixon) Dixon(Goodway)
Mercer Hanley: Tries - Fallon(2): Goals - Irving(2):
CASTLEFORD - Steadman: Ellis T.Smith Anderson Nelson:
Coyne(Fletcher) Ford: Crooks Southernwood Sampson
Morrison(England) Fisher Nikau:
Try - Ford: Goals - Crooks(2):
Referee I Ollerton (Wigan) Att - 12757 H.T. 6 - 6

Wed 3 Mar 1993 ST HELENS away lost 20 - 24
ST HELENS - Lyon(Sullivan): Riley Connolly Loughlin
Hunte: Ropati Griffiths: Harrison O'Donnell Nickle(Cowan)
Joynt Vievers Cooper:
Tries - Ropati Griffiths Nickle Joynt: Goals - Loughlin(4):
CASTLEFORD - Steadman: Middleton T.Smith Ellis
Wray(Paul Fletcher): Anderson Ford: Sampson
Southernwood England(Battye) Morrison Fisher Nikau:
Tries - Steadman Middleton Anderson Ford:
Goals - Steadman(2):
Referee C Steele(Dalton in Furness) Att - 5647 H.T. 6 - 16

Sun 7 Mar 1993 HALIFAX away lost 16 - 28
HALIFAX - Cooper: Sharp Hallas Wilson Preston:
Bailey(McLean) Bishop: Harrison R.Southernwood
Fieldhouse(Fogerty) Lord Perrett Divorty:
Tries - Preston Harrison Fogerty Divorty:
Goals - Bishop(6):
CASTLEFORD - Steadman: C.Smith Middleton Ellis Giles
Boothroyd: Anderson T.Smith: Crooks(S/O) Southernwood
Sampson Neil Battye (Hay) Fisher(CHANCE LEAKE(704))
Nikau: Tries - T.Smith Southernwood:
Goals - Crooks(4):
Referee D Campbell (Widnes) Att - 6874 H.T. 10 - 12

Sun 21 Mar 1993 HULL KINGSTON ROVERS home
won 36 - 18
CASTLEFORD - Steadman: Middleton T.Smith Anderson
Ellis: Coyne(Hay) Ford: Crooks Southernwood Sampson
Morrison(Fisher) Fisher(Ketteridge) Nikau:
Tries - Steadman Smith Ellis Ford Morrison Nikau:
Goals - Crooks(6):
HULL K R - M.Fletcher: Hall Liddiard(P.Fletcher)
Hutchinson Bibby: Parker Chatfield: C.Harrison
Chamberlain D.Harrison(O'Brien) P.Fletcher(Jackson)
Thompson Speckman:
Tries - Hall(2) Liddiard: Goals - M.Fletcher(3):
Referee D Campbell (Widnes) Att - 6874 H.T. 12 - 6

Sun 28 Mar 1993 HALIFAX home won 32 - 16
CASTLEFORD - Steadman: Middleton T.Smith Anderson
Ellis: Coyne(Hay) Ford: Crooks(England) Southernwood
Sampson Morrison Fisher Nikau: Tries - Ford(2)
Middleton Ellis Morrison: Goals - Crooks(6):
HALIFAX - Pilgrim(Sharp): Bentley Cooper Austin Preston:

Bailey Bishop: Harrison R.Southernwood McLean
Lord(Fogerty) Perrett Divorty:
Tries - Bentley Austin Lord: Goals - Bishop(2):
Referee S Cummings (Widnes) Att - 6116 H.T. 20 - 2

Sun 4 Apr 1993 WIGAN home won 26 - 17
CASTLEFORD - Steadman: Middleton T.Smith(B/B) (Hay)
Anderson Ellis: Coyne Ford: Crooks(Hay) Southernwood
Sampson(Ketteridge) Morrison Fisher(Sampson) Nikau:
Tries - Steadman Smith Anderson Crooks:
Goals - Steadman(3) Crooks(2):
WIGAN - Hampson: Robinson Lydon Farrar(Panapa)
Offiah: Botica Edwards: Cowie(Gildart) Dermott
Platt(Cowie) Betts Panapa(Forshaw) Clarke:
Tries - Edwards Cowie: Goals - Botica(4) DermottD/G:
Referee C Steele (Dalton in Furness) Att - 8734 H.T. 6 - 8

Fri 9 Apr 1993 WAKEFIELD TRINITY away won 14 -8
WAKEFIELD T - Spencer: Goddard Mason Benson Wilson:
M.Conway(Jones) Bagnall: Webster(Bell) B.Conway
Thompson Round Flynn Slater:
Try - Round: Goals - M.Conway B.Conway:
CASTLEFORD - Steadman: Middleton T.Smith Anderson
Ellis: Coyne Ford: Crooks Southernwood
Ketteridge(Sampson)(Fisher) Morrison Fisher(Hay) Nikau:
Tries - Crooks Hay: Goals - Crooks(3):
Referee D Atkin (Hull) Att - 4332 H.T. nil - 6

Mon 12 Apr 1993 LEEDS home lost 6 - 10
CASTLEFORD - Steadman: Middleton T.Smith Anderson
Ellis: Coyne Ford: Crooks Southernwood Ketteridge(Hay)
Morrison Fisher(Sampson) Nikau:
Try - Middleton: Goal - Crooks:

LEEDS - Tait: Fallon Iro Innes Irving: Schofield
Stephens(Holroyd: Wane(Harland) Lowes Dixon
Goodway Mercer Hanley:
Tries - Irving Lowes: Goal - Irving:
Referee I Ollerton (Wigan) Att - 7526 H.T. 2 - 10

Sun 18 Apr 1993 WIGAN away lost 18 - 25
WIGAN - Hampson: Robinson Bell Farrar(Mather) Offiah:
Botica Edwards: Flatt Dermott Betts(Forshaw) Panapa
Farrell Clarke:
Tries - Robinson Botica Clarke: Goals - Botica(6) (DG):
CASTLEFORD - Steadman: Middleton T.Smith Anderson
Ellis: Coyne Ford Crooks Southernwood
England(Sampson) Morrison Ketteridge(Fisher) Nikau:
Tries - Ford(2) Morrison: Goals - Crooks(3):
Referee S Cummings (Widnes) Att - 20020 H.T. 6 - 9

Sun 25 Apr 1993 BRADFORD NORTHERN away won 19 – 6 PREMIERSHIP ROUND 1
BRADFORD N - Simpson: Taylor McGowan(D.Powell)
Anderson Kebbie: Summers Fox: Hobbs(Medley) Noble
Hamer R.Powel Fairbank(McGowan) Heron:
Try - Kebbie: Goal - Hobbs:
CASTLEFORD - Steadman: Middleton T.Smith Anderson
Ellis: Coyne Ford: Crooks(England) Southernwood(Fisher)
England(Sampson) Morrison Ketteridge Nikau:
Tries - Smith(2) Ford: Goals - Crooks(3) Steadman(DG):
Referee I Ollerton (Wigan) Att - 4729 H.T. 12 - 6

Fri 2 May 1993 WIGAN away lost 8 - 25 PREMIERSHIP SEMI FINAL
WIGAN - Hampson: Robinson Bell(Forshaw) Farrar Offiah:
Botica Edwards: Cowie(Cassidy) Dermott Skerrett Panapa
Farrell Clarke: Tries - Forshaw Offiah Edwards Farrell:
Goals - Botica(4)D/G:
CASTLEFORD - Steadman: Middleton T.Smith Anderson
Ellis: Peter Coyne Ford: Crooks(Fisher) Graham
Southernwood England(Sampson) Fisher(Hay) Ketteridge
Nikau: Try - Smith: Goals - Steadman Crooks:
Referee S Cummings (Widnes) Att - 12675 H.T. 2 – 14

Tony Morrison
D. No 698
1992-93 to 1994-95

Chris Smith
D. No 699
1992-93 to 1997

Peter Coyne
D. No 701
1992-93

Andy Fisher
D. No 703
1992-93 to 1993-94

SEASON 1992-93

D.N	PLAYER		DEBUT	L MATCH	APP	SUB	T.AP	TRI'S	G'LS	D.G	P'TS
621	ENGLAND	KEITH			10	9	19	1	0	0	4
627	BATTYE	NEIL		07/03/1993	1	1	2	0	0	0	0
636	KETTERIDGE	MARTIN			23	7	30	1	0	0	4
651	IRWIN	SHAUN		16/10/1992	7	1	8	1	0	0	4
657	ANDERSON	GRANT			17	12	29	4	0	0	16
659	BOOTHROYD	GILES		07/03/1993	4	3	7	2	0	0	8
661	SAMPSON	DEAN			21	13	34	2	0	0	8
669	SOUTHERNWOOD	GRAHAM		02/05/1993	17	0	17	1	0	1	5
675	STEADMAN	GRAHAM			24	1	25	9	13	1	63
679	SMITH	TONY			36	0	36	24	0	0	96
680	ELLIS	ST JOHN			36	0	36	11	0	0	44
683	ROEBUCK	NEIL		11/10/1992	6	0	6	1	0	0	4
685	CROOKS	LEE			34	0	34	2	112	0	232
687	HAY	ANDY			0	7	7	1	0	0	4
688	FLETCHER	PAUL		03/03/1993	0	3	3	0	0	0	0
689	WRAY	JON			11	0	11	1	0	0	4
690	NELSON	DAVID			9	2	11	1	0	0	4
691	FORD	MIKE			34	0	34	21	0	0	84
692	NIKAU	TAWERA			36	0	36	2	0	0	8
693	MIDDLETON	SIMON			29	0	29	19	4	0	84
694	SYKES	NATHAN			0	5	5	0	0	0	0
695	BLACKMORE	RICHARD			21	0	21	11	0	0	44
697	WATSON	CHRIS			13	0	13	1	0	0	4
698	MORRISON	TONY	23/08/1992		34	0	34	6	0	0	24
699	SMITH	CHRIS	20/09/1992		2	0	2	0	0	0	0
700	WILLIAMS	DEAN	27/09/1992	27/09/1972	0	1	1	0	0	0	0
701	COYNE	PETER	04/10/1992	02/05/1993	29	0	29	2	1	0	10
702	BLOOM	JAMIE	06/12/1993	06/12/1993	0	1	1	1	0	0	4
703	FISHER	ANDY	24/01/1993		14	2	16	0	0	0	0
704	LEEK	CHANCE	07/03/1993	07/03/1993	0	1	1	0	0	0	0
	30			7	10	468	69	537	125	130	2	762

COMPETITION		P	W	D	L	FOR	AGT
LEAGUE D 1	POSITION 6 OF 14	26	14	1	11	544	401
YORK'S CUP		1	0	0	1	10	16
RL CUP		3	2	0	1	63	34
REGAL TROPHY		4	3	0	1	118	49
CHAMPIONSHIP		2	1	0	1	27	31
PLAYERS RECORDS		36	20	1	15	762	531

After a tremendous run of success in reaching the Final of the Yorkshire Cup last season we came to earth with a bump when we went out in the preliminary round at home to Bradford Northern 16-10.

However, in the League we finished 6th from 14.

The league structure reverted to two divisions, as a result the two bottom teams in Division 1, (Salford and Hull K R) were not relegated, with Featherstone Rovers Oldham promoted from Division 2. The remaining teams were combined into Division 2, with the exception of the three bottom clubs in Division 3 Chorley Borough, Blackpool Gladiators Nottingham City who dropped out of the league.

Fri 20 Aug 1993 HULL home won 22 - 18
KEITH ENGLAND BENEFIT FRIENDLY
CASTLEFORD - Steadman: Ellis Middleton Anderson Wray: T.Smith Ford: Sampson Russell England Fisher Ketteridge Morrison: Subs used - C.Smith Daniels Crooks Smales Hay: Tries - Steadman Ellis Middleton Ford Smales: Goal - Ketteridge:
HULL - O'Donnell: Eastwood Danby Grant Sullivan: Nolan Dearlove: Jones Dixon Walker Divet C.Jackson Busby: Subs used- Hewitt Cassidy A.N.Other:
Tries - Danvy Grant Hewitt: Goals - Eastwood(3): Referee Att - 1850 H.T. 18 - 6

Fri 27 Aug 1993 LEEDS home lost 12 - 21
CASTLEFORD - Steadman: Ellis Middleton Anderson Wray: T.Smith Ford: Crooks(Sampson)RICHARD RUSSELL(705) Sampson(Ketteridge) Morrison (Fisher) IAN SMALES(706) Nikau: Tries - Ellis Anderson: Goals - Crooks(2):
LEEDS - Tait: Fallon Iro Innes Irving: Schofield Gregory(Holroyd): Harmon(Parrish) Lowes Scott Mercer Schultz Hanley: Tries - Hanley(2) Innes Holroyd: Goals - Irving(2) Hanley(DG):
Referee J Connolly (Wigan) Att - 8758 H.T. 2 - 15

Sun 5 Sept 1993 SHEFFIELD EAGLES away won 20 - 11
SHEFFIELD E - Gamson: Stott Price Fraisse Mann: Powell(Sheridan) Aston: Broadbent Cook Laughton Hughes (Farrell) McGuire Carr:
Try - Price: Goals - Aston(3)D/G:
CASTLEFORD - Steadman: Ellis Blackmore Anderson Middleton: T.Smith Ford: Crooks(Sykes) Russell Sampson(Ketteridge) Fisher Smales Nikau: Tries - Smith Steadman Smales Fisher: Goals - Crooks Ketteridge:
Referee J Smith (Halifax) Att - 4000 H.T. 4 - 9

Sun 12 Sept 1993 HULL home won 12 - 4
CASTLEFORD - Steadman: Ellis Blackmore Anderson Middleton: T.Smith Ford: Crooks Russell Sampson(Ketteridge) Fisher Smales Nikau:
Try - Ford: Goals - Crooks(4):
HULL - Gay: Eastwood Danby Grant Sterling: R.Nolan Hasler: Jones(Cassidy) Dixon Walker Divet Sharp(Busby) Busby(Jackson): Try - Gay:
Referee I Ollerton (Wigan) Att - 5771 H.T. 10 - nil

Fri 17 Sept 1993 WIDNES away won 37 - 12
WIDNES - Spruce(Hammond): P.Smith Devereux Ruane Myers: D.Hulme Goulding(Spruce): Ireland McCurrie D.Smith Davidson(Grieve) Faimalo Koloto(Davidson): Tries - Spruce McCurrie: Goals - Goulding(2):
CASTLEFORD - Steadman: Ellis Blackmore Anderson

Middleton: T.Smith Ford: Crooks Russell Ketteridge (Sampson) Fisher(Hay) Smales Nikau: Tries - Ellis(2) Blackmore(2) Russell Hay: Goals - Crooks(6) Ford(DG): Referee J Connolly (Wigan) Att - 3057 H.T. 10 - 12

Sun 26 Sept 1993 ST HELENS home lost 18 - 35
CASTLEFORD - Steadman: Ellis Blackmore Anderson Middleton: T.Smith Ford: Crooks Russell Ketteridge (Sampson) Fisher(Morrison) Smales Nikau:
Tries - Ellis Smith Ford: Goals - Crooks(3):
ST HELENS - Lyon: Riley Veivers Loughlin Quirk: Ropati Griffiths(O'Donnell): Neill(Dannatt) Dwyer Mann Joynt Nickle Cooper: Tries - Veivers Ropati Dwyer Mann Joynt Nickle: Goals - Loughlin(5) O'Donnell(DG):
Referee D Campbell (Widnes) Att - 6303 H.T. 12 - 12

Sun 3 Oct 1993 LEIGH away draw 15 - 15
LEIGH - Winstanley: Sarsfield Booth Clarke Platt: Gunning Donohue: Hansen Rowley Street Pendlebury Collier (Costello) Martin: Tries - Sarsfield Clarke Rowley: Goals - Clarke Donohue(DG):
CASTLEFORD - Steadman: Ellis Blackmore T.Smith (Anderson) Middleton: TONY KEMP(707) Ford: Crooks Russell Sampson(Fisher) Morrison Smales(Sampson) Nikau(S/O):
Tries - Blackmore Smith Ford: Goals - Crooks Ford(DG): Referee B Galress (Bradford) Att - 3025 H.T. 10 - 14

Sun 10 Oct 1993 HULL KINGSTON ROVERS home won 54 - 18
CASTLEFORD - Steadman: Ellis Blackmore T.Smith(Anderson) Middleton: Kemp(T.Smith) Ford: Crooks Russell Ketteridge(England) Morrison Smales Nikau: Tries - Ellis(3) Blackmore(3) Middleton(2) Steadman Nikau: Goals - Crooks(7):
HULL K R - M.Fletcher: Barkworth Hutchinson(Jackson) Bibby Sodje Clark Parker: Hosking(Hutchinson) Chamberlain Jackson(Crane) Harrison Thompson(O'Brien) Leighton:
Tries - Barkworth Clark O'Brien: Goals - M.Fletcher(3): Referee S Nicholson(Whitehaven) Att - 4486 H.T. 20 -14

Tue 12 Oct 1993 NEW ZEALAND won 16 - 4
CASTLEFORD - Steadman: Ellis Blackmore(JASON FLOWERS(708)) Anderson Middleton: Kemp(T.Smith) Ford: Crooks(Sampson) Russell Ketteridge(England) Morrison Hay Smales: Tries - Ellis(3) Middleton:
NEW ZEALAND - P.Edwards: Donnelly Harding Ropati(Williams) M.Edwards: Nixon Whittaker: Piva D.Johnston P.Johnson(Lowrie) Angell(Mackie) Pongia(Lomax) L.Edwards: Try - L.Edwards:
Referee D Campbell (Widnes) Att - 4927 H.T. 8 - nil

Sun 24 Oct 1993 SALFORD away won 34 - nil
SALFORD - Jack(Lee): Evans Critchley Birkett Ford: Blakeley Neil: Young Lee(Reid) O'Connor Tauro(Williams) Potts Burgess:
CASTLEFORD - Steadman: Wray Blackmore Anderson(T.Smith) Middleton (Hay): Kemp Ford: Crooks Russell Ketteridge(Middleton) Morrison Smales Nikau:

Tries - Steadman Wray Blackmore Smales Kemp Ford:
Goals - Crooks(5):
Referee J Smith (Halifax) Att - 3769 H.T. 10 - nil

Sun 31 Oct 1993 WIGAN home won 46 - nil
CASTLEFORD - Steadman: Ellis Blackmore Anderson
Middleton: Kemp(T.Smith) Ford: Crooks Russell
Ketteridge(Hay) Morrison Smales Nikau: Tries - Ellis(3)
Middleton(2) Blackmore Anderson Ford:
Goals - Crooks(7):
WIGAN - Craig(Gildart): Ellison Lydon(Craig)
Connolly(Radlinski) Stevens: Wright Murdock: Skerrett
Hall Platt Cowie Panapa Cassidy:
Referee R Whitfield (Widnes) Att - 7789 H.T. 10 - nil

Sun 7 Nov 1993 HALIFAX away won 35 - 10
HALIFAX - Lay: Bentley Schuster Hallas
Preston(Hampson): Hagan Bishop: Boyd(Harland)
Southernwood Lord Jackson Harland(Perrett) Divorty:
Tries - Hallas(2)   Goal - Bishop:
CASTLEFORD - Steadman: Ellis Blackmore Anderson
Middleton: Kemp(T.Smith) Ford: Sampson(England)
Russell Ketteridge Morrison Smales Nikau:
Tries - Steadman(2) Ellis(2) Anderson Middleton Kemp:
Goals - Steadman(3)D/G:
Referee C Steele(Dalton in Furness) Att - 8088 H.T. 6 - 24

Mon 15 Nov 1993 HULL KINGSTON ROVERS away
won 16 – 12 REGAL TROPHY ROUND 2
HULL K R - M.Fletcher: Barkworth Liddiard Bibby Sodje:
Crane Chatfield: Harrison Chamberlain Jackson P.Fletcher
Hutchinson(Clark) Leighton:
Tries - Chatfield P.Fletcher: Goals - M.Fletcher(2):
CASTLEFORD - Steadman: Ellis Blackmore Anderson
(T.Smith) Middleton: Kemp Ford: Crooks Russell
Ketteridge Morrison Smales Nikau:
Tries - Steadman Middleton Morrison: Goals - Crooks(2):
Referee D Campbell (Widnes) Att - 4500 H.T. nil - 12

Sun 21 Nov 1993 WARRINGTON away lost 10 - 20
WARRINGTON - Penny: Forster Rudd Davies Myler: Ellis
Mackey: Chambers Thursfield Tees(Teitzel) Cullen Gregory
Elliott: Tries - Myler(2) Cullen: Goals - Davies(3)(2D/G):
CASTLEFORD - Steadman: Ellis Blackmore Anderson
Middleton: T.Smith Ford: Crooks(England)(Morrison)
Russell Ketteridge Morrison(Hay)Smales Nikau:
Try - Ford: Goals - Crooks(3):
Referee J Smith (Halifax) Att - 5778 H.T. 10 - 11

Sun 28 Nov 1993 WAKEFIELD TRINITY home
won 34 - 10
CASTLEFORD - Flowers: Ellis Blackmore Anderson
Middleton: Kemp Ford: Crooks Russell Ketteridge(Hay)
Morrison Smales Nikau: Tries - Ellis(2) Flowers Blackmore
Anderson Kemp Smales: Goals - Crooks(3):
WAKEFIELD T - Spencer: Christie Mason Goddard Child:
Hanlan Conway: Durham Bell Marlow(Hirst) Round(Fuller)
Woods Flynn: Tries - Mason Hirst: Goal - Goddard:
Referee R Connolly (Wigan) Att - 5232 H.T. 10 - nil

Sun 5 Dec 1993 BRADFORD NORTHERN home
lost 6 - 13
CASTLEFORD - Steadman: Ellis Blackmore(T.Smith)
Anderson Middleton: Kemp Ford: Crooks Russell
Ketteridge(Sampson) Morrison Smales Nikau:
Try - Ford: Goal - Crooks:
BRADFORD N - Watson: Cordle McGowan Newlove
Kebbie: Summers (Heron) (Summers) Fox: Hobbs Medley
Hamer Powell Dixon Fairbank (Clark):
Tries - Cordle Newlove: Goals - Fox(2)D/G:
Referee D Campbell (Widnes) Att - 6919 H.T. 6 - 8

Mon 13 Dec 1993 LEIGH home won 54 - 14
REGAL TROPHY ROUND 3
CASTLEFORD - Steadman: Ellis T.Smith Anderson
Middleton: Kemp(Hay) Ford: Crooks(Sampson) Russell
Ketteridge Morrison Smales Nikau: Tries - Middleton(3)
Ellis(2) Steadman Smith Ford Morrison Smales:
Goals - Crooks(4) Ketteridge(2) Steadman:
LEIGH - Winstanley(Fletcher): Cawley Davies Martin Pratt:
Gunning Hanger: Costello Rowley Hansen Collier
Booth(Daniel) Baldwin:
Tries - Davies Hanger: Goals - Davies(3):
Referee J Smith (Halifax) Att - 2125 H.T. 30 - 10

Sun 19 Dec 1993 CARLISLE home won 44 - 4
REGAL TROPHY QUARTER FINAL
CASTLEFORD - Steadman: Ellis T.Smith Anderson(Andy
Fisher) Nelson: Kemp Ford(Hay): Sampson Russell
Ketteridge Morrison Smales Nikau:
Tries - Steadman(2) Ellis Anderson Kemp Hay Sampson
Smales: Goals - Ketteridge(6):
CARLISLE - Richardson: Coffey Pape Knox Blake: Graham
Russell: Brierley(Harris) Thomason McMullen Armstrong
Scott(Chorley) Charlton: Try - McMullen:
Referee S Cummings (Widnes) Att - 2624 H.T. 14 - nil

Sun 26 Dec 1993 FEATHERSTONE ROVERS away
won 28 - 18
FEATHERSTONE R - Pearson: Butt Gibson Ropati Simpson:
Maloney(Calland) Daunt: Molloy Gunn(G.S.Price)
Casey(Roebuck) G.S.Price(Casey) G.H.Price Tuuta:
Tries - Ropati Simpson Molloy: Goals - Pearson(3):
CASTLEFORD - Steadman: Ellis T.Smith Anderson
Middleton: Kemp Ford: Crooks(Hay) Russell
Ketteridge(Sampson) Morrison Smales Nikau:
Tries - Ellis(2) Smith Sampson Smales: Goals - Crooks(4):
Referee R Whitfield (Widnes) Att - 6854 H.T. 2 - 10

Sat 1 Jan 1994 BRADFORD NORTHERN away
won 23 – 10 REGAL TROPHY SEMI FINAL
BRADFORD N - Watson: Cordle McGowan Newlove
Kebbie: Summers Fox: Hobbs(Grayshon) Clark(Medley)
Hamer Powell Dixon Heron: Tries - Kebbie(2): Goal - Fox:
CASTLEFORD - Steadman: Ellis T.Smith Anderson
Middleton: Kemp Ford: Crooks Russell
Ketteridge(Sampson) Morrison Smales(Hay) Nikau:
Tries - Steadman Smith Ford Russell:
Goals - Crooks(3)(DG):
Referee J Connolly (Wigan) Att - 8318 H.T. 10 - 4

SEASON 1993-94

Wed 5 Jan 1994 LEEDS away lost 4 - 8
LEEDS - Tait: Fallon Iro(B/B)(Vassilakopoules) Irving
Cummins: Holroyd Stephens: Harmon(Mercer) Lowes
O'Neill(Howard) Eyres Mercer(O'Neill) Hanley:
Goals - Holroyd(4):
CASTLEFORD - Steadman: Ellis T.Smith(B/B)(Nelson)
Anderson Middleton: Kemp Ford: Crooks Russell(Nelson)
Ketteridge Hay Smales(Sampson) Nikau:
Goals - Crooks(2):
Referee I Ollerton (Wigan) Att - 10825 H.T. 4 - nil

Sat 9 Jan 1994 SHEFFIELD EAGLES home won 20 - 18
CASTLEFORD - Steadman: Ellis T.Smith(England)
Anderson(Blackmore) Middleton: Kemp Ford: Crooks
Chris Watson Ketteridge Hay Sampson Nikau:
Tries - Ford(2) Hay: Goals - Crooks(4):
SHEFFIELD E. - Gamson: Stott Price Fraisse Plange: Powell
Aston(Cook)(Hughes): Broadbent Jackson McGuire Carr
Cook(Sheridan) Farrell:
Tries - Aston Jackson Cook: Goals - Aston(2) Fraisse:
Referee J Smith (Halifax) Att - 4269 H.T. 6 - 12

Wed 12 Jan 1994 OLDHAM home won 34 - 16
CASTLEFORD - Steadman: Ellis Blackmore Anderson
(Smales) Middleton Kemp Ford: Crooks(England) Russell
Sampson Hay Morrison Nikau: Tries - Ellis Anderson
Middleton Russell Hay Morrison: Goals - Crooks(5):
OLDHAM - Heslop: Ranson Abram McAllister Jones:
Mitchell Crompton: McDermott Stephenson Parr(Lindner)
Richards(Bradbury) Tupeae Green(Parr):
Tries - Ranson Abram Crompton: Goals - Abram(2):
Referee S Nicholson(Whitehaven) Att - 3806 H.T. 26 -10

Sun 16 Jan 1994 HULL away won 24 - 22
HULL - Gay: Eastwood Nolan(Greenwood) Grant Sterling:
Danby Hasler: Walker(McNamara) Dixon Jackson(Walker)
Divet Sharp Doyle:
Tries - Gay Eastwood Grant Doyle: Goals - Eastwood(3):
CASTLEFORD - Steadman: Ellis Blackmore Anderson
Middleton: Kemp Ford: Crooks Russell Ketteridge
(Sampson) Morrison Smales(Hay) Nikau:
Tries - Blackmore Anderson Kemp Ford Morrison:
Goals - Crooks(2):
Referee D Campbell (St Helens) Att - 4620 H.T. nil - 20

Sat 22 Jan 1994 WIGAN won 33 - 2
REGAL TROPHY FINAL - at HEADINGLEY LEEDS
CASTLEFORD - Steadman: Ellis Blackmore Anderson(Hay)
Middleton: Kemp Ford: Crooks Russell Ketteridge
(Sampson) Morrison Smales Nikau: Tries - Ketteridge(2)
Anderson Crooks Nikau: Goals - Crooks(6) Kemp(DG):
WIGAN - Lydon: Robinson Mather Connolly Offiah: Botica
Edwards(Panapa): Skerrett Dermott Platt Cowie(Cassidy)
Farrell Clarke: Goal - Botica:
Referee D Campbell (St Helens) Att - 15626 H.T. 20 - 2
MAN OF MATCH MARTIN KETTERIDGE

Sun 30 Jan 1994 SALFORD home won 36 - 4
CHALLENGE CUP ROUND 4
CASTLEFORD - Steadman: Ellis Blackmore Anderson
Middleton: Kemp Ford: Crooks(Sampson) Russell
Ketteridge Morrison Smales Nikau(Hay):
Tries - Anderson(3) Ellis Russell Smales:
Goals - Crooks(5 Ketteridge:
SALFORD - Jack: O'Neill Critchley Williams Ford: Blakeley
Gregory: Young Lee O'Connor(Marsden) Forber(Gilfillan)
Tauro Burgess: Try - Blakeley:
Referee R Connolly (Wigan) Att - 5669 H.T. 18 - nil

Sun 6 Feb 1994 ST HELENS away lost 12 - 33
ST HELENS - Prescott(Veivers): Riley Hunte Loughlin
Sullivan: Martyr Griffiths: Dannatt Hodgkinson Neill
Pickavance Nickle(Dwyer) Cooper:
Tries - Griffiths(2) Veivers Sullivan Martyn Pickavance:
Goals - Loughlin(4) MartynD/G:
CASTLEFORD - Flowers: Wray Blackmore Anderson
Middleton: Kemp Ford: Crooks Russell
Ketteridge(England) Morrison(Smales) Smales(Hay) Nikau:
Tries - Anderson Middleton: Goals - Crooks(2):
Referee S Cummings (Widnes) Att - 7605 H.T. 10 - 6

Sun 13 Feb 1994 KEIGHLEY COUGARS away
won 52 – 14 CHALLENGE CUP ROUND 5
KEIGHLEY - Walker: A.Stephenson Farrell P.Stephenson
Race(Butterfield): Wood Eyres: Hill Ramshaw Gately
Hall(Berry) Marr Brooke-Cowden:
Tries - Eyres Hall Brooke-Cowden: Goal - Walker:
CASTLEFORD - Steadman: Ellis Blackmore Anderson
Middleton: Kemp Ford: Crooks(Ketteridge) Russell
(Morrison) Ketteridge(Hay) Morrison(England) Smales
Nikau:
Tries - Middleton(2) Steadman Ellis Blackmore Anderson
Kemp Morrison Smales Nikau: Goals - Crooks(6):
Referee C Morris (Huddersfield) Att - 5680 H.T. 10 - 18

Sun 20 Feb 1994 LEIGH home won 70 - 6
CASTLEFORD - Steadman(Morrison): Ellis Blackmore
Anderson Middleton: Kemp Ford: Sampson Russell
Ketteridge(England) Morrison(Smales) Hay Nikau:
Tries - Ellis(3) Kemp(2) Ford(2) Blackmore Anderson
Sampson Smales Hay Nikau: Goals - Ketteridge(5) Ellis(4):
LEIGH - Cheetham: Pratt Martin(Hall) Sarsfield(Marsh) Hill:
Gunning Hanger: Meadows Rowley Collier Pendlebury
Daniel Baldwin: Try - Daniel: Goal - Baldwin:
Referee R Connolly (Wigan) Att - 3987 H.T. 38 - nil

Sat 26 Feb 1994 WIDNES home won 30 - 6
CHALLENGE CUP QUARTER FINAL
CASTLEFORD - Steadman: Ellis Blackmore Anderson
Middleton: Kemp Ford: Crooks(Ketteridge) Russell
Ketteridge(England) Morrison Smales Nikau(Hay):
Tries - Ford(2) Morrison(2) Steadman: Goals - Crooks(5):
WIDNES - Spruce(Ruane): Myers Hammond Wright
Hadley: D.Hulme Goulding: Ireland(Moriarty) McCurrie
Smith Moriarty(Koloto) Faimalo P.Hulme:
Try - Moriarty: Goal - Goulding:
Referee J Connolly (Wigan) Att - 6076 H.T. 12 - nil

SEASON 1993-94

Wed 2 Mar 1994 WIDNES home won 42 - 6
CASTLEFORD - Steadman(Hay): Ellis Blackmore Anderson Middleton: Kemp Ford: Crooks(England) Russell Ketteridge Morrison Smales Nikau:
Tries - Morrison(2) Steadman Ellis Blackmore Anderson Middleton Russell: Goals - Crooks(3) Ketteridge(2):
WIDNES - Ruane: Myers Hammond Wright Elia: D.Hulme(Makin) Goulding: Smith(Tyrer) McCurrie Faimalo Koloto Russell P.Hulme:
Try - Hammond: Goal - Goulding:
Referee J Smith (Halifax) Att - 3967 H.T. 10 - nil

Sun 6 Mar 1994 HULL KINGSTON ROVERS away won 44 - 24
HULL K R - M.Fletcher: Barkworth Hutchinson Charlesworth(P.Fletcher)Hadi: Wardrobe Parker: Jackson Chamberlain O'Brien P.Fletcher(Glancy)(Halafihi) Harrison Hoe: Tries - O'Brien(2) Parker: Goals - M.Fletcher(6):
CASTLEFORD - Flowers: Ellis Blackmore Hay Middleton: Kemp(T.Smith) Ford: Crooks (Ketteridge) Russell Ketteridge(England) Morrison Smales Nikau:
Tries - Ford(3) Ellis(2) Blackmore(2) Middleton: Goals - Crooks(6):
Referee I Ollerton (Wigan) Att - 2736 H.T. 12 - 24

Thu 12 Mar 1994 WIGAN lost 6 - 20
CHALLENGE CUP SEMI FINAL - at HEADINGLEY LEEDS
CASTLEFORD - Steadman: Ellis Blackmore Anderson Middleton: Kemp Ford: Crooks Russell Ketteridge (England)(Ketteridge)(B/B)(England)(B/B) Morrison(Hay) Smales Nikau: Try - Kemp: Goal - Crooks:
WIGAN - Atcheson: Robinson Mather Connolly Offiah: Botica Edwards: Skerrett(Cowie)(B/B)(Skerrett(B/B)) Dermott(Cassidy) Platt(Bell) Cowie(Platt) Cassidy(Panapa) Farrell: Tries - Atcheson Offiah Botica: Goals - Botica(4):
Referee S Cummings (Widnes) Att - 17049 H.T. nil - 18

Wed 23 Mar 1994 SALFORD home won 22 - 14
CASTLEFORD - Steadman: Nelson Blackmore(Morrison) Ellis Middleton: Anderson Ford: Sampson(Ketteridge) Russell England Hay Smales Nikau: Tries - Blackmore Ellis Middleton Sampson Anderson: Goal - Steadman:
SALFORD - Jack: Critchley Austin Williams Ford(Marsden): Blakeley Gregory(Brown): Young Lee O'Connor Forber Blease Burgess:
Tries - Critchley Williams Blakeley: Goal - Blakeley:
Referee D Atkin (Hull) Att - 3604 H.T. 14 - nil

Sun 26 Mar 1994 HALIFAX home lost 18 - 26
CASTLEFORD - Steadman: Nelson Ellis Anderson Middleton: Kemp(Hay) Ford: Crooks Russell Keith England(Sampson) Morrison Smales Nikau:
Tries - Steadman Hay Sampson: Goals - Crooks(3):
HALIFAX - Hampson: Bentley Schuster Hallas Preston: Hagan Bishop: Harrison Southernwood Fieldhouse(Lord) Round(Boyd) Jackson Divorty: Tries - Schuster Preston Hagan Divorty: Goals - Schuster(5):
Referee R Connolly (Wigan) Att - 6063 H.T. 2 - 16

Fri 1 Apr 1994 FEATHERSTONE ROVERS home won 26 - 6
CASTLEFORD - Steadman: Ellis Blackmore T.Smith Middleton: Anderson(Morrison) Ford: Crooks(Ketteridge) Russell Sampson Morrison Hay(Smales) Nikau:
Tries - Blackmore(2) Ellis Middleton Ford:
Goals - Crooks(3):
FEATHERSTONE R. - Gibson: Butt Bibb Ropati Manning: Pearson Daunt: Molloy(Casey) Gunn Casey(O'Brien) Gary S.Price(G.Southernwood)Gary H.Price Roebuck:
Try - Southernwood: Goal - Pearson:
Referee J Connolly (Wigan) Att - 6280 H.T. 4 - 2

Mon 4 Apr 1994 OLDHAM away won 28 - 10
OLDHAM - Gibson: Heslop Irwin(Topping) Abram Ranson: Liddiard(Kerry)Crompton: Sherratt Clark Parr Lindner Goodway Kuiti: Try - Abram: Goals - Kerry(2) Abram:
CASTLEFORD - Steadman: Ellis Blackmore Hay Middleton: T.Smith Ford: Crooks(Ketteridge) Russell Sampson Morrison Smales Nikau: Tries - Ellis Ford Ketteridge Russell Morrison: Goals - Crooks(3) Ketteridge:
Referee J Smith (Halifax) Att - 4139 H.T. 4 - 10

Fri 8 Apr 1994 BRADFORD NORTHERN away lost 16 - 24
BRADFORD N - Summers: Hall Daio Powell Newlove Cordle: Heron(Holding) Fox: Roy Powell Clark Greenwood(Hamer) Dixon(Greenwood) Medley Fairbank: Tries - Summers D.Powell Newlove Cordle: Goals - Fox(4):
CASTLEFORD - Steadman(C.Smith): Ellis Blackmore Hay Middleton: T.Smith Ford: Crooks Russell Sampson(Ketteridge) Morrison Smales Nikau:
Tries - Ellis Russell Smales: Goals - Crooks(2):
Referee D Campbell (Widnes) Att - 4189 H.T. 6 - 12

Sun 17 Apr 1994 WARRINGTON home lost 16 - 21
CASTLEFORD - Steadman: Ellis Blackmore(Flowers) Hay Middleton: T.Smith Ford: Crooks Russell Sampson Ketteridge(C.Smith) Smales Nikau:
Tries - Hay Crooks: Goals - Crooks(4):
WARRINGTON - Davies: Forster Bateman(Bennett) Roper Harris: Ellis Mackey: Teitzel(Phillips) Thursfield Tees Darbyshire Sanderson Shelford:
Tries - Forster(2) Davies Roper: Goals - Davies(2) (DG):
Referee J Connolly (Wigan) Att - 5994 H.T. 12 - 12

Wed 20 Apr 1994 WIGAN away lost 12 - 21
WIGAN - Connolly: Tuigamala Bell(Lydon) Panapa Offiah: Botica Edwards: Skerrett Dermott Platt(Cowie) Betts Cassidy Farrell: Tries - Tuigamala Offiah Edwards: Goals - Botica(4) Farrell(DG):
CASTLEFORD - Ellis: David Nelson T.Smith Hay Middleton: Steadman Ford(Flowers): Crooks(Sykes) Russell Sampson(Crooks) Ketteridge Smales Nikau:
Tries - Ellis Russell: Goals - Crooks(2):
Referee D Campbell (Widnes) Att - 19896 H.T. 8 - 12

**Sun 24 Apr 1994 WAKEFIELD TRINITY away
won 38 - 24**
WAKEFIELD T - Paul: Wilson Mason Goddard Sodje:
Hanlan Conway: Marlow Fuller Morris Hirst(Eden) Forshaw
Slater(Hirst)(Sheals):
Tries - Paul Mason Sodje Forshaw: Goals - Paul(4):
CASTLEFORD - Ellis: C.Smith Blackmore T.Smith
Middleton: Steadman Ford(Flowers): Crooks Russell
Sampson Ketteridge Smales(Sykes) Nikau:
Tries - Ellis(2) C.Smith(2) Russell Nikau: Goals - Crooks(7):
Referee S Cummings (Widnes) Att - 4235 H.T. 24 - 12

**Fri 6 May 1994 HALIFAX home won 28 - 23
PREMIERSHIP QUARTER FINAL**
CASTLEFORD - Ellis: C.Smith Blackmore T.Smith
Middleton: Steadman Ford: Crooks Russell(Ketteridge)
Sampson(Sykes) Ketteridge(Smales)Hay Nikau:
Tries - Ellis(2) Blackmore(2) Steadman: Goals - Crooks(4):
HALIFAX - Hampson: Sharp Schuster(Fieldhouse) Bentley
Preston: Hagan Bishop: Harrison Southernwood
Fieldhouse(Anderson) Round(Lord) Jackson Divorty:
Tries - Sharp Schuster Preston Divorty:
Goals - Bishop(3)D/G:
Referee D Campbell (Widnes) Att - 4589 H.T. 10 – 10

Richard Russell
D. No 705
1993-94 to 1998

Ian Smales
D. No 706
1993-94 to 1997

Tony Kemp
D. No 707
1993-94 to 1994-95

Jason Flowers
D. No 708
1993-94 to 2001

**Sun 15 May 1994 BRADFORD NORTHERN away
won 24 – 16 PREMIERSHIP SEMI FINAL**
BRADFORD N - Watson: Hall Shelford Newlove Cordle:
Summers Fox: R.Fowell Clark Grayshon(Hamer) Dixon
Medley(Heron) Fairbank:
Tries - Newlove Summers Fairbank: Goals - Fox(2):
CASTLEFORD - Ellis: C.Smith Blackmore T.Smith
Middleton: Steadman(Smales) Ford: Crooks Russell(Sykes)
Sampson Ketteridge Hay Nikau:
Tries - Middleton(3) C.Smith Ford: Goals - Crooks(2):
Referee J Connolly (Wigan) Att - 7603 H.T. 10 - 8

**Sun 22 May 1994 WIGAN lost 20 - 24
PREMIERSHIP FINAL - AT OLD TRAFFORD
MANCHESTER**
WIGAN - Atcheson: Robinson Panapa(Lydon) Connolly
Offiah: Botica Edwards: Skerrett
(Cassidy)(B/B)(Skerrett)(Cowie) Hall Cowie(Cassidy) Betts
Farrell Clarke:
Tries - Panapa Botica Betts Farrell: Goals - Botica(4):
CASTLEFORD - St John Ellis: C.Smith Blackmore T.Smith
Middleton: Steadman Ford: Crooks(Sykes) Russell
Sampson Ketteridge(Smales) Hay(Crooks) Nikau:
Tries - Steadman Sykes Sampson: Goals - Steadman(2)
Crooks(2):
Referee S Cumming (Widnes) Att - 35644 H.T. 8 - 16
**HARRY SUNDERLAND TROPHY WINNER - SAM
PANAPA WIGAN**

**Lee Crooks lifting the Regal Trophy after the
demolition   of Wigan Warriors 33-2**

SEASON 1993-94

D.N	PLAYER		DEBUT	L MATCH	APP	SUB	T.AP	TRI'S	G'LS	D.G	P'TS
621	ENGLAND	KEITH		26/03/1994	2	13	15	0	0	0	0
636	KETTERIDGE	MARTIN			33	7	40	3	18	0	48
657	ANDERSON	GRANT			32	2	34	15	0	0	60
661	SAMPSON	DEAN			19	12	31	6	0	0	24
675	STEADMAN	GRAHAM			40	0	40	16	7	1	79
679	SMITH	TONY			23	7	30	6	0	0	24
680	ELLIS	ST JOHN		22/05/1994	41	0	41	40	4	0	168
685	CROOKS	LEE			39	0	39	2	135	1	279
687	HAY	ANDY			15	18	33	7	0	0	28
689	WRAY	JON			3	0	3	1	0	0	4
690	NELSON	DAVID		20/04/1994	4	1	5	0	0	0	0
691	FORD	MIKE			43	0	43	22	0	2	90
692	NIKAU	TAWERA			42	0	42	6	0	0	24
693	MIDDLETON	SIMON			42	0	42	21	0	0	84
694	SYKES	NATHAN			0	6	6	1	0	0	4
695	BLACKMORE	RICHARD			34	1	35	20	0	0	80
697	WATSON	CHRIS		09/01/1994	1	0	1	0	0	0	0
698	MORRISON	TONY			30	2	32	10	0	0	40
699	SMITH	CHRIS			4	2	6	3	0	0	12
703	FISHER	ANDY		19/12/1993	4	3	7	1	0	0	4
705	RUSSELL	RICHARD	27/08/1993		42	0	42	9	0	0	36
706	SMALES	IAN	27/08/1993		36	6	42	10	0	0	40
707	KEMP	TONY	03/10/1993		27	0	27	9	0	1	37
708	FLOWERS	JASON	12/10/1993		3	4	7	1	0	0	4
	24		**4**	**5**	**559**	**84**	**643**	**209**	**164**	**5**	**1169**

COMPETITION		P	W	D	L	FOR	AGT
LEAGUE D 1	POSITION 4 OF 16	30	19	1	10	787	466
RL CUP		4	3	0	1	124	44
REGAL TROPHY		5	5	0	0	170	42
CHAMPIONSHIP		3	2	0	1	72	63
NEW ZEALAND		1	1	0	0	16	4
PLAYERS RECORDS		**43**	**30**	**1**	**12**	**1169**	**619**

We commenced the season with a new Coach, John Joyner taking over from Darryl Van de Velde.

The Yorkshire Cup Competition was dropped from the fixture list from this season.

In the Regal Trophy we built on last year's good run by going one better and reaching the Final. Playing Wigan at Headingley we proved that our earlier league victory over Wigan by 46–nil was no fluke with another emphatic win of 33–2. With two tries Martin Ketteridge took the Man of the Match award, but he must have been pushed very hard for that honour by Captain Lee Crooks's try and six-goal performance. A team performance to match anything in the Club's history.

The Challenge Cup produced another good run to the semi-final stage. In that semi-final played at Headingley our opponents were again Wigan. Unfortunately we could not repeat our Regal Trophy success and lost 20-6.

The Premiership play off brought another confrontation with Wigan, this time in the Final at Old Trafford Manchester. Losing at half time by 8-16 we then staged a late fight back but eventually ran out of time losing 20-24.

St John Ellis set a new Club record for tries in a season with 40, receiving great service from his centre partner Richard Blackmore who registered 20 touchdowns.

Mike Ford also ended his first spell with the Club and joined St John Ellis and Darryl Van de Velde in Australia.

In the League promotion and relegated again reverted to 'Two Up And Two Down' which resulted in Workington Town and Doncaster being promoted to Division 1. Hull K R and Leigh being relegated to Division 2.

Sun 7 Aug 1994 SHEFFIELD EAGLES away lost 14 -17 DARRYL POWELL TESTIMONIAL FRIENDLY
CASTLEFORD - Goddard: C.Smith Blackmore T.Smith Middleton: Kemp Price: Crooks Russell Ketteridge Morrison Hay Smales: Subs used - Flowers Coventry Sykes Tonks: Tries - T.Smith(2) Kemp: Goal - Crooks: SHEFFIELD - Team and scorers not Known
Referee - Att - H.T.

Sun 21 Aug 1994 WIDNES away won 30 - 16
WIDNES - Spruce: Green Hammond Wright Hadley: Ruane D.Hulme: Ireland McCurrie Smith Halliwell(Tyrer) Hansen P.Hulme(Thorniley):
Tries - D.Hulme(2) Hammond: Goals - Hammond(2):
CASTLEFORD - Steadman: C.Smith Blackmore RICHARD GODDARD(709)(GARETH STEPHENS(710)) Middleton: Kemp T.Smith: Crooks Russell Ketteridge(Hay)Morrison Smales (Ketteridge) Nikau: Tries - Steadman Blackmore Middleton Kemp T.Smith: Goals - Crooks(5):
Referee D Atkin (Hull) Att - 4245 H.T. nil - 16

Sun 28 Aug 1994 WORKINGTON TOWN home won 26 - 14
CASTLEFORD - Steadman: C.Smith Blackmore Goddard Middleton: Kemp T.Smith: Crooks Russell Ketteridge Morrison(Hay) Smales Nikau:
Tries - C.Smith(2) Middleton(2) Kemp: Goals - Crooks(3): WORKINGTON T - Mulligan: Drummond Kay Burns Cocker: Oglanby Marwood: Schubert(Penrice) Pickering(Schubert) McKenzie(Holgate) Holgate (Armstrong) McGinty Hepi
Tries - Kay Marwood: Goals - Marwood(3):
Referee I Ollerton (Wigan) Att - 4870 H.T. 16 - 10

Sun 4 Sep 1994 HULL away won 48 - 18
HULL - O'Donnell: McKenzie G.Nolan Danby Greenwood: R.Nolan(Smirk) Hewitt: Walker Dixon Street Wilson(Sharp) Craven McNamara:
Tries - Craven(2) G.Nolan: Goals - Hewitt(3):
CASTLEFORD - Steadman: C.Smith Blackmore T.Smith Middleton: Kemp Stephens: Crooks(Goddard) Russell Ketteridge Morrison(Hay) Smales Nikau:
Tries - Kemp(3) Steadman T.Smith Middleton Hay Nikau: Goals - Ketteridge(6) Crooks(2):
Referee C Morris (Huddersfield) Att - 5371 H.T. 6 - 18

Sun 11 Sep 1994 SHEFFIELD EAGLES home won 28 -9
CASTLEFORD - Steadman: C.Smith Blackmore T.Smith Middleton: Kemp Stephens: Sampson(Sykes) (Ketteridge)(Sampson)(Goddard) Russell Ketteridge Hay Smales Nikau: Tries - Steadman(2) C.Smith Blackmore Nikau: Goals - Steadman(2) Ketteridge(2):
SHEFFIELD E - Hayes: Stott Mucoe Gamson Sodje: Briggs(Powell) Turner(Mycoe)(Briggs): Broadbent Jackson Thompson(Glancy) Hughes Carr Farrell:
Tries - Broadbent Hughes: Goal - BriggsD/G:
Referee D Campbell (Widnes) Att - 4225 H.T. 10 - 1

Sun 18 Sep 1994 ST HELENS away lost 14 - 47
ST HELENS - Prescott: Hunte Gibbs Loughlin(Veivers) Sullivan: Cooper Goulding: Neill(Dannatt) Casey Fogerty(Dannatt)(Fogerty) Pickavance Nickle Joynt:
Tries - Hunte(4) Sullivan(3) Gibbs:
Goals - Goulding(7)D/G:
CASTLEFORD - Steadman: C.Smith Blackmore T.Smith(Goddard) Middleton: Kemp Stephens: Crooks(Smales) Russell Ketteridge Morrison Hay Nikau:
Tries - Stephens Hay: Goals - Crooks(2) Ketteridge:
Referee J Connolly (Wigan) Att - 7710 H.T. 15 - 8

Fri 23 Sep 1994 WIGAN home lost 28 - 31
CASTLEFORD - Steadman: C.Smith Blackmore Goddard Wray: T.Smith Stephens(Smales): Sampson Russell(Ketteridge) Ketteridge(Sykes) Hay Nikau Kemp:
Tries - Goddard(2) T.Smith Sampson Nikau:
Goals - Ketteridge(3) Steadman:
WIGAN - Atcheson(Botica): Robinson Tuigamala (Atcheson) Connolly Offiah: Paul Edwards: O'Connor (Cassidy) Hall McDermott(O'Connor) Betts Farrell Clarke:
Tries - Paul(2) Robinson Tuigamala Offiah:
Goals - Botica(3) Farrell(2) EdwardsD/G:
Referee D Campbell (Widnes) Att - 6646 H.T. 8 - 13

Fri 30 Sep 1994 LEEDS away draw 14 - 14
LEEDS - Tait: Fallon(Mann)(Fallon) Iro Innes Cummings: Holroyd Entat(Schofield): Faimalo Lowes Mann(Mercer)(Fallon) Mercer(Fozzard) Eyres Hanley(Mann):
Tries - Cummings Hanley: Goals - Holroyd(3):
CASTLEFORD - Steadman: C.Smith Blackmore Goddard Middleton (JAMIE COVENTRY(711)): Kemp T.Smith: Sampson Russell Ketteridge(Crooks) Smales(Ketteridge) Hay Nikau: Tries - Goddard Sampson: Goals - Crooks(3):
Referee J Connolly (Wigan) Att - 12837 H.T. 4 - 6

Sun 9 Oct 1994 SALFORD home won 34 - 6
CASTLEFORD - Steadman: C.Smith Blackmore Goddard Wray: Kemp T.Smith(Coventry)(T.Smith): Crooks Russell Sampson(Sykes) Ketteridge Hay Smales(Coventry):
Tries - Steadman Blackmore T.Smith Crooks Russell Sampson: Goals - Crooks(4) Steadman:
SALFORD - Mahon: Critchley Naylor McAvoy Ford: Blakeley(Webster) Gregory: Young Lee Nicholls(Marsden) Forber Randall Panapa: Try - Randall: Goal - Mahon:
Referee R Connolly (Wigan) Att - 4016 H.T. 12 - nil

Wed 12 Oct 1994 AUSTRALIA lost 12 - 38
CASTLEFORD - Goddard: C.Smith Blackmore PHIL EDEN(712)(Terry McAllister) Wray: Kemp T.Smith: Crooks(Sykes) Russell(PAUL DARLEY(713)) Sampson(LYNTON MORRIS(714)) Ketteridge Hay Smales:
Tries - C.Smith Blackmore Eden:
AUSTRALIA - Brasher(Sailor): Ettingshausen Hill McGregor Wishart Kevin.Walters Langer (Stuart): Lazarus Serdaris Harragon Smith (Menzies) Furner(Furleigh) Florimo:

SEASON 1994-95

Tries - Wishart(2) Ettingshausen Langer McGregor
Serdaris Walters: Goals - Wishart(5):
Referee J Connolly (Wigan) Att - 11091 H.T. 4 - 22

Sun 16 Oct 1994 DONCASTER away lost 28 - 35
DONCASTER - Bloem: Manning Matautia Grobelar
(Carlyle) Evans: Neil Green: Jackson Carlyle (Ellis)
(Grobelar)(Carlyle) Lingard Miller Pennant Turner:
Tries - Bloem(3) Matautia Neil Carlyle:
Goals - Green(5) Turner(DG):
CASTLEFORD - Steadman: C.Smith Blackmore
Goddard(Coventry) Wray: Kemp T.Smith: Sampson Russell
Sykes(Eden) Ketteridge Hay Smales: Tries - Wray(2)
Steadman Sampson Russell: Goals - Ketteridge(4):
Referee S Cross (Hull) Att - 3757 H.T. 18 - 12

Sun 30 Oct 1994 BRADFORD NORTHERN home won 39 - 18
CASTLEFORD - Steadman: C.Smith Blackmore Goddard
Wray: Kemp T.Smith: Sampson Russell(Eden)
Ketteridge(Sykes) Morrison Hay Smales:
Tries - Steadman C.Smith Blackmore Kemp T.Smith
Sampson Hay: Goals - Ketteridge(3) Steadman(2)D/G:
BRADFORD N - Summers: Turpin(Heron) Fraisse Hall
Myers(Turpin): Watson Fox: Powell Medley Bourneville
(Dixon)(Bournville)(B/B) Greenwood(Dixon) McDermott
Fairbank:
Tries - Fraisse Myers Watson Medley: Goal - Fox:
Referee R Connolly (Wigan) Att - 6302 H.T. 26 - 6

Sun 6 Nov 1994 WIDNES home won 26 - 6
CASTLEFORD - Steadman: C.Smith Blackmore Goddard
Wray(Middleton): Kemp T.Smith: Crooks Russell Sampson
Ketteridge Hay(Eden) Smales:
Tries - Eden(2) Blackmore: Goals - Crooks(7):
WIDNES - Spruce: Green Hammond Wright P.Smith:
Ruane P.Hulme: Makin(Barrowe) D.Smith Hansen Collier
Koloto(Kelly) McCurrie: Try - Spruce: Goal - Hammond:
Referee I Ollertron (Wigan) Att - 4174 H.T. 16 - 2

Sun 13 Nov 1994 WORKINGTON TOWN away draw 4 - 4
WORKINGTON T - Mulligan: Drummond Burns Fawcett
Cocker: Ellis Marwood: Pickering(Phillips) McKenzie
(Phillips) Phillips(Williams)(Pickering)(Phillips)(McKenzie)
Armstrong Holgate Hepi: Goals - Marwood(2):
CASTLEFORD - J.Flowers: C.Smith Blackmore Goddard
Wray(Middleton)(Eden): Kemp T.Smith: Crooks Russell
Sampson Ketteridge(Wray) Smales Nikau:
Goals - Crooks(2):
Referee S Cross (Hull) Att - 3285 H.T. 4 - nil

Sun 27 Nov 1994 HULL home won 52 - 10
CASTLEFORD - Steadman: C.Smith Blackmore Middleton
Wray: Kemp(J.Flowers) T.Smith: Crooks Russell Sykes(IAN
TONKS(715)) Sampson Smales Nikau:
Tries - Steadman(2) T.Smith(2) C.Smith Wray Kemp
Sampson: Goals - Crooks(10):
HULL - Stevens: Vaikona Nolan David(Smirk) Sterling:
Endacott Hewitt: Street Richardson McNamara

Wilson(Jackson) Rose Busby:
Tries - Endacott Hewitt: Goal - Hewitt:
Referee S Cummings (Widnes) Att - 4686 H.T. 28 - 6

Sat 3 Dec 1994 HALIFAX home won 32 - 26
REGAL TROPHY ROUND 2
CASTLEFORD - Steadman: C.Smith Blackmore Goddard
Middleton: Kemp T.Smith: Crooks Russell Sampson Hay
Smales(Sykes) Nikau: Tries - C.Smith(2) Blackmore(2)
Kemp Sampson: Goals - Crooks(4):
HALIFAX - Martindale: Bentley Schuster R.Smith
(Fieldhouse) Preston: Hagan Parker (R.Smith): Harrison
R.Southernwood(Rowley) Fieldhouse(Burton) Moriarty
Baldwin Divorty:
Tries - Bentley(2) Moriarty(2):   Goals - Schuster(5):
Referee D Campbell (Widnes) Att - 4680 H.T. 16 - 14

Fri 9 Dec 1994 SHEFFIELD EAGLES away won 27 - 16
SHEFFIELD E - Gamson: Stott Senior Mycoe Sodje: Powell
Price: Broadbent Jackson Glancy(Thompson) Carr Hughes
(Turner) Farrell: Tries -Mycoe Powell Carr: Goals -Stott(2):
CASTLEFORD - Steadman: C.Smith Blackmore Goddard
Middleton: Kemp T.Smith: Crooks Russell(J.Flowers)
Sampson Hay Smales(Sykes) Nikau:
Tries - Blackmore(2) Goddard Middleton T.Smith:
Goals - Crooks(3) SteadmanD/G:
Referee J Connolly (Wigan) Att - 2570 H.T. 20 - 10

Tue 20 Dec 1994 DEWSBURY away won 30 - 2
REGAL TROPHY ROUND 3
DEWSBURY - Graham: Cornforth Marchant Agar Rombo:
Delaney Longo: McElvie(Bonson) Bates Bonson(Worthy)
Fisher Williams(Palmer) Holliday: Goal - Agar:
CASTLEFORD - Steadman: Coventry Blackmore Goddard
Middleton: Kemp T.Smith: Crooks Russell(Sykes) Sampson
Hay Smales((Morrison) Nikau: Tries - Blackmore Goddard
Middleton Kemp T.Smith: Goals - Crooks(3) Steadman(2):
Referee I Ollerton (Wigan) Att - 3850 H.T. 8 - 2

Mon 26 Dec 1994 FEATHERSTONE ROVERS home won 32 - 16
CASTLEFORD - Steadman(J.Flowers): C.Smith Blackmore
Middleton Wray: Kemp T.Smith: Crooks(Sykes) Russell
Sampson Morrison Hay Nikau: Tries - Middleton(2)
Steadman Flowers Wray Kemp: Goals - Crooks(4):
FEATHERSTONE R - Wilson: Butt Gibson Calland Banquet:
Nixon(Simms) Aston: Molloy Gunn(G.S.Price) Casey
Roebuck G.H.Price Tuuta:
Tries - G.S.Price(2) Molloy: Goals - Aston(2):
Referee S Cummings (Widnes) Att - 8862 H.T. 16 - 2

Sat 7 Jan 1995 LEEDS away won 34 - 14
REGAL TROPHY QUARTER FINAL
LEEDS - Tait: Fallon Iro Innes Cummings:
Schofield(Howard) Holroyd: Howard(Mann)Lowes
Faimalo(Harmon) Mercer Eyres Hanley:
Tries - Hanley(2):   Goals - Holroyd(3):
CASTLEFORD - J.Flowers: C.Smith Blackmore Middleton
Wray: Kemp T.Smith: Crooks(Sykes) Russell Sampson
Morrison Hay(Ketteridge) Nikau:

Tries - T.Smith(2) Middleton Sampson Morrison:
Goals - Crooks(5) Ketteridge(2):
Referee S Cummings (Widnes) Att - 10500 H.T. 8 - 14

Sun 15 Jan 1995 WIGAN away lost 6 - 34
REGAL TROPHY SEMI FINAL
WIGAN - Paul: Robinson Tuigamala(O'Connor) Connolly
Offiah: Botica Edwards(Atcheson): O'Connor(Cassidy) Hall
Cowie Betts Farrell Clarke:
Tries - Offiah(3) Robinson Hall: Goals - Botica(7):
CASTLEFORD - J.Flowers: C.Smith Blackmore Middleton
Wray: Kemp T.Smith: Crooks(Sykes) Russell Sampson
Morrison(Ketteridge)(Hay) Hay(Ketteridge) Nikau:
Try - Kemp: Goal - Crooks:
Referee S Cummings (Widnes) Att - 13006 H.T. 6 -14

Wed 18 Jan 1995 WARRINGTON away lost 24 - 25
WARRINGTON - Davies: Forster Harris Roper
Lee(Bennett): Shelford Mackey: McGuire Barlow
Elliott(Wainwright) Sanderson Cullen Darbyshire:
Tries - Davies Roper Cullen: Goals - Davies(5) (3D/G):
CASTLEFORD - J.Flowers: C.Smith Blackmore Goddard
Middleton: Kemp T.Smith: Sampson Russell(Wray)
Sykes(Morrison) Ketteridge Hay Nikau:
Tries - C.Smith(2) Middleton Nikau: Goals - Ketteridge(4):
Referee J Connolly (Wigan) Att - 4551 H.T. 6 - 16

Sun 25 Jan 1995 HALIFAX away lost 24 - 30
HALIFAX - Dean: Bentley Schuster Gillespie Preston:
Hagan Parker: Harrison Southernwood (Rowley)
Fieldhouse(Jackson) Moriarty (Fieldhouse) Baldwin
Divorty(Southernwood): Tries - Preston(2) Schuster
Gillespie Moriarty Divorty: Goals - Schuster(3):
CASTLEFORD - J.Flowers: C.Smith Blackmore Middleton
Wray: Kemp T.Smith: Crooks (Ketteridge) Russell
(Stephens) Sampson(S/O) Morrison Hay Nikau: Tries -
C.Smith Blackmore Kemp Sampson: Goals - Crooks(4):
Referee D Campbell (Widnes) Att - 6018 H.T. 14 - 24

Sun 29 Jan 1995 ST HELENS home won 18 - 16
CASTLEFORD - J.Flowers: C.Smith Blackmore Middleton
Wray: Kemp T.Smith: Crooks Russell Ketteridge(CRAIG
PALMER(716)) Morrison Hay Nikau:
Tries - C.Smith Middleton: Goals - Crooks(5):
ST HELENS - Lyon: Booth Nothey Elia Sullivan: Veivers
Griffiths (Morley): Fogerty Cunningham Pickavance Joynt
Nickle Cooper:
Tries - Veivers(2) Northey : Goals - Sullivan(2):
Referee A Bates (Workington) Att - 5329 H.T. 14 - 6

Sun 5 Feb 1995 WIGAN away lost 6 - 46
WIGAN - Paul: Robinson Tuigamala Connolly Offiah:
Botica Edwards: McDermott(Skerrett)(Atcheson) Hall
Cowie Haughton Cassidy Clarke: Tries - Offiah(3)
Connolly(2) Robinson Cowie: Goals - Botica(9):
CASTLEFORD - J.Flowers: C.Smith Blackmore Middleton
Wray: Kemp Stephens: Crooks SIMON PRICE(717)
Ketteridge(Sykes) Morrison(Coventry) Hay Nikau:
Try - Hay: Goal - Crooks:
Referee D Cambell (Widnes) Att - 14515 H.T. 14 - 6

Sun 12 Feb 1995 WARRINGTON away lost 2 - 17
CHALLENGE CUP ROUND 4
WARRINGTON - Penny: Forster Bateman Davies Harris:
Shelford Mackey: Tees (Bennett) Barlow McGuire(Hilton)
Sanderson Cullen(McGuire)Darbyshire:
Tries - Forster Barlow McGuire: Goals - Davies(2) D/G:
CASTLEFORD - Steadman: C.Smith Blackmore
Middleton(B/B)(Goddard)(Middleton) Jon Wray:
Kemp(Martin Ketteridge) T.Smith: Crooks Darley
Sykes(Goddard) Morrison Hay Nikau: Goal - Crooks:
Referee C Morris (Huddersfield) Att - 5500 H.T. nil - 6

Fri 17 Feb 1995 LEEDS home lost 16 - 22
CASTLEFORD - J.Flowers: C.Smith Blackmore Goddard
Middleton: Steadman(Coventry) T.Smith: Crooks Darley
Sampson Morrison Hay(Sykes) Nikau:
Tries - T.Smith Hay: Goals - Crooks(4):
LEEDS - Tait: Fallon Iro Innes Cummins: Schofield Holroyd:
Harmon(Leatham) Lowes Faimalo
(Vassilakopoulos) Mercer Mann Hanley:
Tries - Tait Cummins Mann Hanley: Goals - Holroyd(3):
Referee C Morris (Huddersfield) Att - 6426 H.T. 8 - 12

Sun 26 Feb 1995 WAKEFIELD TRINITY away
won 36 - 25
WAKEFIELD T - Spencer: Nelson Powell Flynn Child:
Wright Whittaker: Marlow(Thompson) Conway
Thompson(Sheals) Bell Slater(Hanlan) Forshaw: Tries -
Powell Flynn Child Whittaker: Goals - Wright(4)D/G:
CASTLEFORD - Steadman: C.Smith Blackmore Goddard
Middleton: Kemp T.Smith: Crooks(Sykes) Russell
(J.Flowers) Sampson Morrison Sykes(STUART FLOWERS
(718) Nikau: Tries - Blackmore(2) Goddard Middleton
Kemp S.Flowers Nikau: Goals - Crooks(3) Steadman:
Referee S Cross (Hull) Att - 4463 H.T. 19 - 16

Sun 12 Mar 1995 SALFORD away won 48 - 16
SALFORD - Wilson: Critchley Naylor Birkett(Randall) Ford:
Quigley Watson: Young Marshall Eccles(Webster)
Marsden(Birkett) Webster(Blease) Panapa:
Tries - Naylor Ford Marsden Webster:
CASTLEFORD - Steadman: C.Smith Blackmore
Goddard(J.Flowers) Middleton: Kemp T.Smith:
Crooks(S.Flowers) Russell Sampson Morrison Hay Nikau:
Tries - C.Smith(2) Blackmore(2) Hay(2) Steadman
Middleton: Goals - Crooks(7) Kemp:
Referee D Campbell (St Helens) Att - 2950 H.T. 8 - 14

Wed 15 Mar 1995 OLDHAM home won 34 - 14
CASTLEFORD - Steadman: C.Smith Blackmore Goddard
Middleton: Kemp T.Smith: Crooks(Sykes) Russell(LEE
HARLAND(719)) Sampson Morrison Hay Nikau:
Tries - Steadman Blackmore Kemp Sampson Morrison:
Goals - Crooks(6) Steadman:
OLDHAM - Gibson: Belle Topping Abram(Neal) Ransom:
Marsh Crompton: Sherrett(Davidson) Stephenson Temu
Davidson(Lord) Faimalo Kuiti:
Tries - Gibson Marsh: Goals - Marsh(3):
Referee D Asquith (York) Att - 3373 H.T. 16 - 8

SEASON 1994-95

Sun 19 Mar 1995 HALIFAX home won 16 - 13
CASTLEFORD - Steadman: C.Smith Blackmore Goddard
Middleton: Kemp T.Smith: Crooks(Sykes) Russell
Sampson(Crooks) Morrison(Harland) Hay Nikau:
Tries - Kemp Sampson Morrison: Goals - Crooks(2):
HALIFAX - Dean: Bentley Schuster Hallas(Turner) Preston:
Hagan Parker: Ketteridge(Tiffany)(Ketteridge) Rowley
Divorty Moriarty Jackson Baldwin:
Tries - Bentley Jackson: Goals - Schuster(2)D/G:
Referee C Morris (Huddersfield) Att - 5715 H.T. 10 - 10

Fri 31 Mar 1995 WARRINGTON home lost 24 - 37
CASTLEFORD - Steadman(J.Flowers): C.Smith Blackmore
Goddard Middleton: Kemp T.Smith: Crooks Russell
Sampson Morrison(Sykes) Hay Nikau: Tries - Flowers
Middleton T.Smith Morrison: Goals - Crooks(4):
WARRINGTON - Penny: Forster Bateman Davies Roper:
Harris Shelford: Hilton Barlow Tees(Elliott) Sanderson
McGuire(S/O) Wainwright: Tries - Barlow(2) Bateman
Davies Harris Wainwright: Goals - Davies(6)D/G:
Referee C Morris (Huddersfield) Att - 3404 H.T. 14 - 20

Sun 9 Apr 1995 DONCASTER home won 25 - 18
CASTLEFORD - J.Flowers: C.Smith Blackmore Middleton
Coventry: Kemp T.Smith: Crooks Darley Sampson
Morrison(Goddard) Hay(Harland) Nikau:
Tries - T.Smith(4):   Goals - Crooks(4) KempD/G:
DONCASTER - Hayes: Foster Manning Rothwell
Roache(Carlyle): Zelei Eaton: Tuffs Maskill Lingard
Whakarau Pennant(Barrow) Miller:
Tries - Hayes Manning Pennant: Goals - Eaton(3):
Referee P Lee (Tyldesley) Att - 3515 H.T. 14 - 6

**Fri 14 Apr 1995 FEATHERSTONE ROVERS away
won 27 - 6**
FEATHERSTONE R - Gibson: Butt Rodger Calland
Simpson: Tuuta Aston (Gunn): Molloy Southernwood
Casey(Simms) Divet Price Roebuck:
Try - Calland: Goal - Aston:
CASTLEFORD - J.Flowers: C.Smith Blackmore Goddard
Middleton: Kemp(Coventry) T.Smith: Crooks(Morrison)
Russell Sampson(Crooks) Harland Hay Nikau:
Tries - Goddard Kemp Crooks Harland:
Goals - Crooks(4) Middleton KempD/G:
Referee A Bates (Workington) Att - 5033 H.T. 12 - 2

**Sun 17 Apr 1995 WAKEFIELD TRINITY home
won 86 - nil**
CASTLEFORD - J.Flowers: C.Smith Blackmore Goddard
Middleton: Kemp (Russell) T.Smith: Sampson(Morrison)
Russell(Steadman) Sykes Harland Hay(Sampson) Nikau:
Tries - Blackmore(3) C.Smith(2) Middleton(2) Kemp(2)
T.Smith(2)Hay(2) Goddard Steadman Harland Nikau:
Goals - Steadman(6) Kemp(3)
WAKEFIELD T - Spencer: Child Powell Mosley(Hirst)
Knighton: McGowan Flynn: Marlow Conway(Thompson)
Sheals Webster Hicks Bell:
Referee R Connolly (Wigan) Att - 4443 H.T. 30 - nil

Wed 20 Apr 1995 OLDHAM away won 18 - 10
OLDHAM - Ransome(Lord): Jones(Neal) Topping Abrams
Belle: Gartland Burns: Richardson(Kuiti) Stephenson Temu
Lord (Richardson)(B/B) Faimalo Bradbury:
Try - Temu: Goals - Topping(3):
CASTLEFORD - J.Flowers: C.Smith Blackmore Goddard
Middleton: Kemp T.Smith: Crooks Russell(Sykes) Sampson
Harland(Morrison) Hay Nikau:
Tries - C.Smith Morrison Hay: Goals - Crooks(3):
Referee D Campbell (Widnes) Att - 2840 H.T. 12 - 10

**Sun 23 Apr 1995 BRADFORD NORTHERN away
won 40 - 26**
BRADFORD N - Paul: Simpson Hall(Clegg) Newlove
Christie: Summers Fox: Powell Clark Clegg (Greenwood)
(Bournville) Bournville(Medley) Fairbank McDermott:
Tries - Summers(2) Medley(2) Simpson: Goals - Fox(3):
CASTLEFORD - J.Flowers: C.Smith Blackmore Goddard
Middleton: Kemp(Steadman) T.Smith: Crooks(Sykes)
Darley Sampson(Crooks) Morrison(Kemp) Hay Nikau:
Tries - Blackmore(2) T.Smith(2) Nikau(2) Goddard
Steadman: Goals - Crooks(4):
Referee D Campbell (Widnes) Att - 6048 H.T. 10 - 24

**Sun 7 May 1995 WARRINGTON home lost 22 - 30
PREMIERSHIP ROUND 1**
CASTLEFORD - J.Flowers: C.Smith <u>Richard Blackmore</u>
Goddard Middleton: <u>Tony Kemp(S/O)</u> T.Smith: Crooks
Darley Sampson <u>Tony Morrison</u>(Sykes)(Steadman) <u>Andy
Hay</u> Nikau: Tries - Blackmore(2) Goddard Middleton
T.Smith: Goal - Crooks:
WARRINGTON - Penny: Forster Bateman(Sculthorpe)
Davies Rudd: Shelford Harris: Hilton(Tees) Thursfield
Tees(Wainwright) Sanderson McGuire Elliott:
Tries - Bateman Sculthorpe Shelford McGuire:
Goals - Davies(6) (2D/G):
Referee C Morris (Huddersfield) Att - 5462 H.T. 10 - 18

Richard Goddard
D. No 709
1994-95 to 1997

Ian Tonks
D. No 715
1994-95 to 2001

Lee Harland
D. No 719
1994-95 to 2004

SEASON 1994-95

D.N	PLAYER		DEBUT	L MATCH	APP	SUB	T.AP	TRI'S	G'LS	D.G	P'TS
636	KETTERIDGE	MARTIN		12/02/1995	16	4	20	0	25	0	50
661	SAMPSON	DEAN			30	0	30	11	0	0	44
673	McALLISTER	TERRY		12/10/1994	0	1	1	0	0	0	0
675	STEADMAN	GRAHAM			23	3	26	14	16	2	90
679	SMITH	TONY			36	0	36	22	0	0	88
685	CROOKS	LEE			30	1	31	2	111	0	230
687	HAY	ANDY		07/05/1995	31	3	34	10	0	0	40
689	WRAY	JON		12/02/1995	15	1	16	4	0	0	16
692	NIKAU	TAWERA			32	0	32	8	0	0	32
693	MIDDLETON	SIMON			30	2	32	17	1	0	70
694	SYKES	NATHAN			6	19	25	0	0	0	0
695	BLACKMORE	RICHARD		07/05/1995	37	0	37	24	0	0	96
698	MORRISON	TONY		07/05/1995	21	5	26	5	0	0	20
699	SMITH	CHRIS			36	0	36	17	0	0	68
705	RUSSELL	RICHARD			31	0	31	2	0	0	8
706	SMALES	IAN			15	2	17	0	0	0	0
707	KEMP	TONY		07/05/1995	36	0	36	18	4	2	82
708	FLOWERS	JASON			14	6	20	2	0	0	8
709	GODDARD	RICHARD	21/08/1994		25	5	30	10	0	0	40
710	STEPHENS	GARETH	21/08/1994		5	2	7	1	0	0	4
711	COVENTRY	JAMIE	30/09/1994		2	6	8	0	0	0	0
712	EDEN	PHIL	12/10/1994		1	4	5	3	0	0	12
713	DARLEY	PAUL	12/10/1994		5	1	6	0	0	0	0
714	MORRIS	LYNTON	12/10/1994	12/10/1994	0	1	1	0	0	0	0
715	TONKS	IAN	27/11/1994		0	1	1	0	0	0	0
716	PALMER	CRAIG	29/01/1995		0	1	1	0	0	0	0
717	PRICE	SIMON	05/02/1995		1	0	1	0	0	0	0
718	FLOWERS	STUART	26/02/1995		0	2	2	1	0	0	4
719	HARLAND	LEE	15/03/1995		3	3	6	2	0	0	8
	29		11	8	481	73	554	173	157	4	1010

COMPETITION		P	W	D	L	FOR	AGT
LEAGUE D 1	POSITION 3 OF 16	30	20	2	8	872	564
RL CUP		1	0	0	1	2	17
REGAL TROPHY		4	3	0	1	102	76
CHAMPIONSHIP		1	0	0	1	22	30
AUSTRALIA		1	0	0	1	12	38
PLAYERS RECORDS		**37**	**23**	**2**	**12**	**1010**	**725**

In the Regal Trophy we made a determined effort to defend our title. We reached the semi-final where our opponents were last season's beaten finalists Wigan, but we failed to repeat our previous success losing 6-34

Graham Steadman scored his 100th try for the Club in 39-18 home victory over Bradford Bulls on 30 October 1994.

Lee Crooks, with 10 goals in the 52-10 home victory over Hull on 27 November 1994, notched up his 1,000th point for the club.

SEASON 1995-96

STONES BITTER LEAGUE CENTENARY CHAMPIONSHIP

This season the 'Stones Bitter Centenary Championship' was the last season of 'Winter Rugby' in preparation for Sky sponsored Super League. Therefore although Hull and Doncaster finished the bottom two teams in Division 1 and Keighley Cougars and Batley finished the top two teams in Division 2 promotion and relegation was not carried out.

Thu 10 Aug 1995 SHEFFIELD EAGLES home lost 24 – 32 FRIENDLY
CASTLEFORD - J.Flowers: C.Smith Coventry Flynn Middleton: T.Smith Stephens: Crooks Darley Palmer Sykes Tonks Smales: Subs used - Price Marchant Maskill Hill: Tries - Flynn Crooks Sykes Maskill:
Goals - Crooks(2) Maskill(2)
SHEFFIELD E - Team and Scorers not Known
Referee   Att -   H.T.

Sun 20 Aug 1995 OLDHAM home won 28 - 22
CASTLEFORD - J.Flowers: C.Smith Coventry ADRIAN FLYNN(720)(ANDY HILL(721)) Middleton: T.Smith Stephens: Crooks COLIN MASKILL(722) Palmer(Darley) Sykes Tonks(Marchant) Smales: Tries - T.Smith(2) Flowers Middleton: Goals - Crooks(4) Darley(2):
OLDHAM - Gibson: Ranson(Neal) Topping Abram Myler: Maloney Crompton: Sherratt Clarke((Hill) Parr(Richards) Lord Faimalo(Geldart) Green: Tries - Ranson Abram Crompton Lord: Goals - Maloney(3):
Referee K Kirkpatrick (War'gton) Att - 4341 H.T. 2 - 16

Fri 25 Aug 1995 LEEDS home won 22 - 18
CASTLEFORD - J.Flowers: C.Smith Marchant Coventry Middleton: T.Smith Stephens: Crooks Maskill Sykes(Craig Palmer) Harland Hill(Eden) Smales:
Tries - Flowers(2) Maskill(2) Middleton: Goals - Crooks:
LEEDS - Tait: Fallon Iro Innes(Cook) Cummins: Kemp Gibbons: Harmon (Morley) Lowes Fozzard(B/B) (Faimalo) (Fozzard)(Harmon) Mercer(Schofield) Mann Forshaw:
Tries - Iro Kemp Forshaw: Goals - Cummins(3):
Referee S Cummings (Widnes) Att - 5695 H.T. 10 - 18

Sun 3 Sep 1995 SHEFFIELD EAGLES away lost 26 -36
SHEFFIELD E - Banquet: Sodje Price D.Hughes Picksley: Sheridan Turner (Lyon): Broadbent Jackson(Lawless) Glancy(Whakaru) Hay(Lawford) I.Hughes Carr:
Tries - Price(2) Sodje D.Hughes Jackson I.Hughes Carr:
Goals - Banquet(4):
CASTLEFORD - J.Flowers: C.Smith Marchant Flynn Middleton: Coventry(T.Smith) Stephens: Crooks Maskill Sykes Harland Hill(Eden) Smales(S.Flowers):
Tries - Coventry(2) J.Flowers Sykes: Goals - Crooks(5):
Referee C Morris (Hud'field) Att - Est 4000 H.T. 8 - 26

Wed 6 Sep 1995 WORKINGTON TOWN home won 32 - 24
CASTLEFORD – J.Flowers: C.Smith Coventry Flynn Marchant: T.Smith Stephens: Crooks Maskill Sykes Harland(Hill) S.Flowers (ANDREW SCHICK(723)) Smales: Tries - C.Smith(2) Coventry Marchant Maskill:
Goals - Crooks(5) Maskill:
WORKINGTON T - Livett: Pape Burns Fraisse Johnson: Kitchen Marwood: Schubert(Fawcett) Gorley Phillips(McGurk) Armstrong McGinty Holgate (Penrice)
Tries - Livett Johnson Gorley Holgate:
Goals - Marwood(4):
Referee R Connolly (Wigan) Att - 3287 H.T. 16 - 6

Wed 13 Sep 1995 WIGAN away lost 8 - 40
WIGAN - Radlinski(Mather): Robinson Tuigamala(Craig) Connolly Offiah: Paul Edwards: Skerrett(Johnson) Hall(Dermott) Cowie Haughton Cassidy Farrell:
Tries - Mather Tuigamala Offiah Paul Edwards Cassidy:
Goals - Farrell(8):
CASTLEFORD - J.Flowers: C.Smith Marchant(Coventry) Flynn Middleton: T.Smith(Marchant) Stephens: Crooks(Sykes) Maskill Sampson(Eden)Harland(S.Flowers) Schick Smales: Try - Harland: Goals - Crooks Maskill:
Referee S Cummings (Widnes) Att - 12461 H.T. 6 - 16

Sun 17 Sep 1995 ST HELENS away lost 18 - 35
ST HELENS - Prescott(Arnold): Hayes Hammond Loughlin Sullivan: Waring Goulding(Northey): Pickavance(Matautia) Cunningham Dwyer(Perelini) Joynt Nickle Busby:
Tries - Joynt(2) Hammond Loughlin Sullivan Perelini:
Goals - Prescott(4) Goulding HammondD/G:
CASTLEFORD - J.Flowers: C.Smith Marchant Flynn Middleton: Steadman Stephens: Crooks(Sykes) Maskill(Smales) Sampson Schick(Harland)BRENDON TUUTA(724) Nikau: Tries - Flowers Steadman Nikau:
Goals – Crooks(2) Steadman:
Referee R Connolly (Wigan) Att - 7400 H.T. 6 - 24

Sun 24 Sep 1995 WARRINGTON home won 34 - 25
CASTLEFORD - J.Flowers: C.Smith Middleton(Steadman) Flynn Marchant: T.Smith Stephens: Sampson (Crooks) (Sampson) Maskill Sykes(Schick) Harland Tuuta Nikau:
Tries - Marchant(2) Steadman Flynn T.Smith Maskill Harland: Goals - Steadman(2) Maskill:
WARRINGTON - Penny: Forster G.Davies J.Davies Lee: Harris Mackey: Hilton(Chambers)(B/B)(Hilton) Hough Sumner(Chambers) Bennett McGuire(Kettlewell) Sculthorpe: Tries - Sculthorpe(2) J.Davies:
Goals – J Davies(5)D/G Mackey(2D/G):
Referee D Campbell (Widnes) Att - 4346 H.T. 18 - 20

Fri 29 Sep 1995 HALIFAX away lost 10 - 19
HALIFAX - Umaga: Bentley Amone Highton Ekoku: Briggs Parker: Harrison Southernwood Fieldhouse(Ketteridge) Moriarty(Perrett) Gillespie Baldwin(Dean):   Tries - Parker Harrison Gillespie: Goals - Umaga(3) BriggsD/G:
CASTLEFORD - J.Flowers: C.Smith Steadman Goddard Tony Marchant: T.Smith Stephens: Sampson Darley Sykes(Schick) Harland(Smales) Tuuta Nikau:
Try - C.Smith: Goals - Goddard(3):
Referee A Bates (Workington) Att - 3981 H.T. 4 - 19

SEASON 1995-96

Wed 1 Nov 1995 BRADFORD BULLS away won 18 - 12
BRADFORD B - Ellis: Christie Hall Hassan Scales(Turpin):
Paul Fox: Bournville(Boothroyd) Donahue Fairbank Knox
McDermott(Boothroyd)(Powell) Wilson(Medley):
Tries - Paul(2): Goals - Fox(2):
CASTLEFORD - Steadman: C.Smith Goddard J.Flowers
Middleton: T.Smith Stephens: Sampson Darley
Sykes(Tuuta) Harland Schick(Smales)Nikau:
Tries - Goddard T.Smith Nikau: Goals - Goddard(3):
Referee J Connolly (Wigan) Att - 5006 H.T. 18 - 4

Sun 5 Nov 1995 LONDON BRONCOS home lost 8 - 37
CASTLEFORD - Steadman: C.Smith Goddard Flynn
Middleton: T.Smith Stephens(Coventry): Sampson(B/B)
(Harland) Darley Sykes(Smales) Tuuta Smales(Schick)
Nikau(Harland): Tries - Middleton Coventry:
LONDON B - Hauff: Riley McKenna Green
Cochrane(Roskell): Walker(Stevens) Dynevor: Mestrov
O'Donnell(Langer) Shaw Bawden Gill(Pitt)Matterson:
Tries - Dynevor(3) Riley McKenna Green Matterson:
Goals - Matterson(3) Dynevor Walker(DG):
Referee K Kirkpatrick (War'gton) Att - 4099 H.T. 4 - 19

Sun 12 Nov 1995 CARLISLE RAIDERS away
lost 18 – 19 REGAL TROPHY ROUND 2
CARLISLE R - Richardson: Ruddy Thurlow Lynch Manning:
Day(Brierley) Kavanagh: Brierley(Armstrong) Russell Rudd
(Williams) Rhodes Graham Manihera: Tries - Ruddy
Williams Rhodes: Goals - Richardson(3) KavanaghD/G:
CASTLEFORD - Steadman: C.Smith J.Flowers Flynn
Middleton: Coventry Stephens: Sampson Maskill Sykes
Harland(S.Flowers) Tuuta(Schick) Nikau:
Tries - C.Smith J.Flowers Nikau: Goals - Maskill(3):
Referee D Asquith (York) Att - 850 H.T. 10 - 18

Wed 15 Nov 1995 WIGAN home lost 20 - 42
CASTLEFORD – J Flowers: C.Smith Middleton Flynn
Marchant(Goddard): Steadman T.Smith: Crooks(Sykes)
Maskill Sampson Harland S.Flowers (Schick) Nikau:
Tries - Steadman(2) Flynn Maskill:
Goals - Steadman Maskill:
WIGAN - Radlinski: Craig(Cardiss) Tuigamala Connolly
Offiah(Murdock): Paul Edwards: Skerrett Hall O'Connor
(Barrow) Quinnell(Knowles) Cassidy Johnson:
Tries - Paul(3) Cardiss Tuigamala Edwards Hall O'Connor:
Goals - Paul(5):
Referee S Cummings (Widnes) Att - 5657 H.T. nil - 22

Sun 19 Nov 1995 OLDHAM away lost 20 - 25
OLDHAM - Atcheson(Myler): Ranson Topping Abram
Gibson: Gartland Crompton: Sherratt(Faimalo) Green
Temu Lord Davidson Hill(McKinney): Tries - Topping
Abram Gibson McKinney: Goals - Gartland(4)(DG):
CASTLEFORD - J.Flowers: C.Smith Goddard Flynn
Middleton: Steadman(Coventry) T.Smith: Crooks Maskill
Sampson Harland Schick(S.Flowers) Nikau:
Tries - Flynn Middleton T.Smith: Goals - Crooks(4):
Referee R Connolly (Wigan) Att - 2620 H.T. 18 - 12

Wed 29 Nov 1995 WORKINGTON TOWN away
won 22 - 16
WORKINGTON T - Livett: Fraisse Burns(Pape) Fawcett
(Penrice) Johnson: Campbell Kitchen: Schubert(Filipo)
Marwood Phillips McGinty Holgate (Armstrong) Palmado:
Tries - Fraisse Burns: Goals - Marwood(4):
CASTLEFORD - J Flowers: C.Smith Goddard Flynn
Middleton(Coventry): Steadman T.Smith: Crooks(Sykes)
Maskill Sampson(Phil Eden) Harland Schick Nikau:
Tries - J.Flowers Goddard Flynn Maskill: Goals - Crooks(3):
Referee K Kirkpatrick (Warr'ton) Att - 2157 H.T. 2 - 6

Fri 15 Dec 1995 WARRINGTON away lost - 20 - 31
WARRINGTON - Penny: Eckersley Rudd Currier
Thompson: Harris Ford(Mackey): Jones(Hilton) Hough
(Bennett)King Cullen Knott(Barrow) Sculthorpe:
Tries - Penny(2) Eckersley Ford Cullen Knott:
Goals - Harris(3) FordD/G:
CASTLEFORD - J.Flowers: C.Smith Goddard(Stephens)
Flynn Coventry: Steadman T.Smith: Crooks
Maskill(S.Flowers) Sampson(Smales) Harland(Sykes)
Schick Nikau:
Tries - C.Smith Flynn Schick: Goals - Crooks(4):
Referee J Connolly (Wigan) Att - 2229 H.T. 20 - 10

Wed 20 Dec 1995 ST HELENS home won 26 - 18
CASTLEFORD - Steadman: C.Smith Goddard(Smales)
Flynn Coventry (J.Flowers): T.Smith Stephens: Crooks
Darley(S.Flowers) Sykes (Sampson) Harland Schick Nikau:
Tries - T.Smith(2) Steadman C.Smith Goddard:
Goals - Crooks(3):
ST HELENS - Arnold: Booth Gibbs Newlove(Leatham)
Sullivan(Haigh): Hammond Waring(Veivers): Fogerty
Cunningham Pickavance Perelini Busby Northey
(Matautia):
Tries - Leatham Haigh Veivers Matautia: Goal - Arnold:
Referee J Connolly (Wigan) Att - 3567 H.T. 18 - nil

Tue 26 Dec 1995 LEEDS away lost 16 - 28
LEEDS - Gibbons: Fallon Cummings Hall Golden:
Mann(Field) Kemp(Shaw): Harmon Lowes McDermott
(Howard) Morley Field(Schofield) Forshaw: Tries -
Golden(2) Fallon Cummins Hall: Goals - Cummins(4):
CASTLEFORD - Steadman: C.Smith Goddard Flynn
Coventry: T.Smith Stephens: Crooks(Sampson)
Darley(Maskill) Sykes Harland Schick (Smales) Nikau:
Tries - Flynn Coventry Harland: Goals - Steadman Crooks:
Referee C Morris (Huddersfield) Att - 18000 H.T. 10 - 8

Mon 1 Jan 1996 SHEFFIELD EAGLES home lost 12 -42
CASTLEFORD - Steadman: C.Smith Flynn Goddard
Coventry: T.Smith Stephens: Crooks Paul Darley
Sykes(Sampson) Harland(Smales) Schick (S.Flowers)
Nikau: Tries - Steadman(2): Goals - Crooks(2):
SHEFFIELD E - Gamson(Sovatabua): Dakuitoga Stott(Price)
Garcia Sodje: Mycoe Sheridan: Broadbent Lawless
McAllister(Dixon) Hay Hughes(Carr) Cook:
Tries - Sodje(2) Lawless(2) Stott Garcia McAllister Hay:
Goals - Mycoe(5):
Referee K Kirkpatrick (War'ton) Att - 3472 H.T. nil - 20

SEASON 1995-96

Sun 7 Jan 1996 HALIFAX home draw 26 - 26

CASTLEFORD - Steadman: DAVID FURNESS(725) Flynn Goddard Coventry: T.Smith Price: Crooks(Tuuta) Maskill Sykes Smales S.Flowers(SHAUN RICHARDSON(726)) Nikau: Tries - Flynn(2) Furness Smales:
Goals - Crooks(3) Goddard(2):
HALIFAX - Umaga(Gillespie): Tuilagi Moana Ellis Munro: Chester Dean(Briggs): W.Jackson(Anderson) Rowley Ketteridge Amone M.Jackson Perrett:
Tries - Gillespie Munro Chester Amone Perrett:
Goals - Umaga Ketteridge Amone:
Referee R Connolly (Wigan) Att - 3478 H.T. 16 - 10

Fri 12 Jan 1996 BRADFORD BULLS home won 32 - 26

CASTLEFORD - Steadman: Furness Flynn Goddard Coventry: T.Smith Price: Sampson Maskill(Tuuta) Sykes Smales(Richardson) S.Flowers(Schick) Nikau: Tries - Flynn(2) Steadman T.Smith Schick: Goals - Goddard(6):

BRADFORD B - Graham(Summers): Christie Hassan Loughlin Cook: Longo Paul : McDermott(Medley) Donahue Fairbank(Ireland) Donougher(Knox) Nickle Bradley:
Tries - Loughlin(2) Longo Nickle: Goals - Cook(5):
Referee S Cummings(Widnes) Att - 2794 H.T. 18 - 20

Sun 21 Jan 1996 LONDON BRONCOS away won 50 - 44

LONDON B - McRaw: Butt Rosolen Hauff Carroll: Matterson Dynevor: Mestrov Rea Shaw Keating(Bryant) Francis(Bawden) Stevens (Roskell): Tries - McRaw(3) Rosolen Hauff Dynevor Rea Shaw: Goals - Dynevor(6):
CASTLEFORD - Steadman(C.Smith): Furness Flynn Goddard Coventry: T.Smith Simon Price (Stephens): Sampson(Tuuta) Maskill Sykes Smales(Richardson) Schick Nikau: Tries - Schick(3) Furness(2) Coventry T.Smith Sykes Smales: Goals - Goddard(7):
Referee K Kirkpatrick (War'ton) Att - 1465 H.T. 22 – 26

Adrian Flynn
D. No 720
1995-96 to 1997

Andy Hill
D. No 721
1995-96 to 1999

Colin Maskill
D. No 722
1995 96- to 1996

Andrew Schick
D. No 723
1995-96 to 1998

Brendon Tuuta
D. No 724
1995-96 to 1997

David Furness
D. No 725
1995-96 to 1996

Shaun Richardson
D. No 726
1995-96 to 1997

SEASON 1995-96

D.N	PLAYER		DEBUT	L MATCH	APP	SUB	T.AP	TRI'S	G'LS	D.G	P'TS
618	MARCHANT	TONY		29/09/1995	8	1	9	3	0	0	12
661	SAMPSON	DEAN			13	3	16	1	0	0	4
675	STEADMAN	GRAHAM			15	1	16	8	5	0	42
679	SMITH	TONY			18	1	19	9	0	0	36
685	CROOKS	LEE			14	1	15	0	38	0	76
692	NIKAU	TAWERA			16	C	16	3	0	0	12
693	MIDDLETON	SIMON			12	C	12	4	0	0	16
694	SYKES	NATHAN			15	5	20	2	0	0	8
699	SMITH	CHRIS			18	-	19	6	0	0	24
706	SMALES	IAN			9	7	16	1	0	0	4
708	FLOWERS	JASON			14	1	15	7	0	0	28
709	GODDARD	RICHARD			12	1	13	3	21	0	54
710	STEPHENS	GARETH			14	2	16	0	0	0	0
711	COVENTRY	JAMIE			12	4	16	6	0	0	24
712	EDEN	PHIL		29/11/1995	0	4	4	0	0	0	0
713	DARLEY	PAUL		01/01/1996	6	1	7	0	2	0	4
715	TONKS	IAN			1	0	1	0	0	0	0
716	PALMER	CRAIG		25/08/1995	1	1	2	0	0	0	0
717	PRICE	SIMON		21/01/1996	3	0	3	0	0	0	0
718	FLOWERS	STUART			4	7	11	0	0	0	0
719	HARLAND	LEE			15	2	17	3	0	0	12
720	FLYNN	ADRIAN	20/08/1995		18	0	18	10	0	0	40
721	HILL	ANDY	20/08/1995		2	2	4	0	0	0	0
722	MASKILL	COLIN	20/08/1995		15	1	16	6	7	0	38
723	SCHICK	ANDREW	06/09/1995		10	7	17	5	0	0	20
724	TUUTA	BRENDON	17/09/1995		5	4	9	0	0	0	0
725	FURNESS	DAVID	07/01/1996		3	0	3	3	0	0	12
726	RICHARDSON	SHAUN	07/01/1996		0	3	3	0	0	0	0
	28		**7**	**5**	**273**	**60**	**333**	**80**	**73**	**0**	**466**

COMPETITION		P	W	D	L	FOR	AGT
S.B. LEAGUE C.C	POSITION 6 OF 11	20	9	1	10	448	566
REGAL TROPHY		1	0	0	1	18	19
PLAYERS RECORDS		**21**	**9**	**1**	**11**	**466**	**585**

As this was a shortened season which commenced in August 1995 and finished in January 1996, there was no Challenge Cup.

SEASON 1996

SUPER LEAGUE I

This was the first season of 'Super League' and 'Summer Rugby'. The Super league consisted of the top ten teams of the previous seasons Division 1, Wigan Leeds Castleford St Helens Halifax Warrington Bradford Northern Sheffield Eagles Workington Town Oldham plus the London Broncos and a French team Paris St Germain.

Five of the six teams not being admitted to Super league from the 1995/96 Division 1, Featherstone Rovers Salford Wakefield Trinity Widnes Hull were placed into a new Division 1, with Keighley Batley Huddersfield Whitehaven Rochdale Hornets and Dewsbury.

The sixth team omitted Doncaster Rovers found themselves in Division 2 with Hull K R York (who had dropped the prefix Ryedale) Hunslet Hawks Leigh Centurians Swinton Bramley Carlisle Barrow Prescot Panthers (with a change in name from Highfield) plus readmitted Chorley Borough and new club South Wales.

Sun 4 Feb 1996 ST HELENS home lost 16 - 58
CHALENGE CUP ROUND 4
CASTLEFORD - J.Flowers: C.Smith Flynn Goddard Coventry: Steadman <u>Gareth Stephens</u>: Sampson Maskill(Schick) Sykes Smales(Harland Schick(Tuuta) <u>Tawera Nikau</u>:
Tries - Smith Goddard Sampson: Goals - Goddard(2):
ST HELENS - Prescott: Arnold Northey Newlove Sullivan: Hammond Goulding: Perelini(Matautia) Cunningham Leatham(Perilini) Joynt Booth Bushby:
Tries - Newlove(3) Prescott Arnold Sullivan Hammond Joynt Northey Matautia: Goals - Goulding(9):
Referee S Cummings (Widnes) Att - 7023 H.T 16 - 28

Sun 31 Mar 1996 BRADFORD BULLS away lost 18 -30
BRADFORD - Loughlin: Christie(Hassan) Calland Bradley Scales: Paul Tomlinson(Donahue): McDermott(Dwyer) Lowes Fairbank(McDermott) Donougher Nickle Knox(Medley):
Tries Donogher(3) Paul(2) Calland: Goals - Loughlin(3):
CASTLEFORD - Steadman(J.Flowers): C.Smith Goddard(Anderson) Flynn <u>Jamie Coventry</u>: FRANO BOTICA(727) T.Smith: Crooks Russell Sampson(Sykes) Schick Harland Tuuta:
Tries - T.Smith(2) Crooks: Goals - Botica(3):
Referee R Connolly (Wigan) Att - 10027 H.T. 10 - 18

Fri 5 Apr 1996 LEEDS home won 26 - 23
CASTLEFORD - J.Flowers: C.Smith Anderson Flynn Middleton(RICHARD GAY(728)): Botica T.Smith: Crooks (Sampson) Russell Sykes Schick(Smales) Harland Tuuta:
Tries - Flowers Gay Botica Russell Schick: Goals –Botica(3):
LEEDS - A.Gibbons: Fallon Iro Hall (Hasson)(Hall) Gleadhill: Cummings Holroyd: Harmion(McDermott) Shaw Howard(Harmon) Fozzard(D.Gibbons) Mann Schultz:

Tries - Shaw(2) Iro Cummings:
Goals - Holdroyd(3) A.GibbonsD/G:
Referee R Connolly (Wigan) Att - 7179 H.T. 14 - 12

Tue 9 Apr 1996 HALIFAX BLUE SOX away won 34 -30
HALIFAX - Umaga: Hallas Schuster Tuilago(Amone) Ekoku: Moana Dean: Harrison (Anderson) Southernwood W.Jackson(Harrison) Moriarty(W.Jackson) M.Jackson (Gillespie)Parker: Tries - Moana(2) Umaga Dean Anderson: Goals - Schuster(5):
CASTLEFORD - J.Flowers: C.Smith(S.Flowers) Anderson Flynn DICCON EDWARDS(729): Botica(Goddard) T.Smith: Sampson Maskill(Smales) Sykes Schick Harland Tuuta:
Tries - Smales(2) J.Flowers Goddard T.Smith Tuuta: Goals - Goddard(4) Botica:
Referee D Campbell (Widnes) Att - 4791 H.T. 24 - 18

Sun 14 Apr 1996 WIGAN WARRIORS home lost 10 -28
CASTLEFORD - J.Flowers: C.Smith Anderson(Gay) Flynn Edwards: Goddard T.Smith: Sampson Russell(PAUL ROUND(730)) Sykes(S.Flowers) Schick(Smales) Harland Tuuta: Try - T.Smith: Goals - Goddard(3):
WIGAN - Paul(Johnson): Robinson Tuigamala Connolly Radlinski: Edwards Murdock(Smyth): Cowie Hall O'Connor(Skerrett)(O'Connor) Quinnell(Haughton) (Quinnell) Cassidy Farrell: Tries - Robinson Connolly Smyth Hall Farrell: Goals - Farrell(4):
Referee C Morris (Huddersfield) Att – 7985 H.T. 10 - 6

Sat 20 Apr 1996 OLDHAM BEARS home lost 20 - 24
CASTLEFORD - J.Flowers(Gay): C.Smith Anderson(S/O) Flynn Edwards: Botica T.Smith: Sampson Maskill(Sykes) (Crooks) Sykes(Steadman) Smales(J.Flowers) Harland (Goddard) Tuuta:
Tries - Flynn Sampson Smales: Goal - Botica(4):
OLDHAM - Atcheson: Ranson(Hill) Patmore Abram (Topping) Belle: Maloney Crompton(Abram): Faimalo (Davidson) Clarke Temu(Gildart) Munro Bradbury Hill (Lord): Tries - Atcheson(2) Abram Maloney:
Goals - Maloney(4):
Referee C Morris (Huddersfield) Att - 4396 H.T. 14 - 8

Fri 3 May 1996 SHEFFIELD EAGLES away lost 12 - 20
SHEFFIELD - Sovatabua: Sodje(Stott)(Sodje) Grimley Garcia Senior: Sheridan Aston: Broadbent(Dixon) Lawless McAllister(Broadbent) Hay Carr Farrell(Turner):
Tries - Sodje Senior Farrell Turner: Goals - Aston)2):
CASTLEFORD - J.Flowers: C.Smith Goddard(<u>David Furness</u>)(BB) Gay Edwards: Botica .Smith: Crooks Russell Sampson (Sykes) Schick Smales(Tonks)(<u>Stuart Flowers</u>) Tuuta: Tries - C.Smith Schick: Goals - Botica(2):
Referee S Cummings (Widnes) Att - 5486 H.T. 10 - 6

Sun 12 May 1996 WORKINGTON TOWN home won 50 - 16
CASTLEFORD - Gay(Steadman): C.Smith Goddard Flynn(Russell) Middleton: Botica T.Smith: Crooks (J.Flowers) Russell(SPENCER HARGRAVE(731)) Sykes

SEASON 1996

Tonks (Harland) Schick Tuuta: Tries - Flynn(2) Steadman
T.Smith Tonks Harland Schick Tuuta: Goals Botica(9):
WORKINGTON - Campbell: Wallace(Penrice) Allen
Fraisse(Livett) L.Smith: T.Smith Marwood: Armstrong
(Filipo) McKenzie(Kitchen) Phillips Palmada Holgate
Nairn(Armstrong):
Tries - Penrice Kithen Nairn: Goals - Marwood(2):
Referee J Connolly (Wigan) Att - 3605 H.T. 20 - 6

Sun 19 May 1996 LONDON BRONCOS home lost 20 - 21

CASTLEFORD - Steadman(Hargrave)(Botica): C.Smith
Goddard(J.Flowers) Flynn Middleton: Botica(Edwards)
T.Smith: Crooks Russell Sykes(Round) Schick(Hargrave)
Harland Tuuta: Tries - C.Smith Flowers Middleton:
Goals - Botica(3) Crooks:
LONDON - Barwick: Roskell Tollitt Strutton Minto:
McRae(Langer)Dynevor: Mestrov Rea Bawden(Roselen
)(Shaw)(Bawden) Shaw(Brown)(Roselen)(Pitt)Bryant Gill:
Tries - Barwick Tollitt Minto Gill: Goals - Barwick(2)D/G:
Referee S Cummings (Widnes) Att – 3489 H.T. 8 - 14

Mon 27 May 1996 ST HELENS away lost 24 - 62

ST HELENS - Prescott: Arnold Hunte Newlove(Matautia)
Sullivan: Martin(Morley) Goulding: Perelini(Booth)
Cunningham Pickavance Joynt(Haigh) McVey Hammond:
Tries - Prescott(2) Newlove(2) Arnold Matautia Martin
Morley Perelini Haigh: Goals - Goulding(11):
CASTLEFORD - Steadman: C.Smith Anderson(DAVID
CHAPMAN(732)) Flynn(Edwards) Middleton: Botica
T.Smith: Crooks Maskill(Paramore) Sykes Harland
Schick(JUNIOR PARAMORE(733)) (Schick) Tuuta:
Tries - Steadman Middleton T.Smith Sykes:
Goals - Botica(4):
Referee R Connolly (Wigan) Att - 8239 H.T. 26 - 8

Fri 31 May 1996 WARRINGTON WOLVES home lost 17 - 22

CASTLEFORD - Steadman: C.Smith Chapman(Middleton)
Flynn Edwards: Anderson Botica: Crooks(Paramore)
Maskill(Russell) Sykes(Schick) Paramore(Sykes) Harland
(J.Flowers) Tuuta:
Tries - Flynn Edwards Paramore: Goals - Botica(2)D/G:
WARRINGTON - Mafi(Kohe-Love): Forster Kohe-Love(B/B)
(Roper) Roper(Barrow) Henare: Harris Swann: Hilton
Bennett(Watson) Chambers(Jones) Sculthorpe Cullen
Rudd:
Tries - Roper Henare Sculthorpe Rudd: Goals - Harris(3):
Referee S Cummings (Widnes) Att - 2874 H.T. 10 - 10

Fri 7 Jun 1996 PARIS ST GERMAIN away won 54 -22

PARIS - Lucchese: Van Brussell Smith(Wulf) Banquet Yaha:
Brown Entat: Sands Wulf (Devecchi) Parry(Teixido)(Parrt)
Adams(Zenon) Bloomfield(Boudebza) Pech:
Tries - Banquet(2) Brown(2)   Goals - Yaha(3):
CASTLEFORD - Steadman(J.Flowers): C.Smith Chapman
Flynn Edwards: Anderson Botica: Crooks(Sampson)
Maskill Sykes(Russell) Schick(Middleton) Paramore
(Crooks)Tuuta:
Tries - Steadman Flowers Smith Chapman Flynn Anderson

Botica Maskill Schick: Goals - Botica(8) Maskill:
Referee J Connolly (Wigan) Att - 6618 H.T. 42 - 6

Sun 16 Jun 1996 BRADFORD BULLS home won 26 -23

CASTLEFORD - J.Flowers: C.Smith Chapman Flynn
Edwards(JON WELLS(734)): Anderson Botica:
Crooks(Sampson) Maskill(Goddard) Sykes(Crooks)
Paramore(Paul Round) Schick Tuuta:
Tries - Flowers Chapman Flynn Botica: Goals - Botica(5):
BRADFORD - Spruce: Hassan(Tamani) Calland Bradley
Scales(Cook): Tomlinson Paul: McDermott(Nickle)
(Donougher) Lowes Fairbank(Medley) Dwyer Donougher
(Fairbank) McNamara: Tries - Spruce Cook Donougher
Dwyer: Goals - McNamara(3) (DG):
Referee D Campbell (Widnes) Att - 6275 H.T. 8 - 10

Sat 22 Jun 1996 LEEDS away lost 18 - 25

LEEDS - Holroyd(Newton): Golden Cummings(Tait) Hall
Hassan: Kemp Clark: Faimalo(Fozzard) Newton(Shaw)
McDermott(Faimalo) Mann(Mercer) Morley Hulme:
Tries - Golden Hall McDermott Mercer:
Goals - Holroyd(4) (DG):
CASTLEFORD - J.Flowers: C.Smith Chapman Flynn
Edwards: Anderson(Paramore) Botica: Crooks(Sampson)
Maskill(Tonks) Sykes(Crooks) Paramore (T.Smith) Schick
Tuuta: Tries - Flowers Chapman Flynn : Goals - Botica(3):
Referee W Harrigan (Australia) Att - 6242 H.T. 6 - 12

Sun 30 Jun 1996 HALIFAX BLUE SOX home lost 20 -24

CASTLEFORD - J.Flowers: C.Smith Chapman Anderson
Edwards: Botica T.Smith: Crooks (Sykes) Colin
Maskill(Smales) Sykes(Sampson) Schick Paramore(Flynn)
Tuuta: Tries - Flowers(2) Anderson: Goals - Botica(4):
HALIFAX - Amone: Bentley Schuster Hallas Tuilagi: Moana
Briggs(Dean): Ketteridge Rowley Perrett(Marshall)Gillespie
Jackson(Bastian) Baldwin(Chester):   Tries - Bentley(2)
Moana Rowley Jackson: Goals - Schuster(2):
Referee A Bates (Workington) Att - 4194 H.T. 14 - 10

Fri 5 Jul 1996 WIGAN WARRIORS away lost 25 - 26

WIGAN - Robinson: Craig Tuigamala Connolly
Ellison(Long): Edwards(Murdock) Murdock(Wright):
O'Conner(Haughton) Hall Cassidy Haughton(Barrow)
Farrell A.Johnson: Tries - Robinson(2) Tuigamala
A.Johnson: Goals - Farrell(5):
CASTLEFORD - J.Flowers: C.Smith Chapman Flynn
Edwards(Middleton): Botica T.Smith: Crooks(Sykes) Tuuta
Sampson Harland(Richardson) Schick Smales(Paramore):
Tries - T.Smith Crooks Tuuta Paramore:
Goals - Botica(4) (DG):
Rteferee - Mr S Clark (Australia) Att - 8180 H.T. 16 - 12

Sun 14 Jul 1996 OLDHAM BEARS away won 30 - 20

OLDHAM - Atcheson: Belle Hill Topping Ranson(Cowans):
Maloney Crompton: Gildart Clarke(Davidson) Temu
(Faimalo)(Temu) Lord(Crook) Munro Bradbury: Tries -
Atcheson Hill Ranson Crompton: Goals - Maloney(2):
CASTLEFORD - J.Flowers: C.Smith Chapman(Steadman)
Flynn Middleton: Botica T.Smith: Crooks(Chapman) Tuuta
(Paramore) Sampson(Sykes) Schick Harland Smales

SEASON 1996

(Richardson): Tries - C.Smith Flynn Middleton T.Smith
Paramore: Goals - Botica(5):
Referee D Campbell (Widnes) Att - 3480 H.T. 16 - 4

Sun 21 Jul 1996 SHEFFIELD EAGLES home won 36 -31
CASTLEFORD - J.Flowers: C.Smith Flynn (Steadman)
Chapman Middleton: Botica T.Smith: Crooks(Sykes) Tuuta
Sykes(Richardson) Schick(Flynn) Harland Smales:
Tries - C.Smith(3) Chapman Middleton Schick:
Goals - Botica(6):
SHEFFIELD - Sovatabua: Dakuitoga(Crowther) Stott Senior
Garcia: Lawford Aston: Broadbent(Turner)(Mycoe)
Turner(Laughton) Yasa(Lawless) McAllister Farrell Cook
(Broadbent): Tries - Sovatabua(2) Senior Laughton Cook:
Goals - Aston(5) Lawford(DG):
Referee R Connolly (Wigan) Att - 4524 H.T. 16 - 18

Sun 28 Jul 1996 WORKINGTON TOWN away won 46 - 20
WORKINGTON - Penrice: Armswood(Stainton) Allen
Johnson Chilton: Smith Watson: Riley(Prest)(Kithen)
Bethwaite Phillips(S/O) Filipo(Grima) Holgate(More)
Grima(Riley):
Tries - Allen Johnson Grima: Goals - Watson(4):
CASTLEFORD - Steadman(Gay): C.Smith Chapman
J.Flowers Middleton: Botica T.Smith: Crooks(Sykes) Russell
Sampson(Schick) Schick(Harland) Richardson(Paramore)
Smales: Tries - C.Smith(2) Smales(2) Middleton Harland
Richardson: Goals - Botica(9):
Referee R Connolly (Wigan) Att - 1622 H.T. 8 - 20

Fri 2 Aug 1996 ST HELENS home lost 16 - 20
CASTLEFORD - J.Flowers: C.Smith(Gay) Goddard Chapman
Flynn: Botica T.Smith: Crooks(Sampson) Tuuta
Sykes(Crooks) Schick(Junior Paramore)
Harland(Richardson) Smales (Harland):
Tries - Flowers T.Smith: Goals - Botica(4):
ST HELENS - Prescott: Hayes Matautia(Haigh) Newlove
Sullivan: Hammond Goulding Perelini Cunningham
Fogerty(Martin) McVey(Busby) Pickavance Morley:
Tries - Sullivan(2) Newlove Martin: Goals - Goulding(2):
Referee D Campbell (Widnes) Att - 6143 H.T. 10 -10

Sat 10 Aug 1996 WARRINGTON WOLVES away lost 24 - 38
WARRINGTON - Knott: Forster(Mafi) Kohe-Love Roper
Henare(Rudd): Shelford Swann: Jones(Fnau)(Jones)b
Watson Stevens(Cullen) Hulme(Forster) Cullen(Davies)
Sculthorpe: Tries - Henare(2) Mafi Shelford Sculthorpe
Hulme Cullen: Goals - Knott(5):
CASTLEFORD - J.Flowers: Flynn Chapman Goddard
Middleton: Botica T.Smith: Crooks(Gay) Russell
Sykes(Sampson S/O) Schick(Richardson) Smales(Harland)
Tuuta(Sykes): Tries - Flynn Goddard Botica T.Smith
Schick: Goals - Botica(2):
Referee D Campbell (Widnes) Att - 4277 H.T. 20 - 4

Sat 17 Aug 1996 PARIS ST GERMAIN home won 22 - 18
CASTLEFORD - Gay: EDDIE GLAZE(735) Chapman
J.Flowers(CHRIS ALLEN(736)) Wells: Botica T.Smith:
Crooks Russell(LEE BARDAUSKAS(737)) Sykes(Sampson)
Smales Schick(Hargrave) Tuuta:
Tries - Gay Chapman Flowers Botica: Goals - Botica(3):
PARIS - Bird: Bomati Chamorin Vergniol
Wilson(Lucchese): Devecchi Entat: Cabestany (Griffiths)
Wulf Sands (Bloomfield) Pech(Bryant) Bryant(Sands)(Pech)
Smith(Banquet):
Tries - Bird Bomati Vergniol Devecchi: Goal - Banquet
Referee S Gamson (St Helens) Att - 4473 H.T. 12 - 4

Sun 25 Aug 1996 LONDON BRONCOS away lost nil - 56
LONDON - Martin: Roskell(McGuire) Barwick Krause
Offiah(Dynevor): Tollett Langer: Allen(Bawden) Rea
Mestrov Shaw(Allen) Rosolen(Pitt) Gill:
Tries - Barwick(4) Dynevor(2) Gill(2) Martin McGuire
Krause: Goals - Barwick(6):
CASTLEFORD - Gay: C.Smith Chapman(J.Flowers)
J.Flowers(Steadman) Wells: Frano Botica T.Smith:
Crooks(Sampson) Russell(Schick) Sykes(Crooks)
Smales(Richardson) Tuuta Goddard:
Referee S Cummings (Widnes) Att - 3500(est) H.T. nil – 22

Frano Botica
D. No 727
1996

Richard Gay
D. No 728
1996 to 2002

David Chapman
D. No 732
1996 to 1998

Jon Wells
D. No 734
1996 to 2002

SEASON 1996

D.N	PLAYER		DEBUT	L MATCH	APP	SUB	T.AP	TRI'S	G'LS	D.G	P'TS
657	ANDERSON	GRANT			10	1	11	2	0	0	8
661	SAMPSON	DEAN			9	9	18	2	0	0	8
675	STEADMAN	GRAHAM			7	5	12	3	0	0	12
679	SMITH	TONY			18	1	19	10	0	0	40
685	CROOKS	LEE			19	1	20	2	1	0	10
692	NIKAU	TAWERA		04/02/1996	1	0	1	0	0	0	0
693	MIDDLETON	SIMON			8	3	11	5	0	0	20
694	SYKES	NATHAN			18	5	23	1	0	0	4
699	SMITH	CHRIS			21	0	21	10	0	0	40
705	RUSSELL	RICHARD			10	2	12	1	0	0	4
706	SMALES	IAN			11	4	15	5	0	0	20
708	FLOWERS	JASON			17	5	22	10	0	0	40
709	GODDARD	RICHARD			9	3	12	3	9	0	30
710	STEPHENS	GARETH		04/02/1996	1	0	1	0	0	0	0
711	COVENTRY	JAMIE		31/03/1996	2	0	2	0	0	0	0
715	TONKS	IAN			1	2	3	1	0	0	4
718	FLOWERS	STUART		03/05/1996	0	3	3	0	0	0	0
719	HARLAND	LEE			12	4	16	2	0	0	8
720	FLYNN	ADRIAN			18	1	19	9	0	0	36
722	MASKILL	COLIN		30/06/1996	9	0	9	1	1	0	6
723	SCHICK	ANDREW			20	2	22	6	0	0	24
724	TUUTA	BRENDON			21	1	22	3	0	0	12
725	FURNESS	DAVID		03/05/1996	0	1	1	0	0	0	0
726	RICHARDSON	SHAUN			1	5	7	1	0	0	4
727	BOTICA	FRANO	31/03/1996	25/08/1996	21	0	21	5	84	2	190
728	GAY	RICHARD	05/04/1996		4	5	10	2	0	0	8
729	EDWARDS	DICCON	09/04/1996		10	2	12	1	0	0	4
730	ROUND	PAUL	14/04/1996	16/06/1996	0	3	3	0	0	0	0
731	HARGRAVE	SPENCER	12/05/1996		0	3	3	0	0	0	0
732	CHAPMAN	DAVID	27/05/1996		13	1	14	5	0	0	20
733	PARAMORE	JUNIOR	27/05/1996	02/08/1996	5	6	11	3	0	0	12
734	WELLS	JON	16/06/1996		2	1	3	0	0	0	0
735	GLAZE	EDDIE	17/08/1996	17/08/1996	1	0	1	0	0	0	0
736	ALLEN	CHRIS	17/08/1996	17/08/1996	0	1	1	0	0	0	0
737	BARDAUSKAS	LEE	17/08/1996		0	1	1	0	0	0	0
	35		11	11	299	83	382	93	95	2	564

COMPETITION		P	W	D	L	FOR	AGT
S. LEAGUE	POSITION 9 OF 12	22	9	0	13	548	599
RL CUP		1	0	0	1	16	58
PLAYERS RECORDS		**23**	**9**	**0**	**14**	**564**	**657**

With the Challenge Cup Competition being played at the same time of the year as in previous seasons and with the Final still taking place in May, the competition now preceded the League Competition. Super League clubs entered the competition at the fourth round stage, and our tie was against St Helens at home which we lost 16-58.

As a result of the new league structure the Regal Trophy was disbanded.

Frano Botica set a record for most points scored in Super League game at 18 against Workington Town at home on the 12 May 1996 and then increased it to 20, against Paris St Germain away on the 7 June 1996.

SEASON 1997

SUPER LEAGUE II

In Super League Workington Town were relegated into Division 2 being replaced by Salford. In Division 1 Rochdale Hornets and Batley were relegated to Division 2, replaced by Hull K R Swinton Lions. In Division 2 Chorley Borough changed their name to Lancashire Lynx and South Wales dropped out after one season.

Sun 2 Feb 1997 FEATHERSTONE ROVERS home lost 20 – 24 FRIENDLY
CASTLEFORD - Gay: Lewington Chapman Anderson Roach: Vowles Orr: Crooks Russell Sampson Smales Lidden Goddard: Subs used- Steadman Middleton Tuuta Schick Bardauskas Sykes :
Tries - Vowles(2) Lewington Goddard: Goals - Goddard(2):
FEATHERSTONE R - Strange: Gleadhill Irwin Hughes Bargate: Summers Fox: Molloy Maskill Naidole Powell Baker Slater: Subs used- Gunn Jackson Morgan Miller Evans Lambert Kimmel Maher Chapman Handley:
Tries - Hughes(2) Molloy(2) Jackson: Goals - Summers(2):
Referee G Shaw (Dewsbury) Att - 4074 H.T. 6 - 14

Sun 9 Feb 1997 SALFORD REDS home lost 18 - 36 CHALLENGE CUP ROUND 4
CASTLEFORD - Gay(Steadman): C.Smith Chapman Anderson JASON ROACH(738): ADRIAN VOWLES(739) T.Smith: Crooks(Schick) Russell Schick(SEAN McVEAN (741)) JASON LIDDEN(740)(Smales) Tuuta(Flynn) Goddard:
Tries - Roach T.Smith Flynn: Goals - Goddard(3):
SALFORD R - Laurence(Lee): Sini Naylor McAvoy Rogers: Watson Lee(Martin): Platt(Forber) Edwards Eccles (Cartwright) Forber(Savelio) Cartwright(Faimalo) Randall(Hulme): Tries - Rogers(3) Lee Sini Edwards Hulme: Goals - Watson(3) Sini:
Referee D Campbell (Widnes) Att - 5935 H.T. 2 - 10

Sun 2 Mar 1997 WIGAN WARRIORS away lost 14 – 54 FRIENDLY
WIGAN W - Murray: Robinson Radlinski A.Johnson Ellison: Paul Murdock: O'Connor Hall Cowie Haughton Cassidy Farrell: Subs used - P.Johnson Long Holgate Tallec:
Tries - Radlinski(3) Murdock(2) P.Johnson Ellison Tallec Robinson Haughton: Goals Farrell(4) Paul(3):
CASTLEFORD - Steadman: C.Smith Chapman Flynn Middleton: Anderson T.Smith: Sampson St Hilaire Sykes Lidden Smales Goddard:
Subs used - Flowers Crooks Schick Harland:
Tries - Steadman T.Smith Flowers: Goal - Goddard:
Referee S Cummings (Widnes) Att - 3530 H.T. 8 - 30

Fri 7 Mar 1997 WIGAN WARRIORS home won 18 - 8 FRIENDLY
CASTLEFORD - Flowers: C.Smith Goddard(Edwards) Gay Middleton: Vowles(Steadman) Orr: Crooks(Schick) St Hilaire Sykes(Crooks) Lidden Harland(Richardson) Tuuta (Harland):
Tries - C.Smith(2) Middleton: Goals - Crooks(2) Orr:

WIGAN W - Murray(Cardiss): P.Johson A.Johnson Haughton(Murray) Ellison: Long Murdock: Cowie (Knowles) Hall O'Connor(Barrow)Holgate(Tallec) Cassidy Paul: Tries - Cowie: Goals - Paul(2):
Referee K Kirkpatrick (Warrington) Att - 1677 H.T. 6-2

Sun 16 Mar 1997 SALFORD REDS away lost nil - 4
SALFORD R - Rogers: Sini Naylor McAvoy Coussins: Blakeley Lee(Watson) Southern(Savelio) Edwards Eccles Forber Cartwright(Faimalo) Randall(Martin):
Try - Coussins:
CASTLEFORD - Flowers: C.Smith Gay(Tony Smith) Goddard Middleton: Vowles DANNY ORR(742) (Steadman): Crooks(Sykes) LEE ST HILAIRE(743) Sampson (Crooks) Harland(Smales) Richardson(Harland) Tuuta:
Referee S Cummings (Widnes) Att - 5726 H.T. nil - 4

Sun 23 Mar 1997 WIGAN WARRIORS home lost 14-22
CASTLEFORD - Flowers: C.Smith Gay Richard Goddard(Steadman) (Richard Goddard) Middleton: Vowles Orr: Crooks(Sykes) St Hilaire Sampson(Crooks) Lidden(Smales)(Lidden) Harland Tuuta:
Tries - Middleton Lidden: Goals - Crooks(2) Goddard:
WIGAN W - Murray: Robinson Connolly Radlinski A.Johnson: Paul Murdock(Long): Cowie(Holgate) Cassidy(Hall) O'Connor Haughton Tallec Farrel:
Tries - Haughton(2) Robinson Cassidy: Goals - Farrell(3):
Referee D Campbell (Widnes) Att - 4339 H.T. 12 -12

Fri 25 Mar 1997 HALIFAX BLUE SOX away lost 12 -29
HALIFAX B S - Umaga(S/O): Tuilagi Schuster Amone(Dean) Bouveng: Pearson Parker(Chester): Harrison(Gillespie) Rowley Skerret(W.Jackson) Baldwin M.Jackson Moana: Tries - Rowley(2) Umaga Baldwin M.Jackson Bouveng: Goals - Schuster(2)(DG):
CASTLEFORD - Flowers: C.Smith Gay(Flynn) Anderson Middleton: Vowles Orr(Steadman): Crooks(Sykes) St Hilaire Sampson Lidden Harland Tuuta(Schick):
Tries - C.Smith Lidden Flynn:
Referee R Connolly (Wigan) Att - 5421 H.T. 4 - 8

Tue 1 Apr 1997 BRADFORD BULLS home lost 12 -38
CASTLEFORD - Flowers: C.Smith Gay Flynn Middleton: Steadman(Chapman) Vowles: Crooks(Sykes))(PAUL SMITH(744)) St Hilaire Sampson(Crooks) Harland Lidden(Schick) Tuuta:
Tries - Flowers Chapman: Goals - Crooks Vowles:
BRADFORD B - Spruce: Cook Bradley(Calland) Loughlin Christie: Paul Tomlinson: McDermott Lowes Anderson(Reinana) Nickle Jowitt(Graham) McNamara(Knox): Tries - Pual(2) Loughlin McDermott Lowes Jowitt: Goals - Cook(4) McNamara(3):
Referee J Connolly (Wigan) Att - 7882 H.T. 6 - 18

Sun 6 Apr 1997 SHEFFIELD EAGLES away lost 20 -42
SHEFFIELD E - Stott: Crowther Pinkney Senior Garcia (Savatabua): Doyle(Mycoe) Aston: Broadbent(Edmed) Lawless Edmed(Thompson) Carr McAllister Wood(Turner):

SEASON 1997

Tries - Garcia(2) Stott Crowther Pinkney Aston Wood:
Goals - Aston(7):
CASTLEFORD - Flowers: C.Smith Adrian Flynn(Edwards)
Gay Middleton: Steadman(Vowles) Vowles(Hargrave):
Crooks(Harland) Russell Schick Lidden Harland(P.Smith)
Tuuta(Orr):
Tries - Flowers Lidden Orr: Goals - Crooks(2) Orr(2):
Referee R Connolly (Wigan) Att - 4000 H.T. 8 - 16

Sun 13 Apr 1997 WARRINGTON WOLVES home lost 8 - 24

CASTLEFORD - Flowers: C.Smith Goddard(Gay) Anderson
Middleton: Vowles Orr(Ford): Sampson Russell
Sykes(Harland) Lidden(Schick) Harland(Smales)(Lidden)
Tuuta: Tries - Gay: Goals - Goddard(2):
WARRINGTON W - Rudd(Knott): Forster Kohe-Love Roper
Henare: Vagana Shelford: Stephens(Finau)(Darbyshire)
Hulme Chambers(Finau)(Stephens) Tatupu Mann
Sculthorpe:
Tries - Vagana(3) Henare Shelford: Goals - Roper(2):
Referee D Campbell (Widnes) Att - 3546 H.T. 4 - 8

Tue 15 Apr 1997 LEEDS RHINOS away lost 21 - 24

LEEDS R - Gibson: Sterling Blackmore Hassan St
Hilaire(Cummings): Harris Sheridan(Holroyd):
Masella(Fozzard) Collins Mathiou(Field) Morley Farrell
Mercer: Tries - Sterling Cummings Harris Farrell:
Goals - Holroyd(3) Harris:
CASTLEFORD - Flowers: C.Smith Anderson Vowles(Gay)
Middleton: Orr Ford: Sampson(Sykes) Russell
Sykes(P.Smith) Tonks Schick Tuuta: Tries - Anderson
Middleton Russell Schick: Goals - Tonks(2) FordD/G:
Referee S Cummings (Widnes) Att - 10303 H.T. 11 - 6

Sun 20 Apr 1997 HALIFAX BLUE SOX home lost 12 -28

CASTLEFORD - Flowers: C.Smith(Chapman)(Gay) Vowles
Anderson Middleton: Orr Ford Sampson(Sykes) Russell
Sykes(Harland) Tonks(Lidden) Schick Tuuta:
Tries - Vowles Sampson: Goals - Orr Tonks:
HALIFAX B S - Umaga: Amone Pearson Moana Munro:
Chester Parker: Harrison(Skerrett) Rowley
Skerrett(W.Jackson)(Dean) M.Jackson Gillespie(Highton)
(Gillespie)(Highton) Baldwin(Rushforth):   Tries - Pearson
Moana Munro Gillespie: Goals - Pearson(6):
Referee K Kirkpatrick (Warrington) Att - 4304 H.T. 6 - 12

Sun 27 Apr 1997 ST HELENS away lost 16 - 42
AT ANFIELD STADIUM LIVERPOOL

ST HELENS - Prescott: Arnold(Matautia) Haigh Newlove
Sullivan: Martyn(Anderson) Goulding: Perelini
Cunningham O'Neill(Northey) Joynt Morley(Pickavance)
Hammond: Tries - Hammond(3) Newelove(2) Prescott
Martyn: Goals - Goulding(7):
CASTLEFORD - Steadman: Roach(Edwards) Gay Vowles
Middleton: Orr Ford: Sampson Russell Sykes(Tonks)
(Sykes) Lidden(Tonks)(Harland) Schick Tuuta:
Tries - Vowles Middleton Orr: Goals - Orr(2):
Referee J Connolly (Wigan) Att - 12329 H.T. 2 - 18

Sun 11 May 1997 PARIS ST GERMAIN home lost 8 -13

CASTLEFORD - Flowers: Roach Vowles Gay Middleton
Orr(Steadman) Ford(Diccon Edwards): Sampson Russell
Sykes(Anderson)(Tonks) Tonks(Sykes) Richardson
(Harland) Lidden(Richardson):
Try - Steadman: Goals - Orr Tonks:
PARIS S G - Bird: Wall Robinson Evans Bergman:
Olejnik(O'Connor) Martin(Hancock): Menkins(Priddle)
O'Donnell Sands(Menkins)(Sands) Lomax Peters(Hogue)
Chamorin: Try - Bergman O'Donnell:
Goals - Robinson(2) O'Connor(DG):
Referee S Cummings (Widnes) Att - 3098 H.T. 8 - 2

Sun 18 May 1997 SALFOR REDS home won 12 - 10

CASTLEFORD - Flowers: Roach JASON CRITCHLEY(745)
Vowles Simon Middleton Orr Ford(Steadman)(BB):
Sampson Russell Sykes(Crooks)(Sykes) Tonks(Tuuta)
(Anderson)(Steadman) Harland(St Hilaire)
Tuuta(Anderson): Tries - Roach(2):   Goals - Orr(2):
SALFORD R - Broadbent: Sini Martin McAvoy Rogers:
Blakeley Watson(Lee)(Watson): Platt(Southern)
Edwards(Lee)(BB) Eccles(Forber) Forber(Savelio) Faimalo
Hulme(Randall):   Tries - Rogers Blakeley: Goal - Blakely:
Referee J Connoly (Wigan) Att - 3205 H.T. 10 - 10

Fri 23 May 1997 WIGAN WARRIORS away lost 8 -48

WIGAN W - Paul: Robinson Connolly(Cardiss) Radlinski
A.Johnson: Wright Smith: Cowie(Tallec) Hall
O'Connetr(Hansen) Haughton Cassidy(Holgate)
Farrell(Cowie):   Tries - Robinson(2) Connolly(2) Radlinski
Wright Smith Haughton: Goals - Farrell(7) Paul:
CASTLEFORD - Steadman(Orr): Roach Critchley Flowers
Chapman: Orr (Richardson) Ford: Sampson Russell(Lee St
Hilaire) Crooks(Schick) Anderson(Crooks) Tuuta
(Anderson) Vowles: Try - Critchley: Goals - Crooks(2):
Referee D Campbell (Widnes) Att - 7664 H.T. 8 - 14

Mon 26 May 1997 LEEDS RHINOS home draw 30 -30

CASTLEFORD - Flowers: Roach Vowles Critchley
Chapman: Steadman(Orr)Ford: Sampson
Russell(Steadman) Crooks (Shaun Richardson) (Lee
Bardauskas)(Tuuta)(BB) Schick(Crooks)(Tonks)
Tonks(Crooks) Tuuta (Lee Bardauskas):   Tries -
Critchley(2) Flowers Steadman Orr: Goals - Crooks(4) Orr:
LEEDS - St Hilaire: Sterling Blackmore Hassan Cummings:
Harris Holroyd Collins): Massella(Mathiou)(Massella)
Collins(Sheridan) McDermott(Hay)Morley Farrell Mercer:
Tries - Sterling Blackmore Morley Farrell McDermott:
Goals - Harris(3) Holroyd(2):
Referee G Shaw (Dewsbury) Att - 6815 H.T. 8 - 18

Fri 30 May 1997 OLDHAM BEARS away draw 12 -12

OLDHAM - Atcheson: Leuila Abraham Fawcett(Topping)
Myler: Maloney Crompton: Geldart(Temu) Stephnson
(Clarke) Temu Lord: Davidson(Munro) Munro(Hill)
Goodwin: Tries - Atcheson(2):   Goals - Goodwin(2):
CASTLEFORD - Flowers: Roach Vowles Critchley
Chapman: Steadman(C.Smith) Ford: Crooks (Sykes)
(Crooks) Russell Sampson Schick Tonks(Harland)
Tuuta(Orr): Tries - Roach Schick: Goals - Crooks(2):

Referee R Connolly (Wigan) Att - 3620 H.T. 6 - 2

Sun 8 Jun 1997 PERTH WESTERN REDS home lost 16 – 24 WORLD CLUB CHAMPIONSHIP
CASTLEFORD - Flowers: Roach Critchley Chapman
C.Smith: Vowles Ford: Crooks(Lidden)(Orr) Russell(Lidden)
Sampson(Tonks) Schick Tonks(Sykes) Tuuta(Crooks):
Tries - Critchley Chapman Tonks: Goals - Orr Tonks:
PERTH W R - Fleming: Ryan Bell Haron Daylight:
Wilson(Geyer) Rodwell: Green(Kearns)Fuller Kearns
(Ridding)(Green) Shiels(Chapman) Grieve(Shiels)
Higgins(Evans):
Tries - Rodwell Shiels Grieve Wilson: Goals - Ryan(4):
Referee R Connolly (Wigan) Att - 3590 H.T. nil - 18

Sun 15 Jun 1997 HUNTER MARINERS home lost 14 – 42 WORLD CLUB CHAMPIONSHIP
CASTLEFORD - Flowers(Gay): Roach Lidder (Lee Crooks)
Chapman C.Smith: Vowles Ford: Sampson(Tuuta)
Russell(Richard Goddard) Lee Crooks(Sykes) Schick Tonks
Tuuta(Orr): Tries - Ford Schick C.Smith: Goal - Tonks:
HUNTER M - Ross: Thompson Godden K.Iro Carlaw: Hill
Goldthorpe: Maddison(Brann) Kimorley Stone(T.Iro)
(Marquet) T.Iro(Doherty) Marquet(Piccinelli) Poching:
Tries - Ross(2) Carlaw(2) Hill Goldthorpe Stone T.Iro:
Goals Goldthorpe(5):
Referee S Cummings (Widnes) Att - 3087 H.T. 6 - 16

Sun 29 Jun 1997 LONDON BRONCOS away lost 10 -17
LONDON B -Tollett: Roskell Martin Krause(Higgins)
Offiah: White(Thomas) Edwards:Mestov(Dunford)
Beazley(Howard) Dunford(Bawden) Bawden(Gill)
Rosolen(Mestrov) Matterson:
Tries - Tollett Higgins Dunford: Goals - Matterson(2)D/G:
CASTLEFORD - Flowers: Roach Chapman Vowles C.Smith:
BRAD DAVIS(746)(Lidden) Ford: Sampson(McKell)
Russell(Steadman) Sykes(RICHARD McKELL(747))(Sykes)
Lidden(Anderson) Schick Tuuta(Orr):
Tries - Roach Lidden: Goal - Davis:
Referee S Cummings (Widnes) Att - 2500 H T. 4 - 10

Wed 2 Jul 1997 BRADFORD BULLS away lost 20 - 34
BRADFORD B - Spruce: Hodgson Loughlin Calland Scales:
Graham Tomlinson: Wittengerg(Reihana) Lowes Medley
(Anderson) Nickle(Knox)(Nickle) Forshaw McNamara:
Tries - Scales(2) Tomlinson(2) Graham McNamara:
Goals - McNamara(5):
CASTLEFORD - Flowers: Gay Chapman Vowles C.Smith:
Davis Ford(Steadman): Sampson Russell(Orr)
McKell(Sykes)Schick Lidden(Anderson) Tuuta:
Tries - Vowles(2) Flowers Chapman: Goals - Davis Orr:
Referee D Campbell (Widnes) Att - 11873 H T. 6 - 4

Sat 5 Jul 1997 PARIS ST GERMAIN away won 20 - 8
PARIS S G - Bird: Bergman Evans Chamorin Mahoney:
O'Connor(Robinson) Martin: Taylor (Priddle)(Taylor)
O'Donnell(Bellamy)(O'Donnell) Sing Hancock Peters
Lomax: Try - Evans: Goals - O'Connor Robinson:
CASTLEFORD - Flowers: Gay Critchley Chapman C.Smith:
Vowles Davis: Sampson Russell(Orr) McKell(Sykes)(McKell)

Schick Lidden Tuuta(Anderson)(Harland):
Tries - Gay(2) Chapman Lidden: Goals - Davis(1)(2D/G):
Referee J Connolly (Wigan) Att - 1000(est) H.T. 14 - 8

Fri 11 Jul 1997 OLDHAM BEARS home won 25 - 20
CASTLEFORD - Flowers: Gay Chapman Critchley C.Smith:
Vowles(Tuuta) Davis: McKell(Sykes) Russell(Orr) Sykes
(Tonks) Lidden Schick(Harland) Tuuta(Steadman):   Tries -
Critchley(2) Davis Tonks: Goals - Orr(3) Davis(1)D/G:
OLDHAM B - Atcheson: Leuila Hill Goodwin Jones:
Maloney Crompton: Goldspink(Temu) Clarke(Stephenson)
Temu(Lord)(Geldart) Davidson(Munro) Faimalo Munro
(Topping):   Tries - Davidson(2) Goodwin Maloney:
Goals - Goodwin Maloney:
Referee S Cummings (Widnes) Att - 5408 H.T. 2 - 18

Sun 20 Jul 1997 HUNTER MARINERS away lost 8 – 26 WORLD CLUB CHAMPIONSHIP
HUNTER M - Ross: Beauchamp K.Iro Godden(Zisty)
Carlaw: Hill Goldthorpe: Stone(T.Iro) McCormack(Swain)
Brann(Stone)Marquet Doherty(Brann) Piccinelli(Smith):
Tries - Beauchamp(2) Carlaw(2) K.Iro T.Iro:
Goal - Goldthorpe:
CASTLEFORD - Flowers: Gay Vowles C.Smith Critchley:
Davis Ford(Roach): Sampson(McKell) Orr(Russell)
McKell(Sykes)Lidden Schick(Harland) Harland(Tuuta):
Tries - C.Smith Critchley:
Referee T Smith Att - 3379 H.T. 4 - 18

Sun 27 Jul 1997 PERTH WESTERN REDS away lost 14 – 24 WORLD CLUB CHAMPIONSHIP
PERTH W R - Matt Geyer: Brady-Smith Fleming Ryan
Wilshire: Devine Rodwell: Millar Higgins (Shiels) Evans
(Mark Geyer)(Evans) Green(Sapatu)(Chapman) Fuller
Ridding(Sapatu):
Tries - Matt Geyer Mark Geyer Devine: Goals - Devine(6):
CASTLEFORD - Gay: C.Smith Vowles Critchley Jason
Roach(Flowers): Steadman Ford: Sykes(Sampson) Russell
(Orr) McKell Grant Anderson(Lidden) Harland Tuuta
(Sykes): Tries - Critchley Roach Flowers: Goal - Steadman:
Referee B Grant Att - 6114 H.T. nil - 20

Sun 10 Aug 1997 LONDON BRONCOS home lost 13 - 22
CASTLEFORD - Flowers: Gay Critchley Vowles C.Smith:
Davis Ford: Sampson Orr(Russell) McKell(Sykes)(McKell)
Lidden(Orr) Schick(Steadman) Tuuta(Harland):
Tries - Gay Vowles: Goals - Orr(2) Davis(DG):
LONDON B - Mardon: Roskell Martin(Barwick) Krause
Fatnowna: Beazley(White) Edwards: Bawden(Beazley
Matterson Mestov Salter(Howard)(Hamilton)
Toby(Howard) Gill: Tries - Edwards Matterson White:
Goals - Matterson(3) Barwick(2):
Referee R Connolly (Wigan) Att - 4563 H.T. 13 - 6

Sun 17 Aug 1997 ST HELENS home won 35 - 16
CASTLEFORD - Flowers: Gay Vowles Critchley C.Smith:
Davis (Steadman) Ford(Steadman)(BB): Sampson(Tuuta)
Russell(Orr) McKell(Sykes) Lidden Harland Tuuta(Schick):
Tries - Critchley(2) Gay C.Smith Lidden:

Goals - Davis(6)D/G Orr:
ST HELENS - Arnold: Hayes Haigh Newlove(Morley)
(Newlove) Sullivan: Hammond Long: Northey(O'Neill)
Cunningham O'Neill(Pickavance)McVey(Anderson)
Matautia (Morley) Joynt: Tries - Haigh(2) Newlove:
Goals - Long(2):
Referee D Campbell (Widnes) Att - 5909 H.T. 16 - 16

Mon 25 Aug 1997 WARRINGTON WOLVES away lost 14 - 22

WARRINGTON W - Penny: Finau(Murray) Roper Vagana
Forster: Shelford Briers: Chambers Swann(Wainwright)
(Swann) Mann(Eyres) Knott Tatapau Sculthorpe:
Tries - Roper Vagana Forster: Goals - Briers(4)(2D/G):
CASTLEFORD - Flowers(Steadman)(Flowers): Gay Critchley
Vowles C.Smith: Davis Ford: McKell(Schick) Russell(Orr)
Sykes(Ian Smales) Lidden Harland Tuuta(Steadman):
Tries - Critchley Smith Lidden: Goal - Davis:
Referee J Connolly (Wigan) Att - 6078 H.T. 4 - 11

Sun 31 Aug 1997 SHEFFIELD EAGLES home won 12-10

CASTLEFORD - Flowers: Gay Critchley Vowles C.Smith:
Davis Ford: Sykes(Steadman) Russell(Orr)(B/B)
Mckell(Tonks) Lidden(Harland)(McKell) Schick(Orr)
Harland(Tuuta)(B/B)(Lidden):
Tries - Gay(2): Goals - Davis Orr:
SHEFFIELD E - Sovatabua: Pinkney Morganson
Taewa(Senior) Crowther: Wood Aston (Stephens):
Broadbent(Laughton) Lawless(Turner)
Thompson(Broadbent Carr(Lawless)McAllister Doyle:
Try - Wood: Goals - Aston(2) Crowther: :
Referee S Gamson (St Helens) Att - 5916 H.T. nil - 4

Sun 7 Sept 1997 HALIFAX BLUE SOX away won 23 - 18 PREMIERSHIP PRELIMINARY ROUND

HALIFAX B S - Umaga: Tuilagi Schuster Pearson Bouveng:
Chester Dean(Amone): Harrison (Boothroyd) Rowley
W.Jackson(Marshall) Highton(Gillespie) M.Jackson Moana:
Tries - Bouveng Rowley M.Jackson: Goals - Schuster(3):
CASTLEFORD - Flowers: Gay(Steadman) Critchley Vowles
C.Smith: Davis Ford: Sykes(McKell) Russell(Orr)
McKell(Tonks) Lidden(Tuuta) Schick Harland(Sykes):
Tries - Vowles(2) Davis Schick: Goals - Davis(3) Ford(DG):
Referee D Campbell (Widnes) Att - 2382 H.T. 18 - 6

Sun 14 Sept 1997 BRADFORD BULLS away won 25 – 12 PREMIERSHIP QUARTER FINAL

BRADFORD B - Spruce: Calland(S/O) Loughlin(Graham)
Peacock Ekoku: Paul Tomlinson: McDermott (McNamara)
Lowes(McDermott) Reihana(Wittenberg)(Jowitt) Forshaw
Dwyer McNamara(Nickle):
Tries - Lowes Forshaw: Goals - Loughlin McNamara:
CASTLEFORD - Flowers: Gay Vowles(Steadman) Critchley
C.Smith: Davis Ford: McKell(Sykes) Russell(Orr)
Sykes(Tonks) Schick Lidden Tuuta(Harland):
Tries - Critchley C.Smith Davis Tuuta:
Goals - Davis (3) Steadman Ford(D/G):
Referee R Connolly (Wigan) Att - 10300 H.T. 11 - 8

Fri 19 Sept 1997 ST HELENS away lost 18 - 32 PREMIERSHIP SEMI FINAL

ST HELENS - Arnold: Stewart Hunte Newlove Sullivan:
Hammond Long: Leatham (Morley) Cunningham O'Neill
(McVey)(Booth) McVey(Pickavance) Perelini Joynt: Tries -
Newlove(2) Hammond Long Morley: Goals - Long(6):
CASTLEFORD - Flowers: Gay Vowles (Graham Steadman)
Critchley Chris Smith: Davis Ford:
Sykes(Tonks)(BrendonTuuta) Russell(Orr) McKell(Sykes)
Schick Jason Lidden Brendon Tuuta(Harland):
Tries - Vowles Davis Schick: Goals - Davis(3):
Referee J Connolly (Wigan) Att - 5343 H.T. 12 – 2

Adrian Vowles
D. No 739
1997- to 2005

Danny Orr
D. No 742
1997 to 2012

Paul Smith
D. No 744
1997 to 2000

Jason Critchley
D. No 745
1997 to 1998

Brad Davis
D. No 746
1997 to 2006

Richard McKell
D. No 747
1997- to 1998

SEASON 1997

D.N	PLAYER		DEBUT	L MATCH	APP	SUB	T.AP	TRI'S	G'LS	D.G	P'TS
657	ANDERSON	GRANT		27/07/1997	7	5	12	1	0	0	4
661	SAMPSON	DEAN			21	1	22	1	0	0	4
675	STEADMAN	GRAHAM		19/09/1997	7	16	23	2	2	0	12
679	SMITH	TONY		16/03/1997	1	1	2	1	0	0	4
685	CROOKS	LEE		15/06/1997	11	1	12	0	13	0	26
691	FORD	MIKE			21	1	22	1	0	3	7
693	MIDDLETON	SIMON		18/05/1997	11	0	11	3	0	0	12
694	SYKES	NATHAN			14	12	26	0	0	0	0
699	SMITH	CHRIS		19/09/1997	24	1	25	6	0	0	24
705	RUSSELL	RICHARD			24	2	26	1	0	0	4
706	SMALES	IAN		25/08/1997	0	5	5	0	0	0	0
708	FLOWERS	JASON			27	1	28	5	0	0	20
709	GODDARD	RICHARD		23/03/1997	4	1	5	0	6	0	12
715	TONKS	IAN			8	6	14	2	6	0	20
719	HARLAND	LEE			13	9	22	0	0	0	0
720	FLYNN	ADRIAN		06/04/1997	2	3	5	2	0	0	8
723	SCHICK	ANDREW			19	6	25	5	0	0	20
724	TUUTA	BRENDON		19/07/1997	26	3	29	1	0	0	4
726	RICHARDSON	SHAUN		26/05/1997	2	2	4	0	0	0	0
728	GAY	RICHARD			20	4	24	7	0	0	28
729	EDWARDS	DICCON		11/05/1997	0	3	3	0	0	0	0
731	HARGRAVE	SPENCER			0	1	1	0	0	0	0
732	CHAPMAN	DAVID			10	2	12	4	0	0	16
737	BARDAUSKAS	LEE		26/05/1997	0	1	1	0	0	0	0
738	ROACH	JASON	09/02/1997	27/07/1997	11	1	12	6	0	0	24
739	VOWLES	ADRIAN	09/02/1997		30	0	30	8	1	0	34
740	LIDDEN	JASON	09/02/1997	19/09/1997	21	3	24	7	0	0	28
741	McVEAN	SEAN	09/02/1997	09/02/1997	0	1	1	0	0	0	0
742	ORR	DANNY	16/03/1997		12	16	28	3	18	0	48
743	ST HILAIRE	LEE	16/03/1997	23/05/1997	4	2	6	0	0	0	0
744	SMITH	PAUL	01/04/1997		0	3	3	0	0	0	0
745	CRITCHLEY	JASON	18/05/1997		16	0	16	12	0	0	48
746	DAVIS	BRAD	29/06/1997		12	0	12	4	21	5	63
747	McKELL	RICHARD	29/06/1997		12	1	13	0	0	0	0
	34		**10**	**17**	**390**	**114**	**504**	**82**	**67**	**8**	**470**

COMPETITION		P	W	D	L	FOR	AGT
S. LEAGUE	POSITION 10 OF 12	22	5	2	15	334	515
RL CUP		1	0	0	1	18	36
W.C.C.		4	0	0	4	52	116
PLAY OFF		3	2	0	1	66	62
PLAYERS RECORDS		**30**	**7**	**2**	**21**	**470**	**729**

From this season the team became known as the Castleford Tigers

Following defeats in the Challenge Cup and the opening five league games, Coach John Joyner left after a 25-year association with the Club. His last game in charge was the away fixture at Sheffield Eagles. Mick Morgan was installed as Caretaker Coach until a permanent replacement could be recruited.

Mick's reign lasted for only four games, the last being the defeat by St Helens 42-16, played at the Anfield Stadium Liverpool. With the new Coach, Australian Stuart Raper, only arriving in the country on the Thursday prior to the St Helens Sunday fixture, his first game in complete charge was the home defeat by Paris St Germain 13–8.

A World Club Championship was introduced, with Super League Clubs playing Australian Clubs on a home and away basis. Castleford lost to Perth Western Reds 16-24 at home and 14-24 away and Hunter Mariners 14-42 at home and 8-26 away.

Three notable Debutants were Adrian Vowles Danny Orr and Brad Davis.

SEASON 1998

SUPER LEAGUE III

From last seasons Super League Oldham as the bottom club were relegated then folded and subsequently reformed joining Division 2. Paris St Germain then folded and dropped out of the league altogether these two clubs being replaced by Hull Sharks and Huddersfield.Giants.in Division 1 Workington Town were relegated and replaced by Hunslet Hawks, Rochdale Hornets and Leigh Centurians.in Division 2 with the three promotions and only one relegation plus Oldham and Carlisle and Prescot Panthers dropping out of the league the division was reduced to eight teams

Fri 1 Jan 1998 LEEDS RHINOS away draw 22 - 22 FRIENDLY
LEEDS R - Harris: Golden Hughes(Hassan) Cummins Rivett: Kemp(Holroyd) Sheridan: Masella(Field) Cantilon (Lawford) Fleary(Masella) Hay Farrell Morley:
Tries - Golden Hughes Sheridan Farrell:
Goals - Holroyd(2) Harris:
CASTLEFORD - Flowers: Gay Critchley Mather Wells: Maloney(Benn) Ford(Dobson): Sampson(Hill)(Smith) Dobson(Orr) Sykes(Sampson)(S/O) Harland Tonks Hargrave:
Tries - Gay(2) Critchley Maloney: Goals - Maloney(2)Benn:
Referee C Morris (Huddersfield) Att - 8915 H.T. 16 - 10

Sun 1 Feb 1998 SHEFFIELD EAGLES home lost 16 – 22 FRIENDLY
CASTLEFORD - Flowers: Critchley Mather Vowles Wells: Maloney Ford: Sampson Orr McKell Schick Tallec Harland: Subs - Tonks Hargrave Ellison Dobson:
Tries - Critchley Wells Orr: Goals - Maloney(2):
SHEFFIELD E - Sovatabue: Cardoza Morganson Senior Sodje: Stephens Aston: Broadbents Rousso Laughton Carr Shaw Wood: Subs - Doyle Law Wright Edmed Crowther Taewa Thorman :
Tries - Sodje Broadbent Carr Wood: Goals - Aston(3):
Referee R Connolly (Wigan) Att - 4123 H.T. 12 - 4

Sun 8 Feb 1998 HULL SHARKS away won 26 - 22 FRIENDLY
HULL S - Prescott: Seru Baridon Hunte Johnson: Hallas Tomlinson: Temu Donahue Leatham Craven Radford Campbell: Subs - Nolan Gray Smith Wilson Kithing:
Tries - Hunte Johnson Leatham Campbell:
Goals - Hallas(3):
CASTLEFORD - Flowers: Wells Critchley Vowles Gay: Davies Ford: Sampson Orr Sykes Schick Tallec Harland: Subs - McKell Maloney Smith Dobson Hargrave Benn:
Tries - Critchley Gay Davis Schick Maloney:
Goals - Benn(2) Orr:
Referee P Taberner (Wigan) Att - 3836 H.T. 10 - 4

Sat 14 Feb 1998 LEEDS RHINOS away won 15 - 12 CHALLENGE CUP ROUND 4
LEEDS R - Harris: Sterling Blackmore Cummins Rivett: Kemp(Holroyd) Sheridan: Masella(McDermott)(Masella)

Lawford Fleary(Mathoiu) Morley Farrell Glanville(Hay):
Try - Kemp: Goals Harris (4):
CASTLEFORD - Flowers: Gay(Wells) Vowles BARRIE-JON MATHER(748) Critchley: Davis Ford: Sampson Orr (FRANCIS MALONEY(749)) McKell (MICHAEL SMITH (750))(McKell) Sykes(Schick) Schick(GAEL TALLEC(751)) Harland (M.Smith):
Tries - Mather Schick: Goals - Davis(2) Maloney Ford(DG):
Referee J Connolly (Wigan) Att - 7067 H.T. 7 - 2

Sat 28 Feb 1998 BRADFORD BULLS home won 26 -21 CHALLENGE CUP ROUND 5
CASTLEFORD - Flowers: Gay Vowles Mather Critchley: Davis Ford(Maloney): Sampson Orr(Ford) McKell(M.Smith) (McKell) Tallec(DANNY ELLISON(752)) Schick(Tallec) Harland(Tallec):
Tries - Flowers Davis Tallec Ellison: Goals - Davis(5):
BRADFORD B - Spruce: Valkona Calland Peacock (McNamara) Graham: Paul(Donougher) Edwards: McDermott(Rehana)Lowes Jowett(Anderson) (McDermott) Forshaw Bradley McNamara(Nickle):
Tries - Spruce Calland Peacock Lowes:
Goals McNamara(1) LowesD/G:
Referee S Cummings (Widnes) Att -10283 H.T. 20 - 8

Sat 14 Mar 1998 SHEFFILED EAGLES home Lost 22 – 32 CHALLENGE CUP QUARTER FINAL
CASTLEFORD - Flowers: Gay Vowles Mather(Ellison) Critchley: Davis Ford: Sampson (M.Smith) Orr(Maloney) McKell(M.Smith)(McKell) Tallec(Sykes) Schick Harland:
Tries - Davis(2) Mather(2) Vowles: Goal - Maloney:
SHEFFIELD E - Sovatabua: Pinkney Taewa Senior Crowther(Stott): Watson Aston: Broadbent(Laughton) Tuner(Stephens) Laughton(Shaw) Carr Shaw(Jackson) Doyle(Wood : Tries - Senior(2) Crowther(2) Sovatabua Carr: Goals - Aston(4):
Referee R Connolly (Wigan) Att - 7467 H.T. 8 - 16

Sun 5 Apr 1998 WIGAN WARRIORS away lost 4 - 18
WIGAN W - Radlinski: Gilmour Connolly Moore(Cassidy) Robinson: Paul Smith: Cowie(Holgate)(Cowie) McCormack Mestrov(O'Connor) Betts Haughton(Johnson) Farrell:
Tries - Smith(2) Paul: Goals - Farrell(3):
CASTLEFORD - Flowers(Ford): Gay Mather Critchley Ellison: Davis Ford(Maloney): McKell(M.Smith) Russell(Orr) Sykes(Harland) Schick Tallec(McKell) Vowles: Try - Mather:
Referee S Cummings (Widnes) Att - 10920 H.T. 6 - 4

Fri 10 Apr 1998 SHEFFIELD EAGLES home won 19 -6
CASTLEFORD - Flowers: Gay Critchley Mather Wells: Davis(Maloney)(Davis) Ford: Sampson(M.Smith) Russell(Orr)(B/B) Sykes(McKell)(B/B) Schick(Sampson) M.Smith (Harland)(Sykes) Vowles: Tries - Flowers Critchley Orr: Goals - Davis(2) (DG) Maloney:
SHEFFIELD E - Sovatabua: Pinkney Taewa Stott Crowther: Watson(Turner) Aston: Broadbent(Laughton) Lawless Laughton Molloy Carr(Jackson) Shaw(Carr) Doyle(Wood):
Try - Stott: Goal - Aston:
Referee C Morris (Huddersfield) Att - 5248 H.T. 6 - 6

SEASON 1998

Fri 17 Apr 1998 LEEDS RHINOS away lost 10 - 20
LEEDS R - Harris: Sterling Blackmore Godden(St Hilaire)
Cummins: Kemp Sheridan: Masella(Mathiou) Newton
(Holroyd) Fleary(Masella) Morley Farrell Glanville(Powell):
Tries - Harris Kemp Sheridan: Goals - Harris(4):
CASTLEFORD - Flowers: Gay Mather Critchley Wells
(Harland)(McKell): Maloney Davis: Sampson Russell(Orr)
Sykes(M.Smith) M.Smith(Ford) Schick (Harland) Vowles:
Tries - M.Smith Vowles: Goal Davis:
Referee S Cummings (Widnes) Att - 13120 H.T. nil - 6

Sun 26 Apr 1998 HALIFAX BLUE SOX away lost 16 -29
HALIFAX B S - Pearson(Baldwin)(Gillespie): Tuilagi Gibson
Bouveng Powell: Moana Chester(Pearson): Harrison
(Hobson) Rowley Skerratt(Marshall) Clark Gillespie(Marns)
Mercer: Tries - Chester(2) Powell Skerrett Clark:
Goals - Chester(3) PearsonD/G:
CASTLEFORD - Flowers: Gay Mather Vowles Critchley:
Davis Ford(Maloney): Sampson MARTIN HALL(753)(Ford)
Sykes(M.Smith)(Tallec) M.Smith(P.Smith) Schick(McKell)
Harland: Tries - Gay Sykes: Goals - Davis (4):
Referee K Kirkpatrick (Warrington) Att - 5172 H.T. 8 - 16

Sun 10 May 1998 HULL SHARKS home won 31 - 18
CASTLEFORD - Flowers: Gay Critchley Mather Wells:
Maloney(Tallec) Davis(Ford): Sykes(Ellison) Hall
McKell(M.Smith) Schick M.Smith(Harland) Vowles:
Tries - Gay(2) Flowers Critchley Ellison McKell:
Goals - Davis(3) FordD/G:
HULL S - Prescott: Seru Hunte Hallas Baildon: Lester
Nolan: Okesene(Leatham) Stephenson(Johnson) Ireland
Campbell Leatham (Okesene)(Wilson)(Radford) Hepi
(J Smith):
Tries - Radford(2) Stephenson Leatham: Goal - Hallas:
Referee S.Gamson (St Helens) Att - 7722 H.T. 22 - 4

**Sun 17 May 1988 WARRINGTON WOLVES away
lost 18 - 33**
WARRINGTON W - Penny: Rudd(Fawcett) Kohe-Love
Eager Forster: Roper(Doyle) Briers: Chambers(Hilton)
Farrar Nutley McCurrie(Chambers) Tuuta(Morley)
Wainwright: Tries - McCurrie(2) Eager Wainwright Briers:
Goals - Briers(6) (DG):
CASTLEFORD - Flowers(Ellison): Gay Critchley Mather
Wells: Maloney Ford: Sampson(M.Smith) Hall Sykes
(Sampson) M.Smith(Harland) Schick(Tallec) (Chapman)
Vowles: Tries - Ford(2) Mather: Goals - Maloney(3):
Referee J Connolly (Wigan) Att - 4918 H.T. 4 - 13

Fri 22 May 1998 BRADFORD BULLS home lost 10 -52
CASTLEFORD - Flowers(Ellison): Gay Mather Critchley
Wells: Maloney Davis: M.Smith(McKell) Martin
Hall(Ford)(BB) Sykes(Tallec) Tallec(Harland) Harland
(P.Smith) Vowles: Tries - Mather Maloney: Goals Davis:
BRADFORD B - Spruce(Scales): Vaikona Bradley(Spruce)
Peacock Ekoku: Paul Edwards: Donougher Lowes
Reihana(Nickle) Forshaw(Graham) Dwyer(McDermott)
McNamara: Tries - Paul(3) Edwards(2) McDermott(2)
Vaikona Peacock Donougher: Goals McNamara(6):
Referee J Connolly (Wigan) Att - 8043 H.T. nil - 30

Sun 31 May 1998 SALFORD REDS away won 18 - 8
SALFORD R - Broadbent: Hassan Martin McAvoy Rogers:
White(Savello) Crompton: Southern (E Faimalo)(Southern)
Edwards Eccles(Randall) J Faimalo(Forber) Bradbury
(White) Hulme: Tries - Martin Rogers:
CASTLEFORD - Gay: Chapman(JAMIE BENN(754)) Mather
Critchley Wells: Maloney(Tallec) Ford: Sampson(P.Smith)
Davis McKell(Sampson) Tallec(Orr) Harland(Sykes) Vowles:
Tries - Ford Mather Wells: Goals Benn(3):
Referee C Morris (Huddersfield) Att -4143 H.T.12 - 12

Sun 7 Jun 1998 ST HELENS home lost 12 - 34
CASTLEFORD - Flowers: Gay(Benn) Critchley Mather
Wells: Maloney(Davis) Ford: Sykes(Tonks) Davis(Orr)
McKell(Sykes) Harland Tallec(P.Smith) Vowles:
Triy - Flowers: Goals - Davis(2) Maloney Benn:
ST HELENS - Atcheson: C Smith Newlove D Smith(Haigh)
(D Smith)(Haigh)(B/B) Sullivan: Martyn Long: Goldspink
(Pickavance) Cunningham O'Neill(Perelini)(O'Neil)
Joynt(Davidson) Sculthorpe Hammond:
Tries - Newlove(2) Long Perelini Joynt Hammond:
Goals - Long(5):
Referee R Connolly (Wigan) Att - 7192 H.T. 6 - 20

**Sun 14 Jun 1998 HUDDERSFIELD GIANTS home
lost 10 - 16**
CASTLEFORD - Flowers(Benn): Gay Mather Vowles Wells:
Davis Ford: Sampson Orr Mckell(Maloney) M.Smith
(P.Smith) Sykes(M.Smith) Schick(Tonks):
Try - Orr: Goals Davis(3):
HUDDERSFIELD G - Arnold: Hanger King Bunyan
Cheatham: Orr Booth: Harmon(Jackson) (Harmon) Russell
Field(Wittenberg) Richards(Vievers) Wittenberg(Berry)
(Moore) Sturm:
Tries - King Booth Russell: Goals - Booth(2):
Referee S Ganson (St Helens) Att - 5306 H.T. 10 - 6

Sun 21 Jun 1998 LONDON BRONCOS away won 36-16
LONDON B - Godden: Cotton Toshack Ryan Chesney: Gill
Air(Chapman): Young Beasley(Wlliams)(Beasley)
Carroll(Temu) Retchless Best(Higgins)(Best) Mattinson:
Tries - Godden Beasley Mattinson: Goals - Mattinson(2):
CASTLEFORD - Gay: Wells Mather Maloney(M.Smith)
Chapman: Davis Ford: Sampson Orr (P.Smith) McKell
(Sykes) Schick(Tonks) Harland(Orr) Vowles:
Tries - Gay Davis Ford Sampson M.Smith Tonks Vowles:
Goals - Davis(4):
Referee C.Morris (Huddersfield) Att - 2500 H.T. 6 – 10

Sun 28 Jun 1998 WIGAN WARRIORS home lost 4 - 34
CASTLEFORD - Gay: Wells Maloney Vowles
Chapman(Flowers): Davis Ford: Sampson Orr
McKell(M.Smith) Schick(P.Smith)(B/B)(Schick)(P.Smith)
Tonks(Sykes)(Tonks) Harland: Try - P.Smith:
WIGAN W - Radlinski: Robison Connolly Moore(Bell)
Bell(Johnson): Paul Smith (Gilmour): Cowie(Mestrov)
McCormack Mestrov(O'Connor) Betts(Haughton) Cassidy
Farrell: Tries - Paul(2) Johnson Connolly Moore Farrell:
Goals - Farrell(5):
Referee S Cummings (Widnes) Att – 6734 H.T. 18 - 4

SEASON 1998

Fri 3 Jul 1998 SHEFFIELD EAGLES away lost 16 - 22
SHEFFIELD E - Watson(Sovatabua): Stott Morganson
Senior Sodje: Wood Vassilakopoulos(Turner): Broadbent
Stephens Molloy(Laughton)(Molloy) Carr(Taewa) Shaw
(Carr) Doyle:
Tries - Sodje Stephens Taewa: Goals - Wood(4)(2DG):
CASTLEFORD - Gay: Wells Maloney Critchley Ellison: Davis
Ford(Flowers): Sampson(Sykes) Orr Sykes(P.Smith)
Tonks(McKell) Harland Vowles(Tallec)(P.Smith):
Tries - Wells Davis Orr: Goals - Maloney Davis:
Referee K Kirkpatrick(Warr'ton) Att - 3000(Est) H.T. 12 - 12

**Sat 25 Jul 1998 WARRINGTON WOLVES won 23 - 16
at CARDIFF RUFC WALES**
CASTLEFORD - Gay: Ellison(M.Smith) Mather
Critchley(Ford) Chapman: Maloney Davis: Sampson
Orr(Ford)(Orr) Sykes(McKell) P.Smith(Schick)(B/B) Harland
Vowles: Tries - M.Smith Critchley Ford Sampson:
Goals - Maloney(3) Davis(DG):
WARRINGTON W - Penny(Knott): Rudd Kohe-Love
(Fawcett) Eager Roach: Doyle Briers(Causey)(Briers): Hilton
Farrar Nutley McCurrie Tuuta(Chambers) Wainwright:
Tries - Rudd Briers McCurrie: Goals - Rudd(2):
Referee S Ganson (St Helens) Att - 4437 H.T. 10 - 6

Sun 2 Aug 1998 LEEDS RHINOS home won 22 - 16
CASTLEFORD - Flowers: Critchley Maloney Vowles Wells:
Orr Davis: Sampson Harland (Tallec) McKell(M.Smith)
Sykes(P.Smith) M.Smith(Russell)(Ford) Schick(McKell):
Tries - Flowers Wells Orr M.Smith: Goals - Maloney(3):
LEEDS R - St Hilaire: Sterling(Powell) Blackmore Cummins
Rivett: Harris Holroyd: Masella(McDermott)(Masella)
Sheridan Fleary(Mathiou) Farrell(Fleary) Hay Glanville
(Morley):   Tries - Blackmore Cummins: Goals - Harris(4):
Referee S Cummings (Widnes) Att - 8406 H.T. 14 - 14

Sun 9 Aug 1998 HALIFAX BLUE SOX home lost 16 -36
CASTLEFORD - Gay: Flowers Maloney Vowles Wells:
Orr(Harland) Davis: Sampson Russell(Ford) Mckell
(P.Smith) M.Smith(Sykes) Schick(M.Smith) Harland
(Critchley):   Tries - Flowers Gay Mckell: Goals - Orr(2):
HALIFAX B S - Bloem(Marns): Tuilagi Powell Pearson
Bouveng: Chester Clinch: Harrison(Baldwin) Rowley
Skerrett(Marshall) Clark(Moana) Mercer(Harrison)
Moana(Hall):   Tries - Tuilagi Bouveng Chester Clinch
Marshall Clark Moana: Goals - Clinch(3) Pearson:
Referee J Connolly (Wigan) Att - 6820 H.T. 16 - 10

Sun 16 Aug 1998 HULL SHARKS away lost 6 - 18
HULL S - Prescott: Seru Hunte(Baildon) Campbell Hallas:
Lester Murdock: Temu(Wilson) Hepi(Busby) Okesene
(Ireland)(Okesene) Craven Schultz Busby(Nolan):
Tries - Prescott Lester Nolan: Goals - Prescott(3):
CASTLEFORD - Gay: Flowers Critchley Maloney(Tallec)
Wells: Orr(Ford) Davis(Orr): Sampson(Sykes) Russell
(Schick) McKell Sykes(M.Smith) Harland Vowles:
Try - Orr: Goal - Orr:
Referee – Mr K Kirkpatrick(War'ton) Att - 5144 H.T. 6 -10

**Sat 21 Aug 1998 WARRINGTON WOLVES home
won 50 - 24**
CASTLEFORD - Gay: Ellison(Critchley) Mather Maloney
Wells: Orr Davis(Flowers): Sampson Russell(Ford)
Sykes(M.Smith) Schick(Sykes) Harland(Russell) Vowles:
Tries - Wells(2) Ellison Maloney Davis Sampson M.Smith
Schick Vowles: Goals - Orr(7):
WARRINGTON W - Penny: Roach Fawcett Eager Forster:
Wainwright Brie-s: Chambers(Stevens)(Causey)
Farrar(Chambers) Nutley Knott(Tuuta)
Tuuta(Causey)(Pechey) McCurrie:
Tries - Roach(2) Penny Farrar Tuuta: Goals Briers(2):
Referee R Connolly (Wigan) Att - 4130 H.T. 26 - 10

**Mon 31 Aug 1998 BRADFORD BULLS away
lost 8 - 24**
BRADFORD B - Spruce: Vaikona McAvoy(Ekoku) Bradley
Scales: Paul Deacon: McDermott (Harmon) Lowes
Harmon(Howard)(Fielden)(McDermott) Forshaw
Dwyer(Donougher) McNamara:
Tries - Spruce Scales Lowes: Goals - McNamara(6):
CASTLEFORD - Gay: Critchley Mather Maloney(Chapman)
(BB) Wells: Orr Ford: Sampson Russell(M.Smith) McKell
(Sykes)(McKell) Harland M.Smith (Schick)(Flowers) Vowles:
Try - Orr: Goals - Orr(2):
Referee S Cummings (Widnes) Att - 10559 H.T. 8 - 12

Sun 6 Sept 1998 SALFORD REDS home won 30 - 12
CASTLEFORD - Flowers: Wells Mather Maloney
Ellison(Critchley): Orr Davis: Sampson(McKell) Russell
(Ford) McKell(Sykes) M.Smith(Schick) Harland Vowles:
Tries - Orr(2) Davis(2) M.Smith: Goals - Orr(3) Davis(2):
SALFORD R - Broadbent: Martin Naylor Hassan Rogers:
Blakeley Waring: Southern(Savelio) Edwards(Forber)
Eccles(E Faimalo) Highton(J Faimalo) J Faimalo(Randall)
Hulme: Tries - Waring Hulme: Goals - Blakeley(2):
Referee R Conrolly (Wigan) Att - 4865 H.T. 10 - nil

Sun 13 Sept 1998 ST HELENS away draw 32 - 32
ST HELENS - Atcheson: C Smith D Smith Newlove
Sullivan: Martyn Long: Perelini(Pickavance) Cunningham
Goldspink(Matautia) Sculthorpe Davidson(Perelini)
Hammond Tries - Martyn(2) Newlove Pickavance
Goldspink: Goals - Long(6):
CASTLEFORD - Flowers;Wells(David Chapman) Vowles
Maloney Critchley: Orr Davis: Sampson(Ellison)
Russell(Tallec) Mckell(Sykes) M.Smith Schick Harland:
Tries - Sampson(3) Maloney Vowles Tallec:
Goals - Orr(2) Davis(2):
Referee K Kirkpatrick (War'ton) Att - 5887 H.T. 14 - 14

**Sun 20 Sept 1998 HUDDERSFIELD GIANTS away
won 32 - 20**
HUDDERSFIELD G - Arnold: Simpson Hanger(Cheetham)
Loughlin Cheetham(Barton): Orr Goulding:
Wittenberg(King) Russell Field(Adams) King(Richards)
Fielden(Berry) Sturm:
Tries - Arnold Simpson Hanger Orr: Goals - Goulding(2):
CASTLEFORD - Flowers: Wells Maloney Vowles Critchley:
Orr Davis: Sampson Richard Russell(GARETH DOBSON

SEASON 1998

(755)) (Ford) McKell(M.Smith) M.Smith(Sykes)
Tallec(Schick)(BB) Harland(Dobson): Tries - Maloney(2)
Orr(2) Wells Vowles: Goals - Davis(3) Orr:
Referee S Nicholson(Whitehaven) Att - 3791 H.T. 10 -16

**Sun 27 Sept 1998 LONDON BRONCOS home
won 23 - 18**
CASTLEFORD - Flowers: Wells Vowles Maloney Jason
Critchley(Dobson): Orr Davis: Sampson Harland(Andrew
Schick) Richard Mckell(Sykes) Smith(Tallec) Tallec(Tonks)
Andrew Schick(Mike Ford): Tries - Flowers(2) Vowles
Harland: Goals - Orr(3) FordD/G:
LONDON B - Toshack: Smyth Temu Ryan Cotton
(Spencer): Tollett(Jennings) Air: Young Beasley(Salter)
Salter(Thomas)(Peters) Peters(Millard) Retchless Gill:
Tries - Temu Air Gill: Goals - Ryan(3):
Referee K Kirkpatrick (Warrington) Att - 5880 H.T. 2 – 12

Barrie-Jon Mather
D. No 748
1998 to 2002

Francis Maloney
D. No 749
1998 to 2004

Michael Smith
D. No 750
1998 to 2004

Gael Tallec
D. No 751
1998 to 1999

Danny Ellison
D. No 752
1998 to 1999

Martin Hall
D. No 753
1998

Jamie Benn
D. No 754
1998 to 2000

Gareth Dobson
D. No 755
1998 to 2000

SEASON 1998

D.N	PLAYER		DEBUT	L MATCH	APP	SUB	T.AP	TRI'S	G'LS	D.G	P'TS
661	SAMPSON	DEAN			22	0	22	6	0	0	24
691	FORD	MIKE		27/09/1998	14	11	25	5	0	3	23
694	SYKES	NATHAN			15	10	25	1	0	0	4
705	RUSSELL	RICHARD		20/09/1998	10	1	11	0	0	0	0
708	FLOWERS	JASON			19	4	23	8	0	0	32
715	TONKS	IAN			2	4	6	1	0	0	4
719	HARLAND	LEE			20	5	25	1	0	0	4
723	SCHICK	ANDREW		27/09/1998	17	5	22	2	0	0	8
728	GAY	RICHARD			21	0	21	5	0	0	20
732	CHAPMAN	DAVID		13/09/1998	4	3	7	0	0	0	0
734	WELLS	JON			20	1	21	6	0	0	24
739	VOWLES	ADRIAN			26	0	26	7	0	0	28
742	ORR	DANNY			17	5	22	10	21	0	82
744	SMITH	PAUL			1	0	11	1	0	0	4
745	CRITCHLEY	JASON		27/09/1998	20	3	23	3	0	0	12
746	DAVIS	BRAD			24	0	24	8	35	2	104
747	McKELL	RICHARD		27/09/1998	18	6	24	2	0	0	8
748	MATHER	BARRIE-JON	14/02/1998		18	0	18	7	0	0	28
749	MALONEY	FRANCIS	14/02/1998		19	7	26	5	14	0	48
750	SMITH	MICHAEL	14/02/1998		14	9	23	6	0	0	24
751	TALLEC	GAEL	14/02/1998		8	8	16	2	0	0	8
752	ELLISON	DANNY	28/02/1998		5	6	11	3	0	0	12
753	HALL	MARTIN	26/04/1998	22/05/1998	4	0	4	0	0	0	0
754	BENN	JAMIE	31/05/1998		0	3	3	0	4	0	8
755	DOBSON	GARETH	21/09/1998		0	2	2	0	0	0	0
	25		**8**	**7**	**338**	**103**	**441**	**89**	**74**	**5**	**509**

COMPETITION		P	W	D	L	FOR	AGT
S. LEAGUE	POSITION 6 OF 12	23	10	1	12	446	522
RL CUP		3	2	0	1	63	65
PLAYERS RECORDS		**26**	**12**	**1**	**13**	**509**	**587**

In the Challenge Cup we had victories away at Leeds 15-12 in Round 4 through a late try by Andrew Schick, and at home to Bradford Bulls 26-21 in Round 5. We were "KO'd" (pun intended) by a Keith Senior inspired Sheffield Eagles in the quarter-finals, who went on to beat Wigan in the Final 17-8.

With the introduction of the Australian styled Top 5 play-off we just missed out by finishing in sixth place.

SEASON 1999

SUPER LEAGUE IV

In the Super League Wakefield Trinity Wildcats were promoted and new club Gateshead Thunder were admitted.
The previous seasons Divisions 1 and 2 were formed Into one division consisting of eighteen clubs and re-titled The Northern Ford Premiership.

Sat 26 Dec 1998 FEATHERSTONE ROVERS away won 25 – 12 FRIENDLY
FEATHERSTONE R - Bramald: Thompson Law Newlove Stokes: Horsley Handley: Dickens Patrickson Fisher Williamson Padgett Dooler:
Subs used- Scott Riley Okesene Wileman Swinson:
Tries - Horsley Swinson: Goals - Dickens(2)
CASTLEFORD - Kirk: P Wells J Wells Ellis Sibson: Allen Riley: Tonks Dobson Lynch Hill Hargrave Bardauskas:
Subs used - Butterfield Smith Canning Kear McNally:
Tries - Hill(2) Allen McNally: Goals - Tonks(4) Riley(DG):
Referee J McGregor (Hud'field) Att - 3107 H.T. 18 - 2

Fri 1st Jan 1999 LEEDS RHINOS away lost 21 - 26 FRIENDLY
LEEDS R - Harris: Sailor Hughes Godden Cummins: Pratt Sheridan: Field Jackson McDermott Carvell Glanville Sinfield: Subs used - Golden Lawford Ward Chapman:
Tries - Harris(2} Hughes Sheridan Sinfield Sailor:
Goal - Harris:
CASTLEFORD - Flowers: Gay Wells Eagar Rogers: Maloney Orr: Sampson Dobson Sykes Hill Tonks Harland: Subs used - Ellis Riley Tallec Lynch:
Tries - Sampson(2) Rogers Tonks: Goals - Orr Tonks Maloney(DG):
Referee N Oddy (Halifax) Att - 19907 H.T.10 - 4

Fri 29 Jan 1999 GATESHEAD THUNDER home won 18 - 8 FRIENDLY
CASTLEFORD - Flowers: Gay Eagar Maloney Wells: Orr Davis: Sykes Raper Sampson Harland Fritz Vowles:
Subs used- Ellison Tallec Lynch Dobson Rogers Jones Hill:
Tries - Vowles(2) Wells: Goals - Orr(3):
GATESHEAD T - Sammut: Talone Maiden Bird Daylight: Simon Peters: Green Waltert Hick Allwood Wilson Grimaldi: Subs used - Herron Felsch Rutherforth Carney Robinson Collings Singleton Allwood Towari:
Tries - Daylight Hick:
Referee S Cummins (Widnes) Att - 4120 H.T. 12 - 4

Sun 14 Feb 1999 HULL SHARKS home won 36 - 22 CHALLENGE CUP ROUND 4
CASTLEFORD - Flowers: Gay MICHAEL EAGAR(756) Maloney DARREN ROGERS(757): Orr Davis: Sampson AARON RAPER(758)(Hill) Sykes(Tonks) Tonks(ANDY LYNCH(759)) Tallec(Ellison) Vowles(Wells):
Tries - Flowers(2) Davis(2) Gay Orr Rogers:
Goals - Tonks(4):
HULL S - Prescott: Baildon Calland Campbell Saru: Lester Murdock: HarrisonHall Ireland(Smith)(Craven) Craven(Leatham) Holgate Purcell(Hallas)(Purcell):

Tries - Prescott(2) Baildon Hall: Goals - Prescott(3):
Referee R Connolly (Wigan) - Sub Referee after 18 minutes of play - Mr D Ansell (Hud'field Att - 6107 H.T. 14 - 12

Fri 26 Feb 1999 YORK WASPS home won 28 - 2 CHALLENGE CUP ROUND 5
CASTLEFORD - Flowers: Gay Eagar Maloney Rogers: Orr Davis: Sampson Harland (Dobson) JAMES PICKERING(760)(Sykes)(Pickering) DALE FRITZ(761)(Harland) Tonks(Tallec) Vowles(Wells):
Tries - Eagar Maloney Davis Harland: Goals - Orr(6):
YORK W - Benn: Sini Goddard Austerfield Deakin: Cain Strange: Booth(Tichener)(Booth) Pallister(Callaghan) Hill(Hagan)(Hill) Judge Lambert(Ramsden) Edwards:
Goal - Benn:
Referee N Oddy (Halifax) Att - 5411 H.T. 10 - 2

Sun 7 Mar 1999 WAKEFIELD TRINITY home won 12 - 10
CASTLEFORD - Flowers: Gay Maloney Eagar Rogers: Orr Davis: Sykes(Pickering)(Sykes) Raper(Pickering) Sampson Harland(Tonks) Fritz (Tallec) Vowles:
Try - Maloney: Goals - Orr(4):
WAKEFIELD T - Hodgson: Stott Brunker Crouthers Law: Kennard Tomlinson: Stephenson(Watene)(Fisher) Southernwood(Price) Fisher(McDonald) Price(Law) Poching Kemp:
Tries - Crouthers Poching: Goal - Hodgson:
Referee K Kirkpatrick (Warrington) Att - 7233 H.T. 6 - 6

Sat 13 Mar 1999 SALFORD REDS home won 30 - 10 CHALLENGE CUP QUARTER FINAL
CASTLEFORD - Flowers: Gay(Wells) Eagar Maloney Rogers: Orr Davis: Sampson (Sykes) Raper Sykes (Pickering)(Sampson) Fritz(Tonks) Harland (Tallec) Vowles:
Tries - Rogers(2) Maloney Davis Raper: Goals - Orr(5):
SALFORD R - Broadbent: Hayes(Svabic) Thompson(Briggs) Martin Carige: Blakeley Crompton: Baynes(Faimalo) Alker Southern(Highton)(Baynes) Smith Hulme Casey: Try - Broadbent: Goals - Blakeley(3):
Referee S Cummins (Widnes) Att - 5236 H.T. 8 - 4

Sun 21 Mar 1999 WARRINGTON WOLVES away lost 14 - 19
WARRINGTON W - Roper: Roach(Hangar) Kohe-Love Hunte Forster: Wilson Briers: Hilton(Chambers)(Hilton) Farrar Nutley Gillies Knott Wainwright(McCurrie) (Causey):
Tries - Kohe-Love(2) Briers Knott: Goal - Briers (1) (DG):
CASTLEFORD - Flowers: Gay Eagar Vowles Rogers: Orr(Wells) Davis: Sampson(Pickering) (B/B)(Lynch)(Tallec) Raper Sykes(Lynch)(B/B) Fritz Tonks(Sykes) Harland(Pickering): Tries - Gay Eagar Davis: Goal - Orr:
Referee S Ganson (St Helens) Att - 4738 H.T. 6 - 9

Sat 27 Mar 1999 LONDON BRONCOS lost 27 – 33 CHALLENGE CUP SEMI-FINAL - at HEADINGLEY LEEDS
CASTLEFORD - Flowers: Gay Eagar Maloney Rogers: Orr

SEASON 1999

Davis: Sykes(Pickering)(Sykes) Raper Sampson(Lynch)
Tonks(Tallec) Fritz Vowles:
Tries - Gay(2) Eagar(2) Rogers: Goals - Orr(3) (DG):
LONDON B - Tollett: Warton Fleming Timu Offiah:
Hammond Edwards: Retchless Beazley(Callaway)
Millard(Salter)(Millard) Simpson(Salter) Peters Gill:
Tries - Offiah Hammond Edwards Retchless Beazley Gill:
Goals - Warton (4) Beazley(DG):
Referee S Cummins (Widnes) Att - 7561 H.T. 12 - 14

Fri 2 Apr 1999 HALIFAX BLUE SOX home won 14 - 10
CASTLEFORD - Flowers(Wells): Gay Eagar Maloney
Rogers: Orr Davis: Sampson (Tonks) Raper
Sykes(Pickering)(Sampson) Fritz(Sykes) Harland (Tallec)
Vowles: Tries - Eagar(3):   Goal - Orr:
HALIFAX B S - Cardiss(Craig): Gibson Bloem Bouveng
Pinkney: Holroyd (Chester) Clinch: Broadbent Rowley
Marshall Clark(Marns)(Clark) Gillespie Randall:
Tries - Craig Pinkney: Goal - Clinch:
Referee J Connolly (Wigan) Att - 7210 H.T. 4 - 4

Wed 7 Apr 1999 HUDDERSFIELD GIANTS away won 36 - 14
HUDDERSFIELD G - Reilly: Bentley Loughlin Lenihan
Cheetham(Arnold): Weston Goulding(Wright):
Fozzard(Pickavance) Russell Berry(Sturm) Boughton
Sturm(Richards) Tangata-Tpa:
Tries - Weston Wright: Goal - Weston(2) Goulding:
CASTLEFORD - Flowers: Gay Eagar Maloney Rogers: Orr
Davis: Sampson(Tallec) Raper(Wells) Sykes(Pickering)
Harland(Fritz) Fritz(Tonks) Vowles(Sykes):   Tries -
Rogers(2) Maloney(2) Eagar(2) Vowles: Goals - Orr(4):
Referee N Oddy (Halifax) Att - 3882 H.T. 20 - 8

Sun 11 Apr 1999 SALFORD REDS away won 29 - 17
SALFORD R - Carige: Thompson Litter Casey Martin:
Blakeley Briggs: Baynes(Morley)(Faimalo) Lee(Crompton)
Southern(Makin) Smith(Faimalo) (Smith)
Bradbury(Baynes)(Southern) Highton: Tries - Littler
Baynes Faimalo: Goals - Blakeley(2) Briggs(DG):
CASTLEFORD - Flowers: Gay Maloney Eagar
Rogers(Ellison): Orr Davis: Sampson Aaron(Tonks) Sykes
Harland(Fritz) Tallec(Hill) Vowles: Tries - Flowers Gay
Maloney Eagar: Goals - Orr(4) (DG) Tonks(2):
Referee K Kirkpatrick (War'ton) Att - 3663 H.T. 12 - 11

Sun 18 Apr 1999 GATESHEAD THUNDER home lost 14 - 17
CASTLEFORD - Flowers: Wells Eagar Maloney Rogers: Orr
Davis: Sykes(Pickering)(Sykes) Raper Sampson
Harland(Tonks) Fritz(Tallec) Vowles:
Tries - Rogers(2) Davis: Goal - Orr:
GATESHEAD T - Sammut: Herron Collins Simon
Daylight(Grogan): Robinson Peters: Hick(Lee)(Hick)(B/B)
Walters Green(Hick) Felsch Maher(Wilson) Grimaldi:
Tries - Sammut Grimaldi: Goals - Herron(4) Peters(DG):
Referee R Connolly (Wigan) Att 6489 H.T. 4 - 12

Sun 25 Apr 1999 WIGAN WARRIORS away won 24 - 8
WIGAN W - Davies: Robinson Moore(Bretherton)
Connolly Jones: Florimo Smith: Cowie(Reber) Cassidy
Mestrov(O'Connor)(Goldspink) Gilmour Betts(Cowie)
Farrell: Try - Reber: Goals - Farrell(2):
CASTLEFORD - Flowers: Wells Eagar Maloney Rogers: Orr
Davis: Sampson(Sykes) Raper(Fritz) Sykes
(Pickering)(Tallec) Fritz(Tonks) Harland Vowles(Ellison):
Tries - Wells Davis Harland Vowles: Goals - Orr(3) Tonks:
Referee S Ganson (St Helens) Att - 8856 H.T. 12 - 2

Mon 3 May 1999 BRADFORD BULLS home draw 18 - 18
CASTLEFORD - Flowers: Rogers Eagar Maloney Wells:
Orr(Ellison) Davis: Sykes(Pickering) Raper
Sampson(Sykes)(Sampson) Harland Fritz(Tallec) Vowles:
Tries - Rogers Tallec Sampson: Goals - Orr(2) Maloney:
BRADFORD B - Spruce: Vaikona Peacock(Price) McAvoy
Withers: H.Paul (McDermott) R.Paul:
McDermott(McNamara) Lowes Anderson(Fielden)
Forshaw Boyle(Jowett) McNamara(H.Paul):
Tries - R.Paul McNamara: Goals McNamara(5):
Referee S Ganson (St Helens) Att - 10122 H.T. 6 - 10

Sun 9 May 1999 LONDON BRONCOS away draw 12 - 12
LONDON B - Fleming: Smyth(Offiah) Ryan Timu Peters:
Hammond Air: Cram Beazley (Spencer)(Beazley)(Spencer)
Millard Simpson(Callaway) Toshack Gill(Hughes)(Gill):
Tries - Smyth Offiah Callaway:
CASTLEFORD - Flowers: Gay Eagar Rogers Wells: Maloney
Davis: Sampson Raper Sykes(Pickering) (Tallec)(Fritz)
Harland(BRAD HEPI(762))(Ellison) Fritz(Harland) Vowles:
Tries - Rogers Raper: Goals - Maloney(2):
Referee S Cummins (Widnes) Att - 2347 H.T. 6 - 8

Sun 16 May 1999 SHEFFIELD EAGLES home won 10 - 6
CASTLEFORD - Flowers: Gay Eagar Maloney Rogers: Orr
Davis: Sampson Raper(Hepi) Sykes(Pickering)
(Sampson)(Fritz) Tallec(Tonks) Fritz(Tallec) Vowles:
Tries - Maloney Vowles: Goal - Orr:
SHEFFIELD E - Watson: Cardoza Powell(Lovell) Senior
Crowther: Hardy Pearson: Molloy(Laughton)
Lawless(Turner) Shaw(Molloy) Jackson(Shaw) Turner
(Anderson) Doyle: Try - Doyle: Goal - Pearson:
Referee S Nicholson(Whit'aven) Att - 5748 H.T. 10 - nil

Wed 19 May 1999 ST HELENS home lost 14 - 33
CASTLEFORD - Flowers: Gay Vowles
Eagar(Ellison)(Eagar)(Ellison) Rogers: Orr Davis:
Sykes(Pickering)(Sykes) Raper(Hepi) Sampson Tallec
(Tonks) Fritz Harland:
Tries - Gay Rogers Davis: Goal - Tonks:
ST HELENS - Atcheson: Smith Iro Newlove Stewart: Martin
Long: Matautia (Edmondson) Cunningham
O'Neill(Matautia)(Tuilagi) Perelini(O'Neill) Joynt
Sculthorpe(Jonkers): Tries - Smith(3) Newlove(2) Long:
Goals - Long(4) Martin(DG):
Referee S Cummins (Widnes) Att - 6633 H.T. 4 - 14

SEASON 1999

Sun 23 May 1999 HULL SHARKS away won 30 - 2

HULL S - Prescott: Seru Smith Campbell Lee: Lester Murdock(Horne): Harrison(Barrow)(Craven) King(Cooke) Ireland(Barrow) Schultz(King) Craven(Booth): Purcell:
Goal - Prescott:
CASTLEFORD - Flowers: Gay Rogers Vowles Wells: Orr Davis: Sampson(Lynch) Hepi Pickering(Tonks)(Ellison) Sykes(Pickering) Tallec(Hill) Fritz: Tries - Rogers(2) Gay Davis Sampson Hepi: Goals - Tonks(2) Orr:
Referee S Ganson (St Helens) Att - 4564 H.T. 16 - 2

Sun 30 May 1999 LEEDS RHINOS home draw 12 - 12

CASTLEFORD - Flowers: Gay Eagar Rogers Wells: Orr Davis(Ellison): Sykes (Pickering) (B/B)(Pickering) Hepi(Fritz) Sampson(Sykes) Tallec(Harland) Fritz(Tonks) Vowles:
Tries - Eagar Wells: Goals - Orr(2):
LEEDS R - Harris: Sterling Golden Godden(Rivett) Cummins: Powell (St Hilaire) Sheridan: Fleary (McDermott) Jackson McDermott(Mathiou) Morley(Hay) Farrell Glanville(B/B)(Hay)(Glanville)(Powell):
Try - Jackson: Goals - Harris(4):
Referee S Cummings (Widnes) Att - 10462 H.T. 8 - 6

Sun 6 Jun 1999 WAKEFIELD TRINITY WILDCATS away lost 10 - 11

WAKEFIELD T W - Kennard: Stott(Fisher) Brunker Hughes Law: P March Tomlinson: Stephenson (McDonald) (Stephenson) D March Field(Watenic)(B/B)(Field)(Watenic) Price Fisher(Poching) Fawcett(Kemp):
Tries – D March(2): Goal - Hughes Kemp(DG):
CASTLEFORD - Flowers: Gay Eagar Rogers Wells(Ellison): Orr Davis: Sykes(Pickering)(Tonks)(Hill) Hepi Sampson Tallec Fritz Harland:
Tries - Sampson Harland: Goal - Orr:
Referee R Connolly (Wigan) Att - 6596 H.T. 4 - 10

Sun 13 Jun 1999 WARRINGTON WOLVES home won 39 - 6

CASTLEFORD - Flowers: Gay(Ellison) Maloney Eagar Rogers: Orr Davis: Sampson Hepi(Dobson) Sykes(Lynch) Tallec Hill(Pickering)(Hill) Fritz (Hill)(B/B) Tries - Maloney(3) Gay(2) Ellison Orr: Goals - Orr(5) Davis(DG):
WARRINGTON W - Penny: Hangar Kohe-Love Roper Hunte(Roache): Wilson Briers(Duffy): Chambers(Busby) Farrar Nutley(Leatham)(B/B) Busby(Knott) Gillies Wainwright: Tries - Kohe-Love: Goal - Briers:
Referee N Oddy (Halifax) Att - 5561 H.T. 25 - nil

Fri 18 Jun 1999 HALIFAX BLUE SOX away won 24 - nil

HALIFAX B S - Gibson: Pinkney Maona Bouveng Marns: Cardiss Holroyd: Broadbent (Hobson)(Broadbent) Rowley Hobson(Marshall)(Gillespie) Clark Mercer Fearon(Seal)(Fearon):
CASTLEFORD - Flowers: Wells Maloney(Ellison) Eagar(Gay) Rogers: Orr Davis: Sampson(Lynch)(B/B) Hepi(Lynch) Sykes(Lynch)(Hill) Hill (Dobson) Tallec Fritz:
Tries - Flowers Wells Ellison Orr: Goals - Orr(4):
Referee S Nicholson (White'ven) Att - 3582 H.T. 12 - nil

Wed 23 Jun 1999 LEEDS RHINOS away lost 22 - 50

LEEDS R - St Hilaire: Rivett Golden Cummins Sterling: Powell Harris(Pratt): Farrell(McDermott) Newton (Jackson) McDermott(Mathiou) Sinfield Hay (Farrell) Glanville(Newton): Tries - Golden(3) Harris(2) St Hilaire Rivett Sterling Hay: Goals - Harris(5) Sinfield(2):
CASTLEFORD - Flowers: Wells Gay(Hill) Rogers Ellison: Eagar Orr: Sampson Hepi(Dobson) Sykes(Lynch) Hill(Raper) Tallec(Fritz) Fritz(Smith):
Tries - Wells Rogers Eager Orr: Goals - Orr(3):
Referee J Connolly (Wigan) Att - 16371 H.T. 6 - 28

Sun 27 Jun 1999 HUDDERSFIELD GIANTS home won 19 - 10

CASTLEFORD - Flowers: Wells Rogers Eagar Ellison: Orr(Hargrave) Raper: Sampson (Lynch)(B/B) Hepi(Hill) Sykes(Lynch) Hill(Dobson)(Hill)(B/B) Tallec (Smith) (B/B) Fritz:
Tries - Ellison(2) Orr: Goals - Raper(2) Orr Flowers(DG):
HUDDERSFIELD - Reilly: Simpson Lenihan(Bentley)(B/B)Loughlin Cheetham(Bentley): Weston Goulding: Fozzard Hudson(Pickavance)(Neil) Neil(Richards)(Carlton) Boughton Sturm Tangata-Tua:
Tries - Simpson Lenihan: Goal - Goulding:
Referee S Cummings (Widnes) Att - 5379 H.T.14 - 6

Sun 4 Jul 1999 SALFORD REDS home won 38 - 10

CASTLEFORD - Flowers: Gay Rogers Eagar(Smith)(Ellison) Wells: Maloney Raper (Hill)(B/B): Sampson(Andy Hill)(B/B) Hepi Sykes(Smith) Tallec(Dobson) Fritz(Tallec) Vowles:
Tries - Gay(2) Flowers Eagar Hepi Wells:
Goals - Maloney(7):
SALFORD R - Thompson: Svabic Littler(Waeing)(B/B) Carige(Briggs) Johnson: Casey Briggs(Littler): Baynes(Morley) Alker Morley(Faimalo)Highton Bradbury(Russell) Smith:
Tries - Johnson Highton: Goal - Casey:
Referee K Kirkpatrick (Warrington) Att - 5786 H.T. 8 - 5

Sun 11 Jul 1999 GATESHEAD THUNDER away lost 16 - 24

GATESHEAD T - Sammut: Herron Grogan Collins Daylight: Simon Peters: Felsch (Allwood)(B/B) Jenkins (Walters) McAllister Grimaldi Maher(O'Neill)(B/B) Bird(Maiden): Tries - Collins Maher Bird: Goals - Herron(5) Sammut:
CASTLEFORD - Flowers: Gay(Danny Ellison) Eagar Rogers Wells: Maloney Orr: Sampson Raper(Lynch) Tonks(Smith)(Tonks) Tallec(Hepi) Fritz Vowles:
Tries - Flowers Sampson Tonks: Goals - Orr(2):
Referee S Ganson (St Helens) Att - 6108 H.T. 10 - 10

Fri 16 Jul 1999 WIGAN WARRIORS home won 33 - 18

CASTLEFORD - Flowers: Gay Eagar Maloney Rogers: Orr Davis: Sampson(Smith) Raper Sykes(Tonks)(B/B) (Sampson)(Fritz) Harland(Hepi) Fritz(Harland) Vowles:
Tries - Orr(2) Maloney Gay Davis Harland: Goals - Orr(4) Davis(DG):
WIGAN W - Radlinski: Robinson Gilmour(Moore) Connolly Johnson: Smith Clinch: Cowie (O'Connor)(B/B)

Clarke(Chester) O'Connor(Goldspink)(O'Connor) Cassidy Betts Farrell:
Tries - Robinson Clarke Goldspink: Goals - Farrell(3):
Referee S Cummings (Widnes) Att - 7089 H.T.16 - 6

Sun 25 Jul 1999 BRADFORD BULLS away lost 22 - 24

BRADFORD B - Spruce: Vaikona(Withers) Naylor McAvoy(Vaikona) Price: H.Paul Deacon: Anderson (McDermott) Lowes Fielden Dwyer(Peacock)(Jowett) Forshaw(Anderson) McNamara:
Tries - Price McAvoy Paul Lowes: Goals - McNamara(4):
CASTLEFORD - Flowers: Gay Maloney Eagar Rogers: Orr Davis: Sampson(Smith)(Sampson) Raper Sykes(Smith) Harland(Hepi)(B/B) (Tallec) Fritz (Wells) Vowles:
Tries - Gay(2) Maloney Orr: Goals - Orr(3):
Referee J Connolly (Wigan) Att - 13284 H.T. 18 - 12

Sun 1 Aug 1999 LONDON BRONCOS home won 52 - 16

CASTLEFORD - Flowers(Wells)(B/B)(Fritz): Gay Eagar Maloney Rogers: Orr Davis: Sykes(Smith) Raper(Harland) Smith(Tallec) Harland(Lynch) Fritz (Hepi) Vowles:
Tries - Maloney(3) Eagar(2) Davis(2) Gay Harland Vowles: Goals - Orr(6):
LONDON BRONCOS - Fleming: Warton Ryan Timu Smyth: Edwards Air: Seibold(Salter) Callaway(Beazley) Millard Retchless(Spencer) Wynard Gill(Toshack):
Tries - Warton Edwards Spencer: Goals - Warton Millard:
Referee N Oddy (Halifax) Att 5693 - H.T. 28 - nil

Sat 7 Aug 1999 SHEFFIELD EAGLES away won 22 - nil

SHEFFIELD E - Watson: Sodje Cardoza(Molloy) Senior Crowther: Thorman(Hardy) Stephens (Thorman): Molloy(Lovell)(B/B)(Shaw)(Lovell) Lawless Laughton(Jackson) Shaw(Sovatabua) Turner Doyle:
CASTLEFORD - Flowers: Gay Eagar Maloney(Harland) Rogers: Orr(Fritz) Davis: Sykes(Tallec) Raper Sampson (Smith) Harland(Hepi) Fritz (Spencer Hargrave) Vowles(Sampson):
Tries - Rogers(2) Eagar Raper Sampson: Goal - Orr:
Referee K Kirkpatrick (War'ton) Att - 3750 H.T. 14 - nil

Sun 15 Aug 1999 HULL SHARKS home won 44 - 16

CASTLEFORD - Flowers: Gay Eagar Maloney Rogers: Orr Davis: Sampson(Smith) (Sampson) Raper(Wells) Sykes(Tonks) Harland(Fritz) Fritz(Hepi)Vowles:
Tries - Gay(2) Flowers Maloney Rogers Orr Davis Smith: Goals - Orr(6):
HULL S - Poucher: Baildon Parker Campbell Lee: Purcell Windley: Harrison(Leatham) King Craven(Smith) Pickavance(Nolan) Smith(Booth) (Pickavance) Roberts:
Tries - Leatham Pickavance Roberts: Goals - Roberts(2):
Referee S Ganson (St Helens) Att - 6078 H.T. 28 - 4

Fri 20 Aug 1999 WAKEFIELD WILDCATS home won 30 - 18

CASTLEFORD - Flowers: Gay(Wells) Eagar Maloney Rogers: Orr Davis: Sampson(Smith)(Sampson) Raper Sykes(Tonks) Harland(Fritz) Fritz(Hepi) Vowles:

Tries - Vowles(2) Gay Rogers Orr Hepi: Goals - Orr(3):
WAKEFIELD T W - Kennard: Stott Fawcett(McDonald) Hughes Law: Kemp(March) Tomlinson: Stephenson(Watene) Talbot(Kemp) Jackson(Field) Price McDonald(Crouthers) Poching:
Tries - Law March Tomlinson: Goals - Talbot(3):
Referee J Connolly (Wigan) Att - 6322 H.T. 16 - 4

Wed 25 Aug 1999 ST HELENS away lost 14 - 42

ST HELENS - Atcheson(Nickle): Smith Tailigi Newlove Sullivan(Hall): Long Wellens(Martin) (Edmondson)(B/B) Perelini(Edmondson) Cunningham O'Neill(Price)(B/B) Joynt: (Price)(Joynt) Nickle(Price) Scuithorpe:
Tries - Joynt(2) Tailigi Newlove Hall Long Wellens:
Goals - Long(7):
CASTLEFORD - Flowers: Wells Eagar Maloney(Hepi) Rogers: Orr Davis: Sampson Raper(Harland) Sykes(Smith)(Sykes) Harland(Tonks) Tonks (Tallec) Vowles:
Tries - Wells Rogers Davis: Goal - Orr:
Referee S Cummings (Widnes) Att - 7976 H.T. 6 - 30

Sun 29 Aug 1999 WARRINGTON WOLVES away won 3 - 6

WARRINGTON W - Penny: Roach Kohe-Love Roper Forster: Wilson Briers: Hilton(Chambers) Farrar(Highton) Nutley(Hilton)(Nutley)(Hilton) Gillies Knott(McCurrie) Wainwright: Try - Wilson: Goal - Roper:
CASTLEFORD - Flowers: Wells Vowles Eagar Rogers: Orr(Tallec) Davis: Sampson)(Tonks)(B/B) Raper Sykes(Pickering)(Hepi) Fritz Tallec(Tonks) Harland:
Try - Wells: Goals - Orr(2):
Referee S Ganson (St Helens) Att - 4864 H.T. 6 - nil

Sun 5 Sep 1999 HALIFAX BLUE SOX home won 48 - 12

CASTLEFORD - Flowers: Gay Eagar Rogers Wells: Orr Davis: Sampson (Pickering)(Tallec) Raper(Hepi) Tonks(Lynch) Harland Fritz(Hepi)(B/B) Vowles(Pickering):
Tries - Orr(2) Harland(2) Gay Rogers Wells Tallec Vowles:
Goals - Orr(6):
HALIFAX E S - Cardiss(Marns): Pinkney Gibson Craig Hodgson: Moana Dunemann: Broadbent (Marshall)(Broadbent) Rowley Gannon(Hobson) Gillespie(Knox) (Marshall) Mercer Randall:
Tries - Moana Mercer: Goals - Craig(2):
Referee K Kirkpatrick (War'ton) Att - 7367 H.T. 14 - 8

Sun 12 Sep 1999 HUDDERSFIELD GIANTS away won 32 - 10

HUDDERSFIELD G - Reilly: Booth Weston Gleeson Simpson Ngamu Lawford: Berry(Wright) Russell Neill(Hill)(Neill) Slattery Sturm(Carlton) Johnson:
Tries - Gleeson Ngamu: Goal - Ngamu:
CASTLEFORD - Flowers: Gay (Wells) Maloney Eagar Rogers: Orr Davis: Sampson Raper(Harland) Tonks(Pickering)(Tonks) Harland(Hepi) Fritz (Gael Tallec)(E/B)(Tallec) Vowles: Tries - Rogers(3) Wells Eagar Raper Vowles: Goals - Orr(2):
Referee R Connolly (Wigan) Att - 4405 H.T. 20 - 4

SEASON 1999

Sun 19 Sep 1999 WIGAN WARRIORS away
won 14 – 10 TOP FIVE PLAY OFF

WIGAN W - Radlinski: Robinson Gilmour Johnson Moore:
Clinch Smith (Chester): Cowie(Mestrov)
(Goldspink)(O'Connor)(Cowie) Smith(Haughton)
O'Connor(Goldspink) Cassidy Betts Farrell:
Try - Betts: Goals - Farrell(3):
CASTLEFORD - Flowers: Gay Maloney Eagar Rogers: Orr
Davis: Sampson (Pickering)(Sampson) Raper
Sykes(Tonks)(Sykes) Fritz Harland(Hepi) Vowles(Wells):
Tries - Eagar Vowles: Goals - Orr(3):
Referee S Cummings (Widnes) Att – 13374 H.T. 12 - 6

Fri 24 Sep 1999 LEEDS RHINOS away won 23 - 16
TOP FIVE PLAY OFF

LEEDS R - Harris: Sterling Senior Godden Cummings:
Powell(Massella)Sheridan: Massella(McDermott)
Speak(Jackson) Fleary(Hay) Morley Farrell Glanville (St
Hilaire):   Tries - Cummings(2):   Goals - Harris(4):
CASTLEFORD - Flowers: Gay Maloney Eagar Rogers: Orr
Davis: Sampson (Sykes) Raper(Pickering) Sykes
(Tonks)(Fritz) Harland(Sampson) Fritz (Hepi) Vowles:
Tries - Eagar Fritz Vowles: Goals Orr(5) Raper(DG):
Referee S Cummings (Widnes) Att - 16912 H.T. 14 - 2

Sun 3 October 1999 ST HELENS away lost 6 - 36
TOP FIVE PLAY OFF

ST HELENS - Aitcheson: Smith Iro Newlove Sullivan:
Sculthorpe Martyn: Perelini(Hoppi) Cunningham
O'Neill(Long)(Wellens Tuilagi(Matautia)(Neil)
Nickle(Matautia) Joynt: Tries - Martyn(2) Long(2) Sullivan
Joynt: Goals - Long(5) Wellens:
CASTLEFORD - Flowers: Gay(Wells) Maloney Eagar
Rogers: Orr Davis: Sampson (Sykes) Raper
Sykes(Tonks)(James Pickering) Harland(Hepi) Fritz Vowles:
Try - Flowers: Goal - Orr:
Referee S Cummings (Widnes) Att – 11212 H.T. 6 – 10

Michael Eager
D. No 756
1999 to 2005

Darren Rogers
D. No 757
1999 to 2004

Aaron Raper
D. No 758
1999 to 2001

Andy Lynch
D. No 759
1999 to

Dale Fritz
D. No 761
1999 to 2003

Brad Hepi
D. No 762
1999 to 2001

SEASON 1999

D.N	PLAYER		DEBUT	L MATCH	APP	SLB	T.AP	TRI'S	G'LS	D.G	P'TS
661	SAMPSON	DEAN			36	0	36	5	0	0	20
694	SYKES	NATHAN			33	1	34	0	0	0	0
708	FLOWERS	JASON			37	0	37	8	0	1	33
715	TONKS	IAN			8	19	27	1	10	0	24
719	HARLAND	LEE			26	1	27	7	0	0	28
721	HILL	ANDY		04/07/1999	4	5	9	0	0	0	0
728	GAY	RICHARD			30	1	31	19	0	0	76
731	HARGRAVE	SPENCER		07/08/1999	0	2	2	0	0	0	0
734	WELLS	JON			15	15	30	9	0	0	36
739	VOWLES	ADRIAN			32	0	32	10	0	0	40
742	ORR	DANNY			35	0	35	12	97	2	244
744	SMITH	PAUL			1	10	11	1	0	0	4
746	DAVIS	BRAD			33	0	33	14	0	2	58
749	MALONEY	FRANCIS			28	0	28	16	10	0	84
751	TALLEC	GAEL		12/09/1999	14	17	31	2	0	0	8
752	ELLISON	DANNY		11/07/1999	2	13	15	4	0	0	16
755	DOBSON	GARETH			0	6	6	0	0	0	0
756	EAGER	MICHAEL	14/02/1999		36	0	36	19	0	0	76
757	ROGERS	DAREN	14/02/1999		37	0	37	23	0	0	92
758	RAPER	AARON	14/02/1999		30	1	31	4	2	1	21
759	LYNCH	ANDY	14/02/1999		0	11	11	0	0	0	0
760	PICKERING	JAMES	26/02/1999	03/10/1999	2	21	23	0	0	0	0
761	FRITZ	DALE	26/02/1999		34	1	35	1	0	0	4
762	HEPI	BRAD	09/05/1999		8	17	25	3	0	0	12
	24		**7**	**5**	**481**	**141**	**622**	**158**	**119**	**6**	**876**

COMPETITION		P	W	D	L	FOR	AGT
S. LEAGUE	POSITION 5 OF 12	30	19	3	8	712	451
RL CUP		4	3	0	1	121	67
PLAY OFF		3	2	0	1	43	62
PLAYERS RECORDS		**37**	**24**	**3**	**10**	**876**	**580**

The 40/20 rule was introduced, a team that kicked the ball from behind their own 40 metre line and going into touch behind their opponent's 20 metre line, were given the head and feed at the resulting scrum.

In the Challenge Cup we had victories in Round 4 at home to Hull Sharks 36–22, in Round 5 at home to York Wasps 28-2, and in the quarter-final at home to Salford Reds 30-10. The semi-final at Headingley was an end to end pulsating affair against London Broncos, which somehow slipped through our grasp 33–27 in the last seconds of the game, through a Steele Retchless try goaled by Brett Wharton.

By finishing fifth in the League we qualified for the Top 5 play-off and consequently if we were to reach the final we would have to do it the hard way by playing away in every round. In the first play-off round we won at Wigan 14-10, (the first game at the new JJB Stadium) in the second play-off round we won at Leeds Rhinos 23-16 but we ran out of steam in the final play-off round losing away to St Helens 36–6.

Danny Orr equalled the record for points scored in a Super League game at 20 points against Halifax Blue Sox at home on 5 September 1999.

Adrian Vowles our loose forward and Captain became the first Castleford player to win the Man of Steel Award, a just reward for a magnificent season.

A notable Debutant was Andy Lynch.

SEASON 2000

SUPER LEAGUE V

Huddersfield avoided relegation again, due to the merger with Sheffield Eagles to form Huddersfield-Sheffield Giants. Also at the end of this season Gateshead Thunder and Hull Sharks were merged to form Hull F.C. resulting in a twelve team super league

Sun 26 Dec 1999 WAKEFIELD TRINITY WILDCATS home draw 14 - 14 FRIENDLY
CASTLEFORD - McNally: Ellis Wells Rogers: Benn: Orr Briggs: Lynch Dobson Tonks White Smith Goddard; Subs used - Reilly Butterfield Wells Bates Senior Maskill{ Tries - Benn Reilly: Goals Benn(3):
WAKEFIELD T W - Prescott: Sampson Maloney Hughes Law: March Tomlinson: Stephenson Hudson Jackson Jowitt Ellis Bastow: Subs used - Holland Westwood McNamara Shillabeer Mason Garside Handforth Haughey:
Tries - Prescott Hughes Handforth: Goal - McNamaara: Referee R Connolly (Wigan) Att - 6335 H.T. 8 - 5

Sun 2 Jan 2000 LEEDS RHINOS away lost 14 - 26 FRIENDLY
LEEDS R - Cummins: Rivett Walker Senior Pratt: Morton Sheridan: Ward Jackson McDermott Jones-Buchanan Barnhill Sinfield: Subs used - Harris Lawford Carvell Chapman Diskin Cox: Tries - Pratt(2) Cummings Walker McDermott Harris: Goal - Harris:
CASTLEFORD - Benn: McNally Campbell J Wells Ellis: Orr Davis: Tonks Dobson Sampson Shaw Smith Goddard: Subs used - Briggs Reilly Wright Lynch P Wells:
Tries - Goddard Wright: Goals - Benn(3):
Referee S Ganson (St Helens) Att - 10089 H.T. 12 - 8

Fri 28 Jan 2000 HULL F C home won 20 - 14 AVEC CHALLENGE TROPHY FRIENDLY
CASTLEFORD - Benn: Wells Eagar Campbell Rogers: Orr Davis: Sykes Raper Sampson Shaw Fritz Harland: Subs used - Tonks Smith Lynch Wright:
Tries - Benn Eagar Campbell: Goals - Benn(4):
HULL F C - Collins:Herron Bird Simon Daylight: Gene Robinson: Broadbent Jenkins McDonald Felsch Wilson Maiden:Subs used - Home Maher Carney Hick Robets King: Tries - Datlight Jenkins Maiden: Goals - Roberts:
Referee R Connolly (Wigan) Att - 4018 H.T. 8 - 4

Sun 13 Feb 2000 OLDHAM ST ANNES home won 64 - 8 CHALLENGE CUP ROUND 4
OLDHAM ST A - Wright(Akeroyd): Belle Calland Rose Charlesworth(Sykes): Badby Kay:M Taylor(K Deakin)(K Taylor) Crowther M Deakin(Russell) Brierley Kay Mitchell: Tries - M Taylor: Goals - Rose(2):
CASTLEFORD - Benn: Rogers(B/B DEAN ELLIS(765)) Eagar LOGAN CAMPBELL(763) Wells: ANDREW PURCELL(764) Davis: Sykes(DARREN SHAW(766))(Lynch) Raper (Fritz) Sampson Harland Fritz(Smith) Vowles:
Tries - Sampson(3) Eagar(2) Raper(2) Campbell(2) Wells Purcell Davis: Goals - Benn(8):
Referee C Morris (Huddersfield) Att - 3832 H.T. 34 - nil

Sun 27 Feb 2000 HALIFAX BLUE SOX home lost 10 - 11 CHALLENGE CUP ROUND 5
CASTLEFORD - Benn: Wells Campbell Eagar Rogers: Orr(Purcell) Davis:Sampson Raper Sykes(Shaw) Harland(Tonks) Fritz(Harland) Vowles:
Tries - Campbell: Goals - Benn (3):
HALIFAX B S - Cardiss(Tallec)(Holgate): Gibson Bloem: Florimo Golden:Pearson Duneman: Goldspink(Hobson) (Goldspink) Rowley Gannon Mercer Holgate(Hassan) Moana:
Tries - Bloem(2): Goals - Perason(1) D/G:
Referee S Ganson (St Helens) Att - 5516 H.T. 0 - 10

Sun 5 Mar 2000 WIGAN WARRIORS home lost 24 - 30
CASTLEFORD - Benn: Wells Campbell Eagar Rogers: Purcell Davis: Sampson(Shaw)(Sykes) Raper Shaw(Sykes) Harland(Smith)(SampsonB/B)(Harland)Fritz(GRAIG WRIGHT(767)) Vowles:
Tries - Rogers(3) Eagar Sampson: Goals - Benn(2):
WIGAN W - Radlinski(t): Dallas Connolly(Haughton) Renouf Robinson: Smith Peters(Jones): O'Connor(Haughton) (O'Connor) Newton Cowie(Mestrov) Cassidy(Gilmour) Betts Farrell:
Tries - Smith(2) Radlinski Dallas Peters: Goals - Farrell(5):
Referee S Cummins (Widnes) Att - 8812 H.T. 4 - 12

Sun 19 Mar 2000 SALFORD away won 22 - 16
SALFORD - Broadbent: Pinkney Tassell Webber Offiah: Svabic Crompton: Southern(Highton) Acker Makin(Baynes) Smith(Faimalo)(Johnnson)Brown Highton(Hepi)
Tries - Tassell Webber Offiah: Goals - Svabic(2):
CASTLEFORD - Eagar: Wells Vowles Campbell Rogers: Orr Davis: Sampson(Sykes) (Smith) Raper Shaw(Sampson) Harland Fritz(Benn) Purcell(Tonks):
Tries - Vowles Campbell Davis Raper: Goals - Benn(2) Davis:
Referee K Kirkpatrick (Warrington) Att - 5534 H.T. 10 - 6

Sun 2 Apr 2000 LONDON BRONCOS home won 16 - 10
CASTLEFORD - Benn: Rogers Eagar(Smith) Campbell Wells: Orr(Tonks)(Wright) Davis: Sampson(Sykes) Purcell Shaw(Sampson) Harland Fritz Vowles:
Tries - Rogers Orr: Goals - Benn(4):
LONDON B - Fleming: Tollett Moore Toshack Wharton: Hammond Magnus: Seibold(Retchless) Callaway(Clarke) Cram(Davidson) Millard Retchless(Johnson) Wynyard (Napoli) Tries - Fleming(2): Goal - Wharton
Referee S Cummings (Widnes) Att - 6372 H.T. 10 - 6

Sun 9 Apr 2000 BRADFORD BULLS away lost 12 - 44
BRADFORD B - Spruce(t): McAvoy Naylor(Vaikona) Withers Brooker H Paul R Paul: McDermott(Fielden)(Anderson) Lowes Anderson(Fielden) Peacock(Boyle) Forshaw(Radford) Mackay: -

Tries - Lowes(2) Spruce McAvoy Withers H Paul Fielden:
Goals - H Paul (7) D/G Lowes D/G
CASTLEFORD - Benn(DANNY ARNOLD(768)): Rogers
Eagar Campbell Wells: Orr Davis: Sampson(Sykes) Purcell
Shaw(Tonks) Harland(Sampson)(S/O) Fritz Vowles:
Tries - Wells Harland: Goals - Benn(2):
Referee R Connolly (Wigan) Att - 15237 H.T. 6 - 9

Sat 15 Apr 2000 HULL home won 22 - 12
CASTLEFORD - Flowers: Wells Campbell Eagar Rogers: Orr
Davis: Shaw(Tonks) Raper Tonks(Purcell)
Fritz(Sykes)(Smith) Harland(Fritz) Vowles: Tries - Davis(2)
Eagar(2):Goals - Orr(3):
HULL - Sammutt: Carney Collins Simon (Bird)
Daylight(Simon): Robinson Home: Broadbent
(Felsch)(Broadbent) Jenkins(B/B)(King)(Jenkins)
Hick(McDermott) Wilson Grimaldi Maiden:
Tries - Simon Daylight: Goals - Sammutt(2)
Referee J Connolly (Wigan) Att - 8358 H.T. 10 - nil

Thu 20 Apr 2000 WAKEFIELD TRINITY WILDCATS
away won 22 - 12
WAKEFIELD T W - Prescott: Sampson Tatupa Hughes N
Law: P March Goulding:
Stephenson(Massella)(Stephenson)
Hudson(Kemp)(Hudson) Field(Fisher)
Price(Jackson B/B)(Price) Poching(Jackson) McNamara:
Tries - Prescott: Goals - McNamara(4):
CASTLEFORD - Flowers: Wells(Arnold) Campbell Eagar
Rogers: Orr Davis: Sampson(Sykes) Raper
Shaw(Tonks)(Sampson) Harland(Purcell) Fritz(Harland)
Vowles: Tries - Wells Eagar Rogers Orr: Goals - Orr(3):
Referee S Ganson (St Helens) Att - 6138 H.T. 10 - 10

Mon 24 Apr 2000 WIGAN WARRIORS away
lost 16 -30
WIGAN W - Davis: Dallas(Hodgson) Radlinski Gilmour
Robinson:Smith Peters:Malam(O'Connor) Newton(Reber)
Cowie(Haughton) Betts Cassidy Farrell:
Tries - Dallas Hodgson Peters Newton Farrell:
Goals - Farrell(5):
CASTLEFORD - Flowers: Wells(Arnold) Eagar Campbell
Rogers: Orr Davis(Purcell): Sampson Raper Shaw(Sykes)
Harland Fritz(Tonks) Vowles:
Tries - Flowers Davis Sampson: Goals - Orr(2):
Referee S Cummins (Widnes) Att - 10098 H.T. 6 - 12

Tue 2 May 2000 HALIFAX BLUE SOX away
won 20 - 14
HALIFAX B S - Cardiss: Naylor Gibson Golden Marnes:
Dunneman Pearson:Goldspink(Hobson)(Goldspink)
Rowley Gannon Mercer Bloem(Tallec) Moana:
Tries - Tallec Moana: Goals - Pearson(3):
CASTLEFORD - Flowers: Wells Campbell Eagar Rogers: Orr
Raper: Sampson(Lynch) Tonks(Benn) Shaw(Sykes) Harland
Smith Vowles:
Tries - Orr Lynch Smith Harland: Goals - Orr Benn:
Referee J Connolly(Wigan) Att 10008 H.T. 10 - 2

Sun 7 May 2000 ST HELENS home lost 22 - 32
CASTLEFORD - Flowers(Smith): Wells Campbell Eagar
Rogers: Orr Purcell:Sampson Tonks(Lynch) Shaw(Wright)
Harland(Danny Arnold) Smith(Sykes) Vowles:
Tries - Rogers(2) Purcell Shaw: Goals - Orr(3):
ST HELENS - Atcheson(Mike Bennett B/B): Hoppe Iro
Newlove(Perelini) Sullivan:Sculthorpe Martyn:
Perelini(Oneill: Cunningham(Stankevich)
Oneill(Henare B/B)(Oneill)(Henare) Nickle(Smith)
Tuilagi(Bennett) Chris Joynt: Tries - Sullivan(2) Iro Martyn
Stankevich Joint: Goals - Maryn(4):
Referee S Cummings (Widnes) Att - 7564 H.T. 4 - 22

Sun 14 May 2000 HUDDSFIELD/ SHEFFIELD GIANTS
home won 26 - 6
CASTLEFORD - Flowers: Wells Campbell Eagar Rogers: Orr
Purcell: Sykes(Dobson) Tonks(Shaw) Shaw(Lynch)
Smith(Wright)(Smith) Fritz(Benn) Vowles:
Tries - Rogers(2) Purcell Tonks Lynch: Goals - Orr(3):
HUDDERSFIELD/SHEFFIELD G - Ngamu: Reilly(Cardoza)
Lovell Savatabua Cooper: Thorman Clinch(Moxon):
Lomax(Marshall) Lawless Laughton(Molloy B/B) Turner
(Lomax) Bradbury(Turner) Hardy:
Tries - Ngamu: Goals - Ngamu:
Referee S Ganson (St Helens) Att - 7506 H.T. 4 - 6

Sun 21 May 2000 WARRINGTON WOLVES away
won 37 - 26
WARRINGTON W - Penny: Campbell Knott Roper Hunte:
Briers(Highton) Langer: Gee(Hilton B/B) (Nutley) Farrar
Nutley(Hilton)(Gee) Guisset(Noone) McCurrie(Busby)
Nikau: Tries - Guisset(2) Roper Hunte Farrar:
Goals - Roper(2) Briers:
CASTLEFORD - Flowers: Wells(Benn) Campbell Eagar
Rogers (Wrigh B/B): Orr Purcell(Raper): Sykes Tonks(Shaw)
Shaw (Lynch) Smith(Lynch)(Smith) Wright(Mather) Vowles:
Tries - Campbell(2) Eagar Orr Sykes Mather:
Goals - Orr (6) D/G:
Referee S Cummings (Widnes) Att - 5915 H.T. 12 - 14

Fri 26 May 2000 SALFORD REDS home won 30 - 4
CASTLEFORD - Flowers: Mather Campbell Eagar Rogers
(Jamie Benn): Orr Davis:Sykes(Sampson) Raper(Dobson)
Sampson Lynch) Shaw(Wright) Tonks Vowles:
Tries - Flowers Mather Benn Orr Vowles: Goals - Orr(5):
SALFORD R - Broadbent(Lee): Pinkney Littler Tassell
Offiah(Johnson): BrownBlakeley(Makin):
Southern(Faimalo) Alker Baynes(Southern) Smith Highton
Wainwright:
Try - Brown:
Referee J Connolly (Wigan) Att - 6303 H.T. 12 - nil

Wed 31 May 2000 LEEDS RHINOS home lost 18 - 20
CASTLEFORD - Flowers: Wells Campbell Eagar Mather:
Orr Davis: Sampson(Shaw) Raper Sykes(Lynch)(Sykes)
Tonks(Wright)(Sampson) Shaw(Harland) Vowles:
Tries - Davis Sampson Tonks: Goals - Orr(3):
LEEDS R - Cummings: Sterling Blackmore Senior Pratt
(Mackay): Harris Sheridan: Fleary(McDermott) Jackson

SEASON 2000

(Powell B/B) McDermott (Mathiou) Morley Barnhill
(Farrell) Hay(Barnhill):
Tries - Sterling Senior Mackay Sheridan:
Goals - Harris(2):
Referee R Connolly (Wigan) Att - 11702 H.T. 18 - 6

Sun 11 Jun 2000 LONDON BRONCOS away
won 26 -20
LONDON B - Warton: Napoli Crowthers(Air) Toshack
Peters: Lupton Tollett: Dooley(Seibold) Clarke(Callaway)
Retchless Wynyard(Davidson)(Dooley)Johnson(Dooley)
Hammond:
Tries - Tollett Retchless Johnson Hammond:
Goals - Warton(2):
CASTLEFORD - Flowers: Wells Eagar Campbell Mather:
Orr Davis:Sykes(Sampson) Raper Sampson(Shaw)
Harland(Fritz)(Lynch) Fritz(Tonks)(Harland) Vowles
Tries - Eagar(2) Mather Sykes Tonks: Goals - Orr(3):
Referee S Ganson (St Helens) Att - 8067 H.T. 16 - 6

Fri 16 Jun 2000 BRADFORD BULLS home
lost 10 - 39
CASTLEFORD - Flowers: Wells Mather Eagar Rogers: Orr
Davis: Sampson(Shaw)(Tonks) Raper(Purcell)
Sykes(Harland) Tonks(Sampson) Fritz(Campbell) Vowles:
Tries - Davis Sampson: Goal - Orr:
BRADFORD B - H Paul: McAvoy(Wilkinson) Naylor Pryce
Vaikona: R Paul Deacon: Fieldon Lowes McDermott
(Anderson) Boyle(Hudson-Smith)(McDermott) Peacock
Mackey(Radford) Tries - Anderson(2) Naylor R Paul
Deacon Lowes: Goals - H Paul(7) BoyleD/G:
Referee S Cummings (Widnes) Att - 10015 H.T. 6 - 15

Sun 25 Jun 2000 HULL F C away won 18 - 4
HULL F C - Sammutt: Carney Collins Simon Daylight:
Cooke Home: roadbent(Felsch)(Fletcher) Jenkins(Gene)
Hick(King) Maher Grimaldi Maiden: Try - Maher:
CASTLEFORD - Flowers: Wells(Harland) Mather(Smith)
Eagar Rogers: Orr Davis: Shaw(Tonks)(Shaw) Purcell
Tonks(Sampson) Harland(Gay) Fritz(Lynch)(SampsonB/B)
Vowles: Tries - Eagar Orr Rogers: Goals - Orr(3):
Referee S Ganson (St Helens) Att - 6501 H.T. 6 - 4

Sat 1st Jul 2000 LEEDS RHINOS away lost 12 - 20
LEEDS R - Cummings(Mathiou): Mackay Walker Senior
Pratt: Harris Sheridan: Fleary(Raynor) Jackson(Sinfield)
Mathiou
(Farrell) Morley(Barnhill) Sinfield(Powell)(Jackson) Hay:
Tries - Mackay Senior Barnhill Sinfield: Goals - Harris(2):
CASTLEFORD - Flowers: Wells Mather Eagar Rogers: Orr
Davis: Shaw(Sampson)(Smith) Purcell Sykes(Shaw)
Harland(Tonks)(Vowles) Fritz Vowles(Gay):
Tries - Orr Fritz: Goals Orr(2):
Referee S Cummings (Widnes) Att - 14492 H.T. 12 - 8

Sat 8 Jul 2000 WAKEFIELD TRINITY WILDCATS home
won 16 - 12
CASTLEFORD - Gay: Wells Mather Eagar Rogers: Orr
Davis: Shaw(Sampson)(S/O) Purcell(Lynch) Sykes(Shaw)
Tonks(Raper) Flowers(Wright) Vowles:

Tries - Wells(2) Eagar: Goals - Orr(2):
WAKEFIELD T W - Prescott: Sodje Maloney Critchley
Law(Ellis): McNamara(Jackson) Goulding:
Jackson(Massella) Hudson(Speak)
Massella(Poching)(Watene) Field Jowitt(Hudson) Price:
Tries - Field Jowitt: Goals - Goulding(2):
Referee R Connolly (Wigan) Att - 8043 H.T. 10 - 6

Sun 16 Jul 2000 HALIFAX BLUE SOX hom
won 26 - 12
CASTLEFORD - Gay: Wells Mather Eagar Rogers: Orr
Davis: Shaw(Tonks) Raper Sykes(Shaw) Purcell (Harland)
Fritz(Flowers) Vowles(Sykes)
Tries - Wells Mather Rogers Orr Harland: Goals - Orr(3):
HALIFAX B S - Cardiss(Tallec): Scales(Marns) Hassan
Gibson Golden: Florimo Duneman:
Goldspink(Hobson)(Gannon) Rowley
Gannon(Holgate)(Goldspink)Mercer Bloem Moana:
Tries - Gibson Rowley: Goals - Bloem(2):
Referee S Cummings (Widnes) Att - 6827 H.T. 16 - 6

Fri 21 Jul 2000 ST HELENS away lost 18 - 42
St HELENS - Wellen: Hall Iro(West) Hoppe Sullivan: Martin
Long: Perelini(Matautia)(Nickle) Cunningham
Nickle(O'Neill)(Jonkers) JoyntTuilagi(Perelini) Sculthorpe:
Tries - Long(2) Cunningham(2) Wellen Joynt Sculthorpe:
Goals - Long(7):
CASTLEFORD T - Gay: Wells Mather Eagar Rogers: Orr
Davis(Lynch): Sykes(Tonks)(Shaw) Purcell Shaw(Tonks)
Harland(Flowers) Fritz(Harland) Vowles.
Tries - Orr Mather Purcell: Goals - Orr(3):
Referee S Cummings (Widnes) Att - 6979 H.T. 18 - 8

Fri 28 Jul 2000 WARRINGTON WOLVES home
lost 18 - 32
CASTLEFORD - Gay: Wells(Logan Campbell) Mather Eagar
Rogers: Purcell(Orr) Davis: Shaw(Lynch) Tonks (Flowers)
Sykes(Shaw) Harland(Purcell) Fritz Vowles:
Tries - Gay Davis Lynch: Goals - Orr(3):
WARRINTON W - Penny: Smyth Kohe-Love Hunte
Campbell: Briers Langer: Gee Farrell(McCurrie)
Nutley(Hilto)(Peters) Noone McCurrie(Guisset) Nikau:
Tries - Kohe -Love(2) Briers(2) Farrell McCurrie:
Goals - Briers(4):
Referee I Smith (Oldham) Att - 7058 H.T. 6 -14

Sun 6 Aug 2000 HUDDERSFIELD/SHEFFIELD away
won 32 - 16 at Bramall Lane Sheffield
HUDDERSFIELD/SHEFFIELD - Ngamu: Arnold
Dekkiche(Revett) Gardoza Sovatabua: Thorman(Dekkiche)
Clinch: Lomax(Molloy) Lawless(Russell) Laughton(Lomax)
Marshall(Wilkes) Bradbury Hardy:
Tries - Ngamu Arnold Laughton: Goals - Ngamu(2):
CASTLEFORD - Flowers: Gay Mather(Smith) Eagar Rogers:
Orr Davis: Lynch(Tonks)(Wright) Fritz Sykes(Shaw)
Harland(Lynch) Shaw(BARRY EATON(769)) Vowles:
Tries - Rogers(3) Gay Vowles Mather: Goals - Orr(4):
Referee J Connolly (Wigan) Att - 2102 H.T. 20 - nil

SEASON 2000

Fri 11 Aug 2000 BRADFORD BULLS away lost 8 - 28
BRADFORD B - Spruce(Radford): Pryce Naylor(Boyle)
Withers Vaikona: Henry Paul Deacon: McDermott(Fielding
B/B)(McDermott) Lowes Fielden(Anderson) Peacock
(Forshaw) Forshaw(Smith) Mackay: Tries - Spruce Withers
Vaiona Deacon Anderson: Goals - H Paul(4):
CASTLEFORD - Flowers: Wells Vowles Eagar Rogers: Orr
Davis: Sampson(Tonks) Fritz Sykes(Lynch) Shaw(Eaton)
Tonks(Graig Wright) Harland(Smith):
Tries - Eagar Rogers:
Referee J Connolly (Wigan) Att - 11302 H.T. 4 - 24

Fri 18 Aug 2000 LEEDS RHINOS home won 20 - 16
CASTLEFORD - Flowers: Wells Mather Eagar Rogers: Orr
(Eaton) Davis: Sampson(Lynch)(Sykes) Fritz Sykes(Smith)
Shaw(Tonks) Harland Vowles
Tries - Wells(2) Rogers Davis: Goals - Orr Eaton:
LEEDS R - Cummins: Mackay Blackmore Senior Pratt:
Harris Sheridan: Fleary(Farrell) Jackson
McDermott(Mathiou) (McDermott)
Barnhill(Morley)Farrell(Sterling) Hay(Sinfield):
Tries - Harris Sterling: Goals - Harris(4):
Referee Mr S Ganson (St Helens) Att - 9819 H.T. 10 - 8

Sun 27 Aug 2000 HALIFAX BLUE SOX away
lost 16 - 36
HALIFAX B.S. - Cardiss: Greenwood Florimo(Moana)
Gibson Golden: Moana(Halliwell B/B)(Halliwell) Duneman:
Hobson (Thackray)(Tallec)(Hobson)
RowleyGannon(Holgate) Mercer (Gannon) Bloem(Tallec)
Tickle: Tries - Greenwood(2) Gibson(2) Halliwell Tickle
Bloem: Goals - Tickle(4):
CASTLEFORD - Flowers: Wells(WAIN PRYCE(770) Mather
Eagar Rogers: Eaton(Raper B/B) Davis(Harland): Sampson
Shaw Sykes(Lynch) Tonks(Smith B/B) Harland(Smith)
Vowles:
Tries - Wells Mather Davis: Goals - Eaton Tonks:
Referee I Smith (Oldham) Att - 6293 H.T. 24 - 6

Sun 3 Sep 2000 LONDON BRONCOS home
won 30 -16
CASTLEFORD – Flowers(Pryce): Wells Mather Eagar
Rogers: Orr(Barry Eaton) Davis: Sampson(Tonks B/B)
Raper Lynch (Tonks) Shaw(Smith) Harland(Shaw) Vowles:
Tries - Eagar(2) Rogers(2) Flowers Vowles:
Goals - Tonks(2) Eaton:
LONDON B - Warton(Napoli): Toshack Timu Crouthers
Peters(Dooley) Lupton Air: Dooley(Seibold)
Clarke(Callaway) Seibold(Crane) Millard(Davidson)(Millard
B/B) Retchless Johnson: Tries - Timu Davidson Johnson:
Goals - Lupton(2)
Referee R Connolly (Wigan) Att - 6387 H.T. 20 - 10

Sun 10 Sep 2000 HUDDERSFIELD/SHEFFIELD GIANTS
away won 28 - 14
HUDDERSFIELD/SHEFFIELD G - Ngamu(Reilly): Arnold
Crowther Langley Rivett: Thorman Moxon:
Molloy(Laughton) Russell Laughton(Fielden)(Hardy)
Bradbury Lomax(Marshall) (Lomax) Turner:
Tries - Crowther Turner: Goals - Ngamu(2) Crowther:

CASTLEFORD - Vowles: Wells Mather(Purcell) Eagar
Rogers: Orr Davis:Sampson(Smith B/B)(Gareth Dobson)
Raper Lynch
(Pryce) Tonks(Smith) Shaw Harland
Tries - Wells(2 Rogers(2) Pryce: Goals - Orr(4):
Referee J Connolly (Wigan) Att - 2903 H.T. 10 - 8

Sat 16 Sep 2000 WAKEFIELD WILDCATS home
won 20 - 8
CASTLEFORD - Gay(Purcell): Wells Rogers Eagar Pryce:
Orr Davis: SampsonRaper(Shaw)(Smith)
Lynch(Tonks)(Lynch) Harland Purcell(JONATHON
GODDARD(771)) Vowles:
Tries - Wells(2) Gay Orr: Goals - Orr(2):
WAKEFIELD W - N Law: Hughes Westwood G Law Sodje:
P March D March(Speak):Fisher(Watene)
Speak(Handforth) Jackson Field (Mason) Price(Ellis)
Hudson:
Tries - Handforth: Goals - G Law(2):
Referee K Fitzpatrick (Warrington) Att - 6892 H.T. 10 - 4

Sat 23 Sep 2000 LEEDS RHINOS away lost 14 - 22
TOP FIVE PLAY OFF
LEEDS R - Cummins: Sterling(Pratt) Blackmore Senior
Pratt(Mackay): Harris Sheridan: Fleary(Mathiou) Jackson
McDermott(Fleary) Morley Sinfield(Powell) Hay(Farrell):
Tries - Sterling Senior Sheridan Sinfield:
Goals - Harris(3):
CASTLEFORD T - Gay(Flowers)(Pryce): Wells Mather Eagar
Rogers: Orr Davis: Sampson(Tonks B/B) Andrew Purcell
Lynch (Tonks)(Lynch) Harland Shaw(Paul Smith) Vowles:
Tries - Wells Mather Davis: Goal - Orr:
Referee S Cummings (Widnes) Att - 13685 H.T. 10 – 12

Logan Campbell   Andrew Purcell
D. No 763   D. No 764
2000   2000

SEASON 2000

Darren Shaw
D. No 766
2000 to 2001

Waine Pryce
D. No 770
2000 to 2006

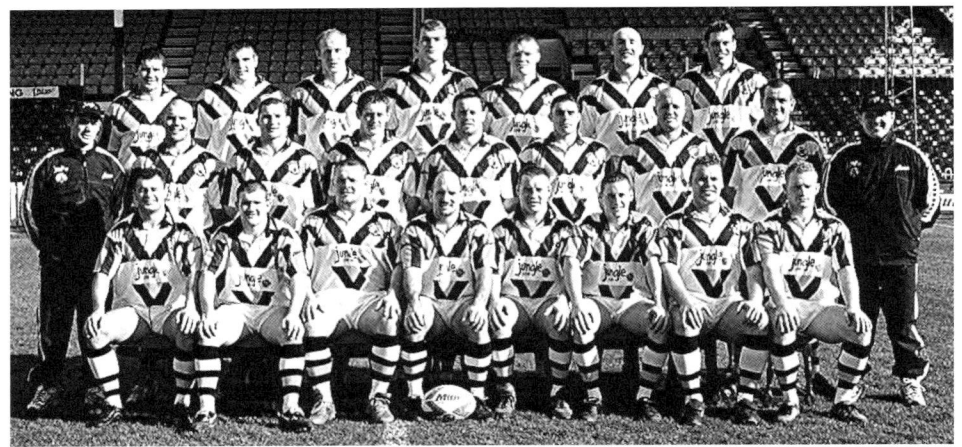

2000 SQUAD
Back Row – Michael Eager Andy Lynch Darren Rogers Paul Smith Lee Harland Nathan Sykes Brad Davis
Middle Row – Graham Steadman (Asst,Coach) Darren Shaw Dale Fritz Jamie Benn Andrew Purcell Logan Campbell
Aaron Raper Graig Wright Stuart Raper (Coach)
Front Row – Richard Gay Danny Orr Dean Sampson Adrian Vowles (Captain) Jason Flowers Andy McNally Ian Tonks
Jon Wells

SEASON 2000

D.N	PLAYER		DEBUT	L MATCH	APP	SUB	T.AP	TRI'S	G'LS	D.G	P'TS
661	SAMPSON	DEAN			21	3	24	7	0	0	28
694	SYKES	NATHAN			17	9	26	2	0	0	8
708	FLOWERS	JASON			19	4	23	3	0	0	12
715	TONKS	IAN			14	15	29	3	3	0	18
719	HARLAND	LEE			24	3	27	3	0	0	12
728	GAY	RICHARD			7	2	9	3	0	0	12
734	WELLS	JON			29	0	29	14	0	0	56
739	VOWLES	ADRIAN			31	0	31	4	0	0	16
742	ORR	DANNY			27	1	28	10	61	1	163
744	SMITH	PAUL		23/09/2000	4	15	19	1	0	0	4
746	DAVIS	BRAD			27	0	27	11	1	0	46
748	MATHER	BARRIE-JON			16	1	17	8	0	0	32
754	BENN	JAMIE		26/05/2000	5	5	10	1	22	0	48
755	DOBSON	GARETH		10/09/2000	0	3	3	0	0	0	0
756	EAGER	MICHAEL			31	0	31	14	0	0	56
757	ROGERS	DAREN			29	0	29	20	0	0	80
758	RAPER	AARON			16	3	19	3	0	0	12
759	LYNCH	ANDY			5	15	20	3	0	0	12
761	FRITZ	DALE			20	0	20	1	0	0	4
763	CAMPBELL	LOGAN	13/02/2000	28/07/2000	16	2	18	6	0	0	24
764	PURCELL	ANDREW	13/02/2000	23/09/2000	16	6	22	4	0	0	16
765	ELLIS	DEAN	13/02/2000	13/02/2000	0	1	1	0	0	0	0
766	SHAW	DARREN	13/02/2000		26	5	31	1	0	0	4
767	WRIGHT	GRAIG	05/03/2000	11/08/2000	1	9	10	0	0	0	0
768	ARNOLD	DANNY	09/04/2000	07/05/2000	0	4	4	0	0	0	0
769	EATON	BARRY	06/08/2000	03/09/2000	1	4	5	0	3	0	6
770	PRYCE	WAINE	27/08/2000		1	4	5	1	0	0	4
771	GODDARD	JONATHON	16/09/2000		0	1	1	0	0	0	0
	28			**9**	**9**	**403**	**115**	**518**	**123**	**90**	**1**

(P'TS total) **673**

COMPETITION		P	W	D	L	FOR	AGT
S. LEAGUE	POSITION 5 OF 12	28	17	0	11	585	571
RL CUP		2	1	0	1	74	19
PLAY OFF		1	0	0	1	14	22
PLAYERS RECORDS		**31**	**18**	**0**	**13**	**673**	**612**

In January the Club announced a sponsorship deal with the Internet retailer Jungle.com and renamed the ground 'The Jungle'

In June we took over 5,000 fans to London Broncos thanks to the new sponsor subsidising buses at £5 per seat.

Darren Rodgers finished joint Super League Top Try scorer with 20 tries - a club Super League record, his centre partner Michael Eager finished with 12 Super League tries and 14 in total

Darren also got a late call up to the England World Cup Squad when Nathon McVoy was injured. Also receiving international call ups were Michael Eager for Ireland, and Darren Shaw, Andrew Purcell and Adrian Vowles for Scotland.

SEASON 2001

SUPER LEAGUE VI

There were 12 Super League teams, the same as in 2000. i.e. Bradford Bulls Castleford Tigers Halifax Blue Sox Huddersfield-Sheffield Giants Leeds Rhinos London Broncos Saint Helens Salford City Reds Wakefield Trinity Wildcats Warrington Wolves Wigan Warriors.

Tue 26 Dec 2000 WAKEFIELD TRINITY WILDCATS home lost 2 – 38 FRIENDLY
CASTLEFORD - Goddard: Pryce Steel Ellis Saxton: Reilly Lennon: Handford Green Lynch Barrow Tonks Thornton: Subs used - Thaler Blakeway Godwin Whelan Maskill Lee Potter: Goal - Lennon:
WAKEFIELD T W – Holland: N Law R Smith Westwood Sovatabua: G Law P March: Jackson D March Watene Hudson Field Haughey: Subs used – Handforth Ellis Feather Mason Brough White Elston Rauter Boles S Smith
Tries – R Smith(2) Westwood(2) Field Ellis Feather Rauter: Goals - G Law P March D Brough:
Referee S Ganson (St Helens) Att – 3200 H.T. 2 - 16

Sun 11 Feb 2001 DEWSBURY RAMS away won 18 - 4 CHALLENGE CUP
DEWSBURY R - Grahame: Godfrey Potter Flynn (Cain) Baker: Agar Eaton: Fisher(Long) Pachnuik Jowitt (McDonald)(Jowitt) Richardson Smith(Fisher) Ball(Spink): Goals - Eaton(2):
CASTLEFORD - MARK LENNON(772): Wells Mather Eager Rogers: Orr MITCH HEALEY(773): Sampson Raper(Sykes) Lynch(GARETH HANDFORD(774))(Tonks) Tonks(JONATHON ROPER(775))(Harland) Harland(Shaw) Vowles: Tries - Healey Sampson Orr: Goals - Orr(3):
Referee K Kirkpatrick (Warrington) Att - 3284 H.T. 6 - 4

Sat 24 Feb 2001 LEEDS RHINOS home lost 12 - 42 CHALLENGE CUP
CASTLEFORD - Gay; Wells Mather Eager Rogers: Orr Raper: Sampson Shaw(Lennon) Lynch(Sykes) (HandfordB/B) Harland(Smith) Tonks(Harland) Vowles: Tries - Rogers(2) Sykes:
LEEDS R - Mullins(St Hilaire): Pratt Carroll Senior Cummins: Harris Sheridan: Fleary(McDermott) Diskin McDermott(Mathiou) Hay(Wrench) Farrell Sinfield: Tries - Harris(2) Sinfield(2) Pratt Carroll Senior McDermott: Goals - Harris(5):
Referee R Connolly (Wigan) Att - 11481 H.T. 4 - 16

Sun 4 Mar 2001 WAKEFIELD WILDCATS home won 22 - 17
WAKEFIELD T W – Holland: N Law(Handforth)(G Law) Tatupu Brooker Sovatabua: Pearson P March: O'Neill(Watene)(O'Neill) Rauter(Hudson) Jackson Field Price Haughey:
Tries - Sovatabua Jackson: Goals - Pearson(4) D/G:
CASTLEFORD - Gay(Lennon): Wells Mather Eager Rogers: Orr Healey(Lennon): Sampson(Handford)(Lynch) Raper Lynch(Smith) Shaw(Sampson) Harland Vowles: Tries - Smith(2) Mather Vowles: Goals - Orr(3):

Referee S Cummings (Widnes) Att - 5130 H.T. nil - 9

Sat 17 Mar 2001 WIGAN WARRIORS home lost 8 - 24
CASTLEFORD - Gay: Wells Mather Eager Rogers: Vowles(Shaw) Orr: Sykes Raper(Smith) Sampson (Handford) Tonks(Fritz) Shaw(Tonks) Harland(Lennon): Try - Vowles: Goals - Orr(2):
WIGAN W - Radlinski: Dallas Johnson Renouf (Connolly) Hodgson: Jones Lam: O'Connor (Cowie B/B) Newton (Smith) Cowie(Stephenson) Betts(Newton) Furner Farrell(Haughton)
Tries - Jones(3) Dallas: Goals - Farrell(2) Jones(2):
Referee S Cummings (Widnes) Att - 7214 H.T. 2 -14

Sun 25 Mar 2001 HULL FC away draw 18 - 18
HULL F C - Prescott(Campbell): C Smith(Gene) Horne Bird Crowther: J Smith T Smith: Broadbent(Craven)(Broadbent) Jackson Felsch(Carvell) Maher Grimaldi Maiden:
Tries - Jackson(2) Bird: Goals - Crowther(3):
CASTLEFORD - Gay: Wells Mather Eager Rogers: Orr Lennon: Sykes(Shaw) Hepi(Fritz) Handford(Lynch) (Handford) Tonks(Smith) Shaw(Pryce) Vowles:
Tries - Eager(2) Orr: Goals - Orr(3):
Referee S Ganson (St Helens) Att - 7460 H.T. 12 - 12

Sat 7 Apr 2001 WARRINGTON WOLVES home won 18 - nil
CASTLEFORD - Gay: Wells Mather Eager Rogers: Orr Healey(Lennon): Handford(Lynch) Raper(Handford) Shaw(Hepi) Fritz Harland Vowles(Smith):
Tries - Wells Orr: Goals - Orr(5):
WARRINGTON W - Hunte: Smyth Sibbett(Kidwell) Kohe-Love Stenhouse: Briers Langer: Gee Highton Nutley (Masella)(Nutley) Busby Mercer Georgallis(McCurrie):
Referee I Smith (Oldham) Att - 6800 H.T. 16 - 0

Fri 13 Apr 2001 SALFORD REDS home lost 22 - 24
CASTLEFORD - Gay: Wells Mather Eager Rogers: Orr Healey(Lennon B/B): Handford(Smith) Raper Sykes(Hepi)(Lennon) Shaw(Sampson) Fritz(Sykes) Harland:
Tries - Fritz Smith Healey Rogers: Goals - Orr(3):
SALFORD R - Tassell: Pinkney Maloney Littler Offiah: Blakeley Goulding: Southern(Driscoll) Alker Driscoll(Hancock)(Coley)(Hancock) Jowitt Highton(Holroyd) Wainwright(Brown):
Tries - Maloney(2) Pinkney Jowitt: Goals - Goulding(4):
Referee S Ganson (St Helens) Att - 6816 H.T. 8 - 12

Mon 16 Apr 2001 LEEDS RHINOS away lost 22 - 32
LEEDS R - Cummins: Calderwood Walker Senior Hilaire: Harris Burrow: Fleary(Farrell)(Ward)(Ferrall) Pratt Mathuiou(Fleary) Farrell(Wrench) Hay(Kirk) Sinfield:
Tries - Hilaire(3) Cummins Farrell Sinfield: Goals - Harris(4):
CASTLEFORD - Gay(Lennon): Wells Mather Eager Rogers: Orr Healey: Sykes(Lynch) Raper Handford(Smith) Shaw(Handford) Fritz(Hepi) Harland;
Tries - Rogers(2) Eager Orr: Goals - Orr(3):

424

SEASON 2001

Referee I Smith (Oldham) Att - 15039 H.T. 16 - 12

Sun 22 Apr 2001 HALIFAX BLUE SOX home won 34 - 24
CASTLEFORD - Gay: Lennon Wells Eager Rogers: Orr
Healey(Pryce): Sykes(Lynch) Raper Sampson(Smith)
Shaw(Sampson)(Sykes) Fritz(Brad Hepi) Harland:
Tries - Eager(2) Gay Wells Smith: Goals - Orr(7):
HALIFAX B S - Donlan: Marns Tickle
Hughes(Lawford)(Ekis) Gibson: Cardiss Clinch:
Goldspink(Davidson) Lawless(Penkywicz) Gannon
Davidson(Bloem) McMenemy(Goldspink) Moana:
Tries - Cardiss(2) Marns Tickle :   Goals - Tickle(4):
Referee K Fitzpatrick (Warrington) Att - 6483 H.T. 18 - 18

Sat 5 May 2001 BRADFORD BULLS home lost 22 - 24
CASTLEFORD - Gay: Wells Mather Eager Rogers: Orr
Lennon: Sykes(Sampson) Aaron Raper(Smith)
Handford(Tonks) Shaw(Flowers) Fritz Harland:
Tries - Gay Wells Orr: Goals - Orr(5):
BRADFORD B - Withers: Vaikona Mackay Gilmour Pryce:
H Paul R Paul: Vagana(Anderson)(McDermott) Lowes
McDermott(Fielden) Peacock Radford
Forshaw(Vagona)(Anderson)(McDermottB/B):
Tries - H Paul R Paul Lowes: Goals - H Paul(6):
Referee S Cummings (Widnes) Att - 8528 H.T. 2 - 8

Wed 9 May 2001 ST HELENS away lost 16 - 36
ST HELENS - Stewart: Hall Iro Hoppe Sullivan: Wellens
Long(West): Fairleigh(Nickle) Cunningham(Matautia)
(Jonkers) Edmondson(Matautia) Shiels Joynt(Edmonson)
Sculthorpe: Tries - Stewart(2) Sullivan Long Nickle
Cunningham Matautia :   Goals - Long(4):
CASTLEFORD - Flowers: Gay Wells Eager Rogers(ANDY
McNALLY(777): Orr Lennon(Pryce): Sampson Fritz
Handford(Lynch) Shaw(ANDY SPEAK(776))(Tonks)
Tonks(Speak) Harland:
Tries - Gay Wells Tonks: Goals - Orr(2):
Referee I Smith (Oldham) Att - 6836 H.T. 6 - 10

Sun 13 May 2001 HUDDERSFIELD GIANTS away won 46 - 26
HUDDERSFIELD G - Appo(Langley)(Appo): Frew Costin
Cardoza Gleeson: Thorman Kusto: Laughton(Crabtree
B/B)(Crabtree) Rowley Marshall (Lomax) Atkins(Rice)
Lomax(Atkins) McNamara: Tries - Frew Cardoza Gleeson
Kusto : Goals - McNamara(5):
CASTLEFORD - Flowers: Gay Eager Wells Pryce(McNally):
Orr Lennon: Sykes(Tonks) Fritz Sampson (Tonks B/B)
(Tonks)(Sampson) Shaw(Speak) Harland(Smith) Vowles:
Tries - Sampson(3) Flowers(2) Tonks(2) Wells Orr:
Goals - Orr(5):
Referee R Silverwood (Mirfield) Att - 3453 H.T. 8 - 20

Sun 20 May 2001 LONDON BRONCOS home lost 12 - 25
CASTLEFORD - Gay(Flowers): Wells Mather(Lennon) Eager
Rogers: Orr Healey: Sykes(Shaw) Fritz Sampson(Tonks
B/B) Shaw (Smith) Harland Vowles(Tonks):
Tries - Flowers Mather: Goals - Orr(2):

LONDON B - Roy: Golden Martin Tollett Peters:
Dymock(Lupton) Moran: Cram(Mestrov) Hetherington
Dooley(Mestrov)(Dooley) Millard Retchless(Johnson)
(Tretchless) Toshack: Tries - Roy Moran Cram Toshack:
Goals - Martin 4) Moran D/G
Referee I Smith (Oldham) Att - 6142 H.T. 6 - 8

Fri 25 May 2001 WIGAN WARRIORS away lost 12 - 54
WIGAN W - Radlinski: Hodgson Johnson Connolly Davies
Johns(Jones) Lam: Cowie(Howard) Newton(Smith)
O'Connor(Cowie) Betts Furner Farrell(Cassidy):
Tries - Radlinski(2) Johnson(2) Newton(2) Hodgson Jones
Farrell: Goals - Farrell(9):
CASTLEFORD - Flowers: Lennon Wells Eager(Pryce)
Rogers: Orr Healey: Sykes(Tonks) Fritz Sampson(Tonks
B/B)(Sykes)(Sampson B/B) Harland(Lynch) Shaw(Smith)
Vowles: Tries Eager Orr: Goals - Orr(2):
Referee S Cummings (Widnes) Att - 10190 H.T. nil - 22

Fri 1 Jun 2001 WAKEFIELD TRINITY WILDCATS home won 26 - 22
CASTLEFORD - Flowers: Gay Wells Rogers Pryce: Orr
Healey: Gareth Handford(Shaw B/B)(Tonks)(Shaw)
Speak(Lennon) Sampson(Lynch B/B)(Sampson)
Tonks(Smith) Fritz Vowles:
Tries - Gay Rogers Pryce Orr Sampson: Goals - Orr(3):
WAKEFIELD T W - Pearson: N Law Westwood Brooker
Sovatabua: Dorahy Davis(Poaching): O'Neill(Watene)
(O'Neill) Rauter Jackson(Mason) Poaching(Price)
Hudson(G Law) Field:
Tries - Sovatabua Dorahy Watene: Goals - Pearson(5):
Referee K Kirkpatrick (Warr'ton) Att - 6309 H.T. 18 - 12

Sat 9 Jun 2001 HULL F C home won 33 - 26
CASTLEFORD - Flowers; Gay (McNally) Wells Rogers
Pryce: Healey Lennon: Sykes(Speak) Speak(Shaw)
Sampson (Tonks)(Harland) Harland(Smith) Fritz Vowles:
Tries - Wells(2) Rogers Lennon Tonks Smith:
Goals - Lennon(4) VowlesD/G:
HULL FC - Prescott: Raynor Bird Parker C Smith: Cooke T
Smith: Craven(Broadbent) Jackson(Gene) Broadbent(King)
Carvell(Fletcher)(Campbell) Grimaldi Maiden:
Tries - Raynor Broadbent King Campbell Maiden:
Goals - Prescott(3):
Referee K Kirkpatrick (War'ton) Att - 6952 H.T. 16 - 10

Sun 17 Jun 2001 WARRINGTON WOLVES away lost 16 - 30
WARRINGTON W - Hunte: Smyth Kidwell Sibbit Alstead:
Briers Langer: Guisset Clarke Nutley(Wood)(Massella)
McCurrie(Noone) Marcer Nikau(Busby)(Nikau):
Tries - Hunte Sibbit Briers Clarke McCurrie:
Goals - Briers(5):
CASTLEFORD - Flowers: Pryce Wells Rogers(Lynch)
SIMON LEWIS(778): Healey Lennon: Shaw(Tonks)
Speak(Shaw) Sykes(McNally) Harland(Smith) Fritz
Vowles(Harland): Tries - Rogers Lewis: Goals - Lennon(4):
Referee S Cummings (Widnes) Att - 6002 H.T. 16 - 14

SEASON 2001

Sun 23 Jun 2001 SALFORD REDS away won 26 - 18
SALFORD R - Broadbent: Pinkney Maloney(Tassell) Littler
Offiah: Blakeley Goulding: Baynes(Makin) Alker
Driscoll(Harmon B/B) Coley(Baynes)(Arnold)
Hancock(Coley) Highton:
Tries - Offiah Coley Tassel: Goals - (Blakeley)(3):
CASTLEFORD - Lennon: Pryce Wells Roper Lewis: Orr
Healey: Sykes(Tonks)(Sykes) Speak(Shaw B/B)
Sampson(Tonks)(Sampson) Smith(Harland) Fritz
Vowles(Flowers B/B)(Smith):
Tries - Smith Roper Sampson Healey: Goals - Orr (5):
Referee R Silverwood (Mirfield) Att - 3530 H.T. 16 - 6

Fri 29 Jun 2001 LEEDS RHINOS home won 28 - 26
CASTLEFORD - Lennon(Flowers): Pryce Wells Roper Lewis:
Orr Healey: Sykes(Lynch)(Sykes) Shaw (Speak)(Shaw)
Sampson (Tonks B/B) Harland Fritz Vowles:
Tries - Lennon Price Roper Lewis Fritz: Goals - Orr(4):
LEEDS - Cummins: St Hilaire Carroll Walker Calderwood:
Harris Burrow: Fleary(Clyde) Mears McDermott(Ward)
(Diskin) Hay Farrell(McDermott) Sinfield: Tries - Carroll(2)
Harris McDermott Farrell: Goals - Harris(3):
Referee S Ganson (St Helens) Att - 10625 H.T. 24 - 6

**Sun 8 Jul 2001 HALIFAX BLUE SOX away
lost 16 - 22**
HALIFAX B S - Cardiss: Marns Hassan(Hughes) Donlan
Gibson: Dunemann Clinch: Goldspink (Hobson)
(Goldspink) Lawless Gannon Bloem(Tickle) Davidson
(Foster B/B) McMenemy: Tries - Bloem Marns Lawless
Hughes: Goals - Bloem(2) Tickle:
CASTLEFORD - Lennon(Flowers): Gay Wells Roper Simon
Lewis: Orr Healey: Sykes(Shaw B/B) Shaw(Andy Speak)
Sampson(Ian Tonks)(Sampson) Harland(Smith B/B) Fritz
Vowles: Tries Lewis Gay Orr: Goals - Orr(2):
Referee R Silverwood (Mirfield) Att - 5041 H.T. 10 - 2

Sun 15 Jul 2001 BRADFORD BULLS away lost 4 - 44
BRADFORD B - Withers(Rigon): Vaikona Naylor Rigon
(Gilmour) McAvoy: Pryce Deacon: Vagana(Anderson)
(Vagana) Lowes McDermott(Fielden) Gartner(Radford)
Peacock Forshaw: Tries - Lowes(2) Naylor(2) Withers
Pryce Deacon: Goals - Deacon(8):
CASTLEFORD - Flowers: Gay Wells(Smith) Roper Pryce:
Healey Lennon: Sykes(Jonathon Goddard) Shaw(WAYNE
GODWIN(779)) Sampson(Lynch)(Sampson) Harland Fritz
Vowles: Try - Fritz:
Referee S Ganson (St Helens) Att - 9287 H.T. 4 - 24

**Sun 22 Jul 2001 HUDDERSFIELD GIANTS home
won 20 - 14**
CASTLEFORD - Flowers(Lennon): Wells(Flowers) Roper
Eager Pryce: Orr(Gay) Healey: Sampson Shaw(Orr)
Smith(Lynch B/B) Harland(Lynch) Fritz Vowles:
Tries - Roper Orr Healey Smith: Goals - Orr Roper:
HUDDERSFIELD G - Reilly: Frew Gene Gleeson Langley:
Costin Kusto: Stone(Walker)(Lomax) Rowley
Marshall(Molloy)(Marshall) Atkins(Thorman)
Lomax(Stone) Mcnamara(Cardoza B/B):
Tries - Frew Kusto Costin: Goal - Costin

Referee R Silverwood (Mirfield) Att - 5697 H.T. 6 - 10

**Sat 28 Jul 2001 LONDON BRONCOS away
lost 10 - 40**
LONDON B - Barnett(Johnson): Sykes Fleming Roy
Houles: Dymock(Gillett) Moran: Mestrov(Dooley) Air
Cram(Toshack) Millard(Cram)(Mestrov) Retchless Parker:
Tries - Houles(2) Air(2) Fleming Gillett: Goals - Sykes(8):
CASTLEFORD - Flowers(Orr): Wells Roper Eager Pryce:
Healey Lennon: Sykes(Smith) Fritz Sampson(Lynch B/B)
Harland(Godwin)(Flowers) Smith(Harland) Vowles:
Tries - Wells Lennon: Goals - Roper:
Referee S Cummins (Widnes) Att - 2342 H.T. nil - 14

Fri 3 Aug 2001 ST HELENS away won 28 - 26
CASTLEFORD - Flowers: Wells Roper Eager Pryce:
Healey(Harland) Lennon(Gay): Smith Shaw Sampson
(Lynch)(Sykes)(Sampson) Harland(Sykes) Fritz Vowles:
Tries - Pryce Healey Harland Fritz Vowles:
Goals - Roper(4):
ST HELENS - Stewart(Bennett): Hall Iro Stankevitch Hoppe:
Martyn Wellens: Nickle(Matautia)(Jonkers) Cunningham
Fairleigh(McDonald)(Matautia) Joynt(Shiels)
Shiels(Fairleigh) Sculthorpe: Tries - Hoppe(2) Iro
Cunningham Shiels: Goals - Sculthorpe(3):
Referee K Kirkpatrick (War'ton) Att - 7054 H.T. 22 - 10

**Sun 12 Aug 2001 WARRINGTON WOLVES away
lost 12 - 27**
WARRINGTON W - Alstead: Smyth(Knott) Kohe-Love
Sibbitt Hunte: Briers Hulse: Massella(Noone)(Massalla)
Clarke Nuttley(Wood)(Nuttley) McCurrie(Smith) Guisset
Nikau: Tries - Kohe-Love(3) Hulse: Goals - Briers(5) D/G:
CASTLEFORD - Flowers(Gay): Rogers Eager Wells
Pryce(Lennon) Roper JAMIE ROONEY(780):
Sampson(DAVID BATES(781)) Shaw Sykes Fritz
Smith(Harland) Vowles: Try - Rogers: Goals - Rooney(4):
Referee R Connolly (Wigan) Att - 5235 H.T. 6 - 14

Sat 18 Aug 2001 LEEDS RHINOS home lost - 10 - 17
CASTLEFORD - Flowers: Wells Roper(Gay) Eager Rogers:
Healey(Rooney) Lennon: Sykes(Sampson) Shaw(Lynch)
Sampson(CHRIS CHARLES(782)) Smith Fritz
Harland(Sykes):   Tries - Wells Eager: Goal - Lennon:
LEEDS R - Cummins: Walker Carroll Senior Calderwood:
Pratt Sheridan: Fleary(Ward) Mears McDermott(Mathiou)
(McDermott) Farrell(Wrench) Mercer(Mathiou) Sinfield:
Tries - Senior Calderwood Pratt:
Goals - Sinfield(2) Cummins D/G:
Referee Mr K Kirkpatrick (War'ton) Att - 7750 H.T. 6 - 2

Sun 26 Aug 2001 BRADFORD BULLS away lost 30 - 56
BRADFORD B - Withers(McAvoy): Vaikona Mackay(Rigon)
Gilmour Pryce: H Paul(Deacon) R Paul: Anderson
(McDermott) Lowes McDermott(Fielden) Gartner(H Paul)
Peacock Forshaw: Tries - Withers(3) McAvoy Vaikona
Deacon R Paul Lowes Gartner: Goals - H Paul(9) Deacon:
CASTLEFORD - Lennon: Gay Wells Eager(Pryce) Rogers:
Roper Jamie Rooney(Flowers): Lynch (Godwin) Shaw
(Charles) Sampson(Lynch) Smith(Charles B/B) Fritz

SEASON 2001

Harland: Tries - Harland(2) Roper Godwin Smith:
Goals - Roper(3) Rooney(2):
Referee S Ganson (St Helens) Att - 10469 H.T. 8 - 38

Fri 31 Aug 2001 ST HELENS away lost 20 - 44
ST HELENS - Stewart: Kirkpatrick Iro(Jonkers) Hoppe Hall:
Sculthorpe Wellens: Fairleigh (Matautia) (McDonald)
Cunningham Nickle(Matautia) Joynt Stankevitch
(Cruckshank) McConnell: Tries - McConnell(3) Hall
Stewart Cunningham Hoppe Nickle: Goals - Sculthorpe(6)
CASTLEFORD - Jason Flowers(Pryce): Gay Wells Roper
Rogers: Vowles Lennon: Sykes(Godwin) Shaw
Sampson(Smith) Smith(Charles) Fritz Harland(Lynch):
Tries - Lennon Roper Smith Vowles: Goals - Lennon:(2):
Rerferee R Silverwood (Mrfield) Att - 7680 H.T. 4 - 22

Sun 9 Sep 2001 WIGAN WARRIORS home lost 22 - 30
CASTLEFORD - Gay(Pryce): Wells Roper Eager Rogers:
Healey(GARY SMITH(783)) Lennon: Sykes(Lynch)(Godwin)
Shaw M Smith(GodwinB/B) Charles(Lynch) Fritz Vowles:
Tries - Roper Charles Lennon M Smith: Goals - Roper(3):
WIGAN W - Radlinski(Dallas): Dallas(Carney) Connolly
Renouf Johnson: Chester Lam: Howard(Cowie) Newton
(Smith) O'Connor(Wilde) Betts Cassidy(Howard) Farrell:
Tries - Connolly Renouf Johnson Lam Radlinski Carney:
Goals - Farrell (3):
Referee S Ganson (St Helens) Att - 7546 H.T. 8 - 16

Sun 16 Sep 2001 WARRINGTON WOLVES home
lost 28 - 31
CASTLEFORD - Wells: Pryce Jonathon Roper Eager
Rogers: Healey Lennon: Lynch(Bates) Darren
Shaw(Godwin) Sampson(Darren Shaw)(Sampson) M
Smith Fritz(Charles) Vowles:
Tries - Pryce(2) Eager Godwin Roper: Goals - Lennon(4):
WARRINGTON W - Hunte: Reddicliffe Crouthers Kohe-
Love Thomas(Tickle): Briers Hulse:
Massella(Parry)(Hill)(Parry) Gleeson Nutley
Noone)(Hill)(Massella) Guisset(Clarke) Nikau:
Tries - Gleeson(2) Clarke Hunte Massella:
Goals - Briers(5) D/G:
Referee P Taberner (Wigan) Att - 6019 H.T. 8 - 14

Mark Lennon
D. Nc 772
2001 to 2003

Mitch Healey
D. No 773
2001 to 2003

Wayne Godwin
D. No 779
2001 to 2004

Chris Charles
D. No 782
2001 to 2007

SEASON 2001

D.N	PLAYER		DEBUT	L MATCH	APP	SUB	T.AP	TRI'S	G'LS	D.G	P'TS
661	SAMPSON	DEAN			23	2	25	6	0	0	24
694	SYKES	NATHAN			20	3	23	1	0	0	4
708	FLOWERS	JASON		31/08/2001	13	6	19	3	0	0	12
715	TONKS	IAN		08/07/2001	6	9	15	4	0	0	16
719	HARLAND	LEE			24	2	26	3	0	0	12
728	GAY	RICHARD			19	4	23	5	0	0	20
734	WELLS	JON			30	0	30	9	0	0	36
739	VOWLES	ADRIAN			23	0	23	4	0	1	17
742	ORR	DANNY			19	1	20	10	60	0	160
748	MATHER	BARRIE-JON			10	0	10	2	0	0	8
750	SMITH	MICHAEL			10	17	27	10	0	0	40
756	EAGER	MICHAEL			22	0	22	8	0	0	32
757	ROGERS	DAREN			22	0	22	9	0	0	36
758	RAPER	AARON		05/05/2001	9	0	9	0	0	0	0
759	LYNCH	ANDY			5	16	21	0	0	0	0
761	FRITZ	DALE			25	2	27	4	0	0	16
762	HEPI	BRAD		22/04/2001	1	4	5	0	0	0	0
766	SHAW	DARREN		16/09/2001	25	4	29	0	0	0	0
770	PRYCE	WAINE			12	7	19	5	0	0	20
771	GODDARD	JONATHON		15/07/2001	0	1	1	0	0	0	0
772	LENNON	MARK	11/02/2001		20	10	30	5	15	0	50
773	HEALEY	MITCH	11/02/2001		21	0	21	5	0	0	20
774	HANDFORD	GARETH	11/02/2001	01/06/2001	7	4	11	0	0	0	0
775	ROPER	JONATHON	11/02/2001	16/09/2001	13	1	14	7	12	0	52
776	SPEAK	ANDY	09/05/2001	08/07/2001	4	4	8	0	0	0	0
777	McNALLY	ANDY	09/05/2001		0	4	4	0	0	0	0
778	LEWIS	SIMON	17/06/2001	08/07/2001	4	0	4	3	0	0	12
779	GODWIN	WAYNE	15/07/2001		0	6	6	2	0	0	8
780	ROONEY	JAMIE	12/08/2001	26/08/2001	2	1	3	0	6	0	12
781	BATES	DAVID	12/08/2001		0	2	2	0	0	0	0
782	CHARLES	CHRIS	18/08/2001		1	4	5	1	0	0	4
783	SMITH	GARY	09/09/2001	09/09/2001	0	1	1	0	0	0	0
	32				**390**	**115**	**505**	**106**	**93**	**1**	**611**
				12	**12**						

COMPETITION		P	W	D	L	FOR	AGT
S. LEAGUE	POSITION 8 OF 12	28	10	1	17	581	777
RL CUP		2	1	0	1	30	46
PLAYERS RECORDS		**30**	**11**	**1**	**18**	**611**	**823**

On 18 May 2001 Stuart Raper left the Club to take over at Wigan. Graham Steadman was appointed Caretaker Coach.

Dean Sampson makes his 400th appearance for the Club in the 20-14 victory against Huddersfield Giants on 22 July 2001.

SUPER LEAGUE VII

Huddersfield Giants were relegated from Super League and replaced with Widnes Vikings.

Wed 26 Dec 2001 LEEDS RHINOS away lost 12 - 56 FRIENDLY
LEEDS R - Cummins: Calderwood C Walker Kirk St Hilaire:B Walker Sheridan: Fleary Diskin McDonald Hay Adamson Vowles: Subs used - Ward Burrow Jones-Buchanan Dowes Morton: Tries - Calderwood(2) B Walker(2) Cummins C Walker Kirk St Hilaire Adamson Burrow: Goals - B Walker(8):
CASTLEFORD - Gay: Saxton Rogers Johnson Pryce: Thaler Bartrim: Sykes Godwin Lynch Smith Bates Hudson: Subs used - Irvine Spedding Elima Blakeway Walker: Tries - Rogers Lynch : Goals - Bartrim(2):
Referee S Cummins (Widnes) Att - 12771 H.T. 0 - 34

Wed 23 Jan 2002 BRADFORD BULLS home lost 12 - 30 FRIENDLY
CASTLEFORD - Gay: Wells Eager Johnson Rogers: Healey Lennon: Sykes Bartrim Lynch Fritz Smith Mercer: Subs used - Pryce Godwin Hudson Harland: Tries - Smith Johnson: Goals - Bartrim(2)
BRADFORD - Withers: Vaikona Naylor Gilmour Vaikikolo: Paul Deacon: Vagana Lowes McDermott Peacock Gartner Forshaw: Subs used - Anderson Fielden Radford Costin McAvoy Pryce Parker Sykes Wilkinson Stanley Myler Langley:
Tries Paul(2) Sykes(2) Gilmour Vainikolo: Goals Deacon(3):
Referee S Cummings (Widnes) Att - 4016 H.T. 6 - 16

Wed 30 Jan 2002 HALIFAX BLUE SOX home won 26 -4 FRIENDLY
CASTLEFORD - Rogers: Wells Johnson Eager Pryce: Healey Lennon: Sykes Bartrim Lynch Smith Fritz Harland: Subs used Hudson Godwin Bates Elima:
Tries Rogers(2) Johnson Pryce Lynch: Goals - Bartrim(3):
HALIFAX B S - Cardiss: Marns Halpenny Donlan Greenwood: Dunemann Clinch: Hobson Penkywicz Thackray Brocklehurst Bloem Hammond:
Subs used - Lawless Mcdowell Gannon Beckett Flowers Birchall Tickle Goldspink Clayton Finn:: Try – Not Known
Referee R Silverwood (Mirfield) Att - 1973 H.T. 14 - 4

Sun 10 Feb 2002 SALFORD CITY REDS home won 19 -6 CHALLENGE CUP ROUND 4
CASTLEFORD - Gay(Lennon): Wells Eager Rogers: Orr Healey: Sykes(RYAN HUDSON(786)) WAYNE BARTRIM(785) Lynch (Sykes)(Smith) Smith(Lynch) Fritz(Godwin) Harland:
Tries - Orr(2) Smith: Goals - Bartrim(3) Healey(DG):
SALFORD C R - Broadbent: Pinkney Hunte Littler Gibson: Holroyd(Arnold) Goulding: Baynes(Shaw) Watson Highton(Ebril) Nicol(Baynes) Jowitt(Wainwright) Treacy: Goals - Goulding(3):
Referee S Ganson (St Helens) Att - 5394 H.T. 12 - 6

Sun 24 Feb 2002 LONDON BROCHOS away won 19 -6 CHALLENGE CUP ROUND 5
LONDON B - Barnett(Purdham B/B): Hall Roy Martin Houles: Gillett Moran: Bawden(Stephenson) (Marshall) (Cram) Budworth Cram(Bawden)(Stephenson) Evans(Retchless B/B) Toshack(Purdham) Dymock: Try - Moran: Goal Martin:
CASTLEFORD - Lennon(Gay): Wells Eager Johnson Rogers: Orr Healey: Sykes(Lynch) Bartrim Lynch(Sampson)(KYLE WARREN(787)) Smith Fritz Harland(Hudson):
Tries - Hudson(2) Gay: Goals - Bartrim(3) Healey(DG):
Referee S Cummins (Widnes) Att - 2436 H.T. 0 - 6

Sun 3 Mar 2002 WAKEFIELD TRINITY WILDCATS away won 28 - 10
WAKEFIELD T W - Holland: Sovatabua Tassell Ellis(G Law B/B) N Law: Davis(G Law) Wood: Broadbent(Feather) Sattery Jackson(Broadbent) Wrench(Handforth) Field(Keating) Knott: Tries - Holland N law: Goal - Knott:
CASTLEFORD - Gay: Wells Eager Johnson Rogers: Orr Healey(Lennon): Sykes(Smith) Bartrim Lynch(Warren) (Sykes) Smith(Sampson)(Lynch B/B) Fritz(Harland) Harland(Hucson):
Tries - Johnson(2) Bartrim(2) Gay: Goals - Bartrim(4):
Referee Mr R Silverwood (Dewsbury) Att - 6174 H.T. 8 - 0

Sun 10 Mar 2002 WIDNES VIKINGS home lost 24 - 31
CASTLEFORD - Gay(Lennon): Wells Johnson Eager Rogers: Orr Healey: Sykes(Warren)(Sykes) Bartrim Lynch(Sampson) (Lynch B/B) Smith Warren(Hudson) Harland:
Tries - Wells Orr Warren Bartrim: Goals - Bartrim(4):
WIDNES V - Spruce: Munro(Atcheson) Demetriou Hughes Percival: Weston Eaton: Relf(Mills)(Stone) Cantilon Stone(O'Neill)(Relf) Farrell(Richardson) McCurrie Frame:
Tries - Spruce Demetriou Percival Weston Eaton: Goals - Eaton(5)(1 D/G)
Referee K Kirkpatrick (Warrington) Att - 8192 H.T. 8 - 30

Sun 17 Mar 2002 DONCASTER DRAGONS home won 32 – 14 CHALLENGE CUP QUARTER FINAL
CASTLEFORD Gay(Lennon): Wells Johnson Eager Rogers: Orr Healey Lynch(Warren)(Sampson) Hudson Sampson(Sykes)(Lynch) Smith Harland Bartrim(Godwin):
Tries - Eager(2) Rogers(2) Wells Orr: Goals - Bartrim(4):
DONCASTER D - Baker: Woodcock Golden Garcia Lee: Mansson Ross: David(Handford) Green(Conway) Handford Forsyth) Atter(Fielden) Ostler(Lawton) (Atter)Moana:
Tries - Golden Ross Fielden: Goals - Ross:
Referee R Silverwood (Dewsbury) Att - 6061 H.T. 22 - 6

Sun 24 Mar 2002 LONDON BRONCHOS home draw 18 - 18
CASTLEFORD - Lennon: Wells(Pryce) Johnson(Wells) Eager Rogers: Orr Healey: Sykes(Hudson) Bartrim Lynch(Bates)(Warren) Smith Fritz(Lynch) Harland:
Tries - Pryce Rogers Bartrim: Goals - Bartrim(3):

SEASON 2002

LONDON B - Barnett: Roy Martin Jackson(Houles) Peters: Purdham(Cram) Moran: Cram(Bawden)(Marshall) Hetherington(Evans B/B) Marshall(Evans) Retchless Toshack Dymock:
Tries - Moran(2) Jackson: Goals - Martin(3):
Referee R Connolly (Wigan) Att - 5578 H.T. 2 - 12

Fri 31 Mar 2002 WIGAN WARRIORS away lost 12 - 34
WilGAN W - Radlinski(Carney): Dallas Ainscough Johnson Hodgson: O'Neill Lam: O'Connor(Bibey) Newton(M Smith) Bibey(Howard) Wild(Haughton) Furner(Wild) Farrell:
Tries - Dallas(2) Wild Radlinski Ainscough Johnson: Goals - Farrell(5):
CASTLEFORD - Lennon: Pryce Eager Wells Rogers: Orr Healey: Sykes(Warren) Bartrim(Hudson) Lynch(Sampson) (Sykes) Fritz Harland(Bartrim B/B)(Godwin) Hudson (Smith):   Tries - Wells Eager Rogers:
Referee S Ganson (St Helens) Att - 10761 H.T. 0 - 18

Tue 2 Apr 2002 LEEDS RHINOS home lost 16 - 36
CASTLEFORD - Lennon: Pryce Eager Wells(Harland) Rogers: Orr Healey: Sykes(Smith) Bartrim Sampson(Lynch) Fritz Harland(Warren) Hudson(Godwin):   Tries - Eager Harland: Goals - Bartrim(4):
LEEDS R - Cummins: St Hilaire Carroll(Calderwood) Senior: C Walker: B Walker Sheridan(Burrow): Ward(McDermott) Diskin McDermott(McDonald)Adamson Poaching(Hay) Sinfield: Tries - Diskin Senior Sheridan B Walker Burrow Calderwood: Goals - B Walker(6):
Referee I Smith (Oldham) Att - 10017 H.T. 4 - 18

Sun 7 Apr 2002 SALFORD CITY REDS away won 74-16
SALFORD C R - Gibson: Pinkney Nicol Hunte Arnold: Blakeley(Holroyd) Goulding: Baynes(Corvo) Alker Shaw(Southern) Jowitt Ebrill Wainwright(Highton):
Tries - Goulding(2) Arnold: Goals - Goulding(2):
CASTLEFORD - Gay: Pryce Rogers Eager Lennon: Orr(Mather) Healey: Sampson Bartrim(Godwin) Lynch(OLIVIER ELIMA(788)) Warren(Harland) Smith Hudson: Tries - Hudson(2) Godwin(2) Rogers(2) Mather Elima Lennon Smith Bartrim Harland Healey:
Goals - Bartrim(7) Lennon(4):
Referee C Morris (Huddersfield) Att – 4101H.T. 4 - 36

Sat 13 Apr 2002 WIGAN WARRIORS lost 10 - 20
SEMI FINAL CHALLENGE CUP - at HEADINGLEY LEEDS
CASTLEFORD - Gay: Pryce Eager Johnson Rogers: Orr Healey: Sykes(Lynch) Bartrim(Godwin)(Lennon) Sampson(Warren) Smith Fritz Hudson(Bartrim):
Tries - Smith Hudson: Goals - Bartrim:
WIGAN W - Radlinski: Carney Connolly Hodgson Dallas((Wild B/B): O'Neill Lam: O'Connor(Bibey)(C Smith) Newton(M Smith) C Smith(Howard)(O'Connor)(C Smith B/B) Haughton(Wild) Cassidy Farrell:
Tries - Newton Dallas Connolly: Goals - Farrell(4)
Referee S Cummings (Widnes) Att - 10380 H.T. 10 - 14

Sun 21 Apr 2002 HULL F C away lost 18 - 48
CASTLEFORD - Gay: Pryce Eager Johnson Rogers:

Orr(Lennon) Healey: Sykes(Sampson) Godwin(GARY MERCER B/B (789)) Sampson(Lynch)(Sykes) Smith Warren(Mather) Hudson:
Tries - Smith Godwin Sampson: Goals - Lennon(2) Orr:
HULL F C - Prescott: Raynor McKay(Bird) Kohe-Love Crowther: Horne(McKay) J Smith(T Smith): Greenhill(King) Jackson Carvell(King B/B) Maher(Logan) Ryan(Ryan) Cooke: Tries - McKay(2) Crowther(2) Kohe-Love(2) Prescott J Smith: Goals - Crowther(8):
Referee R Silverwood (Dewsbury) Att - 8908 H.T. 6 - 30

Fri 3 May 2002 BRADFORD BULLS home lost 8 - 32
CASTLEFORD - Gay: Pryce(Lennon) Johnson Eager Rogers: Orr Healey: Sampson(Lynch)(Sampson) Bartrim(Godwin) Sykes(Sampson B/B) Smith Warren(Mather) Hudson:
Tries - Rogers: Goals - Bartrim(2)
BRADFORD B - Pryce: Vaikona Naylor Gilmour(McAvoy) Vainikolo: Paul Deacon: McDermott(Anderson) (Vagana B/B)(McDermott) Lowes Vagana(Fielden) Gartner(Radford) Peacock(Vagana)Forshaw:
Tries - McAvoy(2) Paul Gilmour: Goals - Deacon(8):
Referee R Connolly (Wigan) Att - 7496 H.T. 2 - 12

Mon 29 Apr 2002 ST HELENS home won 36 - 22
CASTLEFORD - Gay(Johnson): Wells Eager Mather Rogers: Orr Lennon(Healey): Sykes(Hudson) Godwin(Bartrim) Lynch(Sampson) Smith Warren Hudson(Godwin):
Tries - Mather(2) Rogers(2) Hudson Johnson Bartrim:
Goals - Bartrim(4):
ST HELENS - Wellens: Albert Hoppe Gleeson Stewart Sculthorpe Martyn: Britt(Bennett)(Higham)Cunningham Nickle(Edmonson)(Nickle) Joynt Stankevitch Sheils:
Tries - Gleeson(2) Shiels Scunthorpe:
Goals - Sculthorpe(3):
Referee C Morris (Huddersfield) Att - 5947 H.T. 16 - 18

Sun 12 May 2002 HALIFAX BLUE SOX away lost 18 -19
HALIFAX B S - Flowers Halpenny Woods(Cardiss B/B) Donlan Beckett: Dunemann Clinch: Goldspink (Hobson) (Goldspink B/B) Lawless Gannon(Birchall)(Gannon) McMenney Tickle(Thackray) Hammond: Tries - Beckett Halpenny Dunemann: Goals - Tickle(3) Dunemann(D/G):
CASTLEFORD - Rogers: Wells Mather(Warren) Eager Pryce: Orr Healey(Godwin): Sykes(Lynch)(Sykes) Bartrim Lynch(Sampson) Smith Warren(Johnson) Hudson:
Tries - Smith Orr: Goals - Bartrim(5):
Referee R Silverwood (Mirfield) Att - 4450 H.T. 8 - 12

Sun 19 May 2002 WARRINGTON WOLVES home won 46 - 24
CASTLEFORD - Richard Gay(Wells): Pryce Mather Eager Rogers: Orr Healey: Sykes(Warren) Bartrim Lynch (ADRIAN RAINEY(790)) B/B)(Johnson) Smith(Sykes) Warren(Rainey) Hudson(Godwin): Tries - Eager(2) Mather Pryce Hudson Smith Lynch Wells: Goals - Bartrim(7):
WARRINGTON W - Watts: Smyth Burns Halliwell(Appo) Rivett: Briers Hulse(O'Reilly): Laughton(Hilton) Clarke Fozzard(Laughton) Guissett(Wood) Marquet(Fozzard) Domic: Tries - Briers O'Reilly Burns: Goals - Briers(6):
Referee R Connolly (Wigan) Att - 6175 H.T. 22 - 10

SEASON 2002

Sun 26 May 2002 WAKEFIELD TRINITY WILDCATS home lost 18 - 30
CASTLEFORD - Rogers: Wells Mather Eager Pryce: Orr
Healey: Sykes(Warren) Bartrim(Godwin)(Bartrim)
Lynch(Fritz) Smith Rainey(Sykes) Hudson:
Tries - Hudson Mather Orr: Goals - Bartrim(3):
WAKEFIELD T W - Frew: Hassan Tassell Westwood N Law:
Moana Davies(March B/B): Feather(Keating)(Jackson)
Wood Jackson(Feather) Ellis(G Law) Field Knott(Wrench):
Tries - Tassell(3) Westwood Wrench:
Goals - Knott(4) G Law:
Referee I Smith (Oldham) Att - 6338 H.T. 6 - 14

Tue 4 Jun 2002 WIDNES VIKINGS away lost 20 - 26
WIDNES V - Spruce: Demetriou Potter Hughes Percival:
Weston Eaton: Relf(Mills)(Relf) Cantillon
Stone(O'Neill)(Stone)(O'Neill B/B) Farrell(Frame)
McCurrie(Atcheson B/B) Frame(Carter)(Frame B/B):
Tries - Spruce Demetriou Cantillon Mills: Goals - Eaton(5):
CASTLEFORD - Rogers: Wells Mather(Johnson) Eager
Pryce: Orr Healey: Sykes(Sampson) Bartrim(Hudson)
Rainey(Sykes) Smith Fritz(Warren) Hudson(Harland):
Tries - Wells Orr Johnson: Goals - Bartrim(4):
Referee K Kirkpatrick (War'gton) Att - 5671 H.T. 12 - 14

Sun 9 Jun 2002 SALFORD CITY REDS home won 24 - 2
CASTLEFORD - Rogers: Wells Johnson Eager Pryce: Orr
Healey: Rainey(Sykes)(Warren) Bartrim(Hudson)
Sampson(Warren B/B)(Sykes B/B) Smith(Rainey)
Fritz(Mather) Hudson(Harland):
Tries - Wells(2) Bartrim Eager Hudson: Goals - Bartrim(2):
SALFORD C R - Broadbent: Hunte(Watson)
Gibson(Hancock)(Nicol) Littler Arnold: Maloney Holroyd:
Baynes(Southern) Alker Coley(Baynes) Ebrill(Treacy B/B)
Nicol(Treacy) Wainwright: Goal - Holroyd:
Referee C Morris (Huddersfield) Att - 5025 H.T. 2 - 2

Fri 21 Jun 2002 ST HELENS away lost 16 - 26
ST HELENS - Albert: Gardner Stewart Newlove
Kirkpatrick(Stankevitch)(Shiels): Gleeson Martyn(Wellens):
Britt(Nickle B/B) Higham Nickle(Ward)(Stankevitch B/B)
Joynt(Edmondson) Bennett Shiels(Martyn): Tries - Albert
Shiels Gardner: Goals - Wellens(5) Martyn(2):
CASTLEFORD - Warren(TOM SAXTON (791)): Pryce
Mather Johnson Rogers: Orr(Hudson B/B) Healey:
Sykes(Lynch) Bartrim(Sampson) Sampson(Rainey)(Smith)
Smith(Hudson) Fritz Harland:
Tries - Orr Rogers Mather: Goals - Bartrim(2):
Referee K Kirkpatrick (Warrington) Att - 7254 H.T. 16 - 14

Fri 28 Jun 2002 HULL FC home lost 12 - 18
CASTLEFORD - Rogers(Lennon): Pryce Eager Mather
Johnson: Orr Healey: Sykes(Sampson)(Rainey
B/B)(Sampson)(Warren) Bartrim Lynch(Sykes)
Smith(Warren)(Smith) Fritz Harland:
Tries - Healey Orr: Goals - Bartrim(2):
HULL FC - Crowther(Parker): Raynor Kohe-Love Mackay C
Smith: Cooke J Smith: Greenhill(Logan)(Greenhill) Jackson
King(Carvel)(King)(Carvel) Ryan(Bird B/B)(Bird) Maher
Chester:

Tries - Jackson Raynor Kohe-Love: Goals - Crowther(3):
Referee I Smith (Oldham) Att - 6818 H.T. 4 - 12

Sat 6 Jul 2002 LONDON BRONCOS away won 24 - 20
LONDON B - Sykes: Hall Martin Roy Houles(Gillett):
Dymock Moran: Bawden(Gillett B/B)(Stephenson)
Budworth Marshall(Shaw)(Bawden)(Price B/B)
Retchless(Marshall B/B) Toshack Purdham:
Tries - Martin Bawden Roy: Goals - Martin(4):
CASTLEFORD - Lennon(Warren): Pryce Eager(Mather)
Johnson Rogers: Orr Healey: Sykes(Rainey) Bartrim
Lynch(Smith) Warren(Sampson) Fritz Harland:
Tries - Rogers 2) Orr Harland: Goals - Bartrim(4):
Referee R Silverwood (Dewsbury) Att - 3343 H.T. 16 - 6

Fri 12 Jul 2002 LEEDS RHINOS away won 32 - 24
LEEDS R - Cummins: Claderwood Carroll Chev Walker
Kirk: Ben Walker(McGuire) Burrow(Ben Walker):
Adamson(McDonald)(Adamson) Diskin Ward(Bailey) Hay
Poching(Jones -Buchanan) Vowles:
Tries - McGuire(2) Vowles Diskin: Goals - Ben Walker(4):
CASTLEFORD - Rogers: Wells Mather Johnson Pryce:
Orr(Saxton) Healey: Sykes(Lynch) Bartrim(Hudson)
Lynch(Warren)(Bartrim) Smith Fritz(Rainey) Harland:
Tries Wells(2) Rogers Pryce Warren Smith:
Goals - Bartrim(3) Orr:
Referee S Ganson (St Helens) Att - 10062 H.T. 22 - 6

Sat 20 Jul 2002 WIGAN WARRIORS home draw 18 - 18
CASTLEFORD - Rogers: Wells Mather Johnson Pryce: Orr
Healey: Sykes(Lynch) Bartrim
Lynch(Warren)(Sampson)(Sykes B/B)(Fritz)Smith
Fritz(Hudson) Harland:
Tries - Wells(2) Orr: Goals - Bartrim(3):
WIGAN W - Connolly: Carney(M Smith) Aspinwall
Ainscough Briscoe: O'Loughlin Lam(Robinson):
O'Connor(Bibey) Newton C Smith(Howard)(C
Smith)Cassidy O'Connor Tickle Furner:
Tries - Aspinwall Newton Furner: Goals - Furner(3):
Referee I Smith (Oldham) Att - 6804 H.T. 10 - 6

Fri 26 Jul 2002 BRADFORD BULLS away lost 18 - 40
BRADFORD B - Withers: Vaikona Naylor Gilmour
Vainikolo(McAvoy): Paul Deacon: Vagana(McDermott)
Lowes(Price) Felden Gartner(Radford) Peacock(Vagana)
Forshaw(Peacock):Tries - Withers Lowes Vaikona Gilmour
Vainikolo Naylor McDermott: Goals - Deacon(6):
CASTLEFORD - Rogers: Saxton Warren Wells Pryce: Orr
Healey(ADAM THALER (792)): Rainey(David Bates)(Lynch)
Bartrim(Godwin) Lynch(Rainey) Harland Fritz(RICHARD
BLAKEWAY B/3 (793)) Hudson(Bartrim):
Tries - Pryce Rainey Godwin: Goals - Bartrim(3):
Referee R Silverwood (Mirfield) Att - 9316 H.T. 12 - 0

SEASON 2002

Sun 4 Aug 2002 HALIFAX BLUE SOX home
won 38 - 14
CASTLEFORD - Rogers: Pryce Mather Eager Wells: Orr
Healey: Sykes(Warren)(Lynch B/B)(Smith)
Bartrim(Godwin)Lynch(Sykes) Fritz Smith(Rainey)(Bartrim)
Harland:
Tries - Smith(2) Pryce(2) Rogers Eager: Goals - Bartrim(7):
HALIFAX B S - Donlan: Beckett Flowers Halpenny
Halliwell: Clinch Finn: Hobson(Thackray) Penkywicz
(Bloem) Birchall(Gannon) Gannon(Davidson)(Hobson)
McMenemy(Brocklehurst) Lawless:
Tries - Beckett Lawless: Goals - Finn(3):
Referee K Kirkpatrick (Warrington) Att - 5894 H.T. 8 - 14

Sun 11 Aug 2002 WARRINGTON WOLVES away
won 24 - 12
WARRINGTON W - Penny: Smyth Westwood Alstead
Mathers(Appo): Briers N Wood(Mathers): Hilton
(Laughton) Clarke Laughton(P Wood) Marquet(Noone)
P Wood(Fozzard) Burns:
Tries - Wood Briers: Goals - Briers(2):
CASTLEFORD - Rogers: Wells Mather(Johnson) Eager
Pryce: Orr Hudson: Sykes(Adrian Rainey)(Lynch) Bartrim
Lynch(Smith B/B)(Warren) Warren(Smith) Fritz
Harland(Godwin):
Tries - Eager Pryce Johnson Godwin: Goals - Bartrim(4):
Referee I Smith (Oldham) Att - 4667 H.T. 14 - 8

Sun 18 Aug 2002 HALIFAX BLUE SOX away won 40-16
HALIFAX B S - Donlan: Beckett Flowers Woods Halliwell:
Dunermann Clinch: Hobson(Birchall)(Clayton) Lawless
Goldspink(Davidson)(Goldspink) Gannon Thackray
(Bloem)(Thackray) McMenemy:
Tries - Woods Dunermann Donlan: Goals Clinch(2):
CASTLEFORD - Rogers: Wells Johnson Eager Pryce: Orr
Healey: Sykes(Warren) Bartrim(Godwin)(Mather)
Lynch(Smith) Harland(Lynch) Fritz(Bartrim)
Hudson(Bartrim B/B): Tries - Rogers(2) Eager Pryce
Hudson Warren: Goals - Bartrim(5) Orr(3):
Referee P Taberner (Wigan) Att - 3126 H.T. 32 - 4

Sun 25 Aug 2002 BRADFORD BULLS home won 44 -14
CASTLEFORD - Rogers(Saxton): Wells Johnson Eager
Pryce: Orr Healey: Smith(Lynch)(Smith) Bartrim
Lynch(Sykes)(Mather) Harland Fritz Hudson(Lennon):
Tries - Pryce Healey Johnson Wells Mather Orr Harland:
Goals - Bartrim(6) Orr(2):
BRADFORD B - Withers: Vaikona Naylor
Gilmour(Vainikolo) McAvoy: Paul Deacon(Pryce B/B):
Vagana(McDermott)(Radford) Lowes(Pryce B/B)Fielden
Peacock Radford(Anderson)(Vagana)(Anderson) Forshaw:
Tries - Pryce Deacon: Goals – Deacon(2) Withers:
Referee S Ganson (St Helens) Att - 7697 H.T. 16 - 8

Sun 1 Sep 2002 WAKEFIELD TRINITY WILCATS home
won 44 - 6
CASTLEFORD - Rogers(Saxton): Wells Johnson Eager
Pryce: Orr(Blakeway) Healey: Smith(Lynch) Bartrim
Lynch(Mather) Harland(Smith) Fritz Hudson(Lennon):
Tries - Pryce(4) Fritz Wells Orr Lennon: Goals Bartrim(6):

WAKEFIELD T W - Holland: Hassan(G Law) Tassell Bird
Frew: Moana Davis: Broadbent(Keating)
Handforth(March)(Handforth) Feather(Snitch) Ellis
Field(Broadbent) Slattery: Try - Ellis: Goal - Davis:
Referee C Morris (Huddersfield) Att - 7134 H.T.10 - 2

Sun 8 Sep 2002 WARRINGTON WOLVES away
lost 14 - 29
WARRINGTON - O'Reilly: Smyth(Burns B/B) Alstead
Westwood Appo: Briers Wood: Fozzard(Noone) Clarke
Hilton(Stevens)(Hilton) Guisset(Sturm)Busby(Wood)
Burns(Fozzard):
Tries - Appo(2) Burns Clarke: Goals Briers(6) (D/G):
CASTLEFORD - Rogers :Wells Johnson Eager Pryce: Orr
Healey(Lennon B/B): Warren(Sampson B/B)
(Sampson)(Lynch)(Warren) Bartrim Lynch(Saxton) Smith
Fritz Hudson(Lennon):
Tries - Eager(2) Pryce: Goal Bartrim:
Referee I Smith (Oldham) Att - 6103 H.T. 8 - 14

Sun 15 Sep 2002 WIDNES VIKINGS home won 32 - 20
CASTLEFORD - Rogers: Wells Johnson Eager Pryce: Orr
Healey: Sykes(Warren)(Sampson)(Hudson B/B)
Bartrim(Warren) Lynch(Hudson B/B)(Hudson) Smith
Fritz(Mather) Hudson(Lennon): Tries - Eager Rogers
Lennon Johnson Pryce Lynch: Goals - Bartrim(4):
WIDNES V - Spruce: Percival Demetriou Hughes Devlin:
Weston(Atcheson) Eaton: Relf(Stone)(Relf B/B) Cantillon
O'Neill(Mills)(Stone) Potter(Richardson)(Potter) McCurrie
Frame: Tries - McCurrie(2) Spruce: Goals - Hughes(4):
Referee R Silverwood (Dewsbury) Att - 7679 H.T. 16 - 4

Sun 22 Sep 2002 SALFORD CITY REDS away
won 20 - 10
SALFORD C R - Gibson: Reardon Nicol Maloney Arnold:
Blakeway Watson: Baynes(Coley) AlkerP Highton(Baynes)
Wainwright(P Highton) Treacy D Highton(Ebrill):
Try - D Highton: Goals - Blakeway(3):
CASTLEFORD - Rogers: Wells Johnson(Mather) Eager
Pryce:Orr Healey(Hudson): Sykes(Harland) Bartrim
Lynch(Warren B/B) Fritz Smith(Warren) Hudson(Lennon):
Tries - Rogers Bartrim Hudson: Goals Bartrim(4):
Referee R Connolly (Wigan) Att - 5541 H.T. 8 - 6

Sat 28 Sep 2002 WIGAN WARRIORS away lost
14 – 26 TOP 6 ELIMINATION PLAYOFF 3rd v 6th
WIGAN W - Radlinski: Aspiwall Connolly Hodgson
Briscoe: O'Neill Lam: Howard(Bibey)(Howard) Newton(M
Smith) C Smith(Sculthorpe)(C Smith)Tickle Furner(Wild)
Farrell:
Tries - Lam Hodgson Tickle Furner: Goals - Farrell(5):
CASTLEFORD - Rogers: Jon Wells Johnson(Barrie Jon
Mather) Eager Pryce: Orr Lennon: Kyle Warren (Sykes)
(Lynch) Bartrim Lynch(Harland) Fritz Smith(Kyle Warren)
Hudson(Smith):
Tries - Eager(2) Pryce: Goal - Bartrim:
Referee S Ganson (St Helens) Att - 8381 H.T. 14 - 10

Andy Joihnson
D. No 784
2002 to 2003

Wayne Bartrim
D. No 785
2002 to 2003

Ryan Hucson
D. No 786
2002 to 2012

Kyle Warren
D. No 787
2002

Adrian Rainey
D. No 790
2002

Tommy Saxton
D. No 791
2002 to 2007

Richard Blakeway
D. No 793
2002 to 2004

SEASON 2002

D.N	PLAYER		DEBUT	L MATCH	APP	SUB	T.AP	TRI'S	G'LS	D.G	P'TS
661	SAMPSON	DEAN			8	12	20	1	0	0	4
694	SYKES	NATHAN			25	4	29	0	0	0	0
719	HARLAND	LEE			19	5	24	4	0	0	16
728	GAY	RICHARD		19/05/2002	10	1	11	2	0	0	8
734	WELLS	JON		28/09/2002	25	1	26	13	0	0	52
742	ORR	DANNY			33	0	33	13	7	0	66
748	MATHER	BARRIE-JON		28/09/2002	11	11	22	7	0	0	28
750	SMITH	MICHAEL			27	5	32	9	0	0	36
756	EAGER	MICHAEL			29	0	29	15	0	0	60
757	ROGERS	DAREN			33	0	33	18	0	0	72
759	LYNCH	ANDY			26	5	31	2	0	0	8
761	FRITZ	DALE			24	1	25	1	0	0	4
770	PRYCE	WAINE			26	1	27	16	0	0	64
772	LENNON	MARK			8	13	21	3	6	0	24
773	HEALEY	MITCH			30	1	31	3	0	2	14
779	GODWIN	WAYNE			2	14	16	5	0	0	20
781	BATES	DAVID		26/07/2002	0	2	2	0	0	0	0
784	JOHNSON	ANDY	10/02/2002		22	5	27	7	0	0	28
785	BARTRIM	WAYNE	10/02/2002		31	1	32	8	115	0	262
786	HUDSON	RYAN	10/02/2002		22	8	30	11	0	0	44
787	WARREN	KYLE	24/02/2002	28/09/2002	13	17	30	3	0	0	12
788	ELIMA	OLIVIER	07/04/2002	07/04/2002	0	1	1	1	0	0	4
789	MERCER	GARY	21/04/2002	21/04/2002	0	1	1	0	0	0	0
790	RAINEY	ADRIAN	19/05/2002	11/08/2002	4	7	11	1	0	0	4
791	SAXTON	TOMMY	21/06/2002		1	5	6	0	0	0	0
792	THALER	ADAM	26/07/2002	26/07/2008	0	1	1	0	0	0	0
793	BLAKEWAY	RICHARD	26/07/2002		0	2	2	0	0	0	0
	27		**10**	**9**	**429**	**124**	**553**	**143**	**128**	**2**	**830**

COMPETITION		P	W	D	L	FOR	AGT
S. LEAGUE	POSITION 6 OF 12	28	14	2	12	736	615
RL CUP		4	3	0	1	80	46
PLAY OFFS		1	0	0	1	14	26
PLAYERS RECORDS		**33**	**17**	**2**	**14**	**830**	**687**

Graham Steadman was confirmed as Head Coach with Gary Mercer the former New Zealand international his assistant.

In the Challenge Cup we reached the semi-final losing to Wigan Warriors at Headingley 20-10.

With the play-offs increased to six teams we just qualified in sixth place, but lost to third place Wigan Warriors 14–26.

Wayne Bartrim finished with 103 League goals to set a club Super League record and with one play-off and 11 RL Cup goals made a total of 115.

SEASON 2003

SUPER LEAGUE VIII

Salford City Reds were relegated from Super League, being replaced by Huddersfield Giants.

Thu 26 Dec 2002 LEEDS RHINOS away lost 2 - 20 FRIENDLY
LEEDS R - Cummins: Calderwood C Walker Kirk Mathers: Dunemann Burrow: Feather Diskin McDonald Furner Adamson Lupton: Subs used - McGuire Dowes Netherton Jones-Buchanan Bailey: Tries - Mather Burrow Adamson Lupton: Goals - Burrow(2):
CASTLEFORD - Gibson: Pryce Maloney Rogers Saxton: Orr Lennon: Lynch Godwin Jackson Thackray Blakeway Hudson: Subs used - Spears Wray Thaler Spedding Ripley: Goals - Lennon:
Referee R Silverwood (Mirfield) Att - 10366 H.T. 2 - 14

Fri 24 Jan 2003 BRADFORD BULLS home lost 16 - 44   FRIENDLY
CASTLEFORD - Gibson: Saxton Eager Johnson Rogers: Orr Healey: Sykes Bartrim Lynch Thackray Fritz Hudson: Subs used - Lennon Godwin Thaler Jackson Blakeway: Tries - Gibson(2) Thackray: Goals - Bartrim(2):
BRADFORD B - Pryce: Pratt Naylor Hape Vaikikolo: Paul Deacon: Vagana Lowes Fielden Peacock Gartner Radford: Subs used - Gilmour Parker Langley Moore Reardon Wilkinson Smith Bridge Myler: Tries - Paul(2) Radford(2) Pryce Naylor Gartner Reardon: Goals - Deacon(6):
Referee K Kirkpatrick (Warrington) Att - 4908 H.T. 6 - 24

Sat 8 Feb 2003 WAKEFIELD TRINITY WILDCATS away lost 18 – 20 FOURTH ROUND RL CHALLENGE CUP
WAKEFIELD T W - Holland: Wells Ellis Sears Halpenny: Jeffries Davis: O'Brien March Korkidas Hood Knott Vowles: Subs used - Handforth Sovatabua Slattery Wrench: Tries - Ellis Jeffries Sovatabua: Goals - Knott(4):
CASTLEFORD - Lennon: Pryce DAMIAN GIBSON(794) Eager Rogers: Orr Healey: Sykes Bartrim Lynch Smith Fritz Hudson(S/O): Subs used - Harland PAUL JACKSON(795) JAMIE THACKRAY(796): Tries - Lennon(2) Orr: Goals - Bartrim(3):
Referee I Smith (Oldham) Att - 4125 H.T. 6 - 6

Sun 23 Feb 2003 WIGAN WARRIORS home won 19-10
CASTLEFORD - Lennon: Pryce Gibson Eager Rogers: Orr Healey: Sykes Bartrim Lynch Smith Fritz Harland: Subs used - Godwin Jackson Thackray Saxton: Tries - Rogers(2) Pryce: Goals - Bartrim(3) Orr D/G:
WIGAN W - Radlinski: Carney Johnson Hodgson Ainscough: O.Neill Lam: Sculthorpe Newton G Smith Cassidy Farrell O'Loughlin: Subs used - Aspinwall Tickle M Smith Wild: Goals - O'Neill (4) Farrell:
Referee S Ganson (St Helens) Att - 8462 H.T. 6 - 4

Sat 1 Mar 2003 LEIGH CENTURIANS home won 36 - 12 FRIENDLY

CASTLEFORD - Saxton: Pryce Gibson Eager Rogers: Orr Lennon: Sykes Godwin Jackson Smith Thackray Hudson: Subs used - Thaler Blakeway Huby Johnson Lynch: Tries - Godwin(2) Smith Lennon Gibson Rogers Hudson: Goals - Lennon(4):
LEIGH C - Turley: Rivett Munro Cardoza Andrews: Weisner Sanderson: Ball Maddox Henare Richardson Blackwood Bristow: Subs used - Swann Holdstock Alstead Bradbury Woods: Tries - Turley Swann: Goals - Turley(2):
Referee J King (St Helens) Att - 1427 H.T. 26 - 6

Fri 7 Mar 2003 HALIFAX away won 20 - 10
HALIFAX - Finnerty: Greenwood Donlan Clayton Norman: Moana Dorahy: Hobson Lawlless Birchall Cruckshank Brocklehurst McMenemy: Subs used - Cardiss Penkywicz Davidson Seuseu: Try - Dorahy: Goals - Dorahy(3):
CASTLEFORD - Gibson: Pryce Johnson Eager Rogers: Orr Lennon: Sykes Bartrim Lynch Smith Fritz Hudson: Subs used - Maloney Jackson Thackray Godwin: Tries - Maloney Gibson Godwin: Goals - Bartrim(2) Orr(2):
Referee R Silverwood (Mirfield) Att - 4388 H.T. 8 - 8

Fri 21 Mar 2003 ST HELENS away lost 12 - 54
ST HELENS - Wellens: Stewart Smith Newlove Albert: Sculthorpe Long: Britt Higham Jonkers Joynt Stankevitch Hooper: Subs used - Gardner Jones Bennett Edmondson: Tries - Long(3) Newlove(2) Albert Jonkers Higham Jones: Goals - Long(9):
CASTLEFORD - Gibson: Pryce Johnson Eager Rogers: Orr Lennon: Sykes Bartrim Lynch Smith Fritz Hudson: Subs used - Maloney Jackson Harland PAUL MELLOR(797): Try - Lynch: Goals - Bartrim(4)
Referee I Smith (Oldham) Att - 10292 H.T. 12 - 18

Sat 29 Mar 2003 WAKEFIELD TRINITY WILDCATS home lost 14 - 20
CASTLEFORD - Gibson: Pryce Mellor Eager Rogers: Orr Maloney: Sykes Bartrim Lynch Smith Fritz Hudson: Subs used - Johnson Jackson Harland Lennon: Tries - Eager Lennon: Goals - Bartrim(2):
WAKEFIELD T W - Halpenny: Wells Ellis Seers Newlove: Jeffries Davis: Field March Korkidas Slattery Knott Vowles: Subs used - Handforth Elima Snitch Wrench: Tries - Ellis Seers Davis: Goals - Knott(4):
Referee K Kirkpatrick (Warrington) Att - 6853 H.T. 8 - 10

Sun 6 Apr 2003 LONDON BRONCOS away won 24 - 12
LONDON B - Roy: Buchanan King Martin Hall: Dymock Moran: Bawden Budworth Stephenson Retchless Toshack Purdham: Subs used - Marshall Fielden Kennnedy Long: Tries - Martin King: Goals - Martin(2):
CASTLEFORD - Gibson: Pryce Eager Mellor Rogers: Orr Lennon: Sykes Bartrim Lynch Smith Fritz Hudson: Subs used - Godwin Johnson Harland Maloney: Tries - Lennon Pryce Eager: Goals - Bartrim(6):
Referee P Taberner (Wigan) Att - 3013 H.T. 10 - 12

SEASON 2003

Fri 18 Apr 2003 LEEDS RHINOS home lost 14 - 15
CASTLEFORD - Gibson: Pryce Mellor Eager Rogers: Orr
Hudson: Sykes Bartrim Lynch Smith Fritz Harland:
Subs used - Godwin Jackson Thackray:
Try - Lynch: Goals - Bartrim(5):
LEEDS R - Connolly: Calderwood Walker Senior
Cummings: McGuire Dunemann: Mcdermott Diskin Bailey
Furner Poching Sinefield: Subs used - Burrow Jones-
Buchanan Feather McDonald: Tries - Mcguire Poching
Walker: Goals - Sinfield Dunemann D/G:
Referee R Silverwood (Mirfield) Att - 10655 H.T. 10 - 4

**Mon 21 Apr 2003 HUDDERSFIELD GIANTS away
won 29 - 16**
HUDDERSFIELD G - St Hilaire: O'Hare Bailey Cooper
Wilkinson: Costin McNamara: Fleary March Slicker Bloem
O'Doherty Gene: Subs used - Turner Crabtree Grayshon
Whitaker: Tries - Costin O'Hare Bloem:
Goals - McNamara Costin:
CASTLEFORD - Saxton: Pryce Mellor Gibson Rogers: Orr
Maloney: Sykes Hudson Lynch Smith Fritz Harland:
Subs used – Blakeway Godwin Jackson Johnson:
Tries - Smith(2) Hudson Lynch:
Goals - Orr(6) MaloneyD/G:
Referee R Connolly (Wigan) Att - 5139 H.T. 12 - 14

Mon 5 May 2003 HULL FC home draw 26 - 26
CASTLEFORD - Gibson: Pryce Mellor Johnson Rogers: Orr
Healey: Sykes Bartrim Lynch Harland Fritz Hudson:
Subs used - Jackson Eager Blakeway Saxton:
Tries - Orr(2) Eager Gibson: Goals - Bartrim(5):
HULL FC - Prescot: Best Barnett Kohe Love Crowther:
Cooke Horne: Greenhill Last King Ryan Maher Chester:
Subs used - Treister Craven Carvell Yeaman:
Tries - Barnett(2) Prescott Horne Best: Goals - Prescott(3):
Referee R Connolly (Wigan) Att - 8713 H.T. 8 - 14

Sun 11 May 2003 BRADFORD BULLS away lost 10 - 30
BRADFORD B - Paul Vaikona Naylor Hape Vainikolo:
Pryce Deacon: Vagana Lowes Moore Peacock Gartner
Gilmour: Subs used - Pratt Radford Parker Anderson:
Tries - Vaikona(2) Vagana Deacon: Goals - Deacon(7):
CASTLEFORD - Saxton: Pryce Gibson Eager Rogers: Orr
Healey: Sykes Hudson Jackson Smith Fritz Bartrim:
Subs used - Godwin Johnson Blakeway BEN SKERRETT
(798):   Try - Smith: Goals - Bartrim(3):
Referee S Ganson (St Helens) Att - 14749 H.T. 8- 16

Sun 18 May 2003 WIDNES VIKINGS home won 40 - 2
CASTLEFORD - Saxton: Pryce Gibson Eager Rogers: Orr
Healey: Sykes Hudson Smith Johnson Fritz Bartrim:
Subs used - Lynch Blakeway McNally JON HEPWORTH
(799):   Tries - Rogers(2) Hudson Saxton Lynch McNally
Hepworth: Goals - Bartrim(5) Orr:
WIDNES V - Atcheson: Demetriou Frame Hughes Giles:
Lawdford Sheridan: Relf Millard Julian O'Neill Hay
McCurrie Jules O'Neill: Subs used - McDonald Farrell
Cantiillon Potter: Goal - Jules O'Neill:
Referee P Taberner (Wigan) Att - 6516 H.T. 12 - 2

**Sat 24 May 2003 WARRINGTON WOLVES away
won 32 - 16**
WARRINGTON W - Penny: Smytth Groser Sibbit Appo:
Briers N Wood: Fozzard Clarke Hilton Guisset Wainwright
Domic: Subs used - Gleeson Burns P Wood Stevens:
Tries - Burns Briers Smyth: Goals - Briers (2):
CASTLEFORD - Saxton: Pryce Gibson Eager Rogers: Orr
Healey: Sykes Hudson Lynch Johnson Fritz Bartrim:
Subs used - Hepworth Blakeway Smith Sampson:
Tries - Hudson(2) Sampson Pryce Saxton:
Goals - Bartrim(5) Orr:
Referee I Smith (Oldham) Att - 6090 H.T. 18 - 10

**Fri 30 May 2003 HUDDERSFIELD GIANTS home
won 32 - 18**
CASTLEFORD - Saxton: Pryce Gibson Eager Rogers: Orr
Healey: Sykes Hudson Lynch Smith Johnson Bartrim:
Subs used - Hepworth Godwin Blakeway Sampson:
Tries - Eager(2) Orr Rogers Bartrim Johnson:
Goals - Bartrim(4):
HUDDERSFIELD G - Reilly O'Hare Cooper Bailey St Hilaire:
Costin Gene: Fleary March Gannon O'Doherty Morrison
McNamara: Subs used - Turner Slicker Bloem Holroyd:
Tries - Gene Bailey March: Goals - McNamara (3);
Referee P Taberner (Wigan) Att - 5682 H.T. 18 - 6

Sat 7 Jun 2003 LEEDS RHINOS away lost 26 - 39
LEEDS R - Connolly: Calderwood Walker Senior Cummins:
Dunnemann McGuire: McDonald Diskin McDermott
Furner Poching Sinfield: Subs used - Feather Bailey
Burrow Jones-Buchanan: Tries - Cummins(2) McDonald
Calderwood McGuire Burrow Senior:
Goals - Sinfield(5) BurrowD/G:
CASTLEFORD - Saxton: Pryce Gibson Eager Rogers: Orr
Healey: Sampson Hudson Lynch Smith Johnson Bartrim:
Subs used - Godwin CRAIG HUBY(800) Hepworth
Blakeway:
Tries - Pryce(2) Eager Rogers Orr: Goals - Bartrim(3):
Referee R Silverwood (Mirfield) Att - 14488 H.T. 16 - 20

Sun 15 Jun 2003 LONDON BRONCOS home lost 16-28
CASTLEFORD - Saxton: Pryce Gibson Eager Rogers: Orr
Healey: Sykes Hudson Lynch Smith Johnson Bartrim:
Subs used - Mellor Sampson Hepworth Blakeway:
Tries - Eager Rogers: Goals - Bartrim (4):
LONDON B - Moran: Sykes Roy Martin Hall: Purdham
Thorman: Bawden Budworth Retchless Toshack Peden
Dymock: Subs used - Marshall Stephenson Kennedy
Gallagher:
Tries - Moran(2) Martin(2):   Goals - Thorman(6):
Referee R Connolly (Wigan) Att - 5630 H.T. 8 - 8

Fri 20 Jun 2003 HULL FC away lost 14 - 22
HULL FC - Prescott: Best Barnett Yeaman Wilkinson:
Cooke Horne: Greenhill Treister King Ryan Maher Chester:
Subs used - Carvell Dowes Horne Fletcher:
Tries - Treister(2) Yeaman King: Goals - Prescott(3):
CASTLEFORD - Gibson: Pryce Maloney Eager Rogers: Orr
Healey: Sykes Hudson Lynch Smith Fritz Bartrim:
Subs used - Harland Johnson Hepworth Mellor:

Tries - Orr Eager Pryce: Goal - Bartrim:
Referee A Klein (London) Att - 10703 H.T. 6 - 10

Fri 27 Jun 2003 WIGAN WARRIORS away lost 10 - 24
WIGAN W - Briscoe: Carney Aspinwall Johnson Hodgson:
O'Loughlin Lam: O'Connor Newton Smith Cassidy
Graham Farrell:
Subs used - Sculthorpe Pongia Robinson Hock:
Tries - Aspinwall Hodgson Johnson: Goals - Farrell(6):
CASTLEFORD - Rogers: Pryce Mellor Maloney McNally:
Orr Healey: Smith Hudson Sykes Johnson Fritz Harland:
Subs used - Blakeway Huby Hepworth Lynch:
Tries - Orr Mellor: Goal - Orr:
Referee R Laughton (Barnsley) Att - 9884 H.T. 10 - 8

Sun 6 Jul 2003 HALIFAX home won 38 - 12
CASTLEFORD – Rogers: Mellor Maloney Eager Pryce: Orr
Healey: Sykes Hepworth Lynch Blakeway Fritz Johnson:
Subs used - Saxton Godwin Smith Thackray:
Tries - Hepworth(2) Orr Mellor Smith Johnson Thackray:
Goals - Healey(3) Orr(2):
HALIFAX - Cardiss: Greenwood Donlan Frew Norman:
Dorahy Penkywicz: Birchall Lawless Harmon Clayton
Brocklehurst Moana:
Subs used - Hobson Chapman Grix Corcoran:
Tries - Frew Dorahy: Goals - Dorahy(2):
Referee I Smith (Oldham) Att - 5444 H.T. 12 - 12

Sun 13 Jul 2003 ST HELENS home lost 32 - 46
CASTLEFORD - Saxton: Pryce Mellor Maloney Rogers: Orr
Healey: Sykes Hepworth Smith Johnson Fritz Hudson:
Subs used - Eager Godwin Harland Thackray:
Tries - Orr(3) Saxton Smith: Goals - Orr(6):
ST HELENS - Wellens: Abert Gleeson Hooper Stewart:
Long Highham: Britt Cunningham Mason Bennett Smith
Sculthorpe: Subs used - Jonkers Kirkpatrick Joynt
Edmondson: Tries - Higham(2) Wellens(2) Gleeson(2)
Albert Long: Goals - Long(7):
Referee R Silverwood (Dewsbury) Att - 6320 H.T. 14 - 24

**Sat 19 Jul WAKEFIELD TRINITY WILDCATS away
won 32 - 4**
WAKEFIELD T W - Halfpenny: Wells Ellis Spicer Wray:
Jeffries Rooney: Korkidas March Hood Knott Field Vowles:
Subs used - Davis Griffen Snitch Wrench:
Goals - Rooney(2):
CASTLEFORD - Rogers: Gibson Mellor Eager Pryce: Orr
Healey: Thackray Godwin Lynch Smith Fritz Hudson:
Subs used - Johnson Sykes Harland Hepworth:
Tries - Godwin(2) Pryce Fritz Rogers Hudson:
Goals - Orr(3) Healey:
Referee S Ganson (St Helens) Att - 4094 H.T. 14 - 2

Sun 27 Jul 2003 BRADFORD BULLS home lost 20 - 40
CASTLEFORD - Saxton: Rogers Eager Mellor Pryce: Orr
Healey: Sykes Godwin Lynch Smith Fritz Hudson:
Subs used - Johnson Thackray Hepworth TIM
SPEARS(801)
Tries – Pryce(2)Rogers Eager: Goals - Orr Healey:
BRADFORD B - Reardon: Vaikona Naylor Hape Vainikolo:

Pryce Deacon: Vagana Lowes Anderson Gartner Peacock
Forshaw:
Subs used - Gilmour Langley Radford Parker:
Tries - Deacon Pryce Radford Naylor Gartner Gilmour
Vaikona: Goals - Deacon(6):
Referee S Ganson (St Helens) Att - 9081 H.T. 16 - 18

Fri 1 Aug 2003 WIDNES VIKINGS away lost 16 - 27
WIDNES V - Spruce: Potter Bird Hughes Devlin: Jules
O,Neill Sheridan: Relf Millard Julian O'Neill Hay McCurrie
Frame: Subs used - Cantillon Farrell Atcheson Finnigan:
Tries - Devlin(2) Frame Hughes Potter:
Goals - Jules O'Neill(3) D/G:
CASTLEFORD - Rogers: Gibson Mellor Eager Pryce:
Hepworth Healey: Smith Hudson Lynch Harland Fritz
Johnson: Subs used - Saxton Thackray Huby Godwin:
Tries - Healey(2): Goals - Healey (4):
Referee R Connolly (Wigan) Att - 5698 H.T. 8 - 6

**Sun 10 Aug 2003 WARRINGTON WOLVES home
lost 16 - 29**
CASTLEFORD - Rogers: Mellor Maloney Eager Pryce:
Hepworth Healey: Sykes Hudson Lynch Smith Fritz
Harland: Subs used - Johnson Godwin Saxton Huby
Tries - Mellor Johnson Godwin: Goals - Healey (2):
WARRINGTON W - Penny: Grose Sibbit Gaskell: Appo N Wood: Hilton Clarke Fozzard Burns P
Wood Wainwright: Subs used - Domic Hulse Stevens
Guisset: Tries - P Wood N Wood Domic Grose;
Goals - Appo (6) N Wood(D/G):
Referee A Klein (London) Att - 5940 H.T. 4 - 14

Fri 15 Aug 2003 ST HELENS away lost 10 - 26
ST HELENS - Wellens: Stewart Newlove Hooper Gardner:
Long Wilkin: Mason Cunningham Ward Stankevitch
Bennett Jonkers: Subs used - Hill Graham Jones
Hardman: Tries - Stankevitch Newlove Hooper Gardner:
Goals - Long (5):
CASTLEFORD - Saxton: Pryce Eager Mellor Andy McNally:
Maloney Healey: Sykes Godwin Lynch Johnson Fritz
Hudson: Subs used - Gibson Wayne Bartrim Huby
Spears:
Tries - Saxton Pryce: Goal - Healey:
Referee R Connolly (Wigan) Att - 8041 H.T. 6 - 14

Sun 24 Aug 2003 LEEDS RHINOS home won 28 - 20
CASTLEFORD - Saxton: Pryce Gibson Eager Rogers:
Maloney Healey: Sykes Godwin Lynch Mellor Fritz
Hudson: Subs used – Tim Spears Hepworth Huby:
Tries - Healey Rogers Lynch Fritz Maloney Eager:
Goals - Healey(2):
LEEDS - Mathers: Calderwood Cummins Senior Botham:
McGuire Dunemann: Ward Diskin McDermott Furner
Adamson Sinfield: Subs used - Burrow Poaching Feather
McDonald: Tries - Calderwood Senior McGuire Adamson:
Goals - Sinfield (2):
Referee I Smith (Oldham) Att - 8281 H.T. 24 - 4

SEASON 2003

Sun 31 Aug 2003 HUDDERSFIELD GIANTS home won 26 - 18

CASTLEFORD - Saxton: Pryce Gibson Eager Rogers: Maloney Healey: Sykes Godwin Lynch Mellor Fritz Hudson:
Subs used – Orr Smith Huby Johnson
Tries - Pryce(2) Gibson Eager: Goals - Huby(3) Healey(2):
HUDDERSFIELD G - Reilly: O'Hare Bailey Bloem St Hilaire: Gene March: Fleary Turner Gannon Morrison Roarty O'Doherty:
Subs used - Slicker McNamara Cooper Crabtree:
Tries - O'Hare Crabtree: Goals - Bloem(3) McNamara(2):
Referee K Kirkpatrick (Warrington) Att - 5289 H.T. 8 - 12

Sun 7 Sep 2003 HULL FC away lost 12 - 32

HULL FC - Horne: Best Barnett Yeaman Raynor: Cooke J Smith: Greenhill Treister King Maher Ryan Chester:
Subs used - Carvell Dowes Lupton McMenemy:
Tries - Raynor Dowes McMenemy Horne:
Goals - Cooke (7) Greenhill(1):
CASTLEFORD - Saxton: Pryce Maloney Eager Rogers: Orr Healey: Sykes Godwin Lynch Mellor Fritz Hudson:
Subs used - Gibson Smith Vowles Johnson:
Tries - Maloney Lynch: Goals - Orr (2):
Referee R Silverwood (Dewsbury) Att 10631 H.T. 4 - 16

Sun 14 Sep 2003 BRADFORD BULLS away won 28 - 14

BRADFORD B - Reardon: Vaikona Naylor Gilmour Hape: Pryce Deacon: Vagana Lowes Anderson Gartner Peacock Langley: Subs used - Pratt Forshaw Parker Moore:
Tries - Hape Pryce: Goals - Deacon (3):
CASTLEFORD - Saxton: Pryce Mellor Eager Rogers: Orr Healey: Sykes Hudson Lynch Smith Fritz Vowles:
Subs used - Godwin Huby Blakeway Johnson:
Tries - Orr Godwin Lynch Saxton: Goals - Orr(6)
Referee A Klein (London) Att - 13626 H.T. 8 - 6

Sun 21 Sep 2003 WIGAN WARRIORS home lost 16 -23

CASTLEFORD - Saxton: Pryce Gibson Eager Rogers:Orr Mitch Healey: Sykes Hudson Lynch Andy Johnson Dale Fritz Vowles: Subs used - Blakeway Mark Lennon Huby Godwin: Tries - Pryce Johnson Orr: Goals - Orr (2):
WIGAN W - Radlinski: Carney Aspinwall Hodgson Dallas: O'Loughlin Robinson: O'Connor M Smith C Smith: Cassidy Tickle Farrell: Subs used - Lam P Johnson Sculthorpe Hock: Tries - O'Connor Dallas Hodgson Tickle:
Goals - Farrell (3) LamD/G:
Referee S Ganson (St Helens) Att - 7886 H.T. 12 – 6

Damian Gibson
D. No 794
2003 to 2004

Paul Jackson
D. No 795
2003 to 2012

Jamie Thackery
D. No 796
2003 to 2004

Paul Mellor
D. No 797
2003 to 2004

Jon Hepworth
D. No 799
2003 to 2005

Graig Huby
D. No 800
2003 to 2014

SEASON 2003

D.N	PLAYER		DEBUT	L MATCH	APP	SUB	T.AP	TRI'S	G'LS	D.G	P'TS
661	SAMPSON	DEAN			1	3	4	1	0	0	4
694	SYKES	NATHAN			26	1	27	0	0	0	0
719	HARLAND	LEE			7	7	14	0	0	0	0
739	VOWLES	ADRIAN			2	1	3	0	0	0	0
742	ORR	DANNY			24	3	27	13	33	1	119
749	MALONEY	FRANCIS			11	3	14	3	0	1	13
750	SMITH	MICHAEL			21	4	25	5	0	0	20
756	EAGER	MICHAEL			25	2	27	11	0	0	44
757	ROGERS	DAREN			28	0	28	10	0	0	40
759	LYNCH	ANDY			25	2	27	7	0	0	28
761	FRITZ	DALE		21/09/2003	26	0	26	2	0	0	8
770	PRYCE	WAINE			29	0	29	13	0	0	52
772	LENNON	MARK		21/09/2003	5	2	7	4	0	0	16
773	HEALEY	MITCH		21/09/2003	23	0	23	3	16	0	44
777	McNALLY	ANDY		15/08/2003	2	1	3	1	0	0	4
779	GODWIN	WAYNE			6	14	20	5	0	0	20
784	JOHNSON	ANDY		21/09/2003	14	11	25	4	0	0	16
785	BARTRIM	WAYNE		15/08/2003	15	1	16	1	56	0	116
786	HUDSON	RYAN			27	0	27	5	0	0	20
791	SAXTON	TOMMY			15	5	20	5	0	0	20
793	BLAKEWAY	RICHARD			1	11	12	0	0	0	0
794	GIBSON	DAMION	08/02/2003		21	2	23	3	0	0	12
795	JACKSON	PAUL	08/02/2003		1	8	9	0	0	0	0
796	THACKRAY	JAMIE	08/02/2003		1	8	9	1	0	0	4
797	MELLOR	PAUL	21/03/2003		17	3	20	3	0	0	12
798	SKERRETT	BEN	11/05/2003	11/05/2003	0	1	1	0	0	0	0
799	HEPWORTH	JON	18/05/2003		4	10	14	3	0	0	12
800	HUBY	CRAIG	07/06/2003		0	9	9	0	3	0	6
801	SPEARS	TIM	27/07/2003	24/08/2008	0	3	3	0	0	0	0
	29			**8**	**8**	377	113	490	103	108	2	630

	COMPETITION		P	W	D	L	FOR	AGT
	S. LEAGUE	POSITION 8 OF 12	28	12	1	15	612	633
	RL CUP		1	0	0	1	18	20
	PLAYERS RECORDS		**29**	**12**	**1**	**16**	**630**	**653**

New Substitute Rule:
12 exchanges from four players including Blood Bins.

Danny Orr increased the record for most points scored in a Super League game to 24 against St Helens at home on the 13 July 2003.

Andy Lynch topped the Club's 'Apta Stats' for carries, metres, offloads and overall index, and earned himself a place in the Super League Dream Team.

A notable Debutant was Graig Huby.

SEASON 2004

SUPER LEAGUE IX

Halifax were relegated from Super League being replaced by Salford City Reds.

Fri 26 Dec 2003 LEEDS RHINOS away lost 12 - 20 FRIENDLY
LEEDS R - Mathers: Calderwood McKenna Walker Bai: McGuire Burrow: Ward Poaching McDonald Netherton Bailey Jones-Buchanan:
Subs used - Scruton Feather Barker Gallagher Gardner:
Tries - McGuire(2) Calderwood Burrow:
Goals - Burrow(2):
CASTLEFORD - Saxton: Pryce Gibson Maloney Rogers: Hepworth Sheridan: Jackson Godwin Huby Mellor Smith Clayton: Sub used - Thackray Smith Kain Lunt Ripley:
Tries - Godwin(2):   Goals - Maloney(2):
Referee I Smith (Oldham) Att - 13154 H.T. 6 - 10

Sun 25 Jan 2004 BRADFORD BULLS away lost 18 - 56 FRIENDLY - BRIAN MCDERMOTT TESTIMONIAL
BRADFORD B - Withers: Vaikona Johnson Reardon Vainikolo: L Pryce Deacon: Vagana Smith McDermott Peacock Swann Radford:
Subs used - Anderson Langley K Pryce Myler Ferres Bridge Parker Saxton Fielden Moore Western Smith:
Tries - Johnson (4) Langley(2) Withers Deacon Vainikolo K Pryce: Goals - Deacon(5) Bridge(2) Withers:
CASTLEFORD - Saxton: Mellor Maloney Gibson Pryce: Hepworth Sheridan: Greenhill Godwin Sykes Smith Ryan Hudson: Subs used - Rogers Jackson Harland Thackray Smith Huby Lunt:
Tries - Godwin Greenhill Harland: Goals - Maloney(3):
Referee S Ganson (St Helens) Att - 5256 H.T. 0 - 34

Fri 30 Jan 2004 HUDDERSFIELD GIANTS away lost 0 - 36   FRIENDLY
HUDDERSFIELD G – Reilly; O'Hara Donlan Bailey St Hilaire: Gene March: Fleary Penkywicz Roarty Nero Jones Costin:
Subs used – White Crabtree Gannon Slicker Smith Whittaker Cooper Morrison: Tries – Reilly St Hilaire March Penkywicz Whittaker Cooper: Goals - Costin(5) March:
CASTL;EFORD – Saxton: Pryce Maloney Newlove Rogers: Hepworth Sheridan: Greenhill Godwin Sykes Harland Ryan Hudson:
Subs used – Lunt Thackray Jackson Gibson Huby Rudder:
Referee R Connolly (Wigan) Att – 1467 H.T. 0 - 12

Wed 11 Feb 2004 HULL F C home lost 22 - 24 FRENDLY
CASTLEFORD - Gibson: Pryce Clayton Maloney Rogers: Rudder Sheridan: Greenhill Godwin Sykes Harland Thackray Hudson:
Subs used - Smith Hepworth Jackson Saxton Huby:
Tries - Hudson(2) Pryce Sheridan: Goals - Maloney (3):
Hull F C - Briscoe: R Barnett Jnr Best Wilkinson Raynor: Whiting G Horne: Benjafield Lupton Dowes McMenemy McNicholas Cooke:
Subs used - Chester Bailey Last King Carvell:
Tries - Raynor Best Cooke Wilkinson: Goals - Cooke (4)

Referee R Silverwood (Dewsbury) Att - 2666 H.T. 16 - 12

Sun 22 Feb 2004 HUDDERSFIELD GIANTS away lost 22 - 26
HUDDERSFIELD G - Reilly: O'Hare Donlan Bailey St Hilaire: Gene March: Fleary Turner Roarty Nero Jones Costin:
Subs used - Penkywicz Sicker Crabtree:
Tries - St Hilaire(2) March Jones Costin:
Goals - Costin(3):
CASTELFORD - Saxton: Pryce Gibson RYAN CLAYTON(802) Rogers: SEAN RUDDER(803) RYAN SHERIDAN(804): CRAIG GREENHILL(805) Godwin Sykes Thackray Harland Hudson:
Subs used - Jackson Smith Hepworth SEAN RYAN(806):
Tries: - Rogers Pryce Clayton Saxton: Goals - Godwin (3):
Referee R Laughton (Barnsley) Att - 5326 H.T. 12 - 10

Sun 29 Feb 2004 UNION TREIZISTE CATALANE home won 32 – 20 FOURTH ROUND RL CHALLENGE CUP
CASTLEFORD - Saxton: Gibson Clayton Rogers Pryce: Rudder Sheridan: Greenhill Godwin Sykes Harland Ryan Hudson: Subs used - Hepworth Jackson Smith Thackray:
Tries - Thackray(2) Godwin Gibson Rudder Pryce:
Goals - Godwin(3) Hepworth:
UTC - Horne: Hill Howlett Hall Verges: Frayssinous Rinaldi: Bawden Berthezene Felious Jampy Fakir Cologni:
Subs used - Martin Teixido Mounis Bosc:
Tries - Cologni Hall Fakir Howlett: Goals - Frayssinous (2):
Referee A Klein (London) Att - 3435 H.T. 22 - 12

Sun 7 Mar 2004 LEEDS RHINOS home lost 8 - 34
CASTLEFORD - Gibson: Rogers Maloney Clayton Pryce: Rudder Sheridan: Greenhill Godwin Sykes Smith Ryan Hudson: Subs used - Hepworth Jackson Harland Thackray:
Try - Clayton: Goals - Godwin(2):
LEEDS R - Connolly: Bai Walker Senior Calderwood: McGuire Burrow: Bailey Diskin McDermott Furner Poching Sinfield: Subs used - Ward Jones Buchanan McDonald Dunemann:
Tries - McGuire(3) Bai Connolly Senior: Goals - Sinfield(5):
Referee K Kirkpatrick (War'ton) Att - 11731 H.T. 8 - 12

Sun 14 Mar 2004 HULL FC away lost 0 - 26 FIFTH ROUND RL CHALLENGE CUP
HULL FC - Birscoe: Best R Barnett Snr Yeaman R Barnett Jnr: Cooke Horne: King Swain Dowes McMenemy McNicholas Lupton: Sub used - Chester Bailey Whiting Higgins: Tries - Best(3) Whiting: Goals - Cooke(5):
CASTLEFORD - Saxton: Gibson Clayton Maloney Rogers: Rudder Ryan Sheridan: Greenhill Hudson Jackson Smith Ryan Harland:
Subs used - Godwin Lynch Hepworth Thackray:
Referee R Silverwood (Dewsbury) Att - 11443 H.T. 0 - 14

Sun 21 Mar 2004 WARRINGTON WOLVES away lost 18 - 32
WARRINGTON W - Cardiss: Wilshere Grose Noone Sibbit;

SEASON 2004

Briers N Wood: Hilton Clarke P Wood Forshaw
Wainwright Burns: Subs used - Gleeson Stevens Guisset
Lima: Tries - Wilshere(2) Noone Grose P Wood Hilton:
Goals - Briers (4):
CASTLEFORD - Saxton: Rogers Maloney Clayton Gibson:
Rudder Hepworth: Greenhill Godwin Jackson Smith
Thackray Hudson: Subs used - Lynch Ryan Huby:
Tries - Hepworth(2) Hudson: Goals - Godwin (3):
Referee I Smith (Oldham) Att - 8902 H.T. 12 - 10

Fri 2 Apr 2004 ST HELENS home lost 14 - 22
CASTLEFORD - Gibson: Saxton Clayton Maloney Rogers:
Rudder Hepworth: Greenhill Godwin Jackson Smith
Thackray Hudson:
Subs used - DEAN RIPLEY(807) Lynch Ryan Huby:
Tries - Hudson Godwin: Goals - Godwin (3):
ST HELENS - Wellens: Gardner Albert Talau Feaunati:
Hooper Long: Fozard Cunningham Bibey Gilmour Joynt
Sculthorpe:
Subs used - Edmondson Highham Fa'asavalu Wilkin:
Tries - Wellens(2) Cunningham Hooper: Goals - Long (3):
Referee I Smith (Oldham) Att - 6876 H.T. 0 - 12

Thu 8 Apr 2004 HULL FC away lost 4 - 26
HULL FC - Briscoe: Best R Barnett Snr Yeaman R Barnett
Jnr: Cooke Horne: King Swain Carvell McMenemy
McNicholas Lupton:
Subs used - Chester Dowes Whiting Higgns:
Tries - Yeaman Lupton Best Barnett Snr: Goals - Cook (5):
CASTLEFORD - Gibson: Saxton Maloney PAUL
NEWLOVE(808) Rogers: Rudder Hepworth: Greenhill
Godwin Lynch Ryan Smith Hudson: Subs used - Thackray
Jackson Clayton Harland: Try - Smith
Refereee A Klein (London) Att - 10971 H.T. 0 - 22

Tue 13 Apr 2004 LONDON BRONCOS home
lost 34 - 42
CASTLEFORD - Gibson: Saxton Maloney Newlove Rogers:
Rudder Hepworth: Greenhill Hudson Lynch Smith Ryan
Harland: Subs used - Ripley Godwin Jackson Thackray:
Tries - Saxton(2) Newlove Rogers Rudder Hudson Ryan:
Goals - Maloney(3):
LONDON B - Sykes: Wells Haughey Roy Greenwood:
Murrell Moran: Retchless Budworth Springer Brocklehurst
Mbu Dymock: Subs used - Trindall Highton McNally
Williams: Tries - Greenwood(2) Moran(2) Wells Roy
Murrell Mbu: Goals - Sykes(5):
Referee R Laughton (Barnsley) Att - 4710 H.T. 18 - 20

Sun 18 Apr 2004 WAKEFIELD TRINITY WILDCATS
home lost 10 - 42
CASTLEFORD - Saxton: Ripley Clayton Newlove Rogers:
Rudder Maloney: Jackson Hudson Lynch Smith Ryan
Thackray: Subs used - Sykes Hepworth Huby DOMINIC
BRAMBANI(809): Tries - Ryan Ripley: Goal - Maloney:
WAKEFIELD T W - Halpenny: Wainwright Demetriou
Domic Tadulala: Rooney Jeffries: Griffin March Korkidas
Solomona Wrench Ellis: Subs used - Hood Ryder Elima
Talipeau: Tries - Ellis(2) Jeffries(2) Tadulala(2) Demetriou
Korkidas: Goals - Rooney(1) March(4):

Referee R S lverwood (Dewsbury) Att - 5427 H.T. 7 - 10

Sun 25 Apr 2004 WIDNES VIKINGS away lost 18 - 29
WIDNES V - Rowlands: Royle Moule Hughes Giles: Jules
O'Neil Myler: Relf Millard Mills Hay Wozniak Frame:
Subs used - Hobson Bird McCurrie Atcheson:
Tries - Royle Myler McCurrie O'Neil:
Goals - O'Neil(6) D/G:
CASTLEFORD - Saxton: Ripley Rogers Newlove Mellor:
Maloney Hepworth: Greenhill Hudson Lynch Smith
Thackray Ryan:
Subs used - Clayton Jackson Sykes Harland:
Tries - Rogers Saxton Thackray: Goals - Maloney(3):
Referee A Klein (London) Att - 5274 H.T. 6 - 8

Sat 1 May 2004 WIGAN WARRIORS home lost 28 - 42
CASTLEFORD - Saxton: MICHAEL SHENTON(810) Rogers
Clayton Mellor: Maloney Brambani: Greenhill Godwin
Lynch M Smith Harland Hudson:Subs used - Sykes
Hepworth Thackray BYRON SMITH(811): Tries - Mellor(3)
Saxton Thackray: Goals - Godwin(3) Maloney:
WIGAN W - Radlinski: Williams O'Loughlin Brown Dallas:
Orr Lam: Pongia Newton Smith Cassidy Tickle Farrell:
Subs used - O'Connor Sculthorpe Hock Wild:
Tries - Dallas(2) Newton(2) Brown Lam Smith Radlinski:
Goals - Farrell(5)
Referee I Smith (Oldham) Att - 6222 H.T. 8 - 14

Sun 9 May 2004 BRADFORD BULLS away lost 18 - 44
BRADFORD B - Withers: Reardon Pryce Johnson Vinikolo:
Paul Deacon: Anderson Smith Parker Langley Peacock
Swann: Subs used - Bridge Radford Vagana Fielden:
Tries - Reardon(4) Langley(2) Vainikolo(2):
Goals - Deacon(6):
CASTLEFORD - ROB WORRINCY(812): Rogers Clayton
Mellor Hepworth: Maloney Brambani: Greenhill Godwin
Lynch Jamie Thackray Harland Hudson:
Subs used - Jackson B Smith Ryan ANDY KAIN(813):
Tries - Rogers Godwin Mellor: Goals - Godwin(3):
Referee R Laughton (Barnsley) Att – 12877 H.T. 2 - 26

Sun 23 May 2004 SALFORD CITY REDS home
lost 32 - 36
CASTLEFORD - Gibson: Rogers Paul Newlove Maloney
Mellor: Rudder LUKE ROBINSON(814): Greenhill Godwin
Lynch M Smith Harland Hudson: Subs used - Jackson
Hepworth Ryan Kain: Tries - Godwin M Smith Harland
Kain Hudson: Goals - Godwin(6):
SALFORD C R - Caine: McAvoy Littler McGuinness
Stewart: Beverley Clinch: Baynes Alker Highton Rutgerson
Coley Charles: Subs used - Fitzpatrick Johnson Shipway
Haggerty: Tries - Baynes Caine Highton Haggerty Stewart
Johnson: Goals - Caine(6):
Referee K Kirkpatrick (Warrington) Att - 6961 H.T. 14 - 8

Sun 30 May 2004 LONDON BRONCOS away
won 12 - 10
LONDON B - Wells: Greenwood Jackson O'Halloran
Kirkpatrick: Sykes Moran: Retchless Budworth Trindall
Mbu Haughey Dymock:

441

SEASON 2004

Subs used - Stringer Brocklehurst Botham Highton:
Tries - Greenwood Brocklehurst: Goal - Botham:
CASTLEFORD - Hepworth: Pryce Rogers Saxton Mellor:
Kain Robinson: Greenhill Godwin Lynch Harland Ryan
Hudson: Subs used - Rudder Sykes M Smith Jackson:
Tries - Robinson Mellor: Goals - Godwin(2):
Referee R Silverwood (Dewsbury) Att - 2562 H.T. 10 - 8

Sun 6 Jun 2004 HULL FC home lost 18 - 52
CASTLEFORD - Hepworth: Rogers Mellor Saxton Pryce:
MOTU TONY(815) Robinson: Greenhill Godwin _ynch
Ryan Harland Hudson: Subs used - Clayton Rudder Sykes
B Smith: Tries - Clayton Rudder Mellor:
Goals - Hepworth(2) Godwin:
HULL FC - Briscoe: Best Yeaman Eager Raynor: Cooke
Horne: King Swain Dowes McMenemy Chester Smith:
Subs used - Whiting McNicholas Lupton Scruton:
Tries - Raynor(3) Yeaman(2) Horne Smith King Best
Whiting: Goals - Cooke (5) Whiting:
Referee A Klein (London) Att - 8084 H.T. 0 - 24

Fri 11 Jun 2004 ST HELENS away lost 8 - 52
ST HELENS - Wellens: Albert Gleeson Talau Gardner:
Hooper Long: Fozzard Cunningham Mason Wilkin
Stankevitch Sculthorpe:
Subs used - Edmondson Fa'asavalu Joynt Hardman:
Tries - Wellens(2) Albert(2) Joynt(2) Hooper Long
Sculthorpe: Goals - Long(6) Sculthorpe(2):
CASTLEFORD - Hepworth: Pryce Saxton Rogers Mellor:
Kain Robinson: Greenhill Godwin Lynch Ryan Clayton
Hudson: Subs used - Sykes B Smith Rudder Tony:
Try - Hudson: Goals - Godwin(2):
Referee K Kirkpatrick (Warrington) Att - 8397 H.T. 8 - 18

Sun 20 Jun 2004 WARRINGTON WOLVES home
lost 10 - 32
CASTLEFORD - Hepworth: Mellor Saxton Tony Pryce: Sean
Rudder Robinson: Greenhill Godwin Lynch Ryan M Smith
Hudson: Subs used - Jackson Richard Blakeway Gibson
Rogers: Tries - Robinson(2):   Goal - Godwin:
WARRINGTON W - Cardiss: Appo Grose Westwood
Gaskell: Clarke Wood: Lima Noone Hilton Guisset Sibbit
Wainwright: Subs used - Hulse Gleeson Stevens Leikvoll:
Tries - Westwood(3) Gaskell Grose Wood:
Goals - Noone(3) Appo:
Referee A Klein (London) Att - 6111 H.T. 4 - 12

Sun 27 Jun 2004 SALFORD CITY REDS away
lost 14 - 30
CASTLEFORD - Hepworth: Pryce Tony Gibson Mellor:
Davis Robinson: Jackson Godwin Lynch M Smith Ryan
Hudson: Subs used - B Smith Clayton Saxton Ripley:
Tries - Mellor Lynch: Goals - Godwin (3):
SALFORD C R - Flowers: Caine Littler McGuinness Stewart:
Beverley Clinch: Baynes Alker Highton Coley Rutgerson
Charles:
Subs used - Haggerty Fitzpatrick Johnson Shipway:
Tries - Alker(2) Coley Charles Shipway: Goals - Charles (5):
Referee K Kirkpatrick (War'gton) Att - 3313 H.T. 14 - 12

Sun 4 Jul 2004 BRADFORD BULLS home lost 12 - 60
CASTLEFORD - Hepworth: Gibson Tony Mellor Rogers:
Davis Robinson: Jackson Godwin Lynch Sean Ryan M
Smith Clayton: Subs used - Greenhill Sykes B Smith KEVIN
KING (816):   Tries - Godwin Rogers: Goals - Godwin(2):
BRADFORD B - Reardon: Pratt Johnson Hape Vainikolo:
Pryce Deacon: Vagana Paul Fielden Swann Peacock
Radford: Subs used - Smith Langley Parker Anderson:
Tries - Vainikolo(4) Hape(2) Pryce Deacon Peacock Parker:
Goals - Deacon (10):
Referee R Laughton (Barnsley) Att - 6606 H.T. 6 - 32

Fri 9 Jul 2004 LEEDS RHINOS away lost 14 - 46
LEEDS R - Cummins: Calderwood Walker Senior Bai:
McGuire Dunemann: Feather Diskin McDermott McKenna
Adamson Sinfield: Subs used - Ward Jones-Buchanan
Burrow Poching: Tries - Poching(3) McGuire(2) Bai Diskin
Calderwood: Goals - Sinfield(7):
CASTLEFORD - Gibson: Dean Ripley Tony Rogers Mellor:
Davis Robinson: Greenhill Hudson Sykes M Smith Harland
Clayton: Subs used - Godwin Lynch Hepworth Saxton:
Tries - Lynch Greenhill Tony :   Goals - Godwin:
Referee A Klein (London) Att 13922 H.T. 4 - 24

Sun 18 Jul 2004 HUDDERSFIELD GIANTS home
won 24 - 20
CASTLEFORD - Gibson: Pryce Tony Rogers Mellor: Davis
Luke Robinson: Greenhill Godwin Lynch M Smith Harland
Hudson: Subs used - MARK TOOKEY(817) Sykes Clayton
Hepworth: Tries - Mellor Robinson Hudson Rogers:
Goals - Robinson(3) Godwin:
HUDDERSFIELD G - Reilly: O'Hare Nero Evans Donlan:
Costin March: Fleary Penkywicz Gannon Jones Smith
Roarty: Subs used - Grayshon Slicker Crabtree White:
Tries - Evans Penkywicz O'Hare: Goals - Costin(4):
Referee S Ganson (St Helens) Att - 5321 H.T. 6 - 16

Fri 23 Jul 2004 WIGAN WARRIORS away
lost 18 - 48
WIGAN W - Connolly: Varney Wild Aspinwall Dallas:
O'Loughlin Robinson: Farrell Newton Cassidy Tickle Hock
Radlinski: Subs used - Hodgson Smith Beswick Prescott:
Tries - Dallas(4) Newton(2) Robinson Aspinwall:
Goals - Farrell(7) Tickle:
CASTLEFORD - Gibson: MATT GARDNER(818) Saxton
Rogers Pryce: Davis Tony: Sykes Hepworth Lynch Harland
M Smith Hudson:
Subs used - Tookey Clayton B Smith Shenton:
Tries - Pryce Lynch Gardner Rogers: Goal - Hepworth:
Referee I Smith (Oldham) Att - 10032 H.T. 10 - 18

Sat 31 Jul 2004 WIDNES VIKINGS home won 42 - 8
CASTLEFORD - Gibson: Saxton MotuTony Rogers Mellor:
Davis Maloney: Tookey Godwin Lynch Harland M Smith
Hudson: Subs used - Greenhill Sykes B Smith Hepworth:
Tries - Mellor(2) Davis M Smith Hudson Maloney Godwin
Rogers: Goals - Godwin(5):
WIDNES V - Atcheson: Devlin Bird Hughes Giles: Myler
Peters: Hobson Millard Mills Frame Hay Finnigan:
Subs used - McCurrie Whitaker Wozniak Middlehurst:

SEASON 2004

Try - Millard: Goals - Myler(2):
Referee K Kirkpatrick (Warrington) Att - 5517 H.T. 26 - 2

Sun 8 Aug 2004 WAKEFIELD TRINITY WILDCATS away lost 18 - 39
WAKEFIELD T W - M Field: Ryder Demetriou Domic
Tadulala: Rooney Jeffries: MacGillivray March Korkidas
Solomona J Field Ellis: Subs used - Griffin Elima Spicer
Wainwright: Tries - Jeffries(2) Demetriou(2) Domic Ellis:
Goals - Rooney(7) DG:
CASTLEFORD - Gibson: Saxton Maloney Rogers Mellor:
Davis Hepworth: Tookey Godwin Lynch Harland M Smith
Hudson: Subs used - Greenhill Sykes Brambani STEVE
CROUCH(819): Tries - Hepworth Crouch Davis:
Goals - Hepworth(2) Godwin:
Referee R Silverwood (Mirfield) Att - 6673 H.T. 8 - 10

Sun 15 Aug 2004 HUDDERSFIELD GIANTS away won 29 - 12
HUDDERSFIELD G - Donlan: O'Hare Evans Bailey St
Hilaire: Costin March: Gannon Penkywicz Roarty Nero
Jones Gene:
Subs used - Grayston Smith White Fleary:
Tries - White Evans: Goals - Costin(2):
CASTLEFORD - Gibson: Pryce Saxton Rogers Mellor: Davis
Maloney: Sykes Godwin Lynch Harland Crouch Hudson:
Subs used - Greenhill Hepworth Tookey Jackson:
Tries - Pryce(2) Hudson Tookey: Goals - Godwin(6)
Maloney DG:
Referee I Smith (Oldham) Att - 3231 H.T. 14 - 0

Sun 22 Aug 2004 HULL FC home won 21 - 14
CASTLEFORD - Gibson: Pryce Saxton Rogers Mellor: Davis
Maloney: Greenhill Godwin Lynch Harland Crouch
Hudson: Subs used - Sykes Tookey Hepworth Jackson:
Tries - Rogers Gibson:
Goals - Godwin(5) Hepworth Davis DG:
HULL FC - Briscoe: Best Whiting Yeaman R Barnett Jnr:
Cooke R Horne: Dowes Swain King Bailey McMenemy
Smith: Subs used - G Horne Higgins Fletcher Scruton:
Tries - Cooke Yeaman R Barnett Jnr: Goal - Cooke:
Referee R Silverwood (Dewsbury) Att - 8054 H.T. 10 - 4

Fri 27 Aug 2004 LEEDS RHINOS away lost 12 - 64
LEEDS R - Mathers: Bai Walker Senior Calderwood:
Dunemann Burrow: Ward Diskin McDonald Adamason
Lauitiiti Sinfield; Subs used - Bailey Poaching McDermott
Jones-Buchanan Tries - Walker(4) Burrow(2) Poaching(2)
Senior Dunemann McDonald Bai: Goals - Sinfield(8):
CASTLEFORD - Gibson: Pryce Saxton Clayton Rogers:
Davis Hepworth: Greenhill Hudson Jackson Lynch Crouch
Harland: Subs used - Tookey Sykes Shenton B Smith:
Tries - Crouch Davis: Goals - Hepworth (2):
Referee A Klein (London) Att - 14605 H.T. 6 - 34

Sun 5 Sep 2004 SALFORD CITY REDS home lost 22 - 24
CASTLEFORD - Gibson: Pryce Rogers Saxton Mellor: Davis
Maloney: Greenhill Godwin Lynch Harland Crouch
Hudson: Subs used - Sykes Tookey Hepworth Jackson:
Tries - Mellor(3) Maloney: Goals - Godwin(2) Maloney:
SALFORD C R - Fitzpatrick: Caine Littler Beverley Stewart:
McGuinness Clinch: Baynes Alker Highton Coley
Rutgerson Charles:
Subs used - Haggerty Johnson Shipway Baldwin:
Tries - Fitzpatrick(2) Alker Coley: Goals - Charles (4):
Referee S Ganson (St Helens) Att - 5809 H.T. 12 - 6

Sun 12 Sep 2004 WIDNES VIKINGS away won 7 - 6
WIDNES V - Holmes: Devlin Bird Hughes Murphy: Jules
O'Neill Myler: Julian O'Neill Millard McCurrie Frame Hay
Finnigan: Subs used - Whattaker Mills Gallagher
Fa'alogo: Try - Myler: Goal - Jules O'Neill:
CASTLEFORD - Gibson: Pryce Rogers Saxton Mellor: Davis
Maloney: Greenhill Godwin Lynch Harland M Smith
Hudson: Subs used - Sykes Tookey Hepworth Jackson:
Try - Hepworth: Goals - Godwin Maloney DG:
Referee K Kirkpatrick (Warrington) Att - 7005 H.T. 0 - 6

Sun 19 Sep 2004 WAKEFIELD TRINITY WILDCATS home lost 28 - 32
CASTLEFORD - Damian Gibson: Pryce Darren Rogers
Saxton Paul Mellor: Davis Francis Maloney: Craig Greenhill
Wayne Godwin Lynch Lee Harland Michael Smith
Hudson: Subs used - Nathan Sykes Mark Tookey
Hepworth Jackson: Tries - Mellor(2) Gibson Saxton M
Smith Gocwin: Goals - Maloney(2):
WAKEFIELD T W - Field: Halfpenny Demetriou Domic
Tadulala: Ellis Jeffries: Feather March Korkidas Solomona
MacGillvray Spicer: Subs used - Griffin Handforth Elima
Ryder: Tries - Solomona(2) Halfpenny(2) Tadulala
Handforth: Goals - March(3) Handfoth:
Referee I Smith (Oldham) Att 11055 H.T. 18 - 18

Ryan Clayton
D. No 802
2004 to 2010

Sean Rudder
D. No 803
2004

Graig Greenhill
D. No 805
2004

Sean Ryan
D. No 806
2004

Michael Shenton
D. No 810
2004 to

Byron Smith
D. No 811
2004 to 2005

Andy Kain
D. No 813
2004 to 2006

Steve Crouch
D. No 819
2004 to 2005

2004 SQUAD
Back Row.- G Huby T Saxton G Greenhall A Lynch D Rogers P Mellor R Blakeway M Smith S Ryan
Middle Row – B Harrington J Hepworth R Clayton L Harland A Smith P Newlove N Sykes J Thackray P Jackson
G Mercer(Ass.Coach)
Front Row – W Pryce R Sheridan D Gibson S Rudder G Steadman (Coach) R Hudson W Godwin F Maloney A Kain

SEASON 2004

D.N	PLAYER		DEBUT	L MATCH	APP	SUE	T.AP	TRI'S	G'LS	D.G	P'TS
694	SYKES	NATHAN		19/09/2004	6	15	21	0	0	0	0
719	HARLAND	LEE		19/09/2004	20	3	23	1	0	0	4
746	DAVIS	BRAD			13	0	13	3	0	1	13
749	MALONEY	FRANCIS		19/09/2004	18	0	18	2	11	2	32
750	SMITH	MICHAEL		19/09/2004	20	3	23	4	0	0	16
757	ROGERS	DAREN		19/09/2004	28	1	29	9	0	0	36
759	LYNCH	ANDY			23	4	27	3	0	0	12
770	PRYCE	WAINE			16	0	16	5	0	0	20
779	GODWIN	WAYNE		19/09/2004	23	3	26	7	59	0	146
786	HUDSON	RYAN			29	0	29	8	0	0	32
791	SAXTON	TOMMY			23	2	25	6	0	0	24
793	BLAKEWAY	RICHARD		20/06/2004	0	1	1	0	0	0	0
794	GIBSON	DAMION		19/09/2004	22	1	23	3	0	0	12
795	JACKSON	PAUL			7	15	22	0	0	0	0
796	THACKRAY	JAMIE		09/05/2004	6	6	12	4	0	0	16
797	MELLOR	PAUL		19/09/2004	19	0	19	15	0	0	60
799	HEPWORTH	JON			15	15	30	4	9	0	34
800	HUBY	CRAIG			0	3	3	0	0	0	0
802	CLAYTON	RYAN	22/02/2004		13	6	19	3	0	0	12
803	RUDDER	SEAN	22/02/2004	20/06/2004	11	3	14	3	0	0	12
804	SHERIDAN	RYAN	22/02/2004	14/03/2004	4	0	4	0	0	0	0
805	GREENHILL	CRAIG	22/02/2004	19/09/2004	23	4	27	1	0	0	4
806	RYAN	SEAN	22/02/2004	04/07/2004	13	5	18	2	0	0	8
807	RIPLEY	DEAN	02/04/2004	09/07/2004	3	3	6	1	0	0	4
808	NEWLOVE	PAUL	08/04/2004	23/05/2004	5	0	5	1	0	0	4
809	BRAMBANI	DOMINIC	18/04/2004		2	2	4	0	0	0	0
810	SHENTON	MICHAEL	01/05/2004		1	2	3	0	0	0	0
811	SMITH	BYRON	01/05/2004		0	9	9	0	0	0	0
812	WORRINCY	ROB	09/05/2004		1	0	1	0	0	0	0
813	KAIN	ANDY	09/05/2004		2	2	4	1	0	0	4
814	ROBINSON	LUKE	23/05/2004	18/07/2004	9	0	9	4	3	0	22
815	TONY	MOTU	06/06/2004	31/07/2004	8	1	9	1	0	0	4
816	KING	KEVIN	04/07/2004	04/07/2004	0	1	1	0	0	0	0
817	TOOKEY	MARK	18/07/2004	19/09/2004	2	8	10	1	0	0	4
818	GARDNER	MATT	23/07/2004	23/07/2004	1	0	1	1	0	0	4
819	CROUCH	STEVE	08/08/2004		4	1	5	2	0	0	8
	36				**18**	**21**	**390**	**119**	**509**	**95**	**82**	**3**	**547**

COMPETITION		P	W	D	L	FOR	AGT
S. LEAGUE	POSITION 12 OF 12	28	6	0	22	515	924
RL CUP		2	1	0	1	32	46
PLAYERS RECORDS		**30**	**7**	**0**	**23**	**547**	**970**

After losing the first seven League Games the Club dismissed Coach Graham Steadman on 21 April 2004 and his Assistant Gary Mercer was made Caretaker Coach.

On 20 May 2004 Gary Mercer appointed as Head Coach with Ellery Hanley appointed as Consultant Coach, however Hanley left the Club on 6 July 2004.

Australian winger Paul Mellor finished with 15 tries from 19 appearances - a commendable effort.

After a disappointing season with only six victories from 28 league games, the Club finished bottom of Super league and were relegated, the first time in its history that the Club would not be competing in the top flight.

A notable Debutant was Michael Shenton.

SEASON 2005

LHF HEALTHPLAN NATIONAL LEAGUE ONE

Castleford were relegated from Super League being replaced by Leigh Centurions.
The National League 1 consisted of 10 teams – Barrow Batley Castleford Doncaster Featherstone Halifax Hull K R Oldham Rochdale Whitehaven.

Sun 23 Jan 2005 HUNSLET HAWKS home won 62 - 12 FRIENDLY
CASTLEFORD - Platt: Pryce Reid Hepworth Shenton: A Kain Handforth: B Smith Henderson Hamilton Haughey James A Smith: Subs used - Rowe A Watene Huby Worrincy Brambani S Kain Tries - Hepworth (2) Platt(2) A Watene Huby Pryce Handforth Kain Shenton James Worrincy:
Goals - Handforth(3) Huby(3) Hepworth:
HUNSLET H - Rayner: Carey Redfearn Cummins Hunter: D Gibbons Moxon: Staveley Wray Mears Freeman Cawthray Bastow: Subs used - M Gibbons Carbutt Hawley Cass Cook Tepper:
Tries - Moxon Cummins: Goals: - Bastow Rayner:
Referee I Smith (Oldham) Att - 3646 H.T. 18 - 6

Sun 30 Jan 2005 SHEFFIELD EAGLES home won 32 - 10 FRIENDLY
CASTLEFORD - Platt: Pryce ReidS/O Hepworth Shenton: A Kain Brambani: B Smith Henderson: A Watane Huby James Haughey:
Subs - Bird Hamilton Cooke Edwards Cogan:
Tries - Platt(2) Kain Pryce James Cooke: Goals - Huby(4):
SHEFFIELD E - Hurst: Mills A Dickinson Veamatahau: De Chenu: R Dickinson G Brown: Howleson S Collins Molyneux Rice C Brown S Dickinson:
Subs used - Breakingbury K Collins Moore Brentley Morton Turnbull Tillyer North:
Tries - Veamatahau De Chenu: Goals - G Brown:
Referee C Morris (Huddersfield) Att - 2689 H.T. 6 - 6

Sun 13 Feb 2005 YORK CITY KNIGHTS home won 52 – 2 NORTHERN RAIL CUP - GROUP MATCH
CASTLEFORD - MICHAEL PLATT(820): Pryce DAMIEN REID(821) Hepworth Shenton: A Kain PAUL HANDFORTH(822): ADAM WATENE(823) ANDREW HENDERSON(824) Huby TOMMY HAUGHEY(825) Crouch AARON SMITH(826): Subs used - FRANK WATENE(827) B Smith DEON BIRD(828) LEIGH COOKE(829):
Tries - Hepworth(2) A Kain(2) Huby(2) A Smith Shenton Pryce Bird: Goals - Huby(4) Handforth(2):
YOKK C K - Blaymire: Fox Potter Ross Buchanan: Thorman Levy: Sozi Jackson Sullivan Kike Callaghan Patterson:
Subs used - Elston Cain Smith Buckenham:
Goal - Thorman:
Referee B Thaler (Wakefield) Att - 5768 H.T. 12 - 2

Sun 20 Feb 2005 FEATHERSTONE ROVERS away won 22 – 10 NORTHERN RAIL CUP - GROUP MATCH
FEATHERSTONE R - McNally: Powell Maun Newlove Wray: Weeden Ripley: Tonks C Hughes Sykes Dooler Hayes Blakeway: Subs used - Moss Lowe Evans Carlton:

Try - Weeden: Goals - Weeden(3):
CASTLEFORD - Platt: Pryce Reid Hepworth Shenton: A Kain Handforth: F Watene Henderson B Smith Haughey Crouch A Smith: Subs used - Bird Cooke A Watene Huby:
Tries - Shenton A Kain Haughey Platt:
Goals - Handforth(2) Huby:
Referee J King (St Helens) Att - 6353 H.T. 8 - 8

Sun 27 Feb 2005 HUNSLET HAWKS home won 70 - 0 NORTHERN RAIL CUP - GROUP MATCH
CASTLEFORD - Platt: Pryce Reid Hepworth Shenton: A Kain Handforth: B Smith Henderson Huby Haughey JORDAN JAMES(830) A Smith: Subs used - Brambani Cooke A Watene F Watene: Tries - Hepworth(3) Shenton(2) Huby(2) Handforth Reid James F Watene Haughey Platt: Goals - Huby(8) Handforth:
HUNSLET H - Rayner: Amraz A Gibbons Cummins McCelland: D Gibbons Moxon: Staveley Hawley Pryce Freeman Mears Wray:
Subs used - Cass Freeman Carbutt Redfearn:
Referee P Bentham (Warrington) Att - 4483 H.T. 38 - 0

Sun 6 Mar 2005 HUNSLET HAWKS away won 34 - 6 NORTHERN RAIL CUP - GROUP MATCH
HUNSLET H - Raynor: Dyson A Gibbons Redfearn Morton: Cass Moxon: Staveley Hawley Pryce Fletcher Cunnins D Gibbons: Subs used - Carbutt North Norcross Cook:
Try - Moton: Goal - Dyson:
CASTLEFORD - Platt: Pryce Reid Hepworth Shenton: A Kain Handforth: A Watene Henderson F Watene James Huby Haughey: Subs used - Cooke TIM ROBINSON(831) ANTHONY ENGLAND(832) MICHAEL KNOWLES(833):
Tries - Pryce(2) A Kain James Shenton Henderson Reid: Goals - Huby(3):
Referee B Thaler (Wakefield) Att - 1432 H.T. 14 - 6

Sun 13 Mar 2005 HULL DOCKERS home won 72 - 10 R.L. CHALLENGE CUP ROUND 3
CASTLEFORD - STUART KAIN(834): Pryce Reid Hepworth Shenton: A Kain Handforth: A Watene Henderson F Watene James Crouch A Smith: Subs used - Cooke Anthony England Knowles Dean Sampson
Tries - Reid(3) Hepworth(3) A Kain(2) James Pryce F Watene A Watene Shenton: Goals - Handforth(10):
HULL D - Hall: A Walker P Taylor Molly Jones: Stephenson Yeaman: Emerson Sellars Jay Henry Eccles A Taylor:
Subs used - Gardner Ulyatt D Walker Caldwell:
Tries - P Taylor Henry: Goal - Stephenson:
Referee J Leahy (Dewsbury) Att - 3331 H.T. 38 - 4

Sun 20 Mar 2005 YORK CITY KNIGHTS away won 24 – 16 NORTHERN RAIL CUP - GROUP MATCH
YORK C K - Lingard: Fox Callaghan Law Watson: Rhodes P Thorman: Smith Elston Sullivan Ward Friend Liddell: Subs used - Jackson N Thorman Sozi McDowell:
Tries - Watson Lingard: Goals - P Thorman(4):
CASTLEFORD - S Kain: Pryce Reid Hepworth Shenton: A Kain Handforth: A Watene Henderson F Watene Haughey

Crouch A Smith: Subs used - SHAUN LUNT(835) Cooke James B Smith: Tries - Haughey(2) Shenton Henderson A Kain: Goals - Handforth A Kain:
Referee B Thaler (Wakefield) Att - 2340 H.T. 8 - 16

Fri 25 Mar 2005 FEATHERSTONE ROVERS home won 35 – 16 NORTHERN RAIL CUP - GROUP MATCH
CASTLEFORD - S Kain; Pryce Reid Shenton Robinson: A Kain Brambani: B Smith Lunt ALEX ROWE(836) Cooke LANCE HAMILTON(837) James: Subs used - Haughey Rob Worrincy Handforth F Watene: Tries - Pryce(3) S Kain Robinson Shenton; Goals - A Kain(5) D/G:
FEATHERSTONE R - Batty: Powell Maun Newlove Wray: McNally Weedon: Tonks Kay Sykes Houston Lowe Nicholson: Subs used - Moss Evans C Hughes Carlton: Tries - Newlove Lowe McNally Hughes:
Referee G Hewer (Whitehaven) Att - 7338 H.T. 19 - 8

Mon 28 Mar 2005 DONCASTER DRAGONS away won 29 - 10
DONCASTER D - Horne: Colton Farrell Cardoza Mills: Holroyd Tawhai: Handforth Cook Ostler Hay Green Moana: Subs used - Cockayne Lawton O'Loughlin Harland: Tries - Mills Holroyd: Goal - Holroyd:
CASTLEFORD - Platt: Robinson Reid Hepworth Shenton: A Kain Handforth: A Watene Henderson F Watene Haughey Crouch A Smith: Subs used - Lunt James B Smith Rowe: Tries - Robinson Reid Shenton Haughey James - Goals – A Kain(4) D/G:
Referee J King (St Helens) Att - 3371 H.T. 12 - 10

Sun 3 Apr 2005 HALIFAX away lost 14 - 23 R.L. CHALLENGE CUP ROUND 4
HALIFAX - Gibson: Haley Bunyan Blackwood Hadcroft: Corcoran Black: Morley Fisher Birchall Larder Bloem Weisner: Subs used - Attwood Sheriffe McDonald Boults: Tries - Weisner Fisher Bunyan Black:
Goals - Bloem(3) Weisner D/G:
CASTLEFORD - Platt: Pryce Reid Hepworth Shenton: Davis Handforth: A Watene Henderson B Smith Haughey Crouch A Smith: Subs used - Brambani James Lance Hamilton Rowe: Tries - Shenton(2): Goals - Davis(3):
Referee Mr J Leahey (Dewsbury) Att - 3925 H.T. 8 - 14

Sun 10 Apr 2005 ROCHDALE HORNETS home won 36 - 22
CASTLEFORD - Platt: Pryce Reid Hepworth Shenton: Davis Henderson: A Watene A Smith B Smith Haughey James Crouch: Subs used – Dominic Brambani Huby Leigh Cooke Shaun Lunt: Tries - Pryce(2) Shenton(2) James Haughey Platt Hepworth: Goals - Davis(2):
ROCHDALE H - Giles: Saywell McCully Varkulis Cambell: Bowker Goulding: Hopkinson McConnell Price Gorski Doran Farrell:
Subs used - Birdseye Newton Cunliffe Hansen:
Tries - Bowker Saywell Farrell McCully: Goals - McCully(3):
Referee G Hewer (Whitehaven) Att - 4776 H.T. 18 - 4

Sun 17 Apr 2005 OLDHAM away won 32 - 20
OLDHAM - Dodd: Gorey Munro Goddard Johnson: Turner

Mataora: Bibey Barber Wilson Haughton Roberts Hough: Subs used - Kirkland Svabic Hodson Tootill: Tries - Johnson Wilson Dodd: Goals - Turner(3) Barber:
CASTLEFORD - Platt: Pryce Reid Hepworth Shenton: A Kain Davis: A Watene Henderson B Smith Haughey Crouch A Smith:
Subs used - Tim Robinson James Alex Rowe Huby: Tries - Davis(2) Pryce(2) Shenton A Kain: Goals - A Kain(4):
Referee M Dawber (Wigan) Att - 2054 H.T. 22 - 14

Sun 24 Apr 2005 BARROW RAIDERS away won 36 - 22
BARROW R - Zitter: Marshall Roach Muff Nixon: Colley Holt: A Fisher Clark D Fisher Whitehead Horton Atkinson: Subs used - Archer Dancer Osborne Wilcock:
Tries - Nixon Whitehead Muff Marshall: Goals - Holt(3):
CASTLEFORD - Platt: Pryce Reid Hepworth Shenton : A Kain Davis: A Watene Henderson B Smith Haughey Crouch A Smith: Subs used - James Knowles Huby: Tries - Pryce(2) Haughey(2) A Watene Davis Reid:
Goals - Kain(4):
Referee P Taberner (Wigan) Att - 1816 H.T. 16 - 12

Sun 15 May 2005 HULL KINGSTON ROVERS home won 32 - 26
CASTLEFORD - Hepworth: Pryce Reid Bird Shenton: A Kain Henderson: A Watene A Smith B Smith Haughey Crouch RICHARD FLETCHER(838) Subs used - Davis Huby James Handforth: Tries - Davis(2) Shenton A Kain Huby A Watene: Goals - Huby(3) A Kain:
Hull K R - Rivett: Steele Parker Epati Ford: Mansson Webster: Harmon Pickering Tangata-Toa Raleigh Smith Blanchard: Subs used - Ellis Garmston Bovill Aizue: Tries - Epati(3) Mansson Raleigh: Goals - Steel(3):
Referee J King (St Helens) Att - 8078 H.T. 20 - 16

Sun 22 May 2005 HALIFAX away won 48 - 16
HALIFAX - Gibson: Haley Bunyan Blackwood Sheriffe: Corcoran Weisner: Hobson Fisher Boults Larder Spink Ball: Subs used - Bloem Morley MacDonald Tuilagi: Tries - Sheriffe (2) Ball: Goals - Weisner(2):
CASTLEFORD - Platt: Pryce Bird Hepworth Shenton: A Kain Davis: A Watene Henderson Fletcher Haughey Huby Crouch: Subs used - ANDY BAILEY(839) B Smith Handforth James: Tries - Pryce(2) Shenton(2) Bird Henderson Haughey Hepworth Huby;
Goals - Huby(4) Kain(2):
Referee C Morris (Huddersfield) Att - 3259 H.T. 38 - 6

Sun 29 May 2005 FEATHERSTONE ROVERS away won 38 – 14 NORTHERN RAIL CUP - QUARTER FINAL
FEATHERSTONE R - Batty: Kirmond Ripley Newlove Powell: Finn Georgiadis: Evans C Hughes Sykes Hayes Lowe Weedon: Subs used - McNally Tonks Dooler Carlton: Tries - Georgiadis Newlove: Goals - Finn(3):
CASTLEFORD - Platt: Hepworth Bird Haughey Shenton: Handforth Davis: A Watene Henderson Fletcher Huby Crouch A Smith:
Subs used - A Kain Bailey B Smith James:
Tries - Platt(4) Davis Bird: Goals - Handforth(4) Huby(3):
Referee P Taberner (Wigan) Att - 3418 H.T. 18 - 8

SEASON 2005

Sun 5 Jun 2005 WHITEHAVEN home won 42 - 24
CASTLEFORD - Platt: Pryce Bird Hepworth Shenton:
Handforth Davis: A Watene Henderson Fletcher Haughey
Crouch A Smith: Subs used - Huby B Smith Bailey F
Watene: Tries - Pryce(2) Hepworth(2) Crouch Platt Bird
Haughey: Goals - Fletcher(2) Huby(2) Handforth:
WHITEHAVEN - Broadbent: Calvert Wilson Nanyn Lebbon:
Joe Penny: Cox Lester Fatialofa McDermott Hill Rudd:
Subs used - Kirbride Davidson Sice Morton:
Tries - Wilson Fatialofa Sice Lester: Goals - Nanyn(4):
Referee P Bentham (Warrington) Att - 7323 H.T. 36 - 12

**Sun 12 Jun 2005 FEATHERSTONE ROVERS away
won 38 - 34**
FEATHERTONE R - Moss: Kirmond Batty Newlove Powell:
Weeden Finn: Tonks Hughes Houston Hayes Lowe
Dooler: Subs used - Georgiadis Evans Nicholson Carlton:
Tries - Finn(2) Dooler Hughes Weeden: Goals - Finn(7):
CASTLEFORD - Platt: Pryce Bird Hepworth Shenton:
Handforth Davis: Bailey Henderson Fletcher Huby James
A Smith: Subs used - Haughey Crouch B Smith F Watene:
Tries - Handforth Henderson Huby Pryce James Shenton:
Goals - Huby(6) Fletcher:
Referee B Thaler (Wakefield) Att - 3334 H.T. 14 - 26

**Sun 19 Jun 2005 WHITEHAVEN home won 42 - 14
NORTHERN RAIL CUP - SEMI FINAL**
CASTLEFORD - Platt: Pryce Bird Hepworth Shenton:
Handforth Davis: A Watene Henderson Fletcher Haughey
Crouch A Smith: Subs used - Huby B Smith A Kain
F Watene Tries - Haughey Handforth Crouch Pryce Platt
F Watene A Kain: Goals - Huby(5) Fletcher Davis:
WHITEHAVEN - Broadbent: Calvert Seeds Nanyn Wilson:
Joe Penny: Summers Lester Fatialofa McDermott Hill
Rudd: Subs used - Miller Davidson Sice Morton:
Tries - Fatialofa Nanyn Calvert: Goals - Nanyn:
Referee P Bentham (Warrington) Att - 5019 H.T. 24 - 0

Sun 26 Jun 2005 BATLEY BULLDOGS home won 60 -12
CASTLEFORD - Platt: Reid Bird Hepworth Shenton: A Kain
Davis: F Watene Henderson Huby Haughey Crouch A
Smith: Subs used - Bailey James RYAN BOYLE(840) B
Smith: Tries - Bird(2) Shenton(2) Davis Henderson F
Watene Reid Crouch Platt Boyle:
Goals - Huby(5) Davis Kain Boyle:
BATLEY B - Sibson: Stokes Royston Muff Lister: Toohey
Eaton: Morgan Roden Berry Richardson S/O Shillabeer
Marsh: Subs used - Lingard Spears Rourke McLoughlin:
Tries - Lister Lingard: Goals - Eaton(2):
Referee J King (St Helens) Att - 4487 H.T. 24 - 6

**Sun 3 Jul 2005 DONCASTER DRAGONS home
won 40 - 16**
CASTLEFORD - Platt: S Kain Bird Haughey Shenton: A Kain
Handforth: A Watene Henderson Bailey Huby Crouch A
Smith: Subs used - James B Smith Reid F Watene:
Tries - Platt(3) Shenton Bailey F Watene Handforth:
Goals - Huby(3) A Kain(3):
DONCASTER D - Miles: D Mills Wood Farrell Colton:
Cockayne Tawhai: Handforth Cook Fisher Ostler Lawton

Leaf: Subs Used - Green O'Loughlin K Mills Andrews:
Tries - Lawton(2) Colton: Goals - Cockayne Miles:
Referee P Bentham (Warrington) Att - 5005 H.T. 18 - 6

**Sun 10 Jul 2005 ROCHDALE HORNETS away
lost 16 - 17**
ROCHDALE H - Giles Saywell McCully Gorski Campbell:
Bowker Goulding: Hill McConnell Price Varkulis Doran
Farrell: Subs used - Butterworth Anderson Cunliffe Ball:
Tries - Campbell Butterworth: Goals - Goulding(4) D/G:
CASTLEFORD - Platt: Pryce Bird Damien Reid Shenton: A
Kain Davis: Huby Henderson Bailey Haughey Crouch A
Smith: Subs used - Handforth B Smith DOMiNIC
MALONEY(841) F Watene:
Tries - Haughey Reid Davis: Goals - Huby (2):
Referee M Dawber (Wigan) Att - 1728 H.T. 10 - 11

**Sun 17 Jul 2005 HULL KINGSTON ROVERS
lost 16 - 18 NORTHERN RAIL CUP FINAL AT
BLOOMFIELD ROAD BLACKPOOL**
CASTLEFORD - Platt: Pryce Bird Hepworth Shenton:
Handforth Davis: A Watene Henderson Bailey Haughey
Crouch Huby: Subs used - A Kain Fletcher B Smith F
Watene: Tries - Platt Hepworth: Goals - Huby(4):
HULL K R - Rivett: Steel Epati Morton Ford: Mansson
Webster: Garmston Ellis Tangata-Toa Raleigh Netherton
Holdstock: Subs used - Pickering Barker Bovill Aizue:
Tries - Raleigh Ford: Goals - Morton(5):
Referee B Thaler (Wakefield) Att - 9400 H.T. 10 - 2

Sun 24 Jul 2005 OLDHAM home won 32 - 20
CASTLEFORD - Platt: Pryce Bird Eager Shenton: A Kain
Davis: A Watene Henderson Bailey Huby James Crouch:
Subs used - Haughey Stuart Kain Dominic Maloney
Fletcher: Tries - Huby(2) Pryce(2) A Kain Bird:
Goials - Huby(3) Fletcher:
OLDHAM - Doidd: Munro Wilkinson Goddard Johnson:
Turner Hough: Bibey Kirkland Glassie Hodson Roberts
Svabic: Subs used - Barber Wilson Norman Hough:
Tries - Hough Barber Goddard Johnson: Goals - Turner(2):
Referee T Alibert (Albi, France) Att - 4600 H.T. 18 - 16

**Sun 31 Jul 2005 BARROW RAIDERS home
won 76 - 12**
CASTLEFORD - Platt: Pryce Bird Eager Shenton: A Kain
Davis: A Watene Henderson Fletcher Huby James Crouch:
Subs used - Haughey Handforth Bailey F Watene:
Tries - Huby(3) Pryce(3) Shenton(2) James Eager A
Watene Platt Davis Crouch: Goals - Huby(9) Fletcher:
BARROW R - Pate: Marshall Finch Zitter Nixon: Colley
Holt Dancer Clark Tandy Whitehead Osborn Atkinson:
Subs used - Irabor Osborn Wilcock Raftrey:
Tries - Tandy Osborn: Goals - Holt(2):
Referee K Kirkpatrick (Warrington) Att - 4056 H.T. 44 - 0

**Sun 7 Aug 2005 HULL KINGSTON ROVERS away
lost 18 - 46**
HULL K R - Rivett: Steel Epati Morton Ford: Mansson
Webster: Aizue Ellis Tangata-Toa Raleigh Barker

SEASON 2005

Holdstock: Subs used - Pickering Walker Blanchard
Pramil: Tries - Ford Rivett Mansson Barker Ellis Webster
Blanchard Holdstock: Goals - Morton(7):
CASTLEFORD - Platt: Pryce Bird Handforth Shenton: A
Kain Davis: A Watene Henderson Bailey HubyS/O Fletcher
Crouch: Subs used - JASON MOSSOP(842) James B Smith
F Watene:
Tries - James Pryce A Kain: Goals - Huby(2) A Kain:
Referee A Klein (Keighley) Att - 5023 H.T. 6 - 18

Sun 14 Aug 2005 WHITEHAVEN away lost 16 - 19
WHITEHAVEN - Broadbent; Calvert Seeds Nanyn Wilson:
Leroy Penny: Summers Sice Fatialofa Miller Hill Lester:
Subs used - McDermott Rudd Jackson Tandy:
Tries - Sice Penny Seeds: Goals - Nanyn(3) Rudd D/G:
CASTLEFORD - Platt: Pryce Bird Eager Shenton: A Kain
Davis: A Watene Henderson Andy Bailey Huby Haughey
Crouch: Subs used - Hepworth James B Smith F Watene:
Tries Pryce(2) A Kain: Goals - Huby(2):
Referee K Kirkpatrick (Warrington) Att - 4437 H.T. 0 - 18

Sun 21 August 2005 HALIFAX home won 38 - 34
CASTLEFORD - Platt: Pryce Eager Hepworth Shenton: A
Kain Davis: A Watene Henderson F Watene Haughey
Crouch Bird: Subs used - DAMIEN BLANCH(843) James
Fletcher B Smith Tries - Henderson(2) Bird Pryce Fletcher
Blanch: Goals A Kain(6) Fletcher:
HALIFAX - Gibson: Haley Kirk Blackwood Sherrife:
Corcoran Black: Hobson Fisher Boults Larder Spink
Weisner: Subs used - Bloem McDonald Law Reid:
Tries - Black(2) Spink Blackwood Weisner Reid:
Goals - Corcoran(2) Bloem(2) Weisner:
Referee P Bentham (Warrington) Att - 4941 H.T. 22 - 6

**Sun 4 Sep 2005 FEATHERSTONE ROVERS home
won 40 - 6**
CASTLEFORD - Platt: Pryce Eager Hepworth Shenton:
Davis Henderson A Watene A Smith Huby Haughey
Crouch Bird: Subs used - Blanch A Kain B Smith F
Watene: Tries - Haughey(2) Shenton Blanch Crouch Pryce
Bird: Goals - Huby(3) A Kain(3):
FEATHERSTONE R - Moss: Ford Batty Newlove Powell:
Brambani Finn: Tonks Nicholson Dickens Hayes Houston
Dooler: Subs used - P Hughes Evans Lowe Kay:
Try - Moss: Goal - Finn:
Referee M Dawber (Wigan) Att - 5943 H.T. 14 - 2:

Sun 11 Sep 2005 BATLEY BULLDOGS away won 54 -12
CASTLEFORD - Platt: Pryce Eager Hepworth Blanch: Davis
Henderson: A Watene A Smith Huby Haughey Crouch
Bird: Subs used - A Kain Jordan James Fletcher F Watene:
Tries - Haughey(3) A Watene(2) Pryce A Kain James
Hepworth Davis: Goals - Huby(5) Fletcher(2):
BATLEY B - Lingard: Stokes Marsh Jones Sibson: Gallagher
Eaton: Morgan Roden Rourke Spears McClouhlin
Robinson: Subs used - Lythe Shillabeer Berry Richardson:
Tries - Sibson Jones: Goals - Eaton(2):
Referee P Taberner (Wigan) Att - 2230 H.T. 28 - 6

**Sun 25 Sep 2005 WHITEHAVEN away lost 22 - 32
NATIONAL LEAGUE ONE - QUALIFYING SEMI-FINAL**
WHITEHAVEN - Broadbent: Calvert Seeds Nanyn Wilson:
Joe Penny: Tandy Sice Fatialofa Miller Hill Lester:
Subs used - Rudd Summers Chambers Jackson:
Tries - Sice(2) Nanyn(2) Chambers Calvert:
Goals - Nanyn (4):
CASTLEFORD - Platt: Pryce Eager Hepworth Blanch: Davis
Henderson: A Watene A Smith Huby Haughey Crouch
Bird : Subs used - A Kain Vowles Fletcher F Watene:
Tries - Pryce Bird Eager: Goals - Huby(5):
Referee S Ganson (St Helens) Att - 6154 H.T. 18 - 6

**Sun 2 Oct 2005 HALIFAX home won 15 - 12
NATIONAL LEAGUE ONE ELIMINATION SEMI-FINAL**
CASTLEFORD - Platt: Pryce Michael Eager Hepworth
Blanch: Davis Henderson A Watene A Smith Fletcher
Haughey Crouch Bird: Subs used - Handforth Byron
Smith Vowles F Watene: Tries - Platt Blanch:
Goals - Fletcher(2) Crouch HandforthD/G:
HALIFAX - Gibson: Haley Kirk Blackwood Sheriffe: Lawford
Black: Hobson Fisher Boults Larder Ball Weisner:
Subs used - Bloem Spink McDonald Burchall:
Tries - Sheriffe Kirk: Goals - Weisner Bloem;
Referee K Kirkpatrick (Warrington) Att - 6197 H.T. 10 - 2

**Sun 9 Oct 2005 WHITEHAVEN won 36 - 8
NATIONAL LEAGUE ONE GRAND FINAL AT HALTON
STADIUM WIDNES**
CASTLEFORD - Platt: Pryce Shenton Jon Hepworth Blanch:
Davis Henderson: Adam Watene A Smith Fletcher
Haughey Steve Crouch Bird: Subs used - Handforth Huby
Adrian Vowles Frank Watene:
Tries - Davis(2) Huby Crouch Blanch Haughey:
Goals - Fletcher(2) Huby(3) Hepworth:
WHITEHAVEN - Broadbent: Calvert Seeds Nanyn Wilson:
Joe Penny: Tandy Sice Fatialofa Miller Hill Lester:
Tries - Seeds Calvert:
Referee S Ganson (St Helens) Att - 13300 H.T. 26 – 0

Michael Platt
D. No 820
2005 to 2006

Paul Handforth
D. No 822
2005 to 2006

449

SEASON 2005

Adam Watane
D. No 823
2005

Andew Herderson
D. No 824
2005 to 2008

Tommy Haughey
D. No 825
2005 to 2006

Deon Bird
D. No 828
2005 to 2006

Richard Fletcher
D. No 833
2005 to 2006

Ryan Boyle
D. No 840
2005 to 2016

SEASON 2006

Luke Dyer
D. No 844
2006

Viane Gray
D. No 845
2006

Ryan McGoldrick
D. No 846
2006 to 2012

Danny Nutley
D. No 848
2006

Richard Fa'aoso
D. No 850
2006

Danny Ward
D. No 852
2006

450

SEASON 2005

D.N	PLAYER		DEBUT	L MATCH	APP	SLB	T.AP	TRI'S	G'LS	D.G	P'TS
661	SAMPSON	DEAN		13/03/2005	0	1	1	0	0	0	0
739	VOWLES	ADRIAN		09/10/2005	0	3	3	0	0	0	0
746	DAVIS	BRAD			22	1	23	12	7	0	62
756	EAGER	MICHAEL		02/10/2005	8	0	8	2	0	0	8
770	PRYCE	WAINE			28	0	28	31	0	0	124
799	HEPWORTH	JON		09/10/2005	25	1	26	14	1	0	58
800	HUBY	CRAIG			17	8	25	13	85	0	222
809	BRAMBANI	DOMINIC		10/04/2005	1	3	4	0	0	0	0
810	SHENTON	MICHAEL			29	0	29	24	0	0	96
811	SMITH	BYRON		02/10/2005	8	17	25	0	0	0	0
812	WORRINCY	ROB		25/03/2005	0	1	1	0	0	0	0
813	KAIN	ANDY			20	6	26	14	35	2	128
819	CROUCH	STEVE		09/10/2005	28	1	29	6	1	0	26
820	PLATT	MICHAEL	13/02/2005		28	0	28	16	0	0	64
821	REID	DAMIEN	13/02/2005	10/07/2005	15	1	16	9	0	0	36
822	HANDFORTH	PAUL	13/02/2005		15	7	22	4	21	1	59
823	WATENE	ADAM	13/02/2005	09/10/2005	26	2	28	6	0	0	24
824	HENDERSON	ANDREW	13/02/2005		31	0	31	7	0	0	28
825	HAUGHEY	TOMMY	13/02/2005		26	4	30	18	0	0	72
826	SMITH	AARON	13/02/2005		23	0	23	1	0	0	4
827	WATENE	FRANK	13/02/2005	09/10/2005	7	17	24	5	0	0	20
828	BIRD	DEON	13/02/2005		20	2	22	10	0	0	40
829	COOKE	LEIGH	13/02/2005	10/04/2005	1	7	8	0	0	0	0
830	JAMES	JORDAN	27/02/2005	11/09/2005	8	14	22	9	0	0	36
831	ROBINSON	TIM	06/03/2005	17/04/2005	2	2	4	2	0	0	8
832	ENGLAND	ANTHONY	06/03/2005	13/03/2005	0	2	2	0	0	0	0
833	KNOWLES	MICHAEL	06/03/2005		0	3	3	0	0	0	0
834	KAIN	STUART	13/03/2005	24/07/2005	4	1	5	1	0	0	4
835	LUNT	SHAUN	20/03/2005	10/04/2005	1	3	4	0	0	0	0
836	ROWE	ALEX	25/03/2005	17/04/2005	1	3	4	0	0	0	0
837	HAMILTON	LANCE	25/03/2005	03/04/2005	1	1	2	0	0	0	0
838	FLETCHER	RICHARD	15/05/2005		10	5	15	1	13	0	30
839	BAILEY	ANDY	22/05/2005	14/08/2005	7	5	12	1	0	0	4
840	BOYLE	RYAN	26/06/2005		0	1	1	1	1	0	6
841	MALONEY	DOMINIC	10/07/2005	24/07/2005	0	2	2	0	0	0	0
842	MOSSOP	JASON	07/08/2005	07/08/2005	0	1	1	0	0	0	0
843	BLANCH	DAMIEN	21/08/2005		4	2	6	4	0	0	16
	37			24	22	416	127	543	211	164	3	1175

COMPETITION		P	W	D	L	FOR	AGT
N. LEAGUE 1	POSITION 2 OF 10	18	15	0	3	683	368
RL CUP		2	1	0	1	86	33
N.R.C.		9	8	0	1	333	96
PLAY OFF		3	2	0	1	73	52
PLAYERS RECORDS		**32**	**26**	**0**	**6**	**1175**	**549**

Gary Mercer was replaced as Coach by Australian Dave Woods.

With the aim of going straight back to Super League the Club retained a full-time playing squad.

With only three losses in the League, all away from home, at Rochdale, Hull KR and Whitehaven, we finished runners up to Whitehaven who only lost twice. In the National Rail Cup we reached the final losing to Hull KR 16-18.

With the winner of the National League Grand Final being promoted to Super League we lost the qualifying semi-final away at Whitehaven but won through to the Final by beating Halifax at home in the Elimination semi-final. The Final, played at Widnes, was against Whitehaven who were 2-1 up in victories against us. But with a stunning team performance and a brilliant Man of the Match 2-try display from Brad Davies we ran out convincing winners 36–8 to win promotion back to Super League, the Club's aim achieved.

Graig Huby scored 30 points in a National League One game. Barrow Raiders at home on the 31 July 2005

Andy Kane won the National League One Young Player of the Year Award.

A notable Debutant was Andrew Henderson

SEASON 2006

SUPER LEAGUE XI

In Super League the bottom two Widnes Vikings and Leigh Centurions were relegated, they were replaced by promoted Castleford Tigers and newly admitted French Team Catalan Dragons.

Mon 26 Dec 2005 FEATHERSTONE ROVERS home won 28 – 4 FRIENDLY
CASTLEFORD - S Kain: Blanch Shenton Mossop Goodacre: A Kain Handforth: Fletcher Henderson Boyle England Whitaker Edwards: Subs used - Brambani Knowles Payne Lee Maloney Wood: Tries - A Kain(2) Handforth Goodacre Shenton: Goals - Fletcher(3) A Kain:
FEATHERSTONE R - Moss: Mchugh Shillabeer Swinson Close: C Hughes Fawcett: Houston P Hughes Dickens Dooler Carlton Nicholson: Subs used - Kay Larvin Hickman Wray Batty Ellery Sutcliffe Fowler: Try - Sutcliffe:
Referee J Leahy (Dewsbury) Att - 3546 H.T. 12 - 0

Sun 22 Jan 2006 WAKEFIELD TRINITY WILDCATS home won 33 – 20 FRIENDLY
CASTLEFORD - Bird: Pryce Shenton Dyer Blanch: A Kain Handforth: Fletcher Henderson Nutley Whitaker Huby Sculthorpe: Subs used - Manu Mason Fa'aoso Viane B Smith: Tries - Dyer(2) Pryce(2) Shenton(2) Blanch: Goals - Huby A Kain Handforth D/G:
WAKEFIELD T W - Halfpenny: Buchanan Demetriou King Tadulala: Jeffries Speake: Korkidas March McGillivray Elima Ferguson Applegarth:
Subs used - MacDonald Gledhill Samuels Cawthray Walkin Dobek Burnett Mockford Horsefield:
Tries - Demetriou(2) Tadulala Buchanan: Goals - March(2):
Referee R Silverwood (Dewsbury) Att - 4828 H T. 16 - 16

Sun 29 Jan 2006 HUDDERSFIELS GIANTS home lost 22 – 24 FRIENDLY
CASTLEFORD - Bird: Pryce Shenton Dyer Blanch: A Kain Handforth: Mason Henderson Nutley Haughey Fa'aoso Roarty:
Subs used - Huby Fletcher Whitaker McGoldrick Viane:
Tries - Roarty Fletcher A Kain Blanch: Goals Huby(3):
HUDDERSFIELD G - Donlan: Gardner Torrens Aspinwall De Vere: Thorman Paul: McDonald Drew Jackson P Smith Snitch Jones Subs used - Fagborun, March, Nero, Grayson, Raleigh Tries - McDonald Thorman Gardner Paul Drew: Goals - De Vere(2):
Referee P Bentham (Warrington) Att - 3889 H.T. 6 - 10

Fri 10 Feb 2006 HULL F C home lost 18 - 42
CASTLEFORD - Bird: Blanch LUKE DYER(844) GRAY VIANE(845) Shenton: RYAN McGOLDRICK(846) A Kain: DANNY SCULTHORPE(847) Henderson DANNY NUTLEY(848) MATT WHITAKER(849) RICHARD FA'AOSO(850) BEN ROARTY(851): Subs used - DANNY WARD(852) A Smith R Fletcher KEITH MASON(853):
Tries - Viane(2) Fa'aoso McGoldrick: Goals - R Fletcher:
HULL FC - Briscoe: Tony Whiting Yeaman Raynor: Horne Brough: Dowes Swain King Radford Domic Cooke:
Subs used - Carvell Thackray Lupton Blacklock:

Tries - Yeaman(2) Domic Briscoe Cooke Blacklock Raynor Lupton: Goals - Brough(3) Cooke(2):
Referee K Kirkpatrick (War'gton) Att - 10188 H.T. 6 - 18

Fri 17 Feb 2006 ST HELENS away lost 8 - 44
ST HELENS - Wellens: Gardner Lyon Talau Meli: Pryce Long: Fozzard Cunningham Cayless Gilmour Sculthorpe Hooper: Subs used - Roby V Anderson Graham Fa'asavalu: Tries - Gardner Talau Meli Long Wellens Fa'asavalu Gragam Hooper: Goals - Lyon(6):
CASTLEFORD - Platt: Blanch Dyer Viane Shenton: McGoldrick A Kain: Ward Henderson Nutley Fa'aoso Roarty Bird: Subs used - Sculthorpe Huby R Fletcher Arron Smith: Tries - A Kain Viane:
Referee R Laughton (Barnsley) Att - 13528 H.T. 0 - 32

Sun 26 Feb 2006 CATALAN DRAGONS home won 34 - 28
CASTLEFORD - Platt: Pryce Viane Shenton Dyer: McGoldrick A Kain: Sculthorpe Henderson Nutley R Fletcher Huby Roarty: Subs used – Mason Bird Haughey Handforth: Tries - Viane(3) Pryce Huby R Fletcher Shenton: Goals - Huby(2) A Kain:
CATALAN D - Hughes: Murphy Wilson Guigue Verges: Rudder Frayssinous: Beattie Rinaldi Fellous Fakir Guisset Hindmarsh: Subs used - Bosc Chan Touxagas Mouins: Tries - Fakir Bosc Beattie Guigue Wilson: Goals - Frayssinous(4):
Referee S Ganson (St Helens) Att - 5852 H.T. 10 - 22

Sun 5 Mar 2006 LEEDS RHINOS away lost 14 - 66
LEEDS R - Mathers: Donald Walker Senior Williams: McGuire Burrow: Bailey Diskin Peacock Lauitiiti Poching Sinfield: Subs used - Feather Kirke Ablett Millard: Tries - Walker (3) Burrow(2) Poching Kirke McGuire Mathers Lauitiiti Bailey: Goals - Sinfield (11):
CASTLEFORD - Platt: Pryce Shenton Viane Dyer: McGoldrick Handforth: Sculthorpe Henderson Nutley Huby Whitaker Haughey:
Subs used - Bird A Kain Blanch Boyle:
Tries - Haughey McGoldrick: Goals - Huby(3):
Referee P Bentham (Warrington) Att - 16660 H.T. 8 - 42

Sun 12 Mar 2006 HARLEQUINS away won 34 - 20
HARLEQUINS - Clubb: Gafa Luisi Smith Brasley-Qalilawa: Dorn Leuluai: Tookey Weisner Heckenberg Purdham Hopkins Temata:
Subs used - Williams Haumono Mills Lolohea:
Tries - Hopkins(2) Clubb Leuluai: Goals - Gafa(2):
CASTLEFORD - Platt: Pryce Viane Bird Shenton: McGoldrick A Kain: Sculthorpe Henderson Nutley R Fletcher Whitaker Fa'aoso: Subs used - Handforth Huby Ward Dyer: Tries - Pryce McGoldrick Sculthorpe Shenton R Fletcher Henderson: Goals - Huby(5):
Referee S Ganson (St Helens) Att - 3535 H.T. 16 - 20

SEASON 2006

**Sun 19 Mar 2006 WIGAN WARRIORS home
won 38 - 18**
CASTLEFORD - Platt: Pryce Bird Viane Shenton:
McGoldrick A Kain: Sculthorpe Henderson Nutley Fa'aoso
Whitaker R Fletcher: Subs used - Handforth Dyer Ward
WILLIE MANU(854): Tries - Pryce(2) Platt Handforth
Fa'aoso A Kain: Goals A Kain(6) Handforth:
WIGAN W - Ashton: Calderwood Richards Brown Dallas:
Orr Moran: Logan Higham Hargreaves Hansen Prescott
O'Loughlin: Subs used - Fletcher Seuseu Tickle Godwin:
Tries - O'Loughlin(2) Richards: Goals - Tickle(2) Orr:
Referee P Bentham (Warrington) Att - 9021 H.T. 6 - 12

**Sun 26 Mar 2006 HUDDERSFIELD GIANTS home
lost 22 - 36**
CASTLEFORD - Platt: Shenton Bird Viane Dyer:
McGoldrick A Kain: Ward Henderson Nutley Whitaker
Huby R Fletcher: Subs used - Manu Roarty Handforth
GRANT EDWARDS(855) Tries - Manu(2) Dyer Bird:
Goals - A Kain(2) Huby:
HUDDERSFIELD G - Reilly: Donlan Evans Torrens Gardner:
Thorman Paul: Crabtree Drew Jackson Nero Jones Wild:
Subs used - Snitch March McDonald Raleigh:
Tries - Wild(2) Drew Evans Reilly Snitch:
 Goals - Thorman(6):
Referee S Ganson (St Helens) Att - 6881 H.T. 14 - 22

**Sun 2 Apr 2006 WIDNES VIKINGS away lost 4 - 14
R.L. CHALLENGE CUP 3RD ROUND**
WIDNES - Peachey: Dodd Cardiss Nanyn Onyango: Coyle
Durbin: O'Connor Beswick McDermott Cassidy Allen
Smith: Subs used - Summers Heaton Reid Nash:
Tries - Peachey(2):   Goals - Nanyn(3):
CASTLEFORD - Platt: Blanch Dyer Bird Shenton:
McGoldrick A Kain: Fa'aoso Handforth Whitaker Manu
Knowles Haughey: Subs used - Henderson Huby Edwards
Boyle: Try - Haughey:
Referee A Klein (Keighley) Att - 4205 H.T. 4 - 8

**Sat 8 Apr 2006 CATALAN DRAGONS away
lost 14 – 51 At CARCASSONNE**
CATALAN D - Bosc: Murphy Wilson Hughes Verges:
Rudder Dobson: Beattie Rinaldi Guissett Fakir Hindmarsh
Mounis: Subs used - Chan Fellous Berthezene Guigue:
Tries - Verges(3) Guissett(2) Hughes(2) Bosc Murphy:
Goals - Dobson(7) D/G(1):
CASTLEFORD - Platt: Shenton Bird Viane Dyer:
McGoldrick A Kain: Ward Henderson Nutley Fa'aoso
Manu Whitaker:
Subs used - Haughey Handforth R Fletcher Roarty:
Tries - Platt Roarty Dyer: Goal - A Kain:
Referee R Silverwood (Dewsbury) Att - 6109 H.T. 10 - 20

**Fri 14 Apr 2006 WAKEFIELD TRINITY WILDCATS
away lost 26 - 34**
WAKEFIELD T W - Halpenny: Buchanan Demetriou Atkins
Tadulala: Rooney Jeffries: McGillivray Obst Korkidas Elima
Solomona Betham: Sub used - Griffin Field White Catic:
Tries - Solomona Halpenny Atkins Griffin Jeffries White:
Goals - Rooney(5):

CASTLEFORD - Bird: Pryce Shenton Viane Dyer:
McGoldrick Davis: Ward Henderson Nutley Manu R
Fletcher Whitaker:
Subs used - Handforth Roarty PAUL FRANZE(856)
Fa'aoso: Tries - Shenton R Fletcher Pryce Dyer Bird:
Goals - R Fletcher(3):
Referee A Klein (Keighley) Att - 8237 H.T. 16 - 24

**Mon 17 Apr 2006 WARRINGTON WOLVES home
lost 6 - 64**
CASTLEFORD - Platt: Dyer Franze Viane Pryce: McGoldrick
Davis: Ward Henderson Nutley Fa'aoso Manu Bird:
Subs used - A Kain Roarty Huby Whitaker:
Try - Platt: Goal - McGoldrick:
WARRINGTON W - Grose: Fa'afili Martin Gleeson Kohe-
Love Reardon Briers Sullivan: Leikvoll Mark Gleeson
Wood Swann Wainwright Noone:
Subs used - Clarke Rauhihi Parker Grix:
Tries - Fa'afili(2) Martin Gleeson(2) Kohe-Love Clarke
Sillivan Briers Wood Rauhihi Parker: Goals - Briers(10):
Referee R Silverwood (Dewsbury) Att - 5681 H.T. 6 - 28

Fri 21 Apr 2006 LEEDS RHINOS away lost 6 - 42
LEEDS R - Mathers: Donald Gibson Senior Williams:
McGuire Burrow: Bailey Diskin Peacock Jones-Buchanan
Lauitiiti Ellis: Subs used - Tansey Scruton Kirke O'Neill:
Tries - Diskin(2) Senior(2) Ellis Peacock Donald McGuire
Gibson: Goals - Gibson(3):
CASTLEFORD - Platt: Pryce Bird Paul Franze Dyer:
McGoldrick Davis: Ward Henderson Nutley Manu
Whitaker Roarty: Subs used - Fa'aoso Huby Tommy
Haughey A Kain: Try - Platt: Goal - McGoldrick:
Referee R Laughton (Barnsley) Att - 14054 H.T. 6 - 16

**Sun 31 Apr 2006 SALFORD CITY REDS home
won 28 - 26**
CASTLEFORD - Platt: Dyer McGoldrick Shenton Pryce:
PETER LUPTON(857) Davis: Fa'aoso Henderson Nutley
Roarty Manu Bird: Subs used - Ward Huby Viane Blanch:
Tries - Roarty Davis Fa'aoso Nutley Viane Manu:
Goals - Huby(2):
SALFORD C R - Fitzpatrick: Hodgson Langi Moule
Wishere: Dunemann Robinson: Coley Alker Baldwin Littler
Brockelhurst Finnigan: Subs used - Charles Clayton
Haggerty Myler: Tries - Finnigan Moule Wilshere
Hodgson Langi: Goals - Wilshere(3):
Referee P Bentham (Warrington) Att - 6069 H.T. 8 - 16

Fri 5 May 2006 WIGAN WARRIORS away won 30 - 24
WIGAN W - Ashton: Calderwood Goulding McAvoy
Richards: Orr Moran: Logan Godwin Seuseu Tickle
Fletcherr O'Loughlin: Subs used - Paleaaesina Hargreaves
Higham James: Tries - Higham(2) Calderwood McAvoy:
Goals - Richards(3) Tickle:
CASTLEFORD - Platt: Pryce Shenton McGoldrick Dyer:
Lupton Davis: Fa'aoso Henderson Nutley Roarty Manu
Bird:Subs used - Ward Huby Viane Handforth:
Tries - Platt(2) Viane Davis Handforth Manu:
Goals - Davis(2) Huby:
Referee K Kirkpatrick (War'gton) Att - 12484 H.T. 22 - 12

453

SEASON 2006

Sun 14 May 2006 CATALAN DRAGONS home lost 18 - 40

CASTLEFORD - Platt: Dyer Shenton McGoldrick Pryce: Lupton Davis: Fa'aoso Henderson Nutley Manu Roarty Bird: Subs used - Handforth Viane Huby Ward: Tries - Viane(2) Nutley: Goals - McGoldrick(3): CATALAN D - Guigue: Murphy Wilson Hughes Varges: Frayssinous Dobson: Fellous Rinaldi Guisset Hindmarsh Rudder Jamby: Subs used - Cologni Chan Mounis Beattie: Tries - Wilson(3) Hindmarsh Dobson Murphy Cologni: Goals - Dobson(6): Referee K Kirkpatrick (Warrington) Att - 6024 H.T. 6 - 12

Sun 28 May 2006 WARRINGTON WOLVES away lost 28 - 46

WARRINGTON W - Reardon: Fa'afili Martin Gleeson Grose Barnett: Briers Sullivan: Wood Clarke Hilton Swann Wainwright Westwood: Subs used - Mark Gleeson Lima Grix Pickersgill: Tries - Grose (2) Fa'afili Swann Clarke Barnett Wood Briers: Goals - Briers(7): CASTLEFORD - Platt: Pryce Shenton Bird <u>Damien Blanch</u>: McGoldrick Lupton: Ward Henderson Nutley Sculthorpe Manu Huby: Subs used - Handforth <u>Matthew Whitaker</u> Viane Fa'aoso: Tries - Shenton(2) Lupton Bird Sculthorpe: Goals - Huby (3): McGoldrick Referee R Laughton (Barnsley) Att - 9508 H.T. 6 - 26

Sun 11 Jun 2006 BRADFORD BULLS home draw 26 -26

CASTLEFORD - Platt: Pryce Viane Bird Shenton: McGoldrick Lupton: Sculthorpe Henderson Nutley Ward Manu R Fletcher: Subs used - Handforth Huby Fa'aoso ADAM FLETCHER(858):   Tries - Pryce(2) Manu Sculthorpe Shenton: Goals McGoldrick(2) Huby: BRADFORD B - Withers: Vainikolo Hape Harris St Hilaire: Harris Deacon: Fielden Newton Lynch Meyers McvKenna Langley: Subs used - Gene Henderson Ferres Vagana: Tries - Newton(2) Withers Deacon Hape: Goals Deacon(3): Referee P Taberner (Wigan) Att - 7600 H.T. 16 - 12

Sun 18 Jun 2006 HUDDERSFIELD GIANTS home won 32 - 14

CASTLEFORD - Platt: Pryce Viane McGoldrick Shenton: Lupton DANNY BROUGH(859): Sculthorpe Henderson Nutley Ward Manu R Fletcher: Subs used - Huby Roarty Fa'aoso A Fletcher: Tries - Pryce(2) Viane(2) Ward A Fletcher: Goals - Brough(4): HUDDERSFIELD G - Reilly: Gardner Wild Nero Donlan: Thorman Paul: Mason Drew Jackson Smith Raleigh Jones: Subs used - Crabtree Snitch McDonald Hemingway: Tries - Donlan(2) Smith: Goals - Thorman: Referee P Bentham (Warrington) Att - 6502 H.T. 18 - 14:

Fri 23 Jun 2006 HULL F C away lost 10 - 28

HULL FC - Tony: Blacklock Domic Whiting Raynor: Cooke R Horne: Dowes Swain Carvell Radford McMenemy Washbrook: Subs used - G Horne King Wheeldon Lee: Tries - Tony R Horne Domic Lee Blacklock: Goals - Cooke(4): CASTLEFORD - Platt: Pryce Viane McGoldrick Shenton: Lupton Brough: Sculthorpe Henderson Nutley Ward

Nutley Roarty: Subs used - Handforth Huby Fa'aoso A Fletcher: Tries - Henderson Fa'aoso: Goal - Brough: Referee A Klein (Keighley) Att 11360 H.T. 6 - 18

Sun 2 Jul 2006 WARRINGTON WOLVES home won 52 - 26

CASTLEFORD - Platt: Pryce Viane Shenton A Fletcher: McGoldrickS/O Brough: Sculthorpe Henderson Nutley Manu Roarty Lupton: Subs used - Handforth Huby Fa'aoso Ward: Tries - Lupton(2) Pryce Manu Brough Fa'aoso Platt A Fletcher Shenton: Goals - Brough(8): WARRINGTON W - Reardon: Fa'fili Kohe-Love Gleeson Grose: Briers Grix: Leikvoll Sullivan WoodsS/O Westwood Wainwright Parker: Subs used - Noone Pickersgill Bracek Cooper: Tries - Parker Grose Reardon Sullivan Cooper: Goals - Briers(3): Referee S Ganson (St Helens) Att - 5411 H.T. 28 - 14

Sat 8 Jul 2006 HARLEQUINS away lost 16 - 24

HARLEQUINS - McLinden: Smith Gafa Luisi Bradley-Qalilawa: Paul Weisner: Mills Randall Heckenberg Purdham Hopkins Mbu: Subs used - Tookey Lolohea Budworth McCarthy-Scarsbrook: Tries - McLinden(2) Hopkins Randall: Goals - Paul(4): CASTLEFORD - Platt: <u>Waine Pryce</u> Viane Shenton A Fletcher: Lupton Brough: Sculthorpe Henderson Nutley R Fletcher Ward Roarty: Subs used - Fa'aoso Manu Huby Handforth: Tries - Manu Huby Viane: Goals - Brough(2): Referee R Laughton (Barnsley) Att -3656 H.T. 4 - 18

Sun 16 Jul 2006 LEEDS RHINOS home won 31 - 30

CASTLEFORD - Platt: A Fletcher Shenton Viane Dyer: McGoldrick Brough: Sculthorpe Henderson Nutley Manu Ward Lupton: Subs used - Huby Fa'aoso Roarty R Fletcher: Tries - A Fletcher(2) Ward Shenton McGoldrick: Goals - Brough(5) D/G LEEDS R - Smith: Donald Walker Senior Williams: McGuire Burrow: Jones-Buchanan Millard Scruton Peacock Poching Lauititi: Subs used - Diskin Bailey Gibson O'Neill: Tries - McGuire(2) Burrow Donald Millard: Goals - Burrow(5): Referee K Kirkpatrick (Warr'ton) Att - 11016 H.T. 14 - 12

Sun 23 Jul 2006 HUDDERSFIELD GIANTS away lost 10 - 34

HUDDERSFIELD G - Reilly: Aspinwall Brown De Vere Donlan: Thorman Paul: Jackson Drew Gannon Nero Jones Wild: Subs used - Crabtree Snitch Mason Raleigh: Tries - Drew Brown Raleigh Gannon Nero Aspinwall: Goals - De Vere(4) Reilly: CASTLEFORD - Platt: A Fletcher Shenton Viane Dyer: McGoldrick BroughS/O: Sculthorpe Henderson Nutley R Fletcher Ward <u>Ben Roarty</u>: Subs used - Huby Fa'aoso Manu Bird: Tries - A Fletcher Bird: Goals - Brough: Referee J Leaghy (Dewsbury) Att - 5573 H.T. 10 - 12

SEASON 2006

Sat 5 Aug 2006 WAKEFIELD TRINITY WILDCATS home lost 0 - 18
CASTLEFORD - Platt: A Fletcher Shenton Viane Bird: McGoldrick Lupton: Sculthorpe Henderson Nutley Manu Ward R Fletcher:
Subs used - Handforth A Kain Huby Fa'aoso:
WAKEFIELD T W - Halfpenny: Demetriou Evans Atkins Tadulala: Rooney Jeffries: Korkidas March Watene Solomona MacGillvray BethamS/O:
Subs used - Obst Elima CaticS/O Saxton:
Tries - Tadulala Halfpenny Evans Saxton: Goals - Rooney:
Referee R Silverwood (Dewsbury) Att - 7205 H.T.0 - 4

Sun 13 Aug 2006 SAINT HELENS home lost 4 - 72
CASTLEFORD - Platt: A Fletcher Viane Shenton Bird: McGoldrick Handforth: Sculthorpe Henderson Nutley Manu R Fletcher JASON PAYNE(860): Subs used – Andy Kain Grant Edwards Huby Fa'aoso: T ry - Viane:
ST HELENS - Wellens: Gardner Lyon Talua Meli: Pryce Long: Cayless Cunningham P Anderson Sculthorpe Wilkin Hooper: Subs used - Fa'asavalu Fozzard Roby V Anderson: T ries - Wellens(2) Lyon(2) Long(2) Wilkin Talu Sculthorpe Fa'asavalu Cayless Roby: Goals - Lyon(12):
Referee K Kirkpatrick (War'ton) Att - 6369 H.T. 0 - 36

Fri 18 Aug 2006 BADFORD BULLS away lost 10 - 48
BRADFORD B - Withers: Vainakolo Hape B Harris Bai: I Harris Deacon: Vagana Henderson Lynch McKenna Ferres Langley: Subs used - Cook Meyers Gene Pryce:
Tries - B Harris(2) Pryce(2) Vainikolo Mckenna Ferres Gene Meyers: Goals - Deacon(6):
CASTLEFORD - Platt: A Fletcher Viane Shenton Bird: McGoldrick Brough: Ward Hennderson: Nutley Manu Fa'aoso Lupton: Subs used - Huby Knowles Payne Paul Handforth: Tries - Bird A Fletcher: Goal - Brough:
Referee R Silverwood (Dewsbury) Att - 10576 H.T. 4 - 18

Sat 2 Sep 2006 HARLEQUINS home won 27 - 12
CASTLEFORD - Platt: A Fletcher Shenton McGoldrick Dyer: Lupton Brough: Sculthorpe Henderson Nutley Manu Ward R Fletcher Subs used - Bird Viane Fa'aoso Davis:
Tries - Dyer McGoldrick Lupton Manu A Fletcher:
Goals - Brough(3) SculthorpeD/G:
HARLEQUINS - McLinden: Stewart Luisi Smith Bradley-Qalilawa: Sykes Dorn: Heckenberg Randall Mills Hopkins Purdham Paul: Subs used - Budworth Haumono Williams Noone: Tries - Sykes Williams: Goals - Sykes(2):
Referee P Bentham (Warrington) Att - 5531 H.T. 16 - 12

Fri 8 Sep 2006 SALFORD CITY REDS away lost 16 - 26
SALFORD C R - Hodgson: Williams McGuinness Moule Wishere: Dunemann Robinson: Coley Alker Rutgerson Littler Brocklehurst Finnigan: Subs used - Adamson Charles Highton Haggerty: Tries - Alker Williams Robinson Coley Hodgson: Goals - Charles(2) Hodgson:
CASTLEFORD - Platt: A Fletcher Shenton McGoldrick Dyer: Lupton Brough: Sculthorpe Henderson Nutley Manu Ward R Fletcher: Subs used - Bird Viane Fa'aoso Davis:
Tries - Dyer Sculthorpe: Goals - Brough(4):
Referee K Kirkpatrick (Warrington) Att - 6106 H.T. 14 - 8

Sat 16 Sep 2006 WAKEFIELD TRINITY WILDCATS away lost 17 - 29
WAKEFIELD T W - Halpenny: Demetriou Evans Henderson Tadulala: Rooney Jeffries: Korkidas Obst Watene MacGillivray Solomona Betham: Subs used - Catic Latu March Elima: Tries - Evans(2) Demetriou Betham Henderson: Goals - Rooney(4) D/G:
CASTLEFORD – Michael Platt: Fletcher Shenton McGoldrick Luke Dyer: Lupton Brough: Danny Sculthorpe Henderson Danny Nutley Willie Manu Danny Ward Richard Fletcher: Subs used – Deon Bird Gray Viane Richard Fa'aoso Brad Davis:
Tries - Manu A Fletcher Nutley: Goals - Brough(2) D/G:
Referee R Silverwood (Dewsbury) Att -11000 H.T. 11 - 14:

Fri 20 October 2006 MANLY WARRINGAH DISTRICT SELECT home won 36 – 6 FRIENDLY
CASTLEFORD – SCORERS
Tries - Richard Owen(3) Eddie Croft(3) Ryan Boyle:
Goals - Graic Huby :(3) Terry Matterson   Att 1803
Teams and Manly Scorers not Known

Willie Manu
D. No 854
2006

Peter Lupton
D. No 857
2006 to 2008

Adam Fletcher
D No 858
2006 to 2008

Danny Brough
D. No 859
2006 to 2007

SEASON 2006

D.N	PLAYER		DEBUT	L MATCH	APP	SUB	T.AP	TRI'S	G'LS	D.G	P'TS
746	DAVIS	BRAD		16/09/2006	6	3	9	2	2	0	12
770	PRYCE	WAINE		08/07/2006	16	0	16	10	0	0	40
800	HUBY	CRAIG			4	18	22	2	18	0	44
810	SHENTON	MICHAEL			27	0	27	8	0	0	32
813	KAIN	ANDY		13/08/2006	8	5	13	2	10	0	28
820	PLATT	MICHAEL		16/09/2006	27	0	27	7	0	0	28
822	HANDFORTH	PAUL		18/08/2006	3	15	18	2	1	0	10
824	HENDERSON	ANDREW			28	1	29	2	0	0	8
825	HAUGHEY	TOMMY		21/04/2006	2	3	5	2	0	0	8
826	SMITH	AARON		17/02/2006	0	2	2	0	0	0	0
828	BIRD	DEON		16/09/2006	18	6	24	5	0	0	20
833	KNOWLES	MICHAEL			1	1	2	0	0	0	0
838	FLETCHER	RICHARD		16/09/2006	14	4	18	3	4	0	20
840	BOYLE	RYAN			0	2	2	0	0	0	0
843	BLANCH	DAMIEN		28/05/2006	4	2	6	0	0	0	0
844	DYER	LUKE	10/02/2006	16/09/2006	18	2	20	5	0	0	20
845	VIANE	GRAY	10/02/2006	16/09/2006	20	7	27	14	0	0	56
846	McGOLDRICK	RYAN	10/02/2006		28	0	28	5	8	0	36
847	SCULTHORPE	DANNY	10/02/2006	16/09/2006	18	1	19	4	0	1	17
848	NUTLEY	DANNY	10/02/2006	16/09/2006	28	0	28	3	0	0	12
849	WHITAKER	MATTHEW	10/02/2006	28/05/2006	9	2	11	0	0	0	0
850	FA'AOSO	RICHARD	10/02/2006	16/09/2006	11	15	26	5	0	0	20
851	ROARTY	BEN	10/02/2006	23/07/2006	11	6	17	2	0	0	8
852	WARD	DANNY	10/02/2006	16/09/2006	18	7	25	2	0	0	8
853	MASON	KEITH	10/02/2006	26/02/2006	0	2	2	0	0	0	0
854	MANU	WILLIE	19/03/2006	16/09/2006	20	4	24	9	0	0	36
855	EDWARDS	GRANT	26/03/2006	13/08/2006	0	3	3	0	0	0	0
856	FRANZE	PAUL	14/04/2006	21/04/2006	2	1	3	0	0	0	0
857	LUPTON	PETER	31/4/2006		15	0	15	4	0	0	16
858	FLETCHER	ADAM	11/06/2006		10	3	13	8	0	0	32
859	BROUGH	DANNY	18/06/2006		10	0	10	1	31	2	68
860	PAYNE	JASON	13/08/2006		1	1	2	0	0	0	0
	32		**17**	**22**	**377**	**116**	**493**	**107**	**74**	**3**	**579**

COMPETITION		P	W	D	L	FOR	AGT
S. LEAGUE	POS TION 11 OF 12	28	9	1	18	575	968
RL CUP		1	0	0	1	4	14
PLAYERS RECORDS		**29**	**9**	**1**	**19**	**579**	**982**

Coach Dave Woods who led the team to promotion was replaced by former Australian International and London Broncos Captain Terry Matterson.

We were battling relegation all season alongside Wigan and Wakefield. However, Wigan bought themselves out of trouble by replacing Coach Ian Millward with Brian Noble and signing Michael Dobson and Stuart Fielding for £450,000 a Super League record fee. Wigan finished on 22 points to our 19. However, they were deducted four league points in 2007 for breaching the salary cap in 2006.

Wakefield beat us at home on 5 August 0-18 despite having two men sent off. They then repeated the victory at home in the last game of the season, in a 'winner takes all' match.

Thus we finished second from bottom with only one team to be relegated. However the bottom team, Catalan Dragons on 16 points, had been given a two-year dispensation from relegation therefore we were relegated back to National League 1.

SEASON 2007

CO-OPERATIVE NATIONAL LEAGUE 1

Castleford relegated to National League 1, Dewsbury Rams and Sheffield Eagles promoted from Division 2, York City Knights and Oldham Roughyeds relegated to Division 2. This Resulted in a Ten Team League – Batley Bulldogs Castleford Tigers Dewsbury Rams Doncaster Lakers Halifax Leigh Centurions Sheffield Eagles Widnes Vikings Whitehaven.

Tue 26 Dec 2006 FEATHERSTONE ROVERS home lost 8 – 14 FRIENDLY

CASTLEFORD - Owen: Wainwright Dixon M Shenton Jones: Westerman Croft: Higgins Lee Huby Barker Payne Clayton: Subs used - Boyle Knowles A Shenton Cording Kelly Bassinder Duckworth Watts Bryan Massey: Tries - Dixon M Shenton:
FEATHERSTONE R - Moss: Kirmond Whittle Cardoza Wynne: P Handforth Ross: G Handforth Hughes Dickens Field Haughey Blakeway: Subs used - Speake Dye Cawthray Fowler Benn Eadie Binks Dooler: Tries - Kirmond Cardoza Benn: Goal - Dickens: Referee P Bentham (Warrington) Att - 3874 H.T. 0 - 10

Fri 26 Jan 2007 YORK CITY KNIGHTS away won 18 - 16 FRIENDLY

YORK C K - Rayner: Waldron Palmer Spurr Godfrey: Liddell Gargan: Cakacaka Wray McDonald Smith Priestley Grundy: Subs used - Esders Williams Helme Hodgson Mapals Watling:
Tries - Godfrey(2) Raynor: Goals - Palmer Gargan:
CASTLEFORD - Owen: A Shenton Jones Bassinder Ripley: Brough Croft: Boyle Johnson Potter Knowles Payne Westerman: Subs used - Lee Massy Bryan Cording Duckworth Turner Watts: Tries - Brough Payne Knowles: Goals - Brough(2) Westerman:
Referee J Leahy (Dewsbury) Att - 1043 H.T. 8 - 0

Sun 28 Jan 2007 DONCASTER LAKERS home won 42 – 18 FRIENDLY

CASTLEFORD - Saxton: Donlan M Shenton Dixon Wainwright: Lupton Brough: Higgins Henderson Huby Guttenbeil Glassie Charles:
Subs used - Leafa Barker Westerman Owen:
Tries - Dixon(2) Glassie(2) Owen(2) Huby M Shenton: Goals - Brough(4) Huby:
DONCASTER - Wildbore: Cuffe Sheriffe Buttery Mills: Holroyd Turner: Garmston Green Lawton Mbu Lowe McLocklan: Subs used - Rowe Benson Scott Gorton Lynn Robinson Castle Colton Endersby Abebesi Leaf Okul: Tries - Sheriffe Mbu Leaf: Goals - Holroyd(2) Turner: Referee I Smith (Oldham) Att - 3536 H.T. 20 - 12

Sun 4 Feb 2007 HULL FC home lost 24 - 30 FRIENDLY

CASTLEFORD - Saxton: Wainwright Dixon M Shenton Donlan Lupton Brough: Higgins Henderson Leafa Guttenbeil Barker Charles: Subs used - Glassie Boyle Payne Knowles Owen Jones Westerman: Tries - Donlan Barker Dixon M Shenton:

Goals - Brough(2) Westerman(2):
HULL FC - Briscoe: Sing Domic Yeaman Hall: Cooke Lee: Dowes Godwin Carvell Radford Tickle Washbrook: Subs used - McMennemy Maiava Wheeldon Dale Whiting Houghton: Tries - Washbrook Lee Wheeldon Whiting Sing: Goals - Cooke(4) Hall:
Referee B Thaler (Wakefield) Att - 4813 H.T. 12 - 0

Sun 11 Feb 2007 DONCASTER LAKERS away won 30 - 6 NORTHERN RAIL CUP - GROUP MATCH

DONCASTER L - Wildbore: Sheriffe Gorton Buttery Mills: Holroyd Turner: Garmston Green Benson Mbu Lowe McLocklan: Subs used - Rowe Lawton Scott Leaf: Try - Wildbore: Goal - Holroyd:
CASTLEFORD - Saxton: MICHAEL WAINWRIGHT(861) STUART DONLAN(862) McGoldrick RICHARD OWEN(863): Lupton Brough: LIAM HIGGINS(864) Henderson TERE GLASSIE(865) AWEN GUTTENBEIL(866) DWAYNE BARKER(867) Charles: Subs used - Huby MARK LEAFA(868) Clayton JOE WESTERMAN(869): Tries - Henderson(2) Saxton Donlan Owen Barker: Goals - Brough(3):
Referee S Ganson (St Helens) Att - 4180 H.T. 20 - 0

Sun 18 Feb 2007 FEATHERSTONE ROVERS home won 48 – 10 NORTHERN RAIL CUP - GROUP MATCH

CASTLEFORD - Saxton: Wainwright KIRK DIXON(870) Donlan Owen: McGoldrick Brough: Higgins Henderson Huby Guttenbeil Leafa Charles: Subs used - Clayton Barker Boyle Westerman: Tries - Donlan(3) Wainwright(2) Charles(2) Saxton Dixon: Goals - Brough(5) Huby:
FEATHERSTONE R - Benn: Kirmond McHugh Whittle Moss: Ross Handforth: Handford P Hughes Dickens Haughey Dooler Blakeway: Subs used - Bower Ward Houston Tonks: Try - Ross: Goals - Dickens(3): Referee K Kirkpatrick (Warrington) Att - 6871 H.T. 10 - 8

Sun 25 Feb 2007 SHEFFIELD EAGLES home won 38 -12 NORTHERN RAIL CUP - GROUP MATCH

CASTLEFORD - Saxton: Wainwright Dixon Donlan Owen: McGoldrick Brough: Huby Henderson Leafa Clayton Barker Westerman: Subs used - Charles Higgins Boyle Knowles: Tries - Saxton Owen Donlan Henderson Brough McGoldrick Boyle: Goals - Brough(5):
SHEFFIELD E - Woodcock: Hurst Reid Newlove Farrow: Crawford Brambani: Howleson Cook Buckenham Aston Corcoran Edwards:
Subs used - Presley Bravo Law Hepworth:
Tries Hurst Corcoran: Goals Brambani(2):
Referee I Leahy (Dewsbury) att - 5108 H.T. 16 - 0

Sun 4 Mar 2007 FEATHERSTONE ROVERS away won 22 – 16 NORTHERN RAIL CUP - GROUP MATCH

FEATHERSTONE R - Larvin: Kimond McHugh Cardoza Moss: Ross Handforth: Handford P Hughes Dickens Dooler Blakeway Haughey:
Subs used - Swinson Tonks Sutton Houston:
Tries - P Hughes McHugh Handforth: Goals - Dickens(2)

457

SEASON 2007

CASTLEFORD - Owen: Wainwright Dixon Clayton Donlan: McGoldrick Brough: Boyle Henderson(S/O) Huby Guttenbeil Barker Charles:
Subs used - Leafa Westerman Payne Knowles:
Tries - Dixon(2) Henderson Charles: Goals - Brough(3):
Referee G Hewer (Whitehaven) Att - 3229 H.T. 20 - 16

Sun 11 Mar 2007 CASTLEFORD LOCK LANE home won 88 – 10 R.L. CHALLENGE CUP 3RD ROUND
CASTLEFORD - Owen: ALEX SHENTON(871) Barker Knowles ADAM JONES(872): McGoldrick EDDIE CROFT(873): Higgins SEAN JOHNSON(874) Boyle Payne Clayton Westerman:
Subs used - MATTHEW DUCKWORTH(875) NATHAN MASSEY(876) LIAM WATTS(877) GRAIG POTTER(878):
Tries - A Shenton(2) Croft(2) Jones(2) Boyle(2) Westerman Owen Barker Clayton Johnson Watts Knowles Duckworth:
Goals - Westerman(12):
LOCK L;ANE - Bolderson: Bassinder Chen Stockton Bettison: Astbury Mawson: Hardy Wilkinson Jeffels Price Tudor Spears: Subs used - Robinson Crouch Rayner Potts: Tries - Bettison Robinson: Goal - Hardy:
Referee J Child (Dewsbury) Att - 3948 H.T. 36 - 4

Fri 16 Mar 2007 SHEFFIELD EAGLERS away won 44 - 6 NORTHERN RAIL CUP - GROUP MATCH
SHEFFIELD E - Woodcock: Hurst Law Reid Ford: Lindsay Brambani: Howleson Cook Ashton Hepworth Trayler Hayes: Subs used - Bravo Buckenham Pickering Stringer:
Try - Lindsay: Goal - Woodcock:
CASTLEFORD - Saxton: Wainwright Dixon M Shenton Donlan: McGoldrick Brough: Higgins Henderson Leafa Clayton Charles Lupton: Subs used - Boyle Barker Knowles Glassie: Tries - Donlan(2) M Shenton(2) Leafa Brough Barker Lupton: Goals - Brough(6):
Referee G Hewer (Whitehaven) Att - 1897 H.T. 22 - 6

Sun 25 Mar 2007 DONCASTER LAKERS home won 64 – 8 NORTHERN RAIL CUP - GROUP MATCH
CASTLEFORD - Saxton: Wainwright Dixon Clayton Owen: McGoldrick Brough: Higgins Henderson Huby Guttenbeil Barker Lupton: Subs used - Glassie Westerman Knowles Johnson: Tries - Wainwright(2) Guttenbeil(2) Owen(2) Saxton Clayton Barker Lupton Dixon Brough:
Goals - Brough(6) Dixon(2):
DONCASTER L - Wildbore: Sheriffe Gorton Buttery Mills: McLocklan Turner: Lawton Green Benson Robinson Mbu Scott: Subs used - Okul Castle Garmston Endersby:
Try - McLocklan: Goals - Wildbore(2):
Referee R Hicks (Oldham) Att - 4613 H.T. 20 - 8

Fri 30 Mar 2007 BRADORD BULLS away lost 16 - 24 R.L. CHALLENGE CUP 4TH ROUND
BRADFORD BULLS - St Hilaire: McAvoy B Harris Evans Vainikolo: I Harris Deacon: Vangana Newton Lynch Solomona McKenna Morrison:
Subs used - Feather Cook Henderson Burgess:
CASTLEFORD - Saxton: Wainwright Dixon M Shenton Donlan: McGoldrick Brough: Higgins Henderson Huby Guttenbeil Charles Lupton:

Subs used - Leafa Glassie Barker Clayton:
Tries - Wainwright M Shenton Lupton: Goals - Brough (2):
Referee A Klein (Keighley) Att - 6748 H.T. 6 - 18

Fri 6 Apr 2007 HALIFAX home won 46 -22
CASTLEFORD - Saxton: Wainwright Dixon Clayton Donlan: McGoldrick Brough: Higgins Henderson Leafa Guttenbeil Barker Charles: Subs used - Glassie Huby Knowles Owen:
Tries - Huby(2) Saxton Clayton Donlan Wainwright McGoldrick Henderson: Goals - Brough(7):
HALIFAX - Gibson: George Hartley Varkulis Greenwood: White Watson: Southern Penkywicz Wrench Larder Roberts Ball: Subs used - Jones Trinder Joseph Watene:
Tries - Jones(2) Greenwood Penkywicz:
Goals - Hartley(3):
Referee R Hicks (Oldham) Att - 6284 H.T. 28 - 6

Thu 12 Apr 2007 DONCASTER LAKERS away won 66 - 4
CASTLEFORD - Saxton: Wainwright Dixon Barker Donlan: McGoldrick Brough: Huby Henderson Leafa Guttenbeil Clayton Charles: Subs used - Higgins Glassie Westerman Owen: Tries - Dixon(3) Brough(2) Donlan(2) Charles Henderson McGoldrick Barker Wainwright Huby:
Goals - Brough(6) Dixon:
DONCASTER L - Wildbore: Mills Gorton Andrews Sheriffe: McLocklan Penny: Mbu Green Tandy Robinson Lowe Lawton: Subs used - Adebisi Rowe Castle Garmston:
Try - Lowe
Referee J Leahy (Dewsbury) Att - 6528 H.T. 30 - 0

Sun 15 Apr 2007 BATLEY BULLDOGS home won 75- 12
CASTLEFORD - Saxton: Wainwright Dixon Clayton Donlan: McGoldrick Brough: Higgins Johnson Glassie Guttenbeil Barker Charles: Subs used - Westerman Owen Huby Leafa: Tries - Donlan(3) Saxton(2) Owen(2) Brough Glassie Charles McGoldrick Dixon Huby:
Goals - Brough(11) McGoldrick D/G:
BATLEY B - Lingard: Clemie Mossop Langley Marns: Paterson Gordon: Rourke Lythe Stenchion Cooke Spears McLoughlin:
Subs used - Lindsay Henderson Menzies Simpson:
Tries - Lingard Chemie: Goals - Gordon(2):
Referree - Mr R Laughton (Barnsley) Att 5223 H.T. 45 - 0

Sun 22 Apr 2007 WORKINGTON TOWN home won 50 – 24 NORTHERN RAIL CUP - QUALIFYING QUARTER FINAL
CASTLEFORD - Saxton: Wainwright Dixon Donlan Owen: McGoldrick Brough: Higgins Johnson Huby Leafa Glassie Barker: Subs used - Boyle Jason Payne Westerman Knowles: Tries - Saxton(2) Knowles(2) Dixon Barker McGoldrick Owen Leafa: Goals - Brough(7):
WORKINGTON T - Lunt: Woodcok Beattie Frazer Davies: Forber Campbell: McGuinness King Burgess Ormesher Miller Purdham:
Subs used - Whitworth Wilson Kmet Robinson:
Tries Forber(2) Kmet Beattie: Goals - Forber(4)
Referee T Albert (France) Att - 3610 H.T. 22 - 12

458

SEASON 2007

Sun 29 Apr 2007 ROCHDALE HORNETS home won 56 - 6
CASTLEFORD - Saxton: Wainwright Dixon M Shenton
Donlan: McGoldrick Brough: Higgins Charles Leafa
Guttenbeil Clayton Lupton:
Subs used - Barker Sean Johnson Glassie Boyle:
Tries - M Shenton(3) Donlan(2) Dixon(2) Higgins
Guttenbeil Barker Saxton: Goals - Brough(6):
ROCHDALE H - Andrews: Johnson Patterson King
Fagborun: Hasty Hulse: Baldwin McConnell Bailey Gorski
Gledhill Golden: Subs used - Robinson Blanchard
Anderson Norman: Try - Hasty: Goal - King:
Referee G Hewer (Whitehaven) Att - 4645 H.T. 20 - 0

Suneday 6 May 2007 LEIGH CENTURIANS away won 32 - 24
LEIGH C - Greenwood: Rivett Couturier Halliwell Alstead:
Ainscough Heremaia: Wilson Butterworth Stevens Taylor
Roberts Stewart: Subs used - Hughes Bemberton Styles
Astley: Tries - Ainscough(2) Greenwood Heremaia:
Goals - Courturier(4):
CASTLEFORD - Saxton Wainwright Dixon M Shenton
Donlan: McGoldrick Brough: Higgins Henderson
Guttenbeil Barker Charles Lupton: Subs used - Owen
Glassie Leafa Boyle: Tries - Lupton(2) Brough Owen
McGoldrick Dixon: Goals - Brough(4):
Referee M Dawber (Wigan) Att - 2753 H.T. 6 - 12

Thu 17 May 2007 WIDNES VIKINGS home lost 20 - 44
CASTLEFORD - Donlan: Wainwright Dixon M Shenton
Owen: McGoldrick Brough: Higgins Henderson Glassie
Guttenbeil Barker Charles:
Subs used - Boyle Saxton Lupton Leafa:
Tries - Donlan(2) Owen Brough: Goals - Brough(2):
WIDNES V - Grix: Blanch Kirk Nanyn: Dodd Moran
Webster: Cassidy Smith Wilkes Doran Noone Beswick:
Subs used - Summers James Gaskell Price:
Tries - Smith(2) Blanch(2) Dodd James Webster Beswick:
Goals - Nanyn(6)
Referee P Taberner (Wigan) Att - 6007 H.T. 4 - 12

Sun 27 May 2007 LEIGH CENTURIAN home won 42 - 6
NORTHERN RAIL CUP - QUARTER FINAL
CASTLEFORD - Saxton: Wainwright Dixon M Shenton
Donlan: McGoldrick Lupton: Boyle Henderson Leafa
Guttenbeil Barker Charles:
Subs used - Westerman Clayton Knowles Owen:
Tries - Barker(2) Wainwright M Shenton Leafa McGoldrick
Clayton Donlan: Goals - Dixon(5):
LEIGH C - Greenwood: Rivett Couturier Halliwell Alstead:
Ainscough Hermaia: Stevens Butterworth Astley Rudd
Taylor Stewart Subs used - Thomas Styles Cookson
Wilson: Try Couturier: Goals - Couturier:
Referee M Dawber (Wigan) Att - 3205 H.T. 32 - 0

Sun 3 Jun 2007 HALIFAX away won 30 - 14
HALIFAX - Gibson: George Roberts Varkulis Greenwood:
Holroyd Watson: Southern Penkywicz Shikell Joseph
Smith Ball: Subs used - Hoare Larder Heaton Watene:
Tries - George Greenwood Gibson: Goal - Holdroyd:

CASTLEFORD - Saxton: Wainwright Dixon M Shenton
Donlan: McGoldrick Brough: Boyle Henderson Leafa
Guttenbeil Barker Clayton:
Subs used - Charles Westerman Huby Owen:
Tries - M Shenton Leafa Guttenbeil Dixon Huby
Wainwright: Goals - Dixon Brough Charles:
Referee P Taberner (Wigan) Att - 2990 H.T. 20 - 0

Sun 10 Jun 2007 DEWSBURY RAMS home won 56 - 8
CASTLEFORD - Saxton: Wainwright Dixon M Shenton
Donlan: McGoldrick Brough: Boyle Henderson Leafa
Charles Westerman Cayton: Subs used - Knowles Barker
Huby Owen: Tries - McGoldrick(3) Wainwright(2)
Dixon(2) Brough Saxton Barker Knowles:
Goals - Dixon(3) Westerman(2) Brough:
DEWSBURY R - Preece: Buchanan Walker Bostock Maun: F
Maloney Lawford: Hobson Finn D Maloney Crouthers
Robinson Bretherton: Subs used - Haigh Kelly Southwell
Hirst: Tries - Maun Buchanan:
Referee G Hewer (Whitehaven) Att - 4739 H.T. 28 - 0

Fri 15 Jun 2007 SHEFFIELD EAGLES away won 27 - 15
SHEFFIELD E - Woocock: Mills Ford Reid Huirst: Lindsay
Brown: Howieson Pickering Stringer Brown Trayler Hayes:
Subs used - Brambani Morrow Hepi Buckenham:
Tries - Hurst Ford: Goals - Woodcock(3) Brambani D/G:
CASTLEFORD - Saxton: Wainwright Dixon Owen
Donlan:McGoldrick Westerman: Boyle Henderson Leafa
Huby Charles Clayton: Subs used - Michael Knowles
Barker Higgins JAKE BASSINDER(879):
Tries - Huby(2) Wainwright Dixon Henderson:
Goals - Westerman(3) Saxton D/G:
Referee P Taberner (Wigan) Att - 1333 H.T. 4 - 6

Sun 24 Jun 2007 WIDNES VIKINGS away
lost 12 – 18 NORTHERN RAIL CUP - SEMI FINAL
WIDNES V - Grix: Blanch Kohe-Love Nanyn Dodd: Moran
Penny: Cassidy Smith Wilkes Summers Noone Beswick:
Subs used - Webster Doran James Lima:
Tries - Wilkes Nanyn: Goals - Nanyn(5):
CASTLEFORD – Tom Saxton: Wainwright Dixon M
Shenton Donlan: McGoldrick Brough: Leafa Henderson
Huby Guttenbeil Charles Clayton:
Subs used - Westerman Glassie Boyle Higgins:
Tries - Boyle(2): Goals - Brough(2):
Referee G Hewer (Whitehaven) Att - 5388

Sun 1 Jul 2007 WHITEHAVEN home won 44 - 12
CASTLEFORD - Donlan: Wainwright Dixon Clayton M
Shenton: McGoldrick Brough: Leafa Henderson Huby
Guttenbeil Charles Barker:
Subs used - Owen Westerman Boyle Higgins:
Tries - Westerman(2) Barker Leafa M Shenton Boyle Dixon
Owen: Goals - Brough(3) Westerman(2) Dixon:
WHITEHAVEN - Broadbent: Calvert Seeds Elbeck Jackson:
Joe Duffy: Jackson Smith Trindall Miler Fletcher Rudd:
Subs used - Sice Mattinson Dale Teare:
Tries - Duffy Calvert: Goals - Rudd(2):
Referee J Leahy (Dewsbury) Att - 4902 H.T. 16 - 12

SEASON 2007

Sun 8 Jul 2007 DONCASTER LAKERS home won 66 - 4
CASTLEFORD - Donlan: Wainwright Dixon Barker M
Shenton: McGoldrick Lupton: Higgins Henderson Leafa
Guttenbeil Clayton Westerman:
Subs used - Owen Charles Huby Glassie:
Tries - Barker(3) Leafa(2) Wainwright(2) Westerman(2)
McGoldrick Clayton Glassie: Goals - Dixon(8) Westerman:
DONCASTER L - Skelton: Close Munro Woods Brown:
Gale Speak: Rowe Richardson Castle Green Leaf Benson:
Subs used - Mills Potter Burgess Lawton: Try - Munro:
Referee D Merrick (Pontefract) Att - 4109 H.T. 28 - 4

Sun 22 Jul 2007 BATLEY BULLDOGS away won 42 - 6
BATLEY B - Stokes: Doyle Cardiss Marns Lindsay: Colley
Hemingway: Henderson Lythe Stenchion Toohey
Gallagher: Subs used - Spears Menzies Watson Simpson:
Try - Gallagher: Goal - Hemingway:
CASTLEFORD - Donlan: Wainwright Dixon M Shenton
DANNY WILLIAMS(880): Lupton McGoldrick(S/O): Higgins
Henderson Glassie Guttenbeil Charles Clayton:
Subs used - Barker ANTHONY THACKERAY(881) Huby
Boyle: Tries - Williams(3) Dixon(2) Lupton M Shenton
Guttenbeil: Goals - Dixon(5):
Referee G Hewer (Whitehaven) Att - 2378 H.T. 12 - 6

Sun 29 Jul 2007 DEWSBURY RAMS away won 36 - 10
DEWSBURY R - Hall: Powell Domic Maun Buchanan:
Walker Lawford: Hobson Finn Maloney Robinson
Brotherton Weeden: Subs used - Kelly Crouthers Helme
Crawley: Tries - Hobson Buchanan: Goal - Finn:
CASTLEFORD - McGoldrick: Wainwright Dixon M Shenton
Williams: Lupton Thackeray: Higgins Henderson Glassie
Guttenbeil Charles Clayton: Subs used - Donlan
Westerman Boyle Huby: Tries - M Shenton(3) Henderson
Thackeray Lupton Clayton: Goals - Dixon(4):
Referee Dawber (Wigan) Att - 3010 H.T. 26 - 0

**Sun 5 Aug 2007 SHEFFIELD EAGLES home
won 52 - 26**
CASTLEFORD - Donlan: Wainwright Dixon M Shenton
Williams: Thackeray Brough: Higgins Henderson Glassie
Guttenbeil Barker Westerman:
Subs used - Clayton Owen Charles Boyle:
Tries - Thackeray(2) Barker(2) M Shenton(2) Westerman
Williams Dixon: Goals - Dixon(6) Brough(2):
SHEFFIELD E - Worricry: Mills Ford Reid Hurst: G Brown
Brambani: Howieson Pickering Stringer C Brown Trayler
Hayes: Subs used - Lindsay Edwards Newlove Corcoran:
Tries Ford(2) Brown Worricry: Goals - Brambani(5):
Referee J Child (Dewsbury) Att - 4538 H.T. 18 - 14

Thu 9 Aug 2007 WHITEHAVEN away won 20 - 12
WHITEHAVEN - Broadbent: Calvert Seeds R Jackson
Maden: Joe Duffy: Baldwin Mattison Fatialota Miller
Fletcher Rudd: Subs used - Sice Smith M Jackson Hill:
Tries - Fletcher Baldwin: Goals - Rudd(2);
CASTLEFORD - Donlan: Wainwright M Shenton Dixon
Williams: Thackeray Brough: Higgins Henderson Glassie
Charles Clayton Westerman:
Subs used - Owen Barker Boyle Leafa:

Tries - Clayton Dixon Barker: Goals - Brough(4):
Referee I Smith (Oldham) Att - 3366 H.T. 18 - 6

Thu 16 Aug 2007 WIDNES VIKINGS away won 24 - 18
WIDNES V - Grix: Blanch Kohe-Love Nanyn Gaskell:
Moran Penny: Cassidy Smith Wilkes Doran Noone
Beswick: Subs used - Summers James Webster Dodd:
Tries - Nanyn Kohe-Love Dodd: Goals - Nanyn(3):
CASTLEFORD - Donlan: Wainwright Dixon M Shenton
Williams: Thackeray Brough: Higgins Henderson Leafa
Guttenbeil Charles Clayton:
Subs used - Westerman Boyles Glassie Lupton:
Tries Williams Wainwright Dixon: Goals - Brough(6):
Referee A Klein (Keighley) Att - 4598 H.T. 14 - 10

2 Sep 2007 LEIGH CENTURIANS home won 62 - 10
CASTLEFORD - Donlan: Wainwright Dixon M Shenton
Williams: Thackeray Brough: Higgins Henderson Leafa
<u>Tere Glassie</u> Clayton Lupton:
Subs used - Westerman Barker Boyle:
Tries - Thackeray(4) Westerman(2) Dixon Glassie Donlan
Williams Wainwright: Goals - Brough(8) Dixon:
LEIGH C - Giles: Rivett Halliwell Alstead Greenwood:
Hough Heremaia: Astley McConnell Wilson Couturier
Styles Taylor: Subs used - Clough Rudd Kay Martins:
Tries - Halliwell Alstead: Goals - Halliwell:
Referee J Leahy (Dewsbury) Att - 5525 H.T. 16 -10

9 Sep 2007 ROCHDALE HORNETS away won 106 - 0
ROCHDALE H - Attwood: Andrews Marsh McCully
Campbell: Barber Hasty: Ball Corcoran Smith Blanchard
Law Cunliffe
Subs used - Hulse Bailey Robinson Benjafield:
CASTLEFORD - Donlan: Wainwright Dixon M Shenton
Williams: Thackeray Brough: Higgins Henderson Charles
Guttenbeil Clayton Lupton: Subs used - Westerman
<u>Dwayne Barker</u> Boyle:Leafa Tries - M Shenton(3)
Henderson(3) Williams(3) Brough(2) Leafa(2) Guttenbeil
Donlan Boyle Thackeray Westerman Clayton:
Goals - Brough(11) Dixon(3) Charles:
Referee Mr G Halloran (   ) Att 2506 H.T. 50 - 0

**Thu 20 September 2007 WIDNES VIKINGS home
won 26 – 8 CO-OPERATIVE NATIONAL PLAYOFFS -
QUALIFYING SEMI-FINAL**
CASTLEFORD - Donlan: Wainwright Dixon M Shenton
Williams: Thackeray Brough: Higgins Henderson Clayton
Guttenbeil Westerman Lupton: Subs used - McGoldrick
Charles Boyle Leafa: Tries - Westerman(2) Wainwright
Williams: Goals - Brough(5):
WIDNES V - Grix: Blanch Kohe-Love Nanyn Dodd: Moran
Webster: Summers Smith Wilkes Tomkins Noome
Beswick: Subs used - Cassidy James Myler Doran:
Try -Nanyn: Goals - Nanyn(2):
Referee R Silverwood (Dewsbury) Att - 6179 H.T. 4- 4

SEASON 2007

Sunday 7 Oct 2007 WIDNES VIKINGS won 42 - 10
CO-OPERATIVE NATIONAL PLAYOFFS - FINAL at
HEADINGLEY
CASTLEFORD - Donlan: Dixon McGoldrick M Shenton
Danny Williams: Thackeray Danny Brough: Higgins
Henderson Guttenbeil Westerman Clayton Lupton:
Subs used - Chris Charles Boyle Leafa: Wainwright
Tries - Guttenbeil(2) Wainwright McGoldrick M Shenton
Westerman Clayton: Goals - Brough (6): 2D/G
WIDNES V - Grix: Blanch Kohe-Love Nanyn Dodd: Moran
Penny: Cassidy Smith Wilkes Tomkins Noone Beswick:
Subs used - Summers James Webster Doran:
Tries - Nanyn Wilkes: Goal - Nanyn:
Referee P Bentham (Warrington) Att - 20814 H.T. 13 - 4

Michael Wainwright
D. No 861
2007 to 2010

Stuart Donlan
D. No 862
2007 to 2008

Awen Guttenbeil
D. No 866
2007 to 2008

Richard Owen
D. No 863
2007 to 2014

Joe Westerman
D. No 869
2007 to 2010

Liam Higgins
D. No 864
2007 to 2010

Kirk Dixon
D. No 870
2007 to 2014

Nathan Massey
D. No 876
2007 to

SEASON 2007

D.N	PLAYER		DEBUT	L MATCH	APP	SUB	T.AP	TRI'S	G'LS	D.G	P'TS
782	CHARLES	CHRIS		07/10/2007	21	6	27	5	2	0	24
791	SAXTON	TOMMY		24/06/2007	17	1	18	11	0	1	45
800	HUBY	CRAIG			10	8	18	7	1	0	30
802	CLAYTON	RYAN			23	5	28	9	0	0	36
810	SHENTON	MICHAEL			20	0	20	19	0	0	76
824	HENDERSON	ANDREW			27	0	27	11	0	0	44
833	KNOWLES	MICHAEL		15/06/2007	1	9	10	4	0	0	16
840	BOYLE	RYAN			6	18	24	7	0	0	28
846	McGOLDRICK	RYAN			25	1	26	12	0	1	49
857	LUPTON	PETER			14	2	16	7	0	0	28
859	BROUGH	DANNY		07/10/2007	25	0	25	11	122	2	290
860	PAYNE	JASON		22/04/2007	1	2	3	0	0	0	0
861	WAINWRIGHT	MICHAEL	11/02/2007		29	1	30	18	0	0	72
862	DONLAN	STUART	11/02/2007		28	1	29	20	0	0	80
863	OWEN	RICHARD	11/02/2007		9	11	20	11	0	0	44
864	HIGGINS	LIAM	11/02/2007		22	5	27	1	0	0	4
865	GLASSIE	TERE	11/02/2007	02/09/2007	9	10	19	3	0	0	12
866	GUTTENBEIL	AWEN	11/02/2007		23	0	23	8	0	0	32
867	BARKER	DWAYNE	11/02/2007	09/09/2007	16	10	26	17	0	0	68
868	LEAFA	MARK	11/02/2007		16	10	26	9	0	0	36
869	WESTERMAN	JOE	11/02/2007		9	15	24	12	20	0	88
870	DIXON	KIRK	18/02/2007		29	0	29	23	40	0	172
871	SHENTON	ALEX	11/03/2007	11/03/2007	1	0	1	2	0	0	8
872	JONES	ADAM	11/03/2007	11/03/2007	1	0	1	2	0	0	8
873	CROFT	EDDIE	11/03/2007	11/03/2007	1	0	1	2	0	0	8
874	JOHNSON	SEAN	11/03/2007	29/04/2007	3	2	5	1	0	0	4
875	DUCKWORTH	MATTHEW	11/03/2007	11/03/2007	0	1	1	1	0	0	4
876	MASSEY	NATHAN	11/03/2007		0	1	1	0	0	0	0
877	WATTS	LIAM	11/03/2007	11/03/2007	0	1	1	1	0	0	4
878	POTTER	GRAIG	11/03/2007	11/03/2007	0	1	1	0	0	0	0
879	BASSINDER	JAKE	15/06/2007	15/06/2007	0	1	1	0	0	0	0
880	WILLIAMS	DANNY	22/07/2007	07/10/2007	9	0	9	10	0	0	40
881	THACKERAY	ANTHONY	22/07/2007		8	1	9	8	0	0	32
	33		21	16	403	123	526	252	185	4	1382

COMPETITION		P	W	D	L	FOR	AGT
N, LEAGUE 1	POSITION 1 OF 10	18	17	0	1	860	247
RL CUP		2	1	0	1	104	34
N.R.C.		9	8	0	1	350	106
PLAY OFF		2	2	0	0	68	18
PLAYERS RECORDS		**31**	**28**	**0**	**3**	**1382**	**405**

In the National Rail Cup after winning all our group matches and the quarter-final were drawn at Widnes in the semi-final losing 12-18.

In the RL Cup, after an easy win over local amateurs Lock Lane and despite fielding a very youthful team with Nathan Massey making his debut, we lost away to Bradford Bulls in the next round.

Danny Brough equalled the points scored in a National League One game at 20 against Rochdale Hornets on the 8 September 2007.

In the league we vied all season with Widnes Vikings for top spot with each team winning its away game and losing its home game against each other.

With Widnes losing two league games to our one we finished top of the League, and drew Widnes at home in the qualifying semi-final beating them 26-8. Widnes won the Elimination semi-final against Halifax, so we were set to meet again in the Final at Headingley.

In the final we put Widnes to the sword with a magnificent 42–10 victory with Danny Brough and Awen Guttenbeil, the former New Zealand international, producing brilliant performances, thus winning our place back in Super League.

SEASON 2008

SUPER LEAGUE X111

In Super League Castleford Tigers replaced Salford
City Reds In a 12 Team League – Bradford Bulls
Castleford Tigers Catalan Dragons Harlequins
Huddersfield Giants Hull Hull K R Leeds Rhinos St
Helens Wakefield T Wildcats Warrington Wolves
Wigan Warriors.

Wed 26 Dec 2006 FEATHERSTONE ROVERS home
draw 24 – 24 FRIENDLY

CASTLEFORD - Turner: Arundell Cording Dixon Jones:
Westerman Thackeray: Higgins Johnson Korkidas Huby
Haberecht Lee: Subs used - Boyle Massey Bassinger
Duckworth Bryan Davies Swift: Tries - Korkidas Haberecht
Thackeray Westerman: Goals - Dixon(2) Westerman(2):
FEATHERSTONE R - Wildbore: Wilson Kirk McHugh
Lingard: Hughes McLocklan: A Tonks Eadie Dickens Field
Dooler Hesketh: Subs used - Houston Saxton Cawthray
Ellery Larvin Richardson Smith: Tries - Saxton(2) Hughes
Hersketh: Goal - Dickens(2) Wildbore(2):
Referee R Silverwood (Mirfield) Att - 3743 H.T. 12 - 6

Sun 20 Jan 2008 HUDDERSFIELD GIANTS home
lost 16 – 30 FRIENDLY

CASTLEFORD - Donlan: Wainwright Shenton McGoldrick
Owen: Thackeray Sherwin: Huby Henderson Higgins Leafa
Clayton Lupton: Subs used - Westerman Korkidas Moore
Boyle Lee Massey Arundel Dorn Haberecht:
Tries - McGoldrick(2) Wainwright: Goals - Sherwin(2):
HUDDERSFIELD G - Thorman: Lolesi Efford Whatuira
Jenson: Brown Robinson: Mason Hudson Crabtree Snitch
Raleigh Wild: Subs used - Gatis Griffin Jacckson Kirmond
Lawrence Cudjoe Barlow: Tries - Jenson(2) Thorman
Whaturia Wild Gatis: Goals - Thorman(3):
Referee B Thaler (Wakefield) Att - 3749 H.T. 16 - 0

Fri 25 Jan 2008 DEWSBURY RAMS away lost 0 - 60
FRIENDLY

DEWSBURY R - Colleran: Powell Langley Bostock
Buchanan: Weedon Lawford: Trinder Haigh Maloney
Gledhill Crawley Walker: Subs used - Finn Chapman
Wilson Rourke Field Clayton North Broady:
Tries - Langley(3) Powell(3) Weeden Colleran Bostock
Maloney North Broady: Goals - Walker(4) Finn(2):
CASTLEFORD - Turner: R Jones Arundel Cording Shenton:
Schofield Smith: Potter Swift Massey Kelly Bassinger Lee:
Subs used - A Jones Saunders Davies Bryan
Tasker-Howard Duckworth:
Referee M Dawber (Wigan) Att - 742 H.T. 0 - 40

Sun 27 Jan 2008 HULL KINGSTON ROVERS away
lost 10 – 22 FRIENDLY

HULL K R - Briscoe: Fox Cockayne Jake Webster Fitzhenry:
Gene James Webster: Vella Fisher Mills Gatea Chester
Murell: Subs used - Crossman Azue Netherton Menzies
I'Anson Welham:
Tries - Fox(3) Murell: Goals - Murell(2) Webster:
CASTLEFORD - Donlan: Owen Shenton Clayton
Wainwright; Dorn Thackeray: Boyle Henderson Korkidas

Leafa Lupton Westerman:
Subs used - Huby Haberecht Massey Moore:
Tries - Shenton Donlan: Goal - Westerman:
Referee I Smith (Oldham) Att - 5462 H.T. 10 - 6

Fri 9 Feb 2008 CATALAN DRAGONS home
lost 14 - 21

CASTLEFORD - LUKE DORN(882): Donlan McGoldrick
Shenton Wainwright: Thackeray BRENT SHERWIN(883):
Leafa Henderson MICHAEL KORKIDAS(884) Guttenbeil
Lupton Westerman: Subs used - SCOTT MOORE(885)
Huby TOM HABERECHT(886) Boyle:
Tries - Donlan Shenton: Goals - Westerman(3):
CATALAN D - Greenshields: Stacui Baile Wilson Khattabi:
Bosc McGuire: Ferriol Gorrell Chan Gossard Croker
Carlaw: Subs used - Guisset Raguin Mounis Casty:
Tries - Mounis Crocker Bosc: Goals - Bosc(4) D/G:
Referee P Bentham (Warrington) Att - 7060 H.T.12 -2

Fri 15 Feb 2008 WIGAN WARRIORS away lost 16 - 28

WIGAN W - Mathers: Colbon Goulding Carmont Richards:
Barrett Leului: Coley Higham Palea'aesina Hansen Bailey
O'Loughlin:
Subs used - Hock Mcllorum Prescott O'Carroll:
Tries - Leului(2) Richards Colbon: Goals - Richards(6):
CASTLEFORD - Dorn: Owen Shenton McGoldrick
Wainwright Thackeray Sherwin: Leafa Henderson
Korkidas Guttenbeill Lupton Westerman:
Subs used - Higgins Huby Haberecht Fletcher:
Tries - Lupton Haberecht Leafa: Goals - Westerman(2):
Referee I Smith (Oldham) Att - 16667 H.T. 6 - 8

Sun 24 Feb 2008 HUDDERSFIELD GIANTS away
lost 12 - 64

HUDDERSFIELD G - Thorman: Elford Whatuira Lolesi
Jensen: Brown Robinson: Mason Hudson Skandalis
Crabtree Snitch Wild:
Subs used - Gatis Raleigh Jackson Griffen:
Ties - Lolesi(2) Robinson(2) Jensen Brown Snitch Elford
Thortman Whatuira Mason Raleigh: Goals - Thorman(8):
CASTLEFORD - Dorn: Wainwright Dixon McGoldrick
Owen: Thackeray Lupton: Leafa Henderson Huby
Guttenbeil Haberecht Westerman:
Subs used - Higgins Korkidas Boyle Fletcher:
Tries - Lupton Wainwright: Goals Westerman(2):
Referee R Silverwood (Mirfield) Att - 7184 H.T. 6 - 28

Sun 2 Mar 2008 HARLEQUINS RL home lost 16 - 22

CASTLEFORD - McGoldrick: Wainwright Lupton Dixon
Owen: Dorn Sherwin: Huby Moore Korkidas Guttenbeil
Haberecht Westerman:
Subs used - Leafa Henderson Higgins Fletcher:
Tries - McGoldrick Dixon Dorn: Goals - Westerman(2):
HARLEQUINS RL - McLinden: Wellls Gafa Howell Sheriffe:
Orr Randall: McCarthy-Scarsbrook Rinaldi Ward Purdham
Kemata Paul: Subs used - Barker Chubb Heckenberg
Haggerty: Tries – McCarthy-Scarsbrook Orr Wells
Purdham: Goals - Purdham(2) Paul:

SEASON 2008

Referee B Thaler (Wakefield Att - 6268 H.T. 12- 12

Fri 7 Mar 2008 LEEDS RHINOS home won 38 - 20
CASTLEFORD - McGoldrick: Donlan Shenton Dixon
Wainwright: Dorn Sherwin: Huby Moore Korkidas
Guttenbeil Lupton Westerman:
Subs used - Henderson Leafa Higgins Clayton:
Tries - Shenton(2) Dorn(2) Westerman Donlan
McGoldrick: Goals - Westerman(5):
LEEDS R - Webb: Donald Gibson Senior Smith: Tansey
Burrow: Leuluai Diskin Bailey Jones-Buchanan Ellis
Sinfield: Subs used - Lauititi Scruton Ablett Burgess:
Tries - Donald(3) Tansey: Goals - Sinfield(2):
Referee P Bentham (Warrington) Att - 9459 H.T. 14 - 6

Sat 15 Mar 2008 HULL KINGSTON ROVERS away lost 4 - 20
HULL K R - Briscoe: Steel Webster Walker Fitzhenry: Galea
Webster: Vella Netherton Mills Newton Gene Murrell:
Subs used - Aizue Crossman Cockayne Menzies:
Tries - Fitzhenry(2) Cockayne Walker: Goals - Murrell(2):
CASTLEFORD - McGoldrick: Donlan Shenton Dixon
Wainwright: Dorn Sherwin: Huby Moore Korkidas
Guttenbeill Lupton Westerman: Subs used - Leafa
Higgins Clayton Henderson: Try - Huby:
Referee S Ganson (St Helens) Att - 8003 H.T. 0 - 10

Fri 21 Mar 2008 WAKEFIELD TRINITY WILDCATS away lost 16 - 28
WAKEFIELD T W - Blaymire: Gleeson Demetriou Atkins
Murphy: Rooney Brough: Watene Obst Moore Ferres
McGillivray Ferguson Subs used - Bibey Sculthorpe
Henderson Wilkes: Tries - Rooney Murphy Obst Brough
Atkins: Goals - Brough(2) Rooney(2):
CASTLEFORD - McGoldrick: Owen Dorn Dixon Fletcher:
Lupton Sherwin: Higgins Henderson Korkidas Guttenbeil
Huby Clayton:
Subs used - Thackeray Leafa Westerman Boyle:
Tries - Dorn(2) Lupton: Goals Huby Westerman:
Referee I Smith (Oldham) Att - 9287 H.T. 10 - 16

Mon 24 Mar 2008 WARRINGTON WOLVES home lost 31 - 34
CASTLEFORD - McGoldrick: Owen Dorn Dixon Fletcher:
Lupton Sherwin: Leafa Henderson Korkidas Huby Clayton
Westerman: Subs used - Thackeray Higgins Boyle:
Tries Westerman(3) Lupton Owen:
Goals - Westerman(5): SherwinD/G:
WARRINGTON W - Reardon: Hicks Martin Gleeson King
Penny: V Anderson Briers: Morley Clarke Rauhihi L
Anderson Westwood Johnson:
Subs used - Mark Gleeson Parker Pickersgill Bracek:
Tries - Westwood Reardon Martin Gleeson V Anderson L
Anderson: Goals - Briers(2) Hicks(3)
Referee S Ganson (St Helens) Att – 7245 H.T. 12 - 18

Sun 30 Mar 2008 BRADFORD BULLS away lost 4 - 50
BRADFORD B - Halley: Evans Sykes Hape Tadulala: Jeffries
Deacon: Burgess Godwin Lynch Nero Solomona Langley:
Subs used - Kopczak Finnigan Feather Harris:

Tries - Tadulala(3) Godwin Evans Sykes Jeffries Hape
Nero: Goals - Deacon(6) Harris:
CASTLEFORD - McGoldrick: Owen Lupton Dixon
Wainwright: Dorn Sherwin: Huby Henderson Korkidas
Leafa Clayton Westerman: Subs used - Fletcher Higgins
Boyle Massey: Try – Fletcher:
Referee B Thaler (Wakefield) Att - 10119 H.T. 4 - 22

Sun 6 Apr 2008 ST HELENS home won 30 - 24
CASTLEFORD - McGoldrick: Owen Lupton Dixon
Wainwright: Dorn Sherwin: Higgins Henderson Huby
Guttenbeil Clayton Westerman: Subs used - Thackeray
Korkidas Boyle: Tries - Westerman(2) Dixon(2) Owen
Dorn: Goals - Westerman(2) Huby:
ST HELENS - Wellens Gardner Gidley Tyrer Meli: Pryce
Long: Frodsham Roby Cayless Clough Wilkin Flannery:
Subs used - Bennett Fa'asavalu Eastmond Dean:
Tries - Clough Fa'asavalu Gardner Tyrer:
Goals - Long(4):
Referee P Bentham (Warringgton) Att - 7529 H.T. 10 - 16

Fri 11 Apr 2008 HULL F C home lost 12 - 32
CASTLEFORD - Donlan; Owen Shenton Dixon Wainwright:
Dorn Sherwin: Huby Henderson Higgins Guttenbeil
Lupton Westerman: Subs used - MATTHEW COOK(887)
Moore Clayton Boyle: Tries - Cook Lupton:
Goals - Huby(2):
HULL F C - Tony: Byrne Hall Yeaman Raynor: Washbrook
Berrigan: Dowes Lee Cusack Manu Tickle Radford:
Subs used - Wheeldon Houghton Burnett Thackray:
Tries - Hall(2) Wheeldon Tony Thackray:
Goals - Tickle(6):
Referee S Ganson (St Helens) Att - 8136 H.T. 2 - 18

Sat 19 Apr 2008 HARLEQUINS away lost 14 - 44
RL CHALLENGE CUP FOURTH ROUND
HARLEQUINS - Wells: Clubb Gafa Howell Sheriffe: Paul
Orr: Temata Randall Ward: Mbu Worrincy Purdham: Subs
used - Rinaldi Haggerty Grayshon Melling:
Tries- Worrincy Randall Clubb Orr Haggerty Howell Ward:
Goals - Purdham(7) Paul:
CASTLEFORD - Donlan: Fletcher Dixon Shenton
Wainwright: Thackeray Sherwin: Higgins Henderson
Korkidas Huby Clayton Lupton:
Subs used - Moore Boyle McGoldrick Tom Haberecht:
Tries - Shenton Fletcher: Goals - Huby(2) Dixon: Referee
R Silverwood (Dewsbury) Att - 2108 H.T. 14 - 0

Sat 26 Apr 2008 CATALAN DRAGAONS away lost 30 - 38
CATALAN D - Greenshields: Murphy Raguin Mogg Pelo:
Bosc McGuire: Chan Gorrell Guisett Croker Mounis
Carlaw: Subs used - Duport Bentley Casty Touxgas:
Tries - Pelo Guisett Raguin Murphy Greenshields Mounis
Gorrell: Goals - Bosc(5):
CASTLEFORD - Donlan: Fletcher Dixon Shenton Owen:
McGoldrick Sherwin: Higgins Henderson Korkidas Lupton
Cook Westerman: Subs used - Thackeray Boyle Moore
BRENDON HLAD(888): Tries - Shenton Westerman
Korkidas McGoldrick Fletcher: Goals - Dixon(5):

SEASON 2008

Referee P Bentham (Warrington) Att - 8745 H.T.- 18 - 30

Sat 3 May 2008 WAKEFIELD TRINITY WILDCATS lost 16 – 54 PLAYED AT MILLENNIUM STADIUM CARDIFF

CASTLEFORD - McGoldrick: Donlan Shenton Dixon Owen: Dorn Sherwin: Higgins Moore Huby Guttenbeil Cook Westerman:
Subs used - Henderson Korkidas Clayton
NED CATIC(889):
Tries - Owen Westerman Shenton: Goals - Dixon(2):
WAKEFIELD T W - Blaymire: Gleeson Martin Atkins Grix: Rooney Brough: Watene Obst Moore MacGillvray Golden Dale: Subs used - Wilkes Leo-Latu Bibb Blanch:
Tries - Grix(3) Blanch(2) Watene Obst Moore Atkins:
Goals - Brough(9):
Referee I Smith (Oldham) Att - 30628 H.T. 6 - 24

Sun 18 May 2008 BRADFORD BULLS home lost 24 - 46

CASTLEFORD - Donlan: Fletcher Shenton Dixon Wainwright: McGoldrick Dorn: Higgins Moore Huby Guttenbeil Catic Westerman: Subs used - Korkidas Henderson Hlad Owen: Tries - Shenton McGoldrick Westerman Wainwright Dorn: Goals - Dixon Westerman:
Bradford B - Platt: Evans Sykes Nero Tadulala: Jeffries Deacon: Lynch Newton Burgess Solomona Langley Morrison: Subs used - Finnigan Tupou Harris Kopczak:
Tries - Sykes Newton Burgess Morrison Langley Platt Jeffries Finnigan: Goals - Deacon(7):
Referee R Laughton (Barnsley) Att - 7855 H.T. 14 - 28

Mon 26 May 2008 WARRINGTON WOLVES away won 36 - 28

WARRINGTON W - Hicks: Riley Martin Gleeson King Penny: Briers Monaghan: Morley Clarke Rauhihi L Anderson Westwood V Anderson:
Subs used - Mark Gleeson Grix Bracek Harrison:
Tries - Riley(2) V Anderson Penny Hicks: Goals - Hicks(4):
CASTLEFORD - Donlan: Wainwright Owen Shenton Fletcher: McGoldrick Dorn: Huby Moore Guttenbeil Catic Lupton Westerman: Subs used - Henderson Korkidas Higgins Boyle: Tries - Dorn(2) Owen Shenton Fletcher Wainwright Donlan: Goals - Westerman(3) Huby:
Referee I Smith (Oldham) Att - 7788 H.T. 14 - 10

Sun 8 Jun 2008 WAKEFIELD TRINITYT WILDCATS home lost 16 - 32

CASTLEFORD - Donlan: Wainwright Owen Shenton Dixon: McGoldrick Dorn: Higgins Moore Huby Guttenbeil Lupton Westerman: Subs used - Henderson Clayton Boyle Catic:
Tries - Dorn(2) McGoldrick: Goals - Dixon(2):
WAKEFIELD T W - Blaymire: Gleeson Martin Atkins Blanch: Rooney Brough: Wilkes Obst Moore Golden MacGillivray Sculthorpe: Subs used - Bibey Henderson Grix Bibb:
Tries - Blanch(2) Brough Blaymire Rooney:
Goals - Brough(6):
Referee I Smith (Oldham) Att - 8236 H.T. 18 - 10

Sun 15 Jun 2008 HULL F C away lost 14 - 40

HULL FC - Byrne: Sing Horne Yeaman T Briscoe: Washbrook Dykes: Dowes Berrigan Carvell Manu Tickle Radford:

Subs used - Thackray Houghton Hall Wheeldon:
Tries - Hall(3) Yeaman(2) Briscoe: Goals - Tickle(8):
CASTLEFORD - McGoldrick: Donlan Dixon Shenton Wainwright: Dorn Sherwin: Higgins Moore Huby Catic Lupton Westerman: Subs used - Henderson Clayton Boyle Owen: Tries - Huby Catic: Goals - Dixon(3):
Referee- Mr P Bentham (War'ton) Att - 12681 H.T. 8 - 18

Sun 22 Jun 2008 WIGAN WARRIORS home draw 22 - 22

CASTLEFORD - McGoldrick: Donlan Shenton Owen Wainwright: Dorn Sherwin: Higgins Henderson Korkidas Huby Lupton Westerman:
Subs used - Thackeray Boyle Brendon Hlad Catic:
Tries - McGoldrick Henderson Lupton: Goals - Huby(5):
WIGAN W - Mathers: Calderwood Phelps Carmond Richards: Barrett Leuluai: Fielden Higham Coley Hansen Bailey O'Loughlin: Subs used - McIlorum Colbon Palea'aesina Frescott: Tries - Richards Barrett Higham Leuluai: Goals - Richards(3):
Referee B Thaler (Wakefield) Att - 7048 H.T.14 - 6

Sat 28 Jun 2008 LEEDS RHINOS away lost 12 - 18

LEEDS R - Jones-Bishop: Hall Jones-Buchanan Smith Donald: Allar Webb: Leuluai Diskin Burgess Lauitiiti Bailey Worrell: Subs used - Haley Kaye Williams Chandler:
Tries - Smith Diskin Webb: Goals - Smith(3):
CASTLEFORD - Donlan: Adam Fletcher Shenton Owen Wainwright: Dorn Sherwin Huby Henderson Korkidas Lupton Catic McGoldrick: Subs used - Higgins Westerman Boyle Anthony Thackeray:
Tries - Owen Westerman: Goals - Huby(2):
Referee P Bentham (Warrington) Att - 17619 H.T. 6 - 0

Sun 6 Jul 2008 HULL KINGSTON ROVERS home won 18 - 10

CASTLEFORD - Donlan: Wainwright Owen Shenton Dixon: Dorn Sherwin: Higgins Henderson Korkidas Lupton Westerman McGoldrick:
Subs used - Leafa Boyle Moore Catic:
Tries - Dorn Shenton Lupton: Goals - Dixon(3):
HULL K R -Fizhenry: Gomersall Webster Welham Steel: Galea Dobson: Crossman Netherton Mills Gene Chester Cooke: Subs used - Vella Fisher Lovegrove I'Anson:
Tries - Vella Steel: Goal – Cooke
Referee R Silverwood (Mirfiield) Att - 7771 H.T. 18 - 0

Fri 11 Jul 2008 ST HELENS away lost 12 - 68

ST HELENS - Wellens: Gardner Gidley Talu Meli: Pryce Long: Graham Cunningham Hargreaves Gilmour Wilkin Sculthorpe: Subs used - Roby Flannery Clough Fa'asavalu: Tries - Sculthorpe (2) Meli(2) Gidley Long Gilmour Gardner Clough Flannery Wilkin Roby:
Goals - Long (8) Sculthorpe(2):
CASTLEFORD - Donlan: Dixon Shenton Owen Wainwright: McGoldrick Sherwin: Higgins Henderson Korkidas Catic Lupton Westerman: Subs used - Dorn Leafa Boyle Moore:
Tries - Shenton Dixon: Goals - Dixon(2):
Referee P Bentham (Warrington) Att - 8430 H.T. 0 - 46

SEASON 2008

Sun 20 Jul 2008 HARLEQUINS RL away won 66 - 12
HARLEQUINS RL - Melling: Bryan Sharp Purdham
O'Callaghan: Hill Paul: Temata Ranndall Ward Barker
Grayshon Haggerty: Subs used - Skee Heckenberg Tootill
Mbu: Tries Melling Grayshon: Goals - Purdham(2):
CASTLEFORD - Donlan: Owen Shenton Dixon Wainwright:
Dorn Sherwin: Higgins Moore Huby Guttenbeil Lupton
McGoldrick:
Subs used - Westerman Henderson Boyle Catic:
Tries - Owen(3) Shenton(3) Dorn(3) Donlan Catic
McGoldrick Wainwright: Goals - Dixon(7):
Referee B Thaler (Wakefield) Att - 2112 H.T. 28 - 12

Sun 3 Aug 2008 HUDDERRSFIELD GIANTS home lost 14 - 40
CASTLEFORD - Donlan: Owen Shenton Lupton
Wainwright: Dorn Sherwin: Higgins Henderson Huby
Guttenbeil Westerman McGoldrick: Subs used - Korkidas
Boyle MITCHELL SARGENT(890) JOE ARUNDEL(891):
Tries - Owen Dorn: Goals - Westerman(2) Huby:
HUDDERSFIELD G - Cdjoe: Aspinwall Brown Whatuira
Hodgson: Thorman Robinson: Mason Hudsor Griffin Wild
Lolesi Raleigh: Subs used - Crabtree Jones Jackson
Kirmond: Tries - Hodgson Lolesi Hudson Whatuira
Griffin Thorman: Goals - Thorman(8):
Referee R Silverwood (Mirfield) Att - 6935 H.T. 14 - 14

Sun 10 Aug 2008 WAKEFIELD TRINITY WILDCATS away won 48 - 22
WAKEFIELD T W - Blaymire: Blanch Gleeson Atkins Grix:
Rooney Brough: Sculthorpe Obst Wilkes Ferres Golden
Demetriou: Subs used - Leo-Latu Bibey Bibb Henderson:
Tries - Gleeson Obst Atkins Ferres: Goals - Brough(3):
CASTLEFORD - Donlan: Owen Shenton Dixon Wainwright:
Dorn Sherwin: Higgins Moore Huby Guttenbeil Lupton
McGoldrick: Subs used - Henderson Westerman Catic
Sargent: Tries - Donlan(2) Westerman(2) Dorn
Henderson Huby Moore: Goals - Dixon(8)
Referee I Smith (Oldham) Att - 6498 H.T. 24 - 12

Fri 15 Aug 2008 LEEDS RHINOS away lost 12 - 54
LEEDS R - Webb: Smith Ablett senior Gibson: McGuire
Burrow: Leuluai Diskin Peacock Ellis Kirke Sinfield:
Subs used - Scruton Lauitiiti Burgess Tansey :
Tries - Tansey(3) Gibson Burrow Smith Ablett Lautiiti
Webb McGuire: Goals - Sinfield(6) Ellis:
CASTLEFORD - Donlan: Owen Shenton Dixon Wainwright:
McGoldrick Dorn: Higgins Moore Huby Guttenbeil
Lupton Westerman: Subs used - Sargent
Henderson Leafa: Tries - Owen Dorn: Goals - Dixon(2):
Referee T Albert (France) Att - 17354 H.T. 6 - 24

Sun 24 Aug 2008 WARRINGTON WOLVES home won 44 - 24
CASTLEFORD - Donlan: Owen Shenton Dixon Wainwright:
McGoldrick Dorn: Korkidas Henderson Sargent Guttenbeil
Catic Lupton: Subs used - Leafa Boyle Huby Higgins:
Tries - Wainwright(3) Donlan(2) Owen(2) Dorn Catic
Dixon
Goals - Dixon Huby:

WARRINGTON W - Hicks: Riley Gleeson King Welch:
Briers Monaghan: Morley Clarke Parker Mitchell
Westwood Grix:
Subs used - Blythe Bracek Cooper Wood:
Tries - Riley(2) Briers Blythe: Goals - Hicks(4):
Referee I Smith (Oldham) Att - 5912 H.T. 22 - 12

Sun 7 Sep 2008 BRADFORD BULLS home lost 16 - 18
CASTLEFORD – Stuart Donlan: Owen Shenton Dixon
Wainwright: McGoldrick Dorn: Sargent Andrew
Henderson Michael Korkidas Awen Guttenbeil Ned Catic
Peter Lupton:
Subs used – Mark Leafa Boyle Huby Higgins:
Tries - Owen Dixon Boyle: Goals - Dixon(2):
BRADFORD B - Sykes: Halley Evans Nero Tadulala: Jeffries
Deacon: Vagana Newton Lynch Cook Finnigan Langley:
Subs used - Harris Solomona Godwin Kopczak:
Tries - Tadulala(3): Goals - Harris(2) Deacon:
Referee I Smith (Oldham) Att - 8067 H.T. 10 - 10

Luke Dorn
D. No 882
2008 to 2016

Brent Sherwin
D. No 883
2008 to 2010

Michael Korkidas
D. No 884
2008

Scott Moore
D. No 885
2008 to 2015

Matt Cook	Ned Catic	Michel Sargent	Joe Arundel
D. No 887	D. No 889	D. No 890	D. No 891
2008 to	2008	2008 to 2010	2008 to 2012

2008 SQUAD NUMERS AND NAMES
1: LUKE DORN 2: STUART DONLAN 3: MICHAEL SHENTON 4: KIRK DIXON 5: MICHAE_ WAINWRIGHT 6: ANTHONY THACKERY 7: BRENT SHERWIN 8: MARK LEFA 9: ANDREW HENDERSON 10: MICHAEL KORKIDAS 11: AWEN GUTTENBEIL 12: RYAN CLAYTON 13: JOE WESTERMAN 14: LIAM HIGGINS 15: GRAIG HUBY 16: PETER LUPTON 18: RYAN BOYLE 20: SCOTT MOORE 21: RICHARD OWEN 22: NATAN MASSEY 23: RYAN McGOLDRICK 25: BEN GLEDHILL 27: NED CATIC 28: MITCHELL SARGENT 29: JOE ARUNDEL 30: ADAM FLETCHER

SEASON 2008

D.N		PLAYER		DEBUT	L MATCH	APP	SUB	T.AP	TRI'S	G'LS	D.G	P'TS
800	1	HUBY	CRAIG			21	4	25	3	16	0	44
802	2	CLAYTON	RYAN			5	6	11	0	0	0	0
810	3	SHENTON	MICHAEL			22	0	22	13	0	0	52
824	4	HENDERSON	ANDREW		07/09/2008	17	11	28	2	0	0	8
840	5	BOYLE	RYAN			0	20	20	1	0	0	4
846	6	McGOLDRICK	RYAN			26	1	27	7	0	0	28
857	7	LUPTON	PETER		07/09/2008	26	0	26	7	0	0	28
858	8	FLETCHER	ADAM		28/06/2008	7	4	11	4	0	0	16
861	9	WAINWRIGHT	MICHAEL			24	0	24	7	0	0	28
862	10	DONLAN	STUART		07/09/2008	21	0	21	8	0	0	32
863	11	OWEN	RICHARD			22	2	24	13	0	0	52
864	12	HIGGINS	LIAM			16	11	27	0	0	0	0
866	13	GUTTENBEIL	AWEN		07/09/2008	19	0	19	0	0	0	0
868	14	LEAFA	MARK		07/09/2008	5	9	14	1	0	0	4
869	15	WESTERMAN	JOE			21	4	25	12	28	0	104
870	16	DIXON	KIRK			22	0	22	6	39	0	102
876	17	MASSEY	NATHAN			0	1	1	0	0	0	0
881	18	THACKERAY	ANTHONY		28/06/2008	4	6	10	0	0	0	0
882	19	DORN	LUKE	09/02/2008		25	1	26	19	0	0	76
883	20	SHERWIN	BRENT	09/02/2008		21	0	21	0	0	1	1
884	21	KORKIDAS	MICHAEL	09/02/2008	07/09/2008	16	6	22	1	0	0	4
885	22	MOORE	SCOTT	09/02/2008		11	6	17	1	0	0	4
886	23	HABERECHT	TOM	09/02/2008	19/04/2008	2	3	5	1	0	0	4
887	24	COOK	MATTHEW	11/04/2008		2	1	3	1	0	0	4
888	25	HLAD	BRENDAN	26/04/2008	22/06/2008	0	3	3	0	0	0	0
889	26	CATIC	NED	03/05/2008	07/09/2008	7	7	14	3	0	0	12
890	27	SARGENT	MITCHELL	03/08/2008		2	3	5	0	0	0	0
891	28	ARUNDEL	JOE	03/08/2008		0	1	1	0	0	0	0
	28			10	11	364	110	474	110	83	1	607

COMPETITION		P	W	D	L	FOR	AGT
S, LEAGUE	POSITION 12 OF 12	27	7	1	19	593	869
RL CUP		1	0	0	1	14	44
PLAYERS RECORDS		**28**	**7**	**1**	**20**	**607**	**913**

In July 2008 the RL announced the 14 teams to be granted a Super League License for the three seasons commencing 2009. These were: 'A' License; Hull FC, Leeds Rhinos, and Warrington Wolves. 'B' License; Bradford Bulls St Helens and Wigan Warriors 'C' License; Castleford Tigers Celtic Crusaders Catalan Dragons Harlequins Hull KR Huddersfield Giants Salford City Reds and Wakefield Trinity Wildcats.

This decision meant that if any of these teams finished bottom of Super League they would not be relegated.

Thus the pressure was off ourselves, which was just as well as we did finish bottom of the League but this also allowed the Club to build the team gradually without any panic.

Luke Dorn finished with a creditable 19 tries from 26 appearances in his Debut season

SEASON 2009

SUPER LEAGUE XIV

The first year of the three year Licence with no promotion or relegation.

Fri 26 Dec 2008 GATESHEAD THUNDER home won 44 – 18 FRIENDLY
CASTLEFORD - Owen: Ford Dixon Shenton Jones: McGoldrick Chase: Boyle Netherton Massey Davies Huby Westerman:
Subs used - Atkinson Cording Kelly Harris Walker Arundel Turner Fairhead Gledhill Thompson Pountney
Tries - Arundel(2) Chase(2) Westerman Shenton Dixon Pountney Fairhead : Goals - Dixon(2) Huby(2):
GATESHEAD T - Pears; Wilson Neighbour Nash Dack: Thorman Brannigan: Payne Clarke McBride Pybus Clarke Knowles:
Subs used - Vernon Barron Welton Parker Woods:
Tries - Wilson(2) Nash Payne: Goals - Branningan:
Referee G Halloran (Dewsbury) Att - 3008 H.T. 24 - 8

Sun 18 Jan 2009 HUDDERSFIELD GIANTS home lost 20 – 28 FRIENDLY
CASTLEFORD - Owen: Thompson Dixon Shenton Wainwright: McGoldrick Chase: Sargent Hudson Huby Widders Jones Westerman   :Subs used - Higgins Feather Boyle Massey Netherton Arundle Harris:
Tries - Wainwright Owen Harris Feather: Goals - Dixon(2):
HUDDERSFIELD - Cudjoe: Aspinwall Lawrence Whatuira D Hodgson: Brown Robinson: Mason Faiumu Jackson Wild Raleigh Finnigan: Subs used - B Hodgson Crabtree Griffin Korkidas Kirmond Moore Walsh Johnson Lopag Worthington: Tries - D Hodgson(2) Wild Whatura B Hodgson Kirmond: Goals - B Hodgson(2):
Referee Bentham (Warrington) Att - 3713 H.T. 0 - 12

Sun 25 Jan 2009 WAKEFIELD TRINITY WILDCATS home won 32 – 12 FRIENDLY
CASTLEFORD - McGoldrick: Owen Shenton Evans Dixon: Faumuina Chase: Sargent Netherton Higgins Ferres Jones Westerman: Subs used - Wainwright Feather Massey Widders Thompson Huby Walker: Tries - Shenton(3) Faumuina(2) Widders :   Goals - Dixon (4):
WAKEFIELD T W - Blaymire: Blanch Gleeson Martin Potts: Rooney Grix: Wilkes Drew Bibb Snitch Ferguson Demetriou: Subs used - Obst Stosic Pitts Henderson Annakin Davey: Tries - Martin Obst: Goals - Martin(2):
Referee J Child (Dewsbury) Att - 4359 H.T. 20 - 0

Fri 30 Jan 2009 YORK CITY KNIGHTS away lost 14 – 32 FRIENDLY
YORK C K - Faircliffe: Joe Stearman Blaney Jones Stancliffe: Grimshaw Watling: Sullivan Hodgson Woodcock Wilcox-Harrison Barrow Applegarth: Subs used - Hughes Endersby Jack Stearman Hunter Lineman Walton: Tries - Hodgson(3) Joe Stearman(2) Stancliffe: Goals - Fairclough(2) Grimshaw)2):
CASTLEFORD - Ford: Turner Thompson Arundel Atkinson: Helliwell Fairhead Massey Milner Walker Boyle Davies Cording: Subs used - Lynch Shenton Poutney Tosh Jones

Duncan Turner Johnson Kelly Harris Gledhill Hayward: Tries - Fairhead Ford Walker: Goals - Arundel:
Referee R Laughton (Barnsley) Att - 711 H.T. 4 - 20

Sun 1 Feb 2009 FEATHERSTONE ROVERS home won 50 – 10 FRIENDLY
CASTLEFORD - McGoldrick: Dixon Shenton Evans Owen: Faumuina Chase: Feather Hudson Higgins Ferres Jones Westerman: Subs used - Wainwright Netherton Massey Widders Huby Ford: Tries - Ferres(2) Dixon McGoldrick Chase Netherton Huby Wainwright Westerman:
Goals - Dixon(7):
FEATHERSTONE R - S Kain: Pryce Hardiman Saxton Steel: Harris A Kain Tonks Lee Dickens Dale Spears Haughey: Subs used - Hesketh Blakeway McLocklan Houston Smeaton: Tries Pryce Dale: Goal - Harris
Referee D Merrick (Pontefract) Att- 2583 H.T. 24 - 10

Sun 15 Feb 2009 HARLEQUINS RL home lost 8 - 12
CASTLEFORD - McGoldrick: Dixon JAMES EVANS(892) Shenton Owen: SIONE FAUMUINA(893) RANGI CHASE(894) Sargent Hudson Higgins BRETT FERRES(895) STUART JONES(896) Westerman: Subs used - Huby CHRIS FEATHER(897) KIRK NETHERTON(898) DEAN WIDDERS(899): Tries - Evans Owen:
HARLEQUINS RL - Wells: Melling Gafa Howell Sharp: Dorn Orr: Temate Randall Ward Williamson Robinson Purdham: Subs used - McCarthy-Scarsbrook Harrerty Kay Clubb: Tries - Dorn(2):   Goals - Purdham(2):
Referee J Leahy (Dewsbury) Att - 7049 H.T. 4 - 6

Fri 20 Feb 2009 WIGAN WARRIORS away won 28 - 22
WIGAN W - Roberts: Pryce Goulding Carmont Ainscough: Smith Leuluai: Fielden Riddell O,Carroll Hock J Tomkins O'Loughlin: Subs used - Paleaaesina Coley Hansen McIlorium   Tries - Leuluai Pryce Goulding Tomkins Ainscough: Goal - Roberts:
CASTLEFORD - McGoldrick: Dixon Evans Shenton Owen: Faumuina Sherwin: Higgins Hudson Huby Ferres Jones Westerman: Subs used - Chase Sargent Feather Netherton: Tries - Ferres(2) Westerman Dixon Shenton: Goals - Dixon(4):
Referee S Ganson (St Helens) Att - 12079 H.T. 16 - 6

Sat 28 Feb 2009 SALFORD CITY REDS home won 52 - 16
CASTLEFORD - McGoldrick: Wainwright Dixon Shenton Owen: Faumuina Sherwin: Sargent Hudson Huby Ferres Jones Westerman:
Subs used - Chase Widders Feather Netherton:
Tries - Owen(2) Shenton Huby Hudson Westerman Netherton McGoldrick Widders: Goals - Dixon(8):
SALFORD - Fitzpatrick: Wilshere Littler Talua Henry: Smith Myler: Cashmere Alker Stapleton Parker Adamson Swain: Subs used - Paul Sibbit Leuluai Nash:
Tries - Talau Fitzpatrick Henry: Goals - Wilshere(2):
Referee G Hewer (Whitehven) Att - 7052 H.T. 28 - 6

469

SEASON 2009

Sat 7 Mar 2009 CATALAN DRAGONS away won 24 - 22
CATALAN D - Greenshields: Stacul Bell Mogg Pelo: Bosc Perry: Elima McGuirte Guisset Fakir Croker Mounis: Subs used - Casty Ferrol Baile Bird:
Tries - Stacul(2) Greenshields Fakir: Goals - Bosc(3)
CASTLEFORD - McGoldrick: Dixon Evans Shenton Owen: Faumuina Sherwin: Sargent Hudson Huby Ferres Jones Westerman:
Subs used - Chase Widders Feather Netherton:
Tries - Evans(2) Dixon Owens Chase: Goals Dixon(2):
Referee R Silverwood (Dewsbury) Att - 8150 H.T. 12 - 14

Sat 14 Mar 2009 HUDDERSFIELD GIANTS home lost 24 - 26
CASTLEFORD - McGoldrick: Dixon Evans Shenton Owen: Faumuina Sherwin: Sargent Hudson Huby Ferres Jones Westerman:
Subs used - Chase Widders Feather Netherton
Tries - Ferres(2) Huby(2) Evans: Goals Dixon(2):
HUDDERSFIELD G - B Hodgson: Cudjoe Lawrence Whaturia D Hodgson: Brown Robinson: Jackson Moore Mason Wild Lolesi Walsh: Subs used - Kirmond Griffin Larne Lunt: Tries - D Hodgson(3) Lolesi B Hodgson: Goals B Hodgson(3):
Referee S Ganson (St Helens) Att - 6572 H.T. 12 - 14

Fri 20 Mar 2009 HULL FC away won 19 - 18
HULL FC - Hall: Calderwood G Horne Yeaman Briscoe: R Horne Thorman: Dowes Houghton Cusack Manu Tickle Radford: Subs used - Lee Thackray Moa Berrigan:
Tries G Horne(3) R Horn: Goals Tickle:
CASTLEFORD - McGoldrick Dixon Evans Shenton Owen: Chase Sherwin: Sargent Hudson Feather Ferres Jones Faumuina: Subs used - Westerman Huby Higgins Netherton: Tries Dixon Westerman McGoldrick
Goals Dixon(3) Sherwin D/G:
Referee T Albert (France) Att - 14028 H.T. 6 - 10

Sun 29 Mar 2009 BRADFORD BULLS home won 28 - 26
CASTLEFORD - McGoldrick: Wainwright Dixon Shenton Owen: Chase Sherwin: Sargent Hudson Huby Ferres Westerman Faumuina:
Subs used - Feather Massey Netherton Widders:
Tries - Shenton(2) Dixon(2) Chase: Goals Dixon(4):
BRADFORD B - Platt: Sherriffe Sykes Nero Tadulala: Jeffries Deacon: Burgess Newton Lynch Menzies Morrison Langley: Subs used - Halley Worrincy Kopczak Scruton:
Tries - Platt Tadulala Lynch Morrison Haley:
Goals - Deacon(2) Sykes:
Referee G Hewer (Whitehaven) Att - 9185 H.T. 10 - 16

Sun 5 Apr 2009 KEIGHLEY COUGERS away won 64 - 20
R. L CHALLENGE CUP 4th ROUND
KEIGHLEY C - Rayner: Gardner Smith Williams Duffy: Presley Jones: Law Feather Cartledge Gunney Purseglove Nicholson: Subs used - Wray Mapals Hughes Bissell:
Tries - Mapals(3) Presley: Goals - Jones(2):
CASTLEFORD - McGoldrick: Dixon Evans Shenton Owen:

Chase Sherwin: Feather Netherton Massey Huby Widders Westerman: Subs used - Higgins Boyle Faumuina JAMES FORD(900): Tries - Chase(3) Shenton Higgins Dixon Faumuina Evans Owen Ford Netherton: Goals - Dixon(10)
Referee - M Thomason Att - 3255 H.T. 16 - 6

Fri 10 Apr 2009 WAKEFIELD TRINITY WILDCATS home lost 6 - 35
CASTLEFORD - Owen: Dixon Evans Shenton Wainwright: Chase Sherwin: Sargent Hudson Massey Huby Faumuina Westerman: Subs used - Higgins Feather Netherton Widders: Try Westerman: Goal - Dixon:
WAKEFIELD T W - Blaymire: Blanch Gleeson Atkins Murphy: Martin Brough: Wilkes Obst Snitch Pitts Ferguson Demetriou: Subs used - Bibb Sculthorpe Drew Henderson: Tries - Atkins(2) Martin Blaymire Gleeson: Goals Brough(4) Matin(3) Brough D/G:
Referee P Bentham (Warrington) Att - 10155 H.T. 0 - 8

Mon 13 Apr 2009 WARRINGTON WOLVES away won 28 - 6
WARRINGTON W - Hicks: Johnson Grix King Penny: Bridge Monaghan: Morley Higham Carvel L Anderson Westwood Harrison: Subs used - Clarke Rauhhi Wood Blythe: Try - Bridge: Goal - Hicks:
CASTLEFORD - Owen: Dixon Evans Shenton Wainwright: Chase Sherwin: Sargent Hudson Higgins Ferres Faumuina Westerman: Subs used - Huby Feather Netherton Ford: Tries - Chase(2) Ferres Wainwright Shenton:
Goals - Dixon(4):
Referee S Ganson (St Helens) Att - 8202 H.T. 6 - 0

Sun 19 Apr 2009 SAINT HELENS home lost 22 - 68
CASTLEFORD - McGoldrick: Owen Dixon Shenton Wainwright: Chase Sherwin: Sargent Netherton Higgins Huby Faumuina Westerman: Subs used - Clayton Boyle Massey Ford: Tries - Shenton Sargent Dixon Faumuina: Goals - Dixon(3):
ST HELENS - Wellens: Gardner Gidley Dean Meli: Price Long: Graham Cunningham Puletua Gilmour Wilkin Clough: Subs used - Fa'asavalu Roby Hargreaves Ashurst: Tries - Puleua(4) Wilkin(3) Pryce(2) Gardner Hargreaves Fa'asavalu: Goals Long(10):
Referee Mr I Smith (Oldham) Att - 8003 H.T. 6 - 38

Sun 26 Apr 2009 CELTIC CRUSADERS away won 34 -22
CELTIC C - Chalk: Dyer Hannay Dalle Cort Ballard: Quinn Van Dilk: O'Hara Withers Chan Peek Lupton Beasley: Subs used - Bryant Buidworth James Tangata-Toa: Tries - O'Hara(2) Peek Tangata-Toa: Goals - Quinn(3):
CASTLEFORD - Owen: Dixon Evans Shenton Wainwright: Chase Sherwin: Sargent Netherton Higgins Jones Faumuina McGoldrick: Subs used - Ferres Feather Boyle Ford: Tries - Boyle Evans Dixon Wainwright Shenton Sherwin: Goals - Dixon(5):
Referee T Albert (France) Att - 2017 H.T. 12 - 16

SEASON 2009

Sun 3 May 2009 HULL FC lost 16 - 24
AT MURRAYFIELD STADIUM EDINBURGH SCOTLAND
CASTLEFORD - Owen: Dixon Evans Shenton Wainwright:
Chase Sherwin: Sargent Jones Higgins Ferres Faumuina
McGoldrick: Subs used - Feather Boyle Netherton Ford:
Tries - Ford Dixon Evans: Goals - Dixon(2):
HILL FC - R Horne: Calderwood Whiting Yeaman G Horne:
Washbrook Thorman: Dowes Lee Thackray Manu Tickle
Radford: Subs used - Houghton Burnett Cusack Maloney:
Tries - Burnett Cusack Whiting Washbrook:
Goals - Tickle (4):
Referee P Bentham (Warrington)   Att - 30122 H.T. 6 - 6

Sun 10 May 2009 HALIFAX home won 35 -34
RL CHALLENGE CUP 5th ROUND
CASTLEFORD - McGoldrick: Dixon Evans Shenton
Wainwright: Chase Sherwin: Sargent Jones Boyle Ferres
Faumuina Westerman:
Subs used - Clayton Higgins Feather Ford:
Tries - McGoldrick(2) Evans Shenton Dixon Chase
Sherwin: Goals - Dixon(2) Sherwin(1) D/G;
HALIFAX - Greenwood: Paterson Barker Royston Haley:
Penkywicz Black: Wilson Gleeson Tamghart Larder Smith
Beswick:
Subs used - Roberts Watene Cherryholme Wrench:
Tries - Beswick(3) Royston Barker: Goals - Paterson(7):
Referee S Ganson (St Helens) Att - 5595 H.T. 16 - 12
**EXTRA TIME PLAYED UNTIL SHERWIN'S GOLDEN
POINT DROP GOAL WON THE MATCH**

Fri 15 May 2009 LEEDS RHINOS home lost 22 - 24
CASTLEFORD - McGoldrick: Dixon Evans Shenton
Wainwright: Faumuina Sherwin: Sargent Chase Higgins
Ferres Jones Westerman:
Subs used - Feather Boyle Clayton Ford:
Tries - Jones Dixon Chase Shenton: Goals - Dixon(3):
LEEDS R - Webb: Donald Senior Hall: McGuire Burrow:
Leuluai Buderus Peacock Kirke Jones-Buchanan Sinfield:
Subs used - Diskin Lauitiiti Burgess Ablett:
Tries - McGuire(2) Burrow Hall: Goals - Sinfield(4):
Referee I Smith(Oldham) Att - 8082 H.T. 10 - 16

Fri 22 May 2009 HULL KINGSTON ROVERS away
lost 6 - 16
HULL K R - Briscoe: Fox Webster Welham Colbon: Cooke
Dobson: Fozzard Fitzhenry Newton Walker Galea Murrell:
Subs used - Aizue Fisher Wheeldon Dowse:
Tries - Briscoe(2) Fox: Goals Dobson(2):
CASTLEFORD - Ford: Dixon Evans Shenton Wainwright:
Faumuina Sherwin: Sargent Chase Higgins Ferres Jones
Westerman: Subs used - Huby Clayton Feather Boyle:
Try - Sargent: Goal - Dixon
Referee G Hewer (Whitehaven) Att - 8104 H.T. 0 - 4

Sun 31 May 2009 HUDDERSFIELD GIANTS away
lost 14 – 16 RL CHALLENGE CUP QUARTER FINAL
HUDDERSFIELD G - B Hodgson: Aspinwall Lolesi Whatuira
D Hodgson:: Brown Robinson: Mason Moore Jackson
Kirmond Wild Finnigan:
Subs used - Faiumu Crabtree Griffin Raleigh:

Tries - Brown Wild Kirmond: Goals- B Hodgson(2):
CASTLEFORD - Owen: Dixon Evans Shenton Wainwright:
McGoldrick Chase: Sargent Netherton Higgins Ferres
Jones Westerman: Subs used - Huby Clayton Feather
Faumuina: Tries Shenton Ferres: Goals - Dixon(3):
Referee R Silverwood (Dewsbury) Att - 6359 H.T.6 - 6

Fri 5 Jun 2009 WARRINGTON WOLVES home
lost 18 - 34
CASTLEFORD - McGoldrick: Owen Evans Shenton Dixon:
Faumuina Chase; Sargent Netherton Huby Ferres Jones
Clayton:
Subs used - Feather Westerman Widders Higgins:
Tries - Dixon Owen Shenton Evans: Goal - Dixon:
WARRINGTON W - Mathers: Riley Grix King Hicks: Bridge
Briers:Morley Clarke Carvell L Anderson Westwood
Harrison: Subs used - Higham Wood Rauhihi V
Anderson: Tries - Briers(2) V Anderson(2) King L
Anderson Hicks: Goals - Bridge(3):
Referee B Thaler (Normanton) Att - 5628 H.T. 8 - 12

Fri 12 Jun 2009 SAINT HELENS away lost 10 - 50
ST HELENS - Wellens: Lomax Gidley Dean Meli: Pryce
Long: Puletua Cunningham Hargreaves Wilkin Flannery
Gilmour:
Subs used - Clough Eastmond Fa'asavalu Ashurst:
Tries - Eastmon(2) Pryce Dean Cunningham Wilkin Long
Lomax Clough: Goals - Long(3) Eastmond(4):
CASTLEFORD - Owen Wainwright Ferres Dixon Ford:
McGoldrick Chase: Higgins Netherton Huby Widders
Jones Faumuina: Subs used - Sargent Clayton Feather
JORDAN THOMPSON(901):   Tries - Ferres Dixon:
Goal - Dixon:
Referee I Smith (Oldham) Att - 9680 H.T. 6 – 20

Fri 19 Jun 2009 HUDDERSFIELD GIANTS away
won 13 - 6
HUDDERSFIELD G - B Hodgson: Cudjoe Lolesi Whatura D
Hodgson: Brown Robinson: Mason Moore Griffin Wild
Crabtree Finnigan: Subs used - Faiumu Fulton Raleigh
Sculthorpe: Try - Cudjoe: Goal - B Hodgson:
CASTLEFORD - Owen: Wainwright Shenton Widders
Dixon: Faumuina McGoldrick: Sargent Chase Huby Ferres
Jones Westerman:
Subs used - Higgins Boyle Clayton Netherton:
Tries - Dixon McGoldrick: Goals - Dixon(2) ChaseD/G:
Referee S Ganson (St Helens) Att - 6010 H.T. 12 - 0

Sat 27 Jun 2009 CATALAN DRAGONS home
lost 20 - 22
CASTLEFORD - Owen: Dixon Widders Shenton
Wainwright: Sione Faumuina McGoldrick: Sargent Chase
Huby Ferres Jones Westerman:
Subs used - Clayton Higgins Boyle Netherton:
Tries - Owen(2) Ferres: Goals - Westerman(3) Dixon:
CATALAN D - Greenshields: Bell Baile Crocker Pelo: Mogg
Bosc: Ferriol McGuire Guisset Elima Gossard Carlow:
Subs used - Casty Mounis Ryles Perry:
Tries - Pelo Baile Greenshields Carlaw: Goals - Bosc(3):
Referee Smith (Oldham) Att - 5508 H.T. 12 - 12

Sun 5 Jul 2009 BRADFORD BULLS away won 40 - 38
BRADFORD B - Halley: Sheriffe Sykes Nero Tadulala:
Jeffries Deacon: Lynch Newton Scuton Burgess Menzies
Langley: Subs used - Worrincy Godwin Donaldson
Kopczak: Tries - Jeffries(2) Tadulala Halley Scruton
Worrancy Burgess: Goals - Deacon(4) Sykes:
CASTLEFORD - Owen: Thompson Shenton Widders
Wainwright: McGoldrick Chase: Sargent Jones Higgins
Ferres Huby Westerman: Subs used - Boyle Feather
Clayton Netherton: Tries -Shenton(2) Chase(2)
Thompson Westerman Widders: Goals - Westerman(6):
Referee B Thaler (Normanton) Att - 8971 H.T. 12 - 22

Sun 12 Jul 2009 HULL FC home won 40 -18
CASTLEFORD - Owen: Dixon Shenton Widders
Wainwright: McGoldrick Chase: Sargent Hudson Huby
Ferres Clayton Westerman: Subs used - Jones Feather
Netherton Higgins: Tries Chase(2) Wainwright(2) Huby
Hudson Shenton: Goals - Westerman(6):
HULL FC - R Horne: Broughton G Horne Yeaman Raynor:
Thorman Berrigan: King Lee Cordoba Manu Tickle
Radford: Subs used - Houghton Whiting Burnett Moa:
Tries - Manu Yeaman Broughton:
Goals - Whiting(2) Tickle:
Referee J Leahy (Dewsbury) Att- 8297 H.T. 24 - 6

Fri 17 Jul 2009 SALFORD CITY REDS away won 18 - 12
SALFORD C R - Wilshere: Henry Turner Ratchford
McGilvray: Smith Myler: Cashmere Alker Stapleton
Adamason Sislow Swain: Subs used - Littler Leuluai Paul
Jewitt: Tries - McGilvray Ratchford: Goals - Wilshere(2):
CASTLEFORD - Owen: Dixon Shenton Widders
Wainwright: Chase McGoldrick; Sargent Hudson Huby
Ferres Clayton Westerman:
Subs used - Jones Higgins Feather Netherton:
Tries - Ferres Shenton Netherton: Goals - Westerman(3):
Referee G Hewer (Whitehaven) Att - 3487 H.T. 12 - 0

Sun 26 Jul 2009 WAKEFIELD TRINITY WILDCATS away won 20 - 12
WAKEFIELD T W - Blaymire: Grix Gleeson Atkins Murphy:
Demetriou Brough: Bibbey Obst Korkidas Snitch Wilkes
Henderson: Subs used - Stosic Moore Ferguson Drew:
Tries Brough(2) Goals - Brough(2):
CASTLEFORD - Owen: Dixon Shenton Widders
Wainwright: McGoldrick Chase: Sargent Hudson Higgins
Huby Clayton Westerman: Subs used – Evans Jones
Feather Netherton Tries - Widders(2):
Goals - Westerman(6):
Referee -Mr I Smith (Oldham) Att - 8371 H. T. 8 - 6

Sun 2 Aug 2009 HULL KINGSTON ROVERS home lost 28 - 46
CASTLEFORD - Owen: Dixon Shenton Evans Wainwright:
McGoldrick Chase: Huby Hudson Higgins Ferres Jones
Westerman: Subs used - Sargent Feather Netherton
Widders: Tries - Ferres Huby Hudson Netherton:
Goals - Westerman(5) Huby:
HULL KR - Briscoe: Fox Welham Webster Colbon: Cooke
Dobson: Wheeldon Fisher Vella Newtron Galea Murrell:

Subs used - Lovegrove Bibb Fitzhenry Cockayne:
Tries Briscoe(3) Dobson(2) Fox(2) Colbon:
Goals - Dobson(7):
Referee T Albert (France) Att - 8709 H.T. 20 - 18

Fri 14 Aug 2009 LEEDS RHINOS away lost 12 - 76
LEEDS R - Webb: Donald Smith Senior Hall: McGuire
Burrows: Leuluai Diskin Peacock Jones-Buchanan Ablett
Sinfield: Subs used - Lauitiiti Burgess Worrall Ratu:
Tries - Hall(5) Webb(2) Donald Smith Leuluai Burrows
Peacock Ratu Lauitiiti: Goals - Sinfield(10):
CASTLEFORD - McGoldrick: James Ford Shenton Evans
Wainwright Widders Chase: Sargent Hudson Huby Ferres
Clayton Westerman: Subs used Jones Higgins Feather
Netherton: Tries - Evans Chase: Goals - Westerman(2):
Referee B Thaler (Normanton) Att - 16391 H.T. 6 - 26

Sun 23 Aug 2009 WIGAN WARRIORS home lost 26-29
CASTLEFORD - McGoldrick: Dixon Shenton Evans
Wainwright: Chase Sherwin: Sargent Hudson Huby Jones
Ferres Westerman Subs used - Clayton Higgins Boyle
Widders: Tries - Dixon(2) Shenton Ferres Widders:
Goals - Westerman(2) Dixon:
WIGAN - Phelps: Roberts Gleeson Carmont Richards: S
Tomkins Leuluai: Coley Riddell Prescott Hansen J Tomkins
O'Loughlin: Subs used - Fielden Paleasesina Mossop
Flanagan: Tries - S Tomkins(3) Leuluai(2):
Goals - Richards(4) S Tomkins D/G
Referee S Ganson (St Helens) Att - 6,579 H.T. 6 - 14

Sun 30 Aug 2009 HARLEQUINS RL away won 48 - 0
HARLEQUINS RL - Melling: Clubb Gafa Purdham Sharp
Dorn Orr: Ward Randall McCarthy-Scarsbrook Williamson
Esders Golden:
Subs used - Heckenberg Gale Haggerty Bryan:
CASTLEFORD - McGoldrick: Dixon Evans Shenton
Wainwright: Chase Sherwin: Sargent Jones Higgins Huby
Clayton Westerman: Subs used - Ferres Feather
Netherton Widders: Tries - Westerman(3) Dixon(2) Evans
Widders Higgins Ferres: Goals - Westerman(5) Dixon
Referee T Alibert (France) Att - 3824 H.T. 12 - 0

Sun 13 Sep 2009 CELTIC CRUSADERS home won 35 - 22
CASTLEFORD - McGoldrick: Dixon Evans Shenton
Wainwright: Chase Sherwin: Sargent Jones Higgins Ferres
Clayton Westerman:
Subs used - Owen Huby Feather Netherton:
Tries - Shenton(2) Dixon Sargent Wainwright Owen Huby:
Goals - Dixon(2) Westerman SherwinD/G:
CELTIC C - Kear: Bateman Blackwood Tyrer Lennon:
Withers Smith: Ohara Budworth Bryant James Chan
White: Subs used - Flower Tangata-Toa Mills Davies:
Tries - Withers(2) White O'Hara: Goals - Tyrer(3):
Referee Mr J Childs (Dewsbury) First Half Retired Injured
at H.T. Referee Mr P Brook Second Half Att - 6547
H.T. 14 - 16

SEASON 2009

Sun 20 Sep 2009 WIGAN WARRIORS away lost 12 - 18
Elimination Play off Sixth v Seventh
WIGAN W - Phelps: Roberts Gleeson Carmont Richards: S
Tompkins Leuluai: Coley McIlorum Prescott J Tomkins
Hansen O'Loughlin:
Subs used - Fielden Palea'aesina Flanagan Riddell:
Tries - Hansen Carmont Roberts: Goals - Richards(3):
CASTLEFORD - Owen: Dixon Evans Shenton Wainwright:
McGoldrick Sherwin: Sargent Chase Huby Ferres Clayton
Jones:
Subs used - Higgins Chris Feather Netherton Westerman:
Tries - Huby Westerman: Goals Westerman(2):
Referee I Smith (Oldham) Att - 8689 H.T. 0 – 12

James Evans
D. No 892
2009 to 2010

Rangi Chase
D. No 894
2009 to

Brett Ferris
D. No 895
2009 to 2012

Stuart Jones
D. No 896
2009 to 2012

Chris Feather
D. No 897
2009

Kirk Netherton
D. No 898
2009 to 2010

Dean Widders
D. No 899
2009 to 2011

Jordan Thompson
D. No 901
2009 to 2013

SEASON 2009

D.N	PLAYER		DEBUT	L MATCH	APP	SUB	T.AP	TRI'S	G'LS	D.G	P'TS
786	HUDSON	RYAN			15	0	15	3	0	0	12
800	HUBY	CRAIG			21	6	27	7	1	0	30
802	CLAYTON	RYAN			8	10	18	0	0	0	0
810	SHENTON	MICHAEL			30	0	30	19	0	0	76
840	BOYLE	RYAN			1	10	11	1	0	0	4
846	McGOLDRICK	RYAN			28	0	28	5	0	0	20
861	WAINWRIGHT	MICHAEL			24	0	24	5	0	0	20
863	OWEN	RICHARD			24	1	25	9	0	0	36
864	HIGGINS	LIAM			15	12	27	2	0	0	8
869	WESTERMAN	JOE			25	3	28	9	41	0	118
870	DIXON	KIRK			29	0	29	19	66	0	208
876	MASSEY	NATHAN			2	2	4	0	0	0	0
883	SHERWIN	BRENT			19	0	19	2	1	3	13
890	SARGENT	MITCHELL			27	3	30	3	0	0	12
892	EVANS	JAMES	15/02/2009		21	1	22	11	0	0	44
893	FAUMUINA	SIONE	15/02/2009	27/06/2009	19	2	21	2	0	0	8
894	CHASE	RANGI	15/02/2009		27	4	31	14	0	1	57
895	FERRES	BRETT	15/02/2009		25	2	27	12	0	0	48
896	JONES	STUART	15/02/2009		22	4	26	1	0	0	4
897	FEATHER	CHRIS	15/02/2009	20/09/2009	2	25	27	0	0	0	0
898	NETHERTON	KIRK	15/02/2009		6	21	27	4	0	0	16
899	WIDDERS	DEAN	15/02/2009		9	10	19	6	0	0	24
900	FORD	JAMES	05/04/2009	14/08/2009	3	7	10	2	0	0	8
901	THOMPSON	JORDAN	12/06/2009		1	1	2	1	0	0	4
	24		10	3	403	124	527	137	109	4	770

COMPETITION		P	W	D	L	FOR	AGT
S, LEAGUE	POSITION 7 OF 14	27	14	0	13	645	702
RL CUP		3	2	0	1	113	70
PLAY OFF		1	0	0	1	12	18
PLAYERS RECORDS		31	16	0	15	770	790

In June 2009 Coach Terry Matterson signed a two-year contract extension to the end of 2011.

In the RL Challenge Cup, after two good victories, we lost at Halifax by one point 34-35.

With a much better League performance we finished 7th of the 14 teams, thus qualifying for a play-off place.

Drawn at Wigan in the 6th v 7th play off match we lost 12-18

Michael Shenton and Kirk Dixon were joint leaders in the try scoring stakes with 19 each.

SEASON 2010

SUPER LEAGUE XV

The second year of the three year Licence with no promotion or relegation.

Sat. 26 Dec 2009 BRADFORD BULLS home lost 16 - 26 FRIENDLY
CASTLEFORD - Thompson: Lopag Evans Arundel Wainwright: Widders Chase: Higgins Netherton Massey Huby Snitch Clayton: Subs used - Davies Holmes Barber Milner Walker Dawson Brierley Clarke:
Tries - Arundel Widders Davies: Goals - Huby Brierley:
BRADFORD B - Halley: Sheriffe Platt Crooks Reardon: Addy Kearney: Lynch L'Estrange Scruton Hall Whitehead Donaldson: Subs used - Hyde Straughier Olbisn Crossley Tate Helliwell Mackay Itaye Lillycrop T Burgess G Burgess Finnigan Wardle: Tries - Halley Whitehead Straughier Horton(2): Goals - Addy Hyde(2):
Referee R Hicks Att - 2998 H.T. 6 - 10

Sat. 16 Jan 2010 CATALAN DRAGONS away won 14 – 12 FRIENDLY
CATALAN - Greenshields: Bell Raguin Sa Pelo: Mogg Bosc: Casty McGuire Guisset Elima Gossard Fakir: Subs used - Mounis Guasch Barthau Bentley Martins Walker Gigot Stacul Simon Vaccari:
Tries - Bentley Stacul: Goals - Barthau(2):
CASTLEFORD - McGoldrick: Thompson Evans Shenton Wainwright: Widders Netherton: Jackson Hudson Huby Snitch Clayton Jones: Subs used - Sargent Higgins Davies Holmes: Tries - Widders(2) Evans: Goals - Huby:
Referee M Drizza (France) Att - 3800 H.T. 4 - 0

Sun 24 Jan 2010 GATESHEAD THUNDER home won 48 – 22 FRIENDLY
CASTLEFORD - Lynch: Atkinson Arundel Chappell Nathanial: Barber Brierley: Walker Milner Massey Holmes Wilcock Davies: Subs used - Senior Pearson Elkington Thompson Eden Smirk Clarke Dawson Duncan:
Tries - Davies(3) Milner Arundel Senior Lynch Barber Thompson: Goals - Barber(6):
GATESHEAD - Neighbour: Peers Aderiye M Brown Matthews: Duffy Bate: Welton Wall Parker Harvey Humphries O'Sullivan: Subs used - Elliot Atkinson Wilson Watson J Brown Ryan Clarke Walker Rhys Clarke Barron Scott Attard Barron: Tries - Peers(2) Watson J Brown M Brown: Goals - Ryan Clark:
Referee W Turley (   ) Att - 597 H.T. 34 - 4

Sun 31 Jan 2010 HUDDERSFIELD GIANTS home lost 28 – 10 FRIENDLY
CASTLEFORD - McGoldrick: Owen Evans Shenton Wainwright: Widders Chase: Jackson Hudson Huby Snitch Jones Clayton: Subs used - Sargent Higgins Sherwin Ferris Westerman Netherton Thompson Davies Massey: Tries - Wainwright Shenton: Goal - Westerman:
HUDDERSFIELD G - B Hodgson: Cudjoe Lawrence Loesi D Hodgson: Brown Robinson: D Griffin Lunt Raleigh Gilmour Horne Falumu: Subs used - Crabtree Fa'alogo Grix Whatuira Aspinwall Wood Patrick J Griffin McGilvary:

Tries - Robinson Lunt Gilmour Whaturia J Griffin: Goals - B Hodgson(4):
Referee S Ganson (St Helens) Att - 2036 H.T. 0 - 18

Fri 5 Feb 2010 LEEDS RHINOS away won 24 - 10
LEEDS R - Webb: Donald Delaney Senior Hall: McGuire Burrow: Bailey Buderus Peacock Jones-Buchanan Ablett Sinfield: Subs used - Diskin Eastwood Lauitiiti Burgess Tries - McGuire Delaney: Goal - Sinfield:
CASTLEFORD - McGoldrick: Owen Evans Shenton Wainwright: Chase Sherwin: Jackson Hudson Higgins Ferres STEVE SNITCH(902) Westerman: Subs used - Jones Sargent Widders Huby: Tries - Evans Westerman Sherwin Widders: Goals - Westerman(3) Huby:
Referee I Smith (Oldham) Att - 15875 H.T. 6 - 10

Sat. 13 Feb 2010 WARRINGTON WOLVES home lost 16 - 28
CASTLEFORD - McGoldrick: Owen Evans Shenton Wainwright: Chase Sherwin: Jackson Hudson Huby Ferres Snitch Westerman:
Subs used - Sargent Jones Higgins Widders:
Tries - Evans (2) Westerman: Goals - Westerman(2):
WARRINGTON W - Mathers: Riley Bridge Atkins King: Briers Myler: Morley Monaghan Carvell L Anderson Westwood Harrison:
Subs used - Higham Grix Wood V Anderson:
Tries - Myler(2) Grix Riley Briers: Goals - Bridge(3) Briers:
Referee B Thaler (Normanton) Att - 7569 H.T. 10 - 10

Fri 19 Feb 2010 BRADFORD BULLS away lost 22- 41
BRADFORD B - Halley: Sheriffe Sykes Nero Reardon: Kearney Orford: Scruton L'Estrange Lynch Langley Whitehead Menzies: Subs used - Godwin Worrincy Kopczak Hall Tries - Kearney(2) Scruton Sheriffe Whitehead Halley Sykes: Goals - Orford(6) D/G:
CASTLEFORD - McGoldrick: Owen Shenton Evans Wainwright: Snitch Chase: Jackson Hudson Higgins Ferres Jones Westerman: Subs used - Sargent Huby Netherton Clayton: Tries - Shenton Owen Snitch Hudson: Goals Westerman(3):
Referee T Albert (France) Att - 8019 H.T. 10 - 25

Sat. 27 Feb 2010 HULL KINGSTIN ROVERS home lost 20 - 24
CASTLEFORD - McGoldrick: SHAUN AINSCOUGH(903) Evans Shenton Wainwright: Chase Sherwin: Sargent Hudson Jackson Ferres Snitch Westerman:
Subs used - Huby Jones Higgins:
Tries - Ainscough(3) Wainwright: Goals - Westerman(2):
HULL K R - Briscoe: Fox Welham Webster Cockayne: I'Anson Dobson: Lovegrove Murrell Clinton Newton Cook Vella: Subs used - Wheeldon Netherton Fisher Watts: Tries - Murrell Dobson Cockayne Watts: Goals - Dobson(4):
Referee P Bentham (Warrington) Att - 6855 H.T. 10 - 12

SEASON 2010

Fri 5 Mar 2010 HULL FC away lost 22 - 42
HULL FC - Tansey: Calderwood Hall Yeaman Briscoe:
Turner Horne: Dowes Berrigan O'Mealey Manu Tickle
Fitzgibbon: Subs used - Cusack Lauki Whiting Moa:
Tries - Horne(2) Yeaman Manu Cusack Hall Fitzgibbon:
Goals - Tickle(6) Fitzgibbon:
CASTLEFORD - McGoldrick: Ainscough Shenton Evans
Wainwright: Chase Sherwin: Sargent Hudson Jackson
Huby Snitch Clayton: Subs used - Dixon Jones Higgins
Massey: Tries - Hudson Ainscough Chase Evans:
Goals - Huby(2) Dixon:
Referee R Silverwood (Dewsbury) Att 13352 H.T. 12 - 12

Sat. 13 Mar 2010 CATALAN DRAGONS away won 20 - 16
CATALAN D - Greenshields: Bell Raguin Walker Stacu: Sa
McGuire: Ferriol Bentley Carlaw Gossard Elima Johnson:
Subs used - Guisset Fakir Casty Mounis:
Tries - Walker Fakir McGuire: Goals - Mounis(2):
CASTELFORD - McGoldrick: Ainscough Shenton Dixon
Wainwright: Chase Sherwin: Higgins Hudson Huby
Clayton Snitch Westerman: Subs used - Sargent Jones
MICHAEL COOPER(904) JOHN DAVIES (905)
Tries - Cooper Chase Jones Wainwright:
Goals - Westerman(2):
Referee I Smith (Oldham) Att - 6810 H.T. 6 - 10

Sun 21 Mar 2010 WIGAN WARRIORS home Lost 22 -36
CASTLEFORD - McGoldrick: Thompson Shenton Dixon
Wainwright: Westerman Chase: Higgins Hudsor Huby
Snitch Jones Clayton: Subs used - Sargent Cooper
Massey Sherwin: Tries - Shenton(2) Wainwright Cooper:
Goals - Westerman(3):
WIGAN W - Phelps: Roberts Gleeson Carmont Richards: S
Tompkins Leuluai: Coley Riddell Fielden Bailey J Tompkins
O'Loughlin: Tries - Roberts(3) J Tompkins(2) Phelps
Richards: Goals - Richards(4):
Referee J Childs (Dewsbury) Att - 8493 H.T. 12 - 14

Fri 26 Mar 2010 CRUSADERS R L home won 22 - 16
CASTLEFORD - McGoldrick: Thompson Shenton Dixon
Ainscough: Chase Sherwin: Sargent Hudson Higgins
Jones Snitch Westerman: Subs used - Clayton Cooper
CHRIS TUSON(906) Jackson: Tries - Dixon McGoldrick
Westerman Thompson: Goals -Westerman(3):
CRUSADERS RL - Kear Youngquest Martin Mellars Dyer:
Witt Lupton: O'Hara Withers Bryant Chan Hauraki
Trimarch:
Subs used - Thomas Peek Thackray Winterstein:
Tries - Mellars Chan Hauraki: Goals - Winn(2):
Referee I Smith (Oldham) Att - 5299 H.T. 16 - 6

Fri 2 Apr 2010 WAKEFIELD TRINITY WILDCATS away lost 6 - 19
WAKEFIELD T W - Blaymire; Blanch Murphy Millard
Morton: Cooke Jeffries: Korkidas Obst Moore Henderson
Demetriou Morrison:
Subs used - King Leo-Latu Tronc Kirmond:
Tries - Obst Morton Leo-Latu: Goals Cooke(3) D/G:

CASTLEFORD - McGoldrick: Thompson Shenton Dixon
Ainscough: Chase Sherwin: Jackson Jones Huby Tuson
Snitch Westerman: Subs used - Hudson Higgins Clayton
Cooper: Try - Thompson: Goal - Westerman:
Referee J Childs (Dewsbury) Att - 8337 H.T. 6 - 6

Mon 5 Apr 2010 SAINT HELENS home lost 18 - 52
CASTLEFORD - McGoldrick: Ainscough Clayton Shenton
Wainwright: Chase Sherwin: Sargent Hudson Jackson
Jones Tuson Westerman: Subs used - Huby Higgins
Netherton Cooper: Tries - Huby Clayton Westerman
Shenton: Goal - Westerman:
ST HELENS - Pryce: Gardner Gidley Dean Meli: Wikin
Eastmond: Graham Cunningham Fozzard Ashurst
Flannery Puletua: Subs used - Roby Hargreaves Moore
Fa'asavalu
Tries - Estmond(2) Meli(2) Roby(2) Fa'asavalu Puletua
Pryce: Goals - Estmond (8):
Referee P Bentham (Warrington) Att - 6879 H.T. 10 - 16

Fri 9 Apr 2010 HUDDERSFIELD GIANTS away lost 0 - 24
HUDDERSFIELD G - B Hodgson: Lolesi Lawrence Whatuira
D Hodgson: Brown: Brough: Mason Robinson Griffin
Gilmour Fa'alongo Aspinwall;
Subs used - Raleigh Crabtree Faiumu Grix:
Tries -D Hodgson(3) Lolesi: Goals - B Hodgson(4):
CASTLEFORD - Thompson: Shaun Ainscough Shenton
Clayton Wainwright: McGoldrick Netherton: Jackson
Hudson Huby Michael Cooper Snitch Jones:
Subs used - Sargent Higgins OLIVER HOLMES(907) Tuson:
Referee S Ganson(St Helens) Att - 5932 H.T. 0 - 6

Sun 17 Apr 2010 BARROW RAIDERS home lost 28 - 34 R.L.CHALLENGE CUP 4TH ROUND
CASTLEFORD - Thompson: Dixon Clayton Evans
Wainwright: McGoldrick Chase: Jackson Kirk Netherton
Huby Jones Snitch Westerman: Subs used - Sargent
Hudson Holmes Arundel: Tries - Westerman(2)
Thompson Sargent Dixon: Goals - Westerman(4):
BARROW R - Broadbent: Ballard Blackwood Harrison
McGilvary: Coyle Rooney: James Henderson Bracek
Knowles Catic Luisi: Subs used - Noone Roberts
Campbell Ostler: Tries - Rooney(2) McGilvary(2) Ballard
Catic: Goals - Rooney(5)
Referee T Albert (France) Att - 5285 H.T. 18 - 12

Sun 26 Apr 2010 SALFORD CITY REDS home won 30 - 12
CASTLEFORD - McGoldrick: Dixon Evans Thompson
Wainwright: Chase Sherwin: Sargent Hudson Jackson
Huby Jones Westerman: Subs used - Higgins Clayton
Snitch Tuson: Tries - McGoldrick Sargent Thompson
Jones: Goals - Westerman(7):
SALFORD C R - Fitzpatrick: Tyrer Henry Talau
Gibson: Ratchford Holdsworth: Cashmere Alker Boyle
Sidlow Adamson Swain:
Subs used - Littler Jewittt Lealuai Smith:
Tries - Gibson Henry: Goals - Holdsworth(2):
Referee Mr B Thaler (Normanton) Att - 5025 H.T. 12 - 12

SEASON 2010

Sun 2 May 2010 CATALAN DRAGON won 34 - 18
PLAYED AT MURRYFIELD STADIUM EDINBURGH
CASTLEFORD - McGoldrick: Wainwright Evans Thompson
Dixon: Chase Sherwin: Sargent Hudson Jackson Huby
Jones Westerman: Subs used - Snitch Higgins Holmes
Tuson: Tries McGoldrick(2) Sherwin(2) Wainwright Evans:
Goals - Westerman(5):
CATALAN D - Pelo: Bell Raguin Sa Vaccari: Bosc McGuire:
Carlaw Baile Guisset Elima Mounis Johnson:
Subs used - Tpuxagas Bentley Matins Casty:
Tries - Vaccari Elima Mounis Baile: Goals - Mounis:
Referee I Smith (Oldham) Att - 24401 H.T. 16 - 10

Sun 16 May 2010 HALEQUINS away lost 24 - 40
HALEQUINS - Dorn: Penny Clubb Howell Sharp: Gale
Randall: McCarthty-Scarsbrook Orr Temata Purdham
Willaimson Melling: Subs used - Wilkes Mills Esders May:
Tries - Randall(2) Melling Penny Williamson Orr Howell:
Goals - Orr(4) Gale(2):
CASTLEFORD - McGoldrick:Thompson James Evans Ferres
Wainwright: Chase Brent Sherwin: Huby Hudson Higgins
Jones Clayton Westerman: Subs used - Snitch Holmes
Tuson Widders: Tries - Westerman Ferres Higgins Snitch:
Goals Westerman(4):
Referee I Smith (Oldham) Att - 2941 H.T. 18 - 16

Sun 23 May 2010 HULL FC home lost 26 - 34
CASTLEFORD - McGoldrick: Wainwright Shenton Ferres
Arundel: Widders Chase: Higgins Hudson Huby Jones
Snitch Westerman: Subs used - Sargent Clayton Chris
Tuson KYLE WOOD(908): Tries - Wainwright(2) Jones
Arundel Chase: Goals - Westerman(3):
HULL FC - Tansey: Whiting Turner Yeaman Briscoe:
Washbrook Long: Dowes(S/B) Houghton O'Meley
Radford Tickle Fitzgibbon: Subs used - Burnett Hall Moa
McShane: Tries – Yeaman Tansey Long Briscoe
Fitzgibbon Meley: Goals – Tickle(5)
Referee B Thaler (Normanton) Att - 7996 H.T. 16 - 10

Fri 4 Jun 2010 WIGAN WARRIORS away lost 22 - 38
WIGAN - Richards: Goulding Gleeson Carmont Pryce: S
Tomkins Leulua: Fielden McIlorum Prescott Bailey J
Tomkins O'Loughlin: Subs used - Riddell Palea'aesina
Farrell Tuson: Tries - Goulding(3) O'Loughlin(2) Leuluai
Tuson: Goals - Richards(5):
CASTLEFORD - McGoldrick: Dixon Shenton Ferres
Wainwright: Widders Wood: Higgins Hudson Jackson
Huby Clayton Westerman: Subs used - Sargent Jones
Thompson JONATHAN WALKER(909):
Tries - Jackson Jones Ferres Huby: Goals - Westerman(3):
Referee T Albert (France) Att - 14047 H.T. 12 - 16

Tue 15 Jun 2010 CATALAN DRAGONS home
won 24 - 20
CASTLEFORD - Thompson: Dixon Shenton Ferres
Wainwright: Widders Chase: Jackson Hudson Higgins
Huby Jones Westerman:
Subs used - Snitch Wood Arundel Sargent:
Tries - Snitch(2) Wainwright(2): Goals - Westerman(4):
CATALAN D - Bathau: Bell Raguin Gossard Vaccari: Sa

Sherwin: Ferriol McGuire Guisset Elima Carlaw Johnson:
Subs used Mouni Fakir Casty A Bently
Tries - Vaccari(2) McGuire Raguin: Goals - Barthau(2):
Referee R Silverwood (Mirfield) Att - 4209 H.T. 12 - 10

Sun 20 Jun 2010 SALFORD CITY REDS away
won 28 - 22
SALFORD C R - Fitzpatrick: Broughton Talau Gibson Tyrer:
M Smith Holdsworth: Boyle Alker Sidlow Sibbit Littler
Swain: Subs used - Leuilui Adamson J Smith Parker:
Tries - Fitzpatrick Littler Broughton Sibbit:
Goals - Holcsworth (3):
CASTLEFORD - McGoldrick: Dixon Arundel Ferres
Wainwright: Widders Chase: Higgins Hudson Jackson
Huby Snitch Westerman:
Subs used - Sargent Jones Thompson Wood:
Tries - Widders(3) Huby Ferres: Goals - Westerman(4):
Referee S Ganson (St Helens) Att - 3130 H.T. 22 - 6

Sun 27 Jun 2010 BRADBORD BULLS home won 28 - 22
CASTLEFORD - McGoldrick: Dixon Shenton Arundel
Wainwright: Widders Chase: Higgins Hudson Huby Ferres
Snitch Westerman: Subs used - Sargent Jones Jackson
Kyle Wood: Tries - Shenton(3) Chase Dixon:
Goals - Dixon(3) Westerman:
BRADFORD B - Kearney: Sheriffe Platt Nero Halley: Sykes
Southernwood: Lynch L'estrange Hall Whitehead Langley
Menzies: Subs used - Kopczak Worrincy Godwin Addy:
Tries - Whitehead Menzies Kearney Platt: Goals - Sykes(3):
Referee B Thaler (Normanton) Att - 5482 H.T. 8 - 10

Sun 4 Jul 2010 HUDDERSFIELD GIANTS home
won 44 - 18
CASTLEFORD - McGoldrick: Dixon Shenton Ferres
Wainwright: Widders Chase: Huby Hudson Jackson Snitch
Clayton Westerman: Subs used - Sargent ADAM MILNER
(910) Thompson Walker: Tries - Huby(2) Chase(2) Snitch
McGoldrick Dixon: Goals - Westerman(6) Dixon(2):
HUDDERSFIELD G - B Hodgson: Cudjoe Lolesi Lawrence D
Hodgson: Brown Robinson: Griffin Drew Mason Gilmour
Finnigan Lunt: Subs used - Brough Patrick Faiumu Horne:
Tries - Lunt(2) Cudjoe Lolesi: Goal - B Hodgson:
Referee T Albert (France) Att - 5925 H.T. 18 - 14

Sun 11 Ju 2010 WARRINGTOIN WOLVES away
lost 30 - 54
WARRINGTON W - Mathers: Hicks King Atkins Riley: Grix
Myler: Morley Monaghan Carvel L Anderson Westwood
Solomona Subs used - Wood Cooper V Anderson
Clarke:
Tries - Myler(3) Riley Morley Atkins Mathers Hicks
Solomona: Goals - Westwood(9):
CASTLEFCRD - McGoldrick: Dixon Ferres Thompson
Wainwright: Widders Chase: Huby Hudson Jackson Snitch
Clayton Westerman: Subs used - Sargent Jones Walker
Milner: Tries Westerman(2) Dixon Wainwright Clayton
Snitch: Goals - Westerman(3):
Referee P Bentham (Warrington) Att – 10577 H.T. 4 - 30

SEASON 2010

Sun 18 Jul 2010 WAKEFIELD TRINITY WILDCATS home won 40 - 16
CASTLEFORD - McGoldrick: Dixon Shenton Ferres
Wainwright: Widders Chase: Huby Hudson Jackson Snitch
Clayton Westerman:
Subs used - Sargent Higgins Jones Thompson:
Tries - Dixon(2) Widders(2) Wainwright McGoldrick
Hudson: Goals - Westerman(5) Dixon:
WAKEFIELD T W - Blaymire: Gleeson Murphy Millard
Blanch: Cooke Jeffries: Leaeno Rinaldi Moore Demetriou
Johnson Morrison:
Subs used - Korkidas Henderson King Leo-Latu:
Tries - Morrison(2) Blaymire: Goals - Cooke(2)
Referee J Child (Dewsbury) Att - 8517 H.T. 6 - 10

Sun 25 Jul 2010 CRUSADERS RL away lost 24 - 30
Played at The Gnoll Neath
CRUSADERS RL - Schifcofske: Dyer Martin Mellars
Youngquest: Hanbury Sammut: Peek Withers Bryant
Hauraki Chan Lupton: Subs used - Lee James Winterstein
Trimachi: Tries - Hanbury James Hauraki Martin Sammut:
Goals - Schifcofske(5):
CASTLEFORD - McGoldrick: Dixon Shenton Ferres
Wainwright: Widders Chase: Huby Hudson Jackson Snitch
Clayton Westerman: Subs used - Sargent Jones Higgins
Thompson: Tries - Westerman Widders Shenton Chase:
Goals - Westerman(4):
Referee S Ganson (St Helens) Att - 1495 H.T. 12 - 12

Sun 1 Aug 2010 HULL KINGSTON ROVERS away
lost   26 - 28
HULL K R - Briscoe: Fox Charnley Colbon S Latus : Morrell
Dobson: Clinton Fisher Lovegrove Newton Galea Watts:
Subs used - Wheeldon Netherton Hodgson Mariano:
Tries - Charnley(3) Briscoe: Goals - Dobson(6):
CASTLEFORD - McGoldrick: Dixon Shenton Arundel
Wainwright: Widders Chase: Huby Hudson Sargent Ferres
Clayton Westerman:
Subs used - Snitch Jones Holmes Walker:
Tries - Ferres Arundel Chase Jones: Goals - Westerman(5):
Referee P Bentham (Warrington) Att - 8104 H.T. 12 - 18

Fri 13 Aug 2010 LEEDS RHINOS home lost 6 - 38
CASTLEFORD - McGoldrick: Dixon Shenton Arundel
Wainwright: Westerman Chase: Huby Hudson Sargent
Snitch Ryan Clayton Ferres: Subs used - Jones Widders
Walker Higgins: Try - Snitch: Goal - Westerman:
LEEDS R - Webb: Donald Senior Smith Hall: McGuire
Burrow: Leuluai Diskin Peacock Kirke Eastwood Clarkson:
Subs used - McShane Burgess Jones-Buchanan Lauitiiti:
Tries - Hall(2) Clarkson McGuire Burrow Lauitiiti Donald:
Goals - Smith(5):
Referee R Silverwood (Mirfield) Att - 7901 H.T. 0 - 18

Sun 22 Aug 2010 HARLEQUINS home won 40 - 28
CASTLEFORD - McGoldrick: Dixon Shenton Ferres
Wainwright: Widders Chase: Sargent Hudson Higgins
Snitch Jones Westerman: Subs used - Huby Arundel
Walker Milner: Tries - McGoldrick Shenton Hudson
Dixon Huby Milner Sargent: Goals - Westerman(6):

HARLEQUINS - Melling: O'Callaghan Clubb Howell Sharp:
Gale Dorn: Ward Ellis Wilkes Purdham Williamson Golden:
Subs used - McCarthy-Scarsbrook Mills Orr Brian:
Tries - Howell Sharp O'Callaghan Gale Dorn:
Goals - Purdham(4):
Referee P Bentham (Warrington) Att - 5862 H.T. 18 - 6

Sat. 4 Sep 2010 SAINT HELENS away lost 30 - 40
ST HELENS - Wellens: Gardner Gidley Meli Foster: Lomax
Eastmond: Graham Cunningham Puletua Flannery Wilkin
Roby: Subs used - Soliola Hargreaves Moore Clough:
Tries - Wellens Graham Flannery Meli Puletua Gidley
Cunningham: Goals Foster(6):
CASTLEFORD - McGoldrick: Dixon Shenton Ferres Michael
Wainwright: Widders Chase: Mitchell Sargent Hudson
Liam Higgins Jones Snitch Joe Westerman:
Subs used - Huby Milner Walker Arundel
Tries - Widders(2) McGoldrick Milner Shenton Hudson:
Goals - Dixon(2) Westerman:
Referee B Thaler (Normanton) Att - 13978 H.T. 4 - 18

Steve Snitch
D. No 902
2010 to 2012

Oliver Holmes
D. No 907
2010 to

Jonathon Walker
D. No 909
2010 to 2013

Adam Milner
D. No 910
2010 to

SEASON 2010

D.N	PLAYER		DEBUT	L MATCH	APP	SUB	T.AP	TRI'S	G'LS	D.G	P'TS
786	HUDSON	RYAN			26	2	28	5	0	0	20
795	JACKSON	PAUL			18	2	20	1	0	0	4
800	HUBY	CRAIG			21	6	27	6	3	0	30
802	CLAYTON	RYAN		13/08/2010	14	5	19	2	0	0	8
810	SHENTON	MICHAEL			22	0	22	10	0	0	40
846	McGOLDRICK	RYAN			27	0	27	8	0	0	32
861	WAINWRIGHT	MICHAEL		04/09/2010	26	0	26	10	0	0	40
863	OWEN	RICHARD			3	0	3	1	0	0	4
864	HIGGINS	LIAM		04/09/2010	13	11	24	1	0	0	4
869	WESTERMAN	JOE		04/09/2010	26	0	26	10	86	0	212
870	DIXON	KIRK			19	1	20	8	9	0	50
876	MASSEY	NATHAN			0	2	2	0	0	0	0
883	SHERWIN	BRENT		16/05/2010	11	1	12	3	0	0	12
890	SARGENT	MITCHELL		04/09/2010	10	16	26	3	0	0	12
891	ARUNDEL	JOE			5	4	9	2	0	0	8
892	EVANS	JAMES		16/05/2010	9	0	9	5	0	0	20
894	CHASE	RANGI			26	0	26	8	0	0	32
895	FERRES	BRETT			18	0	18	4	0	0	16
896	JONES	STUART			14	13	27	5	0	0	20
898	NETHERTON	KIRK		17/04/2010	2	2	4	0	0	0	0
899	WIDDERS	DEAN			12	4	16	9	0	0	36
901	THOMPSON	JORDAN			10	5	15	4	0	0	16
902	SNITCH	STEVE	05/02/2010		21	5	26	7	0	0	28
903	AINSCOUGH	SHAUN	27/02/2010	09/04/2010	7	0	7	4	0	0	16
904	COOPER	MICHAEL	13/03/2010	09/04/2010	1	5	6	2	0	0	8
905	DAVIES	JOHN	13/03/2010		0	1	1	0	0	0	0
906	TUSON	CHRIS	26/03/2010	23/05/2010	2	6	8	0	0	0	0
907	HOLMES	OLIVER	09/04/2010		0	5	5	0	0	0	0
908	WOOD	KYLE	23/05/2010	27/06/2010	1	4	5	0	0	0	0
909	WALKER	JONATHAN	04/06/2010		0	7	7	0	0	0	0
910	MILNER	ADAM	04/07/2010		0	4	4	2	0	0	8
	31		9	12	364	111	475	120	98	0	676

COMPETITION			P	W	D	L	FOR	AGT
S, LEAGUE	POSITION 9 OF 14		27	11	0	16	648	766
RL CUP			1	0	0	1	28	34
PLAYERS RECORDS			28	11	0	17	676	800

During training for the pre-season friendly win away at Catalan Dragons, Coach Terry Matterson lost a finger in accident as he attempted to jump over a fence to retrieve a ball.

In the RL Challenge Cup we had a very disappointing defeat at home to Division 1 team Barrow Raiders 34-28.

In the League we finished in 9th position, missing out on a play-off spot.

Oliver Holmes and Adam Milner made their Debuts and by the end of their careers they will probable be classed as 'notable debuts'.

SEASON 2011

SUPER LEAGUE XV1

This was the third and final year of the initial Super League Licences with no promotion and relegation.

Sun 26 Dec 2010 BRADFORD BULLS home
FRIENDLY - Cancelled - Snow and Ice

Sun 9 Jan 2011 YORK CITY KNIGHTS home
won 62 – 10 FRIENDLY
CASTLEFORD - Mathers: Dixon Arundel Thompson Youngquest: Chase Orr: Emmitt Hudson Walker Holmes J Davies Milner: Subs used - Picketts Payne Danny Holmes Clark Eden Blackmore Harris Siddons Brierley Orange: Tries - Dixon (2) Chase Milner Youngquest Eden Harris Orange Clark Brierley J Davies:
Goals - Dixon(4) Arundle(5):
YORK C K - Haynes: Sutton Straugheir Bush Wilson: Thorman Priestley: Freer Lee Benson Lewis Barron Esders: Subs used - Stearman Mitchell Stamp Barlow Burns Woods Jones Waterman Garside:
Tries - Straugheir Lewis: Goals - Waterman:
Referee T Roby Att - 1716 H.T. 28 - 4

Sun 16 Jan 2011 YORK CITY KNIGHTS away
won 40 – 26 FRIENDLY - UNDER 20'S
YORK C K - Haynes: Mole Sutton Smith Turflour: Barlow Woods: Burns Stamp Stearman Rice Williams Lewis: Subs used - Gray Worthington Winstanley Brining Holmes Mitchell Mortimer Carmody Hepworth: Tries - Turflour(3) Stearman Williams: Goals - Mole(2) Barlow: CASTLEFORD - Eden: Atkinson Holmes Nathaniel Blackmore: Brierley Johnson: Fleming Clark Thompson Harris J Davies Picketts: Subs used - Orange Siddons Smith Payne Pick Snelgrove Backhouse:
Tries - Atkinson(2) Clark(2) Brierley Eden Thompson: Goals - Brierley(6):
Referee M Kidd Att- 561 H.T. 16 - 16

Sun 23 Jan 2011 BATLEY BULLDOGS home
won 42 – 22 FRIENDLY
CASTLEFORD - Eden: Dixon Thompson Arundle Blackmore: Chase Orr: Fozzard Hudson Walker Huby Snitch Holmes: Subs used - Atkinson Harris J Davies Clark D Holmes Massey Emmitt: Tries - Orr Hudson Holmes Arundel Emmitt Walker Clark: Goals - Dixon(5) Huby(2):
BATLEY B - Preece: Brown Williams Maun Reittie:Mennell Handforth: Smith Lythe Martin Bretherton Walton Toohey: Subs used - Moore Lindsay Potter Hesketh Tootill Campbell Foulstone: Tries - Williams(2) Preece Foulstone: Goals - Moore(2) Mennell
Referee D Merrick Att- 1622 H.T. 18 - 12

Sun 30 Jan 2011 HULL FC home lost 20 - 22
FRIENDLY
CASTLEFORD - Mathers: Dixon Arundel Isa Younquest: Chase Orr: Fozzard Hudson Huby Walker Snitch Ferres: Subs used - Widders Aspinwall Thompson Jackson Holmes McGoldrick Emmitt Jones:

Tries - Chase(2) Arundel Dixon: Goals - Dixon Arundel: HULL FC - Whiting: Sharp Manu Yeaman Briscoe: Turner Long O'Maley Houghton Lauaki Westerman Tickle Fitzgibbon: Subs used - Williams Aldous Moa Cunningham Washbrook Dowes Lyne Kent:
Tries - Whiting Turner Manu Westerman: Goals - Tickle(3): Referee B Thaler Att- 4661 H.T. 8 - 6

Sat 13 Feb 2011 WAKEFIELD TRINITY WILDCATS won
40 – 20 PLAYED AT MILLENNIUM STADIUM CARDIFF
CASTLEFORD - RICHIE MATHERS(911): Dixon Ferres Arundel NICK YOUNGQUEST(912): Chase Orr: Huby Hudson JAKE EMMITT(913) Jones Holmes Snitch: Subs used - Milner Widders Jackson Walker:
Tries - Widders(2) Arundel Ferres Youngquest Chase Milner Jackson: Goals - Dixon (4):
WAKEFIELD T W - Blaymire: Veivers Murphy Dean George: Hyde Obst: Korkidas Rinaldi Johnson Ferguson Morrison Lee: Subs used - Millard King Spiers Henderson:
Tries - Ferguson(2) Rinaldi George: Goals - Veivers(2): Referee J Child Att - 30891 H.T. 18 - 10

Sat 20 Feb 2011 HUDDERSFIELD GIANTS home
won 18 -12
CASTLEFORD - Mathers: Dixon Arundel Ferres Youngquest: Chase Orr: Jackson Milner Huby Emmitt Holmes Jones: Subs used - Walker MARTIN ASPINWALL(914) Widders DARYL CLARK(915):
Tries - Youngquest(2) Arundel: Goals - Dixon(3): HUDDERSFIELD G - Grix: McGillvary Cudjoe Lawrence Hodgson: Brown Brough: Crabtree Carlile Mason Gilmour Fa'aloogo O'Donnell: Subs used - Lunt Faiumu Horne Griffin: Tries - McGillvary(2): Goals - Brough(2): Referee S Ganson Att - 5992 H.T. 8 - 0

Sun 6 Mar 2011 HULL KINGSTONE ROVERS home
won 27 - 14
CASTLEFORD - Mathers: Dixon Arundel Ferres Youngquest: Chase Orr: Jackson Milner Huby Holmes Jones Emmitt: Subs used - Aspinwall Walker Clark Widders: Tries - Holmes Youngquest Clark Dixon: Goals - Dixon (5) Chase D/G:
HULL KR - Briscoe: Fox Hall Welham Colbon: Greren Morrell: Vella Hodgson Watts Newton Galea Netherton: Subs used - Wheeldon Cockayne Taylor Fisher:
Tries - Newton Hall Galea: Goal - Hall:
Referee R Silverwood Att - 8537 H.T. 12 - 14

Sun 13 Mar 2011 CATALAN DRAGONS home
won 34 - 24
CASTLEFORD - Mathers: Dixon Arundel Ferres Youngquest: Chase Orr: Jackson Milner Huby Emmitt Holmes Jones: Subs used - NICK FOZZARD(916) Aspinwall Widders Clark: Tries - Huby Jones Dixon Chase Youngquest Arundel: Goals - Dixon(5):
CATALAN D - Greenshields: Blanch Farrar Millard Stacul: Sa Dureau: Fakir Henderson Pae Menzies Ragui Baitieri:

SEASON 2011

Subs used - Ferriol Casty Mounis Gigot:
Tries - Dureau(2) Blanch Stacul: Goals - Dureau(4):
Referee P Bentham Att - 4889 H.T. 12 - 18

Sun 20 Mar 2011 BRADFORD BULLS away lost 14 - 18
BRADFORD B - Sykes: Ainscough Platt Royston Ah Van:
Kearney Herbert: Lynch Diskin Hargreaves Elima
Whittaker Langley:
Subs used - Scruton L'Estrange Kopczak Olbison:
Tries - Scuton(2) Elima: Goals - Ah Van (3):
CASTLEFORD - Mathers: Dixon Arundel Ferres
Youngquest: Chase Orr: Jackson Milner Huby Holmes
Emmitt Jones:
Subs used - Fozzard Aspinwall Clark WILLIE ISA(917):
Tries - Chase Clark: Goals - Dixon(3):
Referee R Hicks Att - 14348 H.T. 8 - 12

Sun 27 Mar 2011 CRUSADERS home won 56 - 16
CASTLEFORD - Mathers: Dixon Arundel Isa Youngquest:
Chase Orr: Fozzard Milner Huby Jones Aspinwall Ferres:
Subs used - Jackson Emmitt Widders Clark:
Tries - Clark(2) Dixon(2) Widders Ferres Isa Mathers
Youngquest Arundel: Goals - Dixon(8):
CRUSADERS - Schifcofske: Reardon Martin Mellars
Tansey: Witt Sammut: O'Hara Withers Bryant Thomas
Chan Moore: Subs used - Dudson White Flower Murphy:
Tries - Reardon Martin Mellars; Goals - Schifcofske(2):
Referee B Thaler Att - 6030 H.T. 22 - 0

Fri 1 Apr 2011 HULL FC away won 20 - 18
HULL FC - Phelps: Sharp Whiting Yeaman Briscoe: Horne
Long: Moa Houghton Radford Westerman Tickle
Fitzgibbon: Subs used - Obst Manu Lauaki Dowes:
Tries - Yeaman Tickle Fitzgibbon:
Goals - Tickle(2) Westerman:
CASTLEFORD - Mathers: Dixon Arundel Isa Owen: Chase
Orr: Jackson Hudson Emmitt Jones Aspinwall Ferres:
Subs used - Huby Fozzard Widders Clark:
Tries - Isa(2) Owen: Goals - Dixon(4):
Referee J Child Att - 11856 H.T. 10 - 6

**Sun 8 Apr 2011 SALFORD CITY REDS home
won 52 - 20**
CASTLEFORD - Mathers: Owen Dixon Arundel
Youngquest: Chase Orr: Emmitt Hudson Huby Aspinwall
Holmes Ferres: Subs used - Jackson Fozzard Widders
Clark: Tries - Arundel(2) Youngquest(2) Dixon Mathers
Widders Clark Owen: Goals - Dixon(8):
SALFORD C R - Patten: Broughton Nero Ratchford Henry:
Smith Holdsworth: Cashmere Godwin Boyle Adamson
Anderson Wild: Subs used - Sneyd Sidlow Neal
Paleaaesina: Tries - Broughton Anderson Holdsworth
Sidlow: Goals - Holdsworth(2):
Referee P Bentham Att - 6471 H.T. 30 - 10

Fri 15 Apr 2011 HARLEQUINS RL away draw 26 - 26
HARLEQUINS RL - Dorn: O'Callaghan Clubb Howell
Melling: Gale Randall: Ambler Bailey Purdham Wilkes:
Subs used - Williams Bryan Bolger Pryce:
Tries - Clubb(2) Bryan Dorn Ellis: Goals - Gale(3):

CASTLEFORD - Mathers Dixon Arundel Ferres Owen:
Chase Orr: Jackson Hudson Huby Aspinwall Widders
Holmes: Subs used - Emmitt Snitch Fozzard Clark;
Tries - Ower (2) Chase Clark: Goals - Dixon(5):
Referee M Thomason Att - 4128 H.T. 12 - 10

**Fri 22 Apr 2011 WAKEFIELD TRINITY WILDCATS
home lost 24 - 28**
CASTLEFORD - Mathers: Thompson Arundel Dixon Owen:
Chase Orr: Fozzard Hudson Emmitt Jones Ferres
Aspinwall: Subs used - Jackson Huby Widders Clark:
Tries - Mathers Aspinwall Thompson Orr:
Goals - Dixon(4):
WAKEFIELD T W - Blaymires: G Johnson Dean Murphy
Griffin: Hyde Lee: Amor Rinaldi P Johnson Morrison
Mariano Howarth: Subs used - King Henderson Higgins
Wilde: Tries - Dean Hyde Griffin P Johnson Mariano:
Goals - Griffin(4):
Referee J Childs Att - 9020 H.T. 18 - 4

**Mon 25 Apr 2011 SAINT HELENS away lost 20 - 22
PLAYED AT WIDNES RLFC**
ST HELENS - Makinson:Gardner Shenton Meli Foster:
Wilkin Lomax: Graham Roby McCarthy-Scarsbrook
Soliola Ashurst Puletua:
Subs used - Moore Dixon Magennis Armstrong:
Tries - Armstrong(2) Gardner Meli: Goals - Foster(3):
CASTLEFORD - Mathers: Thompson Arundel Dixon Owen:
Chase Orr Jackson Milner Huby Jones Holmes Aspinwall:
Subs used - Hudson Emmitt Snitch Ferres:
Tries - Chase Thompson Jones: Goals - Dixon(4):
Referee P Bentham Att - 8010 H.T. 8 - 12:

Frday 29 Apr 2011 LEEDS RHINOS home lost 6 - 48
CASTLEFORD - Mathers: Thompson Arundel Dixon Owen:
Chase Orr: Jackson Milner Snitch Jones Holmes Ferres:
Subs used - Emmitt Aspinwall McGoldrick Clark:
Try - Arundel: Goal - Dixon:
LEEDS R - Webb: Watkins Delaney Senior Hall: Sinfield
Burrow: Leuluai McShane Burgess Jones-Buchanan
Clarkson Ablett: Subs used - McGuire Peacock Cross
Kirke: Tries - Hall(2) Watkins Jones-Buchanan McGuire
Burrow McShane Kirke: Goals - Sinfield(8):
Referee R Silverwood Att - 9860 H.T. 0 - 12

**Sun 8 May 2011 ROCHDALE HORNETS away
won 72 – 10 RL CHALLENGE CUP 3rd ROUND**
ROCHDALE H - Yates: Bloomfield Strong Gorton Saywell:
Crook Roper: Mervill Ashall Cookson Hobson Bowman
Donoghue: Subs used - Ekis Newton McDermott
English: Tries - Yates Saywell: Goal - Crook:
CASTLEFORD - Owen: Thompson Arundel Dixon GREG
EDEN(918) McGoldrick Chase: Fozzard Milner Emmitt
Holmes Widders Hudson: Subs used - Orr Snitch Massey
Clark: Tries - Dixon(2) Arundel(2) Snitch(2) Clark(2)
Massey(2) Chase Milner Owen: Goals - Dixon(9) Orr:
Referee T Albert Att - 1675 H.T. 22 - 6

SEASON 2011

Fri 13 May 2011 WARRINGTON WOLVES away lost 0 - 62
WARRINGTON W - Hodgson: J Monaghan Bricge Atkins King: Briers O'Brien: Morley M Monaghan: Carvell Anderson Westwood Grix: Subs used - Higham Wood Cooper Solomona: Tries - Briers(2) King(2) Grix(2) O'Brien Hodgson Higham Solomona J Monagham: Goals - Hodgson(7) Briers(2): CASTLEFORD - Mathers: Dixon McGoldrick Arundel Owen: Chase Orr: Massey Hudson Fozzard Ferres Jones Aspinwall: Subs used - Emmitt Milner Holmes Widders: Referee Mr S Ganson Att - 10715 H.T. 0 - 28

Sat 21 May 2011 WAKEFIELD TRINITY away won 20-18 RL CHALLENGE CUP 4th ROUND
WAKEFIELD TW - Veivers: Johnson Murphy Griffin Morton: Hyde Lee: Korkidas Rinaldi Johnson Mcrrison Henderson Howarth: Subs used - Mariano King Amor Wildie: Tries - Morrison Lee: Goals - Veivers(5): CASTLEFORD - Mathers: Dixon Isa Arundel Owen: Chase Orr: Fozzard Hudson Emmitt Holmes Ferres Snitch: Subs used - Massey Thompson Widders Clark: Tries - Ferres Chase Orr: Goals - Dixon(4): Rerferee - Mr R Silverwwod Att - 6604 H.T. 6 - 8
DRAWING 18 - 18 AT THE END OF FULL TIME. GOLDEN POINT RULE OPERATED DIXON KICKED A PENALTY GOAL IN THE 9TH MINUTE OF EXTRA TIME TO WIN THE GAME.

Sun 29 May 2011 HARLEQUINS RL home won 56 - 24
CASTLEFORD - Mathers: Dixon Arundel Isa Owen Chase Orr: Fozzard Milner Emmitt Jones Ferres Snitch: Subs used - Walker Thompson Widders Clark: Tries - Chase(4) Dixon Mathers Thompson Owen Clark Milner: Goals - Dixon(8): HARLEQUINS RL - O'Callaghan: Melling Pryce Chubb Riley: Bailey Gale: Temata Randall Ward Burnett Mitchell Wilkes: Subs used - Ambler Krasniqi Ellis Kouparitsas: Tries - Riley(2) Wilkes(2) O'Callaghan: Goals - Gale(2): Referee R Hicks Att - 7072 H.T. 22 - 18

Sun 5 Jun 2011 HUDDERSFIELD GIANTS away lost 18 – 40 PLAYED AT THE SHAY HALIFAX (GALPHARM BEING RESEEDED)
HUDDERSFIELD G - Gix: McGillvary Warsle Lawrence Hodgson: Cudjoe Brough: Crabtree Robinson Griffin Gilmour Horne Fa'alogo: Subs used - Mason Patrick Kirmond Faiumu: Tries - Cudjoe(2) Crabtree Hodgson Gilmour McGillvary Fa'alogo: Goals - Brough(4) Cudjoe(2): CASTLEFORD - Mathers: Thompson Dixon Arundel Owen: Chase Orr: Jackson Milner Emmitt Jones Ferres Asp nwall: Subs used - Walker Fozzard Widders Clark: Tries - Owen(2) Orr: Goals - Dixon(3): Referee B Thaler Att - 5237 H.T. 6 - 18

Sun 12 Jun WIGAN WARRIORS home draw 22 -22
CASTLEFORD - Mathers Dixon Thompson Arundel Owen: McGoldrick Orr: Jackson Milner Emmitt Ferres Aspinwall Hudson: Subs used - Chase Fozzard Massey Widders: Tries - Arundel(2) Widders Aspinwall Mathers:

Goal - Dixon: WIGAN W - Roberts: Charnley J Tompkins Goulding Richards: Finch Deacon: Mossop Leuluai Lima Hansen Hoffman Tuson: Subs used - McLlorum O'Loughlin Prescott Farrell: Tries - Finch Charnley Prescott J Tompkins: Goals - Richards(3): Referee P Bentham Att - 7263 H.T. 4 - 22

Fri 17 Jun 2011 SALFORD CITY REDS away won 15 - 8
SALFORD C R - Patten: Broughton Ratchford Gleeson Henry: Smith Holdsworth: Cashmere Godwin Boyle Adamson Nero Anderson: Subs used - Jewitt Paleaaesina Sidlow Neal: Tries - Broughton Holdsworth: CASTLEFORD - Mathers: Dixon Thompson Arundel Youngquest: Chase Orr: Jackson Hudson Emmitt Snitch Ferres McGoldrick: Subs used - Fozzard Massey Widders Clark: Tries - Thompson Orr: Goals - Dixon(3) ChaseD/G: Referee P Bentham Att- 3587 H.T. 2 - 4

Sat 25 Jun 2011 CATALAN DRAGONS away lost 20 - 54
CATALAN D - Greenshields: Blanch Baile Millard Vaccari: Sa Dureau: Ferriol Henderson Fakir Menzies Paea Mounis: Subs used - Casty Simon Baitieri Pelissier: Tries - Paea(2) Vaccari(2) Menzies Blanch Dureau Greenshields Baitieri Baile: Goals - Dureau(7): CASTLEFORD - Mathers: Dixon Thompson Arundel Owen: Chase Orr: Jackson Hudson Emmitt Snitch Ferres McGoldrick: Subs used - Fozzard Massey Widders Clark: Tries - Owen(2) Widders Mathers: Goals - Dixon(2): Referee T Albert Att - 8695 H.T. 10 - 26

Fri 1 Jul 2011 WARRINGTON WOLVES home lost 18 - 48
CASTLEFORD - Mathers Eden Arundel Ferres Owen Chase McGoldrick: Fozzard Orr Emmitt Jones Snitch Hudson: Subs Used - Jackson Milner Massey Holmes: Tries - Ferres Chase Hudson Eden: Goal - Orr: WARRINGTON W -Hodgson: J Monaaghan Blythe Atkins King: Bridge Myler: Wood M Monaghan Carvell Grix Westwood Harrison: Subs used - Higham Clarke Cooper Solomona: Tries - King(3) Hodgson(2) Myler Blythe J Monaghan Atkins: Goals - Hodgson(6): Referee J Child Att - 5947 H.T. 0 - 24

Wed 6 Jul 2011 WIGAN WARRIORS away lost 16 - 26
WIGAN W - S Tomkins: Goulding J Tomkins Carmont Charnley: Finch Deacon: Lima Leuluai Mossop Hansen Farrell O'Loughlin: Subs used - McIlorum Hoffman Tuson Hock: Tries - Charnley(2) Farrell Carmont Hoffman: Goals - Deacon(3): CASTLEFORD - McGoldrick: Eden Arundel Ferres Owen: Widders Chase: Fozzard Milner Emmitt Jones Holmes Snitch: Subs used - Massey J Davies Clark ROB PARKER(919): Tries - Jones Owen Davies: Goals - Arundel(2): Referee S Ganson Att - 13096 H.T. 16 - 10

Sun 10 Jul 2011 BRADFORD BULLS home won 34 - 30
CASTLEFORD - McGoldrick: Youngquest Dixon Arundel
Owen: Chase Orr: Jackson Milner Parker Ferres Jones
Hudson: Subs used - Massey Thompson Widders J
Davies: Tries - Arundel(2) Milner Chase Parker Jones:
Goals - Dixon(5):
BRADFORD B - Kearney: Ah Van Sykes Whitehead Raynor:
Jeffries Herbert: Lynch Diskin Burgess Elima Langley
Hargreaves:Subs used - Addy Royston Kopczak Scruton:
Tries - Kearney(2) Raynor Royston Sykes:
Goals - Ah Van(5):
Referee R Silverwood Att - 7004 H.T. 18

Sat 16 Jul 2011 CRUSADERS away won 26 - 20
CRUSADERS - Schifcofske: Reardon Martin Mellars
Tansey: Witt White: O'Hara Withers Moore Winterstein
Chan Cahill: Subs used - James Sammut Williams Flower:
Tries - Chan White Tansey Sammut:
Goals - Schifcofske(2):
CASTLEFORD - Mathers: Youngquest Dixon Arundel
Owen: McGoldrick Orr: Jackson Clark Parker Ferres Jones
Hudson: Subs used - Widders Snitch Thompson BEN
DAVIES(920): Tries - Thompson Youngquest B Davies
Parker: Goals - Dixon(5):
Referee Mr B Thaler Att - 3055 H.T. 6 -14

**Sun 24 Jul 2011 HUDDERSFIELD GIANTS home
won 22 – 18 RL CHALLENGE CUP QUARTER FINAL**
CASTLEFORD - McGoldrick: Youngquest Dixon Arundel
Owen: Chase Orr: Jackson Milner Parker Ferres Jones
Hudson: Subs used - Massey Thompson Clark B Davies:
Tries - Dixon Thompson Orr Hudson: Goals - Dixon(3):
HUDDERSFIELD G - Grix: McGillvary Wardle Gilmour
Hodgson: Cudjoe Brough: Crabtree Robinson Mason
Lawrence Patrick Ferguson:
Subs used - Faiumu Griffin Kirmond Wood:
Tries - Grix McGillvary Cudjoe Lawrence: Goal - Brough:
Referee P Bentham Att - 6336 H.T. 12 - 6

Sun 31 Jul 2011 SAINT HELENS home lost 26 - 46
CASTLEFORD - McGoldrick: Youngquest Dixon Arundel
Owen: Widders Chase: Massey Milner B Davies Ferres
Holmes Thompson: Subs used - Hudson Isa Aspinwall J
Davies: Tries Chase Dixon Youngquest Owen Widders:
Goals - Dixon(3):
ST HELENS - Wellens: Makinson Shenton Eastmond
Foster Pryce Lomax: Graham Roby McCarthy-Scarsbrook
Flannery Wilkin Puletua: Subs used - Moore Magennis
Dixon Gaskell: Tries - Wellens(2) Graham Shenton
McCarthy-Scarsbrook Puletua Gaskell Eastmond:
Goals - Foster (7):
Referee R Hicks Att - 6802 H.T. 16 - 24

**Sun 6 Aug 2011 LEEDS RHINOS lost 8 - 10
RL CHALLENGE CUP SEMI FINAL AT KEEPMOAT
STADIUM DONCASTER**
CASTLEFORD - McGoldrick: Youngquest Dixon Arundel
Owen: Chase Orr: Jackson Milner Parker Ferres Jones
Apinwall: Subs used - Hudson Isa Thompson B Davies:
Try - Chase: Goal - Dixon(2):

LEEDS R - Webb: Jones-Bishop Watkins Ablett Hall:
Sinfield Burrow: Leuluai Buderus Peacock Jones-Buchanan
Delaney Clarkson: Subs used - McGuire Bailey Kirke
Hauraki: Try - Watkins: Goals - Sinfield(3):
Referee P Bentham Att - 13158 H.T. 0- 2
**DRAWING 8-8 AT FULL TIME, GOLDEN POINT RULE
APPLIED LEEDS AWARDED A PENALTY 2ND MINUTE
OF EXTRA TIME SINFIELD KICKING THE GOAL**

Fri 12 Aug 2011 LEEDS RHINOS away lost 0 - 56
LEEDS R - Webb: Jones -Bishop Watkins Ablett Hall:
Sinfield McGuire: Leuluai Buderus Peacock Jones-
Buchanan Hauraki Chlarkson: Subs used - Bailey Kirke
Burrow Lauitiiti: Tries - Webb(2) Burrow(2) Jones-
Buchanan Hall Watkins Jones-Bishop Lauitiiti McGuire:
Goals - Sinfield(6) Burrow(2):
CASTLEFORD - McGoldrick: Youngquest Isa Arundel
Owen: Wicders Orr: Parker Milner B Davies Jones Holmes
Aspinwall: Subs used - Massey Thompson J Davies Clark:
Referee T Alibert Att - 15156 H.T. 0 - 20

**Sat 20 Aug 2011 WAKEFIELD TRINITY WILDCATS
away won 34 - 30**
WAKEFIELD T W - Tongia: Morton Henderson Dean
Tadulala: Smith Lee: Amor Rinaldi Higgins Johnson
Morrison Howarth: Subs used - Wildie Tony Gledhill
Hickey: Tries - Morrison Johnson Wilde Tadulala Dean:
Goals - Morton(5):
CASTLEFORD - McGoldrick: Youngquest Mathers Isa
Owen: Chase Orr: Parker Milner Massey Jones Aspinwall
Hudson: Subs used - Thompson Holmes Widders B
Davies: Tries - Isa(2) Mathers B Davies Youngquest
Widders: Goals - Orr(5):
Referee F. Silverwood Att - 6784 H.T. 22 - 24

Sat 3 Sep 2011 HULL F C home lost 18 - 50
CASTLEFORD - McGoldrick: Youngquest Isa Arundel
Owen: Chase Orr: Massey Hudson Davies Jones Holmes
Martin Aspinwall:
Subs used - Richard Mathers Snitch Fozzard Widders:
Tries - Orr Youngquest Isa: Goals - Orr(3):
HULL FC - Phelps: Whiting Turner Yeaman Briscoe: Horne
Obst: O'Meley Houghton Moa Manu Westerman
Fitzgibbon: Tries - Briscoe(2) Turner(2) Manu(2) Yeaman
Houghton Sharp: Goals - Westerman(7):
Referee S Ganson Att - 7866 H.T. 6 - 22

**Sat 10 Sep 2011 HULL KINGSTON ROVERS away
lost 24 - 26**
HULL K R - Briscoe: Latus Welham Webster Hall: Green
Dobsor: Vella Hodgson Taylor Newton Galea Watts:
Subs used - Fisher Murrell Lovegrove Cox:
Tries - Latus(2) Dobson Vella Webster:
Goals - Dobson(3):
CASTLEFORD - Owen: Arundel Dean Widders Willie Isa
Thompson: Chase Orr: Nick Fozzard Milner Massey Jones
Holmes Hudson:
Subs used - Snitch J Davies Clark Rob Parker:
Tries - Orr Owen Snitch Thompson: Goals - Orr(4):
Referee R Silverwood Att - 8936 H.T. 12 - 18

Richie Mathers
D. No 911
2011

Nick Younquest
D. No 912
2011 to 2012

Jacob Emmitt
D. No 913
2011 to 2013

Martin Aspinwall
D. No 914
2011

Daryl Clark
D. No 915
2011 to 2014

Nick Fozzard
D. No 916
2011

2011 SQUAD
Back Row – Oliver Holmes Ryan McGoldrick Craig Huby Jacob Emmitt Nick Fozzard Jonathan Walker Martin Aspinwall Kirk Dixon
Middle Row – Willie Isa Jordan Thompson Nathan Massey John Davies Paul Jackson Nick Youngquest Joe Arundel Dean Widders
Front Row –Richard Owen Stuart Jones Adam Milner Richard Mathers Ryan Hudson Terry Matterson Danny Orr Steve Snitch Brett Ferris

SEASON 2011

D.N	PLAYER		DEBUT	L MATCH	APP	SUB	T.AP	TRI'S	G'LS	D.G	P'TS
742	ORR	DANNY			28	1	29	7	14	0	56
786	HUDSON	RYAN			18	3	21	2	0	0	8
795	JACKSON	PAUL			16	5	21	1	0	0	4
800	HUBY	CRAIG			9	2	11	1	0	0	4
846	McGOLDRICK	RYAN			15	1	16	0	0	0	0
863	OWEN	RICHARD			24	0	24	13	0	0	52
870	DIXON	KIRK			25	0	25	10	102	0	244
876	MASSEY	NATHAN			5	10	15	2	0	0	8
891	ARUNDEL	JOE			30	0	30	13	2	0	56
894	CHASE	RANGI			28	1	29	15	0	2	62
895	FERRES	BRETT			25	1	26	4	0	0	16
896	JONES	STUART			23	0	23	4	0	0	16
899	WIDDERS	DEAN		10/09/2011	6	19	25	8	0	0	32
901	THOMPSON	JORDAN			10	8	18	7	0	0	28
902	SNITCH	STEVE			8	6	14	3	0	0	12
905	DAVIES	JOHN			0	5	5	1	0	0	4
907	HOLMES	OLIVER			16	3	19	1	0	0	4
909	WALKER	JONATHAN			0	5	5	0	0	0	0
910	MILNER	ADAM			19	3	22	4	0	0	16
911	MATHERS	RICHARD	13/02/2011	03/09/2011	22	1	23	7	0	0	28
912	YOUNGQUEST	NICK	13/02/2011		16	0	16	12	0	0	48
913	EMMITT	JACOB	13/02/2011		17	5	22	0	0	0	0
914	ASPINWALL	MARTIN	20/02/2011	03/09/2011	13	6	19	2	0	0	8
915	CLARKE	DARYL	20/02/2011		1	20	21	9	0	0	36
916	FOZZARD	NICK	13/03/2011	10/09/2011	9	10	19	0	0	0	0
917	ISA	WILLIE	20/03/2011	10/09/2011	8	3	11	6	0	0	24
918	EDEN	GREG	08/05/2011		3	0	3	1	0	0	4
919	PARKER	ROB	06/07/2011	10/09/2011	6	2	8	2	0	0	8
920	DAVIES	BEN	16/07/2011		3	4	7	2	0	0	8
	29		10	6	403	124	527	137	118	2	786

COMPETITION		P	W	D	L	FOR	AGT
S, LEAGUE	POSITION 9 OF 14	27	12	2	13	664	808
RL CUP		4	3	0	1	122	56
PLAYERS RECORDS		**31**	**15**	**2**	**14**	**786**	**864**

In the RL Challenge Cup we made it through to the semi-final, with two away victories in the Round 3 at Rochdale Hornets and the Round 4 at Wakefield Trinity Wildcats but only after a 'Golden Point' penalty conversion by Kirk Dixon after drawing 18 all at full-time. The semi-final, played at the Keepmoat Stadium Doncaster against Leeds, was eight all at full-time after Rangi Chase had put a drop goal attempt wide with only seconds left on the clock. Leeds were awarded a very easy penalty two minutes into extra time and Sinfield slotted the goal over for the victory.

In July Coach Terry Matterson announced that he would be leaving at the end of the season.

Also in July the Rugby League announced that Castleford Tigers had been awarded a 'C' License for seasons 2012 to 2015.

Kirk Dixon equalled the record of points scored in a Super League game at 24 against the Crusaders at home on 27 March 2011.

It could be said that this was the Rangi Chase season. He won the Albert Goldthorpe Medal awarded by the Rugby Leaguer and League Express for Super League's best and fairest player. He also won the 'Super League Man of Steel' award. He represented the 'Exiles' against England, and after pledging his allegiance to England he played for England in all four Tri- Nations games at the end of the season. Chase then signed a contract extension to the end of the 2015 season. Nevertheless he left the Club before the end of his contracted period.

After losing three out of the last four matches after the semi-final defeat we were beaten by one point by Hull for eighth spot thus missing the play offs.

Daryl Clark made his Debut and in the short period he played for the Club he made a significant impact.

SEASON 2012

SUPER LEAGUE XVII

The first season of the second licencing franchise. Celtic crusaders withdrew from the bidding process the day before the announcement of the teams. Widnes had previously been allocated a licence and place therefore the only difference in the make up of the league from the previous season was Widnes for Celtic.

Mon 26 Dec 2011 BRADFORD BULLS home won 28 – 18 FRIENDLY

CASTLEFORD - Clare: Atkinson Thompson Griffin D Holmes McGoldrick Johnson: Nash Milner Massey O Holmes Mitchell Jones: Subs used - Clark Snellgrove Smith Davies Snitch Siddons Brierley: Tries - Griffin(2) Atkinson(2) Johnson Nash: Goals - Griffin Thompson: BRADFORD BULLS - Sykes: Ainscough Platt Walker Crookes Briggs Jeffries; Hargeaves O'Brian Joseph Sibbit Olbison Langley: Subs used - Donaldson Addy Bateman Murphy Hawthorne McVoy Payne: Tries - Crookes Walker Hargreaves Ainscough: Goal - Briggs Referee J Leahy Att - 3296 H.T. 10 - 4

Fri 13 Jan 2012 HUDDERSFIELD GIANTS home won 32 – 22 FRIENDLY

CASTLEFORD - McGoldrick: Clare Griffin Arundel Dixon: Chase Orr: Nash Hudson Massey Holmes Snitch Jones: Subs used - Mitchell Emmitt Shaw Thompson Clark Atkinson Owen Milner Davies: Tries - Hudson Orr Holmes Mitchell Chase Clark: Goals - Dixon(3) Shaw: HUDDERSFIELD G - Eden: McGilvary: Wardle Cudjoe George: Brough Grix: Crabtree Lee A Walker Sarsfield Chan Lunt: Subs used - Gilmour Johnson Fairbank Molly Robinson Mason Coding F Walker: Tries - McGilvary(2) Brough Wardle : Goals - Brough(3): Referee J Childs Att - 2542 H.T. 16 - 12

Sun 22 Jan 2012 WAKEFIELD TRINITY WILDCATS away lost 20 – 40 FRIENDLY

WAKEFIELD T W - Mathers: Fox Collis Mellars Cockayne: John Smith: Amor Alton Southern Kirmond Lauitiiti Washbrook: Subs used - Wood Trout Johnson Slater Walshaw Ellis Tony: Tries - Wasbrook(2) Amor Mathers Cockayne Lauitiiti Mellars Tony: Goals - John(4): CASTLEFORD - Owen: Shaw Arundel Griffin Dixon: Chase Orr: Emmitt Hudson Nash Ferres Holmes McGoldrick: Subs used - Jones Mitchell Clark Milner Thompson Davies: Tries - Ferres Jones Mitchell Nash: Goals - Dixon(2): Referee T Albert Att - 2200 H.T. 4 - 18

Sun 29 Jan 2012 v YORK CITY KNIGHTS away lost 14 – 34 FRIENDLY

YORK C K - Haynes Pryce Ford Elliott Sutton: Thornton Tansey: Sullivan Lee Houston Clarke Smith Aldous: Subs used - Gay Hellewell Broughton Howard Williams Garside Benson: Tries - Sutton(2) Thorman Benson Ford Pryce Gay: Goals - Thorman(3): CASTLEFORD - Clare: Lipori Wilson Grehan Atkinson:

Carroll Johnston: Massey Canterbury Walker J Thompson Siddons Davies: Subs used - Reynolds Fleming Lloyd D Holmes Orange Richards C Thompson Smith: Tries - Grehan J Thompson Lipori: Goal - Reynolds: Referee G Dolan Att - 469 H.T. 0 - 22

Fri 3 Feb 2012 SALFORD CITY REDS away won 24 - 10 FIRST SUPER LEAGUE GAME STAGED AT SALFORDS NEW GROUND 'SALFORD CITY STADIUM'

SALFORD C R - Patten: Broughton Gleeson Moon Williams: Holdsworth Smith: James Godwin Boyle Ashirst Anderson Wild: Subs used - Adamson Palea'aesina Gledhill Howarth: Tries - Smith Ashirst: Goal - Holdsworth: CASTLEFORD - Owen: JOSH GRIFFIN(921) McGoldrick Arundel Dixon: Chase Orr: Emmitt Milner Walker LEE MITCHELL(922) Holmes Jones: Subs used - Clark Ferres Massey STEVE NASH(923): Tries - Owen(2) Griffin Milner: Goals - Dixon(4): Referee T Albert Att - 5242 H.T. 6 - 4

Sun 12 Feb 2012 BRADFORD BULLS home lost 12 - 20

CASTLEFORD - Owen: Dixon Arundel McGoldrick Griffin: Chase Orr: Emmitt Milner Walker Holmes Mitchell Jones: Subs used - Clark Massey Ferres Nash: Tries - Griffin Owen: Goals - Dixon(2): BRADFORD B - Kearney: Crookes Purtell Walker Kear: Sammut Gale: Kopczak Diskin Hargreaves Sibbit Whitehead Langley: Subs used Donaldson Scruton Burgess L'Estrange: Tries - Sammut Burgess Kearney: Goals Gale(4): Referee B Thaler Att - 8054 H.T. 0 - 12

Sat 18 Feb 2012 CATALAN DRAGONS away lost 20 -28

CATALAN D - Greenshields: Blanch Duport Millard Bosc: Pryce Dureau: Paea Henderson Casty Sa Raguin Baitieri: Subs used - Ferriol Menzies Fakir Fisher: Tries - Millard(2) Bosc Duport Baitieri: Goals - Dureau(4): CASTLEFORD - Owen: Dixon Arundel McGoldrick Griffin: Chase Orr: Nash Clark Massey Ferres Holmes Jones: Subs used - Emmitt Snitch Milner Mitchell: Tries - Griffin(3) Arundel: Goals - Dixon(2): Referee T Roby Att - 7455 H.T. 16 - 6

Sun 26 Feb 2012 WIGAN WARRIORS home lost 4 - 46

CASTLEFORD - Owen: Youngquest Dixon McGoldrick Griffin: Chase Orr: Emmitt Milner Nash Holmes Mitchell Jones: Subs used - Clark Snitch Massey JAMES GREHAN(924)   Try - Griffin: WIGAN W - Tomkins: Charnley Goulding Hughes Richards: Finch Leuluai: Lauaki McLlourum Mossop Hansen Hock O'Loughlin: Subs used - Lima Farrell Tuson Spencer Tries - Tomkins(3) Richards(2) Charnley(2) O'Loughlin: Goals - Richards(7): Referee T Alibert Att - 8156 H.T. 4 - 24

Fri 2 Mar 2012 LEEDS RHINOS home lost 14 - 36

CASTLEFORD - Owen: Griffin McGoldrick Dixon Youngquest: Chase Orr: Emmitt Milner GRANT

SEASON 2012

MILLINGTON(925) Ferres Holmes Jones:
Subs used - Clark Snitch Mitchell Massey:
Tries - Clark Dixon Griffin: Goal - Dixon:
LEEDS R - Webb: Jones-Bishop Watkins Hardaker Hall:
Sinfield McGuire: Leuluai Burrow Peacock Pitts Delaney
Ablett: Subs used - Kirke Clarkson Griffin Hood:
Tries - Hall(3) Watkins McGuire Hood: Goals - Sinfield(6):
Referee J Child Att- 9237 H.T. 10 - 18

Sat 10 Mar 2012 LONDON BRONCOS away
lost 16 - 42
LONDON B - Dorn: Robertson Howell Sarginson Colbon:
Witt Gower: Kaufusi Randall Clubb Cook Golden Bailey:
Subs used - Bryant Rinaldi Temata Melling:
Tries - Howell(2) Bailey Gower Cook Sarginson Golden
Melling: Goals Witt(5):
CASTLEFORD - Owen Youngquest: Dixon McGoldrick
Griffin: Chase Orr: Emmitt Milner Millington Mitchell
Holmes Jones: Subs used - Clark Walker Snitch Massey:
Tries - Youngquest Dixon McGoldrick: Goals - Dixon(2):
Referee P Bentham Att - 2381 H.T. 12 -22

Fri 16 Mar HUDDERSFIELD GIANTS away lost 4 - 42
HUDDERSFIELD G - Eden: McGilvary Cudjoe Wardle
George: Grix Brough: Crabtree Robinson Gilmour Chan
Lawrence Brown: Subs used - Fa'alogo Faiumu Patrick
Lee: Tries - George(3) Eden Wardle Patrick Brown
Lawrence: Goals - Brough(5):
CASTLEFORD - Owen: JAMES CLARE (926) Joe Arundel
Dixon Youngquest: McGoldrick Chase: Walker Hudson
Millington Ferres Grehan Snitch: Subs used - Clark
Mitchell Emmitt Massey: Try - Youngquest
Referee S Ganson Att - 6928 H.T. 4 - 26

Sun 25 Mar 2012 HULL FC home lost 28 - 42
CASTLEFORD - Owen: Griffin Grehan Dixon Youngquest:
Chase Orr: Massey Hudson Walker Ferres Holmes Emmitt:
Subs used - Snitch Jones Millington McGoldrick:
Tries - Youngquest Walker Millington Griffin Ferres:
Goals - Dixon(4):
HULL FC - McKinnon: Sharp Martin Turner Briscoe: Horne
Seymour: Moa Houghton Lynch Manu Tickle Aspinwall:
Subs used - Ellis Whiting O,Carroll Bowden:
Tries - Manu(2) Moa Turner Tickle Seymour Briscoe:
Goals - Tickle(7):
Referee M Thomason Att - 9050 H.T. 16 - 20

Fri 30 Mar 2012 HULL KINGSTON ROVERS home
won 34 - 30
CASTLEFORD - Owen: Griffin Dixon Mitchell Youngquest:
Chase Orr: Walker Clark Massey Ferres Holmes Emmitt:
Subs used - Snitch Jones Millington McGoldrick:
Tries - Youngquest(2) Griffin Owen Dixon Snitch:
Goals - Dixon (5):
HULL KR - McDonnell: Salter Horne Welham D Hodgson:
Murrell Dobson: Clinton Withers Wheeldon Mika J
Hodgson Watts: Subs used - Paea Taylor Lovegrove Cox:
Tries - Welham(3) J Hodgson Withers: Goals - Dobson(5):
Referee R Hicks Att - 6396 H.T. 18 - 16

Fri 6 Apr 2012 WAKEFIELD TRINITY WILDCATS away
won 34 - 16
WAKEFIELD T W - Mathers: Fox Mellars Sykes Cockayne:
John Smith Amor Aiton Raleigh Lauitiiti Southern
Washbrook: Subs used - Wood Trout Johnson Wilkes:
Tries - Fox Sykes Wood: Goals - Sykes(2):
CASTLEFORD - Owen: Youngquest Dixon Ferres Griffin:
Chase Orr: Walker Clark Massey Holmes Snitch Emmitt:
Subs used - Jones Mitchell Millington McGoldrick:
Tries - Owen(2) Millington Snitch Ferres Holmes:
Goals - Dixon(5):
Referee S Ganson Att - 9786 H.T. 18 - 10

Mon 9 Apr 2012 SAINT HELENS home lost 12 - 18
CASTLEFORD - Dixon: JOSH ATKINSON(927) Thompson
Ferres Griffin: McGoldrick Milner: Walker Hudson Nash
Mitchell Holmes John Davies: Subs used - Emmitt Snitch
Jones James Grehan: Tries - Ferres(2): Goals - Dixon(2):
ST HELENS - Wellens: Gardner Shenton Jones Meli:
Wheeler Hohaia: Perry Roby Laffranchi Puletua Soliola
Flannery: Subs used - McCarthy-Scarsbrook Flanagan
Clough, Magennis:
Tries - Gardner Soliola Shenton Meli: Goal - Roby:
Referee R Silverwood Att- 6492 H.T. 6 - 8

Sat 14 Apr 2012 FEATHERSTONE ROVERS away
lost 16 – 23 R.L CHALLENNGE CUP 4th ROUND
FEATHERSTONE R - Hardman: Saxton Smeaton
Worthington: Ropati: Briggs Finn: Dickens Kaye Lockwood
Dale Spears Hepworth: Subs used - Kain Haley Grayson
Maloney: Tries - Ropati Briggs Hardman Worthington:
Goals - Finn (3) D/G:
CASTLEFORD - Owen: Youngquest Ferres Dixon Griffin:
Chase Orr: Massey Clark Walker Snitch Holmes Emmitt:
Subs used - Huby Jones Millington McGoldrick:
Tries - Clark Griffin Youngquest: Goals - Dixon Orr:
Referee B Thaler Att - 4165 H.T. 10 - 20

Sun 22 Apr 2012 WARRINGTON WOLVES away
lost 6 - 54
WARRINGTON W - Hodgson: Riley Bridge Atkins J
Monaghan: Briers O'Brien: Hill Higham Wood Waterhouse
Westwood McCarthey: Subs used - Dwyer Grix Cooper
Harrisor: Tries - J Monaghan(2) Hodgson(2) Atkins(2)
Bridge Waterhouse Riley Grix: Goals - Hodgson(7):
CASTLEFORD - Youngquest: Josh Atkinson Thompson
Ferres Griffin: McGoldrick Orr: Massey Milner Walker
Mitchel Holmes Emmitt: Subs used - Huby Jones Clark
Millington: Try - Mitchell: Goal - Orr:
Referee R Hicks   Att - 10590 H.T. 0 - 38

Mon 7 May 2012 WIDNES VIKINGS home won 36 - 12
CASTLEFORD - Owen: Griffin Dixon Ferres Youngquest:
McGoldrick Orr: Massey Hudson Huby Mitchell Millington
Jones: Subs used - Clark Emmitt Walker: Thompson:
Tries - Youngquest(3) Clark(2) Ferres Thompson:
Goals - Orr(2) Huby Griffin:
WIDNES V - Phelps: Flynn Marsh Dean Isa: Hanbury
Mellor Cross Clarke Cahill Winterstein Allen Finnigan:
Subs used - White Davies Pickersgill Leuluai:

SEASON 2012

Tries - Fynn Marsh: Goals - Hanbury (2):
Referee S Ganson Att - 5580 H.T. 10 - 8

Sun 20 May 2012 HULL KINGSTON ROVERS away lost 12 - 70
HULL K R - McDonnell: Latus Hall Welham D Hodgson:
Green Dobson: Paea J Hodgson Taylor Mika Galea
Lovegrove: Subs used - Withers Murrell O'Hara Clinton:
Tries - D Hodgson(4) McDonnell(3) Latus Welham
Withers Mika Hall: Goals - Dobson (11):
CASTLEFORD - Owen: Youngquest Thompson D xon
Griffin: Ferres Milner: Massey Hudson Huby Mitchell
Millington Jones: Subs used - Clark Emmitt Walker
Holmes: Tries - Thompson Griffin: Goals - Dixon(2):
Referee J Child Att - 7312 H.T. 6 - 36

Sat 26 May 2012 WAKEFIELD TRINITY WILDCATS lost 26 – 32 Magic Weekend at Etihad Stadium Manchester
CASTLEFORD - Owen: RYHS WILLIAMS(928) Dixon
Thompson Youngquest: Chase Orr: Jackson Jones Huby
Ferres Holmes Mitchell: Subs used - Walker Milner
Millington Massey: Tries - Thompson Jones Youngquest
Holmes Orr: Goals - Dixon(2) Orr:
WAKEFIELD T W - Mathers: Fox Collis Mellars Cockayne:
Sykes Smith: Amor Aiton Raleigh Mariano Kirmond
Washbrook: Subs used - Wood Lauitiiti Southern James:
Tries - Mellars Mathers Southern Washbrook Fox Smith:
Goals - Sykes(4):
Referee R Hicks H.T. 20 - 24

Mon 4 Jun 2012 BRADFORD BULLS away lost 32 - 46
BRADFORD B - Kearney: Ainscough Platt Lula Pryce:
Jeffries Gale: Manuckafoa L'estrange Hargreaves Bateman
Olbison Elima: Subs Used - Burgess Whitehead S bbit
Addy: Tries - Ainscough(3) Kearney(2) Bateman Lula
Elima: Goals - Gale(7):
CASTLEFORD - Youngquest: Griffin Dixon Thompson
Williams: Chase Orr: Jackson Jones Huby Ferres Holmes
Mitchell: Subs used - Walker McGoldrick Millington
Massey: Tries - Williams(2) Chase(2) Massey Thompson:
Goals - Dixon(4):
Referee B Thaler Att - 10906 H.T. 16 - 34

Sun 10 Jun 2012 SALFORD CITY REDS home won 34 - 30
CASTLEFORD - Owen: Youngquest: Dixon Thompson
Williams: Chase McGoldrick: Walker Milner Huby Ferres
Millington Jones: Subs used - Orr Emmitt Holmes
Massey: Tries - Orr(3) Youngquest Thompson Huby:
Goals - Dixon(3) Huby Orr:
SALFORD C R - Patten: Broughton Moon Gleeson
Williams: Sneyd Smith: McPherson Howarth Sidlow
Ashurst Anderson Wild: Subs used - Nero Owen
Palea'aesina Gledhill: Tries - Anderson Broughton Moon
Wild Gleeson: Goals - Sneyd(5):
Referee G Stokes Att - 5877 H.T. 16 - 12

Sun 24 Jun 2012 LEEDS RHINOS away lost 22 - 40
LEEDS R - Hardaker: Jones-Bishop Watkins Ablett Hall:

Sinfield McGuire: Leuluai Burrow Griffin Jones-Buchanan
Delaney Ward:
Subs used - Moore Lunt Hauraki Bailey: Tries - Jones-
Bishop(2) Burrow(2) Hall(2) Watkins: Goals - Sinfield(6):
CASTLEFORD - Youngquest: Owen Thompson Ferres
Williams: McGoldrick Orr: Massey Milner Huby Millington
Holmes Emmitt: Subs used - Walker Snitch Jones
Jackson: Tries - Ferres(2) Huby Jackson:
Goals - Huby Orr: McGoldrick:
Referee T Roby Att - 16153 H.T. 6 - 22

Mon 2 Jul 2012 WIDNES VIKINGS away lost 10 - 40
WIDNES V - Phelps: Isa Marsh Dean Ah Van: Mellor
Hanbury: Cross Clarke Pickersgill Winterstein Allen Cahill:
Subs used - Davies Kite McShane O'Carroll:
Tries - Marsh Winterstein Davies McShane Mellor
O'Carroll Ah Van: Goals - Ah Van(5) Hanbury:
CASTLEFORD - Youngquest: Clare Griffin Thompson
Williams: Steve Ferres Ryan McGoldrick: Walker Milner
Huby Millington Holmes Snitch:
Subs used - Orr Emmitt Jones Massey:
Tries - Youngquest Jones: Goal - Huby:
Referee S Ganson Att - 4501 H.T. 4 - 18

Sun 8 Jul 2012 HUDDERSFIELD GIANTS home won 52 - 6
CASTLEFORD - Owen: Youngquest Thompson Griffin
Clare: Orr JAMIE ELLIS(929): Jackson Milner Huby
Millington Snitch Emmitt: Subs used - Jones Hudson
Mitchell Massey: Tries - Owen(2) Clare Thompson
Youngquest Griffin Milner Ellis: Goals- Ellis (10):
HUDDERWSFIELD G - Eden: Murphy Cudjoe Lawrence
George: Brough Robinson: Mason Moore Gilmour
O,Donnell Patrick Brown: Subs used - Fa'alogo Lee
Faiumu Chan: Try - Cudjoe: Goal - Brough:
Referee B Thaler Att - 5012 H.T. 22 - 6

Sun 22 Jul 2012 WARRINGTON WOLVES home lost 26 - 40
CASTLEFORD - Owen: Youngquest Thompson Griffin
Williams: Chase Ellis: Jackson Milner Huby Snitch
Millington Emmitt: N Subs used - Orr Jones Mitchell
Massey: Tries - Youngquest(2) Williams Owen Mitchell:
Goals - Orr(2) Ellis:
WARRINGTON W - Hodgson: J Monaghan Blythe Atkins
Riley: Ratchford Myler: Hill Higham Morley McCarthy
Westwood Cooper: Subs used - Wood Solomona Carvel
Monaghan: Tries - Westwood(2) J Monaghan Atkins
Riley Solomona Ratchford: Goals - Hodgson(6):
Referee R Hicks Att - 6167 H.T. 0 - 30

Fri 27 Jul 2012 WIGAN WARRIORS away lost 16 - 40
WIGAN W - Tomkins: Charnley Goulding Carmount
Thornley: Finch Smith: Lauaki McIlorum Mossop Hansen
Hock Flower: Subs used - Lima Farrell Crosby Tuson:
Tries - Lauaki(2) Tomkins(2) Thornley Farrel Carmont
Charnley: Goals - Charnley(4):
CASTLEFORD - Owen: Williams Thompson Jones
Youngquest: Holmes Orr: Jackson Milner Huby Snitch
Millington Emmitt:

488

SEASON 2012

Subs used - Hudson Nash Mitchell Massey:
Tries - Williams Holmes Jones: Goals - Youngquest(2):
Referee G Stokes Att - 13975 H.T. 6 - 20

Sun 5 Aug 2012 WAKEFIELD TRINITY WILDCATS home lost 12 - 40
CASTLEFORD - Owen: Youngquest Griffin Thompson Rhys Williams: Orr Milner: Jackson Hudson Huby Millington Snitch Emmitt: Subs used - Jones Mitchell Massey Ellis:
Tries - Jackson Youngquest: Goals Orr(2):
WAKEFIELD T W - Mathers: Fox Collis L Smith Cockayne: Sykes T Smith: Amor Ellis Raleigh Lauitiiti Kirmond Washbrook: Subs used - Wood Mariano Johnson James:
Tries - Mathers(2) Cockayne T Smith Collis Kirmond L Smith: Goals - Sykes(6);
Referee B Thaler Att - 7050 H.T. 0 - 16

Sun 12 Aug 2012 LONDON BRONCOS home lost 20 - 42
CASTLEFORD - Owen: Youngquest Griffin Snitch Thompson: BEN JOHNSTON(930) Ellis: Millington Orr Huby Mitchell Jones Milner:
Subs used - Emmitt Hudson Massey Holmes:
Tries - Griffin(2) Milner Orr: Goals - Ellis(2)
LONDON B - Dorn: Dixon O'Callaghan Howell Caro: Witt Gower: Kaufusi Randal Wheeldon Melling Bailey Clubb:
Subs used - Rinaldi Bryant Krasniqi Bolger:
Tries - Dorn(4) Bailey Dixon Clubb: Goals - Witt(7):
Referee R Silverwood Att - 5149 H.T. 10 - 30

Fri 17 Aug 2012 SAINT HELENS away lost 12 - 44
ST HELENS - Wellens: Makinson Swift Wheeler Meli: Hohaia Lomax: Perry Roby Laffranchi Soliola Flannery Puletua: Subs used - McCarthy-Scarsbrook Flanagan Clough Dixon: Tries - Makinson(2) Laffranchi Wellens Flannery Wheeler Swift Lomax:
Goals - Makinson(3) Wheeler(3):
CASTLEFORD - Owen: Youngquest Snitch Thompson Josh Griffin: Ben Johnston Orr: Emmitt Hudson Huby Millington Jones Mitchell:
Subs used - Milner Paul Jackson Holmes Massey:
Tries - Jackson Snitch : Goals - Orr(2):
Referee G Stokes Att - 12224 H.T. 6 - 20

Sun 2 Sep 2012 CATALAN DRAGONS home lost 26 - 46
CASTLEFORD - Owen: Youngquest Snitch Stuart Jones Thompson; Chase Ellis: Massey Orr Huby Millington Hudson Milner: Subs used - Clark Mitchell Holmes Steve Nash: Tries - Hudson Jones Youngquest Millington Owen: Goals - Orr(3):
CATALAN D - Greenshields; Blanch MIllard Duport Pala: Bosc Dureau: Mounis Henderson Casty Sa Anderson Baitieri: Subs used - Pelissier Fakir Maria Larroyer:
Tries - Greenshields(3) Blanch(3) Duport Sa:
Goals - Durea(7):
Referee T Roby Att - 5005 H.T. 12 - 30

Sun 9 Sep 2012 HULL FC away lost 10 - 36
HULL FC - Horne: Foster Crooks Yeaman Briscoe: Seymour Heremaia: Watts Houghton Lynch Manu Westerman Pitts: Subs used - O'Meley Aspinwall Tickle Green: Tries - Manu Briscoe Horne Houghton O'Meley Green: Goals - Foster(6):
CASTLEFORD - Owen: Nick Youngquest Steve Snitch Thompson BEN BLACKMORE(931): Chase Danny Orr: Huby Clark Massey Millington Holmes Ryan Hudson:
Subs used - Emmitt Walker Lee Mitchell Milner:
Tries Thompson Holmes: Goal - Orr:
Referee R Hicks Att - 11607 H.T. 6 – 14

Josh Griffin
D. No 921
2012

Lee Mitchell
D. No 922
2012

Grant Millington
D. No 925
2012 to

James Clare
D. No 926
2012 to 2015

Jamie Ellis
D. No 929
2012 to 2014

489

SEASON 2012

D.N	PLAYER		DEBUT	L MATCH	APP	SUB	T.AP	TRI'S	G'LS	D.G	P'TS
742	ORR	DANNY		09/09/2012	22	3	25	6	17	0	58
786	HUDSON	RYAN		09/09/2012	9	3	12	1	0	0	4
795	JACKSON	PAUL		17/08/2012	6	2	8	3	0	0	12
800	HUBY	CRAIG			15	2	17	2	4	0	16
846	McGOLDRICK	RYAN		02/07/2012	13	5	18	1	1	0	6
863	OWEN	RICHARD			24	0	24	10	0	0	40
870	DIXON	KIRK			17	0	17	3	39	0	90
876	MASSEY	NATHAN			11	16	27	1	0	0	4
891	ARUNDEL	JOE		16/03/2012	4	0	4	1	0	0	4
894	CHASE	RANGI			17	0	17	2	0	0	8
895	FERRES	BRETT		02/07/2012	16	2	18	7	0	0	28
896	JONES	STUART		02/09/2012	15	11	26	4	0	0	16
901	THOMPSON	JORDAN			16	1	17	7	0	0	28
902	SNITCH	STEVE		09/09/2012	12	8	20	2	0	0	8
905	DAVIES	JOHN		09/04/2012	1	0	1	0	0	0	0
907	HOLMES	OLIVER			18	5	23	4	0	0	16
909	WALKER	JONATHAN			11	7	18	1	0	0	4
910	MILNER	ADAM			17	4	21	3	0	0	12
912	YOUNGQUEST	NICK		09/09/2012	24	0	24	17	2	0	72
913	EMMITT	JACOB			16	9	25	0	0	0	0
915	CLARK	DARYL			5	10	15	4	0	0	16
921	GRIFFIN	JOSH	03/02/2012	17/08/2012	21	0	21	14	1	0	58
922	MITCHELL	LEE	03/02/2012	09/09/2012	13	10	23	2	0	0	8
923	NASH	STEVE	03/02/2012	02/09/2012	3	4	7	0	0	0	0
924	GREHAN	JAMES	26/02/2012	09/04/2012	2	2	4	0	0	0	0
925	MILLINGTON	GRANT	02/03/2012		16	7	23	3	0	0	12
926	CLARE	JAMES	16/03/2012		3	0	3	1	0	0	4
927	ATKINSON	JOSH	09/04/2012	22/04/2012	2	0	2	0	0	0	0
928	WILLIAMS	RHYS	26/05/2012	05/08/2012	8	0	8	4	0	0	16
929	ELLIS	JAMIE	08/07/2012		4	1	5	1	13	0	30
930	JOHNSTON	BEN	12/08/2012	17/08/2012	2	0	2	0	0	0	0
931	BLACKMORE	BEN	09/12/2012	09/12/2012	1	0	1	0	0	0	0
	32			**11**	**18**	**364**	**112**	**476**	**104**	**77**	**0**	**570**

COMPETITION		P	W	D	L	FOR	AGT
S, LEAGUE	POSITION 13 OF 14	27	6	0	21	554	948
RL CUP		1	0	0	1	16	23
PLAYERS RECORDS		**28**	**6**	**0**	**22**	**570**	**971**

Rule Changes:
Interchanges reduced to 10 from the previous 12
If a player in possession of the ball touches the corner flag, he will no longer be deemed 'in touch'.

Ian Millward replaces Terry Matterson as Head Ccach and Stuart Donlan replaces Andy Hay as Assistant Coach.

Jamie Ellis equalled the points scored in a Super League game at 24 in his debut match against Huddersfield Giants at home on the 8 July 2012.

Following last year's heroics in the Challenge Cup we went out at the first attempt to local rivals and Division 1 team Featherstone Rovers masterminded by their Coach Daryl Powell.

The League campaign was also disappointing. With only six wins we finished second from bottom in thirteenth position.

Grant Millington made his debut and is proving to be one of the best overseas signings.

SEASON 2013

SUPER LEAGUE XV111

The second year of the second franchise with no promotion or relegation

Sun 13 Jan 2013 HULL FC away lost 6 - 26
KIRK YEAMAN TESTIMONIAL MATCH FRIENDLY
HULL FC - First Half - Shaul: Lineham B Crooks Yeaman J Briscoe: Horne Seymour: Green Cunningham Bowden Hadley Whiting Pitts:
Subs used - Starling Wilson Nickles Latus:
Second Half - McDonnell: J Crookes Arundel Yeaman T Briscoe: Holdsworth Heremaia: O'Meley Houghton Lynch Ellis Galea Westerman: Subs used - Mixture of all players:
Tries - Crooks Bowden Heremaia Westerman McDonnell: Goals - Crooks Holdsworh(2):
CASTLEFORD - Owen: Carney Shenton Webster Dixon; Chase Ellis: Walker Clark Huby Millington Hauraki Massey: Subs used - Emmitt Milner Holmes Thompson Nash Johnson Fleming Clare: Try - Webster; Goal - Dixon:
Referee T Roby Att - 5577 H.T. 6 - 10

Sun 20 Jan 2013 FEATHERSTONE ROVERS home won 20 – 10 FRIENDLY
CASTLEFORD - Owen Dixon Shenton Webster Carney: Chase Ellis: Walker Milner Huby Gilmour Hauraki Millington: Subs Used - Clark Emmitt Massey Holmes Thompson Fleming Clare:
Tries - Carney(2) Webster Dixon: Goals - Dixon(2):
FEATHERSTONE R - Hepworth: Scott Hardman Worthington Johnson: Briggs Finn: England Kaye Crossley Lockwood Bryan Dale: Subs used - Ellis Kain Ormondroyd James Bostock Mackay Bussey Holmes:
Tries -Hardman Bussey: Goal - Finn:
Referee J Child Att - 2388 H.T. 0 - 4

Sun 3 Feb 2013 WARRINGTON WOLVES away lost 24 - 40
WARRINGTON W - Hodgson: Riley Atkins Evans J Monaghan: Briers Myler: Morley M Monaghan Hill Grix Westwood Harrison: Subs used - Carvell Waterhouse Higham Ratchford: Tries - Westwood(2) Riley Atkins Evans Myler Carvell: Goals - Hodgson(6):
CASTLEFORD - JORDAN TANSEY(932) JUSTIN CARNEY(933) Shenton JAKE WEBSTER(934) Owen: Chase Ellis: Mason Milner Huby LEE GILMOUR(935) WELLER HAURAKI(936) Holmes:
Subs used - Walker Clark Massey Millington:
Tries - Carney Shenton Owen Webster: Goals - Ellis(4):
Referee R Hicks Att - 10721 H.T. 12 - 34

Sun 10 Feb 2013 LEEDS RHINOS home won 14 - 12
CASTLEFORD - Tansey: Owen Shenton Webster Carney: Chase Ellis: Walker Milner Huby Gilmour Hauraki Holmes: Subs used - Clark Millington Massey Thompson:
Tries - Tansey Webster: Goals Ellis(3):
LEEDS R - Hardaker: Keinhorst Watkins Moon Hall: Sinfield McGuire: Bailey Burrow Peacock Delaney Ablett Jones-Buchanan: Subs used - Kirke McShane Achurch Clarkson: Tries - McGuire Hall: Goals Sinfield(2):

Referee T Roby Att - 9103 H.T. 10 - 6

Sat 16 Feb 2013 BRADFORD BULLS away lost 12 - 38
BRADFORD B - Kearney: Kear Blythe Lulia Foster: Addy Sammut: Scrutton Diskin Manuokafoa Oblison Whitehead Walker: Subs used - L'Estrange Murphy Sidlow Langley: Tries - Kearney(3) Sidlow Blythe Walker: Goals - Foster(7):
CASTLEFORD - Tansey: Dixon Shenton Webster Carney: GARETH O'BRIEN(937) Ellis: Walker Milner Huby Gilmour Hauraki Holmes: Subs used - Clark Millington Massey Thompson: Tries - Ellis Dixon: Goals Ellis(2):
Referee S Ganson Att - 7724 H.T. 6 - 12

Sun 24 Feb 2013 CATALAN DRAGONS home draw 17 - 17
CASTLEFORD - Tansey: Carney Shenton Webster Dixon: Gareth O'Brien Ellis: Walker Clark Mason Gilmour Hauraki Millington:
Subs used - Huby Massey Holmes Thompson:
Tries - Thompson Shenton Dixon:
Goals - Ellis(2) O'Brien D/G:
CATALAN D - Millard: Blanch Menzies Duport Pala: Pryce Bosc: Fakir Henderson Casty Taia Anderson Baitieri: Subs used - Elima Mounis Pelissier Simon:
Tries - Duport Anderson Blanch: Goals Bosc(2) D/G
Referee J Child Att - 5245 H.T. 6 - 12

Sun 3 Mar 2013 WIGAN WARRIORS home lost 22 - 28
CASTLEFORD - Tansey: Carney Webster Shenton Dixon: Chase Ellis: Emmitt Clark Mason Gilmour Hauraki Millington:
Subs used - Huby Massey Holmes Thompson:
Tries - Carney(2) Webster Ellis: Goals - Ellis(3):
WIGAN W - S Tompkins: Charnley Hughes Thornley Richards Green Smith: Flower McIlorum Crosby Tuson Farrell O'Loughlin: Subs used - Dudson Taylor Powell Burke: Tries - Tuson(2) Flower Richards McIlorum:
Goals - Richards(4):
Referee T Alibert Att - 7852 H.T. 4 - 16

Fri 8 Mar 2013 HULL FC away lost 0 - 52
HULL FC - McDonnell: Lineham Arundel Yeaman Briscoe: Holdsworth Horne: O'Meley Houghton Lynch Galea TickleS/O Westerman:
Subs used - Whiting Heremaia Bowden Watts:
Tries - Arundel(3) Lineham(3) Horne Houghton Bowden: Goals - Tickle(5) Holdsworth Westerman Arundel:
CASTLEFORD - Tansey: Dixon Shenton CarneyS/O Clare: Chase E lis: Massey Milner Huby Millington Hauraki Holmes
Subs used - Clark Mason Jordan Thompson Emmitt:
Referee S Ganson Att - 11852 H.T. 0 - 22

Sun 17 Mar 2013 LONDON BRONCHOS home lost 12 - 26
CASTLEFORD - Tansey: Dixon Shenton Webster Owen: Chase Ellis: Emmitt Clark Huby Gilmour Millington Holmes: Subs Used - Walker Massey Thompson DANIEL

FLEMING(938)   Tries - Dixon Huby: Goals - Ellis(2):
LONDON B - Robertson: Colbon Channing Sarginson
Dixon: Witt Gower: Cook Lee Bryant Rodney Eailey
Kaufusi: Subs used - Clubb Lovell Dorn Randall:
Tries - Bailey(2) Robertson Gower: Goals - Witt(5):
Referee T Roby Att - 4521 H.T. 12 - 6

Sun 24 Mar 2013 HULL KINGSTON ROVERS away lost 22 - 26
HULL K R - Eden: Brown Welham Hall D Hodgson: Burns
Dobson: Paea J Hodgson Tuimavave Cox Paterson Griffin:
Subs used - Carlile Horne Maka Beaumont: Tries - Burns
Welham D Hodgson J Hodgson Hall: Goals - Burns(3):
CASTLEFORD - Owen: Thompson Shenton Webster Dixon:
Chase Tansey: Mason Milner Huby Gilmour Hauraki
Holmes: Subs used - Ellis Clark Millington Massey:
Tries - Dixon Webster Owen Clark: Goals - Dixon(3):
Referee J Child Att - 6489 H.T. 16 - 14

Fri 29 Mar 2013 WAKEFIELD TRINITY WILDCATS home lost 16 - 37
CASTLEFORD - Tansey: Owen Shenton Carney Thompson:
Hauraki Ellis: Massey Chase Mason Gilmour Millington
Holmes: Subs used - Walker Clark Huby Emmitt:
Tries - Thompson(2) Owen: Goals - Ellis(2):
WAKEFIELD T W - Mathers: Fox Collis Lyne Cockayne:
Sykes T Smith: Poore Ainton Wilkes Lauitiiti Kirmond
Washbrook: Subs used - L Smith Amor Mellars Annakin:
Tries - Fox(2) T Smith Kirmond Mathers L Smith:
Goals - Sykes(4) D/G L Smith(2)
Referee B Thaler Att - 7705 H.T. 0 - 25
MATCH STOPED WITH 7 MINUTES LEFT DUE TO FLOODLGHT PROBLEM RESULT TO STAND

Mon 1 Apr 2013 SAINT HELENS away lost 18 - 48
ST HELENS - Makinson: Percival Turner Jones Swift:
Wellens Wilkins: Perry Howarth Clough Soliola Flanagan
McCarthay-Scarsbrook: Subs used - Laffranchi Walmsley
Tilley Greenwood: Tries - Perry(2) Greenwood(2)
Flanagan McCarthay-Scarsbrook Makinson Swift Turner:
Goals - Percival(5) Markinson:
CASTLEFORD - Tansey Owen Shenton Carney Clare:
Chase Ellis: Walker Clark Mason Holmes Thompson
Hauraki: Subs used - Jake Emmitt Huby CHARLIE
MARTIN(939) Massey:
Tries - Clark Carney Clare: Goals - Ellis(3):
Referee R Hicks Att - 10943 H.T. 0 - 26

Sat 6 Apr 2013 HUDDERSFIELD GIANTS home lost 24 - 40
CASTLEFORD - Tansey: Owen Shenton Gilmour
Thompson: Chase Ellis: Walker Milner Mason Massey
Hauraki Holmes: Subs used - Clark Huby Fleming Boyle:
Tries - Holmes Milner Clark Walker: Goals - Ellis(4):
HUDERSFIELD G - Grix: McGillvary Cudjoe Wardle
Murphy: Brough Robinson: Fielden Lunt Kopczak Ferres
Lawrence Ferguson: Subs used - George Faiumu Patrick
Cording: Tries - McGillvary(2) Lunt Wardle Murphy
Robinson Ferres: Goals - Brough(6):
Referee P Bentham Att - 3222 H.T. 6 - 28

Sat 13 Apr 2013 WIDNES VIKINGS home won 28 - 26
CASTLEFORD - Tansey: Clare Shenton Thompson Owen:
Chase Ellis: Mason Milner Huby Holmes Hauraki Massey:
Subs used - Walker Clark Martin Boyle:
Tries - Owen(2) Clare Thompson Milner: Goals - Ellis(4):
WIDNES V - Hanbury: Flynn Dean Phelps Ah Van: Brown
Mellor: O'Carroll Clarke Pickersgill Winterstein Leuluai
Gerrard: Subs used - Kavanagh Joseph Lawton White:
Tries - Flynn Hanbury Clarke Phelps Ah Van:
Goals - Ah Van(3):
Referee R Silverwood: Att 3986 H.T. 16 - 26

Fri 19 Apr 2013 LEEDS RHINOS away lost 12 - 28
R L CHALLENGE CUP 4th ROUND
LEEDS R - Hardaker: Watkins Ablett Moon Hall: Sinfield
McGuire: Leuluai Burrow Peacock Ward Delaney Jones-
Buchanan: Subs used - McShane Kirke Clarkson Achurch:
Tries - McGuire(2) Watkins Burrow Clarkson:
Goals - Sinfield(4):
CASTLEFORD - Tansey: Clare Shenton Thompson Carney:
Chase Ellis: Mason Milner Huby Holmes Hauraki Massey:
Subs used - Walker Clark Gilmour Boyle:
Tries Chase Ellis: Goals - Ellis(2):
Referee P Bentham Att 8130 H.T. 6 - 4

Sat 27 Apr 2013 SALFORD CITY REDS away lost 30- 34
SALFORD C R - Sneyd: Broughton Gibson Gleeson
Williams: Fages McGoldrick: Griffin Godwin Emmitt
Ashurst Dixon Wild: Subs used - Foran Mauro A Walne
James: Tries - Ashurst Williams Dixon Mauro Fages
McGoldrick: Goals - Sneyd(5):
CASTLEFORD - Tansey Dixon Shenton Thompson Carney:
Chase Ellis: Mason Milner Huby Holmes Hauraki Massey:
Subs used - Walker Clark Gilmour Boyle: Tries - Massey
Carney Milner Holmes Ellis Thompson: Goals - Ellis(3):
Referee T Alibert Att - 2306 H.T. 14 - 16
SALFORD HAD14 PLAYERS ON THE FIELD FOR LAST 5 MINUTES, DEDUCTED 2 POINTS FOR THE OFFENCE.

Sun 5 May 2013 HULL KINGSTON ROVERS home won 32 - 24
CASTLEFORD - Tansey: Dixon Shenton Thompson Carney:
Chase Ellis: Mason Clark Boyle Holmes Hauraki Massey:
Subs used - Walker Milner Huby Lee Gilmour: Tries -
Carney(2) Boyle Shenton Walker Tansey: Goals - Ellis(4):
HULL K R - Hall: Caro Salter George D Hodgson: Burns
Dobson: Walker Carlile Beaumont Lovegrove J Hodgson
Mika: Subs used - Paea Cox Green Griffin:
Tries - Salter(2) Lovegrove Caro: Goals - Dobson(4):
Referee T Roby Att - 6474 H.T. 12 - 12

Sat 18 May 2013 CATALAN DRAGONS away lost 30 - 39
CATALAN D - Escare: Blanch Menzies Duport Millard:
Pryce Bosc: Simon Henderson Casty Taia Anderson
Mounis: Subs used - Maria Pelissier Larroyer Fakir:
Tries - Millard Duport Anderson Menzies Escare Pelissier:
Goals - Bosc(7) D/G:
CASTLEFORD - Tansey: Dixon Shenton Thompson Carney:
Chase Ellis: Mason Clark Huby Gilmour Holmes Massey:

Subs used - Walker Millington Milner Boyle:
Tries - Carney(2) Tansey Thompson Clark: Goals - Ellis(5);
Referee P Bentham Att - 7083 H.T. 6 - 30

**Sat 25 May 2013 WAKEFIELD TRINITY WILDCATS
won 49 – 24 PLAYED AT ETIHAD STADIUM
MANCHESTER - MAGIC WEEKEND**
CASTLEFORD - Tansey: Dixon Shenton Thompson
Carney: Chase Ellis: Millington Clark Huby Holmes Hauraki
Massey: Subs used - Walker Milner Fleming Boyle:
Tries - Dixon(4) Clark Ellis Huby Carney Thompson:
Goals - Ellis(6) D/G:
WAKEFIELD T W - Mathers: Fox Collis Lyne Cocayne: L
Smith T Smith: Poore Aiton Raleigh Lauitiiti Kirmond
Washbrook: Subs used - Amor Trout Annakin Tautai:
Tries - Collis(2) Kirmond Annakin: Goals - Smith(4):
Referee R Hicks Att - 30793 (Total Day One) H.T 32- 12

Sat 1 Jun 2013 LONDON BRONCOS away draw 30 - 30
LONDON B - Dorn: Melling Mendeika Channing
Robertson: Witt Gower: Wheeldon Fisher Clubb Rodney
Bailey Cook: Subs used - Bryant Krasnigi Bishay Kaufusi:
Tries - Mendeika Wheeldon Melling Bailey Gower:
Goals - Witt(5):
CASTLEFORD - Tansey: Carney Thompson Shenton Dixon:
Chase Ellis: Millington Clark Huby Holmes Hauraki
Massey: Subs used - Walker Milner Fleming Boyle:
Tries - Clark Chase Millington Carney Massey:
Goals - Ellis(5):
Referee B Thaler Att - 1810 H.T. 10 - 16

Fri 7 Jun 2013 LEEDS RHINOS away lost 24 - 42
LEEDS R - Hardaker: Hall Keinhorst Moon Minns: Sinfield
Burrow: Leuluai McShane Peacock Jones-Buchannan
Delaney Bailey: Subs used - Kirke Sutcliffe Achurch
Singleton: Tries - Keinhorst(3) Minns Hardaker Kirke
Moon: Goals - Sinfield(7):
CASTLEFORD - Tansey: Clare Shenton Thompson Dixon:
Chase Ellis: Walker Huby Milner Holmes Hauraki Massey:
Subs used - Millington Clark Fleming Boyle:
Tries - Tansey(2) Hauraki Huby: Goals - Ellis(4):
Referee R Hicks Att - 17035 H.T. 12 - 16

Fri 21 Jun 2013 HULL FC home won 30 - 28
CASTLEFORD - Tansey: Owen Shenton Dixon Clare:
Hauraki Chase: Boyle Milner Huby Holmes Millington
Massey: Subs used - Walker Clark Thompson Davies:
Tries - Owen Chase Clark Walker Clare: Goals - Dixon(5):
HULL FC - McDonnell: Lineham Crooks Arundel Crookes:
Holdsworth Miller: O'Meley Houghton Green Whiting
Westerman Pitts:
Subs used - Galea Lynch Watts Heremaia:
Tries - Crookes(4) Heremaia(2): Goals - Holdswort(2):
Referee J Childs Att - 6022 H.T. 6 - 16

Fri 28 Jun 2013 WIGAN WARRIORS away won 18 - 4
WIGAN W - Tierney: Charnley Goulding Gelling Richards:
Powell Smith: Crosby McIlorum Dudson Hansen Farrell
Burke: Subs used - Hughes Green Tuson Powell:
Try - Charnley:

CASTLEFORD - Tansey: Owen Shenton Dixon Clare:
Hauraki Chase: Boyle Milner Huby Holmes Millington
Massey:
Subs used - Thompson Clark Walker Mason:
Tries - Dixon Millington Clare: Goals - Dixon(3):
Referee P Bentham Att - 12463 H.T. 12 - 0

Sun 7 Jul 2013 SAINT HELENS home lost 24 - 40
CASTLEFORD - Tansey: Owen Shenton Dixon Carney:
Hauraki Chase: Boyle Milner Huby Thompson Millington
Massey: Subs used - Walker Clark Holmes Mason:
Tries - Owen Tansey Hauraki Carney Chase:
Goals - Dixon(2):
ST HELENS - Lomax: Makinson Jones Turner Meli: Wilkin
O'Brien: Puletua Roby Clough Thompson Manu
McCarthy-Scarsbrook: Subs used - Wellens Greenwood
Walmsley Richards: Tries - Makinson(3) Lomax
Thompson Turney Walmsley: Goals - O'Brien(6):
Referee G Stokes Att- 8229 H.T. 16 - 12

**Sun 21 Jul 2013 HUDDERSFIELD GIANTS away
lost 32 - 43**
HUDDERSFIELD G - Grix: Blackmore Cudjoe Wardle
Murphy: Brough Robinson: Crabtree Wood Kopczak
Ferres Ta'ai Ferguson: Subs used - Faiumu Lawrence
Patrick Mullally: Tries - Blackmore(2) Murphy(2) Wardle
Brough Cudjoe Wood: Goals - Brough(8):
CASTLEFORD - Tansey: Owen Shenton Dixon Carney:
Hauraki Chase: Jonathan Walker Milner Huby Holmes
Millington Massey: Subs used - Clark Thompson Fleming
Ben Davies: Tries - Carney(2) Shenton Clark Chase
Hauraki: Goals - Dixon(4)
Referee R Silverwood Att - 5773 H.T. 4 - 36

**Sun 4 Aug 2013 WARRINGTON WOLVES home
lost 30 - 40**
CASTLEFORD - Tansey: Carney MICHAEL CHANNING(940)
Shenton Dixon: Chase Ellis: Boyle Milner Huby Millington
Hauraki Massey: Subs used - Clark Fleming Martin Keith
Mason: Tries - Carney Hauraki Milner Dixon Huby:
Goals - Dixon(5):
WARRINGTON WOLVES - Ratchford: Riley Grix Bridge J
Monaghan: Briers Myler: Wood Higham Hill Waterhouse
Westwood Harrison: Subs used - Morley Carvell Dwyer
Laithwaite: Tries - Higham(2) Briers Carvell Dwyer Myler
J Monaghan: Goals - Ratchford(6):
Referee R Hicks Att - 5980 H.T. 24 - 12

Sun 11 Aug 2013 WIDNES VIKINGS away won 42 - 38
WIDNES V - Hanbury: Isa Marsh Phelps Au Van: Brown
Mellor: O'Carroll Clarke Kavanagh Hock Leului Cahill:
Subs used - Gore Joseph Winterstein Owens:
Tries - Hock(4) Winterstein(2) Mellor Hanbury:
Goals - Marsh(2) Owens:
CASTLEFORD - Owen: Dixon Shenton Channing Carney:
Chase Ellis: Boyle Milner Huby Millington Hauraki Clark:
Subs used - Massey Thompson Fleming Martin:
Tries - Carney(2) Boyle Massey Ellis Milner Hauraki
Channing: Goals - Dixon(5):
Referee R Silverwood Att - 5155 H.T. 24 - 18

SEASON 2013

Sun 18 Aug 2013 BRADFORD BULLS home
won 46 - 34
CASTLEFORD - Tansey: Clare Shenton Dixon Carney:
Chase Ellis: Boyle Milner Huby Millington Hauraki Massey:
Subs used - Clark Fleming Martin: -(Non Playing Sub -
Owen):   Tries - Milner(2) Dixon Carney Chase Tansey
Massey Ellis: Goals - Dixon(7):
BRADFORD B - Kearney: Kear Purtell Lulia Foster: Sammut
Addy: Scruton Diskin Manuokafoa Olbison Blythe Walker:
Subs used - Langley Donaldson O'Brien Evans:
Tries - Sammut(2) Kearney Scruton Kear Addy:
Goals - Foster(5):
Referee R Hicks Att - 6633 H.T. 22 - 12

Sun 1 Sep 2013 SALFORD CITY REDS home
won 44 - 30
CASTLEFORD - Tansey: Carney Shenton Channing Dixon:
Chase Ellis: Boyle Milner Huby Millington Hauraki Massey
Subs used - Clark Thompson Fleming BEN
REYNOLDS(941): Tries - Carney(3) Channing(2) Shenton
Fleming Chase Thompson: Goals - Dixon(3) Ellis:
SALFORD C R - Gaskell: Williams Gibson McGoldrick
Broughton: Sneyd Fages: Griffin Owen Emmitt Ashurst
Dixon Wild:
Subs used - James J Walne A Walne Davies:
Tries - Broughton(3) Williams(2): - Goals Sneyd(5):
Referee C Leatherbarrow Att - 6817 H.T. 14 - 6

Sun 8 Sep 2013 WAKEFIELD TRINITY WILDCATS
away lost 32 - 36
WAKEFIELD T W - Mathers: Fox Collis Mariano Cockayne:
Kay Wilde: Poore Aiton Amor Kirmond Walshaw Trout:
Subs used - Lauitiiti L Smith Wilkes Raleigh:
Tries - Kay(3) Mariano(2) Lauitiiti Trout:
Goals - Cockayne Smith(3):
CASTLEFORD - Tansey Clare Dixon Channing Owen:
Chase Ellis: Boyle Milner Huby Massey Hauraki Clark:
Subs used - Jordan Thompson Fleming Charlie Martin
Reynolds:
Tries - Clare(4) Chase Hauraki: Goals - Dixon(4):
Referee R Hicks Att - 6404 H.T. 20 - 24

Jordan Tansey
D. No 932
2013 to 2015

Justin Carney
D. No 933
2013 to 2015

Jake Webster
D. No 934
2013 to

Weller Hauraki
D. No 936
2013 to 2014

Danial Fleming
D. No 938
2013 to 2014

Michael Channing
D. No 940
2013 to 2015

SEASON 2013

D.N	PLAYER		DEBUT	L MATCH	APP	SUB	T.AP	TRI'S	G'LS	D.G	P'TS
800	HUBY	CRAIG			22	6	28	4	0	0	16
810	SHENTON	MICHAEL			27	0	27	5	0	0	20
840	BOYLE	RYAN			9	8	17	2	0	0	8
853	MASON	KEITH		04/08/2013	12	4	16	0	0	0	0
863	OWEN	RICHARD			14	0	14	7	0	0	28
870	DIXON	KIRK			21	0	21	11	41	0	126
876	MASSEY	NATHAN			19	9	28	4	0	0	16
894	CHASE	RANGI		07/09/2013	26	0	26	8	0	0	32
901	THOMPSON	JORDAN		08/03/2013	13	12	25	8	0	0	32
907	HOLMES	OLIVER			20	3	23	2	0	0	8
909	WALKER	JONATHAN		21/07/2013	7	13	20	3	0	0	12
910	MILNER	ADAM			19	4	23	7	0	0	28
913	EMMITT	JACOB		01/04/2013	2	3	5	0	0	0	0
915	CLARK	DARYL			10	18	28	8	0	0	32
920	DAVIES	BEN		21/07/2013	0	2	2	0	0	0	0
925	MILLINGTON	GRANT			15	6	21	2	0	0	8
926	CLARE	JAMES			9	0	9	8	0	0	32
929	ELLIS	JAMIE			23	1	24	7	59	1	147
932	TANSEY	JORDAN	03/02/2013		27	0	27	7	0	0	28
933	CARNEY	JUSTIN	03/02/2013		20	0	20	21	0	0	84
934	WEBSTER	JAKE	03/02/2013		7	0	7	4	0	0	16
935	GILMOUR	LEE	03/02/2013	05/05/2013	10	3	13	0	0	0	0
936	HAURAKI	WELLER	03/02/2013		26	0	26	6	0	0	24
937	O,BRIEN	GARETH	16/02/2013	24/02/2013	2	0	2	0	0	1	1
938	FLEMING	DANIEL	17/03/2013		0	11	11	1	0	0	4
939	MARTIN	CHARLIE	01/04/2013	08/09/2013	0	6	6	0	0	0	0
940	CHANNING	MICHAEL	04/08/2013		4	0	4	3	0	0	12
941	REYNOLDS	BEN	01/09/2013		0	2	2	0	0	0	0
	28		**10**	**9**	**364**	**111**	**475**	**128**	**100**	**2**	**714**

COMPETITION		P	W	D	L	FOR	AGT
S, LEAGUE	POSITION 12 OF 14	27	9	2	16	702	881
RL CUP		1	0	0	1	12	28
PLAYERS RECORDS		**28**	**9**	**2**	**17**	**714**	**909**

On 9 April 2013 with only one victory and a draw to date Coach Ian Millward stands down as Head Coach with Danny Orr taking over as Caretaker Coach.

On 7 May 2013 Daryl Powell was announced as new Head Coach with Danny Orr as his Assistant.

Daryl brings about an improvement in performance and results and we finish the season in 12th place.

SEASON 2014

SUPER LEAGUE XIX

The third year of the second franchise with no promotion or relegation. Salford City Reds changed their name to Salford Red Devils

Thu 26 Dec 2013 HALIFAX home draw 30 - 30
GRAIG HUBY TESTIMONIAL MATCH FRIENDLY
CASTLEFORD - Tansey: Owen Channing Dixon Clare: Dorn Sneyd: Lynch Clark Huby Gilmour Holmes Wheeldon: Subs used - Fleming Finn Martin Reynolds Howden Maher Day Orr:
Tries - Owen(4) Clark Dixon :   Goals - Dixon(3)
HALIFAX - Fieldhouse: Rettle Tyrer Heaton Potts: Brown Johnson: Tonks Kaye Bracek Manning Adamson Murrell: Subs used - Fairbank Mennell Worrincy Ambler Divorty Brooks Casey Ward:
Tries - Potts(3) Johnson Brooks Brown: Goals - Tyrer(3):
Referee C Leatherbarrow Att - 3621 H.T. 22 - 14

Sun 19 Jan 2014 YORK CITY KNIGHTS home won 62 – 6 FRIENDLY
CASTLEFORD - Tansey: Owen Channing Carney Clare: Sneyd Finn: Fleming Clark Wheeldon Mariano Martin Millington: Subs used - Lynch Huby Holmes Reynolds Seymour Howden Maher Day: Tries - Carney(3) Sneyd(2) Owen Huby Clare Clark Reynolds Millington:
Goals Sneyd(9):
YORK C K - Haynes McDonald Rogers Minikin Dent: B Hardcastle Presley: Bell Smith Joynt Mallender Crowe Pickles; Subs used - Brining Liey Stubbs Orange Backhouse L Hardcastle Nathaniel Pickerill:
Try Brining: Goal - B Hardcastle
Referee A Sweet Att - 1453 H.T. 26 - 6

Sun 26 Jan 2014 FEATHERSTONE ROVERS away POSTPONED WATERLOGGED PITCH FRIENDLY

Sun 2 Feb 2014 BRADFORD BULLS away won 66 - 10 FRIENDLY
BRADFORD B - Foster: Kear Henry Purtell Saltenstall: Addy Gale: Scruton O'Brien Manuofakoa Olbison Ferguson Donaldson: Subs used - Diskin Roberts Sidlow Bates Walker Conroy: Tries - Kear Scruton:
Goal - Foster;
CASTLEFORD - Dorn: Owen Carney Shenton Dixon: Sneyd Finn: Lynch Clark Huby Holmes Hauraki Millington: Subs used - Wheeldon Mariano Milner Gibson Channing Clare Seymour: Tries - Dixon(3) Clark(2) Hauraki(2) Dorn Owen Shenton Milner Mariano: Goals Dixon(9):
Referee R Silverwood Att- 1967 H.T. 26 - 10

Sat 8 Feb 2014 DEWSBURY RAMS away lost 0 - 18 FRIENDLY
DEWSBURY R - Sheriff: Morton Pryce Grady Scott: Hemingway Thackery: Nash Godwin Hepworth Spicer Hale Brown: Subs used - Lillycrop Haggerty Hyde Gallagher Wright Farrell Grayston: Tries - Farrell Gallagher Hale: Goals - Hemingway(2) Gallagher:
CASTLEFORD - Tansey Howden Channing Gibson Owen:

Seymour Ellis: Fleming Milner Martin Mariano Day: Massey: Subs used - Reynolds T Holmes Maher Ellrington Foster Westerman:
Referee - Mr C Leatherbarrow Att - 721 H.T. 0 - 12

Sun 16 Feb 2014 BRADFORD BULLS away won 36 - 18
BRADFORD B - Kearney: Kear Henry Putell Foster: Gaskell Gale: Scruton Diskin Sidlow Olbison Addy Donaldson: Subs used - Walker Manuokofoa O'Brian Bridge:
Tries - Addy Foster Purtell: Goals - Foster(3):
CASTLEFORD - Dorn: Dixon Channing Shenton Carney: MARC SNEYD(942) LIAM FINN(943): Lynch Clark Huby Holmes Hauraki Millington: Subs used - Milner SCOTT WHEELDON(944) FRANKIE MARIANO(945) Fleming
Tries - Hauraki Dixon Clark Carney Dorn Millington:
Goals - Dixon(6):
Referee R Hicks Att - 8774 H.T. 6 - 6

Sun 23 Feb 2014 CATALAN DRAGONS home won 32 - 6
CASTLEFORD - Tansey: Carney Shenton Channing Dixon: Sneyd Finn: Lynch Clark Huby Holmes Hauraki Millington: Subs used - Milner Mariano Wheeldon Fleming:
Tries - Carney(3) Dixon Tansey Clark: Goals - Sneyd(4)
CATALAN D - Webb: Escare Cardace Pomeroy Oldfield: Pryce Dureau: Lema Henderson Bouquet Taia Whitehead Mounis: Subs used - Pelissier Maria Paea Baitieri:
Try - Escare: Goal - Duureau:
Referee T Roby Att - 5104 H.T. 12 - 6

Fri 28 Feb 2014 HULL KINGSTON ROVERS away won 30 - 10
HULL KR - Eden: Cockayne Welham Salter Caro: Burns Keating: J Walker Hodgson Green Larroyer Lovegrove Costigan: Subs used - Carlile Cox Horne A Walker:
Tries - Green Caro: Goal - Burns:
CASTLEFORD - Dorn: Owen Channing Shenton Carney: Sneyd Finn: Lynch Clark Huby Mariano Hauraki Millington: Subs used - Milner Holmes Wheeldon Fleming:
Tries - Owen(3) Mariano Holmes: Goals Sneyd(5):
Referee B Thaler Att - 7022 H.T. 18 - 10

Sun 9 Mar 2014 WIGAN WARRIORS home won 36 -31
CASTLEFORD - Dorn: Dixon Channing Shenton Carney: Sneyd Finn: Lynch Milner Huby Holmes Hauraki Millington: Subs used - Massey Clark Mariano Wheeldon: Tries - Dorn(2) Dixon Milner Clark Channing:
Goals Sneyd(6):
WIGAN W - Bowen: Charnley Sarginson Thornley Burgess: Green Smith: Crosby McIlorum Taylor Farrell Bateman Flower: Subs used – L Tomkins Pettybourne Clubb James Tries - Bowen Green Smith Clubb Burgess Charnley:
Goals Smith(3) D/G:
Referee R Hicks Att - 8604 H.T. 22 - 24

Sun 16 Mar 2014 HULL home won 19- 16
CASTLEFORD - Tansey: Owen Channing Shenton Carney: Sneyd Finn: Lynch Clark Huby Holmes Hauraki Millington:

Sub used - Webster Milner Massey Mariano:
Tries - Shenton Sneyd Mariano: Goals - Sneyd(3) D/G
HULL FC - Shaul: Colbon Crooks Yeaman Talanoa:
Heremaia Horne: Paea Houghton Bowden Ellis Tuson
Westerman:
Subs used - Watts Whiting Thompson Rankin:
Tries - Talanoa Ellis Colbon: Goals - Crooks(2):
Referee T Roby Att - 9867 H.T. 6 - 12

Sun 23 Mar 2014 SALFORD RED DEVILS away lost 16 - 23

SALFORD R D - Mullaney: Johnson Gleeson Sa'u Meli:
Chase Smith: Morley Lee Tasi Hansen Dixon Peletua:
Subs used - Fages Walne Waine McPherson:
Tries - Dixon(2) Gleeson Johnson:
Goals - Mullaney(3) ChaseD/G:
CASTLEFORD - Dorn: Owen Channing Shenton Carney:
Sneyd Finn: Lynch Clark Huby Holmes Hauraki Millington:
Subs used - Webster Milner Massey Mariano:
Tries - Carney Hauraki Dorn: Goals Sneyd(2):
Referee J Childs Att - 5823 H.T. 6 - 10

Thu 27 Mar 2014 LONDON BRONCOS away won 54 - 6

LONDON B - Solomona: O'Callaghan MoKeeken Canton-
Brown Macani: Farrar Drinkwater: Greenwood Moore
Krasniqi Slyney Cook Foster:
Subs used - Vea Griffin Cunningham Woodburn-Hall:
Try McMeekan: Goal - Drinkwater:
CASTLEFORD - Dorn: Clare Channing Shenton Carney:
Ellis Finn: Lynch Clark Huby Holmes Hauraki Millington:
Subs used - Sneyd Massey Mariano Fleming:
Tries - Shenton(2) Carney(2) Channing Holmes Finn Huby
Dorn: Goals - Ellis(9):
Referee B Thaler Att - 1036 H.T. 24 - 0

Sun 6 Apr 2014 BATLEY BULLDOGS away won 48 - 10 R.L. CHALLENGE CUP 4TH ROUND

BATLEY B - Greenwood: Paterson Brotherton Griffin
Finigan: Davies Leatherbarrow: Smith Blake Gledhill
Martin Scott Applegarth: Subs used - Rowe Leek Leary
Chandler: Tries - Griffin Paterson: Goal - Paterson:
CASTLEFORD - Dorn: Clare Channing Shenton Carney:
Sneyd Finn: Lynch Milner Wheeldon Holmes Hauraki
Massey:
Subs Used - Boyle Mariano Ellis Danial Fleming:
Tries - Carney(3) Dorn(2) Sneyd Clare Ellis Wheeldon:
Goals - Sneyd(6):
Referee G Stokes - Att - 2482 H.T. 12 - 6

Fri 11 Apr 2014 SAINT HELENS home lost 28 - 30

CASTLEFORD - Dorn: Clare Webster Shenton Carney:
Sneyd Finn: Lynch Clark Huby Holmes Hauraki Millington:
Subs used - Massey Milner Boyle Mariano:
Tries - Shenton(2) Webster Millington Carney:
Goals - Sneyd(4):
ST HELENS - Lomax Makinson Dawson Turner Swift:
Wilkin Walsh Masoe Roby McCarthy-Scarsbrook Soliola
Manu Jones: Subs used - Wellens Walmsley Greenwood
Laffranchi: Tries - Soliola Lomax Makinson Turner

Wellens Swift: Goals - Walsh(3):
Referee B Thaler Att - 6487 H.T. 24 - 6

Fri 18 Apr 2014 WAKEFIELD TRINITY WILDCATS away won 43 - 20

WAKEFIELD T W - Sammut: Riley Collis Lyne Mathers:
Sykes Siejka: Anderson McShane Scruton Kirmond Ryan
Washbrook:
Subs used - Godinet Moore Annakin Smith:
Tries Sammut(2) McShane Lyne: Goals - Sammut(2):
CASTLEFORD - Clare: Owen Channing Shenton Carney:
Sneyd Finn: Lynch Clark Huby Holmes Hauraki Millington:
Subs used - Milner Boyle Mariano Wheeldon:
Tries - Clark(2) Owen(2) Wheeldon(2) Carney Finn:
Goals - Sneyd(5) D/G
Referee P Bentham Att - 5159 H.T. 26 - 12

Mon 21 Apr 2014 WARRINGTON WOLVES home won 40 - 6

CASTLEFORD - Tansey: Richard Owen ASHLEY
GIBSON(946) Shenton Clare: Sneyd Ellis: Lynch Milner
Wheeldon Mariano Webster Massey:
Subs used : Huby Millington Hauraki Clark.:
Tries - Shenton(3) Clare(2) Ellis Owen: Goals - Sneyd(6):
WARRINGTON W - Russell: J Monaghan Evans Atkins
Penny: O'Brien Ratchford; Hill M Monaghan Asotasi
Waterhouse Laithwaite Harrison:
Subs used - Higham Currie England, Evans:
Try - M Monaghan: Goal - Ratchford :
Referee: R Silverwood Att - 6853 H.T. 18 - 6

Sun 27 Apr 20104 SHEFFIELD EAGLES home won 60 - 16 R.L. CHALLENGE CUP 5TH ROUND

CASTLEFORD - Tansey: Dixon Gibson Shenton Carney:
Ellis Finn: Wheeldon Milner Huby Holmes Webster
Millington: Subs used - Sneyd Massey Clark Mariano:
Tries - Carney(4) Ellis(2) Gibson Millington Dixon Clark
Tansey Holmes: Goals - Dixon(2) Sneyd(4):
SHEFFIELD E - Laulu-Togagae: Turner Hanson Straugheir
Burke: Walker Brambani: Lillycrop Henderson Green
Garside Aspinall Taulapapa:
Subs used - Davey Blagbrough Tagaloa Ashton
Tries - Turner Straugheir Ashton: Goals - Brambani(2):
Referee R Hicks Att - 4648 H.T. 36 - 4

Sun 4 May 2014 HUDDERSFIELD GIANTS away lost 28 - 29

HUDDERSFIELD G - Grix: McGilvary Cudjoe Wardle
Murphy: Brough Robinson: Crabtree Lunt Kopozak Chan
Ta'al Lawrence: Subs used - Bailey Faiumu Wood
Mullally: Tries - Wardle Cudjoe McGilvary Grix Murphy:
Goals - Brough(4) D/G
CASTLEFORD - Clare: Dixon Channing Shenton Carney:
Sneyd Ellis: Lynch Clark Huby Holmes Hauraki Millington:
Subs used - Webster Milner Mariano Wheeldon:
Tries - Shenton Carney Dixon Webster Clark:
Goals - Sneyd(4):
Referee J Child Att - 7196 H.T. 12 - 12

SEASON 2014

Thu 8 May 2014 LEEDS RHINOS home lost 14 - 22
CASTLEFORD - Tansey: Dixon Gibson Shenton Carney:
Sneyd Finn: Lynch Milner Mariano Holmes Webster
Wheeldon: Subs used - Clark Millington Hauraki Huby;
Tries - Dixon Sneyd: Goals - Sneyd(3)
LEEDS R - Hardaker: Jones-Bishop, Watkins Moon
Briscoe; McGuire Ablett: Leuluai Sinfield Peacock Achurch
Clarkson Delaney:
Subs used - Ward Singleton Sutcliffe Bailey:
Tries - Jones-Bishop(2), Watkins(2): Goals - Sinfield(3):
Referee R Silverwood Att - 9208 H.T. 14 - 12

Sun 18 May 2014 WAKEFIELD TRINITY WILDCATS away won 50 – 12 MAGIC WEEKEND AT ETIHEAD STADIUM MANCHESTER
WAKEFIELD T W - Sammut: Mathers Collis Walshaw Riley:
Sykes Siejka: Anderson McShane Scruton Ryan Kirmond
Smith: Subs used - Godinet Moore Washbrook Fairbank:
Tries - Scruton Sykes: Goals Sammut(2):
CASTLEFORD - Tansey: Dixon Webster Shenton Carney:
Sneyd Finn: Lynch Clark Huby Holmes Hauraki Millington::
Subs used - Mariano Wheeldon Ellis LEE JEWITT(947):
Tries - Clark(2) Carney(2) Sneyd(2) Tansey Shenton
Mariano: Goals - Sneyd(7):
Referee J Child Att - 28213 H.T. 22 - 0

Sun 25 May 2014 WIDNES VIKINGS home won 34 - 22
CASTLEFORD - Dorn: Dixon Webster Shenton Carney:
Sneyd Finn: Lynch Clark Huby Holmes Hauraki
Millington: Subs used - Mariano Wheeldon Ellis Jewitt:
Tries - Dorn(2) Shenton Webster Wheeldon Clark:
Goals - Sneyd(5):
WIDNES V - Hanbury: Owens Marsh Phelps Flynn: Brown
Gilmore: Clough White Gerrard Allen Tickle Leuiuai:
Subs used - Gore Isa Johnson Kavanagh:
Tries - Brown Marsh Phelps Gilmore: Goals - Tickle(3):
Referee B Thaler Att - 4476 H.T. 10 - 12

Sun 1 Jun 2014 HULL KINGSTONE ROVERS home won 54 - 12
CASTLEFORD - Dorn: Dixon Channing Shenton Clare:
Sneyd Ellis: Lynch Milner Huby Holmes Hauraki
Millington: Subs used - Webster Clark Mariano
Wheeldon: Tries - Dorn(3) Channing(2) Millington Dixon
Ellis Webster Huby Clare: Goals - Sneyd(5):
HULL K. R - Cockayne: Gardner Horne Welham Ulugia:
Burns Keating: A Walker Hodgson Weyman Larroyer Cox
Costigan: Subs used - J Walker Langley Green
Lovegrove: Tries - Burns Ulugia: Goals - Burns(2):
Referee T Roby Att - 7196 H.T. 28 - 0

Sat 7 Jun 2014 WIGAN WARRIORS away won 16 - 4 R.L. CHALLENGE CUP QUARTER FINAL
WIGAN W - Bowen: Manfriedi Sarginson Gelling Burgess:
Williams Smith: Flower McIlorum Dudson Farrell Batemen
O'Laughlan: Subs used - Hughes Crosby Hampshire
Sutton: Try - Farrell
CASTLEFORD - Dorn: Dixon Webster Shenton Clare:
Sneyd Finn: Lynch Clark Huby Holmes Hauraki Jewitt:
Subs used - Millington Mariano Wheeldon Ellis:

Tries - Clare Dixon Jewitt: Goals - Sneyd(2):
Referee R Silverwood - Att - 8736 H.T. - 6 - 0

Fri 13 Jun 2014 WIGAN WARRIORS away lost 6 - 46
WIGAN W - Bowen: Manfredi Sarginson Gelling Burgess:
Powell Smith: Flower McIlorum Taylor Farrell Hughes
O'Loughlin: Subs used - Hampshire James Crosby
Sutton: Tries - Manfredi(2) Burgess(2) Bowen James
Farrell Mcllorum: Goals - Smiith(7):
CASTLEFORD - Dorn: Dixon Gibson Carney Clare: Ellis
Finn: Jewitt Milner Huby Mariano Hauraki Wheeldon:
Subs used - Millington Massey Holmes Reynolds:
Try - Gibson : Goal - Ellis
Referee P Bentham Att - 11914 H.T. 0- 022

Sun 22 Jun 2014 SAINT HELENS away lost 16 - 38
ST HELENS - Wellens: Makinson Turner Percival: Hohaia
Walsh: Masoe Roby McCathy-Scarsbrook Wilkin Flanagan
Soliola: Subs used - Manu Richards Thompson Savelio:
Tries - Percival(2) Wellens(2) Makinson Turner Walsh:
Goals - Walsh(5):
CASTLEFORD - Dorn: Dixon Webster Shenton Clare:
Sneyd Finn: Lynch Clark Huby Holmes Hauraki Millington:
Subs used - Massey Mariano Ellis Jewitt:
Tries - Dixon Sneyd Dorn: Goals - Sneyd(2):
Referee R Silverwood Att - 12648 H.T. 4 - 22

Sat 28 Jun 2014 SALFORD RED DEVILS home won 14 - 10
CASTLEFORD - Dorn: Dixon Webster Shenton Carney:
Sneyd Finn: Lynch Clark Huby Hauraki Millington
Wheeldon: Subs used - Milner Mariano Jewitt GARETH
CARVELL(948) Tries - Carney Webster: -
Goals - Sneyd(3):
SALFORD R D - Evalds: J Griffin Meli Sa'u Johnson: Chase
Fages: Morley Lee Tasi Ashurts Hock Puletua:
Subs used - Walne Rapira Tompkins Walton:
Tries - Sa'u Hock: Goal - Chase:
Referee T Roby Att - 5937 H.T. 6 - 0

Thu 3 Jul 2014 WIDNES VIKINGS away won 40 - 20
WIDNES V - Hanbury: Flynn Dean Phelps Ah Van: Brown
Mellor: Garrard Clarke Kavanagh Galea Tickle Cahill:
Subs used - Allen White Isa Lauluai:
Tries - Flyn Galea Ah Van Dean: Goals - Tickle(2):
CASTLEFORD - Dorn: Dixon Channing Shenton Carney:
Sneyd Ellis: Lynch Clark Huby Holmes Hauraki Millington:
Subs used - Milner Massey Jewitt Carvell:
Tries - Clark(3) Shenton(2) Dorn Holmes :
Goals - Sneyd(6):
Referee P Bentham Att - 4562 H.T. 22 - 12

Fri 11 Jul 2014 HUDDERSFIELD GIANTS home won 44 - 30
CASTLEFORD - Sneyd: Dixon Webster Shenton Carney:
Ellis Finn: Lynch Clark Huby Holmes Mariano Millington:
Subs used - Milner Massey Wheeldon Jewitt:
Tries - Finn(2) Holmes Carney Milner Dixon Mariano
Millington: Goals - Sneyd(6):
HUDDERSFIELD G - Connor: McGilvary Cudjoe Wardle

SEASON 2014

Broughton: Wood Robinson: Kaufussi Bailey Mullally
Ferres Patrick Lawrence: Subs used - Crabtree Kopozak
Ta'ai Leeming: Tries - Bailey(2) Cudjoe Wardle Crabtree:
Goals - Cudjoe(5):
Referee R Silverwood Att - 5310 H.T. 16 - 12

Thu 17 Jul 2014 LEEDS RHINOS away draw 24 - 24
LEEDS R - Hardaker: Briscoe Watkins Moon Hall: McGuire
Sinfield: Leulaui Aiton Peacock Ablett Ward Delaney:
Subs used - Burrow Jones-Buchanan Bailey Achurch:
Tries - Ablett(2) Briscoe Bailey Goals - Sinfield(4):
CASTLEFORD - Dorn: Dixon Webster Shenton Carney:
Sneyd Finn: Lynch Milner Jewitt Holmes Hauraki
Millington: Subs used - Clark Huby Massey Mariano:
Tries - Shenton Hauraki Massey Millington
Goals - Sneyd(4):
Referee B Thaler Att - 16173 H.T. 18 -18

Thu 24 Jul 2014 HULL F.C. away draw 18 - 18
HULL F C - Shaul: Lineham: Whiting Yeaman Talanoa:
Abdull Rankin: Green Houghton Watts Ellis Hadley
Westerman: Subs used - Heremaia Sa Thompson Paea:
Tries - Talanoa Abdull Yeaman: Goals - Rankin(3):
CASTLEFORD - Dorn: Dixon Gibson Shenton Clare: Sneyd
Finn: Lynch Milner Carvell Mariano Hauraki Massey:
Subs used - Millington Holmes Clark Wheeldon:
Tries - Clare(2) Shenton Sneyd: Goal - Sneyd
Referee J Child Att - 9969 H.T. 18 - 18

**Sun 3 Aug 2014 LONDON BRONCOS home
won 64 - 18**
CASTLEFORD - Dorn: Dixon Gibson Shenton Carney:
Sneyd Finn: Jewitt Milner Huby Holmes Webster Massey:
Subs used - Mariano Ellis Wheeldon Carvell:
Tries - Carney(3) Dorn(2) Dixon(2) Wheeldon Shenton
Carvell Mariano Milner: Goals - Sneyd(8):
LONDON B - Farrar: Atkins Minns Mataitonga Solomona:
Keyes Drinkwater: Slyney Moore Krasniqi McMeeken Vea
Cook: Subs used - Wicks Griffin Wallace Dollapi:
Tries -Krasniqi Dollapi McMeeken: Goals - Drinkwater(3):
Referee J Cobb Att - 5233 H.T. 28 - 12

**Sun 10 Aug 2014 WIDNES VIKINGS away won   28 - 6
R.L CHALLENGE CUP SEMI-FINAL AT LEIGH**
WIDNES V - Hanbury: Flynn Dean Marsh Owens: Brown
Mellor: Gerrard Clarke Kavanagh Galea Tickle Cahill:
Subs used - Allen O'Carroll White Isa:
Try - Owens: Goal - Owens:
CASTLEFORD - Dorn: Dixon Webster Shenton Clare:
Sneyd Finn: Lynch Clark Huby Holmes Mariano Massey:
Subs used - Wheeldon Ellis Jewitt Carvell:
Tries - Finn Clark Dixon Ellis Webster: Goals - Sneyd (4):
Referee R Silverwood Att - 12005 H.T. 14 - 0

**Fri 15 Aug 2014 WARRINGTON WOLVES away
lost 10 - 48**
WARRINGTON W - Russell: J Monaghan Atkins Bridge E
Evans: Ratchford O'Brien: Hill M Monaghan Harrison
Waterhouse Westwood Grix:
Subs used - Higham Wood England Laithwaite:

Tries - Evans(2) Atkins O'Brien Bridge England Ratchford J
Monaghan: Goals - Ratchford(5) Bridge(3): CASTLEFORD
- Ben Reynolds: Tansey Channing Gibson Clare: Ellis
Finn: Lynch Milner Wheeldon Mariano Hauraki Jewitt:
Subs used - Massey Holmes BRAD DAY(949) WILL
MAHER(950): Tries - Clare Holmes: Goal - Finn:
Referee J Chid Att - 8391 H.T. 4 - 18

**Sat 23 Aug 2014 LEEDS RHINOS away lost 10 - 23
R.L. CHALLENGE CUP FINAL AT WEMBLEY**
CASTLEFORD - Dorn: Dixon Webster Shenton Carney:
Sneyd Finn: Lynch Clark Huby Holmes Hauraki Massey:
Subs used - Mariano Wheeldon Ellis Jewitt:
Tries Clark Holmes: Goal - Finn:
LEEDS R - Hardaker: Briscoe Watkins Moon Hall: Sinfield
McGuire: Leuluai Burrow Peacock Delaney Ablett Jones-
Buchanan: Subs used - Aiton Bailey Kirke Sutcliffe:
Tries - Hall(2) Briscoe McGuire:
Goals - Sinfield(3) McGuireD/G
Referee P Bentham Att - 77914 H.T. 4 - 16
LANCE TODD TROPHY WINNER RYAN HALL

Sun 31 Aug 2014 BRADFORD BULLS home won 32 -18
CASTLEFORD - Dorn: Dixon Webster Shenton Clare:
Sneyd Finn: Lynch Clark Jewitt Holmes Hauraki Massey:
Subs used - Mariano Wheeldon Ellis Channing:
Tries - Lynch Clare Dorn Shenton Clark: Goals - Sneyd(6):
BRADFORD - Kearney: George Henry Arundel Williams:
Gaskell Gale: Manuokafoa O'Brien Sidlow Ferguson Pitts
Donaldson: Subs used - Olbison Blythe Fakir Addy:
Tries - Gaskell(3) Goals - Gale(3):
Referee G Stokes Att - 7428 H.T. 24 - 6

**Sun 7 Sep 2014 WAKEFIELD TRINITY WILDCATS
home won 26 - 22**
CASTLEFORD - Dorn: Dixon Webster Shenton Clare:
Sneyd Finn: Lynch Clark Jewitt Holmes Hauraki Massey:
Subs used - Mariano Wheeldon Milner Gareth Carvell:
Tries - Clare(2) Dorn Dixon Webster: Goals - Sneyd(3):
WAKEFIELD T W - Sykes: Owen Gilmour Lyne Riley:
Godinet T Smith: Anderson McShane Raleigh Washbrook
Molloy D Smith:
Subs used - Lauititi Wildie Tautai Annakin:
Tries - Gilmour Riley Wildie Owen: Goals - Sykes(3):
Referee J Child Att - 9182 H.T. 22 - 10

**Sat 13 Sep 2014 CATALAN DRAGONS away
lost 6 - 28**
CATALAN D - Escare: Oldfield Pomeroy Duport Millard:
Bosc Williams: Elima Henderson Anderson Taia
Whitehead Baitieri: Subs used - Lima Maria Pelissier
Garcia: Tries - Escare(2) Taia Henderson Whitehead:
Goals - Bosc(4):
CASTLEFORD - Dorn: Dixon Webster Shenton Clare:
Sneyd Finn: Lynch Clark Jewitt Holmes Hauraki Massey:
Subs used - Huby Millington Wheeldon Ellis:
Try - Dixon Goal - Sneyd:
Rerferee B Thaler Attt - 9223 H.T. 0 - 10

SEASON 2014

Fri 19 Sep 2014 SAINT HELENS away lost 0 - 41
IST ROUND SUPER LEAGUE PLAY OFF

ST HELENNS - Wellens: Makinson Percival Wheeler Swift: Hohaia Flanagan: Richards Roby Amor McCarthy-Scarsbrook Thompson Turner:
Subs used - Masoe Soliola Manu Laffranchi:
Tries - Roby(2) Turner Swift Makinson Amor Masoe:
Goals - Percival(6) Turner D/G:
CASTLEFORD - Dorn: Dixon Webster Shenton Carney: Ellis Finn: Lynch Milner Huby Holmes Hauraki Millington:
Subs used - Massey Clark Wheeldon Channing:
Referee J Child Att - 7548 H.T. 0 - 13

Thu 25 Sep 2014 WARRINGTON WOLVES home
lost 14 - 30   2ND ROUND SUPER LEAGUE PLAY OFF

CASTLEFORD - Dorn: Clare Channing Shenton Carney: Marc Sneyd Jamie Ellis: Lynch Darryl Clark Graig Huby Holmes Weller Hauraki Massey:
Subs used - Kirk Dixon Milner Millington Wheeldon:
Tries - Ellis Dorn Shenton: Goal - Sneyd:
WARRINGTON W - Ratchford: J Monaghan Bridge Atkins Evans: O'Brien Myler: Hill M Monaghan England Laithwaite Waterhouse Harrison: Subs used - Higham Asotasi Currie Wood: Tries - J Monaghan(2) Atkins O'Brien Evans: Goals - Ratchford(5)::
Referee P Bentham Att - 6219 H.T. 4 - 10

Marc Sneyd
D. No 942
2014

Liam Finn
D. No 943
2014 to 2015

Scott Wheeldon
D. No 944
2014 to 2015

Frankie Mariano
D. No 945
2014 to 2016

Ashley Gibson
D. No 946
2014 to 2015

Lee Jewitt
D. No 947
2014 to 2016

Will Maher
D. No 950
2014 to

SEASON 2014

D.N	PLAYER		DEBUT	L MATCH	APP	SUB	T.AP	TRI'S	G'LS	D.G	P'TS
759	LYNCH	ANDY			31	0	31	1	0	0	4
800	HUBY	CRAIG		25/09/2014	25	4	29	2	0	0	8
810	SHENTON	MICHAEL			32	0	32	18	0	0	72
840	BOYLE	RYAN			0	3	3	0	0	0	0
863	OWEN	RICHARD		21/04/2014	5	0	5	6	0	0	24
870	DIXON	KIRK		25/09/2015	24	1	25	15	8	0	76
876	MASSEY	NATHAN			10	13	23	1	0	0	4
882	DORN	LUKE			24	0	24	19	0	0	76
907	HOLMES	OLIVER			28	4	32	7	0	0	28
910	MILNER	ADAM			12	13	25	3	0	0	12
915	CLARK	DARYL		25/09/2014	22	8	30	16	0	0	64
925	MILLINGTON	GRANT			20	7	27	6	0	0	24
926	CLARE	JAMES			17	0	17	11	0	0	44
929	ELLIS	JAMIE		25/09/2014	11	10	21	7	10	0	48
932	TANSEY	JORDAN			7	0	7	3	0	0	12
933	CARNEY	JUSTIN			24	0	24	24	0	0	96
934	WEBSTER	JAKE			18	4	22	7	0	0	28
936	HAURAKI	WELLER		25/09/2014	28	2	30	3	0	0	12
938	FLEMING	DANIEL		06/04/2014	0	5	5	0	0	0	0
940	CHANNING	MICHAEL			14	2	16	4	0	0	16
941	REYNOLDS	BEN		15/08/2014	1	1	2	0	0	0	0
942	SNEYD	MARC	16/02/2014	25/09/2014	29	2	31	7	116	2	262
943	FINN	LIAM	16/02/2014		29	0	29	5	2	0	24
944	WHEELDON	SCOTT	16/02/2014		7	20	27	5	0	0	20
945	MARIANO	FRANKIE	16/02/2014		8	22	30	5	0	0	20
946	GIBSON	ASHLEY	21/04/2014		7	0	7	2	0	0	8
947	JEWITT	LEE	18/05/2014		8	8	16	1	0	0	4
948	CARVELL	GARRETH	28/06/2014	07/09/2014	1	5	6	1	0	0	4
949	DAY	BRAD	15/08/2014	15/08/2014	0	1	1	0	0	0	0
950	MAHER	WILL	15/08/2014		0	1	1	0	0	0	0
	30		**9**	**11**	**442**	**136**	**578**	**179**	**136**	**2**	**990**

COMPETITION		P	W	D	L	FOR	AGT
S, LEAGUE	POSITION 4 OF 14	27	17	2	8	814	583
RL CUP		5	4	0	1	162	59
PLAY OFF		2	0	0	2	14	71
PLAYERS RECORDS		**34**	**21**	**2**	**11**	**990**	**713**

At the end of the season the teams will be reduced to 12 from 14, therefore it will be imperative to finish above the last two places to remain in Super League for 2015.

In the RL Challenge Cup we won through to the Final. With big wins in the first two rounds against Batley Bulldogs and Sheffield Eagles, we then faced Wigan away in the quarter- final. With a magnificent display we outplayed the odds-on favourites to register 16-4 victory. Next up was Widnes Vikings in the semi-final at the Leigh Sports Village. In front of a capacity crowd of 12,005 we totally outplayed our opponents to register a 28-6 victory. The Castleford fans were brilliant in not rising to the bait of the Vikings fans' invasion of the pitch at the end of the game. The Final at Wembley against the Leeds Rhinos was a real disappointment. A poor first half performance meant that we were really never in the game and were beaten 23-10.

In the League we had a brilliant campaign went into the last match away at Catalan Dragons needing a victory to finish top of the League on points difference from St Helens. Unfortunately we were not at our best and we lost 28-6 resulting in us finishing in 4th place. Unfortunately we appeared to have lost our 'mo-jo' and subsequently lost our two play-off games.

Marc Sneyd was top Super League goal scorer with 99 League, one play-off and 16 Cup goals giving 116 in total. Top try scorer was Justin Carney with 24 tries from 24 appearances, closely followed by Luke Dorn with 19 from 24 and Michael Shenton with 18 from 32.

Daryl Clark won both the Man of Steel and Young Man of Steel awards and Daryl Powell won the Coach of the Year award. How we missed out on winning the Club of the Year award to Widnes Vikings we will never know.

SEASON 2015

SUPER LEAGUE XX

Bradford Bulls and London Broncos were relegated from the league to leave a 12 team competition

Sun 28 Dec 2014 FEATHERSTONE ROVERS home won 18 – 0 FRIENDLY

CASTLEFORD - Howden: Clare Channing Gibson Solomona: Tansey Finn: Crossley Milner Moors Cook McMeeken Wheeldon: Subs used - Maher Massey S Moore T Holmes Westerman:
Tries - Solomona Cook Tansey: Goals - Finn(3):
FEATHERSTONE R - Hardman: Blackmore Chappell Minns Johnson: Sykes Moore: James Ellis Baldwinson Lockwood Cording Bussey: Subs used - Irwin Cooper Torks Coventry Walmsley Foster Milner Newbould:
Referee R Silverwood Att – 4800 H.T. 6 - 0

Sun 11 Jan 2015 BRADFORD BULLS home won 22 - 14 FRIENDLY

CASTLEFORD - Dorn: Clare Webster Solomona Carney: Roberts Gale: Lynch Milner Millington O Holmes Cook Massey: Subs used - S Moore Wheeldon Finn Tansey Channing McMeeken Crossley Gibson:
Tries - Carney Gibson Moore McMeeken: Goals - Gale(3):
BRADFORD B - Mullaney: Uaisele Purtell Baile Williams: Gaskell: Siajka: Clough O'Brien Sidlow Walshaw Pitts Walker: Subs used - Tahraoul Addy Brook Olbison Ulugia Shaw Halafihi Davies Mellor:
Tries - Pitts Shaw Purtell: Goal - Siejka:
Referee G Stokes Att - 3844 H.T. 6 - 14

Sun 18 Jan 2015 DONCASTER away won 32 - 12 FRIENDLY

DONCASTER - Scott: Doherty Gilbey Welham Sanderson: Kittrick Wilkinson: Spiers Kesik Carbutt Foster Kel y Wilson: Subs used - Cowling Robinson Clark Waller Waterman Palmer Holt:
Tries - Holt Kittrick: Goals - Sanderson(2):
CASTLEFORD - Tansey: Clair Channing Gibson Solomona: Roberts Finn: Boyle T Holmes Crossley McMeeken Westerman Maher: Subs used - Gale Howden Sheehan Massey Plimmer Wheeldon Webster Lynch:
Tries - Gibson(2) Massey Roberts T Holmes Solomona: Goals - Finn(2) Gale(2):
Referee C Kendall Att - 1200(est) H.T. 10 - 6

Sun 25 Jan 2015 WIDNES VIKINGS home won 20 - 18 FRIENDLY

CASTLEFORD - Dorn: Solomona Gibson Shenton Carney: Roberts Gale: Lynch Moore Millington O Holmes McMeeken Massey: Subs used - Boyle Milner Wheeldon Finn Tansey Crossley Webster:
Tries - Solomona(2) Roberts Finn: Goals - Gale(2):
WIDNES V - Hanbury: Ah Van Phelps Marsh Flynn: Brown Mellor: Dudson White O'Carroll Galea Tickle Isa: Subs used - Hulme Cahill Joseph Manuokafoa Dean Haremia Gore Gilmore Kavanagh Leulaui Craven Gerrard Clarkson: Tries - Flynn(2) Hanbury Brown: Goal Tickle:
Referee B Thaler Att - 2141 H.T. 10 - 14

Sun 8 Feb 2015 WAKEFIELD TRINITY WILDCATS home lost 22 - 24

CASTLEFORD - Tansey: DENNY SOLOMONA(951) Gibson Shenton Carney: LUKE GALE(952) Finn: Lynch Moore Millington O Holmes JUNIOR MOORS(953) Massey: Subs used - STEVE CROSSLEY(954) Milner Boyle Webster:
Tries - Solomona(2) Gale Carney: - Goals -Gale(3):
WAKEFIELD T W - Hall: Riley Collis Lyne Owen: Miller T Smith: Scruton McShane Paea Kirmond Washbrook D Smith: Subs used - Godinet Anderson Annakin Lauitiiti:
Tries - McShane Godinet Lauitiiti Washbrook:
Goals - Hall(4):
Referee R Hicks Att - 10728 H.T. 16 - 6

Sat 14 Feb 2015 CATALAN DRAGONS away lost 12 -13

CATALAN D - Escare: Oldfield Pomery Tonga Duport: Bosc Dureau: Lima Henderson Anderson Taia Whitehead Mounis: Subs Used - Elima Palissier Garcia Baitier:
Tries - Escare Whithead: Goals - Dureau(2) D/G
CASTLEFORD - Tansey: Solomona Channing Shenton Carney: BEN ROBERTS(955) Gale: Lynch Moore Millington O Holmes Moors Massey: Subs used - Webster Wheeldon Finn Crossley: Tries - Carney Tansey:
Goals - Gale(2):
Referee J Child Att - 9169 H.T. 6 - 0

Fri 27 Feb 2015 SAINT HELENS away lost 14 - 21

ST HELENS - Lomax: Makinson Percival Jones Swift: Burns Wilkin: Walmsley Roby Amor Greenwood Vea McCarthy-Scarsbrook: Subs used - Masoe Flanagan Thompson Richards: Tries - Swift Makinson Jones Percival:
Goals - Percival(2) WilkinD/G:
CASTLEFORD - Tansey: Solomona Channing Shenton Carney: Finn Gale: Lynch Moore Millington O Holmes Moors Massey:
Subs used - Milner Cook Boyle MIKE McMEEKEN(956):
Tries - Carney(2) Tansey: Goal – Gale
Referee R Silverwood Att - Not Given H.T. 0 - 10

Fri 6 Mar 2015 WIGAN WARRIORS home won 42 - 14

CASTLEFORD - Dorn: Clare Webster Shenton Carney: Finn Gale: Cook Milner Millington O Holmes Moors Massey: Subs used - Roberts Boyle Wheeldon Crossley:
Tries - Carney(2) Clare Dorn Finn O Holmes Shenton: Goals - Gale(7):
WIGAN W - Bowen: Charnley Gelling Sarginson Manfridi: Powell Smith: Clubb McLlorum Mossop J Tompkins Farrell Bateman: Subs used - Williams Tautai Patrick Greenwood: Tries - Charnley(2) Smith: Goal - Smith:
Referee T Roby Att - 7772 H.T. 22 - 4

Thu 12 Mar 2015 HUDDERSFIELD GIANTS away lost 0 - 22

HUDDERSFIELD G - Grix: McGillvary Cudjoe Wardle Murphy: Brough Ellis: Huby Robinson Kopozak Ferres Hughes Lawrence: Subs used- Crabtree Wood Ta'al Johnson:
Tries - Ellis Ta'al Murphy McGillvary: Goals - Brough(3):

SEASON 2015

CASTLEFORD - Dorn: Clare Channing Webster Carney: Finn Gale: Lynch Moore Millington O Holmes Moors Massey: Subs used - Roberts Cook Wheeldon Crossley: Referee J Child Att 6257 H.T. 0 - 6:

Fri 20 Mar 2015 SALFORD RED DEVILS home won 30 - 16
CASTLEFORD - Dorn: Clare Webster Shenton Carney: Finn Gale: Millington Milner Cook O Holmes Moors Massey: Subs used - Roberts Boyle Wheeldon McMeeken: Tries - Carney(2) Finn Shenton Wheeldon Clare: Goals - Gale(3):
SALFORD R D - Evalds: Jones-Bishop J Griffin Sa'u Johnson: Chase Dobson: Morley Lee Taylor Hansen Hauraki Walne: Subs used - Fages D Griffin Tasi Walton; Tries - Lee Hauraki Jones-Bishop: Goals - J Griffin(2): Referee R Hicks Att 6901 H.T. 22 - 12

Fri 27 Mar 2015 HULL F C home won 20 - 14
CASTLEFORD - Tansey: Clare Gibson Shenton Carney: Finn Gale: Millington Milner Moors O Holmes Webster Wheeldon:
Subs used - Lynch Roberts McMeeken Crossley: Tries - Gale(2) Carney Clare: Goals - Gale(2):
HULL F C - Rankin: Lineham Michaels Logan Talanoa: Pryce Sneyd: Paea Houghton Watts Thompson Minichiello Westerman: Subs used - Hadley Green Bowden Howarth: Tries - Lineham(3): Goal - Sneyd
Referee M Thomason Att - 9774 H.T. 6 - 4

Thu 3 Apr 2015 LEEDS RHINOS home lost 12 - 26
CASTLEFORD - Dorn: Clare Gibson Shenton Carney: Finn Gale: Lynch Moore Millington O Holmes Webster Massey: Subs used - Milner Cook Boyle Wheeldon: Tries - Shenton(2): Goals - Gale(2):
LEEDS R - Hardaker: Handley Watkins Moon Hall: Sutcliffe McGuire: Singleton Aiton Peacock Ward Ablett Cuthbertson: Subs used - Burrow Delaney Achurch Yates: Tries - Hall(2) Moon Ward Cuthbertson: Goals - Sutcliffe(3):
Referee B Thaler Att - 11235 H.T. 6 - 16

Mon 6 Apr 2015 WARRINGTON WOLVES away won 22 - 14
WARRINGTON W - Ratchford: Monaghan Bridge Atkins Penny: O'Brien Myler: Hill Higham Sim Currie Westwood Harrison;
Subs used - Clark Asotasi England Laithwaite
Tries - Ratchford Atkins Penny: Goals - O'Brien (1)
CASTLEFORD - Dorn: Tansey Channing Shenton Carney: Roberts Gale: Lynch Moore Wheeldon Mariano Cook Massey:
Subs used - Milner Millington Boyle Maher: Tries - Tansey Dorn Milner Roberts: Goals - Gale(3)
Referee J Childs Att - 8,580 H.T. 10-10

Sat 11 Apr 2015 HULL KINGSTON ROVERS home won 25 - 4
CASTLEFORD - Tansey: Gibson Channing Shenton Carney: Roberts Gale: Lynch Moore Wheeldon O Holmes Mariano

Massey: Subs - Milner Millington Jewitt Boyle: Tries - Tansey Gale Massey Mariano: Goals – Gale(4) D/G: HULL K R - Dixon: Mantellato Whelham Goulding Siro: Campese Kelly: Walker Lunt Allgood Larroyer Horne McCarthy: Subs used - Cockayne Ollett Green Burke: Try - Sio
Referee B Thaler Att - 6102 H.T. 18 - 4

Sun 19 Apr 2015 WINDES VIKINGS away lost 16 - 46
WIDNES V - Hanbury: Owens Marsh Phelps Ah Van: Brown Gilmore: Dudson White O'Carroll Gales Dean Leulual: Subs used - Gerrard Heremaia Manuokafoa Isa: Tries - Ah Van(2) Hanbury(2) Owens Marsh Brown Phelps: Goals - Owens(7):
CASTLEFORD - Tansey: Clare Channing Shenton Gibson: Roberts Finn: Lynch Moore Wheeldon O Holmes Millington Massey:
Subs used - Milner Jewitt Boyle Steve Crossley: Tries – Roberts O Holmes Shenton: Goals - Finn(2): Referee J Child Att - 6457 H.T. 6 - 28

Sun 26 Apr 2015 SALFORD RED DEVILS away won 22 - 20
SALFORD R D - Evalds: Locke Caton-Brown Gildart Johnson: Fages G Griffin: Taylor Godwin Tasi Hansen Forster Greenwood: Subs used - Morley Lannon Hood Gee: Tries - Locke(2) Fages Taylor: Goals - Locke Johnson:
CASTLEFORD - Tansey: Clare Gibson Shenton ASH ROBSON(957): Roberts Gale: Lynch Moore Wheeldon O Holmes Millington Massey:
Subs used - Milner Jewitt Moors Maher: Tries - Gibson(2) Massey Robson: Goals - Gale(3): Referee - G Stokes Att - 3397 H.T. 10 - 10
(Referee Left the field injured with 6 minute left replaced by C Leatherbarrow)

Sun 3 May 2015 CATALAN DRAGONS home won 36 - 28
CASTLEFORD - Tansey: Gibson Channing Shenton Robson: Finn Gale: Lynch Moore RYAN BAILEY(958) O Holmes Mariano Massey: Subs used - Millington Boyle Maher TOM HOLMES(959): Tries - Gibson Channing Millington Shenton Tansey Moore: Goals - Gale(6): CATALAN D - Escare: Oldfield Carace Tonga Yaha: Bosc Dureau: Anderson Henderson Casty Taia Whitehead Baitieri: Subs used - Pelissier Garcia Bousquet Springer: Tries - Garcia(3) Yaha Tala: Goals - Dureau(4): Referee R Hicks Att - 5704 H.T. 20 - 6

Fri 8 May 2015 WIGAN WARRIORS away lost 0 - 28
WIGAN W - Hampshire: Manfredi J Tompkins Sarginson Burgess: Williams Smith: Crosby McIlorum Mossop Lloyd Bateman O'Loughlin: Subs used - Powell Tautai Patrick Sutton: Tries - Burgess McIlorum Sarginson Manfredi: Goals - Smith(6)
CASTLEFORD - Tansey: Gibson Channing Shenton Clare: Finn Gale: Bailey Milner Boyle Mariano Moors Jewitt: Subs used - Webster Roberts Millington Wheeldon: Referee B Thaler Att - 15002 H.T. 0 - 10

Sat 16 May 2015 HULL F. C. away lost 14 - 40
R.L CHALLENG CUP 6TH ROUND
HULL FC - Rankin: Naughton Talanoa Yeaman Michaels:
Pryce Sneyd: Watts Houghton Pea Minichiello Sa Ellis:
Subs used - Abdull Thompson Green Whiting: Tries -
Naughton(3) Rankin(2) Pea Yeaman: Goals - Sneyd(6):
CASTLEFORD - Tansey: Gibson Webster Shenton James
Clare: Roberts Gale: Lynch Milner Bailey O Holmes Moors
Massey: Subs used - Millington Jewitt McMeeken Finn:
Tries - Gibson Clare McMeeken: Goal - Gale:
Referee J Child   Att - 6715   H.T. 4 - 16

**Thu 21 May 2015 HUDDERSFIELD GIANTS home
lost 16 - 24**
CASTLEFORD - Tansey: Gibson Webster Shenton
Solomona: Roberts Gale: Lynch Milner Bailey O Holmes
Mariano Massey:
Subs used - Millington Jewitt Finn McMeeken:
Tries - Webster Roberts Shenton: Goals - Gale(2):
HUDDERSFIELD G - Grix: McGillvary Murphy Connor
Broughton: Brough: Wood: Mullally Leeming Huby Wardle
Hughes Ferres:
Subs used - Robinson Crabtree Koppczak Ta'a:
Tries - Huby Murphy Ta'a Crabtree: Goals - Brough(4):
Referee R Silverwood   Att - 4634   H.T. 4 - 18

**Sun 31 May 2015 WAKEFIELD TRINITY WILDCATS
away won 56 – 16 MAGIC WEEKEND PLAYED AT
NEWCASTLE UNITED FC**
CASTLEFORD - Tansey: Gibson Webster Shenton
Solomona: Finn Gale: Lynch Moore Millington O Holmes
McMeeken Massey: Subs used - Milner Boyle Moors
Maher: Tries - Solomona(4) Gibson(3) Tansey Shenton
Gale: Goals - Gale(8):
WAKEFIELD T W - Owen: Johnstone Collis Lyne Riley:
Miller T Smith: Scruton McShane Anderson Washbrook
Kirmond Molloy: Subs used - Godinet Ryan Simon D
Smith;   Tries - Johnstone(2) D Smith: Goals - Miller(2):
Referee J Cobb   Att 26917   H.T. 22 - 16

**Fri 5 Jun 2015 HULL KINGSTON ROVERS away
won 30 - 22**
HULL K R - Cockayne: Dixon Welham Salter Sio: Campese
Kelly: Green Boudebza Puletua Larroyer Blair McCarthy:
Subs used - Cox Donaldson Ollett Greenwood:
Tries - Kelly(2) Dixon Ollett: Goals - Dixon(3):
CASTLEFORD - Roberts: Gibson Webster Shenton
Solomona: Finn Gale: Lynch Milner Millington O Holmes
McMeeken Massey: Subs used - Boyle Jordan Tansey
Moors Maher: Tries - Roberts Solomona O Holmes Gale
Finn: Goals - Gale(5):
Referee R Silverwood   Att – 7093   H.T. 24 - 16

Thu 11 Jun 2015 LEEDS RHINOS away won 31 - 24
LEEDS R - Sutcliffe: Handley Watkins Keinhorst Hall:
McGuire Burrow: Singleton Aiton Peacock Ablett Ward
Cuthbertson: Subs used - Sinfield Yates Leuluai (Walters
not used):   Tries - Ablett Hall Cuthbertson Keinhorst:
Goals - Sutcleffe(2) Sinfield(2):
CASTLEFORD - Roberts: Gibson Webster Shenton

Solomona: Finn Gale: Lynch Moore Millington O Holmes
McMeeken Massey: Subs used - Milner Moors Boyle
Bailey: Tries - Solomona(2) Millington Finn Shenton:
Goals - Gale(5) FinnD/G:
Referee J Child   Att - 15089   H.T. 18 - 16

Thu 18 Jun 2015 SAINT HELENS home won 25 - 24
CASTLEFORD - Roberts: Solomona Webster Shenton
Carney: Finn Gale: Lynch Moore Millington O Holmes
McMeeken Massey: Subs used - Milner Cook Moors
Ryan Bailey: Tries - Carney Solomona Webster Cook:
Goals - Gale(4) Roberts D/G:
ST HELENS - McDonnell: Dawson Percival Turner Swift:
Burns Walsh: Amor Roby Walmsley McCartney-
Scarsbrook Wilkin Jones: Subs used - Masoe Richards
Flanagan Greenwood: Tries - Walsh Walmsley
Greenwood McDonnell: Goals - Percival(4):
Referee R Silverwood   Att - 6086   H.T. 10 - 18

Sun 5 Jul 2015 WIDNES VIKINGS home won 34 - 20
CASTLEFORD - Dorn: Solomona Webster Shenton Carney:
Finn Gale: Lynch Milner Millington O Holmes McMeeken
Massey: Subs used - Roberts Cook Moors
GADWIN SPRINGER(960):   Tries - Solomona(3) Webster
Cook Carney: Goals - Gale(5):
WIDNES V - Hanbury: Flynn Dean Craven Owens: Gilmore
Mellor: Manuokafoa Haremaia Gerrard Clarkson Gales
Cahill: Subs used - O'Carroll Leuluai Dudson Isa:
Tries - Owens Clarkson Gilmore Leuluai: Goals - Owens(2);
Referee J Cobb   Att - 7002   H.T. 24 - 10

Sun 12 Jul 2015 HULL F.C. away lost 18 - 21
CASTLEFORD - Dorn: Solomona Webster Shenton Carney:
Finn Roberts: Lynch Milner Millington O Holmes
McMeeken Cook:
Subs used - Boyle Moors Scott Moore Springer:
Tries- Solomona(2) Dorn Roberts: Goal - Finn:
HULL F.C. - Rankin: Lineham Taanoa Logan Michaels:
Pryce Sneyd: Watts Houghton Bowden Hadley Whiting
Westerman:
Subs used - Abdull Thompson Green Fash:
Tries - Lineham(2) Whiting Abdull: Goals - Sneyd(2) D/G:
Referee J Cobb   Att - 10949   H.T. 6 - 14

**Sun 19 Jul 2015 WAKEFIELD TRINITY WILDCATS
away won 58 - 20**
CASTLEFORD - Dorn: Solomona Gibson Shenton Carney:
Finn Gale: Lynch Milner Millington O Holmes McMeeken
Springer: Subs used - Roberts Cook Boyle Moors:
Tries - Carney(4) Dorn(2) Millington Gale McMeeken O
Holmes: Goals- Gale(9):
WAKEFIELD T W - Locke: Tansey Arundel Lyne Johnstone:
Miller T Smith: Scruton Howarth Anderson Lauitiiti Molloy
Simon:
Subs used - McShane Washbrook Walker Mullally:
Tries - Johnstone(2) Lyne Walker :   Goals - Arundel(2):
Referee R Hicks   Att - 6013   H.T. 18 - 12

SEASON 2015

Sun 26 Jul 2015 WARRINGTON WOLVES home lost 6 - 44
CASTLEFORD - Dorn: Gibson Webster Shenton Carney:
Finn Gale: Lynch Milner Millington O Holmes McMeeken
Springer: Subs used - Boyle Cook Moors Roberts:
Try - Moors: Goal - Finn:
WARRINGTON - Russell: Ormsby Ratchford Atkins:
Monaghan: O'Brien Myler: Hill Clark Sims Westwood
Currie Harrison: Subs used - Dwyer Asotasi Wilde
England: Tries - Monaghan(2) Westwood O'Brien
Ormsby Currie Ratchford Wilde Myler: Goals - O'Brien(4):
Referee P Bentham   Att - 7239 H.T. 0 - 30

Fri 7 Aug 2015 HULL F C home won 36 - 30 ROUND 1 SUPER 8
CASTLEFORD - Roberts: Gibson Webster Shenton Carney:
Finn Gale: Lynch PAUL MCSHANE(961) Millington O
Holmes Moors Massey:
Subs used - Milner Cook McMeeken Springer:
Tries - Shenton(4) Gale Gibson: Goals - Gale (6):
HULL F C - Rankin: Lineham Sa Logan Michaels: Sneyd
Abdull: Pea Houghton Watts Whiting Minichiello
Westerman: Subs used - Thompson Palea'aesina Green
Yeaman:Tries - Whiting Rankin Michaels Lineham Logan:
Goals - Sneys(5):
Referee R Hicks   Att - 6760 H.T. 16 - 18

Thu 13 Aug 2015 WARRINGTON WOLVES home won 17 – 16 ROUND 2 SUPER 8
CASTLEFORD - Roberts: Gibson Webster Shenton Carney:
Finn Gale: Lynch Milner Millington O Holmes McMeeken
Massey: Subs used - Dorn Cook Moors Springer:
Tries - Carney(2) Shenton: Goals - Gale (2) FinnD/G
WARRINGTON W - Ratchford: Penny Evans Atkins
Monaghan: Sandow Myler: Hill Clark Sims Westwood
Currie Harrison: Subs used - Asotasi Wheeler Dwyer
King: Tries - Myler(2) Penny: Goals - Sandow(2):
Referee B Thaler   Att - 5212 H.T. 12 - 6

Sat 22 Aug 2015 CATALAN DRAGONS away lost 26 – 44 ROUND 3 SUPER 8
CATALAN D - Escare: Inu Goigot Pomeroy Sigismeau:
Carney Bosc: Elima Pellisier Lima Taia Whitehead Baitieri:
Subs used - Henderson Anderson Garcia Bousquet:
Tries - Gigot(3) Escare(2) Taia Lima Carney:
Goals - Bosc(6):
CASTLEFORD - Roberts: Gibson Channing Shenton Justin
Carney: Liam Finn Gale: Lynch Milner Millington O
Holmes McMeeken Massey:
Subs used - Cook Moors Springer McShane:
Tries - Milner(2) Carney O Holmes Moors: Goals - Gale(3):
Referee B Thaler   Att - 7473 H.T. 6 - 26

Thu 3 Sep 2015 HUDDERSFIELD GIANTS away lost 26 – 40 ROUND 4 SUPER 8
HUDDERSFIELD - Grix: McGillvary Cudjoe Connor
Murphy: Brough Ellis: Crabtree Robinson Huby Wardle
Hughes Ta'ai: Subs used - Lawrence Kopczak Leeming
Smith: Tries - McGillvary(2) Ta'ai Connor Murphy Wardle
Ellis Crabtree: Goals - Brough(2) Ellis(2):

CASTLEFORD - Dorn: Gibson McMeeken Michael
Channing Solomona: Roberts Gale: Lynch Milner
Wheeldon Millington Moors Massey: Subs used - Cook
Boyle Springer McShane: Tries - Gale Gibson Dorn
Roberts Solomona: Goals Gale(3):
Referee R Hicks   Att - 5350 H.T. 10 - 24

Thu 10 Sep 2015 SAINT HELENS home lost 38 - 42 ROUND 5 SUPER 8
CASTLEFORD - Dorn: Gibson McMeeken Shenton
Solomona: Roberts Gale: Lynch Milner Millington O
Holmes Moors Wheeldon: Subs used - Boyle Maher
Springer McShane: Tries - Dorn(2) Roberts(2) Solomona
Moors: Goals - Gale(7):
ST HELENS - Quinlan: Makinson Percival Jones Swift:
Burns Walsh: Amor Roby Walmsley McCarthy-Scarsbrook
Wilkin Turner: Subs used - Richards Greenwood
Flanagan Thompson: Tries - Swift(3) Percival(2) Quinlan
Makinson: Goals - Walsh(7):
Referee B Thaler   Att - 5235 Halftime 18 - 18

Thu 17 Sep 2015 LEEDS RHINOS away won 29 - 22 ROUND 6 SUPER 8
LEEDS R - Hardaker: Briscoe Watkins Moon Hall: Sinfield
McGuire: Cuthbertson Lilley Peacock Ward Ablett
Delaney: Subs used - Walters Leuluai Singleton Garbutt:
Tries - Hall(2) Moon Cuthbertson: Goals - Sinfield(2) Lilley:
CASTLEFORD - Dorn: Gibson McMeeken Shenton
Solomona: Roberts Gale: Lynch Milner Millington O
Holmes Moors Wheeldon: Subs used - Cook Boyle
Maher McShane: Tries - Gale(2) Solomona Dorn Roberts:
Goals - Gale(4) RobertsD/G:
Referee J Child   Att - 15069 H.T. 16 – 16

Fri 25 Sep 2015 WIGAN WARRIORS away lost 12 – 47 ROUND 7 SUPER 8
WIGAN W - Bowen: Charnley Gildart Burgess Manfredi:
Williams Smith: Crosby McIlorum Flower Farrell Tompkins
O'Loughlin: Subs used - Powell Chubb Mossop Patrick:
Tries - Manfredi(4) Bowen Gildart Williams Burgess
Patrick: Goals - Bowen(5):SmithD/G:
CASTLEFORD - Dorn: Ash Robson McMeeken Ashley
Gibson Solomona: Roberts Gale: Lynch Milner Millington
O Holmes Moors Scott Wheeldon:
Subs used - Cook Maher Springer McShane:
Tries - Dorn Moors: Goals - Gale(2):
Referee P Bentham   Att - 15070 H.T. 12 – 10

Denny Solomona
D. No 951
2015 to 2016

Luke Gale
D. No 952
2015 to

Junior Moors
D. No 953
2015 to

Ben Roberts
D. No 955
2015 to

Mike McMeeken
D. No 956
2015 to

Ash Robson
D. No 957
2015

Tom Holmes
D. No 959
2015 to

Gadwin Springer
D. No 960
2015 to

Paul McShane
D. No 961
2015 to

SEASON 2015

D.N	PLAYER		DEBUT	L MATCH	APP	SUB	T.AP	TRI'S	G'LS	D.G	P'TS
759	LYNCH	ANDY			27	1	28	0	0	0	0
810	SHENTON	MICHAEL			28	0	28	14	0	0	56
840	BOYLE	RYAN			1	18	19	0	0	0	0
876	MASSEY	NATHAN			23	0	23	2	0	0	8
882	DORN	LUKE			13	1	14	10	0	0	40
885	MOORE	SCOTT		12/07/2015	13	1	14	1	0	0	4
887	COOK	MATTHEW			4	13	17	2	0	0	8
907	HOLMES	OLIVER			28	0	28	5	0	0	20
910	MILNER	ADAM			17	11	28	3	0	0	12
925	MILLINGTON	GRANT			25	6	31	3	0	0	12
926	CLARE	JAMES		16/05/2015	9	0	9	4	0	0	16
932	TANSEY	JORDAN		05/06/2015	13	1	14	6	0	0	24
933	CARNEY	JUSTIN		22/08/2015	18	0	18	18	0	0	72
934	WEBSTER	JAKE			16	3	19	3	0	0	12
940	CHANNING	MICHAEL		03/09/2015	10	0	10	1	0	0	4
943	FINN	LIAM		22/08/2015	21	3	24	4	4	2	26
944	WHEELDON	SCOTT		25/09/2015	9	6	15	1	0	0	4
945	MARIANO	FRANKIE			5	0	5	1	0	0	4
946	GIBSON	ASHLEY		25/09/2015	22	0	22	9	0	0	36
947	JEWITT	LEE			1	5	6	0	0	0	0
950	MAHER	WILL			0	8	8	0	0	0	0
951	SOLOMONA	DENNY	08/02/2015		15	0	15	18	0	0	72
952	GALE	LUKE	08/02/2015		29	0	29	11	102	1	249
953	MOORS	JUNIOR	08/02/2015		14	11	25	4	0	0	16
954	CROSSLEY	STEVE	08/02/2015	19/04/2015	0	6	6	0	0	0	0
955	ROBERTS	BEN	14/02/2015		18	8	26	9	0	2	38
956	McMEEKEN	MIKE	27/02/2015		14	6	20	2	0	0	8
957	ROBSON	ASH	26/04/2015	25/09/2015	3	0	3	1	0	0	4
958	BAILEY	RYAN	03/05/2015	18/06/2015	4	2	6	0	0	0	0
959	HOLMES	TOM	03/05/2015		0	1	1	0	0	0	0
960	SPRINGER	GADWIN	05/07/2015		2	8	10	0	0	0	0
961	McSHANE	PAUL	07/08/2015		1	5	6	0	0	0	0
	32			**11**	**11**						
					403	**124**	**527**	**132**	**106**	**5**	**745**

COMPETITION		P	W	D	L	FOR	AGT
S, LEAGUE	POSITION 5 OF 12	23	13	0	10	547	505
SUPER 8'S		7	3	0	4	184	241
RL CUP		1	0	0	1	14	40
PLAYERS RECORDS		**31**	**16**	**0**	**15**	**745**	**786**

The 2015 Super League season sees teams play each other home and away, and one team for a third time at the 'Magic Weekend'. After 23 games, the league table is frozen and the teams are split up into "Super 8's". Teams finishing in the top eight will play seven more games each as they compete in the Super League Super 8 group with the top four teams playing off on a knock-out basis for a place in the Grand Final. Teams finishing in the bottom four will join the top four teams from the Championship in the Qualifiers Super 8 group and also play seven more games each for a place in the 2016 Super League competition. The top three teams qualifying as of right, the fourth and fifth teams, playing off, with the winner taking the final place in Super League.

In the RL Challenge Cup, after last season's run to the Final, we had a disappointing loss in our first game at Hull 40-4.

In the League we just failed to make the top four and the play-offs finishing fifth.

Luke Gale, in his Debut season, kicked a century of goals with 101 in the League and Super 8's, being a Club Super League record, and one in the RL Cup giving a total of 102. He also won the League Express Albert Goldthorpe Medal and made the Super League Dream Team, a notable start to hopefully a 'fruitful' career.

Denny Solomona, also in his first season, scored 18 tries from 15 appearances. Justin Carney also scored 18 tries from 18 appearances but missed the last four games through 'Club Suspension' for disciplinary reasons, and subsequently went out on loan to Salford in the Close Season.

Jack Fulton, the Club Chairman, dies in September 2015.

SUPER LEAGUE XXI

Sun 2 Dec 2015 FEATHERSTONE ROVERS home won 42 – 28 FRIENDLY

CASTLEFORD - Robson: Monaghan Crooks Minikin Hitchcox: Hampshire T Holmes: Springer McShane Maher McMeeken Moors Jewitt: Subs used - Cook Westerman Milner Webster Roberts Gill Douglas Sheehan:
Tries - McMeeken(2) Crooks Monaghan Minikin Hampshire Robson: Goals - Hampshire(7):
FEATHERSTONE R - Brown: Johnson Channing Cording Turner: Milner Thackeray: Griffin Wilde Bostock Snitch Davies Tagg: Subs used - Day Cooper Roche Ormondroyd Hill Sowerby Coventry:
Tries – Johnson(2) Day Thackeray Roche
Goals – Thackeray(2) Johnson(2):
Referee S Ansell Att 5274 H.T. 30 - 0

Fri 22 Jan 2016 YORK CITY KNIGHTS away won 20 – 16 FRIENDLY

YORK C K – Turner: Morrison Morland Hey: Dent Presley: Wilkinson Waller Carter Aldous Smith Tonks Emmett: Subs used – Brining Applegarth Spiers Nicholson Mallinder England:
Tries – Emmett Hey Morland: Goals – Wilkinson(2):
CASTLEFORD – Robson: Sheehan Minikin Gill Hitchcox: Hampshire Adamson: Springer Million Boyle W Cook Westerman Maher: Subs used – Douglas Fitzsimmons O'Neil Dickson Diskin: Tries – Hitchcox Fitzsimmons Diskin Minikin: Goals – Hampshire Robson:
Referee J Roberts Att - 854 H.T. 10 – 12

Sun 24 Jan 2016 WAKEFIELD TRINITY WILDCATS home won 32 – 6 FRIENDLY

CASTLEFORD – Dorn: Monaghan Webster Shenton Solomona: Roberts Gale: Lynch McShane Millington Holmes McMeeken Jewitt: Subs used – Milner M Cook Moors Hampshire Crooks: Tries – Solomona(4) Holmes Dorn Monaghan: Goals – Gale(2):
WAKEFIELD T W – Jones–Bishop: Johnstone B Tupou Gibson Lyne: Miller Finn: Scruton Howarth England Kirmond A Tupou Annakin:
Subs used – Tansey Arona Ashurst Arundel Molloy Sio Jowitt Hall Yates Walton: Try – Lyne: Goal – Finn:
Referee R Silverwood Att – 3685 H.T. 14 – 6

Fri 29 Jan 2016 BRADFORD BULLS away lost 8 – 26 FRIENDLY

BRADFORD B – Thomas: Clare Ryan Blythe Caro: Jacks Addy: Haggerty O'Brien Kavanagh Olbison Ferguson Pitts: Subs used – Halifihi Pickersgill Caprice Walshaw Hooley J Mellor Bartle A Mellor Walker Fleming Bentley Kirk Lauski: Tries – Clare Caro A Mellor Hooley Kirk: Goals – Addy(3):
CASTLEFORD – Robson: Sheehan Gill Minikin Hitchcox: Hampshire T Holmes: Springer O'Neil Maher W Cook Westerman Boyle: Subs used – Fitzsimmons Douglas Diskin Johnson Adamson   Tries – Minikin Sheehan
Referee B Thaler Att – 1366 H.T. 4 – 10

Sun 7 Feb 2016 HULL KINGSTONE ROVERS away draw 16 – 16

HULL K R – Cockayne: Sio Mimms Thornley Mantellato: Blair Kelly: Tilse Lawler Allgood Horne Clarkson Greenwood:
Subs used – Mulhern Donaldson Green Boounebza:
Tries – Mantellato(2) Donldson: Goals - Mantellato(2):
CASTLEFORD – Dorn JOEL MONAGHAN(962) BEN CROOKS(963) Shenton Solomona: Roberts Gale: Millington McShane Cook O Holmes McMeeken Jewitt: Subs used – Boyle Milner Moors Webster:
Tries – Webster(2) Solomona: Goals – Gale(2):
Referee R Silverwood Att – 11011 H.T. 6 – 6

Sun 14 Feb 2016 WAKEFIELD TRINITY WILDCATS home won 40 – 6

CASTLEFORD – Dorn: Monaghan Crooks Webster Solomona: Roberts Gale: Lynch McShane Millington O Holmes McMeeken Jewitt: Subs used –Milner Moors Massey Cook: Tries – Solomona(2) O Holmes(2) Roberts Dorn Milner: Goals – Gale(6):
WAKEFIELD T W – Jones-Bishop: Lyne Gibson Arundel B Tupou: Milner Finn: Scruton Howarth England Kirmond Ashurst Arona: Subs used – A Tupou Sio Anderson Walton: Try Howarth: Goal – Finn:
Referee J Child Att - 9761 H.T. 18 – 6

Thu 25 Feb 2016 HULL F C away won 31 – 24

HULL F C – Shaul: Michaels Logan Tuimavave Talanoa: Pryce Sneyd: Taylor Houghton Watts Minichiello Manu Thompson:
Subs used – Ellis Bowden Pritchard Washbrook:
Tries – Shaul(2) Thompson Michaels: Goals – Sneyd(4):
CASTLEFORD – Dorn: JY HITCHCOX(964) Crooks Webster Solomona: Roberts Gale: Lynch McShane Millington O Holmes McMeeken Jewitt:
Subs used – Milner Massey Cook Moors:
Tries – Solomona(3) Hitchcox(2): Goals – Gale(5) D/G:
Referee R Hicks Att – 10247 H.T. 18 – 18

Fri 4 Mar 2016 SAINT HELENS away lost 22 – 28

ST HELENS – McDonnell: Makinson Peyroux Dawson Swift: Turner Walsh: Walmsley Roby Amour Vea Wilkin McCarthy-Scarsbrook: Subs used – Tasi Richards Thompson Fages: Tries – Dawson(2) Swift Vea McCarthy-Scarsbrook: Goals – Walsh(4):
CASTLEFORD – Dorn: Hitchcox Crooks Webster Solomona: Roberts Gale: Lynch McShane Millington Moors McMeeken Jewitt: Subs used – Milner Massey Cook Maher: Tries – Millington McMeeken Milner: Goals – Gale(4) Crooks:
Referee J Child Att – 11298 H.T. 14 – 16

Sun 13 Mar 2016 SALFORD RED DEVILS home lost 16 – 32

CASTLEFORD – Dorn: Monaghan Crooks Webster Solomona: RYAN HAMPSHIRE(965) Gale: Lynch Milner Jewitt McMeeken Cook Massey:

Subs used – McShane Boyle Springer Maher:
Tries – Solomona(3):   Goals – Gale(2):
SALFORD R D – O'Brien: Carney Sa'u J Griffin Johnson: Lui
Dobson: Kopozak Lee G Griffin Murdock-Masila Jones
Lannon: Subs used – Flanagan Walne Tompkins Joseph:
Tries – Carney(2) J Griffin(2) Johnson Goals – O'Brien(6):
Referee P Bentham Att – 8151 H.T. 6 – 8

**Fri 18 Mar 2016 WARRINGTON WOLVES away
lost 12 – 56**
WARRINGTON W – Russell: Penny Evans Atkins Lineham:
Gidley Sandow: Hill Dwyer Sims Currie Hughes
Westerman: Subs used – Ratchford Clark King Cox:
Tries – Sandow(2) Currie(2) Lineham(2) Russell(2) Penny
Atkins Dwyer.   Goals – Gidley(6):
CASTLEFORD – Hitchcox: Monaghan Crooks Webster
Solomona: Hampshire Gale: Lynch Milner Maher
Millington McMeeken Massey:
Subs used – McShane Cook Mariano Springer:
Tries – Monaghan Springer: Goals - Gale(2):
Referee R Hicks Att – 10940 H.T. 0 - 38

Thu 24 Mar 2016 LEEDS RHINOS home won 18 - 14
CASTLEFORD – Solomona: Monaghan Crooks Webster
Hitchcox: Hampshire Gale: Lynch Milner Boyle Millington
McMeeken Massey: Subs used – McShane Springer
Maher GREG MINIKIN(956):
Tries – Webster(2) Lynch: Goals – Gale(3):
LEEDS R – Hardaker: Briscoe Watkins Moon Handley:
Sutcliffe Burrow: Galloway Falloon Cuthbertson Ablett
Ferres Jones-Buchanan:
Subs used – Lilley Mullally Walters Keinhorst:
Tries – Moon Watkins Briscoe: Goal – Sutcliffe:
Referee J Child Att – 11426 H.T. 12 – 14

**Mon 28 Mar 2016 CATALAN DRAGONS away
lost 22 – 41**
CATALAN D – Escare: Broughton Giget Duport Yaha:
Carney Bosc: Taylor Pelissier Bousquet Anderson Stewart
Mounis: Subs used – Aiton Casty Baitieri Mason;
Tries – Escare(2) Carney(2) Broughton Anderson Aiton:
Goals – Bosc(6) EscareD/G:
CASTLEFORD – Solomona: Monaghan Crooks Minikin
Hitchcox: Hampshire Gale: Lynch Milner Boyle Webster
McMeeken Massey:
Subs used – Millington McShane Maher T Holmes:
Tries – Minikin(2) Monaghan(2):   Goals – Gale(3):
Referee B Thaler Att – 10351 H.T. 16-22

**Sun 3 Apr 2016 HUDDERSFIELD GIANTS home
won 38 – 34**
CASTLEFORD – Hampshire: Minikin Crooks Webster
Hitchcox T Holmes Gale: Lynch Milner Jewitt Millington
McMeeken Massey: Subs used – Cook McShane Maher
Boyle: Tries – Hitchcox(3) McMeeken(2) Minikin
Webster: Goals - Gale (5):
HUDDERSFIELD G – Brierley: McGillvary Cudjoe Wardle
Murphy: Brough Connor: Rapira Hinchcliffe Huby
Lawrence Ta'ai Roberts:
Subs used – Crabtree Patrick Mason Wood:

Tries – McGillvary(3) Cudjoe(2) Rapira: Goals – Brough(5):
Referee P Bentham Att – 6631 H.T. 16 – 12

Sun 10 Apr 2016 WIDNES VIKINGS away won 34 – 24
WIDNES V – Hanbury: Thompson Dean Bridge Ah Van:
Brown Mellor: O'Carroll Heremaia Dudson Sa Houston
Leuluai: Subs used – Brooks Gerrard White Whitely
Tries – Ah Van Leuluai Thompson White:
Goals – Bridge(4):
CASTLEFORD – Hampshire: Monaghan Minikin Webster
Solomona: T Holmes Gale: Lynch Milner Jewitt Cook
McMeeken Massey:
Subs used – McShane Maher Ryan Boyle Springer:
Tries – Solomona(3) Boyle Gale McShane: Goals – Gale(5):
Referee J Cobb Att – 5081 H.T. 10 - 18

Fri 15 Apr 2016 WIGAN WARRIORS away lost 12 – 26
WIGAN W – Sarginson: Tierney Bateman Gildart Charnley:
Gregson Smith: Mossop Powell Club J Tompkins Isa
Sutton: Subs used – Crosby Tautai Burke Bretherton:
Tries – Bateman(2) Tierney Gregson: Goals – Smith(5):
CASTLEFORD – Hampshire: Monaghan Minikin Webster
Solomona: T Holmes Gale(S/B): Lynch Milner Jewitt O
Holmes McMeeken Massey:
Subs used – McShane Millington Maher Cook:
Tries – Solomona Millington: Goals – Gale(2):
Referee P Bentham Att – 11849 H.T. 6 – 8

**Sun 24 Apr 2016 HULL KINGSTON ROVERS home
lost 16 - 58**
CASTLEFORD – Solomona: Monaghan Minikin Webster
Hitchcox: Hampshire Gale: Lynch Milner Jewitt Millington
McMeeker Massey:
Subs used – McShane LARNE PATRICK(967) Cook Moors:
Tries – Webster Hampshire Hitchcox: Goals – Gale(2):
HULL K R – Cockayne: Sio Minns Thornley Wardill: Blair
Kelly: Tilse Lunt Mulhern Clarkson Horne Allgood:
Subs used – Green Donaldson Boudebza Walker:
Tries – Minns(3) Thornley(2) Sio(2) Blair Kelly Horne
Allgood: Goals – Cockayne(7):
Referee B Thaler Att – 7106 H.T. 16 - 20

Sun 1 May 2016 SAINT HELENS home lost 20 – 30
CASTLEFORD – Hampshire: Hitchcox Crooks Monaghan
Solomona: Millington Gale: Lynch Milner Jewitt Cook
McMeeken Massey: Subs used – McShane Maher
Springer CONOR FITZSIMMONS(968)
Tries – Monaghan Solomona McMeeken Hitchcox:
Goals – Gale(2):
ST HELENS – McDonnell: Lomax Payroux Percival Owens:
Fages Walsh: Walmsley Roby Amor Vea Greenwood
Wilkin: Subs used – McCarthey-Scarsbrook Tasi Richards
Knowles: Tries – Greenwood(2) McDonnell Amor Lomax:
Goals – Walsh(5):
Referee G Hewer Att – 6658 H.T. 10 – 6

**Sat 7 May 2016 SALFORD RED DEVILS home
won 32 – 18 CHALLENGE CUP Round 6**
CASTLEFORD – Hampshire: Monaghan Crooks Webster
Solomona: Millington McShane: Patrick Milner Jewitt

509

Moors McMeeken Massey: Subs used – Cook DANNY
TICKLE(969) Springer Hitchcox: Tries – McMeeken(2)
Solomona(2) Webster McShane: Goals – McShane(4):
SALFORD R D – O'Brien: Carney Sa'u Jones Vidot: Lui
Dobson: Kopczak Joseph Griffin Murdoch-Masi a Hauraki
Flanagan: Subs used – J Walne A Walne Krasnci Evalds:
Tries – Sa'u(2) Lui: Goals – O'Brien(3):
Referee J Childs Att – 3317 H.T. 18 – 12

Thu 12 May 2016 LEEDS RHINOS away won 52 - 12
CASTLEFORD – Dorn: PADDY FLYNN(970)Crooks
Monaghan Solomona: McShane Gale: Patrick Milner
Jewitt Moors McMeeken Massey: Subs used – Cook
Millington Springer Tickle: Tries – Dorn(3): Solomona(2)
Monaghan Springer Crooks Millington: Goals - Gale(8):
LEEDS R – Golding: Handley Watkins Keinhorst Hardaker:
McGuire Lilley: Galloway Burrow Garbutt Jones-Buchanan
Ferres Cuthbertson: Subs used – Mullally Sutcliffe Walters
Achurch: Tries – Garbutt Handley: Goals – Lilley(2):
Referee R Silverwood Att – 17123 H.T. 30 – 6

**Sat 21 May 2016 WARRINGTON WOLVES away won
34 – 14 MAGIC WEEKEND AT NEWCASTLE UNITED FC**
WARRINGTON W – Russell: Lineham T King Julien
Ormsby: Ratchford Gidley: Hill Clark Sims Currie
Westwood Westerman: Subs used – Cox G King Smith
Bailey: Tries – Ratchford Gidley Currie: Goal – Gidley:
CASTLEFORD – Dorn: Flynn Crooks Monaghan Solomona:
Roberts Gale: Tickle Milner Millington Moors McMeeken
Massey: Subs used – Cook McShane Springer Webster:
Tries – Dorn(2) Solomona(2) Millington McMeeken:
Goals – Gale(5):
Referee G Hewer Att – 39331 H.T. 12 – 14

**Thu 26 May 2016 WIGAN WARRIORS home
lost 26 – 33**
CASTLEFORD – Dorn: Flynn Crooks Webster(S/B)
Solomona: McShane Gale: Patrick Milner Millington
Moors McMeeken Jewitt:
Subs used – Tickle Springer Hampshire Cook:
Tries – Solomona(2) McShane Webster: Goals – Gale(5):
WIGAN W – S Tomkins: Manfredi Sarginson Gildart
Charnley: Williams Smith: Crosby Powell Flower Bateman
Isa J Tomkins: Subs used – Mossop Tautai Sutton Burke:
Tries – Charnley(2) S Tomkins Manfredi Powell:
Goals – Smith(6) D/G:
Referee B Thaler Att – 5558 H.T. 12 - 14

**Fri 1 Jun 2016 HUDDERSFIELD GIANTS away
won 30 – 22**
HUDDERSFIELD – Grix: McGillvary Cudjoe Connor
Murphy: Wood Ellis: Crabtree Hinchcliffe Johnston Wardle
Ta'ai Lawrence:
Subs used – Rapira Mason Roberts Brierley:
Tries – Ellis Cudjoe Brierley Connor: Goals – Ellis(3):
CASTLEFORD – Dorn: Monaghan Crooks Webster
Solomona: McShane Gale: Jewitt Milner Tickle Moors
McMeeken Massey:
Subs used – Millington Cook Hampshire Springer:
Tries – Solomona(2) Webster(2) Gale: Goals – Gale(5):

Referee C Cambell Att – 5741 H.T. 16 – 10

Thu 6 Jun 2016 WIDNES VIKINGS home lost 28 – 38
CASTLEFORD – Solomona: Monaghan Crooks Webster
Flynn: McShane Gale: Jewitt Milner Patrick Moors
McMeeken Massey: Subs used - Millington Springer
Cook Tickle: Tries – Flynn(3) Patrick Gale: Goals – Gale(4):
WIDNES V – Hanbury: Thompson Runciman Bridge Ah
Van: Brown Mellor: Cahill White Buchanan Whitely Dean
Leuluai: Subs used – Chapelhow Manuokafoa Walker
Heremaia: Tries – White(2) Ah Van(2) Leulual Bridge
Mellor: Goals Hanbury(5):
Referee J Smith Att – 4968 H.T. 6 – 14

Sun 19 Jun 2016 HULL F C home lost 22 - 24
CASTLEFORD – Dorn: Flynn Crooks Monaghan Solomona:
McShane Millington: Tickle Milner Patrick Moors Webster
Massey: Subs used – T Holmes Springer Maher Cook:
Tries – Solomona(2) Dorn Webster:Flynn: Goal Tickle:
HULL F C – Shaul: Michaels Fonua Yeaman Naughton:
Tuimavave Sneyd: Taylor Houghton Watts Pritchard
Washbrook Thompson:
Subs used – Hadley Green Pryce Bowden:
Tries – Pritchard Houghton Fonua Shaul: Goals – Sneyd(4)
Referee G Hewer Att – 10790 H.T. 8 – 18

**Sat 25 Jun 2016 WIGAN WARRIORS away
lost 12 – 26 R.L. CHALLENGE CUP Q-FINAL**
WIGAN W – S Tompkins: Charnley Sarginson Gildart
Manfredi: Williams Smith: Mossop Powell Flower Sutton
Isa O'Loughlin: Subs used – J Tompkins Tautai Burkle
Breterton: Tries – Charnley(2) Sarginson S Tompkins
Manfredi: Goals – Smith(3):
CASTLEFORD – Dorn: Monaghan Crooks Minikin
Solomona: Millington Gale: Jewitt McShane Patrick Moors
McMeeken Massey: Subs used – Milner Tickle O Holmes
Cook Tries – Gale Crooks: Goals – Gale(2):
Referee C Campbell Att – 8010 H.T. 0 – 22

Fri 1 Jul 2016 SALFORD RED DEVILS away lost 18 - 22
SALFORD R D – O'Brien: Caton-Brown J Griffin Sa'u
Johnson: Lui Dobson: Kopczak Tomkins Murdock-Maila
Jones Flanagan G Griffin:
Subs used – Hauraki J Walne Kenny A Walne
Tries – O'Brien Dobson Caton-Brown: Goals – O'Brien(5):
CASTLEFORD – Dorn; Monaghan Crooks Webster Flynn: T
Holmes Gale: Tickle McShane Patrick Moors McMeeken
Massey: Subs used – Milner Millington O Holmes
Springer: Tries – Webster(2) Dorn: Goals Gale(3):
Referee J Child Att – 2275 H.T. 12 – 10

**Sun 10 Jul 2016 CATALAN DRAGONS home
won 38 – 24**
CASTLEFORD – Dorn: Hampshire Crooks Minikin
Solomona: McShane Gale: Tickle Milner Patrick O Holmes
Moors Massey: Subs used – Millington Mariano Cook
Springer: Tries – Hampshire(2) Dorn(2) Mariano
McShane O Holmes: Goals – Gale(5):
CATALAN D – Escare:Broughton Gigot Duport Yaha: Bosc
Myler: Maria Da Costa Casty Taylor Horo Garcia:

Subs used – Bousquet Pellissier Mounis Navarrete:
Tries – Horo Yaha Casty Bousquet: Goals – Bosc(3) Gigot:
Referee M Woodhead Att – 5886 H.T. 20 – 6

Sun 17 Jul 2016 WARRINGTON WOLVES home lost 26 – 42

CASTLEFORD – Dorn: Hampshire Crooks Minikin
Solomona: McShane Gale: Danny Tickle Milner Patrick O
Holmes Mariano Moors:
Subs used – Millington Chase Cook Springer:
Tries – Solomona(4) Mariano Crooks: Goal – Gale:
WARRINGTON W – Ratchford: Russell Evans Atkins
Lineham: Gidley Sandow: Hill Clark Sims Currie Hughes
Westerman: Subs used – T King Dwyer Westwood Bailey:
Tries – Evans(2) Ratchford Dwyer Currie T King Clark:
Goals Gidley(3) Sandow(4):
Referee C Kendall Att – 8060 H.T. 18 -16

Sun 24 Jul 2016 WAKEFIELD TRINITY WLIDCATS away won 46 – 20

CASTLEFORD – Hampshire: Flynn Crooks O Holmes
Minikin: McShane Gale: Springer Milner Patrick Mariano
Millington Moors: Subs used – ANDRE SAVELIO(971) T
Holmes Cook Maher: Tries – Minikin(2) O Holmes
Savelio Gale Moors T Holmes Hampshire: Goals – Gale(7):
WAKEFIELD T W – Jowitt Lyne B Tupou Arundel Hall:
Miller Finn: Scruton Sio Fifta Walton Ashurst Molloy:
Subs used – Crowther Arona Moules A Tupou:
Tries – Arundel(2) Miller Lyn: Goals Finn(2):
Referee J Cobb Att – 6855 H.T. 10 – 16

Fri 5 Aug 2016 HULL F C away won 30 – 16 Round 1 Super 8

HULL F C - Shaul: Michaels Tuimavave Yeaman
Naughton: Abdull Sneyd: Taylor Houghton Bowden Manu
Pritchard Ellis:
Subs used – Minichello Green Thompson Washbrook:
Tries – Michaels Washbrook Shaul: Goals - Sneyd(2):
CASTLEFORD – Dorn: Hampshire Crooks Minikin
Solomona: Chase Gale: Springer Milner Patrick O Holmes
Savelio Moors: Subs used – Jewitt McShane Cook
Millington: Tries – Hampshire(2) Minikin Gale Dorn
Milner: Goals – Gale(3):
Referee J Smith Att – 9936 H.T. 20- 0

Fri 12 Aug 2016 WIGAN WARRIORS home won 36 – 22   Round 2 Super 8

CASTLEFORD – Dorn: Hampshire Crooks Minikin
Solomona: Chase Gale: Springer Milner Patrick
O HolmesS/B Savelio Moors: Subs used – Lee Jewitt
McShane Cook Millington: Tries – Solomona(3) McShane
Hampshire O Holmes: Goals – Gale(6):
WIGAN W – Tomkins: Charnley Gelling Sarginson
Manfredi: Williams Smith: CrosbyS/B Powell Flower
Bateman Isa Sutton:
Subs used – Farrell Mossop Tautai Nuuaussla:
Tries – Powell Flower Bateman Mossop: Goals – Smith(3):
Referee J Cobb Att – 6325 H.T. 12 - 6

Sat 20 Aug 2016 WARRINGTON WOLVES away lost 11 – 14 Round 3 Super 8

WARRINGTON W – Ratchford: Russell T King Atkins
Evans: Gidley Sandow: Hill Clark Sims Currie Hughes
Westerman Subs used – Dwyer Westwood King Bailey:
Tries – Westerman Evans Hughes: Goal – Gidley:
CASTLEFORD – Dorn: Hampshire Crooks Minikin
Solomona: Chase Gale: Springer Milner Patrick O Holmes
Savelio Moors: Subs used – Frankie Mariano McShane
Cook Millington: Try – Solomona: Goals – Gale(3) D/G:
Referee C Kendall Att – 9226 H.T. 8 - 6

Fri 2 Sep 2016 WAKEFIELD TRINITY WILDCATS home won 46 – 22 Round 4 Super 8

CASTLEFORD – Dorn: Hampshire Minikin Webster
Solomona: Chase Gale: Patrick Miller Springer O Holmes
Savelio Moors: Subs used – McShane Millington Cook
Maher: Tries – Solomona(3) Chase Dorn McShane
Webster Gale: Goals - Gale(7):
WAKEFIELD T W – Hall: Lyne Arundel B Tupou Johnstone:
Miller Finn: Scruton Moore Arona Molloy A Tupou
Harrison: Subs used – Sio Simon Yates Anderson:
Tries – Johnson(2) Lyne B Tupou Scruton: Goal - Finn:
Referee G Hewer Att – 6283 H.T. 34 – 8

Thu 8 Sep 2016 SAINT HELENS away lost 16 – 40 Round 5 Super 8

ST HELENS – Lomax: Owens Peyroux Fleming Swift:
Turner Walsh: Walmsley Roby Richards Wilkin Greenwood
McCarthy-Scarsbrook:
Subs used – Amor Vea Thompson Knowles:
Tries – Fleming Knowles Amor Thompson McCarthy-
Scarsbrook Swift Walmsley: Goals Walsh(5) Owens:
CASTLEFORD – Dorn: Hampshire Crooks Minikin
Solomona ChaseS/B Gale: Cook McShane Patrick
Webster Moors Milner: Subs used – Maher Fitzsimmons
Flynn BRANDON DOUGLAS(972):
Tries – Dorn Hampshire Maher: Goals - Gale(2):
Referee J Smith Att – 9448 H.T. 10 – 24

Sat 17 Sep 2016 CATALAN DRAGONS away won 34 -28 Round 6 Super 8

CATALAN D – Gogot: Broughton Garcia Duport
Sigismeau; Stewart Myler: Casty Aiton Elima Anderson
Horo Mounis: Subs used – Taylor Bousquet Pellissier
Seguier: Tries – Elima Stewart Pellissier Anderson Myler:
Goals - G got(4):
CASTLEFORD – Dorn: Flynn Minikin Webster Solomona:
Hampshire Gale: Cook McShane Patrick Savelio O Holmes
Milner: Subs used – McMeeken Crooks Maher: Non
Playing Sub Douglas :
Tries - Flynn(2) Solomona(2) Crooks(2): Goals – Gale (5):
Referee P Bentham Att – 7802 H.T. 24 – 10

Sun 25 Sep 2016 WIDNES VIKINGS home won 40 – 26 Round 7 Super 8

CASTLEFORD – Luke Dorn: Paddy Flynn Minikin Webster
Denny Solomona: Ryan Hampshire Gale: Cook
McShaneS/B Springer O Holmes Andre Savelio Milner:
Subs used - Maher Chase Crooks McMeeken:

511

SEASON 2016

Tries – Solomona(3) Dorn Crooks Cook McShane:
Goals - Gale(6):
WIDNES V – Hanbury: Thompson Dean Runciman Ah Van:
Mellor Gilmore: J Chapelhow White Dudson Whiley
FarrellS/B Cahill:
Subs used – T Chapelhow Leuluai Millward Manuokafoa
Tries – Farrell(2) Thompson(2) Ah Van: Goals – White)3):
Referee J Smith Att – 7103 H.T. 16 – 6

Joel Monaghan
D. No 962
2016 to

Ben Crooks
D. No 963
2016

Jy Hitchcox
D. No 964
2016 to

Ryan Hampshire
D. No 965
2016

Greg Minikin
D. No 966
2016 to

Larne Patrick
D. No 967
2016 to

Connor Fitzsimmons
D. No 968
2016 to

Paddy Flynn
D. No 970
2016

Andre Savelio
D. No 971
2016

Brandon Douglas
D. No 972
2016 to

SEASON 2016

D.N	PLAYER		DEBUT	L MATCH	APP	SUB	T.AP	TRI'S	G'LS	D.G	P'TS
759	LYNCH	ANDY			12	0	12	1	0	0	4
810	SHENTON	MICHAEL			1	0	1	0	0	0	0
840	BOYLE	RYAN		10/04/2016	2	4	6	1	0	0	4
876	MASSEY	NATHAN			18	3	21	0	0	0	0
882	DORN	LUKE		25/09/2016	21	0	21	14	0	0	56
887	COOK	MATTHEW			7	22	29	1	0	0	4
894	CHASE	RANGI			5	2	7	1	0	0	4
907	HOLMES	OLIVER			13	2	15	5	0	0	20
910	MILNER	ADAM			26	6	32	3	0	0	12
925	MILLINGTON	GRANT			15	12	27	4	0	0	16
934	WEBSTER	JAKE			21	2	23	14	0	0	56
945	MARIANO	FRANKIE		20/08/2016	2	3	5	2	0	0	8
947	JEWITT	LEE		12/08/2016	16	2	18	0	0	0	0
950	MAHER	WILL			1	14	15	1	0	0	4
951	SOLOMONA	DENNY			29	0	29	42	0	0	168
952	GALE	LUKE			30	0	30	7	120	2	270
953	MOORS	JUNIOR			18	4	22	1	0	0	4
955	ROBERTS	BEN			5	0	5	1	0	0	4
956	McMEEKEN	MIKE			21	2	23	7	0	0	28
957	ROBSON	ASH			0	0	0	0	0	0	0
959	HOLMES	TOM			4	3	7	1	0	0	4
960	SPRINGER	GADWIN			6	15	21	2	0	0	8
961	McSHANE	PAUL			18	14	32	7	4	0	36
962	MONAGHAN	JOEL	07/02/2016		18	0	18	5	0	0	20
963	CROOKS	BEN	07/02/2016		26	2	28	6	1	0	26
964	HITCHCOX	JY	25/02/2016		8	1	9	7	0	0	28
965	HAMPSHIRE	RYAN	13/03/2016	25/09/2016	20	2	22	8	0	0	32
966	MINIKIN	GREG	24/03/2016		16	1	17	6	0	0	24
967	PATRICK	LARNE	24/04/2016		16	1	17	1	0	0	4
968	FITZSIMMONS	CONOR	01/05/2016		0	2	2	0	0	0	0
969	TICKLE	DANNY	07/05/2016	17/07/2016	6	5	11	0	1	0	2
970	FLYNN	PADDY	12/05/2016	25/09/2016	9	1	10	6	0	0	24
971	SAVELIO	ANDRE	24/07/2016	25/09/2016	6	1	7	1	0	0	4
972	DOUGLAS	BRANDON	08/09/2016		0	1	1	0	0	0	0
	34		**11**	**8**	**416**	**127**	**543**	**155**	**126**	**2**	**874**

COMPETITION		P	W	D	L	FOR	AGT
S, LEAGUE	POSITION 5 OF 12	23	10	1	12	617	640
SUPER 8'S		7	5	0	2	213	168
RL CUP		2	1	0	1	44	44
PLAYERS RECORDS		**32**	**16**	**1**	**15**	**874**	**852**

Wakefield Trinity Wildcats beat Bradford Bulls in the 2015 "Million Pound" play-off game to remain in Super League. For 2016 and it was to be the second season featuring the 'Super 8's' and 'Middle 8's'.

The season got off to a bad start injury wise with Ash Robson sustaining a season long leg injury in a pre-season friendly at Bradford and Michael Shenton suffering the same fate in the first match of the season at Hull KR. From there on the injury list progressively got worse.

Despite the injury situation we had a brilliant finish to the season winning five out of seven games (only losing to Warrington in the last seconds) in the Super 8's play-offs to finish 5th in the table.

Denny Solomona broke the Super League try scoring record held jointly by Bradford Bulls' Vainikolo and Leeds Rhinos' McGuire with 40 tries. With two more in the RL Cup for a total of 42 he also claimed the Club Record passing St John Ellis's 1993-94 total of 40. What was also remarkable, Denny achieved this in 29 games whilst St John took 41 games. He also created a Super League Record of six hat tricks in a season.

Luke Gale, for the second successive season, scored a century of goals with 118 League and Super 8's goals increasing the Club Super League record, plus two RL Cup goals for a total of 120. Luke also won the Rugby League Express Albert Goldthorpe Medal for the second year running.

Luke, for the second successive season, and Denny both made the Super League Dream Team.

PLAYERS CAREER STATISTICS UPTO AND INCLUDING SEASON 2016 IN ALPHABETICAL ORDER

D,N:		PLAYER		DEBUT	L. MATCH	APP	SUB	T.AP	TR'S	G'LS	D.G	PTS
416		A N OTHER		23/04/1957	23/04/1957	1	0	1	0	0	0	0
283		A N OTHER		01/05/1946	01/05/1946	1	0	1	0	0	0	0
308		A N OTHER		08/01/1949	26/02/1949	2	0	2	1	0	0	3
92		A.N.OTHER		09/04/1930	09/04/1930	1	0	1	0	0	0	0
105		A.N.OTHER		25/04/1931	25/04/1931	1	0	1	0	0	0	0
118		A.N.OTHER		21/04/1932	21/04/1932	1	0	1	0	0	0	0
615		A.N.OTHER		26/10/1980	26/10/1980	1	0	1	0	0	0	0
153		A.N.OTHER		11/04/1936	11/04/1936	1	0	1	0	0	0	0
522		ACKROYD	ALAN	16/08/1969	23/01/1976	88	26	114	23	56	1	183
316		ADAMS	C A	18/02/1950	04/03/1950	2	0	2	0	0	0	0
133		ADAMS	LESLIE	20/01/1934	02/05/1942	196	0	196	39	0	0	117
903		AINSCOUGH	SHAUN	27/02/2010	09/04/2010	7	0	7	4	0	0	16
312		ALDRED	PERCY	05/11/1949	09/04/1951	63	0	63	14	1	0	44
37		ALDRIDGE	D J	15/01/1927	15/01/1927	1	0	1	0	0	0	0
126		ALLAN	JOSEPH	29/04/1933	29/04/1933	1	0	1	0	0	0	0
736		ALLEN	CHRIS	17/08/1996	17/08/1996	0	1	1	0	0	0	0
152		ALLEN	STANLEY	26/02/1936	18/04/1938	27	0	27	1	2	0	7
202	G	ALLMAN	RICHARD (F'tone))	05/10/1940	02/11/1940	3	0	3	0	0	0	0
324		ANDERSON	COLIN	18/11/1950	28/01/1956	121	0	121	20	5	0	70
657		ANDERSON	GRANT	18/03/1987	27/07/1997	212	22	234	82	0	1	329
306		ANDERSON	JOSEPH	25/12/1948	08/01/1955	204	0	204	8	0	0	24
620		ANDERSON	KEVIN	22/08/1982	08/04/1984	8	3	11	0	1	0	2
100		ANDREWS	GEORGE	17/01/1931	07/03/1931	8	0	8	0	0	0	0
110		ANNABLE	CHARLES	26/09/1931	05/11/1932	30	0	30	1	0	0	3
481		APPLEYARD	DAVID	03/10/1964	05/02/1968	18	1	19	9	0	0	27
354		APPLEYARD	JACKSON	04/04/1953	14/01/1956	2	0	2	0	0	0	0
517		APPLEYARD	ROY	03/01/1969	03/02/1974	63	4	67	17	47	0	145
257		ARCHER		03/02/1945	03/02/1945	1	0	1	0	0	0	0
768		ARNOLD	DANNY	09/04/2000	07/05/2000	0	4	4	0	0	0	0
54		ARNOLD	MACK	28/01/1928	28/01/1928	1	0	1	0	0	0	0
891		ARUNDEL	JOE	03/08/2008	16/03/2012	39	5	44	16	2	0	68
428		ASHALL	NORMAN	22/03/1958	12/04/1958	5	0	5	0	0	0	0
117		ASKIN	AMBROSE	28/03/1932	25/12/1936	89	0	89	7	0	0	21
430		ASKIN	MAURICE	23/04/1958	03/10/1959	11	0	11	1	0	0	3
98		ASKIN	THOMAS C	15/11/1924	07/11/1936	196	0	196	64	0	0	192
914		ASPINWALL	MARTIN	20/02/2011	03/09/2011	13	6	19	2	0	0	8
16		ASQUITH	WILLIAM (NAT)	04/09/1926	25/12/1930	97	0	97	25	0	0	75
191		ASTBURY	ALBERT(JACK)	11/05/1940	02/05/1942	20	0	20	5	3	0	21
630		ATKINS	BRETT	01/02/1984	22/03/1987	42	3	45	21	0	0	84
686		ATKINS	GARY	09/09/1990	05/01/1992	4	5	9	1	0	0	4
21		ATKINSON	ARTHUR	11/09/1926	14/03/1942	431	0	431	157	230	1	933
927		ATKINSON	JOSH	09/04/2012	22/04/2012	2	0	2	0	0	0	0
498		AUSTIN	JACK	15/08/1966	23/09/1969	89	2	91	31	0	0	93
48		BACON	JOSHUA (JIM)	08/10/1927	09/11/2029	41	0	41	7	0	0	21
206		BADDELEY	DENNIS	19/10/1940	02/05/1942	12	0	12	3	0	0	9
839		BAILEY	ANDY	22/05/2005	14/08/2005	7	5	12	1	0	0	4
958		BAILEY	RYAN	03/05/2015	18/06/2015	4	2	6	0	0	0	0
475		BAKER	DENNIS	05/10/1963	21/08/1967	8	0	8	1	0	0	3
595		BALLANTYNE	GEORGE	17/09/1978	11/04/1980	41	4	45	6	0	0	18
190	G	BANKS	GEORGE (Wigan/C.P.)	04/05/1940	02/05/1942	16	0	16	0	0	0	0
150		BANKS	THOMAS	01/02/1936	30/10/1937	30	0	30	2	0	0	6
737		BARDAUSKAS	LEE	17/08/1996	26/05/1997	0	2	2	0	0	0	0
867		BARKER	DWAYNE	11/02/2007	09/09/2007	16	10	26	17	0	0	68
274		BARKER	SIDNEY	12/01/1946	12/01/1946	1	0	1	0	0	0	0
389		BARNES	JACK	07/01/1956	31/10/1964	93	0	93	3	102	0	213
327		BARRACLOUGH	IRVING	03/02/1951	27/09/1952	20	0	20	0	16	2	36
397		BARRETT	FRED	18/08/1956	22/08/1956	2	0	2	0	0	0	0
485		BARTON	PETER	10/10/1964	11/09/1965	15	0	15	8	0	0	24
785		BARTRIM	WAYNE	10/02/2002	15/08/2003	46	2	48	9	171	0	378
879		BASSINDER	JAKE	15/06/2007	15/06/2007	0	1	1	0	0	0	0
278		BASTOW	ARTHUR	23/02/1946	17/11/1951	140	0	140	28	0	0	84
781		BATES	DAVID	12/08/2001	26/07/2002	0	4	4	0	0	0	0
221	G	BATTEN	ERIC (Hunslet)	14/02/1942	14/02/1942	1	0	1	0	0	0	0

514

PLAYERS CAREER STATISTICS UPTO AND INCLUDING SEASON 2016 N ALPHABETICAL ORDER

D,N:		PLAYER		DEBUT	L. MATCH	APP	SUB	T.AP	TR'S	G'LS	D.G	PTS
332		BATTEN	ROBERT	18/08/1951	25/10/1954	93	0	93	15	0	0	45
40		BATTEN	WILLIAM	05/02/1927	09/04/1927	8	0	8	1	0	0	3
427		BATTYE	COLIN	22/03/1958	25/03/1966	173	1	174	75	0	0	225
586		BATTYE	IAN D.(JOE)	30/09/1977	04/04/1979	10	3	13	1	0	0	3
462		BATTYE	MALCOLM	07/04/1962	14/10/1966	46	6	52	8	0	0	24
627		BATTYE	NEIL	21/08/1983	07/03/1993	42	21	63	11	0	0	44
611		BEARDMORE	KEVIN	18/01/1980	06/10/1991	241	6	247	80	0	0	297
608		BEARDMORE	ROBERT	18/11/1979	19/03/1989	279	14	293	99	518	9	1397
662		BEATTIE	MICHAEL	06/09/1987	07/02/1988	20	0	20	10	0	0	40
104		BEAUMONT	BEN	20/04/1931	29/04/1931	3	0	3	0	0	0	0
345		BEAUMONT	STANLEY	20/09/1952	28/04/1953	10	0	10	1	0	0	3
425		BECK	BRIAN	08/03/1958	07/04/1958	4	0	4	0	0	1	2
286		BEDFORD	ARTHUR	16/11/1946	12/04/1947	2	0	2	0	0	0	0
474		BEDFORD	TREVOR	06/05/1963	18/09/1970	94	17	111	6	0	0	18
61		BEDWORTH	MILLWARD	15/09/1928	15/09/1928	1	0	1	0	0	0	0
667		BELCHER	GARY	11/09/1988	20/11/1988	10	1	11	5	0	1	21
507		BELL	JOHN	08/03/1967	08/03/1967	0	1	1	0	0	0	0
476		BELL	ROY	09/11/1963	09/12/1966	45	3	48	4	2	0	16
569		BENCE	ALAN	06/04/1975	10/05/1977	62	4	66	6	0	0	18
754		BENN	JAMIE	31/05/1998	26/05/2000	5	8	13	1	26	0	56
115		BENNETT	ALBERT	16/01/1932	29/03/1932	4	0	4	2	0	0	6
260	G	BENNETT	GEORGE (B'ford)	24/02/1945	24/02/1945	1	0	1	2	0	0	6
299		BENNETT	FRED	17/01/1948	30/04/1949	2	0	2	0	0	0	0
421		BERRY	JOHN	09/11/1957	18/08/1962	32	0	32	1	0	0	3
394		BERRY	ROWLAND	24/03/1956	14/12/1957	43	0	43	1	0	0	3
502		BIBB	HOWARD	16/09/1966	04/05/1970	16	2	18	1	0	0	3
245		BIBBY	JOSEPH	14/10/1944	14/10/1944	1	0	1	0	0	0	0
392		BICKERDYKE	RONALD	17/03/1956	08/09/1956	3	0	3	0	0	0	0
828		BIRD	DEON	13/02/2005	16/09/2006	38	8	46	15	0	0	60
122		BIRD	JOHN	29/10/1932	29/10/1932	1	0	1	0	0	0	0
547		BIRDSALL	CHARLIE	29/01/1972	04/01/1976	38	25	63	4	11	1	35
606		BIRKBY	IAN	23/09/1979	27/03/1983	32	14	46	13	38	1	116
378		BIRKIN	FRANK	12/02/1955	26/12/1955	24	0	24	6	0	0	18
521		BISCOMB	TERRY	16/08/1969	13/12/1975	19	8	27	5	0	0	15
265		BLACK	JAMES C.	07/04/1945	07/09/1946	3	0	3	1	0	0	3
658		BLACKBURN	JOHN	29/03/1987	18/03/1990	8	2	10	0	0	0	0
931		BLACKMORE	BEN	09/12/2012	09/12/2012	1	0	1	0	0	0	0
695		BLACKMORE	RICHARD	29/09/1991	07/05/1995	108	3	111	64	0	0	256
520		BLAKEWAY	GRAHAM	20/04/1969	03/04/1972	18	5	23	2	4	1	16
793		BLAKEWAY	RICHARD	26/07/2002	20/06/2004	1	14	15	0	0	0	0
843		BLANCH	DAMIEN	21/08/2005	28/05/2006	8	4	12	4	0	0	16
672		BLANKLEY	DEAN	30/03/1989	10/09/1989	4	1	5	0	0	0	0
702		BLOEM	JAMIE	06/12/1993	06/12/1993	0	1	1	1	0	0	4
461		BLOOMFIELD	GEOFFREY	07/10/1961	07/10/1961	1	0	1	0	0	0	0
195		BOLTON	EDWARD	07/09/1940	07/09/1940	1	0	1	0	0	0	0
171		BONNER	GORDON	15/01/1938	19/04/1938	2	0	2	0	0	0	0
372		BOOT	JACK	18/08/1954	10/09/1957	53	0	53	0	0	0	0
262		BOOTH	GORDON	02/04/1945	23/10/1948	33	0	33	6	0	0	18
659		BOOTHROYD	GILES	30/08/1987	07/03/1993	47	14	61	24	0	0	96
727		BOTICA	FRANO	31/03/1996	25/08/1996	21	0	21	5	84	2	190
155		BOUCHER	WILFRED (BUCK)	02/05/1936	08/09/1945	14	0	14	3	3	0	15
267	G	BOWDEN	JIM (F'tone)	21/04/1945	21/04/1945	1	0	1	0	0	0	0
187	G	BOWEN	TREVOR (D'bury)	25/11/1939	25/11/1939	1	0	1	0	0	0	0
840		BOYLE	RYAN	26/06/2005	10/04/2016	19	84	103	13	1	0	54
227	G	BRADBURY	JACK (St Helens)	14/03/1942	04/04/1942	4	0	4	2	0	0	6
234	G	BRADBURY	JOSEPH (Salford)	04/04/1942	25/04/1942	3	0	3	0	0	0	0
696		BRADLEY	GRAEME	06/10/1991	10/05/1994	29	4	33	4	0	0	16
393		BRADLEY	RONALD	17/03/1956	24/03/1956	2	0	2	0	0	0	0
363		BRADSHAW	WILLIAM	29/08/1953	26/09/1953	7	0	7	0	0	0	0
581		BRADY	PETER	17/12/1976	14/05/1977	7	5	12	1	0	0	3
682		BRAGGER	IAN	12/11/1989	29/09/1991	24	3	27	4	0	0	16
809		BRAMBANI	DOMINIC	18/04/2004	10/04/2005	3	5	8	0	0	0	0
419		BRIDGES	KEITH	14/09/1957	18/08/1962	110	0	110	4	0	0	12

515

PLAYERS CAREER STATISTICS UPTO AND INCLUDING SEASON 2016 IN ALPHABETICAL ORDER

D,N:	PLAYER		DEBUT	L. MATCH	APP	SUB	T.AP	TR'S	G'LS	D.G	PTS
454	BRIERS	PETER	19/09/1960	18/11/1961	9	0	9	0	30	0	60
587	BRIGGS	DAVID	04/12/1977	27/08/1978	18	2	20	0	0	0	0
269	BRIGGS	GEOFFREY	01/09/1945	26/10/1946	36	0	36	0	59	0	118
493	BRIGGS	TREVOR	16/10/1965	11/11/1977	316	22	338	92	0	0	276
167	BRINDLE	FRED	18/09/1937	23/09/1946	81	0	81	14	0	0	42
550	BROOK	GARY	18/08/1972	01/01/1976	75	17	92	22	0	0	66
199	BROOKES	KENNETH	14/09/1940	01/05/1946	84	0	84	18	41	0	136
859	BROUGH	DANNY	18/06/2006	07/10/2007	35	0	35	12	153	4	358
319	BROUGHTON	GEORGE	04/03/1950	22/11/1952	92	0	92	37	0	0	111
436	BROWN	GEORGE	22/11/1958	24/11/1962	101	0	101	29	0	0	87
466	BROWN	GILBERT	22/08/1962	12/09/1964	10	0	10	1	0	0	3
242	BROWN	LEONARD	16/09/1944	22/09/1951	20	0	20	2	0	0	6
505	BROWN	RICHARD	21/01/1967	14/11/1970	11	5	16	0	0	1	2
22	BROWN	WILLIAM	11/09/1926	11/09/1926	1	0	1	0	0	0	0
437	BROWNLEY	WILLIAM	20/12/1958	22/09/1962	20	0	20	0	0	0	0
272	BRUMMITT	HARRY	01/12/1945	26/01/1946	3	0	3	0	0	0	0
546	BRUNYEE	STEVEN	23/01/1972	22/08/1975	29	7	36	2	0	1	8
410	BRYANT	EDWARD	15/12/1956	16/03/1963	62	0	62	5	0	0	15
426	BRYANT	WILLIAM	08/03/1958	02/12/1969	251	2	253	75	0	0	225
219	G BUCKLE	*(D'bury)*	10/01/1942	10/01/1942	1	0	1	1	0	0	3
519	BULLEN	NORMAN	07/03/1969	12/04/1972	7	4	11	0	0	0	0
584	BURKE	JOHN	11/04/1977	11/09/1977	10	2	12	2	0	0	6
577	BURTON	BRUCE	18/01/1976	30/03/1980	134	1	135	89	41	4	353
380	BURTON	CLIFFORD	19/04/1955	21/04/1959	107	0	107	31	0	0	93
387	BURTON	RAYMOND	24/12/1955	24/12/1955	1	0	1	0	0	0	0
448	BUTTERFIELD	COLIN	12/12/1959	15/04/1963	47	0	47	12	0	0	36
273	BYRNE	JAMES	22/12/1945	25/12/1945	2	0	2	0	0	0	0
201	CADDICK	ALBERT	21/09/1940	21/09/1940	1	0	1	0	0	0	0
763	CAMPBELL	LOGAN	13/02/2000	28/07/2000	16	2	18	6	0	0	24
209	G CARMICHAEL	JOSEPH *(B'ford)*	22/04/1941	22/02/1941	1	0	1	0	0	0	0
933	CARNEY	JUSTIN	03/02/2013	22/08/2015	62	0	62	63	0	0	252
203	CARR	FRANK	12/10/1940	12/10/1940	1	0	1	0	0	0	0
252	G CARRES	RON *(W'field)*	11/11/1944	11/11/1944	1	0	1	0	0	0	0
196	G CARRINGTON	GEORGE *(York)*	07/09/1940	07/09/1940	1	0	1	0	0	0	0
47	CARTER	FRED	01/10/1927	07/11/1928	41	0	41	11	0	0	33
434	CARTWRIGHT	HOWARD	11/10/1963	14/09/1963	18	0	18	6	0	0	18
948	CARVELL	GARRETH	28/06/2014	07/09/2014	1	5	6	1	0	0	4
224	G CASE	DESMOND *(B'ford)*	14/02/1942	14/02/1942	1	0	1	1	0	0	3
69	CASEY	JOHN	25/12/1928	10/09/1932	81	0	81	17	1	0	53
384	CASWELL	BRIAN	29/10/1955	29/10/1955	1	0	1	0	0	0	0
889	CATIC	NED	03/05/2008	07/09/2008	7	7	14	3	0	0	12
81	CAYSER	JOHN	05/10/1929	05/10/1929	1	0	1	0	0	0	0
940	CHANNING	MICHAEL	04/08/2013	03/09/2015	28	2	30	8	0	0	32
634	CHAPMAN	CHRIS	01/01/1985	20/01/1990	57	3	60	26	0	0	104
732	CHAPMAN	DAVID	27/05/1996	13/09/1998	27	6	33	9	0	0	36
58	CHAPMAN	HAROLD	09/04/1928	07/04/1934	111	0	111	31	0	0	93
782	CHARLES	CHRIS	18/08/2001	07/10/2007	22	10	32	6	2	0	28
489	CHARLESWORTH	BARRY	20/02/1965	27/09/1965	22	0	22	2	0	0	6
894	CHASE	RANGI	15/02/2009		129	7	136	48	0	3	195
554	CHAWNER	TREVOR	23/04/1973	26/12/1973	8	6	14	0	0	0	0
154	CHEETHAM	JACK	25/04/1936	02/05/1936	2	0	2	0	0	0	0
235	G CHESTER	ALFRED *(D'bury)*	06/04/1942	06/04/1942	1	0	1	0	0	0	0
277	CHURCH	FRED	02/02/1946	15/10/1947	32	0	32	9	1	0	29
271	CHURM	WILLIAM	20/10/1945	20/10/1945	1	0	1	0	0	0	0
228	G CLAPHAM	THOMAS *(H'field)*	21/03/1942	21/03/1942	1	0	1	0	0	0	0
926	CLARE	JAMES	16/03/2012	16/05/2015	38	0	38	24	0	0	96
915	CLARK	DARYL	20/02/2011	25/09/2014	38	56	94	37	0	0	152
439	CLARK	JOHN	26/12/1958	16/01/1965	58	3	61	14	100	0	242
677	CLARKE	ANDY	10/09/1989	26/12/1991	17	13	30	2	0	0	8
399	CLARKSON	DESMOND	22/08/1956	22/08/1956	1	0	1	0	3	0	6
544	CLAUGHTON	GEORGE	27/12/1971	29/08/1982	117	25	142	13	1	0	41
310	CLAUGHTON	RICHARD	16/04/1949	27/02/1954	45	0	45	6	43	0	104
802	CLAYTON	RYAN	22/02/2004	13/08/2010	63	32	95	14	0	0	56

PLAYERS CAREER STATISTICS UPTO AND INCLUDING SEASON 2016 IN ALPHABETICAL ORDER

D,N:		PLAYER		DEBUT	L. MATCH	APP	SUB	T.AP	TR'S	G'LS	D.G	PTS
255		CLINTON	GEORGE	18/11/1944	05/04/1952	103	0	103	25	4	0	83
259	G	CLINTON	JACK (Wigan)	17/02/1945	10/03/1945	4	0	4	4	0	0	12
395		CLOUGH	ANTHONY	31/03/1956	29/09/1956	5	0	5	0	0	0	0
337		COATES	HERBERT	24/11/1951	29/03/1952	7	0	7	1	0	0	3
622		COEN	DARREN	21/11/1982	14/04/1985	70	7	77	15	0	0	55
183		COLLINS	ALBERT	30/09/1939	06/04/1942	4	0	4	0	0	0	0
604		CONNELL	GARY	30/03/1979	06/04/1985	129	22	151	16	0	0	54
887		COOK	MATTHEW	11/04/2008		13	36	49	4	0	0	16
829		COOKE	LEIGH	13/02/2005	10/04/2005	1	7	8	0	0	0	0
570		COOKLAND	PETER	05/09/1975	02/04/1978	38	11	49	5	0	0	15
573		COOMBS	RONALD	26/09/1975	05/09/1977	0	5	5	0	0	0	0
904		COOPER	MICHAEL	13/03/2010	09/04/2010	1	5	6	2	0	0	8
275		COPLEY	RON	02/02/1946	21/02/1948	59	0	59	15	0	0	45
417		CORBAN	IAN	17/08/1957	08/04/1960	26	0	26	0	0	0	0
160		COTTINGTON	GORDON	24/10/1936	27/04/1946	121	0	121	2	0	0	6
711		COVENTRY	JAMIE	30/09/1994	31/03/1996	16	10	26	6	0	0	24
536		COVENTRY	JOHN	21/11/1970	15/09/1972	20	2	22	0	0	0	0
318		COWES	JOHN	18/02/1950	10/09/1951	8	0	8	0	0	0	0
701		COYNE	PETER	04/10/1992	02/05/1993	29	0	29	2	1	0	10
664		CRABTREE	PAUL	08/11/1987	15/10/1989	10	7	17	1	0	0	4
591		CRAMPTON	JAMES	27/01/1978	12/05/1984	91	5	96	17	0	0	56
149		CRAVEN	DON	30/10/1935	18/01/1936	3	0	3	1	0	0	3
745		CRITCHLEY	JASON	18/05/1997	27/09/1998	36	3	39	15	0	0	60
873		CROFT	EDDIE	11/03/2007	11/03/2007	1	0	1	2	0	0	8
963		CROOKS	BEN	07/02/2016		26	2	28	6	1	0	26
685		CROOKS	LEE	14/01/1990	15/06/1997	215	7	222	18	596	1	1265
605		CROSSLEY	JOHN Jnr	27/04/1979	15/05/1979	4	3	7	3	0	0	9
401		CROSSLEY	JOHN Snr	03/09/1956	15/09/1956	4	0	4	0	0	0	0
136		CROSSLEY	JAMES M.	03/03/1934	23/04/1949	261	0	261	23	6	2	85
954		CROSSLEY	STEVE	08/02/2015	19/04/2015	0	6	6	0	0	0	0
130		CROSTON	ALFRED JAMES	07/10/1933	21/10/1944	283	0	283	150	52	0	554
819		CROUCH	STEVE	08/08/2004	09/10/2005	32	2	34	8	1	0	34
135		CUNNIFFE	BERNARD	03/03/1934	10/11/1945	184	0	184	89	0	0	267
441		DALE	TREVOR	31/03/1959	19/12/1959	6	0	6	0	0	0	0
713		DARLEY	PAUL	12/10/1994	01/01/1996	11	2	13	0	2	0	4
210	G	DARLISON	VICTOR (W,field)	22/02/1941	29/03/194	3	0	3	0	0	1	2
920		DAVIES	BEN	16/07/2011	21/07/2013	3	6	9	2	0	0	8
905		DAVIES	JOHN	13/03/2010	09/04/2013	1	6	7	1	0	0	4
266	G	DAVIES	LADIS (York)	21/04/1945	21/04/1945	1	0	1	0	0	0	0
4		DAVIES	THOMAS	28/08/1926	29/01/1927	19	0	19	1	0	0	3
111		DAVIES	WILLIAM H	26/09/1931	20/02/1937	204	0	204	25	0	5	85
270		DAVIES		29/04/1945	29/04/1945	1	0	1	0	0	0	0
746		DAVIS	BRAD	29/06/1997	16/09/2006	137	4	141	54	66	10	358
949		DAY	BRAD	15/08/2014	15/08/2014	0	1	1	0	0	0	0
515		DAY	MICHAEL	05/10/1968	23/04/1971	21	0	21	5	0	0	15
530		DEAN	TONY	31/01/1970	17/10/1972	28	2	30	9	0	3	33
121		DENNIS	THOMAS	12/10/1932	07/10/1933	8	0	8	0	0	0	0
86		DESMOND	WALLY	21/12/1929	25/12/1929	2	0	2	0	0	0	0
75		DEVONSHIRE	GEORGE H	20/04/1929	11/01/1930	3	0	3	0	0	0	0
644		DIAMOND	STEVE	01/09/1985	26/01/1986	13	3	16	1	6	1	17
542		DICKINSON	ALAN	30/07/1971	03/12/1978	122	17	139	14	0	0	42
25		DICKINSON	ALBERT	18/09/1926	25/08/1928	13	0	13	3	0	0	9
479		DICKINSON	CLIVE	25/01/1964	15/11/1974	303	25	328	29	1	0	89
467		DICKINSON	FRANK	29/09/1962	05/10/1963	22	0	22	0	53	1	108
870		DIXON	KIRK	18/02/2007	25/09/2014	186	2	188	95	344	0	1068
32		DIXON	NORMAN	13/11/1926	11/01/1928	7	0	7	0	0	0	0
755		DOBSON	GARETH	21/09/1998	10/09/2000	0	11	11	0	0	0	0
338		DOLAN	TERRY	01/12/1951	26/12/1951	2	0	2	0	0	0	0
90		DOLAN	WILLIAM	15/03/1930	15/03/1930	1	0	1	0	0	0	0
862		DONLAN	STUART	11/02/2007	07/09/2008	49	1	50	28	0	0	112
368		DOOLER	GEORGE	23/01/1954	23/01/1954	1	0	1	0	0	0	0
882		DORN	LUKE	09/02/2008	25/09/2016	83	2	85	62	0	0	248
972		DOUGLAS	BRANDON	08/09/2016		0	1	1	0	0	0	0

517

D,N:		PLAYER		DEBUT	L. MATCH	APP	SUB	T.AP	TR'S	G'LS	D.G	PTS
561		DOWNHAM	PETER	11/09/1974	11/09/1974	1	0	1	0	0	0	0
875		DUCKWORTH	MATTHEW	11/03/2007	11/03/2007	0	1	1	1	0	0	4
294		DUDLEY	JOEY	18/10/1947	06/09/1952	10	0	10	2	0	0	6
844		DYER	LUKE	10/02/2006	16/09/2006	18	2	20	5	0	0	20
756		EAGER	MICHAEL	14/02/1999	02/10/2005	151	2	153	69	0	0	276
371		EAST	FRANK	18/08/1954	27/12/1958	85	0	85	34	0	0	102
249		EAST	JACK	04/11/1944	15/12/1951	46	0	46	5	0	0	15
769		EATON	BARRY	06/08/2000	03/09/2000	1	4	5	0	3	0	6
143		ECCLESTONE	WILLIAM	01/12/1934	08/12/1934	2	0	2	0	0	0	0
918		EDEN	GREG	08/05/2011	06/07/2011	3	0	3	1	0	0	4
712		EDEN	PHIL	12/10/1994	29/11/1995	1	8	9	3	0	0	12
458		EDWARDS	DEREK	18/02/1961	30/04/1972	305	4	309	38	1	0	116
729		EDWARDS	DICCON	09/04/1996	11/05/1997	10	5	15	1	0	0	4
855		EDWARDS	GRANT	26/03/2006	13/08/2006	0	3	3	0	0	0	0
788		ELIMA	OLIVIER	07/04/2002	07/04/2002	0	1	1	1	0	0	4
765		ELLIS	DEAN	13/02/2000	13/02/2000	0	1	1	0	0	0	0
929		ELLIS	JAMIE	08/07/2012	25/09/2014	38	12	50	15	82	1	225
188	G	ELLIS	JOSEPH (D'bury)	09/03/1940	16/03/1940	2	0	2	0	0	0	0
680		ELLIS	ST JOHN	03/10/1989	22/05/1994	173	2	175	97	17	0	422
752		ELLISON	DANNY	28/02/1998	11/07/1999	7	19	26	7	0	0	28
913		EMMITT	JACOB	13/02/2011	01/04/2013	35	17	52	0	0	0	0
832		ENGLAND	ANTHONY	06/03/2005	13/03/2005	0	2	2	0	0	0	0
139		ENGLAND	ERIC	25/08/1934	16/10/1937	18	0	18	5	0	0	15
621		ENGLAND	KEITH	31/10/1982	26/03/1994	310	36	346	33	0	0	130
101		EVANS	ARTHUR	17/01/1931	29/04/1931	18	0	18	1	0	0	3
892		EVANS	JAMES	15/02/2009	16/05/2010	30	1	31	16	0	0	64
404		EVANS	RONALD	29/09/1956	23/08/1960	90	0	90	8	0	0	24
361		EXLEY	LEN	22/08/1953	22/08/1953	1	0	1	0	0	0	0
850		FA'AOSO	RICHARD	10/02/2006	16/09/2006	11	15	26	5	0	0	20
893		FAUMUINA	SIONE	15/02/2009	27/06/2009	19	2	21	2	0	0	8
897		FEATHER	CHRIS	15/02/2009	20/09/2009	2	25	27	0	0	0	0
24		FELTHAM	ARTHUR	18/09/1926	28/09/1929	60	0	60	3	50	3	115
560		FENTON	STEVE	11/09/1974	16/11/1986	243	9	252	89	0	0	278
321		FERGUSON	ARCHIE	11/03/1950	29/09/1951	28	0	28	4	0	0	12
895		FERRES	BRETT	15/02/2009	02/07/2012	84	5	89	27	0	0	108
385		FEWSTER	RAYMOND	16/11/1955	08/12/1956	36	0	36	7	0	0	21
246	G	FIDDES	ALEX (W'field)	04/11/1944	13/01/1945	2	0	2	0	1	0	2
663		FIFITA	JOHN	06/09/1987	13/03/1988	21	3	24	6	0	0	24
599		FINCH	DAVID	12/11/1978	07/10/1984	100	6	106	42	117	1	364
943		FINN	LIAM	16/02/2014	22/08/2015	50	3	53	9	6	2	50
292		FISHER	ALFRED	27/09/1947	17/11/1951	67	0	67	18	0	0	54
703		FISHER	ANDY	24/01/1993	19/12/1993	18	5	23	1	0	0	4
298		FISHER	ARTHUR (DIAMOND)	26/12/1947	24/11/1951	91	0	91	20	2	0	64
243		FISHER	GEORGE	16/09/1944	16/09/1944	1	0	1	0	0	0	0
571		FISHER	TONY	21/09/1975	11/12/1977	47	0	47	1	0	0	3
968		FITZSIMMONS	CONOR	01/05/2016		0	2	2	0	0	0	0
408		FLANAGAN	WILLIAM	03/11/1956	23/03/1957	22	0	22	1	0	0	3
938		FLEMING	DANIEL	17/03/2013	06/04/2014	0	16	16	1	0	0	4
314		FLEMING	LEO	17/12/1949	30/10/1954	88	0	88	2	0	0	6
858		FLETCHER	ADAM	11/06/2006	28/06/2008	17	7	24	12	0	0	48
640		FLETCHER	IAN	08/04/1985	02/11/1986	6	19	25	1	0	0	4
688		FLETCHER	PAUL	14/10/1990	03/03/1993	13	8	21	2	0	0	8
838		FLETCHER	RICHARD	15/05/2005	16/09/2006	24	9	33	4	17	0	50
708		FLOWERS	JASON	12/10/1993	31/08/2001	163	31	194	47	0	1	189
718		FLOWERS	STUART	26/02/1995	03/05/1996	4	12	16	1	0	0	4
720		FLYNN	ADRIAN	20/08/1995	06/04/1997	38	4	42	21	0	0	84
970		FLYNN	PADDY	12/05/2016		9	1	10	6	0	0	24
900		FORD	JAMES	05/04/2009	14/08/2009	3	7	10	2	0	0	8
691		FORD	MIKE	01/09/1991	27/09/1998	151	12	163	57	0	8	236
297		FOREMAN	DESMOND	13/12/1947	08/01/1949	44	0	44	13	9	0	57
557		FORSTER	CHRIS	01/01/1974	12/04/1975	31	5	36	2	0	0	6
509		FOSTER	DEREK	03/04/1967	09/12/1973	130	1	131	53	0	0	159
471		FOULKES	KENNY	6/03/1963	19/09/1964	14	1	15	6	0	0	18

PLAYERS CAREER STATISTICS UPTO AND INCLUDING SEASON 2016 IN ALPHABETICAL ORDER

D,N:	PLAYER		DEBUT	L. MATCH	APP	SUB	T.AP	TR'S	G'LS	D.G	PTS
540	FOWLER	DENNIS	18/04/1971	03/10/1975	30	7	37	1	0	0	3
510	FOX	FRANK	19/08/1967	31/03/1970	51	14	65	2	0	0	6
284	FOX	HAROLD	31/08/1946	18/02/1950	16	0	16	0	0	0	0
189	FOX	JOHN H.	26/03/1940	05/09/1946	20	0	20	1	0	0	3
916	FOZZARD	NICK	13/03/2011	10/09/2011	9	10	19	0	0	0	0
856	FRANZE	PAUL	14/04/2006	21/04/2006	2	1	3	0	0	0	0
628	FREEMAN	GARY	20/11/1983	28/03/1984	15	2	17	4	0	0	16
678	FRENCH	GARY	17/09/1989	21/04/1991	53	2	55	15	1	1	63
647	FRENCH	IAN	13/10/1985	03/05/1986	20	0	20	11	0	0	44
383	FRETWELL	TONY	24/09/1955	24/09/1955	1	0	1	0	0	0	0
761	FRITZ	DALE	26/02/1999	21/09/2003	129	4	133	9	0	0	36
725	FURNESS	DAVID	07/01/1996	03/05/1996	3	1	4	3	0	0	12
952	GALE	LUKE	08/02/2015		59	0	59	18	222	3	519
465	GAMBLE	JACK	22/08/1962	18/11/1966	100	1	101	39	0	0	117
559	GARBETT	BRIAN	28/04/1974	26/03/1980	2	2	4	0	0	0	0
174	GARBETT	LEONARD	18/04/1938	06/04/1942	8	0	8	1	0	0	3
818	GARDNER	MATT	23/07/2004	23/07/2004	1	0	1	1	0	0	4
728	GAY	RICHARD	05/04/1996	19/05/2002	111	18	129	43	0	0	172
666	GIBBS	RON	28/08/1988	07/01/1990	41	0	41	12	0	0	48
946	GIBSON	ASHLEY	21/04/2014	25/09/2015	29	0	29	11	0	0	44
794	GIBSON	DAMIAN	08/02/2003	19/09/2004	43	3	46	6	0	0	24
670	GIBSON	MARK	11/02/1989	03/10/1989	14	3	17	2	0	0	8
365	GILL	BRIAN	11/11/1953	11/11/1953	1	0	1	1	0	0	3
131	GILL	JAMES	25/12/1933	12/10/1935	19	0	19	7	0	0	21
610	GILL	STEVEN	04/01/1980	08/11/1987	26	1	27	5	0	0	19
935	GILMOUR	LEE	03/02/2013	05/05/2013	10	3	13	0	0	0	0
865	GLASSIE	TERE	11/02/2007	02/09/2007	9	10	19	3	0	0	12
735	GLAZE	EDDIE	17/08/1996	17/08/1996	1	0	1	0	0	0	0
82	GLEDHILL	WILLIAM	12/10/1929	21/12/1929	9	0	9	0	0	0	0
229	G GLOVER	CHARLIE (Wigan)	21/03/1942	02/05/1942	4	0	4	0	3	0	6
771	GODDARD	JONATHON	16/09/2000	15/07/2001	0	2	2	0	0	0	0
709	GODDARD	RICHARD	21/08/1994	23/03/1997	50	10	60	16	36	0	136
779	GODWIN	WAYNE	15/07/2001	19/09/2004	31	37	68	19	59	0	194
233	G GOLBY	JOSEPH (F'stone)	04/04/1942	04/04/1942	1	0	1	0	0	0	0
212	G GOODFELLOW	HERBERT (W'field)	29/03/1941	29/03/1941	1	0	1	0	0	0	0
157	GOODWIN	ALFRED	04/05/1936	04/05/1936	1	0	1	0	0	0	0
80	GORMAN	AUGUSTINE	28/09/1929	10/10/1931	33	0	33	2	0	0	6
355	GRACE	ARNOLD	06/04/1953	25/08/1956	25	0	25	3	1	1	13
472	GRACE	DAVID	27/04/1963	28/12/1963	2	0	2	0	2	0	4
418	GRAHAM	GORDON	07/09/1957	07/09/1957	1	0	1	0	0	0	0
285	GRAHAME	THOMAS	02/11/1946	07/05/1947	24	0	24	4	0	0	12
646	GREATBATCH	NEIL	25/09/1985	22/04/1986	22	2	24	6	0	0	24
411	GREATBATCH	SIDNEY	19/01/1957	19/01/1957	1	0	1	0	0	0	0
162	GREAVES	GEORGE	06/03/1937	01/09/1937	7	0	7	1	0	0	3
161	GREEN	ARTHUR	30/01/1937	06/02/1937	2	0	2	1	0	0	3
449	GREEN	FRANK	09/01/1960	25/04/1964	15	0	15	4	0	0	12
805	GREENHILL	CRAIG	22/02/2004	19/09/2004	23	4	27	1	0	0	4
924	GREHAN	JAMES	26/02/2012	09/04/2012	2	2	4	0	0	0	0
921	GRIFFIN	JOSH	03/02/2012	17/08/2012	21	0	21	14	1	0	58
320	GRONOW	PETER	04/03/1950	04/03/1950	1	0	1	0	0	0	0
524	GUEST	IAN	08/10/1969	18/04/1971	11	0	11	4	0	0	12
179	GUEST	NORMAN	11/04/1939	24/12/1949	139	0	139	41	76	5	285
328	GUNBY	WILLIAM	26/03/1951	20/04/1953	29	0	29	11	0	0	33
402	GUTHRIE	RONALD	15/09/1956	29/09/1956	3	0	3	0	0	0	0
866	GUTTENBEIL	AWEN	11/02/2007	07/09/2008	42	0	42	8	0	0	32
886	HABERECHT	TOM	09/02/2008	19/04/2008	2	3	5	1	0	0	4
344	HAGUE	ROY	10/09/1952	12/11/1955	27	0	27	0	0	0	0
359	HALE	BRIAN	15/08/1953	19/08/1953	2	0	2	0	0	0	0
240	HALE	HAROLD	09/09/1944	21/10/1944	5	0	5	0	0	0	0
123	HALEY	HAROLD	29/10/1932	06/12/1947	338	0	338	11	0	3	39
753	HALL	MARTIN	26/04/1998	22/05/1998	4	0	4	0	0	0	0
84	HALL	WILSON	09/11/1929	08/12/1934	175	0	175	24	0	0	72
594	HALMSHAW	TONY	03/09/1978	04/01/1980	12	5	17	0	0	0	0

PLAYERS CAREER STATISTICS UPTO AND INCLUDING SEASON 2016 IN ALPHABETICAL ORDER

D,N:	PLAYER		DEBUT	L. MATCH	APP	SUB	T.AP	TR'S	G'LS	D.G	PTS
232	HAMER	RAYMOND (F'ne/C.P.)	14/004/1942	07/09/1946	29	0	29	6	0	0	18
837	HAMILTON	LANCE	25/03/2005	03/04/2005	1	1	2	0	0	0	0
965	HAMPSHIRE	RYAN	13/03/2016		20	2	22	8	0	0	32
446	HAMPTON	JOE	31/10/1959	18/03/1961	9	0	9	0	0	0	0
99	HAND	HARRY (MICK)	27/12/1930	30/09/1933	17	0	17	0	0	0	0
774	HANDFORD	GARETH	11/02/2001	01/06/2001	7	4	11	0	0	0	0
822	HANDFORTH	PAUL	13/02/2005	18/08/2006	18	22	40	6	22	1	69
331	HANSELL	DERRICK	24/04/1951	24/04/1951	1	0	1	0	0	0	0
374	HARDCASTLE	TONY	02/10/1954	06/11/1954	5	0	5	0	0	0	0
433	HARDISTY	ALAN	27/09/1958	23/04/1971	400	1	401	206	78	42	858
638	HARDISTY	IAN	08/04/1985	23/04/1985	2	0	2	0	5	0	10
568	HARDY	ALAN	14/03/1975	20/11/1983	96	16	112	4	0	6	18
684	HARDY	JEFF	14/01/1990	21/04/1991	51	0	51	15	0	0	60
147	HARDY	THOMAS	28/09/1935	25/12/1945	186	0	186	45	0	0	135
513	HARGRAVE	DAVID (DANNY)	20/10/1967	03/12/1972	97	27	124	22	0	2	70
731	HARGRAVE	SPENCER	12/05/1996	07/08/1999	0	6	6	0	0	0	0
1	HARGRAVE	WILLIAM	28/08/1926	25/01/1930	108	0	108	22	83	2	236
247	G HARGRAVE	(York)	04/11/1944	04/11/1944	1	0	1	0	0	0	0
719	HARLAND	LEE	15/03/1995	19/09/2004	183	44	227	26	0	0	104
96	HARLING	CLIFFORD	18/10/1930	03/03/1934	22	0	22	2	0	0	6
490	HARRIS	DENNIS	27/03/1965	02/10/1970	33	3	36	14	2	0	46
290	HARRIS	DYL	25/04/1947	24/04/1951	133	0	133	6	0	0	18
41	HARRIS	WILLIAM R.	05/02/1927	12/02/1927	2	0	2	0	0	0	0
617	HARRISON	JOHN	08/11/1981	20/03/1983	2	1	3	0	0	0	0
403	HARRISON	KEITH	22/09/1956	22/09/1956	1	0	1	0	0	0	0
106	HARRISON	WILLIAM	29/04/1931	29/04/1931	1	0	1	0	0	0	0
205	HART	THOMAS	19/10/1940	02/11/1940	3	0	3	0	0	0	0
503	HARTLEY	DENNIS	16/09/1966	04/04/1975	259	9	268	15	1	1	49
641	HARTLEY	IAIN	08/04/1985	16/04/1986	2	1	3	0	0	0	0
415	HATTEE	ARTHUR	22/04/1957	10/10/1959	17	0	17	1	14	0	31
323	HAUGHEY	LESLIE	08/04/1950	27/08/1956	173	0	173	3	0	0	9
825	HAUGHEY	TOMMY	13/02/2005	21/04/2006	28	7	35	20	0	0	80
936	HAURAKI	WELLER	03/02/2013	25/09/2014	54	2	56	9	0	0	36
207	HAWES		09/11/1940	09/11/1940	1	0	1	0	0	0	0
687	HAY	ANDY	06/10/1990	07/05/1995	46	29	75	18	0	0	72
109	HAYES	WILLIAM	09/09/1931	21/04/1945	23	0	23	2	0	0	6
348	HAYNES	JACK	24/01/1953	24/01/1953	1	0	1	0	0	0	0
773	HEALEY	MITCH	11/02/2001	21/09/2003	74	1	75	11	16	2	78
824	HENDERSON	ANDREW	13/02/2005	07/09/2008	103	12	115	22	0	0	88
137	HENSHAW	WILLIAM	17/03/1934	19/04/1934	6	0	6	0	0	0	0
762	HEPI	BRAD	09/05/1999	22/04/2001	9	21	30	3	0	0	12
562	HEPTON	ROY	11/10/1974	22/11/1974	1	2	3	1	0	0	3
799	HEPWORTH	JON	18/05/2003	09/10/2005	44	26	70	21	10	0	104
442	HEPWORTH	KEITH	04/04/1959	05/10/1971	325	4	329	66	4	14	234
598	HIGGINS	BARRY	06/10/1978	16/04/1986	57	28	85	13	0	0	46
864	HIGGINS	LIAM	11/02/2007	04/09/2010	66	39	105	4	0	0	16
538	HIGGINS	PAUL	06/02/1971	12/04/1975	29	8	37	5	0	0	15
94	HIGO	JAMES	30/08/1930	30/08/1930	1	0	1	0	0	0	0
721	HILL	ANDY	20/08/1995	04/07/1999	6	7	13	0	0	0	0
239	HILL	JOHN	03/09/1944	14/01/1956	158	0	158	3	0	0	9
660	HILL	KENNETH	30/08/1987	28/03/1990	17	14	31	1	0	0	4
488	HILL	RONALD	30/01/1965	26/10/1968	81	2	83	14	158	3	364
496	HINCHCLIFFE	JOHN	15/04/1966	02/09/1966	5	0	5	0	0	0	0
398	HINDLEY	KENNETH	22/08/1956	12/04/1958	30	0	30	3	0	0	9
31	HINTON	GEORGE (GAGGER)	23/10/1926	23/04/1927	15	0	15	1	0	0	3
71	HIRST	HARRY	30/03/1929	14/09/1929	8	0	8	0	0	0	0
424	HIRST	JACK	25/12/1957	17/04/1965	178	3	181	7	3	0	27
964	HITCHCOX	JY	25/02/2016		8	1	9	7	0	0	28
888	HLAD	BRENDAN	26/04/2008	22/06/2008	0	3	3	0	0	0	0
42	HOBSON	ERNEST	23/02/1927	23/02/1927	1	0	1	0	0	0	0
65	HODGSON	BENJAMIN T	03/11/1928	10/11/1928	2	0	2	0	0	0	0
178	HOLMES	JOSEPH	10/02/1939	02/03/1940	6	0	6	2	0	0	6
907	HOLMES	OLIVER	09/04/2010		123	22	145	24	0	0	96

PLAYERS CAREER STATISTICS UPTO AND INCLUDING SEASON 2016 IN ALPHABETICAL ORDER

D,N:	PLAYER		DEBUT	L. MATCH	APP	SUB	T.AP	TR'S	G'LS	D.G	PTS
959	HOLMES	TOM	03/05/2015		4	4	8	1	0	0	4
175	HORAN	JOHN	27/08/1938	22/12/1945	23	0	23	1	0	0	3
668	HORO	SHANE	23/10/1988	30/03/1989	17	1	18	11	0	0	44
377	HORSFALL	ALAN	29/01/1955	04/09/1957	53	0	53	3	0	0	9
619	HORTON	STUART	31/03/1982	01/04/1987	76	4	80	10	0	0	39
119	HOULT	JACK	27/08/1932	16/12/1933	52	0	52	19	0	0	57
302	HOWARD	GEORGE (CHARLIE)	23/10/1948	25/04/1959	325	0	325	17	0	0	51
473	HOWE	KEITH	04/05/1963	06/09/1969	162	5	167	109	0	0	327
218	HOYLE		26/12/1941	26/12/1941	1	0	1	0	0	0	0
800	HUBY	CRAIG	07/06/2003	25/09/2014	165	76	241	47	131	0	450
552	HUDDLESTONE	JAMES (SID)	15/10/1972	05/04/1980	41	22	63	6	0	0	18
5	HUDSON	HARRY	28/08/1926	10/09/1932	47	0	47	12	0	0	36
786	HUDSON	RYAN	10/02/2002	09/09/2012	146	16	162	35	0	0	140
38	HUDSON	THOMAS	15/01/1927	15/01/1927	1	0	1	0	0	0	0
144	HUGGETT	WILLIAM	06/04/1935	16/04/1938	10	0	10	0	0	0	0
602	HUGHES	BRIAN	19/11/1978	13/12/1980	42	1	43	3	0	0	9
340	HUGHES	DAVID	25/12/1951	27/12/1958	43	0	43	3	0	0	9
400	HUNT	JAMES	27/08/1956	30/11/1957	5	0	5	1	0	0	3
18	HUNTER	ELIJAH	06/09/1926	09/10/1926	3	0	3	0	1	0	2
601	HYDE	GARY	19/11/1978	04/04/1988	250	21	271	130	216	0	875
173	INNES	GORDON	05/02/1938	26/11/1938	22	0	22	3	0	0	9
444	IREDALE	DOUGLAS	22/08/1959	30/04/1960	24	0	24	13	0	0	39
651	IRWIN	SHAUN	24/08/1986	16/10/1992	130	11	141	41	0	0	164
917	ISA	WILLIE	20/03/2011	10/09/2011	8	3	11	6	0	0	24
795	JACKSON	PAUL	08/02/2003	17/08/2013	48	32	80	5	0	0	20
830	JAMES	JORDAN	27/02/2005	11/09/2005	8	14	22	9	0	0	36
614	JAMES	NEIL	26/03/1980	14/04/1985	82	29	111	17	0	0	60
549	JAMES	RICHARD	24/03/1972	24/03/1972	0	1	1	0	0	0	0
78	JAMES	WILLIAM	07/09/1929	27/04/1935	151	0	151	22	168	2	406
564	JEFF	TONY	29/11/1974	29/11/1974	0	1	1	0	0	0	0
87	JENNINGS	STANLEY	26/12/1929	14/01/1933	42	0	42	3	0	0	9
947	JEWITT	LEE	18/05/2014	12/08/2016	25	15	40	1	0	0	4
653	JOHNS	CHRIS	14/09/1986	01/03/1987	18	0	18	7	0	0	28
477	JOHNSON	ANDREW	14/12/1963	17/04/1965	11	1	12	1	3	0	9
784	JOHNSON	ANDY	10/02/2002	21/09/2003	36	16	52	11	0	0	44
613	JOHNSON	BARRY	14/03/1980	25/09/1988	206	16	222	22	1	0	77
120	JOHNSON	JOHN	17/09/1932	25/11/1933	12	0	12	3	0	0	9
579	JOHNSON	PETER	20/03/1976	26/12/1978	0	7	7	1	0	0	3
526	JOHNSON	PHILIP	31/10/1969	25/03/1981	267	21	288	86	0	0	258
874	JOHNSON	SEAN	11/03/2007	29/04/2007	3	2	5	1	0	0	4
930	JOHNSTON	BEN	12/08/2012	17/08/2012	2	0	2	0	0	0	0
872	JONES	ADAM	11/03/2007	11/03/2007	1	0	1	2	0	0	8
470	JONES	DENIS	10/11/1962	30/03/1964	14	0	14	0	1	0	2
63	JONES	EDWIN	22/09/1928	24/11/1928	7	0	7	0	0	0	0
192	JONES	ERIC	01/06/1940	11/01/1947	119	0	119	10	0	0	30
504	JONES	GLYN	17/12/1966	17/11/1971	48	7	55	5	0	1	17
339	JONES	HARRY	15/12/1951	07/03/1953	38	0	38	10	0	0	30
186	G JONES	J (Leeds)	18/11/1939	18/11/1939	1	0	1	0	0	0	0
300	JONES	JAMES	24/01/1948	10/03/1951	119	0	119	0	0	0	0
642	JONES	KEITH	23/04/1985	17/04/1988	11	10	21	1	2	0	8
626	JONES	KEVIN	21/08/1983	23/12/1984	18	3	21	4	39	0	94
896	JONES	STUART	15/02/2009	02/09/2012	74	28	102	14	0	0	56
529	JORDAN	GARY	10/01/1970	16/09/1970	3	0	3	0	0	0	0
551	JOYNER	JOHN	01/09/1972	20/04/1992	585	28	613	185	0	0	614
97	JUBB	KENNETH	25/10/1930	29/04/1933	67	0	67	8	0	0	24
665	JULIFF	BRIAN	13/12/1987	24/04/1988	8	3	11	3	0	0	12
580	KAHN	PAUL	01/10/1976	15/03/1977	22	2	24	3	0	0	9
813	KAIN	ANDY	09/05/2004	13/08/2006	30	13	43	17	45	2	160
582	KAIN	JOHN	18/02/1977	23/04/1978	19	10	29	7	0	0	21
834	KAIN	STUART	13/03/2005	24/07/2005	4	1	5	1	0	0	4
237	KARLE	EDDIE	02/09/1944	02/09/1944	1	0	1	0	0	0	0
138	KAYE	ROSSLYN	24/03/1934	16/03/1935	2	0	2	1	0	0	3
593	KEAR	BARRY	03/09/1978	13/09/1981	22	2	24	0	0	0	0

D,N:		PLAYER		DEBUT	L. MATCH	APP	SUB	T.AP	TR'S	G'LS	D.G	PTS
200		KEAR	HERBERT	21/09/1940	20/12/1941	5	0	5	0	0	0	0
596		KEAR	JOHN	01/10/1978	11/09/1987	119	14	133	37	0	0	132
624		KELLETT	NEIL	06/03/1983	06/03/1983	1	0	1	0	0	0	0
13		KELLY	JOSEPH (PAT)	28/08/1926	05/03/1927	18	0	18	1	0	0	3
208	G	KELLY	(Hunslet)	15/02/1941	08/03/1941	3	0	3	0	0	0	0
19		KEMP	ALBERT	06/09/1926	30/10/1926	4	0	4	0	0	0	0
707		KEMP	TONY	03/10/1993	07/05/1995	63	0	63	27	4	3	119
102		KENDALL	JOSEPH	03/04/1931	03/10/1931	7	0	7	0	0	0	0
248	G	KENDALL	KENNETH (H'field/C.P.)	04/11/1944	22/04/1946	14	0	14	0	0	0	0
367		KENDRICK	ALAN	02/01/1954	27/02/1954	8	0	8	0	0	0	0
373		KETT	ANDREW	18/09/1954	06/11/1954	3	0	3	0	0	0	0
636		KETTERIDGE	MARTIN	17/02/1985	12/02/1995	263	43	306	14	420	0	896
166		KILLINGBECK	MATTHEW	28/08/1937	16/04/1938	27	0	27	21	10	0	83
816		KING	KEVIN	04/07/2004	04/07/2004	0	1	1	0	0	0	0
43		KINSEY	VICTOR	05/03/1927	25/12/1929	22	0	22	5	0	0	15
456		KIRK	MALCOLM	17/12/1960	24/12/1960	2	0	2	0	0	0	0
523		KIRKBRIDE	WILLIAM	20/09/1969	04/12/1970	43	0	43	3	0	1	11
508		KIRKBRIGHT	JOSEPH	25/03/1967	16/08/1969	6	0	6	1	0	0	3
258	G	KITCHING	JACK (B'ford/C.P.)	10/02/1945	06/10/1951	29	0	29	11	0	0	33
333		KITSON	ARTHUR	25/08/1951	30/10/1954	13	0	13	0	16	0	32
528		KNIGHT	GLEN	26/12/1969	17/03/1974	34	14	48	13	9	0	57
125		KNOWLES	DONALD	17/12/1932	16/11/1935	38	0	38	8	0	0	24
833		KNOWLES	MICHAEL	06/03/2005	15/06/2007	2	13	15	4	0	0	16
108		KNOWLING	FRED	09/09/1931	12/09/1931	2	0	2	0	0	0	0
884		KORKIDAS	MICHAEL	09/02/2008	07/09/2008	16	6	22	1	0	0	4
350		LAMBERT	ROY	28/02/1952	12/12/1953	26	0	26	14	0	1	44
193		LANE	JACK	07/09/1940	14/04/1941	22	0	22	2	0	0	6
280		LANGFIELD	GEORGE	06/04/1946	25/12/1951	228	0	228	62	369	22	968
674		LARDER	STEVE	03/09/1989	21/04/1991	55	4	59	39	10	1	177
216	G	LARGE	ALBANY (St Helens)	29/11/1941	06/12/1941	2	0	2	0	0	0	0
435		LATU	PENI	18/10/1958	18/10/1958	1	0	1	0	0	0	0
261		LAVENDER	EDWARD	24/02/1945	08/11/1947	87	0	87	8	0	0	24
431		LAWSON	JAMES	23/08/1958	23/08/1958	1	0	1	0	0	0	0
868		LEAFA	MARK	11/02/2007	07/09/2008	21	19	40	10	0	0	40
704		LEAKE	CHANCE	07/03/1993	07/03/1993	0	1	1	0	0	0	0
8		LEAKE	JACK	28/08/1926	06/04/1929	72	0	72	13	0	0	39
85		LEESE	ALBERT	09/11/1929	06/01/1934	10	0	10	1	0	0	3
772		LENNON	MARK	11/02/2001	21/09/2003	33	25	58	12	21	0	90
79		LEWIS	GEORGE	21/09/1929	28/10/1944	373	0	373	19	373	11	825
238		LEWIS	RONALD	09/09/1944	07/03/1953	260	0	260	7	2	0	25
778		LEWIS	SIMON	17/06/2001	08/07/2001	4	0	4	3	0	0	12
740		LIDDEN	JASON	09/02/1997	19/09/1997	21	3	24	7	0	0	28
450		LINDLEY	JOHN	09/01/1960	19/04/1960	12	0	12	0	0	0	0
655		LINDNER	BOB	01/01/1987	13/12/1987	19	0	19	9	0	0	36
244	G	LINGARD	F (Batley)	23/09/1944	23/09/1944	1	0	1	0	0	0	0
532		LLOYD	GEOFFREY (SAMMY)	30/03/1970	02/04/1978	209	16	225	44	741	2	1616
176		LLOYD	REGINALD	15/10/1938	17/03/1951	248	0	248	59	0	0	177
497		LOCKWOOD	BRIAN	16/04/1966	07/03/1975	221	10	231	38	8	0	130
220	G	LONGLEY	ALBAN (F'tone)	10/01/1942	21/04/1945	3	0	3	0	0	0	0
558		LONGSTAFF	PAUL	13/04/1974	25/10/1974	7	0	7	0	0	0	0
637		LORD	GARY	20/03/1985	10/04/1988	38	14	52	9	0	0	36
516		LOWNDES	ALAN	13/12/1968	09/01/1977	201	0	201	83	0	0	249
575		LUCAS	DOUG	24/10/1975	02/11/1975	2	0	2	0	0	0	0
429		LUMB	MICHAEL	29/03/1958	05/04/1958	2	0	2	0	0	0	0
341		LUNN	ALBERT	22/03/1952	09/02/1963	363	0	363	40	875	0	1870
835		LUNT	SHAUN	20/03/2005	10/04/2005	1	3	4	0	0	0	0
857		LUPTON	PETER	31/4/2006	07/09/2008	55	2	57	18	0	0	72
351		LYLES	RONALD	07/03/1953	22/08/1953	3	0	3	0	0	0	0
759		LYNCH	ANDY	14/02/1999		154	54	208	17	0	0	68
49		LYONS	WILLIAM E	27/12/1927	27/12/1927	1	0	1	0	0	0	0
180		LYTHGOE	PETER	30/09/1939	25/04/1942	32	0	32	2	11	0	28
950		MAHER	WILL	15/08/2014		1	23	24	1	0	0	4
146		MALKIN	HARRY	08/04/1935	08/04/1935	1	0	1	0	0	0	0

D,N:		PLAYER		DEBUT	L. MATCH	APP	SUB	T.AP	TR'S	G'LS	D.G	PTS
11		MALKIN	JOSEPH	28/08/1926	01/10/1932	79	0	79	11	1	0	35
841		MALONEY	DOMINIC	10/07/2005	24/07/2005	0	2	2	0	0	0	0
749		MALONEY	FRANCIS	14/02/1998	19/09/2004	76	10	86	26	35	3	177
53		MALSOM	EPHRAIM	28/01/1928	31/03/1928	2	0	2	0	0	0	0
29		MANN	CLARENCE	16/10/1926	13/11/1926	3	0	3	0	0	0	0
854		MANU	WILLIE	19/03/2006	16/09/2006	20	4	24	9	0	0	36
362		MARCHANT	ALAN	29/08/1953	29/08/1953	1	0	1	1	0	0	3
618		MARCHANT	TONY	17/03/1982	29/09/1995	262	6	268	101	0	0	386
945		MARIANO	FRANKIE	16/02/2014	20/08/2016	15	25	40	8	0	0	32
452		MARSDEN	BRIAN	13/08/1960	06/04/1963	57	0	57	13	0	0	39
36		MARSHALL	ALBERT	08/01/1927	10/10/1931	28	0	28	1	0	0	3
459		MARSTON	PETER	01/04/1961	03/04/1961	2	0	2	0	0	0	0
939		MARTIN	CHARLIE	01/04/2013	08/09/2013	0	6	6	0	0	0	0
612		MARTIN	PAUL	01/02/1980	22/11/1981	1	1	2	0	0	0	0
722		MASKILL	COLIN	20/08/1995	30/06/1996	24	1	25	7	8	0	44
66		MASKILL	RAYMOND	17/11/1928	03/10/1931	20	0	20	1	0	0	3
853		MASON	KEITH	10/02/2006	04/08/2013	12	6	18	0	0	0	0
876		MASSEY	NATHAN	11/03/2007		88	57	145	10	0	0	40
748		MATHER	BARRIE-JON	14/02/1998	10/02/2002	55	12	67	24	0	0	96
911		MATHERS	RICHARD	13/02/2011	03/09/2011	22	1	23	7	0	0	28
44		MATTICK	ROBERT	23/04/1927	03/09/2029	28	0	28	2	0	0	6
673		McALLISTER	TERRY	09/04/1989	12/10/1994	5	8	13	0	0	0	0
478		McCARTNEY	HAROLD	01/01/1964	06/09/1967	23	5	28	2	0	0	6
230	G	McCUE	THOMAS (Widnes)	21/03/1942	21/03/1942	1	0	1	1	0	0	3
846		McGOLDRICK	RYAN	10/02/2006	02/07/2012	162	8	170	38	9	1	171
114		McGONIGLE	ALBERT	26/12/1931	05/09/1932	7	0	7	1	0	0	3
511		McKALROY	JOHN	15/09/1967	31/03/1970	12	2	14	0	0	0	0
747		McKELL	RICHARD	29/06/1997	27/09/1998	30	7	37	2	0	0	8
164		McMANUS	ANDY	10/04/1937	10/04/1937	1	0	1	0	0	0	0
141		McMANUS	PATRICK B.	25/08/1934	07/05/1947	296	0	296	16	0	0	48
956		McMEEKEN	MIKE	27/02/2015		35	8	43	9	0	0	36
777		McNALLY	ANDY	09/05/2001	15/08/2003	2	5	7	1	0	0	4
961		McSHANE	PAUL	07/08/2015		19	19	38	7	4	0	36
34		McTIGHE	JOSEPH	18/12/1926	21/01/1928	31	0	31	4	1	0	14
741		McVEAN	SEAN	09/02/1997	09/02/1997	0	1	1	0	0	0	0
797		MELLOR	PAUL	21/03/2003	19/09/2004	36	3	39	18	0	0	72
789		MERCER	GARY	21/04/2002	21/04/2002	0	1	1	0	0	0	0
360		METCALFE	ALLAN	22/08/1953	22/08/1953	1	0	1	0	0	0	0
693		MIDDLETON	SIMON	08/09/1991	18/05/1997	159	11	170	83	5	0	342
495		MILLER	TONY	26/02/1966	15/12/1973	119	16	135	15	0	0	45
925		MILLINGTON	GRANT	02/03/2012		91	38	129	18	0	0	68
483		MILLWARD	ROGER	03/10/1964	30/04/1966	34	6	40	16	35	0	118
910		MILNER	ADAM	04/07/2010		110	45	155	25	0	0	100
966		MINIKIN	GREG	24/03/2016		16	1	17	6	0	0	24
3		MINTON	HARRY	28/08/1926	16/10/1926	6	0	6	1	0	0	3
671		MIRFIN	PHIL	19/03/1989	29/10/1989	3	7	10	5	0	0	20
922		MITCHELL	LEE	03/02/2012	09/09/2012	13	10	23	2	0	0	8
304		MOGG	LISTER	04/12/1948	04/09/1951	7	0	7	0	0	0	0
962		MONAGHAN	JOEL	07/02/2016		18	0	18	5	0	0	20
885		MOORE	SCOTT	09/02/2008	12/07/2015	24	7	31	2	0	0	8
953		MOORS	JUNIOR	08/02/2015		32	15	47	5	0	0	20
222	G	MORRELL	CYRIL (Hunslet)	14/02/1942	14/02/1942	1	0	1	0	0	0	0
565		MORRIS	GEOFF	15/12/1974	28/04/1982	69	26	95	12	0	0	36
714		MORRIS	LYNTON	12/10/1994	12/10/1994	0	1	1	0	0	0	0
225	G	MORRIS	OLIVER (Leeds)	14/02/1940	14/02/1940	1	0	1	0	0	0	0
698		MORRISON	TONY	23/08/1992	07/05/1995	85	7	92	21	0	0	84
842		MOSSOP	JASON	07/08/2005	07/08/2005	0	1	1	0	0	0	0
631		MOUNTAIN	DEAN	29/04/1984	03/01/1988	17	32	49	4	0	0	16
217	G	MOXON	HAROLD (F'tone)	13/12/1941	13/12/1941	1	0	1	0	0	0	0
291		MUGGLESTONE	FRANK	30/08/1947	29/09/1951	145	0	145	19	0	4	65
251	G	MURPHY	HARRY (W'field)	04/11/1944	04/11/1944	1	0	1	0	0	0	0
30		MUSCROFT	TONY	23/10/1926	23/10/1926	1	0	1	0	0	0	0
20		NASH	JAMES	06/09/1926	24/03/1928	24	0	24	2	0	0	6

PLAYERS CAREER STATISTICS UPTO AND INCLUDING SEASON 2016 IN ALPHABETICAL ORDER

D,N:	PLAYER		DEBUT	L. MATCH	APP	SUB	T.AP	TR'S	G'LS	D.G	PTS
923	NASH	STEVE	03/02/2012	02/09/2012	3	4	7	0	0	0	0
413	NAYLOR	CHARLES	02/02/1957	01/03/1958	10	0	10	3	0	0	9
555	NAYLOR	JAMES	16/09/1973	10/10/1973	6	0	6	1	0	0	3
6	NEEDHAM	THOMAS	28/08/1926	23/03/1929	77	0	77	13	1	1	43
690	NELSON	DAVID	01/09/1991	20/04/1994	51	3	54	14	0	0	56
263 G	NESS	WILF (Hull)	02/04/1945	02/04/1945	1	0	1	0	0	0	0
898	NETHERTON	KIRK	15/02/2009	17/04/2010	8	23	31	4	0	0	16
808	NEWLOVE	PAUL	08/04/2004	23/05/2004	5	0	5	1	0	0	4
537	NEWTON	RAY	28/11/1970	05/10/1977	171	14	185	46	0	0	138
215	NICHOLLS	JAMES	27/09/1941	01/01/1949	117	0	117	10	0	0	30
9	NICHOLLS	ROBERT	28/08/1926	14/03/1931	92	0	92	4	0	0	12
231 G	NICHOLSON	J (D'bury)	28/03/1942	28/03/1942	1	0	1	0	0	0	0
692	NIKAU	TAWERA	01/09/1991	04/02/1996	164	1	165	25	0	0	100
369	NORBURY	GEORGE	27/02/1954	22/04/1955	12	0	12	4	0	0	12
381	NORTON	DENNIS	27/04/1955	16/11/1955	12	0	12	1	0	0	3
588	NORTON	PAUL	04/12/1977	31/10/1982	96	9	105	7	174	0	369
281	NORTON	ROY	27/04/1946	27/04/1946	1	0	1	0	0	0	0
531	NORTON	STEVE (KNOCKER)	13/03/1970	17/04/1977	170	13	183	56	0	5	177
463	NOWELL	ERIC	12/04/1962	12/10/1963	10	0	10	1	0	0	3
848	NUTLEY	DANNY	10/02/2006	16/09/2006	28	0	28	3	0	0	12
937	O,BRIEN	GARETH	16/02/2013	24/02/2013	2	0	2	0	0	1	1
322	O'CONNOR	LEWIS	08/04/1950	15/04/1950	3	0	3	1	0	0	3
346	ODDY	HAROLD	13/12/1952	22/10/1955	70	0	70	10	0	0	30
386	OLSON	LEN	26/11/1955	10/12/1955	3	0	3	0	0	0	0
742	ORR	DANNY	16/03/1997	09/09/2012	217	28	245	84	328	4	996
578	ORR	PAUL	06/02/1976	11/10/1981	90	18	108	16	38	0	124
609	ORUM	IAN	25/11/1979	13/04/1986	77	36	113	10	0	1	32
583	OULTON	ARTHUR	06/03/1977	21/08/1977	2	0	2	0	5	0	10
35	OWEN	HARRY	27/12/1926	27/08/1927	8	0	8	1	0	0	3
863	OWEN	RICHARD	11/02/2007	21/04/2014	125	14	139	70	0	0	280
301	OWENS	IKE	16/10/1948	15/01/1949	7	0	7	2	0	0	6
716	PALMER	CRAIG	29/01/1995	25/08/1995	1	2	3	0	0	0	0
55	PANTHER	RALPH	18/02/1928	03/03/1928	2	0	2	0	0	0	0
733	PARAMORE	JUNIOR	27/05/1996	02/08/1996	5	6	11	3	0	0	12
50	PARKER	EDWARD	11/01/1928	11/01/1928	1	0	1	0	0	0	0
305	PARKER	HARRY	25/12/1948	22/11/1952	46	0	46	9	0	0	27
182	PARKER	JAMES	30/09/1939	14/04/1941	3	0	3	0	0	0	0
491	PARKER	RICHARD	07/04/1965	30/04/1966	5	2	7	0	0	0	0
919	PARKER	ROB	06/07/2011	10/09/2011	6	2	8	2	0	0	8
967	PATRICK	LARNE	24/04/2016		16	1	17	1	0	0	4
860	PAYNE	JASON	13/08/2006	22/04/2007	2	3	5	0	0	0	0
649	PAYNE	PHILIP	19/01/1986	22/04/1986	15	0	15	3	0	0	12
51	PEARCE	GEORGE	14/01/1928	21/01/1928	2	0	2	0	0	0	0
370	PEASE	KENNETH	14/08/1954	18/08/1954	2	0	2	0	0	0	0
198	PENNINGTON	ERIC	07/09/1940	20/09/1941	28	0	28	5	0	0	15
356	PERRETT	MAURICE	15/04/1953	07/01/1956	25	0	25	0	0	0	0
336	PETCHER	TREVOR	27/10/1951	17/11/1951	4	0	4	0	0	0	0
132	PHILLIPS	JAMES	13/01/1934	13/01/1934	1	0	1	0	0	0	0
574	PICKERILL	CLIVE	17/10/1975	30/03/1978	27	8	35	4	0	0	12
760	PICKERING	JAMES	26/02/1999	03/10/1999	2	21	23	0	0	0	0
553	PINCHER	STEPHEN	22/12/1972	22/12/1972	0	1	1	0	0	0	0
635	PLANGE	DAVID	30/01/1985	14/04/1991	191	2	193	98	5	0	402
820	PLATT	MICHAEL	13/02/2005	16/09/2006	55	0	55	23	0	0	92
39	PLIMMER	JAMES	22/01/1927	07/09/1935	158	0	158	1	0	0	3
128	POLLITT	JOHN	15/09/1933	06/02/1937	31	0	31	1	58	0	119
878	POTTER	GRAIG	11/03/2007	11/03/2007	0	1	1	0	0	0	0
70	POWELL	JAMES	29/03/1929	21/03/1931	12	0	12	0	0	0	0
214 G	POWELL	STAN (St Helens/C.P.)	13/09/1941	15/10/1949	26	0	26	7	12	0	45
676	PRICE	DARREN	10/09/1989	04/02/1990	4	3	7	1	0	0	4
717	PRICE	SIMON	05/02/1995	21/01/1996	4	0	4	0	0	0	0
317	PRITCHARD	WILLIAM T.	18/02/1950	18/02/1950	1	0	1	0	0	0	0
770	PRYCE	WAINE	27/08/2000	08/07/2006	128	12	140	81	0	0	324
764	PURCELL	ANDREW	13/02/2000	23/09/2000	16	6	22	4	0	0	16

PLAYERS CAREER STATISTICS UPTO AND INCLUDING SEASON 2016 IN ALPHABETICAL ORDER

D,N:		PLAYER		DEBUT	L. MATCH	APP	SUB	T.AP	TR'S	G'LS	D.G	PTS
600		PYE	GARY	12/11/1978	12/11/1978	1	0	1	0	0	0	0
422		PYE	JEFFREY	23/11/1957	02/01/1960	14	0	14	2	0	0	6
342		PYE	JOSHUA J.	11/04/1952	13/10/1956	79	0	79	3	1	0	11
330		PYE	KENNETH	21/04/1951	01/09/1962	344	0	344	70	0	0	210
790		RAINEY	ADRIAN	19/05/2002	11/08/2002	4	7	11	1	0	0	4
758		RAPER	AARON	14/02/1999	05/05/2001	55	4	59	7	2	1	33
57		RAYNOR	PERCY	31/03/1928	31/03/1928	1	0	1	0	0	0	0
388		RAYNOR	RAYMOND	27/12/1955	10/03/1956	7	0	7	0	0	0	0
494		REDFEARN	MICHAEL	27/11/1965	25/01/1977	291	29	320	26	375	20	868
254	G	REES	FRANK (R'dale)	18/11/1944	18/11/1944	1	0	1	0	0	0	0
821		REID	DAMIEN	13/02/2005	10/07/2005	15	1	16	9	0	0	36
512		REILLY	MALCOLM	30/09/1967	06/04/1986	294	22	316	68	6	7	230
204		RENNARD	JOSEPH	12/10/1940	25/10/1941	16	0	16	11	0	0	33
10		RENTON	WILLIAM	28/08/1926	24/11/1928	89	0	89	4	0	0	12
941		REYNOLDS	BEN	01/09/2013	15/08/2014	1	3	4	0	0	0	0
566		RHODES	ALAN	04/01/1975	25/04/1975	11	2	13	2	0	0	6
375		RHODES	EDWARD	29/01/1955	15/09/1956	25	0	25	1	0	0	3
447		RHODES	KENNETH	14/11/1959	14/11/1959	1	0	1	0	0	0	0
390		RICHARDSON	FRED	14/01/1956	03/03/1956	5	0	5	1	0	0	3
726		RICHARDSON	SHAUN	07/01/1996	26/05/1997	3	11	14	1	0	0	4
556		RICHARDSON	TERRY	15/12/1973	24/04/1983	233	4	237	102	0	0	306
807		RIPLEY	DEAN	02/04/2004	09/07/2004	3	3	6	1	0	0	4
289		RIPLEY	COLIN	20/05/1947	20/05/1947	1	0	1	0	0	0	0
738		ROACH	JASON	09/02/1997	27/07/1997	11	1	12	6	0	0	24
623		ROACHE	MARK	19/12/1982	26/12/1984	20	0	20	5	0	0	19
851		ROARTY	BEN	10/02/2006	23/07/2005	11	6	17	2	0	0	8
592		ROBBINS	GARY	23/04/1978	25/03/1979	1	1	2	0	0	0	0
955		ROBERTS	BEN	14/02/2015		23	8	31	10	0	2	42
27		ROBERTS	OWEN	02/10/1926	02/10/1926	1	0	1	0	0	0	0
91		ROBINSON	DONALD	26/03/1930	30/08/1930	3	0	3	1	0	0	3
158		ROBINSON	GILBERT	19/09/1936	10/10/1936	2	0	2	0	0	0	0
358		ROBINSON	J	20/04/1953	28/04/1953	2	0	2	0	0	0	0
177		ROBINSON	JAMES	12/11/1938	21/02/1948	157	0	157	25	3	0	81
814		ROBINSON	LUKE	23/05/2004	18/07/2004	9	0	9	4	3	0	22
279		ROBINSON	MAXWELL	23/02/1946	08/01/1949	27	0	27	0	0	0	0
629		ROBINSON	STEVEN	01/02/1984	12/05/1984	15	0	15	5	0	0	20
831		ROBINSON	TIM	06/03/2005	17/04/2005	2	2	4	2	0	0	8
957		ROBSON	ASH	26/04/2015	25/09/2015	3	0	3	1	0	0	4
683		ROEBUCK	NEIL	26/12/1989	11/10/1992	37	25	62	11	0	2	46
757		ROGERS	DAREN	14/02/1999	19/09/2004	177	1	178	89	0	0	356
625		ROOCKLEY	DAVID	10/04/1983	09/04/1989	135	24	159	43	25	2	224
73		ROOKES	WALTER	13/04/1929	13/04/1929	1	0	1	0	0	0	0
780		ROONEY	JAMIE	12/08/2001	26/08/2001	2	1	3	0	6	0	12
775		ROPER	JONATHON	11/02/2001	16/09/2001	13	1	14	7	12	0	52
88		ROSSER	MEL	15/02/1930	15/02/1930	1	0	1	0	0	0	0
730		ROUND	PAUL	14/04/1996	16/06/1996	0	3	3	0	0	0	0
836		ROWE	ALEX	25/03/2005	17/04/2005	1	3	4	0	0	0	0
457		ROWE	BRIAN	07/01/1961	01/05/1961	12	0	12	0	0	0	0
315		ROWLEY	LESLIE	17/12/1949	16/04/1951	7	0	7	1	0	0	3
803		RUDDER	SEAN	22/02/2004	20/06/2004	11	3	14	3	0	0	12
45		RUSHWORTH	A.R.	27/08/1927	22/10/1927	4	0	4	0	0	0	0
46		RUSSELL	BEN	03/09/1927	29/10/1927	3	0	3	0	0	0	0
14		RUSSELL	HARRY (DANNY)	01/09/1926	10/03/1934	226	0	226	8	0	0	24
705		RUSSELL	RICHARD	27/08/1993	20/09/1998	117	5	122	13	0	0	52
806		RYAN	SEAN	22/02/2004	04/07/2004	13	5	18	2	0	0	8
253	G	RYLANCE	RON (W'field)	11/11/1944	11/11/1944	1	0	1	2	1	0	8
134		SADLER	EDWARD L.	03/02/1934	08/06/1940	185	0	185	54	0	0	162
590		SAMPSON	DAVID	22/01/1978	05/10/1980	23	5	28	0	0	0	0
661		SAMPSON	DEAN	30/08/1987	13/03/2005	330	102	432	69	0	0	276
648		SANDY	JAMIE	20/10/1985	03/05/1986	17	1	18	4	0	0	16
890		SARGENT	MITCHELL	03/08/2008	04/09/2010	39	22	61	6	0	0	24
971		SAVELIO	ANDRE	24/07/2016		6	1	7	1	0	0	4
791		SAXTON	TOMMY	21/06/2002	24/06/2007	56	13	69	22	0	1	89

PLAYERS CAREER STATISTICS UPTO AND INCLUDING SEASON 2016 IN ALPHABETICAL ORDER

D,N:		PLAYER		DEBUT	L. MATCH	APP	SUB	T.AP	TR'S	G'LS	D.G	PTS
451		SAYER	BERT	06/02/1960	03/04/1961	30	0	30	1	0	0	3
723		SCHICK	ANDREW	06/09/1995	27/09/1998	66	20	86	18	0	0	72
409		SCHOFIELD	DERRICK	24/11/1956	01/03/1958	37	0	37	3	4	0	17
165		SCHOFIELD	ERNEST	01/05/1937	01/05/1937	1	0	1	0	0	0	0
654		SCOTT	COLIN	01/10/1986	22/03/1987	25	0	25	10	8	1	57
847		SCULTHORPE	DANNY	10/02/2006	16/09/2006	18	1	19	4	0	1	17
256	G	SEARLES	PERCY (F'tone)	18/11/1944	18/11/1944	1	0	1	0	0	0	0
309		SENIOR	ARTHUR	22/01/1949	30/04/1949	3	0	3	0	0	0	0
52		SHAW	ALBERT	21/01/1928	21/01/1928	1	0	1	0	0	0	0
766		SHAW	DARREN	13/02/2000	16/09/2001	51	9	60	1	0	0	4
527		SHAW	LESLIE	22/11/1969	05/10/1973	16	2	18	1	0	0	3
539		SHEARD	LESLIE	26/02/1971	30/10/1971	9	0	9	0	1	0	2
307		SHEEHY	DANNY	28/12/1948	15/01/1949	4	0	4	1	0	0	3
871		SHENTON	ALEX	11/03/2007	11/03/2007	1	0	1	2	0	0	8
810		SHENTON	MICHAEL	01/05/2004		239	2	241	130	0	0	520
576		SHEPPARD	TOM	29/11/1975	14/03/1976	6	2	8	4	0	0	12
382		SHERIDAN	JOHN	20/08/1955	20/11/1965	300	1	301	86	2	1	264
804		SHERIDAN	RYAN	22/02/2004	14/03/2004	4	0	4	0	0	0	0
883		SHERWIN	BRENT	09/02/2008	16/05/2010	51	1	52	5	1	4	26
62		SHERWOOD	ARTHUR	15/09/1928	19/04/1934	183	0	183	8	9	0	42
17		SHERWOOD	THOMAS	04/09/1926	12/11/1927	26	0	26	1	0	0	3
26	G	SHERWOOD	WILLIAM (C.P./F'tone)	25/09/1926	26/04/1941	5	0	5	1	0	0	3
59		SHERWOOD	WILLIAM	01/09/1928	01/09/1928	1	0	1	0	0	0	0
645		SHILLITO	ALAN	01/09/1985	06/12/1987	40	12	52	3	0	0	12
633		SIGSWORTH	RON	23/09/1984	10/04/1985	21	6	27	11	0	0	44
343		SIMPSON	PETER	26/08/1952	11/02/1956	48	0	48	2	0	0	6
2		SKELTON	WILLIAM	28/08/1926	23/04/1927	11	0	11	0	0	0	0
798		SKERRETT	BEN	11/05/2003	11/05/2003	0	1	1	0	0	0	0
295		SKIDMORE	LEONARD	15/11/1947	19/04/1949	66	0	66	9	0	0	27
184		SLATER	HARRY	30/09/1939	03/10/1946	23	0	23	1	0	0	3
652		SLATER	MARTIN	31/08/1986	31/08/1986	1	0	1	0	0	0	0
460		SLATTER	KEITH	22/04/1961	04/12/1965	38	3	41	2	0	0	6
706		SMALES	IAN	27/08/1993	25/08/1997	71	24	95	16	0	0	64
443		SMALES	THOMAS	08/04/1959	25/04/1959	4	0	4	0	0	0	0
438		SMALL	PETER	26/12/1958	17/01/1969	310	5	315	109	0	0	327
364		SMART	DEREK	17/10/1953	29/08/1959	84	0	84	50	0	0	150
826		SMITH	AARON	13/02/2005	17/02/2006	23	2	25	1	0	0	4
811		SMITH	BYRON	01/05/2004	02/10/2005	8	26	34	0	0	0	0
699		SMITH	CHRIS	20/09/1992	19/09/1997	105	4	109	42	0	0	168
468		SMITH	FRANK Jnr	29/09/1962	26/09/1964	45	0	45	25	0	0	75
124		SMITH	FRANK Snr	29/10/1932	20/05/1947	282	0	282	42	13	0	152
783		SMITH	GARY	09/09/2001	09/09/2001	0	1	1	0	0	0	0
145		SMITH	HERBERT	08/04/1935	27/04/1935	3	0	3	0	0	0	0
501		SMITH	JAMES	02/09/1966	31/03/1967	2	0	2	0	0	0	0
750		SMITH	MICHAEL	14/02/1998	19/09/2004	92	38	130	34	0	0	136
589		SMITH	NIGEL	18/12/1977	26/02/1978	2	0	2	0	0	0	0
744		SMITH	PAUL	01/04/1997	23/09/2000	6	38	44	3	0	0	12
407		SMITH	TERENCE	20/10/1956	03/11/1956	3	0	3	1	0	0	3
679		SMITH	TONY	27/09/1989	16/03/1997	173	22	195	90	0	0	360
89		SMITH	WILLIAM	15/03/1930	18/04/1930	3	0	3	1	0	0	3
942		SNEYD	MARC	16/02/2014	25/09/2014	29	2	31	7	116	2	262
902		SNITCH	STEVE	05/02/2010	09/09/2012	41	19	60	12	0	0	48
639		SNOWDEN	SEAN	08/04/1985	14/04/1985	2	0	2	0	0	0	0
951		SOLOMONA	DENNY	03/02/2015		44	0	44	60	0	0	240
669		SOUTHERNWOOD	GRAHAM	30/10/1988	02/05/1993	80	3	83	12	0	1	49
650		SOUTHERNWOOD	ROY	29/01/1986	20/01/1990	38	20	58	9	0	0	36
95		SPAWFORTH	HAROLD	13/09/1930	06/04/1931	6	0	6	0	0	0	0
776		SPEAK	ANDY	09/05/2001	08/07/2001	4	4	8	0	0	0	0
801		SPEARS	TIM	27/07/2003	24/08/2008	0	3	3	0	0	0	0
643		SPEARS	TONY	01/09/1985	04/03/1987	23	7	30	6	0	0	24
616		SPEDDING	PAUL	01/11/1981	08/01/1984	15	12	27	0	0	0	0
960		SPRINGER	GADWIN	05/07/2015		8	23	31	2	0	0	8
518		SPURR	ROBERT	10/01/1969	06/03/1983	299	24	323	45	0	0	135

D,N:		PLAYER		DEBUT	L. MATCH	APP	SUB	T.AP	TR'S	G'LS	D.G	PTS
743		ST HILAIRE	LEE	16/03/1997	23/05/1997	4	2	6	0	0	0	0
77		STAFFORD	GEORGE	03/09/1929	24/12/1932	95	0	95	11	0	0	33
172		STAINES	CHARLES	29/01/1938	06/09/1950	170	0	170	36	83	0	274
347		STANILAND	ARTHUR	13/12/1952	03/03/1956	72	0	72	23	0	0	69
168		STEAD	WILLIAM	16/10/1937	29/08/1945	73	0	73	9	0	0	27
675		STEADMAN	GRAHAM	03/09/1989	19/09/1997	209	28	237	121	174	8	840
492		STENTON	IAN	02/10/1965	17/10/1972	130	8	138	37	14	3	145
514		STEPHENS	DAVID	03/02/1968	12/09/1969	39	1	40	11	0	0	33
710		STEPHENS	GARETH	21/08/1994	04/02/1996	20	4	24	1	0	0	4
525		STEPHENS	GARY	10/10/1969	19/10/1980	262	10	272	78	0	4	240
113		STOBART	J J	28/11/1931	25/12/1931	5	0	5	0	0	0	0
56		STONES	SAMMY	31/03/1928	30/08/1930	52	0	52	4	4	1	22
293		STOREY	GEORGE	11/10/1947	22/12/1951	11	0	11	0	0	0	0
250	G	STOTT	WILLIAM (BILLY) (W'ld)	11/11/1944	10/02/1945	2	0	2	2	3	0	12
197		STREET	JACK	07/09/1940	29/09/1945	25	0	25	1	0	0	3
264	G	SWEETING	SAM (Hull)	02/04/1945	02/04/1945	1	0	1	0	0	0	0
694		SYKES	NATHAN	15/09/1991	19/09/2004	196	95	291	8	0	0	32
33		SYLVESTER	HARRY	20/11/1926	22/09/1928	28	0	28	3	0	0	9
751		TALLEC	GAEL	14/02/1998	12/09/1999	22	25	47	4	0	0	16
932		TANSEY	JORDAN	03/02/2013	05/06/2015	47	1	48	16	0	0	64
211		TAYLOR	B	01/03/1941	01/03/1941	1	0	1	0	0	0	0
406		TAYLOR	COLIN	06/10/1956	25/01/1964	78	0	78	7	0	0	21
15		TAYLOR	HARRY	04/09/1926	23/10/1926	3	0	3	1	0	0	3
329		TAYLOR	JACK	07/04/1951	29/08/1951	2	0	2	0	0	0	0
487		TAYLOR	JOHN	21/11/1964	27/03/1967	61	3	64	8	0	0	24
288		TAYLOR	LEONARD	29/04/1947	07/05/1947	2	0	2	0	0	0	0
597		TAYLOR	PETER	01/10/1978	01/03/1980	3	3	6	1	0	0	3
440		TAYLOR	ROBERT	31/01/1959	30/04/1960	32	0	32	18	0	0	54
163		TAYLOR	ROBERT M	20/03/1937	01/05/1937	8	0	8	0	0	0	0
116		TAYLOR	THOMAS L	19/03/1932	03/04/1946	388	0	388	17	0	0	51
484		TERRY	ABE	03/10/1964	01/04/1966	58	0	58	0	0	0	0
881		THACKERAY	ANTHONY	22/07/2007	28/06/2008	12	7	19	8	0	0	32
796		THACKRAY	JAMIE	08/02/2003	09/05/2004	7	14	21	5	0	0	20
792		THALER	ADAM	26/07/2002	26/07/2008	0	1	1	0	0	0	0
64		THOMAS	EDWIN	20/10/1928	01/10/1932	40	0	40	8	0	0	24
151		THOMAS	HAROLD	08/02/1936	15/02/1936	2	0	2	2	0	0	6
268		THOMAS	JAMES	29/08/1945	15/09/1945	2	0	2	0	0	0	0
506		THOMAS	TONY	04/02/1967	30/01/1971	128	8	136	28	0	0	84
901		THOMPSON	JORDAN	12/06/2009	08/03/2013	50	27	77	27	0	0	108
276		THORNBURROW	JIM	02/02/1946	16/02/1946	3	0	3	0	0	0	0
353		THORNLEY	HARRY	03/04/1953	23/11/1957	27	0	27	1	0	0	3
325		THORNTON	DENNIS	27/01/1951	09/04/1951	10	0	10	0	0	0	0
311		THORNTON	REG	22/10/1949	22/10/1949	1	0	1	0	0	0	0
656		THORNTON	WAYNE	04/03/1987	08/11/1989	3	7	10	0	0	0	0
969		TICKLE	DANNY	07/05/2016	17/07/2016	6	5	11	0	1	0	2
607		TIMSON	ANDY	07/10/1979	14/04/1985	79	19	98	28	0	0	86
420		TONKINSON	ALBERT	28/09/1957	11/01/1964	157	0	157	8	0	0	24
715		TONKS	IAN	27/11/1994	08/07/2001	40	56	96	12	19	0	86
815		TONY	MOTU	06/06/2004	31/07/2004	8	1	9	1	0	0	4
817		TOOKEY	MARK	18/07/2004	19/09/2004	2	8	10	1	0	0	4
76		TOOTLES	THOMAS	03/09/1929	14/09/1929	3	0	3	0	0	0	0
236	G	TOWILL	IDRIS (H'field)	25/04/1942	02/05/1942	2	0	2	0	0	0	0
185		TOWNSLEY	HARRY	21/10/1939	18/04/1949	12	0	12	1	0	0	3
7		TREVIS	ARTHUR	28/08/1926	18/01/1930	88	0	88	8	0	0	24
499		TUCKER	DAVID	15/08/1966	30/11/1968	23	3	26	1	0	0	3
142		TURNER	HAROLD	19/09/1934	22/09/1934	2	0	2	0	0	0	0
223	G	TURTON	RONALD (Hunslet)	14/02/1942	14/02/1942	1	0	1	0	0	0	0
906		TUSON	CHRIS	26/03/2010	23/05/2010	2	6	8	0	0	0	0
724		TUUTA	BRENDON	17/09/1995	19/07/1997	52	8	60	4	0	0	16
567		TYREMAN	GRAHAM	15/02/1975	13/05/1979	29	13	42	3	0	0	9
432		UMPLEBY	PETER	30/08/1958	06/09/1958	2	0	2	0	0	0	0
534		VAN BELLEN	IAN	29/09/1970	25/02/1973	52	2	54	11	5	3	49
845		VIANE	GRAY	10/02/2006	16/09/2006	20	7	27	14	0	0	56

PLAYERS CAREER STATISTICS UPTO AND INCLUDING SEASON 2016 IN ALPHABETICAL ORDER

D,N:	PLAYER		DEBUT	L. MATCH	APP	SUB	T.AP	TR'S	G'LS	D.G	PTS
739	VOWLES	ADRIAN	09/02/1997	09/10/2005	144	4	148	33	1	1	135
500	WADDLE	PETER	29/08/1966	20/10/1967	2	1	3	0	0	0	0
112	WADSWORTH	FRED	26/09/1931	15/04/1933	16	0	16	3	0	0	9
194	WAGSTAFF	FRANK	07/09/1940	21/04/1945	68	0	68	7	0	0	21
282	WAGSTAFF	KENNETH	27/04/1946	27/04/1946	1	0	1	0	0	0	0
861	WAINWRIGHT	MICHAEL	11/02/2007	04/09/2010	103	1	104	40	0	0	160
455	WALKER	JOHN	19/11/1960	01/12/1967	210	10	220	27	0	0	81
909	WALKER	JONATHAN	04/06/2010	21/07/2013	18	32	50	4	0	0	16
74	WALKER	JOSEPH	20/04/1929	14/09/2029	5	0	5	0	0	1	2
148	WALKER	FRANK	19/10/1935	29/11/1941	146	0	146	51	113	0	379
545	WALLIS	CLIFF	31/12/1971	03/02/1974	74	2	76	12	0	4	44
412	WALSH	BARRY	26/01/1957	24/02/1962	85	0	85	29	0	0	87
563	WALSH	JAMIE	29/11/1974	22/11/1981	51	12	63	16	1	0	50
535	WALSH	JOHN	02/10/1970	05/10/1971	15	2	17	2	0	0	6
159	WALSH	THOMAS	24/10/1936	23/02/1946	112	0	112	26	20	5	128
326	WALTER	RONALD	27/01/1951	02/11/1957	44	0	44	4	0	0	12
469	WALTON	DOUGLAS	03/11/1962	31/12/1971	113	0	113	12	2	0	40
23	WALTON	RICHARD	11/09/1926	08/06/1940	208	0	208	9	0	0	27
852	WARD	DANNY	10/02/2006	16/09/2006	18	7	25	2	0	0	8
533	WARD	DENIS	04/05/1970	04/05/1970	1	0	1	0	0	0	0
366	WARD	ERNEST	28/11/1953	26/12/1955	78	0	78	9	153	1	335
349	WARD	FRED	14/02/1953	07/12/1957	152	0	152	37	0	0	111
414	WARD	GEOFFREY G	02/02/1957	24/09/1965	235	1	236	60	1	0	182
226	G WARD	J (R'dale)	14/03/1942	06/04/1942	5	0	5	2	0	0	6
303	WARD	JEFF	13/11/1948	15/10/1949	29	0	29	10	0	0	30
140	WARD	JOHN	25/08/1934	13/04/1935	15	0	15	4	14	2	44
453	WARD	JOHNNY	23/08/1960	16/01/1970	259	3	262	42	0	3	132
603	WARD	KEVIN	14/03/1979	22/04/1990	301	12	313	74	0	0	249
241	WARD	LEN	16/09/1944	17/02/1945	14	0	14	10	0	0	30
480	WARD	ROY	27/05/1964	19/08/1967	19	2	21	1	0	0	3
287	WARD	SIDNEY	29/04/1947	03/04/1948	8	0	8	0	0	0	0
482	WARING	TREVOR	03/10/1964	05/11/1966	8	0	8	4	0	0	12
787	WARREN	KYLE	24/02/2002	28/09/2002	13	17	30	3	0	0	12
213	G WARRIOR	DENNIS (Leeds)	14/04/1941	14/04/1941	1	0	1	0	0	0	0
823	WATENE	ADAM	13/02/2005	09/10/2005	26	2	28	6	0	0	24
827	WATENE	FRANK	13/02/2005	09/10/2005	7	17	24	5	0	0	20
697	WATSON	CHRIS	22/03/1992	09/01/1994	15	0	15	1	0	0	4
877	WATTS	LIAM	11/03/2007	11/03/2007	0	1	1	1	0	0	4
352	WEBSTER	DENZIL	14/03/1953	06/10/1956	98	0	98	63	0	0	189
934	WEBSTER	JAKE	03/02/2013		62	9	71	28	0	0	112
734	WELLS	JON	16/06/1996	28/09/2002	121	18	139	51	0	0	204
334	WELSBY	HAROLD	10/09/1951	22/08/1955	58	0	58	0	0	0	0
869	WESTERMAN	JOE	11/02/2007	04/09/2010	81	22	103	43	175	0	522
585	WESTON	ALF	24/04/1977	11/12/1977	16	3	19	3	0	0	9
72	WHARVILLE	HERBERT	01/04/1929	01/04/2029	1	0	1	0	0	0	0
944	WHEELDON	SCOTT	16/02/2014	25/09/2015	16	26	42	6	0	0	24
156	WHELAN	ROBERT	04/05/1936	04/05/1936	1	0	1	0	0	0	0
849	WHITAKER	MATTHEW	10/02/2006	28/05/2006	9	2	11	0	0	0	0
681	WHITEHEAD	PAUL	03/10/1989	17/03/1992	0	2	2	0	0	0	0
357	WHITEHEAD	TERENCE	18/04/1953	18/04/1953	1	0	1	0	0	0	0
67	WHITEHOUSE	HERBERT	24/11/1928	01/12/1928	2	0	2	0	0	0	0
181	WHITHAM	CYRIL	30/09/1939	15/02/1941	15	0	15	1	0	0	3
296	WHITTLESTONE	THOMAS	13/12/1947	30/04/1949	11	0	11	0	0	0	0
899	WIDDERS	DEAN	15/02/2009	10/09/2011	27	33	60	23	0	0	92
486	WILLETT	RONALD	31/10/1964	25/04/1969	126	2	128	37	284	0	679
170	WILLIAMS	CYRIL	20/11/1937	15/04/1938	23	0	23	5	0	0	15
880	WILLIAMS	DANNY	22/07/2007	07/10/2007	9	0	9	10	0	0	40
700	WILLIAMS	DEAN	27/09/1992	27/09/1992	0	1	1	0	0	0	0
396	WILLIAMS	HARRY	31/03/1956	10/09/1957	17	0	17	0	2	0	4
169	WILLIAMS	ILLTYD (Tubby)	23/10/1937	05/11/1938	9	0	9	2	0	0	6
129	WILLIAMS	J H	30/09/1933	30/09/1933	1	0	1	0	0	0	0
464	WILLIAMS	MAURICE	28/04/1962	02/01/1965	16	0	16	0	0	0	0
928	WILLIAMS	RHYS	26/05/2012	05/08/2012	8	0	8	4	0	0	16

PLAYERS CAREER STATISTICS UPTO AND INCLUDING SEASON 2016 IN ALPHABETICAL ORDER

D,N:	PLAYER		DEBUT	L. MATCH	APP	SUB	T.AP	TR'S	G'LS	D.G	PTS
405	WILMOT	ARTHUR	29/09/1956	24/08/1957	16	0	16	0	0	0	0
445	WILSON	JOHN	17/10/1959	29/10/1960	27	0	27	4	0	0	12
28	WILSON	JOHN (LINA)	09/10/1926	09/10/1926	1	0	1	0	0	0	0
632	WILSON	NIGEL	16/09/1984	12/04/1985	19	4	23	4	0	0	16
376	WINN	BRIAN	29/01/1955	02/04/1955	2	0	2	1	0	0	3
379	WINN	JOHN	02/04/1955	15/09/1956	17	0	17	1	0	0	3
107	WINN	JOHN WILLIAM	29/08/1931	12/09/1931	3	0	3	1	0	0	3
83	WINSTANLEY	JOHN	26/10/1929	18/10/1930	8	0	8	0	0	0	0
93	WINSTANLEY	THOMAS	12/04/1930	12/04/1930	1	0	1	0	0	0	0
335	WINTERBOTTOM	FRED	10/09/1951	22/12/1951	14	0	14	0	0	0	0
103	WOOD	HERBERT	11/04/1931	11/04/1931	1	0	1	0	0	0	0
908	WOOD	KYLE	23/05/2010	27/06/2010	1	4	5	0	0	0	0
548	WOODALL	DEREK	27/02/1972	01/03/1980	43	13	56	0	0	0	0
60	WOODALL	HARRY	01/09/1928	05/09/1928	2	0	2	0	0	0	0
313	WOOLFORD	CYRIL	17/12/1949	16/01/1954	67	0	67	14	0	0	42
391	WOOLLEY	JACK	25/02/1956	03/03/1956	2	0	2	0	0	0	0
12	WORMALD	JACK	28/08/1926	25/12/1929	92	0	92	4	0	0	12
812	WORRINCY	ROB	09/05/2004	25/03/2005	1	1	2	0	0	0	0
541	WORSLEY	KEITH	30/07/1971	09/11/1979	142	11	153	49	0	0	147
572	WRAITH	GEOFFREY	24/09/1975	06/03/1983	203	13	216	42	0	0	126
68	WRAITH	WILLIAM	24/11/1928	26/12/1928	5	0	5	1	0	0	3
689	WRAY	JON	01/01/1991	12/02/1995	54	1	55	14	0	0	56
423	WRIGHT	CHARLIE	30/11/1957	30/03/1959	38	0	38	5	0	0	15
767	WRIGHT	CRAIG	05/03/2000	11/08/2000	1	9	10	0	0	0	0
543	WRIGHT	GEOFF	30/08/1971	30/08/1971	0	1	1	0	0	0	0
127	YOUNG	HAROLD	09/09/1933	11/11/1933	7	0	7	1	0	0	3
912	YOUNGQUEST	NICK	13/02/2011	09/09/2012	40	0	40	29	2	0	120
	49	972			44109	4378	48487	10477	9887	307	56345

The Castleford Tigers Heritage Project

The Castleford Tigers Heritage project was made possible with funding from a Heritage Lottery grant. The project came about through the concern that as the Club looks towards a new purpose-built stadium, some of the history and heritage of Weldon Road may be lost. The project aimed also to tie in with the 90th anniversary of the Club.

With a lot of community backing from supporters, the Club, other local organisations, Castleford Heritage Trust, Castleford Museum, and local activists and Councillors, the Heritage Project began in September 2015. Overseen by Tigers Trust, One to One Development Trust were brought on board to work with volunteers to create a 'Virtual Museum'. A core group of volunteers were recruited to help shape the project and bring in their expertise.

Key supporters of the Heritage Project are the Garbett family who - for four generations - have been an important part of the Club's history. Brothers Roy and Ian have contributed greatly to the Heritage Project by providing excellent records and documentation about the Club and its players since its inception.

Their father Len Garbett, a prolific and well-respected figure at the Club kept detailed logs of matches and players. After his sad passing, Len's Grandson Martin started putting these records into digital format for a database. The family have continued to keep excellent records of the Club and some of these have been subsequently developed for inclusion into the Heritage Project.

Roy and Ian Garbett

The Volunteer Group have been instrumental to the success of the project. A good mix of ages and genders, the group represents the 'family feel' and passionate dedication of fans from the Club. Some members have developed their own personal collections and archives of memorabilia. These have been kindly contributed to the project.
The group have taken on a wide range of tasks including research, curation of

The Castleford Tigers Heritage Project

exhibitions, promotion of the project, audio and video interviews, scanning, entering information into the database and contributing to the look, design and the overall feel of the project. As the project has developed, the group has developed w th it. Now, at the end of the project they are a focused team of people with a common aim of gathering the heritage of this great Club and making it as accessible as possible for future generations. The group have worked very hard, along the way there has been much debate, and a lot of fun.

Sessions were run at the Club, often in the Tiger Bar. They were open to everyone and advertised through the Club and on social media. At times, the amount of material that was available seemed overwhelming. People would arrive with box loads of press cuttings and memorabilia; bin liners of material would be delivered to the Tigers Community office. It was agreed that we would prioritise processing the vast and immediate collections within the core Volunteer Group.

Throughout the project, Castleford Library and Museum offered their support by providing a space where sessions could be run encouraging people to use their records. The museum holds a dedicated exhibition space for Castleford Tigers, and the artefacts and film were updated as part of this project with a midway celebration event. The support of the Library and Museum staff is much appreciated and has really added valuable help to the project.
A photography competition was launched to extend the reach of the project and increase the themes within the Museum. In bitterly cold weather on Boxing Day,

The Castleford Tigers Heritage Project

volunteers promoted the project to fans at a home game. Some great entries were submitted and winners chosen in six categories. Players Michael Shenton and Grant Millington helped judge the competition and the Club awarded prizes to the winners.

Heritage Project Photo Competition Winners

The aim of the project was to create a virtual museum as a space that could hold all the information donated to the project.

A database driven 'Memory Box' was built with extensive search facilities. Volunteer members were trained in updating the database and using it to check the information being uploaded.

As the project has grown, so has the memory box, which currently includes articles written by the group, photographs, press cuttings, scrapbooks, artwork, posters, programmes, artefacts, audio files and films. The memory box can continue to be updated in the future, it is very accessible and can be accessed on computer, tablet devices and phones.

The Castleford Tigers Heritage Project

Photographc Competion Judging Panel

As the project was originally designed to tie in with the new opening of the new stadium (sadly like many large scale development projec:s the timescale has been delayed) the brief was to also create a showcase of the project to include in the new stadium. The Virtual Museum is the showcase.

Designed used game engine technology, the virtual museum is a dedicated online environment laid out like a real museum. The user navigates through it like a video game. There are zones holding different exhibitions, film galleries and interactive experiences like a rugby ball to play with, a spinning glooe showing where players come from across the world, and a lift with players signatures etched into the wall that takes you to a second floor.

The Castleford Tigers Heritage Project

The Virtual Museum is available for download and can be used for projection/large scale display, navigated by keyboard/mouse or a gamepad controller. The Virtual Museum will be sited for installation in the new stadium. It is also possible to explore the Museum through virtual reality using a headset such as the Oculus Rift.

At this stage in technology development within heritage, this piece of work is very cutting edge, particularly in its methodology of involving 'non-tech' people in its

The Castleford Tigers Heritage Project

creation and curation.

The Heritage Project has been a privilege to be involved with. I believe there is a duty to not just to preserve heritage, but to make it accessible, informative and fun for audiences now and in the future — you can never tell the full story as everyone has their own memories and interpretations of the past — but you can try and preserve information in a way that captures the 'spirit' of a place or community. I hope that the Castleford Tigers Heritage project has succeeded in that.

1939 Seven a side competitio Castleford and Leeds teams

Wheldon Road has an amazing history, it's story is full of colour and passion, of characters and drama. There is strength, resilience and great humour in its heritage. As the fans sing their heart out to the adopted club anthem 'Sweet Caroline' even the hardest of Yorkshire spirits couldn't help feel moved by the camaraderie and pass on of the Cas fans.

The Castleford Tigers Heritage Project

There are too many people to thank individually for their contributions to this project, but the Club, it's associated member organisations, past and current players who've supported the project, photographers (amateur and professional) and collectors who've donated material have all been very supportive and given invaluable insight.

Thank you to Steve Ball of Tigers Trust for his vision and commitment in getting the heritage project off the ground, and bringing us in to work on it.
Thank you to my colleagues at One to One Development Trust whose commitment in creating high quality heritage projects
has excelled itself. Speaking on behalf of my team, we are all incredibly proud to be involved with Castleford Tigers and of this project.
The biggest thank you however must go to the fans, especially the Volunteers who've supported this project, their enthusiasm, knowledge and commitment has been truly outstanding.
Judi Alston
One to One Development Trust June 2017

www.onetoonedevelopment.org

For more information about Castleford Tigers Heritage Project, and to search the Memory Box and explore the Virtual Museum please visit

www.castigersheritage.com

A SELECTION OF SPONSORS OF THE CLUB THROUGHOUT THE YEARS

"WARDONIA"
FOR BETTER SHAVES
WARDONIA
"BARREL-HOLE" BLADE
SHEFFIELD - ENGLAND

The Chocolate Box
Carlton Street

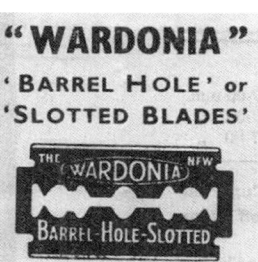

"WARDONIA"
'BARREL HOLE' or
'SLOTTED BLADES'
WARDONIA
BARREL-HOLE-SLOTTED

Stanley Hirst Butchers

DARLEY'S GOLD MEDAL ALES

Can be obtained from the following Houses—
CASTLEFORD
Miners' Arms - Prop. C. H. Fereday
George & Dragon „ B. Teale
Garden House - „ J. Farrar
Golden Cock - „ A. Caswell
Wheldale Hotel „ G. Prince
Hightown Hotel „ C. Parkin
Lancs. & Yorks. „ R. Macfarlane
4, Lumley Street „ L. H. Fitton
NORMANTON
Good Hope Inn „ J. Machin
Junction Inn - „ J. H. Thomas

Co-operative Society Ltd.
SPORTS DEPT

Bp
BRADFORD PERMANENT
BUILDING SOCIETY
Local Agents
HARRY HARRISON & SON

SAM BOLDERSON
Straight Betting

W. Pennington
For
SPORTS GOODS

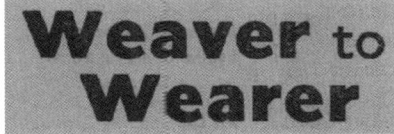

Weaver to Wearer

A SELECTION OF SPONSORS OF THE CLUB THROUGHOUT THE YEARS

SPORTSGEAR
of Huddersfield

FOLLOW YOUR TEAM
with
WALLACE ARNOLD

Bellamy's
POMFRET CAKES

The
Pontefract and
Castleford Express

GET YOUR NEW
or
SECOND HAND CAR
from
J. SIMPSON & SONS

Charles E. Ashton

FUNERAL DIRECTORS

A SELECTION OF SPONSORS OF THE CLUB THROUGHOUT THE YEARS

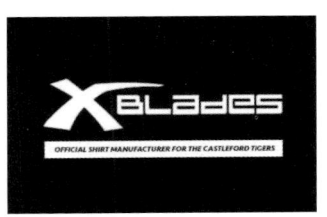